Managerial Accounting for Managers

Managerial Accounting for Managers

Fourth Edition

Eric W. Noreen, Ph.D., CMA

Professor Emeritus
University of Washington

Peter C. Brewer, Ph.D.

Wake Forest University

Ray H. Garrison, D.B.A., CPA

Professor Emeritus
Brigham Young University

Mc Graw Hill Education

MANAGERIAL ACCOUNTING FOR MANAGERS, FOURTH EDITION

This book is printed onacid-free paper.

1 2 3 4 5 6 7 8 9 0 DOW/DOW1 0 9 8 7 6

ISBN 978-1-259-57854-0
MHID 1-259-57854-2

Senior Vice President, Products & Markets: *Kurt L. Strand*
Vice President, General Manager, Products & Markets: *Marty Lange*
Vice President, Content Design & Delivery: *Kimberly Meriwether David*
Managing Director: *Tim Vertovec*
Brand Manager: *Nichole Pullen*
Director, Product Development: *Rose Koos*
Product Developer: *Erin Quinones*
Marketing Manager: *Cheryl Osgood*
Digital Product Developer: *Kevin Moran*
Director, Content Design & Delivery: *Linda Avenarius*
Program Manager: *Daryl Horrocks*
Lead Content Project Managers: *Pat Frederickson* and *Brian Nacik*
Buyer: *Laura M. Fuller*
Senior Designer: *Srdjan Savanovic*
Content Licensing Specialists: *Carrie Burger* and *Jacob Sullivan*
Cover and Chapter Opener Image: © *narvikk/Getty Images*
Compositor: *SPi Global*
Printer: *R. R. Donnelley*

All credits appearing on page xxvi are considered to be an extension of the copyright page.

Library of Congress Cataloging-in-Publication Data

Noreen, Eric W., author.
Managerial accounting for managers / Eric W. Noreen, Peter C. Brewer, Ray H. Garrison. — Fourth Edition.
pages cm
ISBN 978-1-259-57854-0 (alk. paper)
1. Managerial accounting. I. Brewer, Peter C., author. II. Garrison, Ray H., author. III. Title.
HF5657.4.N668 2017
658.15'11—dc23

2015030580

mheducation.com/highered

About the Authors

Eric W. Noreen has held appointments at institutions in the United States, Europe, and Asia. He is emeritus professor of accounting at the University of Washington.

His BA degree is from the University of Washington and his MBA and PhD degrees are from Stanford University. A Certified Management Accountant, he was awarded a Certificate of Distinguished Performance by the Institute of Certified Management Accountants.

Professor Noreen has served as associate editor of *The Accounting Review* and the *Journal of Accounting and Economics.* He has numerous articles in academic journals, including the *Journal of Accounting Research; The Accounting Review;* the *Journal of Accounting and Economics; Accounting Horizons; Accounting, Organizations and Society; Contemporary Accounting Research;* the *Journal of Management Accounting Research;* and the *Review of Accounting Studies.* Professor Noreen has won a number of awards from students for his teaching.

In his spare time, Eric organizes and leads annual hut-to-hut hiking treks for friends in the Alps in Italy, Switzerland, and Austria. ■

Peter C. Brewer is a Lecturer in the Department of Accountancy at Wake Forest University. Prior to joining the faculty at Wake Forest, he was an accounting professor at Miami University for 19 years. He holds a BS degree in accounting from Penn State University, an MS degree in accounting from the University of Virginia, and a PhD from the University of Tennessee. He has published more than 40 articles in a variety of journals, including *Management Accounting Research;* the *Journal of Information Systems; Cost Management; Strategic Finance;* the *Journal of Accountancy; Issues in Accounting Education;* and the *Journal of Business Logistics.*

Professor Brewer is a member of the editorial board of the *Journal of Accounting Education* and has served on the editorial board of *Issues in Accounting Education.* His article "Putting Strategy into the Balanced Scorecard" won the 2003 International Federation of Accountants' Articles of Merit competition, and his articles "Using Six Sigma to Improve the Finance Function" and "Lean Accounting: What's It All About?" were awarded the Institute of Management Accountants' Lybrand Gold and Silver Medals in 2005 and 2006. He has received Miami University's Richard T. Farmer School of Business Teaching Excellence Award.

Prior to joining the faculty at Miami University, Professor Brewer was employed as an auditor for Touche Ross in the firm's Philadelphia office. He also worked as an internal audit manager for the Board of Pensions of the Presbyterian Church (USA).

Pete's recreational interests include fishing, bow hunting, golf, and gardening, He also enjoys biking with his wife spending quality time with his two daughters; and spoiling his two labrador retrievers, Genevieve and Sweet Baby. ■

Ray H. Garrison is emeritus professor of accounting at Brigham Young University, Provo, Utah. He received his BS and MS degrees from Brigham Young University and his DBA degree from Indiana University.

As a certified public accountant, Professor Garrison has been involved in management consulting work with both national and regional accounting firms. He has published articles in *The Accounting Review, Management Accounting,* and other professional journals. Innovation in the classroom has earned Professor Garrison the Karl G. Maeser Distinguished Teaching Award from Brigham Young University. ■

Dedication

To our families and to our many colleagues who use this book.

—Eric W. Noreen, Peter C. Brewer, and Ray H. Garrison

Focus on the Future Manager

with Noreen/Brewer/Garrison

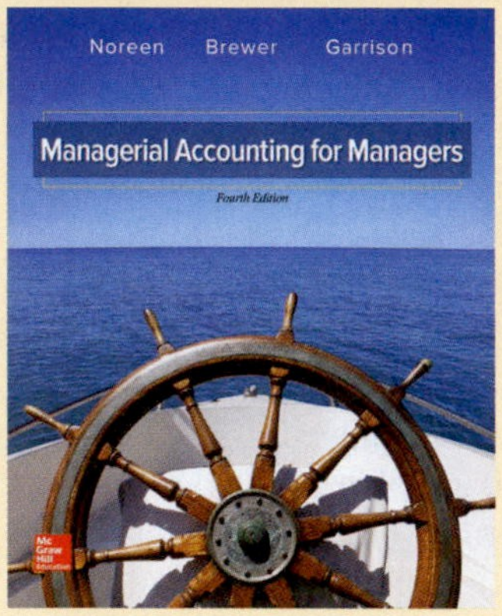

In ***Managerial Accounting for Managers,*** the authors have crafted a streamlined managerial accounting book that is perfect for non-accounting majors who intend to move into managerial positions. The traditional Process Costing, Statement of Cash Flows, and Financial Statement Analysis chapters have been dropped to enable instructors to **focus their attention on the bedrocks of managerial accounting**—planning, control, and decision making. Noreen/Brewer/Garrison focuses on the fundamentals, allowing students to develop the conceptual framework managers need to succeed.

In its fourth edition, *Managerial Accounting for Managers* continues to adhere to three core standards:

FOCUS. Noreen/Brewer/Garrison pinpoint the key managerial concepts students will need in their future careers. With no journal entries or financial accounting topics to worry about, students can focus on the fundamental principles of managerial accounting. The manager approach in Noreen allows students to develop the conceptual framework needed to succeed, with a focus on decision making and analytical skills.

RELEVANCE. Building student interest with its insightful Business Focus vignettes opening each chapter, current In Business examples throughout the text, and tried-and-true end-of-chapter material, students will always see the real-world applicability of Noreen/Brewer/Garrison.

BALANCE. There is more than one type of business, and so Noreen/Brewer/Garrison covers a variety of business models, including non-profit, retail, service, wholesale, and manufacturing organizations. Service company examples are highlighted with icons in the margins of the text.

"It's a very clear book with a healthy focus on decision making and service businesses. Great for non-majors."

—Mark Holtzman, Seton Hall University

"Very well-written and compatible with a user-based approach."

—Kay Poston, University of Indianapolis

"The best introductory management accounting book I have used. It is complete, concise, and written at a level beginning students can understand."

—Christine Haynes, University of West Georgia

New in the Fourth Edition

All Chapters

All chapters (except Chapter 1) have a new Foundational 15 feature.

Chapter 1

This chapter has a new section titled Managerial Accounting: Beyond the Numbers. It has expanded coverage of leadership skills and an expanded set of end-of-chapter exercises.

Chapter 2

The learning objective pertaining to direct and indirect costs has been moved to the front of the chapter to improve the students' ability to understand the material. Appendix 2A has been overhauled to simplify the explanation of how to use Microsoft Excel to perform least-squares regression analysis.

Chapter 3

The assumptions of CVP analysis have been moved from the end of the chapter to the beginning of the chapter. The target profit analysis and break-even analysis learning objectives have been reversed.

Chapter 4

This chapter has added Appendix 3A: Activity-Based Absorption Costing. This material was formerly Appendix 7B in the previous edition of the book. Moving this material to Chapter 3 offers instructors greater flexibility when determining how to cover activity-based costing.

Chapter 5

This chapter has added a new learning objective related to calculating companywide and segment break-even points for companies with traceable fixed costs. It has also added a new appendix related to super-variable costing.

Chapter 6

This chapter has added a new exhibit and accompanying text to better explain key concepts and terminology within the chapter.

Chapter 7

A section illustrating the meaning of a constraint has been added. Also, several new In Business boxes have been created.

Chapter 8

The learning objective pertaining to the payback period has been moved to the front of the chapter. Adopted a Microsoft Excel-based approach for depicting net present value calculations. Added a discussion of the behavioral implications of the simple rate of return method. Completely overhauled Appendix 8C so that students can more easily grasp the impact of income taxes on net present value analysis.

Chapter 9

We added new text and an exhibit to help students better understand how and why a master budget is created and how Microsoft Excel can be used to create a financial planning model that answers "what-if" questions. Two new end-of-chapter exercises that enable students to use Microsoft Excel to answer "what-if" questions have also been added.

Chapter 10

The discussion of the variance analysis cycle and management by exception have been moved into the front of this chapter. This material was previously included in the standard costing chapter. In response to customer feedback, we reversed the headings in the flexible budget performance report. The actual results are shown in the far-left column, and the planning budget is shown in the far-right column.

Chapter 11

In response to customer feedback, we reversed the headings in the general model for standard cost variance analysis. The actual results (AQ × AP) are shown in the far-left column and the flexible budget (SQ × SP) is shown in the far-right column.

Chapter 12

This chapter a new Business Focus feature and two new In Business boxes were added.

Noreen's Powerful Pedagogy

Managerial Accounting for Managers is full of pedagogy designed to make studying productive and hassle-free.

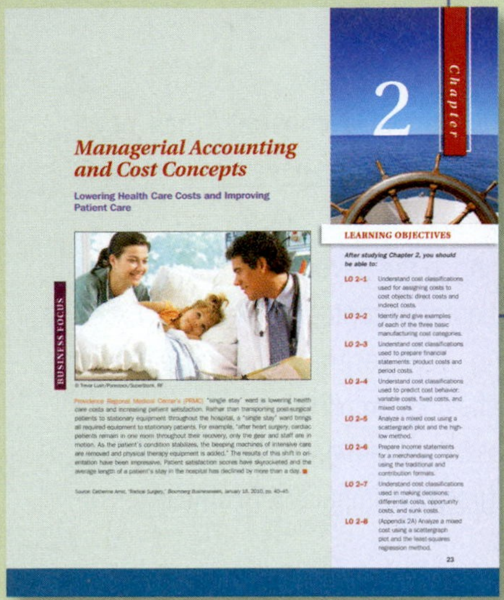

Opening Vignette

Each chapter opens with a **Business Focus** feature that provides a real-world example for students, allowing them to see how the chapter's information and insights apply to the world outside the classroom. **Learning Objectives** alert students to what they should expect as they progress through the chapter.

"Many concepts in accounting are rather abstract if not given some type of context to understand them in. The business focus features help to provide this context and can lead to discussions in class if the instructor wishes."

—Jeffrey Wong, University of Nevada, Reno

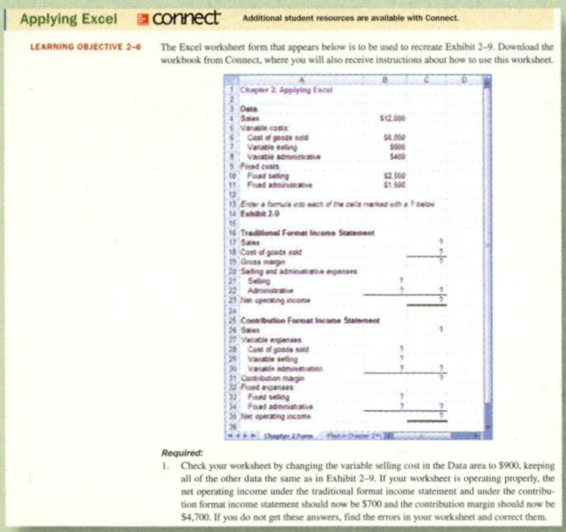

Applying Excel

This exciting end-of-chapter feature **links the power of Excel with managerial accounting concepts** by illustrating how Excel functionality can be used to better understand accounting data. Applying Excel goes beyond plugging numbers into a template by providing students with an opportunity to build their own Excel worksheets and formulas. Students are then asked "what if" questions in which they analyze not only **how** related pieces of accounting data affect each other but **why** they do. Applying Excel immediately precedes the Exercises in eleven of the twelve chapters in the book and is also **integrated with Connect,** allowing students to practice their skills online with algorithmically generated datasets and to watch animated, narrated tutorials on how to use formulas in Excel.

"An excellent pedagogical feature that helps further reinforce students' knowledge of key concepts in the text book, while strengthening students' Excel skills that are so important in the work place."

—Marianne L. James, California State University, Los Angeles

"[Applying Excel is] an excellent way for students to programmatically develop spreadsheet skills without having to be taught spreadsheet techniques by the instructor. A significant associated benefit is that students gain more exposure to the dynamics of accounting information by working with what-if scenarios."

—Earl Godfrey, Gardner–Webb University

The Foundational 15

NEW to the fourth edition of Noreen!

Each chapter now contains one Foundational 15 exercise that includes 15 "building-block" questions related to one concise set of data. These exercises can be used for in-class discussion or as homework assignments. They are found before the Exercises and are available in **Connect.**

Additional student resources are available with Connect. connect **The Foundational 15**

Martinez Company's relevant range of production is 7,500 units to 12,500 units. When it produces and sells 10,000 units, its unit costs are as follows:

LEARNING OBJECTIVES 2–1, 2–2, 2–3, 2–4, 2–6, 2–7

	Amount Per Unit
Direct materials	$6.00
Direct labor	$3.50
Variable manufacturing overhead	$1.50
Fixed manufacturing overhead	$4.00
Fixed selling expense	$3.00
Fixed administrative expense	$2.00
Sales commissions	$1.00
Variable administrative expense	$0.50

In Business Boxes

These helpful boxed features offer a glimpse into how real companies use the managerial accounting concepts discussed within the chapter. Each chapter contains from three to fourteen of these current examples.

IN BUSINESS

© Digital Vision/PunchStock, RF

FOOD PRICES HIT RECORD HIGHS FOR RESTAURANTS

Direct material costs are critically important to restaurants and fast-food chains. In recent years, some food costs have spiked to record highs. For example, unexpected freezing temperatures in the southwestern portion of the United States caused the cost of lettuce to increase 290%. Similarly, the costs of green peppers, tomatoes, and cucumbers jumped 145%, 85%, and 30%, respectively. A large chain such as Subway can withstand these price increases better than smaller competitors because of its buying power and long-term contracts.

Source: Anne VanderMey, "Food For Thought," *Fortune*, May 9, 2011, p. 12.

"I love these. Again, a connection to the real world that adds credence to the course."

—Larry N.Bitner, Shippensburg University

Managerial Accounting in Action Vignettes

These vignettes depict cross-functional teams working together in real-life settings. Using products and services students recognize from their own lives increases engagement and enhances problem-solving skills. Students are shown step-by-step how accounting concepts are implemented in organizations and how these concepts are applied to solve everyday business problems. First, "The Issue" is introduced through a dialogue; the student then walks through the implementation process; finally, "The Wrap-up" summarizes the big picture.

Job-Order Costing—An Example

To introduce job-order costing, we will follow a specific job as it progresses through the manufacturing process. This job consists of two experimental couplings that Yost Precision Machining has agreed to produce for Loops Unlimited, a manufacturer of roller coasters. Couplings connect the cars on the roller coaster and are a critical component in the performance and safety of the ride. Before we begin our discussion, recall from a previous chapter that companies generally classify manufacturing costs into three broad categories: (1) direct materials, (2) direct labor, and (3) manufacturing overhead. As we study the operation of a job-order costing system, we will see how each of these three types of costs is recorded and accumulated.

MANAGERIAL ACCOUNTING IN ACTION
The Issue

YOST Precision Machining

Yost Precision Machining is a small company in Michigan that specializes in fabricating precision metal parts that are used in a variety of applications ranging from deep-sea exploration vehicles to the inertial triggers in automobile air bags. The company's top managers gather every morning at 8:00 A.M. in the company's conference room for the daily planning meeting. Attending the meeting this morning are: Jean Yost, the company's president; David Cheung, the marketing manager; Debbie Turner, the production manager; and Marc White, the company controller. The president opened the meeting:

Jean: The production schedule indicates we'll be starting Job 2B47 today. Isn't that the special order for experimental couplings, David?

David: That's right. That's the order from Loops Unlimited for two couplings for their new roller coaster ride for Magic Mountain.

Debbie: Why only two couplings? Don't they need a coupling for every car?

David: Yes. But this is a completely new roller coaster. The cars will go faster and will be subjected to more twists, turns, drops, and loops than on any other existing roller coaster. To hold up under these stresses, Loops Unlimited's engineers completely

"This element is exceptional. The situations truly reflect real life issues business people would face—not just "textbook" manufactured examples that always have black-and-white answers."

—Ann E. Selk, University of Wisconsin–Green Bay

Applying Excel connect Additional student resources are available with Connect.

LEARNING OBJECTIVES 4–1, 4–2, 4–4

The Excel worksheet form that appears below will reinforce your ability to compute underapplied and overapplied overhead. It is based on the data pertaining to Turbo Crafters Company that was discussed earlier in the chapter. Download the workbook from Connect, where you will also receive instructions about how to use this worksheet.

Exercises connect Additional student resources are available with Connect.

EXERCISE 4–1 Compute the Predetermined Overhead Rate [LO4–1]

Logan Products computes its predetermined overhead rate annually on the basis of direct labor-hours. At the beginning of the year, it estimated that 40,000 direct labor-hours would be required for the period's estimated level of production. The company also estimated $466,000 of fixed manufacturing overhead expenses for the coming period and variable manufacturing overhead of

Problems connect Additional student resources are available with Connect.

PROBLEM 3–19 Break-Even Analysis; Pricing [LO3–1, LO3–4, LO3–5]

Minden Company introduced a new product last year for which it is trying to find an optimal selling price. Marketing studies suggest that the company can increase sales by 5,000 units for each $2 reduction in the selling price. The company's present selling price is $70 per unit, and variable expenses are $40 per unit. Fixed expenses are $540,000 per year. The present annual sales volume

Cases connect Additional student resources are available with Connect.

CASE 3–32 Break-Evens for Individual Products in a Multiproduct Company [LO3–5, LO3–9]

Cheryl Montoya picked up the phone and called her boss, Wes Chan, the vice president of marketing at Piedmont Fasteners Corporation: "Wes, I'm not sure how to go about answering the questions that came up at the meeting with the president yesterday."

"What's the problem?"

End-of-Chapter Material

Building on Garrison/Noreen/Brewer's reputation for having the best end-of-chapter review and discussion material of any text on the market, Noreen's problem and case material continues to conform to AACSB recommendations and makes a great starting point for class discussions and group projects.

Applying Excel integrates key course concepts and Excel—a software students will encounter in the workplace, whether they go into accounting or any other business major. With Applying Excel, students not only gain practice working with Excel software, they also learn how Excel can be used to present accounting data and how that data is interrelated.

"The problem material is still the best I can find."

—Noel McKeon, Florida State College–Jacksonville

"The teaching supplementary materials are excellent for new professors as well as seasoned professors."

—Terence Pitre, University of St. Thomas

Author-Written Supplements

Unlike other managerial accounting texts, the book's authors write all of the major supplements, ensuring a perfect fit between text and supplements. For more information on ***Managerial Accounting for Managers'*** supplements package.

- Instructor's Resource Guide
- Test Bank
- Solutions Manual

Utilizing the Icons

To reflect our service-based economy, the text is replete with examples from service-based businesses. A helpful icon distinguishes service-related examples in the text.

Ethics assignments and examples serve as a reminder that good conduct is vital in business. Icons call out content that relates to ethical behavior for students.

The writing icon denotes problems that require students to use critical thinking as well as writing skills to explain their decisions.

The IFRS icon highlights content that may be affected by the impending change to IFRS and possible convergence between U.S. GAAP and IFRS.

"I strongly recommend this book to colleagues [for the] introductory course in managerial accounting. It fits students without a background in managerial accounting. It is the best textbook in managerial accounting."

—Yousef Jahmani, Savannah State University

"Excellent, comprehensive book. Easy for students to read and understand."

—Sandy Copa, North Hennepin College

"Students can easily understand the book. [Noreen] covers all the pertinent topics needed in Managerial Accounting in a concise, easy to understand format."

—Linda Malgeri, Kennesaw State University

A Market-Leading Book Deserves

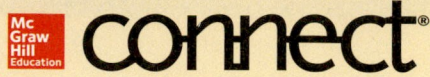

Education is changing . . . and so are we.

McGraw-Hill's Connect is a digital teaching and learning environment that support student's skills in the classroom and beyond. With Connect, instructors use technology to enhance learning by delivering interactive assignments, quizzes, and tests easily online. Connect digital assets focus on concepts, application, and assessment. Students can practice important skills at their own pace and on their own schedule.

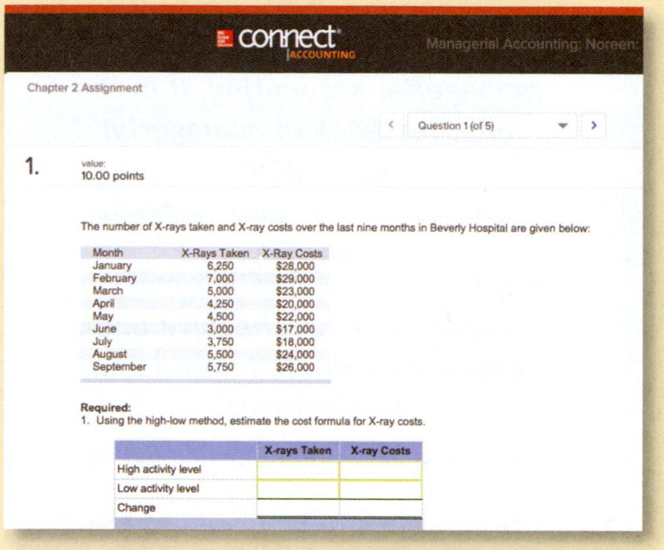

Online Assignments

Connect helps students learn more efficiently by providing feedback and practice material when and where they need it. Connect grades homework automatically, and students benefit from the immediate feedback that they receive, particularly on any questions they may have missed. Furthermore, algorithmic questions provide students with unlimited opportunities for practice.

NEW! Excel Simulations

Simulated Excel questions, assignable within Connect, allow students to practice their Excel skills—such as basic formulas and formatting—within the content of financial accounting. These questions feature animated, narrated Help and Show Me tutorials (when enabled), as well as automatic feedback and grading for both students and professors.

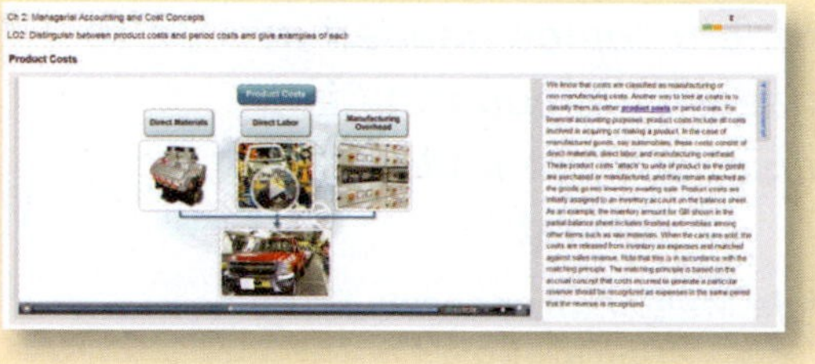

Interactive Presentations

Interactive Presentations, assignable by individual learning objective within Connect, teach the core concepts of the text in an animated, narrated, and interactive multimedia format, bringing the key concepts of the course to life—particularly helpful for online courses and for those audio and visual learners who struggle reading the textbook page by page.

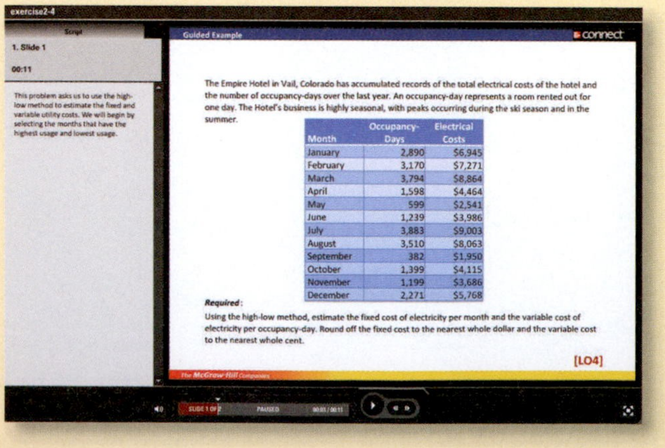

Guided Examples

Guided Examples, available as hints within Connect when enabled by the instructor, provide a narrated, animated, step-by-step walkthrough of select exercises similar to those assigned. These short presentations provide reinforcement when students need it most.

Market-Leading Technology

Less Managing. More Teaching. Greater Learning.

Connect offers a number of powerful tools and features to make managing assignments easier, so faculty can spend more time teaching. With *Connect,* students can engage with their coursework anytime, anywhere, making the learning process more accessible and efficient. Please see the previous page for a description of the student tools available within *Connect.*

connect *Connect* for Instructors

Simple Assignment Management and Smart Grading. With *Connect,* creating assignments is easier than ever, so you can spend more time teaching and less time managing. *Connect* enables you to:

- Create and deliver assignments and assessments easily with selectable static and algorithmic end-of-chapter questions and test bank items.
- Go paperless with online submission and grading of student assignments and by sharing notes through the media-rich eBook.
- Have assignments scored automatically, giving students immediate feedback on their work and comparisons with correct answers and explanations.
- Reinforce classroom concepts by assigning Guided Examples, LearnSmart modules, and Interactive Presentations.

Instructor Library

The *Connect* Instructor Library is your repository for additional resources to improve student engagement in and out of class. You can select and use any asset that enhances your lecture. The *Connect* Instructor Library includes access to the textbook's Solutions Manual, Test Bank, Instructor PowerPoint® Slides, Instructor's Resource Guide, Applying Excel Solutions, Sample Syllabus, and Media-rich eBook.

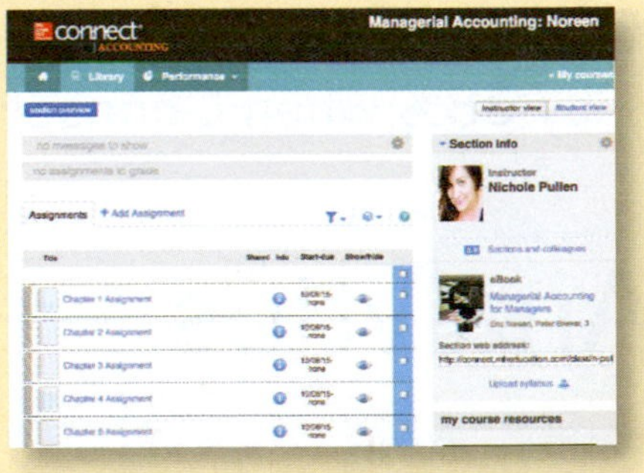

Connect

McGraw-Hill reinvents the textbook learning experience for the modern student with *Connect,* which provides a seamless integration of the eBook and *Connect. Connect* provides all of the *Connect* features, as well as:

- An integrated eBook, allowing for any time, anywhere access to the textbook.
- Dynamic links between the problems or questions you assign to your students and the location in the eBook where the concept related to that problem or question is covered.
- A powerful search function to pinpoint and connect key concepts in a snap.
- Highlighting, note-taking and sharing, and other media-rich capabilities.

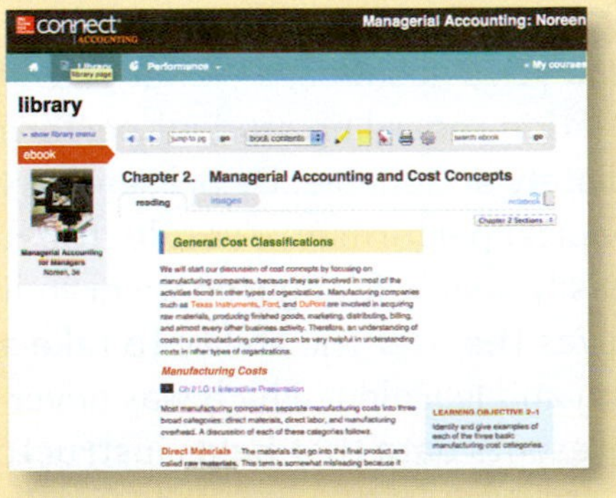

For more information about *Connect,* go to **www.mcgrawhillconnect.com**, or contact your local McGraw-Hill sales representative.

McGraw-Hill Customer Experience

At McGraw-Hill, we understand that getting the most from new technology can be challenging. That's why our services don't stop after you purchase our products. You can e-mail our Product Specialists 24 hours a day to get product training online. Or you can search our knowledge bank of Frequently Asked Questions on our support website. For Customer Support, call 800-331-5094 or visit **www.mhhe.com/support**. One of our Technical Support Analysts will be able to assist you in a timely fashion.

McGraw Hill Education **connect**®

Required=Results

McGraw-Hill Connect®
Learn Without Limits

Connect is a teaching and learning platform that is proven to deliver better results for students and instructors.

Connect empowers students by continually adapting to deliver precisely what they need, when they need it, and how they need it, so your class time is more engaging and effective.

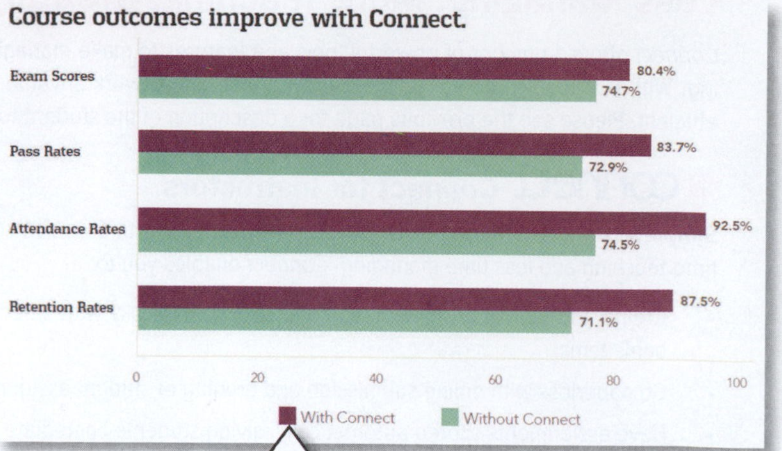

Using **Connect** improves passing rates by **10.8%** and retention by **16.4%.**

88% of instructors who use **Connect** require it; instructor satisfaction **increases** by 38% when **Connect** is required.

Analytics

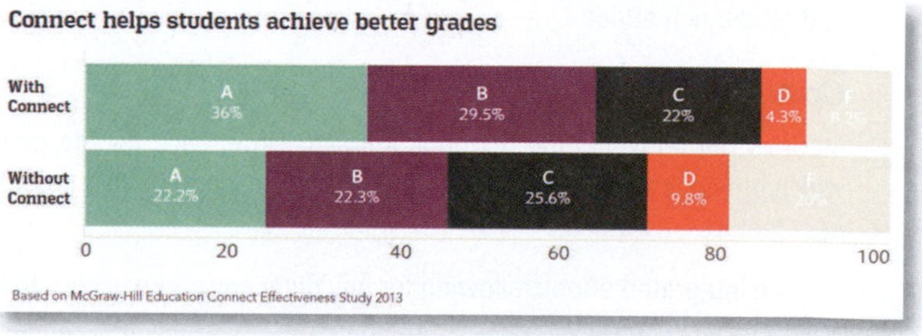

Connect Insight®

Connect Insight is Connect's new one-of-a-kind visual analytics dashboard—that provides at-a-glance information regarding student performance, which is immediately actionable. By presenting assignment, assessment, and topical performance results together with a time metric that is easily visible for aggregate or individual results, Connect Insight gives the user the ability to take a just-in-time approach to teaching and learning, which was never before available. Connect Insight presents data that helps instructors improve class performance in a way that is efficient and effective.

Adaptive

THE FIRST AND ONLY **ADAPTIVE READING EXPERIENCE** DESIGNED TO TRANSFORM THE WAY STUDENTS READ

More students earn **A's** and **B's** when they use McGraw-Hill Education **Adaptive** products.

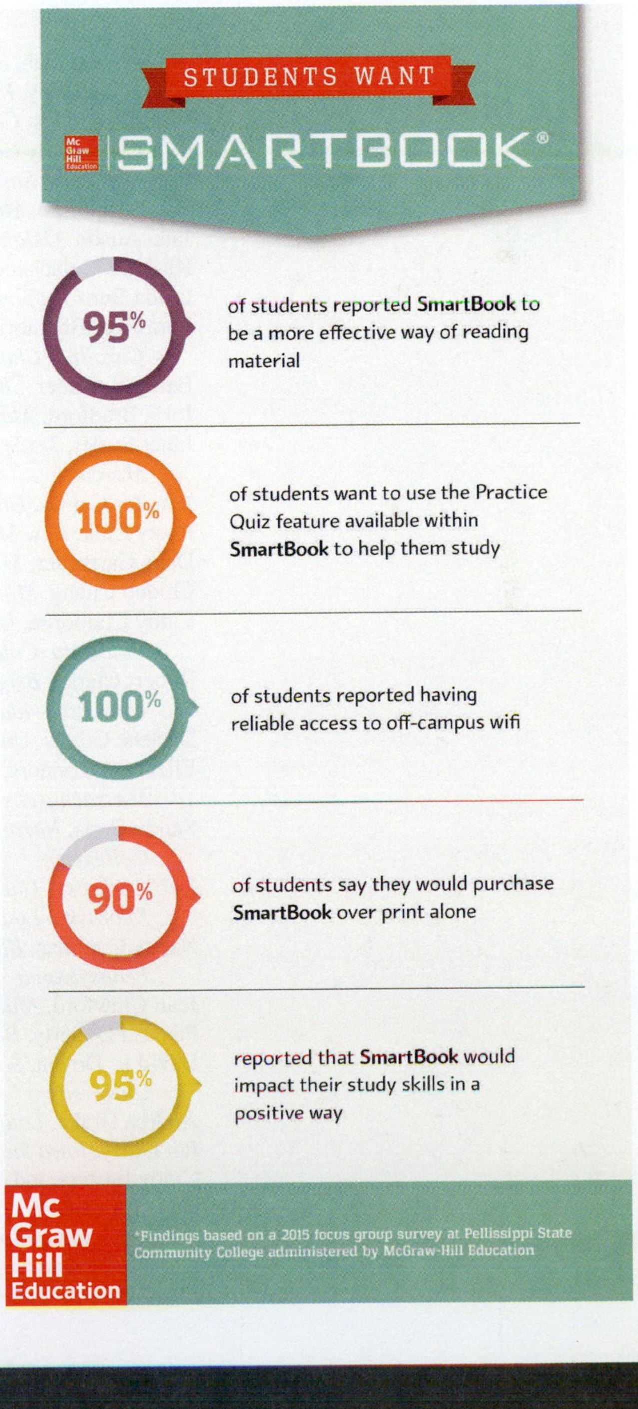
STUDENTS WANT
SMARTBOOK®
95%
of students reported SmartBook to be a more effective way of reading material
100%
of students want to use the Practice Quiz feature available within SmartBook to help them study
100%
of students reported having reliable access to off-campus wifi
90%
of students say they would purchase SmartBook over print alone
95%
reported that SmartBook would impact their study skills in a positive way
Mc Graw Hill Education
*Findings based on a 2015 focus group survey at Pellissippi State Community College administered by McGraw-Hill Education

SmartBook®

Proven to help students improve grades and study more efficiently, SmartBook contains the same content within the print book, but actively tailors that content to the needs of the individual. SmartBook's adaptive technology provides precise, personalized instruction on what the student should do next, guiding the student to master and remember key concepts, targeting gaps in knowledge and offering customized feedback, and driving the student toward comprehension and retention of the subject matter. Available on smartphones and tablets, SmartBook puts learning at the student's fingertips—anywhere, anytime.

Over **4 billion questions** have been answered, making McGraw-Hill Education products more intelligent, reliable, and precise.

Acknowledgments

Suggestions have been received from many of our colleagues throughout the world. Each of those who have offered comments and suggestions has our thanks.

The efforts of many people are needed to develop and improve a text. Among these people are the reviewers and consultants who point out areas of concern, cite areas of strength, and make recommendations for change. In this regard, the following professors provided feedback that was enormously helpful in preparing the fourth edition of ***Managerial Accounting for Managers:***

Wagdy Abdallah, *Seton Hall University*
Linda Abernathy, *Kirkwood Community College*
James Andrews, *Central New Mexico Community College*
Rick Andrews, *Sinclair Community College*
Frank Aquilino, *Montclair State University*
Jane Austin, *Oklahoma City University*
Kashi R. Balachandran, *New York University*
Linda Benz, *Jefferson Technical College*
Surasakdi Bhamornsiri, *University of North Carolina–Charlotte*
Larry N. Bitner, *Shippensburg University*
Jorja Bradford, *Alabama State University*
Janet Butler, *Texas State University-San Marcos*
Jennifer Cainas, *University of South Florida*
Rusty Calk, *New Mexico State University*
Dana Carpenter, *MATC Truax*
Chiaho Chang, *Montlcair State University*
Cathy Claiborne, *University of Colorado–Colorado*
Robert Clarke, *Brigham Young University–Idaho*
Darlene Coarts, *University of Northern Iowa*
Elizabeth Connors, *University of Massachusetts–Boston*
Sandy Copa, *North Hennepin Community College*
Deb Cosgrove, *University of Nebraska–Lincoln*
Nancy Coulmas, *Bloomsburg University of Pennsylvania*
Jean Crawford, *Alabama State University*
Patricia Doherty, *Boston University*
David L. Doyon, *Southern New Hampshire University*
Andrea Drake, *Louisiana Tech University*
Jan Duffy, *Iowa State University*
Cindy Easterwood, *Virginia Tech*
Gene Elrod, *University of North Texas*
Rebecca Evans, *Florida State College–Jacksonville*
Janice Fergusson, *University of South Carolina*
Annette Fisher, *Glendale Community College*
Ananda Ganguly, *Claremont College*
J. Marie Gibson, *University of Nevada Reno*
Olen Greer, *Missouri State University*
Cynthia Greeson, *Ivy Tech Community College*
Richard O. Hanson, *Southern New Hampshire University*
Ken Harmon, *Kennesaw State University*
Christine Haynes, *University of West Georgia*
David Henderson, *College of Charleston*
Kathy Ho, *Niagara University*
Mark Holtzman, *Seton Hall University*
Maggie Houston, *Wright State University*
Tom Hrubec, *Franklin University*
Chuo-Hsuan Lee, *SUNY–Plattsburgh*
Ronald Huefner, *SUNY Buffalo*
Yousef Jahmani, *Savannah State University*
Robyn Jarnagin, *Montana State University*
Iris Jenkel, *St. Norbert College*
Randy Johnston, *Michigan State University*
Nancy Jones, *California State University*
Jai Kang, *San Francisco State University*
Catherine Katagiri, *College of Saint Rose*
Carl Keller, *Indiana Purdue University/Fort Wayne*
Cynthia Khanlarian, *University of North Carolina–Greensboro*
James Kinard, *Ohio State University–Columbus*
Gary Kleinman, *Montclair State University*
Leon Korte, *The University of South Dakota*
Christy Land, *Catawba Valley Community College*
Ron Lazer, *University of Houston*
Candace Leuck, *Clemson University*
Natasha Librizzi, *Milwaukee Area Technical College*
William R. Link, *University of Missouri–St. Louis*

Kathy Long, *University of Tennessee–Chattanooga*
Patti Lopez, *Valencia Community College East*
Mary Loretta Manktelow, *James Madison University*
Jim Lukawitz, *University of Memphis*
Anna Lusher, *Slippery Rock University*
Linda Malgeri, *Kennesaw State University*
Steve Markoff, *Montclair State University*
Melissa Martin, *Arizona State University–Tempe*
Gary McCombs, *College of Charleston*
Noel McKeon, *Florida State College–Jacksonville*
Jim McKittrick, *University of Portland*
Laurie McWhorter, *Mississippi State University*
James Meddaugh, *Ohio University*
Tammy Metzke, *Milwaukee Area Technical College–West Allis*
Tony Mifsud, *Catawba Valley Community College*
Tim Mills, *Eastern Illinois University*
Mark E. Motluck, *Anderson University*
Dennis Mullen, *City College of San Francisco*
Gerald M. Myers, *Pacific Lutheran University*
Michael Newman, *University of Houston–Houston*
Joseph M. Nicassio, *Westmoreland County Community College*
Alfonso R. Oddo, *Niagara University*
Tamara Phelan, *Northern Illinois University*
JoAnn Pinto, *Montclair State University*
Terence Pitre, *University of St. Thomas*
Shirley Polejewski, *University of St. Thomas*
Kay Poston, *University of Indianapolis*
Les Price, *Pierce College*
Kamala Raghavan, *Robert Morris University*
Raul Ramos, *Lorain County Community College*
John Reisch, *East Carolina University*
Michelle Reisch, *East Carolina University*
Therese Rice, *North Hennepin Community College*
Luther L. Ross, Sr., *Central Piedmont Community College*
Pamela Rouse, *Butler University*
Amy Santos, *Manatee Community College*
Rex Schildhouse, *Miramar College*
Ann E. Selk, *University of Wisconsin–Green Bay*
Daniel Sevall, *Lincoln University*
Ken Snow, *Florida State College–Jacksonville*
Vic Stanton, *University of California–Berkeley*
Ellen Sweatt, *Georgia Perimeter College*
Rick Tabor, *Auburn University*
Diane Tanner, *University of North Florida*
Samantha Ternes, *Kirkwood Community College*
Chuck Thompson, *University of Massachusetts*
Dorothy Thompson, *North Central Texas College*
Terri Walsh, *Seminole State College of Florida*
James White, *Boston University*
Michael Wilson, *University of Indianapolis*
Janet Woods, *Macon State College*
Christine Wright, *Seminole State College of Florida*
James Yang, *Montclair State University*
Marjorie Yuschak, *Rutgers University*
Ronald Zhao, *Monmouth University*
Kiran Verma, *University of Massachusetts–Boston*
Jeffrey Wong, *University of Nevada–Reno*
Peter Woodlock, *Youngstown State University*

We are grateful for the outstanding support from McGraw-Hill. In particular, we would like to thank Tim Vertovec, Director; Nichole Pullen, Brand Manager; Erin Quinones, Product Developer; Pat Plumb, Director of Digital Content; Pat Frederickson and Brian Nacik, Lead Content Project Managers; Laura Fuller, Buyer; Srdj Savanovic, Designer; and Carrie Burger and Jacob Sullivan, Content Licensing Specialists.

Thank you to the following individuals who helped prepare the supplements: Jon A. Booker of Tennessee Technological University, Cynthia J. Rooney of the University of New Mexico, and Susan C. Galbreath of Lipscomb University for crafting the Instructor and Student PowerPoint Slides; Ilene Persoff of CW Post Campus/Long Island University for updating the Quizzes and Exams.

Thank you to our Digital Contributor, Margaret Shackell-Dowell (Cornell University), for her many contributions to Connect for Noreen 4e, including Guided Example content, Interactive Presentation review, and accuracy checking. Thank you to Julie Hankins for acting as Lead subject matter expert on Connect content. Patti Lopez (Valencia College) for her efforts as lead subject matter expert on LearnSmart and Jeannie Folk for her review of LearnSmart. Finally, we would like to thank Beth Woods and Helen Roybark for working so hard to ensure an error-free fourth edition.

We are grateful to the Institute of Certified Management Accountants for permission to use questions and/or unofficial answers from past Certificate in Management Accounting (CMA) examinations. Likewise, we thank the American Institute of Certified Public Accountants, the Society of Management Accountants of Canada, and the Chartered Institute of Management Accountants (United Kingdom) for permission to use (or to adapt) selected problems from their examinations. These problems bear the notations CPA, SMA, and CIMA respectively.

Eric W. Noreen • Peter C. Brewer • Ray H. Garrison

Brief Contents

Contents

Chapter 1

Managerial Accounting: An Overview 1

Chapter 2

Managerial Accounting and Cost Concepts 23

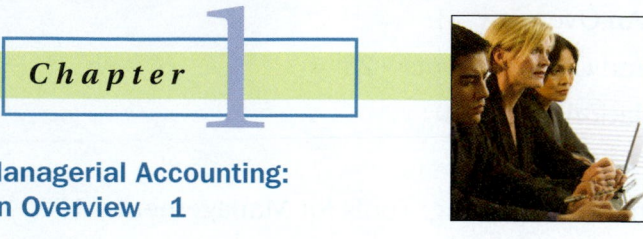

Chapter 3

Chapter 4

Chapter 5

Chapter 6

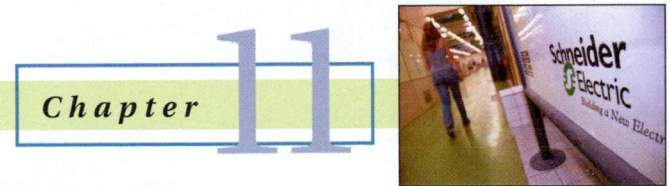

Appendix A

Appendix B

Contents Image Credits: Chapter 1 © Corbis/Superstock, RF; Chapter 2 © Trevor Lush/Purestock/SuperStock, RF; Chapter 3 © Comstock Images, RF; Chapter 4 © Courtesy of University Tees, Inc.; Chapter 5 © Jeff Kowalsky/Bloomberg/Getty Images; Chapter 6 © Brand X Pictures/PunchStock, RF; Chapter 7 © AP Images/Imaginechina/Jhphoto; Chapter 8 © AP Images/David Goldman; Chapter 9 © Sandee Noreen; Chapter 10 © Michael Sears/MCT/Newscom; Chapter 11 © Fabrice Dimier/Bloomberg/Getty Images; Chapter 12 © ZUMA Press, Inc./Alamy.

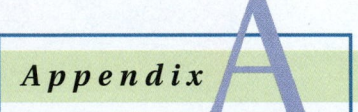

Chapter 1

Managerial Accounting: An Overview

Managerial Accounting: It's More Than Just Crunching Numbers

BUSINESS FOCUS

© Corbis/Superstock, RF

"Creating value through values" is the credo of today's management accountant. It means that management accountants should maintain an unwavering commitment to ethical values while using their knowledge and skills to influence decisions that create value for organizational stakeholders. These skills include managing risks and implementing strategy through planning, budgeting and forecasting, and decision support. Management accountants are strategic business partners who understand the financial and operational sides of the business. They not only report and analyze financial measures, but also nonfinancial measures of process performance and corporate social performance. Think of these responsibilities as profits (financial statements), process (customer focus and satisfaction), people (employee learning and satisfaction), and planet (environmental stewardship). ■

Source: Conversation with Jeff Thomson, president and CEO of the Institute of Management Accountants.

This chapter explains why managerial accounting is important to the future careers of all business students. It begins by answering two questions: (1) What is managerial accounting? and (2) Why does managerial accounting matter to your career? It concludes by discussing six topics—ethics, strategic management, enterprise risk management, corporate social responsibility, process management, and leadership—that define the business context for applying the quantitative aspects of managerial accounting.

What Is Managerial Accounting?

Many students enrolled in this course will have recently completed an introductory *financial accounting* course. **Financial accounting** is concerned with reporting financial information to external parties, such as stockholders, creditors, and regulators. **Managerial accounting** is concerned with providing information to managers for use within the organization. Exhibit 1–1 summarizes seven key differences between financial and managerial accounting. It recognizes that the fundamental difference between financial and managerial accounting is that financial accounting serves the needs of those

EXHIBIT 1–1
Comparison of Financial and Managerial Accounting

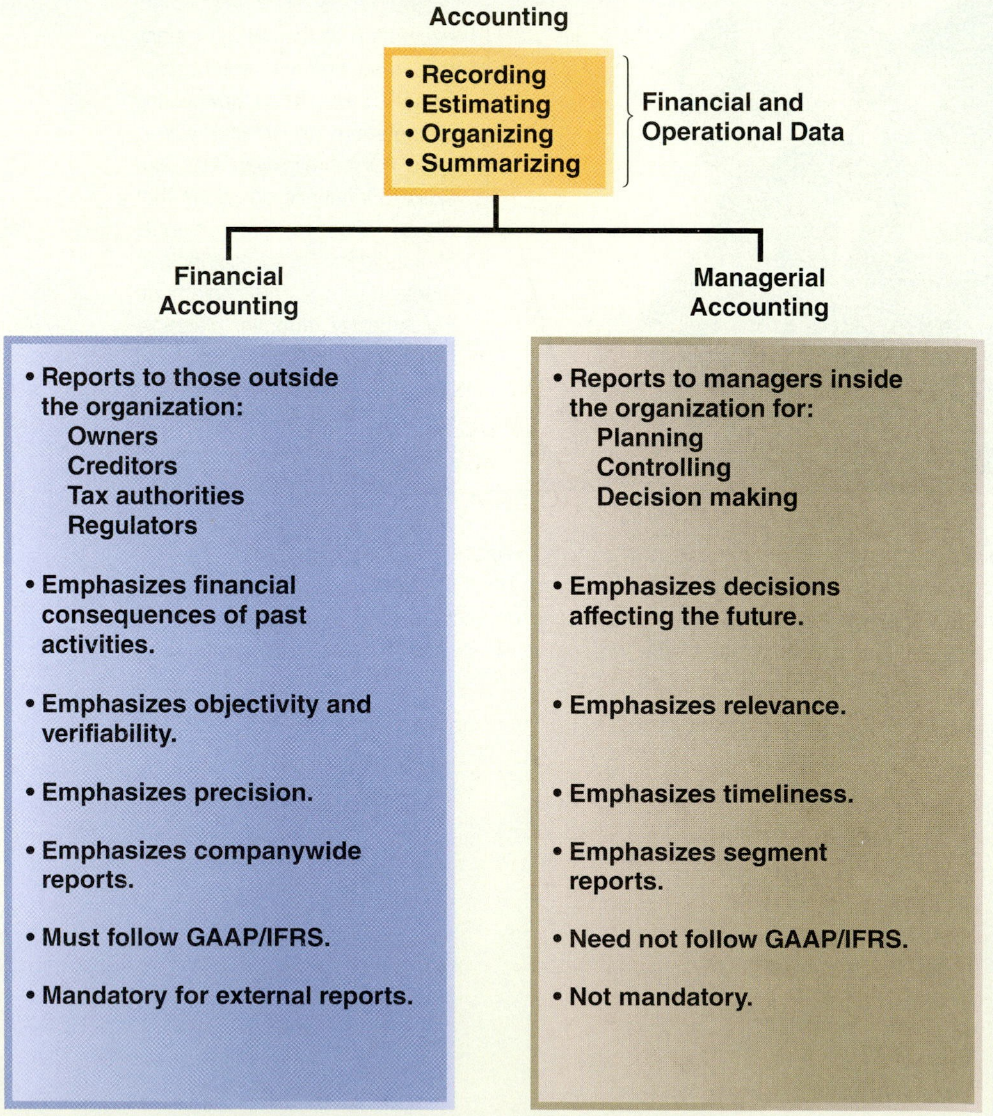

Accounting
• Recording
• Estimating
• Organizing
• Summarizing
Financial and Operational Data
Financial Accounting
Managerial Accounting
• Reports to those outside the organization:
Owners
Creditors
Tax authorities
Regulators
• Emphasizes financial consequences of past activities.
• Emphasizes objectivity and verifiability.
• Emphasizes precision.
• Emphasizes companywide reports.
• Must follow GAAP/IFRS.
• Mandatory for external reports.
• Reports to managers inside the organization for:
Planning
Controlling
Decision making
• Emphasizes decisions affecting the future.
• Emphasizes relevance.
• Emphasizes timeliness.
• Emphasizes segment reports.
• Need not follow GAAP/IFRS.
• Not mandatory.

outside the organization, whereas managerial accounting serves the needs of managers employed *inside* the organization. Because of this fundamental difference in users, financial accounting emphasizes the financial consequences of past activities, objectivity and verifiability, precision, and companywide performance, whereas managerial accounting emphasizes decisions affecting the future, relevance, timeliness, and *segment* performance. A **segment** is a part or activity of an organization about which managers would like cost, revenue, or profit data. Examples of business segments include product lines, customer groups (segmented by age, ethnicity, gender, volume of purchases, etc.), geographic territories, divisions, plants, and departments. Finally, financial accounting is mandatory for external reports and it needs to comply with rules, such as generally accepted accounting principles (GAAP) and international financial reporting standards (IFRS), whereas managerial accounting is not mandatory and it does not need to comply with externally imposed rules.

As mentioned in Exhibit 1–1, managerial accounting helps managers perform three vital activities—*planning, controlling,* and *decision making.* **Planning** involves establishing goals and specifying how to achieve them. **Controlling** involves gathering feedback to ensure that the plan is being properly executed or modified as circumstances change. **Decision making** involves selecting a course of action from competing alternatives. Now let's take a closer look at these three pillars of managerial accounting.

Planning

Assume that you work for Procter & Gamble (P&G) and that you are in charge of the company's campus recruiting for all undergraduate business majors. In this example, your planning process would begin by establishing a goal such as: our goal is to recruit the "best and brightest" college graduates. The next stage of the planning process would require specifying how to achieve this goal by answering numerous questions such as:

- How many students do we need to hire in total and from each major?
- What schools do we plan to include in our recruiting efforts?
- Which of our employees will be involved in each school's recruiting activities?
- When will we conduct our interviews?
- How will we compare students to one another to decide who will be extended job offers?
- What salary will we offer our new hires? Will the salaries differ by major?
- How much money can we spend on our recruiting efforts?

As you can see, there are many questions that need to be answered as part of the planning process. Plans are often accompanied by a *budget.* A **budget** is a detailed plan for the future that is usually expressed in formal quantitative terms. As the head of recruiting at P&G, your budget would include two key components. First, you would have to work with other senior managers inside the company to establish a budgeted amount of total salaries that can be offered to all new hires. Second, you would have to create a budget that quantifies how much you intend to spend on your campus recruiting activities.

Controlling

Once you established and started implementing P&G's recruiting plan, you would transition to the control process. This process would involve gathering, evaluating, and responding to feedback to ensure that this year's recruiting process meets expectations. It would also include evaluating the feedback in search of ways to run a more effective recruiting campaign next year. The control process would involve answering questions such as:

- Did we succeed in hiring the planned number of students within each major and at each school?
- Did we lose too many exceptional candidates to competitors?
- Did each of our employees involved in the recruiting process perform satisfactorily?

- Is our method of comparing students to one another working?
- Did the on-campus and office interviews run smoothly?
- Did we stay within our budget in terms of total salary commitments to new hires?
- Did we stay within our budget regarding spending on recruiting activities?

As you can see, there are many questions that need to be answered as part of the control process. When answering these questions your goal would be to go beyond simple yes or no answers in search of the underlying reasons why performance exceeded or failed to meet expectations. Part of the control process includes preparing *performance reports.* A **performance report** compares budgeted data to actual data in an effort to identify and learn from excellent performance and to identify and eliminate sources of unsatisfactory performance. Performance reports can also be used as one of many inputs to help evaluate and reward employees.

Although this example focused on P&G's campus recruiting efforts, we could have described how planning enables FedEx to deliver packages across the globe overnight, or how it helped Apple develop and market the iPad. We could have discussed how the control process helps Pfizer, Eli Lilly, and Abbott Laboratories ensure that their pharmaceutical drugs are produced in conformance with rigorous quality standards, or how Kroger relies on the control process to keep its grocery shelves stocked. We also could have looked at planning and control failures such as BP's massive oil spill in the Gulf of Mexico. In short, all managers (and that probably includes you someday) perform planning and controlling activities.

Decision Making

Perhaps the most basic managerial skill is the ability to make intelligent, data-driven decisions. Broadly speaking, many of those decisions revolve around the following three questions. *What* should we be selling? *Who* should we be serving? *How* should we execute? Exhibit 1–2 provides examples of decisions pertaining to each of these three categories.

The left-hand column of Exhibit 1–2 suggests that every company must make decisions related to the products and services that it sells. For example, each year Procter & Gamble must decide how to allocate its marketing budget across 23 brands that each generates over $1 billion in sales as well as other brands that have promising growth potential. Mattel must decide what new toys to introduce to the market. Southwest Airlines must decide what ticket prices to establish for each of its thousands of flights per day. General Motors must decide whether to discontinue certain models of automobiles.

EXHIBIT 1–2
Examples of Decisions

What should we be selling?	Who should we be serving?	How should we execute?
What products and services should be the focus of our marketing efforts?	Who should be the focus of our marketing efforts?	How should we supply our parts and services?
What new products and services should we offer?	Who should we start serving?	How should we expand our capacity?
What prices should we charge for our products and services?	Who should pay price premiums or receive price discounts?	How should we reduce our capacity?
What products and services should we discontinue?	Who should we stop serving?	How should we improve our efficiency and effectiveness?

The middle column of Exhibit 1–2 indicates that all companies must make decisions related to the customers that they serve. For example, Sears must decide how to allocate its marketing budget between products that tend to appeal to male versus female customers. FedEx must decide whether to expand its services into new markets across the globe. Hewlett-Packard must decide what price discounts to offer corporate clients that purchase large volumes of its products. A bank must decide whether to discontinue customers that may be unprofitable.

The right-hand column of Exhibit 1–2 shows that companies also make decisions related to how they execute. For example, Boeing must decide whether to rely on outside vendors such as Goodrich, Saab, and Rolls-Royce to manufacture many of the parts used to make its airplanes. Cintas must decide whether to expand its laundering and cleaning capacity in a given geographic region by adding square footage to an existing facility or by constructing an entirely new facility. In an economic downturn, a manufacturer might have to decide whether to eliminate one 8-hour shift at three plants or to close one plant. Finally, all companies have to decide among competing improvement opportunities. For example, a company may have to decide whether to implement a new software system, to upgrade a piece of equipment, or to provide extra training to its employees.

This portion of the chapter has explained that the three pillars of managerial accounting are planning, controlling, and decision making. This book helps prepare you to become an effective manager by explaining how to make intelligent data-driven decisions, how to create financial plans for the future, and how to continually make progress toward achieving goals by obtaining, evaluating, and responding to feedback.

Why Does Managerial Accounting Matter to Your Career?

Many students feel anxious about choosing a major because they are unsure if it will provide a fulfilling career. To reduce these anxieties, we recommend deemphasizing what you cannot control about the future, instead focusing on what you can control right now. More specifically, concentrate on answering the following question: What can you do now to prepare for success in an unknown future career? The best answer is to learn skills that will make it easier for you to adapt to an uncertain future. You need to become adaptable!

Whether you end up working in the United States or abroad, for a large corporation, a small entrepreneurial company, a nonprofit organization, or a governmental entity, you'll need to know how to plan for the future, how to make progress toward achieving goals, and how to make intelligent decisions. In other words, managerial accounting skills are useful in just about any career, organization, and industry. If you commit energy to this course, you'll be making a smart investment in your future—even though you cannot clearly envision it. Next, we will elaborate on this point by explaining how managerial accounting relates to the future careers of business majors and accounting majors.

Business Majors

Exhibit 1–3 provides examples of how planning, controlling, and decision making affect three majors other than accounting—marketing, supply chain management, and human resource management.

The left-hand column of Exhibit 1–3 describes some planning, controlling, and decision-making applications in the marketing profession. For example, marketing managers make planning decisions related to allocating advertising dollars across various communication mediums and to staffing new sales territories. From a control standpoint, they may closely track sales data to see if a budgeted price cut is generating an anticipated increase in unit sales, or they may study inventory levels during the holiday shopping

EXHIBIT 1–3
Relating Managerial Accounting to Three Business Majors

	Marketing	Supply Chain Management	Human Resource Management
Planning	How much should we budget for TV, print, and Internet advertising?	How many units should we plan to produce next period?	How much should we plan to spend for occupational safety training?
	How many sales-people should we plan to hire to serve a new territory?	How much should we budget for next period's utility expense?	How much should we plan to spend on employee recruit-ment advertising?
Controlling	Is the budgeted price cut increasing unit sales as expected?	Did we spend more or less than expected for the units we actually produced?	Is our employee retention rate exceeding our goals?
	Are we accumulating too much inventory during the holiday shopping season?	Are we achieving our goal of reducing the number of defective units produced?	Are we meeting our goal of completing timely performance appraisals?
Decision Making	Should we sell our ser-vices as one bundle or sell them separately?	Should we transfer production of a component part to an overseas supplier?	Should we hire an on-site medical staff to lower our health care costs?
	Should we sell directly to customers or use a distributor?	Should we redesign our manufacturing process to lower inventory levels?	Should we hire tem-porary workers or full-time employees?

season so that they can adjust prices as needed to optimize sales. Marketing managers also make many important decisions such as whether to bundle services together and sell them for one price or to sell each service separately. They may also decide whether to sell products directly to the customer or to sell to a distributor, who then sells to the end consumer.

The middle column of Exhibit 1–3 states that supply chain managers have to plan how many units to produce to satisfy anticipated customer demand. They also need to budget for operating expenses such as utilities, supplies, and labor costs. In terms of control, they monitor actual spending relative to the budget, and closely watch operational measures such as the number of defects produced relative to the plan. Supply chain managers make numerous decisions, such as deciding whether to transfer production of a component part to an overseas supplier. They also decide whether to invest in redesigning a manufacturing process to reduce inventory levels.

The right-hand column of Exhibit 1–3 explains how human resource managers make a variety of planning decisions, such as budgeting how much to spend on occupational safety training and employee recruitment advertising. They monitor feedback related to numerous management concerns, such as employee retention rates and the timely completion of employee performance appraisals. They also help make many important decisions such as whether to hire on-site medical staff in an effort to lower health care costs, and whether to hire temporary workers or full-time employees in an uncertain economy.

For brevity, Exhibit 1–3 does not include all business majors, such as finance, management information systems, and economics. Can you explain how planning, controlling, and decision-making activities would relate to these majors?

Accounting Majors

Many accounting graduates begin their careers working for public accounting firms that provide a variety of valuable services for their clients. Some of these graduates will build successful and fulfilling careers in the public accounting industry; however, most will leave public accounting at some point to work in other organizations. In fact, the Institute of Management Accountants (IMA) estimates that more than 80% of professional accountants in the United States work in nonpublic accounting environments (**www.imanet.org/about_ima/our_mission.aspx**).

The public accounting profession has a strong financial accounting orientation. Its most important function is to protect investors and other external parties by assuring them that companies are reporting historical financial results that comply with applicable accounting rules. Managerial accountants also have strong financial accounting skills. For example, they play an important role in helping their organizations design and maintain financial reporting systems that generate reliable financial disclosures. However, the primary role of managerial accountants is to partner with their co-workers within the organization to improve performance.

Given the 80% figure mentioned above, if you are an accounting major there is a very high likelihood that your future will involve working for a nonpublic accounting employer. Your employer will expect you to have strong financial accounting skills, but more importantly, it will expect you to help improve organizational performance by applying the planning, controlling, and decision-making skills that are the foundation of managerial accounting.

IN BUSINESS

A NETWORKING OPPORTUNITY

The Institute of Management Accountants (IMA) is a network of more than 70,000 accounting and finance professionals from over 120 countries. Every year the IMA hosts a student leadership conference that attracts 300 students from over 50 colleges and universities. Guest speakers at past conferences have discussed topics such as leadership, advice for a successful career, how to market yourself in a difficult economy, and excelling in today's multigenerational workforce. One student who attended the conference said, "I liked that I was able to interact with professionals who are in fields that could be potential career paths for me." For more information on this worthwhile networking opportunity, contact the IMA at the phone number and website shown below.

Source: Conversation with Jodi Ryan, the Institute of Management Accountants' Director, Education/Corporate Partnerships. (201) 474-1556 or visit its website at www.imanet.org.

Professional Certification—A Smart Investment If you plan to become an accounting major, the Certified Management Accountant (CMA) designation is a globally respected credential (sponsored by the IMA) that will increase your credibility, upward mobility, and compensation. Exhibit 1–4 summarizes the topics covered in the two-part CMA exam. For brevity, we are not going to define all the terms included in this exhibit. Its purpose is simply to emphasize that the CMA exam focuses on the planning, controlling, and decision-making skills that are critically important to nonpublic accounting employers. The CMA's internal management orientation is a complement to the highly respected Certified Public Accountant (CPA) exam that focuses on rule-based compliance—assurance standards, financial accounting standards, business law, and the tax code. Information about becoming a CMA is available on the IMA's website (www.imanet.org) or by calling 1-800-638-4427.

EXHIBIT 1–4
CMA Exam Content Specifications

Part 1	*Financial Reporting, Planning, Performance and Control*
	External financial reporting decisions
	Planning, budgeting, and forecasting
	Performance management
	Cost management
	Internal controls
Part 2	*Financial Decision Making*
	Financial statement analysis
	Corporate finance
	Decision analysis
	Risk management
	Investment decisions
	Professional ethics

IN BUSINESS

HOW'S THE PAY?

The Institute of Management Accountants has created the following table that allows individuals to estimate what their salary would be as a management accountant.

			Your Calculation
Start with this base amount		$75,879	$75,879
If you are top-level management	ADD	$48,471	
OR, if you are senior-level management.	ADD	$26,516	
OR, if you are entry-level management.	SUBTRACT	$22,137	
Number of years in the field ______	TIMES	$ 7	
If you have an advanced degree	ADD	$14,662	
If you hold the CMA	ADD	$19,992	
If you hold the CPA	ADD	$15,837	______
Your estimated salary level			______

For example, if you make it to top-level management in 10 years, have an advanced degree and a CMA, your estimated salary would be $159,074 [$75,879 + $48,471 + (10 × 7) + $14,662 + $19,992].

Source: Lee Schiffel, and Coleen Wilder, "IMA 2013 Salary Survey. Rainy Days Persist," *Strategic Finance* June 2014, pp. 23–39.

Managerial Accounting: Beyond the Numbers

Exhibit 1–5 summarizes how each chapter of the book teaches measurement skills that managers use on the job every day. For example, Chapter 9 teaches you the measurement skills that managers use to answer the question—how should I create a financial plan for next year? Chapters 10 and 11 teach you the measurement skills that managers use to answer the question—how well am I performing relative to my plan? Chapter 6 teaches you measurement skills related to product, service, and customer profitability. However, it is vitally important that you also understand managerial accounting involves more than just "crunching numbers." To be successful, managers must complement their

EXHIBIT 1–5
Measurement Skills: A Manager's Perspective

Chapter Number	The Key Question from a Manager's Perspective
Chapter 2	What cost classifications do I use for different management purposes?
Chapter 3	How will my profits change if I change my selling price, sales volume, or costs?
Chapter 4	What is the value of our ending inventory and cost of goods sold for external reporting purposes?
Chapter 5	How should the income statement be presented?
Chapter 6	How profitable is each of our products, services, and customers?
Chapter 7	How do I quantify the profit impact of pursuing one course of action versus another?
Chapter 8	How do I make long-term capital investment decisions?
Chapter 9	How should I create a financial plan for next year?
Chapters 10 & 11	How well am I performing relative to my plan?
Chapter 12	What performance measures should we monitor to ensure that we achieve our strategic goals?

measurement skills with six business management perspectives that "go beyond the numbers" to enable intelligent planning, control, and decision making.

An Ethics Perspective

Ethical behavior is the lubricant that keeps the economy running. Without that lubricant, the economy would operate much less efficiently—less would be available to consumers, quality would be lower, and prices would be higher. In other words, without fundamental trust in the integrity of business, the economy would operate much less efficiently. Thus, for the good of everyone—including profit-making companies—it is vitally important that business be conducted within an ethical framework that builds and sustains trust.

Code of Conduct for Management Accountants The Institute of Management Accountants (IMA) of the United States has adopted an ethical code called the *Statement of Ethical Professional Practice* that describes in some detail the ethical responsibilities of management accountants. Even though the standards were developed specifically for management accountants, they have much broader application. The standards consist of two parts that are presented in full in Exhibit 1–6. The first part provides general guidelines for ethical behavior. In a nutshell, a management accountant has ethical responsibilities in four broad areas: first, to maintain a high level of professional competence; second, to treat sensitive matters with confidentiality; third, to maintain personal integrity; and fourth, to disclose information in a credible fashion. The second part of the standards specifies what should be done if an individual finds evidence of ethical misconduct.

The ethical standards provide sound, practical advice for management accountants and managers. Most of the rules in the ethical standards are motivated by a very practical consideration—if these rules were not generally followed in business, then the economy and all of us would suffer. Consider the following specific examples of the consequences of not abiding by the standards:

- Suppose employees could not be trusted with confidential information. Then top managers would be reluctant to distribute such information within the company and, as a result, decisions would be based on incomplete information and operations would deteriorate.

EXHIBIT 1–6
IMA Statement of Ethical Professional Practice

Members of IMA shall behave ethically. A commitment to ethical professional practice includes: overarching principles that express our values, and standards that guide our conduct.

PRINCIPLES

IMA's overarching ethical principles include: Honesty, Fairness, Objectivity, and Responsibility. Members shall act in accordance with these principles and shall encourage others within their organizations to adhere to them.

STANDARDS

A member's failure to comply with the following standards may result in disciplinary action.

I. COMPETENCE

Each member has a responsibility to:
1. Maintain an appropriate level of professional expertise by continually developing knowledge and skills.
2. Perform professional duties in accordance with relevant laws, regulations, and technical standards.
3. Provide decision support information and recommendations that are accurate, clear, concise, and timely.
4. Recognize and communicate professional limitations or other constraints that would preclude responsible judgment or successful performance of an activity.

II. CONFIDENTIALITY

Each member has a responsibility to:
1. Keep information confidential except when disclosure is authorized or legally required.
2. Inform all relevant parties regarding appropriate use of confidential information. Monitor subordinates' activities to ensure compliance.
3. Refrain from using confidential information for unethical or illegal advantage.

III. INTEGRITY

Each member has a responsibility to:
1. Mitigate actual conflicts of interest. Regularly communicate with business associates to avoid apparent conflicts of interest. Advise all parties of any potential conflicts.
2. Refrain from engaging in any conduct that would prejudice carrying out duties ethically.
3. Abstain from engaging in or supporting any activity that might discredit the profession.

IV. CREDIBILITY

Each member has a responsibility to:
1. Communicate information fairly and objectively.
2. Disclose all relevant information that could reasonably be expected to influence an intended user's understanding of the reports, analyses, or recommendations.
3. Disclose delays or deficiencies in information, timeliness, processing, or internal controls in conformance with organization policy and/or applicable law.

RESOLUTION OF ETHICAL CONFLICT

In applying the Standards of Ethical Professional Practice, you may encounter problems identifying unethical behavior or resolving an ethical conflict. When faced with ethical issues, you should follow your organization's established policies on the resolution of such conflict. If these policies do not resolve the ethical conflict, you should consider the following courses of action:
1. Discuss the issue with your immediate supervisor except when it appears that the supervisor is involved. In that case, present the issue to the next level. If you cannot achieve a satisfactory resolution, submit the issue to the next management level. If your immediate superior is the chief executive officer or equivalent, the acceptable reviewing authority may be a group such as the audit committee, executive committee, board of directors, board of trustees, or owners. Contact with levels above the immediate superior should be initiated only with your superior's knowledge, assuming he or she is not involved. Communication of such problems to authorities or individuals not employed or engaged by the organization is not considered appropriate, unless you believe there is a clear violation of the law.
2. Clarify relevant ethical issues by initiating a confidential discussion with an IMA Ethics Counselor or other impartial advisor to obtain a better understanding of possible courses of action.
3. Consult your own attorney as to legal obligations and rights concerning the ethical conflict.

- Suppose employees accepted bribes from suppliers. Then contracts would tend to go to the suppliers who pay the highest bribes rather than to the most competent suppliers. Would you like to fly in aircraft whose wings were made by the subcontractor who paid the highest bribe? Would you fly as often? What would happen to the airline industry if its safety record deteriorated due to shoddy workmanship on contracted parts and subassemblies?
- Suppose the presidents of companies routinely lied in their annual reports and financial statements. If investors could not rely on the basic integrity of a company's financial statements, they would have little basis for making informed decisions. Suspecting the worst, rational investors would pay less for securities issued by companies and may not be willing to invest at all. As a consequence, companies would have less money for productive investments—leading to slower economic growth, fewer goods and services, and higher prices.

IN BUSINESS

TOYOTA ENCOUNTERS MAJOR PROBLEMS

When Toyota Motor Corporation failed to meet its profit targets, the company set an aggressive goal of reducing the cost of its auto parts by 30%. The quality and safety of the company's automobiles eventually suffered mightily resulting in recalls, litigation, incentive campaigns, and marketing efforts that analysts estimate will cost the company more than $5 billion. The car maker's president, Akio Toyoda, blamed his company's massive quality lapses on an excessive focus on profits and market share. Similarly, Jim Press, Toyota's former top U.S. executive, said the problems were caused by "financially-oriented pirates who didn't have the character to maintain a customer-first focus."

Sources: Yoshio Takahashi, "Toyota Accelerates Its Cost-Cutting Efforts," *The Wall Street Journal*, December 23, 2009, p. B4; Mariko Sanchanta and Yoshio Takahashi, "Toyota's Recall May Top $5 Billion," *The Wall Street Journal*, March 10, 2010, p. B2; and Norihiko Shirouzu, "Toyoda Rues Excessive Profit Focus," *The Wall Street Journal*, March 2, 2010, p. B3.

© Irene Alastruey/Author's Image/ Punchstock, RF

Not only is ethical behavior the lubricant for our economy, it is the foundation of managerial accounting. The numbers that managers rely on for planning, control, and decision making are meaningless unless they have been competently, objectively, and honestly gathered, analyzed, and reported. As your career unfolds, you will inevitably face decisions with ethical implications. Before making such decisions, consider performing the following steps. First, define your alternative courses of action. Second, identify all of the parties that will be affected by your decision. Third, define how each course of action will favorably or unfavorably impact each affected party. Once you have a complete understanding of the decision context, seek guidance from external sources such as the IMA Statement of Ethical Professional Practice, the IMA Ethics Helpline at (800) 245-1383, or a trusted confidant. Before executing your decision ask yourself one final question—would I be comfortable disclosing my chosen course of action on the front page of *The Wall Street Journal?*

A Strategic Management Perspective

Companies do not succeed by sheer luck; instead, they need to develop a *strategy* that defines how they intend to succeed in the marketplace. A **strategy** is a "game plan" that enables a company to attract customers by distinguishing itself from competitors. The focal point of a company's strategy should be its target customers. A company can only succeed if it creates a reason for its target customers to choose it over a competitor. These reasons, or what are more formally called *customer value propositions,* are the essence of strategy.

Customer value propositions tend to fall into three broad categories—*customer intimacy, operational excellence,* and *product leadership.* Companies that adopt a *customer intimacy* strategy are in essence saying to their customers, "You should choose us because we can customize our products and services to meet your individual needs better than our competitors." Ritz-Carlton, Nordstrom, and Virtuoso (a premium service travel agency) rely primarily on a customer intimacy value proposition for their success. Companies that pursue the second customer value proposition, called *operational excellence,* are saying to their target customers, "You should choose us because we deliver products and services faster, more conveniently, and at a lower price than our competitors." Southwest Airlines, Walmart, and Google are examples of companies that succeed first and foremost because of their operational excellence. Companies pursuing the third customer value proposition, called *product leadership,* are saying to their target customers, "You should choose us because we offer higher quality products than our competitors." Apple, Cisco Systems, and W.L. Gore (the creator of GORE-TEX® fabrics) are examples of companies that succeed because of their product leadership.[1]

The plans managers set forth, the variables they seek to control, and the decisions they make are all influenced by their company's strategy. For example, Walmart would not make plans to build ultra-expensive clothing boutiques because these plans would conflict with the company's strategy of operational excellence and "everyday low prices." Apple would not seek to control its operations by selecting performance measures that focus solely on cost-cutting because those measures would conflict with its product leadership customer value proposition. Finally, it is unlikely that Rolex would decide to implement drastic price reductions for its watches even if a financial analysis indicated that establishing a lower price might boost short-run profits. Rolex would oppose this course of action because it would diminish the luxury brand that forms the foundation of the company's product leadership customer value proposition.

IN BUSINESS

© John Foxx Images/Imagestate Media (John Foxx)/Imagestate, RF

A FOUR-YEAR WAITING LIST AT VANILLA BICYCLES

Sacha White started Vanilla Bicycles in Portland, Oregon, in 2001. After eight years in business, he had a four-year backlog of customer orders. He limits his annual production to 40–50 bikes per year that sell for an average of $7,000 each. He uses a silver alloy that costs 20 times as much as brass (which is the industry standard) to join titanium tubes together to form a bike frame. White spends three hours taking a buyer's measurements to determine the exact dimensions of the bike frame. He has resisted expanding production because it would undermine his strategy based on product leadership and customer intimacy. As White said, "If I ended up sacrificing what made Vanilla special just to make more bikes, that wouldn't be worth it to me."

Source: Christopher Steiner, "Heaven on Wheels," *Forbes,* April 13, 2009, p. 75.

An Enterprise Risk Management Perspective

Every strategy, plan, and decision involves risks. **Enterprise risk management** is a process used by a company to identify those risks and develop responses to them that enable it to be reasonably assured of meeting its goals. The left-hand column of Exhibit 1–7 provides 12 examples of the types of business risks that companies face. They range from risks that relate to the weather to risks associated with computer hackers, complying with the law, employee theft, and products harming customers. The right-hand column of Exhibit 1–7 provides an example of a control that could be implemented to help reduce each of the risks mentioned in the left-hand column of the exhibit.[2] Although these types of controls

---

[1] These three customer value propositions were defined by Michael Treacy and Fred Wiersema in "Customer Intimacy and Other Value Disciplines," *Harvard Business Review,* Volume 71 Issue 1, pp. 84–93.

[2] Besides using controls to reduce risks, companies can also chose other risk responses, such as accepting or avoiding a risk.

EXHIBIT 1–7
Identifying and Controlling Business Risks

Examples of Business Risks	Examples of Controls to Reduce Business Risks
• Intellectual assets being stolen from computer files	• Create firewalls that prohibit computer hackers from corrupting or stealing intellectual property
• Products harming customers	• Develop a formal and rigorous new product testing program
• Losing market share due to the unforeseen actions of competitors	• Develop an approach for legally gathering information about competitors' plans and practices
• Poor weather conditions shutting down operations	• Develop contingency plans for overcoming weather-related disruptions
• A website malfunctioning	• Thoroughly test the website before going "live" on the Internet
• A supplier strike halting the flow of raw materials	• Establish a relationship with two companies capable of providing needed raw materials
• A poorly designed incentive compensation system causing employees to make bad decisions	• Create a balanced set of performance measures that motivates the desired behavior
• Financial statements inaccurately reporting the value of inventory	• Count the physical inventory on hand to make sure that it agrees with the accounting records
• An employee stealing assets	• Segregate duties so that the same employee does not have physical custody of an asset and the responsibility of accounting for it
• An employee accessing unauthorized information	• Create password-protected barriers that prohibit employees from obtaining information not needed to do their jobs
• Inaccurate budget estimates causing excessive or insufficient production	• Implement a rigorous budget review process
• Failing to comply with equal employment opportunity laws	• Create a report that tracks key metrics related to compliance with the laws

cannot completely eliminate risks, they enable companies to proactively manage their risks rather than passively reacting to unfortunate events that have already occurred.

In managerial accounting, companies use controls to reduce the risk that their plans will not be achieved. For example, if a company plans to build a new manufacturing facility within a predefined budget and time frame, it will establish and monitor control measures to ensure that the project is concluded on time and within the budget. Risk management is also a critically important aspect of decision making. For example, when a company quantifies the labor cost savings that it can realize by sending jobs overseas, it should complement its financial analysis with a prudent assessment of the accompanying risks. Will the overseas manufacturer use child labor? Will the product's quality decline, thereby leading to more warranty repairs, customer complaints, and lawsuits? Will the elapsed time from customer order to delivery dramatically increase? Will terminating domestic employees diminish morale within the company and harm perceptions within the community? These are the types of risks that managers should incorporate into their decision-making processes.

IN BUSINESS

MANAGING THE RISK OF A POWER OUTAGE

Between January and April of 2010, the United States had 35 major power outages. For business owners, these power outages can be costly. For example, a New York night club called the Smoke Jazz and Supper Club lost an estimated $1,500 in revenue when a power outage shut down its on-line reservation system for one night. George Pauli, the owner of Great Embroidery LLC in Mesa, Arizona, estimates that his company has an average of six power outages every year. Since Pauli's sewing machines cannot resume exactly where they leave off when abruptly shut down, each power outage costs him $120 in lost inventory. Pauli decided to buy $700 worth of batteries to keep his sewing machines running during power outages. The batteries paid for themselves in less than one year.

Source: Sarah E. Needleman, "Lights Out Means Lost Sales," *The Wall Street Journal,* July 22, 2010, p. B8.

A Corporate Social Responsibility Perspective

Companies are responsible for creating strategies that produce financial results that satisfy stockholders. However, they also have a *corporate social responsibility* to serve other stakeholders—such as customers, employees, suppliers, communities, and environmental and human rights advocates—whose interests are tied to the company's performance. **Corporate social responsibility** (CSR) is a concept whereby organizations consider the needs of all stakeholders when making decisions. CSR extends beyond legal compliance to include voluntary actions that satisfy stakeholder expectations. Numerous companies, such as Procter & Gamble, 3M, Eli Lilly and Company, Starbucks, Microsoft, Genentech, Johnson & Johnson, Baxter International, Abbott Laboratories, KPMG, PNC Bank, Deloitte, Southwest Airlines, and Caterpillar, prominently describe their corporate social performance on their websites.

Exhibit 1–8 presents examples of corporate social responsibilities that are of interest to six stakeholder groups.[3] If a company fails to meet the needs of these six stakeholder groups it can adversely affect its financial performance. For example, if a company pollutes the environment or fails to provide safe and humane working conditions for its employees, the negative publicity from environmental and human rights activists could cause the company's customers to defect and its "best and brightest" job candidates to apply elsewhere—both of which are likely to eventually harm financial performance. This explains why in managerial accounting a manager must establish plans, implement controls, and make decisions that consider impacts on all stakeholders.

IN BUSINESS

GREENPEACE LEVERAGES THE POWER OF SOCIAL MEDIA

When Nestlé purchased palm oil from an Indonesian supplier to manufacture Kit-Kat candy bars, Greenpeace International used social media to express its disapproval. Greenpeace claimed that the Indonesian company destroyed rainforest to create its palm oil plantation; therefore, Nestlé's actions were contributing to global warming and endangering orangutans. Greenpeace posted YouTube videos, added comments to Nestlé's Facebook page, and sent Twitter Tweets to communicate its message to supporters. At one point, the number of fans on Nestlé's Facebook page grew to 95,000, most of them being protesters. Nestlé terminated its relationship with the supplier, which provided 1.25% of Nestlé's palm oil needs. A Nestlé spokesperson says the difficulty in responding to social media is to "show that we are listening, which we obviously are, while not getting involved in a shouting match."

Source: Emily Steel, "Nestlé Takes a Beating on Social-Media Sites," *The Wall Street Journal,* March 29, 2010, p. B5.

[3] Many of the examples in Exhibit 1-8 were drawn from Terry Leap and Misty L. Loughry, "The Stakeholder-Friendly Firm," *Business Horizons,* March/April 2004, pp. 27–32.

EXHIBIT 1–8
Examples of Corporate Social Responsibilities

Companies should provide *customers* with:
- Safe, high-quality products that are fairly priced.
- Competent, courteous, and rapid delivery of products and services.
- Full disclosure of product-related risks.
- Easy-to-use information systems for shopping and tracking orders.

Companies should provide *suppliers* with:
- Fair contract terms and prompt payments.
- Reasonable time to prepare orders.
- Hassle-free acceptance of timely and complete deliveries.
- Cooperative rather than unilateral actions.

Companies should provide *stockholders* with:
- Competent management.
- Easy access to complete and accurate financial information.
- Full disclosure of enterprise risks.
- Honest answers to knowledgeable questions.

Companies and their suppliers should provide *employees* with:
- Safe and humane working conditions.
- Nondiscriminatory treatment and the right to organize and file grievances.
- Fair compensation.
- Opportunities for training, promotion, and personal development.

Companies should provide *communities* with:
- Payment of fair taxes.
- Honest information about plans such as plant closings.
- Resources that support charities, schools, and civic activities.
- Reasonable access to media sources.

Companies should provide *environmental and human rights advocates* with:
- Greenhouse gas emissions data.
- Recycling and resource conservation data.
- Child labor transparency.
- Full disclosure of suppliers located in developing countries.

A Process Management Perspective

Most companies organize themselves by functional departments, such as the Marketing Department, the Research and Development Department, and the Accounting Department. These departments tend to have a clearly defined "chain of command" that specifies superior and subordinate relationships. However, effective managers understand that *business processes,* more so than functional departments, serve the needs of a company's most important stakeholders—its customers. A **business process** is a series of steps that are followed in order to carry out some task in a business. These steps often span departmental boundaries, thereby requiring managers to cooperate across functional departments. The term *value chain* is often used to describe how an organization's functional departments interact with one another to form business processes. A **value chain**, as shown in Exhibit 1–9, consists of the major business functions that add value to a company's products and services.

EXHIBIT 1–9
Business Functions Making Up the Value Chain

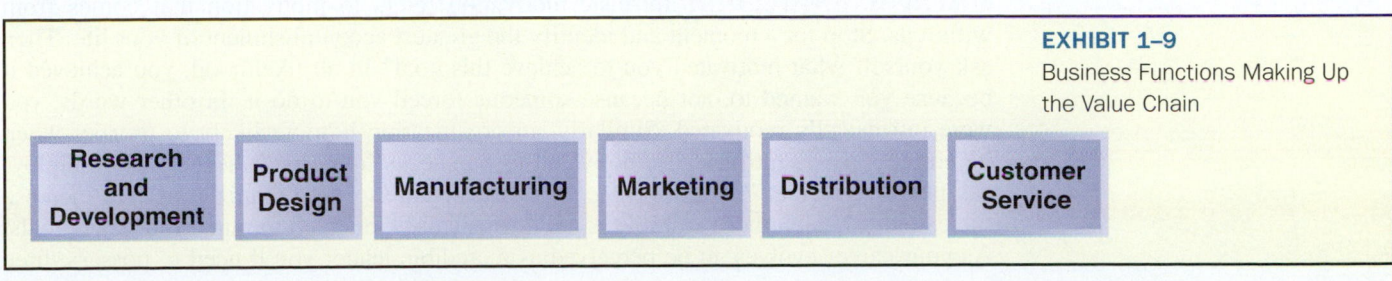

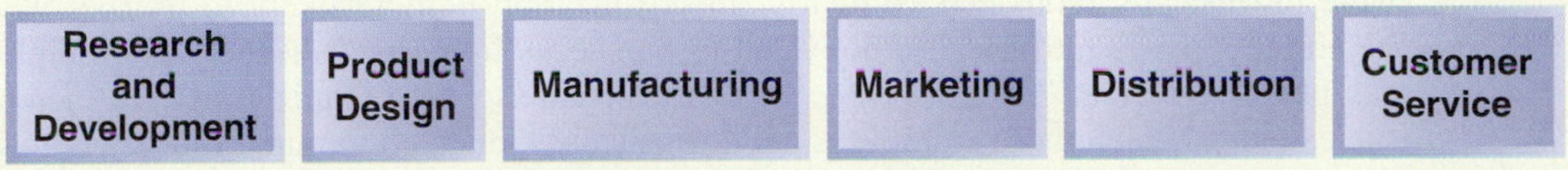

Managers need to understand the value chain to be effective in terms of planning, control, and decision making. For example, if a company's engineers plan to design a new product, they must communicate with the Manufacturing Department to ensure that the product can actually be produced, the Marketing Department to ensure that customers will buy the product, the Distribution Department to ensure that large volumes of the product can be cost-effectively transported to customers, and the Accounting Department to ensure that the product will increase profits. From a control and decision-making standpoint, managers also need to focus on process excellence instead of functional performance. For example, if the Purchasing Department focuses solely on minimizing the cost of purchased materials, this narrowly focused attempt at cost reduction may lead to greater scrap and rework in the Manufacturing Department, more complaints in the Customer Service Department, and greater challenges in the Marketing Department because dissatisfied customers are turning their attention to competitors.

Managers frequently use a process management method known as *lean thinking,* or what is called *Lean Production* in the manufacturing sector. **Lean Production** is a management approach that organizes resources such as people and machines around the flow of business processes and that only produces units in response to customer orders. It is often called *just-in-time* production (or *JIT*) because products are only manufactured in response to customer orders and they are completed just-in-time to be shipped to customers. Lean thinking differs from traditional manufacturing methods, which organize work departmentally and encourage departments to maximize their output even if it exceeds customer demand and bloats inventories. Because lean thinking only allows production in response to customer orders, the number of units produced tends to equal the number of units sold, thereby resulting in minimal inventory. The lean approach also results in fewer defects, less wasted effort, and quicker customer response times than traditional production methods.

IN BUSINESS

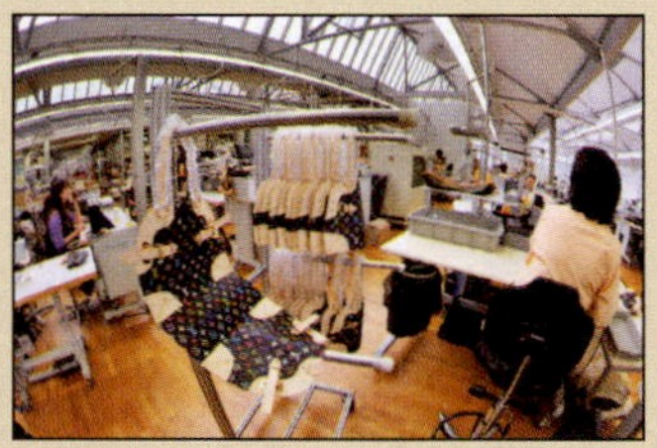

© Miguel Medina/AFP/Getty Images

LOUIS VUITTON IMPLEMENTS LEAN PRODUCTION

Louis Vuitton, headquartered in Paris, France, used lean production to increase its manufacturing capacity without having to build a new factory. It created U-shaped work arrangements for teams of 10 workers, thereby freeing up 10% more floor space in its factories. The company was able to hire 300 more workers without adding any square footage. Louis Vuitton also uses robots and computer programs to reduce wasted leather and the time needed to perform certain tasks.

Source: Christina Passariello, "At Vuitton, Growth in Small Batches," *The Wall Street Journal,* June 27, 2011, pp. B1 and B10.

A Leadership Perspective

An organization's employees bring diverse needs, beliefs, and goals to the workplace. Therefore, an important role for organizational leaders is to unite the behaviors of their fellow employees around two common themes—pursuing strategic goals and making optimal decisions. To fulfill this responsibility, leaders need to understand how *intrinsic motivation, extrinsic incentives,* and *cognitive bias* influence human behavior.

Intrinsic Motivation Intrinsic motivation refers to motivation that comes from within us. Stop for a moment and identify the greatest accomplishment of your life. Then ask yourself what motivated you to achieve this goal? In all likelihood, you achieved it because you wanted to, not because someone forced you to do it. In other words, you were intrinsically motivated. Similarly, an organization is more likely to prosper when its employees are intrinsically motivated to pursue its interests. A leader, who employees perceive as *credible* and *respectful* of their value to the organization, can increase the extent to which those employees are intrinsically motivated to pursue strategic goals. As your career evolves, to be perceived as a credible leader you'll need to possess three attributes—technical competence (that spans the value chain), personal integrity (in terms of work ethic and honesty), and strong communication skills (including oral presentation skills and writing skills). To be perceived as a leader who is respectful of your co-workers' value to the organization, you'll need to possess three more attributes—strong mentoring skills (to help others realize their potential), strong listening skills (to learn from your co-workers and be responsive to their needs), and personal humility (in terms of deferring recognition to all employees who contribute to the organization's success). If you possess these six traits, then you'll have the potential to become a leader who inspires others to readily and energetically channel their efforts toward achieving organizational goals.

Extrinsic Incentives Many organizations use *extrinsic incentives* to highlight important goals and to motivate employees to achieve them. For example, assume a company establishes the goal of reducing the time needed to perform a task by 20%. In addition, assume the company agrees to pay bonus compensation to its employees if they achieve the goal within three months. In this example, the company is using a type of extrinsic incentive known as a bonus to highlight a particular goal and to presumably motivate employees to achieve it.

While proponents of extrinsic incentives rightly assert that these types of rewards can have a powerful influence on employee behavior, many critics warn that they can also produce dysfunctional consequences. For example, suppose the employees mentioned above earned their bonuses by achieving the 20% time reduction goal within three months. However, let's also assume that during those three months the quality of the employees' output plummeted, thereby causing a spike in the company's repair costs, product returns, and customer defections. In this instance, did the extrinsic incentive work properly? The answer is yes and no. The bonus system did motivate employees to attain the time reduction goal; however, it also had the unintended consequences of causing employees to neglect product quality, thereby increasing repair costs, product returns, and customer defections. In other words, what may have seemed like a well-intended extrinsic incentive actually produced dysfunctional results for the company. This example highlights an important leadership challenge that you are likely to face someday—designing financial compensation systems that fairly reward employees for their efforts without inadvertently creating extrinsic incentives that motivate them to take actions that harm the company.

Cognitive Bias Leaders need to be aware that all people (including themselves) possess *cognitive biases,* or distorted thought processes, that can adversely affect planning, controlling, and decision making. To illustrate how cognitive bias works, let's consider the scenario of a television "infomercial" where someone is selling a product with a proclaimed value of $200 for $19.99 if viewers call within the next 30 minutes. Why do you think the seller claims that the product has a $200 value? The seller is relying on a cognitive bias called *anchoring bias* in an effort to convince viewers that a $180 discount is simply too good to pass up. The "anchor" is the false assertion that the product is actually worth $200. If viewers erroneously attach credibility to this contrived piece of information, their distorted analysis of the situation may cause them to spend $19.99 on an item whose true economic value is much less than that amount.

While cognitive biases cannot be eliminated, effective leaders should take two steps to reduce their negative impacts. First, they should acknowledge their own susceptibility to cognitive bias. For example, a leader's judgment might be clouded by optimism bias (being overly optimistic in assessing the likelihood of future outcomes) or self-enhancement bias (overestimating ones strengths and underestimating ones weaknesses relative to others). Second, they should acknowledge the presence of cognitive bias in others and introduce techniques to minimize their adverse consequences. For example, to reduce the risks of confirmation bias (a bias where people pay greater attention to information that confirms their preconceived notions, while devaluing information that contradicts them) or groupthink bias (a bias where some group members support a course of action solely because other group members do), a leader may routinely appoint independent teams of employees to assess the credibility of recommendations set forth by other individuals and groups.

Summary

This chapter defined managerial accounting and explained why it is relevant to business and accounting majors. It also discussed six topics—ethics, strategic management, enterprise risk management, corporate social responsibility, process management, and leadership—that define the context for applying the quantitative aspects of managerial accounting. The most important goal of this chapter was to help you understand that managerial accounting matters to your future career regardless of your major. Accounting is the language of business and you'll need to speak it to communicate effectively with and influence fellow managers.

Glossary

Budget A detailed plan for the future that is usually expressed in formal quantitative terms. (p. 3)

Business process A series of steps that are followed in order to carry out some task in a business. (p. 15)

Controlling The process of gathering feedback to ensure that a plan is being properly executed or modified as circumstances change. (p. 3)

Corporate social responsibility A concept whereby organizations consider the needs of all stakeholders when making decisions. (p. 14)

Decision making Selecting a course of action from competing alternatives. (p. 3)

Enterprise risk management A process used by a company to identify its risks and develop responses to them that enable it to be reasonably assured of meeting its goals. (p. 12)

Financial accounting The phase of accounting that is concerned with reporting historical financial information to external parties, such as stockholders, creditors, and regulators. (p. 2)

Lean Production A management approach that organizes resources such as people and machines around the flow of business processes and that only produces units in response to customer orders. (p. 16)

Managerial accounting The phase of accounting that is concerned with providing information to managers for use within the organization. (p. 2)

Performance report A report that compares budgeted data to actual data to highlight instances of excellent and unsatisfactory performance. (p. 4)

Planning The process of establishing goals and specifying how to achieve them. (p. 3)

Segment A part or activity of an organization about which managers would like cost, revenue, or profit data. (p. 3)

Strategy A company's "game plan" for attracting customers by distinguishing itself from competitors. (p. 11)

Value chain The major business functions that add value to a company's products and services, such as research and development, product design, manufacturing, marketing, distribution, and customer service. (p. 15)

Questions

1–1 How does managerial accounting differ from financial accounting?

1–2 Pick any major television network and describe some planning and control activities that its managers would engage in.

1–3 If you had to decide whether to continue making a component part or to begin buying the part from an overseas supplier, what quantitative and qualitative factors would influence your decision?

1–4 Why do companies prepare budgets?

1–5 Why is managerial accounting relevant to business majors and their future careers?

1–6 Why is managerial accounting relevant to accounting majors and their future careers?

1–7 Pick any large company and describe its strategy using the framework in the chapter.

1–8 Why do management accountants need to understand their company's strategy?

1–9 Pick any large company and describe three risks that it faces and how it responds to those risks.

1–10 Provide three examples of how a company's risks can influence its planning, controlling, and decision-making activities.

1–11 Pick any large company and explain three ways that it could segment its companywide performance.

1–12 Locate the website of any company that publishes a corporate social responsibility report (also referred to as a sustainability report). Describe three nonfinancial performance measures included in the report. Why do you think the company publishes this report?

1–13 Why do companies that implement Lean Production tend to have minimal inventories?

1–14 Why are leadership skills important to managers?

1–15 Why is ethical behavior important to business?

Multiple-choice questions are available with Connect.

Additional student resources are available with Connect. connect

Exercises

EXERCISE 1–1 Planning and Control

Many companies use budgets for three purposes. First, they use them to plan how to deploy resources to best serve customers. Second, they use them to establish challenging goals, or stretch targets, to motivate employees to strive for exceptional results. Third, they use them to evaluate and reward employees.

Assume that you are a sales manager working with your boss to create a sales budget for next year. Once the sales budget is established, it will influence how other departments within the company plan to deploy their resources. For example, the manufacturing manager will plan to produce enough units to meet budgeted unit sales. The sales budget will also be instrumental in determining your pay raise, potential for promotion, and bonus. If actual sales exceed the sales budget, it bodes well for your career. If actual sales are less than budgeted sales, it will diminish your financial compensation and potential for promotion.

Required:

1. Do you think it would be appropriate for your boss to establish the sales budget without any input from you? Why?
2. Do you think the company would be comfortable with allowing you to establish the sales budget without any input from your boss? Why?
3. Assume the company uses its sales budget for only one purpose—planning to deploy resources in a manner that best serves customers. What thoughts would influence your estimate of future sales as well as your boss's estimate of future sales?
4. Assume the company uses its sales budget for only one purpose—motivating employees to strive for exceptional results. What thoughts would influence your estimate of future sales as well as your boss's estimate of future sales?
5. Assume the company uses its sales budget for only one purpose—to determine your pay raise, potential for promotion, and bonus. What thoughts would influence your estimate of future sales as well as your boss's estimate of future sales?
6. Assume the sales budget is used for all three purposes described in requirements 3–5. Describe any conflicts or complications that might arise when using the sales budget for these three purposes.

EXERCISE 1–2 Controlling

Assume that you work for an airline unloading luggage from airplanes. Your boss has said that, on average, each airplane contains 100 pieces of luggage. Furthermore, your boss has stated that you should be able to unload 100 pieces of luggage from an airplane in 10 minutes. Today an airplane arrived with 150 pieces of luggage and you unloaded all of it in 13 minutes. After finishing with the 150 pieces of luggage, your boss yelled at you for exceeding the 10-minute allowance for unloading luggage from an airplane.

Required:

1. How would you feel about being yelled at for taking 13 minutes to unload 150 pieces of luggage?
2. How does this scenario relate to the larger issue of how companies design control systems?

EXERCISE 1–3 Decision Making

Exhibit 1–2 includes 12 questions related to 12 types of decisions that companies often face. In the chapter, these 12 decisions were discussed within the context of for-profit companies; however, they are also readily applicable to nonprofit organizations. To illustrate this point, assume that you are a senior leader, such as a president, provost, or dean, in a university setting.

Required:

For each of the 12 decisions in Exhibit 1–2, provide an example of how that type of decision might be applicable to a university setting.

EXERCISE 1–4 Ethics and the Manager

Richmond, Inc., operates a chain of 44 department stores. Two years ago, the board of directors of Richmond approved a large-scale remodeling of its stores to attract a more upscale clientele.

Before finalizing these plans, two stores were remodeled as a test. Linda Perlman, assistant controller, was asked to oversee the financial reporting for these test stores, and she and other management personnel were offered bonuses based on the sales growth and profitability of these stores. While completing the financial reports, Perlman discovered a sizable inventory of outdated goods that should have been discounted for sale or returned to the manufacturer. She discussed the situation with her management colleagues; the consensus was to ignore reporting this inventory as obsolete because reporting it would diminish the financial results and their bonuses.

Required:

1. According to the IMA's Statement of Ethical Professional Practice, would it be ethical for Perlman *not* to report the inventory as obsolete?
2. Would it be easy for Perlman to take the ethical action in this situation? (CMA, adapted)

EXERCISE 1–5 Strategy

The table below contains the names of six companies.

Required:

For each company, categorize its strategy as being focused on customer intimacy, operational excellence, or product leadership. If you wish to improve your understanding of each company's customer value proposition before completing the exercise, review its most recent annual report. To obtain electronic access to this information, perform an Internet search on each company's name followed by the words "annual report."

Company	Strategy
1. Deere	?
2. FedEx	?
3. State Farm Insurance	?
4. BMW	?
5. Amazon.com	?
6. Charles Schwab	?

EXERCISE 1–6 Enterprise Risk Management

The table below refers to seven industries.

Required:

For each industry, identify one important risk faced by the companies that compete within that industry. Also, describe one control that companies could use to reduce the risk that you have identified.

Industry	Type of Risk	Control to Reduce the Risk
1. Airlines (e.g., Delta Airlines)		
2. Pharmaceutical drugs (e.g., Merck)		
3. Package delivery (e.g., United Parcel Service)		
4. Banking (e.g., Bank of America)		
5. Oil & gas (e.g., ExxonMobil)		
6. E-commerce (e.g., eBay)		
7. Automotive (e.g., Toyota)		

EXERCISE 1–7 Ethics in Business

Consumers and attorney generals in more than 40 states accused a prominent nationwide chain of auto repair shops of misleading customers and selling them unnecessary parts and services, from brake jobs to front-end alignments. Lynn Sharpe Paine reported the situation as follows in "Managing for Organizational Integrity," *Harvard Business Review,* Volume 72, Issue 3:

> In the face of declining revenues, shrinking market share, and an increasingly competitive market . . . management attempted to spur performance of its auto centers. . . . The automotive service advisers were given product-specific sales quotas—sell so many springs, shock absorbers, alignments, or brake jobs per shift—and paid a commission based on sales. . . . [F]ailure to meet quotas could lead to a transfer or a reduction in work hours. Some employees spoke of the "pressure, pressure, pressure" to bring in sales.
>
> This pressure-cooker atmosphere created conditions under which employees felt that the only way to satisfy top management was by selling products and services to customers that they didn't really need.

Suppose all automotive repair businesses routinely followed the practice of attempting to sell customers unnecessary parts and services.

Required:

1. How would this behavior affect customers? How might customers attempt to protect themselves against this behavior?
2. How would this behavior probably affect profits and employment in the automotive service industry?

EXERCISE 1–8 Cognitive Bias

In the 1970s, 1 million college-bound students were surveyed and asked to compare themselves to their peers. Some of the key findings of the survey were as follows:

a. 70% of the students rated themselves as above average in leadership ability, while only 2% rated themselves as below average in this regard.

b. With respect to athletic skills, 60% of the students rated their skills as above the median and only 6% of students rated themselves as below the median.

c. 60% of the students rated themselves in the top 10% in terms of their ability to get along with others, while 25% of the students felt that they were in the top 1% in terms of this interpersonal skill.

Required:

What type of cognitive bias reveals itself in the data mentioned above? How might this cognitive bias adversely influence a manager's planning, controlling, and decision-making activities? What steps could managers take to reduce the possibility that this cognitive bias would adversely influence their actions?

Source: Dan Lovallo and Daniel Kahneman, "Delusions of Success: How Optimism Undermines Executives' Decisions," *Harvard Business Review,* July 2003, pp. 56–63.

EXERCISE 1–9 Ethics and Decision Making

Assume that you are the chairman of the Department of Accountancy at Mountain State University. One of the accounting professors in your department, Dr. Candler, has been consistently and uniformly regarded by students as an awful teacher for more than 10 years. Other accounting professors within your department have observed Dr. Candler's classroom teaching and they concur that his teaching skills are very poor. However, Dr. Candler was granted tenure 12 years ago, thereby ensuring him life-long job security at Mountain State University.

Much to your surprise, today you received a phone from an accounting professor at Oregon Coastal University. During this phone call you are informed that Oregon Coastal University is on the verge of making a job offer to Dr. Candler. However, before extending the job offer, the faculty at Oregon Coastal wants your input regarding Dr. Candler's teaching effectiveness while at Mountain State University.

Required:

How would you respond to the professor from Oregon Coastal University? What would you say about Dr. Candler's teaching ability? Would you describe your answer to this inquiry as being ethical? Why?

EXERCISE 1–10 Corporate Social Responsbility

In his book *Capitalism and Freedom,* economist Milton Friedman wrote on page 133: "There is one and only one social responsibility of business—to use its resources and engage in activities designed to increase its profits so long as it . . . engages in open and free competition, without deception or fraud."

Required:

Explain why you agree or disagree with this quote.

EXERCISE 1–11 Intrinsic Motivation and Extrinsic Incentives

In a *Harvard Business Review* article titled "Why Incentive Plans Cannot Work," (Volume 71, Issue 5) author Alfie Kohn wrote: "Research suggests that, by and large, rewards succeed at securing one thing only: temporary compliance. When it comes to producing lasting change in attitudes and behavior, however, rewards, like punishment, are strikingly ineffective. Once the rewards run out, people revert to their old behaviors. . . . Incentives, a version of what psychologists call extrinsic motivators, do not alter the attitudes that underlie our behaviors. They do not create an enduring *commitment* to any value or action. Rather, incentives merely—and temporarily—change what we do."

Required:

1. Do you agree with this quote? Why?
2. As a manager, how would you seek to motivate your employees?
3. As a manager, would you use financial incentives to compensate your employees? If so, what would be the keys to using them effectively? If not, then how would you compensate your employees?

EXERCISE 1–12 Cognitive Bias and Decision Making

During World War II, the U.S. military was studying its combat-tested fighter planes to determine the parts of the plane that were most vulnerable to enemy fire. The purpose of the study was to identify the most vulnerable sections of each plane and then take steps to reinforce those sections to improve pilot safety and airplane durability. The data gathered by the U.S. military showed that certain sections of its combat-tested fighter planes were consistently hit more often with enemy fire than other sections of the plane.

Required:

1. Would you recommend reinforcing the sections of the plane that were hit most often by enemy fire, or would you reinforce the sections that were hit less frequently by enemy fire? Why?
2. Do you think cognitive bias had the potential to influence the U.S. military's decision-making process with respect to reinforcing its fighter planes?

Source: Jerker Denrell, "Selection Bias and the Perils of Benchmarking," *Harvard Business Review,* Volume 83, Issue 4, pp. 114–119.

EXERCISE 1–13 Ethics and Decision Making

Assume that you just completed a December weekend vacation to a casino within the United States. During your trip you won $10,000 gambling. When the casino exchanged your chips for cash they did not record any personal information, such as your driver's license number or social security number. Four months later while preparing your tax returns for the prior year, you stop to contemplate the fact that the Internal Revenue Service requires taxpayers to report all gambling winnings on Form 1040.

Required:

Would you report your gambling winnings to the Internal Revenue Service so that you could pay federal income taxes on those winnings? Do you believe that your actions are ethical? Why?

Managerial Accounting and Cost Concepts

Lowering Health Care Costs and Improving Patient Care

BUSINESS FOCUS

© Trevor Lush/Purestock/SuperStock, RF

Providence Regional Medical Center's (PRMC) "single stay" ward is lowering health care costs and increasing patient satisfaction. Rather than transporting post-surgical patients to stationary equipment throughout the hospital, a "single stay" ward brings all required equipment to stationary patients. For example, "after heart surgery, cardiac patients remain in one room throughout their recovery, only the gear and staff are in motion. As the patient's condition stabilizes, the beeping machines of intensive care are removed and physical therapy equipment is added." The results of this shift in orientation have been impressive. Patient satisfaction scores have skyrocketed and the average length of a patient's stay in the hospital has declined by more than a day. ■

Source: Catherine Arnst, "Radical Surgery," *Bloomberg Businessweek*, January 18, 2010, pp. 40–45.

LEARNING OBJECTIVES

After studying Chapter 2, you should be able to:

LO 2–1 Understand cost classifications used for assigning costs to cost objects: direct costs and indirect costs.

LO 2–2 Identify and give examples of each of the three basic manufacturing cost categories.

LO 2–3 Understand cost classifications used to prepare financial statements: product costs and period costs.

LO 2–4 Understand cost classifications used to predict cost behavior: variable costs, fixed costs, and mixed costs.

LO 2–5 Analyze a mixed cost using a scattergraph plot and the high-low method.

LO 2–6 Prepare income statements for a merchandising company using the traditional and contribution formats.

LO 2–7 Understand cost classifications used in making decisions: differential costs, opportunity costs, and sunk costs.

LO 2–8 (Appendix 2A) Analyze a mixed cost using a scattergraph plot and the least-squares regression method.

This chapter explains that in managerial accounting the term *cost* is used in many different ways. The reason is that there are many types of costs, and these costs are classified differently according to the immediate needs of management. For example, managers may want cost data to prepare external financial reports, to prepare planning budgets, or to make decisions. Each different use of cost data demands a different classification and definition of costs. For example, the preparation of external financial reports requires the use of historical cost data, whereas decision making may require predictions about future costs. This notion of *different costs for different purposes* is a critically important aspect of managerial accounting.

Exhibit 2–1 summarizes the cost classifications that will be defined in this chapter, namely cost classifications (1) for assigning costs to cost objects, (2) for manufacturing companies, (3) for preparing financial statements, (4) for predicting cost behavior, and (5) for making decisions. As we begin defining the cost terminology related to each of these cost classifications, please refer back to this exhibit to help improve your understanding of the overall organization of the chapter.

EXHIBIT 2–1
Summary of Cost Classifications

Purpose of Cost Classification	Cost Classifications
Assigning costs to cost objects	• Direct cost (can be easily traced) • Indirect cost (cannot be easily traced)

Accounting for costs in manufacturing companies	• Manufacturing costs
	  • Direct materials
	  • Direct labor
	  • Manufacturing overhead
	• Nonmanufacturing costs
	  • Selling costs
	  • Administrative costs

Preparing financial statements	• Product costs (inventoriable) • Period costs (expensed)
Predicting cost behavior in response to changes in activity	• Variable cost (proportional to activity) • Fixed cost (constant in total) • Mixed cost (has variable and fixed elements)
Making decisions	• Differential cost (differs between alternatives) • Sunk cost (should be ignored) • Opportunity cost (foregone benefit)

Cost Classifications for Assigning Costs to Cost Objects

LEARNING OBJECTIVE 2–1
Understand cost classifications used for assigning costs to cost objects: direct costs and indirect costs.

Costs are assigned to cost objects for a variety of purposes including pricing, preparing profitability studies, and controlling spending. A **cost object** is anything for which cost data are desired—including products, customers, jobs, and organizational subunits. For purposes of assigning costs to cost objects, costs are classified as either *direct* or *indirect.*

Direct Cost

A **direct cost** is a cost that can be easily and conveniently traced to a specified cost object. For example, if Reebok is assigning costs to its various regional and national sales offices, then the salary of the sales manager in its Tokyo office would be a direct cost of that office. If a printing company made 10,000 brochures for a specific customer, then the cost of the paper used to make the brochures would be a direct cost of that customer.

Indirect Cost

An **indirect cost** is a cost that cannot be easily and conveniently traced to a specified cost object. For example, a Campbell Soup factory may produce dozens of varieties of canned soups. The factory manager's salary would be an indirect cost of a particular variety such as chicken noodle soup. The reason is that the factory manager's salary is incurred as a consequence of running the entire factory—it is not incurred to produce any one soup variety. *To be traced to a cost object such as a particular product, the cost must be caused by the cost object.* The factory manager's salary is called a *common cost* of producing the various products of the factory. A **common cost** is a cost that is incurred to support a number of cost objects but cannot be traced to them individually. A common cost is a type of indirect cost.

A particular cost may be direct or indirect, depending on the cost object. While the Campbell Soup factory manager's salary is an *indirect* cost of manufacturing chicken noodle soup, it is a *direct* cost of the manufacturing division. In the first case, the cost object is chicken noodle soup. In the second case, the cost object is the entire manufacturing division.

Cost Classifications for Manufacturing Companies

Manufacturing companies such as Texas Instruments, Ford, and DuPont separate their costs into two broad categories—manufacturing and nonmanufacturing costs.

Manufacturing Costs

Most manufacturing companies further separate their manufacturing costs into two direct cost categories, direct materials and direct labor, and one indirect cost category, manufacturing overhead. A discussion of each of these categories follows.

LEARNING OBJECTIVE 2–2
Identify and give examples of each of the three basic manufacturing cost categories.

Direct Materials The materials that go into the final product are called **raw materials**. This term is somewhat misleading because it seems to imply unprocessed natural resources like wood pulp or iron ore. Actually, raw materials refer to any materials that are used in the final product; and the finished product of one company can become the raw materials of another company. For example, the plastics produced by Du Pont are a raw material used by Hewlett-Packard in its personal computers.

Raw materials may include both *direct* and *indirect materials.* **Direct materials** are those materials that become an integral part of the finished product and whose costs can be conveniently traced to the finished product. This would include, for example, the seats that Airbus purchases from subcontractors to install in its commercial aircraft and the electronic components that Apple uses in its iPhones.

Sometimes it isn't worth the effort to trace the costs of relatively insignificant materials to end products. Such minor items would include the solder used to make electrical connections in a Samsung HDTV or the glue used to assemble an Ethan Allen chair. Materials such as solder and glue are called **indirect materials** and are included as part of manufacturing overhead, which is discussed shortly.

Direct Labor **Direct labor** consists of labor costs that can be easily (i.e., physically and conveniently) traced to individual units of product. Direct labor is sometimes

IN BUSINESS

© Digital Vision/PunchStock, RF

FOOD PRICES HIT RECORD HIGHS FOR RESTAURANTS

Direct material costs are critically important to restaurants and fast-food chains. In recent years, some food costs have spiked to record highs. For example, unexpected freezing temperatures in the southwestern portion of the United States caused the cost of lettuce to increase 290%. Similarly, the costs of green peppers, tomatoes, and cucumbers jumped 145%, 85%, and 30%, respectively. A large chain such as Subway can withstand these price increases better than smaller competitors because of its buying power and long-term contracts.

Source: Anne VanderMey, "Food For Thought," *Fortune*, May 9, 2011, p. 12.

called *touch labor* because direct labor workers typically touch the product while it is being made. Examples of direct labor include assembly-line workers at Toyota, carpenters at the home builder KB Home, and electricians who install equipment on aircraft at Bombardier Learjet.

Labor costs that cannot be physically traced to particular products, or that can be traced only at great cost and inconvenience, are termed **indirect labor**. Just like indirect materials, indirect labor is treated as part of manufacturing overhead. Indirect labor includes the labor costs of janitors, supervisors, materials handlers, and night security guards. Although the efforts of these workers are essential, it would be either impractical or impossible to accurately trace their costs to specific units of product. Hence, such labor costs are treated as indirect labor.

Manufacturing Overhead **Manufacturing overhead**, the third manufacturing cost category, includes all manufacturing costs except direct materials and direct labor. Manufacturing overhead includes items such as indirect materials; indirect labor; maintenance and repairs on production equipment; and heat and light, property taxes, depreciation, and insurance on manufacturing facilities. A company also incurs costs for heat and light, property taxes, insurance, depreciation, and so forth, associated with its selling and administrative functions, but these costs are not included as part of manufacturing overhead. Only those costs associated with *operating the factory* are included in manufacturing overhead.

Various names are used for manufacturing overhead, such as *indirect manufacturing cost, factory overhead,* and *factory burden.* All of these terms are synonyms for *manufacturing overhead.*

Nonmanufacturing Costs

Nonmanufacturing costs are often divided into two categories: (1) *selling costs* and (2) *administrative costs.* **Selling costs** include all costs that are incurred to secure customer orders and get the finished product to the customer. These costs are sometimes called *order-getting* and *order-filling costs.* Examples of selling costs include advertising, shipping, sales travel, sales commissions, sales salaries, and costs of finished goods warehouses. Selling costs can be either direct or indirect costs. For example, the cost of an advertising campaign dedicated to one specific product is a direct cost of that product, whereas the salary of a marketing manager who oversees numerous products is an indirect cost with respect to individual products.

Administrative costs include all costs associated with the *general management* of an organization rather than with manufacturing or selling. Examples of administrative costs include executive compensation, general accounting, secretarial, public relations, and similar costs involved in the overall, general administration of the organization *as a whole.* Administrative costs can be either direct or indirect costs. For example, the salary of an accounting manager in charge of accounts receivable collections in the East region is a direct cost of that region, whereas the salary of a chief financial officer who oversees all of a company's regions is an indirect cost with respect to individual regions.

Nonmanufacturing costs are also often called selling, general, and administrative (SG&A) costs or just selling and administrative costs.

Cost Classifications for Preparing Financial Statements

LEARNING OBJECTIVE 2–3
Understand cost classifications used to prepare financial statements: product costs and period costs.

When preparing a balance sheet and an income statement, companies need to classify their costs as *product costs* or *period costs.* To understand the difference between product costs and period costs, we must first discuss the matching principle from financial accounting.

Generally, costs are recognized as expenses on the income statement in the period that benefits from the cost. For example, if a company pays for liability insurance in advance for two years, the entire amount is not considered an expense of the year in which the payment is made. Instead, one-half of the cost would be recognized as an expense each year. The reason is that both years—not just the first year—benefit from the insurance payment. The unexpensed portion of the insurance payment is carried on the balance sheet as an asset called prepaid insurance.

The *matching principle* is based on the *accrual* concept that *costs incurred to generate a particular revenue should be recognized as expenses in the same period that the revenue is recognized.* This means that if a cost is incurred to acquire or make something that will eventually be sold, then the cost should be recognized as an expense only when the sale takes place—that is, when the benefit occurs. Such costs are called *product costs.*

Product Costs

For financial accounting purposes, **product costs** include all costs involved in acquiring or making a product. In the case of manufactured goods, these costs consist of direct materials, direct labor, and manufacturing overhead.[1] Product costs "attach" to units of product as the goods are purchased or manufactured, and they remain attached as the goods go into inventory awaiting sale. Product costs are initially assigned to an inventory account on the balance sheet. When the goods are sold, the costs are released from inventory as expenses (typically called cost of goods sold) and matched against sales revenue on the income statement. Because product costs are initially assigned to inventories, they are also known as **inventoriable costs**.

We want to emphasize that product costs are not necessarily recorded as expenses on the income statement in the period in which they are incurred. Rather, as explained above, they are recorded as expenses in the period in which the related products *are sold.*

Period Costs

Period costs are all the costs that are not product costs. *All selling and administrative expenses are treated as period costs.* For example, sales commissions, advertising, executive salaries, public relations, and the rental costs of administrative offices are all period costs. Period costs are not included as part of the cost of either purchased or manufactured goods; instead, period costs are expensed on the income statement in the period in which they are incurred using the usual rules of accrual accounting. Keep in mind that the period in which a cost is incurred is not necessarily the period in which cash changes

[1] For internal management purposes, product costs may exclude some manufacturing costs. For example, see Appendix 4B and the discussion in Chapter 5.

hands. For example, as discussed earlier, the costs of liability insurance are spread across the periods that benefit from the insurance—regardless of the period in which the insurance premium is paid.

Prime Cost and Conversion Cost

Two more cost categories are often used in discussions of manufacturing costs—*prime cost* and *conversion cost.* **Prime cost** is the sum of direct materials cost and direct labor cost. **Conversion cost** is the sum of direct labor cost and manufacturing overhead cost. The term *conversion cost* is used to describe direct labor and manufacturing overhead because these costs are incurred to convert materials into the finished product.

To improve your understanding of these definitions, consider the following scenario: A company has reported the following costs and expenses for the most recent month:

Direct materials	$69,000
Direct labor	$35,000
Manufacturing overhead	$14,000
Selling expenses	$29,000
Administrative expenses	$50,000

These costs and expenses can be categorized in a number of ways, including product costs, period costs, conversion costs, and prime costs:

Product cost = Direct materials + Direct labor + Manufacturing overhead
= $69,000 + $35,000 + $14,000
= $118,000

Period cost = Selling expenses + Administrative expenses
= $29,000 + $50,000
= $79,000

Conversion cost = Direct labor + Manufacturing overhead
= $35,000 + $14,000
= $49,000

Prime cost = Direct materials + Direct labor
= $69,000 + $35,000
= $104,000

IN BUSINESS

© Zoonar/Michael Roseb/AGE Fotostock

WALMART LOOKS TO REDUCE ITS SHIPPING COSTS

Walmart hopes to lower its shipping costs, thereby enabling it to reduce its "everyday low prices." In years past, suppliers would ship their merchandise to Walmart's distribution centers, and then Walmart would use its own fleet of trucks to ship goods from its distribution centers to its retail store locations. However, now Walmart wants to assume control of transporting merchandise from its suppliers' manufacturing facilities to its distribution centers. Walmart believes it can lower these shipping costs by carrying more merchandise per truck and by taking advantage of volume purchase price discounts for fuel. In exchange for assuming these shipping responsibilities, Walmart is seeking price reductions from suppliers that it can pass along, at least in part, to its customers.

Source: Chris Burritt, Carol Wolf, and Matthew Boyle, "Why Wal-Mart Wants to Take the Driver's Seat," *Bloomberg Businessweek,* May 31–June 6, 2010, pp. 17–18.

Cost Classifications for Predicting Cost Behavior

LEARNING OBJECTIVE 2–4
Understand cost classifications used to predict cost behavior: variable costs, fixed costs, and mixed costs.

It is often necessary to predict how a certain cost will behave in response to a change in activity. For example, a manager at Under Armour may want to estimate the impact a 5 percent increase in sales would have on the company's total direct materials cost. **Cost behavior** refers to how a cost reacts to changes in the level of activity. As the activity level rises and falls, a particular cost may rise and fall as well—or it may remain constant. For planning purposes, a manager must be able to anticipate which of these will happen; and if a cost can be expected to change, the manager must be able to estimate how much it will change. To help make such distinctions, costs are often categorized as *variable, fixed,* or *mixed.* The relative proportion of each type of cost in an organization is known as its **cost structure**. For example, an organization might have many fixed costs but few variable or mixed costs. Alternatively, it might have many variable costs but few fixed or mixed costs.

Variable Cost

A **variable cost** varies, in total, in direct proportion to changes in the level of activity. Common examples of variable costs include cost of goods sold for a merchandising company, direct materials, direct labor, variable elements of manufacturing overhead, such as indirect materials, supplies, and power, and variable elements of selling and administrative expenses, such as commissions and shipping costs.[2]

For a cost to be variable, it must be variable *with respect to something.* That "something" is its *activity base.* An **activity base** is a measure of whatever causes the incurrence of a variable cost. An activity base is sometimes referred to as a *cost driver.* Some of the most common activity bases are direct labor-hours, machine-hours, units produced, and units sold. Other examples of activity bases (cost drivers) include the number of miles driven by salespersons, the number of pounds of laundry cleaned by a hotel, the number of calls handled by technical support staff at a software company, and the number of beds occupied in a hospital. *While there are many activity bases within organizations, throughout this textbook, unless stated otherwise, you should assume that the activity base under consideration is the total volume of goods and services provided by the organization. We will specify the activity base only when it is something other than total output.*

To provide an example of a variable cost, consider Nooksack Expeditions, a small company that provides daylong whitewater rafting excursions on rivers in the North Cascade Mountains. The company provides all of the necessary equipment and experienced guides, and it serves gourmet meals to its guests. The meals are purchased from a caterer for $30 a person for a daylong excursion. The behavior of this variable cost, on both a per unit and a total basis, is shown below:

Number of Guests	Cost of Meals per Guest	Total Cost of Meals
250	$30	$7,500
500	$30	$15,000
750	$30	$22,500
1,000	$30	$30,000

[2] Direct labor costs often can be fixed instead of variable for a variety of reasons. For example, in some countries, such as France, Germany, and Japan, labor regulations and cultural norms may limit management's ability to adjust the labor force in response to changes in activity. In this textbook, always assume that direct labor is a variable cost unless you are explicitly told otherwise.

IN BUSINESS

COST DRIVERS IN THE ELECTRONICS INDUSTRY

Accenture Ltd. estimates that the U.S. electronics industry spends $13.8 billion annually to rebox, restock, and resell returned products. Conventional wisdom is that customers only return products when they are defective, but the data show that this explanation only accounts for 5% of customer returns. The biggest cost drivers that cause product returns are that customers often inadvertently buy the wrong products and that they cannot understand how to use the products that they have purchased. Television manufacturer Vizio Inc. has started including more information on its packaging to help customers avoid buying the wrong product. Seagate Technologies is replacing thick instruction manuals with simpler guides that make it easier for customers to begin using their products.

Source: Christopher Lawton, "The War on Returns," *The Wall Street Journal,* May 8, 2008, pp. D1 and D6.

IN BUSINESS

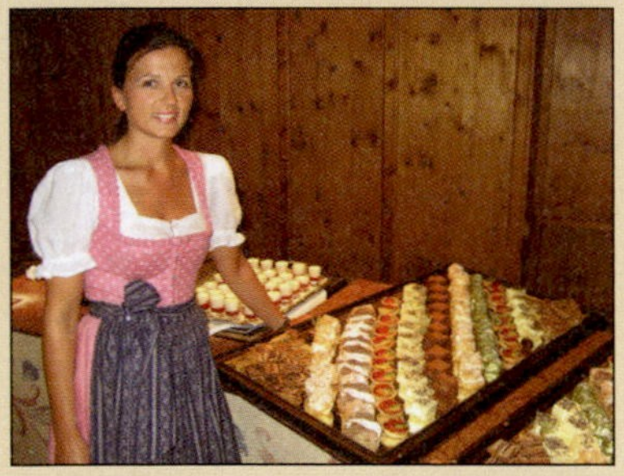

© Sandee Noreen

FOOD COSTS AT A LUXURY HOTEL

The Sporthotel Theresa (http://www.theresa.at/), owned and operated by the Egger family, is a four star hotel located in Zell im Zillertal, Austria. The hotel features access to hiking, skiing, biking, and other activities in the Ziller Alps as well as its own fitness facility and spa.

Three full meals a day are included in the hotel room charge. Breakfast and lunch are served buffet-style while dinner is a more formal affair with as many as six courses. The chef, Stefan Egger, believes that food costs are roughly proportional to the number of guests staying at the hotel; that is, they are a variable cost. He must order food from suppliers two or three days in advance, but he adjusts his purchases to the number of guests who are currently staying at the hotel and their consumption patterns. In addition, guests make their selections from the dinner menu early in the day, which helps Stefan plan which foodstuffs will be required for dinner. Consequently, he is able to prepare just enough food so that all guests are satisfied and yet waste is held to a minimum.

Source: Conversation with Stefan Egger, chef at the Sporthotel Theresa.

While total variable costs change as the activity level changes, it is important to note that a variable cost is constant if expressed on a *per unit* basis. For example, the per unit cost of the meals remains constant at $30 even though the total cost of the meals increases and decreases with activity. The graph in the first part of Exhibit 2–2 illustrates that the total variable cost rises and falls as the activity level rises and falls. At an activity level of 250 guests, the total meal cost is $7,500. At an activity level of 1,000 guests, the total meal cost rises to $30,000.

Fixed Cost

A **fixed cost** is a cost that remains constant, in total, regardless of changes in the level of activity. Examples of fixed costs include straight-line depreciation, insurance, property taxes, rent, supervisory salaries, administrative salaries, and advertising. Unlike variable costs, fixed costs are not affected by changes in activity. Consequently, as the activity level rises and falls, total fixed costs remain constant unless influenced by some outside force, such as a landlord increasing your monthly rental expense. To continue the Nooksack Expeditions example, assume the company rents a building for $500 per month to store its equipment. The total amount of rent paid is the same regardless of the number of guests the company takes on its expeditions during any given month. The concept of a fixed cost is shown graphically in the second part of Exhibit 2–2.

Because total fixed costs remain constant for large variations in the level of activity, the average fixed cost *per unit* becomes progressively smaller as the level of activity

EXHIBIT 2–2
Variable and Fixed Cost Behavior

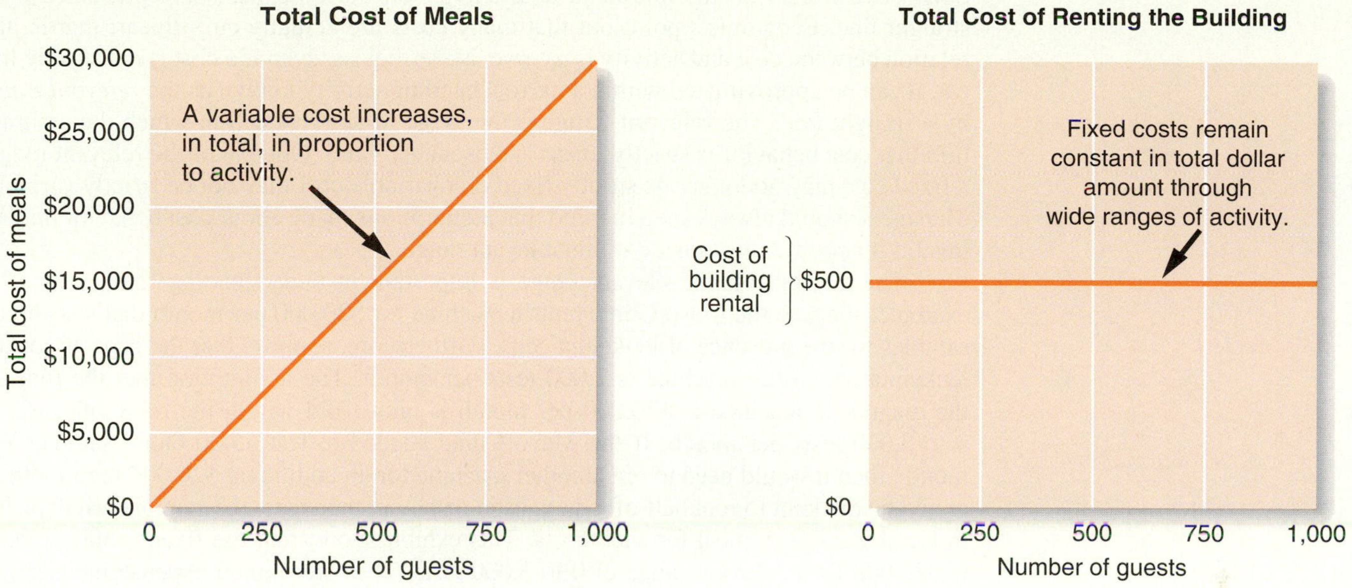

increases. If Nooksack Expeditions has only 250 guests in a month, the $500 fixed rental cost would amount to an average of $2 per guest. If there are 1,000 guests, the fixed rental cost would average only 50 cents per guest. The table below illustrates this aspect of the behavior of fixed costs. Note that as the number of guests increase, the average fixed cost per guest drops.

Monthly Rental Cost	Number of Guests	Average Cost per Guest
$500	250	$2.00
$500	500	$1.00
$500	750	$0.67
$500	1,000	$0.50

As a general rule, *we caution against expressing fixed costs on an average per unit basis in internal reports because it creates the false impression that fixed costs are like variable costs and that total fixed costs actually change as the level of activity changes.*

For planning purposes, fixed costs can be viewed as either *committed* or *discretionary.* **Committed fixed costs** represent organizational investments with a *multiyear* planning horizon that can't be significantly reduced even for short periods of time without making fundamental changes. Examples include investments in facilities and equipment, as well as real estate taxes, insurance expenses, and salaries of top management. Even if operations are interrupted or cut back, committed fixed costs remain largely unchanged in the short term because the costs of restoring them later are likely to be far greater than any short-run savings that might be realized. **Discretionary fixed costs** (often referred to as *managed fixed costs*) usually arise from *annual* decisions by management to spend on certain fixed cost items. Examples of discretionary fixed costs include advertising, research, public relations, management development programs, and internships for students. Discretionary fixed costs can be cut for short periods of time with minimal damage to the long-run goals of the organization.

The Linearity Assumption and the Relevant Range

Management accountants ordinarily assume that costs are strictly linear; that is, the relation between cost on the one hand and activity on the other can be represented by a straight line. Economists point out that many costs are actually curvilinear; that is, the relation between cost and activity is a curve. Nevertheless, even if a cost is not strictly linear, it can be approximated within a narrow band of activity known as the *relevant range* by a straight line. The **relevant range** is the range of activity within which the assumption that cost behavior is strictly linear is reasonably valid. Outside of the relevant range, a fixed cost may no longer be strictly fixed or a variable cost may not be strictly variable. Managers should always keep in mind that assumptions made about cost behavior may be invalid if activity falls outside of the relevant range.

The concept of the relevant range is important in understanding fixed costs. For example, suppose the Mayo Clinic rents a machine for $20,000 per month that tests blood samples for the presence of leukemia cells. Furthermore, suppose that the capacity of the leukemia diagnostic machine is 3,000 tests per month. The assumption that the rent for the diagnostic machine is $20,000 per month is only valid within the relevant range of 0 to 3,000 tests per month. If the Mayo Clinic needed to test 5,000 blood samples per month, then it would need to rent another machine for an additional $20,000 per month. It would be difficult to rent half of a diagnostic machine; therefore, the step pattern depicted in Exhibit 2–3 is typical for such costs. This exhibit shows that the fixed rental expense is $20,000 for a relevant range of 0 to 3,000 tests. The fixed rental expense increases to $40,000 within the relevant range of 3,001 to 6,000 tests. The rental expense increases in discrete steps or increments of 3,000 tests, rather than increasing in a linear fashion per test.

This step-oriented cost behavior pattern can also be used to describe other costs, such as some labor costs. For example, salaried employee expenses can be characterized using a step pattern. Salaried employees are paid a fixed amount, such as $40,000 per year, for providing the capacity to work a prespecified amount of time, such as 40 hours per week for 50 weeks a year (= 2,000 hours per year). In this example, the total salaried employee expense is $40,000 within a relevant range of 0 to 2,000 hours of work. The total salaried employee expense increases to $80,000 (or two employees) if the organization's work requirements expand to a relevant range of 2,001 to 4,000 hours of work. Cost behavior patterns such as salaried employees are often called *step-variable costs.* Step-variable costs can often be adjusted quickly as conditions change. Furthermore, the width of the steps for step-variable costs is generally so narrow that these costs can be treated essentially as variable costs for most purposes. The width of the steps for fixed costs, on the other hand, is so wide that these costs should be treated as entirely fixed within the relevant range.

EXHIBIT 2–3
Fixed Costs and the Relevant Range

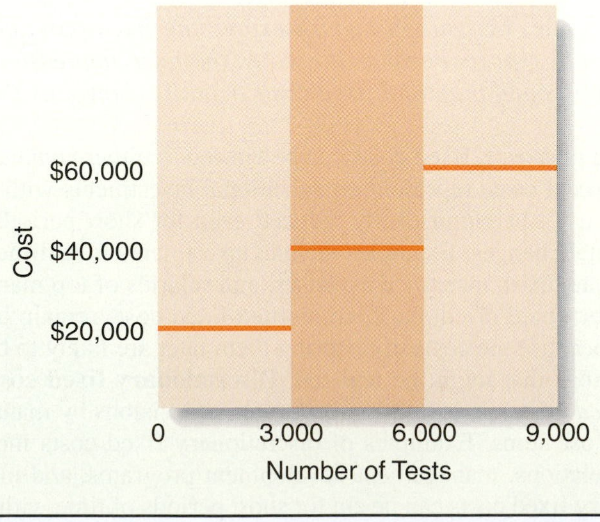

EXHIBIT 2–4
Summary of Variable and Fixed Cost Behavior

	Behavior of the Cost (within the relevant range)	
Cost	**In Total**	**Per Unit**
Variable cost	Total variable cost increases and decreases in proportion to changes in the activity level	Variable cost per unit remains constant
Fixed cost	Total fixed cost is not affected by changes in the activity level within the relevant range	Fixed cost per unit decreases as the activity level rises and increases as the activity level falls

Exhibit 2–4 summarizes four key concepts related to variable and fixed costs. Study it carefully before reading further.

IN BUSINESS

HOW MANY GUIDES?

Majestic Ocean Kayaking, of Ucluelet, British Columbia, is owned and operated by Tracy Morben-Eeftink. The company offers a number of guided kayaking excursions ranging from three-hour tours of the Ucluelet harbor to six-day kayaking and camping trips in Clayoquot Sound. One of the company's excursions is a four-day kayaking and camping trip to The Broken Group Islands in the Pacific Rim National Park. Special regulations apply to trips in the park—including a requirement that one certified guide must be assigned for every five guests or fraction thereof. For example, a trip with 12 guests must have at least three certified guides. Guides are not salaried and are paid on a per-day basis. Therefore, the cost to the company of the guides for a trip is a step-variable cost rather than a fixed cost or a strictly variable cost. One guide is needed for 1 to 5 guests, two guides for 6 to 10 guests, three guides for 11 to 15 guests, and so on.

Sources: Tracy Morben-Eeftink, owner, Majestic Ocean Kayaking. For more information about the company, see www.oceankayaking.com.

Mixed Costs

A **mixed cost** contains both variable and fixed cost elements. Mixed costs are also known as semivariable costs. To continue the Nooksack Expeditions example, the company incurs a mixed cost called fees paid to the state. It includes a license fee of $25,000 per year plus $3 per rafting party paid to the state's Department of Natural Resources. If the company runs 1,000 rafting parties this year, then the total fees paid to the state would be $28,000, made up of $25,000 in fixed cost plus $3,000 in variable cost. Exhibit 2–5 depicts the behavior of this mixed cost.

Even if Nooksack fails to attract any customers, the company will still have to pay the license fee of $25,000. This is why the cost line in Exhibit 2–5 intersects the vertical cost axis at the $25,000 point. For each rafting party the company organizes, the total cost of the state fees will increase by $3. Therefore, the total cost line slopes upward as the variable cost of $3 per party is added to the fixed cost of $25,000 per year.

Because the mixed cost in Exhibit 2–5 is represented by a straight line, the next equation for a straight line can be used to express the relationship between a mixed cost and the level of activity.

EXHIBIT 2–5
Mixed Cost Behavior

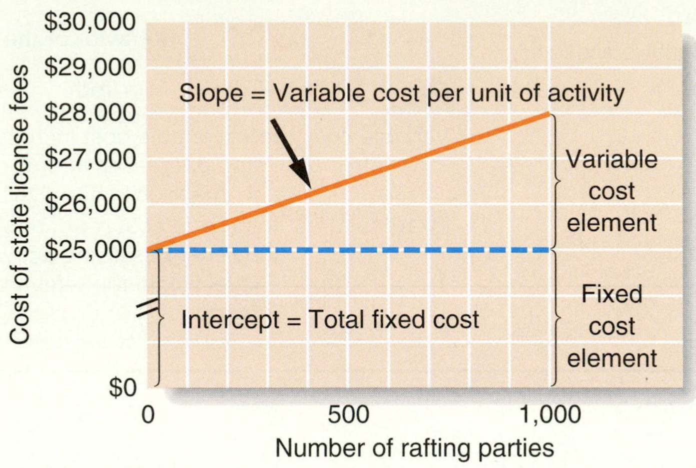

$$Y = a + bX$$

In this equation,

Y = The total mixed cost

a = The total fixed cost (the vertical intercept of the line)

b = The variable cost per unit of activity (the slope of the line)

X = The level of activity

Because the variable cost per unit equals the slope of the straight line, the steeper the slope, the higher the variable cost per unit.

In the case of the state fees paid by Nooksack Expeditions, the equation is written as follows:

$$Y = \$25{,}000 + \$3.00X$$

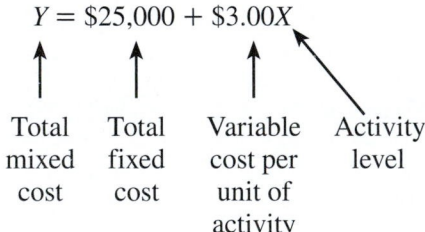

Y	$25,000	$3.00	X
Total mixed cost	Total fixed cost	Variable cost per unit of activity	Activity level

This equation makes it easy to calculate the total mixed cost for any level of activity within the relevant range. For example, suppose that the company expects to organize 800 rafting parties in the next year. The total state fees would be calculated as follows:

$$Y = \$25{,}000 + (\$3.00 \text{ per rafting party} \times 800 \text{ rafting parties})$$
$$= \$27{,}400$$

The Analysis of Mixed Costs

Mixed costs are very common. For example, the overall cost of providing X-ray services to patients at the Harvard Medical School Hospital is a mixed cost. The costs of equipment depreciation and radiologists' and technicians' salaries are fixed, but the costs of X-ray film, power, and supplies are variable. At Southwest Airlines, maintenance costs are a mixed cost. The company incurs fixed costs for renting maintenance facilities and for keeping skilled mechanics on the payroll, but the costs of replacement parts, lubricating oils, tires, and so forth, are variable with respect to how often and how far the company's aircraft are flown.

The fixed portion of a mixed cost represents the minimum cost of having a service *ready and available* for use. The variable portion represents the cost incurred for *actual consumption* of the service, thus it varies in proportion to the amount of service actually consumed.

Managers can use a variety of methods to estimate the fixed and variable components of a mixed cost such as *account analysis,* the *engineering approach,* the *high-low method,* and *least-squares regression analysis.* In **account analysis**, an account is classified as either variable or fixed based on the analyst's prior knowledge of how the cost in the account behaves. For example, direct materials would be classified as variable and a building lease cost would be classified as fixed because of the nature of those costs. The **engineering approach** to cost analysis involves a detailed analysis of what cost behavior should be, based on an industrial engineer's evaluation of the production methods to be used, the materials specifications, labor requirements, equipment usage, production efficiency, power consumption, and so on.

The high-low and least-squares regression methods estimate the fixed and variable elements of a mixed cost by analyzing past records of cost and activity data. We will use an example from Brentline Hospital to illustrate the high-low method calculations and to compare the resulting high-low method cost estimates to those obtained using least-squares regression. Appendix 2A demonstrates how to use Microsoft Excel to perform least-squares regression computations.

Diagnosing Cost Behavior with a Scattergraph Plot

LEARNING OBJECTIVE 2–5
Analyze a mixed cost using a scattergraph plot and the high-low method.

Assume that Brentline Hospital is interested in predicting future monthly maintenance costs for budgeting purposes. The senior management team believes that maintenance cost is a mixed cost and that the variable portion of this cost is driven by the number of patient-days. Each day a patient is in the hospital counts as one patient-day. The hospital's chief financial officer gathered the following data for the most recent seven-month period:

Month	Activity Level: Patient-Days	Maintenance Cost Incurred
January	5,600	$7,900
February	7,100	$8,500
March	5,000	$7,400
April.	6,500	$8,200
May	7,300	$9,100
June	8,000	$9,800
July	6,200	$7,800

The first step in applying the high-low method or the least-squares regression method is to diagnose cost behavior with a scattergraph plot. The scattergraph plot of maintenance costs versus patient-days at Brentline Hospital is shown in Exhibit 2–6. Two things should be noted about this scattergraph:

1. The total maintenance cost, *Y,* is plotted on the vertical axis. Cost is known as the **dependent variable** because the amount of cost incurred during a period depends on the level of activity for the period. (That is, as the level of activity increases, total cost will also ordinarily increase.)
2. The activity, *X* (patient-days in this case), is plotted on the horizontal axis. Activity is known as the **independent variable** because it causes variations in the cost.

From the scattergraph plot, it is evident that maintenance costs do increase with the number of patient-days in an approximately *linear* fashion. In other words, the points lie more or less along a straight line that slopes upward and to the right. Cost behavior is considered **linear** whenever a straight line is a reasonable approximation for the relation between cost and activity.

EXHIBIT 2–6
Scattergraph Method of Cost Analysis

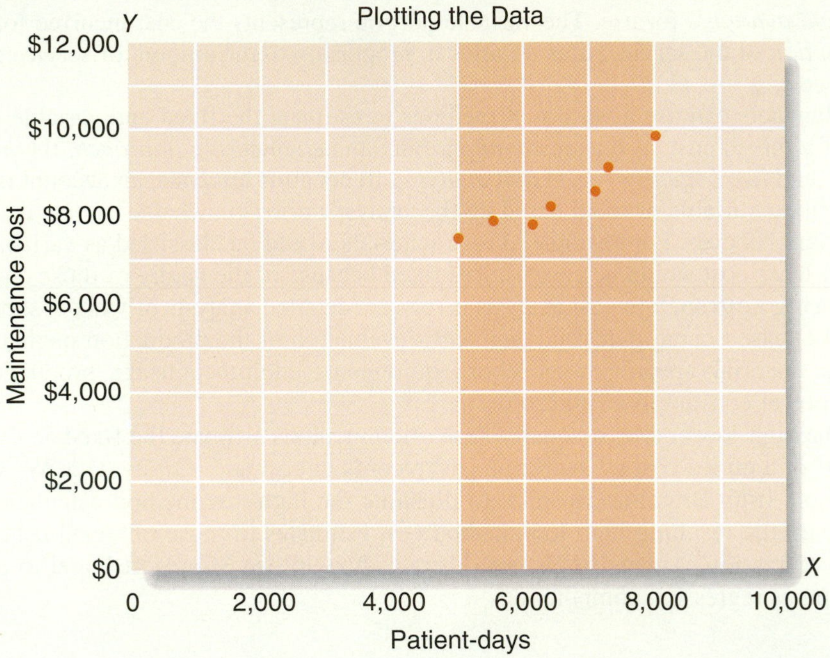

Plotting the data on a scattergraph is an essential diagnostic step that should be performed before performing the high-low method or least-squares regression calculations. If the scattergraph plot reveals linear cost behavior, then it makes sense to perform the high-low or least-squares regression calculations to separate the mixed cost into its variable and fixed components. If the scattergraph plot does not depict linear cost behavior, then it makes no sense to proceed any further in analyzing the data.

The High–Low Method

Assuming that the scattergraph plot indicates a linear relation between cost and activity, the fixed and variable cost elements of a mixed cost can be estimated using the *high-low method* or the *least-squares regression method.* The high-low method is based on the rise-over-run formula for the slope of a straight line. As previously discussed, if the relation between cost and activity can be represented by a straight line, then the slope of the straight line is equal to the variable cost per unit of activity. Consequently, the following formula can be used to estimate the variable cost:

$$\text{Variable cost} = \text{Slope of the line} = \frac{\text{Rise}}{\text{Run}} = \frac{Y_2 - Y_1}{X_2 - X_1}$$

To analyze mixed costs with the **high-low method**, begin by identifying the period with the lowest level of activity and the period with the highest level of activity. The period with the lowest activity is selected as the first point in the above formula and the period with the highest activity is selected as the second point. Consequently, the formula becomes:

$$\text{Variable cost} = \frac{Y_2 - Y_1}{X_2 - X_1} = \frac{\text{Cost at the high activity level} - \text{Cost at the low activity level}}{\text{High activity level} - \text{Low activity level}}$$

or

$$\text{Variable cost} = \frac{\text{Change in cost}}{\text{Change in activity}}$$

Therefore, when the high-low method is used, the variable cost is estimated by dividing the difference in cost between the high and low levels of activity by the change in activity between those two points.

To return to the Brentline Hospital example, using the high-low method, we first identify the periods with the highest and lowest *activity*—in this case, June and March. We then use the activity and cost data from these two periods to estimate the variable cost component as follows:

	Patient-Days	Maintenance Cost Incurred
High activity level (June)	8,000	$9,800
Low activity level (March)	5,000	7,400
Change	3,000	$2,400

$$\text{Variable cost} = \frac{\text{Change in cost}}{\text{Change in activity}} = \frac{\$2,400}{3,000 \text{ patient-days}} = \$0.80 \text{ per patient-day}$$

Having determined that the variable maintenance cost is 80 cents per patient-day, we can now determine the amount of fixed cost. This is done by taking the total cost at *either* the high or the low activity level and deducting the variable cost element. In the computation below, total cost at the high activity level is used in computing the fixed cost element:

$$\begin{aligned}\text{Fixed cost element} &= \text{Total cost} - \text{Variable cost element}\\ &= \$9,800 - (\$0.80 \text{ per patient-day} \times 8,000 \text{ patient-days})\\ &= \$3,400\end{aligned}$$

Both the variable and fixed cost elements have now been isolated. The cost of maintenance can be expressed as $3,400 per month plus 80 cents per patient-day or as:

$$Y = \$3,400 + \$0.80X$$

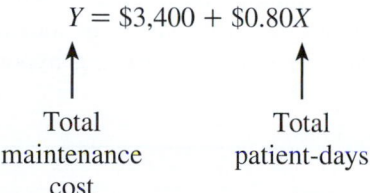

↑ Total maintenance cost (Y)

↑ Total patient-days (X)

The data used in this illustration are shown graphically in Exhibit 2–7. Notice that a straight line has been drawn through the points corresponding to the low and high levels of activity. In essence, that is what the high-low method does—it draws a straight line through those two points.

Sometimes the high and low levels of activity don't coincide with the high and low amounts of cost. For example, the period that has the highest level of activity may not have the highest amount of cost. Nevertheless, the costs at the highest and lowest levels of *activity* are always used to analyze a mixed cost under the high-low method. The reason is that the analyst would like to use data that reflect the greatest possible variation in activity.

The high-low method is very simple to apply, but it suffers from a major (and sometimes critical) defect—it utilizes only two data points. Generally, two data points are not enough to produce accurate results. Additionally, the periods with the highest and lowest activity tend to be unusual. A cost formula that is estimated solely using data from these unusual periods may misrepresent the true cost behavior during normal periods. Such a distortion is evident in Exhibit 2–7. The straight line should probably be shifted down somewhat so that it is closer to more of the data points. For these reasons, least-squares regression will generally be more accurate than the high-low method.

EXHIBIT 2–7
High-Low Method of Cost Analysis

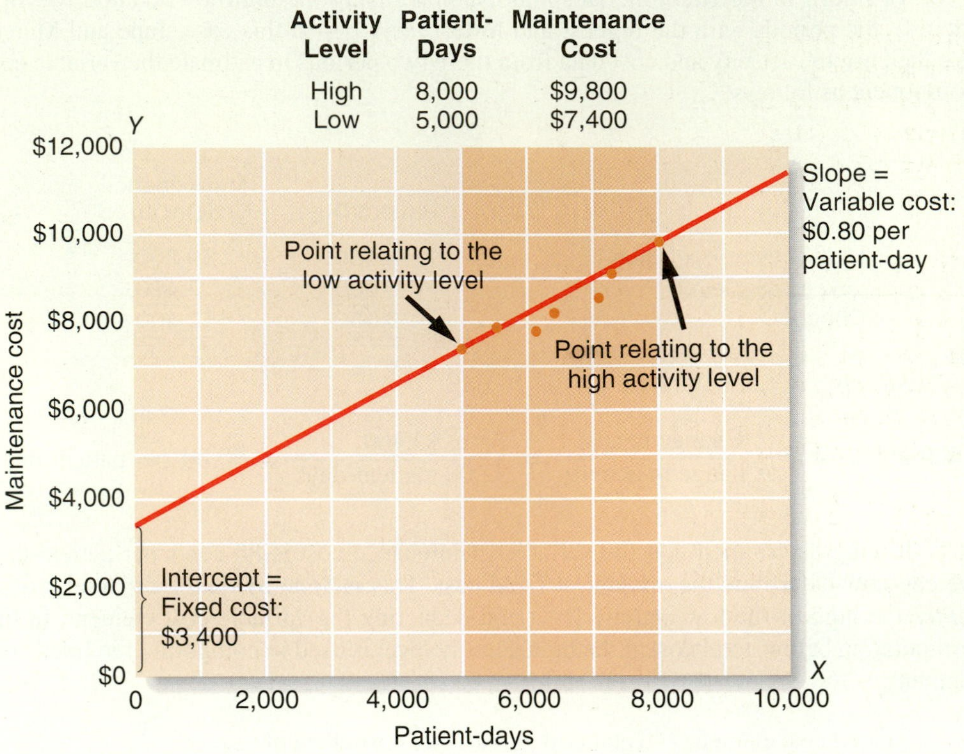

The Least–Squares Regression Method

The **least-squares regression method**, unlike the high-low method, uses all of the data to separate a mixed cost into its fixed and variable components. A *regression line* of the form $Y = a + bX$ is fitted to the data, where a represents the total fixed cost and b represents the variable cost per unit of activity. The basic idea underlying the least-squares regression method is illustrated in Exhibit 2–8 using hypothetical data points. Notice

EXHIBIT 2–8
The Concept of Least-Squares Regression

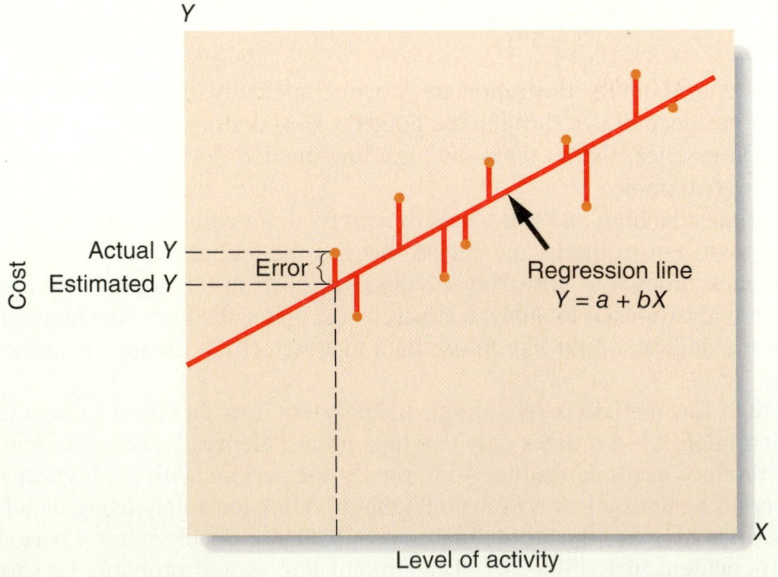

from the exhibit that the deviations from the plotted points to the regression line are measured vertically on the graph. These vertical deviations are called the regression errors. There is nothing mysterious about the least-squares regression method. It simply computes the regression line that minimizes the sum of these squared errors. The formulas that accomplish this are fairly complex and involve numerous calculations, but the principle is simple.

Fortunately, computers are adept at carrying out the computations required by the least-squares regression formulas. The data—the observed values of *X* and *Y*—are entered into the computer, and software does the rest. In the case of the Brentline Hospital maintenance cost data, a statistical software package on a personal computer can calculate the following least-squares regression estimates of the total fixed cost (*a*) and the variable cost per unit of activity (*b*):

$$a = \$3{,}431$$

$$b = \$0.759$$

Therefore, using the least-squares regression method, the fixed element of the maintenance cost is $3,431 per month and the variable portion is 75.9 cents per patient-day.

In terms of the linear equation $Y = a + bX$, the cost formula can be written as

$$Y = \$3{,}431 + \$0.759X$$

where activity (*X*) is expressed in patient-days.

Appendix 2A discusses how to use Microsoft Excel to perform least-squares regression calculations. For now, you only need to understand that least-squares regression analysis generally provides more accurate cost estimates than the high-low method because, rather than relying on just two data points, it uses all of the data points to fit a line that minimizes the sum of the squared errors. The table below compares Brentline Hospital's cost estimates using the high-low method and the least-squares regression method:

	High-Low Method	Least-Squares Regression Method
Variable cost estimate per patient-day	$0.800	$0.759
Fixed cost estimate per month	$3,400	$3,431

When Brentline uses the least-squares regression method to create a straight line that minimizes the sum of the squared errors, it results in estimated fixed costs that are $31 higher than the amount derived using the high-low method. It also decreases the slope of the straight line resulting in a lower variable cost estimate of $0.759 per patient-day rather than $0.80 per patient-day as derived using the high-low method.

IN BUSINESS

THE ZIPCAR COMES TO COLLEGE CAMPUSES

Zipcar is a car sharing service based in Cambridge, Massachusetts. The company serves 13 cities and 120 university campuses. Members pay a $50 annual fee plus $7 an hour to rent a car. They can use their iPhones to rent a car, locate it in the nearest Zipcar parking lot, unlock it using an access code, and drive it off the lot. This mixed cost arrangement is attractive to customers who need a car infrequently and wish to avoid the large cash outlay that comes with buying or leasing a vehicle.

Source: Jefferson Graham, "An iPhone Gets Zipcar Drivers on Their Way," *USA Today,* September 30, 2009, p. 3B.

© Michael Philip O'Malley/Flickr RF/ Getty Images, RF

Traditional and Contribution Format Income Statements

LEARNING OBJECTIVE 2–6
Prepare income statements for a merchandising company using the traditional and contribution formats.

In this section of the chapter, we discuss how to prepare traditional and contribution format income statements for a merchandising company.[3] Merchandising companies do not manufacture the products that they sell to customers. For example, Lowe's and Home Depot are merchandising companies because they buy finished products from manufacturers and then resell them to end consumers.

The Traditional Format Income Statement

Traditional income statements are prepared primarily for external reporting purposes. The left-hand side of Exhibit 2–9 shows a traditional income statement format for merchandising companies. This type of income statement organizes costs into two categories—cost of goods sold and selling and administrative expenses. Sales minus cost of goods sold equals the *gross margin.* The gross margin minus selling and administrative expenses equals net operating income.

The cost of goods sold reports the *product costs* attached to the merchandise sold during the period. The selling and administrative expenses report all *period costs* that have been expensed as incurred. The cost of goods sold for a merchandising company can be computed directly by multiplying the number of units sold by their unit cost or indirectly using the equation below:

$$\text{Cost of goods sold} = \text{Beginning merchandise inventory} + \text{Purchases} - \text{Ending merchandise inventory}$$

For example, let's assume that the company depicted in Exhibit 2–9 purchased $3,000 of merchandise inventory during the period and had beginning and ending merchandise inventory balances of $7,000 and $4,000, respectively. The equation above could be used to compute the cost of goods sold as follows:

EXHIBIT 2–9
Comparing Traditional and Contribution Format Income Statements for Merchandising Companies (all numbers are given)

Traditional Format			Contribution Format		
Sales		$12,000	Sales		$12,000
Cost of goods sold*		6,000	Variable expenses:		
Gross margin		6,000	Cost of goods sold	$6,000	
Selling and administrative expenses:			Variable selling	600	
Selling	$3,100		Variable administrative	400	7,000
Administrative	1,900	5,000	Contribution margin		5,000
Net operating income		$ 1,000	Fixed expenses:		
			Fixed selling	2,500	
			Fixed administrative	1,500	4,000
			Net operating income		$ 1,000

*For a manufacturing company, the cost of goods sold would include some variable costs, such as direct materials, direct labor, and variable overhead, and some fixed costs, such as fixed manufacturing overhead. Income statement formats for manufacturing companies will be explored in greater detail in a subsequent chapter.

[3] Subsequent chapters compare the income statement formats for manufacturing companies.

$$\text{Cost of goods sold} = \text{Beginning merchandise inventory} + \text{Purchases} - \text{Ending merchandise inventory}$$
$$= \$7,000 + \$3,000 - \$4,000$$
$$= \$6,000$$

Although the traditional income statement is useful for external reporting purposes, it has serious limitations when used for internal purposes. It does not distinguish between fixed and variable costs. For example, under the heading "Selling and administrative expenses," both variable administrative costs ($400) and fixed administrative costs ($1,500) are lumped together ($1,900). Internally, managers need cost data organized by cost behavior to aid in planning, controlling, and decision making. The contribution format income statement has been developed in response to these needs.

The Contribution Format Income Statement

The crucial distinction between fixed and variable costs is at the heart of the **contribution approach** to constructing income statements. The unique thing about the contribution approach is that it provides managers with an income statement that clearly distinguishes between fixed and variable costs and therefore aids planning, controlling, and decision making. The right-hand side of Exhibit 2–9 shows a contribution format income statement for merchandising companies.

The contribution approach separates costs into fixed and variable categories, first deducting variable expenses from sales to obtain the *contribution margin.* For a merchandising company, cost of goods sold is a variable cost that gets included in the "Variable expenses" portion of the contribution format income statement. The **contribution margin** is the amount remaining from sales revenues after variable expenses have been deducted. This amount *contributes* toward covering fixed expenses and then toward profits for the period.

The contribution format income statement is used as an internal planning and decision-making tool. Its emphasis on cost behavior aids cost-volume-profit analysis (such as we shall be doing in a subsequent chapter), management performance appraisals, and budgeting. Moreover, the contribution approach helps managers organize data pertinent to numerous decisions such as product-line analysis, pricing, use of scarce resources, and make or buy analysis. All of these topics are covered in later chapters.

Cost Classifications for Decision Making

LEARNING OBJECTIVE 2–7
Understand cost classifications used in making decisions: differential costs, opportunity costs, and sunk costs.

Costs are an important feature of many business decisions. In making decisions, it is essential to have a firm grasp of the concepts *differential cost, opportunity cost,* and *sunk cost.*

Differential Cost and Revenue

Decisions involve choosing between alternatives. In business decisions, each alternative will have costs and benefits that must be compared to the costs and benefits of the other available alternatives. A difference in costs between any two alternatives is known as a **differential cost**. A difference in revenues (usually just sales) between any two alternatives is known as **differential revenue**.

A differential cost is also known as an **incremental cost**, although technically an incremental cost should refer only to an increase in cost from one alternative to another; decreases in cost should be referred to as *decremental costs.* Differential cost is a broader term, encompassing both cost increases (incremental costs) and cost decreases (decremental costs) between alternatives.

The accountant's differential cost concept can be compared to the economist's marginal cost concept. In speaking of changes in cost and revenue, the economist uses the terms *marginal cost* and *marginal revenue.* The revenue that can be obtained from selling one more unit of product is called marginal revenue, and the cost involved in producing one more unit of product is called marginal cost. The economist's marginal concept is basically the same as the accountant's differential concept applied to a single unit of output.

Differential costs can be either fixed or variable. To illustrate, assume that Natural Cosmetics, Inc., is thinking about changing its marketing method from distribution through retailers to distribution by a network of neighborhood sales representatives. Present costs and revenues are compared to projected costs and revenues in the following table:

	Retailer Distribution (present)	Sales Representatives (proposed)	Differential Costs and Revenues
Sales (Variable)......................	$700,000	$800,000	$100,000
Cost of goods sold (Variable).........	350,000	400,000	50,000
Advertising (Fixed)...................	80,000	45,000	(35,000)
Commissions (Variable).............	0	40,000	40,000
Warehouse depreciation (Fixed)......	50,000	80,000	30,000
Other expenses (Fixed)..............	60,000	60,000	0
Total expenses......................	540,000	625,000	85,000
Net operating income	$160,000	$175,000	$ 15,000

According to the above analysis, the differential revenue is $100,000 and the differential costs total $85,000, leaving a positive differential net operating income of $15,000 in favor of using sales representatives.

In general, only the differences between alternatives are relevant in decisions. Those items that are the same under all alternatives and that are not affected by the decision can be ignored. For example, in the Natural Cosmetics, Inc., example above, the "Other expenses" category, which is $60,000 under both alternatives, can be ignored because it has no effect on the decision. If it were removed from the calculations, the sales representatives would still be preferred by $15,000. This is an extremely important principle in management accounting that we will revisit in later chapters.

Opportunity Cost and Sunk Cost

Opportunity cost is the potential benefit that is given up when one alternative is selected over another. For example, assume that you have a part-time job while attending college that pays $200 per week. If you spend one week at the beach during spring break without pay, then the $200 in lost wages would be an opportunity cost of taking the week off to be at the beach. Opportunity costs are not usually found in accounting records, but they are costs that must be explicitly considered in every decision a manager makes. Virtually every alternative involves an opportunity cost.

A **sunk cost** is a cost *that has already been incurred* and that cannot be changed by any decision made now or in the future. Because sunk costs cannot be changed by any decision, they are not differential costs. And because only differential costs are relevant in a decision, sunk costs should always be ignored.

To illustrate a sunk cost, assume that a company paid $50,000 several years ago for a special-purpose machine. The machine was used to make a product that is now obsolete and is no longer being sold. Even though in hindsight purchasing the machine may have been unwise, the $50,000 cost has already been incurred and cannot be undone. And it would be folly to continue making the obsolete product in a misguided attempt to "recover" the original cost of the machine. In short, the $50,000 originally paid for the machine is a sunk cost that should be ignored in current decisions.

IN BUSINESS

THE ECONOMICS OF DRIVING YOUR DREAM CAR

The costs of buying, insuring, repairing, and garaging ultra-luxury vehicles can be very expensive. For example, the purchase price alone for a new Lamborghini or Bentley can easily exceed $300,000. Thus, Gotham Dream Cars offers an alternative to customers who want to drive ultra-luxury cars while avoiding the exorbitant costs of ownership. It sells fractional shares in luxury cars—the minimum price starts at $9,000 for 20 driving-days. George Johnson is a Gotham Dream Cars customer who spent $30,000 for 90 driving-days in two types of ultra-luxury vehicles. He noted that "it's not worth it to buy one of these cars when you have to fix them." In essence, Johnson compared the costs of ownership with the rental costs and decided to rent.

© AP Photo/Damian Dovarganes

Source: David Kiley, "My Lamborghini—Today, Anyway," *BusinessWeek*, January 14, 2008, p. 17.

Summary

In this chapter, we have discussed ways in which managers classify costs. How the costs will be used—for assigning costs to cost objects, preparing external reports, predicting cost behavior, or decision making—will dictate how the costs are classified.

For purposes of assigning costs to cost objects such as products or departments, costs are classified as direct or indirect. Direct costs can be conveniently traced to cost objects. Indirect costs cannot be conveniently traced to cost objects.

For external reporting purposes, costs are classified as either product costs or period costs. Product costs are assigned to inventories and are considered assets until the products are sold. At the point of sale, product costs become cost of goods sold on the income statement. In contrast, period costs are taken directly to the income statement as expenses in the period in which they are incurred.

For purposes of predicting how costs will react to changes in activity, costs are classified into three categories—variable, fixed, and mixed. Variable costs, in total, are strictly proportional to activity. The variable cost per unit is constant. Fixed costs, in total, remain the same as the activity level changes within the relevant range. The average fixed cost per unit decreases as the activity level increases. Mixed costs consist of variable and fixed elements and can be expressed in equation form as $Y = a + bX$, where X is the activity, Y is the total cost, a is the fixed cost element, and b is the variable cost per unit of activity.

If the relation between cost and activity appears to be linear based on a scattergraph plot, then the variable and fixed components of a mixed cost can be estimated using the high-low method, which implicitly draws a straight line through the points of lowest activity and highest activity, or the least-squares regression method, which uses all of the data points to compute a regression line that minimizes the sum of the squares errors.

The traditional income statement format is used primarily for external reporting purposes. It organizes costs using product and period cost classifications. The contribution format income statement aids decision making because it organizes costs using variable and fixed cost classifications.

For purposes of making decisions, the concepts of differential cost and revenue, opportunity cost, and sunk cost are vitally important. Differential costs and revenues are the costs and revenues that differ between alternatives. Opportunity cost is the benefit that is forgone when one alternative is selected over another. Sunk cost is a cost that occurred in the past and cannot be altered. Differential costs and opportunity costs should be carefully considered in decisions. Sunk costs are always irrelevant in decisions and should be ignored.

Review Problem 1: Cost Terms

Many new cost terms have been introduced in this chapter. It will take you some time to learn what each term means and how to properly classify costs in an organization. Consider the following example: Porter Company manufactures furniture, including tables. Selected costs are given below:

1. The tables are made of wood that costs $100 per table.
2. The tables are assembled by workers, at a wage cost of $40 per table.
3. Workers assembling the tables are supervised by a factory supervisor who is paid $38,000 per year.
4. Electrical costs are $2 per machine-hour. Four machine-hours are required to produce a table.
5. The depreciation on the machines used to make the tables totals $10,000 per year. The machines have no resale value and do not wear out through use.
6. The salary of the president of the company is $100,000 per year.
7. The company spends $250,000 per year to advertise its products.
8. Salespersons are paid a commission of $30 for each table sold.
9. Instead of producing the tables, the company could rent its factory space for $50,000 per year.

Required:

Classify these costs according to the various cost terms used in the chapter. *Carefully study the classification of each cost.* If you don't understand why a particular cost is classified the way it is, reread the section of the chapter discussing the particular cost term. The terms *variable cost* and *fixed cost* refer to how costs behave with respect to the number of tables produced in a year.

Solution to Review Problem 1

				Product Cost				
	Variable Cost	Fixed Cost	Period (Selling and Administrative) Cost	Direct Materials	Direct Labor	Manufacturing Overhead	Sunk Cost	Opportunity Cost
1. Wood used in a table ($100 per table)	X			X				
2. Labor cost to assemble a table ($40 per table) . . .	X				X			
3. Salary of the factory supervisor ($38,000 per year)		X				X		
4. Cost of electricity to produce tables ($2 per machine-hour)	X					X		
5. Depreciation of machines used to produce tables ($10,000 per year)		X				X	X*	
6. Salary of the company president ($100,000 per year)		X	X					
7. Advertising expense ($250,000 per year)		X	X					
8. Commissions paid to salespersons ($30 per table sold)	X		X					
9. Rental income forgone on factory space								X†

*This is a sunk cost because the outlay for the equipment was made in a previous period.

†This is an opportunity cost because it represents the potential benefit that is lost or sacrificed as a result of using the factory space to produce tables. Opportunity cost is a special category of cost that is not ordinarily recorded in an organization's accounting records. To avoid possible confusion with other costs, we will not attempt to classify this cost in any other way except as an opportunity cost.

Review Problem 2: High-Low Method

The administrator of Azalea Hills Hospital would like a cost formula linking the administrative costs involved in admitting patients to the number of patients admitted during a month. The Admitting Department's costs and the number of patients admitted during the immediately preceding eight months are given in the following table:

Month	Number of Patients Admitted	Admitting Department Costs
May	1,800	$14,700
June	1,900	$15,200
July	1,700	$13,700
August	1,600	$14,000
September	1,500	$14,300
October	1,300	$13,100
November	1,100	$12,800
December	1,500	$14,600

Required:

1. Use the high-low method to estimate the fixed and variable components of admitting costs.
2. Express the fixed and variable components of admitting costs as a cost formula in the form $Y = a + bX$.

Solution to Review Problem 2

1. The first step in the high-low method is to identify the periods of the lowest and highest activity. Those periods are November (1,100 patients admitted) and June (1,900 patients admitted).

   The second step is to compute the variable cost per unit using those two data points:

Month	Number of Patients Admitted	Admitting Department Costs
High activity level (June)	1,900	$15,200
Low activity level (November)	1,100	12,800
Change	800	$ 2,400

$$\text{Variable cost} = \frac{\text{Change in cost}}{\text{Change in activity}} = \frac{\$2{,}400}{800 \text{ patients admitted}} = \$3 \text{ per patient admitted}$$

The third step is to compute the fixed cost element by deducting the variable cost element from the total cost at either the high or low activity. In the computation below, the high point of activity is used:

$$\begin{aligned}\text{Fixed cost element} &= \text{Total cost} - \text{Variable cost element}\\ &= \$15{,}200 - (\$3 \text{ per patient admitted} \times 1{,}900 \text{ patients admitted})\\ &= \$9{,}500\end{aligned}$$

2. The cost formula is $Y = \$9{,}500 + \$3X$.

Glossary

Account analysis A method for analyzing cost behavior in which an account is classified as either variable or fixed based on the analyst's prior knowledge of how the cost in the account behaves. (p. 35)

Activity base A measure of whatever causes the incurrence of a variable cost. For example, the total cost of X-ray film in a hospital will increase as the number of X-rays taken increases. Therefore, the number of X-rays is the activity base that explains the total cost of X-ray film. (p. 29)

Administrative costs All executive, organizational, and clerical costs associated with the general management of an organization rather than with manufacturing or selling. (p. 26)

Committed fixed costs Investments in facilities, equipment, and basic organizational structure that can't be significantly reduced even for short periods of time without making fundamental changes. (p. 31)

Common cost A cost that is incurred to support a number of cost objects but that cannot be traced to them individually. For example, the wage cost of the pilot of a 747 airliner is a common cost of all of the passengers on the aircraft. Without the pilot, there would be no flight and no passengers. But no part of the pilot's wage is caused by any one passenger taking the flight. (p. 25)

Contribution approach An income statement format that organizes costs by their behavior. Costs are separated into variable and fixed categories rather than being separated into product and period costs for external reporting purposes. (p. 41)

Contribution margin The amount remaining from sales revenues after all variable expenses have been deducted. (p. 41)

Conversion cost Direct labor cost plus manufacturing overhead cost. (p. 28)

Cost behavior The way in which a cost reacts to changes in the level of activity. (p. 29)

Cost object Anything for which cost data are desired. Examples of cost objects are products, customers, jobs, and parts of the organization such as departments or divisions. (p. 24)

Cost structure The relative proportion of fixed, variable, and mixed costs in an organization. (p. 29)

Dependent variable A variable that responds to some causal factor; total cost is the dependent variable, as represented by the letter Y, in the equation $Y = a + bX$. (p. 35)

Differential cost A difference in cost between two alternatives. Also see *Incremental cost.* (p. 41)

Differential revenue The difference in revenue between two alternatives. (p. 41)

Direct cost A cost that can be easily and conveniently traced to a specified cost object. (p. 24)

Direct labor Factory labor costs that can be easily traced to individual units of product. Also called *touch labor.* (p. 25)

Direct materials Materials that become an integral part of a finished product and whose costs can be conveniently traced to it. (p. 25)

Discretionary fixed costs Those fixed costs that arise from annual decisions by management to spend on certain fixed cost items, such as advertising and research. (p. 31)

Engineering approach A detailed analysis of cost behavior based on an industrial engineer's evaluation of the inputs that are required to carry out a particular activity and of the prices of those inputs. (p. 35)

Fixed cost A cost that remains constant, in total, regardless of changes in the level of activity within the relevant range. If a fixed cost is expressed on a per unit basis, it varies inversely with the level of activity. (p. 30)

High-low method A method of separating a mixed cost into its fixed and variable elements by analyzing the change in cost between the high and low activity levels. (p. 36)

Incremental cost An increase in cost between two alternatives. Also see *Differential cost.* (p. 41)

Independent variable A variable that acts as a causal factor; activity is the independent variable, as represented by the letter X, in the equation $Y = a + bX$. (p. 35)

Indirect cost A cost that cannot be easily and conveniently traced to a specified cost object. (p. 25)

Indirect labor The labor costs of janitors, supervisors, materials handlers, and other factory workers that cannot be conveniently traced to particular products. (p. 26)

Indirect materials Small items of material such as glue and nails that may be an integral part of a finished product, but whose costs cannot be easily or conveniently traced to it. (p. 25)

Inventoriable costs Synonym for product costs. (p. 27)

Least-squares regression method A method of separating a mixed cost into its fixed and variable elements by fitting a regression line that minimizes the sum of the squared errors. (p. 38)

Linear cost behavior Cost behavior is said to be linear whenever a straight line is a reasonable approximation for the relation between cost and activity. (p. 35)

Manufacturing overhead All manufacturing costs except direct materials and direct labor. (p. 26)

Mixed cost A cost that contains both variable and fixed cost elements. (p. 33)

Opportunity cost The potential benefit that is given up when one alternative is selected over another. (p. 42)

Period costs Costs that are taken directly to the income statement as expenses in the period in which they are incurred or accrued. (p. 27)

Prime cost Direct materials cost plus direct labor cost. (p. 28)

Product costs All costs that are involved in acquiring or making a product. In the case of manufactured goods, these costs consist of direct materials, direct labor, and manufacturing overhead. Also see *Inventoriable costs.* (p. 27)

Raw materials Any materials that go into the final product. (p. 25)

Relevant range The range of activity within which assumptions about variable and fixed cost behavior are valid. (p. 32)

Selling costs All costs that are incurred to secure customer orders and get the finished product or service into the hands of the customer. (p. 26)

Sunk cost A cost that has already been incurred and that cannot be changed by any decision made now or in the future. (p. 42)

Variable cost A cost that varies, in total, in direct proportion to changes in the level of activity. A variable cost is constant per unit. (p. 29)

Questions

2–1 What are the three major elements of product costs in a manufacturing company?

2–2 Define the following: (*a*) direct materials, (*b*) indirect materials, (*c*) direct labor, (*d*) indirect labor, and (*e*) manufacturing overhead.

2–3 Explain the difference between a product cost and a period cost.

2–4 Distinguish between (*a*) a variable cost, (*b*) a fixed cost, and (*c*) a mixed cost.

2–5 What effect does an increase in volume have on—

a. Unit fixed costs?

b. Unit variable costs?

c. Total fixed costs?

d. Total variable costs?

2–6 Define the following terms: (*a*) cost behavior and (*b*) relevant range.

2–7 What is meant by an *activity base* when dealing with variable costs? Give several examples of activity bases.

2–8 Managers often assume a strictly linear relationship between cost and volume. How can this practice be defended in light of the fact that many costs are curvilinear?

2–9 Distinguish between discretionary fixed costs and committed fixed costs.

2–10 Does the concept of the relevant range apply to fixed costs? Explain.

2–11 What is the major disadvantage of the high-low method?

2–12 Give the general formula for a mixed cost. Which term represents the variable cost? The fixed cost?

2–13 What is meant by the term *least-squares regression?*

2–14 What is the difference between a contribution format income statement and a traditional format income statement?

2–15 What is the contribution margin?

2–16 Define the following terms: differential cost, opportunity cost, and sunk cost.

2–17 Only variable costs can be differential costs. Do you agree? Explain.

Multiple-choice questions are available with Connect.

Applying Excel

connect — **Additional student resources are available with Connect.**

LEARNING OBJECTIVE 2–6

The Excel worksheet form that appears below is to be used to recreate Exhibit 2–9. Download the workbook from Connect, where you will also receive instructions about how to use this worksheet.

	A	B	C	D
1	Chapter 2: Applying Excel			
2				
3	**Data**			
4	Sales	$12,000		
5	Variable costs:			
6	Cost of goods sold	$6,000		
7	Variable selling	$600		
8	Variable administrative	$400		
9	Fixed costs:			
10	Fixed selling	$2,500		
11	Fixed administrative	$1,500		
12				
13	*Enter a formula into each of the cells marked with a ? below*			
14	**Exhibit 2-9**			
15				
16	**Traditional Format Income Statement**			
17	Sales		?	
18	Cost of goods sold		?	
19	Gross margin		?	
20	Selling and administrative expenses:			
21	Selling	?		
22	Administrative	?	?	
23	Net operating income		?	
24				
25	**Contribution Format Income Statement**			
26	Sales		?	
27	Variable expenses:			
28	Cost of goods sold	?		
29	Variable selling	?		
30	Variable administration	?	?	
31	Contribution margin		?	
32	Fixed expenses:			
33	Fixed selling	?		
34	Fixed administrative	?	?	
35	Net operating income		?	
36				

Chapter 2 Form | Filled in Chapter 2 Fo

Required:

1. Check your worksheet by changing the variable selling cost in the Data area to $900, keeping all of the other data the same as in Exhibit 2–9. If your worksheet is operating properly, the net operating income under the traditional format income statement and under the contribution format income statement should now be $700 and the contribution margin should now be $4,700. If you do not get these answers, find the errors in your worksheet and correct them.

   How much is the gross margin? Did it change? Why or why not?

2. Suppose that sales are 10% higher as shown below:

Sales	$13,200
Variable costs:	
Cost of goods sold	$ 6,600
Variable selling	$ 990
Variable administrative	$ 440
Fixed costs:	
Fixed selling	$ 2,500
Fixed administrative	$ 1,500

   Enter this new data into your worksheet. Make sure that you change all of the data that are different—not just the sales. Print or copy the income statements from your worksheet.

   What happened to the variable costs and to the fixed costs when sales increased by 10%? Why? Did the contribution margin increase by 10%? Why or why not? Did the net operating income increase by 10%? Why or why not?

Additional student resources are available with Connect.

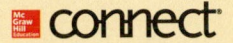

The Foundational 15

LEARNING OBJECTIVES 2–1, 2–2, 2–3, 2–4, 2–6, 2–7

Martinez Company's relevant range of production is 7,500 units to 12,500 units. When it produces and sells 10,000 units, its unit costs are as follows:

	Amount Per Unit
Direct materials	$6.00
Direct labor	$3.50
Variable manufacturing overhead	$1.50
Fixed manufacturing overhead	$4.00
Fixed selling expense	$3.00
Fixed administrative expense	$2.00
Sales commissions	$1.00
Variable administrative expense	$0.50

Required:

1. For financial accounting purposes, what is the total amount of product costs incurred to make 10,000 units?
2. For financial accounting purposes, what is the total amount of period costs incurred to sell 10,000 units?
3. If 8,000 units are sold, what is the variable cost per unit sold?
4. If 12,500 units are sold, what is the variable cost per unit sold?
5. If 8,000 units are sold, what is the total amount of variable costs related to the units sold?
6. If 12,500 units are sold, what is the total amount of variable costs related to the units sold?
7. If 8,000 units are produced, what is the average fixed manufacturing cost per unit produced?
8. If 12,500 units are produced, what is the average fixed manufacturing cost per unit produced?
9. If 8,000 units are produced, what is the total amount of fixed manufacturing cost incurred to support this level of production?
10. If 12,500 units are produced, what is the total amount of fixed manufacturing cost incurred to support this level of production?
11. If 8,000 units are produced, what is the total amount of manufacturing overhead cost incurred to support this level of production? What is this total amount expressed on a per unit basis?
12. If 12,500 units are produced, what is the total amount of manufacturing overhead cost incurred to support this level of production? What is this total amount expressed on a per unit basis?
13. If the selling price is $22 per unit, what is the contribution margin per unit sold?
14. If 11,000 units are produced, what are the total amounts of direct and indirect manufacturing costs incurred to support this level of production?
15. What total incremental cost will Martinez incur if it increases production from 10,000 to 10,001 units?

Additional student resources are available with Connect.

Exercises

EXERCISE 2–1 Identifying Direct and Indirect Costs [LO 2–1]

Northwest Hospital is a full-service hospital that provides everything from major surgery and emergency room care to outpatient clinics.

Required:

For each cost incurred at Northwest Hospital, indicate whether it would most likely be a direct cost or an indirect cost of the specified cost object by placing an *X* in the appropriate column.

Cost		Cost Object	Direct Cost	Indirect Cost
Ex.	Catered food served to patients	A particular patient	X	
1.	The wages of pediatric nurses	The pediatric department		
2.	Prescription drugs	A particular patient		
3.	Heating the hospital	The pediatric department		
4.	The salary of the head of pediatrics	The pediatric department		
5.	The salary of the head of pediatrics	A particular pediatric patient		
6.	Hospital chaplain's salary	A particular patient		
7.	Lab tests by outside contractor	A particular patient		
8.	Lab tests by outside contractor	A particular department		

EXERCISE 2–2 Classifying Manufacturing Costs [LO 2–2]

The PC Works assembles custom computers from components supplied by various manufacturers. The company is very small and its assembly shop and retail sales store are housed in a single facility in a Redmond, Washington, industrial park. Listed below are some of the costs that are incurred at the company.

Required:

For each cost, indicate whether it would most likely be classified as direct labor, direct materials, manufacturing overhead, selling, or an administrative cost.

1. The cost of a hard drive installed in a computer.
2. The cost of advertising in the *Puget Sound Computer User* newspaper.
3. The wages of employees who assemble computers from components.
4. Sales commissions paid to the company's salespeople.
5. The wages of the assembly shop's supervisor.
6. The wages of the company's accountant.
7. Depreciation on equipment used to test assembled computers before release to customers.
8. Rent on the facility in the industrial park.

EXERCISE 2–3 Classification of Costs as Product or Period Cost [LO 2–3]

Suppose that you have been given a summer job as an intern at Issac Aircams, a company that manufactures sophisticated spy cameras for remote-controlled military reconnaissance aircraft. The company, which is privately owned, has approached a bank for a loan to help it finance its growth. The bank requires financial statements before approving such a loan. You have been asked to help prepare the financial statements and were given the following list of costs:

1. Depreciation on salespersons' cars.
2. Rent on equipment used in the factory.
3. Lubricants used for machine maintenance.
4. Salaries of personnel who work in the finished goods warehouse.
5. Soap and paper towels used by factory workers at the end of a shift.
6. Factory supervisors' salaries.
7. Heat, water, and power consumed in the factory.
8. Materials used for boxing products for shipment overseas. (Units are not normally boxed.)
9. Advertising costs.
10. Workers' compensation insurance for factory employees.
11. Depreciation on chairs and tables in the factory lunchroom.
12. The wages of the receptionist in the administrative offices.
13. Cost of leasing the corporate jet used by the company's executives.
14. The cost of renting rooms at a Florida resort for the annual sales conference.
15. The cost of packaging the company's product.

Required:
Classify the above costs as either product costs or period costs for the purpose of preparing the financial statements for the bank.

EXERCISE 2–4 Fixed and Variable Cost Behavior [LO 2–4]

Espresso Express operates a number of espresso coffee stands in busy suburban malls. The fixed weekly expense of a coffee stand is $1,200 and the variable cost per cup of coffee served is $0.22.

Required:
1. Fill in the following table with your estimates of total costs and cost per cup of coffee at the indicated levels of activity for a coffee stand. Round off the cost of a cup of coffee to the nearest tenth of a cent.

	Cups of Coffee Served in a Week		
	2,000	2,100	2,200
Fixed cost	?	?	?
Variable cost	?	?	?
Total cost	?	?	?
Average cost per cup of coffee served	?	?	?

2. Does the average cost per cup of coffee served increase, decrease, or remain the same as the number of cups of coffee served in a week increases? Explain.

EXERCISE 2–5 High-Low Method [LO 2–5]

The Cheyenne Hotel in Big Sky, Montana, has accumulated records of the total electrical costs of the hotel and the number of occupancy-days over the last year. An occupancy-day represents a room rented out for one day. The hotel's business is highly seasonal, with peaks occurring during the ski season and in the summer.

Month	Occupancy-Days	Electrical Costs
January	1,736	$4,127
February	1,904	$4,207
March.	2,356	$5,083
April	960	$2,857
May	360	$1,871
June.	744	$2,696
July.	2,108	$4,670
August.	2,406	$5,148
September	840	$2,691
October.	124	$1,588
November.	720	$2,454
December.	1,364	$3,529

Required:
1. Using the high-low method, estimate the fixed cost of electricity per month and the variable cost of electricity per occupancy-day. Round off the fixed cost to the nearest whole dollar and the variable cost to the nearest whole cent.
2. What other factors other than occupancy-days are likely to affect the variation in electrical costs from month to month?

EXERCISE 2–6 Traditional and Contribution Format Income Statements [LO 2–6]

Cherokee Inc. is a merchandiser that provided the following information:

	Amount
Number of units sold	20,000
Selling price per unit	$30
Variable selling expense per unit	$4
Variable administrative expense per unit	$2
Total fixed selling expense	$40,000
Total fixed administrative expense	$30,000
Beginning merchandise inventory	$24,000
Ending merchandise inventory	$44,000
Merchandise purchases	$180,000

Required:

1. Prepare a traditional income statement.
2. Prepare a contribution format income statement.

EXERCISE 2–7 Differential, Opportunity, and Sunk Costs [LO 2–7]

Northwest Hospital is a full-service hospital that provides everything from major surgery and emergency room care to outpatient clinics. The hospital's Radiology Department is considering replacing an old inefficient X-ray machine with a state-of-the-art digital X-ray machine. The new machine would provide higher quality X-rays in less time and at a lower cost per X-ray. It would also require less power and would use a color laser printer to produce easily readable X-ray images. Instead of investing the funds in the new X-ray machine, the Laboratory Department is lobbying the hospital's management to buy a new DNA analyzer.

Required:

For each of the items below, indicate by placing an *X* in the appropriate column whether it should be considered a differential cost, an opportunity cost, or a sunk cost in the decision to replace the old X-ray machine with a new machine. If none of the categories apply for a particular item, leave all columns blank.

Item	Differential Cost	Opportunity Cost	Sunk Cost
Ex. Cost of X-ray film used in the old machine	X		
1. Cost of the old X-ray machine			
2. The salary of the head of the Radiology Department			
3. The salary of the head of the Pediatrics Department			
4. Cost of the new color laser printer			
5. Rent on the space occupied by Radiology			
6. The cost of maintaining the old machine			
7. Benefits from a new DNA analyzer			
8. Cost of electricity to run the X-ray machines			

EXERCISE 2–8 Cost Behavior; High-Low Method [LO 2–4, LO 2–5]

Hoi Chong Transport, Ltd., operates a fleet of delivery trucks in Singapore. The company has determined that if a truck is driven 105,000 kilometers during a year, the average operating cost is 11.4 cents per kilometer. If a truck is driven only 70,000 kilometers during a year, the average operating cost increases to 13.4 cents per kilometer.

Required:

1. Using the high-low method, estimate the variable and fixed cost elements of the annual cost of the truck operation.
2. Express the variable and fixed costs in the form $Y = a + bX$.
3. If a truck were driven 80,000 kilometers during a year, what total cost would you expect to be incurred?

EXERCISE 2–9 Cost Terminology for Manufacturers [LO 2–2, LO 2–3]

Arden Company reported the following costs and expenses for the most recent month:

Direct materials	$80,000
Direct labor	$42,000
Manufacturing overhead	$19,000
Selling expenses	$22,000
Administrative expenses	$35,000

Required:

1. What is the total amount of product costs?
2. What is the total amount of period costs?
3. What is the total amount of conversion costs?
4. What is the total amount of prime costs?

EXERCISE 2–10 Cost Behavior; Contribution Format Income Statement [LO 2–4, LO 2–6]

Harris Company manufactures and sells a single product. A partially completed schedule of the company's total and per unit costs over the relevant range of 30,000 to 50,000 units produced and sold annually is given below:

	Units Produced and Sold		
	30,000	40,000	50,000
Total costs:			
Variable costs	$180,000	?	?
Fixed costs	300,000	?	?
Total costs	$480,000	?	?
Cost per unit:			
Variable cost	?	?	?
Fixed cost	?	?	?
Total cost per unit	?	?	?

Required:

1. Complete the schedule of the company's total and unit costs above.
2. Assume that the company produces and sells 45,000 units during the year at a selling price of $16 per unit. Prepare a contribution format income statement for the year.

EXERCISE 2–11 High-Low Method; Scattergraph Analysis [LO 2–4, LO 2–5]

The following data relating to units shipped and total shipping expense have been assembled by Archer Company, a wholesaler of large, custom-built air-conditioning units for commercial buildings:

Month	Units Shipped	Total Shipping Expense
January	3	$1,800
February	6	$2,300
March	4	$1,700
April	5	$2,000
May	7	$2,300
June	8	$2,700
July	2	$1,200

Required:

1. Prepare a scattergraph using the data given above. Plot cost on the vertical axis and activity on the horizontal axis. Is there an approximately linear relationship between shipping expense and the number of units shipped?

2. Using the high-low method, estimate the cost formula for shipping expense. Draw a straight line through the high and low data points shown in the scattergraph that you prepared in requirement 1. Make sure your line intersects the *Y* axis.
3. Comment on the accuracy of your high-low estimates assuming a least-squares regression analysis estimated the total fixed costs to be $910.71 per month and the variable cost to be $217.86 per unit. How would the straight line that you drew in requirement 2 differ from a straight line that minimizes the sum of the squared errors?
4. What factors, other than the number of units shipped, are likely to affect the company's shipping expense? Explain.

EXERCISE 2–12 Cost Classification [LO 2–2, LO 2–3, LO 2–4, LO 2–7]

Wollogong Group Ltd. of New South Wales, Australia, acquired its factory building about 10 years ago. For several years, the company has rented out a small annex attached to the rear of the building. The company has received a rental income of $30,000 per year on this space. The renter's lease will expire soon, and rather than renewing the lease, the company has decided to use the space itself to manufacture a new product.

Direct materials cost for the new product will total $80 per unit. To have a place to store finished units of product, the company will rent a small warehouse nearby. The rental cost will be $500 per month. In addition, the company must rent equipment for use in producing the new product; the rental cost will be $4,000 per month. Workers will be hired to manufacture the new product, with direct labor cost amounting to $60 per unit. The space in the annex will continue to be depreciated on a straight-line basis, as in prior years. This depreciation is $8,000 per year.

Advertising costs for the new product will total $50,000 per year. A supervisor will be hired to oversee production; her salary will be $1,500 per month. Electricity for operating machines will be $1.20 per unit. Costs of shipping the new product to customers will be $9 per unit.

To provide funds to purchase materials, meet payrolls, and so forth, the company will have to liquidate some temporary investments. These investments are presently yielding a return of about $3,000 per year.

Required:

Prepare an answer sheet with the following column headings:

Name of the Cost	Variable Cost	Fixed Cost	Product Cost			Period (Selling and Administrative) Cost	Opportunity Cost	Sunk Cost
			Direct Materials	Direct Labor	Manufacturing Overhead			

List the different costs associated with the new product decision down the extreme left column (under Name of the Cost). Then place an *X* under each heading that helps to describe the type of cost involved. There may be *X*'s under several column headings for a single cost. (For example, a cost may be a fixed cost, a period cost, and a sunk cost; you would place an *X* under each of these column headings opposite the cost.)

EXERCISE 2–13 Traditional and Contribution Format Income Statements [LO 2–6]

The Alpine House, Inc., is a large retailer of snow skis. The company assembled the information shown below for the quarter ended March 31:

	Amount
Total sales revenue	$150,000
Selling price per pair of skis	$750
Variable selling expense per pair of skis	$50
Variable administrative expense per pair of skis	$10
Total fixed selling expense	$20,000
Total fixed administrative expense	$20,000
Beginning merchandise inventory	$30,000
Ending merchandise inventory	$40,000
Merchandise purchases	$100,000

Required:

1. Prepare a traditional income statement for the quarter ended March 31.
2. Prepare a contribution format income statement for the quarter ended March 31.
3. What was the contribution toward fixed expenses and profits for each pair of skis sold during the quarter? (State this figure in a single dollar amount per pair of skis.)

EXERCISE 2–14 High-Low Method; Predicting Cost [LO 2–4, LO 2–5]

The Lakeshore Hotel's guest-days of occupancy and custodial supplies expense over the last seven months were:

Month	Guest-Days of Occupancy	Custodial Supplies Expense
March	4,000	$7,500
April.	6,500	$8,250
May.	8,000	$10,500
June	10,500	$12,000
July	12,000	$13,500
August	9,000	$10,750
September.	7,500	$9,750

Guest-days is a measure of the overall activity at the hotel. For example, a guest who stays at the hotel for three days is counted as three guest-days.

Required:

1. Using the high-low method, estimate a cost formula for custodial supplies expense.
2. Using the cost formula you derived above, what amount of custodial supplies expense would you expect to be incurred at an occupancy level of 11,000 guest-days?
3. Prepare a scattergraph using the data given above. Plot custodial supplies expense on the vertical axis and the number of guest-days occupied on the horizontal axis. Draw a straight line through the two data points that correspond to the high and low levels of activity. Make sure your line intersects the *Y*-axis.
4. Comment on the accuracy of your high-low estimates assuming a least-squares regression analysis estimated the total fixed costs to be $3,973.10 per month and the variable cost to be $0.77 per guest-day. How would the straight line that you drew in requirement 3 differ from a straight line that minimizes the sum of the squared errors?
5. Using the least-squares regression estimates given in requirement 4, what custodial supplies expense would you expect to be incurred at an occupancy level of 11,000 guest-days?

EXERCISE 2–15 Classification of Costs as Variable or Fixed and as Product or Period [LO 2–3, LO 2–4]

Below are listed various costs that are found in organizations.

1. Hamburger buns in a Wendy's outlet.
2. Advertising by a dental office.
3. Apples processed and canned by Del Monte.
4. Shipping canned apples from a Del Monte plant to customers.
5. Insurance on a Bausch & Lomb factory producing contact lenses.
6. Insurance on IBM's corporate headquarters.
7. Salary of a supervisor overseeing production of printers at Hewlett-Packard.
8. Commissions paid to automobile salespersons.
9. Depreciation of factory lunchroom facilities at a General Electric plant.
10. Steering wheels installed in BMWs.

Required:

Classify each cost as being either variable or fixed with respect to the number of units produced and sold. Also classify each cost as either a selling and administrative cost or a product cost. Prepare your answer sheet as shown below. Place an *X* in the appropriate columns to show the proper classification of each cost.

	Cost Behavior		Period (Selling and Administrative)	
Cost Item	Variable	Fixed	Cost	Product Cost

Problems

connect Additional student resources are available with Connect.

PROBLEM 2–16 Cost Behavior; High-Low Method; Contribution Format Income Statement [LO 2–4, LO 2–5, LO 2–6]

Morrisey & Brown, Ltd., of Sydney is a merchandising company that is the sole distributor of a product that is increasing in popularity among Australian consumers. The company's income statements for the three most recent months follow:

Morrisey & Brown, Ltd
Income Statements
For the Three Months Ended September 30

	July	August	September
Sales in units	4,000	4,500	5,000
Sales	$400,000	$450,000	$500,000
Cost of goods sold	240,000	270,000	300,000
Gross margin	160,000	180,000	200,000
Selling and administrative expenses:			
Advertising expense	21,000	21,000	21,000
Shipping expense	34,000	36,000	38,000
Salaries and commissions	78,000	84,000	90,000
Insurance expense	6,000	6,000	6,000
Depreciation expense	15,000	15,000	15,000
Total selling and administrative expenses	154,000	162,000	170,000
Net operating income	$ 6,000	$ 18,000	$ 30,000

Required:

1. Identify each of the company's expenses (including cost of goods sold) as either variable, fixed, or mixed.
2. Using the high-low method, separate each mixed expense into variable and fixed elements. State the cost formula for each mixed expense.
3. Redo the company's income statement at the 5,000-unit level of activity using the contribution format.

PROBLEM 2–17 High-Low Method; Predicting Cost [LO 2–4, LO 2–5]

Sawaya Co., Ltd., of Japan is a manufacturing company whose total factory overhead costs fluctuate considerably from year to year according to increases and decreases in the number of direct labor-hours worked in the factory. Total factory overhead costs at high and low levels of activity for recent years are given below:

	Level of Activity	
	Low	High
Direct labor-hours	50,000	75,000
Total factory overhead costs	$14,250,000	$17,625,000

The factory overhead costs above consist of indirect materials, rent, and maintenance. The company has analyzed these costs at the 50,000-hour level of activity as follows:

Indirect materials (variable)	$ 5,000,000
Rent (fixed)	6,000,000
Maintenance (mixed)	3,250,000
Total factory overhead costs	$14,250,000

To have data available for planning, the company wants to break down the maintenance cost into its variable and fixed cost elements.

Required:

1. Estimate how much of the $17,625,000 factory overhead cost at the high level of activity consists of maintenance cost. (*Hint:* To do this, it may be helpful to first determine how much of the $17,625,000 consists of indirect materials and rent. Think about the behavior of variable and fixed costs!)
2. Using the high-low method, estimate a cost formula for maintenance.
3. What total factory overhead costs would you expect the company to incur at an operating level of 70,000 direct labor-hours?

PROBLEM 2–18 Variable and Fixed Costs; Subtleties of Direct and Indirect Costs [LO 2–1, LO 2–4]

Madison Seniors Care Center is a nonprofit organization that provides a variety of health services to the elderly. The center is organized into a number of departments, one of which is the Meals-On-Wheels program that delivers hot meals to seniors in their homes on a daily basis. Below are listed a number of costs of the center and the Meals-On-Wheels program.

example The cost of groceries used in meal preparation
a. The cost of leasing the Meals-On-Wheels van
b. The cost of incidental supplies such as salt, pepper, napkins, and so on
c. The cost of gasoline consumed by the Meals-On-Wheels van
d. The rent on the facility that houses Madison Seniors Care Center, including the Meals-On-Wheels program
e. The salary of the part-time manager of the Meals-On-Wheels program
f. Depreciation on the kitchen equipment used in the Meals-On-Wheels program
g. The hourly wages of the caregiver who drives the van and delivers the meals
h. The costs of complying with health safety regulations in the kitchen
i. The costs of mailing letters soliciting donations to the Meals-On-Wheels program

Required:

For each cost listed above, indicate whether it is a direct or indirect cost of the Meals-On-Wheels program, whether it is a direct or indirect cost of particular seniors served by the program, and whether it is variable or fixed with respect to the number of seniors served. Use the form below for your answer.

		Direct or Indirect Cost of the Meals-on-Wheels Program		Direct or Indirect Cost of Particular Seniors Served by the Meals-on-Wheels Program		Variable or Fixed with Respect to the Number of Seniors Served by the Meals-on-Wheels Program	
Item	Description	Direct	Indirect	Direct	Indirect	Variable	Fixed
Example	The cost of groceries used in meal preparation	X		X		X	

PROBLEM 2–19 Contribution Format versus Traditional Income Statement [LO 2–6]

Marwick's Pianos, Inc., purchases pianos from a large manufacturer and sells them at the retail level. The pianos cost, on the average, $2,450 each from the manufacturer. Marwick's Pianos, Inc., sells the pianos to its customers at an average price of $3,125 each. The selling and administrative costs that the company incurs in a typical month are presented below:

Costs	Cost Formula
Selling:	
Advertising	$700 per month
Sales salaries and commissions	$950 per month, plus 8% of sales
Delivery of pianos to customers	$30 per piano sold
Utilities	$350 per month
Depreciation of sales facilities	$800 per month
Administrative:	
Executive salaries.	$2,500 per month
Insurance	$400 per month
Clerical	$1,000 per month, plus $20 per piano sold
Depreciation of office equipment	$300 per month

During August, Marwick's Pianos, Inc., sold and delivered 40 pianos.

Required:

1. Prepare an income statement for Marwick's Pianos, Inc., for August. Use the traditional format, with costs organized by function.
2. Redo requirement 1 above, this time using the contribution format, with costs organized by behavior. Show costs and revenues on both a total and a per unit basis down through contribution margin.
3. Refer to the income statement you prepared in requirement 2 above. Why might it be misleading to show the fixed costs on a per unit basis?

PROBLEM 2–20 High-Low Method; Predicting Cost [LO 2–4, LO 2–5]

Nova Company's total overhead cost at various levels of activity are presented below:

Month	Machine-Hours	Total Overhead Cost
April.	70,000	$198,000
May	60,000	$174,000
June	80,000	$222,000
July	90,000	$246,000

Assume that the total overhead cost above consists of utilities, supervisory salaries, and maintenance. The breakdown of these costs at the 60,000 machine-hour level of activity is:

Utilities (variable)	$ 48,000
Supervisory salaries (fixed)	21,000
Maintenance (mixed)	105,000
Total overhead cost	$174,000

Nova Company's management wants to break down the maintenance cost into its variable and fixed cost elements.

Required:

1. Estimate how much of the $246,000 of overhead cost in July was maintenance cost. (*Hint:* to do this, it may be helpful to first determine how much of the $246,000 consisted of utilities and supervisory salaries. Think about the behavior of variable and fixed costs!)
2. Using the high-low method, estimate a cost formula for maintenance.
3. Express the company's *total* overhead cost in the linear equation form $Y = a + bX$.
4. What *total* overhead cost would you expect to be incurred at an activity level of 75,000 machine-hours?

PROBLEM 2–21 Cost Classification [LO 2–1, LO 2–3, LO 2–4]

Listed below are costs found in various organizations.

1. Property taxes, factory.
2. Boxes used for packaging detergent produced by the company.
3. Salespersons' commissions.

4. Supervisor's salary, factory.
5. Depreciation, executive autos.
6. Wages of workers assembling computers.
7. Insurance, finished goods warehouses.
8. Lubricants for production equipment.
9. Advertising costs.
10. Microchips used in producing calculators.
11. Shipping costs on merchandise sold.
12. Magazine subscriptions, factory lunchroom.
13. Thread in a garment factory.
14. Billing costs.
15. Executive life insurance.
16. Ink used in textbook production.
17. Fringe benefits, assembly-line workers.
18. Yarn used in sweater production.
19. Wages of receptionist, executive offices.

Required:

Prepare an answer sheet with column headings as shown below. For each cost item, indicate whether it would be variable or fixed with respect to the number of units produced and sold; and then whether it would be a selling cost, an administrative cost, or a manufacturing cost. If it is a manufacturing cost, indicate whether it would typically be treated as a direct cost or an indirect cost with respect to units of product. Three sample answers are provided for illustration.

Cost Item	Variable or Fixed	Selling Cost	Administrative Cost	Manufacturing (Product) Cost	
				Direct	Indirect
Direct labor	V			X	
Executive salaries.	F		X		
Factory rent.	F				X

PROBLEM 2–22 High-Low and Scattergraph Analysis [LO 2–4, LO 2–5]

Pleasant View Hospital of British Columbia has just hired a new chief administrator who is anxious to employ sound management and planning techniques in the business affairs of the hospital. Accordingly, she has directed her assistant to summarize the cost structure of the various departments so that data will be available for planning purposes.

The assistant is unsure how to classify the utilities costs in the Radiology Department because these costs do not exhibit either strictly variable or fixed cost behavior. Utilities costs are very high in the department due to a CAT scanner that draws a large amount of power and is kept running at all times. The scanner can't be turned off due to the long warm-up period required for its use. When the scanner is used to scan a patient, it consumes an additional burst of power. The assistant has accumulated the following data on utilities costs and use of the scanner since the first of the year.

Month	Number of Scans	Utilities Cost
January.	60	$2,200
February.	70	$2,600
March	90	$2,900
April.	120	$3,300
May.	100	$3,000
June	130	$3,600
July	150	$4,000
August	140	$3,600
September.	110	$3,100
October	80	$2,500

The chief administrator has informed her assistant that the utilities cost is probably a mixed cost that will have to be broken down into its variable and fixed cost elements by use of a scattergraph. The assistant feels, however, that if an analysis of this type is necessary, then the high-low method should be used, since it is easier and quicker. The controller has suggested that there may be a better approach.

Required:

1. Using the high-low method, estimate a cost formula for utilities. Express the formula in the form $Y = a + bX$. (The variable rate should be stated in terms of cost per scan.)
2. Prepare a scattergraph by plotting the number of scans and utility cost on a graph. Draw a straight line though the two data points that correspond to the high and low levels of activity. Make sure your line intersects the Y-axis.
3. Comment on the accuracy of your high-low estimates assuming a least-squares regression analysis estimated the total fixed costs to be $1,170.90 per month and the variable cost to be $18.18 per scan. How would the straight line that you drew in requirement 2 differ from a straight line that minimizes the sum of the squared errors?

PROBLEM 2–23 High-Low Method; Contribution Format Income Statement [LO 2–5, LO 2–6]
Milden Company has an exclusive franchise to purchase a product from the manufacturer and distribute it on the retail level. As an aid in planning, the company has decided to start using a contribution format income statement. To have data to prepare such a statement, the company has analyzed its expenses and has developed the following cost formulas:

Cost	Cost Formula
Cost of good sold	$35 per unit sold
Advertising expense	$210,000 per quarter
Sales commissions	6% of sales
Shipping expense	?
Administrative salaries	$145,000 per quarter
Insurance expense	$9,000 per quarter
Depreciation expense	$76,000 per quarter

Management has concluded that shipping expense is a mixed cost, containing both variable and fixed cost elements. Units sold and the related shipping expense over the last eight quarters follow:

Quarter	Units Sold	Shipping Expense
Year 1:		
First	10,000	$119,000
Second	16,000	$175,000
Third	18,000	$190,000
Fourth	15,000	$164,000
Year 2:		
First	11,000	$130,000
Second	17,000	$185,000
Third	20,000	$210,000
Fourth	13,000	$147,000

Milden Company's president would like a cost formula derived for shipping expense so that a budgeted contribution format income statement can be prepared for the next quarter.

Required:

1. Using the high-low method, estimate a cost formula for shipping expense.
2. In the first quarter of Year 3, the company plans to sell 12,000 units at a selling price of $100 per unit. Prepare a contribution format income statement for the quarter.

PROBLEM 2–24 Ethics and the Manager [LO 2–3]

M. K. Gallant is president of Kranbrack Corporation, a company whose stock is traded on a national exchange. In a meeting with investment analysts at the beginning of the year, Gallant had predicted that the company's earnings would grow by 20% this year. Unfortunately, sales have been less than expected for the year, and Gallant concluded within two weeks of the end of the fiscal year that it would be impossible to ultimately report an increase in earnings as large as predicted unless some drastic action was taken. Accordingly, Gallant has ordered that wherever possible, expenditures should be postponed to the new year—including canceling or postponing orders with suppliers, delaying planned maintenance and training, and cutting back on end-of-year advertising and travel. Additionally, Gallant ordered the company's controller to carefully scrutinize all costs that are currently classified as period costs and reclassify as many as possible as product costs. The company is expected to have substantial inventories at the end of the year.

Required:

1. Why would reclassifying period costs as product costs increase this period's reported earnings?
2. Do you believe Gallant's actions are ethical? Why or why not?

PROBLEM 2–25 Cost Classification and Cost Behavior [LO 2–1, LO 2–2, LO 2–3, LO 2–4]

The Dorilane Company specializes in producing a set of wood patio furniture consisting of a table and four chairs. The set enjoys great popularity, and the company has ample orders to keep production going at its full capacity of 2,000 sets per year. Annual cost data at full capacity follow:

Direct labor	$118,000
Advertising	$50,000
Factory supervision	$40,000
Property taxes, factory building	$3,500
Sales commissions	$80,000
Insurance, factory	$2,500
Depreciation, administrative office equipment	$4,000
Lease cost, factory equipment	$12,000
Indirect materials, factory	$6,000
Depreciation, factory building	$10,000
Administrative office supplies (billing)	$3,000
Administrative office salaries	$60,000
Direct materials used (wood, bolts, etc.)	$94,000
Utilities, factory	$20,000

Required:

1. Prepare an answer sheet with the column headings shown below. Enter each cost item on your answer sheet, placing the dollar amount under the appropriate headings. As examples, this has been done already for the first two items in the list above. Note that each cost item is classified in two ways: first, as variable or fixed with respect to the number of units produced and sold; and second, as a selling and administrative cost or a product cost. (If the item is a product cost, it should also be classified as either direct or indirect as shown.)

	Cost Behavior		Period (Selling or Administrative)	Product Cost	
Cost Item	Variable	Fixed	Cost	Direct	Indirect*
Direct labor	$118,000			$118,000	
Advertising		$50,000	$50,000		

*To units of product.

2. Total the dollar amounts in each of the columns in requirement 1 above. Compute the average product cost of one patio set.
3. Assume that production drops to only 1,000 sets annually. Would you expect the average product cost per set to increase, decrease, or remain unchanged? Explain. No computations are necessary.

4. Refer to the original data. The president's brother-in-law has considered making himself a patio set and has priced the necessary materials at a building supply store. The brother-in-law has asked the president if he could purchase a patio set from the Dorilane Company "at cost," and the president agreed to let him do so.
   a. Would you expect any disagreement between the two men over the price the brother-in-law should pay? Explain. What price does the president probably have in mind? The brother-in-law?
   b. Because the company is operating at full capacity, what cost term used in the chapter might be justification for the president to charge the full, regular price to the brother-in-law and still be selling "at cost"?

Cases

CASE 2–26 Mixed Cost Analysis and the Relevant Range [LO 2–4, LO 2–5]

The Ramon Company is a manufacturer that is interested in developing a cost formula to estimate the fixed and variable components of its monthly manufacturing overhead costs. The company wishes to use machine-hours as its measure of activity and has gathered the data below for this year and last year:

	Last Year		This Year	
Month	Machine-Hours	Overhead Costs	Machine-Hours	Overhead Costs
January	21,000	$84,000	21,000	$86,000
February	25,000	$99,000	24,000	$93,000
March	22,000	$89,500	23,000	$93,000
April	23,000	$90,000	22,000	$87,000
May	20,500	$81,500	20,000	$80,000
June	19,000	$75,500	18,000	$76,500
July	14,000	$70,500	12,000	$67,500
August	10,000	$64,500	13,000	$71,000
September	12,000	$69,000	15,000	$73,500
October	17,000	$75,000	17,000	$72,500
November	16,000	$71,500	15,000	$71,000
December	19,000	$78,000	18,000	$75,000

The company leases all of its manufacturing equipment. The lease arrangement calls for a flat monthly fee up to 19,500 machine-hours. If the machine-hours used exceeds 19,500, then the fee becomes strictly variable with respect to the total number of machine-hours consumed during the month. Lease expense is a major element of overhead cost.

Required:

1. Using the high-low method, estimate a manufacturing overhead cost formula.
2. Prepare a scattergraph using all of the data for the two-year period. Fit a straight line or lines to the plotted points using a ruler. Describe the cost behavior pattern revealed by your scattergraph plot.
3. Assume a least-squares regression analysis using all of the given data points estimated the total fixed costs to be $40,102 and the variable costs to be $2.13 per machine-hour. Do you have any concerns about the accuracy of the high-low estimates that you have computed or the least-squares regression estimates that have been provided?
4. Assume that the company consumes 22,500 machine-hours during a month. Using the high-low method, estimate the total overhead cost that would be incurred at this level of activity. Be sure to consider only the data points contained in the relevant range of activity when performing your computations.
5. Comment on the accuracy of your high-low estimates assuming a least-squares regression analysis using only the data points in the relevant range of activity estimated the total fixed costs to be $10,090 and the variable costs to be $3.53 per machine-hour.

CASE 2–27 Scattergraph Analysis; Selection of an Activity Base [LO 2–5]

Angora Wraps of Pendleton, Oregon, makes fine sweaters out of pure angora wool. The business is seasonal, with the largest demand during the fall, the winter, and Christmas holidays. The company must increase production each summer to meet estimated demand.

The company has been analyzing its costs to determine which costs are fixed and variable for planning purposes. Below are data for the company's activity and direct labor costs over the last year.

Month	Thousands of Units Produced	Number of Paid Days	Direct Labor Cost
January	98	20	$14,162
February	76	20	$12,994
March	75	21	$15,184
April	80	22	$15,038
May	85	22	$15,768
June	102	21	$15,330
July	52	19	$13,724
August	136	21	$14,162
September	138	22	$15,476
October	132	23	$15,476
November	86	18	$12,972
December	56	21	$14,074

The number of workdays varies from month to month due to the number of weekdays, holidays, and days of vacation in the month. The paid days include paid vacations (in July) and paid holidays (in November and December). The number of units produced in a month varies depending on demand and the number of workdays in the month.

The company has eight workers who are classified as direct labor.

Required:

1. Plot the direct labor cost and units produced on a scattergraph. (Place cost on the vertical axis and units produced on the horizontal axis.)
2. Plot the direct labor cost and number of paid days on a scattergraph. (Place cost on the vertical axis and the number of paid days on the horizontal axis.)
3. Which measure of actievity—number of units produced or paid days—should be used as the activity base for explaining direct labor cost? Explain.

Appendix 2A: Least-Squares Regression Computations

LEARNING OBJECTIVE 2–8
Analyze a mixed cost using a scattergraph plot and the least-squares regression method.

The least-squares regression method for estimating a linear relationship is based on the equation for a straight line:

$$Y = a + bX$$

As explained in the chapter, least-squares regression selects the values for the intercept a and the slope b that minimize the sum of the squared errors. The following formulas, which are derived in statistics and calculus texts, accomplish that objective:

$$b = \frac{n(\Sigma XY) - (\Sigma X)(\Sigma Y)}{n(\Sigma X^2) - (\Sigma X)^2}$$

$$a = \frac{(\Sigma Y) - b(\Sigma X)}{n}$$

where:

X = The level of activity (independent variable)
Y = The total mixed cost (dependent variable)
a = The total fixed cost (the vertical intercept of the line)
b = The variable cost per unit of activity (the slope of the line)
n = Number of observations
Σ = Sum across all n observations

Manually performing the calculations required by the formulas is tedious at best. Fortunately, Microsoft® Excel can be used to estimate the intercept (fixed cost) and slope (variable cost per unit) that minimize the sum of the squared errors. Excel also provides a statistic called the R^2, which is a measure of "goodness of fit." The $\boldsymbol{R^2}$ tells us the percentage of the variation in the dependent variable (cost) that is explained by variation in the independent variable (activity). The R^2 varies from 0% to 100%, and the higher the percentage, the better. You should always plot the data in a scattergraph, but it is particularly important to check the data visually when the R^2 is low. A quick look at the scattergraph can reveal that there is little relation between the cost and the activity or that the relation is something other than a simple straight line. In such cases, additional analysis would be required.

To illustrate how Excel can be used to prepare a scattergraph plot and to calculate the intercept *a,* the slope *b,* and the R^2, we will use the Brentline Hospital data for patient-days and maintenance costs that was given earlier in the chapter and that is now recreated in Exhibit 2A–1.[1]

To prepare a scattergraph plot, begin by highlighting the data in cells B4 through C10. From the Charts group within the Insert tab, select the "Scatter" subgroup and then click on the choice that has no lines connecting the data points. This should produce a scattergraph plot similar to the one shown in Exhibit 2A–2. Notice that the number of patient-days is plotted on the *X*-axis and the maintenance costs are plotted on the *Y*-axis.[2]

EXHIBIT 2A–1
The Least-Squares Regression Worksheet for Brentline Hospital

	A	B	C
1		Patient	Maintenance
2		Days	Cost
3	*Month*	*X*	*Y*
4	January	5,600	$ 7,900
5	February	7,100	$ 8,500
6	March	5,000	$ 7,400
7	April	6,500	$ 8,200
8	May	7,300	$ 9,100
9	June	8,000	$ 9,800
10	July	6,200	$ 7,800
11			

Least-squares regression

[1] The authors wish to thank Don Schwartz, Professor of Accounting at National University, for providing suggestions that were instrumental in creating this appendix.

[2] To insert labels for the *X*-axis and *Y*-axis, go to the Layout tab in Excel. Then, within the Labels group, select Axis Titles.

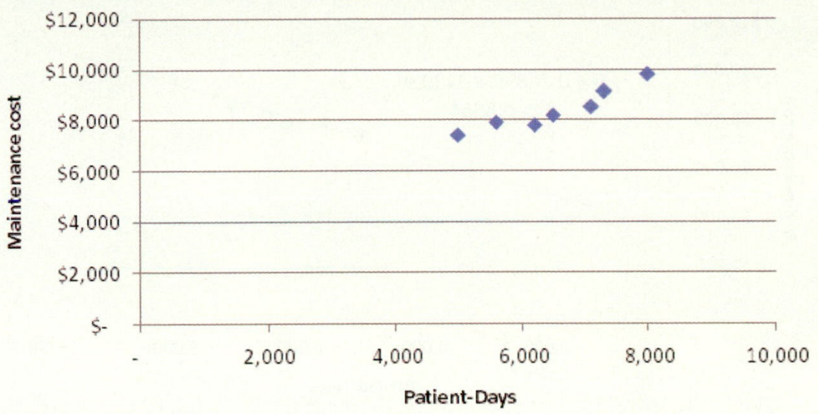

EXHIBIT 2A–2
A Scattergraph Plot for Brentline Hospital

The data is approximately linear, so it makes sense to proceed with estimating a regression equation that minimizes the sum of the squared errors.

To determine the intercept a, the slope b, and the R^2, begin by right clicking on any data point in the scattergraph plot and selecting "Add Trendline." This should produce the screen that is shown in Exhibit 2A–3. Notice that under "Trend/Regression Type" you should select "Linear." Similarly, under "Trendline Name" you should select "Automatic." Next to the word "Backward" you should input the lowest value for the independent variable, which in this example is 5000 patient-days. Taking this particular step instructs Excel to extend your fitted line until it intersects the Y-axis. Finally, you should check the two boxes at the bottom of Exhibit 2A–3 that say "Display Equation on chart" and "Display R-squared value on chart."

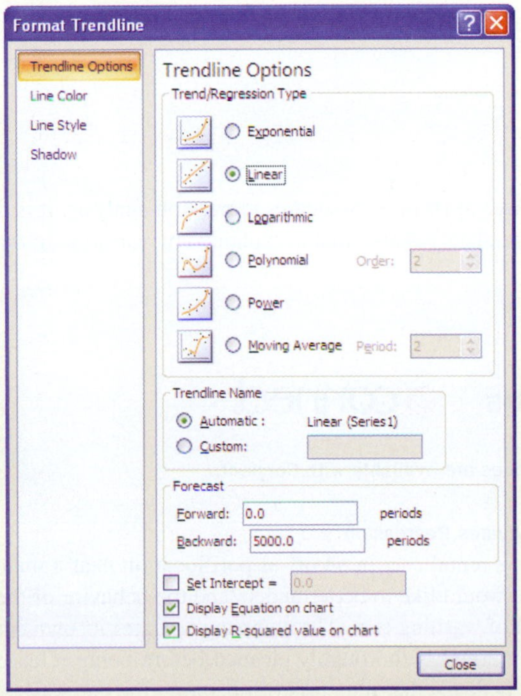

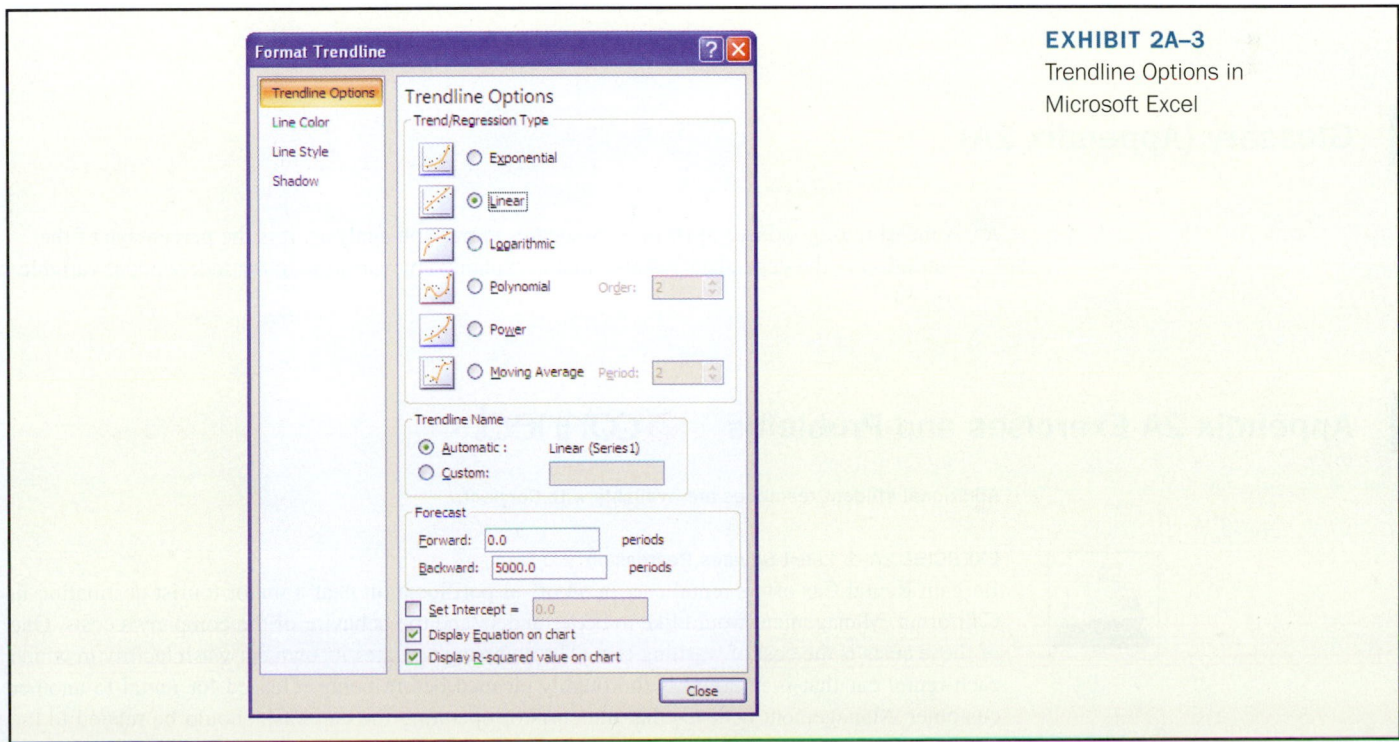

EXHIBIT 2A–3
Trendline Options in Microsoft Excel

EXHIBIT 2A–4
Brentline Hospital: Least-Squares Regression Results

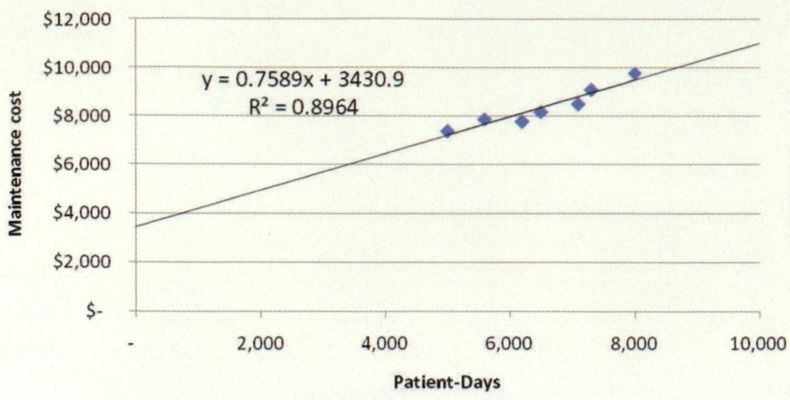

Once you have established these settings, then click "Close." As shown in Exhibit 2A–4, this will automatically insert a line within the scattergraph plot that minimizes the sum of the squared errors. It will also cause the estimated least-squares regression equation and R^2 to be inserted into your scattergraph plot. Instead of depicting the results using the form $Y = a + bX$, Excel uses an equivalent form of the equation depicted as $Y = bX + a$. In other words, Excel reverses the two terms shown to the right of the equals sign. So, in Exhibit 2A–4, Excel shows a least-squares regression equation of $y = 0.7589x + 3{,}430.9$. The slope b in this equation of $0.7589 represents the estimated variable maintenance cost per patient-day. The intercept a in this equation of $3,430.90 (or approximately $3,431) represents the estimated fixed monthly maintenance cost. Note that the R^2 is approximately 0.90, which is quite good and indicates that 90% of the variation in maintenance costs is explained by the variation in patient-days.

Glossary (Appendix 2A)

R^2 A measure of goodness of fit in least-squares regression analysis. It is the percentage of the variation in the dependent variable that is explained by variation in the independent variable. (p. 64)

Appendix 2A Exercises and Problems

connect

Additional student resources are available with Connect.

EXERCISE 2A–1 Least-Squares Regression [LO 2–8]

Bargain Rental Car offers rental cars in an off-airport location near a major tourist destination in California. Management would like to better understand the behavior of the company's costs. One of those costs is the cost of washing cars. The company operates its own car wash facility in which each rental car that is returned is thoroughly cleaned before being released for rental to another customer. Management believes that the costs of operating the car wash should be related to the number of rental returns. Accordingly, the following data have been compiled:

Month	Rental Returns	Car Wash Costs
January.	2,380	$10,825
February.	2,421	$11,865
March	2,586	$11,332
April.	2,725	$12,422
May	2,968	$13,850
June	3,281	$14,419
July	3,353	$14,935
August	3,489	$15,738
September.	3,057	$13,563
October	2,876	$11,889
November	2,735	$12,683
December	2,983	$13,796

Required:

1. Prepare a scattergraph plot. (Place car wash costs on the vertical axis and rental returns on the horizontal axis.)
2. Using least-squares regression, estimate the fixed cost and variable cost elements of monthly car wash costs. The fixed cost element should be estimated to the nearest dollar and the variable cost element to the nearest cent.

EXERCISE 2A–2 Least-Squares Regression [LO 2–4, LO 2–8]

George Caloz & Frères, located in Grenchen, Switzerland, makes prestige high-end custom watches in small lots. One of the company's products, a platinum diving watch, goes through an etching process. The company has observed etching costs as follows over the last six weeks:

Week	Units	Total Etching Cost
1.	4	$ 18
2.	3	17
3.	8	25
4.	6	20
5.	7	24
6.	2	16
	30	$120

For planning purposes, management would like to know the amount of variable etching cost per unit and the total fixed etching cost per week.

Required:

1. Prepare a scattergraph plot. (Place etching costs on the vertical axis and units on the horizontal axis.)
2. Using the least-squares regression method, estimate the variable and fixed elements of etching cost. Express these estimates in the form $Y = a + bX$.
3. If the company processes five units next week, what would be the expected total etching cost?

PROBLEM 2A–3 Least-Squares Regression; Scattergraph; Comparison of Activity Bases [LO 2–4, LO 2–8]

The Hard Rock Mining Company is developing cost formulas for management planning and decision-making purposes. The company's cost analyst has concluded that utilities cost is a mixed cost, and he is attempting to find a base with which the cost might be closely correlated. The controller has suggested that tons mined might be a good base to use in developing a cost formula. The production superintendent disagrees; she thinks that direct labor-hours would be a better base. The cost analyst has decided to try both bases and has assembled the following information:

Quarter	Tons Mined	Direct Labor-Hours	Utilities Cost
Year 1:			
First.	15,000	5,000	$50,000
Second.	11,000	3,000	$45,000
Third	21,000	4,000	$60,000
Fourth.	12,000	6,000	$75,000
Year 2:			
First.	18,000	10,000	$100,000
Second.	25,000	9,000	$105,000
Third	30,000	8,000	$85,000
Fourth.	28,000	11,000	$120,000

Required:

1. Using tons mined as the independent variable, prepare a scattergraph that plots tons mined on the horizontal axis and utilities cost on the vertical axis. Determine a cost formula for utilities cost using least-squares regression. Express this cost formula in the form $Y = a + bX$.
2. Using direct labor-hours as the independent variable, prepare a scattergraph that plots direct labor-hours on the horizontal axis and utilities cost on the vertical axis. Determine a cost formula for utilities cost using least-squares regression. Express this cost formula in the form $Y = a + bX$.
3. Would you recommend that the company use tons mined or direct labor-hours as a base for planning utilities cost?

PROBLEM 2A–4 Least-Squares Regression Method; Scattergraph; Cost Behavior [LO 2–4, LO 2–8]
Professor John Morton has just been appointed chairperson of the Finance Department at Westland University. In reviewing the department's cost records, Professor Morton has found the following total cost associated with Finance 101 over the last several terms:

Term	Number of Sections Offered	Total Cost
Fall, last year	4	$10,000
Winter, last year	6	$14,000
Summer, last year.	2	$7,000
Fall, this year	5	$13,000
Winter, this year	3	$9,500

Professor Morton knows that there are some variable costs, such as amounts paid to graduate assistants, associated with the course. He would like to have the variable and fixed costs separated for planning purposes.

Required:

1. Prepare a scattergraph plot. (Place total cost on the vertical axis and number of sections offered on the horizontal axis.)
2. Using the least-squares regression method, estimate the variable cost per section and the total fixed cost per term for Finance 101. Express these estimates in the linear equation form $Y = a + bX$.
3. Assume that because of the small number of sections offered during the Winter Term this year, Professor Morton will have to offer eight sections of Finance 101 during the Fall Term. Compute the expected total cost for Finance 101. Can you see any problem with using the cost formula from requirement 2 above to derive this total cost figure? Explain.

CASE 2A–5 Analysis of Mixed Costs in a Pricing Decision [LO 2–4, LO 2–8]

Maria Chavez owns a catering company that serves food and beverages at parties and business functions. Chavez's business is seasonal, with a heavy schedule during the summer months and holidays and a lighter schedule at other times.

One of the major events Chavez's customers request is a cocktail party. She offers a standard cocktail party and has estimated the cost per guest as follows:

Food and beverages	$15.00
Labor (0.5 hrs. @ $10.00/hr.)	5.00
Overhead (0.5 hrs. @ $13.98/hr.)	6.99
Total cost per guest	$26.99

The standard cocktail party lasts three hours and Chavez hires one worker for every six guests, so that works out to one-half hour of labor per guest. These workers are hired only as needed and are paid only for the hours they actually work.

When bidding on cocktail parties, Chavez adds a 15% markup to yield a price of about $31 per guest. She is confident about her estimates of the costs of food and beverages and labor but is not as comfortable with the estimate of overhead cost. The $13.98 overhead cost per labor-hour was determined by dividing total overhead expenses for the last 12 months by total labor-hours for the same period. Monthly data concerning overhead costs and labor-hours follow:

Month	Labor-Hours	Overhead Expenses
January	2,500	$ 55,000
February	2,800	59,000
March	3,000	60,000
April	4,200	64,000
May	4,500	67,000
June	5,500	71,000
July	6,500	74,000
August	7,500	77,000
September	7,000	75,000
October	4,500	68,000
November	3,100	62,000
December	6,500	73,000
Total	57,600	$805,000

Chavez has received a request to bid on a 180-guest fund-raising cocktail party to be given next month by an important local charity. (The party would last the usual three hours.) She would like to win this contract because the guest list for this charity event includes many prominent individuals that she would like to land as future clients. Maria is confident that these potential customers would be favorably impressed by her company's services at the charity event.

Required:

1. Prepare a scattergraph plot that puts labor-hours on the *X*-axis and overhead expenses on the *Y*-axis. What insights are revealed by your scattergraph?
2. Use the least-squares regression method to estimate the fixed and variable components of overhead expenses. Express these estimates in the form $Y = a + bX$.
3. Estimate the contribution to profit of a standard 180-guest cocktail party if Chavez charges her usual price of $31 per guest. (In other words, by how much would her overall profit increase?)
4. How low could Chavez bid for the charity event in terms of a price per guest and still not lose money on the event itself?
5. The individual who is organizing the charity's fund-raising event has indicated that he has already received a bid under $30 from another catering company. Do you think Chavez should bid below her normal $31 per guest price for the charity event? Why or why not?

(CMA, adapted)

Chapter 3

LEARNING OBJECTIVES

After studying Chapter 3, you should be able to:

LO3–1 Explain how changes in activity affect contribution margin and net operating income.

LO3–2 Prepare and interpret a cost-volume-profit (CVP) graph and a profit graph.

LO3–3 Use the contribution margin ratio (CM ratio) to compute changes in contribution margin and net operating income resulting from changes in sales volume.

LO3–4 Show the effects on net operating income of changes in variable costs, fixed costs, selling price, and volume.

LO3–5 Determine the break-even point.

LO3–6 Determine the level of sales needed to achieve a desired target profit.

LO3–7 Compute the margin of safety and explain its significance.

LO3–8 Compute the degree of operating leverage at a particular level of sales and explain how it can be used to predict changes in net operating income.

LO3–9 Compute the break-even point for a multiproduct company and explain the effects of shifts in the sales mix on contribution margin and the break-even point.

Cost–Volume–Profit Relationships

Moreno Turns Around the Los Angeles Angels

BUSINESS FOCUS

© Comstock/Getty Images, RF

When Arturo Moreno bought Major League Baseball's Los Angeles Angels in 2003, the team was drawing 2.3 million fans and losing $5.5 million per year. Moreno immediately cut prices to attract more fans and increase profits. In his first spring training game, he reduced the price of selected tickets from $12 to $6. By increasing attendance, Moreno understood that he would sell more food and souvenirs. He dropped the price of draft beer by $2 and cut the price of baseball caps from $20 to $7.

The Angels now consistently draw about 3.4 million fans per year. This growth in attendance helped double stadium sponsorship revenue to $26 million, and it motivated the Fox Sports Network to pay the Angels $500 million to broadcast all of its games for the next ten years. Since Moreno bought the Angels, annual revenues have jumped from $127 million to $212 million, and the team's operating loss of $5.5 million has been transformed to a profit of $10.3 million.

Source: Matthew Craft, "Moreno's Math," *Forbes,* May 11, 2009, pp. 84–87.

Cost–volume–profit (CVP) analysis helps managers make many important decisions such as what products and services to offer, what prices to charge, what marketing strategy to use, and what cost structure to maintain. Its primary purpose is to estimate how profits are affected by the following five factors:

1. Selling prices.
2. Sales volume.
3. Unit variable costs.
4. Total fixed costs.
5. Mix of products sold.

To simplify CVP calculations, managers typically adopt the following assumptions with respect to these factors[1]:

1. Selling price is constant. The price of a product or service will not change as volume changes.
2. Costs are linear and can be accurately divided into variable and fixed elements. The variable element is constant per unit. The fixed element is constant in total over the entire relevant range.
3. In multiproduct companies, the mix of products sold remains constant.

While these assumptions may be violated in practice, the results of CVP analysis are often "good enough" to be quite useful. Perhaps the greatest danger lies in relying on simple CVP analysis when a manager is contemplating a large change in sales volume that lies outside the relevant range. However, even in these situations the CVP model can be adjusted to take into account anticipated changes in selling prices, variable costs per unit, total fixed costs, and the sales mix that arise when the estimated sales volume falls outside the relevant range.

To help explain the role of CVP analysis in business decisions, we'll now turn our attention to the case of Acoustic Concepts, Inc., a company founded by Prem Narayan.

MANAGERIAL ACCOUNTING IN ACTION

The Issue

Prem, who was a graduate student in engineering at the time, started Acoustic Concepts to market a radical new speaker he had designed for automobile sound systems. The speaker, called the Sonic Blaster, uses an advanced microprocessor and proprietary software to boost amplification to awesome levels. Prem contracted with a Taiwanese electronics manufacturer to produce the speaker. With seed money provided by his family, Prem placed an order with the manufacturer and ran advertisements in auto magazines.

The Sonic Blaster was an immediate success, and sales grew to the point that Prem moved the company's headquarters out of his apartment and into rented quarters in a nearby industrial park. He also hired a receptionist, an accountant, a sales manager, and a small sales staff to sell the speakers to retail stores. The accountant, Bob Luchinni, had worked for several small companies where he had acted as a business advisor as well as accountant and bookkeeper. The following discussion occurred soon after Bob was hired:

Prem: Bob, I've got a lot of questions about the company's finances that I hope you can help answer.

Bob: We're in great shape. The loan from your family will be paid off within a few months.

Prem: I know, but I am worried about the risks I've taken on by expanding operations. What would happen if a competitor entered the market and our sales slipped? How far could sales drop without putting us into the red? Another question I've been trying to resolve is how much our sales would have to increase to justify the big marketing campaign the sales staff is pushing for.

Bob: Marketing always wants more money for advertising.

Prem: And they are always pushing me to drop the selling price on the speaker. I agree with them that a lower price will boost our sales volume, but I'm not sure the increased volume will offset the loss in revenue from the lower price.

[1] One additional assumption often used in manufacturing companies is that inventories do not change. The number of units produced equals the number of units sold.

Bob: It sounds like these questions are all related in some way to the relationships among our selling prices, our costs, and our volume. I shouldn't have a problem coming up with some answers.

Prem: Can we meet again in a couple of days to see what you have come up with?

Bob: Sounds good. By then I'll have some preliminary answers for you as well as a model you can use for answering similar questions in the future.

The Basics of Cost-Volume-Profit (CVP) Analysis

Bob Luchinni's preparation for his forthcoming meeting with Prem begins with the contribution income statement. The contribution income statement emphasizes the behavior of costs and therefore is extremely helpful to managers in judging the impact on profits of changes in selling price, cost, or volume. Bob will base his analysis on the following contribution income statement he prepared last month:

Acoustic Concepts, Inc.
Contribution Income Statement
For the Month of June

	Total	Per Unit
Sales (400 speakers)	$100,000	$250
Variable expenses	60,000	150
Contribution margin	40,000	$100
Fixed expenses	35,000	
Net operating income	$ 5,000	

Notice that sales, variable expenses, and contribution margin are expressed on a per unit basis as well as in total on this contribution income statement. The per unit figures will be very helpful to Bob in some of his calculations. Note that this contribution income statement has been prepared for management's use inside the company and would not ordinarily be made available to those outside the company.

Contribution Margin

LEARNING OBJECTIVE 3–1
Explain how changes in activity affect contribution margin and net operating income.

Contribution margin is the amount remaining from sales revenue after variable expenses have been deducted. Thus, it is the amount available to cover fixed expenses and then to provide profits for the period. Notice the sequence here—contribution margin is used *first* to cover the fixed expenses, and then whatever remains goes toward profits. If the contribution margin is not sufficient to cover the fixed expenses, then a loss occurs for the period. To illustrate with an extreme example, assume that Acoustic Concepts sells only one speaker during a particular month. The company's income statement would appear as follows:

Contribution Income Statement
Sales of 1 Speaker

	Total	Per Unit
Sales (1 speaker)	$ 250	$250
Variable expenses	150	150
Contribution margin	100	$100
Fixed expenses	35,000	
Net operating loss	$ (34,900)	

For each additional speaker the company sells during the month, $100 more in contribution margin becomes available to help cover the fixed expenses. If a second speaker is sold, for example, then the total contribution margin will increase by $100 (to a total of $200) and the company's loss will decrease by $100, to $34,800:

Contribution Income Statement
Sales of 2 Speakers

	Total	Per Unit
Sales (2 speakers)	$ 500	$250
Variable expenses	300	150
Contribution margin	200	$100
Fixed expenses	35,000	
Net operating loss	$ (34,800)	

If enough speakers can be sold to generate $35,000 in contribution margin, then all of the fixed expenses will be covered and the company will *break even* for the month—that is, it will show neither profit nor loss but just cover all of its costs. To reach the break-even point, the company will have to sell 350 speakers in a month because each speaker sold yields $100 in contribution margin:

Contribution Income Statement
Sales of 350 Speakers

	Total	Per Unit
Sales (350 speakers)	$87,500	$250
Variable expenses	52,500	150
Contribution margin	35,000	$100
Fixed expenses	35,000	
Net operating income	$ 0	

Computation of the break-even point is discussed in detail later in the chapter; for the moment, note that the **break-even point** is the level of sales at which profit is zero.

Once the break-even point has been reached, net operating income will increase by the amount of the unit contribution margin for each additional unit sold. For example, if 351 speakers are sold in a month, then the net operating income for the month will be $100 because the company will have sold 1 speaker more than the number needed to break even:

Contribution Income Statement
Sales of 351 Speakers

	Total	Per Unit
Sales (351 speakers)	$87,750	$250
Variable expenses	52,650	150
Contribution margin	35,100	$100
Fixed expenses	35,000	
Net operating income	$ 100	

If 352 speakers are sold (2 speakers above the break-even point), the net operating income for the month will be $200. If 353 speakers are sold (3 speakers above the break-even point), the net operating income for the month will be $300, and so forth. To estimate the profit at any sales volume above the break-even point, multiply the number of units sold in excess of the break-even point by the unit contribution margin. The result represents the anticipated profits for the period. Or, to estimate the effect of a planned increase in sales on profits, simply multiply the increase in units sold by the unit contribution margin. The result will be the expected increase in profits. To illustrate, if Acoustic Concepts is currently selling 400 speakers per month and plans to increase sales to 425 speakers per month, the anticipated impact on profits can be computed as follows:

Increased number of speakers to be sold	25
Contribution margin per speaker.	× $100
Increase in net operating income	$2,500

These calculations can be verified as follows:

	Sales Volume			
	400 Speakers	425 Speakers	Difference (25 Speakers)	Per Unit
Sales (@ $250 per speaker)	$100,000	$106,250	$6,250	$250
Variable expenses (@ $150 per speaker)	60,000	63,750	3,750	150
Contribution margin	40,000	42,500	2,500	$100
Fixed expenses.	35,000	35,000	0	
Net operating income	$ 5,000	$ 7,500	$2,500	

To summarize, if sales are zero, the company's loss would equal its fixed expenses. Each unit that is sold reduces the loss by the amount of the unit contribution margin. Once the break-even point has been reached, each additional unit sold increases the company's profit by the amount of the unit contribution margin.

CVP Relationships in Equation Form

The contribution format income statement can be expressed in equation form as follows:

$$\text{Profit} = (\text{Sales} - \text{Variable expenses}) - \text{Fixed expenses}$$

For brevity, we use the term *profit* to stand for net operating income in equations.

When a company has only a *single* product, as at Acoustic Concepts, we can further refine the equation as follows:

$$\text{Sales} = \text{Selling price per unit} \times \text{Quantity sold} = P \times Q$$

$$\text{Variable expenses} = \text{Variable expenses per unit} \times \text{Quantity sold} = V \times Q$$

$$\text{Profit} = (P \times Q - V \times Q) - \text{Fixed expenses}$$

We can do all of the calculations of the previous section using this simple equation. For example, on the previous page we computed that the net operating income (profit) at sales of 351 speakers would be $100. We can arrive at the same conclusion using the above equation as follows:

$$\text{Profit} = (P \times Q - V \times Q) - \text{Fixed expenses}$$

$$\begin{aligned}\text{Profit} &= (\$250 \times 351 - \$150 \times 351) - \$35{,}000\\ &= (\$250 - \$150) \times 351 - \$35{,}000\\ &= (\$100) \times 351 - \$35{,}000\\ &= \$35{,}100 - \$35{,}000 = \$100\end{aligned}$$

It is often useful to express the simple profit equation in terms of the unit contribution margin (Unit CM) as follows:

$$\text{Unit CM} = \text{Selling price per unit} - \text{Variable expenses per unit} = P - V$$

$$\text{Profit} = (P \times Q - V \times Q) - \text{Fixed expenses}$$

$$\text{Profit} = (P - V) \times Q - \text{Fixed expenses}$$

$$\text{Profit} = \text{Unit CM} \times Q - \text{Fixed expenses}$$

We could also have used this equation to determine the profit at sales of 351 speakers as follows:

$$\begin{aligned}\text{Profit} &= \text{Unit CM} \times Q - \text{Fixed expenses}\\ &= \$100 \times 351 - \$35{,}000\\ &= \$35{,}100 - \$35{,}000 = \$100\end{aligned}$$

For those who are comfortable with algebra, the quickest and easiest approach to solving the problems in this chapter may be to use the simple profit equation in one of its forms.

CVP Relationships in Graphic Form

LEARNING OBJECTIVE 3–2
Prepare and interpret a cost-volume-profit (CVP) graph and a profit graph.

The relationships among revenue, cost, profit, and volume are illustrated on a **cost-volume-profit (CVP) graph**. A CVP graph highlights CVP relationships over wide ranges of activity. To help explain his analysis to Prem Narayan, Bob Luchinni prepared a CVP graph for Acoustic Concepts.

Preparing the CVP Graph In a CVP graph (sometimes called a *break-even chart*), unit volume is represented on the horizontal (*X*) axis and dollars on the vertical (*Y*) axis. Preparing a CVP graph involves the three steps depicted in Exhibit 3–1:

EXHIBIT 3–1
Preparing the CVP Graph

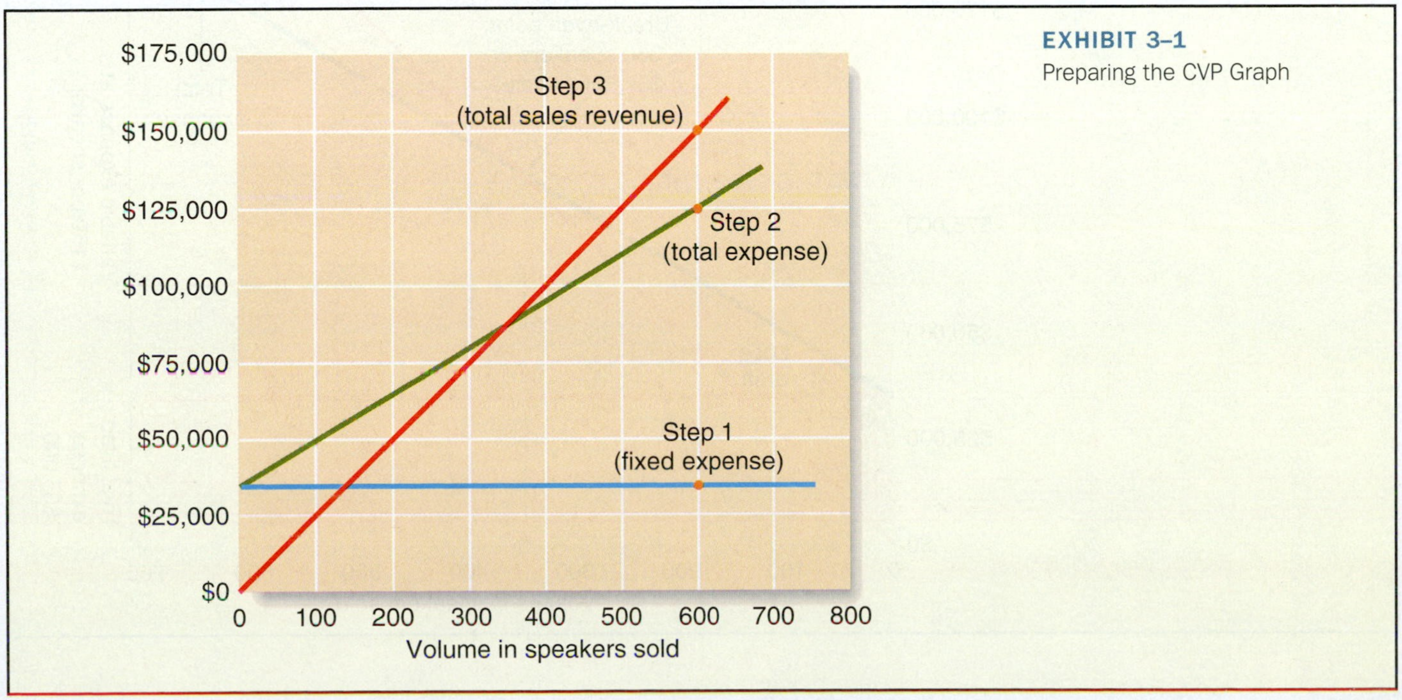

1. Draw a line parallel to the volume axis to represent total fixed expense. For Acoustic Concepts, total fixed expenses are $35,000.
2. Choose some volume of unit sales and plot the point representing total expense (fixed and variable) at the sales volume you have selected. In Exhibit 3–1, Bob Luchinni chose a volume of 600 speakers. Total expense at that sales volume is:

Fixed expense.	$ 35,000
Variable expense (600 speakers × $150 per speaker)	90,000
Total expense	$125,000

   After the point has been plotted, draw a line through it back to the point where the fixed expense line intersects the dollars axis.
3. Again choose some sales volume and plot the point representing total sales dollars at the activity level you have selected. In Exhibit 3–1, Bob Luchinni again chose a volume of 600 speakers. Sales at that volume total $150,000 (600 speakers × $250 per speaker). Draw a line through this point back to the origin.

The interpretation of the completed CVP graph is given in Exhibit 3–2. The anticipated profit or loss at any given level of sales is measured by the vertical distance between the total revenue line (sales) and the total expense line (variable expense plus fixed expense).

The break-even point is where the total revenue and total expense lines cross. The break-even point of 350 speakers in Exhibit 3–2 agrees with the break-even point computed earlier.

EXHIBIT 3–2
The Completed CVP Graph

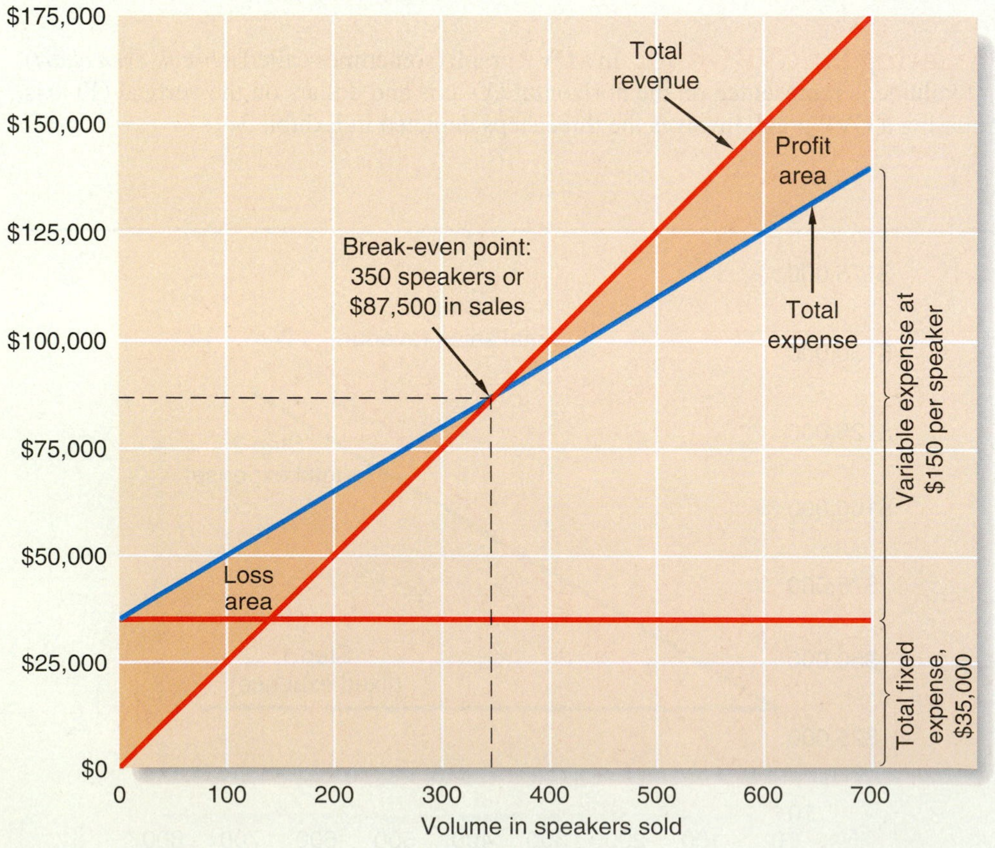

As discussed earlier, when sales are below the break-even point—in this case, 350 units—the company suffers a loss. Note that the loss (represented by the vertical distance between the total expense and total revenue lines) gets bigger as sales decline. When sales are above the break-even point, the company earns a profit and the size of the profit (represented by the vertical distance between the total revenue and total expense lines) increases as sales increase.

An even simpler form of the CVP graph, which we call a profit graph, is presented in Exhibit 3–3. That graph is based on the following equation:

$$\text{Profit} = \text{Unit CM} \times Q - \text{Fixed expenses}$$

In the case of Acoustic Concepts, the equation can be expressed as:

$$\text{Profit} = \$100 \times Q - \$35{,}000$$

Because this is a linear equation, it plots as a single straight line. To plot the line, compute the profit at two different sales volumes, plot the points, and then connect them with a straight line. For example, when the sales volume is zero (i.e., $Q = 0$), the profit is – \$35,000 (= \$100 × 0 – \$35,000). When Q is 600, the profit is \$25,000 (= \$100 × 600 – \$35,000). These two points are plotted in Exhibit 3–3 and a straight line has been drawn through them.

The break-even point on the profit graph is the volume of sales at which profit is zero and is indicated by the dashed line on the graph. Note that the profit steadily increases to the right of the break-even point as the sales volume increases and that the loss becomes steadily worse to the left of the break-even point as the sales volume decreases.

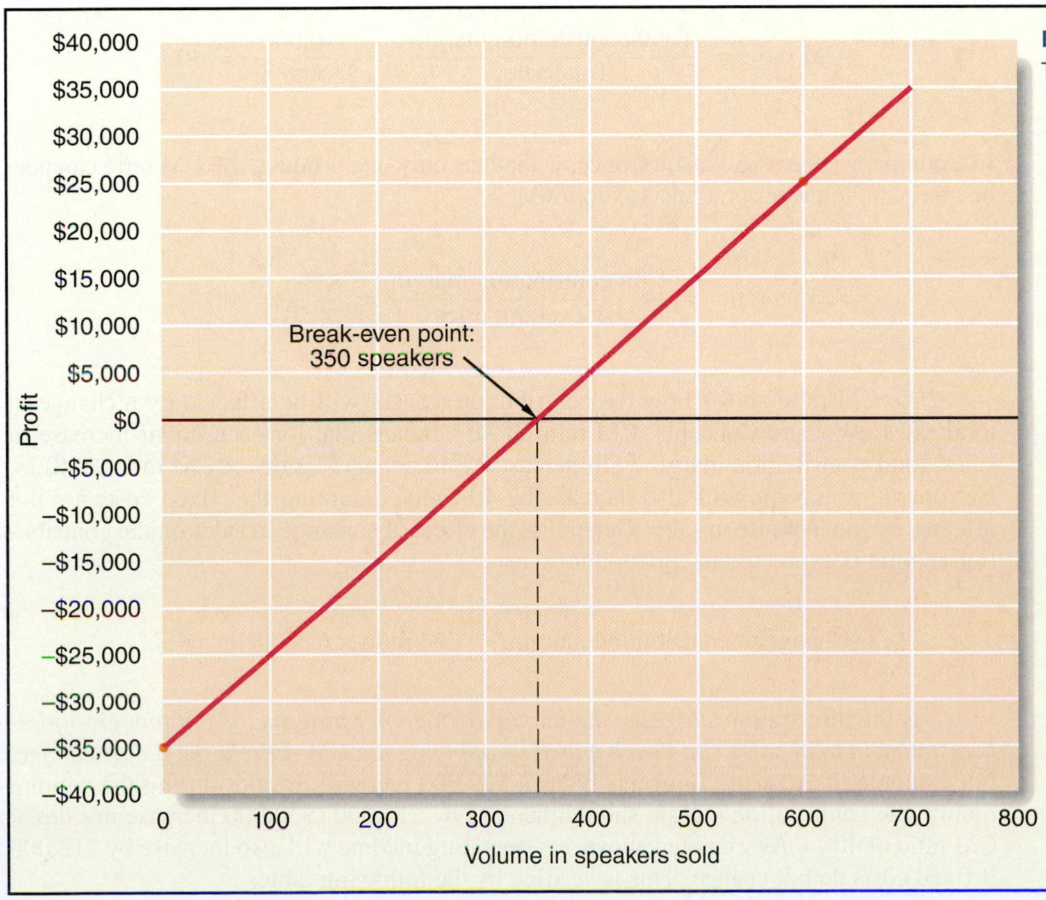

EXHIBIT 3–3
The Profit Graph

LEARNING OBJECTIVE 3–3
Use the contribution margin ratio (CM ratio) to compute changes in contribution margin and net operating income resulting from changes in sales volume.

Contribution Margin Ratio (CM Ratio)

In the previous section, we explored how cost-volume-profit relationships can be visualized. In this section, we show how the *contribution margin ratio* can be used in cost-volume-profit calculations. As the first step, we have added a column to Acoustic Concepts' contribution format income statement in which sales revenues, variable expenses, and contribution margin are expressed as a percentage of sales:

	Total	Per Unit	Percent of Sales
Sales (400 speakers)	$100,000	$250	100%
Variable expenses	60,000	150	60%
Contribution margin	40,000	$100	40%
Fixed expenses	35,000		
Net operating income	$ 5,000		

The contribution margin as a percentage of sales is referred to as the **contribution margin ratio (CM ratio)**. This ratio is computed as follows:

$$\text{CM ratio} = \frac{\text{Contribution margin}}{\text{Sales}}$$

For Acoustic Concepts, the computations are:

$$\text{CM ratio} = \frac{\text{Total contribution margin}}{\text{Total sales}} = \frac{\$40{,}000}{\$100{,}000} = 40\%$$

In a company such as Acoustic Concepts that has only one product, the CM ratio can also be computed on a per unit basis as follows:

$$\text{CM ratio} = \frac{\text{Unit contribution margin}}{\text{Unit selling price}} = \frac{\$100}{\$250} = 40\%$$

The CM ratio shows how the contribution margin will be affected by a change in total sales. Acoustic Concepts' CM ratio of 40% means that for each dollar increase in sales, total contribution margin will increase by 40 cents ($1 sales × CM ratio of 40%). Net operating income will also increase by 40 cents, assuming that fixed costs are not affected by the increase in sales. Generally, the effect of a change in sales on the contribution margin is expressed in equation form as:

$$\text{Change in contribution margin} = \text{CM ratio} \times \text{Change in sales}$$

As this illustration suggests, *the impact on net operating income of any given dollar change in total sales can be computed by applying the CM ratio to the dollar change.* For example, if Acoustic Concepts plans a $30,000 increase in sales during the coming month, the contribution margin should increase by $12,000 ($30,000 increase in sales × CM ratio of 40%). As we noted above, net operating income will also increase by $12,000 if fixed costs do not change. This is verified by the following table:

	Sales Volume			Percent of Sales
	Present	Expected	Increase	
Sales	$100,000	$130,000	$30,000	100%
Variable expenses	60,000	78,000*	18,000	60%
Contribution margin	40,000	52,000	12,000	40%
Fixed expenses	35,000	35,000	0	
Net operating income	$ 5,000	$ 17,000	$12,000	

* $130,000 expected sales ÷ $250 per unit = 520 units. 520 units × $150 per unit = $78,000.

The relation between profit and the CM ratio can also be expressed using the following equations:

$$\text{Profit} = \text{CM ratio} \times \text{Sales} - \text{Fixed expenses}^2$$

or, in terms of changes,

$$\text{Change in profit} = \text{CM ratio} \times \text{Change in sales} - \text{Change in fixed expenses}$$

For example, at sales of $130,000, the profit is expected to be $17,000 as shown below:

$$\begin{aligned}\text{Profit} &= \text{CM ratio} \times \text{Sales} - \text{Fixed expenses}\\ &= 0.40 \times \$130{,}000 - \$35{,}000\\ &= \$52{,}000 - \$35{,}000 = \$17{,}000\end{aligned}$$

Again, if you are comfortable with algebra, this approach will often be quicker and easier than constructing contribution format income statements.

The CM ratio is particularly valuable in situations where the dollar sales of one product must be traded off against the dollar sales of another product. In this situation, products that yield the greatest amount of contribution margin per dollar of sales should be emphasized.

Some Applications of CVP Concepts

LEARNING OBJECTIVE 3–4
Show the effects on net operating income of changes in variable costs, fixed costs, selling price, and volume.

Bob Luchinni, the accountant at Acoustic Concepts, wanted to demonstrate to the company's president Prem Narayan how the concepts developed on the preceding pages can be used in planning and decision making. Bob gathered the following basic data:

	Per Unit	Percent of Sales
Selling price	$250	100%
Variable expenses	150	60%
Contribution margin	$100	40%

[2] This equation can be derived using the basic profit equation and the definition of the CM ratio as follows:

$$\begin{aligned}\text{Profit} &= (\text{Sales} - \text{Variable expenses}) - \text{Fixed expenses}\\ \text{Profit} &= \text{Contribution margin} - \text{Fixed expenses}\\ \text{Profit} &= \frac{\text{Contribution margin}}{\text{Sales}} \times \text{Sales} - \text{Fixed expenses}\\ \text{Profit} &= \text{CM ratio} \times \text{Sales} - \text{Fixed expenses}\end{aligned}$$

Recall that fixed expenses are $35,000 per month. Bob Luchinni will use these data to show the effects of changes in variable costs, fixed costs, sales price, and sales volume on the company's profitability in a variety of situations.

Before proceeding further, however, we need to introduce another concept—the *variable expense ratio.* The **variable expense ratio** is the ratio of variable expenses to sales. It can be computed by dividing the total variable expenses by the total sales, or in a single product analysis, it can be computed by dividing the variable expenses per unit by the unit selling price. In the case of Acoustic Concepts, the variable expense ratio is 0.60; that is, variable expense is 60% of sales. Expressed as an equation, the definition of the variable expense ratio is:

$$\text{Variable expense ratio} = \frac{\text{Variable expenses}}{\text{Sales}}$$

This leads to a useful equation that relates the CM ratio to the variable expense ratio as follows:

$$\text{CM ratio} = \frac{\text{Contribution margin}}{\text{Sales}}$$

$$\text{CM ratio} = \frac{\text{Sales} - \text{Variable expenses}}{\text{Sales}}$$

$$\text{CM ratio} = 1 - \text{Variable expense ratio}$$

Change in Fixed Cost and Sales Volume Acoustic Concepts is currently selling 400 speakers per month at $250 per speaker for total monthly sales of $100,000. The sales manager feels that a $10,000 increase in the monthly advertising budget would increase monthly sales by $30,000 to a total of 520 units. Should the advertising budget be increased? The table below shows the financial impact of the proposed change in the monthly advertising budget.

	Current Sales	Sales with Additional Advertising Budget	Difference	Percent of Sales
Sales.	$100,000	$130,000	$30,000	100%
Variable expenses	60,000	78,000*	18,000	60%
Contribution margin	40,000	52,000	12,000	40%
Fixed expenses.	35,000	45,000†	10,000	
Net operating income	$ 5,000	$ 7,000	$ 2,000	

*520 units × $150 per unit = $78,000.
†$35,000 + additional $10,000 monthly advertising budget = $45,000.

Assuming no other factors need to be considered, the increase in the advertising budget should be approved because it would increase net operating income by $2,000. There are two shorter ways to arrive at this solution. The first alternative solution follows:

Alternative Solution 1

Expected total contribution margin:	
$130,000 × 40% CM ratio	$52,000
Present total contribution margin:	
$100,000 × 40% CM ratio	40,000
Increase in total contribution margin	12,000
Change in fixed expenses:	
Less incremental advertising expense	10,000
Increased net operating income.	$ 2,000

Because in this case only the fixed costs and the sales volume change, the solution can also be quickly derived as follows:

Alternative Solution 2

Incremental contribution margin:	
$30,000 × 40% CM ratio	$12,000
Less incremental advertising expense	10,000
Increased net operating income	$ 2,000

Notice that this approach does not depend on knowledge of previous sales. Also note that it is unnecessary under either shorter approach to prepare an income statement. Both of the alternative solutions involve **incremental analysis**—they consider only the costs and revenues that will change if the new program is implemented. Although in each case a new income statement could have been prepared, the incremental approach is simpler and more direct and focuses attention on the specific changes that would occur as a result of the decision.

Change in Variable Costs and Sales Volume Refer to the original data. Recall that Acoustic Concepts is currently selling 400 speakers per month. Prem is considering the use of higher-quality components, which would increase variable costs (and thereby reduce the contribution margin) by $10 per speaker. However, the sales manager predicts that using higher-quality components would increase sales to 480 speakers per month. Should the higher-quality components be used?

The $10 increase in variable costs would decrease the unit contribution margin by $10—from $100 down to $90.

Solution

Expected total contribution margin with higher-quality components:	
480 speakers × $90 per speaker	$43,200
Present total contribution margin:	
400 speakers × $100 per speaker	40,000
Increase in total contribution margin	$ 3,200

According to this analysis, the higher-quality components should be used. Because fixed costs would not change, the $3,200 increase in contribution margin shown above should result in a $3,200 increase in net operating income.

Change in Fixed Cost, Selling Price, and Sales Volume Refer to the original data and recall again that Acoustic Concepts is currently selling 400 speakers per month. To increase sales, the sales manager would like to cut the selling price by $20 per speaker and increase the advertising budget by $15,000 per month. The sales manager believes that if these two steps are taken, unit sales will increase by 50% to 600 speakers per month. Should the changes be made?

A decrease in the selling price of $20 per speaker would decrease the unit contribution margin by $20 down to $80.

Solution

According to this analysis, the changes should not be made. The $7,000 reduction in net operating income that is shown above can be verified by preparing comparative income statements as shown below.

Expected total contribution margin with lower selling price:	
600 speakers × $80 per speaker	$48,000
Present total contribution margin:	
400 speakers × $100 per speaker	40,000
Incremental contribution margin	8,000
Change in fixed expenses:	
Less incremental advertising expense	15,000
Reduction in net operating income	$ (7,000)

	Present 400 Speakers per Month		Expected 600 Speakers per Month		
	Total	Per Unit	Total	Per Unit	Difference
Sales	$100,000	$250	$138,000	$230	$38,000
Variable expenses	60,000	150	90,000	150	30,000
Contribution margin	40,000	$100	48,000	$ 80	8,000
Fixed expenses	35,000		50,000*		15,000
Net operating income (loss)	$ 5,000		$ (2,000)		$ (7,000)

*35,000 + Additional monthly advertising budget of $15,000 = $50,000.

Change in Variable Cost, Fixed Cost, and Sales Volume Refer to Acoustic Concepts' original data. As before, the company is currently selling 400 speakers per month. The sales manager would like to pay salespersons a sales commission of $15 per speaker sold, rather than the flat salaries that now total $6,000 per month. The sales manager is confident that the change would increase monthly sales by 15% to 460 speakers per month. Should the change be made?

Solution Changing the sales staff's compensation from salaries to commissions would affect both fixed and variable expenses. Fixed expenses would decrease by $6,000, from $35,000 to $29,000. Variable expenses per unit would increase by $15, from $150 to $165, and the unit contribution margin would decrease from $100 to $85.

Expected total contribution margin with sales staff on commissions:	
460 speakers × $85 per speaker	$39,100
Present total contribution margin:	
400 speakers × $100 per speaker	40,000
Decrease in total contribution margin	(900)
Change in fixed expenses:	
Add salaries avoided if a commission is paid	6,000
Increase in net operating income	$ 5,100

According to this analysis, the changes should be made. Again, the same answer can be obtained by preparing comparative income statements:

Change in Selling Price Refer to the original data where Acoustic Concepts is currently selling 400 speakers per month. The company has an opportunity to make a bulk sale of 150 speakers to a wholesaler if an acceptable price can be negotiated. This sale would not disturb the company's regular sales and would not affect the company's total fixed expenses. What price per speaker should be quoted to the wholesaler if Acoustic Concepts is seeking a profit of $3,000 on the bulk sale?

	Present 400 Speakers per Month		Expected 460 Speakers per Month		
	Total	Per Unit	Total	Per Unit	Difference
Sales....................	$100,000	$250	$115,000	$250	$15,000
Variable expenses........	60,000	150	75,900	165	15,900
Contribution margin.......	40,000	$100	39,100	$ 85	900
Fixed expenses	35,000		29,000		(6,000)*
Net operating income.....	$ 5,000		$ 10,100		$ 5,100

*Note: A *reduction* in fixed expenses has the effect of *increasing* net operating income.

Solution

Variable cost per speaker.........	$150
Desired profit per speaker:	
$3,000 ÷ 150 speakers	20
Quoted price per speaker	$170

Notice that fixed expenses are not included in the computation. This is because fixed expenses are not affected by the bulk sale, so all of the additional contribution margin increases the company's profits.

IN BUSINESS

MANAGING RISK IN THE BOOK PUBLISHING INDUSTRY

Greenleaf Book Group is a book publishing company in Austin, Texas, that attracts authors who are willing to pay publishing costs and forgo up-front advances in exchange for a larger royalty rate on each book sold. For example, assume a typical publisher prints 10,000 copies of a new book that it sells for $12.50 per unit. The publisher pays the author an advance of $20,000 to write the book and then incurs $60,000 of expenses to market, print, and edit the book. The publisher also pays the author a 20% royalty (or $2.50 per unit) on each book sold above 8,000 units. In this scenario, the publisher must sell 6,400 books to break even (= $80,000 in fixed costs ÷ $12.50 per unit). If all 10,000 copies are sold, the author earns $25,000 (= $20,000 advance + 2,000 copies × $2.50) and the publisher earns $40,000 (= $125,000 – $60,000 – $20,000 × $5,000).

Greenleaf alters the financial arrangement described above by requiring the author to assume the risk of poor sales. It pays the author a 70% royalty on all units sold (or $8.75 per unit), but the author forgoes the $20,000 advance and pays Greenleaf $60,000 to market, print, and edit the book. If the book flops, the author fails to recover her production costs. If all 10,000 units are sold, the author earns $27,500 (= $10,000 units × $8.75 – $60,000) and Greenleaf earns $37,500 (= 10,000 units × ($12.50 – $8.75)).

Source: Christopher Steiner, "Book It," *Forbes*, September 7, 2009, p. 58.

© Yellow Dog Productions/Digital Vision/ Getty Images, RF

Break-Even and Target Profit Analysis

Managers use break-even and target profit analysis to answer questions such as how much would we have to sell to avoid incurring a loss or how much would we have to sell to make a profit of $10,000 per month? We'll discuss break-even analysis first followed by target profit analysis.

Break–Even Analysis

LEARNING OBJECTIVE 3–5
Determine the break-even point.

Earlier in the chapter we defined the break-even point as *the level of sales at which the company's profit is zero.* To calculate the break-even point (in unit sales and dollar sales), managers can use either of two approaches, the equation method or the formula method. We'll demonstrate both approaches using the data from Acoustic Concepts.

The Equation Method The equation method relies on the basic profit equation introduced earlier in the chapter. Since Acoustic Concepts has only one product, we'll use the contribution margin form of this equation to perform the break-even calculations. Remembering that Acoustic Concepts' unit contribution margin is $100, and its fixed expenses are $35,000, the company's break-even point is computed as follows:

$$\text{Profit} = \text{Unit CM} \times Q - \text{Fixed expense}$$
$$\$0 = \$100 \times Q - \$35{,}000$$
$$\$100 \times Q = \$0 + \$35{,}000$$
$$Q = \$35{,}000 \div \$100$$
$$Q = 350$$

Thus, as we determined earlier in the chapter, Acoustic Concepts will break even (or earn zero profit) at a sales volume of 350 speakers per month.

The Formula Method The formula method is a shortcut version of the equation method. It centers on the idea discussed earlier in the chapter that each unit sold provides a certain amount of contribution margin that goes toward covering fixed expenses. In a single product situation, the formula for computing the unit sales to break even is:

$$\text{Unit sales to break even} = \frac{\text{Fixed expenses}^{3}}{\text{Unit CM}}$$

In the case of Acoustic Concepts, the unit sales needed to break even is computed as follows:

$$\text{Unit sales to break even} = \frac{\text{Fixed expenses}}{\text{Unit CM}}$$
$$= \frac{\$35{,}000}{\$100}$$
$$= 350$$

Notice that 350 units is the same answer that we got when using the equation method. This will always be the case because the formula method and equation method are mathematically equivalent. The formula method simply skips a few steps in the equation method.

Break–Even in Dollar Sales In addition to finding the break-even point in unit sales, we can also find the break-even point in dollar sales using three methods. First, we could solve for the break-even point in *unit* sales using the equation method or formula method and then simply multiply the result by the selling price. In the case of Acoustic Concepts, the break-even point in dollar sales using this approach would be computed as 350 speakers × $250 per speaker, or $87,500 in total sales.

---

[3] This formula can be derived as follows:

$$\begin{aligned} \text{Profit} &= \text{Unit CM} \times Q - \text{Fixed expenses} \\ \$0 &= \text{Unit CM} \times Q - \text{Fixed expenses} \\ \text{Unit CM} + Q &= \$0 + \text{Fixed expenses} \\ Q &= \text{Fixed expenses} \div \text{Unit CM} \end{aligned}$$

Second, we can use the equation method to compute the break-even point in dollar sales. Remembering that Acoustic Concepts' contribution margin ratio is 40% and its fixed expenses are $35,000, the equation method calculates the break-even point in dollar sales as follows:

$$\text{Profit} = \text{CM ratio} \times \text{Sales} - \text{Fixed expenses}$$
$$\$0 = 0.40 \times \text{Sales} - \$35{,}000$$
$$0.40 \times \text{Sales} = \$0 + \$35{,}000$$
$$\text{Sales} = \$35{,}000 \div 0.40$$
$$\text{Sales} = \$87{,}500$$

Third, we can use the formula method to compute the dollar sales needed to break even as shown below:

$$\text{Dollar sales to break even} = \frac{\text{Fixed expenses}^{4}}{\text{CM ratio}}$$

In the case of Acoustic Concepts, the computations are performed as follows:

$$\text{Dollar sales to break even} = \frac{\text{Fixed expenses}}{\text{CM ratio}}$$
$$= \frac{\$35{,}000}{0.40}$$
$$= \$87{,}500$$

Again, you'll notice that the break-even point in dollar sales ($87,500) is the same under all three methods. This will always be the case because these methods are mathematically equivalent.

Target Profit Analysis

LEARNING OBJECTIVE 3–6
Determine the level of sales needed to achieve a desired target profit.

Target profit analysis is one of the key uses of CVP analysis. In **target profit analysis**, we estimate what sales volume is needed to achieve a specific target profit. For example, suppose Prem Narayan of Acoustic Concepts would like to estimate the sales needed to attain a target profit of $40,000 per month. To determine the unit sales and dollar sales needed to achieve a target profit, we can rely on the same two approaches that we have been discussing thus far, the equation method or the formula method.

The Equation Method To compute the unit sales required to achieve a target profit of $40,000 per month, Acoustic Concepts can use the same profit equation that was used for its break-even analysis. Remembering that the company's contribution margin per unit is $100 and its total fixed expenses are $35,000, the equation method could be applied as follows:

$$\text{Profit} = \text{Unit CM} \times Q - \text{Fixed expense}$$
$$\$40{,}000 = \$100 \times Q - \$35{,}000$$
$$\$100 \times Q = \$40{,}000 + \$35{,}000$$
$$Q = \$75{,}000 \div \$100$$
$$Q = 750$$

[4] This formula can be derived as follows:

$$\text{Profit} = \text{CM ratio} \times \text{Sales} - \text{Fixed expenses}$$
$$\$0 = \text{CM ratio} \times \text{Sales} - \text{Fixed expenses}$$
$$\text{CM ratio} \times \text{Sales} = \$0 + \text{Fixed expenses}$$
$$\text{Sales} = \text{Fixed expenses} \div \text{CM ratio}$$

Thus, the target profit can be achieved by selling 750 speakers per month. Notice that the only difference between this equation and the equation used for Acoustic Concepts' break-even calculation is the profit figure. In the break-even scenario, the profit is \$0, whereas in the target profit scenario the profit is \$40,000.

The Formula Method In general, in a single product situation, we can compute the sales volume required to attain a specific target profit using the following formula:

$$\text{Unit sales to attain the target profit} = \frac{\text{Target profit} + \text{Fixed expenses}}{\text{Unit CM}}$$

In the case of Acoustic Concepts, the unit sales needed to attain a target profit of 40,000 is computed as follows:

$$\begin{aligned}\text{Unit sales to attain the target profit} &= \frac{\text{Target profit} + \text{Fixed expenses}}{\text{Unit CM}}\\ &= \frac{\$40{,}000 + \$35{,}000}{\$100}\\ &= 750\end{aligned}$$

Target Profit Analysis in Terms of Dollar Sales When quantifying the dollar sales needed to attain a target profit we can apply the same three methods that we used for calculating the dollar sales needed to break even. First, we can solve for the *unit* sales needed to attain the target profit using the equation method or formula method and then simply multiply the result by the selling price. In the case of Acoustic Concepts, the dollar sales to attain its target profit would be computed as 750 speakers × \$250 per speaker, or \$187,500 in total sales.

Second, we can use the equation method to compute the dollar sales needed to attain the target profit. Remembering that Acoustic Concepts' target profit is \$40,000, its contribution margin ratio is 40%, and its fixed expenses are \$35,000, the equation method calculates the answer as follows:

$$\begin{aligned}\text{Profit} &= \text{CM ratio} \times \text{Sales} - \text{Fixed expenses}\\ \$40{,}000 &= 0.40 \times \text{Sales} - \$35{,}000\\ 0.40 \times \text{Sales} &= \$40{,}000 + \$35{,}000\\ \text{Sales} &= \$75{,}000 \div 0.40\\ \text{Sales} &= \$187{,}500\end{aligned}$$

Third, we can use the formula method to compute the dollar sales needed to attain the target profit as shown below:

$$\text{Dollar sales to attain a target profit} = \frac{\text{Target profit} + \text{Fixed expenses}}{\text{CM ratio}}$$

In the case of Acoustic Concepts, the computations would be:

$$\begin{aligned}\text{Dollar sales to attain a target profit} &= \frac{\text{Target profit} + \text{Fixed expenses}}{\text{CM ratio}}\\ &= \frac{\$40{,}000 + \$35{,}000}{0.40}\\ &= \$187{,}500\end{aligned}$$

Again, you'll notice that the answers are the same regardless of which method we use. This is because all of the methods discussed are simply different roads to the same destination.

IN BUSINESS

SNAP FITNESS GROWS IN A WEAK ECONOMY

When Bally's Total Fitness was filing for bankruptcy, Snap Fitness was expanding to more than 900 clubs in the United States with 400,000 members. The secret to Snap Fitness' success is its "no frills" approach to exercise. Each club typically has five treadmills, two stationary bikes, five elliptical machines, and weight equipment while bypassing amenities such as on-site child care, juice bars, and showers. Each club is usually staffed only 25–40 hours per week and it charges a membership fee of $35 per month.

To open a new Snap Fitness location, each franchise owner has an initial capital outlay of $120,000 for various types of equipment and a one-time licensing fee of $15,000. The franchisee also pays Snap (the parent company) a royalty fee of $400 per month plus $0.50 for each membership. Snap also collects one-time fees of $5 for each new member's "billing setup" and $5 for each security card issued. If a new club attracts 275 members, it can break even in as little as three months. Can you estimate the underlying calculations related to this break-even point?

Source: Nicole Perlroth, "Survival of the Fittest," *Forbes*, January 12, 2009, pp. 54–55.

© AP Images/LM Otero

The Margin of Safety

LEARNING OBJECTIVE 3–7
Compute the margin of safety and explain its significance.

The **margin of safety** is the excess of budgeted or actual sales dollars over the break-even volume of sales dollars. It is the amount by which sales can drop before losses are incurred. The higher the margin of safety, the lower the risk of not breaking even and incurring a loss. The formula for the margin of safety is:

$$\text{Margin of safety in dollars} = \text{Total budgeted (or actual) sales} - \text{Break-even sales}$$

The margin of safety can also be expressed in percentage form by dividing the margin of safety in dollars by total dollar sales:

$$\text{Margin of safety percentage} = \frac{\text{Margin of safety in dollars}}{\text{Total budgeted (or actual) sales in dollars}}$$

The calculation of the margin of safety for Acoustic Concepts is:

Sales (at the current volume of 400 speakers) (a)	$100,000
Break-even sales (at 350 speakers)	87,500
Margin of safety in dollars (b)	$ 12,500
Margin of safety percentage, (b) ÷ (a)	12.5%

This margin of safety means that at the current level of sales and with the company's current prices and cost structure, a reduction in sales of $12,500, or 12.5%, would result in just breaking even.

In a single-product company like Acoustic Concepts, the margin of safety can also be expressed in terms of the number of units sold by dividing the margin of safety in dollars by the selling price per unit. In this case, the margin of safety is 50 speakers ($12,500 ÷ $250 per speaker = 50 speakers).

IN BUSINESS

COMPUTING MARGIN OF SAFETY FOR A SMALL BUSINESS

Sam Calagione owns Dogfish Head Craft Brewery, a microbrewery in Rehobeth Beach, Delaware. He charges distributors as much as $100 per case for his premium beers such as World Wide Stout. The high-priced microbrews bring in $800,000 in operating income on revenue of $7 million. Calagione reports that his raw ingredients and labor costs for one case of World Wide Stout are $30 and $16, respectively. Bottling and packaging costs are $6 per case. Gas and electric costs are about $10 per case.

If we assume that World Wide Stout is representative of all Dogfish microbrews, then we can compute the company's margin of safety in five steps. First, variable cost as a percentage of sales is 62% [($30 + $16 + $6 + $10)/$100]. Second, the contribution margin ratio is 38% (1 – 0.62). Third, Dogfish's total fixed cost is $1,860,000 [($7,000,000 × 0.38) – $800,000]. Fourth, the break-even point in dollar sales is $4,894,737 ($1,860,000/0.38). Fifth, the margin of safety is $2,105,263 ($7,000,000 – $4,894,737).

Source: Patricia Huang, "Château Dogfish," *Forbes*, February 28, 2005, pp. 57–59.

MANAGERIAL ACCOUNTING IN ACTION
The Wrap-Up

ACOUSTIC concepts inc

Prem Narayan and Bob Luchinni met to discuss the results of Bob's analysis.

Prem: Bob, everything you have shown me is pretty clear. I can see what impact the sales manager's suggestions would have on our profits. Some of those suggestions are quite good and others are not so good. I am concerned that our margin of safety is only 50 speakers. What can we do to increase this number?

Bob: Well, we have to increase total sales or decrease the break-even point or both.

Prem: And to decrease the break-even point, we have to either decrease our fixed expenses or increase our unit contribution margin?

Bob: Exactly.

Prem: And to increase our unit contribution margin, we must either increase our selling price or decrease the variable cost per unit?

Bob: Correct.

Prem: So what do you suggest?

Bob: Well, the analysis doesn't tell us which of these to do, but it does indicate we have a potential problem here.

Prem: If you don't have any immediate suggestions, I would like to call a general meeting next week to discuss ways we can work on increasing the margin of safety. I think everyone will be concerned about how vulnerable we are to even small downturns in sales.

CVP Considerations in Choosing a Cost Structure

Cost structure refers to the relative proportion of fixed and variable costs in an organization. Managers often have some latitude in trading off between these two types of costs. For example, fixed investments in automated equipment can reduce variable labor costs. In this section, we discuss the choice of a cost structure. We also introduce the concept of *operating leverage.*

Cost Structure and Profit Stability

Which cost structure is better—high variable costs and low fixed costs, or the opposite? No single answer to this question is possible; each approach has its advantages. To show what we mean, refer to the following contribution format income statements for two blueberry farms. Bogside Farm depends on migrant workers to pick its berries by hand, whereas Sterling Farm has invested in expensive berry-picking machines. Consequently, Bogside Farm has higher variable costs, but Sterling Farm has higher fixed costs:

	Bogside Farm		Sterling Farm	
	Amount	Percent	Amount	Percent
Sales	$100,000	100%	$100,000	100%
Variable expenses	60,000	60%	30,000	30%
Contribution margin	40,000	40%	70,000	70%
Fixed expenses	30,000		60,000	
Net operating income	$ 10,000		$ 10,000	

Which farm has the better cost structure? The answer depends on many factors, including the long-run trend in sales, year-to-year fluctuations in the level of sales, and the attitude of the owners toward risk. If sales are expected to exceed $100,000 in the future, then Sterling Farm probably has the better cost structure. The reason is that its CM ratio is higher, and its profits will therefore increase more rapidly as sales increase. To illustrate, assume that each farm experiences a 10% increase in sales without any increase in fixed costs. The new income statements would be as follows:

	Bogside Farm		Sterling Farm	
	Amount	Percent	Amount	Percent
Sales	$110,000	100%	$110,000	100%
Variable expenses	66,000	60%	33,000	30%
Contribution margin	44,000	40%	77,000	70%
Fixed expenses	30,000		60,000	
Net operating income	$ 14,000		$ 17,000	

Sterling Farm has experienced a greater increase in net operating income due to its higher CM ratio even though the increase in sales was the same for both farms.

What if sales drop below $100,000? What are the farms' break-even points? What are their margins of safety? The computations needed to answer these questions are shown below using the formula method:

	Bogside Farm	Sterling Farm
Fixed expenses	$ 30,000	$ 60,000
Contribution margin ratio	÷ 0.40	÷ 0.70
Dollar sales to break even	$ 75,000	$ 85,714
Total current sales (a)	$100,000	$100,000
Break-even sales	75,000	85,714
Margin of safety in sales dollars (b)	$ 25,000	$ 14,286
Margin of safety percentage (b) ÷ (a)	25.0%	14.3%

Bogside Farm's margin of safety is greater and its contribution margin ratio is lower than Sterling Farm. Therefore, Bogside Farm is less vulnerable to downturns than Sterling Farm. Due to its lower contribution margin ratio, Bogside Farm will not lose contribution margin as rapidly as Sterling Farm when sales decline. Thus, Bogside Farm's profit will be less volatile. We saw earlier that this is a drawback when sales increase, but it provides more protection when sales drop. And because its break-even point is lower, Bogside Farm can suffer a larger sales decline before losses emerge.

To summarize, without knowing the future, it is not obvious which cost structure is better. Both have advantages and disadvantages. Sterling Farm, with its higher fixed costs and lower variable costs, will experience wider swings in net operating income as sales fluctuate, with greater profits in good years and greater losses in bad years. Bogside Farm, with its lower fixed costs and higher variable costs, will enjoy greater profit stability and will be more protected from losses during bad years, but at the cost of lower net operating income in good years.

Operating Leverage

LEARNING OBJECTIVE 3–8
Compute the degree of operating leverage at a particular level of sales and explain how it can be used to predict changes in net operating income.

A lever is a tool for multiplying force. Using a lever, a massive object can be moved with only a modest amount of force. In business, *operating leverage* serves a similar purpose. **Operating leverage** is a measure of how sensitive net operating income is to a given percentage change in dollar sales. Operating leverage acts as a multiplier. If operating leverage is high, a small percentage increase in sales can produce a much larger percentage increase in net operating income.

Operating leverage can be illustrated by returning to the data for the two blueberry farms. We previously showed that a 10% increase in sales (from \$100,000 to \$110,000 in each farm) results in a 70% increase in the net operating income of Sterling Farm (from \$10,000 to \$17,000) and only a 40% increase in the net operating income of Bogside Farm (from \$10,000 to \$14,000). Thus, for a 10% increase in sales, Sterling Farm experiences a much greater percentage increase in profits than does Bogside Farm. Therefore, Sterling Farm has greater operating leverage than Bogside Farm.

The **degree of operating leverage** at a given level of sales is computed by the following formula:

$$\text{Degree of operating leverage} = \frac{\text{Contribution margin}}{\text{Net operating income}}$$

The degree of operating leverage is a measure, at a given level of sales, of how a percentage change in sales volume will affect profits. To illustrate, the degree of operating leverage for the two farms at \$100,000 sales would be computed as follows:

$$\text{Bogside Farm:} \frac{\$40,000}{\$10,000} = 4$$

$$\text{Sterling Farm:} \frac{\$70,000}{\$10,000} = 7$$

Because the degree of operating leverage for Bogside Farm is 4, the farm's net operating income grows four times as fast as its sales. In contrast, Sterling Farm's net operating income grows seven times as fast as its sales. Thus, if sales increase by 10%, then we can expect the net operating income of Bogside Farm to increase by four times this amount, or by 40%, and the net operating income of Sterling Farm to increase by seven times this amount, or by 70%. In general, this relation between the percentage change in sales and the percentage change in net operating income is given by the following formula:

$$\begin{matrix}\text{Percentage change in} \\ \text{net operating income}\end{matrix} = \begin{matrix}\text{Degree of} \\ \text{operating leverage}\end{matrix} \times \begin{matrix}\text{Percentage} \\ \text{change in sales}\end{matrix}$$

Bogside Farm: Percentage change in net operating income = 4 × 10% = 40%
Sterling Farm: Percentage change in net operating income = 7 × 10% = 70%

What is responsible for the higher operating leverage at Sterling Farm? The only difference between the two farms is their cost structure. If two companies have the same total revenue and same total expense but different cost structures, then the company with the higher proportion of fixed costs in its cost structure will have higher operating leverage. Referring back to the original example on page 206, when both farms have sales of $100,000 and total expenses of $90,000, one-third of Bogside Farm's costs are fixed but two-thirds of Sterling Farm's costs are fixed. As a consequence, Sterling's degree of operating leverage is higher than Bogside's.

The degree of operating leverage is not a constant; it is greatest at sales levels near the break-even point and decreases as sales and profits rise. The following table shows the degree of operating leverage for Bogside Farm at various sales levels. (Data used earlier for Bogside Farm are shown in color.)

Sales	$75,000	$80,000	$100,000	$150,000	$225,000
Variable expenses	45,000	48,000	60,000	90,000	135,000
Contribution margin (a)	30,000	32,000	40,000	60,000	90,000
Fixed expenses	30,000	30,000	30,000	30,000	30,000
Net operating income (b)	$ 0	$ 2,000	$ 10,000	$ 30,000	$ 60,000
Degree of operating leverage, (a) ÷ (b)	∞	16	4	2	1.5

Thus, a 10% increase in sales would increase profits by only 15% (10% × 1.5) if sales were previously $225,000, as compared to the 40% increase we computed earlier at the $100,000 sales level. The degree of operating leverage will continue to decrease the farther the company moves from its break-even point. At the break-even point, the degree of operating leverage is infinitely large ($30,000 contribution margin ÷ $0 net operating income = ∞).

The degree of operating leverage can be used to quickly estimate what impact various percentage changes in sales will have on profits, without the necessity of preparing detailed income statements. As shown by our examples, the effects of operating leverage can be dramatic. If a company is near its break-even point, then even small percentage increases in sales can yield large percentage increases in profits. *This explains why management will often work very hard for only a small increase in sales volume.* If the degree of operating leverage is 5, then a 6% increase in sales would translate into a 30% increase in profits.

IN BUSINESS

THE DANGERS OF A HIGH DEGREE OF OPERATING LEVERAGE

In recent years, computer chip manufacturers have poured more than $75 billion into constructing new manufacturing facilities to meet the growing demand for digital devices such as iPhones and BlackBerrys. Because 70% of the costs of running these facilities are fixed, a sharp drop in customer demand forces these companies to choose between two undesirable options. They can slash production levels and absorb large amounts of unused capacity costs, or they can continue producing large volumes of output in spite of shrinking demand, thereby flooding the market with excess supply and lowering prices. Either choice distresses investors who tend to shy away from computer chip makers in economic downturns.

Source: Bruce Einhorn, "Chipmakers on the Edge," *BusinessWeek,* January 5, 2009, pp. 30–31.

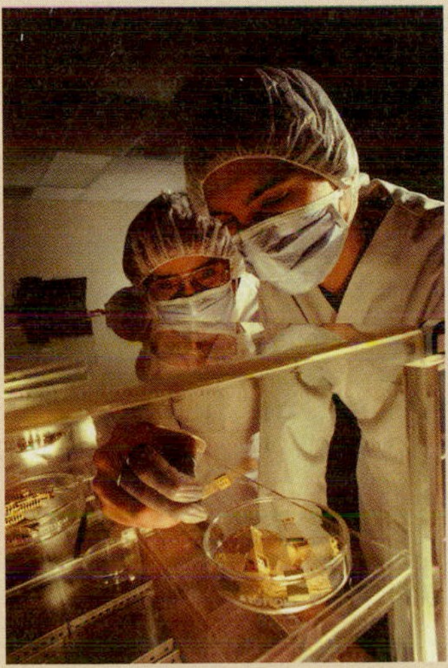

© Digital Stock/Corbis, RF

Structuring Sales Commissions

Companies usually compensate salespeople by paying them a commission based on sales, a salary, or a combination of the two. Commissions based on sales dollars can lead to lower profits. To illustrate, consider Pipeline Unlimited, a producer of surfing equipment. Salespersons sell the company's products to retail sporting goods stores throughout North America and the Pacific Basin. Data for two of the company's surfboards, the XR7 and Turbo models, appear below:

	Model	
	XR7	Turbo
Selling price	$695	$749
Variable expenses	344	410
Contribution margin	$351	$339

Which model will salespeople push hardest if they are paid a commission of 10% of sales revenue? The answer is the Turbo because it has the higher selling price and hence the larger commission. On the other hand, from the standpoint of the company, profits will be greater if salespeople steer customers toward the XR7 model because it has the higher contribution margin.

To eliminate such conflicts, commissions can be based on contribution margin rather than on selling price. If this is done, the salespersons will want to sell the mix of products that maximizes contribution margin. Providing that fixed costs are not affected by the sales mix, maximizing the contribution margin will also maximize the company's profit.[5] In effect, by maximizing their own compensation, salespersons will also maximize the company's profit.

Sales Mix

LEARNING OBJECTIVE 3–9
Compute the break-even point for a multiproduct company and explain the effects of shifts in the sales mix on contribution margin and the break-even point.

Before concluding our discussion of CVP concepts, we need to consider the impact of changes in *sales mix* on a company's profit.

The Definition of Sales Mix

The term **sales mix** refers to the relative proportions in which a company's products are sold. The idea is to achieve the combination, or mix, that will yield the greatest profits. Most companies have many products, and often these products are not equally profitable. Hence, profits will depend to some extent on the company's sales mix. Profits will be greater if high-margin rather than low-margin items make up a relatively large proportion of total sales.

Changes in the sales mix can cause perplexing variations in a company's profits. A shift in the sales mix from high-margin items to low-margin items can cause total profits to decrease even though total sales may increase. Conversely, a shift in the sales mix from low-margin items to high-margin items can cause the reverse effect—total profits may increase even though total sales decrease. It is one thing to achieve a particular sales volume; it is quite another to sell the most profitable mix of products.

[5] This also assumes the company has no production constraint. If it does, the sales commissions should be modified. See the Profitability Appendix at the end of the book.

IN BUSINESS

NETBOOK SALES CANNIBALIZE PC SALES

When computer manufacturers introduced the "netbook," they expected it to serve as a consumer's third computer—complementing home and office personal computers (PCs) rather than replacing them. However, when the economy soured, many customers decided to buy lower-priced netbooks instead of PCs, which in turn adversely affected the financial performance of many companies. For example, when Microsoft failed to achieve its sales goals, the company partially blamed growing netbook sales and declining PC sales for its troubles. Microsoft's Windows operating system for netbooks sells for $15–$25 per device, which is less than half the cost of the company's least expensive Windows operating system for PCs.

Source: Olga Kharif, "Small, Cheap—and Frighteningly Popular," *BusinessWeek*, December 8, 2008, p. 64.

Sales Mix and Break-Even Analysis

If a company sells more than one product, break-even analysis is more complex than discussed to this point. The reason is that different products will have different selling prices, different costs, and different contribution margins. Consequently, the break-even point depends on the mix in which the various products are sold. To illustrate, consider Virtual Journeys Unlimited, a small company that sells two DVDs: the Monuments DVD, a tour of the United States' most popular National Monuments; and the Parks DVD, which tours the United States' National Parks. The company's September sales, expenses, and break-even point are shown in Exhibit 3–4.

As shown in the exhibit, the break-even point is $60,000 in sales, which was computed by dividing the company's fixed expenses of $27,000 by its overall CM ratio of 45%. However, this is the break-even only if the company's sales mix does not change. Currently, the Monuments DVD is responsible for 20% and the Parks DVD for 80% of the company's dollar sales. Assuming this sales mix does not change, if total sales are $60,000, the sales of the Monuments DVD would be $12,000 (20% of $60,000) and the sales of the Parks DVD would be $48,000 (80% of $60,000). As shown in Exhibit 3–4, at these levels of sales, the company would indeed break even. But $60,000 in sales represents the break-even point for the company only if the sales mix does not change. *If the sales mix changes, then the break-even point will also usually change.* This is illustrated by the results for October in which the sales mix shifted away from the more profitable Parks DVD (which has a 50% CM ratio) toward the less profitable Monuments CD (which has a 25% CM ratio). These results appear in Exhibit 3–5.

Although sales have remained unchanged at $100,000, the sales mix is exactly the reverse of what it was in Exhibit 3–4, with the bulk of the sales now coming from the less profitable Monuments DVD. Notice that this shift in the sales mix has caused both the overall CM ratio and total profits to drop sharply from the prior month even though total sales are the same. The overall CM ratio has dropped from 45% in September to only 30% in October, and net operating income has dropped from $18,000 to only $3,000. In addition, with the drop in the overall CM ratio, the company's break-even point is no longer $60,000 in sales. Because the company is now realizing less average contribution margin per dollar of sales, it takes more sales to cover the same amount of fixed costs. Thus, the break-even point has increased from $60,000 to $90,000 in sales per year.

In preparing a break-even analysis, an assumption must be made concerning the sales mix. Usually the assumption is that it will not change. However, if the sales mix is expected to change, then this must be explicitly considered in any CVP computations.

EXHIBIT 3–4

Multiproduct Break-Even Analysis

Virtual Journeys Unlimited
Contribution Income Statement
For the Month of September

	Monuments DVD		Parks DVD		Total	
	Amount	Percent	Amount	Percent	Amount	Percent
Sales	$20,000	100%	$80,000	100%	$100,000	100%
Variable expenses	15,000	75%	40,000	50%	55,000	55%
Contribution margin	$ 5,000	25%	$40,000	50%	45,000	45%
Fixed expenses					27,000	
Net operating income					$ 18,000	

Computation of the break-even point:

$$\frac{\text{Fixed expenses}}{\text{Overall CM ratio}} = \frac{\$27{,}000}{0.45} = \$60{,}000$$

Verification of the break-even point:

	Monuments DVD	Parks DVD	Total
Current dollar sales	$20,000	$80,000	$100,000
Percentage of total dollar sales	20%	80%	100%
Sales at the break-even point	$12,000	$48,000	$60,000

	Monuments DVD		Parks DVD		Total	
	Amount	Percent	Amount	Percent	Amount	Percent
Sales	$12,000	100%	$48,000	100%	$60,000	100%
Variable expenses	9,000	75%	24,000	50%	33,000	55%
Contribution margin	$ 3,000	25%	$24,000	50%	27,000	45%
Fixed expenses					27,000	
Net operating income					$ 0	

EXHIBIT 3–5

Multiproduct Break-Even Analysis: A Shift in Sales Mix (see Exhibit 3–4)

Virtual Journeys Unlimited
Contribution Income Statement
For the Month of October

	Monuments DVD		Parks DVD		Total	
	Amount	Percent	Amount	Percent	Amount	Percent
Sales	$80,000	100%	$20,000	100%	$100,000	100%
Variable expenses	60,000	75%	10,000	50%	70,000	70%
Contribution margin	$20,000	25%	$10,000	50%	30,000	30%
Fixed expenses					27,000	
Net operating income					$ 3,000	

Computation of the break-even point:

$$\frac{\text{Fixed expenses}}{\text{Overall CM ratio}} = \frac{\$27{,}000}{0.30} = \$90{,}000$$

Summary

CVP analysis is based on a simple model of how profits respond to prices, costs, and volume. This model can be used to answer a variety of critical questions such as what is the company's break-even volume, what is its margin of safety, and what is likely to happen if specific changes are made in prices, costs, and volume.

A CVP graph depicts the relationships between unit sales on the one hand and fixed expenses, variable expenses, total expenses, total sales, and profits on the other hand. The profit graph is simpler than the CVP graph and shows how profits depend on sales. The CVP and profit graphs are useful for developing intuition about how costs and profits respond to changes in sales.

The contribution margin ratio is the ratio of the total contribution margin to total sales. This ratio can be used to quickly estimate what impact a change in total sales would have on net operating income. The ratio is also useful in break-even analysis.

Break-even analysis is used to estimate how much sales would have to be to just break even. The unit sales required to break even can be estimated by dividing the fixed expense by the unit contribution margin. Target profit analysis is used to estimate how much sales would have to be to attain a specified target profit. The unit sales required to attain the target profit can be estimated by dividing the sum of the target profit and fixed expense by the unit contribution margin.

The margin of safety is the amount by which the company's current sales exceeds break-even sales.

The degree of operating leverage allows quick estimation of what impact a given percentage change in sales would have on the company's net operating income. The higher the degree of operating leverage, the greater is the impact on the company's profits. The degree of operating leverage is not constant—it depends on the company's current level of sales.

The profits of a multiproduct company are affected by its sales mix. Changes in the sales mix can affect the break-even point, margin of safety, and other critical factors.

Review Problem: CVP Relationships

Voltar Company manufactures and sells a specialized cordless telephone for high electromagnetic radiation environments. The company's contribution format income statement for the most recent year is given below:

	Total	Per Unit	Percent of Sales
Sales (20,000 units)	$1,200,000	$60	100%
Variable expenses	900,000	45	? %
Contribution margin	300,000	$15	? %
Fixed expenses.	240,000		
Net operating income	$ 60,000		

Management is anxious to increase the company's profit and has asked for an analysis of a number of items.

Required:

1. Compute the company's CM ratio and variable expense ratio.
2. Compute the company's break-even point in both unit sales and dollar sales. Use the equation method.
3. Assume that sales increase by $400,000 next year. If cost behavior patterns remain unchanged, by how much will the company's net operating income increase? Use the CM ratio to compute your answer.

4. Refer to the original data. Assume that next year management wants the company to earn a profit of at least $90,000. How many units will have to be sold to meet this target profit?
5. Refer to the original data. Compute the company's margin of safety in both dollar and percentage form.
6. *a.* Compute the company's degree of operating leverage at the present level of sales.
   b. Assume that through a more intense effort by the sales staff, the company's sales increase by 8% next year. By what percentage would you expect net operating income to increase? Use the degree of operating leverage to obtain your answer.
   c. Verify your answer to (*b*) by preparing a new contribution format income statement showing an 8% increase in sales.
7. In an effort to increase sales and profits, management is considering the use of a higher-quality speaker. The higher-quality speaker would increase variable costs by $3 per unit, but management could eliminate one quality inspector who is paid a salary of $30,000 per year. The sales manager estimates that the higher-quality speaker would increase annual sales by at least 20%.
   a. Assuming that changes are made as described above, prepare a projected contribution format income statement for next year. Show data on a total, per unit, and percentage basis.
   b. Compute the company's new break-even point in both unit sales and dollar sales. Use the formula method.
   c. Would you recommend that the changes be made?

Solution to Review Problem

1.

$$\text{CM ratio} = \frac{\text{Unit contribution margin}}{\text{Unit selling price}} = \frac{\$15}{\$60} = 25\%$$

$$\text{Variable expense ratio} = \frac{\text{Variable expense}}{\text{Selling price}} = \frac{\$45}{\$60} = 75\%$$

2.

$$\text{Profit} = \text{Unit CM} \times Q - \text{Fixed expenses}$$
$$\$0 = (\$60 - \$45) \times Q - \$240{,}000$$
$$\$15Q = \$240{,}000$$
$$Q = \$240{,}000 \div \$15$$
$$Q = 16{,}000 \text{ units; or at } \$60 \text{ per unit, } \$960{,}000$$

3.

Increase in sales	$400,000
Multiply by the CM ratio	× 25%
Expected increase in contribution margin	$100,000

Because the fixed expenses are not expected to change, net operating income will increase by the entire $100,000 increase in contribution margin computed above.

4. Equation method:

$$\text{Profit} = \text{Unit CM} \times Q - \text{Fixed expenses}$$
$$\$90{,}000 = (\$60 - \$45) \times Q - \$240{,}000$$
$$\$15Q = \$90{,}000 + \$240{,}000$$
$$Q = \$330{,}000 \div \$15$$
$$Q = 22{,}000 \text{ units}$$

Formula method:

$$\frac{\text{Unit sales to attain}}{\text{the target profit}} = \frac{\text{Target profit} + \text{Fixed expenses}}{\text{Contribution margin per unit}} = \frac{\$90{,}000 + \$240{,}000}{\$15 \text{ per unit}} = 22{,}000 \text{ units}$$

5. Margin of safety in dollars $= \text{Total sales} - \text{Break-even sales}$

$= \$1{,}200{,}000 - \$960{,}000 = \$240{,}000$

$$\text{Margin of safety percentage} = \frac{\text{Margin of safety in dollars}}{\text{Total sales}} = \frac{\$240{,}000}{\$1{,}200{,}000} = 20\%$$

6. *a.* $$\text{Degree of operating leverage} = \frac{\text{Contribution margin}}{\text{Net operating income}} = \frac{\$300{,}000}{\$60{,}000} = 5$$

b.

Expected increase in sales	8%
Degree of operating leverage	× 5
Expected increase in net operating income	40%

c. If sales increase by 8%, then 21,600 units (20,000 × 1.08 = 21,600) will be sold next year. The new contribution format income statement would be as follows:

	Total	Per Unit	Percent of Sales
Sales (21,600 units)	$1,296,000	$60	100%
Variable expenses	972,000	45	75%
Contribution margin	324,000	$15	25%
Fixed expenses	240,000		
Net operating income	$ 84,000		

Thus, the $84,000 expected net operating income for next year represents a 40% increase over the $60,000 net operating income earned during the current year:

$$\frac{\$84{,}000 - \$60{,}000}{\$60{,}000} = \frac{\$24{,}000}{\$60{,}000} = 40\% \text{ increase}$$

Note that the increase in sales from 20,000 to 21,600 units has increased *both* total sales and total variable expenses.

7. *a.* A 20% increase in sales would result in 24,000 units being sold next year: 20,000 units × 1.20 = 24,000 units.

	Total	Per Unit	Percent of Sales
Sales (24,000 units)	$1,440,000	$60	100%
Variable expenses	1,152,000	48*	80%
Contribution margin	288,000	$12	20%
Fixed expenses	210,000†		
Net operating income	$ 78,000		

*$45 + $3 = $48; $48 ÷ $60 = 80%.
†$240,000 – $30,000 = $210,000.

Note that the change in per unit variable expenses results in a change in both the per unit contribution margin and the CM ratio.

b.

$$\text{Unit sales to break even} = \frac{\text{Fixed expenses}}{\text{Unit contribution margin}}$$

$$= \frac{\$210{,}000}{\$12 \text{ per unit}} = 17{,}500 \text{ units}$$

$$\text{Dollar sales to break even} = \frac{\text{Fixed expenses}}{\text{CM ratio}}$$

$$= \frac{\$210{,}000}{0.20} = \$1{,}050{,}000$$

c. Yes, based on these data, the changes should be made. The changes increase the company's net operating income from the present \$60,000 to \$78,000 per year. Although the changes also result in a higher break-even point (17,500 units as compared to the present 16,000 units), the company's margin of safety actually becomes greater than before:

Margin of safety in dollars	=	Total sales − Break-even sales
	=	\$1,440,000 − \$1,050,000 = \$390,000

As shown in (5) above, the company's present margin of safety is only \$240,000. Thus, several benefits will result from the proposed changes.

Glossary

Break-even point The level of sales at which profit is zero. (p. 73)

Contribution margin ratio (CM ratio) A ratio computed by dividing contribution margin by dollar sales. (p. 78)

Cost-volume-profit (CVP) graph A graphical representation of the relationships between an organization's revenues, costs, and profits on the one hand and its sales volume on the other hand. (p. 75)

Degree of operating leverage A measure, at a given level of sales, of how a percentage change in sales will affect profits. The degree of operating leverage is computed by dividing contribution margin by net operating income. (p. 90)

Incremental analysis An analytical approach that focuses only on those costs and revenues that change as a result of a decision. (p. 81)

Margin of safety The excess of budgeted or actual dollar sales over the break-even dollar sales. (p. 87)

Operating leverage A measure of how sensitive net operating income is to a given percentage change in dollar sales. (p. 90)

Sales mix The relative proportions in which a company's products are sold. Sales mix is computed by expressing the sales of each product as a percentage of total sales. (p. 92)

Target profit analysis Estimating what sales volume is needed to achieve a specific target profit. (p. 85)

Variable expense ratio A ratio computed by dividing variable expenses by dollar sales. (p. 80)

Questions

3–1 What is meant by a product's contribution margin ratio? How is this ratio useful in planning business operations?

3–2 Often the most direct route to a business decision is an incremental analysis. What is meant by an *incremental analysis?*

3–3 In all respects, Company A and Company B are identical except that Company A's costs are mostly variable, whereas Company B's costs are mostly fixed. When sales increase, which company will tend to realize the greatest increase in profits? Explain.

3–4 What is meant by the term *operating leverage?*

3–5 What is meant by the term *break-even point?*

3–6 In response to a request from your immediate supervisor, you have prepared a CVP graph portraying the cost and revenue characteristics of your company's product and operations. Explain how the lines on the graph and the break-even point would change if (*a*) the selling price per unit decreased, (*b*) fixed cost increased throughout the entire range of activity portrayed on the graph, and (*c*) variable cost per unit increased.

3–7 What is meant by the margin of safety?

3–8 What is meant by the term *sales mix?* What assumption is usually made concerning sales mix in CVP analysis?

3–9 Explain how a shift in the sales mix could result in both a higher break-even point and a lower net income.

Multiple-choice questions are available with Connect.

Applying Excel

LEARNING OBJECTIVES 3–6, 3–7, 3–8

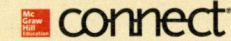

The Excel worksheet form that appears below is to be used to recreate portions of the Review Problem pertaining to Voltar Company that was presented earlier. Download the workbook from Connect, where you will also receive instructions about how to use this worksheet.

	A	B	C	D
1	Chapter 3: Applying Excel			
2				
3	**Data**			
4	Unit sales	20,000	units	
5	Selling price per unit	$60	per unit	
6	Variable expenses per unit	$45	per unit	
7	Fixed expenses	$240,000		
8				
9	*Enter a formula into each of the cells marked with a ? below*			
10	**Review Problem: CVP Relationships**			
11				
12	***Compute the CM ratio and variable expense ratio***			
13	Selling price per unit	?	per unit	
14	Variable expenses per unit	?	per unit	
15	Contribution margin per unit	?	per unit	
16				
17	CM ratio	?		
18	Variable expense ratio	?		
19				
20	***Compute the break-even***			
21	Break-even in unit sales	?	units	
22	Break-even in dollar sales	?		
23				
24	***Compute the margin of safety***			
25	Margin of safety in dollars	?		
26	Margin of safety percentage	?		
27				
28	***Compute the degree of operating leverage***			
29	Sales	?		
30	Variable expenses	?		
31	Contribution margin	?		
32	Fixed expenses	?		
33	Net operating income	?		
34				
35	Degree of operating leverage	?		
36				

Chapter 3 Form | Filled in Chapter 3 Form

You should proceed to the requirements below only after completing your worksheet.

Required:

1. Check your worksheet by changing the fixed expenses to $270,000. If your worksheet is operating properly, the degree of operating leverage should be 10. If you do not get this answer, find the errors in your worksheet and correct them. How much is the margin of safety percentage? Did it change? Why or why not?
2. Enter the following data from a different company into your worksheet:

Unit sales	10,000 units
Selling price per unit	$120 per unit
Variable expenses per unit	$72 per unit
Fixed expenses	$420,000

What is the margin of safety percentage? What is the degree of operating leverage?

3. Using the degree of operating leverage and without changing anything in your worksheet, calculate the percentage change in net operating income if unit sales increase by 15%.
4. Confirm the calculations you made in requirement 3 above by increasing the unit sales in your worksheet by 15%. What is the new net operating income and by what percentage did it increase?
5. Thad Morgan, a motorcycle enthusiast, has been exploring the possibility of relaunching the Western Hombre brand of cycle that was popular in the 1930s. The retro-look cycle would be sold for $10,000 and at that price, Thad estimates 600 units would be sold each year. The variable cost to produce and sell the cycles would be $7,500 per unit. The annual fixed cost would be $1,200,000.
   a. Using your worksheet, what would be the break-even unit sales, the margin of safety in dollars, and the degree of operating leverage?
   b. Thad is worried about the selling price. Rumors are circulating that other retro brands of cycles may be revived. If so, the selling price for the Western Hombre would have to be reduced to $9,000 to compete effectively. In that event, Thad would also reduce fixed expenses by $300,000 by reducing advertising expenses, but he still hopes to sell 600 units per year. Do you think this is a good plan? Explain. Also, explain the degree of operating leverage that appears on your worksheet.

The Foundational 15

connect — Additional student resources are available with Connect.

LEARNING OBJECTIVES 3-1, 3-3, 3-4, 3-5, 3-6, 3-7, 3-8

Oslo Company prepared the following contribution format income statement based on a sales volume of 1,000 units (the relevant range of production is 500 units to 1,500 units):

Sales	$20,000
Variable expenses	12,000
Contribution margin	8,000
Fixed expenses	6,000
Net operating income	$ 2,000

Required:

(Answer each question independently and always refer to the original data unless instructed otherwise.)

1. What is the contribution margin per unit?
2. What is the contribution margin ratio?
3. What is the variable expense ratio?
4. If sales increase to 1,001 units, what would be the increase in net operating income?
5. If sales decline to 900 units, what would be the net operating income?
6. If the selling price increases by $2 per unit and the sales volume decreases by 100 units, what would be the net operating income?
7. If the variable cost per unit increases by $1, spending on advertising increases by $1,500, and unit sales increase by 250 units, what would be the net operating income?
8. What is the break-even point in unit sales?
9. What is the break-even point in dollar sales?
10. How many units must be sold to achieve a target profit of $5,000?
11. What is the margin of safety in dollars? What is the margin of safety percentage?
12. What is the degree of operating leverage?
13. Using the degree of operating leverage, what is the estimated percent increase in net operating income of a 5% increase in sales?
14. Assume that the amounts of the company's total variable expenses and total fixed expenses were reversed. In other words, assume that the total variable expenses are $6,000 and the total fixed expenses are $12,000. Under this scenario and assuming that total sales remain the same, what is the degree of operating leverage?
15. Using the degree of operating leverage that you computed in the previous question, what is the estimated percent increase in net operating income of a 5% increase in sales?

Additional student resources are available with Connect.

Exercises

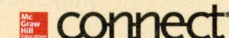

EXERCISE 3–1 Preparing a Contribution Format Income Statement [LO3–1]

Whirly Corporation's most recent income statement is shown below:

	Total	Per Unit
Sales (10,000 units)	$350,000	$35.00
Variable expenses	200,000	20.00
Contribution margin	150,000	$15.00
Fixed expenses	135,000	
Net operating income	$ 15,000	

Required:

Prepare a new contribution format income statement under each of the following conditions (consider each case independently):

1. The sales volume increases by 100 units.
2. The sales volume decreases by 100 units.
3. The sales volume is 9,000 units.

EXERCISE 3–2 Prepare a Cost-Volume-Profit (CVP) Graph [LO3–2]

Karlik Enterprises distributes a single product whose selling price is $24 and whose variable expense is $18 per unit. The company's monthly fixed expense is $24,000.

Required:

1. Prepare a cost-volume-profit graph for the company up to a sales level of 8,000 units.
2. Estimate the company's break-even point in unit sales using your cost-volume-profit graph.

EXERCISE 3–3 Prepare a Profit Graph [LO3–2]

Jaffre Enterprises distributes a single product whose selling price is $16 and whose variable expense is $11 per unit. The company's fixed expense is $16,000 per month.

Required:

1. Prepare a profit graph for the company up to a sales level of 4,000 units.
2. Estimate the company's break-even point in unit sales using your profit graph.

EXERCISE 3–4 Computing and Using the CM Ratio [LO3–3]

Last month when Holiday Creations, Inc., sold 50,000 units, total sales were $200,000, total variable expenses were $120,000, and fixed expenses were $65,000.

Required:

1. What is the company's contribution margin (CM) ratio?
2. Estimate the change in the company's net operating income if it were to increase its total sales by $1,000.

EXERCISE 3–5 Changes in Variable Costs, Fixed Costs, Selling Price, and Volume [LO3–4]

Data for Hermann Corporation are shown below:

	Per Unit	Percent of Sales
Selling price	$90	100%
Variable expenses	63	70%
Contribution margin	$27	30%

Fixed expenses are $30,000 per month and the company is selling 2,000 units per month.

Required:

1. The marketing manager argues that a $5,000 increase in the monthly advertising budget would increase monthly sales by $9,000. Should the advertising budget be increased?
2. Refer to the original data. Management is considering using higher-quality components that would increase the variable expense by $2 per unit. The marketing manager believes that the higher-quality product would increase sales by 10% per month. Should the higher-quality components be used?

EXERCISE 3–6 Compute the Break-Even Point [LO3–5]

Mauro Products distributes a single product, a woven basket whose selling price is $15 and whose variable expense is $12 per unit. The company's monthly fixed expense is $4,200.

Required:

1. Solve for the company's break-even point in unit sales using the equation method.
2. Solve for the company's break-even point in dollar sales using the equation method and the CM ratio.
3. Solve for the company's break-even point in unit sales using the formula method.
4. Solve for the company's break-even point in dollar sales using the formula method and the CM ratio.

EXERCISE 3–7 Compute the Level of Sales Required to Attain a Target Profit [LO3–6]

Lin Corporation has a single product whose selling price is $120 and whose variable expense is $80 per unit. The company's monthly fixed expense is $50,000.

Required:

1. Using the equation method, solve for the unit sales that are required to earn a target profit of $10,000.
2. Using the formula method, solve for the unit sales that are required to earn a target profit of $15,000.

EXERCISE 3–8 Compute the Margin of Safety [LO3–7]

Molander Corporation is a distributor of a sun umbrella used at resort hotels. Data concerning the next month's budget appear below:

Selling price	$30 per unit
Variable expenses	$20 per unit
Fixed expenses	$7,500 per month
Unit sales	1,000 units per month

Required:

1. Compute the company's margin of safety.
2. Compute the company's margin of safety as a percentage of its sales.

EXERCISE 3–9 Compute and Use the Degree of Operating Leverage [LO3–8]

Engberg Company installs lawn sod in home yards. The company's most recent monthly contribution format income statement follows:

	Amount	Percent of Sales
Sales	$ 80,000	100%
Variable expenses	32,000	40%
Contribution margin	48,000	60%
Fixed expenses....................	38,000	
Net operating income.............	$ 10,000	

Required:
1. Compute the company's degree of operating leverage.
2. Using the degree of operating leverage, estimate the impact on net operating income of a 5% increase in sales.
3. Verify your estimate from part (2) above by constructing a new contribution format income statement for the company assuming a 5% increase in sales.

EXERCISE 3–10 Compute the Break-Even Point for a Multiproduct Company [LO3–9]

Lucido Products markets two computer games: Claimjumper and Makeover. A contribution format income statement for a recent month for the two games appears below:

	Claimjumper	Makeover	Total
Sales	$ 30,000	$70,000	$100,000
Variable expenses	20,000	50,000	70,000
Contribution margin	$ 10,000	$20,000	30,000
Fixed expenses			24,000
Net operating income			$ 6,000

Required:
1. Compute the overall contribution margin (CM) ratio for the company.
2. Compute the overall break-even point for the company in dollar sales.
3. Verify the overall break-even point for the company by constructing a contribution format income statement showing the appropriate levels of sales for the two products.

EXERCISE 3–11 Missing Data; Basic CVP Concepts [LO3–1, LO3–9]

Fill in the missing amounts in each of the eight case situations below. Each case is independent of the others. (*Hint:* One way to find the missing amounts would be to prepare a contribution format income statement for each case, enter the known data, and then compute the missing items.)

a. Assume that only one product is being sold in each of the four following case situations:

Case	Units Sold	Sales	Variable Expenses	Contribution Margin per Unit	Fixed Expenses	Net Operating Income (Loss)
1.	15,000	$180,000	$120,000	?	$50,000	?
2.	?	$100,000	?	$10	$32,000	$8,000
3.	10,000	?	$70,000	$13	?	$12,000
4.	6,000	$300,000	?	?	$100,000	$(10,000)

b. Assume that more than one product is being sold in each of the four following case situations:

Case	Sales	Variable Expenses	Average Contribution Margin Ratio	Fixed Expenses	Net Operating Income (Loss)
1.	$500,000	?	20%	?	$7,000
2.	$400,000	$260,000	?	$100,000	?
3.	?	?	60%	$130,000	$20,000
4.	$600,000	$420,000	?	?	$(5,000)

EXERCISE 3–12 Multiproduct Break-Even Analysis [LO3–9]

Olongapo Sports Corporation distributes two premium golf balls—the Flight Dynamic and the Sure Shot. Monthly sales and the contribution margin ratios for the two products follow:

	Product		
	Flight Dynamic	Sure Shot	Total
Sales	$150,000	$250,000	$400,000
CM ratio	80%	36%	?

Fixed expenses total $183,750 per month.

Required:

1. Prepare a contribution format income statement for the company as a whole. Carry computations to one decimal place.
2. Compute the break-even point for the company based on the current sales mix.
3. If sales increase by $100,000 a month, by how much would you expect net operating income to increase? What are your assumptions?

EXERCISE 3–13 Using a Contribution Format Income Statement [LO3–1, LO3–4]

Miller Company's most recent contribution format income statement is shown below:

	Total	Per Unit
Sales (20,000 units)	$300,000	$15.00
Variable expenses	180,000	9.00
Contribution margin	120,000	$ 2.00
Fixed expenses	70,000	
Net operating income	$ 50,000	

Required:

Prepare a new contribution format income statement under each of the following conditions (consider each case independently):

1. The number of units sold increases by 15%.
2. The selling price decreases by $1.50 per unit, and the number of units sold increases by 25%.
3. The selling price increases by $1.50 per unit, fixed expenses increase by $20,000, and the number of units sold decreases by 5%.
4. The selling price increases by 12%, variable expenses increase by 60 cents per unit, and the number of units sold decreases by 10%.

EXERCISE 3–14 Break-Even and Target Profit Analysis [LO3–3, LO3–4, LO3–5, LO3–6]

Lindon Company is the exclusive distributor for an automotive product that sells for $40 per unit and has a CM ratio of 30%. The company's fixed expenses are $180,000 per year. The company plans to sell 16,000 units this year.

Required:

1. What are the variable expenses per unit?
2. Using the equation method:
   a. What is the break-even point in unit sales and in dollar sales?
   b. What amount of unit sales and dollar sales is required to earn an annual profit of $60,000?
   c. Assume that by using a more efficient shipper, the company is able to reduce its variable expenses by $4 per unit. What is the company's new break-even point in unit sales and in dollar sales?
3. Repeat requirement 2 above using the formula method.

EXERCISE 3–15 Operating Leverage [LO3–4, LO3–8]

Magic Realm, Inc., has developed a new fantasy board game. The company sold 15,000 games last year at a selling price of $20 per game. Fixed expenses associated with the game total $182,000 per year, and variable expenses are $6 per game. Production of the game is entrusted to a printing contractor. Variable expenses consist mostly of payments to this contractor.

Required:

1. Prepare a contribution format income statement for the game last year and compute the degree of operating leverage.
2. Management is confident that the company can sell 18,000 games next year (an increase of 3,000 games, or 20%, over last year). Compute:
   a. The expected percentage increase in net operating income for next year.
   b. The expected total dollar net operating income for next year. (Do not prepare an income statement; use the degree of operating leverage to compute your answer.)

EXERCISE 3–16 Break-Even Analysis and CVP Graphing [LO3–2, LO3–4, LO3–5]

The Hartford Symphony Guild is planning its annual dinner-dance. The dinner-dance committee has assembled the following expected costs for the event:

Dinner (per person)	$18
Favors and program (per person)	$2
Band	$2,800
Rental of ballroom	$900
Professional entertainment during intermission	$1,000
Tickets and advertising	$1,300

The committee members would like to charge $35 per person for the evening's activities.

Required:

1. Compute the break-even point for the dinner-dance (in terms of the number of persons who must attend).
2. Assume that last year only 300 persons attended the dinner-dance. If the same number attend this year, what price per ticket must be charged in order to break even?
3. Refer to the original data ($35 ticket price per person). Prepare a CVP graph for the dinner-dance from zero tickets up to 600 tickets sold.

EXERCISE 3–17 Break-Even and Target Profit Analysis [LO3–4, LO3–5, LO3–6]

Outback Outfitters sells recreational equipment. One of the company's products, a small camp stove, sells for $50 per unit. Variable expenses are $32 per stove, and fixed expenses associated with the stove total $108,000 per month.

Required:

1. Compute the break-even point in unit sales and in dollar sales.
2. If the variable expenses per stove increase as a percentage of the selling price, will it result in a higher or a lower break-even point? Why? (Assume that the fixed expenses remain unchanged.)
3. At present, the company is selling 8,000 stoves per month. The sales manager is convinced that a 10% reduction in the selling price would result in a 25% increase in monthly sales of stoves. Prepare two contribution format income statements, one under present operating conditions, and one as operations would appear after the proposed changes. Show both total and per unit data on your statements.
4. Refer to the data in requirement 3 above. How many stoves would have to be sold at the new selling price to yield a minimum net operating income of $35,000 per month?

EXERCISE 3–18 Break-Even and Target Profit Analysis; Margin of Safety; CM Ratio [LO3–1, LO3–3, LO3–5, LO3–6, LO3–7]

Menlo Company distributes a single product. The company's sales and expenses for last month follow:

	Total	Per Unit
Sales	$450,000	$30
Variable expenses	180,000	12
Contribution margin	270,000	$18
Fixed expenses	216,000	
Net operating income	$ 54,000	

Required:

1. What is the monthly break-even point in unit sales and in dollar sales?
2. Without resorting to computations, what is the total contribution margin at the break-even point?
3. How many units would have to be sold each month to earn a target profit of $90,000? Use the formula method. Verify your answer by preparing a contribution format income statement at the target sales level.
4. Refer to the original data. Compute the company's margin of safety in both dollar and percentage terms.
5. What is the company's CM ratio? If sales increase by $50,000 per month and there is no change in fixed expenses, by how much would you expect monthly net operating income to increase?

Problems

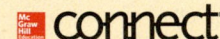

connect **Additional student resources are available with Connect.**

PROBLEM 3–19 Break-Even Analysis; Pricing [LO3–1, LO3–4, LO3–5]

Minden Company introduced a new product last year for which it is trying to find an optimal selling price. Marketing studies suggest that the company can increase sales by 5,000 units for each $2 reduction in the selling price. The company's present selling price is $70 per unit, and variable expenses are $40 per unit. Fixed expenses are $540,000 per year. The present annual sales volume (at the $70 selling price) is 15,000 units.

Required:

1. What is the present yearly net operating income or loss?
2. What is the present break-even point in unit sales and in dollar sales?
3. Assuming that the marketing studies are correct, what is the maximum annual profit that the company can earn? At how many units and at what selling price per unit would the company generate this profit?
4. What would be the break-even point in unit sales and in dollar sales using the selling price you determined in requirement 3 above (e.g., the selling price at the level of maximum profits)? Why is this break-even point different from the break-even point you computed in requirement 2 above?

PROBLEM 3–20 Various CVP Questions: Break-Even Point; Cost Structure; Target Sales [LO3–1, LO3–3, LO3–4, LO3–5, LO3–6, LO3–8]

Northwood Company manufactures basketballs. The company has a ball that sells for $25. At present, the ball is manufactured in a small plant that relies heavily on direct labor workers. Thus, variable expenses are high, totaling $15 per ball, of which 60% is direct labor cost.

Last year, the company sold 30,000 of these balls, with the following results:

Sales (30,000 balls)	$750,000
Variable expenses	450,000
Contribution margin	300,000
Fixed expenses	210,000
Net operating income	$ 90,000

Required:

1. Compute (a) the CM ratio and the break-even point in balls, and (b) the degree of operating leverage at last year's sales level.
2. Due to an increase in labor rates, the company estimates that variable expenses will increase by $3 per ball next year. If this change takes place and the selling price per ball remains constant at $25, what will be the new CM ratio and break-even point in balls?
3. Refer to the data in requirement 2 above. If the expected change in variable expenses takes place, how many balls will have to be sold next year to earn the same net operating income, $90,000, as last year?
4. Refer again to the data in requirement 2 above. The president feels that the company must raise the selling price of its basketballs. If Northwood Company wants to maintain the same CM ratio as last year, what selling price per ball must it charge next year to cover the increased labor costs?
5. Refer to the original data. The company is discussing the construction of a new, automated manufacturing plant. The new plant would slash variable expenses per ball by 40%, but it would cause fixed expenses per year to double. If the new plant is built, what would be the company's new CM ratio and new break-even point in balls?
6. Refer to the data in requirement 5 above.
   a. If the new plant is built, how many balls will have to be sold next year to earn the same net operating income, $90,000, as last year?
   b. Assume the new plant is built and that next year the company manufactures and sells 30,000 balls (the same number as sold last year). Prepare a contribution format income statement and compute the degree of operating leverage.
   c. If you were a member of top management, would you have been in favor of constructing the new plant? Explain.

PROBLEM 3–21 Sales Mix; Multiproduct Break-Even Analysis [LO3–9]

Gold Star Rice, Ltd., of Thailand exports Thai rice throughout Asia. The company grows three varieties of rice—Fragrant, White, and Loonzain. Budgeted sales by product and in total for the coming month are shown below:

	Product							
	White		Fragrant		Loonzain		Total	
Percentage of total sales	20%		52%		28%		100%	
Sales	$150,000	100%	$390,000	100%	$210,000	100%	$750,000	100%
Variable expenses	108,000	72%	78,000	20%	84,000	40%	270,000	36%
Contribution margin	$ 42,000	28%	$312,000	80%	$126,000	60%	480,000	64%
Fixed expenses							449,280	
Net operating income							$ 30,720	

$$\text{Dollar sales to breakeven} = \frac{\text{Fixed expenses}}{\text{CM ratio}} = \frac{\$449,280}{0.64} = \$702,000$$

As shown by these data, net operating income is budgeted at $30,720 for the month and break-even sales at $702,000.

Assume that actual sales for the month total $750,000 as planned. Actual sales by product are: White, $300,000; Fragrant, $180,000; and Loonzain, $270,000.

Required:

1. Prepare a contribution format income statement for the month based on actual sales data. Present the income statement in the format shown above.
2. Compute the break-even point in dollar sales for the month based on your actual data.
3. Considering the fact that the company met its $750,000 sales budget for the month, the president is shocked at the results shown on your income statement in requirement 1 above. Prepare a brief memo for the president explaining why both the operating results and the break-even point in dollar sales are different from what was budgeted.

PROBLEM 3–22 Basics of CVP Analysis; Cost Structure [LO3–1, LO3–3, LO3–4, LO3–5, LO3–6]

Due to erratic sales of its sole product—a high-capacity battery for laptop computers—PEM, Inc., has been experiencing difficulty for some time. The company's contribution format income statement for the most recent month is given below:

Sales (19,500 units × $30 per unit)	$585,000
Variable expenses	409,500
Contribution margin	175,500
Fixed expenses	180,000
Net operating income	$ (4,500)

Required:

1. Compute the company's CM ratio and its break-even point in both unit sales and dollar sales.
2. The president believes that a $16,000 increase in the monthly advertising budget, combined with an intensified effort by the sales staff, will result in an $80,000 increase in monthly sales. If the president is right, what will be the effect on the company's monthly net operating income or loss? (Use the incremental approach in preparing your answer.)
3. Refer to the original data. The sales manager is convinced that a 10% reduction in the selling price, combined with an increase of $60,000 in the monthly advertising budget, will double unit sales. What will the new contribution format income statement look like if these changes are adopted?
4. Refer to the original data. The Marketing Department thinks that a fancy new package for the laptop computer battery would help sales. The new package would increase packaging costs by 75 cents per unit. Assuming no other changes, how many units would have to be sold each month to earn a profit of $9,750?
5. Refer to the original data. By automating, the company could reduce variable expenses by $3 per unit. However, fixed expenses would increase by $72,000 each month.
   a. Compute the new CM ratio and the new break-even point in both unit sales and dollar sales.
   b. Assume that the company expects to sell 26,000 units next month. Prepare two contribution format income statements, one assuming that operations are not automated and one assuming that they are. (Show data on a per unit and percentage basis, as well as in total, for each alternative.)
   c. Would you recommend that the company automate its operations? Explain.

PROBLEM 3–23 Basics of CVP Analysis [LO3–1, LO3–3, LO3–4, LO3–5, LO3–8]

Feather Friends, Inc., distributes a high-quality wooden birdhouse that sells for $20 per unit. Variable expenses are $8 per unit, and fixed expenses total $180,000 per year.

Required:

Answer the following independent questions:

1. What is the product's CM ratio?
2. Use the CM ratio to determine the break-even point in dollar sales.
3. Due to an increase in demand, the company estimates that sales will increase by $75,000 during the next year. By how much should net operating income increase (or net loss decrease) assuming that fixed expenses do not change?

4. Assume that the operating results for last year were:

Sales	$400,000
Variable expenses	160,000
Contribution margin	240,000
Fixed expenses	180,000
Net operating income	$ 60,000

a. Compute the degree of operating leverage at the current level of sales.
b. The president expects sales to increase by 20% next year. By what percentage should net operating income increase?

5. Refer to the original data. Assume that the company sold 18,000 units last year. The sales manager is convinced that a 10% reduction in the selling price, combined with a $30,000 increase in advertising, would increase annual unit sales by one-third. Prepare two contribution format income statements, one showing the results of last year's operations and one showing the results of operations if these changes are made. Would you recommend that the company do as the sales manager suggests?
6. Refer to the original data. Assume again that the company sold 18,000 units last year. The president does not want to change the selling price. Instead, he wants to increase the sales commission by $1 per unit. He thinks that this move, combined with some increase in advertising, would increase annual sales by 25%. By how much could advertising be increased with profits remaining unchanged? Do not prepare an income statement; use the incremental analysis approach.

PROBLEM 3–24 Break-Even and Target Profit Analysis [LO3–5, LO3–6]

The Shirt Works sells a large variety of tee shirts and sweatshirts. Steve Hooper, the owner, is thinking of expanding his sales by hiring high school students, on a commission basis, to sell sweatshirts bearing the name and mascot of the local high school.

These sweatshirts would have to be ordered from the manufacturer six weeks in advance, and they could not be returned because of the unique printing required. The sweatshirts would cost Hooper $8 each with a minimum order of 75 sweatshirts. Any additional sweatshirts would have to be ordered in increments of 75.

Since Hooper's plan would not require any additional facilities, the only costs associated with the project would be the costs of the sweatshirts and the costs of the sales commissions. The selling price of the sweatshirts would be $13.50 each. Hooper would pay the students a commission of $1.50 for each shirt sold.

Required:

1. To make the project worthwhile, Hooper would require a $1,200 profit for the first three months of the venture. What level of unit sales and dollar sales would be required to reach this target net operating income? Show all computations.
2. Assume that the venture is undertaken and an order is placed for 75 sweatshirts. What would be Hooper's break-even point in unit sales and in dollar sales? Show computations and explain the reasoning behind your answer.

PROBLEM 3–25 Changes in Fixed and Variable Expenses; Break-Even and Target Profit Analysis [LO3–4, LO3–5, LO3–6]

Neptune Company produces toys and other items for use in beach and resort areas. A small, inflatable toy has come onto the market that the company is anxious to produce and sell. The new toy will sell for $3 per unit. Enough capacity exists in the company's plant to produce 16,000 units of the toy each month. Variable expenses to manufacture and sell one unit would be $1.25, and fixed expenses associated with the toy would total $35,000 per month.

The company's Marketing Department predicts that demand for the new toy will exceed the 16,000 units that the company is able to produce. Additional manufacturing space can be rented from another company at a fixed expense of $1,000 per month. Variable expenses in the rented facility would total $1.40 per unit, due to somewhat less efficient operations than in the main plant.

Required:

1. Compute the monthly break-even point for the new toy in unit sales and in dollar sales.
2. How many units must be sold each month to make a monthly profit of $12,000?
3. If the sales manager receives a bonus of 10 cents for each unit sold in excess of the break-even point, how many units must be sold each month to earn a return of 25% on the monthly investment in fixed expenses?

PROBLEM 3–26 Basic CVP Analysis; Graphing [LO3–1, LO3–2, LO3–4, LO3–5]

The Fashion Shoe Company operates a chain of women's shoe shops that carry many styles of shoes that are all sold at the same price. Sales personnel in the shops are paid a substantial commission on each pair of shoes sold (in addition to a small base salary) in order to encourage them to be aggressive in their sales efforts.

The following worksheet contains cost and revenue data for Shop 48 and is typical of the company's many outlets:

	Per Pair of Shoes
Selling price	$30.00
Variable expenses:	
Invoice cost	$13.50
Sales commission	4.50
Total variable expenses	$18.00
	Annual
Fixed expenses:	
Advertising	$ 30,000
Rent	20,000
Salaries	100,000
Total fixed expenses	$150,000

Required:

1. Calculate the annual break-even point in unit sales and in dollar sales for Shop 48.
2. Prepare a CVP graph showing cost and revenue data for Shop 48 from zero shoes up to 17,000 pairs of shoes sold each year. Clearly indicate the break-even point on the graph.
3. If 12,000 pairs of shoes are sold in a year, what would be Shop 48's net operating income or loss?
4. The company is considering paying the store manager of Shop 48 an incentive commission of 75 cents per pair of shoes (in addition to the salesperson's commission). If this change is made, what will be the new break-even point in unit sales and in dollar sales?
5. Refer to the original data. As an alternative to requirement 4 above, the company is considering paying the store manager 50 cents commission on each pair of shoes sold in excess of the break-even point. If this change is made, what will be the shop's net operating income or loss if 15,000 pairs of shoes are sold?
6. Refer to the original data. The company is considering eliminating sales commissions entirely in its shops and increasing fixed salaries by $31,500 annually. If this change is made, what will be the new break-even point in unit sales and in dollar sales for Shop 48? Would you recommend that the change be made? Explain.

PROBLEM 3–27 Sales Mix; Break-Even Analysis; Margin of Safety [LO3–7, LO3–9]

Island Novelties, Inc., of Palau makes two products, Hawaiian Fantasy and Tahitian Joy. Present revenue, cost, and sales data for the two products follow:

	Hawaiian Fantasy	Tahitian Joy
Selling price per unit	$15	$100
Variable expenses per unit	$ 9	$ 20
Number of units sold annually	20,000	5,000

Fixed expenses total $475,800 per year.

Required:

1. Assuming the sales mix given above, do the following:
   a. Prepare a contribution format income statement showing both dollar and percent columns for each product and for the company as a whole.
   b. Compute the break-even point in dollar sales for the company as a whole and the margin of safety in both dollars and percent.
2. The company has developed a new product to be called Samoan Delight. Assume that the company could sell 10,000 units at $45 each. The variable expenses would be $36 each. The company's fixed expenses would not change.
   a. Prepare another contribution format income statement, including sales of the Samoan Delight (sales of the other two products would not change).
   b. Compute the company's new break-even point in dollar sales and the new margin of safety in both dollars and percent.
3. The president of the company examines your figures and says, "There's something strange here. Our fixed expenses haven't changed and you show greater total contribution margin if we add the new product, but you also show our break-even point going up. With greater contribution margin, the break-even point should go down, not up. You've made a mistake somewhere." Explain to the president what has happened.

PROBLEM 3–28 Sales Mix; Commission Structure; Multiproduct Break-Even Analysis [LO3–9]

Carbex, Inc., produces cutlery sets out of high-quality wood and steel. The company makes a standard cutlery set and a deluxe set and sells them to retail department stores throughout the country. The standard set sells for $60, and the deluxe set sells for $75. The variable expenses associated with each set are given below.

	Standard	Deluxe
Production costs	$15.00	$30.00
Sales commissions (15% of sales price)	$ 9.00	$11.25

The company's fixed expenses each month are:

Advertising.	$105,000
Depreciation.	$ 21,700
Administrative	$ 63,000

Salespersons are paid on a commission basis to encourage them to be aggressive in their sales efforts. Mary Parsons, the financial vice president, watches sales commissions carefully and has noted that they have risen steadily over the last year. For this reason, she was shocked to find that even though sales have increased, profits for the current month—May—are down substantially from April. Sales, in sets, for the last two months are given below:

	Standard	Deluxe	Total
April.	4,000	2,000	6,000
May	1,000	5,000	6,000

Required:

1. Prepare contribution format income statements for April and May. Use the following headings:

	Standard		Deluxe		Total	
	Amount	Percent	Amount	Percent	Amount	Percent
Sales. . .						
Etc.						

Place the fixed expenses only in the Total column. Do not show percentages for the fixed expenses.

2. Explain the difference in net operating incomes between the two months, even though the same total number of sets was sold in each month.
3. What can be done to the sales commissions to improve the sales mix?
   a. Using April's sales mix, what is the break-even point in dollar sales?
   b. Without doing any calculations, explain whether the break-even points would be higher or lower with May's sales mix than April's sales mix.

PROBLEM 3–29 Changes in Cost Structure; Break-Even Analysis; Operating Leverage; Margin of Safety [LO3–4, LO3–5, LO3–7, LO3–8]

Morton Company's contribution format income statement for last month is given below:

Sales (15,000 units × $30 per unit)	$450,000
Variable expenses	315,000
Contribution margin	135,000
Fixed expenses	90,000
Net operating income	$ 45,000

The industry in which Morton Company operates is quite sensitive to cyclical movements in the economy. Thus, profits vary considerably from year to year according to general economic conditions. The company has a large amount of unused capacity and is studying ways of improving profits.

Required:

1. New equipment has come onto the market that would allow Morton Company to automate a portion of its operations. Variable expenses would be reduced by $9 per unit. However, fixed expenses would increase to a total of $225,000 each month. Prepare two contribution format income statements, one showing present operations and one showing how operations would appear if the new equipment is purchased. Show an Amount column, a Per Unit column, and a Percent column on each statement. Do not show percentages for the fixed expenses.
2. Refer to the income statements in requirement 1 above. For both present operations and the proposed new operations, compute (a) the degree of operating leverage, (b) the break-even point in dollar sales, and (c) the margin of safety in both dollar and percentage terms.
3. Refer again to the data in requirement 1 above. As a manager, what factor would be paramount in your mind in deciding whether to purchase the new equipment? (Assume that enough funds are available to make the purchase.)
4. Refer to the original data. Rather than purchase new equipment, the marketing manager argues that the company's marketing strategy should be changed. Rather than pay sales commissions, which are currently included in variable expenses, the company would pay salespersons fixed salaries and would invest heavily in advertising. The marketing manager claims this new approach would increase unit sales by 30% without any change in selling price; the company's new monthly fixed expenses would be $180,000; and its net operating income would increase by 20%. Compute the break-even point in dollar sales for the company under the new marketing strategy. Do you agree with the marketing manager's proposal?

PROBLEM 3–30 Graphing; Incremental Analysis; Operating Leverage [LO3–2, LO3–4, LO3–5, LO3–6, LO3–8]

Angie Silva has recently opened The Sandal Shop in Brisbane, Australia, a store that specializes in fashionable sandals. Angie has just received a degree in business and she is anxious to apply the principles she has learned to her business. In time, she hopes to open a chain of sandal shops. As a first step, she has prepared the following analysis for her new store:

Required:

1. How many pairs of sandals must be sold each year to break even? What does this represent in total sales dollars?

Sales price per pair of sandals	$40
Variable expenses per pair of sandals	16
Contribution margin per pair of sandals	$24
Fixed expenses per year:	
Building rental	$15,000
Equipment depreciation	7,000
Selling	20,000
Administrative	18,000
Total fixed expense	$60,000

2. Prepare a CVP graph or a profit graph for the store from zero pairs up to 4,000 pairs of sandals sold each year. Indicate the break-even point on your graph.
3. Angie has decided that she must earn at least $18,000 the first year to justify her time and effort. How many pairs of sandals must be sold to reach this target profit?
4. Angie now has two salespersons working in the store—one full time and one part time. It will cost her an additional $8,000 per year to convert the part-time position to a full-time position. Angie believes that the change would bring in an additional $25,000 in sales each year. Should she convert the position? Use the incremental approach. (Do not prepare an income statement.)
5. Refer to the original data. During the first year, the store sold only 3,000 pairs of sandals and reported the following operating results:

Sales (3,000 pairs)	$ 120,000
Variable expenses	48,000
Contribution margin	72,000
Fixed expenses	60,000
Net operating income	$ 12,000

a. What is the store's degree of operating leverage?

b. Angie is confident that with a more intense sales effort and with a more creative advertising program she can increase sales by 50% next year. What would be the expected percentage increase in net operating income? Use the degree of operating leverage to compute your answer.

PROBLEM 3–31 Interpretive Questions on the CVP Graph [LO3–2, LO3–5]

A CVP graph such as the one shown below is a useful technique for showing relationships among an organization's costs, volume, and profits.

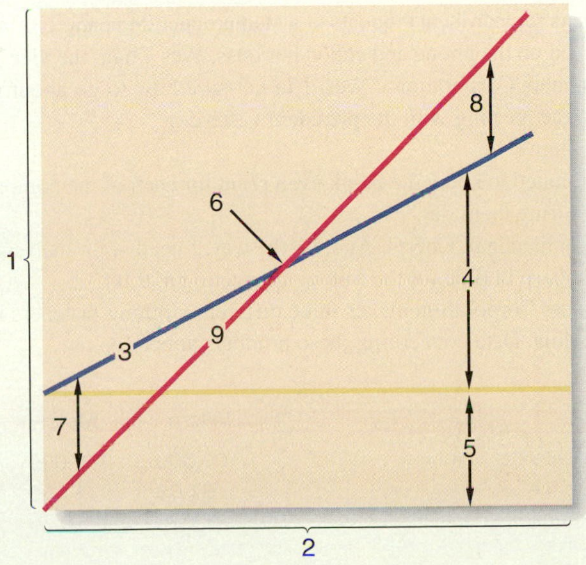

Required:

1. Identify the numbered components in the CVP graph.
2. State the effect of each of the following actions on line 3, line 9, and the break-even point. For line 3 and line 9, state whether the action will cause the line to:
   - Remain unchanged.
   - Shift upward.
   - Shift downward.
   - Have a steeper slope (i.e., rotate upward).
   - Have a flatter slope (i.e., rotate downward).
   - Shift upward *and* have a steeper slope.
   - Shift upward *and* have a flatter slope.
   - Shift downward *and* have a steeper slope.
   - Shift downward *and* have a flatter slope.

   In the case of the break-even point, state whether the action will cause the break-even point to:
   - Remain unchanged.
   - Increase.
   - Decrease.
   - Probably change, but the direction is uncertain.

   Treat each case independently.

   x. *Example.* Fixed expenses are reduced by $5,000 per period.
   Answer (see choices above): Line 3: Shift downward.
   Line 9: Remain unchanged.
   Break-even point: Decrease.

   a. The unit selling price is increased from $18 to $20.
   b. Unit variable expenses are decreased from $12 to $10.
   c. Fixed expenses are increased by $3,000 per period.
   d. Two thousand more units are sold during the period than were budgeted.
   e. Due to paying salespersons a commission rather than a flat salary, fixed expenses are reduced by $8,000 per period and unit variable expenses are increased by $3.
   f. Due to an increase in the cost of materials, both unit variable expenses and the selling price are increased by $2.
   g. Advertising costs are increased by $10,000 per period, resulting in a 10% increase in the number of units sold.
   h. Due to automating an operation previously done by workers, fixed expenses are increased by $12,000 per period and unit variable expenses are reduced by $4.

Cases

connect Additional student resources are available with Connect.

CASE 3–32 Break-Evens for Individual Products in a Multiproduct Company [LO3–5, LO3–9]

Cheryl Montoya picked up the phone and called her boss, Wes Chan, the vice president of marketing at Piedmont Fasteners Corporation: "Wes, I'm not sure how to go about answering the questions that came up at the meeting with the president yesterday."

"What's the problem?"

"The president wanted to know the break-even point for each of the company's products, but I am having trouble figuring them out."

"I'm sure you can handle it, Cheryl. And, by the way, I need your analysis on my desk tomorrow morning at 8:00 sharp in time for the follow-up meeting at 9:00."

Piedmont Fasteners Corporation makes three different clothing fasteners in its manufacturing facility in North Carolina. Data concerning these products appear below:

	Velcro	Metal	Nylon
Normal annual sales volume	100,000	200,000	400,000
Unit selling price	$1.65	$1.50	$0.85
Variable expense per unit	$1.25	$0.70	$0.25

Total fixed expenses are $400,000 per year.

All three products are sold in highly competitive markets, so the company is unable to raise its prices without losing unacceptable numbers of customers.

The company has an extremely effective lean production system, so there are no beginning or ending work in process or finished goods inventories.

Required:

1. What is the company's overall break-even point in dollar sales?
2. Of the total fixed expenses of $400,000, $20,000 could be avoided if the Velcro product is dropped, $80,000 if the Metal product is dropped, and $60,000 if the Nylon product is dropped. The remaining fixed expenses of $240,000 consist of common fixed expenses such as administrative salaries and rent on the factory building that could be avoided only by going out of business entirely.
   a. What is the break-even point in unit sales for each product?
   b. If the company sells exactly the break-even quantity of each product, what will be the overall profit of the company? Explain this result.

CASE 3–33 Cost Structure; Break-Even and Target Profit Analysis [LO3–4, LO3–5, LO3–6]

Pittman Company is a small but growing manufacturer of telecommunications equipment. The company has no sales force of its own; rather, it relies completely on independent sales agents to market its products. These agents are paid a sales commission of 15% for all items sold.

Barbara Cheney, Pittman's controller, has just prepared the company's budgeted income statement for next year. The statement follows:

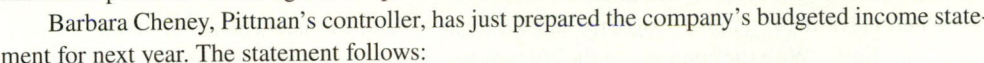

Pittman Company
Budgeted Income Statement
For the Year Ended December 31

Sales		$16,000,000
Manufacturing expenses:		
Variable	$7,200,000	
Fixed overhead	2,340,000	9,540,000
Gross margin		6,460,000
Selling and administrative expenses:		
Commissions to agents	2,400,000	
Fixed marketing expenses	1,20,000*	
Fixed administrative expenses	1,800,000	4,320,000
Net operating income		2,140,000
Fixed interest expenses		540,000
Income before income taxes		1,600,000
Income taxes (30%)		480,000
Net income		$ 1,120,000

*Primarily depreciation on storage facilities.

As Barbara handed the statement to Karl Vecci, Pittman's president, she commented, "I went ahead and used the agents' 15% commission rate in completing these statements, but we've just learned that they refuse to handle our products next year unless we increase the commission rate to 20%."

"That's the last straw," Karl replied angrily. "Those agents have been demanding more and more, and this time they've gone too far. How can they possibly defend a 20% commission rate?"

"They claim that after paying for advertising, travel, and the other costs of promotion, there's nothing left over for profit," replied Barbara.

"I say it's just plain robbery," retorted Karl. "And I also say it's time we dumped those guys and got our own sales force. Can you get your people to work up some cost figures for us to look at?"

"We've already worked them up," said Barbara. "Several companies we know about pay a 7.5% commission to their own salespeople, along with a small salary. Of course, we would have to handle all promotion costs, too. We figure our fixed expenses would increase by $2,400,000 per year, but that would be more than offset by the $3,200,000 (20% × $16,000,000) that we would avoid on agents' commissions."

The breakdown of the $2,400,000 cost follows:

Salaries:	
Sales manager	$ 100,000
Salespersons	600,000
Travel and entertainment	400,000
Advertising	1,300,000
Total	$2,400,000

"Super," replied Karl. "And I noticed that the $2,400,000 is just what we're paying the agents under the old 15% commission rate."

"It's even better than that," explained Barbara. "We can actually save $75,000 a year because that's what we're having to pay the auditing firm now to check out the agents' reports. So our overall administrative expenses would be less."

"Pull all of these numbers together and we'll show them to the executive committee tomorrow," said Karl. "With the approval of the committee, we can move on the matter immediately."

Required:

1. Compute Pittman Company's break-even point in dollar sales for next year assuming:
   a. The agents' commission rate remains unchanged at 15%.
   b. The agents' commission rate is increased to 20%.
   c. The company employs its own sales force.
2. Assume that Pittman Company decides to continue selling through agents and pays the 20% commission rate. Determine the volume of sales that would be required to generate the same net income as contained in the budgeted income statement for next year.
3. Determine the volume of sales at which net income would be equal regardless of whether Pittman Company sells through agents (at a 20% commission rate) or employs its own sales force.
4. Compute the degree of operating leverage that the company would expect to have on December 31 at the end of next year assuming:
   a. The agents' commission rate remains unchanged at 15%.
   b. The agents' commission rate is increased to 20%.
   c. The company employs its own sales force.

Use income *before* income taxes in your operating leverage computation.

5. Based on the data in requirements 1–4 above, make a recommendation as to whether the company should continue to use sales agents (at a 20% commission rate) or employ its own sales force. Give reasons for your answer.

(CMA, adapted)

Job–Order Costing

University Tees: Serving Over 150 Campuses Nationwide

BUSINESS FOCUS

Courtesy of University Tees, Inc.

University Tees was founded in 2003 by two Miami University college students to provide screen-printing, embroidery, and promotional products for fraternities, sororities, and student organizations. Today, the company, which is headquartered in Cleveland, Ohio, employs as many as four Campus Managers on each of over 150 college campuses across America.

Accurately calculating the cost of each potential customer order is critically important to University Tees because the company needs to be sure that the sales price exceeds the cost associated with satisfying the order. The costs include the cost of the blank t-shirts themselves, printing costs (which vary depending on the quantity of shirts produced and the number of colors per shirt), screen costs (which also vary depending on the number of colors included in a design), shipping costs, and the artwork needed to create a design. The company also takes into account its competitors' pricing strategies when developing its own prices.

Given its success on college campuses, University Tees has introduced a sister company called On Point Promos to serve for-profit companies and nonprofit organizations. ■

Source: Conversation with Joe Haddad, cofounder of University Tees.

LEARNING OBJECTIVES

After studying Chapter 4, you should be able to:

LO 4–1 Compute a predetermined overhead rate.

LO 4–2 Apply overhead cost to jobs using a predetermined overhead rate.

LO 4–3 Compute the total cost and average cost per unit of a job.

LO 4–4 Compute underapplied or overapplied overhead cost.

LO 4–5 Use the direct method to determine cost of goods sold.

LO 4–6 Use the indirect method to determine cost of goods sold.

LO 4–7 (Appendix 4A) Use activity-based absorption costing to compute unit product costs.

LO 4–8 (Appendix 4B) Understand the implications of basing the predetermined overhead rate on activity at capacity rather than on estimated activity for the period.

The way in which product and service costs are determined can have a substantial impact on reported profits, as well as on key management decisions.

A managerial costing system should provide cost data to help managers plan, control, and make decisions. Nevertheless, external financial reporting and tax reporting requirements often heavily influence how costs are accumulated and summarized on managerial reports. This is true of product costing. In this chapter we use *absorption costing* to determine product costs. In **absorption costing**, all manufacturing costs, both fixed and variable, are assigned to units of product—units are said to *fully absorb manufacturing costs.*

Most countries—including the United States—require some form of absorption costing for both external financial reports and for tax reports. In addition, the vast majority of companies throughout the world also use absorption costing in their management reports. Because absorption costing is the most common approach to product costing throughout the world, we discuss it first and then discuss the alternatives in subsequent chapters.

Job-Order Costing—An Overview

Under absorption costing, product costs include all manufacturing costs. Some manufacturing costs, such as direct materials, can be directly traced to particular products. For example, the cost of the airbags installed in a Toyota Camry can be easily traced to that particular auto. But what about manufacturing costs like factory rent? Such costs do not change from month to month, whereas the number and variety of products made in the factory may vary dramatically from one month to the next. Because these costs remain unchanged from month to month regardless of what products are made, they are clearly not caused by—and cannot be directly traced to—any particular product. Therefore, these types of costs are assigned to products and services by averaging across time and across products. The type of production process influences how this averaging is done.

Job-order costing is used in situations where many *different* products, each with individual and unique features, are produced each period. For example, a Levi Strauss clothing factory would typically make many different types of jeans for both men and women during a month. A particular order might consist of 1,000 boot-cut men's blue denim jeans, style number A312. This order of 1,000 jeans is called a *job.* In a job-order costing system, costs are traced and allocated to jobs and then the costs of the job are divided by the number of units in the job to arrive at an average cost per unit.

Other examples of situations where job-order costing would be used include large-scale construction projects managed by Bechtel International, commercial aircraft produced by Boeing, greeting cards designed and printed by Hallmark, and airline meals prepared by LSG SkyChefs. All of these examples are characterized by diverse outputs. Each Bechtel project is unique and different from every other—the company may be simultaneously constructing a dam in the Republic of Congo and a bridge in Indonesia. Likewise, each airline orders a different type of meal from LSG SkyChefs' catering service.

Job-order costing is also used extensively in service industries. For example, hospitals, law firms, movie studios, accounting firms, advertising agencies, and repair shops all use a variation of job-order costing to accumulate costs. Although the detailed example of job-order costing provided in the following section deals with a manufacturing company, the same basic concepts and procedures are used by many service organizations.

IN BUSINESS

IS THIS REALLY A JOB?

VBT Bicycling Vacations of Bristol, Vermont, offers deluxe bicycling vacations in the United States, Canada, Europe, and other locations throughout the world. For example, the company offers a 10-day tour of the Puglia region of Italy—the "heel of the boot." The tour price includes international airfare, 10 nights of lodging, most meals, use of a bicycle, and ground transportation as needed. Each tour is led by at least two local tour leaders, one of whom rides with the guests along the tour route. The other tour leader drives a "sag wagon" that carries extra water, snacks, and bicycle repair equipment and is available for a shuttle back to the hotel or up a hill. The sag wagon also transports guests' luggage from one hotel to another.

Each specific tour can be considered a job. For example, Giuliano Astore and Debora Trippetti, two natives of Puglia, led a VBT tour with 17 guests over 10 days in late April. At the end of the tour, Giuliano submitted a report, a sort of job cost sheet, to VBT headquarters. This report detailed the on the ground expenses incurred for this specific tour, including fuel and operating costs for the van, lodging costs for the guests, the costs of meals provided to guests, the costs of snacks, the cost of hiring additional ground transportation as needed, and the wages of the tour leaders. In addition to these costs, some costs are paid directly by VBT in Vermont to vendors. The total cost incurred for the tour is then compared to the total revenue collected from guests to determine the gross profit for the tour.

Sources: Giuliano Astore and Gregg Marston, President, VBT Bicycling Vacations. For more information about VBT, see www.vbt.com.

© Sandee Noreen

© Sandee Noreen

Job-Order Costing—An Example

To introduce job-order costing, we will follow a specific job as it progresses through the manufacturing process. This job consists of two experimental couplings that Yost Precision Machining has agreed to produce for Loops Unlimited, a manufacturer of roller coasters. Couplings connect the cars on the roller coaster and are a critical component in the performance and safety of the ride. Before we begin our discussion, recall from a previous chapter that companies generally classify manufacturing costs into three broad categories: (1) direct materials, (2) direct labor, and (3) manufacturing overhead. As we study the operation of a job-order costing system, we will see how each of these three types of costs is recorded and accumulated.

MANAGERIAL ACCOUNTING IN ACTION

The Issue

YOST Precision Machining

Yost Precision Machining is a small company in Michigan that specializes in fabricating precision metal parts that are used in a variety of applications ranging from deep-sea exploration vehicles to the inertial triggers in automobile air bags. The company's top managers gather every morning at 8:00 A.M. in the company's conference room for the daily planning meeting. Attending the meeting this morning are: Jean Yost, the company's president; David Cheung, the marketing manager; Debbie Turner, the production manager; and Marc White, the company controller. The president opened the meeting:

Jean: The production schedule indicates we'll be starting Job 2B47 today. Isn't that the special order for experimental couplings, David?

David: That's right. That's the order from Loops Unlimited for two couplings for their new roller coaster ride for Magic Mountain.

Debbie: Why only two couplings? Don't they need a coupling for every car?

David: Yes. But this is a completely new roller coaster. The cars will go faster and will be subjected to more twists, turns, drops, and loops than on any other existing roller coaster. To hold up under these stresses, Loops Unlimited's engineers completely

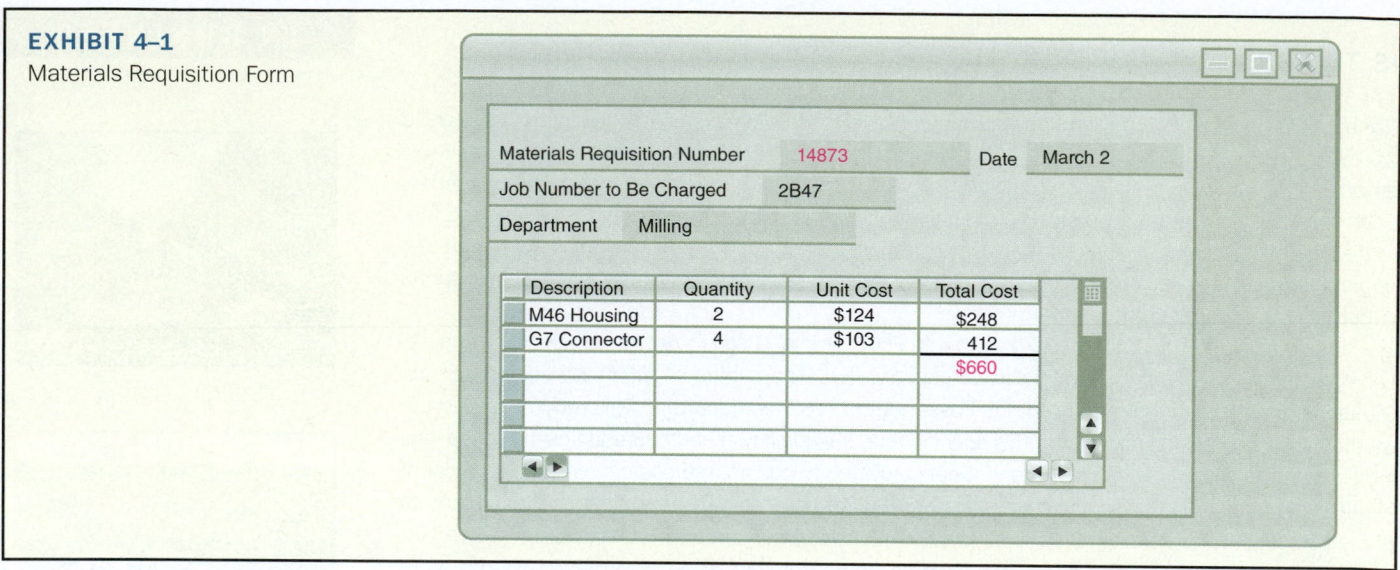

EXHIBIT 4–1
Materials Requisition Form

Materials Requisition Number 14873 Date March 2
Job Number to Be Charged 2B47
Department Milling

Description	Quantity	Unit Cost	Total Cost
M46 Housing	2	$124	$248
G7 Connector	4	$103	412
			$660

redesigned the cars and couplings. They want us to make just two of these new couplings for testing purposes. If the design works, then we'll have the inside track on the order to supply couplings for the whole ride.

Jean: We agreed to take on this initial order at our cost just to get our foot in the door. Marc, will there be any problem documenting our cost so we can get paid?

Marc: No problem. The contract with Loops stipulates that they will pay us an amount equal to our cost of goods sold. With our job-order costing system, I can tell you the cost on the day the job is completed.

Jean: Good. Is there anything else we should discuss about this job at this time? No? Well then let's move on to the next item of business.

Measuring Direct Materials Cost

The blueprints submitted by Loops Unlimited indicate that each experimental coupling will require three parts that are classified as direct materials: two G7 Connectors and one M46 Housing. Since each coupling requires two connectors and one housing, the production of two couplings requires four connectors and two housings. This is a custom product that is being made for the first time, but if this were one of the company's standard products, it would have an established *bill of materials.* A **bill of materials** is a document that lists the type and quantity of each type of direct material needed to complete a unit of product.

When an agreement has been reached with the customer concerning the quantities, prices, and shipment date for the order, a *production order* is issued. The Production Department then prepares a *materials requisition form* similar to the form in Exhibit 4–1. The **materials requisition form** is a document that specifies the type and quantity of materials to be drawn from the storeroom and identifies the job that will be charged for the cost of the materials. The form is used to control the flow of materials into production and also for making entries in the accounting records.

The Yost Precision Machining materials requisition form in Exhibit 4–1 shows that the company's Milling Department has requisitioned two M46 Housings and four G7 Connectors for the Loops Unlimited job, which has been designated as Job 2B47.

Job Cost Sheet

After a production order has been issued, the Accounting Department's job-order costing software system automatically generates a *job cost sheet* like the one presented in Exhibit 4–2. A **job cost sheet** records the materials, labor, and manufacturing overhead costs charged to that job.

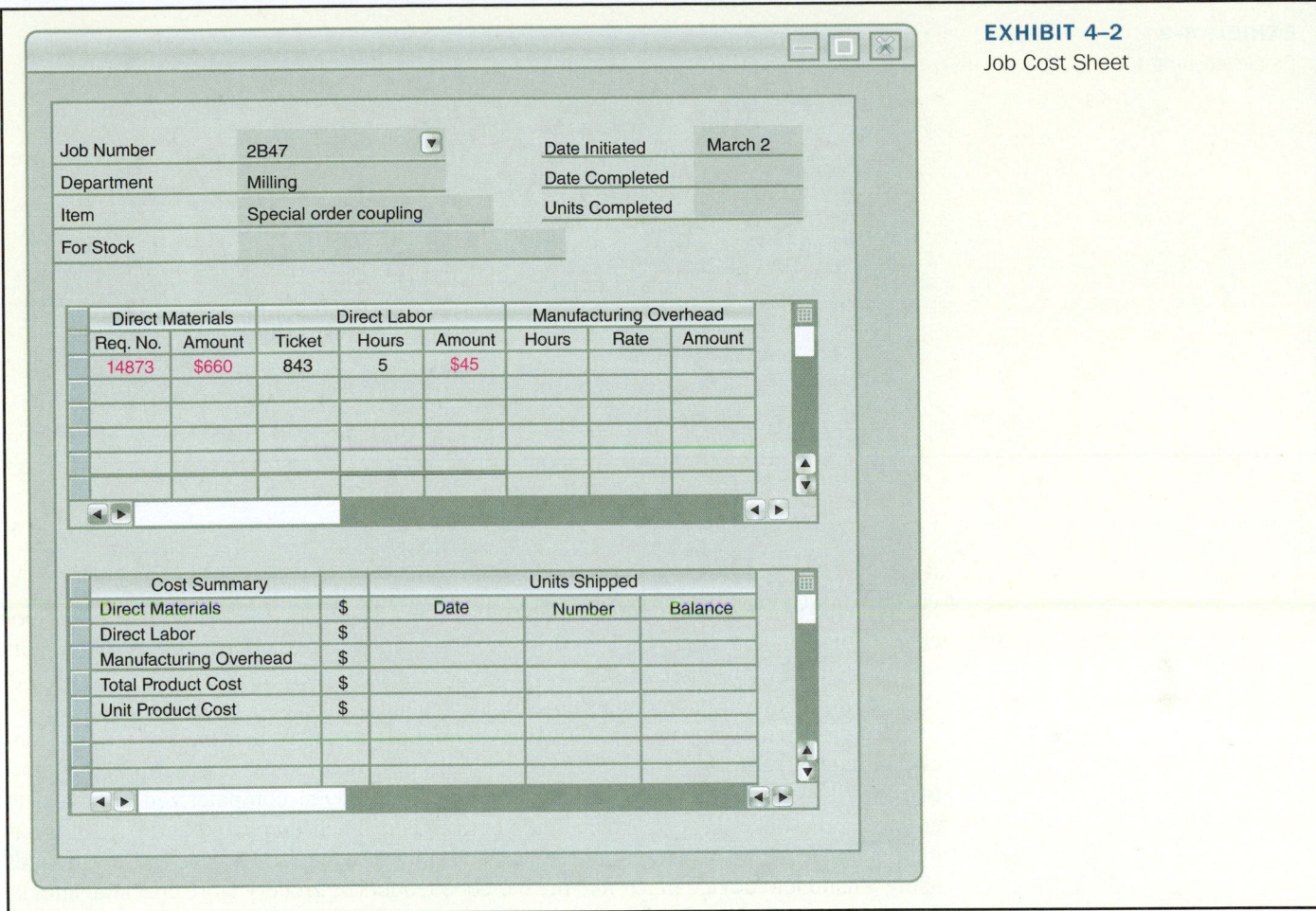

EXHIBIT 4–2
Job Cost Sheet

Job Number	2B47	Date Initiated	March 2
Department	Milling	Date Completed	
Item	Special order coupling	Units Completed	
For Stock			

Direct Materials		Direct Labor			Manufacturing Overhead		
Req. No.	Amount	Ticket	Hours	Amount	Hours	Rate	Amount
14873	$660	843	5	$45			

Cost Summary		Units Shipped		
		Date	Number	Balance
Direct Materials	$			
Direct Labor	$			
Manufacturing Overhead	$			
Total Product Cost	$			
Unit Product Cost	$			

IN BUSINESS

SUPPLY AND DEMAND INFLUENCE LUMBER PRICES

When the housing market crumbled between 2005 and 2009, lumber mills responded by slashing output by 45%. However, in 2010 many home builders decided to expand speculative construction on the belief that an expiring federal tax credit would entice more customers to purchase new homes. The result of plummeting supply coupled with an uptick in demand was predictable-the price of lumber spiked to $279 per thousand board feet, thereby adding about $1,000 to the price of a typical new home. Pulte Homes told investors that it would attempt to offset the increase in direct materials cost by reducing its labor costs.

Home builders use job-order costing systems to accumulate the costs incurred to build each new home. When materials and labor costs fluctuate, job-order costing systems can measure these impacts on each customer's new home construction costs.

Source: Liam Pleven and Lester Aldrich, "Builders Nailed by Lumber Prices," *The Wall Street Journal*, February 16, 2010, pp. C1 and C4.

After direct materials are issued, the cost of these materials are automatically recorded on the job cost sheet. Note from Exhibit 4–2, for example, that the $660 cost for direct materials shown earlier on the materials requisition form has been charged to Job 2B47 on its job cost sheet. The requisition number 14873 from the materials requisition form appears on the job cost sheet to make it easier to identify the source document for the direct materials charge.

EXHIBIT 4–3
Employee Time Ticket

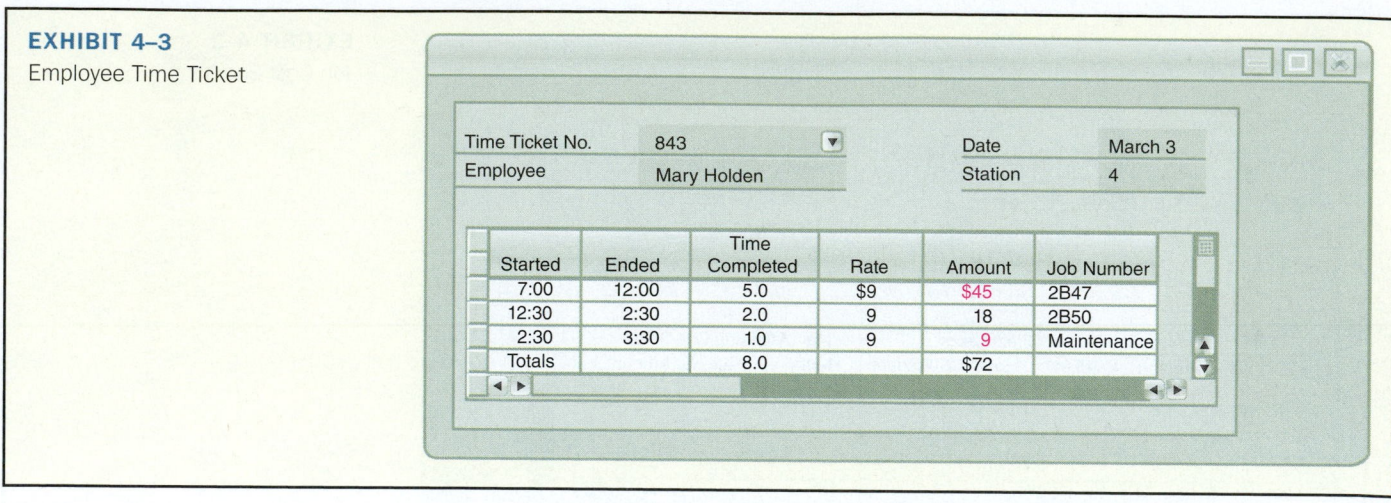

Time Ticket No.	843	Date	March 3
Employee	Mary Holden	Station	4

Started	Ended	Time Completed	Rate	Amount	Job Number
7:00	12:00	5.0	$9	$45	2B47
12:30	2:30	2.0	9	18	2B50
2:30	3:30	1.0	9	9	Maintenance
Totals		8.0		$72	

Measuring Direct Labor Cost

Direct labor consists of labor charges that can be easily traced to a particular job. Labor charges that cannot be easily traced directly to any job are treated as part of manufacturing overhead. As discussed in a previous chapter, this latter category of labor costs is called *indirect labor* and includes tasks such as maintenance, supervision, and cleanup.

Today many companies rely on computerized systems (rather than paper and pencil) to maintain employee *time tickets.* A completed **time ticket** is an hour-by-hour summary of the employee's activities throughout the day. One computerized approach to creating time tickets uses bar codes to capture data. Each employee and each job has a unique bar code. When beginning work on a job, the employee scans three bar codes using a handheld device much like the bar code readers at grocery store checkout stands. The first bar code indicates that a job is being started; the second is the unique bar code on the employee's identity badge; and the third is the unique bar code of the job itself. This information is fed automatically via an electronic network to a computer that notes the time and records all of the data. When the task is completed, the employee scans a bar code indicating the task is complete, the bar code on his or her identity badge, and the bar code attached to the job. This information is relayed to the computer that again notes the time, and a time ticket, such as the one shown in Exhibit 4–3, is automatically prepared. Because all of the source data is already in computer files, the labor costs can be automatically posted to job cost sheets. For example, Exhibit 4–3 shows $45 of direct labor cost related to Job 2B47. This amount is automatically posted to the job cost sheet shown in Exhibit 4–2. The time ticket in Exhibit 4–3 also shows $9 of indirect labor costs related to performing maintenance. This cost is treated as part of manufacturing overhead and does not get posted on a job cost sheet.

Computing Predetermined Overhead Rates

LEARNING OBJECTIVE 4–1
Compute a predetermined overhead rate.

Recall that product costs include manufacturing overhead as well as direct materials and direct labor. Therefore, manufacturing overhead also needs to be recorded on the job cost sheet. However, assigning manufacturing overhead to a specific job involves some difficulties. There are three reasons for this:

1. Manufacturing overhead is an *indirect cost.* This means that it is either impossible or difficult to trace these costs to a particular product or job.
2. Manufacturing overhead consists of many different types of cost ranging from the grease used in machines to the annual salary of the production manager. Some of these costs are variable overhead costs because they vary in direct proportion to changes in the level of production (e.g., indirect materials, supplies, and power) and

some are fixed overhead costs because they remain constant as the level of production fluctuates (e.g., heat and light, property taxes, and insurance).

3. Because of the fixed costs in manufacturing overhead, total manufacturing overhead costs tend to remain relatively constant from one period to the next even though the number of units produced can fluctuate widely. Consequently, the average cost per unit will vary from one period to the next.

Given these problems, allocation is used to assign overhead costs to products. Allocation is accomplished by selecting an *allocation base* that is common to all of the company's products and services. An **allocation base** is a measure such as direct labor-hours (DLH) or machine-hours (MH) that is used to assign overhead costs to products and services. The most widely used allocation bases in manufacturing are direct labor-hours, direct labor cost, machine-hours and (where a company has only a single product) units of product.

Manufacturing overhead is commonly assigned to products using *a predetermined overhead rate*. The **predetermined overhead rate** is computed by dividing the total estimated manufacturing overhead cost for the period by the estimated total amount of the allocation base for the period as follows:

$$\text{Predetermined overhead rate} = \frac{\text{Estimated total manufacturing overhead cost}}{\text{Estimated total amount of the allocation base}}$$

The predetermined overhead rate is computed *before* the period begins using a four-step process. The first step is to estimate the total amount of the allocation base (the denominator) that will be required for next period's estimated level of production. The second step is to estimate the total fixed manufacturing overhead cost for the coming period and the variable manufacturing overhead cost per unit of the allocation base. The third step is to use the cost formula shown below to estimate the total manufacturing overhead cost (the numerator) for the coming period:

$$Y = a + bX$$

where,

Y = The estimated total manufacturing overhead cost
a = The estimated total fixed manufacturing overhead cost
b = The estimated variable manufacturing overhead cost per unit of the allocation base
X = The estimated total amount of the allocation base

The fourth step is to compute the predetermined overhead rate. Notice, the estimated amount of the allocation base is determined before estimating the total manufacturing overhead cost. This needs to be done because total manufacturing overhead cost includes variable overhead costs that depend on the amount of the allocation base.

Applying Manufacturing Overhead

LEARNING OBJECTIVE 4–2
Apply overhead cost to jobs using a predetermined overhead rate.

To repeat, the predetermined overhead rate is computed *before* the period begins. The predetermined overhead rate is then used to apply overhead cost to jobs throughout the period. The process of assigning overhead cost to jobs is called **overhead application**. The formula for determining the amount of overhead cost to apply to a particular job is:

$$\begin{array}{c}\text{Overhead applied to} \\ \text{a particular job}\end{array} = \begin{array}{c}\text{Predetermined} \\ \text{overhead rate}\end{array} \times \begin{array}{c}\text{Amount of the allocation} \\ \text{base incurred by the job}\end{array}$$

For example, if the predetermined overhead rate is \$8 per direct labor-hour, then \$8 of overhead cost is *applied* to a job for each direct labor-hour incurred on the job. When the allocation base is direct labor-hours, the formula becomes:

$$\begin{array}{c}\text{Overhead applied to} \\ \text{a particular job}\end{array} = \begin{array}{c}\text{Predetermined} \\ \text{overhead rate}\end{array} \times \begin{array}{c}\text{Actual direct labor-hours} \\ \text{charged to the job}\end{array}$$

Manufacturing Overhead—A Closer Look

To illustrate the steps involved in computing and using a predetermined overhead rate, let's return to Yost Precision Machining and make the following assumptions. In step one, the company estimated that 40,000 direct labor-hours would be required to support the production planned for the year. In step two, it estimated $220,000 of total fixed manufacturing overhead cost for the coming year and $2.50 of variable manufacturing overhead cost per direct labor-hour. Given these assumptions, in step three the company used the cost formula shown below to estimate its total manufacturing overhead cost for the year:

$$Y = a + bX$$

$$Y = \$220{,}000 + (\$2.50 \text{ per direct labor-hour} \times 40{,}000 \text{ direct labor-hours})$$

$$Y = \$220{,}000 + \$100{,}000$$

$$Y = \$320{,}000$$

In step four, Yost Precision Machining computed its predetermined overhead rate for the year of $8 per direct labor-hour as shown below:

$$\text{Predetermined overhead rate} = \frac{\text{Estimated total manufacturing overhead cost}}{\text{Estimated total amount of the allocation base}}$$

$$= \frac{\$320{,}000}{40{,}000 \text{ direct labor-hours}}$$

$$= \$8 \text{ per direct labor-hour}$$

The job cost sheet in Exhibit 4–4 indicates that 27 direct labor-hours (i.e., DLHs) were charged to Job 2B47. Therefore, a total of $216 of manufacturing overhead cost would be applied to the job:

$$\begin{array}{c}\text{Overhead applied to}\\ \text{Job 2B47}\end{array} = \begin{array}{c}\text{Predetermined}\\ \text{overhead rate}\end{array} \times \begin{array}{c}\text{Actual direct labor-hours}\\ \text{charged to Job 2B47}\end{array}$$

$$= \$8 \text{ per DLH} \times 27 \text{ DLHs}$$

$$= \$216 \text{ of overhead applied to Job 2B47}$$

This amount of overhead has been entered on the job cost sheet in Exhibit 4–4. Note that this is *not* the actual amount of overhead caused by the job. Actual overhead costs are *not* assigned to jobs—if that could be done, the costs would be direct costs, not overhead. The overhead assigned to the job is simply a share of the total overhead that was estimated at the beginning of the year. A **normal cost system**, which we have been describing, applies overhead to jobs by multiplying a predetermined overhead rate by the actual amount of the allocation base incurred by the jobs.

The Need for a Predetermined Rate

Instead of using a predetermined rate based on estimates, why not base the overhead rate on the *actual* total manufacturing overhead cost and the *actual* total amount of the allocation base incurred on a monthly, quarterly, or annual basis? If an actual rate is computed monthly or quarterly, seasonal factors in overhead costs or in the allocation base can produce fluctuations in the overhead rate. For example, the costs of heating and cooling a factory in Illinois will be highest in the winter and summer months and lowest in the spring and fall. If the overhead rate is recomputed at the end of each month or each quarter based on actual costs and activity, the overhead rate would go up in the winter and summer and down in the spring and fall. As a result, two identical jobs, one completed in the winter and one completed in the spring, would be assigned different manufacturing overhead costs. Many managers believe that such fluctuations in product costs serve no useful purpose. To avoid such fluctuations, actual overhead rates could be computed on an annual or less-frequent basis. However, if the overhead rate is computed annually based on the actual costs and activity for the year, the manufacturing overhead assigned

EXHIBIT 4–4
A Completed Job Cost Sheet

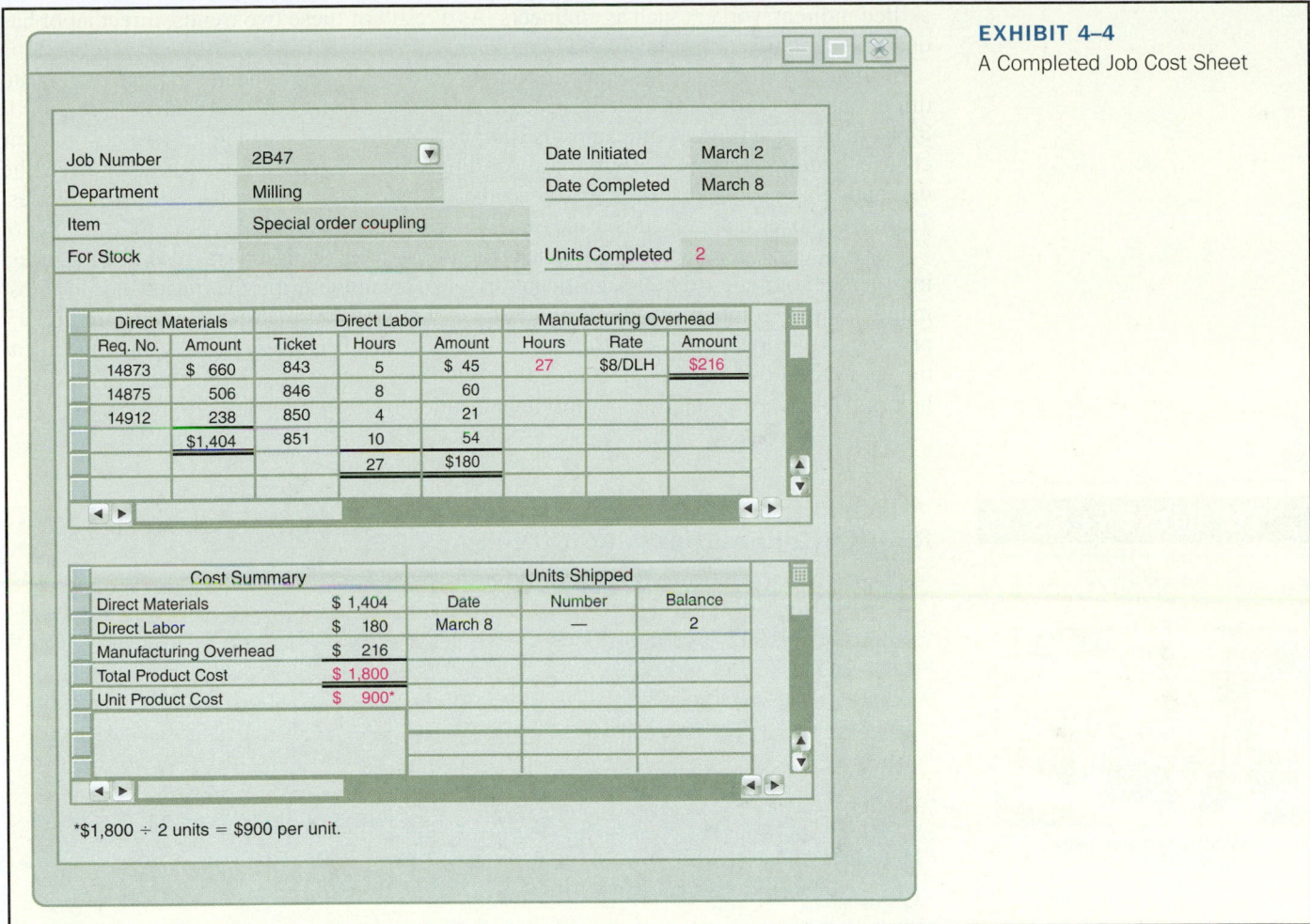

Job Number	2B47	Date Initiated	March 2
Department	Milling	Date Completed	March 8
Item	Special order coupling		
For Stock		Units Completed	2

Direct Materials		Direct Labor			Manufacturing Overhead		
Req. No.	Amount	Ticket	Hours	Amount	Hours	Rate	Amount
14873	$ 660	843	5	$ 45	27	$8/DLH	$216
14875	506	846	8	60			
14912	238	850	4	21			
	$1,404	851	10	54			
			27	$180			

Cost Summary		Units Shipped		
		Date	Number	Balance
Direct Materials	$ 1,404	March 8	—	2
Direct Labor	$ 180			
Manufacturing Overhead	$ 216			
Total Product Cost	$ 1,800			
Unit Product Cost	$ 900*			

*$1,800 ÷ 2 units = $900 per unit.

to any particular job would not be known until the end of the year. For example, the cost of Job 2B47 at Yost Precision Machining would not be known until the end of the year, even though the job will be completed and shipped to the customer in March. For these reasons, most companies use predetermined overhead rates rather than actual overhead rates in their cost accounting systems.

Choice of an Allocation Base for Overhead Cost

Ideally, the allocation base in the predetermined overhead rate should *drive* overhead cost. A **cost driver** is a factor, such as machine-hours, beds occupied, computer time, or flight-hours, that causes overhead costs. If the base in the predetermined overhead rate does not "drive" overhead costs, product costs will be distorted. For example, if direct labor-hours is used to allocate overhead, but in reality overhead has little to do with direct labor-hours, then products with high direct labor-hour requirements will be overcosted.

Most companies use direct labor-hours or direct labor cost as the allocation base for manufacturing overhead. In the past, direct labor accounted for up to 60% of the cost of many products, with overhead cost making up only a portion of the remainder. This situation has changed for two reasons. First, sophisticated automated equipment has taken over functions that used to be performed by direct labor workers. Because the costs of acquiring and maintaining such equipment are classified as overhead, this increases overhead while decreasing direct labor. Second, products are becoming more sophisticated and complex and are modified more frequently. This increases the need for highly skilled indirect workers such as engineers. As a result of these two trends, direct labor has decreased relative to overhead as a component of product costs.

In companies where direct labor and overhead costs have been moving in opposite directions, it would be difficult to argue that direct labor "drives" overhead costs. Accordingly, managers in some companies use *activity-based costing* principles to redesign their cost accounting systems. Activity-based costing is designed to more accurately reflect the demands that products, customers, and other cost objects make on overhead resources. The activity-based approach is discussed in more detail in Appendix 4A and in Chapter 6.

Although direct labor may not be an appropriate allocation base in some industries, in others it continues to be a significant driver of manufacturing overhead. Indeed, most manufacturing companies in the United States continue to use direct labor as the primary or secondary allocation base for manufacturing overhead. The key point is that the allocation base used by the company should really drive, or cause, overhead costs, and direct labor is not always the most appropriate allocation base.

IN BUSINESS

© Keith Brofsky/Photodisc/Getty Images, RF

REDUCING HEALTH-DAMAGING BEHAVIORS

Cianbro is an industrial construction company headquartered in Pittsfield, Maine, whose goal is "to be the healthiest company in America." It introduced a corporate wellness program to attack employee behaviors that drive up health-care costs. The table below summarizes the number of employees in five health risk categories as of 2003 and 2005. The decreases in the number of employees in these high-risk categories are evidence that the wellness program was effective in helping employees make positive lifestyle changes. This should result in reduced health-care costs for the company.

	Number of Employees		
Health Risk Category	January 2003	March 2005	Decrease
Obesity	432	353	79
High cholesterol	637	515	122
Tobacco use	384	274	110
Inactivity	354	254	100
High blood pressure	139	91	48

Source: Cianbro, WELCOA's *Absolute Advantage* Magazine, 2006.

Computation of Unit Costs

LEARNING OBJECTIVE 4–3
Compute the total cost and average cost per unit of a job.

With the application of Yost Precision Machining's $216 of manufacturing overhead to the job cost sheet in Exhibit 4–4, the job cost sheet is complete except for two final steps. First, the totals for direct materials, direct labor, and manufacturing overhead are transferred to the Cost Summary section of the job cost sheet and added together to obtain the total cost for the job.[1] Then the total product cost ($1,800) is divided by the number of units (2) to obtain the unit product cost ($900). This unit product cost information is used for valuing unsold units in ending inventory and for determining cost of goods sold. As indicated earlier, *this unit product cost is an average cost and should not be interpreted as the cost that would actually be incurred if another unit were produced.* The incremental cost of an additional unit is something less than the average unit cost of $900 because much of the actual overhead costs would not change if another unit were produced.

[1] Notice, we are assuming that Job 2B47 required direct materials and direct labor beyond the charges shown in Exhibits 4–1 and 4–3.

MANAGERIAL ACCOUNTING IN ACTION
The Wrap-Up

YOST Precision Machining

In the 8:00 A.M. daily planning meeting on March 9, Jean Yost, the president of Yost Precision Machining, once again drew attention to Job 2B47, the experimental couplings:

Jean: I see Job 2B47 is completed. Let's get those couplings shipped immediately to Loops Unlimited so they can get their testing program under way. Marc, how much are we going to bill Loops for those two units?

Marc: Because we agreed to sell the experimental couplings at cost, we will be charging Loops Unlimited just $900 a unit.

Jean: Fine. Let's hope the couplings work out and we make some money on the big order later.

IN BUSINESS

ONE-OF-A-KIND MASTERPIECE

In a true job-order costing environment, every job is unique. For example, Purdey manufactures 80–90 shotguns per year with each gun being a specially commissioned one-of-a-kind masterpiece. The prices start at $110,000 because every detail is custom built, engraved, assembled, and polished by a skilled craftsman. The hand engraving can take months to complete and may add as much as $100,000 to the price. The guns are designed to shoot perfectly straight and their value increases over time even with heavy use. One Purdey gun collector said "when I shoot my Purdeys I feel like an orchestra conductor waving my baton."

Source: Eric Arnold, "Aim High," *Forbes,* December 28, 2009, p. 86.

Job-Order Costing—The Flow of Costs

We are now ready to discuss the flow of costs through a job-order costing system. Exhibit 4–5 provides a conceptual overview of these cost flows. It highlights the fact that *product costs* flow through inventories on the balance sheet and then on to cost of goods sold in the income statement. More specifically, raw materials purchases are recorded in the *Raw Materials* inventory account. **Raw materials** include any materials that go into the final product. When raw materials are used in production, their costs are transferred to the *Work in Process* inventory account as direct materials.[2] **Work in process** consists of units of product that are only partially complete and will require further work before they are ready for sale to the customer. Notice that direct labor costs are added directly to Work in Process—they do not flow through Raw Materials inventory. Manufacturing overhead costs are applied to Work in Process by multiplying the predetermined overhead rate by the actual quantity of the allocation base consumed by each job.[3] When goods are completed, their costs are transferred from Work in Process to *Finished Goods.* **Finished goods** consist of completed units of product that have not yet been sold to customers. The amount transferred from Work in Process to Finished Goods is referred to as the *cost of goods manufactured.* The **cost of goods manufactured** includes the manufacturing costs associated with the goods that were finished during the period. As goods are sold, their costs are transferred from Finished Goods to Cost of Goods Sold. At this point, the various costs required to make the product are finally recorded as an expense. Until that point, these costs are in inventory accounts on the balance sheet. Period costs (or selling and administrative expenses) do not flow through inventories on the balance sheet. They are recorded as expenses on the income statement in the period incurred.

[2] Indirect material costs are accounted for as part of manufacturing overhead.

[3] For simplicity, Exhibit 4–5 assumes that Cost of Goods Sold does not need to be adjusted as discussed later in the chapter.

EXHIBIT 4–5
Cost Flows and Classifications in a Manufacturing Company

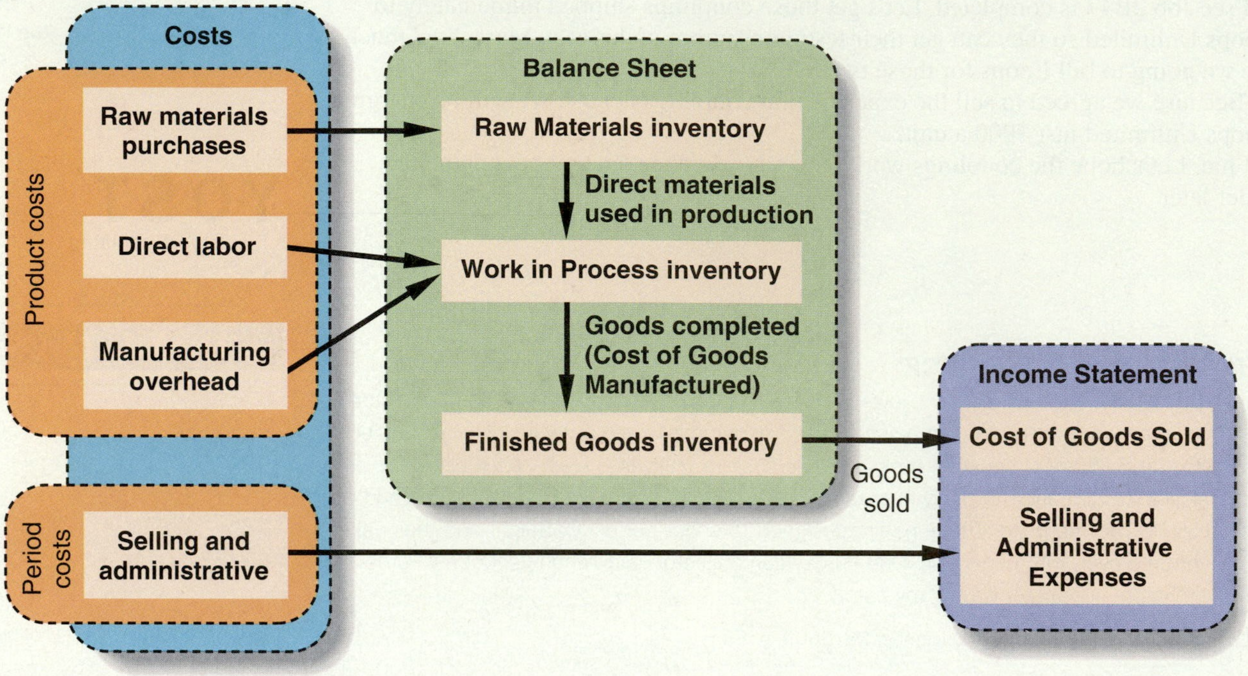

Job cost sheets are the basis for valuing inventory in a job-order costing system. Before a job is completed, its cost from the job cost sheet is included in work in process inventory. When a job is completed, it is part of finished goods inventory. When completed products are sold, their costs from their job cost sheets become part of cost of goods sold.

We are now ready to take a more detailed look at the flow of costs in job-order costing. To illustrate, let's consider activity for the month of April at Rand Company, a producer of gold and silver commemorative medallions. At the beginning of the month, Rand Company had no finished goods inventory and one job in process—Job A, a special minting of 1,000 gold medallions commemorating the invention of motion pictures. Some work had been completed on this job prior to April; therefore, a total of $30,000 in manufacturing costs had already been recorded on Job A's cost sheet. This job will be completed in April. In addition, Job B, an order for 10,000 silver medallions commemorating the fall of the Berlin Wall, will be started in April and completed in a subsequent month.

In this example, we will track the flow of Rand Company's raw materials, labor, and overhead costs for April and prepare an income statement for the month.

Direct and Indirect Materials

During April, $52,000 in raw materials were requisitioned from the storeroom for use in production. These raw materials included $28,000 of direct materials for Job A, $22,000 of direct materials for Job B, and $2,000 of indirect materials. As shown in Exhibit 4–6, these costs are recorded on the appropriate job cost sheets and in an account we will call Manufacturing Overhead Incurred. Specifically, $28,000 of direct materials is charged to Job A's cost sheet and $22,000 is charged to Job B's cost sheet. Note that the $2,000 of indirect materials has *not* been assigned to either of the two jobs—instead, it is charged to the account we call Manufacturing Overhead Incurred. We will be charging all of the actual manufacturing overhead costs that are incurred to this account.

EXHIBIT 4–6
Raw Materials Cost Flows

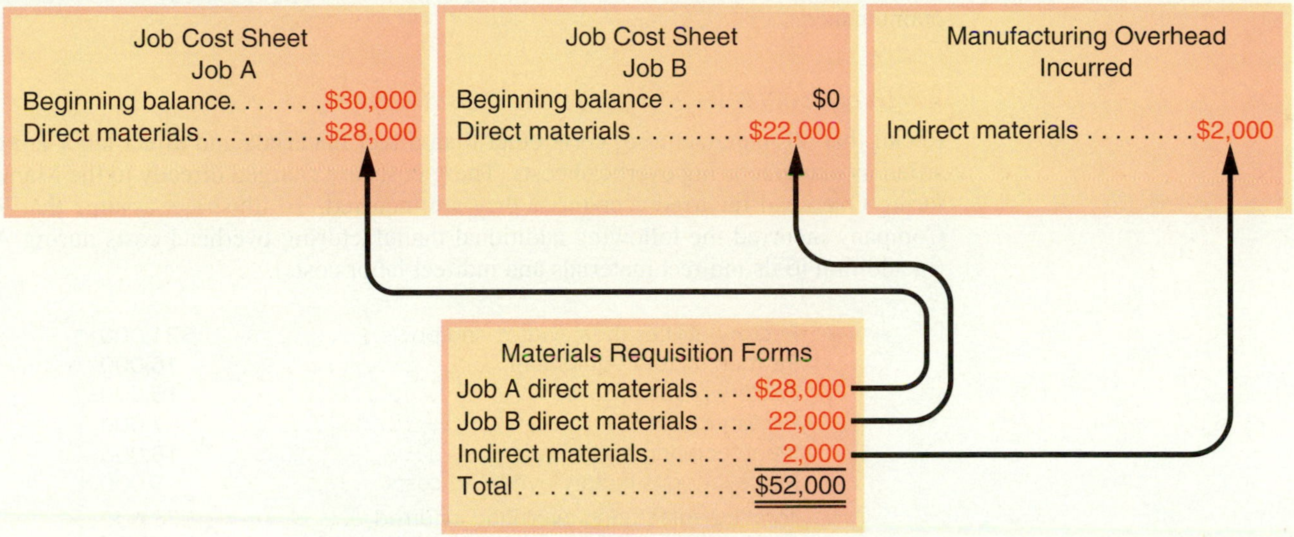

Notice from Exhibit 4–6 that the job cost sheet for Job A contains a beginning balance of $30,000. We stated earlier that this balance represents the cost of work done on this job prior to April. This cost would be classified on the company's balance sheet as Work in Process inventory at the beginning of April.

Labor Cost

Employee time tickets are filled out by workers, collected, and forwarded to the Accounting Department. In the Accounting Department, wages are computed and the resulting costs are classified as either direct or indirect labor. In April, Rand Company incurred $40,000 of direct labor cost for Job A, $20,000 of direct labor cost for Job B, and $15,000 of indirect labor cost. Exhibit 4–7 shows that during April, $40,000 of direct labor cost

EXHIBIT 4–7
Labor Cost Flows

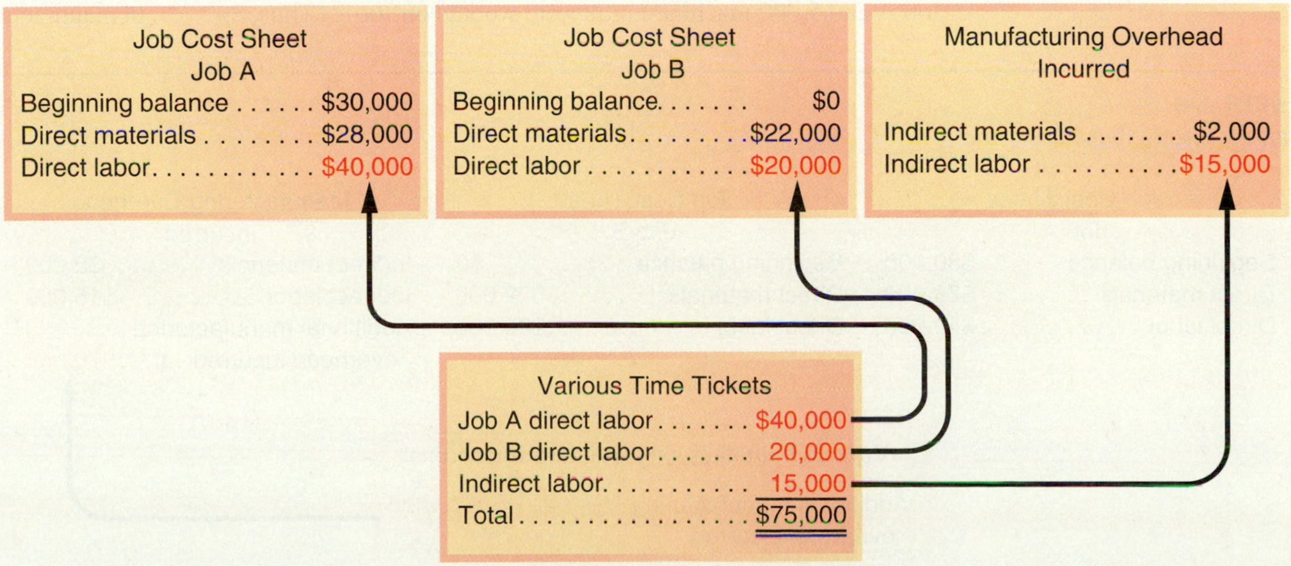

was charged to Job A and $20,000 to Job B on their job cost sheets. The $15,000 of indirect labor costs charged to the Manufacturing Overhead Incurred account represent the indirect labor costs incurred during April, such as supervision, janitorial work, and maintenance.

Manufacturing Overhead Cost

Recall that all manufacturing costs other than direct materials and direct labor are classified as manufacturing overhead costs. These costs are charged directly to the Manufacturing Overhead Incurred account as they are incurred. To illustrate, assume that Rand Company incurred the following additional manufacturing overhead costs during April (in addition to its indirect materials and indirect labor costs):

Factory utilities (heat, water, and power)	$21,000
Rent on factory equipment	16,000
Factory property taxes	13,000
Factory insurance	7,000
Manufacturing depreciation	18,000
Miscellaneous factory overhead costs	3,000
Total manufacturing overhead incurred	$78,000

Exhibit 4–8 shows how these costs are recorded.

Applying Manufacturing Overhead

Because actual manufacturing costs are charged to the Manufacturing Overhead Incurred account rather than to the job cost sheets, how are manufacturing overhead costs assigned to jobs? The answer is, by means of the predetermined overhead rate. Recall from our discussion earlier in the chapter that a predetermined overhead rate is established at the beginning of each year. The rate is calculated by dividing the estimated total manufacturing overhead cost for the year by the estimated amount of the allocation base (measured in machine-hours, direct labor-hours, or some other base). The predetermined overhead rate is then used to apply overhead costs to jobs. For example, if machine-hours is the allocation base, overhead cost is applied to each job by multiplying the predetermined overhead rate by the number of machine-hours charged to the job. To illustrate, assume that Rand Company's predetermined overhead rate is $6 per machine-hour. Also assume that during April, 10,000 machine-hours were worked on Job A and 5,000 machine-hours were worked on Job B. Thus, $60,000 in manufacturing

EXHIBIT 4–8
Manufacturing Overhead Cost Flows

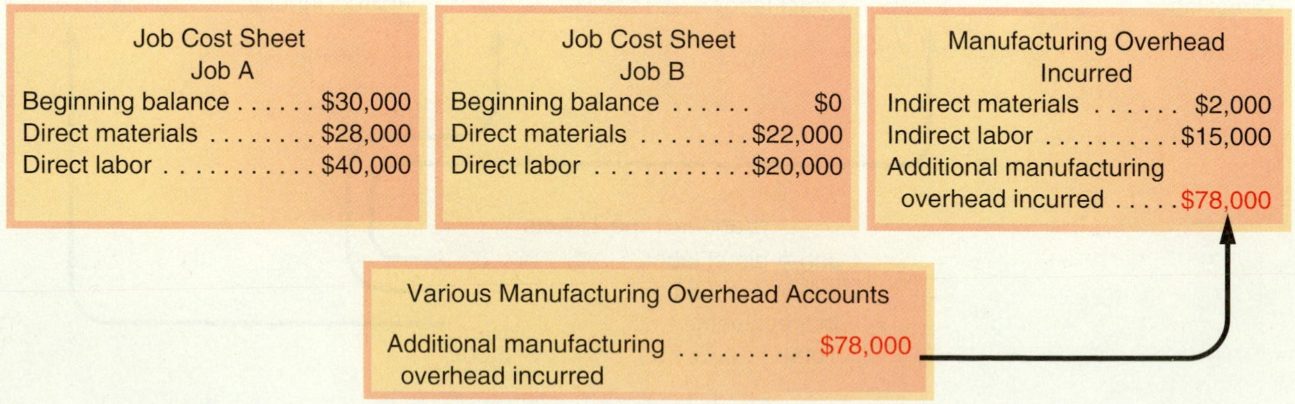

EXHIBIT 4–9
Applying Manufacturing Overhead to Jobs

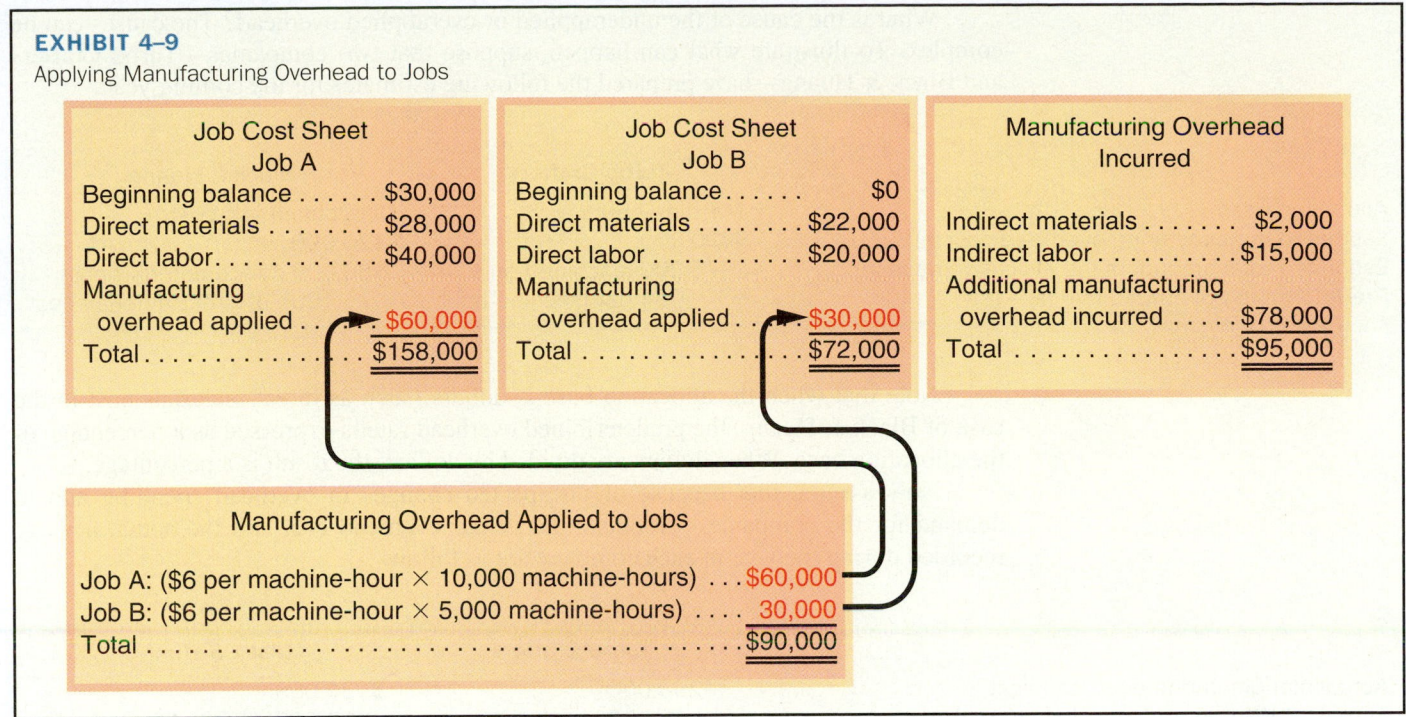

Job Cost Sheet Job A	
Beginning balance	$30,000
Direct materials	$28,000
Direct labor	$40,000
Manufacturing overhead applied	$60,000
Total	$158,000

Job Cost Sheet Job B	
Beginning balance	$0
Direct materials	$22,000
Direct labor	$20,000
Manufacturing overhead applied	$30,000
Total	$72,000

Manufacturing Overhead Incurred	
Indirect materials	$2,000
Indirect labor	$15,000
Additional manufacturing overhead incurred	$78,000
Total	$95,000

Manufacturing Overhead Applied to Jobs	
Job A: ($6 per machine-hour × 10,000 machine-hours)	$60,000
Job B: ($6 per machine-hour × 5,000 machine-hours)	30,000
Total	$90,000

overhead cost ($6 per machine-hour × 10,000 machine-hours) would be applied to Job A and $30,000 in manufacturing overhead cost ($6 per machine-hour × 5,000 machine-hours) would be applied to Job B. Exhibit 4–9 shows how these costs are applied to jobs.

Notice that Job A has been assigned total manufacturing costs of $158,000. Since Job A was completed in April, we can now compute the unit product cost for each of the 1,000 gold medallions included in the job. The unit product cost for Job A is $158 ($158,000 ÷ 1,000 units). This figure will be referred to later when we turn our attention to computing Rand Company's cost of goods sold. Also notice in Exhibit 4–9 that Job B has been assigned $72,000 of manufacturing costs; however, its unit product cost cannot be determined yet because the job is still in progress at the end of April. The $72,000 assigned to Job B will be reported as Work in Process inventory on the balance sheet at the end of April.

Underapplied or Overapplied Overhead

LEARNING OBJECTIVE 4–4
Compute underapplied or overapplied overhead cost.

You may have noticed a discrepancy in Exhibit 4–9. The actual manufacturing overhead incurred during April was $95,000, but only $90,000 in manufacturing overhead cost was applied to the two jobs in process during the month. This discrepancy occurs because the manufacturing overhead applied to jobs is based on the predetermined overhead rate, which is itself based on estimates of the total manufacturing overhead cost and the total machine-hours that were made before the month began. Except under very special circumstances, if either of these estimates is off, the actual manufacturing overhead costs that are incurred will not equal the manufacturing overhead cost that is applied to jobs using the predetermined overhead rate.

The difference between the manufacturing overhead cost applied to jobs and the actual manufacturing overhead costs of a period is called either **underapplied** or **overapplied overhead**. For Rand Company, overhead was underapplied by $5,000 because the applied cost ($90,000) was $5,000 less than the actual cost ($95,000). If the situation had been reversed and the company had applied $95,000 in manufacturing overhead cost to jobs while incurring actual manufacturing overhead costs of only $90,000, then the overhead would have been overapplied.

What is the cause of the underapplied or overapplied overhead? The causes can be complex. To illustrate what can happen, suppose that two companies—Turbo Crafters and Black & Huang—have prepared the following estimates for the coming year:

	Turbo Crafters	Black & Huang
Allocation base	Machine-hours	Direct materials cost
Estimated manufacturing overhead cost (a)	$300,000	$120,000
Estimated total amount of the allocation base (b)	75,000 machine-hours	$80,000 direct materials cost
Predetermined overhead rate (a) ÷ (b)	$4 per machine-hour	150% of direct materials cost

Note that when the allocation base is dollars (such as direct materials cost in the case of Black & Huang) the predetermined overhead rate is expressed as a percentage of the allocation base. When dollars are divided by dollars, the result is a percentage.

Now assume that because of unexpected changes in overhead spending and in demand for the companies' products, the *actual* overhead cost and the actual activity recorded during the year in each company are as follows:

	Turbo Crafters	Black & Huang
Actual manufacturing overhead cost	$290,000	$130,000
Actual total amount of the allocation base	68,000 machine-hours	$90,000 direct materials cost

For each company, note that the actual data for both the cost and the allocation base differ from the estimates used in computing the predetermined overhead rate. This results in underapplied and overapplied overhead as follows:

	Turbo Crafters	Black & Huang
Actual manufacturing overhead cost	$290,000	$130,000
Manufacturing overhead cost applied to jobs during the year:		
Predetermined overhead rate (a)	$4 per machine-hour	150% of direct materials cost
Actual total amount of the allocation base (b)	68,000 machine-hours	$ 90,000 direct materials cost
Manufacturing overhead applied (a) × (b)	$272,000	$135,000
Underapplied (overapplied) manufacturing overhead	$ 18,000	$ (5,000)

For Turbo Crafters, the $272,000 of manufacturing overhead cost applied to jobs is less than the $290,000 actual manufacturing overhead cost for the year. Therefore, overhead is underapplied. Notice that the original $300,000 estimate of manufacturing overhead for Turbo Crafters is not directly involved in this computation. Its impact is felt only through the $4 predetermined overhead rate.

For Black & Huang, the $135,000 of manufacturing overhead cost applied to jobs is greater than the $130,000 actual manufacturing overhead cost for the year, so overhead is overapplied. A summary of the concepts discussed above is presented in Exhibit 4–10.

Disposition of Underapplied or Overapplied Overhead

Note that the manufacturing overhead cost that is applied to jobs is an estimate—it does not represent actual costs incurred. The company's accounts must be adjusted at the end of the period so that they reflect actual costs rather than this estimate. This is accomplished in one of two ways: either (1) the underapplied or overapplied overhead at the

EXHIBIT 4–10
Summary of Overhead Concepts

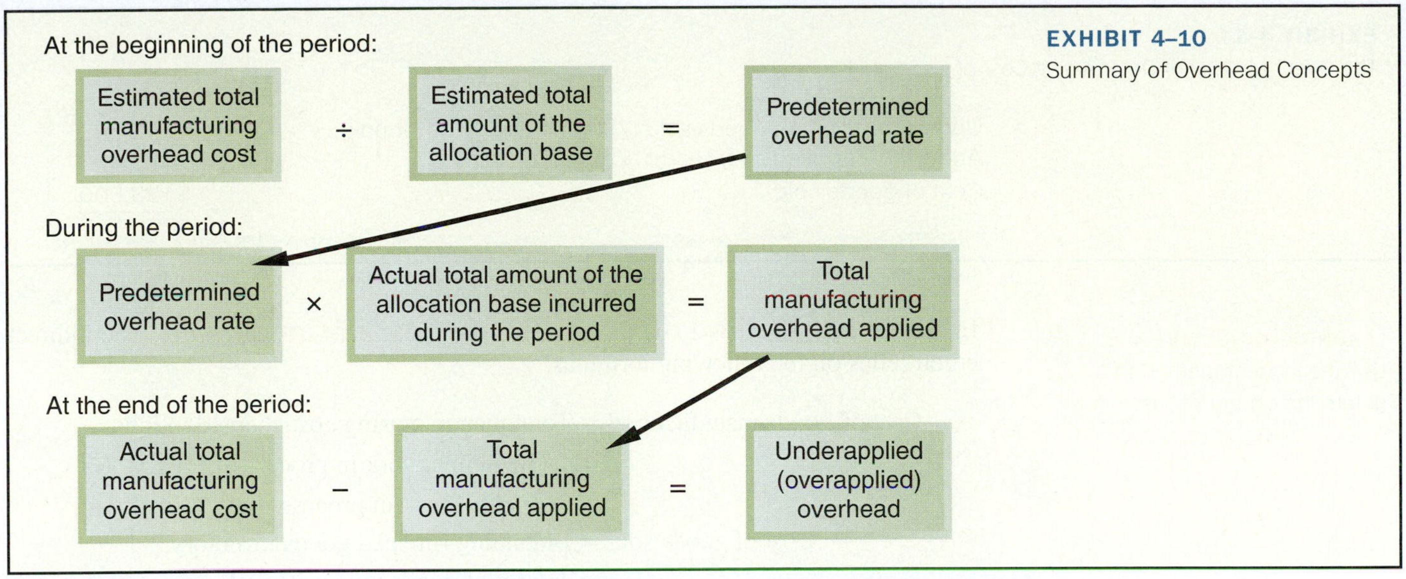

end of a period is closed out to Cost of Goods Sold; or (2) it is allocated among Work in Process, Finished Goods, and Cost of Goods Sold in proportion to the overhead applied during the current period that is in the ending balances of these accounts. The latter method takes us further into the details of bookkeeping than we would like to go in this book, so we will always assume that the underapplied or overapplied overhead is closed out to Cost of Goods Sold. In other words, Cost of Goods Sold is adjusted for the amount of underapplied or overapplied overhead.

The procedure for closing out underapplied or overapplied overhead to Cost of Goods Sold is quite simple. Underapplied overhead is added to Cost of Goods Sold. Overapplied overhead is deducted from Cost of Goods Sold. The reasoning is that if overhead is underapplied, not enough manufacturing overhead was applied to jobs and hence their costs are understated. Therefore, Cost of Goods Sold must be increased to compensate for this understatement. Likewise, if overhead is overapplied, too much manufacturing overhead was applied to jobs and hence their costs are overstated. Therefore, Cost of Goods Sold must be decreased to compensate for this overstatement. In short, adding to or deducting from Cost of Goods Sold corrects the misstatement of cost that occurs as a result of using a predetermined overhead rate.

Prepare an Income Statement

Cost of Goods Sold

LEARNING OBJECTIVE 4–5
Use the direct method to determine cost of goods sold.

Recall from Chapter 2 that Cost of Goods Sold consists of the costs of the products sold to customers. It can be determined directly or indirectly. The direct method is simpler and quicker when the necessary data are available. We will illustrate both approaches for Rand Company.

The Direct Method of Determining Cost of Goods Sold Recall that Job A, which consisted of 1,000 gold medallions, was completed during April, but Job B was not completed. Also recall that the unit product cost for each of the 1,000 gold medallions included in Job A was $158 ($158,000 ÷ 1,000 units). If we assume that 750 of the 1,000 gold medallions included in Job A were shipped to customers by the end of April, then the cost of the medallions sold to customers was $118,500 (750 units × $158 per unit). This amount must be adjusted for the $5,000 underapplied overhead to arrive at the cost of goods sold for the period. Exhibit 4–11 illustrates the direct method of determining the cost of goods sold.

EXHIBIT 4–11
The Direct Method of Determining Cost of Goods Sold

Unadjusted cost of goods sold (750 units × $158 per unit)	$118,500
Add: Underapplied overhead	5,000
Cost of goods sold	$123,500

LEARNING OBJECTIVE 4–6
Use the indirect method to determine cost of goods sold.

The Indirect Method of Determining Cost of Goods Sold

The indirect method relies on the following formulas:

Cost of goods manufactured = Total manufacturing cost charged to jobs
+ Beginning work in process inventory
− Ending work in process inventory

Cost of goods sold = Beginning finished goods inventory
+ Cost of goods manufactured
− Ending finished goods inventory

To determine the cost of goods sold with these formulas, we will need to know five items: (1) the beginning work in process inventory; (2) the total manufacturing cost charged to jobs for the period; (3) the ending work in process inventory; (4) the beginning finished goods inventory; and (5) the ending finished goods inventory. These costs for Rand Company are detailed below:

1. The beginning work in process inventory was $30,000—the beginning balance on Job A's job cost sheet from Exhibit 4–6.
2. The total manufacturing cost charged to jobs consists of direct materials, direct labor, and manufacturing overhead charged to jobs during the period. From Exhibit 4–9, the total manufacturing cost can be determined as follows:

	Job A	Job B	Total
Direct materials	$28,000	$22,000	$ 50,000
Direct labor	$40,000	$20,000	60,000
Manufacturing overhead applied	$60,000	$30,000	90,000
Total manufacturing cost charged to jobs			$200,000

3. The ending work in process inventory consists of $72,000—the accumulated cost of Job B from Exhibit 4–9.
4. At the start of the Rand Company example, we stated that the company had no beginning finished goods inventories.
5. The ending finished goods inventory consists of the costs of any completed units that have not been sold at the end of the month. Job A consisted of 1,000 units, 750 of which were sold. Therefore, the ending finished goods inventory consists of 250 units (1,000 units – 750 units). Recall that the unit product cost of Job A is $158 per unit. Consequently, the total cost of these 250 unsold, but completed, units is $39,500 (250 units × $158 per unit).

Using these data, Exhibit 4–12 illustrates the indirect method of determining the cost of goods sold.

Note two things from Exhibit 4–11 and Exhibit 4–12. First, the cost of goods sold is identical under the two methods—and always will be. Second, under both methods,

EXHIBIT 4–12
The Indirect Method of Determining Cost of Goods Sold

Manufacturing costs charged to jobs:	
Direct materials	$ 50,000
Direct labor	60,000
Manufacturing overhead applied	90,000
Total manufacturing cost charged to jobs	200,000
Add: Beginning work in process inventory	30,000
	230,000
Deduct: Ending work in process inventory	72,000
Cost of goods manufactured	$158,000
Beginning finished goods inventory	$ 0
Add: Cost of goods manufactured (see above)	158,000
Goods available for sale	158,000
Deduct: Ending finished goods inventory	39,500
Unadjusted cost of goods sold	118,500
Add: Underapplied overhead	5,000
Cost of goods sold	$123,500

the underapplied overhead is added to the unadjusted cost of goods sold to determine the cost of goods sold. Remember the reason for this. Underapplied overhead means that not enough overhead was applied to jobs—the actual manufacturing overhead exceeded the amount of manufacturing overhead applied to jobs using the predetermined overhead rate. We must add the underapplied overhead to the unadjusted cost of goods sold to remove this discrepancy.

Income Statement

Now that we know the cost of goods sold ($123,500), all we need to construct the company's income statement for April is the total sales revenue and the selling and administrative expenses. We will assume that Rand Company's total sales revenue is $225,000 and that it has supplied the following data concerning its selling and administrative expenses in April:

Rand Company
Selling and Administrative Expenses
For the Month Ending April 30

Salaries expense	$30,000
Depreciation expense	7,000
Advertising expense	42,000
Other expense	8,000
Total selling and administrative expense	$87,000

Exhibit 4–13 combines these selling and administrative expenses with the sales and cost of goods sold data to create the company's income statement for the month.

EXHIBIT 4–13
Income Statement

Rand Company Income Statement For the Month Ending April 30	
Sales	$225,000
Cost of goods sold	123,500
Gross margin	101,500
Selling and administrative expense	87,000
Net operating income	$ 14,500

Multiple Predetermined Overhead Rates

Our discussion in this chapter has assumed that there is a single predetermined overhead rate for an entire factory called a **plantwide overhead rate**. This is a fairly common practice—particularly in smaller companies. But in larger companies, *multiple predetermined overhead rates* are often used. In a **multiple predetermined overhead rate** system each production department may have its own predetermined overhead rate. Such a system, while more complex, is more accurate because it can reflect differences across departments in how overhead costs are incurred. For example, in departments that are relatively labor intensive overhead might be allocated based on direct labor-hours and in departments that are relatively machine intensive overhead might be allocated based on machine-hours. When multiple predetermined overhead rates are used, overhead is applied in each department according to its own overhead rate as jobs proceed through the department.

Job-Order Costing in Service Companies

Job-order costing is used in service organizations such as law firms, movie studios, hospitals, and repair shops, as well as in manufacturing companies. In a law firm, for example, each client is a "job," and the costs of that job are accumulated on a job cost sheet as the client's case is handled by the firm. Legal forms and similar inputs represent the direct materials for the job; the time expended by attorneys is like direct labor; and the costs of secretaries and legal aids, rent, depreciation, and so forth, represent the overhead.

In a movie studio such as Columbia Pictures, each film produced by the studio is a "job," and costs of direct materials (costumes, props, film, etc.) and direct labor (actors, directors, and extras) are charged to each film's job cost sheet. A share of the studio's overhead costs, such as utilities, depreciation of equipment, wages of maintenance workers, and so forth, is also charged to each film.

In sum, job-order costing is a versatile and widely used costing method that may be encountered in virtually any organization that provides diverse products or services.

IN BUSINESS

COMPUTING JOB COSTS AT FAST WRAP

In 2007, Michael Enos founded Fast Wrap, a company that shrink-wraps everything from jet skis and recreation vehicles (RVs) to entire buildings. Today, the company has 64 locations across America and generates more $6 million in annual sales. The company's revenues far-exceed its direct materials and direct labor costs. For example, Fast Wrap charges customers $400 to wrap a 20-foot boat that requires $25 worth of plastic and $30 worth of labor. Larger jobs are even more profitable. For example, Fast Wrap signed a $250,000 contract to shrink-wrap a 244,000-square-foot hospital under construction in Fontana, California. The materials and labor for this job cost Fast Wrap $44,000.

Source: Susan Adams, "It's a Wrap," *Forbes*, March 15, 2010, pp. 36–38.

Summary

Job-order costing is used to cost products in situations where the organization offers many different products or services, such as in furniture manufacturing, hospitals, and legal firms.

Materials requisition forms and labor time tickets are used to assign direct materials and direct labor costs to jobs in a job-order costing system. Manufacturing overhead costs are assigned to jobs using a predetermined overhead rate. All of the costs are recorded on a job cost sheet.

The predetermined overhead rate is determined before the period begins by dividing the estimated total manufacturing cost for the period by the estimated total amount of the allocation base for the period. The most frequently used allocation bases are direct labor-hours and machine-hours. Overhead is applied to jobs by multiplying the predetermined overhead rate by the actual amount of the allocation base recorded for the job.

Because the predetermined overhead rate is based on estimates, the actual overhead cost incurred during a period may be more or less than the amount of overhead cost applied to production. Such a difference is referred to as underapplied or overapplied overhead. The underapplied or overapplied overhead for a period can be either closed out to Cost of Goods Sold or allocated between Work in Process, Finished Goods, and Cost of Goods Sold. When overhead is underapplied, manufacturing overhead costs have been understated and therefore inventories and/or expenses must be adjusted upwards. When overhead is overapplied, manufacturing overhead costs have been overstated and therefore inventories and/or expenses must be adjusted downward.

Review Problem: Job-Order Costing

Hogle Corporation uses job-order costing and applies overhead cost to jobs on the basis of machine-hours worked. For the just completed year, the company estimated that it would work 75,000 machine-hours and incur $450,000 in manufacturing overhead cost. The company actually worked 80,000 machine-hours.

The company has provided the following financial data concerning its actual operations for the year:

Direct materials	$360,000
Indirect materials	$20,000
Direct labor	$75,000
Indirect labor	$110,000
Sales commissions	$90,000
Administrative salaries	$200,000
General selling expenses	$17,000
Factory utility costs	$43,000
Advertising costs	$180,000
Factory depreciation	$280,000
Selling and administrative depreciation	$70,000
Factory insurance	$7,000
Selling and administrative insurance	$3,000
Cost of goods sold (not adjusted for underapplied or overapplied overhead)	$ 870,000
Sales	$1,500,000

Required:

1. Is overhead underapplied or overapplied for the year? By how much?
2. Prepare an income statement for the year.

Solution to Review Problem

1. To determine the underapplied or overapplied overhead for the year, we must know the actual manufacturing overhead cost incurred and the manufacturing overhead applied to jobs. The actual manufacturing overhead cost incurred can be determined by adding together all of the manufacturing overhead items in the financial data provided by the company as follows:

Manufacturing overhead costs incurred:	
Indirect materials	$ 20,000
Indirect labor	110,000
Factory utility costs	43,000
Factory depreciation	280,000
Factory insurance	7,000
Total manufacturing overhead cost incurred	$460,000

The predetermined overhead rate for the year is computed as follows:

$$\text{Predetermined overhead rate} = \frac{\text{Estimated total manufacturing overhead cost}}{\text{Estimated total amount of the allocation base}}$$

$$= \frac{\$450{,}000}{75{,}000 \text{ machine-hours}}$$

$$= \$6 \text{ per machine-hour}$$

Based on the 80,000 machine-hours actually worked during the year, the company applied $480,000 in overhead cost to production ($6 per machine-hour × 80,000 machine hours). The actual manufacturing overhead cost incurred was $460,000, whereas the manufacturing overhead applied to jobs using the company's predetermined overhead rate was $480,000. Therefore, overhead was overapplied by $20,000 ($480,000 – $460,000).

2. To construct the income statement, we will need the sales (which is given), the adjusted cost of goods sold, and the total selling and administrative expenses. The latter can be determined as follows:

Selling and administrative expenses incurred:	
Sales commissions	$ 90,000
Administrative salaries	200,000
General selling expenses	17,000
Advertising costs	180,000
Selling and administrative depreciation	70,000
Selling and administrative insurance	3,000
Total selling and administrative expense	$560,000

The adjusted cost of goods sold is determined as follows:

Unadjusted cost of goods sold	$870,000
Deduct: Overapplied overhead	20,000
Cost of goods sold	$850,000

Finally, the income statement is constructed as follows:

Hogle Corporation Income Statement	
Sales	$1,500,000
Cost of goods sold	850,000
Gross margin	650,000
Selling and administrative expense	560,000
Net operating income	$ 90,000

Glossary

Absorption costing A costing method that includes all manufacturing costs—direct materials, direct labor, and both variable and fixed manufacturing overhead—in unit product costs. (p. 118)

Allocation base A measure of activity such as direct labor-hours or machine-hours that is used to assign costs to cost objects. (p. 123)

Bill of materials A document that shows the quantity of each type of direct material required to make a product. (p. 120)

Cost driver A factor, such as machine-hours, beds occupied, computer time, or flight-hours, that causes overhead costs. (p. 125)

Cost of goods manufactured The manufacturing costs associated with the goods that were finished during the period. (p. 127)

Finished goods Units of product that have been completed but not yet sold to customers. (p. 127)

Job cost sheet A form that records the materials, labor, and manufacturing overhead costs charged to a job. (p. 120)

Job-order costing A costing system used in situations where many different products, jobs, or services are produced each period. (p. 118)

Materials requisition form A document that specifies the type and quantity of materials to be drawn from the storeroom and that identifies the job that will be charged for the cost of those materials. (p. 120)

Multiple predetermined overhead rates A costing system with multiple overhead cost pools and a different predetermined overhead rate for each cost pool, rather than a single predetermined overhead rate for the entire company. Each production department may be treated as a separate overhead cost pool. (p. 136)

Normal cost system A costing system in which overhead costs are applied to a job by multiplying a predetermined overhead rate by the actual amount of the allocation base incurred by the job. (p. 124)

Overapplied overhead A credit balance in the Manufacturing Overhead account that occurs when the amount of overhead cost applied to Work in Process exceeds the amount of overhead cost actually incurred during a period. (p. 131)

Overhead application The process of charging manufacturing overhead cost to job cost sheets and to the Work in Process account. (p. 123)

Plantwide overhead rate A single predetermined overhead rate that is used throughout a plant. (p. 136)

Predetermined overhead rate A rate used to charge manufacturing overhead cost to jobs that is established in advance for each period. It is computed by dividing the estimated total manufacturing overhead cost for the period by the estimated total amount of the allocation base for the period. (p. 123)

Raw materials Any materials that go into the final product. (p. 127)

Time ticket A document that is used to record the amount of time an employee spends on various activities. (p. 122)

Underapplied overhead A debit balance in the Manufacturing Overhead account that occurs when the amount of overhead cost actually incurred exceeds the amount of overhead cost applied to Work in Process during a period. (p. 131)

Work in process Units of product that are only partially complete and will require further work before they are ready for sale to the customer. (p. 127)

Questions

4–1 Why aren't actual manufacturing overhead costs traced to jobs just as direct materials and direct labor costs are traced to jobs?

4–2 What is the purpose of the job cost sheet in a job-order costing system?

4–3 What is a predetermined overhead rate, and how is it computed?

4–4 Explain how a sales order, a production order, a materials requisition form, and a labor time ticket are involved in producing and costing products.

4–5 Explain why some production costs must be assigned to products through an allocation process.

4–6 Why do companies use predetermined overhead rates rather than actual manufacturing overhead costs to apply overhead to jobs?

4–7 What factors should be considered in selecting a base to be used in computing the predetermined overhead rate?

4–8 If a company fully allocates all of its overhead costs to jobs, does this guarantee that a profit will be earned for the period?

4–9 Would you expect the amount of overhead applied for a period to equal the actual overhead costs of the period? Why or why not?

4–10 What is underapplied overhead? Overapplied overhead? What disposition is made of these amounts at the end of the period?

4–11 Provide two reasons why overhead might be underapplied in a given year.

4–12 What adjustment to cost of goods sold is made for underapplied overhead? What adjustment is made for overapplied overhead?

4–13 What is a plantwide overhead rate? Why are multiple overhead rates, rather than a plantwide overhead rate, used in some companies?

4–14 What happens to overhead rates based on direct labor when automated equipment replaces direct labor?

Multiple-choice questions are available with Connect.

Applying Excel

connect **Additional student resources are available with Connect.**

LEARNING OBJECTIVES 4–1, 4–2, 4–4

The Excel worksheet form that appears below will reinforce your ability to compute underapplied and overapplied overhead. It is based on the data pertaining to Turbo Crafters Company that was discussed earlier in the chapter. Download the workbook from Connect, where you will also receive instructions about how to use this worksheet.

	A	B	C
1	Chapter 4: Applying Excel		
2			
3	**Data**		
4	Allocation base	Machine-hours	
5	Estimated manufacturing overhead cost	$300,000	
6	Estimated total amount of the allocation base	75,000	machine-hours
7	Actual manufacturing overhead cost	$290,000	
8	Actual total amount of the allocation base	68,000	machine-hours
9			
10	*Enter a formula into each of the cells marked with a ? below*		
11			
12	**Computation of the predetermined overhead rate**		
13	Estimated manufacturing overhead cost	?	
14	Estimated total amount of the allocation base	?	machine-hours
15	Predetermined overhead rate	?	per machine-hour
16			
17	**Computation of underapplied or overapplied manufacturing overhead**		
18	Actual manufacturing overhead cost	?	
19	Manufacturing overhead cost applied to Work in Process during the year:		
20	Predetermined overhead rate	?	per machine-hour
21	Actual total amount of the allocation base	?	machine-hours
22	Manufacturing overhead applied	?	
23	Underapplied (overapplied) manufacturing overhead	?	
24			

Chapter 4 Form / Filled in Chapter 4 Form / Chapter 4 Formulas

You should proceed to the requirements below only after completing your worksheet.

Required:

1. Check your worksheet by changing the estimated total amount of the allocation base in the Data area to 60,000 machine-hours, keeping all of the other data the same as in the original example. If your worksheet is operating properly, the predetermined overhead rate should now be $5.00 per machine-hour. If you do not get this answer, find the errors in your worksheet and correct them.

   How much is the underapplied (overapplied) manufacturing overhead? Did it change? Why or why not?
2. Determine the underapplied (overapplied) manufacturing overhead for a different company with the following data:

Allocation base	Machine-hours
Estimated manufacturing overhead cost	$100,000
Estimated total amount of the allocation base	50,000 machine-hours
Actual manufacturing overhead cost	$90,000
Actual total amount of the allocation base	40,000 machine-hours

3. What happens to the underapplied (overapplied) manufacturing overhead from part (2) if the estimated total amount of the allocation base is changed to 40,000 machine-hours and everything else remains the same? Why is the amount of underapplied (overapplied) manufacturing overhead different from part (2)?
4. Change the estimated total amount of the allocation base back to 50,000 machine-hours so that the data look exactly like they did in part (2). Now change the actual manufacturing overhead cost to $100,000. What is the underapplied (overapplied) manufacturing overhead now? Why is the amount of underapplied (overapplied) manufacturing overhead different from part (2)?

Additional student resources are available with Connect. connect

The Foundational 15

LEARNING OBJECTIVES 4–1, 4–2, 4–3, 4–4, 4–5, 4–6

Sweeten Company had no jobs in progress at the beginning of March and no beginning inventories. It started only two jobs during March—Job P and Job Q. Job P was completed and sold by the end of March and Job Q was incomplete at the end of March. The company uses a plantwide predetermined overhead rate based on direct labor-hours. The following additional information is available for the company as a whole and for Jobs P and Q (all data and questions relate to the month of March):

Estimated total fixed manufacturing overhead	$10,000
Estimated variable manufacturing overhead per direct labor-hour	$1.00
Estimated total direct labor hours to be worked	2,000
Total actual manufacturing overhead costs incurred	$12,500

	Job P	Job Q
Direct materials	$13,000	$8,000
Direct labor cost	$21,000	$7,500
Actual direct labor hours worked	1,400	500

(Answer each question independently by always referring to the original data.)

1. What is the company's predetermined overhead rate?
2. How much manufacturing overhead was applied to Job P and Job Q?
3. What is the direct labor hourly wage rate?
4. If Job P includes 20 units, what is its unit product cost?

5. What is the total amount of manufacturing cost assigned to Job Q as of the end of March (including applied overhead)?
6. What is the amount of underapplied or overapplied overhead?
7. Will your answer to question 6 increase or decrease unadjusted cost of goods sold?
8. If Sweeten Company requisitioned $24,000 from raw materials inventory during March, then how much indirect materials cost would be included in Manufacturing Overhead Incurred?
9. If Sweeten Company's labor time tickets totaled $33,000 for the month of March, then how much indirect labor cost would be included in Manufacturing Overhead Incurred?
10. Calculate the cost of goods sold using the direct method.
11. Calculate the cost of goods manufactured using the indirect method.
12. Calculate the cost of goods sold using the indirect method.
13. How would you revise your answer to question 11 if the company had beginning work in process inventory of $8,000?
14. How would you revise your answer to question 12 if the company had beginning finished goods inventory of $12,000?
15. Assume that Job P includes 20 units that each sell for $3,000 and that the company's selling and administrative expenses in March were $14,000. Prepare an absorption costing income statement for March.

Exercises

connect Additional student resources are available with Connect.

EXERCISE 4–1 Compute the Predetermined Overhead Rate [LO4–1]

Logan Products computes its predetermined overhead rate annually on the basis of direct labor-hours. At the beginning of the year, it estimated that 40,000 direct labor-hours would be required for the period's estimated level of production. The company also estimated $466,000 of fixed manufacturing overhead expenses for the coming period and variable manufacturing overhead of $3.00 per direct labor-hour. Logan's actual manufacturing overhead for the year was $713,400 and its actual total direct labor was 41,000 hours.

Required:

Compute the company's predetermined overhead rate for the year.

EXERCISE 4–2 Apply Overhead [LO4–2]

Westan Corporation uses a predetermined overhead rate of $23.10 per direct labor-hour. This predetermined rate was based on a cost formula that estimated $277,200 of total manufacturing overhead for an estimated activity level of 12,000 direct labor-hours.

The company incurred actual total manufacturing overhead costs of $266,000 and 12,600 total direct labor-hours during the period.

Required:

Determine the amount of manufacturing overhead that would have been applied to all jobs during the period.

EXERCISE 4–3 Computing Job Costs [LO4–3]

Weaver Company's predetermined overhead rate is $18.00 per direct labor-hour and its direct labor wage rate is $12.00 per hour. The following information pertains to Job A-200:

Direct materials	$200
Direct labor.	$120

Required:

1. What is the total manufacturing cost assigned to Job A-200?
2. If Job A-200 consists of 50 units, what is the average cost assigned to each unit included in the job?

EXERCISE 4–4 Determine Underapplied or Overapplied Overhead [LO4–4]

Kirkaid Company recorded the following transactions for the just completed month:

a. $84,000 in raw materials were requisitioned for use in production. Of this amount, $72,000 was for direct materials and the remainder was for indirect materials.
b. Total labor wages of $108,000 were incurred. Of this amount, $105,000 was for direct labor and the remainder was for indirect labor.
c. Additional actual manufacturing overhead costs of $197,000 were incurred.
d. A total of $218,000 in manufacturing overhead was applied to jobs.

Required:

Determine the underapplied or overapplied overhead for the month.

EXERCISE 4–5 Direct Method of Determining Cost of Goods Sold [LO4–5]

Morrow Corporation had only one job in process during May—Job X32Z—and had no finished goods inventory on May 1. Job X32Z was started in April and finished during May. Data concerning that job appear below:

	Job X32Z
Beginning balance	$5,000
Charged to the job during May	
Direct materials........................	$8,000
Direct labor	$2,000
Manufacturing overhead applied........	$4,000
Units completed	100
Units in process at the end of May	0
Units sold during May	40

In May, overhead was overapplied by $300. The company adjusts its cost of goods sold every month for the amount of the overhead that was underapplied or overapplied.

Required:

1. Using the direct method, what is the cost of goods sold for May?
2. What is the total value of the finished goods inventory at the end of May?
3. What is the total value of the work in process inventory at the end of May?

EXERCISE 4–6 Indirect Method of Determining Cost of Goods Sold [LO4–6]

Refer to the data for Morrow Corporation in Exercise 4–5.

Required:

Using the indirect method, determine the cost of goods sold for May.

EXERCISE 4–7 Predetermined Overhead Rate; Applying Overhead; Underapplied or Overapplied Overhead [LO4–1, LO4–2, LO4–4]

Medusa Products uses a job-order costing system. Overhead costs are applied to jobs on the basis of machine-hours. At the beginning of the year, management estimated that the company would work 85,000 machine-hours and incur $170,000 in manufacturing overhead costs for the year.

Required:

1. Compute the company's predetermined overhead rate.
2. Assume that during the year the company actually worked only 80,000 machine-hours and incurred $168,000 of manufacturing overhead costs. Compute the amount of underapplied or overapplied overhead for the year.
3. Explain why the manufacturing overhead was underapplied or overapplied for the year.

EXERCISE 4–8 Computing Predetermined Overhead Rates and Job Costs [LO4–1, LO4–2, LO4–3, LO4–4]

Kody Corporation uses a job-order costing system with a plantwide overhead rate based on machine-hours. At the beginning of the year, the company made the following estimates:

Machine-hours required to support estimated production	150,000
Fixed manufacturing overhead cost..................................	$750,000
Variable manufacturing overhead cost per machine-hour...............	$4.00

Required:

1. Compute the predetermined overhead rate.
2. During the year Job 500 was started and completed. The following information was available with respect to this job:
   Compute the total manufacturing cost assigned to Job 500.

Direct materials requisitioned..................	$350
Direct labor cost	$230
Machine-hours used..........................	30

3. During the year the company worked a total of 147,000 machine-hours on all jobs and incurred actual manufacturing overhead costs of $1,325,000. What is the amount of underapplied or overapplied overhead for the year? If this amount were closed out entirely to Cost of Goods Sold, would net operating income increase or decrease?

EXERCISE 4–9 Departmental Overhead Rates [LO4–1, LO4–2, LO4–3]

Diewold Company has two departments, Milling and Assembly. The company uses a job-order costing system and computes a predetermined overhead rate in each department. The Milling Department bases its rate on machine-hours, and the Assembly Department bases its rate on direct labor-hours. At the beginning of the year, the company made the following estimates:

	Department	
	Milling	**Assembly**
Direct labor-hours	8,000	80,000
Machine-hours..	60,000	3,000
Total fixed manufacturing overhead cost	$390,000	$500,000
Variable manufacturing overhead per machine-hour..............	$2.00	—
Variable manufacturing overhead per direct labor-hour	—	$3.75

Required:

1. Compute the predetermined overhead rate to be used in each department.
2. Assume that the overhead rates you computed in requirement 1 are in effect. The job cost sheet for Job 407, which was started and completed during the year, showed the following:

	Department	
	Milling	**Assembly**
Direct labor-hours	5	20
Machine-hours.......................	90	4
Materials requisitioned...............	$800	$370
Direct labor cost	$45	$160

   Compute the total manufacturing cost assigned to Job 407.
3. Would you expect substantially different amounts of overhead cost to be charged to some jobs if the company used a plantwide overhead rate based on direct labor-hours instead of using departmental rates? Explain. No computations are necessary.

EXERCISE 4–10 Applying Overhead; Computing Unit Product Cost [LO4–2, LO4–3]

A company assigns overhead cost to completed jobs on the basis of 120% of direct labor cost. The job cost sheet for Job 413 shows that $12,000 in direct materials has been used on the job and that $8,000 in direct labor cost has been incurred. A total of 200 units were produced in Job 413.

Required:

What is the total manufacturing cost assigned to Job 413? What is the unit product cost for Job 413?

EXERCISE 4–11 Underapplied and Overapplied Overhead [LO4–4]

Cretin Enterprises uses a predetermined overhead rate of $21.40 per direct labor-hour. This predetermined rate was based on a cost formula that estimated $171,200 of total manufacturing overhead for an estimated activity level of 8,000 direct labor-hours.

The company incurred actual total manufacturing overhead costs of $172,500 and 8,250 total direct labor-hours during the period.

Required:

1. Determine the amount of underapplied or overapplied manufacturing overhead for the period.
2. Assuming that the entire amount of the underapplied or overapplied overhead is closed out to cost of goods sold, what would be the effect of the underapplied or overapplied overhead on the company's gross margin for the period?

EXERCISE 4–12 Applying Overhead; Cost of Goods Manufactured [LO4–2, LO4–4, LO4–6]

The following cost data relate to the manufacturing activities of Black Company during the just completed year:

Manufacturing overhead costs incurred:	
Property taxes, factory	$ 3,000
Utilities, factory	5,000
Indirect labor	10,000
Depreciation, factory	24,000
Insurance, factory	6,000
Total actual manufacturing overhead costs	$48,000
Other costs incurred:	
Purchases of raw materials	$32,000
Direct labor cost	$40,000
Inventories:	
Raw materials, beginning	$ 8,000
Raw materials, ending	$ 7,000
Work in process, beginning	$ 6,000
Work in process, ending	$ 7,500

The company uses a predetermined overhead rate to apply overhead cost to jobs. The rate for the year was $5 per machine-hour; a total of 10,000 machine-hours was recorded for the year. All raw materials ultimately become direct materials—none are classified as indirect materials.

Required:

1. Compute the amount of underapplied or overapplied overhead cost for the year.
2. Prepare a schedule of cost of goods manufactured for the year using the indirect method.

EXERCISE 4–13 Varying Predetermined Overhead Rates [LO4–1, LO4–2, LO4–3]

Javadi Company makes a single product that is subject to wide seasonal variations in demand. The company uses a job-order costing system and computes predetermined overhead rates on a quarterly basis using the number of units to be produced as the allocation base. Its estimated costs, by quarter, for the coming year are given below:

	Quarter			
	First	Second	Third	Fourth
Direct materials	$240,000	$120,000	$ 60,000	$180,000
Direct labor	96,000	48,000	24,000	72,000
Manufacturing overhead	228,000	204,000	192,000	?
Total manufacturing costs (a)	$564,000	$372,000	$276,000	$?
Number of units to be produced (b)	80,000	40,000	20,000	60,000
Estimated unit product cost (a) ÷ (b)	$7.05	$9.30	$13.80	?

Management finds the variation in quarterly unit product costs to be confusing and difficult to work with. It has been suggested that the problem lies with manufacturing overhead because it is the largest element of total manufacturing cost. Accordingly, you have been asked to find a more appropriate way of assigning manufacturing overhead cost to units of product.

Required:

1. Using the high-low method, estimate the fixed manufacturing overhead cost per quarter and the variable manufacturing overhead cost per unit. Create a cost formula to estimate the total manufacturing overhead cost for the fourth quarter. Compute the total manufacturing cost and unit product cost for the fourth quarter.
2. What is causing the estimated unit product cost to fluctuate from one quarter to the next?
3. How would you recommend stabilizing the company's unit product cost? Support your answer with computations that adapt the cost formula you created in requirement 1.

EXERCISE 4–14 Apply Overhead to a Job [LO4–2]

Winston Company applies overhead cost to jobs on the basis of direct labor cost. Job X, which was started and completed during the current period, shows charges of $18,000 for direct materials, $10,000 for direct labor, and $15,000 for overhead on its job cost sheet. Job Q, which is still in process at year-end, shows charges of $20,000 for direct materials, and $8,000 for direct labor.

Required:

Should any overhead cost be added to Job Q at year-end? If so, how much? Explain.

EXERCISE 4–15 Plantwide and Departmental Overhead Rates; Job Costs [LO4–1, LO4–2, LO4–3]

Smithson Company uses a job-order costing system and has two manufacturing departments—Molding and Fabrication. The company provided the following estimates at the beginning of the year:

	Molding	Fabrication	Total
Machine-hours	20,000	30,000	50,000
Fixed manufacturing overhead costs	$800,000	$300,000	$1,100,000
Variable manufacturing overhead per machine-hour	$5.00	$5.00	

During the year, the company had no beginning or ending inventories and it started, completed, and sold only two jobs—Job D-75 and Job C-100. It provided the following information related to those two jobs:

Job D-75:	Molding	Fabrication	Total
Direct materials cost	$375,000	$325,000	$700,000
Direct labor cost	$200,000	$160,000	$360,000
Machine-hours	15,000	5,000	20,000

Job C-100:	Molding	Fabrication	Total
Direct materials cost	$300,000	$250,000	$550,000
Direct labor cost	$175,000	$225,000	$400,000
Machine-hours	5,000	25,000	30,000

Smithson had no overapplied or underapplied manufacturing overhead during the year.

Required:

1. Assume Smithson uses a plantwide overhead rate based on machine-hours.
   a. Compute the predetermined plantwide overhead rate.
   b. Compute the total manufacturing costs assigned to Job D-75 and Job C-100.
   c. If Smithson establishes bid prices that are 150% of total manufacturing costs, what bid price would it have established for Job D-75 and Job C-100?
   d. What is Smithson's cost of goods sold for the year?
2. Assume Smithson uses departmental overhead rates based on machine-hours.
   a. Compute the predetermined departmental overhead rates.
   b. Compute the total manufacturing costs assigned to Job D-75 and Job C-100.
   c. If Smithson establishes bid prices that are 150% of total manufacturing costs, what bid price would it have established for Job D-75 and Job C-100?
   d. What is Smithson's cost of goods sold for the year?
3. What managerial insights are revealed by the computations that you performed in this problem? (***Hint:*** Do the cost of goods sold amounts that you computed in requirements 1 and 2 differ from one another? Do the bid prices that you computed in requirements 1 and 2 differ from one another? Why?)

Additional student resources are available with Connect. connect **Problems**

PROBLEM 4–16 Applying Overhead in a Service Company [LO4–1, LO4–2, LO4–3]

Pearson Architectural Design uses a job-order costing system and applies studio overhead to jobs on the basis of direct staff costs. Because Pearson Architectural Design is a service firm, the names of the accounts it uses are different from the names used in manufacturing companies. The following costs were recorded in January:

Cost of subcontracted work (comparable to direct materials)	$90,000
Direct staff costs (comparable to direct labor)	$200,000
Studio overhead (comparable to manufacturing overhead cost applied)	$320,000
Cost of work completed (comparable to cost of goods manufactured)	$570,000

There were no beginning inventories in January.

At the end of January, only job was still in process. This job (the Krimmer Corporation Headquarters project) had been charged with $13,500 in direct staff costs.

Required:

1. Compute the predetermined overhead rate that was used during January.
2. Complete the following job cost sheet for the partially completed Krimmer Corporation Headquarters project. (***Hint:*** Cost of goods manufactured equals beginning work in process inventory plus manufacturing costs incurred less ending work in process inventory.)

Job Cost Sheet Krimmer Corporation Headquarters Project	
Costs of subcontracted work	$?
Direct staff costs	?
Studio overhead	?
Total cost to January 31	$?

PROBLEM 4–17 Applying Overhead; Underapplied or Overapplied Overhead; Income Statement [LO4–2, LO4–4, LO4–5]

Durham Company uses a job-order costing system. The following transactions took place last year:

a. Raw materials requisitioned for use in production, $40,000 (80% direct and 20% indirect).

b. Factory utility costs incurred, $14,600.
c. Depreciation recorded on plant and equipment, $28,000. Three-fourths of the depreciation relates to factory equipment, and the remainder relates to selling and administrative equipment.
d. Costs for salaries and wages were incurred as follows:

Direct labor.	$40,000
Indirect labor	$18,000
Sales commissions	$10,400
Administrative salaries	$25,000

e. Insurance costs incurred, $3,000 (80% relates to factory operations, and 20% relates to selling and administrative activities).
f. Miscellaneous selling and administrative expenses incurred, $18,000.
g. Manufacturing overhead was applied to production. The company applies overhead on the basis of 150% of direct labor cost.
h. Goods that cost $130,000 to manufacture according to their job cost sheets were transferred to the finished goods warehouse.
i. Goods that had cost $120,000 to manufacture according to their job cost sheets were sold for $200,000.

Required:

1. Determine the underapplied or overapplied overhead for the year.
2. Prepare an income statement for the year. (***Hint:*** No calculations are required to determine the cost of goods sold before any adjustment for underapplied or overapplied overhead.)

PROBLEM 4–18 Applying Overhead in a Service Company [LO4–2, LO4–4, LO4–5]

Heritage Gardens provides complete garden design and landscaping services. The company uses a job-order costing system to track the costs of its landscaping projects. The table below provides data concerning the three landscaping projects that were in progress during May. There was no work in process at the beginning of May.

	Project		
	Williams	Chandler	Nguyen
Designer-hours	200	80	120
Direct materials	$4,800	$1,800	$3,600
Direct labor	$2,400	$1,000	$1,500

Actual overhead costs were $16,000 for May. Overhead costs are applied to projects on the basis of designer-hours because most of the overhead is related to the costs of the garden design studio. The predetermined overhead rate is $45 per designer-hour. The Williams and Chandler projects were completed in May; the Nguyen project was not completed by the end of the month. No other jobs were in process during May.

Required:

1. Compute the amount of overhead cost that would have been applied to each project during May.
2. Determine the cost of goods manufactured for May.
3. What is the accumulated cost of the work in process at the end of the month?
4. Determine the underapplied or overapplied overhead for May.

PROBLEM 4–19 Predetermined Overhead Rate; Applying Overhead; Underapplied or Overapplied Overhead [LO4–2, LO4–4, LO4–5]

Ravsten Company uses a job-order costing system.

The company applies overhead cost to jobs on the basis of machine-hours. For the current year, the company estimated that it would work 36,000 machine-hours and incur $153,000 in manufacturing overhead cost. The following transactions occurred during the year:

a. Raw materials requisitioned for use in production, $190,000 (80% direct and 20% indirect).
b. The following costs were incurred for employee services:

Direct labor	$160,000
Indirect labor	$18,000
Sales commissions	$10,000
Administrative salaries	$25,000

c. Heat, power, and water costs incurred in the factory, $42,000.
d. Insurance costs, $10,000 (90% relates to factory operations, and 10% relates to selling and administrative activities).
e. Advertising costs incurred, $50,000.
f. Depreciation recorded for the year, $60,000 (85% relates to factory operations, and 15% relates to selling and administrative activities).
g. The company used 40,000 machine-hours during the year.
h. Goods that cost $480,000 to manufacture according to their job cost sheets were transferred to the finished goods warehouse.
i. Sales for the year totaled $700,000. The total cost to manufacture these goods according to their job cost sheets was $475,000.

Required:

1. Determine the underapplied or overapplied overhead for the year.
2. Prepare an income statement for the year. (***Hint:*** No calculations are required to determine the cost of goods sold before any adjustment for underapplied or overapplied overhead.)

PROBLEM 4–20 Predetermined Overhead Rate; Disposition of Underapplied or Overapplied Overhead [LO4–1, LO4–4, LO4–5]

Savallas Company is highly automated and uses computers to control manufacturing operations. The company uses a job-order costing system and applies manufacturing overhead cost to products on the basis of computer-hours. The following estimates were used in preparing the predetermined overhead rate at the beginning of the year:

Computer-hours	85,000
Fixed manufacturing overhead cost	$1,275,000
Variable manufacturing overhead per computer-hour	$3.00

During the year, a severe economic recession resulted in cutting back production and a buildup of inventory in the company's warehouse. The company's cost records revealed the following actual cost and operating data for the year:

Computer-hours	60,000
Manufacturing overhead cost	$1,350,000
Inventories at year-end:	
Raw materials	$400,000
Work in process	$160,000
Finished goods	$1,040,000
Cost of goods sold	$2,800,000

Required:

1. Compute the company's predetermined overhead rate for the year.
2. Compute the underapplied or overapplied overhead for the year.
3. Determine the cost of goods sold for the year after any adjustment for underapplied or overapplied overhead.

PROBLEM 4–21 Multiple Departments; Applying Overhead [LO4–1, LO4–2, LO4–3, LO4–4]

WoodGrain Technology makes home office furniture from fine hardwoods. The company uses a job-order costing system and predetermined overhead rates to apply manufacturing overhead cost to jobs. The predetermined overhead rate in the Preparation Department is based on machine-hours, and the rate in the Fabrication Department is based on direct labor-hours. At the beginning of the year, the company's management made the following estimates for the year:

	Department	
	Preparation	Fabrication
Machine-hours	80,000	21,000
Direct labor-hours	35,000	50,000
Direct materials cost	$190,000	$400,000
Direct labor cost	$280,000	$530,000
Fixed manufacturing overhead cost	$256,000	$520,000
Variable manufacturing overhead per machine-hour	$2.00	—
Variable manufacturing overhead per direct labor-hour	—	$4.00

Job 127 was started on April 1 and completed on May 12. The company's cost records show the following information concerning the job:

	Department	
	Preparation	Fabrication
Machine-hours	350	70
Direct labor-hours	80	130
Direct materials cost	$940	$1,200
Direct labor cost	$710	$980

Required:

1. Compute the predetermined overhead rate used during the year in the Preparation Department. Compute the rate used in the Fabrication Department.
2. Compute the total overhead cost applied to Job 127.
3. What would be the total cost recorded for Job 127? If the job contained 25 units, what would be the unit product cost?
4. At the end of the year, the records of WoodGrain Technology revealed the following *actual* cost and operating data for all jobs worked on during the year:

	Department	
	Preparation	Fabrication
Machine-hours	73,000	24,000
Direct labor-hours	30,000	54,000
Direct materials cost	$165,000	$420,000
Manufacturing overhead cost	$390,000	$740,000

What was the amount of underapplied or overapplied overhead in each department at the end of the year?

PROBLEM 4–22 Multiple Departments; Overhead Rates; Underapplied or Overapplied Overhead [LO4–1, LO4–2, LO4–3, LO4–4]

Winkle, Kotter, and Zale is a small law firm that contains 10 partners and 10 support persons. The firm employs a job-order costing system to accumulate costs chargeable to each client, and it is organized into two departments—the Research and Documents Department and the Litigation

Department. The firm uses predetermined overhead rates to charge the costs of these departments to its clients. At the beginning of the current year, the firm's management made the following estimates for the year:

	Department	
	Research and Documents	Litigation
Research-hours	20,000	—
Direct attorney-hours	9,000	16,000
Materials and supplies	$18,000	$5,000
Direct attorney cost	$430,000	$800,000
Departmental overhead cost	$700,000	$320,000

The predetermined overhead rate in the Research and Documents Department is based on research-hours, and the rate in the Litigation Department is based on direct attorney cost.

The costs charged to each client are made up of three elements: materials and supplies used, direct attorney costs incurred, and an applied amount of overhead from each department in which work is performed on the case.

Case 618-3 was initiated on February 10 and completed on June 30. During this period, the following costs and time were recorded on the case:

	Department	
	Research and Documents	Litigation
Research-hours	18	—
Direct attorney-hours	9	42
Materials and supplies	$50	$30
Direct attorney cost	$410	$2,100

Required:

1. Compute the predetermined overhead rates used during the year in the Research and Documents Department and the Litigation Department.
2. Using the rates you computed in requirement 1, compute the total overhead cost applied to Case 618–3.
3. What would be the total cost charged to Case 618–3? Show computations by department and in total for the case.
4. At the end of the year, the firm's records revealed the following *actual* cost and operating data for all cases handled during the year:

	Department	
	Research and Documents	Litigation
Research-hours	23,000	—
Direct attorney-hours	8,000	15,000
Materials and supplies	$19,000	$6,000
Direct attorney cost	$400,000	$775,000
Departmental overhead cost	$770,000	$300,000

Determine the amount of underapplied or overapplied overhead cost in each department for the year.

PROBLEM 4–23 Direct Method of Determining Cost of Goods Sold [LO4–5]

Techuxia Corporation worked on four jobs during October: Job A256, Job A257, Job A258, and Job A260. At the end of October, the job cost sheets for these jobs contained the following data:

	Job A256	Job A257	Job A258	Job A260
Beginning balance	$1,200	$500	$0	$0
Charged to the jobs during October:				
Direct materials	$2,600	$3,500	$1,400	$3,500
Direct labor	$800	$1,000	$600	$400
Manufacturing overhead applied	$1,200	$1,500	$900	$600
Units completed	100	0	200	0
Units in process at the end of October	0	400	0	500
Units sold during October	80	0	40	0

Jobs A256 and A258 were completed during October. The other two jobs had not yet been completed at the end of October. There was no finished goods inventory on October 1.

In October, overhead was overapplied by $800. The company adjusts its cost of goods sold every month for the amount of the underapplied or overapplied overhead.

Required:

1. Using the direct method, what is the cost of goods sold for October?
2. What is the total value of the finished goods inventory at the end of October?
3. What is the total value of the work in process inventory at the end of October?

PROBLEM 4–24 Indirect Method of Determining Cost of Goods Sold [LO4–6]

Refer to the data for Techuxia Corporation in Problem 4–23.

Required:

Using the indirect method, what is the cost of goods sold for October?

Cases connect

Additional student resources are available with Connect.

CASE 4–25 Plantwide versus Departmental Overhead Rates; Underapplied or Overapplied Overhead [LO4–1, LO4–2, LO4–3, LO4–4]

"Don't tell me we've lost another bid!" exclaimed Sandy Kovallas, president of Lenko Products, Inc. "I'm afraid so," replied Doug Martin, the operations vice president. "One of our competitors underbid us by about $10,000 on the Hastings job." "I just can't figure it out," said Kovallas. "It seems we're either too high to get the job or too low to make any money on half the jobs we bid anymore. What's happened?"

Lenko Products manufactures specialized goods to customers' specifications and operates a job-order costing system. Manufacturing overhead cost is applied to jobs on the basis of direct labor cost. The following estimates were made at the beginning of the year:

	Department			
	Cutting	Machining	Assembly	Total Plant
Direct labor	$300,000	$200,000	$400,000	$ 900,000
Manufacturing overhead	$540,000	$800,000	$100,000	$1,440,000

Jobs require varying amounts of work in the three departments. The Hastings job, for example, would have required manufacturing costs in the three departments as follows:

	Department			
	Cutting	Machining	Assembly	Total Plant
Direct materials	$12,000	$900	$5,600	$18,500
Direct labor	$6,500	$1,700	$13,000	$21,200
Manufacturing overhead	?	?	?	?

The company uses a plantwide overhead rate to apply manufacturing overhead cost to jobs.

Required:

1. Assuming the use of a plantwide overhead rate:
   a. Compute the rate for the current year.
   b. Determine the amount of manufacturing overhead cost that would have been applied to the Hastings job.
2. Suppose that instead of using a plantwide overhead rate, the company had used a separate predetermined overhead rate in each department. Under these conditions:
   a. Compute the rate for each department for the current year.
   b. Determine the amount of manufacturing overhead cost that would have been applied to the Hastings job.
3. Explain the difference between the manufacturing overhead that would have been applied to the Hastings job using the plantwide rate in requirement 1(b) and using the departmental rates in requirement 2(b).
4. Assume that it is customary in the industry to bid jobs at 150% of total manufacturing cost (direct materials, direct labor, and applied overhead). What was the company's bid price on the Hastings job? What would the bid price have been if departmental overhead rates had been used to apply overhead cost?
5. At the end of the year, the company assembled the following *actual* cost data relating to all jobs worked on during the year:

	Department			
	Cutting	Machining	Assembly	Total Plant
Direct materials	$760,000	$ 90,000	$ 410,000	$1,260,000
Direct labor.	$320,000	$ 210,000	$340,000	$870,000
Manufacturing overhead	$560,000	$830,000	$92,000	$1,482,000

Compute the underapplied or overapplied overhead for the year (*a*) assuming that a plantwide overhead rate is used, and (*b*) assuming that departmental overhead rates are used.

CASE 4–26 Ethics and the Manager [LO4–1, LO4–2, LO4–4]

Cristin Madsen has recently been transferred to the Appliances Division of Solequin Corporation. Shortly after taking over her new position as divisional controller, she was asked to develop the division's predetermined overhead rate for the upcoming year. The accuracy of the rate is important because it is used throughout the year and any overapplied or underapplied overhead is closed out to Cost of Goods Sold at the end of the year. Solequin Corporation uses direct labor-hours in all of its divisions as the allocation base for manufacturing overhead.

To compute the predetermined overhead rate, Cristin divided her estimate of the total manufacturing overhead for the coming year by the production manager's estimate of the total direct labor-hours for the coming year. She took her computations to the division's general manager for approval but was quite surprised when he suggested a modification in the base. Her conversation with the general manager of the Appliances Division, Lance Jusic, went like this:

Madsen: Here are my calculations for next year's predetermined overhead rate. If you approve, we can enter the rate into the computer on January 1 and be up and running in the job-order costing system right away this year.

Jusic: Thanks for coming up with the calculations so quickly, and they look just fine. There is, however, one slight modification I would like to see. Your estimate of the total direct labor-hours for the year is 110,000 hours. How about cutting that to about 105,000 hours?

Madsen: I don't know if I can do that. The production manager says she will need about 110,000 direct labor-hours to meet the sales projections for next year. Besides, there are going to be over 108,000 direct labor-hours during the current year and sales are projected to be higher next year.

Jusic: Cristin, I know all of that. I would still like to reduce the direct labor-hours in the base to something like 105,000 hours. You probably don't know that I had an agreement with your predecessor as divisional controller to shave 5% or so off the estimated direct labor-hours every year. That way, we kept a reserve that usually resulted in a big boost to net operating income at the end of the fiscal year in December. We called it our Christmas bonus.

Corporate headquarters always seemed as pleased as punch that we could pull off such a miracle at the end of the year. This system has worked well for many years, and I don't want to change it now.

Required:

1. Explain how shaving 5% off the estimated direct labor-hours in the base for the predetermined overhead rate usually results in a big boost in net operating income at the end of the fiscal year.
2. Should Cristin Madsen go along with the general manager's request to reduce the direct labor-hours in the predetermined overhead rate computation to 105,000 direct labor-hours?

CASE 4–27 Critical Thinking; Interpretation of Manufacturing Overhead Rates [LO4–1, LO4–2]

Sharpton Fabricators Corporation manufactures a variety of parts for the automotive industry. The company uses a job-order costing system with a plantwide predetermined overhead rate based on direct labor-hours. On December 10, 2015, the company's controller made a preliminary estimate of the predetermined overhead rate for 2016. The new rate was based on the estimated total manufacturing overhead cost of \$2,475,000 and the estimated 52,000 total direct labor-hours for 2016:

$$\text{Predetermined overhead rate} = \frac{\$2{,}475{,}000}{52{,}000 \text{ hours}}$$
$$= \$47.60 \text{ per direct labor-hour}$$

This new predetermined overhead rate was communicated to top managers in a meeting on December 11. The rate did not cause any comment because it was within a few pennies of the overhead rate that had been used during 2015. One of the subjects discussed at the meeting was a proposal by the production manager to purchase an automated milling machine built by Central Robotics. The president of Sharpton Fabricators, Kevin Reynolds, agreed to meet with the regional sales representative from Central Robotics to discuss the proposal.

On the day following the meeting, Mr. Reynolds met with Jay Warner, Central Robotics' sales representative. The following discussion took place:

Reynolds: Larry Winter, our production manager, asked me to meet with you because he is interested in installing an automated milling machine. Frankly, I am skeptical. You're going to have to show me this isn't just another expensive toy for Larry's people to play with.

Warner: That shouldn't be too difficult, Mr. Reynolds. The automated milling machine has three major advantages. First, it is much faster than the manual methods you are using. It can process about twice as many parts per hour as your present milling machines. Second, it is much more flexible. There are some up-front programming costs, but once those have been incurred, almost no setup is required on the machines for standard operations. You just punch in the code of the standard operation, load the machine's hopper with raw material, and the machine does the rest.

Reynolds: Yeah, but what about cost? Having twice the capacity in the milling machine area won't do us much good. That center is idle much of the time anyway.

Warner: I was getting there. The third advantage of the automated milling machine is lower cost. Larry Winters and I looked over your present operations, and we estimated that the automated equipment would eliminate the need for about 6,000 direct labor-hours a year. What is your direct labor cost per hour?

Reynolds: The wage rate in the milling area averages about \$21 per hour. Fringe benefits raise that figure to about \$30 per hour.

Warner: Don't forget your overhead.

Reynolds: Next year the overhead rate will be about \$48 per hour.

Warner: So including fringe benefits and overhead, the cost per direct labor-hour is about \$78.

Reynolds: That's right.

Warner: Since you save 6,000 direct labor-hours per year, the cost savings would amount to about \$468,000 a year.

Reynolds: That's pretty impressive, but you aren't giving away this equipment are you?

Warner: Several options are available, including leasing and outright purchase. Just for comparison purposes, our 60-month lease plan would require payments of only \$300,000 per year.

Reynolds: Sold! When can you install the equipment?

Shortly after this meeting, Mr. Reynolds informed the company's controller of the decision to lease the new equipment, which would be installed over the Christmas vacation period. The controller realized that this decision would require a recomputation of the predetermined overhead rate for the year 2016 since the decision would affect both the manufacturing overhead and the direct labor-hours for the year. After talking with both the production manager and the sales representative from Central Robotics, the controller discovered that in addition to the annual lease cost of $300,000, the new machine would also require a skilled technician/programmer who would have to be hired at a cost of $45,000 per year to maintain and program the equipment. Both of these costs would be included in factory overhead. There would be no other changes in total manufacturing overhead cost, which is almost entirely fixed. The controller assumed that the new machine would result in a reduction of 6,000 direct labor-hours for the year from the levels that had initially been planned.

When the revised predetermined overhead rate for the year 2016 was circulated among the company's top managers, there was considerable dismay.

Required:

1. Recompute the predetermined overhead rate assuming that the new machine will be installed. Explain why the new predetermined overhead rate is higher (or lower) than the rate that was originally estimated for the year 2016.
2. What effect (if any) would this new rate have on the cost of jobs that do not use the new automated milling machine?
3. Why would managers be concerned about the new overhead rate?
4. After seeing the new predetermined overhead rate, the production manager admitted that he probably wouldn't be able to eliminate all of the 6,000 direct labor-hours. He had been hoping to accomplish the reduction by not replacing workers who retire or quit, but that would not be possible. As a result, the real labor savings would be only about 2,000 hours—one worker. Given this additional information, evaluate the original decision to acquire the automated milling machine from Central Robotics.

Appendix 4A: Activity-Based Absorption Costing

LEARNING OBJECTIVE 4–7
Use activity-based absorption costing to compute unit product costs.

Chapter 4 described how manufacturing companies use traditional absorption costing systems to calculate unit product costs for the purpose of valuing inventories and determining cost of goods sold for external financial reports. In this appendix, we contrast traditional absorption costing with an alternative approach called *activity-based absorption costing*. **Activity-based absorption costing** assigns all manufacturing overhead costs to products based on the *activities* performed to make those products. An **activity** is an event that causes the consumption of manufacturing overhead resources. Rather than relying on plantwide or departmental cost pools, the activity-based approach accumulates each activity's overhead costs in *activity cost pools*. An **activity cost pool** is a "bucket" in which costs are accumulated that relate to a single activity. Each activity cost pool has one *activity measure*. An **activity measure** is an allocation base that is used as the denominator for an activity cost pool. The costs accumulated in the numerator of an activity cost pool divided by the quantity of the activity measure in its denominator equals what is called an *activity rate*. An activity rate is used to assign costs from an activity cost pool to products.

Activity-based absorption costing differs from traditional absorption costing in two ways. First, the activity-based approach uses more cost pools than a traditional approach. Second, the activity-based approach includes some activities and activity measures that *do not* relate to the volume of units produced, whereas the traditional approach relies exclusively on allocation bases that are driven by the volume of production. For example, the activity-based approach may include *batch-level activities*. A **batch-level activity** is performed each time a batch is handled or processed, regardless of how many units are in the batch. Batch-level activities include tasks such as placing purchase orders, setting up equipment, and transporting batches of component parts. Costs at the batch level depend on the number of batches processed rather than the number of units produced. The activity-based approach may also include *product-level activities.* A **product-level activity** relates to specific products and typically must be carried out regardless of how many batches are run or units of product are produced and sold. Product-level activities include tasks such as designing a product and making engineering design changes to a product. Costs at the product-level depend on the number of products supported rather than the number of batches run or the number of units of product produced and sold.

To illustrate the differences between traditional and activity-based absorption costing, we'll use an example focused on Maxtar Industries, a manufacturer of high-quality smoker/barbecue units. The company has two product lines—Premium and Standard. The company has traditionally applied manufacturing overhead costs to these products using a plantwide predetermined overhead rate based on direct labor-hours. Exhibit 4A–1 details how the unit product costs of the two product lines are computed using the company's traditional costing system. The unit product cost of the Premium product line is $71.60 and the unit product cost of the Standard product line is $53.70 according to this traditional costing system.

Maxtar Industries has recently experimented with an activity-based absorption costing system that has three activity cost pools: (1) supporting direct labor; (2) setting up machines; and (3) parts administration. The top of Exhibit 4A–2 displays basic data concerning these activity cost pools. Note that the total estimated overhead cost in these three costs pools, $1,520,000, agrees with the total estimated overhead cost in the company's traditional costing system. The company's activity-based approach simply provides an alternative way to allocate the company's manufacturing overhead across the two products.

EXHIBIT 4A–1
Maxtar Industries' Traditional Costing System

Basic Data

Total estimated manufacturing overhead cost	$1,520,000
Total estimated direct labor-hours	400,000 DLHs

	Premium	Standard
Direct materials per unit	$40.00	$30.00
Direct labor per unit	$24.00	$18.00
Direct labor-hours per unit	2.0 DLHs	1.5 DLHs
Units produced	50,000 units	200,000 units

Computation of the Predetermined Overhead Rate

$$\text{Predetermined overhead rate} = \frac{\text{Total estimated manufacturing overhead}}{\text{Total estimated amount of the allocation base}}$$

$$= \frac{\$1{,}520{,}000}{400{,}000 \text{ DLHs}}$$

$$= \$3.80 \text{ per DLH}$$

Traditional Unit Product Costs

	Premium	Standard
Direct materials	$40.00	$30.00
Direct labor	24.00	18.00
Manufacturing overhead (2.0 DLHs × $3.80 per DLH; 1.5 DLHs × $3.80 per DLH)	7.60	5.70
Unit product cost	$71.60	$53.70

EXHIBIT 4A–2
Maxtar Industries' Activity-Based Absorption Costing System

Basic Data

Activity Cost Pools and Activity Measures	Estimated Overhead Cost	Expected Activity		
		Premium	Standard	Total
Supporting direct labor (DLHs)	$ 800,000	100,000	300,000	400,000
Setting up machines (setups)	480,000	600	200	800
Parts administration (part types)	240,000	140	60	200
Total manufacturing overhead cost	$1,520,000			

Computation of Activity Rates

Activity Cost Pools	(a) Estimated Overhead Cost	(b) Total Expected Activity	(a) ÷ (b) Activity Rate
Supporting direct labor	$800,000	400,000 DLHs	$2 per DLH
Setting up machines	$480,000	800 setups	$600 per setup
Parts administration	$240,000	200 part types	$1,200 per part type

Assigning Overhead Costs to Products

Overhead Cost for the Premium Product

Activity Cost Pools	(a) Activity Rate	(b) Activity	(a) × (b) ABC Cost
Supporting direct labor	$2 per DLH	100,000 DLHs	$200,000
Setting up machines	$600 per setup	600 setups	360,000
Parts administration	$1,200 per part type	140 part types	168,000
Total			$728,000

Overhead Cost for the Standard Product

Activity Cost Pools	(a) Activity Rate	(b) Activity	(a) × (b) ABC Cost
Supporting direct labor	$2 per DLH	300,000 DLHs	$600,000
Setting up machines	$600 per setup	200 setups	120,000
Parts administration	$1,200 per part type	60 part types	72,000
Total			$792,000

Activity-Based Absorption Costing Product Costs

	Premium	Standard
Direct materials	$40.00	$30.00
Direct labor	24.00	18.00
Manufacturing overhead ($728,000 ÷ 50,000 units; $792,000 ÷ 200,000 units)	14.56	3.96
Unit product cost	$78.56	$51.96

The activity rates for the three activity cost pools are computed in the second table in Exhibit 4A–2. For example, the total cost in the "setting up machines" activity cost pool, $480,000, is divided by the total activity associated with that cost pool, 800 setups, to determine the activity rate of $600 per setup.

The activity rates are used to allocate overhead costs to the two products in the third table in Exhibit 4A–2. For example, the activity rate for the "setting up machines" activity cost pool, $600 per setup, is multiplied by the Premium product line's 600 setups to determine the $360,000 machine setup cost allocated to the Premium product line.

The table at the bottom of Exhibit 4A–2 displays the overhead costs per unit and the activity-based unit product costs. The overhead cost per unit is determined by dividing the total overhead cost by the number of units produced. For example, the Premium product line's total overhead cost of $728,000 is divided by 50,000 units to determine the $14.56 overhead cost per unit. Note that the unit product costs differ from those computed using the company's traditional costing system in Exhibit 4A–1. Because the activity-based approach contains both a batch-level (setting up machines) and a product-level (parts administration) activity cost pool, the unit product costs under the activity-based approach follow the usual pattern in which overhead costs are shifted from the high-volume to the low-volume product. The unit product cost of the Standard product line, the high-volume product, has gone down from $53.70 under the traditional costing system to $51.96 under activity-based costing. In contrast, the unit product cost of the Premium product line, the low-volume product, has increased from $71.60 under the traditional costing system to $78.56 under activity-based costing. Instead of using direct labor-hours (which moves in tandem with the volume of the production) to assign all manufacturing overhead costs to products, the activity-based approach uses a batch-level activity measure and a product-level activity measure to assign the batch-level and product-level activity cost pools to the two products.

Glossary (Appendix 4A)

Activity An event that causes the consumption of overhead resources in an organization. (p. 155)

Activity-based absorption costing A costing method that assigns all manufacturing overhead costs to products based on the *activities* performed to make those products. (p. 155)

Activity cost pool A "bucket" in which costs are accumulated that relate to a single activity measure in an activity-based costing system. (p. 155)

Activity measure An allocation base in an activity-based costing system; ideally, a measure of the amount of activity that drives the costs in an activity cost pool. (p. 155)

Batch-level activity An activity that is performed each time a batch is handled or processed, regardless of how many units are in the batch. The amount of resources consumed depends on the number of batches run rather than on the number of units in the batch. (p. 155)

Product-level activity An activity that relates to specific products and typically must be carried out regardless of how many batches are run or units of product are produced and sold. (p. 156)

Appendix 4A Exercises, Problems, and Case

connect

Additional student resources are available with Connect.

EXERCISE 4A–1 Activity-Based Absorption Costing [LO4–7]

Fogerty Company makes two products, titanium Hubs and Sprockets. Data regarding the two products follow:

	Direct Labor-Hours per Unit	Annual Production
Hubs	0.80	10,000 units
Sprockets.	0.40	40,000 units

Additional information about the company follows:

a. Hubs require $32 in direct materials per unit, and Sprockets require $18.
b. The direct labor wage rate is $15 per hour.
c. Hubs are more complex to manufacture than Sprockets and they require special processing.
d. The company's activity-based absorption costing system has the following activity cost pools:

Activity Cost Pool (and Activity Measure)	Estimated Overhead Cost	Expected Activity		
		Hubs	Sprockets	Total
Machine setups (number of setups)	$72,000	100	300	400
Special processing (machine-hours) . . .	$200,000	5,000	0	5,000
General factory (direct labor-hours)	$ 816,000	8,000	16,000	24,000

Required:

1. Compute the activity rate for each activity cost pool.
2. Compute the unit product cost for Hubs and Sprockets using activity-based absorption costing.

EXERCISE 4A–2 Activity-Based Absorption Costing as an Alternative to Traditional Product Costing [LO4–7]

Harrison Company makes two products and uses a traditional costing system in which a single plantwide predetermined overhead rate is computed based on direct labor-hours. Data for the two products for the upcoming year follow:

	Rascon	Parcel
Direct materials cost per unit	$13.00	$22.00
Direct labor cost per unit	$6.00	$3.00
Direct labor-hours per unit.	0.40	0.20
Number of units produced.	20,000	80,000

These products are customized to some degree for specific customers.

Required:

1. The company's manufacturing overhead costs for the year are expected to be $576,000. Using the company's traditional costing system, compute the unit product costs for the two products.
2. Management is considering an activity-based absorption costing system in which half of the overhead would continue to be allocated on the basis of direct labor-hours and half would be allocated on the basis of engineering design time. This time is expected to be distributed as follows during the upcoming year:

	Rascon	Parcel	Total
Engineering design time (in hours)	3,000	3,000	6,000

   Compute the unit product costs for the two products using the proposed activity-based absorption costing system.
3. Explain why the product costs differ between the two systems.

EXERCISE 4A–3 Activity-Based Absorption Costing as an Alternative to Traditional Product Costing [LO4–7]

Stillicum Corporation makes ultra light-weight backpacking tents. Data concerning the company's two product lines appear below:

	Deluxe	Standard
Direct materials per unit.	$72.00	$53.00
Direct labor per unit	$12.00	$9.60
Direct labor-hours per unit.	1.0 DLHs	0.8 DLHs
Estimated annual production.	10,000 units	50,000 units

The company has a traditional costing system in which manufacturing overhead is applied to units based on direct labor-hours. Data concerning manufacturing overhead and direct labor-hours for the upcoming year appear below:

Estimated total manufacturing overhead	$325,000
Estimated total direct labor-hours	50,000 DLHs

Required:

1. Determine the unit product costs of the Deluxe and Standard products under the company's traditional costing system.
2. The company is considering replacing its traditional costing system with an activity-based absorption costing system that would have the following three activity cost pools:

Activity Cost Pools and Activity Measures	Estimated Overhead Cost	Expected Activity		
		Deluxe	Standard	Total
Supporting direct labor (direct labor-hours).	$200,000	10,000	40,000	50,000
Batch setups (setups).	75,000	200	100	300
Safety testing (tests).	50,000	30	70	100
Total manufacturing overhead cost.	$325,000			

Determine the unit product costs of the Deluxe and Standard products under the activity-based absorption costing system.

PROBLEM 4A–4 Activity-Based Absorption Costing as an Alternative to Traditional Product Costing [LO4–7]

Ellix Company manufactures two models of ultra-high fidelity speakers, the X200 model and the X99 model. Data regarding the two products follow:

Product	Direct Labor-Hours	Annual Production	Total Direct Labor-Hours
X200. . . .	1.8 DLHs per unit	5,000 units	9,000 DLHs
X99.	0.9 DLHs per unit	30,000 units	27,000 DLHs
			36,000 DLHs

Additional information about the company follows:

a. Model X200 requires $72 in direct materials per unit, and model X99 requires $50.
b. The direct labor rate is $10 per hour.
c. The company has always used direct labor-hours as the base for applying manufacturing overhead cost to products.
d. Model X200 is more complex to manufacture than model X99 and requires the use of special equipment.
e. Because of the special work required in part (d) above, the company is considering the use of activity-based absorption costing to apply manufacturing overhead cost to products. Three activity cost pools have been identified as follows:

Activity Cost Pool	Activity Measure	Estimated Total Cost	Estimated Total Activity		
			X200	X99	Total
Machine setups	Number of setups	$ 360,000	50	100	150
Special processing	Machine-hours	180,000	12,000	0	12,000
General factory	Direct labor-hours	1,260,000	9,000	27,000	36,000
		$1,800,000			

Required:

1. Assume that the company continues to use direct labor-hours as the base for applying overhead cost to products.
   a. Compute the predetermined overhead rate.
   b. Compute the unit product cost of each model.
2. Assume that the company decides to use activity-based absorption costing to apply overhead cost to products.
   a. Compute the activity rate for each activity cost pool and determine the amount of overhead cost that would be applied to each model using the activity-based approach.
   b. Compute the unit product cost of each model.
3. Explain why overhead cost shifted from the high-volume model to the low-volume model under the activity-based approach.

PROBLEM 4A–5 Activity-Based Absorption Costing as an Alternative to Traditional Product Costing [LO4–7]

Siegel Company manufactures a product that is available in both a deluxe model and a regular model. The company has manufactured the regular model for years. The deluxe model was introduced several years ago to tap a new segment of the market. Since introduction of the deluxe model, the company's profits have steadily declined and management has become increasingly concerned about the accuracy of its costing system. Sales of the deluxe model have been increasing rapidly.

Manufacturing overhead is assigned to products on the basis of direct labor-hours. For the current year, the company has estimated that it will incur $900,000 in manufacturing overhead cost and produce 5,000 units of the deluxe model and 40,000 units of the regular model. The deluxe model requires two hours of direct labor time per unit, and the regular model requires one hour. Material and labor costs per unit are as follows:

	Model	
	Deluxe	Regular
Direct materials.	$40	$25
Direct labor	$14	$7

Required:

1. Using direct labor-hours as the base for assigning overhead cost to products, compute the predetermined overhead rate. Using this rate and other data from the problem, determine the unit product cost of each model.
2. Management is considering using activity-based absorption costing to apply manufacturing overhead cost to products. The activity-based system would have the following four activity cost pools:

Activity Cost Pool	Activity Measure	Estimated Overhead Cost
Purchasing.	Purchase orders issued	$204,000
Processing.	Machine-hours	182,000
Scrap/rework.	Scrap/rework orders issued	379,000
Shipping.	Number of shipments	135,000
		$900,000

	Expected Activity		
Activity Measure	Deluxe	Regular	Total
Purchase orders issued.	200	400	600
Machine-hours	20,000	15,000	35,000
Scrap/rework orders issued	1,000	1,000	2,000
Number of shipments	250	650	900

Determine the predetermined overhead rate for each of the four activity cost pools.

3. Using the predetermined overhead rates you computed in requirement 2, do the following:
   a. Compute the total amount of manufacturing overhead cost that would be applied to each model using the activity-based absorption costing system. After these totals have been computed, determine the amount of manufacturing overhead cost per unit of each model.
   b. Compute the unit product cost of each model (direct materials, direct labor, and manufacturing overhead).
4. From the data you have developed in parts requirements 1 through 3, identify factors that may account for the company's declining profits.

CASE 4A–6 Activity-Based Absorption Costing and Pricing [LO4–7]

Java Source, Inc. (JSI), is a processor and distributor of a variety of blends of coffee. The company buys coffee beans from around the world and roasts, blends, and packages them for resale. JSI offers a large variety of different coffees that it sells to gourmet shops in one-pound bags. The major cost of the coffee is raw materials. However, the company's predominantly automated roasting, blending, and packing processes require a substantial amount of manufacturing overhead. The company uses relatively little direct labor.

Some of JSI's coffees are very popular and sell in large volumes, while a few of the newer blends sell in very low volumes. JSI prices its coffees at manufacturing cost plus a markup of 25%, with some adjustments made to keep the company's prices competitive.

For the coming year, JSI's budget includes estimated manufacturing overhead cost of $2,200,000. JSI assigns manufacturing overhead to products on the basis of direct labor-hours. The expected direct labor cost totals $600,000, which represents 50,000 hours of direct labor time. Based on the sales budget and expected raw materials costs, the company will purchase and use $5,000,000 of raw materials (mostly coffee beans) during the year.

The expected costs for direct materials and direct labor for one-pound bags of two of the company's coffee products appear below.

	Kenya Dark	Viet Select
Direct materials.	$4.50	$2.90
Direct labor (0.02 hours per bag).	$0.24	$0.24

JSI's controller believes that the company's traditional costing system may be providing misleading cost information. To determine whether or not this is correct, the controller has prepared an analysis of the year's expected manufacturing overhead costs, as shown in the following table:

Activity Cost Pool	Activity Measure	Expected Activity for the Year	Expected Cost for the Year
Purchasing.	Purchase orders	2,000 orders	$ 560,000
Material handling	Number of setups	1,000 setups	193,000
Quality control.	Number of batches	500 batches	90,000
Roasting	Roasting hours	95,000 roasting hours	1,045,000
Blending.	Blending hours	32,000 blending hours	192,000
Packaging	Packaging hours	24,000 packaging hours	120,000
Total manufacturing overhead cost.			$2,200,000

Data regarding the expected production of Kenya Dark and Viet Select coffee are presented below.

	Kenya Dark	Viet Select
Expected sales	80,000 pounds	4,000 pounds
Batch size	5,000 pounds	500 pounds
Setups	2 per batch	2 per batch
Purchase order size	20,000 pounds	500 pounds
Roasting time per 100 pounds	1.5 roasting hours	1.5 roasting hours
Blending time per 100 pounds	0.5 blending hour	0.5 blending hour
Packaging time per 100 pounds	0.3 packaging hour	0.3 packaging hour

Required:

1. Using direct labor-hours as the base for assigning manufacturing overhead cost to products, do the following:
   a. Determine the predetermined overhead rate that will be used during the year.
   b. Determine the unit product cost of one pound of the Kenya Dark coffee and one pound of the Viet Select coffee.
2. Using activity-based absorption costing as the basis for assigning manufacturing overhead cost to products, do the following:
   a. Determine the total amount of manufacturing overhead cost assigned to the Kenya Dark coffee and to the Viet Select coffee for the year.
   b. Using the data developed in requirement 2*a*, compute the amount of manufacturing overhead cost per pound of the Kenya Dark coffee and the Viet Select coffee. Round all computations to the nearest whole cent.
   c. Determine the unit product cost of one pound of the Kenya Dark coffee and one pound of the Viet Select coffee.
3. Write a brief memo to the president of JSI explaining what you have found in requirements 1 and 2 above and discussing the implications to the company of using direct labor as the base for assigning manufacturing overhead cost to products.

(CMA, adapted)

Appendix 4B: The Predetermined Overhead Rate and Capacity

LEARNING OBJECTIVE 4–8
Understand the implications of basing the predetermined overhead rate on activity at capacity rather than on estimated activity for the period.

Companies typically base their predetermined overhead rates on the estimated, or budgeted, amount of the allocation base for the upcoming period. This is the method that is used in the chapter, but it is a practice that is often criticized based on the accounting for fixed manufacturing overhead costs.[1] As we shall see, the critics argue that, in general, too much fixed manufacturing overhead cost is applied to products. To focus on this issue, we will make two simplifying assumptions in this appendix: (1) we will consider only fixed manufacturing overhead; and (2) we will assume that the actual fixed manufacturing overhead at the end of the period is the same as the estimated, or budgeted, fixed manufacturing overhead at the beginning of the period. Neither of these assumptions is entirely realistic. Ordinarily, some manufacturing overhead is variable and even fixed costs can differ from what was expected at the beginning of the period, but making those assumptions enables us to focus on the primary issues the critics raise.

An example will help us to understand the controversy. Prahad Corporation manufactures music CDs for local recording studios. The company's CD duplicating machine is capable of producing a new CD every 10 seconds from a master CD. The company leases the CD duplicating machine for $180,000 per year, and this is the company's only manufacturing overhead cost. With allowances for setups and maintenance, the machine is theoretically capable of producing up to 900,000 CDs per year. However, due to weak retail sales of CDs, the company's commercial customers are unlikely to order more than 600,000 CDs next year. The company uses machine time as the allocation base for applying manufacturing overhead to CDs. These data are summarized below:

Prahad Corporation Data	
Total manufacturing overhead cost	$180,000 per year
Allocation base—machine time per CD.	10 seconds per CD
Capacity	900,000 CDs per year
Budgeted output for next year	600,000 CDs

[1] Statement of Financial Accounting Standards No. 151: *Inventory Costs* and International Accounting Standard 2: *Inventories* require allocating fixed manufacturing overhead costs to products based on normal capacity. Normal capacity reflects the level of output expected to be produced over numerous periods under normal circumstances. This definition mirrors the language used in this book that refers to basing the predetermined overhead rate on the estimated, or budgeted, amount of the allocation base for the upcoming period.

If Prahad follows common practice and computes its predetermined overhead rate using estimated or budgeted figures, then its predetermined overhead rate for next year would be \$0.03 per second of machine time computed as follows:

$$\text{Predetermined overhead rate} = \frac{\text{Estimated total manufacturing overhead cost}}{\text{Estimated total amount of the allocation base}}$$

$$= \frac{\$180{,}000}{600{,}000\ \text{CDs} \times 10\ \text{seconds per CD}}$$

$$= \$0.03\ \text{per second}$$

Because each CD requires 10 seconds of machine time, each CD will be charged for \$0.30 of overhead cost.

Critics charge that there are two problems with this procedure. First, if predetermined overhead rates are based on budgeted activity and overhead includes significant fixed costs, then the unit product costs will fluctuate depending on the budgeted level of activity for the period. For example, if the budgeted output for the year was only 300,000 CDs, the predetermined overhead rate would be \$0.06 per second of machine time or \$0.60 per CD rather than \$0.30 per CD. In general, if budgeted output falls, the overhead cost per unit will increase; it will appear that the CDs cost more to make. Managers may then be tempted to increase prices at the worst possible time—just as demand is falling.

Second, critics charge that under the traditional approach, products are charged for resources that they don't use. When the fixed costs of capacity are spread over estimated activity, the units that are produced must shoulder the costs of unused capacity. That is why the applied overhead cost per unit increases as the level of activity falls. The critics argue that products should be charged only for the capacity that they use; they should not be charged for the capacity they don't use. This can be accomplished by basing the predetermined overhead rate on capacity as follows:

$$\begin{matrix}\text{Predetermined overhead}\\ \text{rate based on capacity}\end{matrix} = \frac{\text{Estimated total manufacturing overhead cost at capacity}}{\text{Estimated total amount of the allocation base at capacity}}$$

$$= \frac{\$180{,}000}{900{,}000\ \text{CDs} \times 10\ \text{seconds per CD}}$$

$$= \$0.02\ \text{per second}$$

It is important to realize that the numerator in this predetermined overhead rate is the estimated total manufacturing overhead cost *at capacity.* In general, the numerator in a predetermined overhead rate is the estimated total manufacturing overhead cost for the level of activity in the denominator. Ordinarily, the estimated total manufacturing overhead cost *at capacity* will be larger than the estimated total manufacturing overhead cost *at the estimated level of activity.* The estimated level of activity in this case was 600,000 CDs (or 6 million seconds of machine time), whereas capacity is 900,000 CDs (or 9 million seconds of machine time). The estimated total manufacturing overhead cost at 600,000 CDs was \$180,000. This also happens to be the estimated total manufacturing overhead cost at 900,000 CDs, but that only happens because we have assumed that the manufacturing overhead is entirely fixed. If manufacturing overhead contained any variable element, the total manufacturing overhead would be larger at 900,000 CDs than at 600,000 CDs and, in that case, the predetermined overhead rate should reflect that fact.

At any rate, returning to the computation of the predetermined overhead rate based on capacity, the predetermined overhead rate is \$0.02 per second and so the overhead cost applied to each CD would be \$0.20. This charge is constant and would not be affected by the level of activity during a period. If output falls, the charge would still be \$0.20 per CD.

This method will almost certainly result in underapplied overhead. If actual output at Prahad Corporation is 600,000 CDs, then only \$120,000 of overhead cost would be applied to products ($0.20 per CD × 600,000 CDs). Because the actual overhead cost is $180,000, overhead would be underapplied by $60,000. Because we are assuming that manufacturing overhead is entirely fixed and that actual manufacturing overhead equals the manufacturing overhead as estimated at the beginning of the year, the underapplied overhead represents the cost of unused capacity. In other words, if there had been no unused capacity, there would have been no underapplied overhead. The critics suggest that the underapplied overhead that results from unused capacity should be separately disclosed on the income statement as the Cost of Unused Capacity—a period expense. Disclosing this cost as a lump sum on the income statement, rather than burying it in Cost of Goods Sold or ending inventories, makes it much more visible to managers. An example of such an income statement appears below:

Prahad Corporation
Income Statement
For the Year Ended December 31

Sales[1]		$1,200,000
Cost of goods sold[2]		1,080,000
Gross margin		120,000
Other expenses:		
Cost of unused capacity[3]	$60,000	
Selling and administrative expenses[4]	90,000	150,000
Net operating loss		$ (30,000)

[1] Assume sales of 600,000 CDs at $2 per CD.
[2] Assume the unit product cost of the CDs is $1.80, including $0.20 for manufacturing overhead.
[3] See the calculations in the text above. Underapplied overhead is $60,000.
[4] Assume selling and administrative expenses total $90,000.

connect Appendix 4B Exercises, Problem, and Case

Additional student resources are available with Connect.

EXERCISE 4B–1 Overhead Rate Based on Capacity [LO 4–8]

Samanca Cabinets makes custom wooden cabinets for high-end stereo systems from specialty woods. The company uses a job-order costing system. The capacity of the plant is determined by the capacity of its constraint, which is time on the automated bandsaw that makes finely beveled cuts in wood according to the preprogrammed specifications of each cabinet. The bandsaw can operate up to 150 hours per month. The estimated total manufacturing overhead at capacity is $11,000 per month. The company bases its predetermined overhead rate on capacity, so its predetermined overhead rate is $74 per hour of bandsaw use.

The results of a recent month's operations appear below:

Sales	$39,860
Beginning inventories	$0
Ending inventories	$0
Direct materials	$4,820
Direct labor (all variable)	$9,640
Manufacturing overhead incurred	$10,870
Selling and administrative expense	$9,350
Actual hours of bandsaw use	124

Required:

1. Prepare an income statement following the example in Appendix 4B in which any underapplied overhead is directly recorded on the income statement as an expense.
2. Why is overhead ordinarily underapplied when the predetermined overhead rate is based on capacity?

EXERCISE 4B–2 Overhead Rates and Capacity Issues [LO 4–1, LO 4–2, LO 4–4, LO 4–8]

Estate Pension Services helps clients to set up and administer pension plans that are in compliance with tax laws and regulatory requirements. The firm uses a job-order costing system in which overhead is applied to clients' accounts on the basis of professional staff hours charged to the accounts. Data concerning two recent years appear below:

	2016	2017
Estimated professional staff hours to be charged to clients' accounts	2,400	2,250
Estimated overhead cost	$144,000	$144,000
Professional staff hours available	3,000	3,000

"Professional staff hours available" is a measure of the capacity of the firm. Any hours available that are not charged to clients' accounts represent unused capacity. All of the firm's overhead is fixed.

Required:

1. Jennifer Miyami is an established client whose pension plan was set up many years ago. In both 2016 and 2017, only five hours of professional staff time were charged to Ms. Miyami's account. If the company bases its predetermined overhead rate on the estimated overhead cost and the estimated professional staff hours to be charged to clients, how much overhead cost would have been applied to Ms. Miyami's account in 2016? In 2017?
2. Suppose that the company bases its predetermined overhead rate on the estimated overhead cost and the estimated professional staff hours to be charged to clients as in requirement 1. Also suppose that the actual professional staff hours charged to clients' accounts and the actual overhead costs turn out to be exactly as estimated in both years. By how much would the overhead be underapplied or overapplied in 2016? In 2017?
3. Refer back to the data concerning Ms. Miyami in requirement 1. If the company bases its predetermined overhead rate on the professional staff hours available, how much overhead cost would have been applied to Ms. Miyami's account in 2016? In 2017?
4. Suppose that the company bases its predetermined overhead rate on the professional staff hours available as in requirement 3. Also, suppose that the actual professional staff hours charged to clients' accounts and the actual overhead costs turn out to be exactly as estimated in both years. By how much would the overhead be underapplied or overapplied in 2016? In 2017?

PROBLEM 4B–3 Predetermined Overhead Rate and Capacity [LO 4–1, LO 4–2, LO 4–4, LO 4–8]

Skid Road Recording, Inc., is a small audio recording studio located in Seattle. The company handles work for advertising agencies—primarily for radio ads—and has a few singers and bands as clients. Skid Road Recording handles all aspects of recording from editing to making a digital master from which CDs can be copied. The competition in the audio recording industry in Seattle has always been tough, but it has been getting even tougher over the last several years. The studio has been losing customers to newer studios that are equipped with more up-to-date equipment and that are able to offer very attractive prices and excellent service. Summary data concerning the last two years of operations follow:

	2016	2017
Estimated hours of studio service	1,000	750
Estimated studio overhead cost	$90,000	$90,000
Actual hours of studio service provided	900	600
Actual studio overhead cost incurred	$90,000	$90,000
Hours of studio service at capacity	1,800	1,800

The company applies studio overhead to recording jobs on the basis of the hours of studio service provided. For example, 30 hours of studio time were required to record, edit, and master the Slug Fest music CD for a local band. All of the studio overhead is fixed, and the actual overhead cost incurred was exactly as estimated at the beginning of the year in both 2016 and 2017.

Required:

1. Skid Road Recording computes its predetermined overhead rate at the beginning of each year based on the estimated studio overhead and the estimated hours of studio service for the year. How much overhead would have been applied to the Slug Fest job if it had been done in 2016? In 2017? By how much would overhead have been underapplied or overapplied in 2016? In 2017?
2. The president of Skid Road Recording has heard that some companies in the industry have changed to a system of computing the predetermined overhead rate at the beginning of each year based on the hours of studio service that could be provided at capacity. He would like to know what effect this method would have on job costs. How much overhead would have been applied using this method to the Slug Fest job if it had been done in 2016? In 2017? By how much would overhead have been underapplied or overapplied in 2016 using this method? In 2017?
3. How would you interpret the underapplied or overapplied overhead that results from using studio hours at capacity to compute the predetermined overhead rate?
4. What fundamental business problem is Skid Road Recording facing? Which method of computing the predetermined overhead rate is likely to be more helpful in facing this problem? Explain.

CASE 4B–4 Ethics; Predetermined Overhead Rate and Capacity [LO 4–2, LO 4–4, LO 4–8]

Melissa Ostwerk, the new controller of TurboDrives, Inc., has just returned from a seminar on the choice of the activity level in the predetermined overhead rate. Even though the subject did not sound exciting at first, she found that there were some important ideas presented that should get a hearing at her company. After returning from the seminar, she arranged a meeting with the production manager, Jan Kingman, and the assistant production manager, Lonny Chan.

Melissa: I ran across an idea that I wanted to check out with both of you. It's about the way we compute predetermined overhead rates.

Jan: We're all ears.

Melissa: We compute the predetermined overhead rate by dividing the estimated total factory overhead for the coming year, which is all a fixed cost, by the estimated total units produced for the coming year.

Lonny: We've been doing that as long as I've been with the company.

Jan: And it has been done that way at every other company I've worked at, except at most places they divide by direct labor-hours.

Melissa: We use units because it is simpler and we basically make one product with minor variations. But, there's another way to do it. Instead of basing the overhead rate on the estimated total units produced for the coming year, we could base it on the total units produced at capacity.

Lonny: Oh, the Marketing Department will love that. It will drop the costs on all of our products. They'll go wild over there cutting prices.

Melissa: That is a worry, but I wanted to talk to both of you first before going over to Marketing.

Jan: Aren't you always going to have a lot of underapplied overhead?

Melissa: That's correct, but let me show you how we would handle it. Here's an example based on our budget for next year.

Budgeted (estimated) production	80,000 units
Budgeted sales	80,000 units
Capacity	100,000 units
Selling price	$70 per unit
Variable manufacturing cost	$18 per unit
Total manufacturing overhead cost (all fixed)	$2,000,000
Selling and administrative expenses (all fixed)	$1,950,000
Beginning inventories	$0

Traditional approach to computing the predetermined overhead rate:

$$\text{Predetermined overhead rate} = \frac{\text{Estimated total manufacturing overhead cost}}{\text{Estimated total amount of the allocation base}}$$

$$= \frac{\$2{,}000{,}000}{80{,}000 \text{ units}} = \$25 \text{ per unit}$$

Budgeted Income Statement		
Revenue (80,000 units × $70 per unit)		$5,600,000
Cost of goods sold:		
Variable manufacturing (80,000 units × $18 per unit)	$1,440,000	
Manufacturing overhead applied (80,000 units × $25 per unit)	2,000,000	3,440,000
Gross margin		2,160,000
Selling and administrative expenses		1,950,000
Net operating income		$ 210,000

New approach to computing the predetermined overhead rate using capacity in the denominator:

$$\text{Predetermined overhead rate} = \frac{\text{Estimated total manufacturing overhead cost at capacity}}{\text{Estimated total amount of the allocation base at capacity}}$$

$$= \frac{\$2{,}000{,}000}{100{,}000 \text{ units}} = \$20 \text{ per unit}$$

Budgeted Income Statement		
Revenue (80,000 units × $70 per unit)		$5,600,000
Cost of goods sold:		
Variable manufacturing (80,000 units × $18 per unit)	$1,440,000	
Manufacturing overhead applied (80,000 units × $20 per unit)	1,600,000	3,040,000
Gross margin		2,560,000
Cost of unused capacity [(100,000 units – 80,000 units) × $20 per unit]		400,000
Selling and administrative expenses		1,950,000
Net operating income		$ 210,000

Jan: Whoa!! I don't think I like the looks of that "Cost of unused capacity." If that thing shows up on the income statement, someone from headquarters is likely to come down here looking for some people to lay off.

Lonny: I'm worried about something else, too. What happens when sales are not up to expectations? Can we pull the "hat trick"?

Melissa: I'm sorry, I don't understand.

Jan: Lonny's talking about something that happens fairly regularly. When sales are down and profits look like they are going to be lower than the president told the owners they were going to be, the president comes down here and asks us to deliver some more profits.

Lonny: And we pull them out of our hat.

Jan: Yeah, we just increase production until we get the profits we want.

Melissa: I still don't understand. You mean you increase sales?

Jan: Nope, we increase production. We're the production managers, not the sales managers.
Melissa: I get it. Because you have produced more, the sales force has more units it can sell.
Jan: Nope, the marketing people don't do a thing. We just build inventories and that does the trick.

Required:

In all of the forthcoming questions, assume that the predetermined overhead rate under the traditional method is $25 per unit, and under the new method it is $20 per unit. Also, assume that under the traditional method any underapplied or overapplied overhead is taken directly to the income statement as an adjustment to Cost of Goods Sold.

1. Suppose actual production is 80,000 units. Compute the net operating incomes that would be realized under the traditional and new methods if actual sales are 75,000 units and everything else turns out as expected.
2. How many units would have to be produced under each of the methods in order to realize the budgeted net operating income of $210,000 if actual sales are 75,000 units and everything else turns out as expected?
3. What effect does the new method based on capacity have on the volatility of net operating income?
4. Will the "hat trick" be easier or harder to perform if the new method based on capacity is used?
5. Do you think the "hat trick" is ethical?

Chapter 5

Variable Costing and Segment Reporting: Tools for Management

Misguided Incentives in the Auto Industry

BUSINESS FOCUS

© Jeff Kowalsky/Bloomberg/Getty Images

When the economy tanks, automakers, such as General Motors and Chrysler, often "flood the market" with a supply of vehicles that far exceeds customer demand. They pursue this course of action even though it tarnishes their brand image and increases their auto storage costs, tire replacement costs, customer rebate costs, and advertising costs. This begs the question why would managers knowingly produce more vehicles than are demanded by customers?

In the auto industry, a manager's bonus is often influenced by her company's reported profits; thus, there is a strong incentive to boost profits by producing more units. How can this be done you ask? It would seem logical that producing more units would have no impact on profits unless the units were sold, right? Wrong! As we will discover in this chapter, absorption costing—the most widely used method of determining product costs—can artificially increase profits when managers choose to increase the quantity of units produced. ■

Source: Marielle Segarra, *"Lots of Trouble,"* CFO, March 2012, pp. 29–30.

LEARNING OBJECTIVES

After studying Chapter 5, you should be able to:

LO 5–1 Explain how variable costing differs from absorption costing and compute unit product costs under each method.

LO 5–2 Prepare income statements using both variable and absorption costing.

LO 5–3 Reconcile variable costing and absorption costing net operating incomes and explain why the two amounts differ.

LO 5–4 Prepare a segmented income statement that differentiates traceable fixed costs from common fixed costs and use it to make decisions.

LO 5–5 Compute companywide and segment break-even points for a company with traceable fixed costs.

LO 5–6 *(Appendix 5A)* Prepare an income statement using super-variable costing and reconcile this approach with variable costing.

This chapter describes two applications of the contribution format income statements that were introduced in earlier chapters. First, it explains how manufacturing companies can prepare *variable costing* income statements, which rely on the contribution format, for internal decision making purposes. The variable costing approach will be contrasted with *absorption costing* income statements, which were discussed in Chapter 4 and are generally used for external reports. Ordinarily, variable costing and absorption costing produce different net operating income figures, and the difference can be quite large. In addition to showing how these two methods differ, we will describe the advantages of variable costing for internal reporting purposes and we will show how management decisions can be affected by the costing method chosen.

Second, the chapter explains how the contribution format can be used to prepare segmented income statements. In addition to companywide income statements, managers need to measure the profitability of individual *segments* of their organizations. A **segment** is a part or activity of an organization about which managers would like cost, revenue, or profit data. This chapter explains how to create contribution format income statements that report profit data for business segments, such as divisions, individual stores, geographic regions, customers, and product lines.

Overview of Variable and Absorption Costing

LEARNING OBJECTIVE 5–1
Explain how variable costing differs from absorption costing and compute unit product costs under each method.

As you begin to read about variable and absorption costing income statements in the coming pages, focus your attention on three key concepts. First, both income statement formats include product costs and period costs, although they define these cost classifications differently. Second, variable costing income statements are grounded in the contribution format. They categorize expenses based on cost behavior—variable expenses are reported separately from fixed expenses. Absorption costing income statements ignore variable and fixed cost distinctions. Third, as mentioned in the paragraph above, variable and absorption costing net operating income figures often differ from one another. The reason for these differences always relates to the fact the variable costing and absorption costing income statements account for fixed manufacturing overhead differently. *Pay very close attention to the two different ways that variable costing and absorption costing account for fixed manufacturing overhead.*

Variable Costing

Under **variable costing**, only those manufacturing costs that vary with output are treated as product costs. This would usually include direct materials, direct labor, and the variable portion of manufacturing overhead. Fixed manufacturing overhead is not treated as a product cost under this method. Rather, fixed manufacturing overhead is treated as a period cost and, like selling and administrative expenses, it is expensed in its entirety each period. Consequently, the cost of a unit of product in inventory or in cost of goods sold under the variable costing method does not contain any fixed manufacturing overhead cost. Variable costing is sometimes referred to as *direct costing* or *marginal costing*.

Absorption Costing

As discussed in Chapter 4, **absorption costing** treats *all* manufacturing costs as product costs, regardless of whether they are variable or fixed. The cost of a unit of product under the absorption costing method consists of direct materials, direct labor, and *both* variable and fixed manufacturing overhead. Thus, absorption costing allocates a portion of fixed manufacturing overhead cost to each unit of product, along with the variable manufacturing costs. Because absorption costing includes all manufacturing costs in product costs, it is frequently referred to as the *full cost* method.

Selling and Administrative Expenses

Selling and administrative expenses are never treated as product costs, regardless of the costing method. Thus, under absorption and variable costing, variable and fixed selling and administrative expenses are always treated as period costs and are expensed as incurred.

Summary of Differences The essential difference between variable costing and absorption costing, as illustrated in Exhibit 5–1, is how each method accounts for fixed manufacturing overhead costs—all other costs are treated the same under the two methods. In absorption costing, fixed manufacturing overhead costs are included as part of the costs of work in process inventories. When units are completed, these costs are transferred to finished goods and only when the units are sold do these costs flow through to the income statement as part of cost of goods sold. In variable costing, fixed manufacturing overhead costs are considered to be period costs—just like selling and administrative costs—and are taken immediately to the income statement as period expenses.

EXHIBIT 5–1
Variable Costing versus Absorption Costing

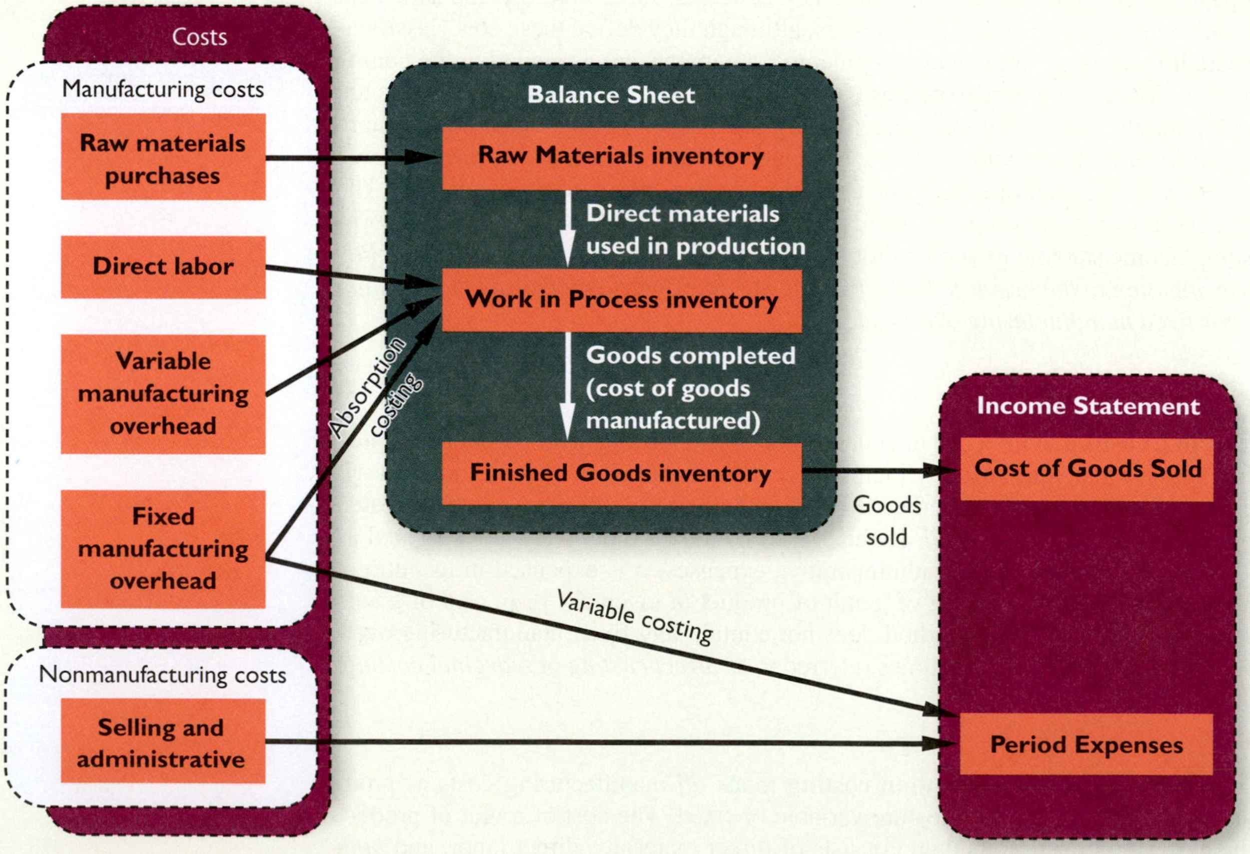

Variable and Absorption Costing—An Example

To illustrate the difference between variable costing and absorption costing, consider Weber Light Aircraft, a company that produces light recreational aircraft. Data concerning the company's operations appear below:

	Per Aircraft	Per Month
Selling price	$100,000	
Direct materials	$19,000	
Direct labor	$5,000	
Variable manufacturing overhead	$1,000	
Fixed manufacturing overhead		$70,000
Variable selling and administrative expenses	$10,000	
Fixed selling and administrative expenses		$20,000

	January	February	March
Beginning inventory	0	0	1
Units produced	1	2	4
Units sold	1	1	5
Ending inventory	0	1	0

As you review the data above, it is important to realize that for the months of January, February, and March, the selling price per aircraft, variable cost per aircraft, and total monthly fixed expenses never change. The only variables that change in this example are the number of units produced (January = 1 unit produced; February = 2 units produced; March = 4 units produced) and the number of units sold (January = 1 unit sold; February = 1 unit sold; March = 5 units sold).

We will first construct the company's variable costing income statements for January, February, and March. Then we will show how the company's net operating income would be determined for the same months using absorption costing.

Variable Costing Contribution Format Income Statement

LEARNING OBJECTIVE 5–2
Prepare income statements using both variable and absorption costing.

To prepare the company's variable costing income statements for January, February, and March we begin by computing the unit product cost. Under variable costing, product costs consist solely of variable production costs. At Weber Light Aircraft, the variable production cost per unit is $25,000, determined as follows:

Variable Costing Unit Product Cost	
Direct materials	$19,000
Direct labor	5,000
Variable manufacturing overhead	1,000
Variable costing unit product cost	$25,000

Since each month's variable production cost is $25,000 per aircraft, the variable costing cost of goods sold for all three months can be easily computed as follows:

Variable Costing Cost of Goods Sold	January	February	March
Variable production cost (a)	$25,000	$25,000	$25,000
Units sold (b)	1	1	5
Variable cost of goods sold (a) × (b)	$25,000	$25,000	$125,000

And the company's total selling and administrative expense would be derived as follows:

Selling and Administrative Expenses	January	February	March
Variable selling and administrative expense (@ $10,000 per unit sold)	$10,000	$10,000	$50,000
Fixed selling and administrative expense	20,000	20,000	20,000
Total selling and administrative expense	$30,000	$30,000	$70,000

Putting it all together, the variable costing income statements would appear as shown in Exhibit 5–2. Notice, the contribution format has been used in these income statements. Also, the monthly fixed manufacturing overhead costs ($70,000) have been recorded as a period expense in the month incurred.

EXHIBIT 5–2
Variable Costing Income Statements

Variable Costing Contribution Format Income Statements	January	February	March
Sales	$100,000	$100,000	$500,000
Variable expenses:			
Variable cost of goods sold	25,000	25,000	125,000
Variable selling and administrative expense	10,000	10,000	50,000
Total variable expenses	35,000	35,000	175,000
Contribution margin	65,000	65,000	325,000
Fixed expenses:			
Fixed manufacturing overhead	70,000	70,000	70,000
Fixed selling and administrative expense	20,000	20,000	20,000
Total fixed expenses	90,000	90,000	90,000
Net operating income (loss)	$ (25,000)	$ (25,000)	$235,000

A simple method for understanding how Weber Light Aircraft computed its variable costing net operating income figures is to focus on the contribution margin per aircraft sold, which is computed as follows:

Contribution Margin per Aircraft Sold		
Selling price per aircraft		$100,000
Variable production cost per aircraft	$25,000	
Variable selling and administrative expense per aircraft	10,000	35,000
Contribution margin per aircraft		$ 65,000

The variable costing net operating income for each period can always be computed by multiplying the number of units sold by the contribution margin per unit and then subtracting total fixed costs. For Weber Light Aircraft these computations would appear as follows:

	January	February	March
Number of aircraft sold	1	1	5
Contribution margin per aircraft	× $ 65,000	× $ 65,000	× $ 65,000
Total contribution margin	$ 65,000	$ 65,000	$325,000
Total fixed expenses	90,000	90,000	90,000
Net operating income (loss)	$(25,000)	$(25,000)	$235,000

Notice, January and February have the same net operating loss. This occurs because one aircraft was sold in each month and, as previously mentioned, the selling price per aircraft, variable cost per aircraft, and total monthly fixed expenses remain constant.

Absorption Costing Income Statement

As we begin the absorption costing portion of the example, remember that the only reason absorption costing income differs from variable costing is that the methods account for fixed manufacturing overhead differently. Under absorption costing, fixed manufacturing overhead is included in product costs. In variable costing, fixed manufacturing overhead is not included in product costs and instead is treated as a period expense just like selling and administrative expenses.

The first step in preparing Weber's absorption costing income statements for January, February, and March is to determine the company's unit product costs for each month as follows[1]:

Absorption Costing Unit Product Cost	January	February	March
Direct materials	$19,000	$19,000	$19,000
Direct labor	5,000	5,000	5,000
Variable manufacturing overhead	1,000	1,000	1,000
Fixed manufacturing overhead ($70,000 ÷ 1 unit produced in January; $70,000 ÷ 2 units produced in February; $70,000 ÷ 4 units produced in March)	70,000	35,000	17,500
Absorption costing unit product cost	$95,000	$60,000	$42,500

Notice that in each month, Weber's fixed manufacturing overhead cost of $70,000 is divided by the number of units produced to determine the fixed manufacturing overhead cost per unit.

Given these unit product costs, the company's absorption costing net operating income in each month would be determined as shown in Exhibit 5–3.

The sales for all three months in Exhibit 5–3 are the same as the sales shown in the variable costing income statements. The January cost of goods sold consists of one unit produced during January at a cost of $95,000 according to the absorption costing system. The February cost of goods sold consists of one unit produced during February at a cost of $60,000 according to the absorption costing system. The March cost of goods

EXHIBIT 5–3
Absorption Costing Income Statements

Absorption Costing Income Statements	January	February	March
Sales	$100,000	$100,000	$500,000
Cost of goods sold ($95,000 × 1 unit; $60,000 × 1 unit; $60,000 × 1 unit + $42,500 × 4 units)	95,000	60,000	230,000
Gross margin	5,000	40,000	270,000
Selling and administrative expenses	30,000	30,000	70,000
Net operating income (loss)	$ (25,000)	$ 10,000	$200,000

[1] For simplicity, we assume in this section that an actual costing system is used in which actual costs are spread over the units produced during the period. If a predetermined overhead rate were used, the analysis would be similar, but more complex.

sold ($230,000) consists of one unit produced during February at an absorption cost of $60,000 plus four units produced in March with a total absorption cost of $170,000 (= 4 units produced × $42,500 per unit). The selling and administrative expenses equal the amounts reported in the variable costing income statements; however they are reported as one amount rather than being separated into variable and fixed components.

Note that even though sales were exactly the same in January and February and the cost structure did not change, net operating income was $35,000 higher in February than in January under absorption costing. This occurs because one aircraft produced in February is not sold until March. This aircraft has $35,000 of fixed manufacturing overhead attached to it that was incurred in February, but will not be recorded as part of cost of goods sold until March.

Contrasting the variable costing and absorption costing income statements in Exhibits 5–2 and 5–3, note that net operating income is the same in January under variable costing and absorption costing, but differs in the other two months. We will discuss this in some depth shortly. Also note that the format of the variable costing income statement differs from the absorption costing income statement. An absorption costing income statement categorizes costs by function—manufacturing versus selling and administrative. All of the manufacturing costs flow through the absorption costing cost of goods sold and all of the selling and administrative expenses are listed separately as period expenses. In contrast, in the contribution approach, costs are categorized according to how they behave. All of the variable expenses are listed together and all of the fixed expenses are listed together. The variable expenses category includes manufacturing costs (i.e., variable cost of goods sold) as well as selling and administrative expenses. The fixed expenses category also includes both manufacturing costs and selling and administrative expenses.

IN BUSINESS

THE BEHAVIORAL SIDE OF CALCULATING UNIT PRODUCT COSTS

Andreas STIHL, a manufacturer of chain saws and other landscaping products, asked its U.S. subsidiary, STIHL Inc., to replace its absorption costing income statements with the variable costing approach. From a computer systems standpoint, the change was not disruptive because STIHL used an enterprise system called SAP that accommodates both absorption and variable costing. However, from a behavioral standpoint, STIHL felt the change could be very disruptive. For example, STIHL's senior managers were keenly aware that the variable costing approach reported lower unit product costs than the absorption costing approach. Given this reality, the sales force might be inclined to erroneously conclude that each product had magically become more profitable, thereby justifying ill-advised price reductions. Because of behavioral concerns such as this, STIHL worked hard to teach its employees how to interpret a variable costing income statement.

Source: Carl S. Smith, "Going for GPK: STIHL Moves Toward This Costing System in the United States," *Strategic Finance,* April 2005, pp. 36–39.

Reconciliation of Variable Costing with Absorption Costing Income

LEARNING OBJECTIVE 5–3
Reconcile variable costing and absorption costing net operating incomes and explain why the two amounts differ.

As noted earlier, variable costing and absorption costing net operating incomes may not be the same. In the case of Weber Light Aircraft, the net operating incomes are the same in January, but differ in the other two months. These differences occur because under absorption costing some fixed manufacturing overhead is capitalized in inventories (i.e., included in product costs) rather than being immediately expensed on the income statement. If inventories increase during a period, under absorption costing some of the fixed manufacturing overhead of the current period will be *deferred* in ending inventories. For example, in February two aircraft were produced and each carried with it $35,000 (= $70,000 ÷ 2 aircraft produced) in fixed manufacturing overhead. Since only one aircraft was sold, $35,000 of this fixed manufacturing overhead was on February's absorption costing income statement as part of cost of goods sold, but $35,000 would have been on the balance sheet as part of finished goods inventories. In contrast, under variable costing *all* of the $70,000 of fixed manufacturing overhead appeared on the February income statement as a period expense. Consequently, net operating income was higher under absorption costing than under variable costing by $35,000 in February. This was reversed in March when four units were produced, but five were sold. In March, under absorption costing $105,000 of fixed manufacturing overhead was included in cost of goods sold ($35,000 for the unit produced in February and sold in March plus $17,500 for each of the four units produced and sold in March), but only $70,000 was recognized as a period expense under variable costing. Hence, the net operating income in March was $35,000 lower under absorption costing than under variable costing.

In general, when the units produced exceed unit sales and hence inventories increase, net operating income is higher under absorption costing than under variable costing. This occurs because some of the fixed manufacturing overhead of the period is *deferred* in inventories under absorption costing. In contrast, when unit sales exceed the units produced and hence inventories decrease, net operating income is lower under absorption costing than under variable costing. This occurs because some of the fixed manufacturing overhead of previous periods is *released* from inventories under absorption costing. When the units produced and unit sales are equal, no change in inventories occurs and absorption costing and variable costing net operating incomes are the same.[2]

Variable costing and absorption costing net operating incomes can be reconciled by determining how much fixed manufacturing overhead was deferred in, or released from, inventories during the period:

Fixed Manufacturing Overhead Deferred in, or Released from, Inventories under Absorption Costing

	January	February	March
Fixed manufacturing overhead in ending inventories	$0	$35,000	$ 0
Fixed manufacturing overhead in beginning inventories	0	0	35,000
Fixed manufacturing overhead deferred in (released from) inventories	$0	$35,000	$(35,000)

In equation form, the fixed manufacturing overhead that is deferred in or released from inventories can be determined as follows:

Manufacturing overhead deferred in (released from) inventory = Fixed manufacturing overhead in ending inventories − Fixed manufacturing overhead in beginning inventories

The reconciliation would then be reported as shown in Exhibit 5–4.

Again note that the difference between variable costing net operating income and absorption costing net operating income is entirely due to the amount of fixed manufacturing overhead that is deferred in, or released from, inventories during the period under absorption costing. Changes in inventories affect absorption costing net operating income—they do not affect variable costing net operating income, providing that variable manufacturing costs per unit are stable.

[2] These general statements about the relation between variable costing and absorption costing net operating income assume LIFO is used to value inventories. Even when LIFO is not used, the general statements tend to be correct. Although U.S. GAAP allows LIFO and FIFO inventory flow assumptions, International Financial Reporting Standards do not allow a LIFO inventory flow assumption.

EXHIBIT 5–4
Reconciliation of Variable Costing and Absorption Costing Net Operating Incomes

Reconciliation of Variable Costing and Absorption Costing Net Operating Incomes

	January	February	March
Variable costing net operating income (loss)	$(25,000)	$(25,000)	$235,000
Add (deduct) fixed manufacturing overhead deferred in (released from) inventory under absorption costing	0	35,000	(35,000)
Absorption costing net operating income (loss)	$(25,000)	$ 10,000	$200,000

The reasons for differences between variable and absorption costing net operating incomes are summarized in Exhibit 5–5. When the units produced equal the units sold, as in January for Weber Light Aircraft, absorption costing net operating income will equal variable costing net operating income. This occurs because when production equals sales, all of the fixed manufacturing overhead incurred in the current period flows through to the income statement under both methods. For companies that use Lean Production, the number of units produced tends to equal the number of units sold. This occurs because goods are produced in response to customer orders, thereby eliminating finished goods inventories and reducing work in process inventory to almost nothing. So, when a company uses Lean Production differences in variable costing and absorption costing net operating income will largely disappear.

When the units produced exceed the units sold, absorption costing net operating income will exceed variable costing net operating income. This occurs because inventories have increased; therefore, under absorption costing some of the fixed manufacturing overhead incurred in the current period is deferred in ending inventories on the balance sheet, whereas under variable costing all of the fixed manufacturing overhead incurred in the current period flows through to the income statement. In contrast, when the units produced are less than the units sold, absorption costing net operating income will be less than variable costing net operating income. This occurs because inventories have

EXHIBIT 5–5
Comparative Income Effects—Absorption and Variable Costing

Relation between Production and Sales for the Period	Effect on Inventories	Relation between Absorption and Variable Costing Net Operating Incomes
Units produced = Units sold	No change in inventories	Absorption costing net operating income = Variable costing net operating income
Units produced > Units sold	Inventories increase	Absorption costing net operating income > Variable costing net operating income*
Units produced < Units sold	Inventories decrease	Absorption costing net operating income < Variable costing net operating income†

*Net operating income is higher under absorption costing because fixed manufacturing overhead cost is *deferred* in inventory under absorption costing as inventories increase.
†Net operating income is lower under absorption costing because fixed manufacturing overhead cost is *released* from inventory under absorption costing as inventories decrease.

decreased; therefore, under absorption costing fixed manufacturing overhead that had been deferred in inventories during a prior period flows through to the current period's income statement together with all of the fixed manufacturing overhead incurred during the current period. Under variable costing, just the fixed manufacturing overhead of the current period flows through to the income statement.

IN BUSINESS

LEAN MANUFACTURING SHRINKS INVENTORIES

Conmed, a surgical device maker in Utica, New York, switched to lean manufacturing by replacing its assembly lines with U-shaped production cells. It also started producing only enough units to satisfy customer demand rather than producing as many units as possible and storing them in warehouses. The company calculated that its customers use one of its disposable surgical devices every 90 seconds, so that is precisely how often it produces a new unit. Its assembly area for fluid-injection devices used to occupy 3,300 square feet of space and contained $93,000 worth of parts. Now the company produces its fluid-injection devices in 660 square feet of space while maintaining only $6,000 of parts inventory.

When Conmed adopted lean manufacturing, it substantially reduced its finished goods inventories. What impact do you think this initial reduction in inventories may have had on net operating income? Why?

Source: Pete Engardio, "Lean and Mean Gets Extreme," *BusinessWeek*, March 23 and 30, 2009, pp. 60–62.

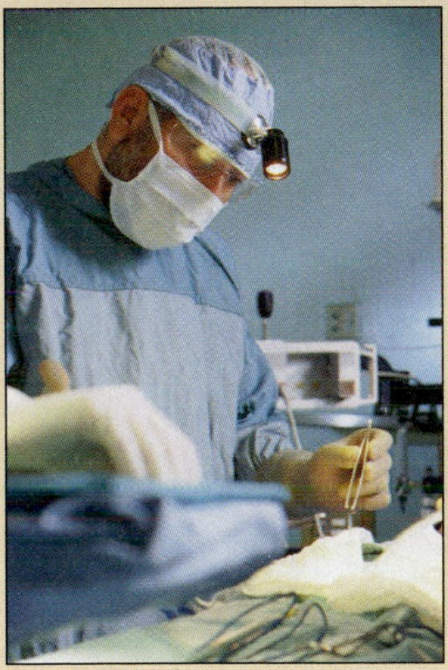

© Photodisc/Getty Images, RF

Advantages of Variable Costing and the Contribution Approach

Variable costing, together with the contribution approach, offers appealing advantages for internal reports. This section discusses three of those advantages.

Enabling CVP Analysis

CVP analysis requires that we break costs down into their fixed and variable components. Because variable costing income statements categorize costs as fixed and variable, it is much easier to use this income statement format to perform CVP analysis than attempting to use the absorption costing format, which mixes together fixed and variable costs.

Moreover, absorption costing net operating income may or may not agree with the results of CVP analysis. For example, let's suppose that you are interested in computing the sales that would be necessary to generate a target profit of $235,000 at Weber Light Aircraft. A CVP analysis based on the January variable costing income statement from Exhibit 5–2 would proceed as follows:

Sales (a).	$100,000
Contribution margin (b).	$65,000
Contribution margin ratio (b) ÷ (a).	65%
Total fixed expenses	$90,000

$$\text{Dollar sales to attain target profit} = \frac{\text{Target profit} + \text{Fixed expenses}}{\text{CM ratio}}$$

$$= \frac{\$235{,}000 + \$90{,}000}{0.65} = \$500{,}000$$

Thus, a CVP analysis based on the January variable costing income statement predicts that the net operating income would be $235,000 when sales are $500,000. And indeed, the net operating income under variable costing *is* $235,000 when the sales are $500,000 in March. However, the net operating income under absorption costing is *not* $235,000 in March, even though the sales are $500,000. Why is this? The reason is that under absorption costing, net operating income can be distorted by changes in inventories. In March, inventories decreased, so some of the fixed manufacturing overhead that had been deferred in February's ending inventories was released to the March income statement, resulting in a net operating income that is $35,000 lower than the $235,000 predicted by CVP analysis. If inventories had increased in March, the opposite would have occurred—the absorption costing net operating income would have been higher than the $235,000 predicted by CVP analysis.

Explaining Changes in Net Operating Income

The variable costing income statements in Exhibit 5–2 are clear and easy to understand. All other things the same, when sales go up, net operating income goes up. When sales go down, net operating income goes down. When sales are constant, net operating income is constant. The number of units produced does not affect net operating income.

Absorption costing income statements can be confusing and are easily misinterpreted. Look again at the absorption costing income statements in Exhibit 5–3; a manager might wonder why net operating income went up from January to February even though sales were exactly the same. Was it a result of lower selling costs, more efficient operations, or was it some other factor? In fact, it was simply because the number of units produced exceeded the number of units sold in February and so some of the fixed manufacturing overhead costs were deferred in inventories in that month. These costs have not gone away—they will eventually flow through to the income statement in a later period when inventories go down. There is no way to tell this from the absorption costing income statements.

To avoid mistakes when absorption costing is used, readers of financial statements should be alert to changes in inventory levels. Under absorption costing, if inventories increase, fixed manufacturing overhead costs are deferred in inventories, which in turn increases net operating income. If inventories decrease, fixed manufacturing overhead costs are released from inventories, which in turn decreases net operating income. Thus, when absorption costing is used, fluctuations in net operating income can be caused by changes in inventories as well as changes in sales.

Supporting Decision Making

The variable costing method correctly identifies the additional variable costs that will be incurred to make one more unit. It also emphasizes the impact of fixed costs on profits. The total amount of fixed manufacturing costs appears explicitly on the income statement, highlighting that the whole amount of fixed manufacturing costs must be covered for the company to be truly profitable. In the Weber Light Aircraft example, the variable costing income statements correctly report that the cost of producing another unit is $25,000 and they explicitly recognize that $70,000 of fixed manufactured overhead must be covered to earn a profit.

Under absorption costing, fixed manufacturing overhead costs appear to be variable with respect to the number of units sold, but they are not. For example, in January, the absorption unit product cost at Weber Light Aircraft is $95,000, but the variable portion of this cost is only $25,000. The fixed overhead costs of $70,000 are commingled with variable production costs, thereby obscuring the impact of fixed overhead costs on profits. Because absorption unit product costs are stated on a per unit basis, managers may mistakenly believe that if another unit is produced, it will cost the company $95,000. But of course it would not. The cost of producing another unit would be only $25,000. Misinterpreting absorption unit product costs as variable can lead to many problems, including inappropriate pricing decisions and decisions to drop products that are in fact profitable.

Segmented Income Statements and the Contribution Approach

LEARNING OBJECTIVE 5–4
Prepare a segmented income statement that differentiates traceable fixed costs from common fixed costs and use it to make decisions.

In the remainder of the chapter, we'll learn how to use the contribution approach to construct income statements for business segments. These segmented income statements are useful for analyzing the profitability of segments, making decisions, and measuring the performance of segment managers.

Traceable and Common Fixed Costs and the Segment Margin

You need to understand three new terms to prepare segmented income statements using the contribution approach—*traceable fixed cost, common fixed cost,* and *segment margin.*

A **traceable fixed cost** of a segment is a fixed cost that is incurred because of the existence of the segment—if the segment had never existed, the fixed cost would not have been incurred; and if the segment were eliminated, the fixed cost would disappear. Examples of traceable fixed costs include the following:

- The salary of the Fritos product manager at PepsiCo is a *traceable* fixed cost of the Fritos business segment of PepsiCo.
- The maintenance cost for the building in which Boeing 747s are assembled is a *traceable* fixed cost of the 747 business segment of Boeing.
- The liability insurance at Disney World is a *traceable* fixed cost of the Disney World business segment of The Walt Disney Corporation.

A **common fixed cost** is a fixed cost that supports the operations of more than one segment, but is not traceable in whole or in part to any one segment. Even if a segment were entirely eliminated, there would be no change in a true common fixed cost. For example:

- The salary of the CEO of General Motors is a *common* fixed cost of the various divisions of General Motors.
- The cost of heating a Safeway or Kroger grocery store is a *common* fixed cost of the store's various departments—groceries, produce, bakery, meat, and so forth.
- The cost of the receptionist's salary at an office shared by a number of doctors is a *common* fixed cost of the doctors. The cost is traceable to the office, but not to individual doctors.

To prepare a segmented income statement, variable expenses are deducted from sales to yield the contribution margin for the segment. The contribution margin tells us what happens to profits as volume changes—holding a segment's capacity and fixed costs constant. The contribution margin is especially useful in decisions involving temporary uses of capacity such as special orders. These types of decisions often involve only variable costs and revenues—the two components of contribution margin.

The **segment margin** is obtained by deducting the traceable fixed costs of a segment from the segment's contribution margin. It represents the margin available after a segment has covered all of its own costs. *The segment margin is the best gauge of the long-run profitability of a segment* because it includes only those costs that are caused by the segment. If a segment can't cover its own costs, then that segment probably should be dropped (unless it has important side effects on other segments). Notice, common fixed costs are not allocated to segments.

From a decision-making point of view, the segment margin is most useful in major decisions that affect capacity such as dropping a segment. By contrast, as we noted earlier, the contribution margin is most useful in decisions involving short-run changes in volume, such as pricing special orders that involve temporary use of existing capacity.

IN BUSINESS

© TRBfoto/Photodisc /Getty Images, RF

HAS THE INTERNET KILLED CATALOGS?

Smith & Hawken, an outdoor-accessories retailer, has experienced growing Internet sales and declining catalog sales. These trends seem consistent with conventional wisdom, which suggests that the Internet will make catalogs obsolete. Yet, Smith & Hawken, like many retailers with growing Internet sales, has no plans to discontinue its catalogs. In fact, the total number of catalogs mailed in the United States by all companies has jumped from 16.6 billion in 2002 to 19.2 billion in 2005. Why?

Catalog shoppers and Internet shoppers are not independent customer segments. Catalog shoppers frequently choose to complete their sales transactions online rather than placing telephone orders. This explains why catalogs remain a compelling marketing medium even though catalog sales are declining for many companies. If retailers separately analyze catalog sales and Internet sales, they may discontinue the catalogs segment while overlooking the adverse impact of this decision on Internet segment margins.

Source: Louise Lee, "Catalogs, Catalogs, Everywhere," *BusinessWeek*, December 4, 2006, pp. 32–34.

Identifying Traceable Fixed Costs

The distinction between traceable and common fixed costs is crucial in segment reporting because traceable fixed costs are charged to segments and common fixed costs are not. In an actual situation, it is sometimes hard to determine whether a cost should be classified as traceable or common.

The general guideline is to treat as traceable costs *only those costs that would disappear over time if the segment itself disappeared.* For example, if one division within a company were sold or discontinued, it would no longer be necessary to pay that division manager's salary. Therefore the division manager's salary would be classified as a traceable fixed cost of the division. On the other hand, the president of the company undoubtedly would continue to be paid even if one of many divisions was dropped. In fact, he or she might even be paid more if dropping the division was a good idea. Therefore, the president's salary is common to the company's divisions and should not be charged to them.

When assigning costs to segments, the key point is to resist the temptation to allocate costs (such as depreciation of corporate facilities) that are clearly common and that will continue regardless of whether the segment exists or not. *Any allocation of common costs to segments reduces the value of the segment margin as a measure of long-run segment profitability and segment performance.*

Traceable Costs Can Become Common Costs

Fixed costs that are traceable to one segment may be a common cost of another segment. For example, United Airlines might want a segmented income statement that shows the segment margin for a particular flight from Chicago to Paris further broken down into first-class, business-class, and economy-class segment margins. The airline must pay a substantial landing fee at Charles DeGaulle airport in Paris. This fixed landing fee is a traceable cost of the flight, but it is a common cost of the first-class, business-class, and economy-class segments. Even if the first-class cabin is empty, the entire landing fee must be paid. So the landing fee is not a traceable cost of the first-class cabin. But on the other hand, paying the fee is necessary in order to have any first-class, business-class, or economy-class passengers. So the landing fee is a common cost of these three classes.

IN BUSINESS

SEGMENT REPORTING AT THE VILAR PERFORMING ARTS CENTER

The Vilar Performing Arts Center is a 535-seat theater located in Beaver Creek, Colorado, that presents an unusually wide variety of performances categorized into six business segments—Family Series, Broadway Series, Theatre/Comedy Series, Dance Series, Classical Series, and Concert Series. The executive director of the Vilar, Kris Sabel, must decide which shows to book, what financial terms to offer to the artists, what contributions are likely from underwriters (i.e., donors), and what prices to charge for tickets. He evaluates the profitability of the segments using segmented income statements that include traceable costs (such as the costs of transporting, lodging, and feeding the artists) and exclude common costs (such as the salaries of Kris and his staff, depreciation on the theater, and general marketing expenses).

Data concerning the Classical Series segment for one season appears below:

Number of shows	4
Number of seats budgeted	863
Number of seats sold	655
Average seats sold per show	164
Ticket sales	$ 46,800
Underwriting (donors)	65,000
Total income	$ 111,800
Artists fees	78,870
Other traceable expenses	11,231
Classical Series segment margin	$ 21,699

Although the Classical Series sold an average of only 164 seats per show, its overall segment margin ($21,699) is positive thanks to $65,000 of underwriting revenues from donors. Had common costs been allocated to the Classical Series, it may have appeared unprofitable and been discontinued—resulting in fewer shows during the season; less diverse programming; disappointment among a small, but dedicated, number of fans; and lower overall income for the Vilar due to the loss of its Classical Series segment margin.

Segmented Income Statements—An Example

ProphetMax, Inc., is a rapidly growing computer software company. Exhibit 5–6 shows its variable costing income statement for the most recent month. As the company has grown, its senior managers have asked for segmented income statements that could be used to make decisions and evaluate managerial performance. ProphetMax's controller

EXHIBIT 5–6
ProphetMax, Inc. Variable Costing Income Statement

ProphetMax, Inc.
Variable Costing Income Statement

Sales	$500,000
Variable expenses:	
Variable cost of goods sold	180,000
Other variable expenses	50,000
Total variable expenses	230,000
Contribution margin	270,000
Fixed expenses	256,500
Net operating income	$ 13,500

responded by creating examples of contribution format income statements segmented by the company's divisions, product lines, and sales channels. She created Exhibit 5–7 to explain that ProphetMax's profits can be segmented into its two divisions—the Business Products Division and the Consumer Products Division. The Consumer Products Division's profits can be further segmented into the Clip Art and Computer Games product lines. Finally, the Computer Games product line's profits (within the Consumer Products Division) can be segmented into the Online and Retail Stores sales channels.

Levels of Segmented Income Statements

Exhibit 5–8 contains the controller's segmented income statements for the segments depicted in Exhibit 5–7. The contribution format income statement for the entire company appears at the very top of the exhibit under the column labeled Total Company. Notice, the net operating income shown in this column ($13,500) is the same as the net operating income shown in Exhibit 5–6. Immediately to the right of the Total Company column are two columns—one for each of the two divisions. We can see that the Business Products Division's traceable fixed expenses are $90,000 and the Consumer Products Division's are $81,000. These $171,000 of traceable fixed expenses (as shown in the Total Company column) plus the $85,500 of common fixed expenses not traceable to individual divisions equals ProphetMax's total fixed expenses ($256,500) as shown in Exhibit 5–6. We can also see that the Business Products Division's segment margin is $60,000 and the Consumer Products Division's is $39,000. These segment margins show the company's divisional managers how much each of their divisions is contributing to the company's profits.

The middle portion of Exhibit 5–8 further segments the Consumer Products Division into its two product lines, Clip Art and Computer Games. The dual nature of some

EXHIBIT 5–7
ProphetMax, Inc.: Examples of Business Segments

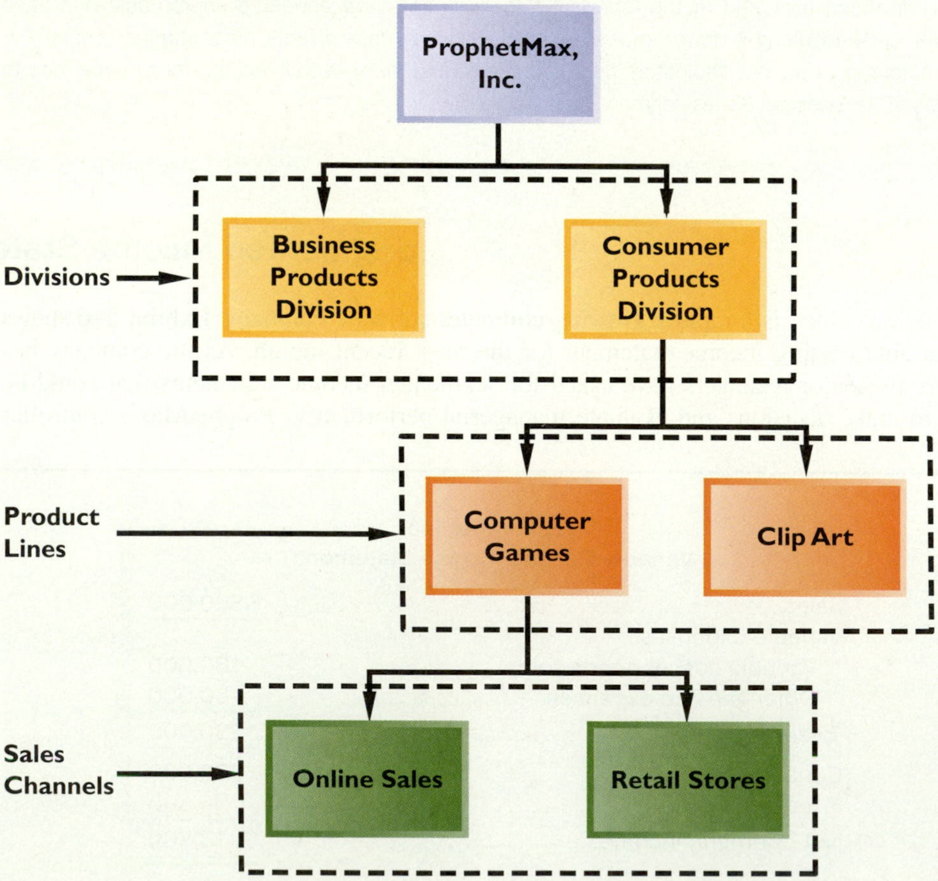

EXHIBIT 5–8
ProphetMax, Inc.—Segmented Income Statements in the Contribution Format

Segments Defined as Divisions

		Divisions	
	Total Company	Business Products Division	Consumer Products Division
Sales	$500,000	$300,000	$200,000
Variable expenses:			
Variable cost of goods sold	180,000	120,000	60,000
Other variable expenses	50,000	30,000	20,000
Total variable expenses	230,000	150,000	80,000
Contribution margin	270,000	150,000	120,000
Traceable fixed expenses	171,000	90,000	81,000
Divisional segment margin	99,000	$ 60,000	$ 39,000
Common fixed expenses not traceable to individual divisions	85,000		
Net operating income	$ 13,500		

Segments Defined as Product Lines of the Consumer Products Division

		Product Line	
	Consumer Products Division	Clip Art	Computer Games
Sales	$200,000	$75,000	$125,000
Variable expenses:			
Variable cost of goods sold	60,000	20,000	40,000
Other variable expenses	20,000	5,000	15,000
Total variable expenses	80,000	25,000	55,000
Contribution margin	120,000	50,000	70,000
Traceable fixed expenses	70,000	30,000	40,000
Product-line segment margin	50,000	$20,000	$ 30,000
Common fixed expenses not traceable to individual product lines	11,000		
Divisional segment margin	$ 39,000		

Segments Defined as Sales Channels for One Product Line, Computer Games, of the Consumer Products Division

		Sales Channels	
	Computer Games	Online Sales	Retail Stores
Sales	$125,000	$100,000	$25,000
Variable expenses:			
Variable cost of goods sold	40,000	32,000	8,000
Other variable expenses	15,000	5,000	10,000
Total variable expenses	55,000	37,000	18,000
Contribution margin	70,000	63,000	7,000
Traceable fixed expenses	25,000	15,000	10,000
Sales-channel segment margin	45,000	$ 48,000	$ (3,000)
Common fixed expenses not traceable to individual sales channels	15,000		
Product-line segment margin	$ 30,000		

fixed costs can be seen in this portion of the exhibit. Notice, in the top portion of Exhibit 5–8 when segments are defined as divisions, the Consumer Products Division has $81,000 in traceable fixed expenses. However, when we drill down to the product lines (in the middle portion of the exhibit), only $70,000 of the $81,000 cost that was traceable to the Consumer Products Division is traceable to the product lines. The other $11,000 becomes a common fixed cost of the two product lines of the Consumer Products Division.

Why would $11,000 of traceable fixed costs become a common fixed cost when the division is divided into product lines? The $11,000 is the monthly depreciation expense on a machine that is used to encase products in tamper-proof packages for the consumer market. The depreciation expense is a traceable cost of the Consumer Products Division as a whole, but it is a common cost of the division's two product lines. Even if one of the product lines were discontinued entirely, the machine would still be used to wrap the remaining products. Therefore, none of the depreciation expense can really be traced to individual products. Conversely, the $70,000 traceable fixed cost can be traced to the individual product lines because it consists of the costs of product-specific advertising. A total of $30,000 was spent on advertising clip art and $40,000 was spent on advertising computer programs.

The bottom portion of Exhibit 5–8 further segments the Computer Games product line into two sales channels, Online Sales and Retail Stores. The dual nature of some fixed costs can also be seen in this portion of the exhibit. In the middle portion of Exhibit 5–8 when segments are defined as product lines, the Computer Games product line has $40,000 in traceable fixed expenses. However, when we look at the sales channels in the bottom portion of the exhibit, only $25,000 of the $40,000 that was traceable to Computer Games is traceable to the sales channels. The other $15,000 becomes a common fixed cost of the two sales channels for the Computer Games product line.

Segmented Income Statements—Decision Making and Break-Even Analysis

Once a company prepares contribution format segmented income statements, it can use those statements to make decisions and perform break-even analysis.

Decision Making

Let's refer again to the bottom portion of Exhibit 5–8 to illustrate how segmented income statements support decision making. Notice that the Online Sales segment has a segment margin of $48,000 and the Retail Stores segment has a segment margin of $(3,000). Let's assume that ProphetMax wants to know the profit impact of discontinuing the sale of computer games through its Retail Stores sales channel. The company believes that online sales of its computer games will increase 10% if it discontinues the Retail Stores sales channel. It also believes that the Business Products Division and Clip Art product line will be unaffected by this decision. How would you compute the profit impact of this decision?

The first step is to calculate the profit impact of the Retail Stores sales channel disappearing. If this sales channel disappears, we assume its sales, variable expenses, and traceable fixed expenses would all disappear. The quickest way to summarize these financial impacts is to focus on the Retail Stores' segment margin. In other words, if the Retail Stores sales channel disappears, then its negative segment margin of $3,000 would also disappear. This would increase ProphetMax's net operating income by $3,000. The second step is to calculate the profit impact of increasing online sales of computer games by 10%. To perform this calculation, we assume that the Online Sales total traceable fixed expenses ($15,000) remain constant and its contribution margin ratio remains constant at 63% (= $63,000 ÷ $100,000). If online sales increase $10,000 (= $100,000 × 10%), then the Online Sales segment's contribution margin will increase by $6,300 (= $10,000 × 63%). The overall profit impact of discontinuing the Retail Stores sales channel can be summarized as follows:

Avoidance of the retail segment's loss	$3,000
Online Sales additional contribution margin	6,300
Increase in ProphetMax's net operating income	$9,300

Break–Even Analysis

LEARNING OBJECTIVE 5–5
Compute companywide and segment break-even points for a company with traceable fixed costs.

In Chapter 3, we learned how to compute a companywide break-even point for a multiproduct company with no traceable fixed expenses. Now we are going to use the ProphetMax, Inc., data in Exhibit 5–8 to explain how to compute companywide and segment break-even points for a company with traceable fixed expenses. The formula for computing a companywide break-even point is as follows:

$$\text{Dollar sales for company to break even} = \frac{\text{Traceable fixed expenses} + \text{Common fixed expenses}}{\text{Overall CM ratio}}$$

In the case of ProphetMax, we should begin by reviewing the information in the Total Company column in the top portion of Exhibit 5–8. This column of data indicates that ProphetMax's total traceable fixed expenses are $171,000 and its total common fixed expenses are $85,500. Furthermore, the company's overall contribution margin of $270,000 divided by its total sales of $500,000 equals its overall CM ratio of 0.54. Given this information, ProphetMax's companywide break-even point is computed as follows:

$$\text{Dollar sales for company to break even} = \frac{\text{Traceable fixed expenses} + \text{Common fixed expenses}}{\text{Overall CM ratio}}$$

$$= \frac{\$171{,}000 + \$85{,}500}{0.54}$$

$$= \frac{\$256{,}500}{0.54}$$

$$= \$475{,}000$$

It is important to emphasize that this computation assumes a constant sales mix. In other words, in the ProphetMax example, it assumes that 60% of the total sales ($300,000 ÷ $500,000) will always come from the Business Products Division and 40% of the total sales ($200,000 ÷ $500,000) will always come from the Consumer Products Division.

To compute the break-even point for a business segment, the formula is as follows:

$$\text{Dollar sales for a segment to break even} = \frac{\text{Segment traceable fixed expenses}}{\text{Segment CM ratio}}$$

In the case of ProphetMax's Business Products Division, we should begin by reviewing the information in the Business Products Division column in the top portion of Exhibit 5–8. This column of data indicates that the Business Products Division's traceable fixed expenses are $90,000 and its CM ratio is 0.50 ($150,000 ÷ $300,000). Given this information, the Business Products Division's break-even point is computed as follows:

$$\text{Dollar sales for a segment to break even} = \frac{\text{Segment traceable fixed expenses}}{\text{Segment CM ratio}}$$

$$= \frac{\$90{,}000}{0.50}$$

$$= \$180{,}000$$

The same calculation can be performed for the Consumer Products Division using data from the Consumer Products Division column in the top portion of Exhibit 5–8.

Given that the Consumer Products Division's traceable fixed expenses are $81,000 and its CM ratio is 0.60 ($120,000 ÷ $200,000), its break-even point is computed as follows:

$$\text{Dollar sales for a segment to break even} = \frac{\text{Segment traceable fixed expenses}}{\text{Segment CM ratio}}$$

$$= \frac{\$81{,}000}{0.60}$$

$$= \$135{,}000$$

Notice that the sum of the segment break-even sales figures of $315,000 ($180,000 + $135,000) is less than the companywide break-even point of $475,000. This occurs because the segment break-even calculations *do not include the company's common fixed expenses.* The exclusion of the company's common fixed expenses can be verified by preparing income statements based on each segment's break-even dollar sales as follows:

	Total Company	Business Products Division	Consumer Products Division
Sales	$315,000	$180,000	$135,000
Variable expenses	144,000	90,000	54,000
Contribution margin	171,000	90,000	81,000
Traceable fixed expenses	171,000	90,000	81,000
Segment margin	0	$ 0	$ 0
Common fixed expenses	85,500		
Net operating loss	$ (85,500)		

When each segment achieves its break-even point, the company's overall net operating loss of $85,500 equals its common fixed expenses of $85,500. This reality can often lead managers astray when making decisions. In an attempt to "cover the company's common fixed expenses," managers will often allocate common fixed expenses to business segments when performing break-even calculations and making decisions. *This is a mistake!* Allocating common fixed expenses to business segments artificially inflates each segment's break-even point. This may cause managers to erroneously discontinue business segments where the inflated break-even point appears unobtainable. The decision to retain or discontinue a business segment should be based on the sales and expenses that would disappear if the segment were dropped. Because common fixed expenses *will persist even if a business segment is dropped,* they should not be allocated to business segments when making decisions.

Segmented Income Statements—Common Mistakes

All of the costs attributable to a segment—and only those costs—should be assigned to the segment. Unfortunately, companies often make mistakes when assigning costs to segments. They omit some costs, inappropriately assign traceable fixed costs, and arbitrarily allocate common fixed costs.

Omission of Costs

The costs assigned to a segment should include all costs attributable to that segment from the company's entire value chain. All of these functions, from research and development, through product design, manufacturing, marketing, distribution, and customer service, are required to bring a product or service to the customer and generate revenues.

However, only manufacturing costs are included in product costs under absorption costing, which is widely regarded as required for external financial reporting. To avoid having to maintain two costing systems and to provide consistency between internal and external reports, many companies also use absorption costing for their internal reports such as segmented income statements. As a result, such companies omit from their profitability analysis part or all of the "upstream" costs in the value chain, which consist of research and development and product design, and the "downstream" costs, which consist of marketing, distribution, and customer service. Yet these nonmanufacturing costs are just as essential in determining product profitability as are the manufacturing costs. These upstream and downstream costs, which are usually included in selling and administrative expenses on absorption costing income statements, can represent half or more of the total costs of an organization. If either the upstream or downstream costs are omitted in profitability analysis, then the product is undercosted and management may unwittingly develop and maintain products that in the long run result in losses.

Inappropriate Methods for Assigning Traceable Costs among Segments

In addition to omitting costs, many companies do not correctly handle traceable fixed expenses on segmented income statements. First, they do not trace fixed expenses to segments even when it is feasible to do so. Second, they use inappropriate allocation bases to allocate traceable fixed expenses to segments.

Failure to Trace Costs Directly Costs that can be traced directly to a specific segment should be charged directly to that segment and should not be allocated to other segments. For example, the rent for a branch office of an insurance company should be charged directly to the branch office rather than included in a companywide overhead pool and then spread throughout the company.

Inappropriate Allocation Base Some companies use arbitrary allocation bases to allocate costs to segments. For example, some companies allocate selling and administrative expenses on the basis of sales revenues. Thus, if a segment generates 20% of total company sales, it would be allocated 20% of the company's selling and administrative expenses as its "fair share." This same basic procedure is followed if cost of goods sold or some other measure is used as the allocation base.

Costs should be allocated to segments for internal decision-making purposes only when the allocation base actually drives the cost being allocated (or is very highly correlated with the real cost driver). For example, sales should be used to allocate selling and administrative expenses only if a 10% increase in sales will result in a 10% increase in selling and administrative expenses. To the extent that selling and administrative expenses are not driven by sales volume, these expenses will be improperly allocated—with a disproportionately high percentage of the selling and administrative expenses assigned to the segments with the largest sales.

Arbitrarily Dividing Common Costs among Segments

The third business practice that leads to distorted segment costs is the practice of assigning nontraceable costs to segments. For example, some companies allocate the common costs of the corporate headquarters building to products on segment reports. However, in a multiproduct company, no single product is likely to be responsible for any significant amount of this cost. Even if a product were eliminated entirely, there would usually be no significant effect on any of the costs of the corporate headquarters building. In short, there is no cause-and-effect relation between the cost of the corporate headquarters building and the existence of any one product. As a consequence, any allocation of the cost of the corporate headquarters building to the products must be arbitrary.

Common costs like the costs of the corporate headquarters building are necessary, of course, to have a functioning organization. The practice of arbitrarily allocating common costs to segments is often justified on the grounds that "someone" has to "cover the common costs." While it is undeniably true that a company must cover its common costs to earn a profit, arbitrarily allocating common costs to segments does not ensure that this will happen. In fact, adding a share of common costs to the real costs of a segment may make an otherwise profitable segment appear to be unprofitable. If a manager eliminates the apparently unprofitable segment, the real traceable costs of the segment will be saved, but its revenues will be lost. And what happens to the common fixed costs that were allocated to the segment? They don't disappear; they are reallocated to the remaining segments of the company. That makes all of the remaining segments appear to be less profitable—possibly resulting in dropping other segments. The net effect will be to reduce the overall profits of the company and make it even more difficult to "cover the common costs."

Additionally, common fixed costs are not manageable by the manager to whom they are arbitrarily allocated; they are the responsibility of higher-level managers. When common fixed costs are allocated to managers, they are held responsible for those costs even though they cannot control them.

Income Statements—An External Reporting Perspective

Companywide Income Statements

Practically speaking, absorption costing is required for external reports according to U.S. generally accepted accounting principles (GAAP).[3] Furthermore, International Financial Reporting Standards (IFRS) explicitly require companies to use absorption costing. Probably because of the cost and possible confusion of maintaining two separate costing systems—one for external reporting and one for internal reporting—most companies use absorption costing for their external and internal reports.

With all of the advantages of the contribution approach, you may wonder why the absorption approach is used at all. While the answer is partly due to adhering to tradition, absorption costing is also attractive to many accountants and managers because they believe it better matches costs with revenues. Advocates of absorption costing argue that *all* manufacturing costs must be assigned to products in order to properly match the costs of producing units of product with their revenues when they are sold. The fixed costs of depreciation, taxes, insurance, supervisory salaries, and so on, are just as essential to manufacturing products as are the variable costs.

Advocates of variable costing argue that fixed manufacturing costs are not really the costs of any particular unit of product. These costs are incurred to have the *capacity* to make products during a particular period and will be incurred even if nothing is made during the period. Moreover, whether a unit is made or not, the fixed manufacturing costs will be exactly the same. Therefore, variable costing advocates argue that fixed manufacturing costs are not part of the costs of producing a particular unit of product, and thus, the matching principle dictates that fixed manufacturing costs should be charged to the current period.

---

[3] The Financial Accounting Standards Board (FASB) has created a single source of authoritative nongovernmental U.S. generally accepted accounting principles (GAAP) called the FASB Accounting Standards Codification (FASB codification). Although the FASB codification does not explicitly disallow variable costing, it does explicitly prohibit companies from excluding all manufacturing overhead costs from product costs. It also provides an in-depth discussion of fixed overhead allocation to products, thereby implying that absorption costing is required for external reports. Although some companies expense significant elements of fixed manufacturing costs on their external reports, practically speaking, U.S. GAAP requires absorption costing for external reports.

Segmented Financial Information

U.S. GAAP and IFRS require that publicly traded companies include segmented financial and other data in their annual reports and that the segmented reports prepared for external users *must use the same methods and definitions that the companies use in internal segmented reports that are prepared to aid in making operating decisions.* This is a very unusual stipulation because companies are not ordinarily required to report the same data to external users that are used for internal decision-making purposes. This requirement creates incentives for publicly traded companies to avoid using the contribution format for internal segmented reports. Segmented contribution format income statements contain vital information that companies are often very reluctant to release to the public (and hence competitors). In addition, this requirement creates problems in reconciling internal and external reports.

IN BUSINESS

3M REPORTS SEGMENTED PROFITABILITY TO SHAREHOLDERS

In 2009, 3M Company reported segmented profitability to its shareholders by product lines and geographic areas. A portion of the company's segmented information is summarized below (all numbers are in millions):

	Net Sales	Net Operating Income
Product Lines:		
Industrial and transportation	$7,116	$1,238
Health care	$4,294	$1,350
Consumer and office	$3,471	$748
Safety, security, and protection services	$3,180	$745
Display and graphics	$3,132	$590
Electro and communications	$2,276	$322
Geographic Areas:		
United States	$8,509	$1,640
Asia Pacific	$6,120	$1,528
Europe, Middle East, and Africa	$5,972	$1,003
Latin America and Canada	$2,516	$631

3M's annual report does not report the gross margins or contribution margins for its business segments. Why do you think this is the case?

Source: 3M Company, 2009 Annual Report.

© Duncan Smith/Photodisc/Getty Images, RF

Summary

Variable and absorption costing are alternative methods of determining unit product costs. Under variable costing, only those manufacturing costs that vary with output are treated as product costs. This includes direct materials, variable overhead, and ordinarily direct labor. Fixed manufacturing overhead is treated as a period cost and it is expensed on the income statement as incurred. By contrast, absorption costing treats fixed manufacturing overhead as a product cost, along with direct materials, direct labor, and variable overhead. Under both costing methods, selling and administrative expenses are treated as period costs and they are expensed on the income statement as incurred.

Because absorption costing treats fixed manufacturing overhead as a product cost, a portion of fixed manufacturing overhead is assigned to each unit as it is produced. If units of product are unsold at the end of a period, then the fixed manufacturing overhead cost attached to those units is carried with them into the inventory account and deferred to a future period. When these units are later sold, the fixed manufacturing overhead cost attached to them is released from the inventory account and charged against income as part of cost of goods sold. Thus, under absorption costing, it is possible to defer a portion of the fixed manufacturing overhead cost from one period to a future period through the inventory account.

Unfortunately, this shifting of fixed manufacturing overhead cost between periods can cause erratic fluctuations in net operating income and can result in confusion and unwise decisions. To guard against mistakes when they interpret income statement data, managers should be alert to changes in inventory levels or unit product costs during the period.

Segmented income statements provide information for evaluating the profitability and performance of divisions, product lines, sales territories, and other segments of a company. Under the contribution approach, variable costs and fixed costs are clearly distinguished from each other and only those costs that are traceable to a segment are assigned to the segment. A cost is considered traceable to a segment only if the cost is caused by the segment and could be avoided by eliminating the segment. Fixed common costs are not allocated to segments. The segment margin consists of revenues, less variable expenses, less traceable fixed expenses of the segment.

The dollar sales required for a segment to break even is computed by dividing the segment's traceable fixed expenses by its contribution margin ratio. A company's common fixed expenses should not be allocated to segments when performing break-even calculations because they will not change in response to segment-level decisions.

Review Problem 1: Contrasting Variable and Absorption Costing

Dexter Corporation produces and sells a single product, a wooden hand loom for weaving small items such as scarves. Selected cost and operating data relating to the product for two years are given below:

Selling price per unit	$50
Manufacturing costs:	
Variable per unit produced:	
Direct materials	$11
Direct labor	$6
Variable manufacturing overhead	$3
Fixed manufacturing overhead per year	$120,000
Selling and administrative expenses:	
Variable per unit sold	$4
Fixed per year	$70,000

	Year 1	Year 2
Units in beginning inventory	0	2,000
Units produced during the year	10,000	6,000
Units sold during the year	8,000	8,000
Units in ending inventory	2,000	0

Required:

1. Assume the company uses absorption costing.
   a. Compute the unit product cost in each year.
   b. Prepare an income statement for each year.
2. Assume the company uses variable costing.
   a. Compute the unit product cost in each year.
   b. Prepare an income statement for each year.
3. Reconcile the variable costing and absorption costing net operating incomes.

Solution to Review Problem 1

1. *a.* Under absorption costing, all manufacturing costs, variable and fixed, are included in unit product costs:

	Year 1	Year 2
Direct materials	$11	$11
Direct labor	6	6
Variable manufacturing overhead	3	3
Fixed manufacturing overhead		
($120,000 ÷ 10,000 units)	12	
($120,000 ÷ 6,000 units)		20
Absorption costing unit product cost	$32	$40

b. The absorption costing income statements follow:

	Year 1	Year 2
Sales (8,000 units × $50 per unit)	$400,000	$400,000
Cost of goods sold (8,000 units × $32 per unit); (2,000 units × $32 per unit) + (6,000 units × $40 per unit)	256,000	304,000
Gross margin	144,000	96,000
Selling and administrative expenses (8,000 units × $4 per unit + $70,000)	102,000	102,000
Net operating income (loss)	$ 42,000	$ (6,000)

2. *a.* Under variable costing, only the variable manufacturing costs are included in unit product costs:

	Year 1	Year 2
Direct materials	$11	$11
Direct labor	6	6
Variable manufacturing overhead	3	3
Variable costing unit product cost	$20	$20

b. The variable costing income statements follow:

	Year 1		Year 2	
Sales (8,000 units × $50 per unit)		$400,000		$400,000
Variable expenses:				
Variable cost of goods sold (8,000 units × $20 per unit)	$160,000		$160,000	
Variable selling and administrative expenses (8,000 units × $4 per unit)	32,000	192,000	32,000	192,000
Contribution margin		208,000		208,000
Fixed expenses:				
Fixed manufacturing overhead	120,000		120,000	
Fixed selling and administrative expenses	70,000	190,000	70,000	190,000
Net operating income		$ 18,000		$ 18,000

3. The reconciliation of the variable and absorption costing net operating incomes follows:

	Year 1	Year 2
Fixed manufacturing overhead in ending inventories	$24,000	$ 0
Fixed manufacturing overhead in beginning inventories.....	0	24,000
Fixed manufacturing overhead deferred in (released from) inventories	$24,000	$(24,000)

	Year 1	Year 2
Variable costing net operating income.....................	$18,000	$18,000
Add fixed manufacturing overhead costs deferred in inventory under absorption costing (2,000 units × $12 per unit)...........................	24,000	
Deduct fixed manufacturing overhead costs released from inventory under absorption costing (2,000 units × $12 per unit)...........................		(24,000)
Absorption costing net operating income (loss)..............	$42,000	$ (6,000)

Review Problem 2: Segmented Income Statements

The business staff of the law firm Frampton, Davis & Smythe has constructed the following report that breaks down the firm's overall results for last month into two business segments—family law and commercial law:

	Company Total	Family Law	Commercial Law
Revenues from clients..........	$1,000,000	$400,000	$600,000
Variable expenses	220,000	100,000	120,000
Contribution margin............	780,000	300,000	480,000
Traceable fixed expenses	670,000	280,000	390,000
Segment margin................	110,000	20,000	90,000
Common fixed expenses.........	60,000	24,000	36,000
Net operating income (loss)	$ 50,000	$ (4,000)	$ 54,000

However, this report is not quite correct. The common fixed expenses such as the managing partner's salary, general administrative expenses, and general firm advertising have been allocated to the two segments based on revenues from clients.

Required:

1. Redo the segment report, eliminating the allocation of common fixed expenses. Would the firm be better off financially if the family law segment were dropped? (***Note:*** Many of the firm's commercial law clients also use the firm for their family law requirements such as drawing up wills.)
2. The firm's advertising agency has proposed an ad campaign targeted at boosting the revenues of the family law segment. The ad campaign would cost $20,000, and the advertising agency claims that it would increase family law revenues by $100,000. The managing partner of Frampton, Davis & Smythe believes this increase in business could be accommodated without any increase in fixed expenses. Estimate the effect this ad campaign would have on the family law segment margin and on the firm's overall net operating income.

3. Compute the companywide break-even point in dollar sales and the dollar sales required for each business segment to break even.

Solution to Review Problem 2

1. The corrected segmented income statement appears below:

	Company Total	Family Law	Commercial Law
Revenues from clients	$1,000,000	$400,000	$600,000
Variable expenses	220,000	100,000	120,000
Contribution margin	780,000	300,000	480,000
Traceable fixed expenses	670,000	280,000	390,000
Segment margin	110,000	$ 20,000	$ 90,000
Common fixed expenses	60,000		
Net operating income	$ 50,000		

No, the firm would not be financially better off if the family law practice were dropped. The family law segment is covering all of its own costs and is contributing $20,000 per month to covering the common fixed expenses of the firm. While the segment margin for family law is much lower than for commercial law, it is still profitable. Moreover, family law may be a service that the firm must provide to its commercial clients in order to remain competitive.

2. The ad campaign would increase the family law segment margin by $55,000 as follows:

Increased revenues from clients	$100,000
Family law contribution margin ratio ($300,000 ÷ $400,000)	× 75%
Incremental contribution margin	$ 75,000
Less cost of the ad campaign	20,000
Increased segment margin	$ 55,000

Because there would be no increase in fixed expenses (including common fixed expenses), the increase in overall net operating income is also $55,000.

3. The companywide break-even point is computed as follows:

$$\text{Dollar sales for company to break even} = \frac{\text{Traceable fixed expenses} + \text{Common fixed expenses}}{\text{Overall CM ratio}}$$

$$= \frac{\$670{,}000 + \$60{,}000}{0.78}$$

$$= \frac{\$730{,}000}{0.78}$$

$$= \$935{,}897 \text{ (rounded)}$$

The break-even point for the family law segment is computed as follows:

$$\text{Dollar sales for a segment to break even} = \frac{\text{Segment traceable fixed expenses}}{\text{Segment CM ratio}}$$

$$= \frac{\$280{,}000}{0.75}$$

$$= \$373{,}333 \text{ (rounded)}$$

The break-even point for the commercial law segment is computed as follows:

$$\text{Dollar sales for a segment to break even} = \frac{\text{Segment traceable fixed expenses}}{\text{Segment CM ratio}}$$

$$= \frac{\$390{,}000}{0.80}$$

$$= \$487{,}500$$

Glossary

Absorption costing A costing method that includes all manufacturing costs—direct materials, direct labor, and both variable and fixed manufacturing overhead—in unit product costs. (p. 171)

Common fixed cost A fixed cost that supports more than one business segment, but is not traceable in whole or in part to any one of the business segments. (p. 181)

Segment Any part or activity of an organization about which managers seek cost, revenue, or profit data. (p. 171)

Segment margin A segment's contribution margin less its traceable fixed costs. It represents the margin available after a segment has covered all of its own traceable costs. (p. 181)

Traceable fixed cost A fixed cost that is incurred because of the existence of a particular business segment and that would be eliminated if the segment were eliminated. (p. 181)

Variable costing A costing method that includes only variable manufacturing costs—direct materials, direct labor, and variable manufacturing overhead—in unit product costs. (p. 171)

Questions

5–1 What is the basic difference between absorption costing and variable costing?

5–2 Are selling and administrative expenses treated as product costs or as period costs under variable costing?

5–3 Explain how fixed manufacturing overhead costs are shifted from one period to another under absorption costing.

5–4 What are the arguments in favor of treating fixed manufacturing overhead costs as product costs?

5–5 What are the arguments in favor of treating fixed manufacturing overhead costs as period costs?

5–6 If the units produced and unit sales are equal, which method would you expect to show the higher net operating income, variable costing or absorption costing? Why?

5–7 If the units produced exceed unit sales, which method would you expect to show the higher net operating income, variable costing or absorption costing? Why?

5–8 If fixed manufacturing overhead costs are released from inventory under absorption costing, what does this tell you about the level of production in relation to the level of sales?

5–9 Under absorption costing, how is it possible to increase net operating income without increasing sales?

5–10 How does Lean Production reduce or eliminate the difference in reported net operating income between absorption and variable costing?

5–11 What is a segment of an organization? Give several examples of segments.

5–12 What costs are assigned to a segment under the contribution approach?

5–13 Distinguish between a traceable cost and a common cost. Give several examples of each.

5–14 Explain how the segment margin differs from the contribution margin.

5–15 Why aren't common costs allocated to segments under the contribution approach?

5–16 How is it possible for a cost that is traceable to a segment to become a common cost if the segment is divided into further segments?

5–17 Should a company allocate its common fixed expenses to business segments when computing the break-even point for those segments? Why?

Multiple-choice questions are provided in Connect.

Applying Excel

connect

Additional student resources are available with Connect.

LEARNING OBJECTIVE 5–2

The Excel worksheet form that follows is to be used to recreate portions of Review Problem 1. Download the workbook containing this form from Connect. *On the website you will also receive instructions about how to use this worksheet form.*

	A	B	C	D	E	F
1	Chapter 5: Applying Excel					
2						
3	**Data**					
4	Selling price per unit	$50				
5	Manufacturing costs:					
6	Variable per unit produced:					
7	Direct materials	$11				
8	Direct labor	$6				
9	Variable manufacturing overhead	$3				
10	Fixed manufacturing overhead per year	$120,000				
11	Selling and administrative expenses:					
12	Variable per unit sold	$4				
13	Fixed per year	$70,000				
14						
15		Year 1	Year 2			
16	Units in beginning inventory	0				
17	Units produced during the year	10,000	6,000			
18	Units sold during the year	8,000	8,000			
19						
20	*Enter a formula into each of the cells marked with a ? below*					
21	**Review Problem 1: Contrasting Variable and Absorption Costing**					
22						
23	***Compute the Ending Inventory***					
24		Year 1	Year 2			
25	Units in beginning inventory	0	?			
26	Units produced during the year	?	?			
27	Units sold during the year	?	?			
28	Units in ending inventory	?	?			
29						
30	***Compute the Absorption Costing Unit Product Cost***					
31		Year 1	Year 2			
32	Direct materials	?	?			
33	Direct labor	?	?			
34	Variable manufacturing overhead	?	?			
35	Fixed manufacturing overhead	?	?			
36	Absorption costing unit product cost	?	?			
37						
38	***Construct the Absorption Costing Income Statement***					
39		Year 1	Year 2			
40	Sales	?	?			
41	Cost of goods sold	?	?			
42	Gross margin	?	?			
43	Selling and administrative expenses	?	?			
44	Net operating income	?	?			
45						
46	***Compute the Variable Costing Unit Product Cost***					
47		Year 1	Year 2			
48	Direct materials	?	?			
49	Direct labor	?	?			
50	Variable manufacturing overhead	?	?			
51	Variable costing unit product cost	?	?			
52						
53	***Construct the Variable Costing Income Statement***					
54		Year 1		Year 2		
55	Sales		?		?	
56	Variable expenses:					
57	Variable cost of goods sold	?		?		
58	Variable selling and administrative expenses	?	?	?	?	
59	Contribution margin		?		?	
60	Fixed expenses:					
61	Fixed manufacturing overhead	?		?		
62	Fixed selling and administrative expenses	?	?	?	?	
63	Net operating income		?		?	
64						

Chapter 5 Form / Filled in Chapter 5 Form / Chapter 5

You should proceed to the requirements below only after completing your worksheet. The LIFO inventory flow assumption is used throughout this problem.

Required:

1. Check your worksheet by changing the units sold in the Data to 6,000 for Year 2. The cost of goods sold under absorption costing for Year 2 should now be $240,000. If it isn't, check cell C41. The formula in this cell should be =IF(C26 < C27,C26*C36+(C27-C26)*B36,C27*C36). If your worksheet is operating properly, the net operating income under both absorption costing and variable costing should be $(34,000) for Year 2. That is, the loss in Year 2 is $34,000 under both systems. If you do not get these answers, find the errors in your worksheet and correct them.

   Why is the absorption costing net operating income now equal to the variable costing net operating income in Year 2?

2. Enter the following data from a different company into your worksheet:

Data		
Selling price per unit	$75	
Manufacturing costs:		
Variable per unit produced:		
Direct materials	$12	
Direct labor	$5	
Variable manufacturing overhead	$7	
Fixed manufacturing overhead per year	$150,000	
Selling and administrative expenses:		
Variable per unit sold	$1	
Fixed per year	$60,000	
	Year 1	Year 2
Units in beginning inventory	0	
Units produced during the year	15,000	10,000
Units sold during the year	12,000	12,000

Is the net operating income under variable costing different in Year 1 and Year 2? Why or why not? Explain the relation between the net operating income under absorption costing and variable costing in Year 1. Explain the relation between the net operating income under absorption costing and variable costing in Year 2.

3. At the end of Year 1, the company's board of directors set a target for Year 2 of net operating income of $500,000 under absorption costing. If this target is met, a hefty bonus would be paid to the CEO of the company. Keeping everything else the same from requirement 2, change the units produced in Year 2 to 50,000 units. Would this change result in a bonus being paid to the CEO? Do you think this change would be in the best interests of the company? What is likely to happen in Year 3 to the absorption costing net operating income if sales remain constant at 12,000 units per year?

The Foundational 15

connect **Additional student resources are available with Connect.**

LEARNING OBJECTIVE 5–1, 5–2, 5–3, 5–4

Diego Company manufactures one product that is sold for $80 per unit in two geographic regions—the East and West regions. The following information pertains to the company's first year of operations in which it produced 40,000 units and sold 35,000 units.

Variable costs per unit:	
Manufacturing:	
Direct materials	$24
Direct labor	$14
Variable manufacturing overhead	$2
Variable selling and administrative	$4
Fixed costs per year:	
Fixed manufacturing overhead	$800,000
Fixed selling and administrative expenses	$496,000

The company sold 25,000 units in the East region and 10,000 units in the West region. It determined that $250,000 of its fixed selling and administrative expenses is traceable to the West region, $150,000 is traceable to the East region, and the remaining $96,000 is a common fixed cost. The company will continue to incur the total amount of its fixed manufacturing overhead costs as long as it continues to produce any amount of its only product.

Required:

Answer each question independently based on the original data unless instructed otherwise. You do not need to prepare a segmented income statement until requirement 13.

1. What is the unit product cost under variable costing?
2. What is the unit product cost under absorption costing?
3. What is the company's total contribution margin under variable costing?
4. What is the company's net operating income under variable costing?
5. What is the company's total gross margin under absorption costing?
6. What is the company's net operating income under absorption costing?
7. What is the amount of the difference between the variable costing and absorption costing net operating incomes? What is the cause of this difference?
8. What is the company's break-even point in unit sales? Is it above or below the actual sales volume? Compare the break-even sales volume to your answer for requirement 6 and comment.
9. If the sales volumes in the East and West regions had been reversed, what would be the company's overall break-even point in unit sales?
10. What would have been the company's variable costing net operating income if it had produced and sold 35,000 units? You do not need to perform any calculations to answer this requirement.
11. What would have been the company's absorption costing net operating income if it had produced and sold 35,000 units? You do not need to perform any calculations to answer this requirement.
12. If the company produces 5,000 fewer units than it sells in its second year of operations, will absorption costing net operating income be higher or lower than variable costing net operating income in Year 2? Why? No calculations are necessary.
13. Prepare a contribution format segmented income statement that includes a Total column and columns for the East and West regions.
14. Diego is considering eliminating the West region because an internally generated report suggests the region's total *gross margin* in the first year of operations was $50,000 less than its traceable fixed selling and administrative expenses. Diego believes that if it drops the West region, the East region's sales will grow by 5% in Year 2. Using the contribution approach for analyzing segment profitability and assuming all else remains constant in Year 2, what would be the profit impact of dropping the West region in Year 2?
15. Assume the West region invests $30,000 in a new advertising campaign in Year 2 that increases its unit sales by 20%. If all else remains constant, what would be the profit impact of pursuing the advertising campaign?

Exercises

EXERCISE 5–1 Variable and Absorption Costing Unit Product Costs [LO 5–1]

Ida Sidha Karya Company is a family-owned company located in the village of Gianyar on the island of Bali in Indonesia. The company produces a handcrafted Balinese musical instrument called a gamelan that is similar to a xylophone. The gamelans are sold for $850. Selected data for the company's operations last year follow:

Units in beginning inventory	0
Units produced	250
Units sold	225
Units in ending inventory	25
Variable costs per unit:	
Direct materials	$100
Direct labor	$320
Variable manufacturing overhead	$40
Variable selling and administrative	$20
Fixed costs:	
Fixed manufacturing overhead	$60,000
Fixed selling and administrative	$20,000

Required:

1. Assume that the company uses absorption costing. Compute the unit product cost for one gamelan.
2. Assume that the company uses variable costing. Compute the unit product cost for one gamelan.

EXERCISE 5–2 Variable Costing Income Statement; Explanation of Difference in Net Operating Income [LO 5–2]

Refer to the data in Exercise 5–1 for Ida Sidha Karya Company. The absorption costing income statement prepared by the company's accountant for last year appears below:

Sales	$191,250
Cost of goods sold	157,500
Gross margin	33,750
Selling and administrative expense	24,500
Net operating income	$ 9,250

Required:

1. Determine how much of the ending inventory consists of fixed manufacturing overhead cost deferred in inventory to the next period.
2. Prepare an income statement for the year using variable costing. Explain the difference in net operating income between the two costing methods.

EXERCISE 5–3 Reconciliation of Absorption and Variable Costing Net Operating Incomes [LO 5–3]

Jorgansen Lighting, Inc., manufactures heavy-duty street lighting systems for municipalities. The company uses variable costing for internal management reports and absorption costing for external reports to shareholders, creditors, and the government. The company has provided the following data:

	Year 1	Year 2	Year 3
Inventories:			
Beginning (units)	200	170	180
Ending (units)	170	180	220
Variable costing net operating income	$1,080,400	$1,032,400	$996,400

The company's fixed manufacturing overhead per unit was constant at $560 for all three years.

Required:

1. Determine each year's absorption costing net operating income. Present your answer in the form of a reconciliation report.
2. In Year 4, the company's variable costing net operating income was $984,400 and its absorption costing net operating income was $1,012,400. Did inventories increase or decrease during Year 4? How much fixed manufacturing overhead cost was deferred or released from inventory during Year 4?

EXERCISE 5–4 Basic Segmented Income Statement [LO 5–4]

Royal Lawncare Company produces and sells two packaged products, Weedban and Greengrow. Revenue and cost information relating to the products follow:

	Product	
	Weedban	Greengrow
Selling price per unit	$6.00	$7.50
Variable expenses per unit	$2.40	$5.25
Traceable fixed expenses per year	$45,000	$21,000

Common fixed expenses in the company total $33,000 annually. Last year the company produced and sold 15,000 units of Weedban and 28,000 units of Greengrow.

Required:

Prepare a contribution format income statement segmented by product lines.

EXERCISE 5–5 Companywide and Segment Break-Even Analysis [LO 5–5]

Piedmont Company segments its business into two regions—North and South. The company prepared the contribution format segmented income statement shown below:

	Total Company	North	South
Sales	$600,000	$400,000	$200,000
Variable expenses	360,000	280,000	80,000
Contribution margin	240,000	120,000	120,000
Traceable fixed expenses	120,000	60,000	60,000
Segment margin	120,000	$ 60,000	$ 60,000
Common fixed expenses	50,000		
Net operating income	$ 70,000		

Required:

1. Compute the companywide break-even point in dollar sales.
2. Compute the break-even point in dollar sales for the North region.
3. Compute the break-even point in dollar sales for the South region.

EXERCISE 5–6 Variable and Absorption Costing Unit Product Costs and Income Statements [LO 5–1, LO 5–2]

Lynch Company manufactures and sells a single product. The following costs were incurred during the company's first year of operations:

Variable costs per unit:	
Manufacturing:	
Direct materials	$6
Direct labor	$9
Variable manufacturing overhead	$3
Variable selling and administrative	$4
Fixed costs per year:	
Fixed manufacturing overhead	$300,000
Fixed selling and administrative	$190,000

During the year, the company produced 25,000 units and sold 20,000 units. The selling price of the company's product is $50 per unit.

Required:

1. Assume that the company uses absorption costing:
   a. Compute the unit product cost.
   b. Prepare an income statement for the year.
2. Assume that the company uses variable costing:
   a. Compute the unit product cost.
   b. Prepare an income statement for the year.

EXERCISE 5–7 Segmented Income Statement [LO 5–4]

Shannon Company segments its income statement into its North and South Divisions. The company's overall sales, contribution margin ratio, and net operating income are $500,000, 46%, and $10,000, respectively. The North Division's contribution margin and contribution margin ratio are $150,000 and 50%, respectively. The South Division's segment margin is $30,000. The company has $90,000 of common fixed expenses that cannot be traced to either division.

Required:

Prepare an income statement for Shannon Company that uses the contribution format and is segmented by divisions. In addition, for the company as a whole and for each segment, show each item on the segmented income statements as a percent of sales.

EXERCISE 5–8 Deducing Changes in Inventories [LO 5–3]

Parker Products Inc, a manufacturer, reported $123 million in sales and a loss of $18 million in its annual report to shareholders. According to a CVP analysis prepared for management, the company's break-even point is $115 million in sales.

Required:

Assuming that the CVP analysis is correct, is it likely that the company's inventory level increased, decreased, or remained unchanged during the year? Explain.

EXERCISE 5–9 Variable and Absorption Costing Unit Product Costs and Income Statements [LO 5–1, LO 5–2, LO 5–3]

Walsh Company manufactures and sells one product. The following information pertains to each of the company's first two years of operations:

Variable costs per unit:	
Manufacturing:	
Direct materials	$25
Direct labor	$15
Variable manufacturing overhead	$5
Variable selling and administrative	$2
Fixed costs per year:	
Fixed manufacturing overhead	$250,000
Fixed selling and administrative expenses	$80,000

During its first year of operations, Walsh produced 50,000 units and sold 40,000 units. During its second year of operations, it produced 40,000 units and sold 50,000 units. The selling price of the company's product is $60 per unit.

Required:

1. Assume the company uses variable costing:
   a. Compute the unit product cost for Year 1 and Year 2.
   b. Prepare an income statement for Year 1 and Year 2.
2. Assume the company uses absorption costing:
   a. Compute the unit product cost for Year 1 and Year 2.
   b. Prepare an income statement for Year 1 and Year 2.
3. Explain the difference between variable costing and absorption costing net operating income in Year 1. Also, explain why the two net operating income figures differ in Year 2.

EXERCISE 5–10 Companywide and Segment Break-Even Analysis [LO 5–5]

Crossfire Company segments its business into two regions—East and West. The company prepared the contribution format segmented income statement shown below:

	Total Company	East	West
Sales	$900,000	$600,000	$300,000
Variable expenses	675,000	480,000	195,000
Contribution margin	225,000	120,000	105,000
Traceable fixed expenses	141,000	50,000	91,000
Segment margin	84,000	$ 70,000	$ 14,000
Common fixed expenses	59,000		
Net operating income	$ 25,000		

Required:

1. Compute the companywide break-even point dollar in sales.
2. Compute the break-even point in dollar sales for the East region.
3. Compute the break-even point in dollar sales for the West region.
4. Prepare a new segmented income statement based on the break-even dollar sales that you computed in requirements 2 and 3. Use the same format as shown above. What is Crossfire's net operating income in your new segmented income statement?
5. Do you think that Crossfire should allocate its common fixed expenses to the East and West regions when computing the break-even points for each region? Why?

EXERCISE 5–11 Segmented Income Statement [LO 5–4]

Wingate Company, a wholesale distributor of electronic equipment, has been experiencing losses for some time, as shown by its most recent monthly contribution format income statement, which follows:

Sales	$1,000,000
Variable expenses	390,000
Contribution margin	610,000
Fixed expenses	625,000
Net operating income (loss)	$ (15,000)

In an effort to isolate the problem, the president has asked for an income statement segmented by division. Accordingly, the Accounting Department has developed the following information:

	Division		
	East	Central	West
Sales	$250,000	$400,000	$350,000
Variable expenses as a percentage of sales	52%	30%	40%
Traceable fixed expenses	$160,000	$200,000	$175,000

Required:

1. Prepare a contribution format income statement segmented by divisions, as desired by the president.
2. As a result of a marketing study, the president believes that sales in the West Division could be increased by 20% if monthly advertising in that division were increased by $15,000. Would you recommend the increased advertising? Show computations to support your answer.

EXERCISE 5–12 Variable Costing Income Statement; Reconciliation [LO 5–2, LO 5–3]

Whitman Company has just completed its first year of operations. The company's absorption costing income statement for the year appears below:

Whitman Company Income Statement	
Sales (35,000 units × $25 per unit)	$875,000
Cost of goods sold (35,000 units × $16 per unit)	560,000
Gross margin	315,000
Selling and administrative expenses	280,000
Net operating income	$ 35,000

The company's selling and administrative expenses consist of $210,000 per year in fixed expenses and $2 per unit sold in variable expenses. The $16 per unit product cost given above is computed as follows:

Direct materials	$5
Direct labor	6
Variable manufacturing overhead	1
Fixed manufacturing overhead ($160,000 ÷ 40,000 units)	4
Absorption costing unit product cost	$16

Required:

1. Redo the company's income statement in the contribution format using variable costing.
2. Reconcile any difference between the net operating income on your variable costing income statement and the net operating income on the absorption costing income statement above.

EXERCISE 5–13 Inferring Costing Method; Unit Product Cost [LO 5–1]

Sierra Company incurs the following costs to produce and sell a single product.

Variable costs per unit:	
Direct materials	$9
Direct labor	$10
Variable manufacturing overhead	$5
Variable selling and administrative expenses	$3
Fixed costs per year:	
Fixed manufacturing overhead	$150,000
Fixed selling and administrative expenses	$400,000

During the last year, 25,000 units were produced and 22,000 units were sold. The Finished Goods inventory account at the end of the year shows a balance of $72,000 for the 3,000 unsold units.

Required:

1. Is the company using absorption costing or variable costing to cost units in the Finished Goods inventory account? Show computations to support your answer.
2. Assume that the company wishes to prepare financial statements for the year to issue to its stockholders.
   a. Is the $72,000 figure for Finished Goods inventory the correct amount to use on these statements for external reporting purposes? Explain.
   b. At what dollar amount *should* the 3,000 units be carried in the inventory for external reporting purposes?

EXERCISE 5–14 Variable Costing Unit Product Cost and Income Statement; Break-Even [LO 5–1, LO 5–2]

Chuck Wagon Grills, Inc., makes a single product—a handmade specialty barbecue grill that it sells for $210. Data for last year's operations follow:

Units in beginning inventory	0
Units produced	20,000
Units sold	19,000
Units in ending inventory	1,000
Variable costs per unit:	
Direct materials	$ 50
Direct labor	80
Variable manufacturing overhead	20
Variable selling and administrative	10
Total variable cost per unit	$160
Fixed costs:	
Fixed manufacturing overhead	$700,000
Fixed selling and administrative	285,000
Total fixed costs	$985,000

Required:

1. Assume that the company uses variable costing. Compute the unit product cost for one barbecue grill.
2. Assume that the company uses variable costing. Prepare a contribution format income statement for the year.
3. What is the company's break-even point in terms of the number of barbecue grills sold?

EXERCISE 5–15 Absorption Costing Unit Product Cost and Income Statement [LO 5–1, LO 5–2]

Refer to the data in Exercise 5–14 for Chuck Wagon Grills. Assume in this exercise that the company uses absorption costing.

Required:

1. Compute the unit product cost for one barbecue grill.
2. Prepare an income statement.

EXERCISE 5–16 Working with a Segmented Income Statement; Break-Even Analysis [LO 5–4, LO 5–5]

Raner, Harris, & Chan is a consulting firm that specializes in information systems for medical and dental clinics. The firm has two offices—one in Chicago and one in Minneapolis. The firm classifies the direct costs of consulting jobs as variable costs. A contribution format segmented income statement for the company's most recent year is given below:

	Total Company		Office: Chicago		Office: Minneapolis	
Sales	$450,000	100%	$150,000	100%	$300,000	100%
Variable expenses	225,000	50%	45,000	30	180,000	60
Contribution margin	225,000	50%	105,000	70	120,000	40
Traceable fixed expenses	126,000	28%	78,000	52	48,000	16
Office segment margin	99,000	22%	$ 27,000	18%	$ 72,000	24%
Common fixed expenses not traceable to offices	63,000	14%				
Net operating income	$ 36,000	8%				

Required:

1. Compute the companywide break-even point in dollar sales. Also, compute the break-even point for the Chicago office and for the Minneapolis office. Is the companywide break-even point greater than, less than, or equal to the sum of the Chicago and Minneapolis break-even points? Why?
2. By how much would the company's net operating income increase if Minneapolis increased its sales by $75,000 per year? Assume no change in cost behavior patterns.
3. Refer to the original data. Assume that sales in Chicago increase by $50,000 next year and that sales in Minneapolis remain unchanged. Assume no change in fixed costs.
   a. Prepare a new segmented income statement for the company using the above format. Show both amounts and percentages.
   b. Observe from the income statement you have prepared that the contribution margin ratio for Chicago has remained unchanged at 70% (the same as in the above data) but that the segment margin ratio has changed. How do you explain the change in the segment margin ratio?

EXERCISE 5–17 Working with a Segmented Income Statement [LO 5–4]

Refer to the data in Exercise 5–16. Assume that Minneapolis' sales by major market are:

The company would like to initiate an intensive advertising campaign in one of the two market segments during the next month. The campaign would cost $5,000. Marketing studies indicate that such a campaign would increase sales in the Medical market by $40,000 or increase sales in the Dental market by $35,000.

	Minneapolis		Market: Medical		Market: Dental	
Sales	$300,000	100%	$200,000	100%	$100,000	100%
Variable expenses	180,000	60%	128,000	64%	52,000	52%
Contribution margin	120,000	40%	72,000	36%	48,000	48%
Traceable fixed expenses	33,000	11%	12,000	6%	21,000	21%
Market segment margin	87,000	29%	$ 60,000	30%	$ 27,000	27%
Common fixed expenses not traceable to markets	15,000	5%				
Office segment margin	$ 72,000	24%				

Required:

1. In which of the markets would you recommend that the company focus its advertising campaign? Show computations to support your answer.
2. In Exercise 5–16, Minneapolis shows $48,000 in traceable fixed expenses. What happened to the $48,000 in this exercise?

Problems

connect Additional student resources are available with Connect.

PROBLEM 5–18 Variable and Absorption Costing Unit Product Costs and Income Statements [LO 5–1, LO 5–2]

Haas Company manufactures and sells one product. The following information pertains to each of the company's first three years of operations:

Variable costs per unit:	
Manufacturing:	
Direct materials	$20
Direct labor	$12
Variable manufacturing overhead	$4
Variable selling and administrative	$2
Fixed costs per year:	
Fixed manufacturing overhead	$960,000
Fixed selling and administrative expenses	$240,000

During its first year of operations, Haas produced 60,000 units and sold 60,000 units. During its second year of operations, it produced 75,000 units and sold 50,000 units. In its third year, Haas produced 40,000 units and sold 65,000 units. The selling price of the company's product is $58 per unit.

Required:

1. Compute the company's break-even point in units sold.
2. Assume the company uses variable costing:
   a. Compute the unit product cost for Year 1, Year 2, and Year 3.
   b. Prepare an income statement for Year 1, Year 2, and Year 3.
3. Assume the company uses absorption costing:
   a. Compute the unit product cost for Year 1, Year 2, and Year 3.
   b. Prepare an income statement for Year 1, Year 2, and Year 3.
4. Compare the net operating income figures that you computed in requirements 2 and 3 to the break-even point that you computed in requirement 1. Which net operating income figures seem counterintuitive? Why?

PROBLEM 5–19 Variable Costing Income Statement; Reconciliation [LO 5–2, LO 5–3]

During Heaton Company's first two years of operations, the company reported absorption costing net operating income as follows:

	Year 1	Year 2
Sales (@ $25 per unit)	$1,000,000	$1,250,000
Cost of goods sold (@ $18 per unit)	720,000	900,000
Gross margin	280,000	350,000
Selling and administrative expenses*	210,000	230,000
Net operating income	$ 70,000	$ 120,000

*$2 per unit variable; $130,000 fixed each year.

The company's $18 unit product cost is computed as follows:

Direct materials	$ 4
Direct labor	7
Variable manufacturing overhead	1
Fixed manufacturing overhead ($270,000 ÷ 45,000 units)	6
Absorption costing unit product cost	$18

Forty percent of fixed manufacturing overhead consists of wages and salaries; the remainder consists of depreciation charges on production equipment and buildings.

Production and cost data for the two years are:

	Year 1	Year 2
Units produced	45,000	45,000
Units sold	40,000	50,000

Required:

1. Prepare a variable costing contribution format income statement for each year.
2. Reconcile the absorption costing and the variable costing net operating income figures for each year.

PROBLEM 5–20 Variable and Absorption Costing Unit Product Costs and Income Statements; Explanation of Difference in Net Operating Income [LO 5–1, LO 5–2, LO 5–3]

High Country, Inc., produces and sells many recreational products. The company has just opened a new plant to produce a folding camp cot that will be marketed throughout the United States. The following cost and revenue data relate to May, the first month of the plant's operation:

Beginning inventory	0
Units produced	10,000
Units sold	8,000
Selling price per unit	$75
Selling and administrative expenses:	
Variable per unit	$6
Fixed (per month)	$200,000
Manufacturing costs:	
Direct materials cost per unit	$20
Direct labor cost per unit	$8
Variable manufacturing overhead cost per unit	$2
Fixed manufacturing overhead cost (per month)	$100,000

Management is anxious to see how profitable the new camp cot will be and has asked that an income statement be prepared for May.

Required:

1. Assume that the company uses absorption costing.
   a. Determine the unit product cost.
   b. Prepare an income statement for May.

2. Assume that the company uses variable costing.
   a. Determine the unit product cost.
   b. Prepare a contribution format income statement for May.
3. Explain the reason for any difference in the ending inventory balances under the two costing methods and the impact of this difference on reported net operating income.

PROBLEM 5–21 Segment Reporting and Decision-Making [LO 5–4]

Vulcan Company's contribution format income statement for June is given below:

Vulcan Company Income Statement For the Month Ended June 30	
Sales	$750,000
Variable expenses	336,000
Contribution margin	414,000
Fixed expenses	378,000
Net operating income	$ 36,000

Management is disappointed with the company's performance and is wondering what can be done to improve profits. By examining sales and cost records, you have determined the following:

a. The company is divided into two sales territories—Northern and Southern. The Northern territory recorded $300,000 in sales and $156,000 in variable expenses during June; the remaining sales and variable expenses were recorded in the Southern territory. Fixed expenses of $120,000 and $108,000 are traceable to the Northern and Southern territories, respectively. The rest of the fixed expenses are common to the two territories.

b. The company is the exclusive distributor for two products—Paks and Tibs. Sales of Paks and Tibs totaled $50,000 and $250,000, respectively, in the Northern territory during June. Variable expenses are 22% of the selling price for Paks and 58% for Tibs. Cost records show that $30,000 of the Northern territory's fixed expenses are traceable to Paks and $40,000 to Tibs, with the remainder common to the two products.

Required:

1. Prepare contribution format segmented income statements first showing the total company broken down between sales territories and then showing the Northern territory broken down by product line. In addition, for the company as a whole and for each segment, show each item on the segmented income statements as a percent of sales.
2. Look at the statement you have prepared showing the total company segmented by sales territory. What insights revealed by this statement should be brought to the attention of management?
3. Look at the statement you have prepared showing the Northern territory segmented by product lines. What insights revealed by this statement should be brought to the attention of management?

PROBLEM 5–22 Prepare and Reconcile Variable Costing Statements [LO 5–1, LO 5–2, LO 5–3]

Denton Company manufactures and sells a single product. Cost data for the product are given below:

Variable costs per unit:	
Direct materials	$ 7
Direct labor	10
Variable manufacturing overhead	5
Variable selling and administrative	3
Total variable costs per unit	$25
Fixed costs per month:	
Fixed manufacturing overhead	$315,000
Fixed selling and administrative	245,000
Total fixed cost per month	$560,000

The product sells for $60 per unit. Production and sales data for July and August, the first two months of operations, follow:

	Units Produced	Units Sold
July.	17,500	15,000
August.	17,500	20,000

The company's Accounting Department has prepared absorption costing income statements for July and August as presented below:

	May	June
Sales	$900,000	$1,200,000
Cost of goods sold	600,000	800,000
Gross margin	300,000	400,000
Selling and administrative expenses	290,000	305,000
Net operating income.	$ 10,000	$ 95,000

Required:

1. Determine the unit product cost under:
   a. Absorption costing.
   b. Variable costing.
2. Prepare contribution format variable costing income statements for July and August.
3. Reconcile the variable costing and absorption costing net operating income figures.
4. The company's Accounting Department has determined the company's break-even point to be 16,000 units per month, computed as follows:

$$\frac{\text{Fixed cost per month}}{\text{Unit contribution margin}} = \frac{\$560{,}000}{\$35 \text{ per unit}} = 16{,}000 \text{ units}$$

"I'm confused," said the president. "The accounting people say that our break-even point is 16,000 units per month, but we sold only 15,000 units in July, and the income statement they prepared shows a $10,000 profit for that month. Either the income statement is wrong or the break-even point is wrong." Prepare a brief memo for the president, explaining what happened on the July absorption costing income statement.

PROBLEM 5–23 Absorption and Variable Costing; Production Constant, Sales Fluctuate [LO 5–1, LO 5–2, LO 5–3]

Tami Tyler opened Tami's Creations, Inc., a small manufacturing company, at the beginning of the year. Getting the company through its first quarter of operations placed a considerable strain on Ms. Tyler's personal finances. The following income statement for the first quarter was prepared by a friend who has just completed a course in managerial accounting at State University.

Tami's Creations, Inc. Income Statement For the Quarter Ended March 31		
Sales (28,000 units)		$1,120,000
Variable expenses:		
Variable cost of goods sold	$462,000	
Variable selling and administrative.	168,000	630,000
Contribution margin		490,000
Fixed expenses:		
Fixed manufacturing overhead	300,000	
Fixed selling and administrative	200,000	500,000
Net operating loss		$ (10,000)

Ms. Tyler is discouraged over the loss shown for the quarter, particularly because she had planned to use the statement as support for a bank loan. Another friend, a CPA, insists that the company should be using absorption costing rather than variable costing and argues that if absorption costing had been used the company probably would have reported at least some profit for the quarter.

At this point, Ms. Tyler is manufacturing only one product, a swimsuit. Production and cost data relating to the swimsuit for the first quarter follow:

Units produced	30,000
Units sold	28,000
Variable costs per unit:	
Direct materials	$3.50
Direct labor	$12.80
Variable manufacturing overhead	$1.00
Variable selling and administrative	$6.00

Required:

1. Complete the following:
   a. Compute the unit product cost under absorption costing.
   b. Redo the company's income statement for the quarter using absorption costing.
   c. Reconcile the variable and absorption costing net operating income (loss) figures.
2. Was the CPA correct in suggesting that the company really earned a "profit" for the quarter? Explain.
3. During the second quarter of operations, the company again produced 30,000 units but sold 32,000 units. (Assume no change in total fixed costs.)
   a. Prepare a contribution format income statement for the quarter using variable costing.
   b. Prepare an income statement for the quarter using absorption costing.
   c. Reconcile the variable costing and absorption costing net operating incomes.

PROBLEM 5–24 Companywide and Segment Break-Even Analysis; Decision Making [LO 5–4, LO 5–5]
Toxaway Company is a merchandiser that segments its business into two divisions—Commercial and Residential. The company's accounting intern was asked to prepare segmented income statements that the company's divisional managers could use to calculate their break-even points and make decisions. She took the prior month's companywide income statement and prepared the absorption format segmented income statement shown below:

	Total Company	Commercial	Residential
Sales	$750,000	$250,000	$500,000
Cost of goods sold	500,000	140,000	360,000
Gross margin	250,000	110,000	140,000
Selling and administrative expenses	240,000	104,000	136,000
Net operating income	$ 10,000	$ 6,000	$ 4,000

In preparing these statements, the intern determined that Toxaway's only variable selling and administrative expense is a 10% sales commission on all sales. The company's total fixed expenses include $72,000 of common fixed expenses that would continue to be incurred even if the Commercial or Residential segments are discontinued, $38,000 of fixed expenses that would be avoided if the Residential segment is dropped, and $55,000 of fixed expenses that would be avoided if the Commericial segment is dropped.

Required:

1. Do you agree with the intern's decision to use an absorption format for her segmented income statement? Why?

2. Based on the intern's segmented income statement, can you determine how she allocated the company's common fixed expenses to the Commercial and Residential segments? Do you agree with her decision to allocate the common fixed expenses to the Commercial and Residential segments?
3. Redo the intern's segmented income statement using the contribution format.
4. Compute the companywide break-even point in dollar sales.
5. Compute the break-even point in dollar sales for the Commercial Division and for the Residential Division.
6. Assume the company decided to pay its sales representatives in the Commercial and Residential Divisions a total monthly salary of $15,000 and $30,000, respectively, and to lower its companywide sales commission percentage from 10% to 5%. Calculate the new break-even point in dollar sales for the Commercial Division and the Residential Division.

PROBLEM 5–25 Prepare and Interpret Income Statements; Changes in Both Sales and Production; Lean Production [LO 5–1, LO 5–2, LO 5–3]

Starfax, Inc., manufactures a small part that is widely used in various electronic products such as home computers. Operating results for the first three years of activity were as follows (absorption costing basis):

	Year 1	Year 2	Year 3
Sales	$800,000	$640,000	$800,000
Cost of goods sold	580,000	400,000	620,000
Gross margin	220,000	240,000	180,000
Selling and administrative expenses	190,000	180,000	190,000
Net operating income (loss)	$ 30,000	$ 60,000	$ (10,000)

In the latter part of Year 2, a competitor went out of business and in the process dumped a large number of units on the market. As a result, Starfax's sales dropped by 20% during Year 2 even though production increased during the year. Management had expected sales to remain constant at 50,000 units; the increased production was designed to provide the company with a buffer of protection against unexpected spurts in demand. By the start of Year 3, management could see that inventory was excessive and that spurts in demand were unlikely. To reduce the excessive inventories, Starfax cut back production during Year 3, as shown below:

	Year 1	Year 2	Year 3
Production in units	50,000	60,000	40,000
Sales in units	50,000	40,000	50,000

Additional information about the company follows:

a. The company's plant is highly automated. Variable manufacturing expenses (direct materials, direct labor, and variable manufacturing overhead) total only $2 per unit, and fixed manufacturing overhead expenses total $480,000 per year.

b. Fixed manufacturing overhead costs are applied to units of product on the basis of each year's production. That is, a new fixed manufacturing overhead rate is computed each year.

c. Variable selling and administrative expenses were $1 per unit sold in each year. Fixed selling and administrative expenses totaled $140,000 per year.

d. The company uses a FIFO inventory flow assumption.

Starfax's management can't understand why profits doubled during Year 2 when sales dropped by 20% and why a loss was incurred during Year 3 when sales recovered to previous levels.

Required:

1. Prepare a contribution format variable costing income statement for each year.
2. Refer to the absorption costing income statements above.
   a. Compute the unit product cost in each year under absorption costing. (Show how much of this cost is variable and how much is fixed.)
   b. Reconcile the variable costing and absorption costing net operating income figures for each year.
3. Refer again to the absorption costing income statements. Explain why net operating income was higher in Year 2 than it was in Year 1 under the absorption approach, in light of the fact that fewer units were sold in Year 2 than in Year 1.
4. Refer again to the absorption costing income statements. Explain why the company suffered a loss in Year 3 but reported a profit in Year 1 although the same number of units was sold in each year.
5. a. Explain how operations would have differed in Year 2 and Year 3 if the company had been using Lean Production, with the result that ending inventory was zero.
   b. If Lean Production had been used during Year 2 and Year 3 and the predetermined overhead rate is based on 50,000 units per year, what would the company's net operating income (or loss) have been in each year under absorption costing? Explain the reason for any differences between these income figures and the figures reported by the company in the statements above.

PROBLEM 5–26 Restructuring a Segmented Income Statement [LO 5–4]

Losses have been incurred at Millard Corporation for some time. In an effort to isolate the problem and improve the company's performance, management has requested that the monthly income statement be segmented by sales region. The company's first effort at preparing a segmented statement is given below. This statement is for May, the most recent month of activity.

	Sales Region		
	West	Central	East
Sales	$450,000	$800,000	$ 750,000
Regional expenses (traceable):			
Cost of goods sold	162,900	280,000	376,500
Advertising	108,000	200,000	210,000
Salaries	90,000	88,000	135,000
Utilities	13,500	12,000	15,000
Depreciation	27,000	28,000	30,000
Shipping expense	17,100	32,000	28,500
Total regional expenses	418,500	640,000	795,000
Regional income (loss) before corporate expenses	31,500	160,000	(45,000)
Corporate expenses:			
Advertising (general)	18,000	32,000	30,000
General administrative expense	50,000	50,000	50,000
Total corporate expenses	68,000	82,000	80,000
Net operating income (loss)	$ (36,500)	$ 78,000	$(125,000)

Cost of goods sold and shipping expense are both variable; other costs are all fixed.

Millard Corporation is a wholesale distributor of office products. It purchases office products from manufacturers and distributes them in the three regions given above. The three regions are about the same size, and each has its own manager and sales staff. The products that the company distributes vary widely in profitability.

Required:

1. List any disadvantages or weaknesses that you see to the statement format illustrated on the previous page.
2. Explain the basis that is apparently being used to allocate the corporate expenses to the regions. Do you agree with these allocations? Explain.
3. Prepare a new contribution format segmented income statement for May. Show a Total column as well as data for each region. In addition, for the company as a whole and for each sales region, show each item on the segmented income statement as a percent of sales.
4. Analyze the statement that you prepared in requirement 3. What points that might help to improve the company's performance would you bring to management's attention?

PROBLEM 5–27 Incentives Created by Absorption Costing; Ethics and the Manager [LO 5–2]

Carlos Cavalas, the manager of Echo Products' Brazilian Division, is trying to set the production schedule for the last quarter of the year. The Brazilian Division had planned to sell 3,600 units during the year, but by September 30 only the following activity had been reported:

	Units
Inventory, January 1	0
Production	2,400
Sales	2,000
Inventory, September 30	400

The division can rent warehouse space to store up to 1,000 units. The minimum inventory level that the division should carry is 50 units. Mr. Cavalas is aware that production must be at least 200 units per quarter in order to retain a nucleus of key employees. Maximum production capacity is 1,500 units per quarter.

Demand has been soft, and the sales forecast for the last quarter is only 600 units. Due to the nature of the division's operations, fixed manufacturing overhead is a major element of product cost.

Required:

1. Assume that the division is using variable costing. How many units should be scheduled for production during the last quarter of the year? (The basic formula for computing the required production for a period in a company is: Expected sales + Desired ending inventory − Beginning inventory = Required production.) Show computations and explain your answer. Will the number of units scheduled for production affect the division's reported income or loss for the year? Explain.
2. Assume that the division is using absorption costing and that the divisional manager is given an annual bonus based on divisional operating income. If Mr. Cavalas wants to maximize his division's operating income for the year, how many units should be scheduled for production during the last quarter? [See the formula in requirement 1.] Explain.
3. Identify the ethical issues involved in the decision Mr. Cavalas must make about the level of production for the last quarter of the year.

PROBLEM 5–28 Basic Segment Reporting; Activity-Based Cost Assignment [LO 5–4]

Diversified Products, Inc., has recently acquired a small publishing company that offers three books for sale—a cookbook, a travel guide, and a handy speller. Each book sells for $10. The publishing company's most recent monthly income statement follows.

The following additional information is available about the company:

a. Only printing costs and sales commissions are variable; all other costs are fixed. The printing costs (which include materials, labor, and variable overhead) are traceable to the three product lines as shown in the statement above. Sales commissions are 10% of sales for any product.

b. The same equipment is used to produce all three books, so the equipment depreciation cost has been allocated equally among the three product lines. An analysis of the company's activities indicates that the equipment is used 30% of the time to produce cookbooks, 50% of the time to produce travel guides, and 20% of the time to produce handy spellers.

		Product Line		
	Total Company	Cookbook	Travel Guide	Handy Speller
Sales	$300,000	$90,000	$150,000	$60,000
Expenses:				
Printing costs	102,000	27,000	63,000	12,000
Advertising	36,000	13,500	19,500	3,000
General sales	18,000	5,400	9,000	3,600
Salaries	33,000	18,000	9,000	6,000
Equipment depreciation	9,000	3,000	3,000	3,000
Sales commissions	30,000	9,000	15,000	6,000
General administration	42,000	14,000	14,000	14,000
Warehouse rent	12,000	3,600	6,000	2,400
Depreciation—office facilities	3,000	1,000	1,000	1,000
Total expenses	285,000	94,500	139,500	51,000
Net operating income (loss)	$ 15,000	$ (4,500)	$ 10,500	$ 9,000

c. The warehouse is used to store finished units of product, so the rental cost has been allocated to the product lines on the basis of sales dollars. The warehouse rental cost is $3 per square foot per year. The warehouse contains 48,000 square feet of space, of which 7,200 square feet is used by the cookbook line, 24,000 square feet by the travel guide line, and 16,800 square feet by the handy speller line.

d. The general sales cost above includes the salary of the sales manager and other sales costs not traceable to any specific product line. This cost has been allocated to the product lines on the basis of sales dollars.

e. The general administration cost and depreciation of office facilities both relate to administration of the company as a whole. These costs have been allocated equally to the three product lines.

f. All other costs are traceable to the three product lines in the amounts shown on the statement above.

The management of Diversified Products, Inc., is anxious to improve the publishing company's 5% return on sales.

Required:

1. Prepare a new contribution format segmented income statement for the month. Adjust allocations of equipment depreciation and of warehouse rent as indicated by the additional information provided.
2. After seeing the income statement in the main body of the problem, management has decided to eliminate the cookbook because it is not returning a profit, and to focus all available resources on promoting the travel guide.
   a. Based on the statement you have prepared, do you agree with the decision to eliminate the cookbook? Explain.
   b. Based on the statement you have prepared, do you agree with the decision to focus all available resources on promoting the travel guide? Assume that an ample market is available for all three product lines. (*Hint:* Compute the contribution margin ratio for each product.)

Cases

Connect — Additional student resources are available with Connect.

CASE 5–29 Variable and Absorption Costing Unit Product Costs and Income Statements [LO 5–1, LO 5–2]
O'Brien Company manufactures and sells one product. The following information pertains to each of the company's first three years of operations:

Variable costs per unit:	
Manufacturing	
Direct materials	$32
Direct labor	$20
Variable manufacturing overhead	$4
Variable selling and administrative	$3
Fixed costs per year:	
Fixed manufacturing overhead	$660,000
Fixed selling and administrative expenses	$120,000

During its first year of operations, O'Brien produced 100,000 units and sold 80,000 units. During its second year of operations, it produced 75,000 units and sold 90,000 units. In its third year, O'Brien produced 80,000 units and sold 75,000 units. The selling price of the company's product is $75 per unit.

Required:

1. Assume the company uses variable costing and a FIFO inventory flow assumption (FIFO means first-in first-out. In other words, it assumes that the oldest units in inventory are sold first):
   a. Compute the unit product cost for Year 1, Year 2, and Year 3.
   b. Prepare an income statement for Year 1, Year 2, and Year 3.
2. Assume the company uses variable costing and a LIFO inventory flow assumption (LIFO means last-in first-out. In other words, it assumes that the newest units in inventory are sold first):
   a. Compute the unit product cost for Year 1, Year 2, and Year 3.
   b. Prepare an income statement for Year 1, Year 2, and Year 3.
3. Assume the company uses absorption costing and a FIFO inventory flow assumption (FIFO means first-in first-out. In other words, it assumes that the oldest units in inventory are sold first):
   a. Compute the unit product cost for Year 1, Year 2, and Year 3.
   b. Prepare an income statement for Year 1, Year 2, and Year 3.
4. Assume the company uses absorption costing and a LIFO inventory flow assumption (LIFO means last-in first-out. In other words, it assumes that the newest units in inventory are sold first):
   a. Compute the unit product cost for Year 1, Year 2, and Year 3.
   b. Prepare an income statement for Year 1, Year 2, and Year 3.

CASE 5–30 Service Organization; Segment Reporting [LO 5–4]

Music Teachers, Inc., is an educational association for music teachers that has 20,000 members. The association operates from a central headquarters but has local membership chapters throughout the United States. Monthly meetings are held by the local chapters to discuss recent developments on topics of interest to music teachers. The association's journal, Teachers' Forum, is issued monthly with features about recent developments in the field. The association publishes books and reports and also sponsors professional courses that qualify for continuing professional education credit. The association's statement of revenues and expenses for the current year is presented below.

Music Teachers, Inc.
Statement of Revenues and Expenses
For the Year Ended November 30

Revenues	$3,275,000
Expenses:	
Salaries	920,000
Personnel costs	230,000
Occupancy costs	280,000
Reimbursement of member costs to local chapters	600,000
Other membership services	500,000
Printing and paper	320,000
Postage and shipping	176,000
Instructors' fees	80,000
General and administrative	38,000
Total expenses	3,144,000
Excess of revenues over expenses	$ 131,000

The board of directors of Music Teachers, Inc., has requested that a segmented income statement be prepared showing the contribution of each segment to the association. The association has four segments: Membership Division, Magazine Subscriptions Division, Books and Reports Division, and Continuing Education Division. Mike Doyle has been assigned responsibility for preparing the segmented income statement, and he has gathered the following data prior to its preparation.

a. Membership dues are $100 per year, of which $20 is considered to cover a one-year subscription to the association's journal. Other benefits include membership in the association and chapter affiliation. The portion of the dues covering the magazine subscription ($20) should be assigned to the Magazine Subscription Division.
b. One-year subscriptions to Teachers' Forum were sold to nonmembers and libraries at $30 per subscription. A total of 2,500 of these subscriptions were sold last year. In addition to subscriptions, the magazine generated $100,000 in advertising revenues. The costs per magazine subscription were $7 for printing and paper and $4 for postage and shipping.
c. A total of 28,000 technical reports and professional texts were sold by the Books and Reports Division at an average unit selling price of $25. Average costs per publication were $4 for printing and paper and $2 for postage and shipping.
d. The association offers a variety of continuing education courses to both members and nonmembers. The one-day courses had a tuition cost of $75 each and were attended by 2,400 students. A total of 1,760 students took two-day courses at a tuition cost of $125 for each student. Outside instructors were paid to teach some courses.
e. Salary costs and space occupied by division follow:

	Salaries	Space Occupied (square feet)
Membership	$210,000	2,000
Magazine Subscriptions	150,000	2,000
Books and Reports	300,000	3,000
Continuing Education	180,000	2,000
Corporate staff	80,000	1,000
Total	$920,000	10,000

Personnel costs are 25% of salaries in the separate divisions as well as for the corporate staff. The $280,000 in occupancy costs includes $50,000 in rental cost for a warehouse used by the Books and Reports Division for storage purposes.

f. Printing and paper costs other than for magazine subscriptions and for books and reports relate to the Continuing Education Division.
g. General and administrative expenses include costs relating to overall administration of the association as a whole. The company's corporate staff does some mailing of materials for general administrative purposes.

The expenses that can be traced or assigned to the corporate staff, as well as any other expenses that are not traceable to the segments, will be treated as common costs. It is not necessary to distinguish between variable and fixed costs.

Required:

1. Prepare a contribution format segmented income statement for Music Teachers, Inc. This statement should show the segment margin for each division as well as results for the association as a whole.
2. Give arguments for and against allocating all costs of the association to the four divisions.

(CMA, adapted)

Appendix 5A: Super-Variable Costing

LEARNING OBJECTIVE 5–6
Prepare an income statement using super-variable costing and reconcile this approach with variable costing.

In the discussion of variable costing in this chapter we have assumed that direct labor and a portion of manufacturing overhead are variable costs that should be attached to products. However, these assumptions about cost behavior may not be true. For example, it may be easier and more accurate to assume that *all* manufacturing overhead costs are fixed costs because the variable portion of these costs is insignificant or too difficult to estimate. Furthermore, many companies' labor costs (including direct and indirect labor) are more fixed than variable due to labor regulations, labor contracts, or management policy. In countries such as France, Germany, Spain, and Japan, management often has little flexibility in adjusting the labor force to changes in business activity. Even in countries such as the United States and the United Kingdom, where management usually has greater latitude to adjust the size of its labor force, many managers choose to view labor as a fixed cost. They make this choice because the cost savings from terminating or laying off employees during a short-term business downturn may be swamped by the negative effects on employee morale and by the costs of later finding and training suitable replacements. Moreover, treating employees as variable costs subtly fosters the attitude that employees are expendable and replaceable like materials rather than unique, difficult-to-replace assets.

Super-variable costing is a variation on variable costing in which direct labor and manufacturing overhead costs are considered to be fixed. **Super-variable costing** classifies all direct labor and manufacturing overhead costs as fixed period costs and *only direct materials as a variable product cost.* To simplify, in this appendix we also assume that selling and administrative expenses are entirely fixed.

Super–Variable Costing and Variable Costing—An Example

To illustrate the difference between treating direct labor as a fixed cost (as in super-variable costing) and treating direct labor as a variable cost (as in variable costing), we will use a modified version of the Weber Light Aircraft example from the main body of the chapter. Data concerning the company's operations appear below:

	Per Aircraft	Per Month
Selling price	$100,000	
Direct materials	$19,000	
Direct labor		$20,000
Fixed manufacturing overhead		$74,000
Fixed selling and administrative expense		$40,000

	January	February	March
Beginning inventory	0	0	1
Units produced	2	2	2
Units sold	2	1	3
Ending inventory	0	1	0

The key thing to notice here is that direct labor is a fixed cost—$20,000 per month. Also, notice that Weber Light Aircraft has no variable manufacturing overhead costs and no variable selling and administrative expenses. For the months of January, February, and March, the company's selling price per aircraft, variable cost per aircraft, monthly production in units, and total monthly fixed expenses never change. The only thing that changes in this example is the number of units sold (January = 2 units sold; February = 1 unit sold; March = 3 units sold).

We will first construct the company's super-variable costing income statements for January, February, and March. Then we will show how the company's net operating income would be determined for the same months using variable costing if it were incorrectly assumed that direct labor is a variable cost. As you'll see, both income statements rely on the contribution format.

Super–Variable Costing Income Statements

To prepare the company's super-variable costing income statements for each month we follow four steps. First, we compute sales by multiplying the number of units sold by the selling price per unit, which in this example is $100,000 per unit. Second, we compute the variable cost of goods sold by multiplying the number of units sold by the unit product cost, which in this example is the direct materials cost of $19,000 per unit. Third, we compute the contribution margin by subtracting the variable cost of goods sold from sales. Fourth, we compute net operating income by subtracting all fixed expenses from the contribution margin.

Using these four steps, Weber's super-variable costing income statements for each month would appear as shown in Exhibit 5A–1. Notice that the only variable expense is variable cost of goods sold, which is the $19,000 of direct materials per unit sold. For example, in March, the unit product cost of $19,000 is multiplied by three units sold to obtain the variable cost of goods sold of $57,000. The total monthly fixed manufacturing expenses of $94,000 include $20,000 of direct labor and $74,000 of fixed manufacturing overhead.

EXHIBIT 5A–1
Super-Variable Costing Income Statements

	January	February	March
Sales (@ $100,000 per unit)	$200,000	$100,000	$300,000
Variable cost of goods sold (@ $19,000 per unit)	38,000	19,000	57,000
Contribution margin	162,000	81,000	243,000
Fixed expenses:			
Fixed manufacturing expenses	94,000	94,000	94,000
Fixed selling and administrative expenses	40,000	40,000	40,000
Total fixed expenses	134,000	134,000	134,000
Net operating income (loss)	$ 28,000	$ (53,000)	$109,000

Variable Costing Income Statements

The variable costing income statements in this example differ from the super-variable costing income statements in one important respect—we will assume that direct labor is incorrectly classified as a variable cost and is included in unit product costs. Because the monthly direct labor cost is $20,000 and two aircraft are produced each month, if direct labor costs are included in unit product costs, then Weber Light Aircraft will assign $10,000 of direct labor cost to each aircraft that it produces. Thus, the company's unit product costs under variable costing would be computed as follows:

	January	February	March
Direct materials	$19,000	$19,000	$19,000
Direct labor	10,000	10,000	10,000
Unit product cost	$29,000	$29,000	$29,000

Given these unit product cost figures, the company's variable costing income statements would be computed as shown in Exhibit 5A–2. For example, in March, the unit product cost of $29,000 is multiplied by three units sold to obtain the variable cost of goods sold of $87,000. The total fixed manufacturing overhead of $74,000 and total fixed selling and administrative expenses of $40,000 are both recorded as period expenses.

EXHIBIT 5A–2
Variable Costing Income Statements

	January	February	March
Sales (@ $100,000 per unit)	$200,000	$100,000	$300,000
Variable cost of goods sold (@ $29,000 per unit)	58,000	29,000	87,000
Contribution margin	142,000	71,000	213,000
Fixed expenses:			
Fixed manufacturing overhead	74,000	74,000	74,000
Fixed selling and administrative expenses	40,000	40,000	40,000
Total fixed expenses	114,000	114,000	114,000
Net operating income (loss)	$ 28,000	$(43,000)	$ 99,000

Reconciliation of Super–Variable Costing and Variable Costing Income

The super-variable costing and variable costing net operating incomes are both $28,000 in January. However, in February, the super-variable costing income is $10,000 lower than the variable costing income and the opposite holds true in March. In other words, the super-variable costing income in March is $10,000 higher than the variable costing income.

Why do these two costing methods produce different net operating incomes? The answer can be found in the accounting for direct labor costs. Super-variable costing treats direct labor as a fixed period expense whereas variable costing treats direct labor as a variable product cost. In other words, super-variable costing records the entire direct labor cost of $20,000 as an expense on each month's income statement. Conversely, variable costing assigns $10,000 of direct labor cost to each unit produced. The $10,000 assigned to each unit produced remains in inventory on the balance sheet until the unit is sold—at which point the $10,000 assigned to it is transferred to variable cost of goods sold on the income statement. Given this background, the super-variable costing and variable costing incomes for each month can be reconciled as follows:

	January	February	March
Direct labor cost in ending inventory (@ $10,000 per unit)	$ 0	$10,000	$ 0
– Direct labor cost in beginning inventory (@ $10,000 per unit)	0	0	10,000
= Direct labor cost deferred in (released from) inventory	$ 0	$10,000	$(10,000)

	January	February	March
Super-variable costing net operating income (loss)	$28,000	$(53,000)	$109,000
Direct labor deferred in (released from) inventory	0	10,000	(10,000)
Variable costing net operating income (loss)	$28,000	$(43,000)	$ 99,000

In January, both costing methods report the same net operating income ($28,000). This occurs because each method expenses $20,000 of direct labor in the income statement. In February, super-variable costing income is $10,000 less than variable costing income. This difference arises because super-variable costing expenses $20,000 of direct labor in the income statement, whereas variable costing expenses only $10,000 of direct labor in the income statement ($10,000 per unit × 1 unit sold) and defers $10,000 of direct labor on the balance sheet ($10,000 per unit × 1 unit produced but not sold). In March, super-variable costing income is $10,000 greater than variable costing income. This difference arises because super-variable costing expenses $20,000 of direct labor on the income statement, whereas variable costing expenses $30,000 of direct labor on the income statement ($10,000 per unit × 3 unit sold). Notice that one of the units sold in March was actually produced in February. Under variable costing, the $10,000 of direct labor attached to the unit produced in February is released from inventory and included in variable cost of goods sold for March.

In summary, the key issue considered in this appendix is how a company treats direct labor costs. If a company treats direct labor as a variable cost, the cost system may encourage managers to treat labor costs as an expense to be minimized when sales decline and this may result in reduced morale and eventual problems when business picks up. Second, in practice management may have little ability to adjust the direct labor force even if they wanted to, resulting in a situation in which direct labor costs are in fact fixed. In either case, treating direct labor costs as variable can lead to bad decisions. The super-variable costing approach overcomes this problem by treating labor costs as fixed costs.

Glossary (Appendix 5A)

Super-variable costing A costing method that classifies all direct labor and manufacturing overhead costs as fixed period costs and *only direct materials as a variable product cost.* (p. 217)

Appendix 5A Exercises and Problems connect

Additional student resources are available with Connect.

EXERCISE 5A–1 Super-Variable Costing Income Statement [LO 5–6]

Zola Company manufactures and sells one product. The following information pertains to the company's first year of operations:

Variable cost per unit:	
Direct materials	$18
Fixed costs per year:	
Direct labor	$200,000
Fixed manufacturing overhead	$250,000
Fixed selling and administrative expenses	$80,000

The company does not incur any variable manufacturing overhead costs or variable selling and administrative expenses. During its first year of operations, Zola produced 25,000 units and sold 20,000 units. The selling price of the company's product is $50 per unit.

Required:

1. Assume the company uses super-variable costing:
   a. Compute the unit product cost for the year.
   b. Prepare an income statement for the year.

EXERCISE 5A–2 Super-Variable Costing and Variable Costing Unit Product Costs and Income Statements [LO 5–2, LO 5–6]

Lyons Company manufactures and sells one product. The following information pertains to the company's first year of operations:

Variable cost per unit:	
Direct materials	$13
Fixed costs per year:	
Direct labor	$750,000
Fixed manufacturing overhead	$420,000
Fixed selling and administrative expenses	$110,000

The company does not incur any variable manufacturing overhead costs or variable selling and administrative expenses. During its first year of operations, Lyons produced 60,000 units and sold 52,000 units. The selling price of the company's product is $40 per unit.

Required:

1. Assume the company uses super-variable costing:
   a. Compute the unit product cost for the year.
   b. Prepare an income statement for the year.
2. Assume the company uses a variable costing system that assigns $12.50 of direct labor cost to each unit produced:
   a. Compute the unit product cost for the year.
   b. Prepare an income statement for the year.
3. Prepare a reconciliation that explains the difference between the super-variable costing and variable costing net operating incomes.

EXERCISE 5A–3 Super-Variable Costing and Variable Costing Unit Product Costs and Income Statements [LO 5–2, LO 5–6]

Kelly Company manufactures and sells one product. The following information pertains to each of the company's first two years of operations:

Variable cost per unit:	
Direct materials	$12
Fixed costs per year:	
Direct labor	$500,000
Fixed manufacturing overhead	$450,000
Fixed selling and administrative expenses	$180,000

The company does not incur any variable manufacturing overhead costs or variable selling and administrative expenses. During its first year of operations, Kelly produced 50,000 units and sold 40,000 units. During its second year of operations, it produced 50,000 units and sold 60,000 units. The selling price of the company's product is $50 per unit.

Required:

1. Assume the company uses super-variable costing:
   a. Compute the unit product cost for Year 1 and Year 2.
   b. Prepare an income statement for Year 1 and Year 2.
2. Assume the company uses a variable costing system that assigns $10 of direct labor cost to each unit produced:
   a. Compute the unit product cost for Year 1 and Year 2.
   b. Prepare an income statement for Year 1 and Year 2.
3. Prepare a reconciliation that explains the difference between the super-variable costing and variable costing net operating incomes in Years 1 and 2.

PROBLEM 5A–4 Super-Variable Costing and Variable Costing Unit Product Costs and Income Statements [LO 5–2, LO 5–6]

Ogilvy Company manufactures and sells one product. The following information pertains to each of the company's first three years of operations:

Variable cost per unit:	
Direct materials	$16
Fixed costs per year:	
Direct labor	$540,000
Fixed manufacturing overhead	$822,000
Fixed selling and administrative expenses	$370,000

The company does not incur any variable manufacturing overhead costs or variable selling and administrative expenses. During its first year of operations, Ogilvy produced 60,000 units and sold 60,000 units. During its second year of operations, it produced 60,000 units and sold 55,000 units. In its third year, Ogilvy produced 60,000 units and sold 65,000 units. The selling price of the company's product is $45 per unit.

Required:

1. Assume the company uses super-variable costing:
   a. Compute the unit product cost for Year 1, Year 2, and Year 3.
   b. Prepare an income statement for Year 1, Year 2, and Year 3.
2. Assume the company uses a variable costing system that assigns $9 of direct labor cost to each unit produced:
   a. Compute the unit product cost for Year 1, Year 2, and Year 3.
   b. Prepare an income statement for Year 1, Year 2, and Year 3.
3. Prepare a reconciliation that explains the difference between the super-variable costing and variable costing net operating incomes in Years 1, 2, and 3.

PROBLEM 5A–5 Super-Variable Costing, Variable Costing, and Absorption Costing Income Statements [LO 5–2, LO 5–6]

Bracey Company manufactures and sells one product. The following information pertains to the company's first year of operations:

Variable cost per unit:	
Direct materials	$19
Fixed costs per year:	
Direct labor	$250,000
Fixed manufacturing overhead	$300,000
Fixed selling and administrative expenses	$90,000

The company does not incur any variable manufacturing overhead costs or variable selling and administrative expenses. During its first year of operations, Bracey produced 20,000 units and sold 18,000 units. The selling price of the company's product is $55 per unit.

Required:

1. Assume the company uses super-variable costing:
   a. Compute the unit product cost for the year.
   b. Prepare an income statement for the year.
2. Assume the company uses a variable costing system that assigns $12.50 of direct labor cost to each unit produced:
   a. Compute the unit product cost for the year.
   b. Prepare an income statement for the year.
3. Assume the company uses an absorption costing system that assigns $12.50 of direct labor cost and $15.00 of fixed manufacturing overhead cost to each unit produced:
   a. Compute the unit product cost for the year.
   b. Prepare an income statement for the year.
4. Prepare a reconciliation that explains the difference between the super-variable costing and variable costing net operating incomes. Prepare another reconciliation that explains the difference between the super-variable costing and absorption costing net operating incomes.

Activity-Based Costing: A Tool to Aid Decision Making

Managing Product Complexity

BUSINESS FOCUS

© Brand X Pictures/PunchStock, RF

Managers often understand that increasing the variety of raw material inputs used in their products increases costs. For example, General Mills studied its 50 varieties of Hamburger Helper and concluded that it could lower costs by discontinuing half of them without alienating customers. Seagate studied seven varieties of its computer hard drives and found that only 2% of their parts could be shared by more than one hard drive. The engineers fixed the problem by redesigning the hard drives so that they used more common component parts. Instead of using 61 types of screws to make the hard drives, the engineers reduced the number of screws needed to 19. Eventually all Seagate products were designed so that 75% of their component parts were shared with other product lines.

Activity-based costing systems quantify the increase in costs, such as procurement costs, material handling costs, and assembly costs that are caused by inefficient product designs and other factors. ■

Sources: Mina Kimes, "Cereal Cost Cutters," *Fortune,* November 10, 2008, p. 24; Erika Brown, "Drive Fast, Drive Hard," *Forbes,* January 9, 2006, pp. 92–96.

LEARNING OBJECTIVES

After studying Chapter 6, you should be able to:

LO 6–1 Understand activity-based costing and how it differs from a traditional costing system.

LO 6–2 Assign costs to cost pools using a first-stage allocation.

LO 6–3 Compute activity rates for cost pools.

LO 6–4 Assign costs to a cost object using a second-stage allocation.

LO 6–5 Use activity-based costing to compute product and customer margins.

LO 6–6 (Appendix 6A) Prepare an action analysis report using activity-based costing data and interpret the report.

This chapter introduces the concept of *activity-based costing,* which has been embraced by a wide variety of organizations including Charles Schwab, Citigroup, Lowe's, Coca-Cola, J&B Wholesale, Fairchild Semiconductor, Assan Aluminum, Sysco Foods, Fisher Scientific International, and Peregrine Outfitters. **Activity-based costing (ABC)** is a costing method that is designed to provide managers with cost information for strategic and other decisions that potentially affect capacity and therefore "fixed" as well as variable costs. Activity-based costing is ordinarily used as a supplement to, rather than as a replacement for, a company's usual costing system. Most organizations that use activity-based costing have two costing systems—the official costing system that is used for preparing external financial reports and the activity-based costing system that is used for internal decision making and for managing activities.

This chapter focuses primarily on ABC applications in manufacturing to provide a contrast with the material presented in earlier chapters. More specifically, Chapter 4 focused on traditional absorption costing systems used by manufacturing companies to calculate unit product costs for the purpose of valuing inventories and determining cost of goods sold for external financial reports. In contrast, this chapter explains how manufacturing companies can use activity-based costing rather than traditional methods to calculate unit product costs for the purposes of managing overhead and making decisions. Chapter 5 had a similar purpose. That chapter focused on how to use variable costing to aid decisions that do not affect fixed costs. This chapter extends that idea to show how activity-based costing can be used to aid decisions that potentially affect fixed costs as well as variable costs.

Activity-Based Costing: An Overview

LEARNING OBJECTIVE 6–1
Understand activity-based costing and how it differs from a traditional costing system.

As stated above, traditional absorption costing is designed to provide data for external financial reports. In contrast, activity-based costing is designed to be used for internal decision making. As a consequence, activity-based costing differs from traditional absorption costing in three ways. In activity-based costing:

1. Nonmanufacturing as well as manufacturing costs may be assigned to products, but only on a cause-and-effect basis.
2. Some manufacturing costs may be excluded from product costs.
3. Numerous overhead cost pools are used, each of which is allocated to products and other cost objects using its own unique measure of activity.

Each of these departures from traditional absorption costing will be discussed in turn.

Nonmanufacturing Costs and Activity-Based Costing

In traditional absorption costing, manufacturing costs are assigned to products and nonmanufacturing costs are not assigned to products. Conversely, in activity-based costing, we recognize that many nonmanufacturing costs relate to selling, distributing, and servicing specific products. Thus, ABC includes manufacturing *and* nonmanufacturing costs when calculating the entire cost of a product rather than just its manufacturing cost.

There are two types of nonmanufacturing costs that ABC systems assign to products. First, ABC systems trace all direct nonmanufacturing costs to products. Commissions paid to salespersons, shipping costs, and warranty repair costs are examples of nonmanufacturing costs that can be directly traced to individual products. Second, ABC systems allocate indirect nonmanufacturing costs to products whenever the products have presumably caused the costs to be incurred. In fact, in this chapter, we emphasize this point by expanding the definition of *overhead* to include all indirect costs—manufacturing and nonmanufacturing.

In summary, ABC product cost calculations include all direct costs that can be traced to products and all indirect costs that are caused by products. The need to distinguish between manufacturing and nonmanufacturing costs disappears—which is very different from earlier chapters that focused solely on determining the manufacturing cost of a product.

Manufacturing Costs and Activity–Based Costing

In traditional absorption costing systems, *all* manufacturing costs are assigned to products—even manufacturing costs that are not caused by the products. For example, in Chapter 4 we learned that a predetermined plantwide overhead rate is computed by dividing *all* budgeted manufacturing overhead costs by a measure of budgeted activity such as direct labor-hours. This approach spreads *all* manufacturing overhead costs across products based on each product's direct labor-hour usage. In contrast, activity-based costing systems purposely do not assign two types of manufacturing overhead costs to products.

Manufacturing overhead includes costs such as the factory security guard's wages, the plant controller's salary, and the cost of supplies used by the plant manager's secretary. These types of costs are assigned to products in a traditional absorption costing system even though they are totally unaffected by which products are made during a period. In contrast, activity-based costing systems do not arbitrarily assign these types of costs, which are called *organization-sustaining* costs, to products. Activity-based costing treats these types of costs as period expenses rather than product costs.

Additionally, in a traditional absorption costing system, the costs of unused, or idle, capacity are assigned to products. If the budgeted level of activity declines, the overhead rate and unit product costs increase as the increasing costs of idle capacity are spread over a smaller base. In contrast, in activity-based costing, products are only charged for the costs of the capacity they use—not for the costs of capacity they don't use. This provides more stable unit product costs and is consistent with the goal of assigning to products only the costs of the resources that they use.[1]

Exhibit 6–1 summarizies the two departures from traditional absorption costing that we have discussed thus far. The top portion of the exhibit shows that traditional absorption costing treats all manufacturing costs as product costs and all nonmanufacturing costs as period costs. The bottom portion of the exhibit shows that activity-based costing expands the definition of *overhead* to include all indirect costs—manufacturing and nonmanufacturing. The overhead costs that are caused by products are allocated to them, whereas any overhead costs that are not caused by products are treated as period costs. It also shows that ABC treats direct nonmanufacturing costs as product costs rather than period costs.

Now we turn our attention to the third and final difference between traditional absorption costing and activity-based costing.

Cost Pools, Allocation Bases, and Activity–Based Costing

Throughout the 19th century and most of the 20th century, cost system designs were simple and satisfactory. Typically, either one plantwide overhead cost pool or a number of departmental overhead cost pools were used to assign overhead costs to products. The plantwide and departmental approaches always had one thing in common—they relied on allocation bases such as direct labor-hours and machine-hours for allocating overhead costs to products. In the labor-intensive production processes of many years ago, direct labor was the most common choice for an overhead allocation base because it represented a large component of product costs, direct labor-hours were closely tracked, and many managers believed that direct labor-hours, the total volume of units produced, and overhead costs were highly correlated. (Three variables, such as direct labor-hours, the total

[1] Appendix 4B discusses how the costs of idle capacity can be accounted for as a period cost in an income statement. This treatment highlights the cost of idle capacity rather than burying it in inventory and cost of goods sold. The procedures laid out in this chapter for activity-based costing have the same end effect.

EXHIBIT 6–1
Differences between Traditional Absorption Costing and Activity-Based Costing

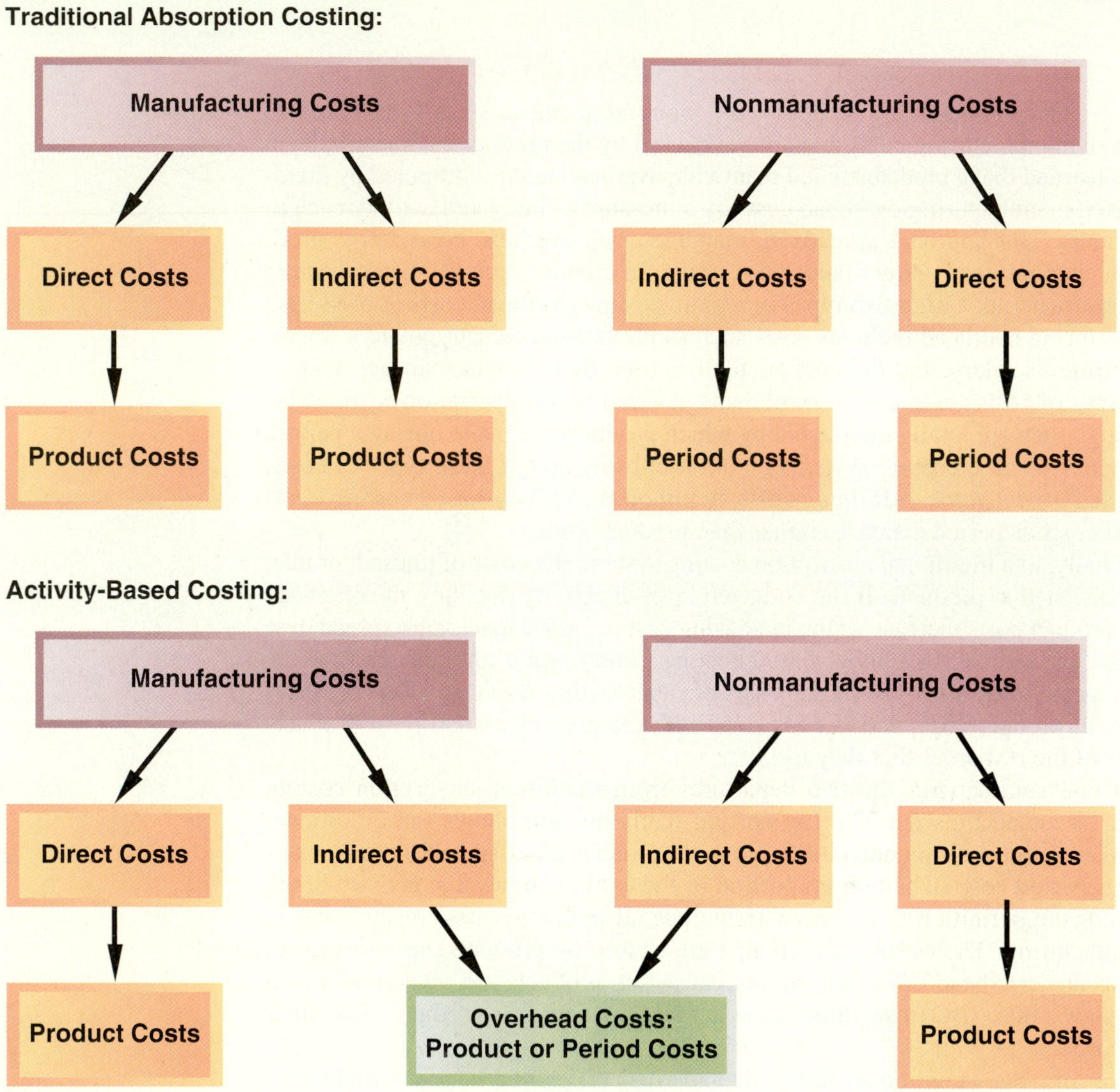

volume of units produced, and overhead costs, are highly correlated if they tend to move together.) Given that most companies at the time were producing a very limited variety of products that required similar resources to produce, allocation bases such as direct labor-hours, or even machine-hours, worked fine because, in fact, there was probably little difference in the overhead costs attributable to different products.

Then conditions began to change. As a percentage of total cost, direct labor began declining and overhead began increasing. Many tasks previously done by direct laborers were being performed by automated equipment—a component of overhead. Companies began creating new products and services at an ever-accelerating rate that differed in volume, batch size, and complexity. Managing and sustaining this product diversity required investing in many more overhead resources, such as production schedulers and product design engineers, that had no obvious connection to direct labor-hours or machine-hours. In this new environment, continuing to rely exclusively on a limited number of overhead cost pools and traditional allocation bases posed the risk that reported unit product costs would be distorted and, therefore, misleading when used for decision-making purposes.

Activity-based costing, thanks to advances in technology that make more complex cost systems feasible, provides an alternative to the traditional plantwide and departmental approaches to defining cost pools and selecting allocation bases. The activity-based approach has appeal in today's business environment because it uses more cost pools and unique measures of activity to better understand the costs of managing and sustaining product diversity.

In activity-based costing, an **activity** is any event that causes the consumption of overhead resources. An **activity cost pool** is a "bucket" in which costs are accumulated that relate to a single activity measure in the ABC system. An **activity measure** is an allocation base in an activity-based costing system. The term *cost driver* is also used to refer to an activity measure because the activity measure should "drive" the cost being allocated. The two most common types of activity measures are *transaction drivers* and *duration drivers.* **Transaction drivers** are simple counts of the number of times an activity occurs, such as the number of bills sent out to customers. **Duration drivers** measure the amount of time required to perform an activity, such as the time spent preparing individual bills for customers. In general, duration drivers are more accurate measures of resource consumption than transaction drivers, but they take more effort to record. For that reason, transaction drivers are often used in practice.

IN BUSINESS

A CRITICAL PERSPECTIVE OF ABC

Marconi is a Portuguese telecommunications company that encountered problems with its ABC system. The company's production managers felt that 23% of the costs included in the system were common costs that should not be allocated to products and that allocating these costs to products was not only inaccurate, but also irrelevant to their operational cost reduction efforts. Furthermore, Marconi's front-line workers resisted the ABC system because they felt it might be used to weaken their autonomy and to justify downsizing, outsourcing, and work intensification. They believed that ABC created a "turkeys queuing for Christmas syndrome" because they were expected to volunteer information to help create a cost system that could eventually lead to their demise. These two complications created a third problem—the data necessary to build the ABC cost model was provided by disgruntled and distrustful employees. Consequently, the accuracy of the data was questionable at best. In short, Marconi's experiences illustrate some of the challenges that complicate real-world ABC implementations.

Source: Maria Major and Trevor Hopper, "Managers Divided: Implementing ABC in a Portuguese Telecommunications Company," *Management Accounting Research,* June 2005, pp. 205–229.

Traditional cost systems rely exclusively on allocation bases that are driven by the volume of production. On the other hand, activity-based costing defines five levels of activity—unit-level, batch-level, product-level, customer-level, and organization-sustaining—that largely do *not* relate to the volume of units produced. The costs and corresponding activity measures for unit-level activities do relate to the volume of units produced; however, the remaining categories do not. These levels are described as follows:[2]

1. **Unit-level activities** are performed each time a unit is produced. The costs of unit-level activities should be proportional to the number of units produced. For example, providing power to run processing equipment would be a unit-level activity because power tends to be consumed in proportion to the number of units produced.
2. **Batch-level activities** are performed each time a batch is handled or processed, regardless of how many units are in the batch. For example, tasks such as placing

[2] Robin Cooper, "Cost Classification in Unit-Based and Activity-Based Manufacturing Cost Systems," *Journal of Cost Management,* Fall 1990, pp. 4–14.

purchase orders, setting up equipment, and arranging for shipments to customers are batch-level activities. They are incurred once for each batch (or customer order). Costs at the batch level depend on the number of batches processed rather than on the number of units produced, the number of units sold, or other measures of volume. For example, the cost of setting up a machine for batch processing is the same regardless of whether the batch contains one or thousands of items.

3. **Product-level activities** relate to specific products and typically must be carried out regardless of how many batches are run or units of product are produced or sold. For example, activities such as designing a product, advertising a product, and maintaining a product manager and staff are all product-level activities.
4. **Customer-level activities** relate to specific customers and include activities such as sales calls, catalog mailings, and general technical support that are not tied to any specific product.
5. **Organization-sustaining activities** are carried out regardless of which customers are served, which products are produced, how many batches are run, or how many units are made. This category includes activities such as heating the factory, cleaning executive offices, providing a computer network, arranging for loans, preparing annual reports to shareholders, and so on.

Many companies throughout the world continue to base overhead allocations on direct labor-hours or machine-hours. In situations where overhead costs and direct labor-hours are highly correlated or in situations where the goal of the overhead allocation process is to prepare external financial reports, this practice makes sense. However, if plantwide overhead costs do not move in tandem with plantwide direct labor-hours or machine-hours, product costs will be distorted—with the potential of distorting decisions made within the company.

IN BUSINESS

© Sandee Noreen

DINING IN THE CANYON

Western River Expeditions (www.westernriver.com) runs river rafting trips on the Colorado, Green, and Salmon rivers. One of its most popular trips is a six-day trip down the Grand Canyon, which features famous rapids such as Crystal and Lava Falls as well as the awesome scenery accessible only from the bottom of the Grand Canyon. The company runs trips of one or two rafts, each of which carries two guides and up to 18 guests. The company provides all meals on the trip, which are prepared by the guides.

In terms of the hierarchy of activities, a guest can be considered as a unit and a raft as a batch. In that context, the wages paid to the guides are a batch-level cost because each raft requires two guides regardless of the number of guests in the raft. Each guest is given a mug to use during the trip and to take home at the end of the trip as a souvenir. The cost of the mug is a unit-level cost because the number of mugs given away is strictly proportional to the number of guests on a trip.

What about the costs of food served to guests and guides—is this a unit-level cost, a batch-level cost, a product-level cost, or an organization-sustaining cost? At first glance, it might be thought that food costs are a unit-level cost—the greater the number of guests, the higher the food costs. However, that is not quite correct. Standard menus have been created for each day of the trip. For example, the first night's menu might consist of shrimp cocktail, steak, cornbread, salad, and cheesecake. The day before a trip begins, all of the food needed for the trip is taken from the central warehouse and packed in modular containers. It isn't practical to finely adjust the amount of food for the actual number of guests planned to be on a trip—most of the food comes prepackaged in large lots. For example, the shrimp cocktail menu may call for two large bags of frozen shrimp per raft and that many bags will be packed regardless of how many guests are expected on the raft. Consequently, the costs of food are not a unit-level cost that varies with the number of guests actually on a trip. Instead, the costs of food are a batch-level cost.

Source: Conversations with Western River Expeditions personnel.

Designing an Activity-Based Costing (ABC) System

There are three essential characteristics of a successful activity-based costing implementation. First, top managers must strongly support the ABC implementation because their leadership is instrumental in properly motivating all employees to embrace the need to change. Second, top managers should ensure that ABC data is linked to how people are evaluated and rewarded. If employees continue to be evaluated and rewarded using traditional (non-ABC) cost data, they will quickly get the message that ABC is not important and they will abandon it. Third, a cross-functional team should be created to design and implement the ABC system. The team should include representatives from each area that will use ABC data, such as the marketing, production, engineering, and accounting departments. These cross-functional employees possess intimate knowledge of many parts of an organization's operations that is necessary for designing an effective ABC system. Furthermore, tapping the knowledge of cross-functional managers lessens their resistance to ABC because they feel included in the implementation process. Time after time, when accountants have attempted to implement an ABC system on their own without top-management support and cross-functional involvement, the results have been ignored.

IN BUSINESS

IMPLEMENTING ACTIVITY-BASED COSTING IN CHINA

Xu Ji Electric Company is publicly traded on China's Shen Zhen Stock Exchange. From 2001–2003, it successfully implemented an activity-based costing (ABC) system because top-level managers continuously supported the new system—particularly during a challenging phase when the ABC software encountered problems. The ABC adoption was also aided by Xu Ji's decision to drive the implementation using a top-down approach, which is aligned with the company's cultural norm of deferring to and supporting the hierarchical chain of command.

Xu Ji's experience is similar to Western ABC implementations that have consistently recognized the necessity of top-level management support. However, contrary to Xu Ji's experience, many Western managers do not readily support the top-down implementation of new management innovations in their organizations. They prefer to be involved in the decision-making processes that introduce change into their organizations.

Source: Lana Y.J. Liu and Fei Pan, "The Implementation of Activity-Based Costing in China: An Innovation Action Research Approach," *The British Accounting Review* 39, 2007, pp. 249–264.

MANAGERIAL ACCOUNTING IN ACTION
The Issue

Classic Brass, Inc., makes two main product lines for luxury yachts—standard stanchions and custom compass housings. The president of the company, John Towers, recently attended a management conference at which activity-based costing was discussed. Following the conference, he called a meeting of the company's top managers to discuss what he had learned. Attending the meeting were production manager Susan Richter, the marketing manager Tom Olafson, and the accounting manager Mary Goodman. He began the conference by distributing the company's income statement that Mary Goodman had prepared a few hours earlier (see Exhibit 6–2):

John: Well, it's official. Our company has sunk into the red for the first time in its history—a loss of $1,250.

Tom: I don't know what else we can do! Given our successful efforts to grow sales of the custom compass housings, I was expecting to see a boost to our bottom line, not a net loss. Granted, we have been losing even more bids than usual for standard stanchions because of our recent price increase, but . . .

John: Do you think our prices for standard stanchions are too high?

Tom: No, I don't think our prices are too high. I think our competitors' prices are too low. In fact, I'll bet they are pricing below their cost.

Susan: Why would our competitors price below their cost?

Tom: They are out to grab market share.

EXHIBIT 6–2
Classic Brass Income Statement

Classic Brass Income Statement Year Ended December 31, 2016		
Sales		$3,200,000
Cost of goods sold:		
Direct materials	$ 975,000	
Direct labor	351,250	
Manufacturing overhead*	1,000,000	2,326,250
Gross margin		873,750
Selling and administrative expenses:		
Shipping expenses	65,000	
General administrative expenses	510,000	
Marketing expenses	300,000	875,000
Net operating loss		$ (1,250)

*The company's traditional cost system allocates manufacturing overhead to products using a plantwide overhead rate and machine-hours as the allocation base. Inventory levels did not change during the year.

Susan: What good is more market share if they are losing money on every unit sold?

John: I think Susan has a point. Mary, what is your take on this?

Mary: If our competitors are pricing standard stanchions below cost, shouldn't they be losing money rather than us? If our company is the one using accurate information to make informed decisions while our competitors are supposedly clueless, then why is our "bottom line" taking a beating? Unfortunately, I think we may be the ones relying on distorted cost data, not our competitors.

John: Based on what I heard at the conference that I just attended, I am inclined to agree. One of the presentations at the conference dealt with activity-based costing. As the speaker began describing the usual insights revealed by activity-based costing systems, I was sitting in the audience getting an ill feeling in my stomach.

Mary: Honestly John, I have been claiming for years that our existing cost system is okay for external reporting, but it is dangerous to use it for internal decision making. It sounds like you are on board now, right?

John: Yes.

Mary: Well then, how about if all of you commit the time and energy to help me build a fairly simple activity-based costing system that may shed some light on the problems we are facing?

John: Let's do it. I want each of you to appoint one of your top people to a special "ABC team" to investigate how we cost products.

Like most other ABC implementations, the ABC team decided that its new ABC system would supplement, rather than replace, the existing cost accounting system, which would continue to be used for external financial reports. The new ABC system would be used to prepare special reports for management decisions such as bidding on new business.

The accounting manager drew the chart appearing in Exhibit 6–3 to explain the general structure of the ABC model to her team members. Cost objects such as products generate activities. For example, a customer order for a custom compass housing requires the activity of preparing a production order. Such an activity consumes resources. A production order uses a sheet of paper and takes time to fill out. And consumption of resources causes costs. The greater the number of sheets used to fill out production orders and the greater the amount of time devoted to filling out such orders, the greater the cost. Activity-based costing attempts to trace through these relationships to identify how products and customers affect costs.

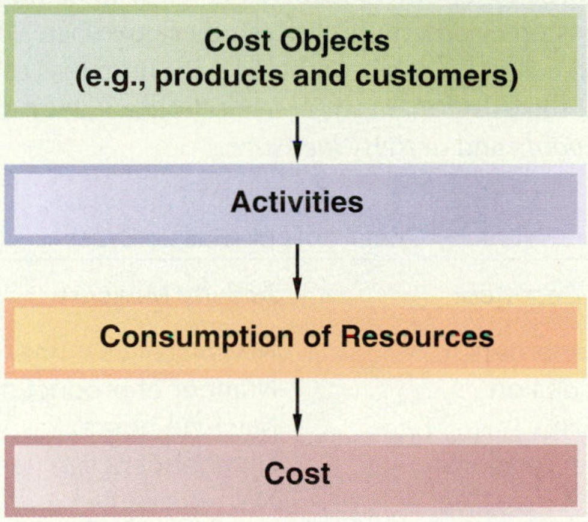

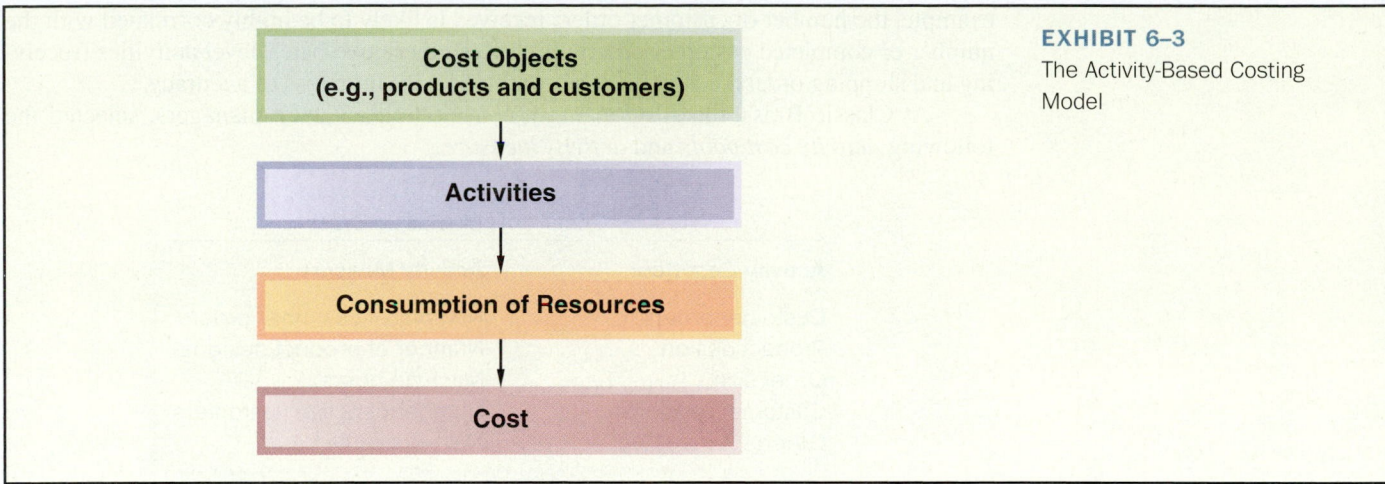

EXHIBIT 6–3
The Activity-Based Costing Model

As in most other companies, the ABC team at Classic Brass felt that the company's traditional cost accounting system adequately measured the direct materials and direct labor costs of products because these costs are directly traced to products. Therefore, the ABC study would be concerned solely with the other costs of the company—manufacturing overhead and selling and administrative costs.

The team felt it was important to carefully plan how it would go about implementing the new ABC system at Classic Brass. Accordingly, it broke down the implementation process into five steps:

Steps for Implementing Activity–Based Costing:

1. Define activities, activity cost pools, and activity measures.
2. Assign overhead costs to activity cost pools.
3. Calculate activity rates.
4. Assign overhead costs to cost objects using the activity rates and activity measures.
5. Prepare management reports.

Step 1: Define Activities, Activity Cost Pools, and Activity Measures

The first major step in implementing an ABC system is to identify the activities that will form the foundation for the system. This can be difficult and time-consuming and involves a great deal of judgment. A common procedure is for the individuals on the ABC implementation team to interview people who work in overhead departments and ask them to describe their major activities. Ordinarily, this results in a very long list of activities.

The length of such lists of activities poses a problem. On the one hand, the greater the number of activities tracked in the ABC system, the more accurate the costs are likely to be. On the other hand, a complex system involving large numbers of activities is costly to design, implement, maintain, and use. Consequently, the original lengthy list of activities is usually reduced to a handful by combining similar activities. For example, several actions may be involved in handling and moving raw materials—from receiving raw materials on the loading dock to sorting them into the appropriate bins in the storeroom. All of these activities might be combined into a single activity called material handling.

When combining activities in an ABC system, activities should be grouped together at the appropriate level. Batch-level activities should not be combined with unit-level activities or product-level activities with batch-level activities and so on. In general, it is best to combine only those activities that are highly correlated with each other within a level. For example, the number of customer orders received is likely to be highly correlated with the number of completed customer orders shipped, so these two batch-level activities (receiving and shipping orders) can usually be combined with little loss of accuracy.

At Classic Brass, the ABC team, in consultation with top managers, selected the following *activity cost pools* and *activity measures:*

Activity Cost Pools at Classic Brass

Activity Cost Pool	Activity Measure
Customer orders.	Number of customer orders
Product design	Number of product designs
Order size.	Machine-hours
Customer relations	Number of active customers
Other.	Not applicable

The *Customer Orders* cost pool will be assigned all costs of resources that are consumed by taking and processing customer orders, including costs of processing paperwork and any costs involved in setting up machines for specific orders. The activity measure for this cost pool is the number of customer orders received. This is a batch-level activity because each order generates work that occurs regardless of whether the order is for one unit or 1,000 units.

The *Product Design* cost pool will be assigned all costs of resources consumed by designing products. The activity measure for this cost pool is the number of products designed. This is a product-level activity because the amount of design work on a new product does not depend on the number of units ultimately ordered or batches ultimately run.

The *Order Size* cost pool will be assigned all costs of resources consumed as a consequence of the number of units produced, including the costs of miscellaneous factory supplies, power to run machines, and some equipment depreciation. This is a unit-level activity because each unit requires some of these resources. The activity measure for this cost pool is machine-hours.

The *Customer Relations* cost pool will be assigned all costs associated with maintaining relations with customers, including the costs of sales calls and the costs of entertaining customers. The activity measure for this cost pool is the number of customers the company has on its active customer list. The Customer Relations cost pool represents a customer-level activity.

The *Other* cost pool will be assigned all overhead costs that are not associated with customer orders, product design, the size of the orders, or customer relations. These costs mainly consist of organization-sustaining costs and the costs of unused, idle capacity. These costs *will not* be assigned to products because they represent resources that are *not* consumed by products.

It is unlikely that any other company would use exactly the same activity cost pools and activity measures that were selected by Classic Brass. Because of the amount of judgment involved, the number and definitions of the activity cost pools and activity measures used by companies vary considerably.

The Mechanics of Activity-Based Costing

LEARNING OBJECTIVE 6–2
Assign costs to cost pools using a first-stage allocation.

Step 2: Assign Overhead Costs to Activity Cost Pools

Exhibit 6–4 shows the annual overhead costs (both manufacturing and nonmanufacturing) that Classic Brass intends to assign to its activity cost pools. Notice the data in the exhibit are organized by department (e.g., Production, General Administrative, and Marketing). This is because the data have been extracted from the company's general ledger. General ledgers usually classify costs within the departments where the costs are incurred. For example,

EXHIBIT 6–4
Annual Overhead Costs (Both Manufacturing and Nonmanufacturing) at Classic Brass

Production Department:		
Indirect factory wages	$500,000	
Factory equipment depreciation	300,000	
Factory utilities	120,000	
Factory building lease	80,000	$1,000,000
General Administrative Department:		
Administrative wages and salaries	400,000	
Office equipment depreciation	50,000	
Administrative building lease	60,000	510,000
Marketing Department:		
Marketing wages and salaries	250,000	
Selling expenses	50,000	300,000
Total overhead cost		$1,810,000

salaries, supplies, rent, and so forth incurred in the marketing department are charged to that department. The functional orientation of the general ledger mirrors the presentation of costs in the absorption income statement in Exhibit 6–2. In fact, you'll notice the total costs for the Production Department in Exhibit 6–4 ($1,000,000) equal the total manufacturing overhead costs from the income statement in Exhibit 6–2. Similarly, the total costs for the General Administrative and Marketing Departments in Exhibit 6–4 ($510,000 and $300,000) equal the marketing and general and administrative expenses shown in Exhibit 6–2.

Three costs included in the income statement in Exhibit 6–2: direct materials, direct labor, and shipping—are excluded from the costs shown in Exhibit 6–4. The ABC team purposely excluded these costs from Exhibit 6–4 because the existing cost system can accurately trace direct materials, direct labor, and shipping costs to products. There is no need to incorporate these direct costs in the activity-based allocations of indirect costs.

Classic Brass's activity-based costing system will divide the nine types of overhead costs in Exhibit 6–4 among its activity cost pools via an allocation process called *first-stage allocation.* The **first-stage allocation** in an ABC system is the process of assigning functionally organized overhead costs derived from a company's general ledger to the activity cost pools.

First-stage allocations are usually based on the results of interviews with employees who have first-hand knowledge of the activities. For example, Classic Brass needs to allocate $500,000 of indirect factory wages to its five activity cost pools. These allocations will be more accurate if the employees who are classified as indirect factory workers (e.g., supervisors, engineers, and quality inspectors) are asked to estimate what percentage of their time is spent dealing with customer orders, with product design, with processing units of product (i.e., order size), and with customer relations. These interviews are conducted with considerable care. Those who are interviewed must thoroughly understand what the activities encompass and what is expected of them in the interview. In addition, departmental managers are typically interviewed to determine how the non-personnel costs should be distributed across the activity cost pools. For example, the Classic Brass production manager would be interviewed to determine how the $300,000 of factory equipment depreciation (shown in Exhibit 6–4) should be allocated to the activity cost pools. The key question that the production manager would need to answer is "What percentage of the available machine capacity is consumed by each activity such as the number of customer orders or the number of units processed (i.e., size of orders)?"

The results of the interviews at Classic Brass are displayed in Exhibit 6–5. For example, factory equipment depreciation is distributed 20% to Customer Orders, 60% to Order Size, and 20% to the Other cost pool. The resource in this instance is machine time. According to the estimates made by the production manager, 60% of the total available machine time was used to actually process units to fill orders. This percentage is entered in the Order Size column. Each customer order requires setting up, which also requires machine time. This activity consumes 20% of the total available machine time and is entered under the Customer Orders column. The remaining 20% of available machine time represents idle time and is entered under the Other column.

IN BUSINESS

AN ABC APPLICATION IN THE CONSTRUCTION INDUSTRY

Researchers from the United States and the Republic of Korea studied how a Korean manufacturer assigned the indirect costs of supplying reinforced steel bars (also called *rebar*) to various construction projects. The company's traditional cost system assigned all indirect costs to projects using rebar tonnage as the allocation base. Its ABC system had 10 activities that assigned indirect costs to projects using activity measures such as number of orders, number of sheets, number of distributing runs, number of production runs, and number of inspections.

The traditional and ABC systems assigned the following overhead costs to three construction projects called Commercial, High-Rise Condo, and Heavy Civil:

	Commercial	High-Rise Condo	Heavy Civil
Traditional cost system allocations	$ 64,587	$ 50,310	$91,102
ABC allocations......................	90,466	61,986	53,548
Difference	$(25,879)	$(11,676)	$37,554

Notice that the traditional cost system was undercosting the Commercial and High-Rise Condo projects relative to the ABC system. It was also overcosting the Heavy Civil project by $37,554 when compared to the ABC system.

Source: Yong-Woo Kim, Seungheon Han, "Sungwon Shin, and Kunhee Choi, "A Case Study of Activity-Based Costing in Allocation Rebar Fabrication Costs to Projects," *Construction Management and Economics,* May 2010, pp. 449–461.

Exhibit 6–5 and many of the other exhibits in this chapter are presented in the form of Excel spreadsheets. All of the calculations required in activity-based costing can be done by hand. Nevertheless, setting up an activity-based costing system on a spreadsheet or using special ABC software can save a lot of work—particularly in situations involving many activity cost pools and in organizations that periodically update their ABC systems.

We will not go into the details of how all of the percentages in Exhibit 6–5 were determined. However, note that 100% of the factory building lease has been assigned to the Other cost pool. Classic Brass has a single production facility. It has no plans to expand or to sublease any excess space. The cost of this production facility is treated as an organization-sustaining cost because there is no way to avoid even a portion of this cost if a particular product or customer were to be dropped. (Remember that organization-sustaining costs are assigned to the Other cost pool and are not allocated to products.) In contrast, some companies have separate facilities for manufacturing specific products. The costs of these separate facilities could be directly traced to the specific products.

Once the percentage distributions in Exhibit 6–5 have been established, it is easy to allocate costs to the activity cost pools. The results of this first-stage allocation are displayed in Exhibit 6–6. Each cost is allocated across the activity cost pools by multiplying it by the percentages in Exhibit 6–5. For example, the indirect factory wages of $500,000 are multiplied by the 25% entry under Customer Orders in Exhibit 6–5 to arrive at the $125,000 entry under Customer Orders in Exhibit 6–6. Similarly, the indirect factory wages of $500,000 are multiplied by the 40% entry under Product Design in Exhibit 6–5 to arrive at the $200,000 entry under Product Design in Exhibit 6–6. All of the entries in Exhibit 6–6 are computed in this way.

Now that the first-stage allocations to the activity cost pools have been completed, the next step is to compute the activity rates.

EXHIBIT 6–5
Results of Interviews: Distribution of Resource Consumption across Activity Cost Pools

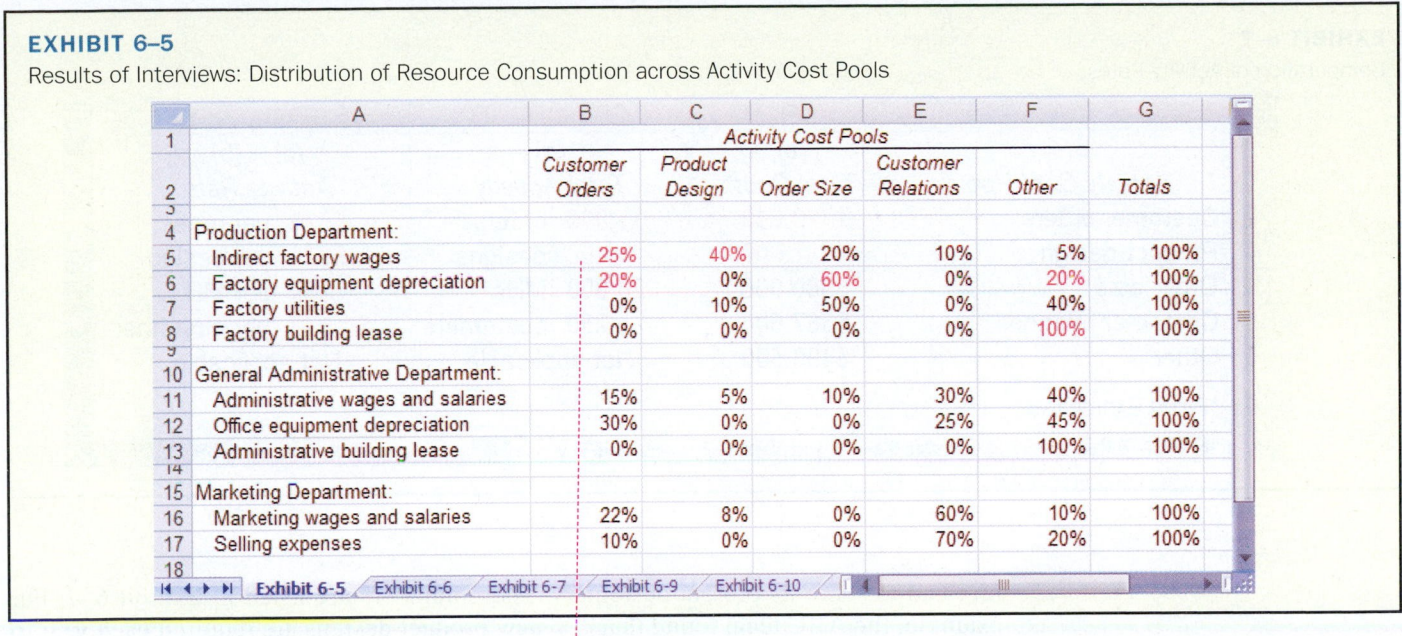

	Customer Orders	Product Design	Order Size	Customer Relations	Other	Totals
Production Department:						
Indirect factory wages	25%	40%	20%	10%	5%	100%
Factory equipment depreciation	20%	0%	60%	0%	20%	100%
Factory utilities	0%	10%	50%	0%	40%	100%
Factory building lease	0%	0%	0%	0%	100%	100%
General Administrative Department:						
Administrative wages and salaries	15%	5%	10%	30%	40%	100%
Office equipment depreciation	30%	0%	0%	25%	45%	100%
Administrative building lease	0%	0%	0%	0%	100%	100%
Marketing Department:						
Marketing wages and salaries	22%	8%	0%	60%	10%	100%
Selling expenses	10%	0%	0%	70%	20%	100%

(Activity Cost Pools: Customer Orders, Product Design, Order Size, Customer Relations, Other)

Exhibit 6-5 | Exhibit 6-6 | Exhibit 6-7 | Exhibit 6-9 | Exhibit 6-10

EXHIBIT 6–6
First-Stage Allocations to Activity Cost Pools

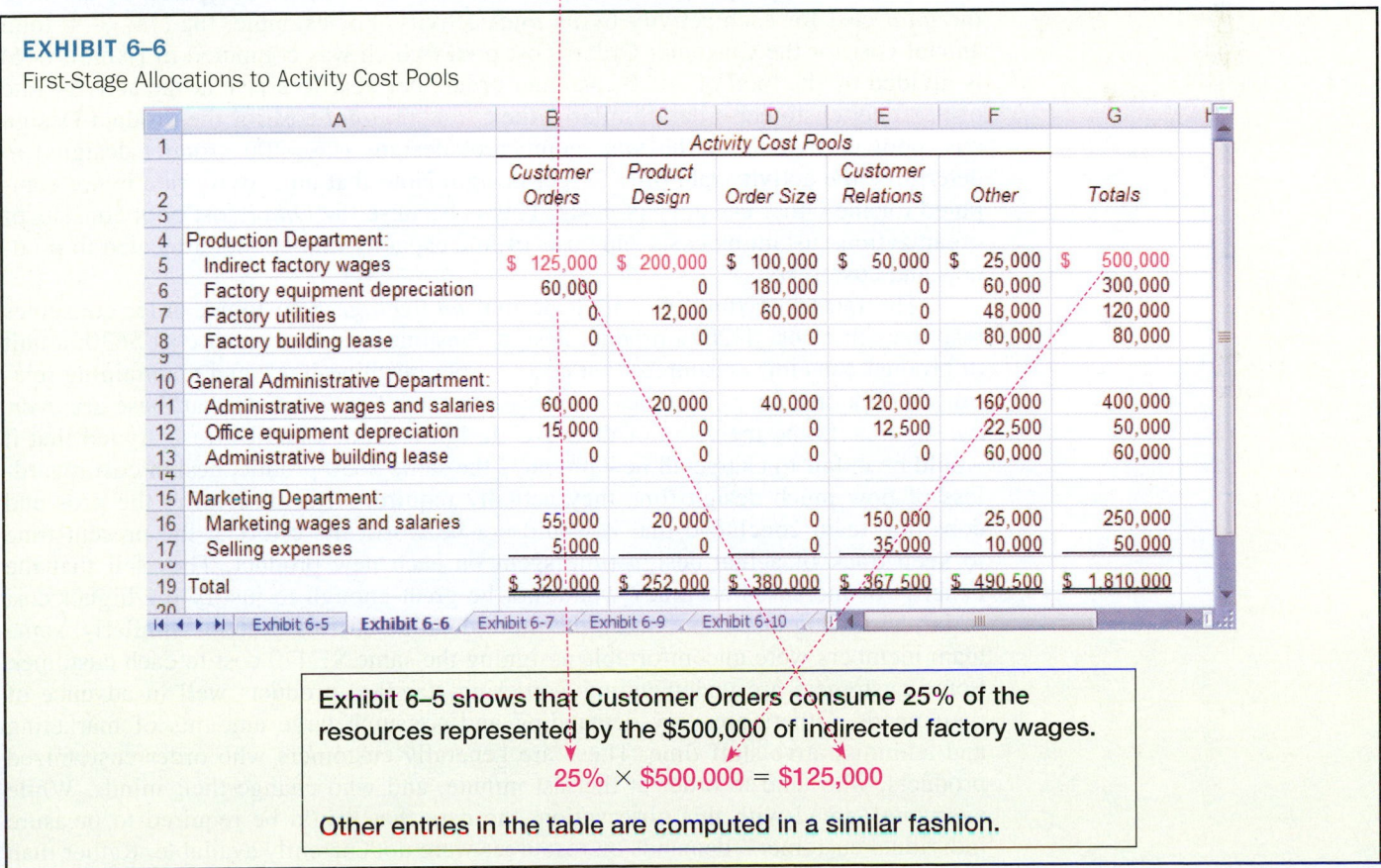

	Customer Orders	Product Design	Order Size	Customer Relations	Other	Totals
Production Department:						
Indirect factory wages	$ 125,000	$ 200,000	$ 100,000	$ 50,000	$ 25,000	$ 500,000
Factory equipment depreciation	60,000	0	180,000	0	60,000	300,000
Factory utilities	0	12,000	60,000	0	48,000	120,000
Factory building lease	0	0	0	0	80,000	80,000
General Administrative Department:						
Administrative wages and salaries	60,000	20,000	40,000	120,000	160,000	400,000
Office equipment depreciation	15,000	0	0	12,500	22,500	50,000
Administrative building lease	0	0	0	0	60,000	60,000
Marketing Department:						
Marketing wages and salaries	55,000	20,000	0	150,000	25,000	250,000
Selling expenses	5,000	0	0	35,000	10,000	50,000
Total	$ 320,000	$ 252,000	$ 380,000	$ 367,500	$ 490,500	$ 1,810,000

(Activity Cost Pools: Customer Orders, Product Design, Order Size, Customer Relations, Other)

Exhibit 6-5 | Exhibit 6-6 | Exhibit 6-7 | Exhibit 6-9 | Exhibit 6-10

Exhibit 6–5 shows that Customer Orders consume 25% of the resources represented by the $500,000 of indirected factory wages.

25% × $500,000 = $125,000

Other entries in the table are computed in a similar fashion.

Step 3: Calculate Activity Rates

LEARNING OBJECTIVE 6–3
Compute activity rates for cost pools.

The activity rates that will be used for assigning overhead costs to products and customers are computed in Exhibit 6–7. The ABC team determined the total activity for each cost pool that would be required to produce the company's present product

EXHIBIT 6–7
Computation of Activity Rates

	A	B	C	D	E	F
1	*Activity Cost Pools*	*(a)* *Total Cost**	*(b)* *Total Activity*		*(a) ÷ (b)* *Activity Rate*	
2	Customer orders	$320,000	1,000	orders	$320	per order
3	Product design	$252,000	400	designs	$630	per design
4	Order size	$380,000	20,000	MHs	$19	per MH
5	Customer relations	$367,500	250	customers	$1,470	per customer
6	Other	$490,500	Not applicable		Not applicable	
7						
8	*From Exhibit 6-6.					

Exhibit 6-5 | Exhibit 6-6 | **Exhibit 6-7** | Exhibit 6-9

mix and to serve its present customers. These numbers are listed in Exhibit 6–7. For example, the ABC team found that 400 new product designs are required each year to serve the company's present customers. The activity rates are computed by dividing the *total* cost for each activity by its *total* activity. For example, the $320,000 total annual cost for the Customer Orders cost pool (which was computed in Exhibit 6–6) is divided by the total of 1,000 customer orders per year to arrive at the activity rate of $320 per customer order. Similarly, the $252,000 *total* cost for the Product Design cost pool is divided by the *total* number of designs (i.e., 400 product designs) to determine the activity rate of $630 per design. Note that an activity rate is not computed for the Other category of costs. This is because the *Other* cost pool consists of organization-sustaining costs and costs of idle capacity that are not allocated to products and customers.

The rates in Exhibit 6–7 indicate that *on average* a customer order consumes resources that cost $320; a product design consumes resources that cost $630; a unit of product consumes resources that cost $19 per machine-hour; and maintaining relations with a customer consumes resources that cost $1,470. Note that these are *average* figures. Some members of the ABC design team at Classic Brass argued that it would be unfair to charge all new products the same $630 product design cost regardless of how much design time they actually require. After discussing the pros and cons, the team concluded that it would not be worth the effort at the present time to keep track of actual design time spent on each new product. They felt that the benefits of increased accuracy would not be great enough to justify the higher cost of implementing and maintaining the more detailed costing system. Similarly, some team members were uncomfortable assigning the same $1,470 cost to each customer. Some customers are undemanding—ordering standard products well in advance of their needs. Others are very demanding and consume large amounts of marketing and administrative staff time. These are generally customers who order customized products, who tend to order at the last minute, and who change their minds. While everyone agreed with this observation, the data that would be required to measure individual customers' demands on resources were not currently available. Rather than delay implementation of the ABC system, the team decided to defer such refinements to a later date.

Before proceeding further, it would be helpful to get a better idea of the overall process of assigning costs to products and other cost objects in an ABC system. Exhibit 6–8 provides a visual perspective of the ABC system at Classic Brass. We recommend that you carefully go over this exhibit. In particular, note that the Other category, which contains organization-sustaining costs and costs of idle capacity, is not allocated to products or customers.

EXHIBIT 6–8
The Activity-Based Costing Model at Classic Brass

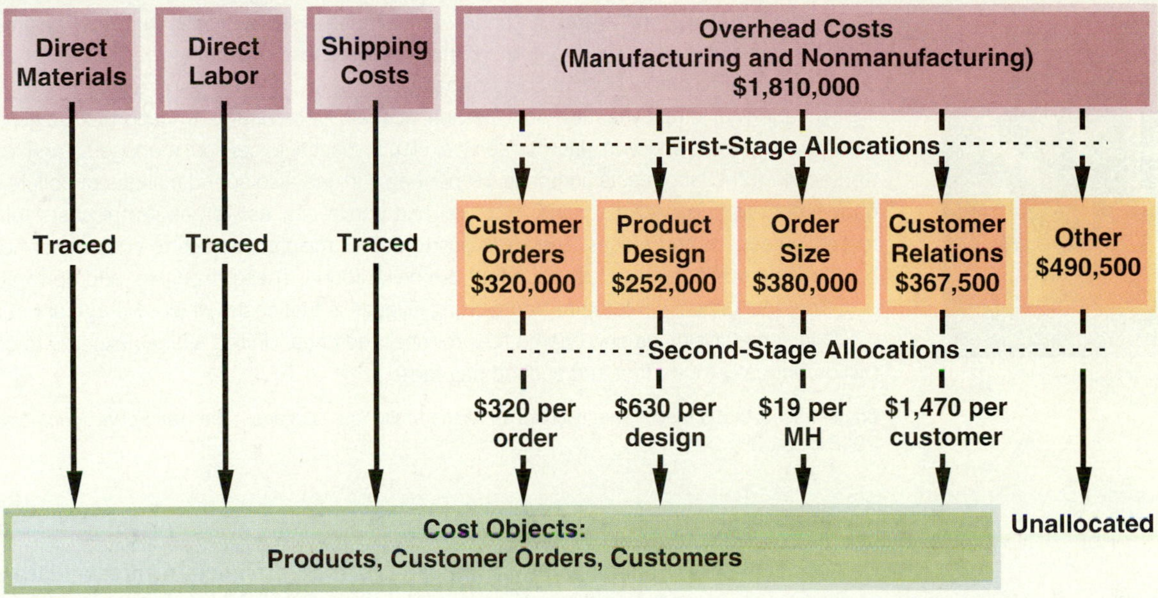

Step 4: Assign Overhead Costs to Cost Objects

LEARNING OBJECTIVE 6–4
Assign costs to a cost object using a second-stage allocation.

The fourth step in the implementation of activity-based costing is called *second-stage allocation.* In the **second-stage allocation,** activity rates are used to apply overhead costs to products and customers. First, we will illustrate how to assign costs to products followed by an example of how to assign costs to customers.

The data needed by the ABC team to assign overhead costs to Classic Brass's two products—standard stanchions and custom compass housings—are as follows:

Standard Stanchions

1. This product line does not require any new design resources.
2. 30,000 units were ordered during the year, comprising 600 separate orders.
3. Each stanchion requires 35 minutes of machine time for a total of 17,500 machine-hours.

Custom Compass Housings

1. This is a custom product that requires new design resources.
2. There were 400 orders for custom compass housings. Orders for this product are placed separately from orders for standard stanchions.
3. There were 400 custom designs prepared. One custom design was prepared for each order.
4. Because some orders were for more than one unit, a total of 1,250 custom compass housings were produced during the year. A custom compass housing requires an average of 2 machine-hours for a total of 2,500 machine-hours.

Notice, 600 customer orders were placed for standard stanchions and 400 customer orders were placed for custom compass housings, for a total of 1,000 customer orders. All 400 product designs related to custom compass housings; none related to standard stanchions. Producing 30,000 standard stanchions required 17,500 machine-hours and producing 1,250 custom compass housings required 2,500 machine-hours, for a total of 20,000 machine-hours.

IN BUSINESS

© Ryan McVay/Photodisc/ Getty Images, RF

HOW MUCH DOES IT COST TO HANDLE A PIECE OF LUGGAGE?

It costs an airline about $15 to carry a piece of checked luggage from one destination another. The activity "transporting luggage" consists of numerous sub-activities such as tagging bags, sorting them, placing them on carts, transporting bags planeside, loading them into the airplane, and delivering them to carousels and connecting flights.

A variety of employees invest a portion of their labor hours "transporting luggage" including ground personnel, check-in agents, service clerks, baggage service managers, and maintenance workers. In total, labor costs comprise $9 per bag. Airlines also spend millions of dollars on baggage equipment, sorting systems, carts, tractors, and conveyors, as well as rental costs related to bag rooms, carousels, and offices. They also pay to deliver misplaced bags to customers' homes and to compensate customers for lost bags that are never found. These expenses add up to about $4 per bag. The final expense related to transporting luggage is fuel costs, which average about $2 per bag.

Many major airlines now charge fees for checked bags. United Airlines expects to collect $275 million annually for its first and second bag fees.

Source: Scott McCartney, "What It Costs an Airline to Fly Your Luggage," *The Wall Street Journal,* November 25, 2008, p. D1 and D8.

Exhibit 6–9 illustrates how overhead costs are assigned to the standard stanchions and custom compass housings. For example, the exhibit shows that $192,000 of overhead costs are assigned from the Customer Orders activity cost pool to the standard stanchions ($320 per order × 600 orders). Similarly, $128,000 of overhead costs are assigned from the Customer Orders activity cost pool to the custom compass housings ($320 per order × 400 orders). The Customer Orders cost pool contained a total of $320,000 (see Exhibit 6–6 or 6–7) and this total amount has been assigned to the two products ($192,000 + $128,000 = $320,000).

Exhibit 6–9 shows that a total of $952,000 of overhead costs is assigned to Classic Brass's two product lines—$524,500 to standard stanchions and $427,500 to custom compass housings. This amount is less than the $1,810,000 of overhead costs included in the ABC system. Why? The total amount of overhead assigned to products does not match the total amount of overhead cost in the ABC system because the ABC team purposely did not assign the $367,500 of Customer Relations and $490,500 of Other costs to products. The Customer Relations activity is a customer-level activity and the Other activity is an organization-sustaining activity—neither activity is caused by products. As shown below, when the Customer Relations and Other activity costs are added to the $952,000 of overhead costs assigned to products, the total is $1,810,000.

	Standard Stanchions	Custom Compass Housings	Total
Overhead Costs Assigned to Products			
Customer orders	$192,000	$128,000	$ 320,000
Product design	0	252,000	252,000
Order size	332,500	47,500	380,000
Subtotal	$524,500	$427,500	952,000
Overhead Costs Not Assigned to Products			
Customer relations			367,500
Other			490,500
Subtotal			858,000
Total overhead cost			$1,810,000

EXHIBIT 6–9
Assigning Overhead Costs to Products

	A	B	C	D	E	F
1	**Overhead Cost for the Standard Stanchions**					
2	*Activity Cost Pools*	*(a) Activity Rate**		*(b) Activity*		*(a) × (b) ABC Cost*
3	Customer orders	$320	per order	600	orders	$ 192,000
4	Product design	$630	per design	0	designs	0
5	Order size	$19	per MH	17,500	MHs	332,500
6	Total					$ 524,500
7						
8	**Overhead Cost for the Custom Compass Housing**					
9	*Activity Cost Pools*	*(a) Activity Rate**		*(b) Activity*		*(a) × (b) ABC Cost*
10	Customer orders	$320	per order	400	orders	$ 128,000
11	Product design	$630	per design	400	designs	252,000
12	Order size	$19	per MH	2,500	MHs	47,500
13	Total					$ 427,500
14						
15	*From Exhibit 6-7.					

Exhibit 6-6 | Exhibit 6-7 | Exhibit 6-9 | Exhibit 6-10

Next, we describe another example of second-stage allocation—assigning activity costs to customers. The data needed by Classic Brass to assign overhead costs to one of its customers—Windward Yachts—are as follows:

Windward Yachts

1. The company placed a total of three orders.
   a. Two orders were for 150 standard stanchions per order.
   b. One order was for a single custom compass housing unit.
2. A total of 177 machine-hours were used to fulfill the three customer orders.
   a. The 300 standard stanchions required 175 machine-hours.
   b. The custom compass housing required 2 machine-hours.
3. Windward Yachts is one of 250 customers served by Classic Brass.

Exhibit 6–10 illustrates how the ABC system assigns overhead costs to this customer. As shown in Exhibit 6–10, the ABC team calculated that $6,423 of overhead costs should be assigned to Windward Yachts. The exhibit shows that Windward Yachts is assigned $960 ($320 per order × 3 orders) of overhead costs from the Customer Orders activity cost pool; $630 ($630 per design × 1 design) from the Product Design cost pool; $3,363 ($19 per machine-hour × 177 machine-hours) from the Order Size cost pool; and $1,470 ($1,470 per customer × 1 customer) from the Customer Relations cost pool.

With second-stage allocations complete, the ABC design team was ready to turn its attention to creating reports that would help explain the company's first ever net operating loss.

EXHIBIT 6–10
Assigning Overhead Costs to Customers

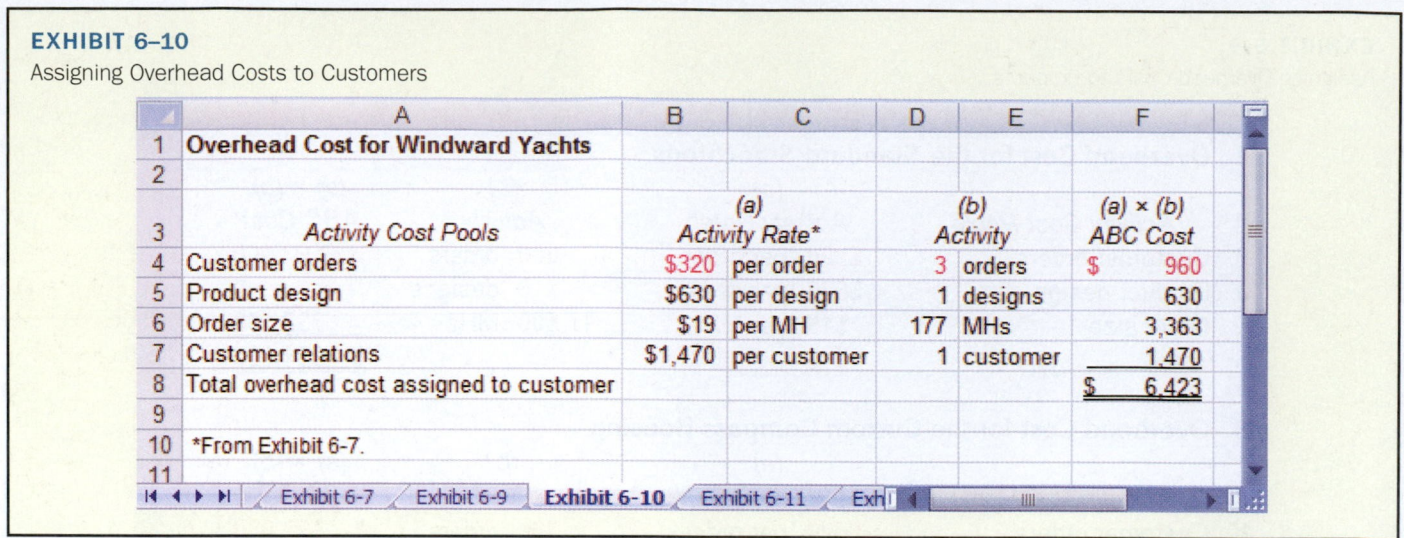

	A	B	C	D	E	F
1	**Overhead Cost for Windward Yachts**					
2						
3	*Activity Cost Pools*		*(a) Activity Rate**		*(b) Activity*	*(a) × (b) ABC Cost*
4	Customer orders	$320	per order	3	orders	$ 960
5	Product design	$630	per design	1	designs	630
6	Order size	$19	per MH	177	MHs	3,363
7	Customer relations	$1,470	per customer	1	customer	1,470
8	Total overhead cost assigned to customer					$ 6,423
9						
10	*From Exhibit 6-7.					
11						

Exhibit 6-7 / Exhibit 6-9 / **Exhibit 6-10** / Exhibit 6-11 / Exh

Step 5: Prepare Management Reports

LEARNING OBJECTIVE 6–5
Use activity-based costing to compute product and customer margins.

The most common management reports prepared with ABC data are product and customer profitability reports. These reports help companies channel their resources to their most profitable growth opportunities while at the same time highlighting products and customers that drain profits. We begin by illustrating a product profitability report followed by a customer profitability report.

The Classic Brass ABC team realized that the profit from a product, also called the *product margin,* is a function of the product's sales and the direct and indirect costs that the product causes. The ABC cost allocations shown in Exhibit 6–9 only summarize each product's indirect (i.e., overhead) costs. Therefore, to compute a product's profit (i.e., product margin), the design team needed to gather each product's sales and direct costs in addition to the overhead costs previously computed. The pertinent sales and direct cost data for each product are shown below. Notice the numbers in the total column agree with the income statement in Exhibit 6–2.

	Standard Stanchions	Custom Compass Housings	Total
Sales	$2,660,000	$540,000	$3,200,000
Direct costs:			
Direct materials	$905,500	$69,500	$975,000
Direct labor	$263,750	$87,500	$351,250
Shipping	$60,000	$5,000	$65,000

Having gathered the above data, the design team created the product profitability report shown in Exhibit 6–11. The report revealed that standard stanchions are profitable, with a positive product margin of $906,250, whereas the custom compass housings are unprofitable, with a negative product margin of $49,500. Keep in mind that the product profitability report purposely does not include the costs in the Customer Relations and Other activity cost pools. These costs, which total $858,000, were excluded from the report because they are not caused by the products. Customer Relations costs are caused by customers, not products. The Other costs are organization-sustaining costs and unused capacity costs that are not caused by any particular product.

EXHIBIT 6–11
Product Margins—Activity-Based Costing

	A	B	C	D	E	F
1	**Product Margins—Activity-Based Costing**					
2		*Standard Stanchions*			*Custom Compass Housings*	
3	Sales		$ 2,660,000			$ 540,000
4	Costs:					
5	Direct materials	$ 905,500			$ 69,500	
6	Direct labor	263,750			87,500	
7	Shipping	60,000			5,000	
8	Customer orders (from Exhibit 6-9)	192,000			128,000	
9	Product design (from Exhibit 6-9)	-			252,000	
10	Order size (from Exhibit 6-9)	332,500			47,500	
11	Total cost		1,753,750			589,500
12	Product margin		$ 906,250			$ (49,500)
13						

Exhibit 6-7 | Exhibit 6-9 | Exhibit 6-10 | **Exhibit 6-11** | Exhibit 6-

The product margins can be reconciled with the company's net operating loss as follows:

	Standard Stanchions	Custom Compass Housings	Total
Sales (See Exhibit 6–11)	$2,660,000	$540,000	$3,200,000
Total costs (See Exhibit 6–11)	1,753,750	589,500	2,343,250
Product margins (See Exhibit 6–11)	$ 906,250	$ (49,500)	856,750
Overhead costs not assigned to products:			
Customer relations			367,500
Other			490,500
Total			858,000
Net operating loss			$ (1,250)

Next, the design team created a customer profitability report for Windward Yachts. Similar to the product profitability report, the design team needed to gather data concerning sales to Windward Yachts and the direct material, direct labor, and shipping costs associated with those sales. Those data are presented below:

	Windward Yachts
Sales	$11,350
Direct costs:	
Direct material costs	$2,123
Direct labor costs	$1,900
Shipping costs	$205

Using these data and the data from Exhibit 6–10, the design team created the customer profitability report shown in Exhibit 6–12. The report revealed that the customer margin for Windward Yachts is $699. A similar report could be prepared for each of Classic Brass's 250 customers, thereby enabling the company to cultivate relationships with its most profitable customers, while taking steps to reduce the negative impact of unprofitable customers.

IN BUSINESS

IS ACTIVITY-BASED COSTING STILL BEING USED?

Researchers surveyed 348 managers to determine which costing methods their companies use. The table below shows the percentage of respondents whose companies use the various costing methods to assign departmental costs to cost objects such as products.

	Departments						
Costing Method	Research and Development	Product and Process Design	Production	Sales and Marketing	Distribution	Customer Service	Shared Services
Activity-based	13.0%	14.7%	18.3%	17.3%	17.2%	21.8%	23.0%
Standard[1]	17.6%	20.7%	42.0%	18.1%	28.4%	18.5%	23.0%
Normal[2]	4.6%	8.6%	9.9%	7.9%	6.0%	8.1%	5.6%
Actual[3]	23.1%	25.0%	23.7%	23.6%	26.7%	16.9%	15.9%
Other	1.9%	0.9%	0.0%	0.8%	0.9%	1.6%	2.4%
Not allocated	39.8%	30.2%	6.1%	32.3%	20.7%	33.1%	30.2%

[1]Standard costing is used for the variance computations in Chapter 10.
[2]Normal costing is used for the job-order costing computations in Chapter 3.
[3]Actual costing is used to create the absorption and variable costing income statements in Chapter 6.

The results show that 18.3% of respondents use ABC to allocate production costs to cost objects and 42% use standard costing for the same purpose. ABC is used by at least 13% of respondents within all functional departments across the value chain. Many companies do not allocate nonproduction costs to cost objects.

Source: William O. Stratton, Denis Desroches, Raef Lawson, and Toby Hatch, "Activity-Based Costing: Is It Still Relevant?" *Management Accounting Quarterly*, Spring 2009, pp. 31–40.

EXHIBIT 6–12
Customer Margin—Activity-Based Costing

	A	B	C
1	**Customer Margin—Activity-Based Costing**		
2		*Windward Yachts*	
3	Sales		$ 11,350
4	Costs:		
5	Direct materials	$ 2,123	
6	Direct labor	1,900	
7	Shipping	205	
8	Customer orders (from Exhibit 6-10)	960	
9	Product design (from Exhibit 6-10)	630	
10	Order size (from Exhibit 6-10)	3,363	
11	Customer relations (from Exhibit 6-10)	1,470	10,651
12	Customer margin		$ 699
13			

Exhibit 6-12 / Exhibit 6-13 / Exhibit 6-14 / Exhibit 6A

Comparison of Traditional and ABC Product Costs

The ABC team used a two-step process to compare its traditional and ABC product costs. First, the team reviewed the product margins reported by the traditional cost system. Then, it contrasted the differences between the traditional and ABC product margins.

Product Margins Computed Using the Traditional Cost System

Classic Brass's traditional cost system assigns only manufacturing costs to products—this includes direct materials, direct labor, and manufacturing overhead. Selling and administrative costs are not assigned to products. Exhibit 6–13 shows the product margins reported by Classic Brass's traditional cost system. We will explain how these margins were calculated in three steps. First, the sales and direct materials and direct labor cost data are the same numbers used by the ABC team to prepare Exhibit 6–11. In other words, the traditional cost system and the ABC system treat these three pieces of revenue and cost data identically.

Second, the traditional cost system uses a plantwide overhead rate to assign manufacturing overhead costs to products. The numerator for the plantwide overhead rate is $1,000,000, which is the total amount of manufacturing overhead shown on the income statement in Exhibit 6–2. The footnote in Exhibit 6–2 mentions that the traditional cost system uses machine-hours to assign manufacturing overhead costs to products. The Order Size activity in Exhibit 6–7 used 20,000 machine-hours as its level of activity. These same 20,000 machine-hours would be used in the denominator of the plantwide overhead rate, which is computed as follows:

$$\text{Plantwide overhead rate} = \frac{\text{Total estimated manufacturing overhead}}{\text{Total estimated machine-hours}}$$

$$= \frac{\$1{,}000{,}000}{20{,}000 \text{ machine-hours}}$$

$$= \$50 \text{ per machine-hour}$$

Because 17,500 machine-hours were worked on standard stanchions, this product line is assigned $875,000 (17,500 machine-hours × $50 per machine-hour) of manufacturing overhead cost. Similarly, the custom compass housings required 2,500 machine-hours, so this product line is assigned $125,000 (2,500 machine-hours × $50 per machine-hour) of manufacturing overhead cost. The sales of each product minus its cost of goods sold equals the product margin of $615,750 for standard stanchions and $258,000 for custom compass housings.

Notice, the net operating loss of $1,250 shown in Exhibit 6–13 agrees with the loss reported in the income statement in Exhibit 6–2 and with the loss shown in the table beneath Exhibit 6–11. The company's *total* sales, *total* costs, and its resulting net operating loss are the same regardless of whether you are looking at the absorption income statement in Exhibit 6–2, the ABC product profitability analysis, or the traditional

EXHIBIT 6–13
Product Margins—Traditional Costing System

	A	B	C	D	E	F	G	H	I
1	**Product Margins—Traditional Cost System**								
2		*Standard Stanchions*			*Custom Compass Housings*			*Total*	
3	Sales		$2,660,000			$ 540,000			$3,200,000
4	Cost of goods sold:								
5	Direct materials	$ 905,500			$ 69,500			$ 975,000	
6	Direct labor	263,750			87,500			351,250	
7	Manufacturing overhead	875,000	2,044,250		125,000	282,000		1,000,000	2,326,250
8	Product margin		$ 615,750			$ 258,000			873,750
9	Selling and administrative								875,000
10	Net operating income								$ (1,250)

Exhibit 6-12 | Exhibit 6-13 | Exhibit 6-14 | Exhibit 6A-1 | Exhibit 6A-2 | Exhibit 6A-3A

product profitability analysis in Exhibit 6–13. Although the "total pie" remains constant across the traditional and ABC systems, what differs is how the pie is divided between the two product lines. The traditional product margin calculations suggest that standard stanchions are generating a product margin of $615,750 and the custom compass housings a product margin of $258,000. However, these product margins differ from the ABC product margins reported in Exhibit 6–11. Indeed, the traditional cost system is sending misleading signals to Classic Brass's managers about each product's profitability. Let's explain why.

The Differences between ABC and Traditional Product Costs

The changes in product margins caused by switching from the traditional cost system to the activity-based costing system are shown below:

	Standard Stanchions	Custom Compass Housings
Product margins—traditional	$615,750	$ 258,000
Product margins—ABC	906,250	(49,500)
Change in reported product margins	$290,500	$(307,500)

The traditional cost system overcosts the standard stanchions and consequently reports an artificially low product margin for this product. The switch to an activity-based view of product profitability increases the product margin on standard stanchions by $290,500. In contrast, the traditional cost system undercosts the custom compass housings and reports an artificially high product margin for this product. The switch to activity-based costing decreases the product margin on custom compass housings by $307,500.

The reasons for the change in reported product margins between the two costing methods are revealed in Exhibit 6–14. The top portion of the exhibit shows each product's direct and indirect cost assignments as reported by the traditional cost system in Exhibit 6–13. For example, Exhibit 6–14 includes the following costs for standard stanchions: direct materials, $905,500; direct labor, $263,750; and manufacturing overhead, $875,000. Each of these costs corresponds with those reported in Exhibit 6–13. Notice, the selling and administrative costs of $875,000 are purposely not allocated to products because these costs are considered to be period costs when using traditional costing. Similarly, the bottom portion of Exhibit 6–14 summarizes the direct and indirect cost assignments as reported by the activity-based costing system in Exhibit 6–11. The only new information in Exhibit 6–14 is shown in the two columns of percentages. The first column of percentages shows the percentage of each cost assigned to standard stanchions. For example, the $905,500 of direct materials cost traced to standard stanchions is 92.9% of the company's total direct materials cost of $975,000. The second column of percentages does the same thing for custom compass housings.

There are three reasons why the traditional and activity-based costing systems report different product margins. First, Classic Brass's traditional cost system allocates all manufacturing overhead costs to products. This forces both products to absorb all manufacturing overhead costs regardless of whether they actually consumed the costs that were allocated to them. The ABC system does not assign the manufacturing overhead costs consumed by the Customer Relations activity to products because these costs are caused by customers, not specific products. It also does not assign the manufacturing overhead costs included in the Other activity to products because these organization-sustaining and unused capacity costs are not caused by any particular

EXHIBIT 6–14
A Comparison of Traditional and Activity-Based Cost Assignments

	A	B	C	D	E	F	G	H	I
1			*Standard Stanchions*			*Custom Compass Housings*			
2	**Traditional Cost System**		(a) Amount	(a) ÷ (c) %*		(b) Amount	(b) ÷ (c) %*		(c) Total
3	Direct materials		$ 905,500	92.9%		$ 69,500	7.1%		$ 975,000
4	Direct labor		263,750	75.1%		87,500	24.9%		351,250
5	Manufacturing overhead		875,000	87.5%		125,000	12.5%		1,000,000
6	Total cost assigned to products		$2,044,250			$282,000			2,326,250
7	Selling and administrative								875,000
8	Total cost								$3,201,250
9									
10	**Activity-Based Costing System**								
11	Direct costs:								
12	Direct materials		$ 905,500	92.9%		$ 69,500	7.1%		$ 975,000
13	Direct labor		263,750	75.1%		87,500	24.9%		351,250
14	Shipping		60,000	92.3%		5,000	7.7%		65,000
15	Indirect costs:								
16	Customer orders		192,000	60.0%		128,000	40.0%		320,000
17	Product design		-	0.0%		252,000	100.0%		252,000
18	Order size		332,500	87.5%		47,500	12.5%		380,000
19	Total cost assigned to products		$1,753,750			$589,500			2,343,250
20									
21	Costs not assigned to products:								
22	Customer relations								367,500
23	Other								490,500
24	Total cost								$3,201,250
25									
26	*The percentages are rounded to the nearest tenth of a percent.								
27									

Exhibit 6-12 | Exhibit 6-13 | **Exhibit 6-14** | Exhibit 6A-1 | Exhibit 6

product. From an ABC point of view, assigning these costs to products is inherently arbitrary and counterproductive.

Second, Classic Brass's traditional cost system allocates all of the manufacturing overhead costs using a volume-related allocation base—machine-hours—that may or may not reflect what actually causes the costs. In other words, in the traditional system, 87.5% of each manufacturing overhead cost is implicitly assigned to standard stanchions and 12.5% is assigned to custom compass housings. For example, the traditional cost system inappropriately assigns 87.5% of the costs of the Customer Orders activity (a batch-level activity) to standard stanchions even though the ABC system revealed that standard stanchions caused only 60% of these costs. Conversely, the traditional cost system assigns only 12.5% of these costs to custom compass housings even though this product caused 40% of these costs. Similarly, the traditional cost system assigns 87.5% of the costs of the Product Design activity (a product-level activity) to standard stanchions even though the standard stanchions caused none (0%) of these costs. All (100%) of the costs of the Product Design activity, rather than just 12.5%, should be assigned to custom compass housings. The result is that traditional cost systems overcost high-volume products (such as the standard stanchions) and undercost low-volume products (such as the custom compass housings) because they assign batch-level and product-level costs using volume-related allocation bases.

The third reason the product margins differ between the two cost systems is that the ABC system assigns the nonmanufacturing overhead costs caused by products to those products on a cause-and-effect basis. The traditional cost system disregards these costs because they are classified as period costs. The ABC system directly traces shipping costs to products and includes the nonmanufacturing overhead costs caused by products in the activity cost pools that are assigned to products.

MANAGERIAL ACCOUNTING IN ACTION

The Wrap-Up

The ABC design team presented the results of its work in a meeting attended by all of the top managers of Classic Brass, including the president John Towers, the production manager Susan Richter, the marketing manager Tom Olafson, and the accounting manager Mary Goodman. The ABC team brought with them copies of the chart showing the ABC design (Exhibit 6–8), and the table comparing the traditional and ABC cost assignments (Exhibit 6–14). After the formal presentation by the ABC team, the following discussion took place:

John: I would like to personally thank the ABC team for all of the work they have done and for an extremely interesting presentation. I am now beginning to wonder about a lot of the decisions we have made in the past using our old cost accounting system. According to the ABC analysis, we had it all backwards. We are losing money on the custom products and making a fistful on the standard products.

Mary: I have to admit that I had no idea that the Product Design work for custom compass housings was so expensive! I knew burying these costs in our plantwide overhead rate was penalizing standard stanchions, but I didn't understand the magnitude of the problem.

Susan: I never did believe we were making a lot of money on the custom jobs. You ought to see all of the problems they create for us in production.

Tom: I hate to admit it, but the custom jobs always seem to give us headaches in marketing, too.

John: If we are losing money on custom compass housings, why not suggest to our customers that they go elsewhere for that kind of work?

Tom: Wait a minute, we would lose a lot of sales.

Susan: So what, we would save a lot more costs.

Mary: Maybe yes, maybe no. Some of the costs would not disappear if we were to drop the custom business.

Tom: Like what?

Mary: Well Tom, I believe you said that about 10% of your time is spent dealing with new products. As a consequence, 10% of your salary was allocated to the Product Design cost pool. If we were to drop all of the products requiring design work, would you be willing to take a 10% pay cut?

Tom: I trust you're joking.

Mary: Do you see the problem? Just because 10% of your time is spent on custom products doesn't mean that the company would save 10% of your salary if the custom products were dropped. Before we take a drastic action like dropping the custom products, we should identify which costs are really relevant.

John: I think I see what you are driving at. We wouldn't want to drop a lot of products only to find that our costs really haven't changed much. It is true that dropping the products would free up resources like Tom's time, but we had better be sure we have some good use for those resources *before* we take such an action.

As this discussion among the managers of Classic Brass illustrates, caution should be exercised before taking action based on an ABC analysis such as the one shown in Exhibit 6–11 and Exhibit 6–12. The product and customer margins computed in these exhibits are a useful starting point for further analysis, but managers need to know what costs are really affected before taking any action such as dropping a product or customer or changing the prices of products or services. Appendix 6A shows how an *action analysis report* can be constructed to help managers make such decisions. An **action analysis report** provides more detail about costs and how they might adjust to changes in activity than the ABC analysis presented in Exhibit 6–11 and Exhibit 6–12.

IN BUSINESS

AN ABC IMPLEMENTATION IN THAILAND

APS, a parawood furniture factory located in the Songkhla Province of Southern Thailand, employs over 250 workers to make more than 100 types of furniture. The company's traditional cost system assigns indirect manufacturing costs to products based on each product's total sales. Its ABC system relies on various volume-related and non–volume-related activity measures, such as direct labor-hours, number of setups, and number of trips, to assign overhead costs to products.

The company's traditional and ABC systems assigned per-unit overhead costs to its five best-selling products as follows:

	Tile Top Table	Side Chair	Telephone Table	Plant Tree with Grooves	Computer Desk
Traditional cost system allocations	$7.08	$2.21	$3.53	$3.65	$ 4.53
ABC allocations	2.18	1.13	1.32	1.80	6.07
Difference	$4.90	$1.08	$2.21	$1.85	$(1.54)

Given that all five of these products have high sales volumes, it is not surprising to see that the traditional cost system has overcosted four of them.

Source: Sakesun Suthummanon, Wanida Ratanamanee, Nirachara Boonyanuwat, and Pieanpon Saritprit, "Applying Activity-Based Costing (ABC) to a Parawood Furniture Factory," *The Engineering Economist,* Volume 56 (2011), pp. 80–93.

Targeting Process Improvements

Activity-based costing can also be used to identify activities that would benefit from process improvements. When used in this way, activity-based costing is often called *activity-based management.* Basically, **activity-based management (ABM)** involves focusing on activities to eliminate waste, decrease processing time, and reduce defects. Activity-based management is used in organizations as diverse as manufacturing companies, hospitals, and the U.S. Marine Corps.

The first step in any improvement program is to decide what to improve. The activity rates computed in activity-based costing can provide valuable clues concerning where there is waste and opportunity for improvement. For example, looking at the activity rates in Exhibit 6–7, managers at Classic Brass may conclude that $320 to process a customer order is far too expensive for an activity that adds no value to the product. As a consequence, they may target their process improvement efforts toward the Customer Orders activity.[3]

Benchmarking is another way to leverage the information in activity rates. **Benchmarking** is a systematic approach to identifying the activities with the greatest room for improvement. It is based on comparing the performance in an organization with the performance of other, similar organizations known for their outstanding performance. If a particular part of the organization performs far below the world-class standard, managers will be likely to target that area for improvement.

Activity-Based Costing and External Reports

Although activity-based costing generally provides more accurate product costs than traditional costing methods, it is infrequently used for external reports for a number of reasons. First, external reports are less detailed than internal reports prepared for decision

[3] In Chapter 7, we introduce the Theory of Constraints, which is a powerful tool that helps companies target their process improvement efforts on the most profitable opportunities.

making. On the external reports, individual product costs are not reported. Cost of goods sold and inventory valuations are disclosed, but they are not broken down by product. If some products are undercosted and some are overcosted, the errors tend to offset each other when the product costs are added together.

Second, it is often very difficult to make changes in a company's accounting system. The official cost accounting systems in most large companies are usually embedded in complex computer programs that have been modified in-house over the course of many years. It is extremely difficult to make changes in such computer programs without causing numerous bugs.

Third, an ABC system such as the one described in this chapter does not conform to generally accepted accounting principles (GAAP). As discussed in prior chapters, product costs computed for external reports must include all of the manufacturing costs and only manufacturing costs; but in an ABC system as described in this chapter, product costs exclude some manufacturing costs and include some nonmanufacturing costs. It is possible to adjust the ABC data at the end of the period to conform to GAAP, but that requires more work.

Fourth, auditors are likely to be uncomfortable with allocations that are based on interviews with the company's personnel. Such subjective data can be easily manipulated by management to make earnings and other key variables look more favorable.

For all of these reasons, most companies confine their ABC efforts to special studies for management, and they do not attempt to integrate activity-based costing into their formal cost accounting systems.

The Limitations of Activity-Based Costing

Implementing an activity-based costing system is a major project that requires substantial resources. And once implemented, an activity-based costing system is more costly to maintain than a traditional costing system—data concerning numerous activity measures must be periodically collected, checked, and entered into the system. The benefits of increased accuracy may not outweigh these costs.

Activity-based costing produces numbers, such as product margins, that are at odds with the numbers produced by traditional costing systems. But managers are accustomed to using traditional costing systems to run their operations and traditional costing systems are often used in performance evaluations. Essentially, activity-based costing changes the rules of the game. It is a fact of human nature that changes in organizations, particularly those that alter the rules of the game, inevitably face resistance. This underscores the importance of top management support and the full participation of line managers, as well as the accounting staff, in any activity-based costing initiative. If activity-based costing is viewed as an accounting initiative that does not have the full support of top management, it is doomed to failure.

In practice, most managers insist on fully allocating all costs to products, customers, and other costing objects in an activity-based costing system—including the costs of idle capacity and organization-sustaining costs. This results in overstated costs and understated margins and mistakes in pricing and other critical decisions.

Activity-based costing data can easily be misinterpreted and must be used with care when used in making decisions. Costs assigned to products, customers, and other cost objects are only *potentially* relevant. Before making any significant decisions using activity-based costing data, managers must identify which costs are really relevant for the decision at hand. See Appendix 6A for more details.

As discussed in the previous section, reports generated by the best activity-based costing systems do not conform to external reporting requirements. Consequently, an organization involved in activity-based costing should have two cost systems—one for internal use and one for preparing external reports. This is costlier than maintaining just one system and may cause confusion about which system is to be believed and relied on.

Summary

Traditional cost accounting methods suffer from several defects that can result in distorted costs for decision-making purposes. All manufacturing costs—even those that are not caused by any specific product—are allocated to products. Nonmanufacturing costs that are caused by products are not assigned to products. And finally, traditional methods tend to place too much reliance on unit-level allocation bases such as direct labor and machine-hours. This results in overcosting high-volume products and undercosting low-volume products and can lead to mistakes when making decisions.

Activity-based costing estimates the costs of the resources consumed by cost objects such as products and customers. The activity-based costing approach assumes that cost objects generate activities that in turn consume costly resources. Activities form the link between costs and cost objects. Activity-based costing is concerned with overhead—both manufacturing overhead and selling and administrative overhead. The accounting for direct labor and direct materials is usually the same under traditional and ABC costing methods.

To build an ABC system, companies typically choose a small set of activities that summarize much of the work performed in overhead departments. Associated with each activity is an activity cost pool. To the extent possible, overhead costs are directly traced to these activity cost pools. The remaining overhead costs are allocated to the activity cost pools in the first-stage allocation. Interviews with managers often form the basis for these allocations.

An activity rate is computed for each cost pool by dividing the costs assigned to the cost pool by the measure of activity for the cost pool. Activity rates provide useful information to managers concerning the costs of performing overhead activities. A particularly high cost for an activity may trigger efforts to improve the way the activity is carried out in the organization.

In the second-stage allocation, activity rates are used to apply costs to cost objects such as products and customers. The costs computed under activity-based costing are often quite different from the costs generated by a company's traditional cost accounting system. While the ABC system is almost certainly more accurate, managers should nevertheless exercise caution before making decisions based on the ABC data. Some of the costs may not be avoidable and hence would not be relevant.

Review Problem: Activity-Based Costing

Ferris Corporation makes a single product—a fire-resistant commercial filing cabinet—that it sells to office furniture distributors. The company has a simple ABC system that it uses for internal decision making. The company has two overhead departments whose costs are listed below:

Manufacturing overhead	$500,000
Selling and administrative overhead	300,000
Total overhead costs	$800,000

The company's ABC system has the following activity cost pools and activity measures:

Activity Cost Pool	Activity Measure
Assembling units	Number of units
Processing orders	Number of orders
Supporting customers	Number of customers
Other	Not applicable

Costs assigned to the "Other" activity cost pool have no activity measure; they consist of the costs of unused capacity and organization-sustaining costs—neither of which are assigned to orders, customers, or the product.

Ferris Corporation distributes the costs of manufacturing overhead and selling and administrative overhead to the activity cost pools based on employee interviews, the results of which are reported below:

Distribution of Resource Consumption across Activity Cost Pools	Assembling Units	Processing Orders	Supporting Customers	Other	Total
Manufacturing overhead	50%	35%	5%	10%	100%
Selling and administrative overhead	10%	45%	25%	20%	100%
Total activity	1,000 units	250 orders	100 customers		

Required:

1. Perform the first-stage allocation of overhead costs to the activity cost pools as in Exhibit 6–6.
2. Compute activity rates for the activity cost pools as in Exhibit 6–7.
3. OfficeMart is one of Ferris Corporation's customers. Last year, OfficeMart ordered filing cabinets four different times. OfficeMart ordered a total of 80 filing cabinets during the year. Construct a table as in Exhibit 6–10 showing the overhead costs attributable to OfficeMart.
4. The selling price of a filing cabinet is $595. The cost of direct materials is $180 per filing cabinet, and direct labor is $50 per filing cabinet. What is the customer margin of OfficeMart? See Exhibit 6–12 for an example of how to complete this report.

Solution to Review Problem

1. The first-stage allocation of costs to the activity cost pools appears below:

	Activity Cost Pools				
	Assembling Units	Processing Orders	Supporting Customers	Other	Total
Manufacturing overhead	$250,000	$175,000	$ 25,000	$ 50,000	$500,000
Selling and administrative overhead.................	30,000	135,000	75,000	60,000	300,000
Total cost....................	$280,000	$310,000	$100,000	$110,000	$800,000

2. The activity rates for the activity cost pools are:

Activity Cost Pools	(a) Total Cost	(b) Total Activity	(a) ÷ (b) Activity Rate
Assembling units	$280,000	1,000 units	$280 per unit
Processing orders...........	$310,000	250 orders	$1,240 per order
Supporting customers.........	$100,000	100 customers	$1,000 per customer

3. The overhead cost attributable to OfficeMart would be computed as follows:

Activity Cost Pools	(a) Activity Rate	(b) Activity	(a) × (b) ABC Cost
Assembling units	$280 per unit	80 units	$22,400
Processing orders............	$1,240 per order	4 orders	$4,960
Supporting customers.........	$1,000 per customer	1 customer	$1,000

4. The customer margin can be computed as follows:

Sales ($595 per unit × 80 units)		$47,600
Costs:		
Direct materials ($180 per unit × 80 units)	$14,400	
Direct labor ($50 per unit × 80 units)	4,000	
Assembling units (above)	22,400	
Processing orders (above)	4,960	
Supporting customers (above)	1,000	46,760
Customer margin		$ 840

Glossary

Action analysis report A report showing what costs have been assigned to a cost object, such as a product or customer, and how difficult it would be to adjust the cost if there is a change in activity. (p. 246)

Activity An event that causes the consumption of overhead resources in an organization. (p. 227)

Activity-based costing (ABC) A costing method based on activities that is designed to provide managers with cost information for strategic and other decisions that potentially affect capacity and therefore fixed as well as variable costs. (p. 224)

Activity-based management (ABM) A management approach that focuses on managing activities as a way of eliminating waste and reducing delays and defects. (p. 247)

Activity cost pool A "bucket" in which costs are accumulated that relate to a single activity measure in an activity-based costing system. (p. 227)

Activity measure An allocation base in an activity-based costing system; ideally, a measure of the amount of activity that drives the costs in an activity cost pool. (p. 227)

Batch-level activities Activities that are performed each time a batch of goods is handled or processed, regardless of how many units are in the batch. The amount of resource consumed depends on the number of batches run rather than on the number of units in the batch. (p. 227)

Benchmarking A systematic approach to identifying the activities with the greatest potential for improvement. (p. 247)

Customer-level activities Activities that are carried out to support customers, but that are not related to any specific product. (p. 228)

Duration driver A measure of the amount of time required to perform an activity. (p. 227)

First-stage allocation The process by which overhead costs are assigned to activity cost pools in an activity-based costing system. (p. 233)

Organization-sustaining activities Activities that are carried out regardless of which customers are served, which products are produced, how many batches are run, or how many units are made. (p. 228)

Product-level activities Activities that relate to specific products that must be carried out regardless of how many units are produced and sold or batches run. (p. 228)

Second-stage allocation The process by which activity rates are used to apply costs to products and customers in activity-based costing. (p. 237)

Transaction driver A simple count of the number of times an activity occurs. (p. 227)

Unit-level activities Activities that are performed each time a unit is produced. (p. 227)

Questions

6–1 In what fundamental ways does activity-based costing differ from traditional costing methods such as job-order costing as described in Chapter 4?

6–2 Why is direct labor a poor base for allocating overhead in many companies?

6–3 Why are top management support and cross-functional involvement crucial when attempting to implement an activity-based costing system?

6–4 What are unit-level, batch-level, product-level, customer-level, and organization-sustaining activities?

6–5 What types of costs should not be assigned to products in an activity-based costing system?

6–6 Why are there two stages of allocation in activity-based costing?

6–7 Why is the first stage of the allocation process in activity-based costing often based on interviews?

6–8 When activity-based costing is used, why do manufacturing overhead costs often shift from high-volume products to low-volume products?

6–9 How can the activity rates (i.e., cost per activity) for the various activities be used to target process improvements?

6–10 Why is the activity-based costing described in this chapter unacceptable for external financial reports?

Multiple-choice questions are available with Connect.

Applying Excel

connect — Additional student resources are available with Connect.

LEARNING OBJECTIVES 6–1, 6–2, 6–3, 6–4

The Excel worksheet form that follows is to be used to recreate the Review Problem relating to Ferris Corporation that was presented earlier. Download the workbook containing this form from Connect. *On the website you will also receive instructions about how to use this worksheet form.*

You should proceed to the requirements below only after completing your worksheet.

Required:

1. Check your worksheet by doubling the units ordered in cell B16 to 160. The customer margin under activity-based costing should now be $7,640 and the traditional costing product margin should be $(21,600). If you do not get these results, find the errors in your worksheet and correct them.
   a. Why has the customer margin under activity-based costing more than doubled when the number of units ordered is doubled?
   b. Why has the traditional costing product margin exactly doubled from a loss of $10,800 to a loss of $21,600?
   c. Which costing system, activity-based costing or traditional costing, provides a more accurate picture of what happens to profits as the number of units ordered increases? Explain.
2. Let's assume that OfficeMart places different orders next year, purchasing higher-end filing cabinets more frequently, but in smaller quantities per order. Enter the following data into your worksheet:

Data				
Manufacturing overhead.	$500,000			
Selling and administrative overhead.	$300,000			
	Assembling Units	Processing Orders	Supporting Customers	Other
Manufacturing overhead	50%	35%	5%	10%
Selling and administrative overhead	10%	45%	25%	20%
Total activity.	1,000 units	250 orders	100 customers	
OfficeMart orders:				
Customers	1 customer			
Orders	20 orders			
Total number of filing cabinets ordered . . .	80 units			
Selling price.	$795			
Direct materials.	$185			
Direct labor	$90			

	A	B	C	D	E	F
1	**Chapter 6: Applying Excel**					
2						
3	**Data**					
4	Manufacturing overhead	$500,000				
5	Selling and administrative overhead	$300,000				
6						
7		*Assembling Units*	*Processing Orders*	*Supporting Customers*	*Other*	
8	Manufacturing overhead	50%	35%	5%	10%	
9	Selling and administrative overhead	10%	45%	25%	20%	
10	Total activity	1,000	250	100		
11		units	orders	customers		
12						
13	OfficeMart orders:					
14	Customers	1	customer			
15	Orders	4	orders			
16	Number of filing cabinets ordered in total	80	units			
17	Selling price	$595				
18	Direct materials	$180				
19	Direct labor	$50				
20						
21	*Enter a formula into each of the cells marked with a ? below*					
22	**Review Problem: Activity-Based Costing**					
23						
24	***Perform the first stage allocations***					
25		*Assembling Units*	*Processing Orders*	*Supporting Customers*	*Other*	*Total*
26	Manufacturing overhead	?	?	?	?	?
27	Selling and administrative overhead	?	?	?	?	?
28	Total cost	?	?	?	?	?
29						
30	***Compute the activity rates***					
31	*Activity Cost Pools*	*Total Cost*	*Total Activity*		*Activity Rate*	
32	Assembling units	?	?	units	?	per unit
33	Processing orders	?	?	orders	?	per order
34	Supporting customers	?	?	customers	?	per customer
35						
36	***Compute the overhead cost attributable to the OfficeMart orders***					
37	*Activity Cost Pools*	*Activity Rate*		*Activity*		*ABC Cost*
38	Assembling units	?	per unit	?	units	?
39	Processing orders	?	per order	?	orders	?
40	Supporting customers	?	per customer	?	customer	?
41						
42	***Determine the customer margin for the OfficeMart orders under Activity-Based Costing***					
43	Sales		?			
44	Costs:					
45	Direct materials	?				
46	Direct labor	?				
47	Unit-related overhead	?				
48	Order-related overhead	?				
49	Customer-related overhead	?	?			
50	Customer margin		?			
51						
52	***Determine the product margin for the OfficeMart orders under a traditional cost system***					
53	Manufacturing overhead	?				
54	Total activity	?	units			
55	Manufacturing overhead per unit	?	per unit			
56						
57	Sales		?			
58	Costs:					
59	Direct materials	?				
60	Direct labor	?				
61	Manufacturing overhead	?	?			
62	Traditional costing product margin		?			

Chapter 6 Form | Filled in Chapter 6 Form | Chapter 6 Formulas

a. What is the customer margin under activity-based costing?

b. What is the product margin under the traditional cost system?

c. Explain why the profitability picture looks much different now than it did when OfficeMart was ordering less expensive filing cabinets less frequently, but in larger quantities per order.

3. Using the data you entered in requirement 2, change the percentage of selling and administrative overhead attributable to processing orders from 45% to 30% and the percentage attributable to supporting customers from 25% to 40%. That portion of the worksheet should look like this:

	Assembling Units	Processing Orders	Supporting Customers	Other
Manufacturing overhead.	50%	35%	5%	10%
Selling and administrative overhead.	10%	30%	40%	20%
Total activity.	1,000 units	250 orders	100 customers	

a. Relative to the results from requirement 2, what has happened to the customer margin under activity-based costing? Why?

b. Relative to the results from requirement 2, what has happened to the product margin under the traditional cost system? Why?

The Foundational 15

connect Additional student resources are available with Connect.

LEARNING OBJECTIVES 6–1, 6–3, 6–4

Hickory Company manufactures two products—14,000 units of Product Y and 6,000 units of Product Z. The company uses a plantwide overhead rate based on direct labor-hours. It is considering implementing an activity-based costing (ABC) system that allocates all of its manufacturing overhead to four cost pools. The following additional information is available for the company as a whole and for Products Y and Z:

Activity Cost Pool	Activity Measure	Estimated Overhead Cost	Expected Activity
Machining	Machine-hours	$200,000	10,000 MHs
Machine setups.	Number of setups	$100,000	200 setups
Product design	Number of products	$84,000	2 products
General factory.	Direct labor-hours	$300,000	12,000 DLHs

Activity Measure	Product Y	Product Z
Machine-hours.	7,000	3,000
Number of setups	50	150
Number of products	1	1
Direct labor-hours	8,000	4,000

Required:

1. What is the company's plantwide overhead rate?
2. Using the plantwide overhead rate, how much manufacturing overhead cost is allocated to Product Y? How much is allocated to Product Z?
3. What is the activity rate for the Machining activity cost pool?
4. What is the activity rate for the Machine Setups activity cost pool?
5. What is the activity rate for the Product Design activity cost pool?
6. What is the activity rate for the General Factory activity cost pool?
7. Which of the four activities is a batch-level activity? Why?
8. Which of the four activities is a product-level activity? Why?

9. Using the ABC system, how much total manufacturing overhead cost would be assigned to Product Y?
10. Using the ABC system, how much total manufacturing overhead cost would be assigned to Product Z?
11. Using the plantwide overhead rate, what percentage of the total overhead cost is allocated to Product Y? What percentage is allocated to Product Z?
12. Using the ABC system, what percentage of the Machining costs is assigned to Product Y? What percentage is assigned to Product Z? Are these percentages similar to those obtained in requirement 11? Why?
13. Using the ABC system, what percentage of Machine Setups cost is assigned to Product Y? What percentage is assigned to Product Z? Are these percentages similar to those obtained in requirement 11? Why?
14. Using the ABC system, what percentage of the Product Design cost is assigned to Product Y? What percentage is assigned to Product Z? Are these percentages similar to those obtained in requirement 11? Why?
15. Using the ABC system, what percentage of the General Factory cost is assigned to Product Y? What percentage is assigned to Product Z? Are these percentages similar to those obtained in requirement 11? Why?

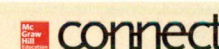

Additional student resources are available with Connect. connect **Exercises**

EXERCISE 6–1 ABC Cost Hierarchy [LO6–1]

The following activities occur at Greenwich Corporation, a company that manufactures a variety of products.

a. Receive raw materials from suppliers.
b. Manage parts inventories.
c. Do rough milling work on products.
d. Interview and process new employees in the personnel department.
e. Design new products.
f. Perform periodic preventive maintenance on general-use equipment.
g. Use the general factory building.
h. Issue purchase orders for a job.

Required:

Classify each of the activities above as either a unit-level, batch-level, product-level, or organization-sustaining activity.

EXERCISE 6–2 First Stage Allocation [LO6–2]

SecuriCorp operates a fleet of armored cars that make scheduled pickups and deliveries in the Los Angeles area. The company is implementing an activity-based costing system that has four activity cost pools: Travel, Pickup and Delivery, Customer Service, and Other. The activity measures are miles for the Travel cost pool, number of pickups and deliveries for the Pickup and Delivery cost pool, and number of customers for the Customer Service cost pool. The Other cost pool has no activity measure because it is an organization-sustaining activity. The following costs will be assigned using the activity-based costing system:

Driver and guard wages	$ 720,000
Vehicle operating expense	280,000
Vehicle depreciation	120,000
Customer representative salaries and expenses	160,000
Office expenses	30,000
Administrative expenses	320,000
Total cost	$1,630,000

The distribution of resource consumption across the activity cost pools is as follows:

	Travel	Pickup and Delivery	Customer Service	Other	Totals
Driver and guard wages	50%	35%	10%	5%	100%
Vehicle operating expense	70%	5%	0%	25%	100%
Vehicle depreciation	60%	15%	0%	25%	100%
Customer representative salaries and expenses	0%	0%	90%	10%	100%
Office expenses	0%	20%	30%	50%	100%
Administrative expenses	0%	5%	60%	35%	100%

Required:
Complete the first stage allocations of costs to activity cost pools as illustrated in Exhibit 6–6.

EXERCISE 6–3 Compute Activity Rates [LO6–3]
Green Thumb Gardening is a small gardening service that uses activity-based costing to estimate costs for pricing and other purposes. The proprietor of the company believes that costs are driven primarily by the size of customer lawns, the size of customer garden beds, the distance to travel to customers, and the number of customers. In addition, the costs of maintaining garden beds depends on whether the beds are low maintenance beds (mainly ordinary trees and shrubs) or high maintenance beds (mainly flowers and exotic plants). Accordingly, the company uses the five activity cost pools listed below:

Activity Cost Pool	Activity Measure
Caring for lawn	Square feet of lawn
Caring for garden beds—low maintenance	Square feet of low maintenance beds
Caring for garden beds—high maintenance	Square feet of high maintenance beds
Travel to jobs	Miles
Customer billing and service	Number of customers

The company has already completed its first stage allocations of costs and has summarized its annual costs and activity as follows:

Activity Cost Pool	Estimated Overhead Cost	Expected Activity
Caring for lawn	$72,000	150,000 square feet of lawn
Caring for garden beds—low maintenance	$26,400	20,000 square feet of low maintenance beds
Caring for garden beds—high maintenance	$41,400	15,000 square feet of high maintenance beds
Travel to jobs	$3,250	12,500 miles
Customer billing and service	$8,750	25 customers

Required:
Compute the activity rate for each of the activity cost pools.

EXERCISE 6–4 Second-Stage Allocation [LO6–4]
Klumper Corporation is a diversified manufacturer of industrial goods. The company's activity-based costing system contains the following six activity cost pools and activity rates:

Activity Cost Pool	Activity Rates
Supporting direct labor	$6.00 per direct labor-hour
Machine processing	$4.00 per machine-hour
Machine setups	$50.00 per setup
Production orders	$90.00 per order
Shipments	$14.00 per shipment
Product sustaining	$840.00 per product

Activity data have been supplied for the following two products:

	Total Expected Activity	
	K425	M67
Number of units produced per year	200	2,000
Direct labor-hours	80	500
Machine-hours	100	1,500
Machine setups	1	4
Production orders	1	4
Shipments	1	10
Product sustaining	1	1

Required:

Determine the total overhead cost that would be assigned to each of the products listed above in the activity-based costing system.

EXERCISE 6–5 Product and Customer Profitability Analysis [LO6–4, LO6–5]

Thermal Rising, Inc., makes paragliders for sale through specialty sporting goods stores. The company has a standard paraglider model, but also makes custom-designed paragliders. Management has designed an activity-based costing system with the following activity cost pools and activity rates:

Activity Cost Pool	Activity Rate
Supporting direct labor	$26 per direct labor-hour
Order processing	$284 per order
Custom design processing	$186 per custom design
Customer service	$379 per customer

Management would like an analysis of the profitability of a particular customer, Big Sky Outfitters, which has ordered the following products over the last 12 months:

	Standard Model	Custom Design
Number of gliders	20	3
Number of orders	1	3
Number of custom designs	0	3
Direct labor-hours per glider	26.35	28.00
Selling price per glider	$1,850	$2,400
Direct materials cost per glider	$564	$634

The company's direct labor rate is $19.50 per hour.

Required:

Using the company's activity-based costing system, compute the customer margin of Big Sky Outfitters.

EXERCISE 6–6 Cost Hierarchy [LO6–1]

CD Express, Inc., provides CD duplicating services to software companies. The customer provides a master CD from which CD Express makes copies. An order from a customer can be for a single copy or for thousands of copies. Most jobs are broken down into batches to allow smaller jobs, with higher priorities, to have access to the machines.

A number of activities carried out at CD Express are listed below.

a. Sales representatives' periodic visits to customers to keep them informed about the services provided by CD Express.
b. Ordering labels from the printer for a particular CD.
c. Setting up the CD duplicating machine to make copies from a particular master CD.
d. Loading the automatic labeling machine with labels for a particular CD.
e. Visually inspecting CDs and placing them by hand into protective plastic cases prior to shipping.
f. Preparation of the shipping documents for the order.
g. Periodic maintenance of equipment.
h. Lighting and heating the company's production facility.
i. Preparation of quarterly financial reports.

Required:

Classify each of the activities above as either a unit-level, batch-level, product-level, customer-level, or organization-sustaining activity. An order to duplicate a particular CD is a product-level activity. Assume the order is large enough that it must be broken down into batches.

EXERCISE 6–7 First-Stage Allocations [LO6–2]

The operations vice president of Security Home Bank has been interested in investigating the efficiency of the bank's operations. She has been particularly concerned about the costs of handling routine transactions at the bank and would like to compare these costs at the bank's various branches. If the branches with the most efficient operations can be identified, their methods can be studied and then replicated elsewhere. While the bank maintains meticulous records of wages and other costs, there has been no attempt thus far to show how those costs are related to the various services provided by the bank. The operations vice president has asked your help in conducting an activity-based costing study of bank operations. In particular, she would like to know the cost of opening an account, the cost of processing deposits and withdrawals, and the cost of processing other customer transactions.

The Westfield branch of Security Home Bank has submitted the following cost data for last year:

Teller wages	$160,000
Assistant branch manager salary	75,000
Branch manager salary	80,000
Total	$315,000

Virtually all other costs of the branch—rent, depreciation, utilities, and so on—are organization-sustaining costs that cannot be meaningfully assigned to individual customer transactions such as depositing checks.

In addition to the cost data above, the employees of the Westfield branch have been interviewed concerning how their time was distributed last year across the activities included in the activity-based costing study. The results of those interviews appear below:

	Distribution of Resource Consumption across Activities				
	Opening Accounts	Processing Deposits and Withdrawals	Processing Other Customer Transactions	Other Activities	Totals
Teller wages	5%	65%	20%	10%	100%
Assistant branch manager salary	15%	5%	30%	50%	100%
Branch manager salary	5%	0%	10%	85%	100%

Required:
Prepare the first-stage allocation for the activity-based costing study. (See Exhibit 6–6 for an example of a first-stage allocation.)

EXERCISE 6–8 Computing and Interpreting Activity Rates [LO6–3]

(This exercise is a continuation of Exercise 6–7; it should be assigned *only* if Exercise 6–7 is also assigned.) The manager of the Westfield branch of Security Home Bank has provided the following data concerning the transactions of the branch during the past year:

Activity	Total Activity at the Westfield Branch
Opening accounts	500 new accounts opened
Processing deposits and withdrawals	100,000 deposits and withdrawals processed
Processing other customer transactions	5,000 other customer transactions processed

The lowest costs reported by other branches for these activities are displayed below:

Activity	Lowest Cost among All Security Home Bank Branches
Opening accounts	$26.75 per new account
Processing deposits and withdrawals	$1.24 per deposit or withdrawal
Processing other customer transactions	$11.86 per other customer transaction

Required:
1. Using the first-stage allocation from Exercise 6–7 and the above data, compute the activity rates for the activity-based costing system. (Use Exhibit 6–7 as a guide.) Round all computations to the nearest whole cent.
2. What do these results suggest to you concerning operations at the Westfield branch?

EXERCISE 6–9 Second-Stage Allocation to an Order [LO6–4]
Durban Metal Products, Ltd., of the Republic of South Africa makes specialty metal parts used in applications ranging from the cutting edges of bulldozer blades to replacement parts for Land Rovers. The company uses an activity-based costing system for internal decision-making purposes. The company has four activity cost pools as listed below:

Activity Cost Pool	Activity Measure	Activity Rate
Order size	Number of direct labor-hours	$16.85 per direct labor-hour
Customer orders	Number of customer orders	$320.00 per customer order
Product testing	Number of testing hours	$89.00 per testing hour
Selling	Number of sales calls	$1,090.00 per sales call

The managing director of the company would like information concerning the cost of a recently completed order for heavy-duty trailer axles. The order required 200 direct labor-hours, 4 hours of product testing, and 2 sales calls.

Required:
Prepare a report summarizing the overhead costs assigned to the order for heavy-duty trailer axles. What is the total overhead cost assigned to the order?

EXERCISE 6–10 Customer Profitability Analysis [LO6–3, LO6–4, LO6–5]

Worley Company buys surgical supplies from a variety of manufacturers and then resells and delivers these supplies to hundreds of hospitals. Worley sets its prices for all hospitals by marking up its cost of goods sold to those hospitals by 5%. For example, if a hospital buys supplies from Worley that had cost Worley $100 to buy from manufacturers, Worley would charge the hospital $105 to purchase these supplies.

For years, Worley believed that the 5% markup covered its selling and administrative expenses and provided a reasonable profit. However, in the face of declining profits Worley decided to implement an activity-based costing system to help improve its understanding of customer profitability. The company broke its selling and administrative expenses into five activities as shown below:

Activity Cost Pool (Activity Measure)	Total Cost	Total Activity
Customer deliveries (Number of deliveries)	$ 500,000	5,000 deliveries
Manual order processing (Number of manual orders).	248,000	4,000 orders
Electronic order processing (Number of electronic orders).	200,000	12,500 orders
Line item picking (Number of line items picked)	450,000	450,000 line items
Other organization-sustaining costs (None)	602,000	
Total selling and administrative expenses	$2,000,000	

Worley gathered the data below for two of the many hospitals that it serves—University and Memorial (both hospitals purchased a total quantity of medical supplies that had cost Worley $30,000 to buy from its manufacturers):

	Activity	
Activity Measure	University	Memorial
Number of deliveries	10	25
Number of manual orders	0	30
Number of electronic orders	15	0
Number of line items picked	120	250

Required:

1. Compute the total revenue that Worley would receive from University and Memorial.
2. Compute the activity rate for each activity cost pool.
3. Compute the total activity costs that would be assigned to University and Memorial.
4. Compute Worley's customer margin for University and Memorial. (***Hint:*** Do not overlook the $30,000 cost of goods sold that Worley incurred serving each hospital.)
5. Describe the purchasing behaviors that are likely to characterize Worley's least profitable customers.

EXERCISE 6–11 Second-Stage Allocation and Margin Calculations [LO6–4, LO6–5]

Foam Products, Inc., makes foam seat cushions for the automotive and aerospace industries. The company's activity-based costing system has four activity cost pools, which are listed below along with their activity measures and activity rates:

Activity Cost Pool	Activity Measure	Activity Rate
Supporting direct labor	Number of direct labor-hours	$5.55 per direct labor-hour
Batch processing.	Number of batches	$107.00 per batch
Order processing.	Number of orders	$275.00 per order
Customer service.	Number of customers	$2,463.00 per customer

The company just completed a single order from Interstate Trucking for 1,000 custom seat cushions. The order was produced in two batches. Each seat cushion required 0.25 direct labor-hours. The selling price was $20 per unit, the direct materials cost was $8.50 per unit, and the direct labor cost was $6.00 per unit. This was Interstate Trucking's only order during the year.

Required:

Using Exhibit 6–12 as a guide, prepare a report showing the customer margin on sales to Interstate Trucking for the year.

EXERCISE 6–12 Activity Measures [LO6–1]

Various activities at Ming Corporation, a manufacturing company, are listed below. Each activity has been classified as a unit-level, batch-level, product-level, or customer-level activity.

	Activity	Level of Activity	Examples of Activity Measures
a.	Direct labor workers assemble a product.	Unit	
b.	Products are designed by engineers.	Product	
c.	Equipment is set up	Batch	
d.	Machines are used to shape and cut materials	Unit	
e.	Monthly bills are sent out to regular customers.	Customer	
f.	Materials are moved from the receiving dock to production lines.	Batch	
g.	All completed units are inspected for defects	Unit	

Required:

Complete the table by providing an example of an activity measure for each activity.

EXERCISE 6–13 Computing ABC Product Costs [LO6–3, LO6–4]

Fogerty Company makes two products, titanium Hubs and Sprockets. Data regarding the two products follow:

	Direct Labor-Hours per Unit	Annual Production
Hubs	0.80	10,000 units
Sprockets	0.40	40,000 units

Additional information about the company follows:

a. Hubs require $32 in direct materials per unit, and Sprockets require $18.
b. The direct labor wage rate is $15 per hour.
c. Hubs are more complex to manufacture than Sprockets and they require special equipment.
d. The ABC system has the following activity cost pools:

		Activity		
Activity Cost Pool (Activity Measure)	Estimated Overhead Cost	Hubs	Sprockets	Total
Machine setups (number of setups).	$72,000	100	300	400
Special processing (machine-hours)	$200,000	5,000	0	5,000
General factory (organization-sustaining) . . .	$816,000	NA	NA	NA

Required:

1. Compute the activity rate for each activity cost pool. Did you compute an activity rate for all of the activity cost pools? Why?
2. Determine the unit product cost of each product according to the ABC system.

EXERCISE 6–14 Calculating and Interpreting Activity-Based Costing Data [LO6–3, LO6–4]

Hiram's Lakeside is a popular restaurant located on Lake Washington in Seattle. The owner of the restaurant has been trying to better understand costs at the restaurant and has hired a student intern to conduct an activity-based costing study. The intern, in consultation with the owner, identified three major activities and then completed the first-stage allocations of costs to the activity cost pools. The results appear below.

Activity Cost Pool	Activity Measure	Total Cost	Total Activity
Serving a party of diners	Number of parties served	$33,000	6,000 parties
Serving a diner.	Number of diners served	$138,000	15,000 diners
Serving a drink.	Number of drinks ordered	$24,000	10,000 drinks

The above costs include all of the costs of the restaurant except for organization-sustaining costs such as rent, property taxes, and top-management salaries.

A group of diners who ask to sit at the same table are counted as a party. Some costs, such as the costs of cleaning linen, are the same whether one person is at a table or the table is full. Other costs, such as washing dishes, depend on the number of diners served.

Prior to the activity-based costing study, the owner knew very little about the costs of the restaurant. She knew that the total cost for the month (including organization-sustaining costs) was $240,000 and that 15,000 diners had been served. Therefore, the average cost per diner was $16.

Required:

1. According to the activity-based costing system, what is the total cost of serving each of the following parties of diners?
   a. A party of four diners who order three drinks in total.
   b. A party of two diners who do not order any drinks.
   c. A lone diner who orders two drinks.
2. Convert the total costs you computed in (1) above to costs per diner. In other words, what is the average cost per diner for serving each of the following parties?
   a. A party of four diners who order three drinks in total.
   b. A party of two diners who do not order any drinks.
   c. A lone diner who orders two drinks.
3. Why do the costs per diner for the three different parties differ from each other and from the overall average cost of $16 per diner?

EXERCISE 6–15 Comprehensive Activity-Based Costing Exercise [LO6–2, LO6–3, LO6–4, LO6–5]

Advanced Products Corporation has supplied the following data from its activity-based costing system:

Overhead Costs	
Wages and salaries.	$300,000
Other overhead costs	100,000
Total overhead costs	$400,000

Activity Cost Pool	Activity Measure	Total Activity for the Year
Supporting direct labor. . . .	Number of direct labor-hours	20,000 DLHs
Order processing	Number of customer orders	400 orders
Customer support	Number of customers	200 customers
Other.	This is an organization-sustaining activity	Not applicable

	Distribution of Resource Consumption across Activities				
	Supporting Direct Labor	Order Processing	Customer Support	Other	Total
Wages and salaries.	40%	30%	20%	10%	100%
Other overhead costs.	30%	10%	20%	40%	100%

During the year, Advanced Products completed one order for a new customer, Shenzhen Enterprises. This customer did not order any other products during the year. Data concerning that order follow:

Data Concerning the Shenzhen Enterprises Order	
Units ordered	10 units
Direct labor-hours	2 DLHs per unit
Selling price	$300 per unit
Direct materials	$180 per unit
Direct labor	$50 per unit

Required:

1. Using Exhibit 6–6 as a guide, prepare a report showing the first-stage allocations of overhead costs to the activity cost pools.
2. Using Exhibit 6–7 as a guide, compute the activity rates for the activity cost pools.
3. Prepare a report showing the overhead costs for the order from Shenzhen Enterprises including customer support costs.
4. Using Exhibit 6–12 as a guide, prepare a report showing the customer margin for Shenzhen Enterprises.

Additional student resources are available with Connect. connect **Problems**

PROBLEM 6–16 Comparing Traditional and Activity-Based Product Margins [LO6–1, LO6–3, LO6–4, LO6–5]

Hi-Tek Manufacturing Inc. makes two types of industrial component parts—the B300 and the T500. An absorption costing income statement for the most recent period is shown below:

Hi-Tek Manufacturing Inc. Income Statement	
Sales	$2,100,000
Cost of goods sold	1,600,000
Gross margin	500,000
Selling and administrative expenses	550,000
Net operating loss	$ (50,000)

Hi-Tek produced and sold 70,000 units of B300 at a price of $20 per unit and 17,500 units of T500 at a price of $40 per unit. The company's traditional cost system allocates manufacturing overhead to products using a plantwide overhead rate and direct labor dollars as the allocation base. Additional information relating to the company's two product lines is shown below:

	B300	T500	Total
Direct materials	$436,300	$251,700	$ 688,000
Direct labor	$200,000	$104,000	304,000
Manufacturing overhead			608,000
Cost of goods sold			$1,600,000

The company has created an activity-based costing system to evaluate the profitability of its products. Hi-Tek's ABC implementation team concluded that $50,000 and $100,000 of the company's advertising expenses could be directly traced to B300 and T500, respectively. The remainder of the selling and administrative expenses was organization-sustaining in nature.

The ABC team also distributed the company's manufacturing overhead to four activities as shown below:

Activity Cost Pool (and Activity Measure)	Manufacturing Overhead	Activity		
		B300	T500	Total
Machining (machine-hours)...............	$213,500	90,000	62,500	152,500
Setups (setup hours)	157,500	75	300	375
Product-sustaining (number of products) ...	120,000	1	1	2
Other (organization-sustaining costs)......	117,000	NA	NA	NA
Total manufacturing overhead cost........	$608,000			

Required:

1. Using Exhibit 6–13 as a guide, compute the product margins for the B300 and T500 under the company's traditional costing system.
2. Using Exhibit 6–11 as a guide, compute the product margins for B300 and T500 under the activity-based costing system.
3. Using Exhibit 6–14 as a guide, prepare a quantitative comparison of the traditional and activity-based cost assignments. Explain why the traditional and activity-based cost assignments differ.

PROBLEM 6–17 Comparing Traditional and Activity-Based Product Margins [LO6–1, LO6–3, LO6–4, LO6–5]
Smoky Mountain Corporation makes two types of hiking boots—Xtreme and the Pathfinder. Data concerning these two product lines appear below:

	Xtreme	Pathfinder
Selling price per unit	$140.00	$99.00
Direct materials per unit.......................	$72.00	$53.00
Direct labor per unit..........................	$24.00	$12.00
Direct labor-hours per unit	2.0 DLHs	1.0 DLHs
Estimated annual production and sales	20,000 units	80,000 units

The company has a traditional costing system in which manufacturing overhead is applied to units based on direct labor-hours. Data concerning manufacturing overhead and direct labor-hours for the upcoming year appear below:

Estimated total manufacturing overhead	$1,980,000
Estimated total direct labor-hours	120,000 DLHs

Required:

1. Using Exhibit 6–13 as a guide, compute the product margins for the Xtreme and the Pathfinder products under the company's traditional costing system.
2. The company is considering replacing its traditional costing system with an activity-based costing system that would assign its manufacturing overhead to the following four activity cost pools (the Other cost pool includes organization-sustaining costs and idle capacity costs):

Activities (and Activity Measures)	Estimated Overhead Cost	Expected Activity		
		Xtreme	Pathfinder	Total
Supporting direct labor (direct labor-hours)....	$ 783,600	40,000	80,000	120,000
Batch setups (setups)	495,000	200	100	300
Product sustaining (number of products)	602,400	1	1	2
Other	99,000	NA	NA	NA
Total manufacturing overhead cost...........	$1,980,000			

Using Exhibit 6–11 as a guide, compute the product margins for the Xtreme and the Pathfinder products under the activity-based costing system.

3. Using Exhibit 6–14 as a guide, prepare a quantitative comparison of the traditional and activity-based cost assignments. Explain why the traditional and activity-based cost assignments differ.

PROBLEM 6–18 Activity-Based Costing and Bidding on Jobs [LO6–2, LO6–3, LO6–4]

Mercer Asbestos Removal Company removes potentially toxic asbestos insulation and related products from buildings. There has been a long-simmering dispute between the company's estimator and the work supervisors. The on-site supervisors claim that the estimators do not adequately distinguish between routine work such as removal of asbestos insulation around heating pipes in older homes and nonroutine work such as removing asbestos-contaminated ceiling plaster in industrial buildings. The on-site supervisors believe that nonroutine work is far more expensive than routine work and should bear higher customer charges. The estimator sums up his position in this way: "My job is to measure the area to be cleared of asbestos. As directed by top management, I simply multiply the square footage by $2.50 to determine the bid price. Since our average cost is only $2.175 per square foot, that leaves enough cushion to take care of the additional costs of nonroutine work that shows up. Besides, it is difficult to know what is routine or not routine until you actually start tearing things apart."

To shed light on this controversy, the company initiated an activity-based costing study of all of its costs. Data from the activity-based costing system follow:

Activity Cost Pool	Activity Measure	Total Activity
Removing asbestos	Thousands of square feet	800 thousand square feet
Estimating and job setup	Number of jobs	500 jobs
Working on nonroutine jobs	Number of nonroutine jobs	100 nonroutine jobs
Other (costs of idle capacity and organization-sustaining costs)	None	

Note: The 100 nonroutine jobs are included in the total of 500 jobs. Both nonroutine jobs and routine jobs require estimating and setup.

Costs for the Year	
Wages and salaries	$ 300,000
Disposal fees	700,000
Equipment depreciation	90,000
On-site supplies	50,000
Office expenses	200,000
Licensing and insurance	400,000
Total cost	$1,740,000

	Distribution of Resource Consumption across Activities				
	Removing Asbestos	Estimating and Job Setup	Working on Nonroutine Jobs	Other	Total
Wages and salaries	50%	10%	30%	10%	100%
Disposal fees	60%	0%	40%	0%	100%
Equipment depreciation	40%	5%	20%	35%	100%
On-site supplies	60%	30%	10%	0%	100%
Office expenses	10%	35%	25%	30%	100%
Licensing and insurance	30%	0%	50%	20%	100%

Required:

1. Using Exhibit 6–6 as a guide, perform the first-stage allocation of costs to the activity cost pools.
2. Using Exhibit 6–7 as a guide, compute the activity rates for the activity cost pools.
3. Using the activity rates you have computed, determine the total cost and the average cost per thousand square feet of each of the following jobs according to the activity-based costing system.
   a. A routine 1,000-square-foot asbestos removal job.
   b. A routine 2,000-square-foot asbestos removal job.
   c. A nonroutine 2,000-square-foot asbestos removal job.
4. Given the results you obtained in (3) above, do you agree with the estimator that the company's present policy for bidding on jobs is adequate?

PROBLEM 6–19 Second Stage Allocations and Product Margins [LO6–4, LO6–5]

Pixel Studio, Inc., is a small company that creates computer-generated animations for films and television. Much of the company's work consists of short commercials for television, but the company also does realistic computer animations for special effects in movies.

The young founders of the company have become increasingly concerned with the economics of the business—particularly since many competitors have sprung up recently in the local area. To help understand the company's cost structure, an activity-based costing system has been designed. Three major activities are carried out in the company: animation concept, animation production, and contract administration. The animation concept activity is carried out at the contract proposal stage when the company bids on projects. This is an intensive activity that involves individuals from all parts of the company in creating story boards and prototype stills to be shown to the prospective client. Once a project is accepted by the client, the animation goes into production and contract administration begins. Almost all of the work involved in animation production is done by the technical staff, whereas the administrative staff is largely responsible for contract administration. The activity cost pools and their activity measures are listed below:

Activity Cost Pool	Activity Measure	Activity Rate
Animation concept	Number of proposals	$6,040 per proposal
Animation production	Minutes of completed animation	$7,725 per minute
Contract administration	Number of contracts	$6,800 per contract

These activity rates include all of the company's costs, except for the costs of idle capacity and organization-sustaining costs. There are no direct labor or direct materials costs.

Preliminary analysis using these activity rates has indicated that the local commercial segment of the market may be unprofitable. This segment is highly competitive. Producers of local commercials may ask three or four companies like Pixel Studio to bid, which results in an unusually low ratio of accepted contracts to bids. Furthermore, the animation sequences tend to be much shorter for local commercials than for other work. Since animation work is billed at fairly standard rates according to the running time of the completed animation, this means that the revenues from these short projects tend to be below average. Data concerning activity in the local commercial market appear below:

Activity Measure	Local Commercials
Number of proposals	25
Minutes of completed animation	5
Number of contracts	10

The total sales from the 10 contracts for local commercials was $180,000.

Required:

1. Determine the cost of serving the local commercial market.
2. Prepare a report showing the margin earned serving the local commercial market. (Remember, this company has no direct materials or direct labor costs.)
3. What would you recommend to management concerning the local commercial market?

PROBLEM 6–20 Evaluating the Profitability of Services [LO6–2, LO6–3, LO6–4, LO6–5]

Gallatin Carpet Cleaning is a small, family-owned business operating out of Bozeman, Montana. For its services, the company has always charged a flat fee per hundred square feet of carpet cleaned. The current fee is $28 per hundred square feet. However, there is some question about whether the company is actually making any money on jobs for some customers—particularly those located on remote ranches that require considerable travel time. The owner's daughter, home for the summer from college, has suggested investigating this question using activity-based costing. After some discussion, a simple system consisting of four activity cost pools seemed to be adequate. The activity cost pools and their activity measures appear below:

Activity Cost Pool	Activity Measure	Activity for the Year
Cleaning carpets	Square feet cleaned (00s)	20,000 hundred square feet
Travel to jobs.	Miles driven	60,000 miles
Job support.	Number of jobs	2,000 jobs
Other (costs of idle capacity and organization-sustaining costs) . . .	None	Not applicable

The total cost of operating the company for the year is $430,000, which includes the following costs:

Wages.	$150,000
Cleaning supplies	40,000
Cleaning equipment depreciation.	20,000
Vehicle expenses	80,000
Office expenses.	60,000
President's compensation	80,000
Total cost.	$430,000

Resource consumption is distributed across the activities as follows:

	Distribution of Resource Consumption across Activities				
	Cleaning Carpets	Travel to Jobs	Job Support	Other	Total
Wages.	70%	20%	0%	10%	100%
Cleaning supplies	100%	0%	0%	0%	100%
Cleaning equipment depreciation.	80%	0%	0%	20%	100%
Vehicle expenses	0%	60%	0%	40%	100%
Office expenses.	0%	0%	45%	55%	100%
President's compensation	0%	0%	40%	60%	100%

Job support consists of receiving calls from potential customers at the home office, scheduling jobs, billing, resolving issues, and so on.

Required:

1. Using Exhibit 6–6 as a guide, prepare the first-stage allocation of costs to the activity cost pools.
2. Using Exhibit 6–7 as a guide, compute the activity rates for the activity cost pools.
3. The company recently completed a 5 hundred square foot carpet-cleaning job at the Flying N ranch—a 75-mile round-trip journey from the company's offices in Bozeman. Compute the cost of this job using the activity-based costing system.
4. The revenue from the Flying N ranch was $140 (5 hundred square feet @ $28 per hundred square feet). Using Exhibit 6–12 as a guide, prepare a report showing the margin from this job.
5. What do you conclude concerning the profitability of the Flying N ranch job? Explain.
6. What advice would you give the president concerning pricing jobs in the future?

Appendix 6A: ABC Action Analysis

LEARNING OBJECTIVE 6–6
Prepare an action analysis report using activity-based costing data and interpret the report.

A conventional ABC analysis, such as the one presented in Exhibit 6–11 and Exhibit 6–12 in the chapter, has several important limitations. Referring back to Exhibit 6–11, recall that the custom compass housings show a negative product margin of $49,500. Because of this apparent loss, managers were considering dropping this product. However, as the discussion among the managers revealed, it is unlikely that all of the $589,500 cost of the product would be avoided if it were dropped. Some of these costs would continue even if the product were totally eliminated. *Before* taking action, it is vital to identify which costs would be avoided and which costs would continue. Only those costs that can be avoided are relevant in the decision. Moreover, many of the costs are managed costs that would require explicit management action to eliminate. If the custom compass housings product line were eliminated, the direct materials cost would be avoided without any explicit management action—the materials simply wouldn't be ordered. On the other hand, if the custom compass housings were dropped, explicit management action would be required to eliminate the salaries of overhead workers that are assigned to this product.

Simply shifting these managed costs to other products would not solve anything. These costs would have to be eliminated or redeployed to increase sales to have any benefit to the company. While eliminating the cost is obviously beneficial, redeploying the resources is only beneficial if the resources are used to expand the output of a work center that has been operating at full capacity. If the resources are redeployed to a work center with idle capacity, the additional resources would only increase the excess capacity in that work center—which has no direct benefit to the company.

In addition, if some overhead costs need to be eliminated as a result of dropping a product, specific managers must be held responsible for eliminating those costs or the reductions are unlikely to occur. If no one is specifically held responsible for eliminating the costs, they will almost certainly continue to be incurred. Without external pressure, managers usually avoid cutting costs in their areas of responsibility. The action analysis report developed in this appendix is intended to help top managers identify what costs are relevant in a decision and to place responsibility for the elimination of those costs on the appropriate managers.

Activity Rates—Action Analysis Report

Constructing an action analysis report begins with the results of the first-stage allocation, which is reproduced as Exhibit 6A–1. In contrast to the conventional ABC analysis covered in the chapter, the calculation of the activity rates for an action analysis report is a bit more involved. In addition to computing an overall activity rate for each activity cost pool, an activity rate is computed for each cell in Exhibit 6A–1. The computations of activity rates for the action analysis are carried out in Exhibit 6A–2. For example, the $125,000 cost of indirect factory wages for the Customer Orders cost pool is divided by the total activity for that cost pool—1,000 orders—to arrive at the activity rate of $125 per customer order for indirect factory wages. Similarly, the $200,000 cost of indirect factory wages for the Product Design cost pool is divided by the total activity for that cost pool—400 designs—to arrive at the activity rate of $500 per design for indirect factory wages. Note that the totals at the bottom of Exhibit 6A–2 agree with the overall activity rates in Exhibit 6–7 in the chapter. Exhibit 6A–2, which shows the activity rates for the action analysis report, contains more detail than Exhibit 6–7, which contains the activity rates for the conventional ABC analysis.

Assignment of Overhead Costs to Products—Action Analysis Report

Computing the overhead costs to be assigned to products for an action analysis report also involves more detail than for a conventional ABC analysis. The computations for Classic Brass are carried out in Exhibit 6A–3. For example, the activity rate of $125 per customer

EXHIBIT 6A–1
First-Stage Allocations to Activity Cost Pools

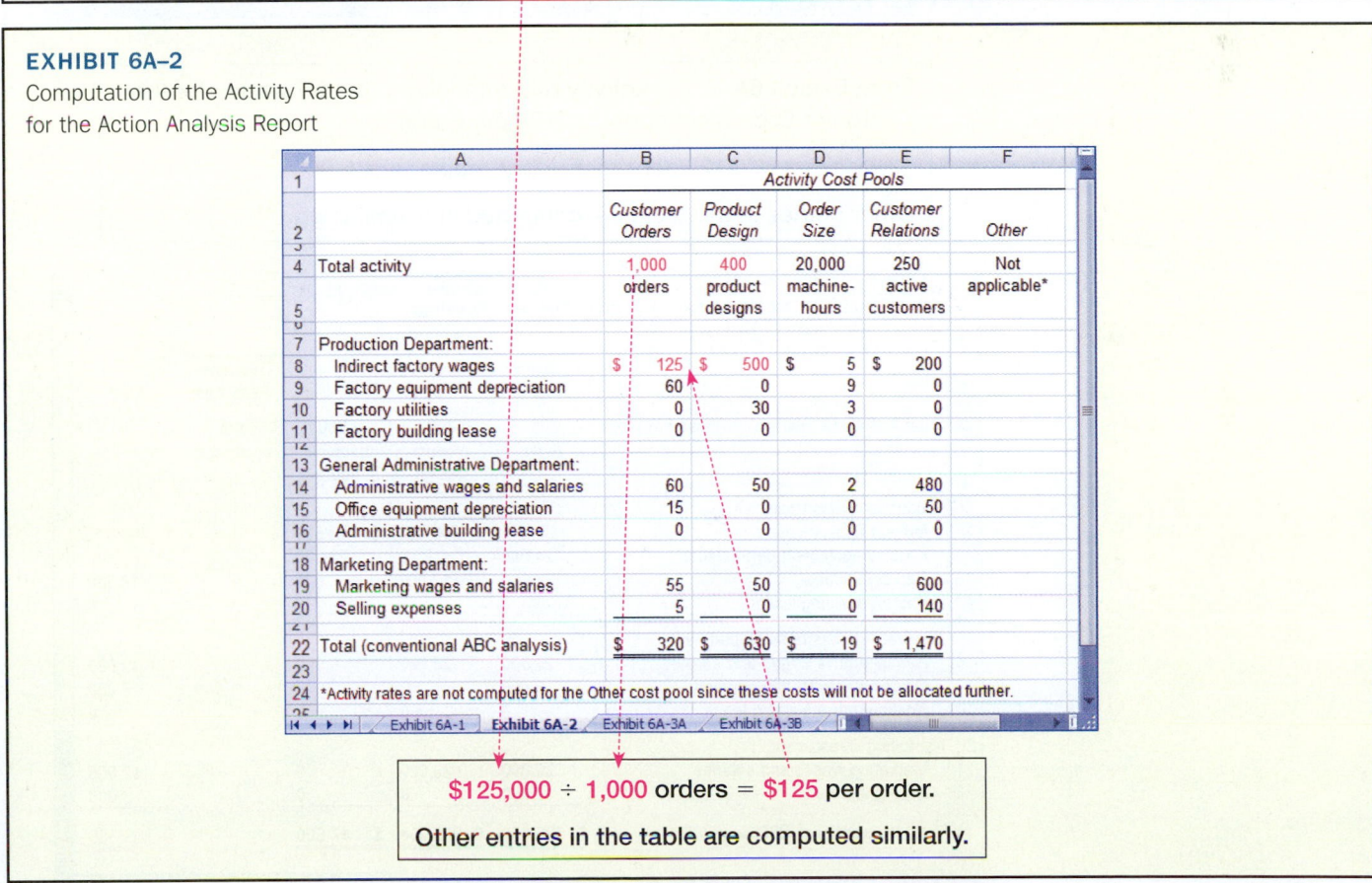

	Activity Cost Pools					
	Customer Orders	*Product Design*	*Order Size*	*Customer Relations*	*Other*	*Total*
Production Department:						
Indirect factory wages	$ 125,000	$ 200,000	$ 100,000	$ 50,000	$ 25,000	$ 500,000
Factory equipment depreciation	60,000	0	180,000	0	60,000	300,000
Factory utilities	0	12,000	60,000	0	48,000	120,000
Factory building lease	0	0	0	0	80,000	80,000
General Administrative Department:						
Administrative wages and salaries	60,000	20,000	40,000	120,000	160,000	400,000
Office equipment depreciation	15,000	0	0	12,500	22,500	50,000
Administrative building lease	0	0	0	0	60,000	60,000
Marketing Department:						
Marketing wages and salaries	55,000	20,000	0	150,000	25,000	250,000
Selling expenses	5,000	0	0	35,000	10,000	50,000
Total cost	$ 320,000	$ 252,000	$ 380,000	$ 367,500	$ 490,500	$ 1,810,000

EXHIBIT 6A–2
Computation of the Activity Rates for the Action Analysis Report

	Activity Cost Pools				
	Customer Orders	*Product Design*	*Order Size*	*Customer Relations*	*Other*
Total activity	1,000 orders	400 product designs	20,000 machine-hours	250 active customers	Not applicable*
Production Department:					
Indirect factory wages	$ 125	$ 500	$ 5	$ 200	
Factory equipment depreciation	60	0	9	0	
Factory utilities	0	30	3	0	
Factory building lease	0	0	0	0	
General Administrative Department:					
Administrative wages and salaries	60	50	2	480	
Office equipment depreciation	15	0	0	50	
Administrative building lease	0	0	0	0	
Marketing Department:					
Marketing wages and salaries	55	50	0	600	
Selling expenses	5	0	0	140	
Total (conventional ABC analysis)	$ 320	$ 630	$ 19	$ 1,470	

*Activity rates are not computed for the Other cost pool since these costs will not be allocated further.

$125,000 ÷ 1,000 orders = $125 per order.

Other entries in the table are computed similarly.

order for indirect factory wages is multiplied by 600 orders for the standard stanchions to arrive at the cost of $75,000 for indirect factory wages in Exhibit 6A–3. Instead of just a single cost number for each cost pool as in the conventional ABC analysis, we now have an entire cost matrix showing much more detail. Note that the column totals for the cost matrix in Exhibit 6A–3 agree with the ABC costs for standard stanchions in Exhibit 6–9. Indeed, the conventional ABC analysis of Exhibit 6–11 can be easily constructed using the column totals at the bottom of the cost matrices in Exhibit 6A–3. In contrast, the

EXHIBIT 6A–3
Action Analysis Cost Matrices

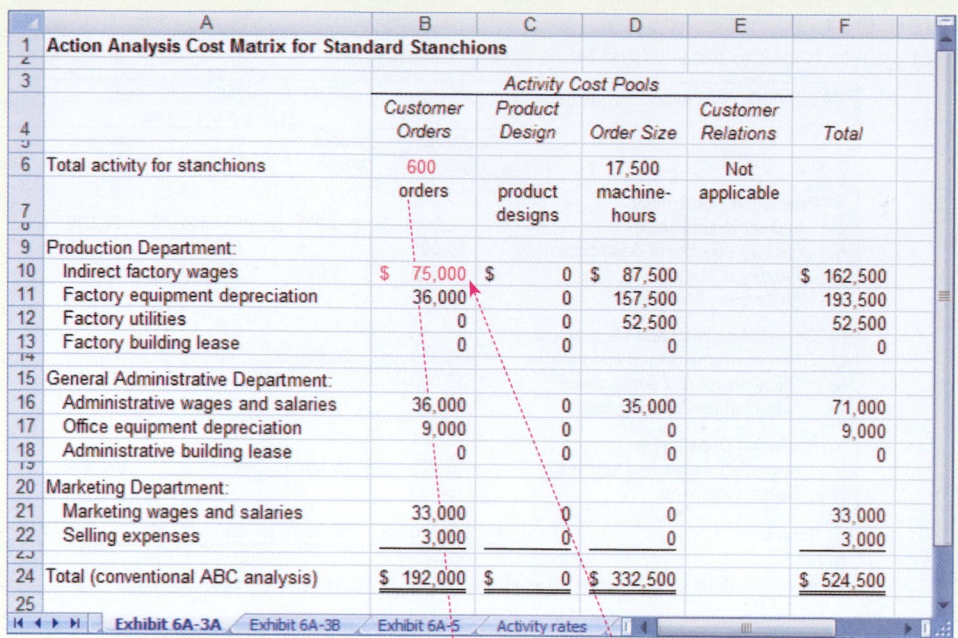

Action Analysis Cost Matrix for Standard Stanchions

	Customer Orders	Product Design	Order Size	Customer Relations	Total
	Activity Cost Pools				
Total activity for stanchions	600 orders	product designs	17,500 machine-hours	Not applicable	
Production Department:					
Indirect factory wages	$ 75,000	$ 0	$ 87,500		$ 162,500
Factory equipment depreciation	36,000	0	157,500		193,500
Factory utilities	0	0	52,500		52,500
Factory building lease	0	0	0		0
General Administrative Department:					
Administrative wages and salaries	36,000	0	35,000		71,000
Office equipment depreciation	9,000	0	0		9,000
Administrative building lease	0	0	0		0
Marketing Department:					
Marketing wages and salaries	33,000	0	0		33,000
Selling expenses	3,000	0	0		3,000
Total (conventional ABC analysis)	$ 192,000	$ 0	$ 332,500		$ 524,500

From Exhibit 6A–2, the activity rate for indirect factory wages for the Customer Orders cost pool is $125 per order.

$125 per order × 600 orders = $75,000

Other entries in the table are computed in a similar way.

Action Analysis Cost Matrix for the Custom Compass Housings

	Customer Orders	Product Design	Order Size	Customer Relations	Total
	Activity Cost Pools				
Total activity for custom compass housings	400 order	400 product design	2,500 machine-hours	Not applicable	
Production Department:					
Indirect factory wages	$ 50,000	$ 200,000	$ 12,500		$ 262,500
Factory equipment depreciation	24,000	0	22,500		46,500
Factory utilities	0	12,000	7,500		19,500
Factory building lease	0	0	0		0
General Administrative Department:					
Administrative wages and salaries	24,000	20,000	5,000		49,000
Office equipment depreciation	6,000	0	0		6,000
Administrative building lease	0	0	0		0
Marketing Department:					
Marketing wages and salaries	22,000	20,000	0		42,000
Selling expenses	2,000	0	0		2,000
Total (conventional ABC analysis)	$ 128,000	$ 252,000	$ 47,500		$ 427,500

From Exhibit 6A–2, the activity rate for indirect factory wages for the Customer Orders cost pool is $125 per order.

$125 per order × 400 orders = $50,000

Other entries in the table are computed in a similar way.

action analysis report will be based on the row totals at the right of the cost matrices in Exhibit 6A–3. In addition, the action analysis report will include a simple color-coding scheme that will help managers identify how easily the various costs can be adjusted.

Ease of Adjustment Codes

The ABC team constructed Exhibit 6A–4 to aid managers in the use of the ABC data. In this exhibit, each cost has been assigned an *ease of adjustment code*—Green, Yellow, or Red. The **ease of adjustment code** reflects how easily the cost could be adjusted to changes in activity.[4] "Green" costs are those costs that would adjust more or less automatically to changes in activity without any action by managers. For example, direct materials costs would adjust to changes in orders without any action being taken by managers. If a customer does not order stanchions, the direct materials for the stanchions would not be required and would not be ordered. "Yellow" costs are those costs that could be adjusted in response to changes in activity, but such adjustments require management action; the adjustment is not automatic. The ABC team believes, for example, that direct labor costs should be included in the Yellow category. Managers must make difficult decisions and take explicit action to increase or decrease, in aggregate, direct labor costs—particularly because the company has a no lay-off policy. "Red" costs are costs that could be adjusted to changes in activity only with a great deal of difficulty, and the adjustment would require management action. The building leases fall into this category because it would be very difficult and expensive to break the leases.

The Action Analysis View of the ABC Data

Looking at Exhibit 6A–3, the totals on the right-hand side of the table indicate that the $427,500 of overhead cost for the custom compass housings consists of $262,500 of indirect factory wages, $46,500 of factory equipment depreciation, and so on. These data are displayed in Exhibit 6A–5, which shows an action analysis of the custom compass housings product. An action analysis report shows what costs have been assigned to the

EXHIBIT 6A–4
Ease of Adjustment Codes

Green: *Costs that adjust automatically to changes in activity without management action.*
- Direct materials
- Shipping costs

Yellow: *Costs that could, in principle, be adjusted to changes in activity, but management action would be required.*
- Direct labor
- Indirect factory wages
- Factory utilities
- Administrative wages and salaries
- Office equipment depreciation
- Marketing wages and salaries
- Selling expenses

Red: *Costs that would be very difficult to adjust to changes in activity and management action would be required.*
- Factory equipment depreciation
- Factory building lease
- Administrative building lease

[4] The idea of using colors to code how easily costs can be adjusted was suggested to us at a seminar put on by Boeing and by an article by Alfred King, "Green Dollars and Blue Dollars: The Paradox of Cost Reduction," *Journal of Cost Management,* Fall 1993, pp. 44–52.

EXHIBIT 6A–5
Action Analysis of Custom Compass Housings: Activity-Based Costing System

	A	B	C
1	**Custom Compass Housings**		
2	Sales (from Exhibit 6-11)		$ 540,000
3			
4	Green costs:		
5	Direct materials (from Exhibit 6-11)	$ 69,500	
6	Shipping (from Exhibit 6-11)	5,000	74,500
7	Green margin		465,500
8			
9	Yellow costs:		
10	Direct labor (from Exhibit 6-11)	87,500	
11	Indirect factory wages (from Exhibit 6A-3)	262,500	
12	Factory utilities (from Exhibit 6A-3)	19,500	
13	Administrative wages and salaries (from Exhibit 6A-3)	49,000	
14	Office equipment depreciation (from Exhibit 6A-3)	6,000	
15	Marketing wages and salaries (from Exhibit 6A-3)	42,000	
16	Selling expenses (from Exhibit 6A-3)	2,000	468,500
17	Yellow margin		(3,000)
18			
19	Red costs:		
20	Factory equipment depreciation (from Exhibit 6A-3)	46,500	
21	Factory building lease (from Exhibit 6A-3)	0	
22	Administrative building lease (from Exhibit 6A-3)	0	46,500
23	Red margin		$ (49,500)
24			

Exhibit 6A-5 | Activity rates | Stanchions | Co

cost object, such as a product or customer, and how difficult it would be to adjust the cost if there is a change in activity. Note that the Red margin at the bottom of Exhibit 6A–5, $(49,500), is exactly the same as the product margin for the custom compass housings in Exhibit 6–11 in the chapter.

The cost data in the action analysis in Exhibit 6A–5 are arranged by the color coded ease of adjustment. All of the Green costs—those that adjust more or less automatically to changes in activity—appear together at the top of the list of costs. These costs total $74,500 and are subtracted from the sales of $540,000 to yield a Green margin of $465,500. The same procedure is followed for the Yellow and Red costs. This action analysis indicates what costs would have to be cut and how difficult it would be to cut them if the custom compass housings product were dropped. Prior to making any decision about dropping products, the managers responsible for the costs must agree to either eliminate the resources represented by those costs or to transfer the resources to an area in the organization that really needs the resources. If managers do not make such a commitment, it is likely that the costs would continue to be incurred. As a result, the company would lose the sales from the products without really eliminating the costs.

MANAGERIAL ACCOUNTING IN ACTION
The Wrap-Up

After the action analysis was prepared by the ABC team, top management at Classic Brass met once again to review the results of the ABC analysis.

John: When we last met, we had discussed the advisability of discontinuing the custom compass housings product line. I understand that the ABC team has done some additional analysis to help us in making this decision.

Mary: That's right. The action analysis report we put together indicates how easy it would be to adjust each cost and where specific cost savings would have to come from if we were to drop the custom compass housings.

John: What's this red margin at the bottom of the action analysis? Isn't that a product margin?

Mary: Yes, it is. However, we call it a red margin because we should stop and think very, very carefully before taking any actions based on that margin.

John: Why is that?

Mary: As an example, we subtracted the costs of factory equipment depreciation to arrive at that red margin. We doubt that we could avoid any of that cost if we were to drop custom orders. We use the same machines on custom orders that we use on standard products. The factory equipment has no resale value, and it does not wear out through use.

John: What about this yellow margin?

Mary: Yellow means proceed with a great deal of caution. To get to the yellow margin we deducted from sales numerous costs that could be adjusted only if the managers involved are willing to eliminate resources or shift them to another department in an effort to grow sales.

John: If I understand the yellow margin correctly, the apparent loss of $3,000 on the custom compass housings is the result of the indirect factory wages of $262,500.

Susan: Right, that's basically the wages of our design engineers.

John: I am uncomfortable with the idea of laying off any of our designers for numerous reasons. So where does that leave us?

Mary: What about raising prices on our custom products?

Tom: We should be able to do that. We have been undercutting the competition to make sure that we won bids on custom work because we thought it was a very profitable thing to do.

John: Why don't we just charge directly for design work?

Tom: Some of our competitors already do that. However, I don't think we would be able to charge enough to cover our design costs.

John: Can we do anything to make our design work more efficient so it costs us less? I'm not going to lay anyone off, but if we make the design process more efficient, we could lower the charge for design work and spread those costs across more customers.

Susan: That may be possible. I'll form a process improvement team to look at it.

John: Let's get some benchmark data on design costs. If we set our minds to it, I'm sure we can be world class in no time.

Susan: Okay. Mary, will you help with the benchmark data?

Mary: Sure.

John: Let's meet again in about a week to discuss our progress. Is there anything else on the agenda for today?

The points raised in the preceding discussion are extremely important. By measuring the resources consumed by products (and other cost objects), an ABC system provides a much better basis for decision making than a traditional cost accounting system that spreads overhead costs around without much regard for what might be causing the overhead. A well-designed ABC system provides managers with estimates of potentially relevant costs that can be a very useful starting point for management analysis.

Summary (Appendix 6A)

The action analysis report illustrated in this appendix is a valuable addition to the ABC toolkit. An action analysis report provides more information for decision making than a conventional ABC analysis. The action analysis report makes it clear where costs would have to be adjusted in the organization as a result of an action. In a conventional ABC analysis, a cost such as $320 for processing an order represents costs from many parts of the organization. If an order is dropped, there will be little pressure to actually eliminate the $320 cost unless it is clear where the costs are incurred and which managers would be responsible for reducing the cost. In contrast, an action analysis report traces the costs to where they are incurred in the organization and makes it much easier to assign responsibility to managers for reducing costs. In addition, an action analysis report provides information concerning how easily a cost can be adjusted. Costs that cannot be adjusted are not relevant in a decision.

EXHIBIT 6A–6
Summary of the Steps to Produce an Action Analysis Report

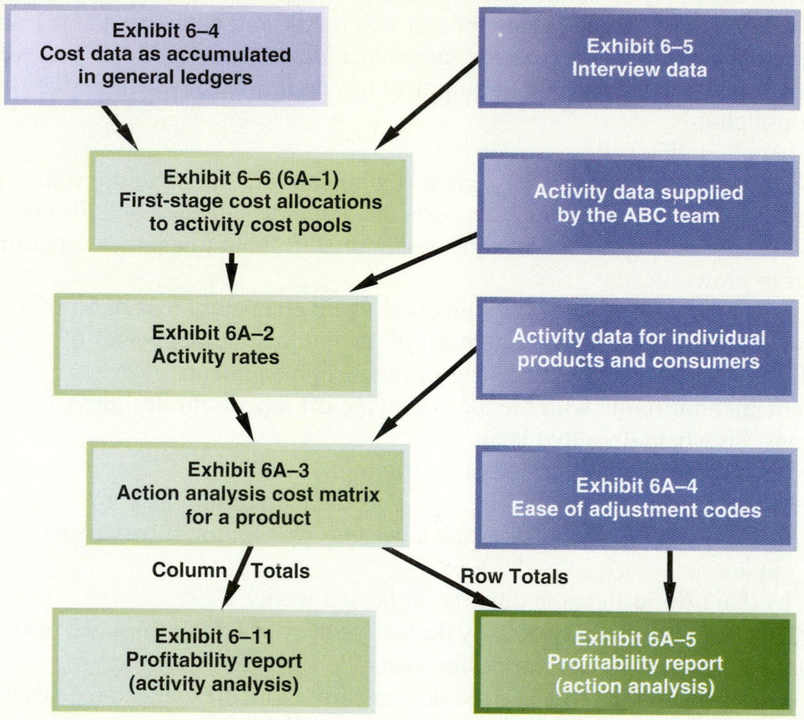

Exhibit 6A–6 summarizes all of the steps required to create both an action analysis report as illustrated in this appendix and an activity analysis as shown in the chapter.

Review Problem: Activity Analysis Report

Refer to the data for Ferris Corporation in the Review Problem at the end of the chapter.

Required:

1. Compute activity rates for Ferris Corporation as in Exhibit 6A–2.
2. Using Exhibit 6A–3 as a guide, construct a table showing the overhead costs for the OfficeMart orders described in requirement (3) of the Review Problem at the end of the chapter.
3. The management of Ferris Corporation has assigned ease of adjustment codes to costs as follows:

Cost	Ease of Adjustment Code
Direct materials.	Green
Direct labor	Yellow
Manufacturing overhead	Yellow
Selling and administrative overhead	Red

Using Exhibit 6A–5 as a guide, prepare an action analysis of the OfficeMart orders.

Solution to Review Problem

1. The activity rates for the activity cost pools are:

	Assembling Units	Processing Orders	Supporting Customers
Total activity	1,000 units	250 orders	100 customers
Manufacturing overhead	$250	$ 700	$ 250
Selling and administrative overhead	30	540	750
Total	$280	$1,240	$1,000

2. The overhead cost for the four orders of a total of 80 filing cabinets would be computed as follows:

	Assembling Units	Processing Orders	Supporting Customers	Total
Activity	80 units	4 orders	1 customer	
Manufacturing overhead	$20,000	$2,800	$ 250	$23,050
Selling and administrative overhead	2,400	2,160	750	5,310
Total	$22,400	$4,960	$1,000	$28,360

3. The action analysis report is:

Sales		$47,600
Green costs:		
Direct materials	$14,400	14,400
Green margin		33,200
Yellow costs:		
Direct labor	4,000	
Manufacturing overhead	23,050	27,050
Yellow margin		6,150
Red costs:		
Selling and administrative overhead	5,310	5,310
Red margin		$ 840

Glossary (Appendix 6A)

Ease of adjustment codes Costs are coded as Green, Yellow, or Red—depending on how easily the cost could be adjusted to changes in activity. "Green" costs adjust automatically to changes in activity. "Yellow" costs could be adjusted in response to changes in activity, but such adjustments require management action; the adjustment is not automatic. "Red" costs could be adjusted to changes in activity only with a great deal of difficulty and would require management action. (p. 271)

Appendix 6A Exercises and Problems

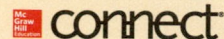

Additional student resources are available with Connect.

EXERCISE 6A–1 Preparing an Action Analysis Report [LO6–6]

Fairway Golf Corporation produces private label golf clubs for pro shops throughout North America. The company uses activity-based costing to evaluate the profitability of serving its customers. This analysis is based on categorizing the company's costs as follows, using the ease of adjustment color coding scheme described in Appendix 6A:

	Ease of Adjustment Code
Direct materials	Green
Direct labor	Yellow
Indirect labor	Yellow
Factory equipment depreciation	Red
Factory administration	Red
Selling and administrative wages and salaries	Red
Selling and administrative depreciation	Red
Marketing expenses	Yellow

Management would like to evaluate the profitability of a particular customer—Shaker Run Golf Club of Lebanon, Ohio. Over the last twelve months this customer submitted one order for 100 golf clubs that had to be produced in four batches due to differences in product labeling requested by the customer. Summary data concerning the order appear below:

Number of clubs	100
Number of orders	1
Number of batches	4
Direct labor-hours per club	0.3
Selling price per club	$50.00
Direct materials cost per club	$29.50
Direct labor rate per hour	$20.50

A cost analyst working in the controller's office at the company has already produced the action analysis cost matrix for the Shaker Run Golf Club that appears below:

Action Analysis Cost Matrix for Shaker Run Golf Club

	Activity Cost Pools				
	Supporting Direct labor	Batch Processing	Order Processing	Customer Service	Total
Activity	30 direct labor-hours	4 batches	1 order	1 customer	
Manufacturing overhead:					
Indirect labor	$ 35.40	$53.70	$ 6.80	$ 0.00	$ 95.90
Factory equipment depreciation	102.80	0.90	0.00	0.00	103.70
Factory administration	18.50	0.50	12.00	228.00	259.00
Selling and administrative overhead:					
Wages and salaries	11.00	0.00	36.00	382.00	429.00
Depreciation	0.00	0.00	6.00	24.00	30.00
Marketing expenses	117.70	0.00	54.00	369.00	540.70
Total	$285.40	$55.10	$114.80	$1,003.00	$1,458.30

Required:

Prepare an action analysis report showing the profitability of the Shaker Run Golf Club. Include direct materials and direct labor costs in the report. Use Exhibit 6A–5 as a guide for organizing the report.

EXERCISE 6A–2 Second-Stage Allocation Using the Action Analysis Approach [LO6–4, LO6–6]

This exercise should be assigned in conjunction with Exercise 6–9.

The results of the first-stage allocation of the activity-based costing system at Durban Metal Products, Ltd., in which the activity rates were computed, appear below:

	Order Size	Customer Orders	Product Testing	Selling
Manufacturing overhead:				
Indirect labor	$ 8.25	$180.00	$30.00	$ 0.00
Factory depreciation	8.00	0.00	40.00	0.00
Factory utilities	0.10	0.00	1.00	0.00
Factory administration.	0.00	48.00	18.00	30.00
Selling and administrative:				
Wages and salaries	0.50	80.00	0.00	800.00
Depreciation	0.00	12.00	0.00	40.00
Taxes and insurance	0.00	0.00	0.00	20.00
Selling expenses.	0.00	0.00	0.00	200.00
Total overhead cost	$16.85	$320.00	$89.00	$1,090.00

Required:

1. Using Exhibit 6A–3 as a guide, prepare a report showing the overhead cost of the order for heavy-duty trailer axles discussed in Exercise 6–9. What is the total overhead cost of the order according to the activity-based costing system?
2. Explain the two different perspectives this report gives to managers concerning the nature of the overhead costs involved in the order. (*Hint:* Look at the row and column totals of the report you have prepared.)

EXERCISE 6A–3 Second-Stage Allocations and Margin Calculations Using the Action Analysis Approach [LO6–4, LO6–6]

Refer to the data for Foam Products, Inc., in Exercise 6–11 and the following additional details concerning the activity rates in the activity-based costing system:

	Activity Rates			
	Supporting Direct Labor	Batch Processing	Order Processing	Customer Service
Manufacturing overhead:				
Indirect labor.	$0.60	$ 60.00	$ 20.00	$ 0.00
Factory equipment depreciation . . .	4.00	17.00	0.00	0.00
Factory administration.	0.10	7.00	25.00	150.00
Selling and administrative overhead:				
Wages and salaries	0.40	20.00	160.00	1,600.00
Depreciation	0.00	3.00	10.00	38.00
Marketing expenses	0.45	0.00	60.00	675.00
Total	$5.55	$107.00	$275.00	$2,463.00

Management has provided its ease of adjustment codes for the purpose of preparing action analyses.

	Ease of Adjustment Codes
Direct materials	Green
Direct labor	Yellow
Manufacturing overhead:	
Indirect labor	Yellow
Factory equipment depreciation	Red
Factory administration	Red
Selling and administrative overhead:	
Wages and salaries	Red
Depreciation	Red
Marketing expenses	Yellow

Required:

Using Exhibit 6A–5 as a guide, prepare an action analysis report for Interstate Trucking similar to those prepared for products.

EXERCISE 6A–4 Comprehensive Activity-Based Costing Exercise [LO6–2, LO6–3, LO6–4, LO6–6]

Refer to the data for Advanced Products Corporation in Exercise 6–15.

Required:

1. Using Exhibit 6A–1 as a guide, prepare a report showing the first-stage allocations of overhead costs to the activity cost pools.
2. Using Exhibit 6A–2 as a guide, compute the activity rates for the activity cost pools.
3. Using Exhibit 6A–3 as a guide, prepare a report showing the overhead costs for the order from Shenzhen Enterprises including customer support costs.
4. Using Exhibit 6–12 as a guide, prepare a report showing the customer margin for Shenzhen Enterprises.
5. Using Exhibit 6A–5 as a guide, prepare an action analysis report showing the customer margin for Shenzhen Enterprises. Direct materials should be coded as a Green cost, direct labor and wages and salaries as Yellow costs, and other overhead costs as a Red cost.
6. What action, if any, do you recommend as a result of the above analyses?

EXERCISE 6A–5 Second Stage Allocations and Product Margins [LO6–4, LO6–6]

Refer to the data for Pixel Studio, Inc., in PROBLEM 6–19. In addition, the company has provided the following details concerning its activity rates:

	Activity Rates		
	Animation Concept	Animation Production	Contract Administration
Technical staff salaries	$4,000	$6,000	$1,600
Animation equipment depreciation	360	1,125	0
Administrative wages and salaries	1,440	150	4,800
Supplies costs	120	300	160
Facility costs	120	150	240
Total	$6,040	$7,725	$6,800

Management has provided the following ease of adjustment codes for the various costs:

	Ease of Adjustment Code
Technical staff salaries	Red
Animation equipment depreciation	Red
Administrative wages and salaries	Yellow
Supplies costs	Green
Facility costs	Red

These codes created some controversy. In particular, some administrators objected to coding their own salaries Yellow, while the technical staff salaries were coded Red. However, the founders of the firm overruled these objections by pointing out that "our technical staff is our most valuable asset. Good animators are extremely difficult to find, and they would be the last to go if we had to cut back."

Required:

1. Using Exhibit 6A–3 as a guide, determine the cost of the local commercials market. (Think of the local commercial market as a product.)
2. Using Exhibit 6A–5 as a guide, prepare an action analysis report concerning the local commercial market. (This company has no direct materials or direct labor costs.)
3. What would you recommend to management concerning the local commercial market?

Differential Analysis: The Key to Decision Making

LEARNING OBJECTIVES

After studying Chapter 7, you should be able to:

LO 7–1 Identify relevant and irrelevant costs and benefits in a decision.

LO 7–2 Prepare an analysis showing whether a product line or other business segment should be added or dropped.

LO 7–3 Prepare a make or buy analysis.

LO 7–4 Prepare an analysis showing whether a special order should be accepted.

LO 7–5 Determine the most profitable use of a constrained resource.

LO 7–6 Determine the value of obtaining more of the constrained resource.

LO 7–7 Prepare an analysis showing whether joint products should be sold at the split-off point or processed further.

BUSINESS FOCUS

Moving Manufacturing Operations Overseas

© AP Images/Imaginechina/Jhphoto

A survey from Ventoro Institute LLC found that many companies expect to realize an 80% cost savings when moving manufacturing operations overseas. However, in this same survey, companies reported an average actual cost savings of less than 10%. Some of the problems encountered by these companies included miscommunications with offshore manufacturers, shipping delays, intellectual property infringement, and substandard product quality. William Botts, vice chairman of Vegas Valley Angels (an angel-investing group), suggests that companies with labor-intensive manufacturing processes are most likely to benefit from sending manufacturing operations overseas because the bulk of potential cost savings relate to labor costs. ■

Source: Small Talk, "Kelly Spors Answers Questions on Protecting Ideas, Cutting Off Junk Mail, and Overseas Manufacturing," *The Wall Street Journal*, March 17, 2008, p. R2.

Managers must decide what products to sell, whether to make or buy component parts, what prices to charge, what channels of distribution to use, whether to accept special orders at special prices, and so forth. Making such decisions is often a difficult task that is complicated by numerous alternatives and massive amounts of data, only some of which may be relevant.

Every decision involves choosing from among at least two alternatives. In making a decision, the costs and benefits of one alternative must be compared to the costs and benefits of other alternatives. The key to making such comparisons is *differential analysis*—focusing on the costs and benefits that *differ* between the alternatives. A difference in cost between any two alternatives is known as a **differential cost**. A difference in revenue between any two alternatives is known as **differential revenue**. Differential costs and revenues are relevant to decision making, whereas costs and revenues that do not differ between alternatives are irrelevant to decision making. Because differential costs and differential revenues are the only inputs that are relevant to decision making, they are also often referred to as **relevant costs** and **relevant benefits**.

Distinguishing between relevant and irrelevant costs and benefits is critical for two reasons. First, irrelevant data can be ignored—saving decision makers tremendous amounts of time and effort. Second, bad decisions can easily result from erroneously including irrelevant costs and benefits when analyzing alternatives. To be successful in decision making, managers must be able to tell the difference between relevant and irrelevant data and must be able to correctly use the relevant data in analyzing alternatives. The purpose of this chapter is to develop these skills by illustrating their use in a wide range of decision-making situations. These decision-making skills are as important in your personal life as they are to managers. After completing your study of this chapter, you should be able to think more clearly about decisions in many facets of your life.

Cost Concepts for Decision Making

Identifying Relevant Costs and Benefits

LEARNING OBJECTIVE 7–1
Identify relevant and irrelevant costs and benefits in a decision.

Only those costs and benefits that differ in total between alternatives are relevant in a decision. If the total amount of a cost will be the same regardless of the alternative selected, then the decision has no effect on the cost, so the cost can be ignored. To elaborate on this point, we'd like to define the terms *avoidable cost, sunk cost,* and *opportunity cost,* and illustrate the concept of *future costs that do not differ between alternatives.*

Assume you are trying to decide whether to go to a movie or rent a DVD for the evening. The rent on your apartment is irrelevant. Whether you go to a movie or rent a DVD, the rent on your apartment will be exactly the same and is therefore irrelevant to the decision. On the other hand, the cost of the movie ticket and the cost of renting the DVD would be relevant in the decision because they are *avoidable costs.*

An **avoidable cost** is a cost that can be eliminated by choosing one alternative over another. By choosing the alternative of going to the movie, the cost of renting the DVD can be avoided. By choosing the alternative of renting the DVD, the cost of the movie ticket can be avoided. Therefore, the cost of the movie ticket and the cost of renting the DVD are both avoidable costs. On the other hand, the rent on your apartment is not an avoidable cost of either alternative. You would continue to rent your apartment under either alternative. Avoidable costs are relevant costs. Unavoidable costs are irrelevant costs.

To refine the notion of relevant costs a little further, two broad categories of costs are never relevant in decisions—sunk costs and future costs that do not differ between the alternatives. As we learned in Chapter 2, **sunk cost** is a cost that has already been incurred and cannot be avoided regardless of what a manager decides to do. For example, suppose a company purchased a five-year-old truck for $12,000. The amount paid for the truck is a sunk cost because it has already been incurred and the transaction cannot be undone. Even though it is perhaps counterintuitive, the amount the company paid for the truck is irrelevant in making decisions such as whether to keep, sell, or replace the truck. Furthermore, any depreciation expense related to the truck is *irrelevant in making decisions.* This is true because depreciation is a noncash expense that simply spreads the cost of the truck over its useful life.[1] Sunk costs are always the same no matter what alternatives are being considered; therefore, they are irrelevant and should be ignored when making decisions.

Future costs that do not differ between alternatives should also be ignored. Continuing with the example discussed earlier, suppose you plan to order a pizza after you go to the movie theater or you rent a DVD. If you are going to buy the same pizza regardless of your choice of entertainment, the cost of the pizza is irrelevant to the choice of whether you go to the movie theater or rent a DVD. Notice, the cost of the pizza is not a sunk cost because it has not yet been incurred. Nonetheless, the cost of the pizza is irrelevant to the entertainment decision because it is a future cost that does not differ between the alternatives.

Opportunity costs also need to be considered when making decisions. An **opportunity cost** is the potential benefit that is given up when one alternative is selected over another. For example, if you were considering giving up a high-paying summer job to travel overseas, the forgone wages would be an opportunity cost of traveling abroad. Opportunity costs are not usually found in accounting records, but they are costs that must be explicitly considered in every decision a manager makes.

To summarize, only those costs and benefits that differ between alternatives are relevant in a decision. Differential costs are also referred to as relevant costs or avoidable costs. The key to successful decision making is to focus on relevant costs and benefits as well as opportunity costs while ignoring everything else—including sunk costs and future costs and benefits that do not differ between the alternatives.

IN BUSINESS

INDUSTRIAL MOTION HEADS EAST

Eric Kozlowski and Brian Pfeifer founded Industrial Motion Inc. in Rancho Santa Margarita, California; however, after 10 years in California, they decided to cut costs by relocating the company to Mooresville, North Carolina. In Mooresville, the company's 42 employees are paid salaries of $35,000–$45,000 instead of the $60,000 paid to employees in California; furthermore, workers' compensation insurance is one-tenth of the amount paid in California. Property taxes and the cost of real estate are 50% less in Mooresville compared to Rancho Santa Margarita. Even the company's security system in Mooresville costs only $25 per month instead of $280 per month in California.

Source: Simona Covel, "Moving Across the Country to Cut Costs," *The Wall Street Journal,* January 10, 2008, p. B4.

Different Costs for Different Purposes

We need to recognize a fundamental concept from the outset of our discussion—costs that are relevant in one decision situation are not necessarily relevant in another. This means that *managers need different costs for different purposes.* For one purpose, a particular group of costs may be relevant; for another purpose, an entirely different group of costs may be relevant. Thus, *each* decision situation must be carefully analyzed to isolate the relevant costs. Otherwise, irrelevant data may cloud the situation and lead to a bad decision.

The concept of "different costs for different purposes" is basic to managerial accounting; we shall frequently see its application in the pages that follow.

An Example of Identifying Relevant Costs and Benefits

Cynthia is currently a student in an MBA program in Boston and would like to visit a friend in New York City over the weekend. She is trying to decide whether to drive or take the train. Because she is on a tight budget, she wants to carefully consider the costs of the two alternatives. If one alternative is far less expensive than the other, that may be decisive in

[1] See Appendix 8C for a discussion of how depreciation expense impacts decisions when tax implications are considered.

her choice. By car, the distance between her apartment in Boston and her friend's apartment in New York City is 230 miles. Cynthia has compiled the following list of items to consider:

Automobile Costs

	Item	Annual Cost of Fixed Items	Cost per Mile (based on 10,000 miles per year)
(a)	Annual straight-line depreciation on car [($24,000 original cost − $10,000 estimated resale value in 5 years)/5 years]	$2,800	$0.280
(b)	Cost of gasoline ($3.30 per gallon ÷ 33 miles per gallon).		0.100
(c)	Annual cost of auto insurance and license.	$1,380	0.138
(d)	Maintenance and repairs		0.065
(e)	Parking fees at school ($45 per month × 8 months)	$360	0.036
(f)	Total average cost per mile		$0.619

Additional Data

	Item	
(g)	Reduction in the resale value of car due solely to wear and tear	$0.026 per mile
(h)	Cost of round-trip train ticket from Boston to New York City.	$104
(i)	Benefit of relaxing and being able to study during the train ride rather than having to drive	?
(j)	Cost of putting the dog in a kennel while gone. . .	$40
(k)	Benefit of having a car available in New York City. . .	?
(l)	Hassle of parking the car in New York City.	?
(m)	Cost of parking the car in New York City.	$25 per day

Which costs and benefits are relevant in this decision? Remember, only those costs and benefits that differ between alternatives are relevant. Everything else is irrelevant and can be ignored.

Start at the top of the list with item (a): the original cost of the car is a sunk cost. This cost has already been incurred and therefore can never differ between alternatives. Consequently, it is irrelevant and should be ignored. The same is true of the accounting depreciation of $2,800 per year, which simply spreads the sunk cost across five years.

Item (b), the cost of gasoline consumed by driving to New York City, is a relevant cost. If Cynthia takes the train, this cost would not be incurred. Hence, the cost differs between alternatives and is therefore relevant.

Item (c), the annual cost of auto insurance and license, is not relevant. Whether Cynthia takes the train or drives on this particular trip, her annual auto insurance premium and her auto license fee will remain the same.[2]

Item (d), the cost of maintenance and repairs, is relevant. While maintenance and repair costs have a large random component, over the long run they should be more or less proportional to the number of miles the car is driven. Thus, the average cost of $0.065 per mile is a reasonable estimate to use.

[2] If Cynthia has an accident while driving to New York City or back, this might affect her insurance premium when the policy is renewed. The increase in the insurance premium would be a relevant cost of this particular trip, but the normal amount of the insurance premium is not relevant in any case.

Item (e), the monthly fee that Cynthia pays to park at her school during the academic year is not relevant. Regardless of which alternative she selects—driving or taking the train—she will still need to pay for parking at school.

Item (f) is the total average cost of $0.619 per mile. As discussed above, some elements of this total are relevant, but some are not relevant. Because it contains some irrelevant costs, it would be incorrect to estimate the cost of driving to New York City and back by simply multiplying the $0.619 by 460 miles (230 miles each way × 2). This erroneous approach would yield a cost of driving of $284.74. Unfortunately, such mistakes are often made in both personal life and in business. Because the total cost is stated on a per-mile basis, people are easily misled. Often people think that if the cost is stated as $0.619 per mile, the cost of driving 100 miles is $61.90. But it is not. Many of the costs included in the $0.619 cost per mile are sunk and/or fixed and will not increase if the car is driven another 100 miles. The $0.619 is an average cost, not an incremental cost. Beware of such unitized costs (i.e., costs stated in terms of a dollar amount per unit, per mile, per direct labor-hour, per machine-hour, and so on)—they are often misleading.

Item (g), the decline in the resale value of the car that occurs as a consequence of driving more miles, is relevant in the decision. Because she uses the car, its resale value declines, which is a real cost of using the car that should be taken into account. Cynthia estimated this cost by accessing the *Kelly Blue Book* website at www.kbb.com. The reduction in resale value of an asset through use or over time is often called *real* or *economic depreciation.* This is different from accounting depreciation, which attempts to match the sunk cost of an asset with the periods that benefit from that cost.

Item (h), the $104 cost of a round-trip ticket on the train, is relevant in this decision. If she drives, she would not have to buy the ticket.

Item (i) is relevant to the decision, even if it is difficult to put a dollar value on relaxing and being able to study while on the train. It is relevant because it is a benefit that is available under one alternative but not under the other.

Item (j), the cost of putting Cynthia's dog in the kennel while she is gone, is irrelevant in this decision. Whether she takes the train or drives to New York City, she will still need to put her dog in a kennel.

Like item (i), items (k) and (l) are relevant to the decision even if it is difficult to measure their dollar impacts.

Item (m), the cost of parking in New York City, is relevant to the decision.

Bringing together all of the relevant data, Cynthia would estimate the relevant costs of driving and taking the train as follows:

Relevant financial cost of driving to New York City:	
Gasoline (460 miles × $0.100 per mile)	$ 46.00
Maintenance and repairs (460 miles × $0.065 per mile)	29.90
Reduction in the resale value of car due solely to wear and tear (460 miles × $0.026 per mile)	11.96
Cost of parking the car in New York City (2 days × $25 per day)	50.00
Total	$137.86
Relevant financial cost of taking the train to New York City:	
Cost of round-trip train ticket from Boston to New York City	$104.00

What should Cynthia do? From a purely financial standpoint, it would be cheaper by $33.86 ($137.86 − $104.00) to take the train than to drive. Cynthia has to decide if the convenience of having a car in New York City outweighs the additional cost and the disadvantages of being unable to relax and study on the train and the hassle of finding parking in the city.

In this example, we focused on identifying the relevant costs and benefits—everything else was ignored. In the next example, we include all of the costs and benefits—relevant or not. Nonetheless, we'll still get the correct answer because the irrelevant costs and benefits will cancel out when we compare the alternatives.

IN BUSINESS

UNDERSTANDING THE IMPORTANCE OF QUALITATIVE FACTORS

SAS is a privately held $2.26 billion company located on a 200-acre campus in Cary, North Carolina. The company has an on-site medical facility (including a lab for blood tests) that is staffed by doctors, nurse practitioners, physical therapists, and a nutritionist. The company also has an infant day care, a Montessori school, a hair salon, a dry cleaning shop, a fitness center, and jogging and biking trails on campus. Employees that use the day care pay $360 per month per child for the service and SAS covers the remaining $720 per month per child that it costs to retain 120 teachers and staffers.

Although it may be difficult to quantify the benefits of these investments, SAS firmly believes that retaining happy and healthy employees is instrumental to its success. Mary Simmons, a SAS software developer says, "At lunch I will go out and bike 20 miles. Then I'll get back and all of a sudden a thought comes to my brain, and I solve something I was struggling with."

Source: Christopher Tkaczyk, "Offer Affordable (Awesome) Day Care," *Fortune,* August 17, 2009, p. 26.

Reconciling the Total and Differential Approaches

Oak Harbor Woodworks is considering a new labor-saving machine that rents for $3,000 per year. The machine will be used on the company's butcher block production line. Data concerning the company's annual sales and costs of butcher blocks with and without the new machine are shown below:

	Current Situation	Situation with the New Machine
Units produced and sold	5,000	5,000
Selling price per unit	$40	$40
Direct materials cost per unit	$14	$14
Direct labor cost per unit	$8	$5
Variable overhead cost per unit	$2	$2
Fixed expenses, other	$62,000	$62,000
Fixed expenses, rental of new machine	—	$3,000

Given the data above, the net operating income for the product under the two alternatives can be computed as shown in Exhibit 7–1.

Note that the net operating income is $12,000 higher with the new machine, so that is the better alternative. Note also that the $12,000 advantage for the new machine can be obtained in two different ways. It is the difference between the $30,000 net operating income with the new machine and the $18,000 net operating income for the current situation. It is also the sum of the differential costs and benefits as shown in the last column of Exhibit 7–1 ($15,000 + $(3,000) = $12,000). A positive number in the Differential Costs and Benefits column indicates that the difference between the alternatives favors the new machine; a negative number indicates that the difference favors the current situation. A zero in that column simply means that the total amount for the item is exactly the same for both alternatives. Thus, because the difference in the net operating incomes equals the sum of the differences for the individual items, any cost or benefit that is the same for both alternatives will have no impact on which alternative is preferred. This is the reason that costs and benefits that do not differ between alternatives are irrelevant and can be ignored. If we properly account for them, they will cancel out when we compare the alternatives.

EXHIBIT 7–1
Total and Differential Costs

	Current Situation	Situation with New Machine	Differential Costs and Benefits
Sales (5,000 units × $40 per unit)	$200,000	$200,000	$ 0
Variable expenses:			
Direct materials (5,000 units × $14 per unit)	70,000	70,000	0
Direct labor (5,000 units × $8 per unit; 5,000 units × $5 per unit)	40,000	25,000	15,000
Variable overhead (5,000 units × $2 per unit)	10,000	10,000	0
Total variable expenses	120,000	105,000	
Contribution margin	80,000	95,000	
Fixed expenses:			
Other	62,000	62,000	0
Rental of new machine	0	3,000	(3,000)
Total fixed expenses	62,000	65,000	
Net operating income	$ 18,000	$ 30,000	$12,000

We could have arrived at the same solution much more quickly by completely ignoring the irrelevant costs and benefits.

- The selling price per unit and the number of units sold do not differ between the alternatives. Therefore, the total sales revenues are exactly the same for the two alternatives as shown in Exhibit 7–1. Because the sales revenues are exactly the same, they have no effect on the difference in net operating income between the two alternatives. That is shown in the last column in Exhibit 7–1, which shows a $0 differential benefit.
- The direct materials cost per unit, the variable overhead cost per unit, and the number of units produced and sold do not differ between the alternatives. Consequently, the total direct materials cost and the total variable overhead cost are the same for the two alternatives and can be ignored.
- The "other" fixed expenses do not differ between the alternatives, so they can be ignored as well.

Indeed, the only costs that do differ between the alternatives are direct labor costs and the fixed rental cost of the new machine. Hence, the two alternatives can be compared based only on these relevant costs:

Net Advantage of Renting the New Machine	
Decrease in direct labor costs (5,000 units at a cost savings of $3 per unit)	$15,000
Increase in fixed expenses	(3,000)
Net annual cost savings from renting the new machine	$12,000

If we focus on just the relevant costs and benefits, we get exactly the same answer as when we listed all of the costs and benefits—including those that do not differ between the alternatives and, hence, are irrelevant. We get the same answer because the only costs and benefits that matter in the final comparison of the net operating incomes are those that differ between the two alternatives and, hence, are not zero in the last column of

Exhibit 7–1. Those two relevant costs are both included in the above analysis that quantifies the net advantage of renting the new machine.

Why Isolate Relevant Costs?

In the preceding example, we used two different approaches to analyze the alternatives. First, we considered all costs, both those that were relevant and those that were not; and second, we considered only the relevant costs. We obtained the same answer under both approaches. It would be natural to ask, "Why bother to isolate relevant costs when total costs will do the job just as well?" Isolating relevant costs is desirable for at least two reasons.

First, only rarely will enough information be available to prepare a detailed income statement for both alternatives. Assume, for example, that you are called on to make a decision relating to a portion of a single business process in a multidepartmental, multi-product company. Under these circumstances, it would be virtually impossible to prepare an income statement of any type. You would have to rely on your ability to recognize which costs are relevant and which are not in order to assemble the data necessary to make a decision.

Second, mingling irrelevant costs with relevant costs may cause confusion and distract attention from the information that is really critical. Furthermore, the danger always exists that an irrelevant piece of data may be used improperly, resulting in an incorrect decision. The best approach is to ignore irrelevant data and base the decision entirely on relevant data.

Relevant cost analysis, combined with the contribution approach to the income statement, provides a powerful tool for making decisions. We will investigate various uses of this tool in the remaining sections of this chapter.

Adding and Dropping Product Lines and Other Segments

LEARNING OBJECTIVE 7–2
Prepare an analysis showing whether a product line or other business segment should be added or dropped.

Decisions relating to whether product lines or other segments of a company should be dropped and new ones added are among the most difficult that a manager has to make. In such decisions, many qualitative and quantitative factors must be considered. Ultimately, however, any final decision to drop a business segment or to add a new one hinges primarily on the impact the decision will have on net operating income. To assess this impact, costs must be carefully analyzed.

An Illustration of Cost Analysis

Exhibit 7–2 provides sales and cost information for the preceding month for the Discount Drug Company and its three major product lines—drugs, cosmetics, and housewares. A quick review of this exhibit suggests that dropping the housewares segment would increase the company's overall net operating income by $8,000. However, this would be a flawed conclusion because the data in Exhibit 7–2 do not distinguish between fixed expenses that can be avoided if a product line is dropped and common fixed expenses that cannot be avoided by dropping any particular product line.

In this scenario, the two alternatives under consideration are keeping the housewares product line and dropping the housewares product line. Therefore, only those costs that differ between these two alternatives (i.e., that can be avoided by dropping the housewares product line) are relevant. In deciding whether to drop housewares, it is crucial to identify which costs can be avoided, and hence are relevant to the decision, and which costs cannot be avoided, and hence are irrelevant. The decision should be analyzed as follows.

If the housewares line is dropped, then the company will lose $20,000 per month in contribution margin, but by dropping the line it may be possible to avoid some fixed costs such as salaries or advertising costs. If dropping the housewares line enables the company to avoid more in fixed costs than it loses in contribution margin, then its overall

EXHIBIT 7–2
Discount Drug Company
Product Lines

		Product Line		
	Total	Drugs	Cosmetics	Housewares
Sales	$250,000	$125,000	$75,000	$50,000
Variable expenses	105,000	50,000	25,000	30,000
Contribution margin	145,000	75,000	50,000	20,000
Fixed expenses:				
Salaries	50,000	29,500	12,500	8,000
Advertising	15,000	1,000	7,500	6,500
Utilities	2,000	500	500	1,000
Depreciation—fixtures	5,000	1,000	2,000	2,000
Rent	20,000	10,000	6,000	4,000
Insurance	3,000	2,000	500	500
General administrative	30,000	15,000	9,000	6,000
Total fixed expenses	125,000	59,000	38,000	28,000
Net operating income (loss)	$ 20,000	$ 16,000	$12,000	$ (8,000)

net operating income will improve by eliminating the product line. On the other hand, if the company is not able to avoid as much in fixed costs as it loses in contribution margin, then the housewares line should be kept. In short, the manager should ask, "What costs can I avoid if I drop this product line?"

As we have seen from our earlier discussion, not all costs are avoidable. For example, some of the costs associated with a product line may be sunk costs. Other costs may be allocated fixed costs that will not differ in total regardless of whether the product line is dropped or retained.

To show how to proceed in a product-line analysis, suppose that Discount Drug Company has analyzed the fixed costs being charged to the three product lines and determined the following:

1. The salaries expense represents salaries paid to employees working directly on the product. All of the employees working in housewares would be discharged if the product line is dropped.
2. The advertising expense represents advertisements that are specific to each product line and are avoidable if the line is dropped.
3. The utilities expense represents utilities costs for the entire company. The amount charged to each product line is an allocation based on space occupied and is not avoidable if the product line is dropped.
4. The depreciation expense represents depreciation on fixtures used to display the various product lines. Although the fixtures are nearly new, they are custom-built and will have no resale value if the housewares line is dropped.
5. The rent expense represents rent on the entire building housing the company; it is allocated to the product lines on the basis of sales dollars. The monthly rent of $20,000 is fixed under a long-term lease agreement.
6. The insurance expense is for insurance carried on inventories within each of the three product lines. If housewares is dropped, the related inventories will be liquidated and the insurance premiums will decrease proportionately.
7. The general administrative expense represents the costs of accounting, purchasing, and general management, which are allocated to the product lines on the basis of sales dollars. These costs will not change if the housewares line is dropped.

With this information, management can determine that $15,000 of the fixed expenses associated with the housewares product line are avoidable and $13,000 are not:

Fixed Expenses	Total Cost Assigned to Housewares	Not Avoidable*	Avoidable
Salaries	$ 8,000		$ 8,000
Advertising	6,500		6,500
Utilities	1,000	$ 1,000	
Depreciation—fixtures	2,000	2,000	
Rent	4,000	4,000	
Insurance	500		500
General administrative	6,000	6,000	
Total	$28,000	$13,000	$15,000

*These fixed costs represent either sunk costs or future costs that will not change whether the housewares line is retained or discontinued.

As stated earlier, if the housewares product line were dropped, the company would lose the product's contribution margin of $20,000, but would save its associated avoidable fixed expenses. We now know that those avoidable fixed expenses total $15,000. Therefore, dropping the housewares product line would result in a $5,000 *reduction* in net operating income as shown below:

Contribution margin lost if the housewares line is discontinued (see Exhibit 7–2)	$(20,000)
Fixed expenses that can be avoided if the housewares line is discontinued (see above)	15,000
Decrease in overall company net operating income	$ (5,000)

In this case, the fixed costs that can be avoided by dropping the housewares product line ($15,000) are less than the contribution margin that will be lost ($20,000). Therefore, based on the data given, the housewares line should not be discontinued unless a more profitable use can be found for the floor and counter space that it is occupying.

A Comparative Format

This decision can also be approached by preparing comparative income statements showing the effects of either keeping or dropping the product line. Exhibit 7–3 contains such an analysis for the Discount Drug Company. As shown in the last column of the exhibit, if the housewares line is dropped, then overall company net operating income will decrease by $5,000 each period. This is the same answer, of course, as we obtained when we focused just on the lost contribution margin and avoidable fixed costs.

Beware of Allocated Fixed Costs

Go back to Exhibit 7–2. Does this exhibit suggest that the housewares product line should be kept—as we have just concluded? No, it does not. Exhibit 7–2 suggests that the housewares product line is losing money. Why keep a product line that is showing a loss? The explanation for this apparent inconsistency lies in part with the common fixed costs that are being allocated to the product lines. One of the great dangers in allocating common fixed costs is that such allocations can make a product line (or other business segment) look less profitable than it really is. In this instance, allocating the common fixed costs among all product lines makes the housewares product line appear to be unprofitable. However, as we have just shown, dropping the product line would result in a decrease in the company's overall net operating income. This point can be seen clearly if we redo Exhibit 7–2 by eliminating the allocation of the common fixed costs. Exhibit 7–4 uses the segmented approach from Chapter 6 to estimate the profitability of the product lines.

EXHIBIT 7–3
A Comparative Format for Product-Line Analysis

	Keep Housewares	Drop Housewares	Difference: Net Operating Income Increase (or Decrease)
Sales	$50,000	$ 0	$(50,000)
Variable expenses	30,000	0	30,000
Contribution margin	20,000	0	(20,000)
Fixed expenses:			
Salaries	8,000	0	8,000
Advertising	6,500	0	6,500
Utilities	1,000	1,000	0
Depreciation—fixtures	2,000	2,000	0
Rent	4,000	4,000	0
Insurance	500	0	500
General administrative	6,000	6,000	0
Total fixed expenses	28,000	13,000	15,000
Net operating loss	$ (8,000)	$(13,000)	$ (5,000)

Exhibit 7–4 gives us a much different perspective of the housewares line than does Exhibit 7–2. As shown in Exhibit 7–4, the housewares line is covering all of its own traceable fixed costs and generating a $3,000 segment margin toward covering the common

EXHIBIT 7–4
Discount Drug Company Product Lines—Recast in Contribution Format (from Exhibit 7–2)

		Product Line		
	Total	Drugs	Cosmetics	Housewares
Sales	$250,000	$125,000	$75,000	$50,000
Variable expenses	105,000	50,000	25,000	30,000
Contribution margin	145,000	75,000	50,000	20,000
Traceable fixed expenses:				
Salaries	50,000	29,500	12,500	8,000
Advertising	15,000	1,000	7,500	6,500
Depreciation—fixtures	5,000	1,000	2,000	2,000
Insurance	3,000	2,000	500	500
Total traceable fixed expenses	73,000	33,500	22,500	17,000
Product-line segment margin	72,000	$ 41,500	$27,500	$ 3,000*
Common fixed expenses:				
Utilities	2,000			
Rent	20,000			
General administrative	30,000			
Total common fixed expenses	52,000			
Net operating income	$ 20,000			

*If the housewares line is dropped, the company will lose the $3,000 segment margin generated by this product line. In addition, we have seen that the $2,000 depreciation on the fixtures is a sunk cost that cannot be avoided. The sum of these two figures ($3,000 + $2,000 = $5,000) would be the decrease in the company's overall profits if the housewares line were discontinued. Of course, the company may later choose to drop the product if circumstances change—such as a pending decision to replace the fixtures.

fixed costs of the company. Unless another product line can be found that will generate a segment margin greater than $3,000, the company would be better off keeping the housewares line. By keeping the product line, the company's overall net operating income will be higher than if the product line were dropped.

Additionally, managers may choose to retain an unprofitable product line if the line helps sell other products, or if it serves as a "magnet" to attract customers. Bread, for example, may not be an especially profitable line in some food stores, but customers expect it to be available, and many of them would undoubtedly shift their buying elsewhere if a particular store decided to stop carrying it.

IN BUSINESS

POOR ECONOMY LEADS TO SEGMENT DISCONTINUATIONS

When the economy declines, many companies must decide whether to retain or discontinue struggling products and services. For example, Condé Nast Publications reacted to a steep drop in advertising revenues by cutting 180 jobs and discontinuing four magazines—*Gourmet, Modern Bride, Elegant Bride,* and *Cookie.* It also cut the budgets of its remaining magazines by 20–25%. Pioneer Corp.'s annual plasma television sales dropped from 460,000 units to 290,000 units. The company responded to its shrinking customer demand by cutting thousands of jobs and withdrawing from the plasma television business.

Sources: Russell Adams, "Ax Falls on Four Condé Nast Titles," *The Wall Street Journal,* October 6, 2009, p. B1; and Daisuke Wakabayashi, "Pioneer Unplugs Its TV Business," *The Wall Street Journal,* February 13, 2009, p. B1.

The Make or Buy Decision

LEARNING OBJECTIVE 7–3
Prepare a make or buy analysis.

Providing a product or service to a customer involves many steps. For example, consider all of the steps that are necessary to develop and sell a product such as tax preparation software in retail stores. First the software must be developed, which involves highly skilled software engineers and a great deal of project management effort. Then the product must be put into a form that can be delivered to customers. This involves burning the application onto a blank CD or DVD, applying a label, and packaging the result in an attractive box. Then the product must be distributed to retail stores. Then the product must be sold. And finally, help lines and other forms of after-sale service may have to be provided. And we should not forget that the blank CD or DVD, the label, and the box must of course be made by someone before any of this can happen. All of these activities, from development, to production, to after-sales service are called a *value chain.*

Separate companies may carry out each of the activities in the value chain or a single company may carry out several. When a company is involved in more than one activity in the entire value chain, it is **vertically integrated**. Some companies control all of the activities in the value chain from producing basic raw materials right up to the final distribution of finished goods and provision of after-sales service. Other companies are content to integrate on a smaller scale by purchasing many of the parts and materials that go into their finished products. A decision to carry out one of the activities in the value chain internally, rather than to buy externally from a supplier, is called a **make or buy decision**. Quite often these decisions involve whether to buy a particular part or to make it internally. Make or buy decisions also involve decisions concerning whether to outsource development tasks, after-sales service, or other activities.

Strategic Aspects of the Make or Buy Decision

Vertical integration provides certain advantages. An integrated company is less dependent on its suppliers and may be able to ensure a smoother flow of parts and materials for production than a nonintegrated company. For example, a strike against a major parts supplier can interrupt the operations of a nonintegrated company for many months, whereas an integrated company that is producing its own parts would be able to continue operations. Also, some companies feel that they can control quality better by producing their own parts and materials, rather than by relying on the quality control standards of outside suppliers. In addition, an integrated company realizes profits from the parts and materials that it is "making" rather than "buying," as well as profits from its regular operations.

The advantages of vertical integration are counterbalanced by the advantages of using external suppliers. By pooling demand from a number of companies, a supplier may be able to enjoy economies of scale. These economies of scale can result in higher quality and lower costs than would be possible if the company were to attempt to make the parts or provide the service on its own. A company must be careful, however, to retain control over activities that are essential to maintaining its competitive position. For example, Hewlett-Packard controls the software for laser printers that it makes in cooperation with Canon Inc. of Japan. The present trend appears to be toward less vertical integration, with companies like Oracle and Hewlett-Packard concentrating on hardware and software design and relying on outside suppliers for almost everything else in the value chain.

An Example of Make or Buy

To provide an illustration of a make or buy decision, consider Mountain Goat Cycles. The company is now producing the heavy-duty gear shifters used in its most popular line of mountain bikes. The company's Accounting Department reports the following costs of producing 8,000 units of the shifter internally each year:

	Per Unit	8,000 Units
Direct materials	$ 6	$ 48,000
Direct labor	4	32,000
Variable overhead	1	8,000
Supervisor's salary	3	24,000
Depreciation of special equipment	2	16,000
Allocated general overhead	5	40,000
Total cost	$21	$168,000

An outside supplier has offered to sell 8,000 shifters a year to Mountain Goat Cycles for a price of only $19 each, or a total of $152,000 (= 8,000 shifters × $19 each). Should the company stop producing the shifters internally and buy them from the outside supplier? As always, the focus should be on the relevant costs—those that differ between the alternatives. And the costs that differ between the alternatives consist of the costs that could be avoided by purchasing the shifters from the outside supplier. If the costs that can be avoided by purchasing the shifters from the outside supplier total less than $152,000, then the company should continue to manufacture its own shifters and reject the outside supplier's offer.

IN BUSINESS

© Asia Images Group/PictureIndia/Getty Images, RF

OUTSOURCING TASKS RATHER THAN JOBS

Pfizer saved 4,000 of its managers 66,500 hours of work by enabling them to outsource their tedious, time-consuming tasks to companies in India. With the click of a mouse the managers go to a website called PfizerWorks to prepare online work orders for services such as PowerPoint slide preparation, spreadsheet preparation, or basic market research. The requests are sent overseas and completed by a services-outsourcing firm. This outsourcing enables Pfizer's managers to spend their time on higher value work such as motivating teams, creating new products, and strategy formulation.

Source: Jena McGregor, "The Chore Goes Offshore," *BusinessWeek*, March 23 & 30, 2009, p. 50–51.

On the other hand, if the costs that can be avoided by purchasing the shifters from the outside supplier total more than $152,000 the outside supplier's offer should be accepted.

Note that depreciation of special equipment is listed as one of the costs of producing the shifters internally. Because the equipment has already been purchased, this depreciation is a sunk cost and is therefore irrelevant. If the equipment could be sold, its salvage value would be relevant. Or if the machine could be used to make other products, this could be relevant as well. However, we will assume that the equipment has no salvage value and that it has no other use except making the heavy-duty gear shifters.

Also note that the company is allocating a portion of its general overhead costs to the shifters. Any portion of this general overhead cost that would actually be eliminated if the gear shifters were purchased rather than made would be relevant in the analysis. However, it is likely that the general overhead costs allocated to the gear shifters are in fact common to all items produced in the factory and would continue unchanged even if the shifters were purchased from the outside. Such allocated common costs are not relevant costs (because they do not differ between the make or buy alternatives) and should be eliminated from the analysis along with the sunk costs.

The variable costs of producing the shifters can be avoided by buying the shifters from the outside supplier so they are relevant costs. We will assume in this case that the variable costs include direct materials, direct labor, and variable overhead. The supervisor's salary is also relevant if it could be avoided by buying the shifters. Exhibit 7–5 contains the relevant cost analysis of the make or buy decision assuming that the supervisor's salary can indeed be avoided.

EXHIBIT 7–5
Mountain Goat Cycles
Make or Buy Analysis

	Total Relevant Costs—8,000 units	
	Make	Buy
Direct materials (8,000 units × $6 per unit)	$ 48,000	
Direct labor (8,000 units × $4 per unit)	32,000	
Variable overhead (8,000 units × $1 per unit)	8,000	
Supervisor's salary	24,000	
Depreciation of special equipment (not relevant)		
Allocated general overhead (not relevant)		
Outside purchase price		$152,000
Total cost	$112,000	$152,000
Difference in favor of continuing to make	$40,000	

Because the avoidable costs related to making the shifters is $40,000 less than the total amount that would be paid to buy them from the outside supplier, Mountain Goat Cycles should reject the outside supplier's offer. However, the company may wish to consider one additional factor before coming to a final decision—the opportunity cost of the space now being used to produce the shifters.

Opportunity Cost

If the space now being used to produce the shifters *would otherwise be idle,* then Mountain Goat Cycles should continue to produce its own shifters and the supplier's offer should be rejected, as stated above. Idle space that has no alternative use has an opportunity cost of zero.

But what if the space now being used to produce shifters could be used for some other purpose? In that case, the space would have an opportunity cost equal to the segment margin that could be derived from the best alternative use of the space.

To illustrate, assume that the space now being used to produce shifters could be used to produce a new cross-country bike that would generate a segment margin of $60,000 per year. Under these conditions, Mountain Goat Cycles should accept the supplier's offer and use the available space to produce the new product line:

	Make	Buy
Total annual cost (see Exhibit 7–5)	$112,000	$152,000
Opportunity cost—segment margin forgone on a potential new product line	60,000	
Total cost	$172,000	$152,000
Difference in favor of purchasing from the outside supplier	$20,000	

Opportunity costs are not recorded in the organization's general ledger because they do not represent actual dollar outlays. Rather, they represent economic benefits that are *forgone* as a result of pursuing some course of action. The opportunity cost for Mountain Goat Cycles is sufficiently large in this case to change the decision.

IN BUSINESS

IS THERE SUCH A THING AS A $1 BUS TICKET?

When Megabus and Greyhound's Bolt Bus sell tickets for $1 it begs the question—how can that be profitable? The answer lies in understanding the concept of opportunity costs. The bus companies use computer algorithms to determine how many empty seats ordinarily exist on a given bus route. Since the incremental cost of allowing a customer to occupy a seat that would otherwise be empty is zero, the $1 price provides bus companies with additional contribution margin. Of course, only a few $1 tickets are available for each trip on a given bus route. Furthermore, these deeply discounted tickets must be purchased well in advance of the travel date. All other customers pay a higher fare that enables the bus company to earn a profit on its routes.

Source: Anne VanderMey, "What's Up With $1 Bus Tickets?" *Fortune,* November 7, 2011, p. 27.

Special Orders

LEARNING OBJECTIVE 7–4
Prepare an analysis showing whether a special order should be accepted.

Managers must often evaluate whether a *special order* should be accepted, and if the order is accepted, the price that should be charged. A **special order** is a one-time order that is not considered part of the company's normal ongoing business. To illustrate, Mountain Goat Cycles has just received a request from the Seattle Police Department to produce 100 specially modified mountain bikes at a price of $558 each. The bikes would be used to patrol some of the more densely populated residential sections of the city. Mountain Goat Cycles can easily modify its City Cruiser model to fit the specifications of the Seattle Police. The normal selling price of the City Cruiser bike is $698, and its unit product cost is $564 as shown below:

Direct materials	$372
Direct labor	90
Manufacturing overhead	102
Unit product cost	$564

The variable portion of the above manufacturing overhead is $12 per unit. The order would have no effect on the company's total fixed manufacturing overhead costs.

The modifications requested by the Seattle Police Department consist of welded brackets to hold radios, nightsticks, and other gear. These modifications would require $34 in incremental variable costs. In addition, the company would have to pay a graphics design studio $2,400 to design and cut stencils that would be used for spray painting the Seattle Police Department's logo and other identifying marks on the bikes.

This order should have no effect on the company's other sales. The production manager says that she can handle the special order without disrupting any of the company's regular scheduled production.

What effect would accepting this order have on the company's net operating income?

Only the incremental costs and benefits are relevant. Because the existing fixed manufacturing overhead costs would not be affected by the order, they are not relevant. The incremental net operating income can be computed as follows:

	Per Unit	Total 100 Bikes
Incremental revenue	$558	$55,800
Less incremental costs:		
Variable costs:		
Direct materials	372	37,200
Direct labor	90	9,000
Variable manufacturing overhead	12	1,200
Special modifications	34	3,400
Total variable cost	$508	50,800
Fixed cost:		
Purchase of stencils		2,400
Total incremental cost		53,200
Incremental net operating income		$ 2,600

Therefore, even though the $558 price on the special order is below the normal $564 unit product cost and the order would require additional costs, the order would increase net operating income. In general, a special order is profitable if the incremental revenue from the special order exceeds the incremental costs of the order. However, it is important to make sure that there is indeed idle capacity and that the special order does not cut into normal unit sales or undercut prices on normal sales. For example, if the company was operating at capacity, opportunity costs would have to be taken into account, as well as the incremental costs that have already been detailed above.

Utilization of a Constrained Resource

What Is a Constraint?

A **constraint** is anything that prevents you from getting more of what you want. Every individual and every organization faces at least one constraint, so it is not difficult to find examples of constraints. You may not have enough time to study thoroughly for every subject *and* to go out with your friends on the weekend, so time is your constraint. United Airlines has only a limited number of loading gates available at its busy Chicago O'Hare hub, so its constraint is loading gates. Vail Resorts has only a limited amount of land to develop as homesites and commercial lots at its ski areas, so its constraint is land.

As an example, long waiting periods for surgery are a chronic problem in the National Health Service (NHS), the government-funded provider of health care in the United Kingdom. A simplified version of the steps followed by an NHS surgery patient accompanied by a summary of the number of patients who can be processed through each of these steps is shown below:

Step	Steps for Processing Patients	Number of Patients That Can Be Processed per Day
1.	General practitioner referral	100
2.	Appointment made	100
3.	Outpatient visit.	50
4.	Add to surgery waiting list	150
5.	Surgery	15
6.	Follow-up visit	60
7.	Discharge	140

The constraint, or **bottleneck**, in the NHS system is determined by the step that limits total output because it has the smallest capacity—in this case surgery (step 5). The total number of patients processed through the entire system cannot exceed 15 per day—the maximum number of patients who can be treated in surgery. No matter how hard managers, doctors, and nurses try to improve the processing rate elsewhere in steps 1 through 4 or steps 6 and 7, they will never succeed in driving down wait lists until the capacity of surgery is increased. In fact, improvements elsewhere in the system—particularly before the constraint in steps 1 through 4—are likely to result in even longer waiting times and more frustrated patients and health care providers. Thus, to be effective, improvement efforts must be focused on the constraint. A business process, such as the process for serving surgery patients, is like a chain. If you want to increase the strength of a chain, what is the most effective way to do this? Should you concentrate your efforts on strengthening the strongest link, all the links, or the weakest link? Clearly, focusing your effort on the weakest link will bring the biggest benefit.

The procedure to follow to strengthen the chain is clear. First, identify the weakest link, which is the constraint. In the case of the NHS, the constraint is surgery. Second, do not place a greater strain on the system than the weakest link can handle—if you do, the chain will break. In the case of the NHS, more referrals than surgery can accommodate lead to unacceptably long waiting lists. Third, concentrate improvement efforts on strengthening the weakest link. In the case of the NHS, this means finding ways to increase the number of surgeries that can be performed in a day. Fourth, if the improvement efforts are successful, eventually the weakest link will improve to the point where it is no longer the weakest link. At that point, the new weakest link (i.e., the new constraint) must be identified, and improvement efforts must be shifted over to that link. This simple sequential process provides a powerful strategy for optimizing business processes.

Contribution Margin per Unit of the Constrained Resource

LEARNING OBJECTIVE 7–5
Determine the most profitable use of a constrained resource.

Managers routinely face the problem of deciding how constrained resources are going to be used. A department store, for example, has a limited amount of floor space and therefore cannot stock every product that may be available. A manufacturer has a limited number of machine-hours and a limited number of direct labor-hours at its disposal. Because the company cannot fully satisfy demand, managers must decide which products or services should be cut back. In other words, managers must decide which products or services make the best use of the constrained resource. Fixed costs are usually unaffected by such choices, so the course of action that will maximize the company's total contribution margin should ordinarily be selected.

If some products must be cut back because of a constraint, the key to maximizing the total contribution margin may seem obvious—favor the products with the highest unit contribution margins. Unfortunately, that is not quite correct. Rather, the correct solution is to favor the products that provide the highest *contribution margin per unit of the constrained resource.* To illustrate, in addition to its other products, Mountain Goat Cycles makes saddlebags for bicycles called *panniers.* These panniers come in two models—a touring model and a mountain model. Cost and revenue data for the two models of panniers follow:

	Mountain Pannier	Touring Pannier
Selling price per unit.	$25	$30
Variable cost per unit	10	18
Contribution margin per unit	$15	$12
Contribution margin (CM) ratio . .	60%	40%

The mountain pannier appears to be much more profitable than the touring pannier. It has a $15 per unit contribution margin as compared to only $12 per unit for the touring model, and it has a 60% CM ratio as compared to only 40% for the touring model.

But now let us add one more piece of information—the plant that makes the panniers is operating at capacity. This does not mean that every machine and every person in the plant is working at the maximum possible rate. Because machines have different capacities, some machines will be operating at less than 100% of capacity. However, if the plant as a whole cannot produce any more units, some machine or process must be operating at capacity. The machine or process that is limiting overall output is called the bottleneck—it is the constraint.

At Mountain Goat Cycles, the bottleneck (i.e., constraint) is a stitching machine. The mountain pannier requires two minutes of stitching time per unit, and the touring pannier requires one minute of stitching time per unit. The stitching machine is available for 12,000 minutes per month, and the company can sell up to 4,000 mountain panniers and 7,000 touring panniers per month. Producing up to this demand for both products would require 15,000 minutes, as shown below:

	Mountain Pannier	Touring Pannier	Total
Monthly demand (a)	4,000 units	7,000 units	
Stitching machine time required to produce one unit (b)	2 minutes	1 minute	
Total stitching time required (a) × (b)	8,000 minutes	7,000 minutes	15,000 minutes

Producing up to demand would require 15,000 minutes, but only 12,000 minutes are available. This simply confirms that the stitching machine is the bottleneck. By definition, because the stitching machine is a bottleneck, the stitching machine does not have enough capacity to satisfy the existing demand for mountain panniers and touring panniers Therefore, some orders for the products will have to be turned down. Naturally, managers will want to know which product is less profitable. To answer this question, they should focus on the contribution margin per unit of the constrained resource. This figure is computed by dividing a product's contribution margin per unit by the amount of the constrained resource required to make a unit of that product. These calculations are carried out below for the mountain and touring panniers:

	Mountain Pannier	Touring Pannier
Contribution margin per unit (a)	$15.00	$12.00
Stitching machine time required to produce one unit (b)	2 minutes	1 minute
Contribution margin per unit of the constrained resource, (a) ÷ (b)	$7.50 per minute	$12.00 per minute

It is now easy to decide which product is less profitable and should be deemphasized. Each minute on the stitching machine that is devoted to the touring pannier results in an increase of $12.00 in contribution margin and profits. The comparable figure for the mountain pannier is only $7.50 per minute. Therefore, the touring model should be emphasized. Even though the mountain model has the larger contribution margin per unit and the larger CM ratio, the touring model provides the larger contribution margin in relation to the constrained resource.

To verify that the touring model is indeed the more profitable product, suppose an hour of additional stitching time is available and that unfilled orders exist for both products. The additional hour on the stitching machine could be used to make either 30 mountain panniers (60 minutes ÷ 2 minutes per mountain pannier) or 60 touring panniers (60 minutes ÷ 1 minute per touring pannier), with the following profit implications:

	Mountain Pannier	Touring Pannier
Contribution margin per unit	$ 15	$ 12
Additional units that can be processed in one hour	× 30	× 60
Additional contribution margin	$450	$720

Because the additional contribution margin would be $720 for the touring panniers and only $450 for the mountain panniers, the touring panniers make the most profitable use of the company's constrained resource—the stitching machine.

The stitching machine is available for 12,000 minutes per month, and producing the touring panniers is the most profitable use of the stitching machine. Therefore, to maximize profits, the company should produce all of the touring panniers the market will demand (7,000 units) and use any remaining capacity to produce mountain panniers. The computations to determine how many mountain panniers can be produced are as follows:

Monthly demand for touring panniers (a)	7,000 units
Stitching machine time required to produce one touring pannier (b)	1 minute
Total stitching time required to produce touring panniers (a) × (b)	7,000 minutes
Remaining stitching time available (12,000 minutes − 7,000 minutes) (c)	5,000 minutes
Stitching machine time required to produce one mountain pannier (d)	2 minutes
Production of mountain panniers (c) ÷ (d)	2,500 units

IN BUSINESS

© McGraw-Hill Education/Andrew Resek

BOEING IS CONSTRAINED BY A SUPPLIER

Boeing Co. had to delay delivery of its model 777 airplanes to Emirates airline because the German supplier Sell GmbH could not provide the equipment for cooking galleys to Boeing on time. The production bottleneck forced Emirates to repeatedly postpone its planned expansion into the U.S. west coast. It also forced Boeing to accept payment delays for airplanes that sell for more than $200 million apiece. In response, Sell GmbH hired 250 more employees and invested millions of euros in new machine tools and factory space to expand its production capacity.

Source: Daniel Michaels and J. Lynn Lunsford, "Lack of Seats, Galleys Stalls Boeing, Airbus," *The Wall Street Journal,* August 8, 2008, pp. B1 and B4.

Therefore, profit would be maximized by producing 7,000 touring panniers and then using the remaining capacity to produce 2,500 mountain panniers.

This example clearly shows that looking at each product's unit contribution margin alone is not enough; the contribution margin must be viewed in relation to the amount of the constrained resource each product requires.

Managing Constraints

LEARNING OBJECTIVE 7–6
Determine the value of obtaining more of the constrained resource.

Effectively managing an organization's constraints is a key to increased profits. As discussed above, when a constraint exists in the production process, managers can increase profits by producing the products with the highest contribution margin per unit of the constrained resource. However, they can also increase profits by increasing the capacity of the bottleneck operation.

When a manager increases the capacity of the bottleneck, it is called **relaxing (or elevating) the constraint**. In the case of Mountain Goat Cycles, the company is currently working one eight-hour shift. To relax the constraint, the stitching machine operator could be asked to work overtime. No one else would have to work overtime. Because all of the other operations involved in producing panniers have excess capacity, up to a point, the additional panniers processed through the stitching machine during overtime could be finished during normal working hours in the other operations.

The benefits from relaxing the constraint are often enormous and can be easily quantified—the key is the contribution margin per unit of the constrained resource that we have already computed. This number, which was originally stated in terms of minutes in the Mountain Goat Cycles example, is restated below in terms of hours for easier interpretation:

	Mountain Pannier	Touring Pannier
Contribution margin per unit of the constrained resource (in minutes) . . .	\$7.50 per minute × 60 minutes per hour	\$12.00 per minute × 60 minutes per hour
Contribution margin per unit of the constrained resource (in hours)	= \$450 per hour	= \$720 per hour

So what is the value of relaxing the constraint—the time on the stitching machine? The manager should first ask, "What would I do with additional capacity at the bottleneck if it were available?" If the time were to be used to make additional mountain panniers, it would be worth \$450 per hour. If the time were to be used to make additional touring panniers, it would be worth \$720 per hour. In this latter case, the company should be willing to pay an overtime *premium* to the stitching machine operator of up to \$720 per hour! Suppose, for example, that the stitching machine operator is paid \$20 per hour during normal working hours and time-and-a-half, or \$30 per hour, for overtime. In this case, the premium for overtime is only \$10 per hour, whereas in principle, the company should be willing to pay a premium of up to \$720 per hour. The difference between what the company should be willing to pay as a premium, \$720 per hour, and what it would actually have to pay, \$10 per hour, is pure profit of \$710 per hour.

To reinforce this concept, suppose that there are only unfilled orders for the mountain pannier. How much would it be worth to the company to run the stitching machine overtime in this situation? Because the additional capacity would be used to make the mountain pannier, the value of that additional capacity would drop to \$7.50 per minute or \$450 per hour. Nevertheless, the value of relaxing the constraint would still be quite high and the company should be willing to pay an overtime premium of up to \$450 per hour.

These calculations indicate that managers should pay great attention to the bottleneck operation. If a bottleneck machine breaks down or is ineffectively utilized, the losses to the company can be quite large. In our example, for every minute the stitching machine is down due to breakdowns or setups, the company loses between \$7.50 and \$12.00.[3] The losses on an hourly basis are between \$450 and \$720! In contrast, there is no such loss of contribution margin if time is lost on a machine that is not a bottleneck—such machines have excess capacity anyway.

The implications are clear. Managers should focus much of their attention on managing the bottleneck. As we have discussed, managers should emphasize products that most profitably utilize the constrained resource. They should also make sure that products are processed smoothly through the bottleneck, with minimal lost time due to breakdowns and setups. And they should try to find ways to increase the capacity at the bottleneck.

The capacity of a bottleneck can be effectively increased in a number of ways, including:

- Working overtime on the bottleneck.
- Subcontracting some of the processing that would be done at the bottleneck.
- Investing in additional machines at the bottleneck.
- Shifting workers from processes that are not bottlenecks to the process that is the bottleneck.
- Focusing business process improvement efforts on the bottleneck.
- Reducing defective units. Each defective unit that is processed through the bottleneck and subsequently scrapped takes the place of a good unit that could have been sold.

The last three methods of increasing the capacity of the bottleneck are particularly attractive because they are essentially free and may even yield additional cost savings.

The Problem of Multiple Constraints

What does a company do if it has more than one potential constraint? For example, a company may have limited raw materials, limited direct labor-hours available, limited floor space, and limited advertising dollars to spend on product promotion. How would it determine the right combination of products to produce? The proper combination or "mix" of products can be found by use of a quantitative method known as *linear programming,* which is covered in quantitative methods and operations management courses.

Joint Product Costs and the Contribution Approach

LEARNING OBJECTIVE 7–7
Prepare an analysis showing whether joint products should be sold at the split-off point or processed further.

In some industries, a number of end products are produced from a single raw material input. For example, in the petroleum refining industry a large number of products are extracted from crude oil, including gasoline, jet fuel, home heating oil, lubricants, asphalt, and various organic chemicals. Another example is provided by the Santa Maria Wool Cooperative of New Mexico. The company buys raw wool from local sheepherders, separates the wool into three grades—coarse, fine, and superfine—and then dyes the wool using traditional methods that rely on pigments from local materials. Exhibit 7–6 contains a diagram of the production process.

At Santa Maria Wool Cooperative, coarse wool, fine wool, and superfine wool are produced from one input—raw wool. Two or more products that are produced from a common input are known as **joint products**. The **split-off point** is the point in the manufacturing process at which the joint products can be recognized as separate products. This does not occur at Santa Maria Wool Cooperative until the raw wool has gone through the separating process. The term **joint cost** is used to describe the costs incurred up to the split-off point. At Santa Maria Wool Cooperative, the joint costs are the \$200,000 cost of

[3] Setups are required when production switches from one product to another. For example, consider a company that makes automobile side panels. The panels are painted before shipping them to an automobile manufacturer for final assembly. The customer might require 100 blue panels, 50 black panels, and 20 yellow panels. Each time the color is changed, the painting equipment must be purged of the old paint color, cleaned with solvents, and refilled with the new paint color. This takes time. In fact, some equipment may require such lengthy and frequent setups that it is unavailable for actual production more often than not.

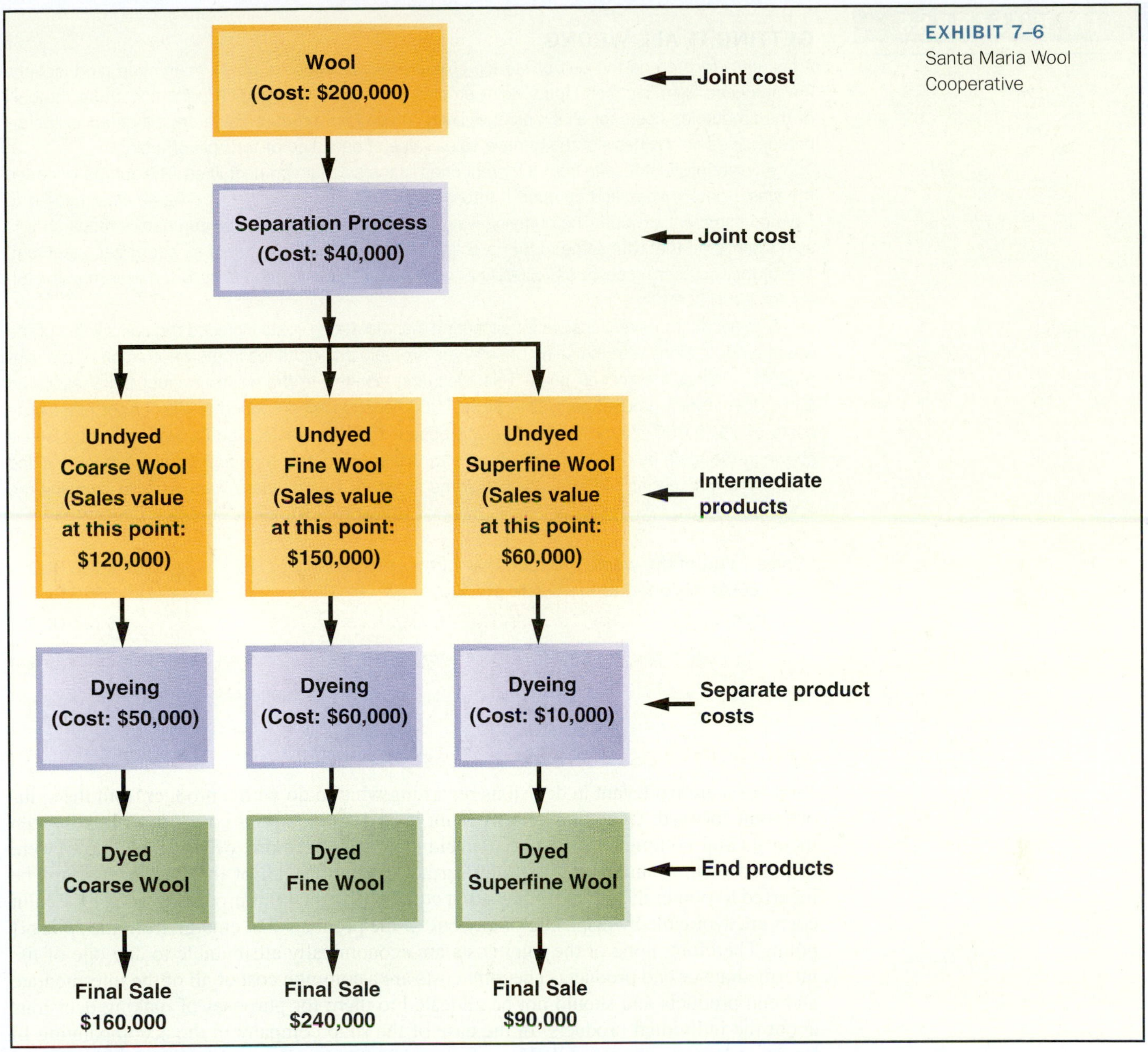

EXHIBIT 7–6
Santa Maria Wool Cooperative

the raw wool and the $40,000 cost of separating the wool. The undyed wool is called an *intermediate product* because it is not finished at this point. Nevertheless, a market does exist for undyed wool—although at a significantly lower price than finished, dyed wool.

The Pitfalls of Allocation

Joint costs are common costs that are incurred to simultaneously produce a variety of end products. These joint costs are often allocated among the different products at the split-off point. A typical approach is to allocate the joint costs according to the relative sales value of the end products.

Although allocation of joint product costs is needed for some purposes, such as balance sheet inventory valuation, allocations of this kind are extremely misleading for decision making. The In Business box "Getting It All Wrong" (see below) illustrates an incorrect decision that resulted from using such an allocated joint cost. You should stop now and read that box before proceeding further.

IN BUSINESS

GETTING IT ALL WRONG

A company located on the Gulf of Mexico produces soap products. Its six main soap product lines are produced from common inputs. Joint product costs up to the split-off point constitute the bulk of the production costs for all six product lines. These joint product costs are allocated to the six product lines on the basis of the relative sales value of each line at the split-off point.

A waste product results from the production of the six main product lines. The company loaded the waste onto barges and dumped it into the Gulf of Mexico because the waste was thought to have no commercial value. The dumping was stopped, however, when the company's research division discovered that with some further processing the waste could be sold as a fertilizer ingredient. The further processing costs $175,000 per year. The waste was then sold to fertilizer manufacturers for $300,000.

The accountants responsible for allocating manufacturing costs included the sales value of the waste product along with the sales value of the six main product lines in their allocation of the joint product costs at the split-off point. This allocation resulted in the waste product being allocated $150,000 in joint product cost. This $150,000 allocation, when added to the further processing costs of $175,000 for the waste, made it appear that the waste product was unprofitable—as shown in the table below. When presented with this analysis, the company's management decided that further processing of the waste should be stopped. The company went back to dumping the waste in the Gulf.

Sales value of the waste product after further processing	$300,000
Less costs assigned to the waste product	325,000
Net loss	$ (25,000)

Sell or Process Further Decisions

Joint costs are irrelevant in decisions regarding what to do with a product from the split-off point forward. Once the split-off point is reached, the joint costs have already been incurred and nothing can be done to avoid them. Furthermore, even if the product were disposed of in a landfill without any further processing, all of the joint costs must be incurred to obtain the other products that come out of the joint process. None of the joint costs are avoidable by disposing of any one of the products that emerge from the split-off point. Therefore, none of the joint costs are economically attributable to any one of the intermediate or end products. The joint costs are a common cost of all of the intermediate and end products and should not be allocated to them for purposes of making decisions about the individual products. In the case of the soap company in the accompanying In Business box "Getting It All Wrong," the $150,000 in allocated joint costs should not have influenced what was done with the waste product from the split-off point forward. Even ignoring the negative environmental impact of dumping the waste in the Gulf of Mexico, a correct analysis would have shown that the company was making money by further processing the waste into a fertilizer ingredient. The analysis should have been done as follows:

	Dump in Gulf	Process Further
Sales value of fertilizer ingredient	0	$300,000
Additional processing costs	0	175,000
Contribution margin	0	$125,000
Advantage of processing further	$125,000	

Decisions of this type are known as **sell or process further decisions**. It is profitable to continue processing a joint product after the split-off point *so long as the incremental revenue from such processing exceeds the incremental processing cost incurred after the split-off point.* Joint costs that have already been incurred up to the split-off point are always irrelevant in decisions concerning what to do from the split-off point forward.

To provide a detailed example of the sell or process further decision, return to the data for Santa Maria Wool Cooperative in Exhibit 7–6. We can answer several important questions using this data. First, is the company making money if it runs the entire process from beginning to end? Assuming there are no costs other than those displayed in Exhibit 7–6, the company is indeed making money as follows:

Analysis of the profitability of the overall operation:		
Combined final sales value ($160,000 + $240,000 + $90,000)		$490,000
Less costs of producing the end products:		
Cost of wool	$200,000	
Cost of separating wool	40,000	
Combined costs of dyeing ($50,000 + $60,000 + $10,000)	120,000	360,000
Profit		$130,000

Note that the joint costs of buying the wool and separating the wool *are* relevant when considering the profitability of the entire operation. This is because these joint costs *could* be avoided if the entire operation were shut down. However, these joint costs are *not* relevant when considering the profitability of any one product. As long as the process is being run to make the other products, no additional joint costs are incurred to make the specific product in question.

Even though the company is making money overall, it may be losing money on one or more of the products. If the company buys wool and runs the separation process, it will get all three intermediate products. Nothing can be done about that. However, each of these products can be sold *as is* without further processing. It may be that the company would be better off selling one or more of the products prior to dyeing to avoid the dyeing costs. The appropriate way to make this choice is to compare the incremental revenues to the incremental costs from further processing as follows:

Analysis of sell or process further:	Coarse Wool	Fine Wool	Superfine Wool
Final sales value after further processing	$160,000	$240,000	$90,000
Less sales value at the split-off point	120,000	150,000	60,000
Incremental revenue from further processing	40,000	90,000	30,000
Less cost of further processing (dyeing)	50,000	60,000	10,000
Profit (loss) from further processing	$ (10,000)	$ 30,000	$20,000

As this analysis shows, the company would be better off selling the undyed coarse wool as is rather than processing it further. The other two products should be processed further and dyed before selling them.

Note that the joint costs of the wool ($200,000) and of the wool separation process ($40,000) play no role in the decision to sell or further process the intermediate products. These joint costs are relevant in a decision of whether to buy wool and to run the wool separation process, but they are not relevant in decisions about what to do with the intermediate products once they have been separated.

Activity-Based Costing and Relevant Costs

As discussed in an earlier chapter, activity-based costing can be used to help identify potentially relevant costs for decision-making purposes. Activity-based costing improves the traceability of costs by focusing on the activities caused by a product or other segment. However, managers should exercise caution against reading more into this "traceability" than really exists. People have a tendency to assume that if a cost is traceable to a segment, then the cost is automatically an avoidable cost. That is not true because the costs provided by a well-designed activity-based costing system are only *potentially* relevant. Before making a decision, managers must still decide which of the potentially relevant costs are actually avoidable. Only those costs that are avoidable are relevant and the others should be ignored.

To illustrate, refer again to the data relating to the housewares line in Exhibit 7–4. The $2,000 fixtures depreciation is a traceable cost of the housewares lines because it directly relates to activities in that department. We found, however, that the $2,000 is not avoidable if the housewares line is dropped. The key lesson here is that the method used to assign a cost to a product or other segment does not change the basic nature of the cost. A sunk cost such as depreciation of old equipment is still a sunk cost regardless of whether it is traced directly to a particular segment on an activity basis, allocated to all segments on the basis of labor-hours, or treated in some other way in the costing process. Regardless of the method used to assign costs to products or other segments, the principles discussed in this chapter must be applied to determine the costs that are avoidable in each situation.

Summary

Everything in this chapter consists of applications of one simple but powerful idea—only those costs and benefits that differ between alternatives are relevant in a decision. All other costs and benefits are irrelevant and should be ignored. In particular, sunk costs are irrelevant as are future costs that do not differ between alternatives.

This simple idea was applied in a variety of situations including decisions that involve adding or dropping a product line, making or buying a component, accepting or rejecting a special order, using a constrained resource, and processing a joint product further. This list includes only a small sample of the possible applications of the relevant cost concept. Indeed, any decision involving costs hinges on the proper identification and analysis of the costs that are relevant. We will continue to focus on the concept of relevant costs in the following chapter where long-term investment decisions are considered.

Review Problem: Relevant Costs

Charter Sports Equipment manufactures round, rectangular, and octagonal trampolines. Sales and expense data for the past month follow:

Management is concerned about the continued losses shown by the round trampolines and wants a recommendation as to whether or not the line should be discontinued. The special equipment used to produce the trampolines has no resale value. If the round trampoline model is dropped, the two line supervisors assigned to the model would be discharged.

Required:

1. Should production and sale of the round trampolines be discontinued? The company has no other use for the capacity now being used to produce the round trampolines. Show computations to support your answer.
2. Recast the above data in a format that would be more useful to management in assessing the profitability of the various product lines.

		Trampoline		
	Total	Round	Rectangular	Octagonal
Sales	$1,000,000	$140,000	$500,000	$360,000
Variable expenses	410,000	60,000	200,000	150,000
Contribution margin	590,000	80,000	300,000	210,000
Fixed expenses:				
Advertising—traceable	216,000	41,000	110,000	65,000
Depreciation of special equipment	95,000	20,000	40,000	35,000
Line supervisors' salaries	19,000	6,000	7,000	6,000
General factory overhead*	200,000	28,000	100,000	72,000
Total fixed expenses	530,000	95,000	257,000	178,000
Net operating income (loss)	$ 60,000	$ (15,000)	$ 43,000	$ 32,000

*A common fixed cost that is allocated on the basis of sales dollars.

Solution to Review Problem

1. No, production and sale of the round trampolines should not be discontinued. Computations to support this answer follow:

Contribution margin lost if the round trampolines are discontinued		$(80,000)
Less fixed expenses that can be avoided:		
Advertising—traceable	$41,000	
Line supervisors' salaries	6,000	47,000
Decrease in net operating income for the company as a whole		$(33,000)

The depreciation of the special equipment is a sunk cost, and therefore, it is not relevant to the decision. The general factory overhead is allocated and will presumably continue regardless of whether or not the round trampolines are discontinued; thus, it is not relevant.

2. If management wants a clearer picture of the profitability of the segments, the general factory overhead should not be allocated. It is a common cost and, therefore, should be deducted from the total product-line segment margin. A more useful income statement format would be as follows:

		Trampoline		
	Total	Round	Rectangular	Octagonal
Sales	$1,000,000	$140,000	$500,000	$360,000
Variable expenses	410,000	60,000	200,000	150,000
Contribution margin	590,000	80,000	300,000	210,000
Traceable fixed expenses:				
Advertising—traceable	216,000	41,000	110,000	65,000
Depreciation of special equipment	95,000	20,000	40,000	35,000
Line supervisors' salaries	19,000	6,000	7,000	6,000
Total traceable fixed expenses	330,000	67,000	157,000	106,000
Product-line segment margin	260,000	$ 13,000	$143,000	$104,000
Common fixed expenses	200,000			
Net operating income	$ 60,000			

Glossary

Avoidable cost A cost that can be eliminated by choosing one alternative over another in a decision. This term is synonymous with *differential cost* and *relevant cost.* (p. 281)

Bottleneck A machine or some other part of a process that limits the total output of the entire system. (p. 296)

Constraint A limitation under which a company must operate, such as limited available machine time or raw materials, that restricts the company's ability to satisfy demand. (p. 295)

Differential cost A difference in cost between two alternatives. Also see *Incremental cost.* (p. 281)

Differential revenue A difference in revenue between two alternatives. (p. 281)

Joint costs Costs that are incurred up to the split-off point in a process that produces joint products. (p. 300)

Joint products Two or more products that are produced from a common input. (p. 300)

Make or buy decision A decision concerning whether an item should be produced internally or purchased from an outside supplier. (p. 291)

Opportunity cost The potential benefit that is given up when one alternative is selected over another. (p. 282)

Relaxing (or elevating) the constraint An action that increases the amount of a constrained resource. Equivalently, an action that increases the capacity of the bottleneck. (p. 299)

Relevant benefit A benefit that differs between alternatives in a decision. *Differential revenue* is a *relevant benefit.* (p. 281)

Relevant cost A difference in cost between any two alternatives. Synonyms are *avoidable cost, differential cost,* and *incremental cost.* (p. 281)

Sell or process further decision A decision as to whether a joint product should be sold at the split-off point or sold after further processing. (p. 303)

Special order A one-time order that is not considered part of the company's normal ongoing business. (p. 294)

Split-off point That point in the manufacturing process where some or all of the joint products can be recognized as individual products. (p. 300)

Sunk cost A cost that has already been incurred and that cannot be changed by any decision made now or in the future. (p. 281)

Vertical integration The involvement by a company in more than one of the activities in the entire value chain from development through production, distribution, sales, and after-sales service. (p. 291)

Questions

7–1 What is a *relevant cost?*

7–2 Define the following terms: *incremental cost, opportunity cost,* and *sunk cost.*

7–3 Are variable costs always relevant costs? Explain.

7–4 "Sunk costs are easy to spot—they're the fixed costs associated with a decision." Do you agree? Explain.

7–5 "Variable costs and differential costs mean the same thing." Do you agree? Explain.

7–6 "All future costs are relevant in decision making." Do you agree? Why?

7–7 Prentice Company is considering dropping one of its product lines. What costs of the product line would be relevant to this decision? What costs would be irrelevant?

7–8 "If a product is generating a loss, then it should be discontinued." Do you agree? Explain.

7–9 What is the danger in allocating common fixed costs among products or other segments of an organization?

7–10 How does opportunity cost enter into a make or buy decision?

7–11 Give at least four examples of possible constraints.

7–12 How will relating product contribution margins to the amount of the constrained resource they consume help a company maximize its profits?

7–13 Define the following terms: *joint products, joint costs,* and *split-off point.*

7–14 From a decision-making point of view, should joint costs be allocated among joint products?

7–15 What guideline should be used in determining whether a joint product should be sold at the split-off point or processed further?

7–16 Airlines sometimes offer reduced rates during certain times of the week to members of a businessperson's family if they accompany him or her on trips. How does the concept of relevant costs enter into the decision by the airline to offer reduced rates of this type?

Multiple-choice questions are available with Connect.

Applying Excel

LEARNING OBJECTIVE 7–7

The Excel worksheet form that appears below is to be used to recreate an example earlier in the chapter. Download the workbook containing this form from Connect. *On the website you will also receive instructions about how to use this worksheet form.*

	A	B	C	D	E
1	Chapter 7: Applying Excel				
2					
3	**Data**				
4	**Exhibit 7-6 Santa Maria Wool Cooperative**				
5	Cost of wool	$200,000			
6	Cost of separation process	$40,000			
7	Sales value of intermediate products at split-off point:				
8	Undyed coarse wool	$120,000			
9	Undyed fine wool	$150,000			
10	Undyed superfine wool	$60,000			
11	Costs of further processing (dyeing) intermediate products:				
12	Undyed coarse wool	$50,000			
13	Undyed fine wool	$60,000			
14	Undyed superfine wool	$10,000			
15	Sales value of end products:				
16	Dyed coarse wool	$160,000			
17	Dyed fine wool	$240,000			
18	Dyed superfine wool	$90,000			
19					
20	*Enter a formula into each of the cells marked with a ? below*				
21	**Example: Joint Product Costs and the Contribution Approach**				
22					
23	***Analysis of the profitability of the overall operation:***				
24	Combined final sales value		?		
25	Less costs of producing the end products:				
26	Cost of wool	?			
27	Cost of separation process	?			
28	Combined costs of dyeing	?	?		
29	Profit		?		
30					
31	***Analysis of sell or process further:***				
32		*Coarse*	*Fine*	*Superfine*	
33		*Wool*	*Wool*	*Wool*	
34	Final sales value after further processing	?	?	?	
35	Less sales value at the split-off point	?	?	?	
36	Incremental revenue from further processing	?	?	?	
37	Less cost of further processing (dyeing)	?	?	?	
38	Profit (loss) from further processing	?	?	?	
39					

Chapter 7 Form / Filled in Chapter 7 Form / Chapter 7

You should proceed to the requirements below only after completing your worksheet.

Required:

1. Check your worksheet by changing the cost of further processing undyed coarse wool in cell B12 to $30,000. The overall profit from processing all intermediate products into final products should now be $150,000 and the profit from further processing coarse wool should now be $10,000. If you do not get these answers, find the errors in your worksheet and correct them.

   How should operations change in response to this change in cost?

2. In industries that process joint products, the costs of the raw materials inputs and the sales values of intermediate and final products are often volatile. Change the data area of your worksheet to match the following:
   a. What is the overall profit if all intermediate products are processed into final products?
   b. What is the profit from further processing each of the intermediate products?
   c. With these new costs and selling prices, what recommendations would you make concerning the company's operations? If your recommendation is followed, what should be the overall profit of the company?

Data
Exhibit 7–6 Santa Maria Wool Cooperative

Cost of wool	$290,000
Cost of separation process	$40,000
Sales value of intermediate products at split-off point:	
Undyed coarse wool	$100,000
Undyed fine wool	$110,000
Undyed superfine wool	$90,000
Costs of further processing (dyeing) intermediate products:	
Undyed coarse wool	$50,000
Undyed fine wool	$60,000
Undyed superfine wool	$10,000
Sales value of end products:	
Dyed coarse wool	$180,000
Dyed fine wool	$210,000
Dyed superfine wool	$90,000

The Foundational 15

connect® Additional student resources are available with Connect.

LEARNING OBJECTIVES 7–2, 7–3, 7–4, 7–5, 7–6

Cane Company manufactures two products called Alpha and Beta that sell for $120 and $80, respectively. Each product uses only one type of raw material that costs $6 per pound. The company has the capacity to annually produce 100,000 units of each product. Its unit costs for each product at this level of activity are given below:

	Alpha	Beta
Direct materials	$ 30	$12
Direct labor	20	15
Variable manufacturing overhead	7	5
Traceable fixed manufacturing overhead	16	18
Variable selling expenses	12	8
Common fixed expenses	15	10
Total cost per unit	$100	$68

The company considers its traceable fixed manufacturing overhead to be avoidable, whereas its common fixed expenses are deemed unavoidable and have been allocated to products based on sales dollars.

Required:

(Answer each question independently unless instructed otherwise.)

1. What is the total amount of traceable fixed manufacturing overhead for the Alpha product line and for the Beta product line?
2. What is the company's total amount of common fixed expenses?
3. Assume that Cane expects to produce and sell 80,000 Alphas during the current year. One of Cane's sales representatives has found a new customer that is willing to buy 10,000 additional Alphas for a price of $80 per unit. If Cane accepts the customer's offer, how much will its profits increase or decrease?
4. Assume that Cane expects to produce and sell 90,000 Betas during the current year. One of Cane's sales representatives has found a new customer that is willing to buy 5,000 additional Betas for a price of $39 per unit. If Cane accepts the customer's offer, how much will its profits increase or decrease?
5. Assume that Cane expects to produce and sell 95,000 Alphas during the current year. One of Cane's sales representatives has found a new customer that is willing to buy 10,000 additional Alphas for a price of $80 per unit. If Cane accepts the customer's offer, it will decrease Alpha sales to regular customers by 5,000 units. Should Cane accept this special order?
6. Assume that Cane normally produces and sells 90,000 Betas per year. If Cane discontinues the Beta product line, how much will profits increase or decrease?

7. Assume that Cane normally produces and sells 40,000 Betas per year. If Cane discontinues the Beta product line, how much will profits increase or decrease?
8. Assume that Cane normally produces and sells 60,000 Betas and 80,000 Alphas per year. If Cane discontinues the Beta product line, its sales representatives could increase sales of Alpha by 15,000 units. If Cane discontinues the Beta product line, how much would profits increase or decrease?
9. Assume that Cane expects to produce and sell 80,000 Alphas during the current year. A supplier has offered to manufacture and deliver 80,000 Alphas to Cane for a price of $80 per unit. If Cane buys 80,000 units from the supplier instead of making those units, how much will profits increase or decrease?
10. Assume that Cane expects to produce and sell 50,000 Alphas during the current year. A supplier has offered to manufacture and deliver 50,000 Alphas to Cane for a price of $80 per unit. If Cane buys 50,000 units from the supplier instead of making those units, how much will profits increase or decrease?
11. How many pounds of raw material are needed to make one unit of Alpha and one unit of Beta?
12. What contribution margin per pound of raw material is earned by Alpha and Beta?
13. Assume that Cane's customers would buy a maximum of 80,000 units of Alpha and 60,000 units of Beta. Also assume that the company's raw material available for production is limited to 160,000 pounds. How many units of each product should Cane produce to maximize its profits?
14. If Cane follows your recommendation in requirement 13, what total contribution margin will it earn?
15. If Cane uses its 160,000 pounds of raw materials as you recommended in requirement 13, up to how much should it be willing to pay per pound for additional raw materials?

Additional student resources are available with Connect. connect

Exercises

EXERCISE 7–1 Identifying Relevant Costs [LO 7–1]

A number of costs are listed below that may be relevant in decisions faced by the management of Svahn, AB, a Swedish manufacturer of sailing yachts:

		Case 1		Case 2	
	Item	Relevant	Not Relevant	Relevant	Not Relevant
a.	Sales revenue				
b.	Direct materials.				
c.	Direct labor				
d.	Variable manufacturing overhead				
e.	Depreciation—Model B100 machine				
f.	Book value—Model B100 machine.				
g.	Disposal value—Model B100 machine. . .				
h.	Market value—Model B300 machine (cost).				
i.	Fixed manufacturing overhead (general) .				
j.	Variable selling expense.				
k.	Fixed selling expense				
l.	General administrative overhead				

Required:

Copy the information above onto your answer sheet and place an X in the appropriate column to indicate whether each item is relevant or not relevant in the following situations. Requirement 1 relates to Case 1 above, and requirement 2 relates to Case 2.

1. The company chronically has no idle capacity and the old Model B100 machine is the company's constraint. Management is considering purchasing a Model B300 machine to use in addition to the company's present Model B100 machine. The old Model B100 machine will continue to be used to capacity as before, with the new Model B300 machine being used to expand production. This will increase the company's production and sales. The increase in

volume will be large enough to require increases in fixed selling expenses and in general administrative overhead, but not in the fixed manufacturing overhead.

2. The old Model B100 machine is not the company's constraint, but management is considering replacing it with a new Model B300 machine because of the potential savings in direct materials with the new machine. The Model B100 machine would be sold. This change will have no effect on production or sales, other than some savings in direct materials costs due to less waste.

EXERCISE 7–2 Dropping or Retaining a Segment [LO 7–2]

The Regal Cycle Company manufactures three types of bicycles—a dirt bike, a mountain bike, and a racing bike. Data on sales and expenses for the past quarter follow:

	Total	Dirt Bikes	Mountain Bikes	Racing Bikes
Sales	$300,000	$90,000	$150,000	$60,000
Variable manufacturing and selling expenses	120,000	27,000	60,000	33,000
Contribution margin	180,000	63,000	90,000	27,000
Fixed expenses:				
Advertising, traceable	30,000	10,000	14,000	6,000
Depreciation of special equipment	23,000	6,000	9,000	8,000
Salaries of product-line managers	35,000	12,000	13,000	10,000
Allocated common fixed expenses*	60,000	18,000	30,000	12,000
Total fixed expenses	148,000	46,000	66,000	36,000
Net operating income (loss)	$ 32,000	$17,000	$ 24,000	$ (9,000)

*Allocated on the basis of sales dollars.

Management is concerned about the continued losses shown by the racing bikes and wants a recommendation as to whether or not the line should be discontinued. The special equipment used to produce racing bikes has no resale value and does not wear out.

Required:

1. Should production and sale of the racing bikes be discontinued? Explain. Show computations to support your answer.
2. Recast the above data in a format that would be more usable to management in assessing the long-run profitability of the various product lines.

EXERCISE 7–3 Make or Buy a Component [LO 7–3]

Troy Engines, Ltd., manufactures a variety of engines for use in heavy equipment. The company has always produced all of the necessary parts for its engines, including all of the carburetors. An outside supplier has offered to sell one type of carburetor to Troy Engines, Ltd., for a cost of $35 per unit. To evaluate this offer, Troy Engines, Ltd., has gathered the following information relating to its own cost of producing the carburetor internally:

	Per Unit	15,000 Units per Year
Direct materials	$14	$210,000
Direct labor	10	150,000
Variable manufacturing overhead	3	45,000
Fixed manufacturing overhead, traceable	6*	90,000
Fixed manufacturing overhead, allocated	9	135,000
Total cost	$42	$630,000

*One-third supervisory salaries; two-thirds depreciation of special equipment (no resale value).

Required:

1. Assuming that the company has no alternative use for the facilities that are now being used to produce the carburetors, should the outside supplier's offer be accepted? Show all computations.
2. Suppose that if the carburetors were purchased, Troy Engines, Ltd., could use the freed capacity to launch a new product. The segment margin of the new product would be $150,000 per year. Should Troy Engines, Ltd., accept the offer to buy the carburetors for $35 per unit? Show all computations.

EXERCISE 7–4 Evaluating a Special Order [LO 7–4]

Imperial Jewelers is considering a special order for 20 handcrafted gold bracelets to be given as gifts to members of a wedding party. The normal selling price of a gold bracelet is $189.95 and its unit product cost is $149.00 as shown below:

Direct materials	$ 84.00
Direct labor	45.00
Manufacturing overhead	20.00
Unit product cost	$149.00

Most of the manufacturing overhead is fixed and unaffected by variations in how much jewelry is produced in any given period. However, $4.00 of the overhead is variable with respect to the number of bracelets produced. The customer who is interested in the special bracelet order would like special filigree applied to the bracelets. This filigree would require additional materials costing $2.00 per bracelet and would also require acquisition of a special tool costing $250 that would have no other use once the special order is completed. This order would have no effect on the company's regular sales and the order could be fulfilled using the company's existing capacity without affecting any other order.

Required:

What effect would accepting this order have on the company's net operating income if a special price of $169.95 per bracelet is offered for this order? Should the special order be accepted at this price?

EXERCISE 7–5 Utilizing a Constrained Resource [LO 7–5]

Outdoor Luggage Inc. makes high-end hard-sided luggage for sports equipment. Data concerning three of the company's most popular models appear below.

	Ski Guard	Golf Guard	Fishing Guard
Selling price per unit	$200	$300	$255
Variable cost per unit	$60	$140	$55
Plastic injection molding machine processing time required to produce one unit	2 minutes	5 minutes	4 minutes
Pounds of plastic pellets per unit	7 pounds	4 pounds	8 pounds

Required:

1. The total time available on the plastic injection molding machine is the constraint in the production process. Which product would be the most profitable use of this constraint? Which product would be the least profitable use of this constraint?
2. A severe shortage of plastic pellets has required the company to cut back its production so much that the plastic injection molding machine is no longer the bottleneck. Instead, the constraint is the total available pounds of plastic pellets. Which product would be the most profitable use of this constraint? Which product would be the least profitable use of this constraint?
3. Which product has the largest unit contribution margin? Why wouldn't this product be the most profitable use of the constrained resource in either case?

EXERCISE 7–6 Managing a Constrained Resource [LO 7–6]

Portsmouth Company makes fine colonial reproduction furniture. Upholstered furniture is one of its major product lines and the bottleneck on this production line is time in the upholstery shop. Upholstering is a craft that takes years of experience to master and the demand for upholstered furniture far exceeds the company's capacity in the upholstering shop. Information concerning three of the company's upholstered chairs appears below:

	Recliner	Sofa	Love Seat
Selling price per unit	$1,400	$1,800	$1,500
Variable cost per unit.	$800	$1,200	$1,000
Upholstery shop time required to produce one unit	8 hours	10 hours	5 hours

Required:

1. More time could be made available in the upholstery shop by asking the employees who work in this shop to work overtime. Assuming that this extra time would be used to produce sofas, up to how much should the company be willing to pay per hour to keep the upholstery shop open after normal working hours?
2. A small nearby upholstering company has offered to upholster furniture for Portsmouth at a fixed charge of $45 per hour. The management of Portsmouth is confident that this upholstering company's work is high quality and their craftsmen should be able to work about as quickly as Portsmouth's own craftsmen on the simpler upholstering jobs such as the love seat. Should management accept this offer? Explain.

EXERCISE 7–7 Sell or Process Further [LO 7–7]

Dorsey Company manufactures three products from a common input in a joint processing operation. Joint processing costs up to the split-off point total $350,000 per quarter. The company allocates these costs to the joint products on the basis of their relative sales value at the split-off point. Unit selling prices and total output at the split-off point are as follows:

Product	Selling Price	Quarterly Output
A	$16 per pound	15,000 pounds
B	$8 per pound	20,000 pounds
C	$25 per gallon	4,000 gallons

Each product can be processed further after the split-off point. Additional processing requires no special facilities. The additional processing costs (per quarter) and unit selling prices after further processing are given below:

Product	Additional Processing Costs	Selling Price
A	$63,000	$20 per pound
B	$80,000	$13 per pound
C	$36,000	$32 per gallon

Required:

Which product or products should be sold at the split-off point and which product or products should be processed further? Show computations.

EXERCISE 7–8 Utilization of a Constrained Resource [LO 7–5, LO 7–6]

Barlow Company manufactures three products: A, B, and C. The selling price, variable costs, and contribution margin for one unit of each product follow:

	Product		
	A	B	C
Selling price.	$180	$270	$240
Variable expenses:			
Direct materials.	24	72	32
Other variable expenses.	102	90	148
Total variable expenses.	126	162	180
Contribution margin.	$ 54	$108	$ 60
Contribution margin ratio	30%	40%	25%

The same raw material is used in all three products. Barlow Company has only 5,000 pounds of raw material on hand and will not be able to obtain any more of it for several weeks due to a strike in its supplier's plant. Management is trying to decide which product(s) to concentrate on next week in filling its backlog of orders. The material costs $8 per pound.

Required:

1. Compute the amount of contribution margin that will be obtained per pound of material used in each product.
2. Which orders would you recommend that the company work on next week—the orders for product A, product B, or product C? Show computations.
3. A foreign supplier could furnish Barlow with additional stocks of the raw material at a substantial premium over the usual price. If there is unfilled demand for all three products, what is the highest price that Barlow Company should be willing to pay for an additional pound of materials? Explain.

EXERCISE 7–9 Special Order [LO 7–4]

Delta Company produces a single product. The cost of producing and selling a single unit of this product at the company's normal activity level of 60,000 units per year is:

Direct materials.	$5.10
Direct labor	$3.80
Variable manufacturing overhead	$1.00
Fixed manufacturing overhead	$4.20
Variable selling and administrative expense	$1.50
Fixed selling and administrative expense	$2.40

The normal selling price is $21 per unit. The company's capacity is 75,000 units per year. An order has been received from a mail-order house for 15,000 units at a special price of $14.00 per unit. This order would not affect regular sales.

Required:

1. If the order is accepted, by how much will annual profits be increased or decreased? (The order will not change the company's total fixed costs.)
2. Assume the company has 1,000 units of this product left over from last year that are inferior to the current model. The units must be sold through regular channels at reduced prices. What unit cost is relevant for establishing a minimum selling price for these units? Explain.

EXERCISE 7–10 Make or Buy a Component [LO 7–3]

For many years Futura Company has purchased the starters that it installs in its standard line of farm tractors. Due to a reduction in output, the company has idle capacity that could be used to produce the starters. The chief engineer has recommended against this move, however, pointing out that the cost to produce the starters would be greater than the current $8.40 per unit purchase price:

	Per Unit	Total
Direct materials	$3.10	
Direct labor	2.70	
Supervision	1.50	$60,000
Depreciation	1.00	$40,000
Variable manufacturing overhead	0.60	
Rent	0.30	$12,000
Total production cost	$9.20	

A supervisor would have to be hired to oversee production of the starters. However, the company has sufficient idle tools and machinery that no new equipment would have to be purchased. The rent charge above is based on space utilized in the plant. The total rent on the plant is $80,000 per period. Depreciation is due to obsolescence rather than wear and tear.

Required:

Prepare computations showing how much profits will increase or decrease as a result of making the starters.

EXERCISE 7–11 Make or Buy a Component [LO 7–3]

Han Products manufactures 30,000 units of part S-6 each year for use on its production line. At this level of activity, the cost per unit for part S-6 is:

Direct materials	$ 3.60
Direct labor	10.00
Variable manufacturing overhead	2.40
Fixed manufacturing overhead	9.00
Total cost per part	$25.00

An outside supplier has offered to sell 30,000 units of part S-6 each year to Han Products for $21 per part. If Han Products accepts this offer, the facilities now being used to manufacture part S-6 could be rented to another company at an annual rental of $80,000. However, Han Products has determined that two-thirds of the fixed manufacturing overhead being applied to part S-6 would continue even if part S-6 were purchased from the outside supplier.

Required:

Prepare computations showing how much profits will increase or decrease if the outside supplier's offer is accepted.

EXERCISE 7–12 Utilization of a Constrained Resource [LO 7–5]

Benoit Company produces three products, A, B, and C. Data concerning the three products follow (per unit):

	Product		
	A	B	C
Selling price	$80	$56	$70
Variable expenses:			
Direct materials	24	15	9
Other variable expenses	24	27	40
Total variable expenses	48	42	49
Contribution margin	$32	$14	$21
Contribution margin ratio	40%	25%	30%

Demand for the company's products is very strong, with far more orders each month than the company can produce with the available raw materials. The same material is used in each product. The material costs $3 per pound with a maximum of 5,000 pounds available each month.

Required:

Which orders would you advise the company to accept first, those for A, for B, or for C? Which orders second? Third?

EXERCISE 7–13 Sell or Process Further [LO 7–7]

Wexpro, Inc., produces several products from processing 1 ton of clypton, a rare mineral. Material and processing costs total $60,000 per ton, one-fourth of which is allocated to product X15. Seven thousand units of product X15 are produced from each ton of clypton. The units can either be sold at the split-off point for $9 each, or processed further at a total cost of $9,500 and then sold for $12 each.

Required:

Should product X15 be processed further or sold at the split-off point?

EXERCISE 7–14 Identification of Relevant Costs [LO 7–1]

Kristen Lu purchased a used automobile for $8,000 at the beginning of last year and incurred the following operating costs:

Depreciation ($8,000 ÷ 5 years)	$1,600
Insurance	$1,200
Garage rent	$360
Automobile tax and license	$40
Variable operating cost	$0.14 per mile

The variable operating cost consists of gasoline, oil, tires, maintenance, and repairs. Kristen estimates that, at her current rate of usage, the car will have zero resale value in five years, so the annual straight-line depreciation is $1,600. The car is kept in a garage for a monthly fee.

Required:

1. Kristen drove the car 10,000 miles last year. Compute the average cost per mile of owning and operating the car.
2. Kristen is unsure about whether she should use her own car or rent a car to go on an extended cross-country trip for two weeks during spring break. What costs above are relevant in this decision? Explain.
3. Kristen is thinking about buying an expensive sports car to replace the car she bought last year. She would drive the same number of miles regardless of which car she owns and would rent the same parking space. The sports car's variable operating costs would be roughly the same as the variable operating costs of her old car. However, her insurance and automobile tax and license costs would go up. What costs are relevant in estimating the incremental cost of owning the more expensive car? Explain.

EXERCISE 7–15 Dropping or Retaining a Segment [LO 7–2]

Thalassines Kataskeves, S.A., of Greece makes marine equipment. The company has been experiencing losses on its bilge pump product line for several years. The most recent quarterly contribution format income statement for the bilge pump product line follows:

Discontinuing the bilge pump product line would not affect sales of other product lines and would have no effect on the company's total general factory overhead or total Purchasing Department expenses.

Thalassines Kataskeves, S.A. Income Statement—Bilge Pump For the Quarter Ended March 31		
Sales		$850,000
Variable expenses:		
Variable manufacturing expenses	$330,000	
Sales commissions	42,000	
Shipping	18,000	
Total variable expenses		390,000
Contribution margin		460,000
Fixed expenses:		
Advertising	270,000	
Depreciation of equipment (no resale value)	80,000	
General factory overhead	105,000*	
Salary of product-line manager	32,000	
Insurance on inventories	8,000	
Purchasing department	45,000†	
Total fixed expenses		540,000
Net operating loss		$ (80,000)

*Common costs allocated on the basis of machine-hours.
†Common costs allocated on the basis of sales dollars.

Required:

Would you recommend that the bilge pump product line be discontinued? Support your answer with appropriate computations.

EXERCISE 7–16 Identification of Relevant Costs [LO 7–1]

Bill has just returned from a duck hunting trip. He has brought home eight ducks. Bill's friend, John, disapproves of duck hunting, and to discourage Bill from further hunting, John has presented him with the following cost estimate per duck:

Camper and equipment:	
Cost, $12,000; usable for eight seasons; 10 hunting trips per season	$150
Travel expense (pickup truck):	
100 miles at $0.31 per mile (gas, oil, and tires—$0.21 per mile; depreciation and insurance—$0.10 per mile)	31
Shotgun shells (two boxes)	20
Boat:	
Cost, $2,320, usable for eight seasons; 10 hunting trips per season	29
Hunting license:	
Cost, $30 for the season; 10 hunting trips per season	3
Money lost playing poker:	
Loss, $24 (Bill plays poker every weekend)	24
Bottle of whiskey:	
Cost, $15 (used to ward off the cold)	15
Total cost	$272
Cost per duck ($272 ÷ 8 ducks)	$ 34

Required:

1. Assuming that the duck hunting trip Bill has just completed is typical, what costs are relevant to a decision as to whether Bill should go duck hunting again this season?
2. Suppose that Bill gets lucky on his next hunting trip and shoots 10 ducks in the amount of time it took him to shoot 8 ducks on his last trip. How much would it have cost him to shoot the last two ducks? Explain.
3. Which costs are relevant in a decision of whether Bill should give up hunting? Explain.

EXERCISE 7–17 Dropping or Retaining a Segment [LO 7–2]

Bed & Bath, a retailing company, has two departments, Hardware and Linens. The company's most recent monthly contribution format income statement follows:

		Department	
	Total	Hardware	Linens
Sales	$4,000,000	$3,000,000	$1,000,000
Variable expenses	1,300,000	900,000	400,000
Contribution margin	2,700,000	2,100,000	600,000
Fixed expenses	2,200,000	1,400,000	800,000
Net operating income (loss)	$ 500,000	$ 700,000	$ (200,000)

A study indicates that $340,000 of the fixed expenses being charged to Linens are sunk costs or allocated costs that will continue even if the Linens Department is dropped. In addition, the elimination of the Linens Department will result in a 10% decrease in the sales of the Hardware Department.

Required:

If the Linens Department is dropped, what will be the effect on the net operating income of the company as a whole?

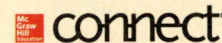

Additional student resources are available with Connect. connect

Problems

PROBLEM 7–18 Relevant Cost Analysis in a Variety of Situations [LO 7–2, LO 7–3, LO 7–4]

Andretti Company has a single product called a Dak. The company normally produces and sells 60,000 Daks each year at a selling price of $32 per unit. The company's unit costs at this level of activity are given below:

Direct materials	$10.00	
Direct labor	4.50	
Variable manufacturing overhead	2.30	
Fixed manufacturing overhead	5.00	($300,000 total)
Variable selling expenses	1.20	
Fixed selling expenses	3.50	($210,000 total)
Total cost per unit	$26.50	

A number of questions relating to the production and sale of Daks follow. Each question is independent.

Required:

1. Assume that Andretti Company has sufficient capacity to produce 90,000 Daks each year without any increase in fixed manufacturing overhead costs. The company could increase its sales by 25% above the present 60,000 units each year if it were willing to increase the fixed selling expenses by $80,000. Would the increased fixed selling expenses be justified?
2. Assume again that Andretti Company has sufficient capacity to produce 90,000 Daks each year. A customer in a foreign market wants to purchase 20,000 Daks. Import duties on the Daks would be $1.70 per unit, and costs for permits and licenses would be $9,000. The only selling costs that would be associated with the order would be $3.20 per unit shipping cost. Compute the per unit break-even price on this order.
3. The company has 1,000 Daks on hand that have some irregularities and are therefore considered to be "seconds." Due to the irregularities, it will be impossible to sell these units at the normal price through regular distribution channels. What unit cost figure is relevant for setting a minimum selling price? Explain.
4. Due to a strike in its supplier's plant, Andretti Company is unable to purchase more material for the production of Daks. The strike is expected to last for two months. Andretti Company

has enough material on hand to operate at 30% of normal levels for the two-month period. As an alternative, Andretti could close its plant down entirely for the two months. If the plant were closed, fixed manufacturing overhead costs would continue at 60% of their normal level during the two-month period and the fixed selling expenses would be reduced by 20%. What would be the impact on profits of closing the plant for the two-month period?

5. An outside manufacturer has offered to produce Daks and ship them directly to Andretti's customers. If Andretti Company accepts this offer, the facilities that it uses to produce Daks would be idle; however, fixed manufacturing overhead costs would be reduced by 75%. Because the outside manufacturer would pay for all shipping costs, the variable selling expenses would be only two-thirds of their present amount. Compute the unit cost that is relevant for comparison to the price quoted by the outside manufacturer.

PROBLEM 7–19 Dropping or Retaining a Segment [LO 7–2]

Jackson County Senior Services is a nonprofit organization devoted to providing essential services to seniors who live in their own homes within the Jackson County area. Three services are provided for seniors—home nursing, Meals On Wheels, and housekeeping. Data on revenue and expenses for the past year follow:

	Total	Home Nursing	Meals On Wheels	House-keeping
Revenues	$900,000	$260,000	$400,000	$240,000
Variable expenses	490,000	120,000	210,000	60,000
Contribution margin	410,000	140,000	190,000	80,000
Fixed expenses:				
Depreciation	68,000	8,000	40,000	20,000
Liability insurance	42,000	20,000	7,000	15,000
Program administrators' salaries	115,000	40,000	38,000	37,000
General administrative overhead*	180,000	52,000	80,000	48,000
Total fixed expenses	405,000	120,000	165,000	120,000
Net operating income (loss)	$ 5,000	$ 20,000	$ 25,000	$ (40,000)

*Allocated on the basis of program revenues.

The head administrator of Jackson County Senior Services, Judith Miyama, is concerned about the organization's finances and considers the net operating income of $5,000 last year to be razor-thin. (Last year's results were very similar to the results for previous years and are representative of what would be expected in the future.) She feels that the organization should be building its financial reserves at a more rapid rate in order to prepare for the next inevitable recession. After seeing the above report, Ms. Miyama asked for more information about the financial advisability of perhaps discontinuing the housekeeping program.

The depreciation in housekeeping is for a small van that is used to carry the housekeepers and their equipment from job to job. If the program were discontinued, the van would be donated to a charitable organization. None of the general administrative overhead would be avoided if the housekeeping program were dropped, but the liability insurance and the salary of the program administrator would be avoided.

Required:

1. Should the Housekeeping program be discontinued? Explain. Show computations to support your answer.
2. Recast the above data in a format that would be more useful to management in assessing the long-run financial viability of the various services.

PROBLEM 7–20 Sell or Process Further [LO 7–7]

(Prepared from a situation suggested by Professor John W. Hardy.) Lone Star Meat Packers is a major processor of beef and other meat products. The company has a large amount of T-bone steak on hand, and it is trying to decide whether to sell the T-bone steaks as they are initially cut or to process them further into filet mignon and the New York cut.

If the T-bone steaks are sold as initially cut, the company figures that a 1-pound T-bone steak would yield the following profit:

Selling price ($2.25 per pound)	$2.25
Less joint costs incurred up to the split-off point where T-bone steak can be identified as a separate product	1.80
Profit per pound	$0.45

As mentioned above, instead of being sold as initially cut, the T-bone steaks could be further processed into filet mignon and New York cut steaks. Cutting one side of a T-bone steak provides the filet mignon, and cutting the other side provides the New York cut. One 16-ounce T-bone steak cut in this way will yield one 6-ounce filet mignon and one 8-ounce New York cut; the remaining ounces are waste. The cost of processing the T-bone steaks into these cuts is $0.25 per pound. The filet mignon can be sold for $4.00 per pound, and the New York cut can be sold for $2.80 per pound.

Required:

1. Determine the profit per pound from processing the T-bone steaks into filet mignon and New York cut steaks.
2. Would you recommend that the T-bone steaks be sold as initially cut or processed further? Why?

PROBLEM 7–21 Dropping or Retaining a Flight [LO 7–2]

Profits have been decreasing for several years at Pegasus Airlines. In an effort to improve the company's performance, consideration is being given to dropping several flights that appear to be unprofitable.

A typical income statement for one round-trip of one such flight (flight 482) is as follows:

Ticket revenue (175 seats × 40% occupancy × $200 ticket price)	$14,000	100.0%
Variable expenses ($15 per person)	1,050	7.5
Contribution margin	12,950	92.5%
Flight expenses:		
Salaries, flight crew	1,800	
Flight promotion	750	
Depreciation of aircraft	1,550	
Fuel for aircraft	5,800	
Liability insurance	4,200	
Salaries, flight assistants	1,500	
Baggage loading and flight preparation	1,700	
Overnight costs for flight crew and assistants at destination	300	
Total flight expenses	17,600	
Net operating loss	$ (4,650)	

The following additional information is available about flight 482:

a. Members of the flight crew are paid fixed annual salaries, whereas the flight assistants are paid based on the number of round trips they complete.
b. One-third of the liability insurance is a special charge assessed against flight 482 because in the opinion of the insurance company, the destination of the flight is in a "high-risk" area. The remaining two-thirds would be unaffected by a decision to drop flight 482.
c. The baggage loading and flight preparation expense is an allocation of ground crews' salaries and depreciation of ground equipment. Dropping flight 482 would have no effect on the company's total baggage loading and flight preparation expenses.
d. If flight 482 is dropped, Pegasus Airlines has no authorization at present to replace it with another flight.
e. Aircraft depreciation is due entirely to obsolescence. Depreciation due to wear and tear is negligible.
f. Dropping flight 482 would not allow Pegasus Airlines to reduce the number of aircraft in its fleet or the number of flight crew on its payroll.

Required:

1. Prepare an analysis showing what impact dropping flight 482 would have on the airline's profits.
2. The airline's scheduling officer has been criticized because only about 50% of the seats on Pegasus' flights are being filled compared to an industry average of 60%. The scheduling officer has explained that Pegasus' average seat occupancy could be improved considerably by eliminating about 10% of its flights, but that doing so would reduce profits. Explain how this could happen.

PROBLEM 7–22 Accept or Reject a Special Order [LO 7–4]

Polaski Company manufactures and sells a single product called a Ret. Operating at capacity, the company can produce and sell 30,000 Rets per year. Costs associated with this level of production and sales are given below:

	Unit	Total
Direct materials	$15	$ 450,000
Direct labor	8	240,000
Variable manufacturing overhead	3	90,000
Fixed manufacturing overhead	9	270,000
Variable selling expense	4	120,000
Fixed selling expense	6	180,000
Total cost	$45	$1,350,000

The Rets normally sell for $50 each. Fixed manufacturing overhead is constant at $270,000 per year within the range of 25,000 through 30,000 Rets per year.

Required:

1. Assume that due to a recession, Polaski Company expects to sell only 25,000 Rets through regular channels next year. A large retail chain has offered to purchase 5,000 Rets if Polaski is willing to accept a 16% discount off the regular price. There would be no sales commissions on this order; thus, variable selling expenses would be slashed by 75%. However, Polaski Company would have to purchase a special machine to engrave the retail chain's name on the 5,000 units. This machine would cost $10,000. Polaski Company has no assurance that the retail chain will purchase additional units in the future. Determine the impact on profits next year if this special order is accepted.
2. Refer to the original data. Assume again that Polaski Company expects to sell only 25,000 Rets through regular channels next year. The U.S. Army would like to make a one-time-only purchase of 5,000 Rets. The Army would pay a fixed fee of $1.80 per Ret, and it would reimburse Polaski Company for all costs of production (variable and fixed) associated with the units. Because the army would pick up the Rets with its own trucks, there would be no variable selling expenses associated with this order. If Polaski Company accepts the order, by how much will profits increase or decrease for the year?
3. Assume the same situation as that described in requirement 2, except that the company expects to sell 30,000 Rets through regular channels next year. Thus, accepting the U.S. Army's order would require giving up regular sales of 5,000 Rets. If the Army's order is accepted, by how much will profits increase or decrease from what they would be if the 5,000 Rets were sold through regular channels?

PROBLEM 7–23 Make or Buy Decision [LO 7–3]

Silven Industries, which manufactures and sells a highly successful line of summer lotions and insect repellents, has decided to diversify in order to stabilize sales throughout the year. A natural area for the company to consider is the production of winter lotions and creams to prevent dry and chapped skin.

After considerable research, a winter products line has been developed. However, Silven's president has decided to introduce only one of the new products for this coming winter. If the product is a success, further expansion in future years will be initiated.

The product selected (called Chap-Off) is a lip balm that will be sold in a lipstick-type tube. The product will be sold to wholesalers in boxes of 24 tubes for $8 per box. Because of excess capacity, no additional fixed manufacturing overhead costs will be incurred to produce the product. However, a $90,000 charge for fixed manufacturing overhead will be absorbed by the product under the company's absorption costing system.

Using the estimated sales and production of 100,000 boxes of Chap-Off, the Accounting Department has developed the following cost per box:

Direct material	$3.60
Direct labor	2.00
Manufacturing overhead	1.40
Total cost	$7.00

The costs above include costs for producing both the lip balm and the tube that contains it. As an alternative to making the tubes, Silven has approached a supplier to discuss the possibility of purchasing the tubes for Chap-Off. The purchase price of the empty tubes from the supplier would be $1.35 per box of 24 tubes. If Silven Industries accepts the purchase proposal, direct labor and variable manufacturing overhead costs per box of Chap-Off would be reduced by 10% and direct materials costs would be reduced by 25%.

Required:

1. Should Silven Industries make or buy the tubes? Show calculations to support your answer.
2. What would be the maximum purchase price acceptable to Silven Industries? Explain.
3. Instead of sales of 100,000 boxes, revised estimates show a sales volume of 120,000 boxes. At this new volume, additional equipment must be acquired to manufacture the tubes at an annual rental of $40,000. Assuming that the outside supplier will not accept an order for less than 120,000 boxes, should Silven Industries make or buy the tubes? Show computations to support your answer.
4. Refer to the data in requirement 3. Assume that the outside supplier will accept an order of any size for the tubes at $1.35 per box. How, if at all, would this change your answer? Show computations.
5. What qualitative factors should Silven Industries consider in determining whether they should make or buy the tubes?

(CMA, adapted)

PROBLEM 7–24 Shutting Down or Continuing to Operate a Plant [LO 7–2]

(Note: This type of decision is similar to keeping or dropping a product line.)

Birch Company normally produces and sells 30,000 units of RG-6 each month. RG-6 is a small electrical relay used as a component part in the automotive industry. The selling price is $22 per unit, variable costs are $14 per unit, fixed manufacturing overhead costs total $150,000 per month, and fixed selling costs total $30,000 per month.

Employment-contract strikes in the companies that purchase the bulk of the RG-6 units have caused Birch Company's sales to temporarily drop to only 8,000 units per month. Birch Company estimates that the strikes will last for two months, after which time sales of RG-6 should return to normal. Due to the current low level of sales, Birch Company is thinking about closing down its own plant during the strike, which would reduce its fixed manufacturing overhead costs by $45,000 per month and its fixed selling costs by 10%. Start-up costs at the end of the shutdown period would total $8,000. Because Birch Company uses Lean Production methods, no inventories are on hand.

Required:

1. Assuming that the strikes continue for two months, would you recommend that Birch Company close its own plant? Explain. Show computations.
2. At what level of sales (in units) for the two-month period should Birch Company be indifferent between closing the plant or keeping it open? Show computations. (***Hint:*** This is a type of break-even analysis, except that the fixed cost portion of your break-even computation should include only those fixed costs that are relevant [i.e., avoidable] over the two-month period.)

PROBLEM 7–25 Utilization of a Constrained Resource [LO 7–5, LO 7–6]

The Walton Toy Company manufactures a line of dolls and a doll dress sewing kit. Demand for the dolls is increasing, and management requests assistance from you in determining an economical sales and production mix for the coming year. The company has provided the following data:

Product	Demand Next Year (units)	Selling Price per Unit	Direct Materials	Direct Labor
Debbie	50,000	$13.50	$4.30	$3.20
Trish	42,000	$5.50	$1.10	$2.00
Sarah	35,000	$21.00	$6.44	$5.60
Mike	40,000	$10.00	$2.00	$4.00
Sewing kit	325,000	$8.00	$3.20	$1.60

The following additional information is available:

a. The company's plant has a capacity of 130,000 direct labor-hours per year on a single-shift basis. The company's present employees and equipment can produce all five products.

b. The direct labor rate of $8 per hour is expected to remain unchanged during the coming year.

c. Fixed costs total $520,000 per year. Variable overhead costs are $2 per direct labor-hour.

d. All of the company's nonmanufacturing costs are fixed.

e. The company's finished goods inventory is negligible and can be ignored.

Required:

1. Determine the contribution margin per direct labor-hour expended on each product.
2. Prepare a schedule showing the total direct labor-hours that will be required to produce the units estimated to be sold during the coming year.
3. Examine the data you have computed in requirements 1 and 2. How would you allocate the 130,000 direct labor-hours of capacity to Walton Toy Company's various products?
4. What is the highest total contribution margin that the company can earn if it makes optimal use of its constrained resource?
5. What is the highest price, in terms of a rate per hour, that Walton Toy Company would be willing to pay for additional capacity (that is, for added direct labor time)?
6. Assume again that the company does not want to reduce sales of any product. Identify ways in which the company could obtain the additional output.

(CMA, adapted)

PROBLEM 7–26 Close or Retain a Store [LO 7–2]

Superior Markets, Inc., operates three stores in a large metropolitan area. A segmented absorption costing income statement for the company for the last quarter is given below:

Superior Markets, Inc.
Income Statement
For the Quarter Ended September 30

	Total	North Store	South Store	East Store
Sales......................	$3,000,000	$720,000	$1,200,000	$1,080,000
Cost of goods sold...........	1,657,200	403,200	660,000	594,000
Gross margin................	1,342,800	316,800	540,000	486,000
Selling and administrative expenses:				
Selling expenses	817,000	231,400	315,000	270,600
Administrative expenses....	383,000	106,000	150,900	126,100
Total expenses	1,200,000	337,400	465,900	396,700
Net operating income (loss) ...	$ 142,800	$ (20,600)	$ 74,100	$ 89,300

The North Store has consistently shown losses over the past two years. For this reason, management is giving consideration to closing the store. The company has asked you to make a recommendation as to whether the store should be closed or kept open. The following additional information is available for your use:

a. The breakdown of the selling and administrative expenses is as follows:

	Total	North Store	South Store	East Store
Selling expenses:				
Sales salaries	$239,000	$ 70,000	$ 89,000	$ 80,000
Direct advertising	187,000	51,000	72,000	64,000
General advertising*	45,000	10,800	18,000	16,200
Store rent	300,000	85,000	120,000	95,000
Depreciation of store fixtures	16,000	4,600	6,000	5,400
Delivery salaries	21,000	7,000	7,000	7,000
Depreciation of delivery equipment	9,000	3,000	3,000	3,000
Total selling expenses	$817,000	$231,400	$315,000	$270,600

*Allocated on the basis of sales dollars.

	Total	North Store	South Store	East Store
Administrative expenses:				
Store management salaries	$ 70,000	$ 21,000	$ 30,000	$ 19,000
General office salaries*	50,000	12,000	20,000	18,000
Insurance on fixtures and inventory	25,000	7,500	9,000	8,500
Utilities	106,000	31,000	40,000	35,000
Employment taxes	57,000	16,500	21,900	18,600
General office—other*	75,000	18,000	30,000	27,000
Total administrative expenses	$383,000	$106,000	$150,900	$126,100

*Allocated on the basis of sales dollars.

b. The lease on the building housing the North Store can be broken with no penalty.
c. The fixtures being used in the North Store would be transferred to the other two stores if the North Store were closed.
d. The general manager of the North Store would be retained and transferred to another position in the company if the North Store were closed. She would be filling a position that would otherwise be filled by hiring a new employee at a salary of $11,000 per quarter. The general manager of the North Store would be retained at her normal salary of $12,000 per quarter. All other employees in the store would be discharged.
e. The company has one delivery crew that serves all three stores. One delivery person could be discharged if the North Store were closed. This person's salary is $4,000 per quarter. The delivery equipment would be distributed to the other stores. The equipment does not wear out through use, but does eventually become obsolete.
f. The company's employment taxes are 15% of salaries.
g. One-third of the insurance in the North Store is on the store's fixtures.
h. The "General office salaries" and "General office—other" relate to the overall management of Superior Markets, Inc. If the North Store were closed, one person in the general office could be discharged because of the decrease in overall workload. This person's compensation is $6,000 per quarter.

Required:

1. Prepare a schedule showing the change in revenues and expenses and the impact on the company's overall net operating income that would result if the North Store were closed.

2. Assuming that the store space can't be subleased, what recommendation would you make to the management of Superior Markets, Inc.?
3. Disregard requirement 2. Assume that if the North Store were closed, at least one-fourth of its sales would transfer to the East Store, due to strong customer loyalty to Superior Markets. The East Store has enough capacity to handle the increased sales. You may assume that the increased sales in the East Store would yield the same gross margin as a percentage of sales as present sales in that store. What effect would these factors have on your recommendation concerning the North Store? Show all computations to support your answer.

PROBLEM 7–27 Sell or Process Further [LO 7–7]

Come-Clean Corporation produces a variety of cleaning compounds and solutions for both industrial and household use. While most of its products are processed independently, a few are related, such as the company's Grit 337 and its Sparkle silver polish.

Grit 337 is a coarse cleaning powder with many industrial uses. It costs $1.60 a pound to make, and it has a selling price of $2.00 a pound. A small portion of the annual production of Grit 337 is retained in the factory for further processing. It is combined with several other ingredients to form a paste that is marketed as Sparkle silver polish. The silver polish sells for $4.00 per jar.

This further processing requires one-fourth pound of Grit 337 per jar of silver polish. The additional direct costs involved in the processing of a jar of silver polish are:

Other ingredients	$0.65
Direct labor	1.48
Total direct cost	$2.13

Overhead costs associated with processing the silver polish are:

Variable manufacturing overhead cost	25% of direct labor cost
Fixed manufacturing overhead cost (per month):	
Production supervisor	$3,000
Depreciation of mixing equipment	$1,400

The production supervisor has no duties other than to oversee production of the silver polish. The mixing equipment is special-purpose equipment acquired specifically to produce the silver polish. Its resale value is negligible and it does not wear out through use.

Direct labor is a variable cost at Come-Clean Corporation.

Advertising costs for the silver polish total $4,000 per month. Variable selling costs associated with the silver polish are 7.5% of sales.

Due to a recent decline in the demand for silver polish, the company is wondering whether its continued production is advisable. The sales manager feels that it would be more profitable to sell all of the Grit 337 as a cleaning powder.

Required:

1. What is the incremental contribution margin per jar from further processing of Grit 337 into silver polish?
2. What is the minimum number of jars of silver polish that must be sold each month to justify the continued processing of Grit 337 into silver polish? Explain. Show all computations.

(CMA, adapted)

PROBLEM 7–28 Make or Buy Analysis [LO 7–3]

"In my opinion, we ought to stop making our own drums and accept that outside supplier's offer," said Wim Niewindt, managing director of Antilles Refining, N.V., of Aruba. "At a price of $18 per drum, we would be paying $5 less than it costs us to manufacture the drums in our own plant. Since we use 60,000 drums a year, that would be an annual cost savings of $300,000." Antilles Refining's current cost to manufacture one drum is given below (based on 60,000 drums per year):

Direct materials	$10.35
Direct labor	6.00
Variable overhead	1.50
Fixed overhead ($2.80 general company overhead, $1.60 depreciation and, $0.75 supervision)	5.15
Total cost per drum	$23.00

A decision about whether to make or buy the drums is especially important at this time because the equipment being used to make the drums is completely worn out and must be replaced. The choices facing the company are:

Alternative 1: Rent new equipment and continue to make the drums. The equipment would be rented for $135,000 per year.

Alternative 2: Purchase the drums from an outside supplier at $18 per drum.

The new equipment would be more efficient than the equipment that Antilles Refining has been using and, according to the manufacturer, would reduce direct labor and variable overhead costs by 30%. The old equipment has no resale value. Supervision cost ($45,000 per year) and direct materials cost per drum would not be affected by the new equipment. The new equipment's capacity would be 90,000 drums per year.

The company's total general company overhead would be unaffected by this decision.

Required:

1. To assist the managing director in making a decision, prepare an analysis showing the total cost and the cost per drum for each of the two alternatives given above. Assume that 60,000 drums are needed each year. Which course of action would you recommend to the managing director?
2. Would your recommendation in requirement 1 be the same if the company's needs were: (a) 75,000 drums per year or (b) 90,000 drums per year? Show computations to support your answer, with costs presented on both a total and a per unit basis.
3. What other factors would you recommend that the company consider before making a decision?

Additional student resources are available with Connect.

Cases

CASE 7–29 Sell or Process Further Decision [LO 7–7]

The Scottie Sweater Company produces sweaters under the "Scottie" label. The company buys raw wool and processes it into wool yarn from which the sweaters are woven. One spindle of wool yarn is required to produce one sweater. The costs and revenues associated with the sweaters are given below:

		Per Sweater
Selling price		$30.00
Cost to manufacture:		
Raw materials:		
Buttons, thread, lining	$ 2.00	
Wool yarn	16.00	
Total raw materials	18.00	
Direct labor	5.80	
Manufacturing overhead	8.70	32.50
Manufacturing profit (loss)		$ (2.50)

Originally, all of the wool yarn was used to produce sweaters, but in recent years a market has developed for the wool yarn itself. The yarn is purchased by other companies for use in production of wool blankets and other wool products. Since the development of the market for the wool yarn, a continuing dispute has existed in the Scottie Sweater Company as to whether the yarn should be sold simply as yarn or processed into sweaters. Current cost and revenue data on the yarn are given below:

		Per Spindle of Yarn
Selling price		$20.00
Cost to manufacture:		
Raw materials (raw wool)	$7.00	
Direct labor	3.60	
Manufacturing overhead	5.40	16.00
Manufacturing profit		$ 4.00

The market for sweaters is temporarily depressed, due to unusually warm weather in the western states where the sweaters are sold. This has made it necessary for the company to discount the selling price of the sweaters to $30 from the normal $40 price. Since the market for wool yarn has remained strong, the dispute has again surfaced over whether the yarn should be sold outright rather than processed into sweaters. The sales manager thinks that the production of sweaters should be discontinued; she is upset about having to sell sweaters at a $2.50 loss when the yarn could be sold for a $4.00 profit. However, the production superintendent does not want to close down a large portion of the factory. He argues that the company is in the sweater business, not the yarn business, and that the company should focus on its core strength.

All of the manufacturing overhead costs are fixed and would not be affected even if sweaters were discontinued. Manufacturing overhead is assigned to products on the basis of 150% of direct labor cost. Materials and direct labor costs are variable.

Required:

1. Would you recommend that the wool yarn be sold outright or processed into sweaters? Support your answer with appropriate computations and explain your reasoning.
2. What is the lowest price that the company should accept for a sweater? Support your answer with appropriate computations and explain your reasoning.

CASE 7–30 Ethics and the Manager; Shut Down or Continue Operations [LO 7–2]

Haley Romeros had just been appointed vice president of the Rocky Mountain Region of the Bank Services Corporation (BSC). The company provides check processing services for small banks. The banks send checks presented for deposit or payment to BSC, which records the data on each check in a computerized database. BSC then sends the data electronically to the nearest Federal Reserve Bank check-clearing center where the appropriate transfers of funds are made between banks. The Rocky Mountain Region has three check processing centers, which are located in Billings, Montana; Great Falls, Montana; and Clayton, Idaho. Prior to her promotion to vice president, Ms. Romeros had been the manager of a check processing center in New Jersey.

Immediately after assuming her new position, Ms. Romeros requested a complete financial report for the just-ended fiscal year from the region's controller, John Littlebear. Ms. Romeros specified that the financial report should follow the standardized format required by corporate headquarters for all regional performance reports. That report follows:

Upon seeing this report, Ms. Romeros summoned John Littlebear for an explanation.

Romeros: What's the story on Clayton? It didn't have a loss the previous year did it?

Littlebear: No, the Clayton facility has had a nice profit every year since it was opened six years ago, but Clayton lost a big contract this year.

Romeros: Why?

Littlebear: One of our national competitors entered the local market and bid very aggressively on the contract. We couldn't afford to meet the bid. Clayton's costs—particularly their facility expenses—are just too high. When Clayton lost the contract, we had to lay off a lot of employees, but we could not reduce the fixed costs of the Clayton facility.

Romeros: Why is Clayton's facility expense so high? It's a smaller facility than either Billings or Great Falls and yet its facility expense is higher.

Littlebear: The problem is that we are able to rent suitable facilities very cheaply at Billings and Great Falls. No such facilities were available at Clayton; we had them built. Unfortunately, there were big cost overruns. The contractor we hired was inexperienced at this kind of work and in fact went bankrupt before the project was completed. After hiring another contractor

Bank Services Corporation (BSC)
Rocky Mountain Region
Financial Performance

		Check Processing Centers		
	Total	Billings	Great Falls	Clayton
Sales	$50,000,000	$20,000,000	$18,000,000	$12,000,000
Operating expenses:				
Direct labor	32,000,000	12,500,000	11,000,000	8,500,000
Variable overhead	850,000	350,000	310,000	190,000
Equipment depreciation	3,900,000	1,300,000	1,400,000	1,200,000
Facility expense	2,800,000	900,000	800,000	1,100,000
Local administrative expense*	450,000	140,000	160,000	150,000
Regional administrative expense†	1,500,000	600,000	540,000	360,000
Corporate administrative expense‡	4,750,000	1,900,000	1,710,000	1,140,000
Total operating expense	46,250,000	17,690,000	15,920,000	12,640,000
Net operating income (loss)	$ 3,750,000	$ 2,310,000	$ 2,080,000	$ (640,000)

*Local administrative expenses are the administrative expenses incurred at the check processing centers.
†Regional administrative expenses are allocated to the check processing centers based on sales.
‡Corporate administrative expenses are charged to segments of the company such as the Rocky Mountain Region and the check processing centers at the rate of 9.5% of their sales.

to finish the work, we were way over budget. The large depreciation charges on the facility didn't matter at first because we didn't have much competition at the time and could charge premium prices.

Romeros: Well we can't do that anymore. The Clayton facility will obviously have to be shut down. Its business can be shifted to the other two check processing centers in the region.

Littlebear: I would advise against that. The $1,200,000 in depreciation at the Clayton facility is misleading. That facility should last indefinitely with proper maintenance. And it has no resale value; there is no other commercial activity around Clayton.

Romeros: What about the other costs at Clayton?

Littlebear: If we shifted Clayton's business over to the other two processing centers in the region, we wouldn't save anything on direct labor or variable overhead costs. We might save $90,000 or so in local administrative expense, but we would not save any regional administrative expense and corporate headquarters would still charge us 9.5% of our sales as corporate administrative expense.

In addition, we would have to rent more space in Billings and Great Falls in order to handle the work transferred from Clayton; that would probably cost us at least $600,000 a year. And don't forget that it will cost us something to move the equipment from Clayton to Billings and Great Falls. And the move will disrupt service to customers.

Romeros: I understand all of that, but a money-losing processing center on my performance report is completely unacceptable.

Littlebear: And if you shut down Clayton, you are going to throw some loyal employees out of work.

Romeros: That's unfortunate, but we have to face hard business realities.

Littlebear: And you would have to write off the investment in the facilities at Clayton.

Romeros: I can explain a write-off to corporate headquarters; hiring an inexperienced contractor to build the Clayton facility was my predecessor's mistake. But they'll have my head at headquarters if I show operating losses every year at one of my processing centers. Clayton has to go. At the next corporate board meeting, I am going to recommend that the Clayton facility be closed.

Required:

1. From the standpoint of the company as a whole, should the Clayton processing center be shut down and its work redistributed to other processing centers in the region? Explain.
2. Do you think Haley Romeros's decision to shut down the Clayton facility is ethical? Explain.
3. What influence should the depreciation on the facilities at Clayton have on prices charged by Clayton for its services?

CASE 7–31 Integrative Case: Relevant Costs; Pricing [LO 7–1, LO 7–4]

Wesco Incorporated's only product is a combination fertilizer/weedkiller called GrowNWeed. GrowNWeed is sold nationwide to retail nurseries and garden stores.

Zwinger Nursery plans to sell a similar fertilizer/weedkiller compound through its regional nursery chain under its own private label. Zwinger does not have manufacturing facilities of its own, so it has asked Wesco (and several other companies) to submit a bid for manufacturing and delivering a 20,000-pound order of the private brand compound to Zwinger. While the chemical composition of the Zwinger compound differs from that of GrowNWeed, the manufacturing processes are very similar.

The Zwinger compound would be produced in 1,000-pound lots. Each lot would require 25 direct labor-hours and the following chemicals:

Chemicals	Quantity in Pounds
AG-5	300
KL-2	200
CW-7	150
DF-6	175

The first three chemicals (AG-5, KL-2, and CW-7) are all used in the production of GrowNWeed. DF-6 was used in another compound that Wesco discontinued several months ago. The supply of DF-6 that Wesco had on hand when the other compound was discontinued was not discarded. Wesco could sell its supply of DF-6 at the prevailing market price less $0.10 per pound selling and handling expenses.

Wesco also has on hand a chemical called BH-3, which was manufactured for use in another product that is no longer produced. BH-3, which cannot be used in GrowNWeed, can be substituted for AG-5 on a one-for-one basis without affecting the quality of the Zwinger compound. The BH-3 in inventory has a salvage value of $600.

Inventory and cost data for the chemicals that can be used to produce the Zwinger compound are shown below:

Raw Material	Pounds in Inventory	Actual Price per Pound When Purchased	Current Market Price per Pound
AG-5	18,000	$1.15	$1.20
KL-2	6,000	$1.10	$1.05
CW-7	7,000	$1.35	$1.35
DF-6	3,000	$0.80	$0.70
BH-3	3,500	$0.90	(Salvage)

The current direct labor wage rate is $14 per hour. The predetermined overhead rate is based on direct labor-hours (DLH). The predetermined overhead rate for the current year, based on a two-shift capacity with no overtime, is as follows:

Variable manufacturing overhead	$ 3.00 per DLH
Fixed manufacturing overhead	10.50 per DLH
Combined predetermined overhead rate	$13.50 per DLH

Wesco's production manager reports that the present equipment and facilities are adequate to manufacture the Zwinger compound. Therefore, the order would have no effect on total fixed manufacturing overhead costs. However, Wesco is within 400 hours of its two-shift capacity this month. Any additional hours beyond the 400 hours must be done in overtime. If need be, the Zwinger compound could be produced on regular time by shifting a portion of GrowNWeed production to overtime. Wesco's direct labor wage rate for overtime is $21 per hour. There is no allowance for any overtime premium in the predetermined overhead rate.

Required:

1. Wesco has decided to submit a bid for the 20,000 pound order of Zwinger's new compound. The order must be delivered by the end of the current month. Zwinger has indicated that this is a one-time order that will not be repeated. Calculate the lowest price that Wesco could bid for the order without reducing its net operating income.
2. Refer to the original data. Assume that Zwinger Nursery plans to place regular orders for 20,000-pound lots of the new compound. Wesco expects the demand for GrowNWeed to remain strong. Therefore, the recurring orders from Zwinger would put Wesco over its two-shift capacity. However, production could be scheduled so that 90% of each Zwinger order could be completed during regular hours. As another option, some GrowNWeed production could be shifted temporarily to overtime so that the Zwinger orders could be produced on regular time. Current market prices are the best available estimates of future market prices.

   Wesco's standard markup policy for new products is 40% of the full manufacturing cost, including fixed manufacturing overhead. Calculate the price that Wesco, Inc., would quote Zwinger Nursery for each 20,000 pound lot of the new compound, assuming that it is to be treated as a new product and this pricing policy is followed.

(CMA, adapted)

CASE 7–32 Make or Buy; Utilization of a Constrained Resource [LO 7–1, LO 7–3, LO 7–5]

TufStuff, Inc., sells a wide range of drums, bins, boxes, and other containers that are used in the chemical industry. One of the company's products is a heavy-duty corrosion-resistant metal drum, called the WVD drum, used to store toxic wastes. Production is constrained by the capacity of an automated welding machine that is used to make precision welds. A total of 2,000 hours of welding time is available annually on the machine. Because each drum requires 0.4 hours of welding machine time, annual production is limited to 5,000 drums. At present, the welding machine is used exclusively to make the WVD drums. The accounting department has provided the following financial data concerning the WVD drums:

WVD Drums		
Selling price per drum		$149.00
Cost per drum:		
Direct materials	$52.10	
Direct labor ($18 per hour)	3.60	
Manufacturing overhead	4.50	
Selling and administrative expense	29.80	90.00
Margin per drum		$ 59.00

Management believes 6,000 WVD drums could be sold each year if the company had sufficient manufacturing capacity. As an alternative to adding another welding machine, management has considered buying additional drums from an outside supplier. Harcor Industries, Inc., a supplier of quality products, would be able to provide up to 4,000 WVD-type drums per year at a price of $138 per drum, which TufStuff would resell to its customers at its normal selling price after appropriate relabeling.

Megan Flores, TufStuff's production manager, has suggested that the company could make better use of the welding machine by manufacturing bike frames, which would require only 0.5 hours of welding machine time per frame and yet sell for far more than the drums. Megan believes that TufStuff could sell up to 1,600 bike frames per year to bike manufacturers at a price of $239 each. The accounting department has provided the following data concerning the proposed new product:

Bike Frames		
Selling price per frame		$239.00
Cost per frame:		
Direct materials	$99.40	
Direct labor ($18 per hour)	28.80	
Manufacturing overhead	36.00	
Selling and administrative expense	47.80	212.00
Margin per frame		$ 27.00

The bike frames could be produced with existing equipment and personnel. Manufacturing overhead is allocated to products on the basis of direct labor-hours. Most of the manufacturing overhead consists of fixed common costs such as rent on the factory building, but some of it is variable. The variable manufacturing overhead has been estimated at $1.35 per WVD drum and $1.90 per bike frame. The variable manufacturing overhead cost would not be incurred on drums acquired from the outside supplier.

Selling and administrative expenses are allocated to products on the basis of revenues. Almost all of the selling and administrative expenses are fixed common costs, but it has been estimated that variable selling and administrative expenses amount to $0.75 per WVD drum whether made or purchased and would be $1.30 per bike frame.

All of the company's employees—direct and indirect—are paid for full 40-hour workweeks and the company has a policy of laying off workers only in major recessions.

Required:

1. Would you be comfortable relying on the financial data provided by the accounting department for making decisions related to the WVD drums and bike frames? Why?
2. Compute the contribution margin per unit for:
   a. Purchased WVD drums.
   b. Manufactured WVD drums.
   c. Manufactured bike frames.
3. Determine the number of WVD drums (if any) that should be purchased and the number of WVD drums and/or bike frames (if any) that should be manufactured. What is the increase in net operating income that would result from this plan over current operations?

   As soon as your analysis was shown to the top management team at TufStuff, several managers got into an argument concerning how direct labor costs should be treated when making this decision. One manager argued that direct labor is always treated as a variable cost in textbooks and in practice and has always been considered a variable cost at TufStuff. After all, "direct" means you can directly trace the cost to products. "If direct labor is not a variable cost, what is?" Another manager argued just as strenuously that direct labor should be considered a fixed cost at TufStuff. No one had been laid off in over a decade, and for all practical purposes, everyone at the plant is on a monthly salary. Everyone classified as direct labor works a regular 40-hour workweek and overtime has not been necessary since the company adopted Lean Production techniques. Whether the welding machine is used to make drums or frames, the total payroll would be exactly the same. There is enough slack, in the form of idle time, to accommodate any increase in total direct labor time that the bike frames would require.
4. Redo requirements (2) and (3) making the opposite assumption about direct labor from the one you originally made. In other words, if you treated direct labor as a variable cost, redo the analysis treating it as a fixed cost. If you treated direct labor as a fixed cost, redo the analysis treating it as a variable cost.
5. What do you think is the correct way to treat direct labor cost in this situation—as variable or as fixed? Explain.

CASE 7–33 Plant Closing Decision [LO 7–1, LO 7–2]

QualSupport Corporation manufactures seats for automobiles, vans, trucks, and various recreational vehicles. The company has a number of plants around the world, including the Denver Cover Plant, which makes seat covers.

Ted Vosilo is the plant manager of the Denver Cover Plant but also serves as the regional production manager for the company. His budget as the regional manager is charged to the Denver Cover Plant.

Vosilo has just heard that QualSupport has received a bid from an outside vendor to supply the equivalent of the entire annual output of the Denver Cover Plant for $35 million. Vosilo was astonished at the low outside bid because the budget for the Denver Cover Plant's operating costs for the upcoming year was set at $52 million. If this bid is accepted, the Denver Cover Plant will be closed down.

The budget for Denver Cover's operating costs for the coming year is presented below.

Denver Cover Plant
Annual Budget for Operating Costs

Materials		$14,000,000
Labor:		
Direct	$13,100,000	
Supervision	900,000	
Indirect plant	4,000,000	18,000,000
Overhead:		
Depreciation—equipment	3,200,000	
Depreciation—building	7,000,000	
Pension expense	5,000,000	
Plant manager and staff	800,000	
Corporate expenses*	4,000,000	20,000,000
Total budgeted costs		$52,000,000

*Fixed corporate expenses allocated to plants and other operating units based on total budgeted wage and salary costs.

Additional facts regarding the plant's operations are as follows:

a. Due to Denver Cover's commitment to use high-quality fabrics in all of its products, the Purchasing Department was instructed to place blanket purchase orders with major suppliers to ensure the receipt of sufficient materials for the coming year. If these orders are canceled as a consequence of the plant closing, termination charges would amount to 20% of the cost of direct materials.

b. Approximately 400 plant employees will lose their jobs if the plant is closed. This includes all of the direct laborers and supervisors as well as the plumbers, electricians, and other skilled workers classified as indirect plant workers. Some would be able to find new jobs while many others would have difficulty. All employees would have difficulty matching Denver Cover's base pay of $18.80 per hour, which is the highest in the area. A clause in Denver Cover's contract with the union may help some employees; the company must provide employment assistance to its former employees for 12 months after a plant closing. The estimated cost to administer this service would be $1.5 million for the year.

c. Some employees would probably choose early retirement because QualSupport has an excellent pension plan. In fact, $3 million of the annual pension expense would continue whether Denver Cover is open or not.

d. Vosilo and his staff would not be affected by the closing of Denver Cover. They would still be responsible for administering three other area plants.

e. If the Denver Cover Plant were closed, the company would realize about $3.2 million salvage value for the equipment and building. If the plant remains open, there are no plans to make any significant investments in new equipment or buildings. The old equipment is adequate and should last indefinitely.

Required:

1. Without regard to costs, identify the advantages to QualSupport Corporation of continuing to obtain covers from its own Denver Cover Plant.
2. QualSupport Corporation plans to prepare a financial analysis that will be used in deciding whether or not to close the Denver Cover Plant. Management has asked you to identify:

a. The annual budgeted costs that are relevant to the decision regarding closing the plant (show the dollar amounts).

b. The annual budgeted costs that are *not* relevant to the decision regarding closing the plant and explain why they are not relevant (again show the dollar amounts).

c. Any nonrecurring costs that would arise due to the closing of the plant, and explain how they would affect the decision (again show any dollar amounts).

3. Looking at the data you have prepared in requirement 2, should the plant be closed? Show computations and explain your answer.
4. Identify any revenues or costs not specifically mentioned in the problem that QualSupport should consider before making a decision.

(CMA, adapted)

Chapter 8

Capital Budgeting Decisions

Commercial Delivery Fleets Adopt Electric Trucks

BUSINESS FOCUS

© AP Images/David Goldman

Staples, Frito-Lay, and AT&T have begun purchasing electric delivery trucks even though they cost $30,000 more than diesel delivery trucks. Staples is willing to make the more expensive up-front investment because it expects each electric truck to incur lower operating costs. For example, it estimates that electric trucks will save $2,450 per year in maintenance costs and $6,500 per year in fuel costs. It also expects to replace each electric truck's brakes every four or five years instead of every one or two years with diesel trucks. In total, Staples expects each electric delivery truck to save $60,000 over its 10-year useful life. ■

Source: Mike Ramsey, "As Electric Vehicles Arrive, Firms See Payback in Trucks," *The Wall Street Journal*, December 8, 2010, pp. B1–B2.

LEARNING OBJECTIVES

After studying Chapter 8, you should be able to:

LO 8–1 Determine the payback period for an investment.

LO 8–2 Evaluate the acceptability of an investment project using the net present value method.

LO 8–3 Evaluate the acceptability of an investment project using the internal rate of return method.

LO 8–4 Evaluate an investment project that has uncertain cash flows.

LO 8–5 Rank investment projects in order of preference.

LO 8–6 Compute the simple rate of return for an investment.

LO 8–7 (Appendix 8A) Understand present value concepts and the use of present value tables.

LO 8–8 (Appendix 8C) Include income taxes in a net present value analysis.

Managers often consider decisions that involve an investment today in the hope of realizing future profits. For example, Yum! Brands, Inc., makes an investment when it opens a new Pizza Hut restaurant. L.L. Bean makes an investment when it installs a new computer to handle customer billing. Ford makes an investment when it redesigns a vehicle such as the F-150 pickup truck.Merck & Co. invests in medical research. Amazon.com makes an investment when it redesigns its website. All of these investments require spending now with the expectation of additional future net cash inflows.

The term **capital budgeting** is used to describe how managers plan significant investments in projects that have long-term implications such as the purchase of new equipment or the introduction of new products. Most companies have many more potential projects than can actually be funded. Hence, managers must carefully select those projects that promise the greatest future return. How well managers make these capital budgeting decisions is a critical factor in the long-run financial health of the organization. This chapter discusses four methods for making capital budgeting decisions—the *payback method,* the *net present value method,* the *internal rate of return method,* and the *simple rate of return method.*

Capital Budgeting—An Overview

Typical Capital Budgeting Decisions

Any decision that involves a cash outlay now in order to obtain a future return is a capital budgeting decision. Typical capital budgeting decisions include:

1. Cost reduction decisions. Should new equipment be purchased to reduce costs?
2. Expansion decisions. Should a new plant, warehouse, or other facility be acquired to increase capacity and sales?
3. Equipment selection decisions. Which of several available machines should be purchased?
4. Lease or buy decisions. Should new equipment be leased or purchased?
5. Equipment replacement decisions. Should old equipment be replaced now or later?

Capital budgeting decisions fall into two broad categories—*screening decisions* and *preference decisions.* **Screening decisions** relate to whether a proposed project is acceptable—whether it passes a preset hurdle. For example, a company may have a policy of accepting projects only if they provide a return of at least 20% on the investment. The required rate of return is the minimum rate of return a project must yield to be acceptable. **Preference decisions**, by contrast, relate to selecting from among several acceptable alternatives. To illustrate, a company may be considering several different machines to replace an existing machine on the assembly line. The choice of which machine to purchase is a preference decision.

Cash Flows versus Net Operating Income

The first three capital budgeting methods discussed in the chapter—the payback method, the net present value method, and internal rate of return method—all focus on analyzing the *cash flows* associated with capital investment projects, whereas the simple rate of return method focuses on *incremental net operating income.* To better prepare you to apply the payback, net present value, and internal rate of return methods, we'd like to define the most common types of cash outflows and cash inflows that accompany capital investment projects.

Typical Cash Outflows Most projects have at least three types of cash outflows. First, they often require an immediate cash outflow in the form of an initial investment in equipment, other assets, and installation costs. Any salvage value realized from the sale of old equipment can be recognized as a reduction in the initial investment or as a cash inflow. Second, some projects require a company to expand its working capital. **Working capital** is current assets (e.g., cash, accounts receivable, and inventory) less current liabilities. When a company takes on a new project, the balances in the current asset accounts often increase. For example, opening a new Nordstrom's department store requires additional cash in sales registers and more inventory. These additional working capital needs are treated as part of the initial investment in a project. Third, many projects require periodic outlays for repairs and maintenance and additional operating costs.

Typical Cash Inflows Most projects also have at least three types of cash inflows. First, a project will normally increase revenues or reduce costs. Either way, the amount involved should be treated as a cash inflow for capital budgeting purposes. Notice that from a cash flow standpoint, a reduction in costs is equivalent to an increase in revenues. Second, cash inflows are also frequently realized from selling equipment for its salvage value when a project ends, although the company may actually have to pay to dispose of some low-value or hazardous items. Third, any working capital that was tied up in the project can be released for use elsewhere at the end of the project and should be treated as a cash inflow at that time. Working capital is released, for example, when a company sells off its inventory or collects its accounts receivable.

The Time Value of Money

Beyond defining a capital project's cash outflows and inflows, it is also important to consider when those cash flows occur. For example, if someone offered to give you $1,000 dollars today that you could save toward your eventual retirement or $1,000 dollars a year from now that you could save toward your future retirement, which alternative would you choose? In all likelihood, you would choose to receive $1,000 today because you could invest it and have more than $1,000 dollars a year from now. This simple example illustrates an important capital budgeting concept known as *the time value of money.* The **time value of money** recognizes that a dollar today is worth more than a dollar a year from now if for no other reason than you could put the dollar in a bank today and have more than a dollar a year from now. Because of the time value of money, capital investments that promise earlier cash flows are preferable to those that promise later cash flows.

Although the payback method focuses on cash flows, it does not recognize the time value of money. In other words, it treats a dollar received today as being of equal value to a dollar received at any point in the future. Conversely, the net present value and internal rate of return methods not only focus on cash flows, but they also recognize the time value of those cash flows. These two methods use a technique called *discounting cash flows* to translate the value of future cash flows to their lesser present value. If you are not familiar with the concept of discounting cash flows and the use of present value tables, you should read Appendix 8A: The Concept of Present Value, at the end of the chapter, before studying the net present value and internal rate of return methods.

IN BUSINESS

INVESTING IN A VINEYARD: A CASH FLOWS PERSPECTIVE

When Michael Evans was contemplating moving to Buenos Aires, Argentina, to start a company called the Vines of Mendoza, he had to estimate the project's initial cash outlays and compare them to its future net cash inflows. The initial cash outlays included $2.9 million to buy 1,046 acres of land and to construct a tasting room, $300,000 for a well and irrigation system, $30,000 for underground power lines, and $285,000 for 250,000 grape plants. The annual operating costs included $1,500 per acre for pruning, mowing, and irrigation and $114 per acre for harvesting.

In terms of future cash inflows, Evans hopes to sell his acreage to buyers who want to grow their own grapes and make their own wine while avoiding the work involved with doing so. He intends to charge buyers a one-time fee of $55,000 per planted acre. The buyers would also reimburse Evans for his annual operating costs per acre plus a 25% markup. In a good year, buyers should be able to get 250 cases of wine from their acre of grapevines.

Source: Helen Coster, "Planting Roots," *Forbes*, March 1, 2010, pp. 42–44.

© Digital Stock/Corbis, RF

The Payback Method

LEARNING OBJECTIVE 8–1
Determine the payback period for an investment.

The payback method of evaluating capital budgeting projects focuses on the *payback period.* The **payback period** is the length of time that it takes for a project to recover its initial cost from the net cash inflows that it generates. This period is sometimes referred to as "the time that it takes for an investment to pay for itself." The basic premise of the payback method is that the more quickly the cost of an investment can be recovered, the more desirable is the investment.

The payback period is expressed in years. *When the annual net cash inflow is the same every year,* the following formula can be used to compute the payback period:

$$\text{Payback period} = \frac{\text{Investment required}}{\text{Annual net cash inflow}} \quad (1)$$

To illustrate the payback method, consider the following data:

Example A: York Company needs a new milling machine. The company is considering two machines: machine A and machine B. Machine A costs $15,000, has a useful life of ten years, and will reduce operating costs by $5,000 per year. Machine B costs only $12,000, will also reduce operating costs by $5,000 per year, but has a useful life of only five years.

Required:
Which machine should be purchased according to the payback method?

$$\text{Machine A payback period} = \frac{\$15{,}000}{\$5{,}000} = 3.0 \text{ years}$$

$$\text{Machine B payback period} = \frac{\$12{,}000}{\$5{,}000} = 2.4 \text{ years}$$

According to the payback calculations, York Company should purchase machine B because it has a shorter payback period than machine A.

Evaluation of the Payback Method

The payback method is not a true measure of the profitability of an investment. Rather, it simply tells a manager how many years are required to recover the original investment. Unfortunately, a shorter payback period does not always mean that one investment is more desirable than another.

To illustrate, refer back to Example A on the previous page. Machine B has a shorter payback period than machine A, but it has a useful life of only 5 years rather than 10 years for machine A. Machine B would have to be purchased twice—once immediately and then again after the fifth year—to provide the same service as just one machine A. Under these circumstances, machine A would probably be a better investment than machine B, even though machine B has a shorter payback period. Unfortunately, the payback method ignores all cash flows that occur after the payback period.

A further criticism of the payback method is that it does not consider the time value of money. A cash inflow to be received several years in the future is weighed the same as a cash inflow received right now. To illustrate, assume that for an investment of $8,000 you can purchase either of the two following streams of cash inflows:

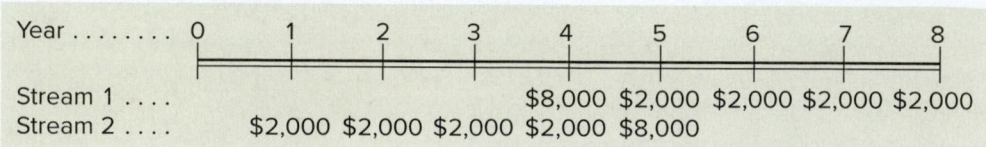

Year	0	1	2	3	4	5	6	7	8
Stream 1					$8,000	$2,000	$2,000	$2,000	$2,000
Stream 2		$2,000	$2,000	$2,000	$2,000	$8,000			

Which stream of cash inflows would you prefer to receive in return for your $8,000 investment? Each stream has a payback period of 4.0 years. Therefore, if payback alone is used to make the decision, the streams would be considered equally desirable. However, from a time value of money perspective, stream 2 is much more desirable than stream 1.

On the other hand, under certain conditions the payback method can be very useful. For one thing, it can help identify which investment proposals are in the "ballpark." That is, it can be used as a screening tool to help answer the question, "Should I consider this proposal further?" If a proposal doesn't provide a payback within some specified period, then there may be no need to consider it further. In addition, the payback period is often important to new companies that are "cash poor." When a company is cash poor, a project with a short payback period but a low rate of return might be preferred over another project with a high rate of return but a long payback period. The reason is that the company may simply need a faster return of its cash investment. And finally, the payback method is sometimes used in industries where products become obsolete very rapidly—such as consumer electronics. Because products may last only a year or two, the payback period on investments must be very short.

IN BUSINESS

THE ECONOMICS OF HYBRID VEHICLES

The table below shows the price premiums (after tax credits) that customers must pay to buy four types of hybrid vehicles. It also depicts the annual gas savings that customers realize by driving a hybrid version of the vehicle instead of a standard model of the same vehicle (assuming the vehicles are driven 15,000 miles per year and gas costs $2.79 a gallon). Dividing the price premium by the annual gas savings yields the payback period when purchasing the hybrid version of the vehicle.

Make and Model	Price Premium	Annual Gas Savings	Payback Period
Ford Escape	$1,364	$438	3.1
Honda Civic	$1,482	$317	4.7
Toyota Camry	$3,763	$310	12.1
Toyota Highlander	$4,372	$388	11.3

The above payback figures highlight the dilemma faced by customers who want to make environmentally friendly purchases, but are constrained by limited financial resources.

Source: Mike Spector, "The Economics of Hybrids," *The Wall Street Journal*, October 29, 2007, pp. R5–R6.

An Extended Example of Payback

As shown by formula (1) above, the payback period is computed by dividing the investment in a project by the project's annual net cash inflows. If new equipment is replacing old equipment, then any salvage value to be received when disposing of the old equipment should be deducted from the cost of the new equipment, and only the *incremental* investment should be used in the payback computation. In addition, any depreciation deducted in arriving at the project's net operating income must be added back to obtain the project's expected annual net cash inflow. To illustrate, consider the following data:

Example B: Goodtime Fun Centers, Inc., operates amusement parks. Some of the vending machines in one of its parks provide very little revenue, so the company is considering removing the machines and installing equipment to dispense soft ice cream. The equipment would cost $80,000 and have an eight-year useful life with no salvage value. Incremental annual revenues and costs associated with the sale of ice cream would be as follows:

Sales	$150,000
Variable expenses	90,000
Contribution margin	60,000
Fixed expenses:	
Salaries	27,000
Maintenance	3,000
Depreciation	10,000
Total fixed expenses	40,000
Net operating income	$ 20,000

The vending machines can be sold for a $5,000 scrap value. The company will not purchase equipment unless it has a payback period of three years or less. Does the ice cream dispenser pass this hurdle?

Exhibit 8–1 computes the payback period for the ice cream dispenser. Several things should be noted. First, depreciation is added back to net operating income to obtain the annual net cash inflow from the new equipment. Depreciation is not a cash outlay; thus, it must be added back to adjust net operating income to a cash basis. Second, the payback computation deducts the salvage value of the old machines from the cost of the new equipment so that only the incremental investment is used in computing the payback period.

Because the proposed equipment has a payback period of less than three years, the company's payback requirement has been met.

Payback and Uneven Cash Flows

When the cash flows associated with an investment project change from year to year, the simple payback formula that we outlined earlier cannot be used. Instead, the payoff period can be computed as follows (assuming that cash inflows occur evenly throughout the year): Payback period = Number of years up to the year in which the investment is paid off + (Unrecovered investment at the beginning of the year in which the investment

EXHIBIT 8–1
Computation of the Payback Period

Step 1: *Compute the annual net cash inflow.* Because the annual net cash inflow is not given, it must be computed before the payback period can be determined:

Net operating income	$20,000
Add: Noncash deduction for depreciation	10,000
Annual net cash inflow	$30,000

Step 2: *Compute the payback period.* Using the annual net cash inflow from above, the payback period can be determined as follows:

Cost of the new equipment	$80,000
Less salvage value of old equipment	5,000
Investment required	$75,000

$$\text{Payback period} = \frac{\text{Investment required}}{\text{Annual net cash inflow}}$$

$$= \frac{\$75{,}000}{\$30{,}000} = 2.5 \text{ years}$$

is paid off ÷ Cash inflow in the period in which the investment is paid off). To illustrate how to apply this formula, consider the following data:

Year	Investment	Cash Inflow
1	$4,000	$1,000
2		$0
3		$2,000
4	$2,000	$1,000
5		$500
6		$3,000
7		$2,000

What is the payback period on this investment? The answer is 5.5 years, computed as follows: 5 + ($1,500 ÷ $3,000) = 5.5 years. In essence, we are tracking the unrecovered investment year by year as shown in Exhibit 8–2. By the middle of the sixth year, sufficient cash inflows will have been realized to recover the entire investment of $6,000 ($4,000 + $2,000).

EXHIBIT 8–2
Payback and Uneven Cash Flows

Year	Investment	Cash Inflow	Unrecovered Investment*
1	$4,000	$1,000	$3,000
2		$0	$3,000
3		$2,000	$1,000
4	$2,000	$1,000	$2,000
5		$500	$1,500
6		$3,000	$0
7		$2,000	$0

*Year X unrecovered investment = Year X-1 unrecovered investment + Year X investment – Year X cash inflow

The Net Present Value Method

LEARNING OBJECTIVE 8–2
Evaluate the acceptability of an investment project using the net present value method.

As previously mentioned, the *net present value method* and the *internal rate of return method* use discounted cash flows to analyze capital budgeting decisions. The net present value method is discussed in this section followed by a discussion of the internal rate of return method.

The Net Present Value Method Illustrated

The net present value method compares the present value of a project's cash inflows to the present value of its cash outflows. The difference between the present value of these cash flows, called the **net present value**, determines whether or not a project is an acceptable investment.

When performing net present value analysis, managers usually make two important assumptions. First, they assume that all cash flows other than the initial investment occur at the end of periods. This assumption is somewhat unrealistic because cash flows typically occur *throughout* a period rather than just at its end; however, it simplifies the computations considerably. Second, managers assume that all cash flows generated by an investment project are immediately reinvested at a rate of return equal to the rate used to discount the future cash flows, also known as the *discount rate*. If this condition is not met, the net present value computations will not be accurate.

To illustrate net present analysis, consider the following data:

Example C: Harper Company is contemplating the purchase of a machine capable of performing some operations that are now performed manually. The machine will cost $50,000, and it will last for five years. At the end of the five-year period, the machine will be sold for its salvage value of $5,000. Use of the machine will reduce labor costs by $18,000 per year. Harper Company requires a minimum pretax return of 18% on all investment projects.[1]

Should the machine be purchased? Harper Company must determine whether a cash investment now of $50,000 can be justified if it will result in an $18,000 reduction in cost in each of the next five years. It may appear that the answer is obvious because the total cost savings is $90,000 ($18,000 per year × 5 years). However, the company can earn an 18% return by investing its money elsewhere. It is not enough that the cost reductions cover just the original cost of the machine; they must also yield a return of at least 18% or the company would be better off investing the money elsewhere.

To determine whether the investment is desirable, the stream of annual $18,000 cost savings and the machine's salvage value of $5,000 should be discounted to their present values and then compared to the cost of the new machine. Exhibit 8–3 demonstrates a four-step approach for performing these computations. First, it calculates the present value of the initial investment by multiplying $50,000 by 1.000, the present value factor for any cash flow that occurs immediately. Second, it calculates the present value of the annual cost savings by multiplying $18,000 by 3.127, the present value factor of a five-year annuity at the discount rate of 18%, to obtain $56,286. Third, it calculates the present value of the machine's salvage value by multiplying $5,000 by 0.437, the present value factor of a single sum to be received in five years at the discount rate of 18%, to obtain $2,185. Finally, cells B8 through D8 are added together to derive the net present value of $8,471.[2]

Exhibit 8–4 demonstrates an alternative approach for performing these same calculations. This alternative approach also begins by calculating the present value of the initial investment by multiplying $50,000 by 1.000, the present value factor for any cash flow that occurs immediately. However, rather than calculating the present value of the annual cost savings using a discount factor of 3.127 from Exhibit 8B–2, it discounts the annual cost savings in Years 1–5 and the machine's salvage value in Year 5 to their present values using the discount factors from Exhibit 8B–1. For example, the $18,000 cost savings in Year 3 is multiplied by the discount factor of 0.609 to derive this future

EXHIBIT 8–3
Net Present Value Analysis Using Discount Factors from Exhibits 8B–1 and 8B–2 in Appendix 8B

	A	B	C	D
1			Year(s)	
2		Now	1-5	5
3	Initial investment	$ (50,000)		
4	Annual cost savings		$ 18,000	
5	Salvage value of the new machine			$ 5,000
6	Total cash flows (a)	$ (50,000)	$ 18,000	$ 5,000
7	Discount factor (18%) (b)	1.000	3.127	0.437
8	Present value of the cash flows (a) × (b)	$ (50,000)	$ 56,286	$ 2,185
9	Net present value (SUM B8:D8)	$ 8,471		
10				
11	Note: The discount factors comes from Exhibits 8B-1 and 8B-2 in Appendix 8B.			

Exhibit 8-3 | Exhibit 8-4 | Exhibit 8-5

[1] For simplicity, we ignore inflation and taxes. The impact of income taxes on capital budgeting decisions is discussed in Appendix 8C.

[2] In this chapter, we use the discount factors from Appendix 8B, which have been rounded to three decimal places, for all present value calculations. However, Microsoft Excel can also be used to calculate discount factors that are not rounded to three decimal places. These unrounded discount factors provide solutions that slightly differ from those derived using the tables in Appendix 8B.

EXHIBIT 8–4
Net Present Value Analysis Using Discount Factors from Exhibit 8B–1 in Appendix 8B

	A	B	C	D	E	F	G
1					Year		
2		Now	1	2	3	4	5
3	Initial investment	$ (50,000)					
4	Annual labor cost savings		$ 18,000	$ 18,000	$ 18,000	$ 18,000	$ 18,000
5	Salvage value of new machine						$ 5,000
6	Total cash flows (a)	$ (50,000)	$ 18,000	$ 18,000	$ 18,000	$ 18,000	$ 23,000
7	Discount factor (18%) (b)	1.000	0.847	0.718	0.609	0.516	0.437
8	Present value of cash flows (a) × (b)	$ (50,000)	$ 15,246	$ 12,924	$ 10,962	$ 9,288	$ 10,051
9	Net present value (SUM B8:G8)	$ 8,471					
10							
11	Note: The discount factors come from Exhibit 8B-1 in Appendix 8B.						
12							

Exhibit 8-3 | Exhibit 8-4 | Exhibit 8-5 | Exhibit 8-6 | Exhibit 8-7 | Exhibit 8

cash flow's present value of $10,962. As another example, the $23,000 of total cash flows in Year 5 is multiplied by the discount factor of 0.437 to determine these future cash flows' present value of $10,051. The present values in cells B8 through G8 are then added together to compute the project's net present value of $8,471.

The methods described in Exhibits 8–3 and 8–4 are mathematically equivalent—they both produced a net present value of $8,471. The only difference between these two exhibits relates to the discounting of the annual labor cost savings. In Exhibit 8–3, the labor cost savings are discounted to their present value using the annuity factor of 3.127, whereas in Exhibit 8–4, these cost savings are discounted using five separate factors that sum to 3.127 (0.847 + 0.718 + 0.609 + 0.516 + 0.437 = 3.127). In other words, the calculations are equivalent.

While you should feel free to use either of these methods when performing net present value calculations, from this point forward we'll be emphasizing the approach used in Exhibit 8–4 for two reasons. First, most managers use an approach similar to Exhibit 8–4 when performing net present value calculations. They use Microsoft Excel to summarize each year's cash flows in a separate column and then they discount each year's cash flows to their present values using the factors shown in Exhibit 8B–1. Second, many students believe that the approach shown in Exhibit 8–4 is easier to understand than competing methods when the net present value computations become increasingly complex.

Once you have computed a net present value using either of the approaches that we just demonstrated, you'll need to interpret your findings. For example, because Harper Company's proposed project has a positive net present value of $8,471, it implies that the company should purchase the new machine. A positive net present value indicates that the project's return exceeds the discount rate. A negative net present value indicates that the project's return is less than the discount rate. Therefore, if the company's minimum required rate of return is used as the discount rate, a project with a positive net present value has a return that exceeds the minimum required rate of return and is acceptable. Conversely, a project with a negative net present value has a return that is less than the minimum required rate of return and is unacceptable. In sum:

If the Net Present Value Is . . .	Then the Project Is . . .
Positive	Acceptable because its return is greater than the required rate of return.
Zero	Acceptable because its return is equal to the required rate of return.
Negative	Not acceptable because its return is less than the required rate of return.

To improve your understanding of the minimum required rate of return, it bears emphasizing that a company's *cost of capital* is usually regarded as its minimum required rate of return. The **cost of capital** is the average rate of return that the company must pay to its long-term creditors and its shareholders for the use of their funds. If a project's rate of return is less than the cost of capital, the company does not earn enough to compensate its creditors and shareholders. Therefore, any project with a rate of return less than the cost of capital should be rejected.

The cost of capital serves as a *screening device.* When the cost of capital is used as the discount rate in net present value analysis, any project with a negative net present value does not cover the company's cost of capital and should be discarded as unacceptable.

Recovery of the Original Investment

The net present value method automatically provides for return of the original investment. Whenever the net present value of a project is positive, the project will recover the original cost of the investment plus sufficient excess cash inflows to compensate the organization for tying up funds in the project. To demonstrate this point, consider the following situation:

Example D: Carver Hospital is considering the purchase of an attachment for its X-ray machine that will cost $3,169. The attachment will be usable for four years, after which time it will have no salvage value. It will increase net cash inflows by $1,000 per year in the X-ray department. The hospital's board of directors requires a rate of return of at least 10% on such investments.

A net present value analysis of the desirability of purchasing the X-ray attachment is presented in Exhibit 8–5. Notice that the attachment has exactly a 10% return on the original investment because the net present value is zero at a 10% discount rate.

Each annual $1,000 cash inflow arising from use of the attachment is made up of two parts. One part represents a recovery of a portion *of* the original $3,169 paid for the attachment, and the other part represents a return *on* this investment. The breakdown of each year's $1,000 cash inflow between recovery *of* investment and return *on* investment is shown in Exhibit 8–6.

The first year's $1,000 cash inflow consists of a return *on* investment of $317 (a 10% return *on* the $3,169 original investment), plus a $683 return *of* that investment. Because the amount of the unrecovered investment decreases each year, the dollar amount of the return on investment also decreases each year. By the end of the fourth year, all $3,169 of the original investment has been recovered.

EXHIBIT 8–5

Carver Hospital—Net Present Value Analysis of X-Ray Attachment

	A	B	C	D	E	F
1				Year		
2		Now	1	2	3	4
3	Initial investment	$ (3,169)				
4	Annual net cash inflow		$ 1,000	$ 1,000	$ 1,000	$ 1,000
5	Total cash flows (a)	$ (3,169)	$ 1,000	$ 1,000	$ 1,000	$ 1,000
6	Discount factor (10%) (b)	1.000	0.909	0.826	0.751	0.683
7	Present value of cash flows (a) × (b)	$ (3,169)	$ 909	$ 826	$ 751	$ 683
8	Net present value (SUM B7:F7)	$ 0				
9						
10	Note: The discount factors come from Exhibit 8B-1 in Appendix 8B.					

Exhibit 8-3 | Exhibit 8-4 | Exhibit 8-5

EXHIBIT 8–6

Carver Hospital—Breakdown of Annual Cash Inflows

	A	B	C	D	E	F
1		(1)	(2)	(3)	(4)	(5)
2	Year	Investment Outstanding during the Year	Cash Inflow	Return on Investment (1) × 10%	Recovery of Investment during the Year (2) − (3)	Unrecovered Investment at the End of the Year (1) − (4)
3	1	$3,169	$1,000	$317	$683	$2,486
4	2	$2,486	$1,000	$249	$751	$1,735
5	3	$1,735	$1,000	$174	$826	$909
6	4	$909	$1,000	$91	$909	$0
7	Total investment recovered				$3,169	

Exhibit 8-3 | Exhibit 8-4 | Exhibit 8-5 | Exhibit 8-6 | Exhibit

IN BUSINESS

COOLING SERVERS NATURALLY

Google consumes more than 2 terawatt hours of electricity per year, which is greater than the annual electricity consumption of 200,000 American homes. A large part of Google's electricity consumption relates to running and cooling its huge number of servers. In an effort to lower its electricity bill, Google invested €200 million to build a server storage facility in the Baltic Sea coastal community of Hamina, Finland. Hamina's low electricity rates coupled with its persistently low ambient air temperatures will lower Google's annual electricity bills considerably. Shortly after Google's facility opened in Hamina, Facebook opened a five-acre data center in Luleå, Sweden, where the average temperature is 35 degrees Fahrenheit.

Source: Sven Grunberg and Niclas Rolander, "For Data Center, Google Goes for the Cold," *The Wall Street Journal*, September 12, 2011, p. B10.

An Extended Example of the Net Present Value Method

Example E provides an extended example of how the net present value method is used to analyze a proposed project. This example helps tie together and reinforce many of the ideas discussed thus far.

Example E: Under a special licensing arrangement, Swinyard Corporation has an opportunity to market a new product for a five-year period. The product would be purchased from the manufacturer, with Swinyard responsible for promotion and distribution costs. The licensing arrangement could be renewed at the end of the five-year period. After careful study, Swinyard estimated the following costs and revenues for the new product:

Cost of equipment needed	$60,000
Working capital needed	$100,000
Overhaul of the equipment in four years	$5,000
Salvage value of the equipment in five years	$10,000
Annual revenues and costs:	
Sales revenues	$200,000
Cost of goods sold	$125,000
Out-of-pocket operating costs (for salaries, advertising, and other direct costs)	$35,000

EXHIBIT 8–7

The Net Present Value Method—An Extended Example

	A	B	C	D	E	F	G
1					Year		
2		Now	1	2	3	4	5
3	Purchase of equipment	$ (60,000)					
4	Investment in working capital	$ (100,000)					
5	Sales		$ 200,000	$ 200,000	$ 200,000	$ 200,000	$ 200,000
6	Cost of goods sold		$ (125,000)	$ (125,000)	$ (125,000)	$ (125,000)	$ (125,000)
7	Out-of-pocket costs for salaries, advertising, etc.		$ (35,000)	$ (35,000)	$ (35,000)	$ (35,000)	$ (35,000)
8	Overhaul of equipment					$ (5,000)	
9	Salvage value of the equipment						$ 10,000
10	Working capital released						$ 100,000
11	Total cash flows (a)	$ (160,000)	$ 40,000	$ 40,000	$ 40,000	$ 35,000	$ 150,000
12	Discount factor (14%) (b)	1.000	0.877	0.769	0.675	0.592	$ 0.519
13	Present value of cash flows (a) × (b)	$ (160,000)	$ 35,080	$ 30,760	$ 27,000	$ 20,720	$ 77,850
14	Net present value (SUM B13:G13)	$ 31,410					
15							
16	Note: The discount factors come from Exhibit 8B-1 in Appendix 8B.						

Exhibit 8-4 Exhibit 8-5 Exhibit 8-6 **Exhibit 8-7** Exhibit 8-8

At the end of the five-year period, if Swinyard decides not to renew the licensing arrangement the working capital would be released for investment elsewhere. Swinyard uses a 14% discount rate. Would you recommend that the new product be introduced?

This example involves a variety of cash inflows and cash outflows. The solution is given in Exhibit 8–7.

Notice how the working capital is handled in this exhibit. It is counted as a cash outflow at the beginning of the project and as a cash inflow when it is released at the end of the project. Also notice how the sales revenues, cost of goods sold, and out-of-pocket costs are handled. **Out-of-pocket costs** are actual cash outlays for salaries, advertising, and other operating expenses.

Because the net present value of the proposal is positive, the new product is acceptable.

IN BUSINESS

ECONOMIC WOES SHRINK CAPITAL BUDGETS

When the health of the economy is uncertain, capital spending declines. Rite Aid CEO Mary Sammons cut her company's capital budget by $50 million due to uncertain economic conditions. PetroHawk Energy responded to a weak economy by slashing its $1.5 billion capital budget by one-third. Estee Lauder tightened its belt by challenging managers to defend what they must have and define what they can give up. YUM! Brands (owner of Pizza Hut, KFC, and Taco Bell) navigated the difficult economy by abandoning projects that "might come true" in favor of a "must have" capital budgeting mentality.

Source: Matthew Boyle, "The Budget Knives Come Out," *BusinessWeek*, October 13, 2008, p. 30.

The Internal Rate of Return Method

LEARNING OBJECTIVE 8–3

Evaluate the acceptability of an investment project using the internal rate of return method.

The **internal rate of return** is the rate of return of an investment project over its useful life. The internal rate of return is computed by finding the discount rate that equates the present value of a project's cash outflows with the present value of its cash inflows. In other words, the internal rate of return is the discount rate that results in a net present value of zero.

The Internal Rate of Return Method Illustrated

To illustrate the internal rate of return method, consider the following data:

Example F: Glendale School District is considering the purchase of a large tractor-pulled lawn mower. At present, the lawn is mowed using a small hand-pushed gas mower. The large, tractor-pulled mower will cost $21,630 and will have a useful life of 5 years. It will have a negligible scrap value, which can be ignored. The tractor-pulled mower would do the job faster than the old mower, resulting in labor savings of $6,000 per year.

To compute the internal rate of return of the new mower, we must find the discount rate that will result in a zero net present value. How do we do this? The simplest and most direct approach *when the net cash inflow is the same every year* is to divide the investment in the project by the expected annual net cash inflow. This computation yields a factor from which the internal rate of return can be determined. The formula is as follows:

$$\text{Factor of the internal rate of return} = \frac{\text{Investment required}}{\text{Annual net cash inflow}} \quad (2)$$

The factor derived from formula (2) is then located in the present value tables to see what rate of return it represents. Using formula (2) and the data for the Glendale School District's proposed project, we get:

$$\frac{\text{Investment required}}{\text{Annual net cash inflow}} = \frac{\$21{,}630}{\$6{,}000} = 3.605$$

Thus, the discount factor that will equate a series of $6,000 cash inflows with a present investment of $21,630 is 3.605. Now we need to find this factor in Exhibit 8B–2 in Appendix 8B to see what rate of return it represents. We should use the 5-period line in Exhibit 8B–2 because the cash flows for the project continue for 5 years. If we scan along the 5-period line, we find that a factor of 3.605 represents a 12% rate of return. Therefore, the internal rate of return of the mower project is 12%. We can verify this by computing the project's net present value using a 12% discount rate as shown in Exhibit 8–8.

Notice that the net present value in Exhibit 8–8 is zero, confirming that the project's internal rate of return equals 12%. However, you'll also notice that the discount factors used in Exhibit 8–8 come from Exhibit 8B–1 in Appendix 8B, whereas the discount factor cited above (3.605) comes from Exhibit 8B–2 in Appendix 8B. Although these approaches to discounting cash flows appear to differ from one another, they are actually mathematically equivalent. To prove this fact, notice that the sum of the discount factors used in Exhibit 8–8 equals 3.605 (0.893 + 0.797 + 0.712 + 0.636 + 0.567 = 3.605). The five discount factors in Exhibit 8–8 are being used to discount five annual cash flows of $6,000 per year to their present value of $21,630, whereas the discount factor of 3.605 discounts the entire five-year annuity stream to its present value of $21,630.

EXHIBIT 8–8

Evaluation of the Mower Using a 12% Discount Rate

	A	B	C	D	E	F	G
1					Year		
2		Now	1	2	3	4	5
3	Initial investment	$ (21,630)					
4	Annual labor cost savings		$ 6,000	$ 6,000	$ 6,000	$ 6,000	$ 6,000
5	Total cash flows (a)	$ (21,630)	$ 6,000	$ 6,000	$ 6,000	$ 6,000	$ 6,000
6	Discount factor (12%) (b)	1.000	0.893	0.797	0.712	0.636	0.567
7	Present value of cash flows (a) × (b)	$ (21,630)	$ 5,358	$ 4,782	$ 4,272	$ 3,816	$ 3,402
8	Net present value (SUM B7:G7)	$ 0					
9							
10	Note: The discount factors come from Exhibit 8B-1 in Appendix 8B.						

Exhibit 8-5 | Exhibit 8-6 | Exhibit 8-7 | Exhibit 8-8

Once the Glendale School District computes the project's internal rate of return of 12%, it would accept or reject the project by comparing this percentage to the school district's minimum required rate of return. If the internal rate of return is equal to or greater than the required rate of return, then the project is acceptable. If the internal rate of return is less than the required rate of return, then the project is rejected. For example, if we assume that Glendale's minimum required rate of return is 15%, then the school district would reject this project because the 12% internal rate of return does not clear the 15% *hurdle rate*.

Comparison of the Net Present Value and Internal Rate of Return Methods

This section compares the net present value and internal rate of return methods in three ways. First, both methods use the cost of capital to screen out undesirable investment projects. When the internal rate of return method is used, the cost of capital is used as the hurdle rate that a project must clear for acceptance. If the internal rate of return of a project is not high enough to clear the cost of capital hurdle, then the project is ordinarily rejected. When the net present value method is used, the cost of capital is the discount rate used to compute the net present value of a proposed project. Any project yielding a negative net present value is rejected unless other factors are significant enough to warrant its acceptance.

Second, the net present value method is often simpler to use than the internal rate of return method, particularly when a project does not have identical cash flows every year. For example, if a project has some salvage value at the end of its life in addition to its annual cash inflows, the internal rate of return method requires a trial-and-error process to find the rate of return that will result in a net present value of zero. While computer software can be used to perform this trial-and-error process in seconds, it is still a little more complex than using spreadsheet software to perform net present value analysis.

Third, the internal rate of return method makes a questionable assumption. Both methods assume that cash flows generated by a project during its useful life are immediately reinvested elsewhere. However, the two methods make different assumptions concerning the rate of return that is earned on those cash flows. The net present value method assumes the rate of return is the discount rate, whereas the internal rate of return method assumes the rate of return earned on cash flows is the internal rate of return on the project. Specifically, if the internal rate of return of the project is high, this assumption may not be realistic. It is generally more realistic to assume that cash inflows can be reinvested at a rate of return equal to the discount rate—particularly if the discount rate is the company's cost of capital or an opportunity rate of return. For example, if the discount rate is the company's cost of capital, this rate of return can be actually realized by paying off the company's creditors and buying back the company's stock with cash flows from the project. In short, when the net present value method and the internal rate of return method do not agree concerning the attractiveness of a project, it is best to go with the net present value method. Of the two methods, it makes the more realistic assumption about the rate of return that can be earned on cash flows from the project.

Expanding the Net Present Value Method

So far, all of our examples have involved an evaluation of a single investment project. In the following section we use the *total-cost approach* to explain how the net present value method can be used to evaluate two alternative projects.

The total-cost approach is the most flexible method for comparing competing projects. To illustrate the mechanics of the approach, consider the following data:

Example G: Harper Ferry Company operates a high-speed passenger ferry service across the Mississippi River. One of its ferryboats is in poor condition. This ferry can be renovated at an immediate cost of $200,000. Further repairs and an overhaul of the motor will be needed three years from now at a cost of $80,000. In all, the ferry will be usable for 5 years if this work is done. At the end of 5 years, the ferry will have to be scrapped at a salvage value of

EXHIBIT 8–9

The Total-Cost Approach to Project Selection

	A	B	C	D	E	F	G
1	Keep the old ferry:				Year		
2		Now	1	2	3	4	5
3	Renovation	$ (200,000)					
4	Annual revenues		$ 400,000	$ 400,000	$ 400,000	$ 400,000	$ 400,000
5	Annual cash operating costs		$ (300,000)	$ (300,000)	$ (300,000)	$ (300,000)	$ (300,000)
6	Repairs in three years				$ (80,000)		
7	Salvage value of old ferry						$ 60,000
8	Total cash flows (a)	$ (200,000)	$ 100,000	$ 100,000	$ 20,000	$ 100,000	$ 160,000
9	Discount factor (14%) (b)	1.000	0.877	0.769	0.675	0.592	0.519
10	Present value of cash flows (a) × (b)	$ (200,000)	$ 87,700	$ 76,900	$ 13,500	$ 59,200	$ 83,040
11	Net present value (SUM B10:G10)	$ 120,340					
12							
13	Buy the new ferry:				Year		
14		Now	1	2	3	4	5
15	Initial investment	$ (360,000)					
16	Salvage value of the old ferry	$ 70,000					
17	Annual revenues		$ 400,000	$ 400,000	$ 400,000	$ 400,000	$ 400,000
18	Annual cash operating costs		$ (210,000)	$ (210,000)	$ (210,000)	$ (210,000)	$ (210,000)
19	Repairs in three years				$ (30,000)		
20	Salvage value of new ferry						$ 60,000
21	Total cash flows (a)	$ (290,000)	$ 190,000	$ 190,000	$ 160,000	$ 190,000	$ 250,000
22	Discount factor (14%) (b)	1.000	0.877	0.769	0.675	0.592	0.519
23	Present value of cash flows (a) × (b)	$ (290,000)	$ 166,630	$ 146,110	$ 108,000	$ 112,480	$ 129,750
24	Net present value (SUM B23:G23)	$ 372,970					
25							
26	Net present value in favor of buying the new ferry (B24-B11)	$ 252,630					
27							
28	Note: The discount factors come from Exhibit 8B-1 in Appendix 8B.						
29							

Exhibit 8-7 Exhibit 8-8 Exhibit 8-9 Exhibit 8-10 Exhibit 8-11

$60,000. The scrap value of the ferry right now is $70,000. It will cost $300,000 each year to operate the ferry, and revenues will total $400,000 annually.

As an alternative, Harper Ferry Company can purchase a new ferryboat at a cost of $360,000. The new ferry will have a life of 5 years, but it will require some repairs costing $30,000 at the end of 3 years. At the end of 5 years, the ferry will have a scrap value of $60,000. It will cost $210,000 each year to operate the ferry, and revenues will total $400,000 annually.

Harper Ferry Company requires a return of at least 14% on all investment projects.

Should the company purchase the new ferry or renovate the old ferry? Exhibit 8–9 shows the solution using the total-cost approach.

Two points should be noted from the exhibit. First, *all* cash inflows and *all* cash outflows are included in the solution under each alternative. No effort has been made to isolate those cash flows that are relevant to the decision and those that are not relevant. The inclusion of all cash flows associated with each alternative gives the approach its name—the *total-cost* approach.

Second, notice that a net present value is computed for each alternative. This is a strength of the total-cost approach because an unlimited number of alternatives can be compared side by side to determine the best option. For example, another alternative for Harper Ferry Company would be to get out of the ferry business entirely. If management desired, the net present value of this alternative could be computed to compare with the alternatives shown in Exhibit 8–9. Still other alternatives might be available to the company. In the case at hand, given only two alternatives, the data indicate that the net present value in favor of buying the new ferry is $252,630.[3]

Least–Cost Decisions

Some decisions do not involve any revenues. For example, a company may be trying to decide whether to buy or lease an executive jet. The choice would be made on the basis of

3 The alternative with the highest net present value is not always the best choice, although it is the best choice in this case. For further discussion, see the section Preference Decisions—The Ranking of Investment Projects.

which alternative—buying or leasing—would be least costly. In situations such as these, where no revenues are involved, the most desirable alternative is the one with the *least total cost* from a present value perspective. Hence, these are known as least-cost decisions. To illustrate a least-cost decision, consider the following data:

Example H: Val-Tek Company is considering replacing an old threading machine with a new threading machine that would substantially reduce annual operating costs. Selected data relating to the old and new machines are presented below:

	Old Machine	New Machine
Purchase cost when new	$200,000	$250,000
Salvage value now	$30,000	—
Annual cash operating costs	$150,000	$90,000
Overhaul needed immediately.	$40,000	—
Salvage value in six years	$0	$50,000
Remaining life	6 years	6 years

Val-Tek Company uses a 10% discount rate.

IN BUSINESS

© Ingram Publishing/SuperStock, RF

HOME CONSTRUCTION GOES GREEN—OR DOES IT?

Many homebuyers like the idea of building environmentally friendly homes until they get the bill. Specpan, an Indianapolis research firm, estimates a "green" home costs 10%–19% more than a comparable conventional home. For example, installing solar-electric glass-faced tiles on a roof costs $15,000 per 100 square feet compared to $1,200 per 100 square feet for standard fiber-cement tiles. Environmentally friendly interior paint costs $35–$42 per gallon compared to $20–$32 per gallon for standard latex paint. To further complicate this least-cost decision, the average homeowner lives in a house only seven years before moving. Within this time frame, many green investments appear to be financially unattractive. Nonetheless, the American Institute of Architects reports that 63% of their clients expressed an interest in renewable flooring materials such as cork and bamboo, up from 53% a year earlier.

Source: June Fletcher, "The Price of Going Green," *The Wall Street Journal*, February 29, 2008, p. W8.

Exhibit 8–10 analyzes the alternatives using the total-cost approach. Because this is a least-cost decision, the present values are negative for both alternatives. However, the present value of the alternative of buying the new machine is $109,440 higher than the other alternative. Therefore, buying the new machine is the less costly alternative.

Uncertain Cash Flows

LEARNING OBJECTIVE 8–4
Evaluate an investment project that has uncertain cash flows.

Thus far, we have assumed that all future cash flows are known with certainty. However, future cash flows are often uncertain or difficult to estimate. A number of techniques are available for handling this complication. Some of these techniques are quite technical—involving computer simulations or advanced mathematical skills—and are beyond the scope of this book. However, we can provide some very useful information to without getting too technical.

An Example

As an example of difficult-to-estimate future cash flows, consider the case of investments in automated equipment. The up-front costs of automated equipment and the tangible

EXHIBIT 8–10

Least-Cost Decision: A Net Present Value Analysis

	A	B	C	D	E	F	G	H
1	Keep the old machine:				Year			
2		Now	1	2	3	4	5	6
3	Overhaul needed now	$ (40,000)						
4	Annual cash operating costs		$ (150,000)	$ (150,000)	$ (150,000)	$ (150,000)	$ (150,000)	$ (150,000)
5	Total cash flows (a)	$ (40,000)	$ (150,000)	$ (150,000)	$ (150,000)	$ (150,000)	$ (150,000)	$ (150,000)
6	Discount factor (10%) (b)	1.000	0.909	0.826	0.751	0.683	0.621	0.564
7	Present value of cash flows (a) × (b)	$ (40,000)	$ (136,350)	$ (123,900)	$ (112,650)	$ (102,450)	$ (93,150)	$ (84,600)
8	Net present value (SUM B7:H7)	$ (693,100)						
9								
10	Buy the new machine:				Year			
11		Now	1	2	3	4	5	6
12	Initial investment	$ (250,000)						
13	Salvage value of the old machine	$ 30,000						
14	Annual cash operating costs		$ (90,000)	$ (90,000)	$ (90,000)	$ (90,000)	$ (90,000)	$ (90,000)
15	Salvage value of new machine							$ 50,000
16	Total cash flows (a)	$ (220,000)	$ (90,000)	$ (90,000)	$ (90,000)	$ (90,000)	$ (90,000)	$ (40,000)
17	Discount factor (10%) (b)	1.000	0.909	0.826	0.751	0.683	0.621	0.564
18	Present value of cash flows (a) × (b)	$ (220,000)	$ (81,810)	$ (74,340)	$ (67,590)	$ (61,470)	$ (55,890)	$ (22,560)
19	Net present value (SUM B18:H18)	$ (583,660)						
20								
21	Net present value in favor of buying the new machine	$ 109,440						
22								
23	Note: The discount factors come from Exhibit 8B-1 in Appendix 8B.							
24								

Exhibit 8-7 Exhibit 8-8 Exhibit 8-9 Exhibit 8-10 Exhibit 8-11 Exhibit 8

benefits, such as reductions in operating costs and waste, tend to be relatively easy to estimate. However, the intangible benefits, such as greater reliability, greater speed, and higher quality, are more difficult to quantify in terms of future cash flows. These intangible benefits certainly impact future cash flows—particularly in terms of increased sales and perhaps higher selling prices—but the cash flow effects are difficult to estimate. What can be done?

A fairly simple procedure can be followed when the intangible benefits are likely to be significant. Suppose, for example, that a company with a 12% discount rate is considering purchasing automated equipment that would have a 10-year useful life. Also suppose that a discounted cash flow analysis of just the tangible costs and benefits shows a negative net present value of $226,000. Clearly, if the intangible benefits are large enough, they could turn this negative net present value into a positive net present value. In this case, the amount of additional cash flow per year from the intangible benefits that would be needed to make the project financially attractive can be computed as follows:

Net present value excluding the intangible benefits (negative)	$(226,000)
Present value factor for an annuity at 12% for 10 periods (from Exhibit 8B–2 in Appendix 8B)	5.650

$$\frac{\text{Negative net present value to be offset, \$226,000}}{\text{Present value factor, 5.650}} = \$40,000$$

Thus, if the intangible benefits of the automated equipment are worth at least $40,000 a year to the company, then the automated equipment should be purchased. If, in the judgment of management, these intangible benefits are not worth $40,000 a year, then the automated equipment should not be purchased.

This technique can be used in other situations in which future cash flows are difficult to estimate. For example, this technique can be used when the salvage value is difficult to estimate. To illustrate, suppose that all of the cash flows from an investment in a supertanker have been estimated—other than its salvage value in 20 years. Using a discount rate of 12%, management has determined that the net present value of all of these cash flows is a negative $1.04 million. This negative net present value would be offset by the salvage value of the supertanker. How large would the salvage value have to be to make this investment attractive?

Net present value excluding salvage value (negative)	$(1,040,000)
Present value factor at 12% for 20 periods (from Exhibit 8B–1 in Appendix 8B)	0.104

$$\frac{\text{Negative net present value to be offset, \$1,040,000}}{\text{Present value factor, 0.104}} = \$10{,}000{,}000$$

Thus, if the salvage value of the tanker in 20 years is at least $10 million, its net present value would be positive and the investment would be made. However, if management believes the salvage value is unlikely to be as large as $10 million, the investment should not be made.

Preference Decisions—The Ranking of Investment Projects

LEARNING OBJECTIVE 8–5
Rank investment projects in order of preference.

Recall that when considering investment opportunities, managers must make two types of decisions—screening decisions and preference decisions. Screening decisions, which come first, pertain to whether or not a proposed investment is acceptable. Preference decisions come *after* screening decisions and attempt to answer the following question: "How do the remaining investment proposals, all of which have been screened and provide an acceptable rate of return, rank in terms of preference? That is, which one(s) would be *best* for the company to accept?"

Sometimes preference decisions are called rationing decisions, or ranking decisions. Limited investment funds must be rationed among many competing alternatives. Hence, the alternatives must be ranked. Either the internal rate of return method or the net present value method can be used in making preference decisions. However, as discussed earlier, if the two methods are in conflict, it is best to use the net present value method, which is more reliable.

Internal Rate of Return Method

When using the internal rate of return method to rank competing investment projects, the preference rule is: *The higher the internal rate of return, the more desirable the project.* An investment project with an internal rate of return of 18% is usually considered preferable to another project that has a return of only 15%. Internal rate of return is widely used to rank projects.

Net Present Value Method

The net present value of one project cannot be directly compared to the net present value of another project unless the initial investments are equal. For example, assume that a company is considering two competing investments, as shown below:

	Investment	
	A	B
Investment required	$(10,000)	$(5,000)
Present value of cash inflows	11,000	6,000
Net present value	$ 1,000	$ 1,000

Although each project has a net present value of $1,000, the projects are not equally desirable if the funds available for investment are limited. The project requiring an investment of only $5,000 is much more desirable than the project requiring an investment of $10,000. This fact can be highlighted by dividing the net present value of the project by the investment required. The result, shown below in equation form, is called the **project profitability index**.

$$\text{Project profitability index} = \frac{\text{Net present value of the project}}{\text{Investment required}} \quad (3)$$

The project profitability indexes for the two investments above would be computed as follows:

	Investment	
	A	B
Net present value (a)	$1,000	$1,000
Investment required (b).	$10,000	$5,000
Project profitability index, (a) ÷ (b).	0.10	0.20

When using the project profitability index to rank competing investments projects, the preference rule is: *The higher the project profitability index, the more desirable the project.*[4] Applying this rule to the two investments above, investment B should be chosen over investment A.

The project profitability index is an application of the techniques for utilizing constrained resources discussed in an earlier chapter. In this case, the constrained resource is the limited funds available for investment, and the project profitability index is similar to the contribution margin per unit of the constrained resource.

A few details should be clarified with respect to the computation of the project profitability index. The "Investment required" refers to any cash outflows that occur at the beginning of the project, reduced by any salvage value recovered from the sale of old equipment. The "Investment required" also includes any investment in working capital that the project may need.

The Simple Rate of Return Method

LEARNING OBJECTIVE 8–6
Compute the simple rate of return for an investment.

The **simple rate of return** method is the final capital budgeting technique discussed in the chapter. This method is also often referred to as the accounting rate of return or the unadjusted rate of return. We will begin by explaining how to compute the simple rate of return followed by a discussion of this method's limitations and its impact on the behavior of investment center managers.

To obtain the simple rate of return, the annual incremental net operating income generated by a project is divided by the initial investment in the project, as shown below.

$$\text{Simple rate of return} = \frac{\text{Annual incremental net operating income}}{\text{Initial investment}} \quad (4)$$

The annual incremental net operating income included in the numerator should be reduced by the depreciation charges that result from making the investment. Furthermore,

[4] Because of the "lumpiness" of projects, the project profitability index ranking may not be perfect. Nevertheless, it is a good starting point. For further details, see the Profitability Analysis Appendix at the end of the book.

the initial investment shown in the denominator should be reduced by any salvage value realized from the sale of old equipment.

Example I: Brigham Tea, Inc., is a processor of low-acid tea. The company is contemplating purchasing equipment for an additional processing line that would increase revenues by $90,000 per year. Incremental cash operating expenses would be $40,000 per year. The equipment would cost $180,000 and have a nine-year life with no salvage value.

To apply the formula for the simple rate of return, we must first determine the annual incremental net operating income from the project:

Annual incremental revenues		$90,000
Annual incremental cash operating expenses	$40,000	
Annual depreciation ($180,000 – $0)/9	20,000	
Annual incremental expenses		60,000
Annual incremental net operating income		$30,000

Given that the annual incremental net operating income from the project is $30,000 and the initial investment is $180,000, the simple rate of return is 16.7% as shown below:

$$\text{Simple rate of return} = \frac{\text{Annual incremental net operating income}}{\text{Initial investment}}$$

$$= \frac{\$30{,}000}{\$180{,}000}$$

$$= 16.7\%$$

Example J: Midwest Farms, Inc., hires people on a part-time basis to sort eggs. The cost of hand sorting is $30,000 per year. The company is investigating an egg-sorting machine that would cost $90,000 and have a 15-year useful life. The machine would have negligible salvage value, and it would cost $10,000 per year to operate and maintain. The egg-sorting equipment currently being used could be sold now for a scrap value of $2,500.

This project is slightly different from the preceding project because it involves cost reductions with no additional revenues. Nevertheless, the annual incremental net operating income can be computed by treating the annual cost savings as if it were incremental revenues as follows:

Annual incremental cost savings		$30,000
Annual incremental cash operating expenses	$10,000	
Annual depreciation ($90,000–$0)/15	6,000	
Annual incremental expenses		16,000
Annual incremental net operating income		$14,000

Thus, even though the new equipment would not generate any additional revenues, it would reduce costs by $14,000 a year. This would have the effect of increasing net operating income by $14,000 a year.

Finally, the salvage value of the old equipment offsets the initial cost of the new equipment as follows:

Cost of the new equipment	$90,000
Less salvage value of the old equipment	2,500
Initial investment	$87,500

Given the annual incremental net operating income of $14,000 and the initial investment of $87,500, the simple rate of return is 16.0% computed as follows:

$$\text{Simple rate of return} = \frac{\text{Annual incremental net operating income}}{\text{Initial investment}}$$

$$= \frac{\$14{,}000}{\$87{,}500}$$

$$= 16.0\%$$

The simple rate of return suffers from two important limitations. First, it focuses on accounting net operating income rather than cash flows. Thus, if a project does not have constant incremental revenues and expenses over its useful life, the simple rate of return will fluctuate from year to year, thereby possibly causing the same project to appear desirable in some years and undesirable in others. Second, the simple rate of return method does not involve discounting cash flows. It considers a dollar received 10 years from now to be as valuable as a dollar received today.

Given these limitations, it is reasonable to wonder why we bothered discussing this method. First of all, in spite of its limitations, some companies use the simple rate of return to evaluate capital investment proposals. Therefore, you should be familiar with this approach so that you can properly critique it in the event that you encounter it in practice. More importantly, you need to understand how the simple rate of return method influences the behavior of investment center managers who are evaluated and rewarded based on their return on investment (ROI).

For example, assume the following three facts. First, assume that you are an investment center manager whose pay raises are based solely on ROI. Second, assume that last year your division had an ROI of 20%. Third, assume that your division has the chance to pursue a capital budgeting project that will have a positive net present value and a simple rate of return of 17%. Given these three assumptions, would you choose to accept this project or reject it? Although the company would want you to accept it because of its positive net present value, you would probably choose to reject it because the simple rate of return of 17% is less than your prior year's ROI of 20%. This basic example illustrates how a project's simple rate of return can influence the decisions made by investment center managers. It also highlights an important challenge faced by organizations, namely designing performance measurement systems that align employee actions with organizational goals.

Postaudit of Investment Projects

After an investment project has been approved and implemented, a *postaudit* should be conducted. A **postaudit** involves checking whether or not expected results are actually realized. This is a key part of the capital budgeting process because it helps keep managers honest in their investment proposals. Any tendency to inflate the benefits or downplay the costs in a proposal should become evident after a few postaudits have been conducted. The postaudit also provides an opportunity to reinforce and possibly expand successful projects and to cut losses on floundering projects.

The same capital budgeting method should be used in the postaudit as was used in the original approval process. That is, if a project was approved on the basis of a net present value analysis, then the same procedure should be used in performing the postaudit. However, the data used in the postaudit analysis should be *actual observed data* rather than estimated data. This gives management an opportunity to make a side-by-side comparison to see how well the project has succeeded. It also helps assure that estimated data received on future proposals will be carefully prepared because the persons submitting the data knows that their estimates will be compared to actual results in the postaudit process. Actual results that are far out of line with original estimates should be carefully reviewed.

IN BUSINESS

© Ruth Peterkin/Shutterstock.com, RF

ROYAL CARIBBEAN CRUISES LAUNCHES *OASIS OF THE SEAS*

Royal Caribbean Cruises invested $1.4 billion to build the *Oasis of the Seas,* a cruise ship that carries 5,400 passengers and stands 20 stories above the sea. The vessel is a third larger than any other cruise ship and contains 21 pools, 24 restaurants, 13 retail shops, and 300-foot water slides. The company hopes the ship's extraordinary amenities will attract large numbers of customers willing to pay premium prices. However, the economic downturn has caused many customers to refrain from spending on lavish vacations.

Source: Mike Esterl, "Huge Cruise Ships Prepare for Launch but Face Uncertain Waters," *The Wall Street Journal,* December 4, 2009, pp. B1–B2.

Summary

The payback method of evaluating capital investment projects focuses on the payback period. The payback period is the length of time that it takes for a project to recover its initial cost from the net cash inflows that it generates. The basic premise of the payback method is that the more quickly the cost of an investment can be recovered, the more desirable is the investment.

Investment decisions should take into account the time value of money because a dollar today is more valuable than a dollar received in the future. The net present value and internal rate of return methods both reflect this fact. In the net present value method, future cash flows are discounted to their present value. The difference between the present value of the cash inflows and the present value of the cash outflows is called a project's net present value. If the net present value of a project is negative, the project is rejected. The discount rate in the net present value method is usually based on a minimum required rate of return such as a company's cost of capital.

The internal rate of return is the rate of return that equates the present value of the cash inflows and the present value of the cash outflows, resulting in a zero net present value. If the internal rate of return is less than a company's minimum required rate of return, the project is rejected.

After rejecting projects whose net present values are negative or whose internal rates of return are less than the minimum required rate of return, more projects may remain than can be supported with available funds. The remaining projects can be ranked using either the project profitability index or internal rate of return. The project profitability index is computed by dividing the net present value of the project by the required initial investment.

The simple rate of return is determined by dividing a project's accounting net operating income by the initial investment in the project. While this method has important limitations, it can influence the decision-making process of investment center managers who are evaluated and rewarded based on their return on investment (ROI).

Review Problem: Comparison of Capital Budgeting Methods

Lamar Company is considering a project that would have a five-year life and require a $2,400,000 investment in equipment. At the end of five years, the project would terminate and the equipment would have no salvage value. The project would provide net operating income each year as follows:

Sales		$3,200,000
Variable expenses		1,800,000
Contribution margin		1,400,000
Fixed expenses:		
Advertising, salaries, and other fixed out-of-pocket costs	$700,000	
Depreciation	300,000	
Total fixed expenses		1,000,000
Net operating income		$ 400,000

The company's discount rate is 12%.

Required:

1. Compute the annual net cash inflow from the project.
2. Compute the project's net present value. Is the project acceptable?
3. Find the project's internal rate of return to the nearest whole percent.
4. Compute the project's payback period.
5. Compute the project's simple rate of return.

Solution to Review Problem

1. The annual net cash inflow can be computed by deducting the cash expenses from sales:

Sales	$3,200,000
Variable expenses	1,800,000
Contribution margin	1,400,000
Advertising, salaries, and other fixed out-of-pocket costs	700,000
Annual net cash inflow	$ 700,000

Or the annual net cash inflow can be computed by adding depreciation back to net operating income:

Net operating income	$400,000
Add: Noncash deduction for depreciation	300,000
Annual net cash inflow	$700,000

2. The net present value is computed as follows:

	A	B	C	D	E	F	G
1					Year		
2		Now	1	2	3	4	5
3	Initial investment	$ (2,400,000)					
4	Sales		$ 3,200,000	$ 3,200,000	$ 3,200,000	$ 3,200,000	$ 3,200,000
5	Variable expenses		$ (1,800,000)	$ (1,800,000)	$ (1,800,000)	$ (1,800,000)	$ (1,800,000)
6	Fixed out-of-pocket costs		$ (700,000)	$ (700,000)	$ (700,000)	$ (700,000)	$ (700,000)
7	Total cash flows (a)	$ (2,400,000)	$ 700,000	$ 700,000	$ 700,000	$ 700,000	$ 700,000
8	Discount factor (12%) (b)	1.000	0.893	0.797	0.712	0.636	0.567
9	Present value of cash flows (a) × (b)	$ (2,400,000)	$ 625,100	$ 557,900	$ 498,400	$ 445,200	$ 396,900
10	Net present value (SUM B9:G9)	$ 123,500					
11							
12	Note: The discount factors comes from Exhibit 8B-1 in Appendix 8B.						

Sheet1 Sheet2 Sheet3

Or, it can also be computed as follows:

	A	B	C
1			Years
2		Now	1-5
3	Initial investment	$ (2,400,000)	
4	Sales		$ 3,200,000
5	Variable expenses		$ (1,800,000)
6	Fixed out-of-pocket costs		$ (700,000)
7	Total cash flows (a)	$ (2,400,000)	$ 700,000
8	Discount factor (12%) (b)	1.000	3.605
9	Present value of the cash flows (a) × (b)	$ (2,400,000)	$2,523,500
10	Net present value (SUM B9:C9)	$123,500	
11			
12	Note: The discount factors comes from Exhibit 8B-2 in Appendix 8B.		

Sheet1 Sheet2 Sheet3

Yes, the project is acceptable because it has a positive net present value.

3. The formula for computing the factor of the internal rate of return is:

$$\text{Factor of the internal rate of return} = \frac{\text{Investment required}}{\text{Annual net cash inflow}}$$

$$= \frac{\$2{,}400{,}000}{\$700{,}000} = 3.429$$

Looking in Exhibit 8B–2 in Appendix 8B at the end of the chapter and scanning along the 5-period line, we find that a factor of 3.429 represents a rate of return of about 14%.

4. The formula for the payback period is:

$$\text{Payback period} = \frac{\text{Investment required}}{\text{Annual net cash flow}}$$

$$= \frac{\$2{,}400{,}000}{\$700{,}000}$$

$$= 3.4 \text{ years}$$

5. The formula for the simple rate of return is:

$$\text{Simple rate of return} = \frac{\text{Annual incremental net operating income}}{\text{Initial investment}}$$

$$= \frac{\$400{,}000}{\$2{,}400{,}000}$$

$$= 16.7\%$$

Glossary

Capital budgeting The process of planning significant investments in projects that have long-term implications such as the purchase of new equipment or the introduction of a new product. (p. 334)

Cost of capital The average rate of return a company must pay to its long-term creditors and shareholders for the use of their funds. (p. 342)

Internal rate of return The discount rate at which the net present value of an investment project is zero; the rate of return of a project over its useful life. (p. 344)

Net present value The difference between the present value of an investment project's cash inflows and the present value of its cash outflows. (p. 339)

Out-of-pocket costs Actual cash outlays for salaries, advertising, repairs, and similar costs. (p. 344)

Payback period The length of time that it takes for a project to fully recover its initial cost out of the net cash inflows that it generates. (p. 336)

Postaudit The follow-up after a project has been approved and implemented to determine whether expected results were actually realized. (p. 353)

Preference decision A decision in which the alternatives must be ranked. (p. 334)

Project profitability index The ratio of the net present value of a project's cash flows to the investment required. (p. 351)

Screening decision A decision as to whether a proposed investment project is acceptable. (p. 334)

Simple rate of return The rate of return computed by dividing a project's annual incremental accounting net operating income by the initial investment required. (p. 351)

Time value of money The concept that a dollar today is worth more than a dollar a year from now. (p. 335)

Working capital Current assets less current liabilities. (p. 335)

Questions

8–1 What is the difference between capital budgeting screening decisions and capital budgeting preference decisions?

8–2 What is meant by the term *time value of money?*

8–3 What is meant by the term *discounting?*

8–4 Why isn't accounting net income used in the net present value and internal rate of return methods of making capital budgeting decisions?

8–5 Why are discounted cash flow methods of making capital budgeting decisions superior to other methods?

8–6 What is net present value? Can it ever be negative? Explain.

8–7 Identify two simplifying assumptions associated with discounted cash flow methods of making capital budgeting decisions.

8–8 If a company has to pay interest of 14% on long-term debt, then its cost of capital is 14%. Do you agree? Explain.

8–9 What is meant by an investment project's internal rate of return? How is the internal rate of return computed?

8–10 Explain how the cost of capital serves as a screening tool when using (*a*) the net present value method and (*b*) the internal rate of return method.

8–11 As the discount rate increases, the present value of a given future cash flow also increases. Do you agree? Explain.

8–12 Refer to Exhibit 8–7. Is the return on this investment proposal exactly 14%, more than 14%, or less than 14%? Explain.

8–13 How is the project profitability index computed, and what does it measure?

8–14 What is meant by the term *payback period?* How is the payback period determined? How can the payback method be useful?

8–15 What is the major criticism of the payback and simple rate of return methods of making capital budgeting decisions?

Multiple-choice questions are available with Connect.

Additional student resources are available with Connect. connect

Applying Excel

LEARNING OBJECTIVES 8–1, 8–3

The Excel worksheet form that follows is to be used to recreate Example E and Exhibit 8–7. Download the workbook containing this form from Connect. *On the website you will also receive instructions about how to use this worksheet form.*

	A	B	C	D	E	F	G
1	Chapter 8: Applying Excel						
2							
3	**Data**						
4	**Example E**						
5	Cost of equipment needed	$60,000					
6	Working capital needed	$100,000					
7	Overhaul of equipment in four years	$5,000					
8	Salvage value of the equipment in five year:	$10,000					
9	Annual revenues and costs:						
10	Sales revenues	$200,000					
11	Cost of goods sold	$125,000					
12	Out-of-pocket operating costs	$35,000					
13	Discount rate	14%					
14							
15	*Enter a formula into each of the cells marked with a ? below*						
16	**Exhibit 8-6**						
17					Years		
18		Now	1	2	3	4	5
19	Purchase of equipment	?					
20	Investment in working capital	?					
21	Sales		?	?	?	?	?
22	Cost of goods sold		?	?	?	?	?
23	Out-of-pocket operating costs		?	?	?	?	?
24	Overhaul of equipment					?	
25	Salvage value of the equipment						?
26	Working capital released						?
27	Total cash flows (a)	?	?	?	?	?	?
28	Discount factor (14%) (b)	?	?	?	?	?	?
29	Present value of cash flows (a) x (b)	?	?	?	?	?	?
30	Net present value	?					
31							
32	*Use the formulas from Appendix 13B:						
33	Present value of $1 = 1/(1+r)^n						
34	Present value of an annuity of $1 = (1/r)*(1-(1/(1+r)^n))						
35	where n is the number of years and r is the discount rate						
36							

Chapter 8 Form / Filled in Chapter 8 Form / Chapter 8 Formulas / Chap

You should proceed to the requirements below only after completing your worksheet. Note that you may get a slightly different net present value from that shown in the text due to the precision of the calculations.

Required:

1. Check your worksheet by changing the discount rate to 10%. The net present value should now be between $56,495 and $56,518—depending on the precision of the calculations. If you do not get an answer in this range, find the errors in your worksheet and correct them.
   Explain why the net present value has increased as a result of reducing the discount rate from 14% to 10%.
2. The company is considering another project involving the purchase of new equipment. Change the data area of your worksheet to match the following:
   a. What is the net present value of the project?

Data	
Example E	
Cost of equipment needed	$120,000
Working capital needed	$80,000
Overhaul of equipment in four years	$40,000
Salvage value of the equipment in five years	$20,000
Annual revenues and costs:	
Sales revenues	$255,000
Cost of goods sold	$160,000
Out-of-pocket operating costs	$50,000
Discount rate	14%

   b. Experiment with changing the discount rate in one percent increments (e.g., 13%, 12%, 15%, etc.). At what interest rate does the net present value turn from negative to positive?

c. The internal rate of return is between what two whole discount rates (e.g., between 10% and 11%, between 11% and 12%, between 12% and 13%, between 13% and 14%, etc.)?

d. Reset the discount rate to 14%. Suppose the salvage value is uncertain. How large would the salvage value have to be to result in a positive net present value?

Additional student resources are available with Connect. connect

The Foundational 15

LEARNING OBJECTIVES 8–1, 8–2, 8–3, 8–5, 8–6

Cardinal Company is considering a five-year project that would require a $2,975,000 investment in equipment with a useful life of five years and no salvage value. The company's discount rate is 14%. The project would provide net operating income in each of five years as follows:

Sales		$2,735,000
Variable expenses		1,000,000
Contribution margin		1,735,000
Fixed expenses:		
Advertising, salaries, and other fixed out-of-pocket costs	$735,000	
Depreciation	595,000	
Total fixed expenses		1,330,000
Net operating income		$ 405,000

Required:

(Answer each question by referring to the original data unless instructed otherwise.)

1. Which item(s) in the income statement shown above will not affect cash flows?
2. What are the project's annual net cash inflows? Using the correct discount factor from Exhibit 8B–2 in Appendix 8B, what is the present value of the project's annual net cash inflows?
3. Using the format shown in Exhibit 8–7, what is the project's net present value?
4. Does your answer to requirement 2 differ from the present value of the annual net cash inflows that you computed in requirement 3? Why?
5. What is the project profitability index for this project? (Round your answer to the nearest whole percent.)
6. What is the project's internal rate of return to the nearest whole percent?
7. What is the project's payback period?
8. What is the project's simple rate of return for each of the five years?
9. If the company's discount rate was 16% instead of 14%, would you expect the project's net present value to be higher than, lower than, or the same as your answer to requirement 4? No computations are necessary
10. If the equipment had a salvage value of $300,000 at the end of five years, would you expect the project's payback period to be higher than, lower than, or the same as your answer to requirement 7? No computations are necessary.
11. If the equipment had a salvage value of $300,000 at the end of five years, would you expect the project's net present value to be higher than, lower than, or the same as your answer to requirement 3? No computations are necessary.
12. If the equipment had a salvage value of $300,000 at the end of five years, would you expect the project's simple rate of return to be higher than, lower than, or the same as your answer to requirement 8? No computations are necessary.
13. Assume a postaudit showed that all estimates (including total sales) were exactly correct except for the variable expense ratio, which actually turned out to be 45%. What was the project's actual net present value?
14. Assume a postaudit showed that all estimates (including total sales) were exactly correct except for the variable expense ratio, which actually turned out to be 45%. What was the project's actual payback period?
15. Assume a postaudit showed that all estimates (including total sales) were exactly correct except for the variable expense ratio, which actually turned out to be 45%. What was the project's actual simple rate of return?

Exercises

connect Additional student resources are available with Connect.

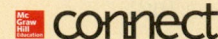

EXERCISE 8–1 Payback Method [LO 8–1]

The management of Unter Corporation, an architectural design firm, is considering an investment with the following cash flows:

Year	Investment	Cash Inflow
1	$15,000	$1,000
2	$8,000	$2,000
3		$2,500
4		$4,000
5		$5,000
6		$6,000
7		$5,000
8		$4,000
9		$3,000
10		$2,000

Required:

1. Determine the payback period of the investment.
2. Would the payback period be affected if the cash inflow in the last year were several times as large?

EXERCISE 8–2 Net Present Value Method [LO 8–2]

The management of Kunkel Company is considering the purchase of a $27,000 machine that would reduce operating costs by $7,000 per year. At the end of the machine's five-year useful life, it will have zero scrap value. The company's required rate of return is 12%.

Required:

1. Determine the net present value of the investment in the machine.
2. What is the difference between the total, undiscounted cash inflows and cash outflows over the entire life of the machine?

EXERCISE 8–3 Internal Rate of Return [LO 8–3]

Wendell's Donut Shoppe is investigating the purchase of a new $18,600 donut-making machine. The new machine would permit the company to reduce the amount of part-time help needed, at a cost savings of $3,800 per year. In addition, the new machine would allow the company to produce one new style of donut, resulting in the sale of 1,000 dozen more donuts each year. The company realizes a contribution margin of $1.20 per dozen donuts sold. The new machine would have a six-year useful life.

Required:

1. What would be the total annual cash inflows associated with the new machine for capital budgeting purposes?
2. Find the internal rate of return promised by the new machine to the nearest whole percent.
3. In addition to the data given previously, assume that the machine will have a $9,125 salvage value at the end of six years. Under these conditions, compute the internal rate of return to the nearest whole percent. (***Hint:*** You may find it helpful to use the net present value approach; find the discount rate that will cause the net present value to be closest to zero.)

EXERCISE 8–4 Uncertain Future Cash Flows [LO 8–4]

Lukow Products is investigating the purchase of a piece of automated equipment that will save $400,000 each year in direct labor and inventory carrying costs. This equipment costs $2,500,000 and is expected to have a 15-year useful life with no salvage value. The company's required rate of return is 20% on all equipment purchases. Management anticipates that this equipment will provide intangible benefits such as greater flexibility and higher-quality output that will result in additional future cash inflows.

Required:
What dollar value per year would these intangible benefits have to have to make the equipment an acceptable investment?

EXERCISE 8–5 Preference Ranking [LO 8–5]
Information on four investment proposals is given below:

	Investment Proposal			
	A	B	C	D
Investment required	$(90,000)	$(100,000)	$(70,000)	$(120,000)
Present value of cash inflows	126,000	138,000	105,000	160,000
Net present value	$ 36,000	$ 38,000	$ 35,000	$ 40,000
Life of the project	5 years	7 years	6 years	6 years

Required:
1. Compute the project profitability index for each investment proposal.
2. Rank the proposals in terms of preference.

EXERCISE 8–6 Simple Rate of Return Method [LO 8–6]
The management of Ballard MicroBrew is considering the purchase of an automated bottling machine for $120,000. The machine would replace an old piece of equipment that costs $30,000 per year to operate. The new machine would cost $12,000 per year to operate. The old machine currently in use could be sold now for a scrap value of $40,000. The new machine would have a useful life of 10 years with no salvage value.

Required:
Compute the simple rate of return on the new automated bottling machine.

EXERCISE 8–7 Net Present Value Analysis of Two Alternatives [LO 8–2]
Perit Industries has $100,000 to invest. The company is trying to decide between two alternative uses of the funds. The alternatives are:

	Project A	Project B
Cost of equipment required	$100,000	$0
Working capital investment required	$0	$100,000
Annual cash inflows	$21,000	$16,000
Salvage value of equipment in six years	$8,000	$0
Life of the project 6 years	6 years	6 years

The working capital needed for project B will be released at the end of six years for investment elsewhere. Perit Industries' discount rate is 14%.

Required:
Which investment alternative (if either) would you recommend that the company accept? Show all computations using the net present value format. Prepare separate computations for each project.

EXERCISE 8–8 Payback Period and Simple Rate of Return [LO 8–1, LO 8–6]

Nick's Novelties, Inc., is considering the purchase of new electronic games to place in its amusement houses. The games would cost a total of $300,000, have an eight-year useful life, and have a total salvage value of $20,000. The company estimates that annual revenues and expenses associated with the games would be as follows:

Revenues		$200,000
Less operating expenses:		
Commissions to amusement houses	$100,000	
Insurance	7,000	
Depreciation	35,000	
Maintenance	18,000	160,000
Net operating income		$ 40,000

Required:

1. Assume that Nick's Novelties, Inc., will not purchase new games unless they provide a payback period of five years or less. Would the company purchase the new games?
2. Compute the simple rate of return promised by the games. If the company requires a simple rate of return of at least 12%, will the games be purchased?

EXERCISE 8–9 Net Present Value Analysis and Simple Rate of Return [LO 8–2, LO 8–6]

Derrick Iverson is a divisional manager for Holston Company. His annual pay raises are largely determined by his division's return on investment (ROI), which has been above 20% each of the last three years. Derrick is considering a capital budgeting project that would require a $3,000,000 investment in equipment with a useful life of five years and no salvage value. Holston Company's discount rate is 15%. The project would provide net operating income each year for five years as follows:

Sales		$2,500,000
Variable expenses		1,000,000
Contribution margin		1,500,000
Fixed expenses:		
Advertising, salaries, and other fixed out-of-pocket costs	$600,000	
Depreciation	600,000	
Total fixed expenses		1,200,000
Net operating income		$ 300,000

Required:

1. Compute the project's net present value.
2. Compute the project's simple rate of return.
3. Would the company want Derrick to pursue this investment opportunity? Would Derrick be inclined to pursue this investment opportunity? Explain.

EXERCISE 8–10 Basic Net Present Value Analysis [LO 8–2]

Kathy Myers frequently purchases stocks and bonds, but she is uncertain how to determine the rate of return that she is earning. For example, three years ago she paid $13,000 for 200 shares of Malti Company's common stock. She received a $420 cash dividend on the stock at the end of each year for three years. At the end of three years, she sold the stock for $16,000. Kathy would like to earn a return of at least 14% on all of her investments. She is not sure whether the Malti Company stock provided a 14% return and would like some help with the necessary computations.

Required:

Using the net present value method, determine whether or not the Malti Company stock provided a 14% return. Round all computations to the nearest whole dollar.

EXERCISE 8–11 Preference Ranking of Investment Projects [LO 8–5]

Oxford Company has limited funds available for investment and must ration the funds among four competing projects. Selected information on the four projects follows:

Project	Investment Required	Net Present Value	Life of the Project (years)	Internal Rate of Return (percent)
A	$160,000	$44,323	7	18%
B	$135,000	$42,000	12	16%
C	$100,000	$35,035	7	20%
D	$175,000	$38,136	3	22%

The net present values above have been computed using a 10% discount rate.

The company wants your assistance in determining which project to accept first, second, and so forth.

Required:

1. Compute the project profitability index for each project.
2. In order of preference, rank the four projects in terms of:
   a. Net present value.
   b. Project profitability index.
   c. Internal rate of return.
3. Which ranking do you prefer? Why?

EXERCISE 8–12 Uncertain Cash Flows [LO 8–4]

The Cambro Foundation, a nonprofit organization, is planning to invest $104,950 in a project that will last for three years. The project will produce net cash inflows as follows:

Year 1	$30,000
Year 2	$40,000
Year 3	?

Required:

Assuming that the project will yield exactly a 12% rate of return, what is the expected net cash inflow for Year 3?

EXERCISE 8–13 Basic Payback Period and Simple Rate of Return Computations [LO 8–1, LO 8–6]

A piece of laborsaving equipment has just come onto the market that Mitsui Electronics, Ltd., could use to reduce costs in one of its plants in Japan. Relevant data relating to the equipment follow:

Purchase cost of the equipment	$432,000
Annual cost savings that will be provided by the equipment	$90,000
Life of the equipment	12 years

Required:

1. Compute the payback period for the equipment. If the company requires a payback period of four years or less, would the equipment be purchased?
2. Compute the simple rate of return on the equipment. Use straight-line depreciation based on the equipment's useful life. Would the equipment be purchased if the company's required rate of return is 14%?

EXERCISE 8–14 Comparison of Projects Using Net Present Value [LO 8–2]

Labeau Products, Ltd., of Perth, Australia, has $35,000 to invest. The company is trying to decide between two alternative uses for the funds as follows:

	Invest in Project X	Invest in Project Y
Investment required	$35,000	$35,000
Annual cash inflows	$12,000	$90,000
Single cash inflow at the end of 6 years		$90,000
Life of the project	6 years	6 years

The company's discount rate is 18%.

Required:

Which alternative would you recommend that the company accept? Show all computations using the net present value approach. Prepare separate computations for each project.

EXERCISE 8–15 Internal Rate of Return and Net Present Value [LO 8–2, LO 8–3]

Henrie's Drapery Service is investigating the purchase of a new machine for cleaning and blocking drapes. The machine would cost $137,280, including freight and installation. Henrie's has estimated that the new machine would increase the company's cash inflows, net of expenses, by $40,000 per year. The machine would have a five-year useful life and no salvage value.

Required:

1. Compute the machine's internal rate of return to the nearest whole percent.
2. Compute the machine's net present value. Use a discount rate of 14%. Why do you have a zero net present value?
3. Suppose that the new machine would increase the company's annual cash inflows, net of expenses, by only $37,150 per year. Under these conditions, compute the internal rate of return to the nearest whole percent.

Problems

connect Additional student resources are available with Connect.

PROBLEM 8–16 Basic Net Present Value Analysis [LO 8–2]

Windhoek Mines, Ltd., of Namibia, is contemplating the purchase of equipment to exploit a mineral deposit on land to which the company has mineral rights. An engineering and cost analysis has been made, and it is expected that the following cash flows would be associated with opening and operating a mine in the area:

Cost of new equipment and timbers	$275,000
Working capital required	$100,000
Annual net cash receipts	$120,000*
Cost to construct new roads in three years	$40,000
Salvage value of equipment in four years	$65,000

*Receipts from sales of ore, less out-of-pocket costs for salaries, utilities, insurance, and so forth.

The mineral deposit would be exhausted after four years of mining. At that point, the working capital would be released for reinvestment elsewhere. The company's required rate of return is 20%.

Required:

Determine the net present value of the proposed mining project. Should the project be accepted? Explain.

PROBLEM 8–17 Net Present Value Analysis; Internal Rate of Return; Simple Rate of Return [LO 8–2, LO 8–3, LO 8–6]

Casey Nelson is a divisional manager for Pigeon Company. His annual pay raises are largely determined by his division's return on investment (ROI), which has been above 20% each of the last three years. Casey is considering a capital budgeting project that would require a $3,500,000 investment in equipment with a useful life of five years and no salvage value. Pigeon Company's discount rate is 16%. The project would provide net operating income each year for five years as follows:

Sales		$3,400,000
Variable expenses		1,600,000
Contribution margin		1,800,000
Fixed expenses:		
Advertising, salaries, and other fixed out-of-pocket costs	$700,000	
Depreciation	700,000	
Total fixed expenses		1,400,000
Net operating income		$ 400,000

Required:

1. What is the project's net present value?
2. What is the project's internal rate of return to the nearest whole percent?
3. What is the project's simple rate of return?
4. Would the company want Casey to pursue this investment opportunity? Would Casey be inclined to pursue this investment opportunity? Explain.

PROBLEM 8–18 Net Present Value Analysis [LO 8–2]

Oakmont Company has an opportunity to manufacture and sell a new product for a four-year period. The company's discount rate is 15%. After careful study, Oakmont estimated the following costs and revenues for the new product:

Cost of equipment needed	$130,000
Working capital needed	$60,000
Overhaul of the equipment in two years	$8,000
Salvage value of the equipment in four years	$12,000
Annual revenues and costs:	
Sales revenues	$250,000
Variable expenses	$120,000
Fixed out-of-pocket operating costs	$70,000

When the project concludes in four years the working capital will be released for investment elsewhere within the company.

Required:

Calculate the net present value of this investment opportunity.

PROBLEM 8–19 Simple Rate of Return; Payback [LO 8–1, LO 8–6]

Paul Swanson has an opportunity to acquire a franchise from The Yogurt Place, Inc., to dispense frozen yogurt products under The Yogurt Place name. Mr. Swanson has assembled the following information relating to the franchise:

a. A suitable location in a large shopping mall can be rented for $3,500 per month.
b. Remodeling and necessary equipment would cost $270,000. The equipment would have a 15-year life and an $18,000 salvage value. Straight-line depreciation would be used, and the salvage value would be considered in computing depreciation.
c. Based on similar outlets elsewhere, Mr. Swanson estimates that sales would total $300,000 per year. Ingredients would cost 20% of sales.
d. Operating costs would include $70,000 per year for salaries, $3,500 per year for insurance, and $27,000 per year for utilities. In addition, Mr. Swanson would have to pay a commission to The Yogurt Place, Inc., of 12.5% of sales.

Required:

1. Prepare a contribution format income statement that shows the expected net operating income each year from the franchise outlet.

2. Compute the simple rate of return promised by the outlet. If Mr. Swanson requires a simple rate of return of at least 12%, should he acquire the franchise?
3. Compute the payback period on the outlet. If Mr. Swanson wants a payback of four years or less, will he acquire the franchise?

PROBLEM 8–20 Net Present Value Analysis; Uncertain Cash Flows [LO 8–2, LO 8–4]

"I'm not sure we should lay out $250,000 for that automated welding machine," said Jim Alder, president of the Superior Equipment Company. "That's a lot of money, and it would cost us $80,000 for software and installation, and another $3,000 every month just to maintain the thing. In addition, the manufacturer admits that it would cost $45,000 more at the end of three years to replace worn-out parts."

"I admit it's a lot of money," said Franci Rogers, the controller. "But you know the turnover problem we've had with the welding crew. This machine would replace six welders at a cost savings of $108,000 per year. And we would save another $6,500 per year in reduced material waste. When you figure that the automated welder would last for six years, I'm sure the return would be greater than our 16% required rate of return."

"I'm still not convinced," countered Mr. Alder. "We can only get $12,000 scrap value out of our old welding equipment if we sell it now, and in six years the new machine will only be worth $20,000 for parts. But have your people work up the figures and we'll talk about them at the executive committee meeting tomorrow."

Required:

1. Compute the annual net cost savings promised by the automated welding machine.
2. Using the data from requirement 1 and other data from the problem, compute the automated welding machine's net present value. Would you recommend purchasing the automated welding machine? Explain.
3. Assume that management can identify several intangible benefits associated with the automated welding machine, including greater flexibility in shifting from one type of product to another, improved quality of output, and faster delivery as a result of reduced throughput time. What dollar value per year would management have to attach to these intangible benefits in order to make the new welding machine an acceptable investment?

PROBLEM 8–21 Preference Ranking of Investment Projects [LO 8–5]

The management of Revco Products is exploring four different investment opportunities. Information on the four projects under study follows:

	Project Number			
	1	2	3	4
Investment required	$(270,000)	$(450,000)	$(360,000)	$(480,000)
Present value of cash inflows at a 10% discount rate	336,140	522,970	433,400	567,270
Net present value	$ 66,140	$ 72,970	$ 73,400	$ 87,270
Life of the project	6 years	3 years	12 years	6 years
Internal rate of return	18%	19%	14%	16%

Because the company's required rate of return is 10%, a 10% discount rate has been used in the present value computations above. Limited funds are available for investment, so the company can't accept all of the available projects.

Required:

1. Compute the project profitability index for each investment project.
2. Rank the four projects according to preference, in terms of:
   a. Net present value
   b. Project profitability index
   c. Internal rate of return
3. Which ranking do you prefer? Why?

PROBLEM 8–22 Basic Net Present Value Analysis [LO 8–2]

The Sweetwater Candy Company would like to buy a new machine that would automatically "dip" chocolates. The dipping operation is currently done largely by hand. The machine the company is considering costs $120,000. The manufacturer estimates that the machine would be usable for five years but would require the replacement of several key parts at the end of the third year. These parts would cost $9,000, including installation. After five years, the machine could be sold for $7,500.

The company estimates that the cost to operate the machine will be $7,000 per year. The present method of dipping chocolates costs $30,000 per year. In addition to reducing costs, the new machine will increase production by 6,000 boxes of chocolates per year. The company realizes a contribution margin of $1.50 per box. A 20% rate of return is required on all investments.

Required:

1. What are the annual net cash inflows that will be provided by the new dipping machine?
2. Compute the new machine's net present value. Round all dollar amounts to the nearest whole dollar.

PROBLEM 8–23 Comprehensive Problem [LO 8–1, LO 8–2, LO 8–3, LO 8–5, LO 8–6]

Lou Barlow, a divisional manager for Sage Company, has an opportunity to manufacture and sell one of two new products for a five-year period. His annual pay raises are determined by his division's return on investment (ROI), which has exceeded 18% each of the last three years. He has computed the cost and revenue estimates for each product as follows:

	Product A	Product B
Initial investment:		
Cost of equipment (zero salvage value)	$170,000	$380,000
Annual revenues and costs:		
Sales revenues	$250,000	$350,000
Variable expenses	$120,000	$170,000
Depreciation expense	$34,000	$76,000
Fixed out-of-pocket operating costs	$70,000	$50,000

The company's discount rate is 16%.

Required:

1. Calculate the payback period for each product.
2. Calculate the net present value for each product.
3. Calculate the internal rate of return for each product.
4. Calculate the project profitability index for each product.
5. Calculate the simple rate of return for each product.
6. Which of the two products should Lou's division pursue? Why?

PROBLEM 8–24 Simple Rate of Return; Payback; Internal Rate of Return [LO 8–1, LO 8–3, LO 8–6]

The Elberta Fruit Farm of Ontario has always hired transient workers to pick its annual cherry crop. Francie Wright, the farm manager, has just received information on a cherry picking machine that is being purchased by many fruit farms. The machine is a motorized device that shakes the cherry tree, causing the cherries to fall onto plastic tarps that funnel the cherries into bins. Ms. Wright has gathered the following information to decide whether a cherry picker would be a profitable investment for the Elberta Fruit Farm:

a. Currently, the farm is paying an average of $40,000 per year to transient workers to pick the cherries.
b. The cherry picker would cost $94,500, and it would have an estimated 12-year useful life. The farm uses straight-line depreciation on all assets and considers salvage value in computing depreciation deductions. The estimated salvage value of the cherry picker is $4,500.
c. Annual out-of-pocket costs associated with the cherry picker would be: cost of an operator and an assistant, $14,000; insurance, $200; fuel, $1,800; and a maintenance contract, $3,000.

Required:

1. Determine the annual savings in cash operating costs that would be realized if the cherry picker were purchased.
2. Compute the simple rate of return expected from the cherry picker. Would the cherry picker be purchased if Elberta Fruit Farm's required rate of return is 16%?
3. Compute the payback period on the cherry picker. The Elberta Fruit Farm will not purchase equipment unless it has a payback period of five years or less. Would the cherry picker be purchased?
4. Compute (to the nearest whole percent) the internal rate of return promised by the cherry picker. Based on this computation, does it appear that the simple rate of return is an accurate guide in investment decisions?

PROBLEM 8–25 Net Present Value Analysis of a Lease or Buy Decision [LO 8–2]

The Riteway Ad Agency provides cars for its sales staff. In the past, the company has always purchased its cars from a dealer and then sold the cars after three years of use. The company's present fleet of cars is three years old and will be sold very shortly. To provide a replacement fleet, the company is considering two alternatives:

Annual cost of servicing, taxes, and licensing	$3,000
Repairs, first year	$1,500
Repairs, second year	$4,000
Repairs, third year	$6,000

Purchase alternative: The company can purchase the cars, as in the past, and sell the cars after three years of use. Ten cars will be needed, which can be purchased at a discounted price of $17,000 each. If this alternative is accepted, the following costs will be incurred on the fleet as a whole:

At the end of three years, the fleet could be sold for one-half of the original purchase price.

Lease alternative: The company can lease the cars under a three-year lease contract. The lease cost would be $55,000 per year (the first payment due at the end of Year 1). As part of this lease cost, the owner would provide all servicing and repairs, license the cars, and pay all the taxes. Riteway would be required to make a $10,000 security deposit at the beginning of the lease period, which would be refunded when the cars were returned to the owner at the end of the lease contract.

Riteway Ad Agency's required rate of return is 18%.

Required:

1. Use the total-cost approach to determine the present value of the cash flows associated with each alternative. Round all dollar amounts to the nearest whole dollar.
2. Which alternative should the company accept?

PROBLEM 8–26 Simple Rate of Return; Payback [LO 8–1, LO 8–6]

Sharkey's Fun Center contains a number of electronic games as well as a miniature golf course and various rides located outside the building. Paul Sharkey, the owner, would like to construct a water slide on one portion of his property. Mr. Sharkey has gathered the following information about the slide:

a. Water slide equipment could be purchased and installed at a cost of $330,000. According to the manufacturer, the slide would be usable for 12 years after which it would have no salvage value.
b. Mr. Sharkey would use straight-line depreciation on the slide equipment.
c. To make room for the water slide, several rides would be dismantled and sold. These rides are fully depreciated, but they could be sold for $60,000 to an amusement park in a nearby city.
d. Mr. Sharkey has concluded that about 50,000 more people would use the water slide each year than have been using the rides. The admission price would be $3.60 per person (the same price that the Fun Center has been charging for the old rides).

e. Based on experience at other water slides, Mr. Sharkey estimates that annual incremental operating expenses for the slide would be: salaries, $85,000; insurance, $4,200; utilities, $13,000; and maintenance, $9,800.

Required:

1. Prepare an income statement showing the expected net operating income each year from the water slide.
2. Compute the simple rate of return expected from the water slide. Based on this computation, would the water slide be constructed if Mr. Sharkey requires a simple rate of return of at least 14% on all investments?
3. Compute the payback period for the water slide. If Mr. Sharkey accepts any project with a payback period of five years or less, would the water slide be constructed?

PROBLEM 8–27 Net Present Value Analysis [LO 8–2]

In five years, Kent Duncan will retire. He is exploring the possibility of opening a self-service car wash. The car wash could be managed in the free time he has available from his regular occupation, and it could be closed easily when he retires. After careful study, Mr. Duncan has determined the following:

a. A building in which a car wash could be installed is available under a five-year lease at a cost of $1,700 per month.
b. Purchase and installation costs of equipment would total $200,000. In five years the equipment could be sold for about 10% of its original cost.
c. An investment of an additional $2,000 would be required to cover working capital needs for cleaning supplies, change funds, and so forth. After five years, this working capital would be released for investment elsewhere.
d. Both a wash and a vacuum service would be offered with a wash costing $2.00 and the vacuum costing $1.00 per use.
e. The only variable costs associated with the operation would be 20 cents per wash for water and 10 cents per use of the vacuum for electricity.
f. In addition to rent, monthly costs of operation would be: cleaning, $450; insurance, $75; and maintenance, $500.
g. Gross receipts from the wash would be about $1,350 per week. According to the experience of other car washes, 60% of the customers using the wash would also use the vacuum.
Mr. Duncan will not open the car wash unless it provides at least a 10% return.

Required:

1. Assuming that the car wash will be open 52 weeks a year, compute the expected annual net cash receipts (gross cash receipts less cash disbursements) from its operation. (Do not include the cost of the equipment, the working capital, or the salvage value in these computations.)
2. Would you advise Mr. Duncan to open the car wash? Show computations using the net present value method of investment analysis. Round all dollar figures to the nearest whole dollar.

PROBLEM 8–28 Net Present Value [LO 8–2]

Bilboa Freightlines, S.A., of Panama, has a small truck that it uses for intracity deliveries. The truck is worn out and must be either overhauled or replaced with a new truck. The company has assembled the following information:

	Present Truck	New Truck
Purchase cost new	$21,000	$30,000
Remaining book value	$11,500	
Overhaul needed now	$7,000	
Annual cash operating costs	$10,000	$6,500
Salvage value-now	$9,000	
Salvage value-five years from now	$1,000	$4,000

If the company keeps and overhauls its present delivery truck, then the truck will be usable for five more years. If a new truck is purchased, it will be used for five years, after which it will be traded in on another truck. The new truck would be diesel-operated, resulting in a substantial reduction in annual operating costs, as shown above.

The company computes depreciation on a straight-line basis. All investment projects are evaluated using a 16% discount rate.

Required:

Should Bilboa Freightlines keep the old truck or purchase the new one? Use the total-cost approach to net present value in making your decision. Round to the nearest whole dollar.

PROBLEM 8–29 Net Present Value Analysis of Securities [LO 8–2]

Linda Clark received $175,000 from her mother's estate. She placed the funds into the hands of a broker, who purchased the following securities on Linda's behalf:

a. Common stock was purchased at a cost of $95,000. The stock paid no dividends, but it was sold for $160,000 at the end of three years.

b. Preferred stock was purchased at its par value of $30,000. The stock paid a 6% dividend (based on par value) each year for three years. At the end of three years, the stock was sold for $27,000.

c. Bonds were purchased at a cost of $50,000. The bonds paid annual interest of $6,000. After three years, the bonds were sold for $52,700.

The securities were all sold at the end of three years so that Linda would have funds available to open a new business venture. The broker stated that the investments had earned more than a 16% return, and he gave Linda the following computations to support his statement:

Common stock:	
Gain on sale ($160,000 − $95,000)	$65,000
Preferred stock:	
Dividends paid (6% × $30,000 × 3 years)	5,400
Loss on sale ($27,000 − $30,000)	(3,000)
Bonds:	
Interest paid ($6,000 × 3 years)	18,000
Gain on sale ($52,700 − $50,000)	2,700
Net gain on all investments	$88,100

$$\frac{\$88{,}100 \div 3 \text{ years}}{\$172{,}000} = 16.8\%$$

Required:

1. Using a 16% discount rate, compute the net present value of each of the three investments. On which investment(s) did Linda earn a 16% rate of return? (Round computations to the nearest whole dollar.)
2. Considering all three investments together, did Linda earn a 16% rate of return? Explain.
3. Linda wants to use the $239,700 proceeds ($160,000 + $27,000 + $52,700 = $239,700) from sale of the securities to open a retail store under a 12-year franchise contract. What annual net cash inflow must the store generate for Linda to earn a 14% return over the 12-year period? Round computations to the nearest whole dollar.

PROBLEM 8–30 Net Present Value; Uncertain Future Cash Flows; Postaudit [LO 8–2, LO 8–4]

Saxon Products, Inc., is investigating the purchase of a robot for use on the company's assembly line. Selected data relating to the robot are provided below:

Cost of the robot	$1,600,000
Installation and software	$450,000
Annual savings in labor costs	?
Annual savings in inventory carrying costs	$210,000
Monthly increase in power and maintenance costs	$2,500
Salvage value in 5 years	$70,000
Useful life	5 years

Engineering studies suggest that use of the robot will result in a savings of 25,000 direct labor-hours each year. The labor rate is $16 per hour. Also, the smoother work flow made possible by the use of automation will allow the company to reduce the amount of inventory on hand by $400,000. This inventory reduction will take place at the end of the first year of operation; the released funds will be available for use elsewhere in the company. Saxon Products has a 20% required rate of return.

Shelly Martins, the controller, has noted that all of Saxon's competitors are automating their plants. She is pessimistic, however, about whether Saxon's management will allow it to automate. In preparing the proposal for the robot, she stated to a colleague, "Let's just hope that reduced labor and inventory costs can justify the purchase of this automated equipment. Otherwise, we'll never get it. You know how the president feels about equipment paying for itself out of reduced costs."

Required:

1. Determine the *annual net* cost savings if the robot is purchased. (Do not include the $400,000 inventory reduction or the salvage value in this computation.)
2. Compute the net present value of the proposed investment in the robot. Based on these data, would you recommend that the robot be purchased? Explain.
3. Assume that the robot is purchased. At the end of the first year, Shelly Martins has found that some items didn't work out as planned. Due to unforeseen problems, software and installation costs were $75,000 more than estimated and direct labor has been reduced by only 22,500 hours per year, rather than by 25,000 hours. Assuming that all other cost data were accurate, does it appear that the company made a wise investment? Show computations using the net present value format as in requirement 2. (***Hint:*** It might be helpful to place yourself back at the beginning of the first year with the new data.)
4. Upon seeing your analysis in requirement 3, Saxon's president stated, "That robot is the worst investment we've ever made. And now we'll be stuck with it for years."
   a. Explain to the president what benefits other than cost savings might accrue from using the new automated equipment.
   b. Compute for the president the dollar amount of cash inflow that would be needed each year from the benefits in part (*a*) for the automated equipment to yield a 20% rate of return.

Cases

CASE 8–31 ETHICS AND THE MANAGER

The Fore Corporation is an integrated food processing company that has operations in over two dozen countries. Fore's corporate headquarters is in Chicago, and the company's executives frequently travel to visit Fore's foreign and domestic facilities.

Fore has a fleet of aircraft that consists of two business jets with international range and six smaller turboprop aircraft that are used on shorter flights. Company policy is to assign aircraft to trips on the basis of minimizing cost, but the practice is to assign the aircraft based on the organizational rank of the traveler. Fore offers its aircraft for short-term lease or for charter by other organizations whenever Fore itself does not plan to use the aircraft. Fore surveys the market often in order to keep its lease and charter rates competitive.

William Earle, Fore's vice president of finance, has claimed that a third business jet can be justified financially. However, some people in the controller's office have surmised that the real reason for a third business jet was to upgrade the aircraft used by Earle. Presently, the people outranking Earle keep the two business jets busy with the result that Earle usually flies in smaller turboprop aircraft.

The third business jet would cost $11 million. A capital expenditure of this magnitude requires a formal proposal with projected cash flows and net present value computations using Fore's minimum required rate of return. If Fore's president and the finance committee of the board of directors approve the proposal, it will be submitted to the full board of directors. The board has final approval on capital expenditures exceeding $5 million and has established a firm policy of rejecting any discretionary proposal that has a negative net present value.

Earle asked Rachel Arnett, assistant corporate controller, to prepare a proposal on a third business jet. Arnett gathered the following data:

- Acquisition cost of the aircraft, including instrumentation and interior furnishing.
- Operating cost of the aircraft for company use.
- Projected avoidable commercial airfare and other avoidable costs from company use of the plane.
- Projected value of executive time saved by using the third business jet.
- Projected contribution margin from incremental lease and charter activity.
- Estimated resale value of the aircraft.

When Earle reviewed Arnett's completed proposal and saw the large negative net present value figure, he returned the proposal to Arnett. With a glare, Earle commented, "You must have made an error. The proposal should look better than that."

Feeling some pressure, Arnett went back and checked her computations; she found no errors. However, Earle's message was clear. Arnett discarded her projections that she believed were reasonable and replaced them with figures that had a remote chance of actually occurring but were more favorable to the proposal. For example, she used first-class airfares to refigure the avoidable commercial airfare costs, even though company policy was to fly coach. She found revising the proposal to be distressing.

The revised proposal still had a negative net present value. Earle's anger was evident as he told Arnett to revise the proposal again, and to start with a $100,000 positive net present value and work backwards to compute supporting projections.

Required:

1. Explain whether Rachel Arnett's revision of the proposal was in violation of the IMA's Statement of Ethical Professional Practice.
2. Was William Earle in violation of the IMA's Statement of Ethical Professional Practice by telling Arnett specifically how to revise the proposal? Explain your answer.
3. Identify specific internal controls that Fore Corporation could implement to prevent unethical behavior on the part of the vice president of finance.

(CMA, adapted)

CASE 8–32 Net Present Value Analysis of a New Product [LO 8–2]

Matheson Electronics has just developed a new electronic device that it believes will have broad market appeal. The company has performed marketing and cost studies that revealed the following information:

a. New equipment would have to be acquired to produce the device. The equipment would cost $315,000 and have a six-year useful life. After six years, it would have a salvage value of about $15,000.

b. Sales in units over the next six years are projected to be as follows:

Year	Sales in Units
1	9,000
2	15,000
3	18,000
4–6	22,000

c. Production and sales of the device would require working capital of $60,000 to finance accounts receivable, inventories, and day-to-day cash needs. This working capital would be released at the end of the project's life.

d. The devices would sell for $35 each; variable costs for production, administration, and sales would be $15 per unit.

e. Fixed costs for salaries, maintenance, property taxes, insurance, and straight-line depreciation on the equipment would total $135,000 per year. (Depreciation is based on cost less salvage value.)

f. To gain rapid entry into the market, the company would have to advertise heavily. The advertising program would be:

Year	Amount of Yearly Advertising
1–2	\$180,000
3	\$150,000
4–6	\$120,000

g. The company's required rate of return is 14%.

Required:

1. Compute the net cash inflow (cash receipts less yearly cash operating expenses) anticipated from sale of the device for each year over the next six years.
2. Using the data computed in (1) above and other data provided in the problem, determine the net present value of the proposed investment. Would you recommend that Matheson accept the device as a new product?

Appendix 8A: The Concept of Present Value

LEARNING OBJECTIVE 8–7
Understand present value concepts and the use of present value tables.

A dollar received today is more valuable than a dollar received a year from now for the simple reason that if you have a dollar today, you can put it in the bank and have more than a dollar a year from now. Because dollars today are worth more than dollars in the future, cash flows that are received at different times must be valued differently.

The Mathematics of Interest

If a bank pays 5% interest, then a deposit of \$100 today will be worth \$105 one year from now. This can be expressed as follows:

$$F_1 = P(1 + r) \quad (1)$$

where F_1 = the balance at the end of one period, P = the amount invested now, and r = the rate of interest per period.

In the case where \$100 is deposited in a savings account that earns 5% interest, P = \$100 and $r = 0.05$. Under these conditions, F_1 = \$105.

The \$100 present outlay is called the **present value** of the \$105 amount to be received in one year. It is also known as the *discounted value* of the future \$105 receipt. The \$100 represents the value in present terms of \$105 to be received a year from now when the interest rate is 5%.

Compound Interest What if the \$105 is left in the bank for a second year? In that case, by the end of the second year the original \$100 deposit will have grown to \$110.25:

Original deposit	\$100.00
Interest for the first year: \$100 × 0.05	5.00
Balance at the end of the first year	105.00
Interest for the second year: \$105 × 0.05	5.25
Balance at the end of the second year	\$110.25

Notice that the interest for the second year is $5.25, as compared to only $5.00 for the first year. This difference arises because interest is being paid on interest during the second year. That is, the $5.00 interest earned during the first year has been left in the account and has been added to the original $100 deposit when computing interest for the second year. This is known as **compound interest**. In this case, the compounding is annual. Interest can be compounded on a semiannual, quarterly, monthly, or even more frequent basis. The more frequently compounding is done, the more rapidly the balance will grow.

We can determine the balance in an account after n periods of compounding using the following equation:

$$F_n = P(1 + r)^n \tag{2}$$

where n = the number of periods of compounding.

If $n = 2$ years and the interest rate is 5% per year, then the balance in two years will be computed as follows:

$$F_2 = \$100(1 + 0.05)^2$$
$$F_2 = \$110.25$$

Present Value and Future Value Exhibit 8A–1 shows the relationship between present value and future value. As shown in the exhibit, if $100 is deposited in a bank at 5% interest compounded annually, it will grow to $127.63 by the end of five years.

EXHIBIT 8A–1
The Relationship between Present Value and Future Value

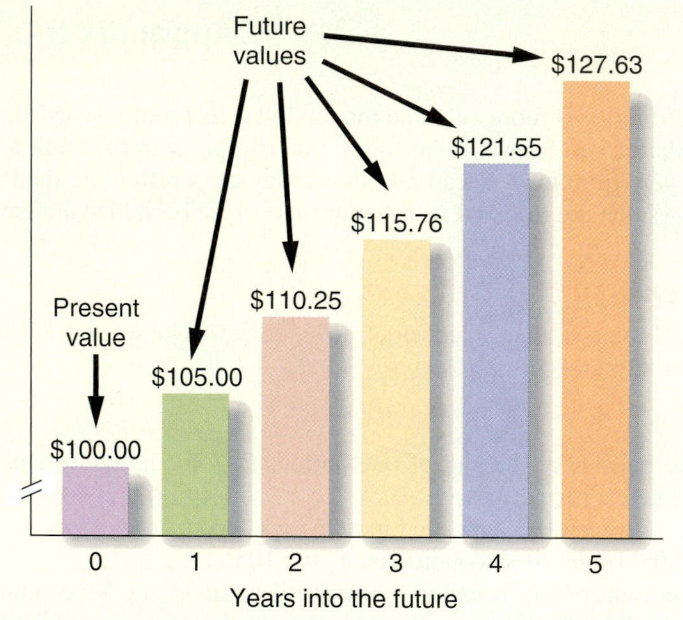

Computation of Present Value

An investment can be viewed in two ways—either in terms of its future value or in terms of its present value. We have seen from our computations above that if we know the present value of a sum (such as our $100 deposit), the future value in n years can be computed by using equation (2). But what if the situation is reversed and we know the *future* value of some amount but we do not know its present value?

For example, assume that you are to receive $200 two years from now. You know that the future value of this sum is $200 because this is the amount that you will be receiving in two years. But what is the sum's present value—what is it worth *right now?* The present value of any sum to be received in the future can be computed by turning equation (2) around and solving for P:

$$P = \frac{F_n}{(1 + r)^n} \tag{3}$$

In our example, $F_n = \$200$ (the amount to be received in the future), $r = 0.05$ (the annual rate of interest), and $n = 2$ (the number of years in the future that the amount will be received).

$$P = \frac{\$200}{(1 + 0.05)^2}$$

$$P = \frac{\$200}{1.1025}$$

$$P = \$181.40$$

As shown by the computation above, the present value of a \$200 amount to be received two years from now is \$181.40 if the interest rate is 5%. In effect, \$181.40 received *right now* is equivalent to \$200 received two years from now.

The process of finding the present value of a future cash flow, which we have just completed, is called **discounting**. We have *discounted* the \$200 to its present value of \$181.40. The 5% interest that we have used to find this present value is called the **discount rate**. Discounting future sums to their present value is a common practice in business, particularly in capital budgeting decisions.

If you have a power key (y^x) on your calculator, the above calculations are fairly easy. However, some of the present value formulas we will be using are more complex. Fortunately, tables are available in which many of the calculations have already been done. For example, Exhibit 8B–1 in Appendix 8B shows the discounted present value of \$1 to be received at various periods in the future at various interest rates. The table indicates that the present value of \$1 to be received two periods from now at 5% is 0.907. Because in our example we want to know the present value of \$200 rather than just \$1, we need to multiply the factor in the table by \$200:

$$\$200 \times 0.907 = \$181.40$$

This answer is the same as we obtained earlier using the formula in equation (3).

Present Value of a Series of Cash Flows

Although some investments involve a single sum to be received (or paid) at a single point in the future, other investments involve a *series* of cash flows. A series of identical cash flows is known as an **annuity**. To provide an example, assume that a company has just purchased some government bonds. The bonds will yield interest of \$15,000 each year and will be held for five years. What is the present value of the stream of interest receipts from the bonds? As shown in Exhibit 8A–2, if the discount rate is 12%, the present value of this stream is \$54,075. The discount factors used in this exhibit were taken from Exhibit 8B–1 in Appendix 8B.

Exhibit 8A–2 illustrates two important points. First, the present value of the \$15,000 interest declines the further it is into the future. The present value of \$15,000 received a year from now is \$13,395, as compared to only \$8,505 if received five years from now. This point underscores the time value of money.

EXHIBIT 8A–2
Present Value of a Series of Cash Receipts

Year	Factor at 12% (Exhibit 8B–1)	Interest Received	Present Value
1	0.893	\$15,000	\$13,395
2	0.797	\$15,000	11,955
3	0.712	\$15,000	10,680
4	0.636	\$15,000	9,540
5	0.567	\$15,000	8,505
			\$54,075

The second point is that the computations used in Exhibit 8A–2 involved unnecessary work. The same present value of $54,075 could have been obtained more easily by referring to Exhibit 8B–2 in Appendix 8B. Exhibit 8B–2 contains the present value of $1 to be received each year over a *series* of years at various interest rates. Exhibit 8B–2 has been derived by simply adding together the factors from Exhibit 8B–1, as follows:

Year	Factors at 12% (from Exhibit 8B–1)
1	0.893
2	0.797
3	0.712
4	0.636
5	0.567
	3.605

The sum of these five factors is 3.605. Notice from Exhibit 8B–2 that the factor for $1 to be received each year for five years at 12% is also 3.605. If we use this factor and multiply it by the $15,000 annual cash inflow, then we get the same $54,075 present value that we obtained earlier in Exhibit 8A–2.

$$\$15{,}000 \times 3.605 = \$54{,}075$$

Therefore, when computing the present value of a series of equal cash flows that begins at the end of period 1, Exhibit 8B–2 should be used.

To summarize, the present value tables in Appendix 8B should be used as follows:

Exhibit 8B–1: This table should be used to find the present value of a single cash flow (such as a single payment or receipt) occurring in the future.

Exhibit 8B–2: This table should be used to find the present value of a series of identical cash flows beginning at the end of the current period and continuing into the future.

The use of both of these tables is illustrated in various exhibits in the main body of the chapter. *When a present value factor appears in an exhibit, you should take the time to trace it back into either or to get acquainted with the tables and how they work.*

Review Problem: Basic Present Value Computations

Each of the following situations is independent. Work out your own solution to each situation, and then check it against the solution provided.

1. John plans to retire in 12 years. Upon retiring, he would like to take an extended vacation, which he expects will cost at least $40,000. What lump-sum amount must he invest now to have $40,000 at the end of 12 years if the rate of return is:
   a. 8%?
   b. 12%?
2. The Morgans would like to send their daughter to a music camp at the end of each of the next five years. The camp costs $1,000 a year. What lump-sum amount would have to be invested now to have $1,000 at the end of each year if the rate of return is:
   a. 8%?
   b. 12%?
3. You have just received an inheritance from a relative. You can either receive a $200,000 lump-sum amount at the end of 10 years or receive $14,000 at the end of each year for the next 10 years. If your discount rate is 12%, which alternative would you prefer?

Solution to Review Problem

1. *a.* The amount that must be invested now would be the present value of the $40,000, using a discount rate of 8%. From Exhibit 8B–1 in Appendix 8B, the factor for a discount rate of 8% for 12 periods is 0.397. Multiplying this discount factor by the $40,000 needed in 12 years will give the amount of the present investment required: $40,000 × 0.397 = $15,880.

   b. We will proceed as we did in (*a*) above, but this time we will use a discount rate of 12%. From Exhibit 8B–1 in Appendix 8B, the factor for a discount rate of 12% for 12 periods is 0.257. Multiplying this discount factor by the $40,000 needed in 12 years will give the amount of the present investment required: $40,000 × 0.257 = $10,280.

   Notice that as the discount rate (desired rate of return) increases, the present value decreases.

2. This part differs from part (1) in that we are now dealing with an annuity rather than with a single future sum. The amount that must be invested now is the present value of the $1,000 needed at the end of each year for five years. Because we are dealing with an annuity, or a series of annual cash flows, we must refer to Exhibit 8B–2 in Appendix 8B for the appropriate discount factor.

   a. From Exhibit 8B–2 in Appendix 8B, the discount factor for 8% for five periods is 3.993. Therefore, the amount that must be invested now to have $1,000 available at the end of each year for five years is $1,000 × 3.993 = $3,993.

   b. From Exhibit 8B–2 in Appendix 8B, the discount factor for 12% for five periods is 3.605. Therefore, the amount that must be invested now to have $1,000 available at the end of each year for five years is $1,000 × 3.605 = $3,605.

   Again, notice that as the discount rate increases, the present value decreases. When the rate of return increases, less must be invested today to yield a given amount in the future.

3. For this part we will need to refer to both Exhibits 8B–1 and 8B–2 in Appendix 8B. From Exhibit 8B–1, we will need to find the discount factor for 12% for 10 periods, then apply it to the $200,000 lump sum to be received in 10 years. From Exhibit 8B–2, we will need to find the discount factor for 12% for 10 periods, then apply it to the series of $14,000 payments to be received over the 10-year period. Whichever alternative has the higher present value is the one that should be selected.

$$\$200{,}000 \times 0.322 = \$64{,}400$$

$$\$14{,}000 \times 5.650 = \$79{,}100$$

   Thus, you should prefer to receive the $14,000 per year for 10 years rather than the $200,000 lump sum. This means that you could invest the $14,000 received at the end of each year at 12% and have *more* than $200,000 at the end of 10 years.

Glossary (Appendix 8A)

Annuity A series of identical cash flows. (p. 375)
Compound interest The process of paying interest on interest in an investment. (p. 374)
Discount rate The rate of return that is used to find the present value of a future cash flow. (p. 375)
Discounting The process of finding the present value of a future cash flow. (p. 375)
Present value The value now of an amount that will be received in some future period. (p. 373)

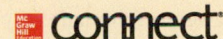

connect Appendix 8A Exercises

Additional student resources are available with Connect.

EXERCISE 8A–1 Basic Present Value Concepts [LO 8–7]
Annual cash inflows that will arise from two competing investment projects are given below:

Year	Investment A	Investment B
1	$ 3,000	$12,000
2	6,000	9,000
3	9,000	6,000
4	12,000	3,000
	$30,000	$30,000

The discount rate is 18%.

Required:

Compute the present value of the cash inflows for each investment.

EXERCISE 8A–2 Basic Present Value Concepts [LO 8–7]

Julie has just retired. Her company's retirement program has two options as to how retirement benefits can be received. Under the first option, Julie would receive a lump sum of $150,000 immediately as her full retirement benefit. Under the second option, she would receive $14,000 each year for 20 years plus a lump-sum payment of $60,000 at the end of the 20-year period.

Required:

If she can invest money at 12%, which option would you recommend that she accept? Use present value analysis.

EXERCISE 8A–3 Basic Present Value Concepts [LO 8–7]

In three years, when he is discharged from the Air Force, Steve wants to buy an $8,000 power boat.

Required:

What lump-sum amount must Steve invest now to have the $8,000 at the end of three years if he can invest money at:

1. 10%?
2. 14%?

EXERCISE 8A–4 Basic Present Value Concepts [LO 8–7]

Fraser Company will need a new warehouse in five years. The warehouse will cost $500,000 to build.

Required:

What lump-sum amount should the company invest now to have the $500,000 available at the end of the five-year period? Assume that the company can invest money at:

1. 10%.
2. 14%.

EXERCISE 8A–5 Basic Present Value Concepts [LO 8–7]

The Atlantic Medical Clinic can purchase a new computer system that will save $7,000 annually in billing costs. The computer system will last for eight years and have no salvage value.

Required:

Up to how much should the Atlantic Medical Clinic be willing to pay for the new computer system if the clinic's required rate of return is:

1. 16%?
2. 20%?

EXERCISE 8A–6 Basic Present Value Concepts [LO 8–7]

The Caldwell Herald newspaper reported the following story: Frank Ormsby of Caldwell is the state's newest millionaire. By choosing the six winning numbers on last week's state lottery, Mr. Ormsby has won the week's grand prize totaling $1.6 million. The State Lottery Commission has indicated that Mr. Ormsby will receive his prize in 20 annual installments of $80,000 each.

Required:

1. If Mr. Ormsby can invest money at a 12% rate of return, what is the present value of his winnings?
2. Is it correct to say that Mr. Ormsby is the "state's newest millionaire"? Explain your answer.

Appendix 8B: Present Value Tables

EXHIBIT 8B–1

Present Value of $1; $\frac{1}{(1 + r)^n}$

Periods	4%	5%	6%	7%	8%	9%	10%	11%	12%	13%	14%	15%	16%	17%	18%	19%	20%	21%	22%	23%	24%	25%
1	0.962	0.952	0.943	0.935	0.926	0.917	0.909	0.901	0.893	0.885	0.877	0.870	0.862	0.855	0.847	0.840	0.833	0.826	0.820	0.813	0.806	0.800
2	0.925	0.907	0.890	0.873	0.857	0.842	0.826	0.812	0.797	0.783	0.769	0.756	0.743	0.731	0.718	0.706	0.694	0.683	0.672	0.661	0.650	0.640
3	0.889	0.864	0.840	0.816	0.794	0.772	0.751	0.731	0.712	0.693	0.675	0.658	0.641	0.624	0.609	0.593	0.579	0.564	0.551	0.537	0.524	0.512
4	0.855	0.823	0.792	0.763	0.735	0.708	0.683	0.659	0.636	0.613	0.592	0.572	0.552	0.534	0.516	0.499	0.482	0.467	0.451	0.437	0.423	0.410
5	0.822	0.784	0.747	0.713	0.681	0.650	0.621	0.593	0.567	0.543	0.519	0.497	0.476	0.456	0.437	0.419	0.402	0.386	0.370	0.355	0.341	0.328
6	0.790	0.746	0.705	0.666	0.630	0.596	0.564	0.535	0.507	0.480	0.456	0.432	0.410	0.390	0.370	0.352	0.335	0.319	0.303	0.289	0.275	0.262
7	0.760	0.711	0.665	0.623	0.583	0.547	0.513	0.482	0.452	0.425	0.400	0.376	0.354	0.333	0.314	0.296	0.279	0.263	0.249	0.235	0.222	0.210
8	0.731	0.677	0.627	0.582	0.540	0.502	0.467	0.434	0.404	0.376	0.351	0.327	0.305	0.285	0.266	0.249	0.233	0.218	0.204	0.191	0.179	0.168
9	0.703	0.645	0.592	0.544	0.500	0.460	0.424	0.391	0.361	0.333	0.308	0.284	0.263	0.243	0.225	0.209	0.194	0.180	0.167	0.155	0.144	0.134
10	0.676	0.614	0.558	0.508	0.463	0.422	0.386	0.352	0.322	0.295	0.270	0.247	0.227	0.208	0.191	0.176	0.162	0.149	0.137	0.126	0.116	0.107
11	0.650	0.585	0.527	0.475	0.429	0.388	0.350	0.317	0.287	0.261	0.237	0.215	0.195	0.178	0.162	0.148	0.135	0.123	0.112	0.103	0.094	0.086
12	0.625	0.557	0.497	0.444	0.397	0.356	0.319	0.286	0.257	0.231	0.208	0.187	0.168	0.152	0.137	0.124	0.112	0.102	0.092	0.083	0.076	0.069
13	0.601	0.530	0.469	0.415	0.368	0.326	0.290	0.258	0.229	0.204	0.182	0.163	0.145	0.130	0.116	0.104	0.093	0.084	0.075	0.068	0.061	0.055
14	0.577	0.505	0.442	0.388	0.340	0.299	0.263	0.232	0.205	0.181	0.160	0.141	0.125	0.111	0.099	0.088	0.078	0.069	0.062	0.055	0.049	0.044
15	0.555	0.481	0.417	0.362	0.315	0.275	0.239	0.209	0.183	0.160	0.140	0.123	0.108	0.095	0.084	0.074	0.065	0.057	0.051	0.045	0.040	0.035
16	0.534	0.458	0.394	0.339	0.292	0.252	0.218	0.188	0.163	0.141	0.123	0.107	0.093	0.081	0.071	0.062	0.054	0.047	0.042	0.036	0.032	0.028
17	0.513	0.436	0.371	0.317	0.270	0.231	0.198	0.170	0.146	0.125	0.108	0.093	0.080	0.069	0.060	0.052	0.045	0.039	0.034	0.030	0.026	0.023
18	0.494	0.416	0.350	0.296	0.250	0.212	0.180	0.153	0.130	0.111	0.095	0.081	0.069	0.059	0.051	0.044	0.038	0.032	0.028	0.024	0.021	0.018
19	0.475	0.396	0.331	0.277	0.232	0.194	0.164	0.138	0.116	0.098	0.083	0.070	0.060	0.051	0.043	0.037	0.031	0.027	0.023	0.020	0.017	0.014
20	0.456	0.377	0.312	0.258	0.215	0.178	0.149	0.124	0.104	0.087	0.073	0.061	0.051	0.043	0.037	0.031	0.026	0.022	0.019	0.016	0.014	0.012
21	0.439	0.359	0.294	0.242	0.199	0.164	0.135	0.112	0.093	0.077	0.064	0.053	0.044	0.037	0.031	0.026	0.022	0.018	0.015	0.013	0.011	0.009
22	0.422	0.342	0.278	0.226	0.184	0.150	0.123	0.101	0.083	0.068	0.056	0.046	0.038	0.032	0.026	0.022	0.018	0.015	0.013	0.011	0.009	0.007
23	0.406	0.326	0.262	0.211	0.170	0.138	0.112	0.091	0.074	0.060	0.049	0.040	0.033	0.027	0.022	0.018	0.015	0.012	0.010	0.009	0.007	0.006
24	0.390	0.310	0.247	0.197	0.158	0.126	0.102	0.082	0.066	0.053	0.043	0.035	0.028	0.023	0.019	0.015	0.013	0.010	0.008	0.007	0.006	0.005
25	0.375	0.295	0.233	0.184	0.146	0.116	0.092	0.074	0.059	0.047	0.038	0.030	0.024	0.020	0.016	0.013	0.010	0.009	0.007	0.006	0.005	0.004
26	0.361	0.281	0.220	0.172	0.135	0.106	0.084	0.066	0.053	0.042	0.033	0.026	0.021	0.017	0.014	0.011	0.009	0.007	0.006	0.005	0.004	0.003
27	0.347	0.268	0.207	0.161	0.125	0.098	0.076	0.060	0.047	0.037	0.029	0.023	0.018	0.014	0.011	0.009	0.007	0.006	0.005	0.004	0.003	0.002
28	0.333	0.255	0.196	0.150	0.116	0.090	0.069	0.054	0.042	0.033	0.026	0.020	0.016	0.012	0.010	0.008	0.006	0.005	0.004	0.003	0.002	0.002
29	0.321	0.243	0.185	0.141	0.107	0.082	0.063	0.048	0.037	0.029	0.022	0.017	0.014	0.011	0.008	0.006	0.005	0.004	0.003	0.002	0.002	0.002
30	0.308	0.231	0.174	0.131	0.099	0.075	0.057	0.044	0.033	0.026	0.020	0.015	0.012	0.009	0.007	0.005	0.004	0.003	0.003	0.002	0.002	0.001
40	0.208	0.142	0.097	0.067	0.046	0.032	0.022	0.015	0.011	0.008	0.005	0.004	0.003	0.002	0.001	0.001	0.001	0.000	0.000	0.000	0.000	0.000

EXHIBIT 8B–2

Present Value of an Annuity of $1 in Arrears; $\frac{1}{r}\left[1 - \frac{1}{(1+r)^n}\right]$

Periods	4%	5%	6%	7%	8%	9%	10%	11%	12%	13%	14%	15%	16%	17%	18%	19%	20%	21%	22%	23%	24%	25%
1	0.962	0.952	0.943	0.935	0.926	0.917	0.909	0.901	0.893	0.885	0.877	0.870	0.862	0.855	0.847	0.840	0.833	0.826	0.820	0.813	0.806	0.800
2	1.886	1.859	1.833	1.808	1.783	1.759	1.736	1.713	1.690	1.668	1.647	1.626	1.605	1.585	1.566	1.547	1.528	1.509	1.492	1.474	1.457	1.440
3	2.775	2.723	2.673	2.624	2.577	2.531	2.487	2.444	2.402	2.361	2.322	2.283	2.246	2.210	2.174	2.140	2.106	2.074	2.042	2.011	1.981	1.952
4	3.630	3.546	3.465	3.387	3.312	3.240	3.170	3.102	3.037	2.974	2.914	2.855	2.798	2.743	2.690	2.639	2.589	2.540	2.494	2.448	2.404	2.362
5	4.452	4.329	4.212	4.100	3.993	3.890	3.791	3.696	3.605	3.517	3.433	3.352	3.274	3.199	3.127	3.058	2.991	2.926	2.864	2.803	2.745	2.689
6	5.242	5.076	4.917	4.767	4.623	4.486	4.355	4.231	4.111	3.998	3.889	3.784	3.685	3.589	3.498	3.410	3.326	3.245	3.167	3.092	3.020	2.951
7	6.002	5.786	5.582	5.389	5.206	5.033	4.868	4.712	4.564	4.423	4.288	4.160	4.039	3.922	3.812	3.706	3.605	3.508	3.416	3.327	3.242	3.161
8	6.733	6.463	6.210	5.971	5.747	5.535	5.335	5.146	4.968	4.799	4.639	4.487	4.344	4.207	4.078	3.954	3.837	3.726	3.619	3.518	3.421	3.329
9	7.435	7.108	6.802	6.515	6.247	5.995	5.759	5.537	5.328	5.132	4.946	4.772	4.607	4.451	4.303	4.163	4.031	3.905	3.786	3.673	3.566	3.463
10	8.111	7.722	7.360	7.024	6.710	6.418	6.145	5.889	5.650	5.426	5.216	5.019	4.833	4.659	4.494	4.339	4.192	4.054	3.923	3.799	3.682	3.571
11	8.760	8.306	7.887	7.499	7.139	6.805	6.495	6.207	5.938	5.687	5.453	5.234	5.029	4.836	4.656	4.486	4.327	4.177	4.035	3.902	3.776	3.656
12	9.385	8.863	8.384	7.943	7.536	7.161	6.814	6.492	6.194	5.918	5.660	5.421	5.197	4.988	4.793	4.611	4.439	4.278	4.127	3.985	3.851	3.725
13	9.986	9.394	8.853	8.358	7.904	7.487	7.103	6.750	6.424	6.122	5.842	5.583	5.342	5.118	4.910	4.715	4.533	4.362	4.203	4.053	3.912	3.780
14	10.563	9.899	9.295	8.745	8.244	7.786	7.367	6.982	6.628	6.302	6.002	5.724	5.468	5.229	5.008	4.802	4.611	4.432	4.265	4.108	3.962	3.824
15	11.118	10.380	9.712	9.108	8.559	8.061	7.606	7.191	6.811	6.462	6.142	5.847	5.575	5.324	5.092	4.876	4.675	4.489	4.315	4.153	4.001	3.859
16	11.652	10.838	10.106	9.447	8.851	8.313	7.824	7.379	6.974	6.604	6.265	5.954	5.668	5.405	5.162	4.938	4.730	4.536	4.357	4.189	4.033	3.887
17	12.166	11.274	10.477	9.763	9.122	8.544	8.022	7.549	7.120	6.729	6.373	6.047	5.749	5.475	5.222	4.990	4.775	4.576	4.391	4.219	4.059	3.910
18	12.659	11.690	10.828	10.059	9.372	8.756	8.201	7.702	7.250	6.840	6.467	6.128	5.818	5.534	5.273	5.033	4.812	4.608	4.419	4.243	4.080	3.928
19	13.134	12.085	11.158	10.336	9.604	8.950	8.365	7.839	7.366	6.938	6.550	6.198	5.877	5.584	5.316	5.070	4.843	4.635	4.442	4.263	4.097	3.942
20	13.590	12.462	11.470	10.594	9.818	9.129	8.514	7.963	7.469	7.025	6.623	6.259	5.929	5.628	5.353	5.101	4.870	4.657	4.460	4.279	4.110	3.954
21	14.029	12.821	11.764	10.836	10.017	9.292	8.649	8.075	7.562	7.102	6.687	6.312	5.973	5.665	5.384	5.127	4.891	4.675	4.476	4.292	4.121	3.963
22	14.451	13.163	12.042	11.061	10.201	9.442	8.772	8.176	7.645	7.170	6.743	6.359	6.011	5.696	5.410	5.149	4.909	4.690	4.488	4.302	4.130	3.970
23	14.857	13.489	12.303	11.272	10.371	9.580	8.883	8.266	7.718	7.230	6.792	6.399	6.044	5.723	5.432	5.167	4.925	4.703	4.499	4.311	4.137	3.976
24	15.247	13.799	12.550	11.469	10.529	9.707	8.985	8.348	7.784	7.283	6.835	6.434	6.073	5.746	5.451	5.182	4.937	4.713	4.507	4.318	4.143	3.981
25	15.622	14.094	12.783	11.654	10.675	9.823	9.077	8.422	7.843	7.330	6.873	6.464	6.097	5.766	5.467	5.195	4.948	4.721	4.514	4.323	4.147	3.985
26	15.983	14.375	13.003	11.826	10.810	9.929	9.161	8.488	7.896	7.372	6.906	6.491	6.118	5.783	5.480	5.206	4.956	4.728	4.520	4.328	4.151	3.988
27	16.330	14.643	13.211	11.987	10.935	10.027	9.237	8.548	7.943	7.409	6.935	6.514	6.136	5.798	5.492	5.215	4.964	4.734	4.524	4.332	4.154	3.990
28	16.663	14.898	13.406	12.137	11.051	10.116	9.307	8.602	7.984	7.441	6.961	6.534	6.152	5.810	5.502	5.223	4.970	4.739	4.528	4.335	4.157	3.992
29	16.984	15.141	13.591	12.278	11.158	10.198	9.370	8.650	8.022	7.470	6.983	6.551	6.166	5.820	5.510	5.229	4.975	4.743	4.531	4.337	4.159	3.994
30	17.292	15.372	13.765	12.409	11.258	10.274	9.427	8.694	8.055	7.496	7.003	6.566	6.177	5.829	5.517	5.235	4.979	4.746	4.534	4.339	4.160	3.995
40	19.793	17.159	15.046	13.332	11.925	10.757	9.779	8.951	8.244	7.634	7.105	6.642	6.233	5.871	5.548	5.258	4.997	4.760	4.544	4.347	4.166	3.999

Appendix 8C: Income Taxes and the Net Present Value Method

LEARNING OBJECTIVE 8–8
Include income taxes in a capital budgeting analysis.

This appendix discusses the impact of income taxes on the net present value method of making capital budgeting decisions. We ignored income taxes throughout the chapter for two reasons. First, many organizations do not pay income taxes. Nonprofit organizations, such as hospitals and charitable foundations, and government agencies are exempt from income taxes. Second, capital budgeting is complex and best absorbed in small doses. Now that we have a solid foundation in the concept of discounting cash flows, we can explore the impact of income taxes on the net present value method.

To keep this discussion within reasonable bounds, we make a number of simplifying assumptions. We assume that a company's taxable income equals its net income for financial reporting purposes and that straight-line depreciation with zero salvage value is used. We also assume that the tax rate is a flat percentage of taxable income and that there are no gains or losses on the sale of noncurrent assets.

Key Concepts

This appendix takes everything that you have already learned about the net present value method and simply adds one more type of cash flow to the computations—it adds income tax expense as a *cash outflow.* To calculate the amount of income tax expense associated with a capital budgeting project, we'll be using a two-step process. The first step is to calculate the incremental net income earned during each year of the project. The second step is to multiply each year's incremental net income by the tax rate to determine the income tax expense. Each year's income tax expense is then discounted to its present value along with all other cash flows realized over the life of the project.

A capital budgeting project's incremental net income computation *includes* annual revenues minus annual cash operating expenses (including variable expenses and fixed out-of-pocket costs), annual depreciation expense, and any one-time expenses. Notice that *depreciation expense is included in the computation of incremental net income.* Although depreciation expense is a noncash expense, it does impact the computation of taxable income, which in turn affects the cash outflows pertaining to income tax expense. A capital budgeting project's incremental net income computation *does not include* immediate cash outflows in the form of initial investments in equipment, other assets, and installation costs. It also *does not include* investments in working capital, the release of working capital at the end of a project, and the proceeds from selling a noncurrent asset when no gain or loss is realized on the sale. To summarize, the items that should be included and excluded from a capital budgeting project's incremental net income computations are as follows:

Include in the computation of incremental net income:
Annual revenues
Annual cash operating expenses
Annual depreciation expense
One-time expenses

Exclude from the computation of incremental net income:
Initial investments in equipment, other assets, and installation costs
Investment in working capital
Release of working capital at the end of a project
Proceeds from selling noncurrent assets when no gain or loss is realized

Income Taxes and Net Present Value Analysis: An Example

Holland Company owns the mineral rights to land that has a deposit of ore. The company is uncertain if it should purchase equipment and open a mine on the property. After careful study, the company gathered the following data:

Initial investment in equipment	\$275,000
Initial investment in working capital	\$50,000
Estimated annual sales of ore	\$250,000
Estimated annual cash operating expenses	\$150,000
Cost of road repairs needed in 3 years	\$30,000

The ore in the mine would be exhausted after five years, at which time the mine would be closed and the working capital would be released and redeployed by the company. The equipment has a useful life of five years and a salvage value of zero. The company uses straight-line depreciation for financial reporting and tax purposes. Its after-tax cost of capital is 12% and its tax rate is 30%. To be consistent, when we take the net present value of after-tax cash flows, we use the *after-tax* cost of capital as the discount rate.

Should Holland Company purchase the equipment and open a mine on the property? Exhibit 8C–1 shows a net present value analysis that incorporates the impact of income taxes on this decision. The top portion of the exhibit computes the project's incremental net income for Years 1–5 and the income tax expense for each of those years. The incremental net income computations include the annual sales (\$250,000), the annual cash operating expenses (\$150,000), the road repairs in Year 3 (\$30,000), and the annual depreciation expense of \$55,000 (\$275,000 ÷ 5 years = \$55,000 per year). Each year's incremental net income is multiplied by the tax rate of 30% to determine the income tax expense.

The bottom portion of Exhibit 8C–1 calculates the net present value of the mining project. The cash flows summarized in this portion of the exhibit include the initial outlays for the purchase of equipment (\$275,000) and the investment in working capital

EXHIBIT 8C–1
Holland Company: Income Taxes and Net Present Value Analysis

	A	B	C	D	E	F	G
1					Year		
2		Now	1	2	3	4	5
3	*Calculate the annual tax expense:*						
4	Sales		\$ 250,000	\$ 250,000	\$ 250,000	\$ 250,000	\$ 250,000
5	Cash operating expenses		\$ (150,000)	\$(150,000)	\$(150,000)	\$(150,000)	\$(150,000)
6	Road repairs				\$ (30,000)		
7	Depreciation expense		\$ (55,000)	\$ (55,000)	\$ (55,000)	\$ (55,000)	\$ (55,000)
8	Incremental net income		\$ 45,000	\$ 45,000	\$ 15,000	\$ 45,000	\$ 45,000
9	Tax rate		30%	30%	30%	30%	30%
10	Income tax expense		\$ (13,500)	\$ (13,500)	\$ (4,500)	\$ (13,500)	\$ (13,500)
11							
12	*Calculate the net present value:*						
13	Purchase of equipment	\$(275,000)					
14	Investment in working capital	\$ (50,000)					
15	Sales		\$ 250,000	\$ 250,000	\$ 250,000	\$ 250,000	\$ 250,000
16	Cash operating expenses		\$ (150,000)	\$(150,000)	\$(150,000)	\$(150,000)	\$(150,000)
17	Road repairs				\$ (30,000)		
18	Release of working capital						\$ 50,000
19	Income tax expense		\$ (13,500)	\$ (13,500)	\$ (4,500)	\$ (13,500)	\$ (13,500)
20	Total cash flows (a)	\$(325,000)	\$ 86,500	\$ 86,500	\$ 65,500	\$ 86,500	\$ 136,500
21	Discount factor (12%) (b)	1.000	0.893	0.797	0.712	0.636	0.567
22	Present value of cash flows (a) × (b)	\$(325,000)	\$ 77,245	\$ 68,941	\$ 46,636	\$ 55,014	\$ 77,396
23	Net present value (SUM B22:G22)	\$ 231					
24							
25	Note: The discount factors come from Exhibit 8B-1 in Appendix 8B.						
26							

Exhibit 8-9 Exhibit 8-10 Exhibit 8-11 Exhibit 8C-1

($50,000), the annual sales ($250,000), the annual cash operating expenses ($150,000), the road repairs in Year 3 ($30,000), the release of working capital in Year 5 ($50,000), and the annual income tax expense. Notice that the amounts of income tax expense shown in cells C19 through G19 come directly from the calculations previously performed in cells C10 through G10. Each year's total cash flows in cells B20 through G20 are multiplied by the appropriate discount factor for 12% to compute their present value. The present values in cells B22 through G22 are combined to determine the project's net present value of $231. Because the net present value is positive, it indicates that Holland Company should proceed with the mining project.

Summary (Appendix 8C)

Unless the organization is tax-exempt, such as a nonprofit school or a governmental body, income taxes should be considered when using net present value analysis to make capital budgeting decisions. Calculating the amount of income tax expense associated with a capital budgeting project is a two-step process. The first step is to calculate the incremental net income earned during each year of the project. The second step is to multiply each year's incremental net income by the tax rate to determine the income tax expense. Each year's income tax expense is then discounted to its present value along with all other cash flows realized over the life of the project.

A capital budgeting project's incremental net income computation includes annual revenues minus annual cash operating expenses, annual depreciation expense, and any one-time expenses. It does not include immediate cash outflows in the form of initial investments in equipment, other assets, and installation costs, as well as investments in working capital, the release of working capital at the end of a project, and the proceeds from selling a noncurrent asset where no gain or loss is realized on the sale.

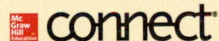

connect Appendix 8C Exercises and Problems

Additional student resources are available with Connect.

EXERCISE 8C–1 Income Taxes and Net Present Value Analysis [LO 8–8]

Gaston Company is considering a capital budgeting project that would require a $2,000,000 investment in equipment with a useful life of five years and no salvage value. The company's tax rate is 30% and its after-tax cost of capital is 13%. It uses the straight-line depreciation method for financial reporting and tax purposes. The project would provide net operating income each year for five years as follows:

Sales		$2,800,000
Variable expenses		1,600,000
Contribution margin		1,200,000
Fixed expenses:		
Advertising, salaries, and other fixed out-of-pocket costs	$500,000	
Depreciation	400,000	
Total fixed expenses		900,000
Net operating income		$ 300,000

Required:
Compute the project's net present value.

EXERCISE 8C–2 Income Taxes and Net Present Value Analysis [LO 8–8]
Winthrop Company has an opportunity to manufacture and sell a new product for a five-year period. To pursue this opportunity, the company would need to purchase a piece of equipment for $130,000. The equipment would have a useful life of five years and zero salvage value. It would be depreciated for financial reporting and tax purposes using the straight-line method. After careful study, Winthrop estimated the following annual costs and revenues for the new product:

Annual revenues and costs:	
Sales revenues	$250,000
Variable expenses	$120,000
Fixed out-of-pocket operating costs	$70,000

The company's tax rate is 30% and its after-tax cost of capital is 15%.

Required:
Calculate the net present value of this investment opportunity.

PROBLEM 8C–3 Income Taxes and Net Present Value Analysis [LO 8–8]
Lander Company has an opportunity to pursue a capital budgeting project with a five-year time horizon. After careful study, Lander estimated the following costs and revenues for the project:

Cost of equipment needed	$250,000
Working capital needed	$60,000
Overhaul of the equipment in two years	$18,000
Annual revenues and costs:	
Sales revenues	$350,000
Variable expenses	$180,000
Fixed out-of-pocket operating costs	$80,000

The piece of equipment mentioned above has a useful life of five years and zero salvage value. Lander uses straight-line depreciation for financial reporting and tax purposes. The company's tax rate is 30% and its after-tax cost of capital is 12%. When the project concludes in five years the working capital will be released for investment elsewhere within the company.

Required:
Calculate the net present value of this investment opportunity.

PROBLEM 8C–4 Income Taxes and Net Present Value Analysis [LO 8–8]
Rosman Company has an opportunity to pursue a capital budgeting project with a five-year time horizon. After careful study, Rosman estimated the following costs and revenues for the project:

Cost of new equipment needed	$420,000
Sale of old equipment no longer needed	$80,000
Working capital needed	$65,000
Equipment maintenance in each of Years 3 and 4	$20,000
Annual revenues and costs:	
Sales revenues	$410,000
Variable expenses	$175,000
Fixed out-of-pocket operating costs	$100,000

The new piece of equipment mentioned above has a useful life of five years and zero salvage value. The old piece of equipment mentioned above would be sold at the beginning of the project and there would be no gain or loss realized on its sale. Rosman uses the straight-line depreciation method for financial reporting and tax purposes. The company's tax rate is 30% and its after-tax cost of capital is 12%. When the project concludes in five years the working capital will be released for investment elsewhere within the company.

Required:
Calculate the net present value of this investment opportunity.

PROBLEM 8C–5 Income Taxes and Net Present Value Analysis [LO 8–5, LO 8–8]

Shimano Company has an opportunity to manufacture and sell one of two new products for a five-year period. The company's tax rate is 30% and its after-tax cost of capital is 14%. The cost and revenue estimates for each product are as follows:

	Product A	Product B
Initial investment in equipment	$400,000	$550,000
Initial investment in working capital	$85,000	$60,000
Annual sales	$370,000	$390,000
Annual cash operating expenses	$200,000	$170,000
Cost of repairs needed in three years	$45,000	$70,000

The equipment pertaining to both products has a useful life of five years and no salvage value. The company uses the straight-line depreciation method for financial reporting and tax purposes. At the end of five years, each product's working capital will be released for investment elsewhere within the company.

Required:
1. What is the net present value of each investment opportunity?
2. Which of the two products should the company pursue? Why?

LEARNING OBJECTIVES

After studying Chapter 9, you should be able to:

LO 9–1 Understand why organizations budget and the processes they use to create budgets.

LO 9–2 Prepare a sales budget, including a schedule of expected cash collections.

LO 9–3 Prepare a production budget.

LO 9–4 Prepare a direct materials budget, including a schedule of expected cash disbursements for purchases of materials.

LO 9–5 Prepare a direct labor budget.

LO 9–6 Prepare a manufacturing overhead budget.

LO 9–7 Prepare a selling and administrative expense budget.

LO 9–8 Prepare a cash budget.

LO 9–9 Prepare a budgeted income statement.

LO 9–10 Prepare a budgeted balance sheet.

Master Budgeting

Planning for a Crisis—Civil War Trust

BUSINESS FOCUS

© Sandee Noreen

The Civil War Trust (CWT) is a private, nonprofit organization with 70,000 members that works to preserve the nation's remaining Civil War battlefields—many of which are threatened by commercial development such as shopping centers, houses, industrial parks, and casinos. To forestall development, the CWT typically purchases the land or development rights to the land. The CWT has saved over 25,000 acres from development, including, for example, 698 acres of battlefield at Gettysburg.

CWT's management team was particularly concerned about the budget proposal for 2009, which was to be presented to the board of directors in the fall of 2008. The CWT is wholly supported by contributions from its members and many of those members had been adversely affected by the ongoing financial crisis that followed the collapse of the subprime mortgage market. Consequently, the funds that would be available for operations in 2009 were particularly difficult to predict. Accordingly, the budget for 2009 contained three variations based on progressively pessimistic economic assumptions. The more pessimistic budgets were called contingent budgets. As 2008 progressed and member contributions declined somewhat from previous levels, CWT switched to the first contingent budget. This contingent budget required a number of actions to reduce costs including a hiring freeze and a salary freeze, but maintained an aggressive program of protecting battlefield acreage through purchases of land and development rights. Fortunately, the CWT did not have to switch to the most pessimistic budget—which would have involved layoffs and other extraordinary cost-saving measures.

Instead of reacting in a panic mode to unfavorable developments, CWT used the budgeting process to carefully plan in advance for a number of possible contingencies. ■

Source: Communications with James Lighthizer, president, and David Duncan, director of membership and development, Civil War Trust; and the CWT website, www.civilwar.org.

In this chapter, we describe how organizations strive to achieve their financial goals by preparing a number of budgets that together form an integrated business plan known as the *master budget.* The master budget is an essential management tool that communicates management's plans throughout the organization, allocates resources, and coordinates activities.

What Is a Budget?

LEARNING OBJECTIVE 9–1
Understand why organizations budget and the processes they use to create budgets.

A **budget** is a detailed plan for the future that is usually expressed in formal quantitative terms. Individuals sometimes create household budgets that balance their income and expenditures for food, clothing, housing, and so on while providing for some savings. Once the budget is established, actual spending is compared to the budget to make sure the plan is being followed. Companies use budgets in a similar way, although the amount of work and underlying details far exceed a personal budget.

Budgets are used for two distinct purposes—*planning* and *control.* **Planning** involves developing goals and preparing various budgets to achieve those goals. **Control** involves gathering feedback to ensure that the plan is being properly executed or modified as circumstances change. To be effective, a good budgeting system must provide for both planning and control. Good planning without effective control is a waste of time and effort.

Advantages of Budgeting

Organizations realize many benefits from budgeting, including:

1. Budgets *communicate* management's plans throughout the organization.
2. Budgets force managers to *think about* and *plan* for the future. In the absence of the necessity to prepare a budget, many managers would spend all of their time dealing with day-to-day emergencies.
3. The budgeting process provides a means of *allocating resources* to those parts of the organization where they can be used most effectively.
4. The budgeting process can uncover potential *bottlenecks* before they occur.
5. Budgets *coordinate* the activities of the entire organization by *integrating* the plans of its various parts. Budgeting helps to ensure that everyone in the organization is pulling in the same direction.
6. Budgets define goals and objectives that can serve as *benchmarks* for evaluating subsequent performance.

IN BUSINESS

EXECUTING STRATEGY WITH BUDGETS

Robert DeMartini, the CEO of New Balance, set a goal of tripling his company's revenues to $3 billion in four years. He tripled the company's annual advertising budget and doubled its consumer research budget in an effort to attract more young customers. These decisions represented a strategic shift for New Balance, which usually spends less than $20 million per year in advertising compared to competitors such as Nike and Adidas, which annually invest $184 million and $80 million, respectively.

One reason companies prepare budgets is to allocate resources across departments in a manner that supports strategic priorities. DeMartini used the budget to send a clear signal that his marketing department was expected to play a huge role in achieving the company's revenue growth targets. As time progresses, he will compare the company's actual revenue growth from young consumers to the marketing department's expenditures to see if his strategy is working or requires adjustment.

Source: Stephanie Kang, "New Balance Steps up Marketing Drive," *The Wall Street Journal,* March 21, 2008, p. B3.

Responsibility Accounting

Most of what we say in this chapter and in the next three chapters is concerned with *responsibility accounting*. The basic idea underlying? **responsibility accounting** is that a manager should be held responsible for those items—and *only* those items—that the manager can actually control to a significant extent. Each line item (i.e., revenue or cost) in the budget is the responsibility of a manager who is held responsible for subsequent deviations between budgeted goals and actual results. In effect, responsibility accounting *personalizes* accounting information by holding individuals responsible for revenues and costs. This concept is central to any effective planning and control system. Someone must be held responsible for each cost or else no one will be responsible and the cost will inevitably grow out of control.

What happens if actual results do not measure up to the budgeted goals? The manager is not necessarily penalized. However, the manager should take the initiative to understand the sources of significant favorable or unfavorable discrepancies, should take steps to correct unfavorable discrepancies and to exploit and replicate favorable discrepancies, and should be prepared to explain discrepancies and the steps taken to correct or exploit them to higher management. The point of an effective responsibility accounting system is to make sure that nothing "falls through the cracks," that the organization reacts quickly and appropriately to deviations from its plans, and that the organization learns from the feedback it gets by comparing budgeted goals to actual results. The point is *not* to penalize individuals for missing targets.

IN BUSINESS

SMALL BUSINESSES ARE CUTTING THE NUMBER OF EMPLOYEES

Costume Specialists had to decrease its workforce by 20% when the economy tanked. However, when sales began to surge the company did not budget for a workforce expansion because it had learned to function more efficiently with fewer employees. Many other small businesses have also "tightened their budgeting belts" by choosing to operate with fewer employees. In some cases, these companies have used methods such as cross-training their employees to improve efficiency. However, in other cases they are using contract workers instead of hiring full-time employees to avoid the cost of providing full-time employees with fringe benefits such as health insurance.

Source: Sarah E. Needleman, "Entrepreneurs Prefer to Keep Staffs Lean," *The Wall Street Journal*, March 2, 2010, p. B5.

Choosing a Budget Period

Operating budgets ordinarily cover a one-year period corresponding to the company's fiscal year. Many companies divide their budget year into four quarters. The first quarter is then subdivided into months, and monthly budgets are developed. The last three quarters may be carried in the budget as quarterly totals only. As the year progresses, the figures for the second quarter are broken down into monthly amounts, then the third-quarter figures are broken down, and so forth. This approach has the advantage of requiring periodic review and reappraisal of budget data throughout the year.

Continuous or *perpetual budgets* are sometimes used. A **continuous** or **perpetual budget** is a 12-month budget that rolls forward one month (or quarter) as the current month (or quarter) is completed. In other words, one month (or quarter) is added to the end of the budget as each month (or quarter) comes to a close. This approach keeps managers focused at least one year ahead so that they do not become too narrowly focused on short-term results.

In this chapter, we will look at one-year operating budgets. However, using basically the same techniques, operating budgets can be prepared for periods that extend over many years. It may be difficult to accurately forecast sales and other data much beyond a year, but even rough estimates can be invaluable in uncovering potential problems and opportunities that would otherwise be overlooked.

The Self–Imposed Budget

The success of a budget program is largely determined by the way a budget is developed. Oftentimes, the budget is imposed from above, with little participation by lower-level managers. However, in the most successful budget programs, managers actively participate in preparing their own budgets. Imposing expectations from above and then penalizing employees who do not meet those expectations will generate resentment rather than cooperation and commitment. In fact, many managers believe that being empowered to create their own *self-imposed budgets* is the most effective method of budget preparation. A **self-imposed** or **participative budget** is a budget that is prepared with the full cooperation and participation of managers at all levels.

Self-imposed budgets have a number of advantages:

1. Individuals at all levels of the organization are recognized as members of the team whose views and judgments are valued by top management.
2. Budget estimates prepared by front-line managers are often more accurate and reliable than estimates prepared by top managers who have less intimate knowledge of markets and day-to-day operations.
3. Motivation is generally higher when individuals participate in setting their own goals than when the goals are imposed from above. Self-imposed budgets create commitment.
4. A manager who is not able to meet a budget that has been imposed from above can always say that the budget was unrealistic and impossible to meet. With a self-imposed budget, this claim cannot be made.

Self-imposed budgeting has two important limitations. First, lower-level managers may make suboptimal budgeting recommendations if they lack the broad strategic perspective possessed by top managers. Second, self-imposed budgeting may allow lower-level managers to create too much *budgetary slack*. Because the manager who creates the budget will be held accountable for actual results that deviate from the budget, the manager will have a natural tendency to submit a budget that is easy to attain (i.e., the manager will build slack into the budget). For this reason, budgets prepared by lower-level managers should be scrutinized by higher levels of management. Questionable items should be discussed and modified as appropriate. Without such a review, self-imposed budgets may fail to support the organization's strategy or may be too slack, resulting in suboptimal performance.

Unfortunately, many companies do not use self-imposed budgeting. Instead, top managers often initiate the budgeting process by issuing profit targets. Lower-level managers are directed to prepare budgets that meet those targets. The difficulty is that the targets set by top managers may be unrealistically high or may allow too much slack. If the targets are too high and employees know they are unrealistic, motivation will suffer. If the targets allow too much slack, waste will occur. Unfortunately, top managers are often not in a position to know whether the targets are appropriate. Admittedly, a self-imposed budgeting system may lack sufficient strategic direction and lower-level managers may be tempted to build slack into their budgets. Nevertheless, because of the motivational advantages of self-imposed budgets, top managers should be cautious about imposing inflexible targets from above.

Human Factors in Budgeting

The success of a budget program also depends on whether top management uses the budget to pressure or blame employees. Using budgets to blame employees breeds hostility, tension, and mistrust rather than cooperation and productivity. Unfortunately, the budget is too often used as a pressure device and excessive emphasis is placed on "meeting the budget" under all circumstances. Rather than being used as a weapon, the budget should be used as a positive instrument to assist in establishing goals, measuring operating results, and isolating areas that need attention.

The budgeting process is also influenced by the fact that bonuses are often based on meeting and exceeding budgets. Typically, no bonus is paid unless the budget is met. The bonus often increases when the budget target is exceeded, but the bonus is usually capped out at some level. For obvious reasons, managers who have such a bonus plan or whose performance is evaluated based on meeting budget targets usually prefer to be evaluated based on highly achievable budgets. Moreover, highly achievable budgets may help build a manager's confidence and generate greater commitment to the budget while also reducing the likelihood that a manager will engage in undesirable behavior at the end of budgetary periods to secure bonus compensation. So, while some experts argue that budget targets should be very challenging and should require managers to stretch to meet their goals, in practice, most companies set their budget targets at "highly achievable" levels.

The Master Budget: An Overview

The **master budget** consists of a number of separate but interdependent budgets that formally lay out the company's sales, production, and financial goals. The master budget culminates in a cash budget, a budgeted income statement, and a budgeted balance sheet. Exhibit 9–1 provides an overview of the various parts of the master budget and how they are related.

EXHIBIT 9–1
The Master Budget Interrelationships

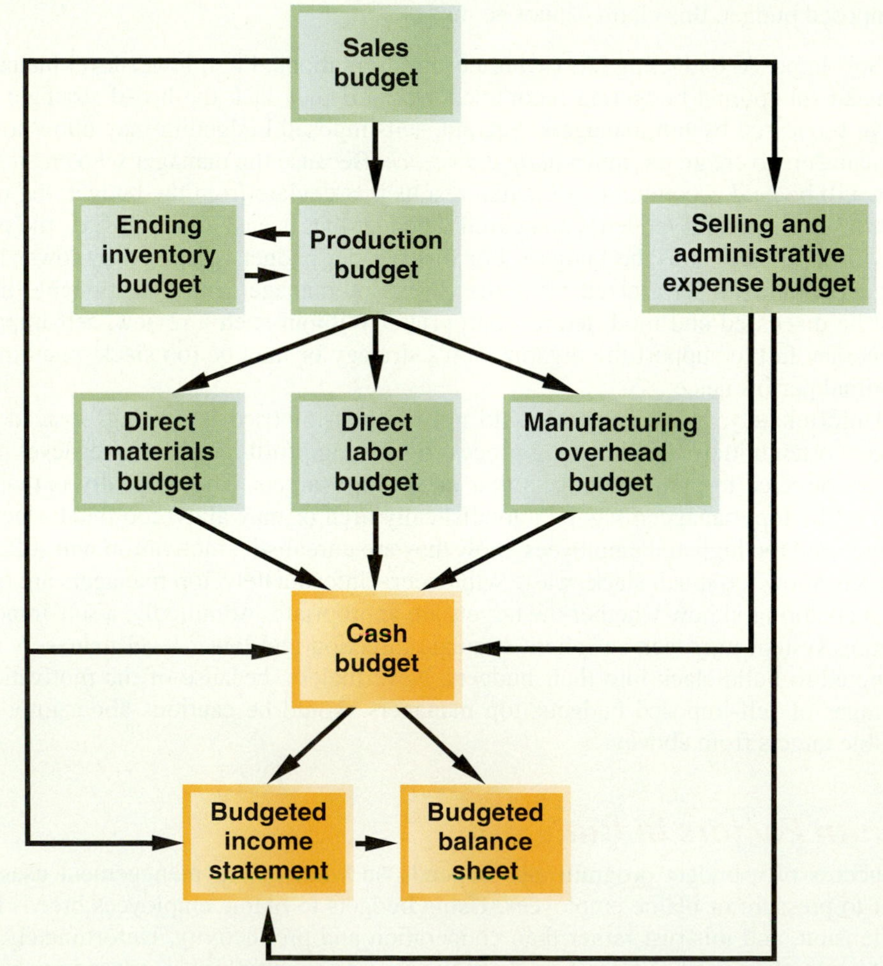

The first step in the budgeting process is the preparation of the **sales budget**, which is a detailed schedule showing the expected sales for the budget period. An accurate sales budget is the key to the entire budgeting process. As illustrated in Exhibit 9–1, all other parts of the master budget depend on the sales budget. If the sales budget is inaccurate, the rest of the budget will be inaccurate. The sales budget is based on the company's sales forecast, which may require the use of sophisticated mathematical models and statistical tools that are beyond the scope of this course.

The sales budget influences the variable portion of the selling and administrative expense budget and it feeds into the production budget, which defines how many units need to be produced during the budget period. The production budget in turn is used to determine the direct materials, direct labor, and manufacturing overhead budgets. Once a company has prepared these three manufacturing cost budgets, it can prepare the ending finished goods inventory budget.

The master budget concludes with the preparation of a cash budget, income statement, and balance sheet. Information from the sales budget, selling and administrative expense budget, and the manufacturing cost budgets all influence the preparation of the *cash budget*. A **cash budget** is a detailed plan showing how cash resources will be acquired and used. The budgeted income statement provides an estimate of net income for the budget period and it relies on information from the sales budget, ending finished goods inventory budget, selling and administrative expense budget, and the cash budget. The final schedule of the master budget is the balance sheet, which estimates a company's assets, liabilities, and stockholders' equity at the end of a budget period.

Seeing the Big Picture

The 10 schedules contained in a master budget can be overwhelming; therefore, it is important to see the big picture in two respects. First, a master budget for a manufacturing company is designed to answer 10 key questions as follows:

1. How much sales revenue will we earn?
2. How much cash will we collect from customers?
3. How much raw material will we need to purchase?
4. How much manufacturing cost (including direct materials, direct labor, and manufacturing overhead) will we incur?
5. How much cash will we pay to our suppliers and our direct laborers, and how much will we pay for manufacturing overhead resources?
6. What is the total cost that will be transferred from finished goods inventory to cost of goods sold?
7. How much selling and administrative expense will we incur and how much cash will we pay related to those expenses?
8. How much money will we borrow from or repay to lenders—including interest?
9. How much net operating income will we earn?
10. What will our balance sheet look like at the end of the budget period?

Second, it is important to understand that many of the schedules in a master budget hinge on a variety of estimates and assumptions that managers must make when preparing those schedules. Exhibit 9–2 summarizes the questions that underlie these estimates and assumptions for seven of the schedules included in a master budget. As you study the forthcoming budget schedules, keep these two "big picture" insights in mind—that the budget is designed to answer 10 key questions and that it is based on various estimates and assumptions—because they will help you understand *why* and *how* a master budget is created.

EXHIBIT 9–2
Estimates and Assumptions for a Master Budget

Sales budget:
1. What are the budgeted unit sales?
2. What is the budgeted selling price per unit?
3. What percentage of accounts receivable will be collected in the current and subsequent periods?

Production budget:
1. What percentage of next period's unit sales needs to be maintained in ending finished goods inventory?

Direct materials budget:
1. How many units of raw material are needed to make one unit of finished goods?
2. What is the budgeted cost for one unit of raw material?
3. What percentage of next period's production needs should be maintained in ending raw materials inventory?
4. What percentage of raw material purchases will be paid in the current and subsequent periods?

Direct labor budget:
1. How many direct labor-hours are required per unit of finished goods?
2. What is the budgeted direct labor wage rate per hour?

Manufacturing overhead budget:
1. What is the budgeted variable overhead cost per unit of the allocation base?
2. What is the total budgeted fixed overhead cost per period?
3. What is the budgeted depreciation expense on factory assets per period?

Selling and administrative expense budget:
1. What is the budgeted variable selling and administrative expense per unit sold?
2. What is the total budgeted fixed selling and administrative expense per period?
3. What is the budgeted depreciation expense on non-factory assets per period?

Cash budget:
1. What is the budgeted minimum cash balance?
2. What are our estimated expenditures for noncurrent asset purchases and dividends?
3. What is the estimated interest rate on borrowed funds?

Preparing the Master Budget

MANAGERIAL ACCOUNTING IN ACTION
The Issue

Hampton Freeze Inc.

Tom Wills is the majority stockholder and chief executive officer of Hampton Freeze, Inc., a company he started in 2015. The company makes premium popsicles using only natural ingredients and featuring exotic flavors such as tangy tangerine and minty mango. The company's business is highly seasonal, with most of the sales occurring in spring and summer.

In 2016, the company's second year of operations, a major cash crunch in the first and second quarters almost forced the company into bankruptcy. In spite of this cash crunch, 2016 turned out to be a very successful year in terms of both cash flow and net income. Partly as a result of that harrowing experience, Tom decided toward the end of 2016 to hire a professional financial manager. Tom interviewed several promising candidates for the job and settled on Larry Giano, who had considerable experience in the packaged foods industry. In the job interview, Tom questioned Larry about the steps he would take to prevent a recurrence of the 2016 cash crunch:

Tom: As I mentioned earlier, we are going to end 2016 with a very nice profit. What you may not know is that we had some very big financial problems this year.
Larry: Let me guess. You ran out of cash sometime in the first or second quarter.
Tom: How did you know?

Larry: Most of your sales are in the second and third quarter, right?

Tom: Sure, everyone wants to buy popsicles in the spring and summer, but nobody wants them when the weather turns cold.

Larry: So you don't have many sales in the first quarter?

Tom: Right.

Larry: And in the second quarter, which is the spring, you are producing like crazy to fill orders?

Tom: Sure.

Larry: Do your customers, the grocery stores, pay you the day you make your deliveries?

Tom: Are you kidding? Of course not.

Larry: So in the first quarter, you don't have many sales. In the second quarter, you are producing like crazy, which eats up cash, but you aren't paid by your customers until long after you have paid your employees and suppliers. No wonder you had a cash problem. I see this pattern all the time in food processing because of the seasonality of the business.

Tom: So what can we do about it?

Larry: The first step is to predict the magnitude of the problem before it occurs. If we can predict early in the year what the cash shortfall is going to be, we can go to the bank and arrange for credit before we really need it. Bankers tend to be leery of panicky people who show up begging for emergency loans. They are much more likely to make the loan if you look like you are in control of the situation.

Tom: How can we predict the cash shortfall?

Larry: You can put together a cash budget. In fact, while you're at it, you might as well do a master budget. You'll find it well worth the effort because we can use a master budget to estimate the financial statement implications of numerous "what-if" questions. For example, with the click of a mouse we can answer questions such as: What-if unit sales are 10% less than our original forecast, what will be the impact on profits? Or, what if we increase our selling price by 15% and unit sales drop by 5%, what will be the impact on profits?

Tom: That sounds great Larry! Not only do we need a cash budget, but I would love to have a master budget that could quickly answer the types of "what-if" questions that you just described. As far as I'm concerned, the sooner you get started, the better.

With the full backing of Tom Wills, Larry Giano set out to create a master budget for the company for the year 2017. In his planning for the budgeting process, Larry drew up the following list of documents that would be a part of the master budget:

1. A sales budget, including a schedule of expected cash collections.
2. A production budget (a merchandise purchases budget would be used in a merchandising company).
3. A direct materials budget, including a schedule of expected cash disbursements for purchases of materials.
4. A direct labor budget.
5. A manufacturing overhead budget.
6. An ending finished goods inventory budget.
7. A selling and administrative expense budget.
8. A cash budget.
9. A budgeted income statement.
10. A budgeted balance sheet.

Larry felt it was important to have everyone's cooperation in the budgeting process, so he asked Tom to call a companywide meeting to explain the budgeting process. At the meeting there was initially some grumbling, but Tom was able to convince nearly everyone of the necessity for planning and getting better control over spending. It helped that the cash crisis earlier in the year was still fresh in everyone's minds. As much as some people disliked the idea of budgets, they liked their jobs more.

In the months that followed, Larry worked closely with all of the managers involved in the master budget, gathering data from them and making sure that they understood and fully supported the parts of the master budget that would affect them.

The interdependent documents that Larry Giano prepared for Hampton Freeze are Schedules 1 through 10 of the company's master budget. In this section, we will study these schedules as well as the beginning balance sheet and the budgeting assumptions that Larry included in his master budget to help answer the types of "what-if" questions that he discussed with Tom Wills.

The Beginning Balance Sheet

Exhibit 9–3 shows the first tab included in Larry's Microsoft Excel master budget file. It contains Hampton Freeze's beginning balance sheet as of December 31, 2016. Larry included this balance sheet in his master budget file so that he could link some of this data to subsequent schedules. For example, as you'll eventually see, he used cell references within Excel to link the beginning accounts receivable balance of $90,000 to the schedule of expected cash collections. He also used cell references to link the beginning cash balance of $42,500 to the cash budget.

The Budgeting Assumptions

Exhibit 9–4 shows the second tab included in Larry's master budget file. It is labeled Budgeting Assumptions and it contains all of Hampton Freeze's answers to the questions summarized in Exhibit 9–2. The data included in Exhibit 9–4 summarize the estimates and assumptions that provide the foundation for Hampton Freeze's entire master budget,

EXHIBIT 9–3
Hampton Freeze: The Beginning Balance Sheet

	A	B	C
1	**Hampton Freeze, Inc.**		
2	**Balance Sheet**		
3	**December 31, 2016**		
4			
5	**Assets**		
6	Current assets:		
7	Cash	$ 42,500	
8	Accounts receivable	90,000	
9	Raw materials inventory (21,000 pounds)	4,200	
10	Finished goods inventory (2,000 cases)	26,000	
11	Total current assets		$162,700
12	Plant and equipment:		
13	Land	80,000	
14	Buildings and equipment	700,000	
15	Accumulated depreciation	(292,000)	
16	Plant and equipment, net		488,000
17	Total assets		$650,700
18			
19	**Liabilities and Stockholders' Equity**		
20	Current liabilities:		
21	Accounts payable		$ 25,800
22	Stockholders' equity:		
23	Common stock	$ 175,000	
24	Retained earnings	449,900	
25	Total stockholders' equity		624,900
26	Total liabilities and stockholders' equity		$650,700
27			

Beginning Balance Sheet / Budgeting Assump

EXHIBIT 9–4

Hampton Freeze: Budgeting Assumptions

	A	B	C	D	E	F
1		**Hampton Freeze, Inc.**				
2		**Budgeting Assumptions**				
3		**For the Year Ended December 31, 2017**				
4						
5		*All 4 Quarters*	*Quarter*			
6	*Sales Budget*		*1*	*2*	*3*	*4*
7	Budgeted sales in cases		10,000	30,000	40,000	20,000
8	Selling price per case	$ 20.00				
9	Percentage of sales collected in the quarter of sale	70%				
10	Percentage of sales collected in the quarter after sale	30%				
11						
12	*Production Budget*					
13	Percentage of next quarter's sales in ending finished goods inventory	20%				
14						
15	*Direct Materials Budget*					
16	Pounds of sugar per case	15				
17	Cost per pound of sugar	$ 0.20				
18	Percentage of next quarter's production needs in ending inventory	10%				
19	Percentage of purchases paid in the quarter purchased	50%				
20	Percentage of purchases paid in the quarter after purchase	50%				
21						
22	*Direct Labor Budget*					
23	Direct labor-hours required per case	0.40				
24	Direct labor cost per hour	$ 15.00				
25						
26	*Manufacturing Overhead Budget*					
27	Variable manufacturing overhead per direct labor-hour	$ 4.00				
28	Fixed manufacturing overhead per quarter	$ 60,600				
29	Depreciation per quarter	$ 15,000				
30						
31						
32	*Selling and Administrative Expense Budget*					
33	Variable selling and administrative expense per case	$ 1.80				
34	Fixed selling and administrative expense per quarter:					
35	Advertising	$ 20,000				
36	Executive salaries	$ 55,000				
37	Insurance	$ 10,000				
38	Property tax	$ 4,000				
39	Depreciation	$ 10,000				
40						
41	*Cash Budget*					
42	Minimum cash balance	$ 30,000				
43	Equipment purchases		$ 50,000	$ 40,000	$ 20,000	$ 20,000
44	Dividends	$ 8,000				
45	Simple interest rate per quarter	3%				
46						

Beginning Balance Sheet | **Budgeting Assumptions** | Schedule 1 | Schedule 2 | Sche

*For simplicity, we assume that all quarterly estimates, except quarterly unit sales and equipment purchases, will be the same for all four quarters.

so it is important to familiarize yourself with this information now. Beginning with the estimates underlying the sales budget, Exhibit 9–4 shows that Hampton Freeze's budgeted quarterly unit sales are 10,000, 30,000, 40,000, and 20,000 cases. Its budgeted selling price is $20 per case. The company expects to collect 70% of its credit sales in the quarter of sale, and the remaining 30% of credit sales will be collected in the quarter after sale.

Exhibit 9–4 also shows that the production budget is based on the assumption that Hampton Freeze will maintain ending finished goods inventory equal to 20% of the next quarter's unit sales. In terms of the company's only direct material, high fructose sugar, it budgets 15 pounds of sugar per case of popsicles at a cost of $0.20 per pound.[1] It expects to maintain ending raw materials inventory equal to 10% of the raw materials needed to

[1] While popsicle manufacturing is likely to involve other raw materials, such as popsicle sticks and packaging materials, for simplicity, we have limited our scope to high fructose sugar.

satisfy the following quarter's production. In addition, the company plans to pay for 50% of its material purchases within the month of purchase and the remaining 50% in the following month.

Continuing with a summary of Exhibit 9–4, the two key assumptions underlying the direct labor budget are that 0.40 direct labor-hours are required per case of popsicles and the direct labor cost per hour is $15. The manufacturing overhead budget is based on three underlying assumptions—the variable overhead cost per direct labor-hour is $4.00, the total fixed overhead per quarter is $60,600, and the quarterly depreciation on factory assets is $15,000. Exhibit 9–4 also shows that the budgeted variable selling and administrative expense per case of popsicles is $1.80 and the fixed selling and administrative expenses per quarter include advertising ($20,000), executive salaries ($55,000), insurance ($10,000), property tax ($4,000), and depreciation expense ($10,000). The remaining budget assumptions depicted in Exhibit 9–4 pertain to the cash budget. The company expects to maintain a minimum cash balance each quarter of $30,000; it plans to make quarterly equipment purchases of $50,000, $40,000, $20,000, and $20,000;[2] it plans to pay quarterly dividends of $8,000; and it expects to pay simple interest on borrowed money of 3% per quarter.

Before reading further, it is important to understand why Larry created the Budgeting Assumptions tab shown in Exhibit 9–4. He did it because it simplifies the process of using a master budget to answer "what-if" questions. For example, assume that Larry wanted to answer the question: What-if we increase the selling price per unit by $2 and expect sales to drop by 1,000 units per quarter, what would be the impact on profits? With a properly constructed Budgeting Assumptions tab, Larry would only need to make a few adjustments to the data within this tab and the formulas embedded in each of the budget schedules would automatically update the projected financial results. This is much simpler than attempting to adjust data inputs within each of the master budget schedules.

The Sales Budget

LEARNING OBJECTIVE 9–2
Prepare a sales budget, including a schedule of expected cash collections.

Schedule 1 contains Hampton Freeze's sales budget for 2017. As you study this schedule, keep in mind that all of its numbers are derived from cell references to the Budgeting Assumptions tab and formulas—none of the numbers appearing in the schedule were actually keyed into their respective cells. Furthermore, it bears emphasizing that all remaining schedules in the master budget are prepared in the same fashion—they rely almost exclusively on cell references and formulas.

For the year, Hampton Freeze expects to sell 100,000 cases of popsicles at a price of $20 per case for total budgeted sales of $2,000,000. The budgeted unit sales for each quarter (10,000, 30,000, 40,000, and 20,000) come from cells C7 through F7 in the Budgeting Assumptions tab shown in Exhibit 9–4, and the selling price per case ($20.00) comes from cell B8 in the Budgeting Assumptions tab. Schedule 1 also shows that the company's expected cash collections for 2017 are $1,970,000. The accounts receivable balance of $90,000 that is collected in the first quarter comes from cell B8 of the beginning balance sheet shown in Exhibit 9–3. All other cash collections rely on the estimated cash collection percentages from cells B9 and B10 of the Budgeting Assumptions tab. For example, Schedule 1 shows that the budgeted sales for the first quarter equal $200,000. In the first quarter, Hampton Freeze expects to collect 70% of this amount, or $140,000. In the second quarter, the company expects to collect the remaining 30% of this amount, or $60,000.

The Production Budget

LEARNING OBJECTIVE 9–3
Prepare a production budget.

The production budget is prepared after the sales budget. The **production budget** lists the number of units that must be produced to satisfy sales needs and to provide for the desired ending finished goods inventory. Production needs can be determined as follows:

[2] For simplicity, we assume that depreciation on these newly acquired assets is included in the quarterly depreciation estimates included in the Budgeting Assumptions tab.

SCHEDULE 1

Hampton Freeze, Inc.
Sales Budget
For the Year Ended December 31, 2017

	Quarter				
	1	2	3	4	Year
Budgeted unit sales (in cases)	10,000	30,000	40,000	20,000	100,000
Selling price per unit	$ 20.00	$ 20.00	$ 20.00	$ 20.00	$ 20.00
Total sales	$200,000	$600,000	$800,000	$400,000	$2,000,000
	70%	30%			

Schedule of Expected Cash Collections

	1	2	3	4	Year
Beginning accounts receivable[1]	$ 90,000				$ 90,000
First-quarter sales[2]	140,000	$ 60,000			200,000
Second-quarter sales[3]		420,000	$180,000		600,000
Third-quarter sales[4]			560,000	$240,000	800,000
Fourth-quarter sales[5]	-	-	-	280,000	280,000
Total cash collections[6]	$230,000	$480,000	$740,000	$520,000	$1,970,000

Budgeting Assumptions | Schedule 1 | Schedule 2 | Schedule 3 | Sc

[1]Cash collections from last year's fourth-quarter sales. See the beginning balance sheet in Exhibit 9–3.
[2]$200,000 × 70%; $200,000 × 30%.
[3]$600,000 × 70%; $600,000 × 30%.
[4]$800,000 × 70%; $800,000 × 30%.
[5]$400,000 × 70%.
[6]Uncollected fourth-quarter sales ($120,000) appear as accounts receivable on the company's end-of-year budgeted balance sheet (see Schedule 10).

Budgeted unit sales	XXXX
Add desired units of ending finished goods inventory	XXXX
Total needs	XXXX
Less units of beginning finished goods inventory	XXXX
Required production in units	XXXX

Note the production requirements are influenced by the desired level of the ending finished goods inventory. Inventories should be carefully planned. Excessive inventories tie up funds and create storage problems. Insufficient inventories can lead to lost sales or last-minute, high-cost production efforts.

Schedule 2 contains the production budget for Hampton Freeze. The budgeted sales data come from cells B7 through E7 of the sales budget. The desired ending finished goods inventory for the first quarter of 6,000 cases is computed by multiplying budgeted sales from the second quarter (30,000 cases) by the desired ending finished goods inventory percentage (20%) shown in cell B13 of the Budgeting Assumptions tab. The total needs for the first quarter (16,000 cases) are determined by adding together the budgeted sales of 10,000 cases for the quarter and the desired ending inventory of 6,000 cases. As discussed above, the ending inventory is intended to provide some cushion in the event that problems develop in production or sales increase unexpectedly. Because the company already has 2,000 cases in beginning finished goods inventory (as shown in the beginning balance sheet in Exhibit 9–3), only 14,000 cases need to be produced in the first quarter.

SCHEDULE 2

Hampton Freeze, Inc.
Production Budget
For the Year Ended December 31, 2017
(in cases)

	Quarter 1	Quarter 2	Quarter 3	Quarter 4	Year
Budgeted unit sales (Schedule 1)	10,000	30,000	40,000	20,000	100,000
Add desired units of ending finished goods inventory*	6,000	8,000	4,000	3,000	3,000
Total needs	16,000	38,000	44,000	23,000	103,000
Less units of beginning finished goods inventory†	2,000	6,000	8,000	4,000	2,000
Required production in units	14,000	32,000	36,000	19,000	101,000

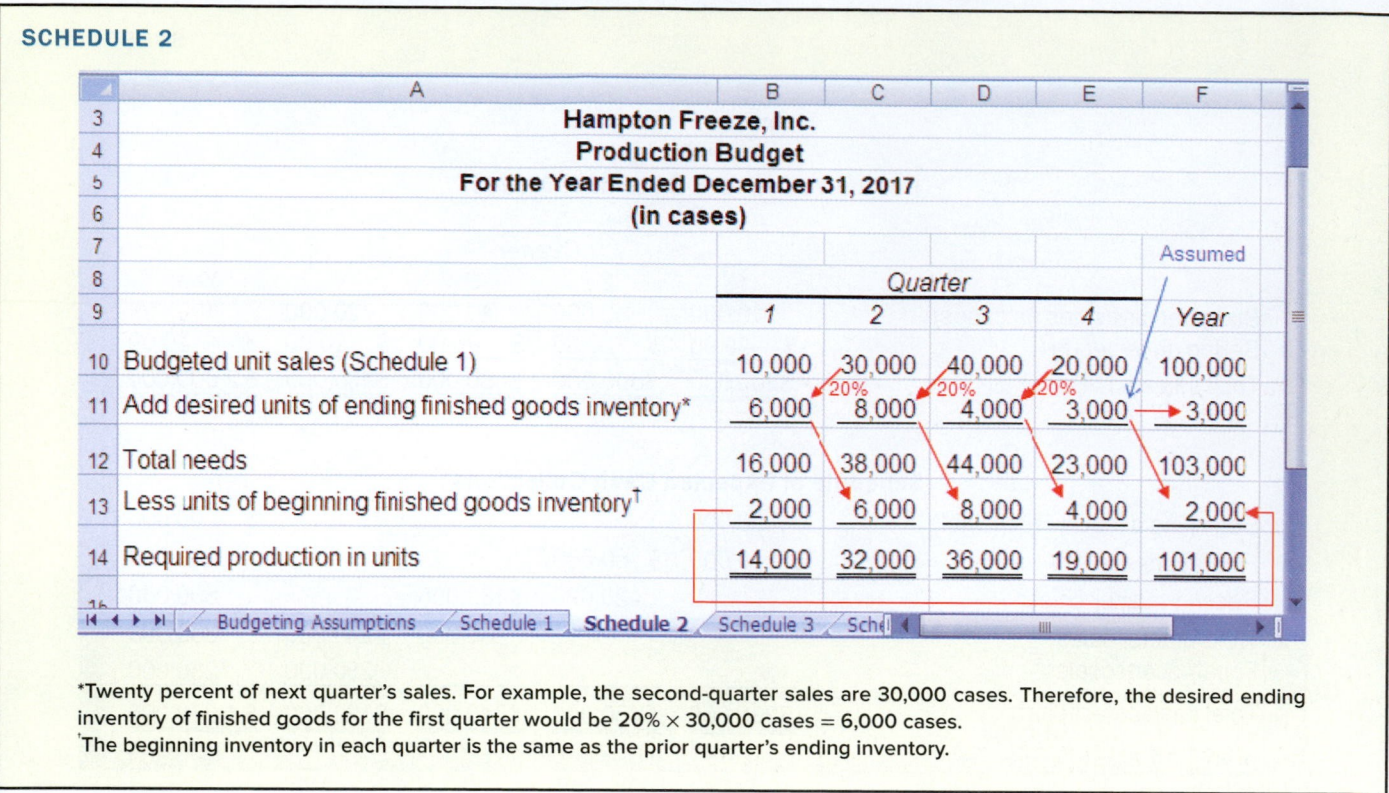

*Twenty percent of next quarter's sales. For example, the second-quarter sales are 30,000 cases. Therefore, the desired ending inventory of finished goods for the first quarter would be 20% × 30,000 cases = 6,000 cases.
†The beginning inventory in each quarter is the same as the prior quarter's ending inventory.

Pay particular attention to the Year column to the right of the production budget in Schedule 2. In some cases (e.g., budgeted sales, total needs, and required production), the amount listed for the year is the sum of the quarterly amounts for the item. In other cases, (e.g., desired units of ending finished goods inventory and units of beginning finished goods inventory), the amount listed for the year is not simply the sum of the quarterly amounts. From the standpoint of the entire year, the beginning finished goods inventory is the same as the beginning finished goods inventory for the first quarter—it is *not* the sum of the beginning finished goods inventories for all four quarters. Similarly, from the standpoint of the entire year, the ending finished goods inventory, which Larry Giano assumed to be 3,000 units, is the same as the ending finished goods inventory for the fourth quarter—it is *not* the sum of the ending finished goods inventories for all four quarters. It is important to pay attention to such distinctions in all schedules that follow.

Inventory Purchases—Merchandising Company

Hampton Freeze prepares a production budget because it is a *manufacturing* company. If it were a *merchandising* company, instead it would prepare a **merchandise purchases budget** showing the amount of goods to be purchased from suppliers during the period.

The format of the merchandise purchases budget is shown below:

Budgeted cost of goods sold	XXXX
Add desired ending merchandise inventory	XXXX
Total needs	XXXX
Less beginning merchandise inventory	XXXX
Required purchases	XXXX

A merchandising company would prepare a merchandise purchases budget, such as the one above, for each item carried in stock. The merchandise purchases budget can be expressed in dollars (as shown above) or in units. The top line of a merchandise purchases budget based on units would say Budgeted unit sales instead of Budgeted cost of goods sold.

A merchandise purchases budget is usually accompanied by a schedule of expected cash disbursements for merchandise purchases. The format of this schedule mirrors the approach used for the schedule of expected cash disbursements for purchases of materials that is illustrated at the bottom of Schedule 3.

The Direct Materials Budget

LEARNING OBJECTIVE 9–4
Prepare a direct materials budget, including a schedule of expected cash disbursements for purchases of materials.

A *direct materials budget* is prepared after the production requirements have been computed. The **direct materials budget** details the raw materials that must be purchased to fulfill the production budget and to provide for adequate inventories. The required purchases of raw materials are computed as follows:

Required production in units of finished goods	XXXX
Units of raw materials needed per unit of finished goods	XXXX
Units of raw materials needed to meet production	XXXX
Add desired units of ending raw materials inventory	XXXX
Total units of raw materials needed	XXXX
Less units of beginning raw materials inventory	XXXX
Units of raw materials to be purchased	XXXX
Unit cost of raw materials	XXXX
Cost of raw materials to be purchased	XXXX

Schedule 3 contains the direct materials budget for Hampton Freeze. The first line of this budget contains the required production for each quarter, which is taken directly from cells B14 through E14 of the production budget (Schedule 2). The second line of the direct materials budget recognizes that 15 pounds of sugar (see cell B16 from the Budgeting Assumptions tab) are required to make one case of popsicles. The third line of the budget presents the raw materials needed to meet production. For example, in the first quarter, the required production of 14,000 cases is multiplied by 15 pounds to equal 210,000 pounds of sugar needed to meet production. The fourth line shows the desired units of ending raw materials inventory. For the first quarter this amount is computed by multiplying the raw materials needed to meet production in the second quarter of 480,000 pounds by the desired ending inventory percentage of 10% as shown in cell B18 of the Budgeting Assumptions tab. The desired units of ending raw materials inventory of 48,000 pounds is added to 210,000 pounds to provide the total units of raw materials needed of 258,000 pounds. However, because the company already has 21,000 pounds of sugar in beginning inventory (as shown in cell A9 in the beginning balance sheet in Exhibit 9–3), only 237,000 pounds of sugar need to be purchased in the first quarter. Because the budgeted cost of raw materials per pound is $0.20 (see cell B17 from the Budgeting Assumptions tab), the cost of raw material to be purchased in the first quarter is $47,400. For the entire year, the company plans to purchase $303,300 of raw materials.

Schedule 3 also shows that the company's expected cash disbursements for material purchases for 2017 are $301,200. The accounts payable balance of $25,800 that is paid in the first quarter comes from cell C21 of the beginning balance sheet shown in Exhibit 9–3. All other cash disbursement computations rely on the estimated cash payment percentages (both of which are 50%) from cells B19 and B20 of the Budgeting Assumptions tab. For example, Schedule 3 shows that the budgeted raw material purchases for the first quarter equal $47,400. In the first quarter, Hampton Freeze expects to pay 50% of this amount, or $23,700. In the second quarter, the company expects to pay the remaining 50% of this amount, or $23,700.

SCHEDULE 3

Hampton Freeze, Inc.
Direct Materials Budget
For the Year Ended December 31, 2017

	Quarter 1	2	3	4	Year
Required production in cases (Schedule 2)	14,000	32,000	36,000	19,000	101,000
Units of raw materials needed per case	15	15	15	15	15
Units of raw materials needed to meet production	210,000	480,000	540,000	285,000	1,515,000
Add desired units of ending raw materials inventory[1]	48,000	54,000	28,500	22,500	22,500
Total units of raw materials needed	258,000	534,000	568,500	307,500	1,537,500
Less units of beginning raw materials inventory	21,000	48,000	54,000	28,500	21,000
Units of raw materials to be purchased	237,000	486,000	514,500	279,000	1,516,500
Cost of raw materials per pound	$ 0.20	$ 0.20	$ 0.20	$ 0.20	$ 0.20
Cost of raw materials to be purchased	$47,400	$97,200	$102,900	$55,800	$ 303,300

Schedule of Expected Cash Disbursements for Purchases of Materials

	Quarter 1	2	3	4	Year
Beginning accounts payable[2]	$25,800				$ 25,800
First-quarter purchases[3]	23,700	$23,700			47,400
Second-quarter purchases[4]		48,600	$ 48,600		97,200
Third-quarter purchases[5]			51,450	$51,450	102,900
Fourth-quarter purchases[6]	-	-	-	27,900	27,900
Total cash disbursements for materials	$49,500	$72,300	$100,050	$79,350	$ 301,200

[1]Ten percent of the next quarter's production needs. For example, the second-quarter production needs are 480,000 pounds. Therefore, the desired ending inventory for the first quarter would be 10% × 480,000 pounds = 48,000 pounds.

[2]Cash payments for last year's fourth-quarter purchases. See the beginning-of-year balance sheet in Exhibit 9–3 on page 394.

[3]$47,400 × 50%; $47,400 × 50%.

[4]$97,200 × 50%; $97,200 × 50%.

[5]$102,900 × 50%; $102,900 × 50%.

[6]$55,800 × 50%. Unpaid fourth-quarter purchases ($27,900) appear as accounts payable on the company's end-of-year budgeted balance sheet (see Schedule 10).

The Direct Labor Budget

LEARNING OBJECTIVE 9–5
Prepare a direct labor budget.

The **direct labor budget** shows the direct labor-hours required to satisfy the production budget. By knowing in advance how much labor time will be needed throughout the budget year, the company can develop plans to adjust the labor force as the situation requires. Companies that neglect the budgeting process run the risk of facing labor shortages or having to hire and lay off workers at awkward times. Erratic labor policies lead to insecurity, low morale, and inefficiency.

The direct labor budget for Hampton Freeze is shown in Schedule 4. The first line in the direct labor budget consists of the required production for each quarter, which is taken directly from cells B14 through E14 of the production budget (Schedule 2). The direct labor requirement for each quarter is computed by multiplying the number of units to be produced in each quarter by the 0.40 direct labor-hours required to make one unit (see cell B23 from the Budgeting Assumptions tab). For example, 14,000 cases are to be produced in the first quarter and each case requires 0.40 direct labor-hours, so a total of 5,600 direct labor-hours (14,000 cases × 0.40 direct labor-hours per case) will be required in the first quarter. The direct labor requirements are then translated into budgeted direct labor costs. How this is done will depend on the company's labor policy. In Schedule 4, Hampton Freeze has assumed that the direct labor force will be adjusted as the work requirements change from quarter to quarter. In that case, the direct labor cost is computed by simply multiplying the direct labor-hour requirements by the direct labor rate of $15 per hour

SCHEDULE 4

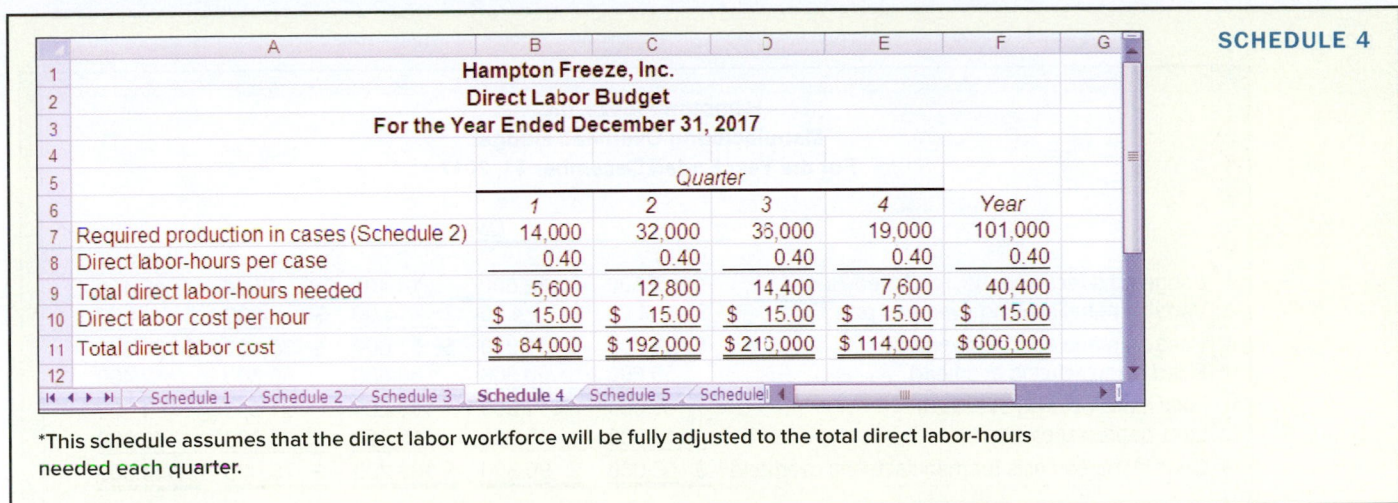

	A	B	C	D	E	F
1	Hampton Freeze, Inc.					
2	Direct Labor Budget					
3	For the Year Ended December 31, 2017					
4						
5		Quarter				
6		1	2	3	4	Year
7	Required production in cases (Schedule 2)	14,000	32,000	36,000	19,000	101,000
8	Direct labor-hours per case	0.40	0.40	0.40	0.40	0.40
9	Total direct labor-hours needed	5,600	12,800	14,400	7,600	40,400
10	Direct labor cost per hour	$ 15.00	$ 15.00	$ 15.00	$ 15.00	$ 15.00
11	Total direct labor cost	$ 84,000	$ 192,000	$ 216,000	$ 114,000	$ 606,000
12						

Schedule 1 | Schedule 2 | Schedule 3 | Schedule 4 | Schedule 5 | Schedule

*This schedule assumes that the direct labor workforce will be fully adjusted to the total direct labor-hours needed each quarter.

(see cell B24 from the Budgeting Assumptions tab). For example, the direct labor cost in the first quarter is $84,000 (5,600 direct labor-hours × $15 per direct labor-hour).

However, many companies have employment policies or contracts that prevent them from laying off and rehiring workers as needed. Suppose, for example, that Hampton Freeze has 25 workers who are classified as direct labor, but each of them is guaranteed at least 480 hours of pay each quarter at a rate of $15 per hour. In that case, the minimum direct labor cost for a quarter would be computed as follows:

$$25 \text{ workers} \times 480 \text{ hours per worker} \times \$15 \text{ per hour} = \$180{,}000$$

Note that in this case the direct costs shown in the first and fourth quarters of Schedule 4 would have to be increased to $180,000.

IN BUSINESS

MANAGING LABOR COSTS IN A DIFFICULT ECONOMY

When the economy sours, many companies choose to lay off employees. While this tactic lowers costs in the short run, it also lowers the morale and productivity of retained employees, sacrifices the institutional knowledge possessed by terminated employees, and increases future recruiting and training costs. Hypertherm Inc. has not fired a permanent employee since its founding in 1968, instead responding to economic hardship by eliminating overtime, cutting temporary staff, delaying capital investments, shifting cross-trained employees to new job responsibilities, and implementing a four-day work week. Hypertherm's employees regularly share their process improvement ideas with the company because they know if they eliminate non-value-added portions of their job responsibilities the company will redeploy them rather than eliminate non-value-added labor costs by firing them.

Source: Cari Tuna, "Some Firms Cut Costs Without Resorting to Layoffs," *The Wall Street Journal*, December 15, 2008, p. B4.

The Manufacturing Overhead Budget

LEARNING OBJECTIVE 9–6
Prepare a manufacturing overhead budget.

The **manufacturing overhead budget** lists all costs of production other than direct materials and direct labor. Schedule 5 shows the manufacturing overhead budget for Hampton Freeze. At Hampton Freeze, manufacturing overhead is separated into variable and fixed components. As shown in the Budgeting Assumptions tab (Exhibit 9–4), the variable component is $4 per direct labor-hour and the fixed component is $60,600 per quarter. Because the variable component of manufacturing overhead depends on direct labor, the first line in the manufacturing overhead budget consists of the budgeted direct labor-hours from cells B9 through E9 of the direct labor budget (Schedule 4). The budgeted direct labor-hours in each quarter are multiplied by the variable rate to determine the variable component of manufacturing overhead. For example, the variable manufacturing

SCHEDULE 5

	A	B	C	D	E	F
1	**Hampton Freeze, Inc.**					
2	**Manufacturing Overhead Budget**					
3	**For the Year Ended December 31, 2017**					
4						
5		*Quarter*				
6		*1*	*2*	*3*	*4*	*Year*
7	Budgeted direct labor-hours (Schedule 4)	5,600	12,800	14,400	7,600	40,400
8	Variable manufacturing overhead rate	$ 4.00	$ 4.00	$ 4.00	$ 4.00	$ 4.00
9	Variable manufacturing overhead	$ 22,400	$ 51,200	$ 57,600	$ 30,400	$ 161,600
10	Fixed manufacturing overhead	60,600	60,600	60,600	60,600	242,400
11	Total manufacturing overhead	83,000	111,800	118,200	91,000	404,000
12	Less depreciation	15,000	15,000	15,000	15,000	60,000
13	Cash disbursements for manufacturing overhead	$ 68,000	$ 96,800	$ 103,200	$ 76,000	$ 344,000
14						
15	Total manufacturing overhead (a)					$ 404,000
16	Budgeted direct labor-hours (b)					40,400
17	Predetermined overhead rate for the year (a)÷(b)					$10.00
18						

Schedule 3 | Schedule 4 | **Schedule 5** | Schedule 6 | Schedule 7 | Schedule 8

overhead for the first quarter is $22,400 (5,600 direct labor-hours × $4.00 per direct labor-hour). This is added to the fixed manufacturing overhead for the quarter to determine the total manufacturing overhead for the quarter of $83,000 ($22,400 + $60,600).

A few words about fixed costs and the budgeting process are in order. In most cases, fixed costs are the costs of supplying capacity to make products, process purchase orders, handle customer calls, and so on. The amount of capacity that will be required depends on the expected level of activity for the period. If the expected level of activity is greater than the company's current capacity, then fixed costs may have to be increased. Or, if the expected level is appreciably below the company's current capacity, then it may be desirable to decrease fixed costs if possible. However, once the level of the fixed costs has been determined in the budget, the costs really are fixed. The time to adjust fixed costs is during the budgeting process. An activity-based costing system can help to determine the appropriate level of fixed costs at budget time by answering questions like, "How many clerks will we need to process the anticipated number of purchase orders next year?" For simplicity, all of the budgeting examples in this book assume that the appropriate levels of fixed costs have already been determined.

The last line of Schedule 5 for Hampton Freeze shows the budgeted cash disbursements for manufacturing overhead. Because some of the overhead costs are not cash outflows, the total budgeted manufacturing overhead costs must be adjusted to determine the cash disbursements for manufacturing overhead. At Hampton Freeze, the only significant noncash manufacturing overhead cost is depreciation, which is $15,000 per quarter (see cell B29 in the Budgeting Assumptions tab). These noncash depreciation charges are deducted from the total budgeted manufacturing overhead to determine the expected cash disbursements. Hampton Freeze pays all overhead costs involving cash disbursements in the quarter incurred. Note that the company's predetermined overhead rate for the year is $10 per direct labor-hour, which is determined by dividing the total budgeted manufacturing overhead for the year by the total budgeted direct labor-hours for the year.

The Ending Finished Goods Inventory Budget

After completing Schedules 1–5, Larry Giano had all of the data he needed to compute the unit product cost for the units produced during the budget year. This computation was needed for two reasons: first, to help determine cost of goods sold on the budgeted income statement; and second, to value ending inventories on the budgeted balance

SCHEDULE 6

Hampton Freeze, Inc.
Ending Finished Goods Inventory Budget
(absorption costing basis)
For the Year Ended December 31, 2017

Item	*Quantity*		*Cost*		*Total*
Production cost per case:					
Direct materials	15.00	pounds	$ 0.20	per pound	$ 3.00
Direct labor	0.40	hours	$15.00	per hour	6.00
Manufacturing overhead	0.40	hours	$10.00	per hour	4.00
Unit product cost					$ 13.00
Budgeted finished goods inventory:					
Ending finished goods inventory in cases (Schedule 2)					3,000
Unit product cost (see above)					$ 13.00
Ending finished goods inventory in dollars					$ 39,000

Schedule 3 | Schedule 4 | Schedule 5 | **Schedule 6** | Sch

sheet. The cost of unsold units is computed on the **ending finished goods inventory budget**.[3]

Larry Giano considered using variable costing to prepare Hampton Freeze's budget statements, but he decided to use absorption costing instead because the bank would very likely require absorption costing. He also knew that it would be easy to convert the absorption costing financial statements to a variable costing basis later. At this point, the primary concern was to determine what financing, if any, would be required in 2017 and then to arrange for that financing from the bank.

The unit product cost computations are shown in Schedule 6. For Hampton Freeze, the absorption costing unit product cost is $13 per case of popsicles—consisting of $3 of direct materials, $6 of direct labor, and $4 of manufacturing overhead. The manufacturing overhead is applied to units of product at the rate of $10 per direct labor-hour. The budgeted carrying cost of the ending inventory is $39,000.

The Selling and Administrative Expense Budget

LEARNING OBJECTIVE 9–7
Prepare a selling and administrative expense budget.

The **selling and administrative expense budget** lists the budgeted expenses for areas other than manufacturing. In large organizations, this budget would be a compilation of many smaller, individual budgets submitted by department heads and other persons responsible for selling and administrative expenses. For example, the marketing manager would submit a budget detailing the advertising expenses for each budget period.

Schedule 7 contains the selling and administrative expense budget for Hampton Freeze. Like the manufacturing overhead budget, the selling and administrative expense budget is divided into variable and fixed cost components. Consequently, budgeted sales in cases for each quarter are entered at the top of the schedule. These data are taken from

3 For simplicity, the beginning balance sheet and the ending finished goods inventory budget both report a unit product cost of $13. For purposes of answering "what-if" questions, this schedule would assume a FIFO inventory flow. In other words, the ending inventory would consist solely of units that are produced during the budget year.

SCHEDULE 7

	A	B	C	D	E	F
1	Hampton Freeze, Inc.					
2	Selling and Administrative Expense Budget					
3	For the Year Ended December 31, 2017					
4						
5		Quarter				
6		1	2	3	4	Year
7	Budgeted units sales (Schedule 1)	10,000	30,000	40,000	20,000	100,000
8	Variable selling and administrative expense per case	$ 1.80	$ 1.80	$ 1.80	$ 1.80	$ 1.80
9	Variable selling and administrative expense	$ 18,000	$ 54,000	$ 72,000	$ 36,000	$180,000
10	Fixed selling and administrative expenses:					
11	Advertising	20,000	20,000	20,000	20,000	80,000
12	Executive salaries	55,000	55,000	55,000	55,000	220,000
13	Insurance	10,000	10,000	10,000	10,000	40,000
14	Property taxes	4,000	4,000	4,000	4,000	16,000
15	Depreciation	10,000	10,000	10,000	10,000	40,000
16	Total fixed selling and administrative expenses	99,000	99,000	99,000	99,000	396,000
17	Total selling and administrative expenses	117,000	153,000	171,000	135,000	576,000
18	Less depreciation	10,000	10,000	10,000	10,000	40,000
19	Cash disbursements for selling and administrative expenses	$107,000	$143,000	$161,000	$125,000	$536,000
20						

Schedule 5 / Schedule 6 / **Schedule 7** / Schedule 8 / Schedule 9 / Schedule 10

cells B7 through E7 of the sales budget (Schedule 1). The budgeted variable selling and administrative expenses are determined by multiplying the budgeted cases sold by the variable selling and administrative expense of $1.80 per case (see cell B33 from the Budgeting Assumptions tab). For example, the budgeted variable selling and administrative expense for the first quarter is $18,000 (10,000 cases × $1.80 per case). The fixed selling and administrative expenses of $99,000 per quarter (see cells B35 through B39 from the Budgeting Assumptions tab) are then added to the variable selling and administrative expenses to arrive at the total budgeted selling and administrative expenses. Finally, to determine the cash disbursements for selling and administrative items, the total budgeted selling and administrative expense is adjusted by subtracting any noncash selling and administrative expenses (in this case, just depreciation).[4]

The Cash Budget

LEARNING OBJECTIVE 9–8
Prepare a cash budget.

The cash budget is composed of four major sections:

1. The receipts section.
2. The disbursements section.
3. The cash excess or deficiency section.
4. The financing section.

The receipts section lists all of the cash inflows, except from financing, expected during the budget period. Generally, the major source of receipts is from sales. The disbursements section summarizes all cash payments that are planned for the budget period. These payments include raw materials purchases, direct labor payments, manufacturing overhead costs, and so on, as contained in their respective budgets. In addition, other cash disbursements such as equipment purchases and dividends are listed.

[4] Other adjustments might need to be made for differences between cash flows on the one hand and revenues and expenses on the other hand. For example, if property taxes are paid twice a year in installments of $8,000 each, the expense for property tax would have to be "backed out" of the total budgeted selling and administrative expenses and the cash installment payments added to the appropriate quarters to determine the cash disbursements. Similar adjustments might also need to be made in the manufacturing overhead budget. We generally ignore these complications in this chapter.

IN BUSINESS

MISMATCHED CASH FLOWS—CLIMBING THE HILLS AND VALLEYS

The Washington Trails Association (WTA) is a private, nonprofit organization primarily concerned with protecting and maintaining hiking trails in the state of Washington. Some 2,000 WTA volunteer workers donate more than 80,000 hours per year maintaining trails in rugged landscapes on federal, state, and private lands. The organization is supported by membership dues, voluntary contributions, grants, and some contract work for government.

The organization's income and expenses are erratic—although somewhat predictable—over the course of the year as shown in the chart below. Expenses tend to be highest in the spring and summer when most of the trail maintenance work is done. However, income spikes in December well after the expenses have been incurred. With cash outflows running ahead of cash inflows for much of the year, it is very important for the WTA to carefully plan its cash budget and to maintain adequate cash reserves to be able to pay its bills.

© Eric Noreen

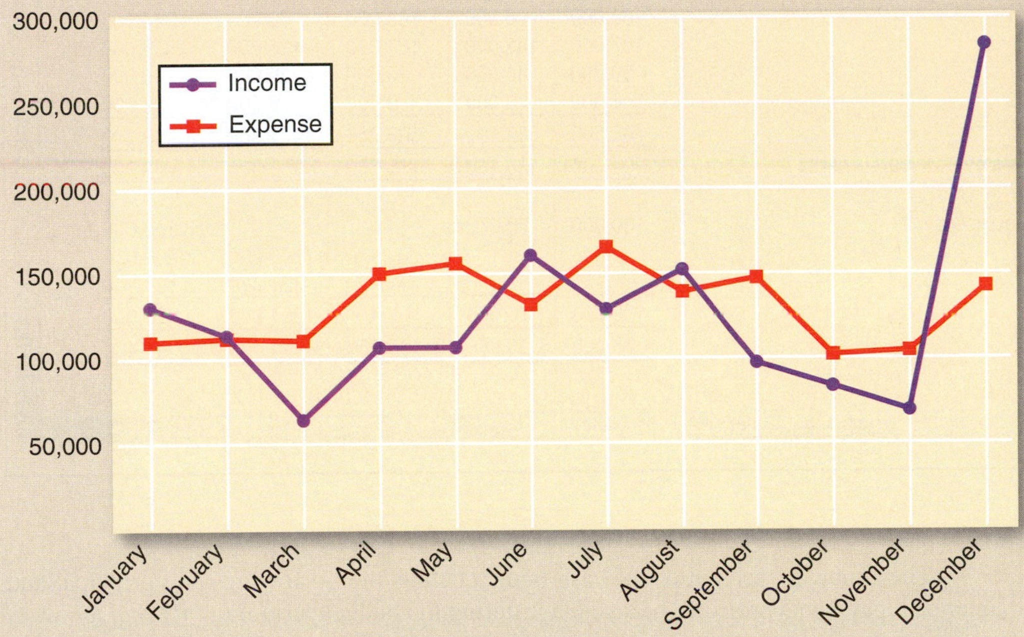

Note: Total income and total expense are approximately equal over the course of the year.

Sources: Conversation with Elizabeth Lunney, President of the Washington Trails Association; WTA documents; and the WTA website www.wta.org.

The cash excess or deficiency section is computed as follows:

Beginning cash balance	XXXX
Add cash receipts	XXXX
Total cash available	XXXX
Less cash disbursements	XXXX
Excess (deficiency) of cash available over disbursements	XXXX

If a cash deficiency exists during any budget period or if there is a cash excess during any budget period that is less than the minimum required cash balance, the company will need to borrow money. Conversely, if there is a cash excess during any budget period that is greater than the minimum required cash balance, the company can invest the excess funds or repay principal and interest to lenders.

SCHEDULE 8

Hampton Freeze, Inc.
Cash Budget
For the Year Ended December 31, 2017

		Quarter				
	Schedule	*1*	*2*	*3*	*4*	*Year*
Beginning cash balance		$ 42,500	$ 36,000	$ 33,900	$ 165,650	$ 42,500
Add cash receipts:						
Collections from customers	1	230,000	480,000	740,000	520,000	1,970,000
Total cash available		272,500	516,000	773,900	685,650	2,012,500
Less cash disbursements:						
Direct materials	3	49,500	72,300	100,050	79,350	301,200
Direct labor	4	84,000	192,000	216,000	114,000	606,000
Manufacturing overhead	5	68,000	96,800	103,200	76,000	344,000
Selling and administrative	7	107,000	143,000	161,000	125,000	536,000
Equipment purchases		50,000	40,000	20,000	20,000	130,000
Dividends		8,000	8,000	8,000	8,000	32,000
Total cash disbursements		366,500	552,100	608,250	422,350	1,949,200
Excess (deficiency) of cash available over disbursements		(94,000)	(36,100)	165,650	263,300	63,300
Financing:						
Borrowings (at the beginnings of quarters)		130,000	70,000	-	-	200,000
Repayments (at end of the year)		-	-	-	(200,000)	(200,000)
Interest		-	-	-	(21,900)	(21,900)
Total financing		130,000	70,000	-	(221,900)	(21,900)
Ending cash balance		$ 36,000	$ 33,900	$ 165,650	$ 41,400	$ 41,400

Schedule 5 | Schedule 6 | Schedule 7 | **Schedule 8** | Schedule 9 | Schedule 10

The financing section of the cash budget details the borrowings and principal and interest repayments projected to take place during the budget period. *In this chapter, we'll always assume that all borrowings take place on the first day of the borrowing period and all repayments take place on the last day of the final period included in the cash budget.* To calculate borrowings and interest payments, you'll need to pay attention to the company's desired minimum cash balance and to the terms of the company's loan agreement with the bank. For example, Hampton Freeze's desired minimum cash balance is $30,000 (see cell B42 in the Budgeting Assumptions tab). Furthermore, *we are going to assume that Hampton Freeze's loan agreement stipulates that it must borrow money in increments of $10,000* and that it must pay simple interest of 3% per quarter (as shown in cell B43 of the Budgeting Assumptions tab).[5]

The cash balances at both the beginning and end of the year may be adequate even though a serious cash deficit occurs at some point during the year. Consequently, the cash budget should be broken down into time periods that are short enough to capture major fluctuations in cash balances. While a monthly cash budget is most common, some organizations budget cash on a weekly or even daily basis. At Hampton Freeze, Larry Giano has prepared a quarterly cash budget that can be further refined as necessary. This budget appears in Schedule 8.[6]

[5] We use simple interest rather than compound interest throughout the chapter for simplicity.

[6] The format for the statement of cash flows, which is discussed in a later chapter, may also be used for the cash budget.

The beginning cash balance in the first quarter of $42,500 agrees with cell B7 of the beginning balance sheet in Exhibit 9–3. Each quarter's collections from customers come from cells B18 through E18 of the schedule of expected cash collections in Schedule 1. Each quarter's beginning cash balance plus the collections from customers equals the total cash available. For example, in the first quarter, the beginning cash balance of $42,500 plus the collections from customers of $230,000 equals the total cash available of $272,500.

The disbursements section of the cash budget includes six types of cash disbursements. Each quarter's cash disbursements for direct materials come from cells B27 through E27 of the schedule of expected cash disbursements for materials (see Schedule 3). The quarterly cash payments for direct labor were calculated in cells B11 through E11 of the direct labor budget (see Schedule 4), whereas the quarterly cash payments related to manufacturing overhead were calculated in cells B13 through E13 of the manufacturing overhead budget (see Schedule 5). The quarterly cash payments for selling and administrative expenses come from cells B19 through E19 of the selling and administrative expense budget (see Schedule 7). So putting it all together, in the first quarter, the cash disbursements for direct materials ($49,500), direct labor ($84,000), manufacturing overhead ($68,000), and selling and administrative expenses ($107,000), plus equipment purchases of $50,000 and a dividend of $8,000 (see cells C43 and B44 from the Budgeting Assumptions tab) equals the total cash disbursements of $366,500.

Each quarter's total cash available minus its total disbursements equals the excess (deficiency) of cash available over disbursements. For example, in the first quarter the total cash available of $272,500 minus the total disbursements of $366,500 results in a cash deficiency of $94,000. The excess or deficiency of cash directly influences whether Hampton Freeze will need to borrow money as shown in the Financing section of the cash budget.

The first row in the financing section of the cash budget relates to projected borrowings. In any period where a company's excess of cash available over disbursements is greater than its desired minimum cash balance, the company will not need to borrow money during that period. In the case of Hampton Freeze, the company wants to maintain a minimum cash balance of $30,000; therefore, it will not need to borrow money in any quarter where its excess of cash available over disbursements is greater than $30,000. However, in the first quarter of 2017 Hampton Freeze estimates that it will have a cash deficiency of $94,000; consequently, the company's minimum required borrowings at the beginning of the first quarter would be computed as follows:

Required Borrowings at the Beginning of the First Quarter	
Desired ending cash balance	$ 30,000
Plus deficiency of cash available over disbursements	94,000
Minimum required borrowings	$124,000

Recall that the bank requires that loans be made in increments of $10,000. Because Hampton Freeze needs to borrow at least $124,000, it will have to borrow $130,000.

In the second quarter of 2017 Hampton Freeze estimates that it will have another cash deficiency of $36,100; therefore, the company's minimum required borrowings at the beginning of the second quarter would be computed as follows:

Required Borrowings at the Beginning of the Second Quarter	
Desired ending cash balance	$30,000
Plus deficiency of cash available over disbursements	36,100
Minimum required borrowings	$66,100

Again, recall that the bank requires that loans be made in increments of $10,000. Because Hampton Freeze needs to borrow at least $66,100 at the beginning of the second quarter, the company will have to borrow $70,000 from the bank.

In the third and fourth quarters, Hampton Freeze has an excess of cash available over disbursements that is greater than $30,000, so it will not need to borrow money in these two quarters. Notice that in the third quarter Hampton Freeze has excess cash of $165,650, yet the cash budget does not include any principal or interest repayments during this quarter. This occurs because in this chapter, we always assume that the company will, as far as it is able, repay the loan plus accumulated interest on the *last day of the final period* included in the cash budget. Because Hampton Freeze has excess cash of $263,300 in the fourth quarter, on the last day of the fourth quarter, it would be able to repay the $200,000 that it borrowed from the lender plus $21,900 of interest computed as follows:

Interest on the $130,000 borrowed at the beginning of the first quarter:	
$130,000 × 0.01 per month × 12 months*	$15,600
Interest on the $70,000 borrowed at the beginning of the second quarter:	
$70,000 × 0.01 per month × 9 months*	6,300
Total interest accrued to the end of the fourth quarter..................	$21,900

* Simple, rather than compounded, interest is assumed for simplicity.

The ending cash balance for each period is computed by taking the excess (deficiency) of cash available over disbursements plus the total financing. For example, in the first quarter, Hampton Freeze's cash deficiency of $(94,000) plus its total financing of $130,000 equals its ending cash balance of $36,000. The ending cash balance for each quarter then becomes the beginning cash balance for the next quarter. Also notice that the amounts under the Year column in the cash budget are not always the sum of the amounts for the four quarters. In particular, the beginning cash balance for the year is the same as the beginning cash balance for the first quarter and the ending cash balance for the year is the same as the ending cash balance for the fourth quarter.

IN BUSINESS

© AP Images/Stew Milne

NEW INSPECTIONS PINCH CASH FLOWS

Herald Metal and Plastic Works is a Chinese toy manufacturer that produces Star Wars action figures and G.I. Joes for Hasbro Inc. in the United States. The company used to ship its toys to America immediately after they rolled off the production line. However, this changed when American consumers discovered that some Chinese companies were using poisonous lead-based paint in their manufacturing processes. The Chinese government now requires toy manufacturers to store finished goods in warehouses for anywhere from three weeks to two months until its inspectors certify them for export.

Herald Metal and Plastic Works borrows money from lenders to buy raw materials and pay laborers to make its toys. The company is struggling to repay its loans because the government's inspection process delays cash receipts from customers.

Source: Chi-Chu Tschang, "Bottlenecks in Toyland," *BusinessWeek*, October 15, 2007, p. 52.

The Budgeted Income Statement

LEARNING OBJECTIVE 9–9
Prepare a budgeted income statement.

Schedule 9 contains the budgeted income statement for Hampton Freeze. All of the revenues and expenses shown on the budgeted income statement come from the data in the beginning balance sheet and the data developed in Schedules 1–8. The sales of $2,000,000 come from cell F9 of the sales budget (Schedule 1). The cost of goods sold of $1,300,000 is computed in two steps. First, cost of goods sold includes the 2,000 units of finished goods inventory from the beginning balance sheet, which have a total cost of $26,000 (see Exhibit 9–3). Second, it includes 98,000 units produced and sold in 2014 multiplied by $13 per unit (see Schedule 6), for a total of $1,274,000. Combining these

SCHEDULE 9

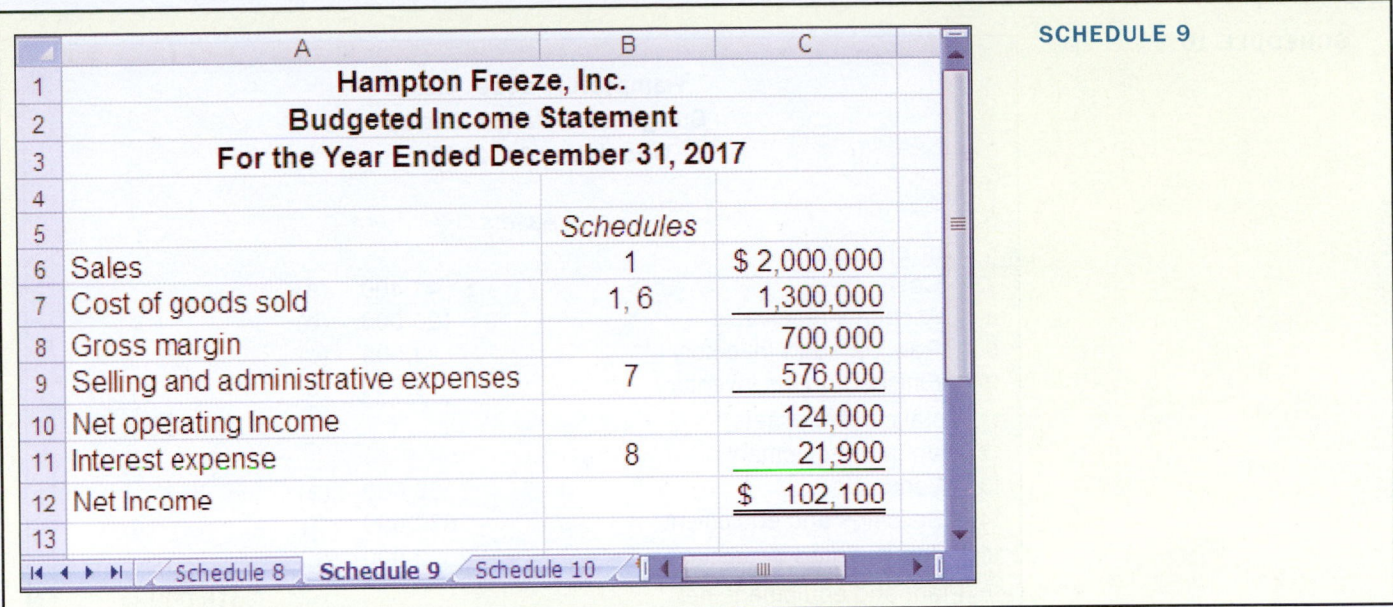

	A	B	C
1	Hampton Freeze, Inc.		
2	Budgeted Income Statement		
3	For the Year Ended December 31, 2017		
4			
5		*Schedules*	
6	Sales	1	$ 2,000,000
7	Cost of goods sold	1, 6	1,300,000
8	Gross margin		700,000
9	Selling and administrative expenses	7	576,000
10	Net operating Income		124,000
11	Interest expense	8	21,900
12	Net Income		$ 102,100
13			

Schedule 8 | **Schedule 9** | Schedule 10

two steps, the total cost of the 100,000 units sold (see Schedule 1) is $1,300,000 ($26,000 + $1,274,000).[7] The selling and administrative expenses of $576,000 come from cell F17 of the selling and administrative expenses budget (Schedule 7). Finally, the interest expense of $21,900 comes from cell G23 of the cash budget (Schedule 8).

The budgeted income statement is one of the key schedules in the budget process. It shows the company's planned profit and serves as a benchmark against which subsequent company performance can be measured. Because Larry Giano created a Budgeting Assumptions tab in his Excel file and linked all of his budget schedules together using properly constructed Excel formulas, he can make changes to his underlying budgeting assumptions and instantly see the impact of the change on all of the schedules and on net income. For example, if Larry wanted to estimate the profit impact if fourth quarter sales are 18,000 cases instead of 20,000 cases, he would simply change the 20,000 cases shown in cell F7 of his Budgeting Assumptions worksheet to 18,000 cases. The revised net income of $87,045 would instantly appear in cell C12 of the budgeted income statement.

The Budgeted Balance Sheet

LEARNING OBJECTIVE 9–10
Prepare a budgeted balance sheet.

The budgeted balance sheet is developed using data from the balance sheet from the beginning of the budget period (see Exhibit 9–3) and data contained in the various schedules. Hampton Freeze's budgeted balance sheet accompanied by explanations of how the numbers were derived is presented in Schedule 10.

After completing the master budget, Larry Giano took the documents to Tom Wills, chief executive officer of Hampton Freeze, for his review.

MANAGERIAL ACCOUNTING IN ACTION
The Wrap-Up

Larry: Here's the budget. Overall, the income is excellent, and the net cash flow for the entire year is positive.

Tom: Yes, but I see on this cash budget that we have the same problem with negative cash flows in the first and second quarters that we had last year.

Larry: That's true. I don't see any way around that problem. However, there is no doubt in my mind that if you take this budget to the bank today, they'll approve an open line of credit that will allow you to borrow enough money to make it through the first two quarters without any problem.

Hampton Freeze Inc.

[7] This explanation assumes a FIFO inventory flow assumption.

SCHEDULE 10

	A	B	C	D	E
1	**Hampton Freeze, Inc.**				
2	**Budgeted Balance Sheet**				
3	**December 31, 2017**				
4					
5	*Assets*				
6	Current assets:				
7	Cash	$ 41,400	(a)		
8	Accounts receivable	120,000	(b)		
9	Raw materials inventory	4,500	(c)		
10	Finished goods inventory	39,000	(d)		
11	Total current assets			$ 204,900	
12	Plant and equipment:				
13	Land	80,000	(e)		
14	Buildings and equipment	830,000	(f)		
15	Accumulated depreciation	(392,000)	(g)		
16	Plant and equipment, net			518,000	
17	Total assets			$ 722,900	
18					
19	*Liabilities and Stockholders' Equity*				
20	Current liabilities:				
21	Accounts payable (raw materials)			$ 27,900	(h)
22	Stockholders' equity:				
23	Common stock, no par	$ 175,000	(i)		
24	Retained earnings	520,000	(j)		
25	Total stockholders' equity			695,000	
26	Total liabilities and stockholders' equity			$ 722,900	
27					

Schedule 8 / Schedule 9 / **Schedule 10**

Explanations of December 31, 2017, balance sheet figures:

(a) From cell G25 of the cash budget (Schedule 8).

(b) Thirty percent of fourth-quarter sales, from Schedule 1 ($400,000 × 30% = $120,000).

(c) From the direct materials budget (Schedule 3). Cell E12 multiplied by cell E16. In other words, 22,500 pounds × $0.20 per pound = $4,500.

(d) From cell H16 of the ending finished goods inventory budget (Schedule 6).

(e) From cell B13 of the beginning balance sheet (Exhibit 9–3).

(f) Cell B14 of the beginning balance sheet (Exhibit 9–3) plus cell G16 from the cash budget (Schedule 8). In other words, $700,000 + $130,000 = $830,000.

(g) The beginning balance of $292,000 (from cell B15 of the beginning balance sheet in Exhibit 9–3) plus the depreciation of $60,000 included in cell F12 of the manufacturing overhead budget (Schedule 5) plus depreciation expense of $40,000 included in cell F18 in the selling and administrative expense budget (Schedule 8). In other words, $292,000 + $60,000 + $40,000 = $392,000.

(h) One-half of fourth-quarter raw materials purchases, from Schedule 3.

(i) From cell B23 of the beginning balance sheet (Exhibit 9–3).

(j)

December 31, 2016, balance	$449,900
Add net income, from cell C12 of Schedule 9	102,100
	552,000
Deduct dividends paid, from cell G17 of Schedule 8	32,000
December 31, 2017, balance	$520,000

Tom: Are you sure? They didn't seem very happy to see me last year when I came in for an emergency loan.

Larry: Did you repay the loan on time?

Tom: Sure.

Larry: I don't see any problem. You won't be asking for an emergency loan this time. The bank will have plenty of warning. And with this budget, you have a solid plan that shows when and how you are going to pay off the loan. Trust me, they'll go for it. Also, keep in mind that the master budget contains all the embedded formulas you'll need to answer the types of "what-if" questions that we discussed earlier. If you want to calculate the financial impact of changing any of your master budget's underlying estimates or assumptions, you can do it with the click of a mouse!

Tom: This sounds fabulous Larry. Thanks for all of your work on this project.

IN BUSINESS

LOCAL MUNICIPALITIES CLOSE BUDGET DEFICITS

Municipalities across the Unites States face a combined budget deficit of $56 to $86 billion. Many cities are responding to their budget shortfalls by outsourcing services to avoid the crushing cost of providing employee benefits. For example, San Jose, California, decided to put a dent in its $118 million budget deficit by outsourcing its janitorial services. The town of Lakewood, California, contracts 40% of its municipal services to outside vendors. Maywood, California, took the drastic step of outsourcing all of its public services to outside contractors. This small town of 40,000 residents terminated all municipal employees and hired the Los Angeles County Sheriff to oversee public safety.

Sources: Tamara Audi, "Cities Rent Police, Janitors to Save Cash," *The Wall Street Journal*, July 19, 2010, p. A3.

Summary

This chapter describes the budgeting process and shows how the various operating budgets relate to each other. The sales budget is the foundation for a master budget. Once the sales budget has been set, the production budget and the selling and administrative expense budget can be prepared because they depend on how many units are to be sold. The production budget determines how many units are to be produced, so after it is prepared, the various manufacturing cost budgets can be prepared. All of these budgets feed into the cash budget and the budgeted income statement and balance sheet. The parts of the master budget are connected in many ways. For example, the schedule of expected cash collections, which is completed in connection with the sales budget, provides data for both the cash budget and the budgeted balance sheet.

The material in this chapter is just an introduction to master budgeting. In later chapters, we will see how budgets are used to control day-to-day operations and how they are used in performance evaluation.

Review Problem: Budget Schedules

Mynor Corporation manufactures and sells a seasonal product that has peak sales in the third quarter. The following information concerns operations for Year 2—the coming year—and for the first two quarters of Year 3:

a. The company's single product sells for $8 per unit. Budgeted unit sales for the next six quarters are as follows (all sales are on credit):

	Year 2 Quarter				Year 3 Quarter	
	1	2	3	4	1	2
Budgeted unit sales	40,000	60,000	100,000	50,000	70,000	80,000

b. Sales are collected in the following pattern: 75% in the quarter the sales are made, and the remaining 25% in the following quarter. On January 1, Year 2, the company's balance sheet showed $65,000 in accounts receivable, all of which will be collected in the first quarter of the year. Bad debts are negligible and can be ignored.

c. The company desires an ending finished goods inventory at the end of each quarter equal to 30% of the budgeted unit sales for the next quarter. On December 31, Year 1, the company had 12,000 units on hand.

d. Five pounds of raw materials are required to complete one unit of product. The company requires ending raw materials inventory at the end of each quarter equal to 10% of the following quarter's production needs. On December 31, Year 1, the company had 23,000 pounds of raw materials on hand.

e. The raw material costs $0.80 per pound. Raw material purchases are paid for in the following pattern: 60% paid in the quarter the purchases are made, and the remaining 40% paid in the following quarter. On January 1, Year 2, the company's balance sheet showed $81,500 in accounts payable for raw material purchases, all of which will be paid for in the first quarter of the year.

Required:

Prepare the following budgets and schedules for the year, showing both quarterly and total figures:

1. A sales budget and a schedule of expected cash collections.
2. A production budget.
3. A direct materials budget and a schedule of expected cash payments for purchases of materials.

Solution to Review Problem

1. The sales budget is prepared as follows:

	Year 2 Quarter				
	1	2	3	4	Year
Budgeted unit sales	40,000	60,000	100,000	50,000	250,000
Selling price per unit	× $8	× $8	× $8	× $8	× $8
Total sales	$320,000	$480,000	$800,000	$400,000	$2,000,000

Based on the budgeted sales above, the schedule of expected cash collections is prepared as follows:

	Year 2 Quarter				
	1	2	3	4	Year
Beginning accounts receivable	$ 65,000				$ 65,000
First-quarter sales ($320,000 × 75%, 25%).	240,000	$ 80,000			320,000
Second-quarter sales ($480,000 × 75%, 25%)		360,000	$120,000		480,000
Third-quarter sales ($800,000 × 75%, 25%).			600,000	$200,000	800,000
Fourth-quarter sales ($400,000 × 75%)				300,000	300,000
Total cash collections.	$305,000	$440,000	$720,000	$500,000	$1,965,000

2. Based on the sales budget in units, the production budget is prepared as follows:

	Year 2 Quarter					Year 3 Quarter	
	1	2	3	4	Year	1	2
Budgeted unit sales	40,000	60,000	100,000	50,000	250,000	70,000	80,000
Add desired ending finished goods inventory*	18,000	30,000	15,000	21,000†	21,000	24,000	
Total needs	58,000	90,000	115,000	71,000	271,000	94,000	
Less beginning finished goods inventory	12,000	18,000	30,000	15,000	12,000	21,000	
Required production	46,000	72,000	85,000	56,000	259,000	73,000	

*30% of the following quarter's budgeted unit sales.
†30% of the budgeted Year 3 first-quarter sales.

3. Based on the production budget, raw materials will need to be purchased during the year as follows:

	Year 2 Quarter					Year 3 Quarter
	1	2	3	4	Year 2	1
Required production in units of finished goods	46,000	72,000	85,000	56,000	259,000	73,000
Units of raw materials needed per unit of finished goods	× 5	× 5	× 5	× 5	× 5	× 5
Units of raw materials needed to meet production	230,000	360,000	425,000	280,000	1,295,000	365,000
Add desired units of ending raw materials inventory*	36,000	42,500	28,000	36,500†	36,500	
Total units of raw materials needed	266,000	402,500	453,000	316,500	1,331,500	
Less units of beginning raw materials inventory	23,000	36,000	42,500	28,000	23,000	
Units of raw materials to be purchased	243,000	366,500	410,500	288,500	1,308,500	
Unit cost of raw materials	× $0.80	× $0.80	× $0.80	× $0.80	× $0.80	
Cost of raw materials to be purchased	$194,400	$293,200	$328,400	$230,800	$1,046,800	

*10% of the following quarter's production needs in pounds.
†10% of the Year 3 first-quarter production needs in pounds.

Based on the raw material purchases above, expected cash payments are computed as follows:

	Year 2 Quarter				
	1	2	3	4	Year 2
Beginning accounts payable	$ 81,500				$ 81,500
First-quarter purchases ($194,400 × 60%, 40%)	116,640	$ 77,760			194,400
Second-quarter purchases ($293,200 × 60%, 40%)		175,920	$117,280		293,200
Third-quarter purchases ($328,400 × 60%, 40%)			197,040	$131,360	328,400
Fourth-quarter purchases ($230,800 × 60%)				138,480	138,480
Total cash disbursements	$198,140	$253,680	$314,320	$269,840	$1,035,980

Glossary

Budget A detailed plan for the future that is usually expressed in formal quantitative terms. (p. 387)

Cash budget A detailed plan showing how cash resources will be acquired and used over a specific time period. (p. 391)

Continuous budget A 12-month budget that rolls forward one month as the current month is completed. (p. 388)

Control The process of gathering feedback to ensure that a plan is being properly executed or modified as circumstances change. (p. 387)

Direct labor budget A detailed plan that shows the direct labor-hours required to fulfill the production budget. (p. 400)

Direct materials budget A detailed plan showing the amount of raw materials that must be purchased to fulfill the production budget and to provide for adequate inventories. (p. 399)

Ending finished goods inventory budget A budget showing the dollar amount of unsold finished goods inventory that will appear on the ending balance sheet. (p. 403)

Manufacturing overhead budget A detailed plan showing the production costs, other than direct materials and direct labor, that will be incurred over a specified time period. (p. 401)

Master budget A number of separate but interdependent budgets that formally lay out the company's sales, production, and financial goals and that culminates in a cash budget, budgeted income statement, and budgeted balance sheet. (p. 390)

Merchandise purchases budget A detailed plan used by a merchandising company that shows the amount of goods that must be purchased from suppliers during the period. (p. 398)

Participative budget See *Self-imposed budget.* (p. 389)

Perpetual budget See *Continuous budget.* (p. 388)

Planning Developing goals and preparing budgets to achieve those goals. (p. 387)

Production budget A detailed plan showing the number of units that must be produced during a period in order to satisfy both sales and inventory needs. (p. 396)

Responsibility accounting A system of accountability in which managers are held responsible for those items of revenue and cost—and only those items—over which they can exert significant control. The managers are held responsible for differences between budgeted and actual results. (p. 388)

Sales budget A detailed schedule showing expected sales expressed in both dollars and units. (p. 391)

Self-imposed budget A method of preparing budgets in which managers prepare their own budgets. These budgets are then reviewed by higher-level managers, and any issues are resolved by mutual agreement. (p. 389)

Selling and administrative expense budget A detailed schedule of planned expenses that will be incurred in areas other than manufacturing during a budget period. (p. 403)

Questions

9–1 What is a budget? What is budgetary control?

9–2 Discuss some of the major benefits to be gained from budgeting.

9–3 What is meant by the term *responsibility accounting?*

9–4 What is a master budget? Briefly describe its contents.

9–5 Why is the sales forecast the starting point in budgeting?

9–6 "As a practical matter, planning and control mean exactly the same thing." Do you agree? Explain.

9–7 Why is it a good idea to create a "Budgeting Assumptions" tab when creating a master budget in Microsoft Excel?

9–8 What is a self-imposed budget? What are the major advantages of self-imposed budgets? What caution must be exercised in their use?

9–9 How can budgeting assist a company in planning its workforce staffing levels?

9–10 "The principal purpose of the cash budget is to see how much cash the company will have in the bank at the end of the year." Do you agree? Explain.

Multiple-choice questions are available with Connect.

Additional student resources are available with Connect. **connect**

Applying Excel

LEARNING OBJECTIVES 9–2, 9–3, 9–4

The Excel worksheet form that follows is to be used to recreate the Review Problem related to Mynor Corporation. Download the workbook containing this form at from Connect. *On the website you will also receive instructions about how to use this worksheet form.*

	A	B	C	D	E	F	G	H
1	Chapter 9: Applying Excel							
2								
3	**Data**		*Year 2 Quarter*			*Year 3 Quarter*		
4		*1*	*2*	*3*	*4*	*1*	*2*	
5	Budgeted unit sales	40,000	60,000	100,000	50,000	70,000	80,000	
6								
7	• Selling price per unit	$8	per unit					
8	• Accounts receivable, beginning balance	$65,000						
9	• Sales collected in the quarter sales are made	75%						
10	• Sales collected in the quarter after sales are made	25%						
11	• Desired ending finished goods inventory is	30%	of the budgeted unit sales of the next quarter					
12	• Finished goods inventory, beginning	12,000	units					
13	• Raw materials required to produce one unit	5	pounds					
14	• Desired ending inventory of raw materials is	10%	of the next quarter's production needs					
15	• Raw materials inventory, beginning	23,000	pounds					
16	• Raw material costs	$0.80	per pound					
17	• Raw materials purchases are paid	60%	in the quarter the purchases are made					
18	and	40%	in the quarter following purchase					
19	• Accounts payable for raw materials, beginning balance	$81,500						
20								
21	*Enter a formula into each of the cells marked with a ? below*							
22	**Review Problem: Budget Schedules**							
23								
24	***Construct the sales budget***		*Year 2 Quarter*			*Year 3 Quarter*		
25		*1*	*2*	*3*	*4*	*1*	*2*	
26	Budgeted unit sales	?	?	?	?	?	?	
27	Selling price per unit	?	?	?	?	?	?	
28	Total sales	?	?	?	?	?	?	
29								
30	***Construct the schedule of expected cash collections***		*Year 2 Quarter*					
31		*1*	*2*	*3*	*4*	*Year*		
32	Accounts receivable, beginning balance	?				?		
33	First-quarter sales	?	?			?		
34	Second-quarter sales		?	?		?		
35	Third-quarter sales			?	?	?		
36	Fourth-quarter sales				?	?		
37	Total cash collections	?	?	?	?	?		
38								
39	***Construct the production budget***		*Year 2 Quarter*				*Year 3 Quarter*	
40		*1*	*2*	*3*	*4*	*Year*	*1*	*2*
41	Budgeted unit sales	?	?	?	?	?	?	?
42	Add desired finished goods inventory	?	?	?	?	?	?	
43	Total needs	?	?	?	?	?	?	
44	Less beginning inventory	?	?	?	?	?	?	
45	Required production	?	?	?	?	?	?	
46								
47	***Construct the raw materials purchases budget***		*Year 2 Quarter*				*Year 3 Quarter*	
48		*1*	*2*	*3*	*4*	*Year*	*1*	
49	Required production (units)	?	?	?	?	?	?	
50	Raw materials required to produce one unit	?	?	?	?	?	?	
51	Production needs (pounds)	?	?	?	?	?	?	
52	Add desired ending inventory of raw materials (pounds)	?	?	?	?	?		
53	Total needs (pounds)	?	?	?	?	?		
54	Less beginning inventory of raw materials (pounds)	?	?	?	?	?		
55	Raw materials to be purchased	?	?	?	?	?		
56	Cost of raw materials per pound	?	?	?	?	?		
57	Cost of raw materials to be purchased	?	?	?	?	?		
58								
59	***Construct the schedule of expected cash payments***		*Year 2 Quarter*					
60		*1*	*2*	*3*	*4*	*Year*		
61	Accounts payable, beginning balance	?				?		
62	First-quarter purchases	?	?			?		
63	Second-quarter purchases		?	?		?		
64	Third-quarter purchases			?	?	?		
65	Fourth-quarter purchases				?	?		
66	Total cash disbursements	?	?	?	?	?		
67								

Chapter 9 Form / Filled in Chapter 9 Form / Chapter 9 Formulas / Chapter 9 Requirement

You should proceed to the requirements below only after completing your worksheet.

Required:

1. Check your worksheet by changing the budgeted unit sales in Quarter 2 of Year 2 in cell C5 to 75,000 units. The total expected cash collections for the year should now be $2,085,000. If you do not get this answer, find the errors in your worksheet and correct them. Have the total cash disbursements for the year changed? Why or why not?
2. The company has just hired a new marketing manager who insists that unit sales can be dramatically increased by dropping the selling price from $8 to $7. The marketing manager would like to use the following projections in the budget:

Data	Year 2 Quarter 1	2	3	4	Year 3 Quarter 1	2
Budgeted unit sales	50,000	70,000	120,000	80,000	90,000	100,000
Selling price per unit	$7					

a. What are the total expected cash collections for the year under this revised budget?
b. What is the total required production for the year under this revised budget?
c. What is the total cost of raw materials to be purchased for the year under this revised budget?
d. What are the total expected cash disbursements for raw materials for the year under this revised budget?
e. After seeing this revised budget, the production manager cautioned that due to the limited availability of a complex milling machine, the plant can produce no more than 90,000 units in any one quarter. Is this a potential problem? If so, what can be done about it?

The Foundational 15

connect Additional student resources are available with Connect.

LEARNING OBJECTIVES 9–2, 9–3, 9–4, 9–5, 9–7, 9–9, 9–10

Morganton Company makes one product and it provided the following information to help prepare the master budget for its first four months of operations:

a. The budgeted selling price per unit is $70. Budgeted unit sales for June, July, August, and September are 8,400, 10,000, 12,000, and 13,000 units, respectively. All sales are on credit.
b. Forty percent of credit sales are collected in the month of the sale and 60% in the following month.
c. The ending finished goods inventory equals 20% of the following month's unit sales.
d. The ending raw materials inventory equals 10% of the following month's raw materials production needs. Each unit of finished goods requires 5 pounds of raw materials. The raw materials cost $2.00 per pound.
e. Thirty percent of raw materials purchases are paid for in the month of purchase and 70% in the following month.
f. The direct labor wage rate is $15 per hour. Each unit of finished goods requires two direct labor-hours.
g. The variable selling and administrative expense per unit sold is $1.80. The fixed selling and administrative expense per month is $60,000.

Required:

1. What are the budgeted sales for July?
2. What are the expected cash collections for July?
3. What is the accounts receivable balance at the end of July?
4. According to the production budget, how many units should be produced in July?
5. If 61,000 pounds of raw materials are needed to meet production in August, how many pounds of raw materials should be purchased in July?
6. What is the estimated cost of raw materials purchases for July?
7. If the cost of raw material purchases in June is $88,880, what are the estimated cash disbursements for raw materials purchases in July?
8. What is the estimated accounts payable balance at the end of July?
9. What is the estimated raw materials inventory balance at the end of July?
10. What is the total estimated direct labor cost for July assuming the direct labor workforce is adjusted to match the hours required to produce the forecasted number of units produced?
11. If the company always uses an estimated predetermined plantwide overhead rate of $10 per direct labor-hour, what is the estimated unit product cost?
12. What is the estimated finished goods inventory balance at the end of July?
13. What is the estimated cost of goods sold and gross margin for July?
14. What is the estimated total selling and administrative expense for July?
15. What is the estimated net operating income for July?

Exercises

EXERCISE 9–1 Schedule of Expected Cash Collections [LO9–2]

Silver Company makes a product that is very popular as a Mother's Day gift. Thus, peak sales occur in May of each year, as shown in the company's sales budget for the second quarter given below:

	April	May	June	Total
Budgeted sales (all on account)	$300,000	$500,000	$200,000	$1,000,000

From past experience, the company has learned that 20% of a month's sales are collected in the month of sale, another 70% are collected in the month following sale, and the remaining 10% are collected in the second month following sale. Bad debts are negligible and can be ignored. February sales totaled $230,000, and March sales totaled $260,000.

Required:

1. Prepare a schedule of expected cash collections from sales, by month and in total, for the second quarter.
2. Assume that the company will prepare a budgeted balance sheet as of June 30. Compute the accounts receivable as of that date.

EXERCISE 9–2 Production Budget [LO9–3]

Down Under Products, Ltd., of Australia has budgeted sales of its popular boomerang for the next four months as follows:

	Sales in Units
April	50,000
May	75,000
June	90,000
July	80,000

The company is now in the process of preparing a production budget for the second quarter. Past experience has shown that end-of-month inventory levels must equal 10% of the following month's sales. The inventory at the end of March was 5,000 units.

Required:

Prepare a production budget for the second quarter; in your budget, show the number of units to be produced each month and for the quarter in total.

EXERCISE 9–3 Direct Materials Budget [LO9–4]

Three grams of musk oil are required for each bottle of Mink Caress, a very popular perfume made by a small company in western Siberia. The cost of the musk oil is $1.50 per gram. Budgeted production of Mink Caress is given below by quarters for Year 2 and for the first quarter of Year 3:

	Year 2				Year 3
	First	Second	Third	Fourth	First
Budgeted production, in bottles	60,000	90,000	150,000	100,000	70,000

Musk oil has become so popular as a perfume ingredient that it has become necessary to carry large inventories as a precaution against stock-outs. For this reason, the inventory of musk oil at the end of a quarter must be equal to 20% of the following quarter's production needs. Some 36,000 grams of musk oil will be on hand to start the first quarter of Year 2.

Required:

Prepare a direct materials budget for musk oil, by quarter and in total, for Year 2. At the bottom of your budget, show the amount of purchases for each quarter and for the year in total.

EXERCISE 9–4 Direct Labor Budget [LO9–5]

The production manager of Rordan Corporation has submitted the following forecast of units to be produced by quarter for the upcoming fiscal year:

	1st Quarter	2nd Quarter	3rd Quarter	4th Quarter
Units to be produced	8,000	6,500	7,000	7,500

Each unit requires 0.35 direct labor-hours, and direct laborers are paid $12.00 per hour.

Required:

1. Construct the company's direct labor budget for the upcoming fiscal year, assuming that the direct labor workforce is adjusted each quarter to match the number of hours required to produce the forecasted number of units produced.
2. Construct the company's direct labor budget for the upcoming fiscal year, assuming that the direct labor workforce is not adjusted each quarter. Instead, assume that the company's direct labor workforce consists of permanent employees who are guaranteed to be paid for at least 2,600 hours of work each quarter. If the number of required direct labor-hours is less than this number, the workers are paid for 2,600 hours anyway. Any hours worked in excess of 2,600 hours in a quarter are paid at the rate of 1.5 times the normal hourly rate for direct labor.

EXERCISE 9–5 Manufacturing Overhead Budget [LO9–6]

The direct labor budget of Yuvwell Corporation for the upcoming fiscal year contains the following details concerning budgeted direct labor-hours:

	1st Quarter	2nd Quarter	3rd Quarter	4th Quarter
Budgeted direct labor-hours......	8,000	8,200	8,500	7,800

The company's variable manufacturing overhead rate is $3.25 per direct labor-hour and the company's fixed manufacturing overhead is $48,000 per quarter. The only noncash item included in fixed manufacturing overhead is depreciation, which is $16,000 per quarter.

Required:

1. Construct the company's manufacturing overhead budget for the upcoming fiscal year.
2. Compute the company's manufacturing overhead rate (including both variable and fixed manufacturing overhead) for the upcoming fiscal year. Round off to the nearest whole cent.

EXERCISE 9–6 Selling and Administrative Expense Budget [LO9–7]

The budgeted unit sales of Weller Company for the upcoming fiscal year are provided below:

	1st Quarter	2nd Quarter	3rd Quarter	4th Quarter
Budgeted unit sales	15,000	16,000	14,000	13,000

The company's variable selling and administrative expense per unit is $2.50. Fixed selling and administrative expenses include advertising expenses of $8,000 per quarter, executive salaries of $35,000 per quarter, and depreciation of $20,000 per quarter. In addition, the company will make insurance payments of $5,000 in the first quarter and $5,000 in the third quarter. Finally, property taxes of $8,000 will be paid in the second quarter.

Required:

Prepare the company's selling and administrative expense budget for the upcoming fiscal year.

EXERCISE 9–7 Cash Budget [LO9–8]

Garden Depot is a retailer that is preparing its budget for the upcoming fiscal year. Management has prepared the following summary of its budgeted cash flows:

	1st Quarter	2nd Quarter	3rd Quarter	4th Quarter
Total cash receipts	$180,000	$330,000	$210,000	$230,000
Total cash disbursements	$260,000	$230,000	$220,000	$240,000

The company's beginning cash balance for the upcoming fiscal year will be $20,000. The company requires a minimum cash balance of $10,000 and may borrow any amount needed from a local bank at a quarterly interest rate of 3%. The company may borrow any amount at the beginning of any quarter and may repay its loans, or any part of its loans, at the end of any quarter. Interest payments are due on any principal at the time it is repaid. For simplicity, assume that interest is not compounded.

Required:
Prepare the company's cash budget for the upcoming fiscal year.

EXERCISE 9–8 Budgeted Income Statement [LO9–9]

Gig Harbor Boating is the wholesale distributor of a small recreational catamaran sailboat. Management has prepared the following summary data to use in its annual budgeting process:

Budgeted unit sales	460
Selling price per unit	$1,950
Cost per unit.	$1,575
Variable selling and administrative expenses (per unit)	$75
Fixed selling and administrative expenses (per year)	$105,000
Interest expense for the year	$14,000

Required:
Prepare the company's budgeted income statement. Use the absorption costing income statement format shown in Schedule 9.

EXERCISE 9–9 Budgeted Balance Sheet [LO9–10]

The management of Mecca Copy, a photocopying center located on University Avenue, has compiled the following data to use in preparing its budgeted balance sheet for next year:

	Ending Balances
Cash	?
Accounts receivable	$8,100
Supplies inventory	$3,200
Equipment	$34,000
Accumulated depreciation	$16,000
Accounts payable	$1,800
Common stock	$5,000
Retained earnings.	?

The beginning balance of retained earnings was $28,000, net income is budgeted to be $11,500, and dividends are budgeted to be $4,800.

Required:
Prepare the company's budgeted balance sheet.

EXERCISE 9–10 Production and Direct Materials Budgets [LO9–3, LO9–4]

Pearl Products Limited of Shenzhen, China, manufactures and distributes toys throughout South East Asia. Three cubic centimeters (cc) of solvent H300 are required to manufacture each unit of Supermix, one of the company's products. The company is now planning raw materials needs for the third quarter, the quarter in which peak sales of Supermix occur. To keep production and sales moving smoothly, the company has the following inventory requirements:

a. The finished goods inventory on hand at the end of each month must be equal to 3,000 units of Supermix plus 20% of the next month's sales. The finished goods inventory on June 30 is budgeted to be 10,000 units.
b. The raw materials inventory on hand at the end of each month must be equal to one-half of the following month's production needs for raw materials. The raw materials inventory on June 30 is budgeted to be 54,000 cc of solvent H300.
c. The company maintains no work in process inventories.

A sales budget for Supermix for the last six months of the year follows.

	Budgeted Sales in Units
July	35,000
August	40,000
September	50,000
October	30,000
November	20,000
December	10,000

Required:

1. Prepare a production budget for Supermix for the months July, August, September, and October.
2. Examine the production budget that you prepared in requirement 1. Why will the company produce more units than it sells in July and August, and fewer units than it sells in September and October?
3. Prepare a direct materials budget showing the quantity of solvent H300 to be purchased for July, August, and September, and for the quarter in total.

EXERCISE 9–11 Cash Budget Analysis [LO9–8]

A cash budget, by quarters, is given below for a retail company (000 omitted). The company requires a minimum cash balance of at least $5,000 to start each quarter.

	Quarter				
	1	2	3	4	Year
Cash balance, beginning	$ 6	$?	$?	$?	$?
Add collections from customers	?	?	96	?	323
Total cash available	71	?	?	?	?
Less disbursements:					
Purchase of inventory	35	45	?	35	?
Selling and administrative expenses	?	30	30	?	113
Equipment purchases	8	8	10	?	36
Dividends	2	2	2	2	?
Total disbursements	?	85	?	?	?
Excess (deficiency) of cash available over disbursements	(2)	?	11	?	?
Financing:					
Borrowings	?	15	—	—	?
Repayments (including interest)*	—	—	(?)	(17)	(?)
Total financing	?	?	?	?	?
Cash balance, ending	$?	$?	$?	$?	$?

*Interest will total $1,000 for the year.

Required:
Fill in the missing amounts in the above table.

EXERCISE 9–12 Schedules of Expected Cash Collections and Disbursements; Income Statement; Balance Sheet [LO9–2, LO9–4, LO9–9, LO9–10]

Beech Corporation is a merchandising company that is preparing a master budget for the third quarter of the calendar year. The company's balance sheet as of June 30 is shown below:

Beech Corporation Balance Sheet June 30	
Assets	
Cash	$ 90,000
Accounts receivable	136,000
Inventory	62,000
Plant and equipment, net of depreciation	210,000
Total assets	$498,000
Liabilities and Stockholders' Equity	
Accounts payable	$ 71,100
Common stock	327,000
Retained earnings	99,900
Total liabilities and stockholders' equity	$498,000

Beech's managers have made the following additional assumptions and estimates:

1. Estimated sales for July, August, September, and October will be $210,000, $230,000, $220,000, and $240,000, respectively.
2. All sales are on credit and all credit sales are collected. Each month's credit sales are collected 35% in the month of sale and 65% in the month following the sale. All of the accounts receivable at June 30 will be collected in July.
3. Each month's ending inventory must equal 30% of the cost of next month's sales. The cost of goods sold is 60% of sales. The company pays for 40% of its merchandise purchases in the month of the purchase and the remaining 60% in the month following the purchase. All of the accounts payable at June 30 will be paid in July.
4. Monthly selling and administrative expenses are always $60,000. Each month $5,000 of this total amount is depreciation expense and the remaining $55,000 relates to expenses that are paid in the month they are incurred.
5. The company does not plan to borrow money or pay or declare dividends during the quarter ended September 30. The company does not plan to issue any common stock or repurchase its own stock during the quarter ended September 30.

Required:
1. Prepare a schedule of expected cash collections for July, August, and September. Also compute total cash collections for the quarter ended September 30.
2. *a.* Prepare a merchandise purchases budget for July, August, and September. Also compute total merchandise purchases for the quarter ended September 30.
   b. Prepare a schedule of expected cash disbursements for merchandise purchases for July, August, and September. Also compute total cash disbursements for merchandise purchases for the quarter ended September 30.
3. Prepare an income statement for the quarter ended September 30. Use the absorption format shown in Schedule 9.
4. Prepare a balance sheet as of September 30.

EXERCISE 9–13 Schedules of Expected Cash Collections and Disbursements; Income Statement; Balance Sheet [LO9–2, LO9–4, LO9–9, LO9–10]

Refer to the data for Beech Corporation in Exercise 9–12. The company is considering making the following changes to the assumptions underlying its master budget:

1. Each month's credit sales are collected 45% in the month of sale and 55% in the month following the sale.
2. Each month's ending inventory must equal 20% of the cost of next month's sales.
3. The company pays for 30% of its merchandise purchases in the month of the purchase and the remaining 70% in the month following the purchase.

All other information from Exercise 9–12 that is not mentioned above remains the same.

Required:

Using the new assumptions described above, complete the following requirements:

1. Prepare a schedule of expected cash collections for July, August, and September. Also compute total cash collections for the quarter ended September 30.
2. *a.* Prepare a merchandise purchases budget for July, August, and September. Also compute total merchandise purchases for the quarter ended September 30.
   b. Prepare a schedule of expected cash disbursements for merchandise purchases for July, August, and September. Also compute total cash disbursements for merchandise purchases for the quarter ended September 30.
3. Prepare an income statement for the quarter ended September 30. Use the absorption format shown in Schedule 9.
4. Prepare a balance sheet as of September 30.

EXERCISE 9–14 Sales and Production Budgets [LO9–2, LO9–3]

The marketing department of Jessi Corporation has submitted the following sales forecast for the upcoming fiscal year (all sales are on account):

	1st Quarter	2nd Quarter	3rd Quarter	4th Quarter
Budgeted unit sales	11,000	12,000	14,000	13,000

The selling price of the company's product is $18.00 per unit. Management expects to collect 65% of sales in the quarter in which the sales are made, 30% in the following quarter, and 5% of sales are expected to be uncollectible. The beginning balance of accounts receivable, all of which is expected to be collected in the first quarter, is $70,200.

The company expects to start the first quarter with 1,650 units in finished goods inventory. Management desires an ending finished goods inventory in each quarter equal to 15% of the next quarter's budgeted sales. The desired ending finished goods inventory for the fourth quarter is 1,850 units.

Required:

1. Prepare the company's sales budget and schedule of expected cash collections.
2. Prepare the company's production budget for the upcoming fiscal year.

EXERCISE 9–15 Direct Labor and Manufacturing Overhead Budgets [LO9–5, LO9–6]

The Production Department of Hruska Corporation has submitted the following forecast of units to be produced by quarter for the upcoming fiscal year:

	1st Quarter	2nd Quarter	3rd Quarter	4th Quarter
Units to be produced	12,000	10,000	13,000	14,000

Each unit requires 0.2 direct labor-hours and direct laborers are paid $12.00 per hour.

In addition, the variable manufacturing overhead rate is $1.75 per direct labor-hour. The fixed manufacturing overhead is $86,000 per quarter. The only noncash element of manufacturing overhead is depreciation, which is $23,000 per quarter.

Required:

1. Prepare the company's direct labor budget for the upcoming fiscal year, assuming that the direct labor workforce is adjusted each quarter to match the number of hours required to produce the forecasted number of units produced.
2. Prepare the company's manufacturing overhead budget.

EXERCISE 9–16 Direct Materials and Direct Labor Budgets [LO9–4, LO9–5]

The production department of Zan Corporation has submitted the following forecast of units to be produced by quarter for the upcoming fiscal year:

	1st Quarter	2nd Quarter	3rd Quarter	4th Quarter
Units to be produced	5,000	8,000	7,000	6,000

In addition, the beginning raw materials inventory for the 1st Quarter is budgeted to be 6,000 grams and the beginning accounts payable for the 1st Quarter is budgeted to be $2,880.

Each unit requires 8 grams of raw material that costs $1.20 per gram. Management desires to end each quarter with an inventory of raw materials equal to 25% of the following quarter's production needs. The desired ending inventory for the 4th Quarter is 8,000 grams. Management plans to pay for 60% of raw material purchases in the quarter acquired and 40% in the following quarter. Each unit requires 0.20 direct labor-hours and direct laborers are paid $11.50 per hour.

Required:

1. Prepare the company's direct materials budget and schedule of expected cash disbursements for purchases of materials for the upcoming fiscal year.
2. Prepare the company's direct labor budget for the upcoming fiscal year, assuming that the direct labor workforce is adjusted each quarter to match the number of hours required to produce the forecasted number of units produced.

Additional student resources are available with Connect. connect **Problems**

PROBLEM 9–17 Cash Budget; Income Statement; Balance Sheet [LO9–2, LO9–4, LO9–8, LO9–9, LO9–10]

Minden Company is a wholesale distributor of premium European chocolates. The company's balance sheet as of April 30 is given below:

Minden Company Balance Sheet April 30	
Assets	
Cash	$ 9,000
Accounts receivable	54,000
Inventory	30,000
Buildings and equipment, net of depreciation	207,000
Total assets	$300,000
Liabilities and Stockholders' Equity	
Accounts payable	$ 63,000
Note payable	14,500
Common stock	180,000
Retained earnings	42,500
Total liabilities and stockholders' equity	$300,000

The company is in the process of preparing a budget for May and has assembled the following data:

a. Sales are budgeted at $200,000 for May. Of these sales, $60,000 will be for cash; the remainder will be credit sales. One-half of a month's credit sales are collected in the month the sales are made, and the remainder is collected in the following month. All of the April 30 accounts receivable will be collected in May.
b. Purchases of inventory are expected to total $120,000 during May. These purchases will all be on account. Forty percent of all purchases are paid for in the month of purchase; the remainder are paid in the following month. All of the April 30 accounts payable to suppliers will be paid during May.
c. The May 31 inventory balance is budgeted at $40,000.
d. Selling and administrative expenses for May are budgeted at $72,000, exclusive of depreciation. These expenses will be paid in cash. Depreciation is budgeted at $2,000 for the month.
e. The note payable on the April 30 balance sheet will be paid during May, with $100 in interest. (All of the interest relates to May.)
f. New refrigerating equipment costing $6,500 will be purchased for cash during May.
g. During May, the company will borrow $20,000 from its bank by giving a new note payable to the bank for that amount. The new note will be due in one year.

Required:

1. Prepare a cash budget for May. Support your budget with a schedule of expected cash collections from sales and a schedule of expected cash disbursements for merchandise purchases.
2. Prepare a budgeted income statement for May. Use the absorption costing income statement format as shown in Schedule 9.
3. Prepare a budgeted balance sheet as of May 31.

PROBLEM 9–18 Cash Budget; Income Statement; Balance Sheet; Changing Assumptions [LO9–2, LO9–4, LO9–8, LO9–9, LO9–10]

Refer to the data for Minden Company in Problem 9–17. The company is considering making the following changes to the assumptions underlying its master budget:

1. Sales are budgeted for $220,000 for May.
2. Each month's credit sales are collected 60% in the month of sale and 40% in the month following the sale.
3. The company pays for 50% of its merchandise purchases in the month of the purchase and the remaining 50% in the month following the purchase.

All other information from Problem 9–17 that is not mentioned above remains the same.

Required:

Using the new assumptions described above, complete the following requirements:

1. Prepare a cash budget for May. Support your budget with a schedule of expected cash collections from sales and a schedule of expected cash disbursements for merchandise purchases.
2. Prepare a budgeted income statement for May. Use the absorption costing income statement format as shown in Schedule 9.
3. Prepare a budgeted balance sheet as of May 31.

PROBLEM 9–19 Schedules of Expected Cash Collections and Disbursements [LO9–2, LO9–4, LO9–8]

You have been asked to prepare a December cash budget for Ashton Company, a distributor of exercise equipment. The following information is available about the company's operations:

a. The cash balance on December 1 is $40,000.
b. Actual sales for October and November and expected sales for December are as follows:

	October	November	December
Cash sales	$65,000	$70,000	$83,000
Sales on account.	$400,000	$525,000	$600,000

Sales on account are collected over a three-month period as follows: 20% collected in the month of sale, 60% collected in the month following sale, and 18% collected in the second month following sale. The remaining 2% is uncollectible.

c. Purchases of inventory will total $280,000 for December. Thirty percent of a month's inventory purchases are paid during the month of purchase. The accounts payable remaining from November's inventory purchases total $161,000, all of which will be paid in December.
d. Selling and administrative expenses are budgeted at $430,000 for December. Of this amount, $50,000 is for depreciation.
e. A new web server for the Marketing Department costing $76,000 will be purchased for cash during December, and dividends totaling $9,000 will be paid during the month.
f. The company maintains a minimum cash balance of $20,000. An open line of credit is available from the company's bank to bolster the cash position as needed.

Required:

1. Prepare a schedule of expected cash collections for December.
2. Prepare a schedule of expected cash disbursements for merchandise purchases for December.
3. Prepare a cash budget for December. Indicate in the financing section any borrowing that will be needed during the month. Assume that any interest will not be paid until the following month.

PROBLEM 9–20 Evaluating a Company's Budget Procedures [LO9–1]

Springfield Corporation operates on a calendar-year basis. It begins the annual budgeting process in late August, when the president establishes targets for total sales dollars and net operating income before taxes for the next year.

The sales target is given to the Marketing Department, where the marketing manager formulates a sales budget by product line in both units and dollars. From this budget, sales quotas by product line in units and dollars are established for each of the corporation's sales districts.

The marketing manager also estimates the cost of the marketing activities required to support the target sales volume and prepares a tentative marketing expense budget.

The executive vice president uses the sales and profit targets, the sales budget by product line, and the tentative marketing expense budget to determine the dollar amounts that can be devoted to manufacturing and corporate office expense. The executive vice president prepares the budget for corporate expenses, and then forwards to the Production Department the product-line sales budget in units and the total dollar amount that can be devoted to manufacturing.

The production manager meets with the factory managers to develop a manufacturing plan that will produce the required units when needed within the cost constraints set by the executive vice president. The budgeting process usually comes to a halt at this point because the Production Department does not consider the financial resources allocated to it to be adequate.

When this standstill occurs, the vice president of finance, the executive vice president, the marketing manager, and the production manager meet to determine the final budgets for each of the areas. This normally results in a modest increase in the total amount available for manufacturing costs, while the marketing expense and corporate office expense budgets are cut. The total sales and net operating income figures proposed by the president are seldom changed. Although the participants are seldom pleased with the compromise, these budgets are final. Each executive then develops a new detailed budget for the operations in his or her area.

None of the areas has achieved its budget in recent years. Sales often run below the target. When budgeted sales are not achieved, each area is expected to cut costs so that the president's profit target can still be met. However, the profit target is seldom met because costs are not cut enough. In fact, costs often run above the original budget in all functional areas. The president is disturbed that Springfield has not been able to meet the sales and profit targets. He hired a consultant with considerable relevant industry experience. The consultant reviewed the budgets for the past four years. He concluded that the product-line sales budgets were reasonable and that the cost and expense budgets were adequate for the budgeted sales and production levels.

Required:

1. Discuss how the budgeting process as employed by Springfield Corporation contributes to the failure to achieve the president's sales and profit targets.
2. Suggest how Springfield Corporation's budgeting process could be revised to correct the problem.
3. Should the functional areas be expected to cut their costs when sales volume falls below budget? Explain your answer.

(CMA, adapted)

PROBLEM 9–21 Schedule of Expected Cash Collections; Cash Budget [LO9–2, LO9–8]

The president of the retailer Prime Products has just approached the company's bank with a request for a $30,000, 90-day loan. The purpose of the loan is to assist the company in acquiring inventories. Because the company has had some difficulty in paying off its loans in the past, the loan officer has asked for a cash budget to help determine whether the loan should be made. The following data are available for the months April through June, during which the loan will be used:

a. On April 1, the start of the loan period, the cash balance will be $24,000. Accounts receivable on April 1 will total $140,000, of which $120,000 will be collected during April and $16,000 will be collected during May. The remainder will be uncollectible.

b. Past experience shows that 30% of a month's sales are collected in the month of sale, 60% in the month following sale, and 8% in the second month following sale. The other 2% represents bad debts that are never collected. Budgeted sales and expenses for the three-month period follow:

	April	May	June
Sales (all on account)	$300,000	$400,000	$250,000
Merchandise purchases	$210,000	$160,000	$130,000
Payroll	$20,000	$20,000	$18,000
Lease payments	$22,000	$22,000	$22,000
Advertising	$60,000	$60,000	$50,000
Equipment purchases	—	—	$65,000
Depreciation	$15,000	$15,000	$15,000

c. Merchandise purchases are paid in full during the month following purchase. Accounts payable for merchandise purchases during March, which will be paid during April, total $140,000.

d. In preparing the cash budget, assume that the $30,000 loan will be made in April and repaid in June. Interest on the loan will total $1,200.

Required:

1. Prepare a schedule of expected cash collections for April, May, and June, and for the three months in total.
2. Prepare a cash budget, by month and in total, for the three-month period.
3. If the company needs a minimum cash balance of $20,000 to start each month, can the loan be repaid as planned? Explain.

PROBLEM 9–22 Cash Budget with Supporting Schedules [LO9–2, LO9–4, LO9–8]

Garden Sales, Inc., sells garden supplies. Management is planning its cash needs for the second quarter. The company usually has to borrow money during this quarter to support peak sales of lawn care equipment, which occur during May. The following information has been assembled to assist in preparing a cash budget for the quarter:

a. Budgeted monthly absorption costing income statements for April–July are:

	April	May	June	July
Sales	$ 600,000	$900,000	$500,000	$400,000
Cost of goods sold	420,000	630,000	350,000	280,000
Gross margin	180,000	270,000	150,000	120,000
Selling and administrative expenses:				
Selling expense	79,000	120,000	62,000	51,000
Administrative expense*	45,000	52,000	41,000	38,000
Total selling and administrative expenses	124,000	172,000	103,000	89,000
Net operating income	$ 56,000	$ 98,000	$ 47,000	$ 31,000

*Includes $20,000 of depreciation each month.

b. Sales are 20% for cash and 80% on account.
c. Sales on account are collected over a three-month period with 10% collected in the month of sale; 70% collected in the first month following the month of sale; and the remaining 20% collected in the second month following the month of sale. February's sales totaled $200,000, and March's sales totaled $300,000.
d. Inventory purchases are paid for within 15 days. Therefore, 50% of a month's inventory purchases are paid for in the month of purchase. The remaining 50% is paid in the following month. Accounts payable at March 31 for inventory purchases during March total $126,000.
e. Each month's ending inventory must equal 20% of the cost of the merchandise to be sold in the following month. The merchandise inventory at March 31 is $84,000.
f. Dividends of $49,000 will be declared and paid in April.
g. Land costing $16,000 will be purchased for cash in May.
h. The cash balance at March 31 is $52,000; the company must maintain a cash balance of at least $40,000 at the end of each month.
i. The company has an agreement with a local bank that allows the company to borrow in increments of $1,000 at the beginning of each month, up to a total loan balance of $200,000. The interest rate on these loans is 1% per month and for simplicity we will assume that interest is not compounded. The company would, as far as it is able, repay the loan plus accumulated interest at the end of the quarter.

Required:

1. Prepare a schedule of expected cash collections for April, May, and June, and for the quarter in total.
2. Prepare the following for merchandise inventory:
   a. A merchandise purchases budget for April, May, and June.
   b. A schedule of expected cash disbursements for merchandise purchases for April, May, and June, and for the quarter in total.
3. Prepare a cash budget for April, May, and June as well as in total for the quarter.

PROBLEM 9–23 Cash Budget with Supporting Schedules; Changing Assumptions [LO9–2, LO9–4, LO9–8]

Refer to the data for Garden Sales, Inc., in Problem 9–22. The company's president is interested in knowing how reducing inventory levels and collecting accounts receivable sooner will impact the cash budget. He revises the cash collection and ending inventory assumptions as follows:

1. Sales continue to be 20% for cash and 80% on credit. However, credit sales from April, May, and June are collected over a three-month period with 25% collected in the month of sale, 65% collected in the month following sale, and 10% in the second month following sale. Credit sales from February and March are collected during the second quarter using the collection percentages specified in Problem 9–22.
2. The company maintains its ending inventory levels for April, May, and June at 15% of the cost of merchandise to be sold in the following month. The merchandise inventory at March 31 remains $84,000 and accounts payable for inventory purchases at March 31 remains $126,000.

All other information from Problem 9–22 that is not referred to above remains the same.

Required:

1. Using the president's new assumptions in requirement 1, prepare a schedule of expected cash collections for April, May, and June and for the quarter in total.
2. Using the president's new assumptions in requirement 2, prepare the following for merchandise inventory:
   a. A merchandise purchases budget for April, May, and June.
   b. A schedule of expected cash disbursements for merchandise purchases for April, May, and June and for the quarter in total.
3. Using the president's new assumptions, prepare a cash budget for April, May, and June, and for the quarter in total.
4. Prepare a brief memorandum for the president explaining how his revised assumptions affect the cash budget.

PROBLEM 9–24 Behavioral Aspects of Budgeting; Ethics and the Manager [LO9–1]

Norton Company, a manufacturer of infant furniture and carriages, is in the initial stages of preparing the annual budget for next year. Scott Ford has recently joined Norton's accounting staff and is interested to learn as much as possible about the company's budgeting process. During a recent lunch with Marge Atkins, sales manager, and Pete Granger, production manager, Ford initiated the following conversation.

Ford: Since I'm new around here and am going to be involved with the preparation of the annual budget, I'd be interested to learn how the two of you estimate sales and production numbers.

Atkins: We start out very methodically by looking at recent history, discussing what we know about current accounts, potential customers, and the general state of consumer spending. Then, we add that usual dose of intuition to come up with the best forecast we can.

Granger: I usually take the sales projections as the basis for my projections. Of course, we have to make an estimate of what this year's ending inventories will be, which is sometimes difficult.

Ford: Why does that present a problem? There must have been an estimate of ending inventories in the budget for the current year.

Granger: Those numbers aren't always reliable because Marge makes some adjustments to the sales numbers before passing them on to me.

Ford: What kind of adjustments?

Atkins: Well, we don't want to fall short of the sales projections so we generally give ourselves a little breathing room by lowering the initial sales projection anywhere from 5% to 10%.

Granger: So, you can see why this year's budget is not a very reliable starting point. We always have to adjust the projected production rates as the year progresses and, of course, this changes the ending inventory estimates. By the way, we make similar adjustments to expenses by adding at least 10% to the estimates; I think everyone around here does the same thing.

Required:

1. Marge Atkins and Pete Granger have described the use of what is sometimes called *budgetary slack*.
   a. Explain why Atkins and Granger behave in this manner and describe the benefits they expect to realize from the use of budgetary slack.
   b. Explain how the use of budgetary slack can adversely affect Atkins and Granger.
2. As a management accountant, Scott Ford believes that the behavior described by Marge Atkins and Pete Granger may be unethical. By referring to the IMA's Statement of Ethical Professional Practice in Chapter 1, explain why the use of budgetary slack may be unethical.

(CMA, adapted)

PROBLEM 9–25 Schedule of Expected Cash Collections; Cash Budget [LO9–2, LO9–8]

Herbal Care Corp., a distributor of herb-based sunscreens, is ready to begin its third quarter, in which peak sales occur. The company has requested a $40,000, 90-day loan from its bank to help meet cash requirements during the quarter. Since Herbal Care has experienced difficulty in paying off its loans in the past, the loan officer at the bank has asked the company to prepare a cash budget for the quarter. In response to this request, the following data have been assembled:

a. On July 1, the beginning of the third quarter, the company will have a cash balance of $44,500.

b. Actual sales for the last two months and budgeted sales for the third quarter follow (all sales are on account):

May (actual)	$250,000
June (actual)	$300,000
July (budgeted)	$400,000
August (budgeted)	$600,000
September (budgeted)	$320,000

Past experience shows that 25% of a month's sales are collected in the month of sale, 70% in the month following sale, and 3% in the second month following sale. The remainder is uncollectible.

c. Budgeted merchandise purchases and budgeted expenses for the third quarter are given below:

	July	August	September
Merchandise purchases.	$240,000	$350,000	$175,000
Salaries and wages.	$45,000	$50,000	$40,000
Advertising	$130,000	$145,000	$80,000
Rent payments.	$9,000	$9,000	$9,000
Depreciation.	$10,000	$10,000	$10,000

Merchandise purchases are paid in full during the month following purchase. Accounts payable for merchandise purchases on June 30, which will be paid during July, total $180,000.

d. Equipment costing $10,000 will be purchased for cash during July.

e. In preparing the cash budget, assume that the $40,000 loan will be made in July and repaid in September. Interest on the loan will total $1,200.

Required:

1. Prepare a schedule of expected cash collections for July, August, and September and for the quarter in total.
2. Prepare a cash budget, by month and in total, for the third quarter.
3. If the company needs a minimum cash balance of $20,000 to start each month, can the loan be repaid as planned? Explain.

PROBLEM 9–26 Cash Budget with Supporting Schedules [LO9–2, LO9–4, LO9–7, LO9–8]

Westex Products is a wholesale distributor of industrial cleaning products. When the treasurer of Westex Products approached the company's bank late in the current year seeking short-term financing, he was told that money was very tight and that any borrowing over the next year would have to be supported by a detailed statement of cash collections and disbursements. The treasurer also was told that it would be very helpful to the bank if borrowers would indicate the quarters in which they would be needing funds, as well as the amounts that would be needed, and the quarters in which repayments could be made.

Because the treasurer is unsure as to the particular quarters in which bank financing will be needed, he has assembled the following information to assist in preparing a detailed cash budget:

a. Budgeted sales and merchandise purchases for next year, as well as actual sales and purchases for the last quarter of the current year, are:

	Sales	Merchandise Purchases
Current Year:		
Fourth quarter actual	$200,000	$126,000
Next year:		
First quarter estimated	$300,000	$186,000
Second quarter estimated	$400,000	$246,000
Third quarter estimated	$500,000	$305,000
Fourth quarter estimated	$200,000	$126,000

b. All sales are on account. The company normally collects 65% of a quarter's sales before the quarter ends and another 33% in the following quarter. The remainder is uncollectible. This pattern of collections is now being experienced in the current year's fourth-quarter actual data.

c. Eighty percent of a quarter's merchandise purchases are paid for within the quarter. The remainder is paid for in the following quarter.

d. Selling and administrative expenses for next year are budgeted at $50,000 per quarter plus 15% of sales. Of the fixed amount, $20,000 each quarter is depreciation.

e. The company will pay $10,000 in dividends each quarter.

f. Land purchases of $75,000 will be made in the second quarter, and purchases of $48,000 will be made in the third quarter. These purchases will be for cash.

g. The Cash account contained $10,000 at the end of the current year. The treasurer feels that this represents a minimum balance that must be maintained.
h. The company has an agreement with a local bank that allows the company to borrow in increments of $1,000 at the beginning of each quarter, up to a total loan balance of $100,000. The interest rate on these loans is 2.5% per quarter and for simplicity we will assume that interest is not compounded. The company would, as far as it is able, repay the loan plus accumulated interest at the end of the year.
i. At present, the company has no loans outstanding.

Required:

1. Prepare the following by quarter and in total for next year:
   a. A schedule of expected cash collections.
   b. A schedule of expected cash disbursements for merchandise purchases.
2. Compute the expected cash disbursements for selling and administrative expenses, by quarter and in total, for next year.
3. Prepare a cash budget, by quarter and in total, for next year.

PROBLEM 9–27 Completing a Master Budget [LO9–2, LO9–4, LO9–7, LO9–8, LO9–9, LO9–10]

The following data relate to the operations of Shilow Company, a wholesale distributor of consumer goods:

Current assets as of March 31:	
Cash	$8,000
Accounts receivable	$20,000
Inventory	$36,000
Buildings and equipment, net	$120,000
Accounts payable	$21,750
Capital stock	$150,000
Retained earnings	$12,250

a. The gross margin is 25% of sales.
b. Actual and budgeted sales data:

March (actual)	$50,000
April	$60,000
May	$72,000
June	$90,000
July	$48,000

c. Sales are 60% for cash and 40% on credit. Credit sales are collected in the month following sale. The accounts receivable at March 31 are a result of March credit sales.
d. Each month's ending inventory should equal 80% of the following month's budgeted cost of goods sold.
e. One-half of a month's inventory purchases is paid for in the month of purchase; the other half is paid for in the following month. The accounts payable at March 31 are the result of March purchases of inventory.
f. Monthly expenses are as follows: commissions, 12% of sales; rent, $2,500 per month; other expenses (excluding depreciation), 6% of sales. Assume that these expenses are paid monthly. Depreciation is $900 per month (includes depreciation on new assets).
g. Equipment costing $1,500 will be purchased for cash in April.
h. Management would like to maintain a minimum cash balance of at least $4,000 at the end of each month. The company has an agreement with a local bank that allows the company to borrow in increments of $1,000 at the beginning of each month, up to a total loan balance of $20,000. The interest rate on these loans is 1% per month and for simplicity we will assume that interest is not compounded. The company would, as far as it is able, repay the loan plus accumulated interest at the end of the quarter.

Required:

Using the preceding data:

1. Complete the following schedule:

Schedule of Expected Cash Collections	April	May	June	Quarter
Cash sales	$36,000			
Credit sales	20,000			
Total collections	$56,000			

2. Complete the following:

Merchandise Purchases Budget	April	May	June	Quarter
Budgeted cost of goods sold	$45,000*	$54,000		
Add desired ending inventory	43,200†			
Total needs	88,200			
Less beginning inventory	36,000			
Required purchases	$52,200			

*For April sales: $60,000 sales × 75% cost ratio = $45,000.
†$54,000 × 80% = $43,200

Schedule of Expected Cash Disbursements—Merchandise Purchases	April	May	June	Quarter
March purchases	$21,750			$21,750
April purchases	26,100	$26,100		52,200
May purchases				
June purchases				
Total disbursements	$47,850			

3. Complete the following cash budget:

Cash Budget	April	May	June	Quarter
Beginning cash balance	$8,000			
Add cash collections	56,000			
Total cash available	64,000			
Less cash disbursements:				
For inventory	47,850			
For expenses	13,300			
For equipment	1,500			
Total cash disbursements	62,650			
Excess (deficiency) of cash	1,350			
Financing				
Etc.				

4. Prepare an absorption costing income statement, similar to the one shown in Schedule 9 in the chapter, for the quarter ended June 30.
5. Prepare a balance sheet as of June 30.

PROBLEM 9–28 Integration of the Sales, Production, and Direct Materials Budgets [LO9–2, LO9–3, LO9–4]

Milo Company manufactures beach umbrellas. The company is preparing detailed budgets for the third quarter and has assembled the following information to assist in the budget preparation:

a. The Marketing Department has estimated sales as follows for the remainder of the year (in units):

July	30,000	October	20,000
August	70,000	November	10,000
September	50,000	December	10,000

The selling price of the beach umbrellas is $12 per unit.

b. All sales are on account. Based on past experience, sales are collected in the following pattern:

30% in the month of sale
65% in the month following sale
5% uncollectible

Sales for June totaled $300,000.

c. The company maintains finished goods inventories equal to 15% of the following month's sales. This requirement will be met at the end of June.

d. Each beach umbrella requires 4 feet of Gilden, a material that is sometimes hard to acquire. Therefore, the company requires that the ending inventory of Gilden be equal to 50% of the following month's production needs. The inventory of Gilden on hand at the beginning and end of the quarter will be:

June 30	72,000 feet
September 30	? feet

e. Gilden costs $0.80 per foot. One-half of a month's purchases of Gilden is paid for in the month of purchase; the remainder is paid for in the following month. The accounts payable on July 1 for purchases of Gilden during June will be $76,000.

Required:

1. Prepare a sales budget, by month and in total, for the third quarter. (Show your budget in both units and dollars.) Also prepare a schedule of expected cash collections, by month and in total, for the third quarter.
2. Prepare a production budget for each of the months July–October.
3. Prepare a direct materials budget for Gilden, by month and in total, for the third quarter. Also prepare a schedule of expected cash disbursements for Gilden, by month and in total, for the third quarter.

PROBLEM 9–29 Completing a Master Budget [LO9–2, LO9–4, LO9–7, LO9–8, LO9–9, LO9–10]

Hillyard Company, an office supplies specialty store, prepares its master budget on a quarterly basis. The following data have been assembled to assist in preparing the master budget for the first quarter:

a. As of December 31 (the end of the prior quarter), the company's general ledger showed the following account balances:

	Debits	Credits
Cash	$ 48,000	
Accounts receivable	224,000	
Inventory	60,000	
Buildings and equipment (net)	370,000	
Accounts payable		$ 93,000
Common stock		500,000
Retained earnings		109,000
	$702,000	$702,000

b. Actual sales for December and budgeted sales for the next four months are as follows:

December (actual)	$280,000
January	$400,000
February	$600,000
March	$300,000
April	$200,000

c. Sales are 20% for cash and 80% on credit. All payments on credit sales are collected in the month following sale. The accounts receivable at December 31 are a result of December credit sales.

d. The company's gross margin is 40% of sales. (In other words, cost of goods sold is 60% of sales.)

e. Monthly expenses are budgeted as follows: salaries and wages, $27,000 per month: advertising, $70,000 per month; shipping, 5% of sales; other expenses, 3% of sales. Depreciation, including depreciation on new assets acquired during the quarter, will be $42,000 for the quarter.

f. Each month's ending inventory should equal 25% of the following month's cost of goods sold.

g. One-half of a month's inventory purchases is paid for in the month of purchase; the other half is paid in the following month.

h. During February, the company will purchase a new copy machine for $1,700 cash. During March, other equipment will be purchased for cash at a cost of $84,500.

i. During January, the company will declare and pay $45,000 in cash dividends.

j. Management wants to maintain a minimum cash balance of $30,000. The company has an agreement with a local bank that allows the company to borrow in increments of $1,000 at the beginning of each month. The interest rate on these loans is 1% per month and for simplicity we will assume that interest is not compounded. The company would, as far as it is able, repay the loan plus accumulated interest at the end of the quarter.

Required:

Using the data above, complete the following statements and schedules for the first quarter:

1. Schedule of expected cash collections:

	January	February	March	Quarter
Cash sales	$ 80,000			
Credit sales	224,000			
Total cash collections	$304,000			

2. *a.* Merchandise purchases budget:

	January	February	March	Quarter
Budgeted cost of goods sold	$240,000*	$360,000		
Add desired ending inventory	90,000†			
Total needs	330,000			
Less beginning inventory	60,000			
Required purchases	$270,000			

*$400,000 sales × 60% cost ratio = $240,000.
†$360,000 × 25% = $90,000.

b. Schedule of expected cash disbursements for merchandise purchases:

	January	February	March	Quarter
December purchases	$ 93,000			$ 93,000
January purchases	135,000	135,000		270,000
February purchases	—			
March purchases	—			
Total cash disbursements for purchases	$228,000			

3. Cash budget:

	January	February	March	Quarter
Beginning cash balance	$48,000			
Add cash collections	304,000			
Total cash available	352,000			
Less cash disbursements:				
Purchases of inventory	228,000			
Selling and administrative expenses	129,000			
Purchases of equipment	—			
Cash dividends	45,000			
Total cash disbursements	402,000			
Excess (deficiency) of cash	(50,000)			
Financing:				
Etc				

4. Prepare an absorption costing income statement for the quarter ending March 31 as shown in Schedule 9 in the chapter.
5. Prepare a balance sheet as of March 31.

Cases

connect — **Additional student resources are available with Connect.**

CASE 9–30 Evaluating a Company's Budget Procedures [LO9–1]

Tom Emory and Jim Morris strolled back to their plant from the administrative offices of Ferguson & Son Manufacturing Company. Tom is manager of the machine shop in the company's factory; Jim is manager of the equipment maintenance department.

The men had just attended the monthly performance evaluation meeting for plant department heads. These meetings had been held on the third Tuesday of each month since Robert Ferguson, Jr., the president's son, had become plant manager a year earlier.

As they were walking, Tom Emory spoke: "Boy, I hate those meetings! I never know whether my department's accounting reports will show good or bad performance. I'm beginning to expect the worst. If the accountants say I saved the company a dollar, I'm called 'Sir,' but if I spend even a little too much—boy, do I get in trouble. I don't know if I can hold on until I retire."

Tom had just been given the worst evaluation he had ever received in his long career with Ferguson & Son. He was the most respected of the experienced machinists in the company. He had been with Ferguson & Son for many years and was promoted to supervisor of the machine shop when the company expanded and moved to its present location. The president (Robert Ferguson, Sr.) had often stated that the company's success was due to the high-quality work of machinists like Tom. As supervisor, Tom stressed the importance of craftsmanship and told his workers that he wanted no sloppy work coming from his department.

When Robert Ferguson, Jr., became the plant manager, he directed that monthly performance comparisons be made between actual and budgeted costs for each department. The departmental budgets were intended to encourage the supervisors to reduce inefficiencies and to seek cost reduction opportunities. The company controller was instructed to have his staff "tighten" the budget slightly whenever a department attained its budget in a given month; this was done to reinforce the plant manager's desire to reduce costs. The young plant manager often stressed the importance of continued progress toward attaining the budget; he also made it known that he kept a file of these performance reports for future reference when he succeeded his father.

Tom Emory's conversation with Jim Morris continued as follows:

Emory: I really don't understand. We've worked so hard to meet the budget, and the minute we do so they tighten it on us. We can't work any faster and still maintain quality. I think my men are ready to quit trying. Besides, those reports don't tell the whole story. We always seem to be interrupting the big jobs for all those small rush orders. All that setup and machine adjustment time is killing us. And quite frankly, Jim, you were no help. When our hydraulic press broke down last month, your people were nowhere to be found. We had to take it apart ourselves and got stuck with all that idle time.

Morris: I'm sorry about that, Tom, but you know my department has had trouble making budget, too. We were running well behind at the time of that problem, and if we'd spent a day on that old machine, we would never have made it up. Instead we made the scheduled inspections of the forklift trucks because we knew we could do those in less than the budgeted time.

Emory: Well, Jim, at least you have some options. I'm locked into what the scheduling department assigns to me and you know they're being harassed by sales for those special orders. Incidentally, why didn't your report show all the supplies you guys wasted last month when you were working in Bill's department?

Morris: We're not out of the woods on that deal yet. We charged the maximum we could to other work and haven't even reported some of it yet.

Emory: Well, I'm glad you have a way of getting out of the pressure. The accountants seem to know everything that's happening in my department, sometimes even before I do. I thought all that budget and accounting stuff was supposed to help, but it just gets me into trouble. It's all a big pain. I'm trying to put out quality work; they're trying to save pennies.

Required:

1. Identify the problems that appear to exist in Ferguson & Son Manufacturing Company's budgetary control system and explain how the problems are likely to reduce the effectiveness of the system.
2. Explain how Ferguson & Son Manufacturing Company's budgetary control system could be revised to improve its effectiveness.

(CMA, adapted)

CASE 9–31 Master Budget with Supporting Schedules [LO9–2, LO9–4, LO9–8, LO9–9, LO9–10]

You have just been hired as a new management trainee by Earrings Unlimited, a distributor of earrings to various retail outlets located in shopping malls across the country. In the past, the company has done very little in the way of budgeting and at certain times of the year has experienced a shortage of cash.

Since you are well trained in budgeting, you have decided to prepare comprehensive budgets for the upcoming second quarter in order to show management the benefits that can be gained from an integrated budgeting program. To this end, you have worked with accounting and other areas to gather the information assembled below.

The company sells many styles of earrings, but all are sold for the same price—$10 per pair. Actual sales of earrings for the last three months and budgeted sales for the next six months follow (in pairs of earrings):

January (actual)	20,000	June (budget)	50,000
February (actual)	26,000	July (budget)	30,000
March (actual)	40,000	August (budget)	28,000
April (budget)	65,000	September (budget)	25,000
May (budget)	100,000		

The concentration of sales before and during May is due to Mother's Day. Sufficient inventory should be on hand at the end of each month to supply 40% of the earrings sold in the following month.

Suppliers are paid $4 for a pair of earrings. One-half of a month's purchases is paid for in the month of purchase; the other half is paid for in the following month. All sales are on credit, with no discount, and payable within 15 days. The company has found, however, that only 20% of a month's sales are collected in the month of sale. An additional 70% is collected in the following month, and the remaining 10% is collected in the second month following sale. Bad debts have been negligible.

Monthly operating expenses for the company are given below:

Variable:	
Sales commissions	4% of sales
Fixed:	
Advertising	$200,000
Rent	$18,000
Salaries	$106,000
Utilities	$7,000
Insurance	$3,000
Depreciation	$14,000

Insurance is paid on an annual basis, in November of each year.

The company plans to purchase $16,000 in new equipment during May and $40,000 in new equipment during June; both purchases will be for cash. The company declares dividends of $15,000 each quarter, payable in the first month of the following quarter.

A listing of the company's ledger accounts as of March 31 is given below:

Assets	
Cash	$ 74,000
Accounts receivable ($26,000 February sales; $320,000 March sales)	346,000
Inventory	104,000
Prepaid insurance	21,000
Property and equipment (net)	950,000
Total assets	$1,495,000
Liabilities and Stockholders' Equity	
Accounts payable	$ 100,000
Dividends payable	15,000
Common stock	800,000
Retained earnings	580,000
Total liabilities and stockholders' equity	$1,495,000

The company maintains a minimum cash balance of $50,000. All borrowing is done at the beginning of a month; any repayments are made at the end of a month.

The company has an agreement with a bank that allows the company to borrow in increments of $1,000 at the beginning of each month. The interest rate on these loans is 1% per month and for simplicity we will assume that interest is not compounded. At the end of the quarter, the company would pay the bank all of the accumulated interest on the loan and as much of the loan as possible (in increments of $1,000), while still retaining at least $50,000 in cash.

Required:

Prepare a master budget for the three-month period ending June 30. Include the following detailed budgets:

1. *a.* A sales budget, by month and in total.
   b. A schedule of expected cash collections from sales, by month and in total.
   c. A merchandise purchases budget in units and in dollars. Show the budget by month and in total.
   d. A schedule of expected cash disbursements for merchandise purchases, by month and in total.
2. A cash budget. Show the budget by month and in total. Determine any borrowing that would be needed to maintain the minimum cash balance of $50,000.
3. A budgeted income statement for the three-month period ending June 30. Use the contribution approach.
4. A budgeted balance sheet as of June 30.

Flexible Budgets and Performance Analysis

LEARNING OBJECTIVES

After studying Chapter 10, you should be able to:

LO 10–1 Prepare a flexible budget.

LO 10–2 Prepare a report showing activity variances.

LO 10–3 Prepare a report showing revenue and spending variances.

LO 10–4 Prepare a performance report that combines activity variances and revenue and spending variances.

LO 10–5 Prepare a flexible budget with more than one cost driver.

LO 10–6 Understand common errors made in preparing performance reports based on budgets and actual results.

Why Do Companies Need Flexible Budgets?

BUSINESS FOCUS

© Michael Sears/MCT/Newscom

The difficulty of accurately predicting future financial performance can be readily understood by reading the annual report of any publicly traded company. For example, Nucor Corporation, a steel manufacturer headquartered in Charlotte, North Carolina, cites numerous reasons why its actual results may differ from expectations, including the following: (1) changes in the supply and cost of raw materials; (2) changes in the availability and cost of electricity and natural gas; (3) changes in the market demand for steel products; (4) fluctuations in currency conversion rates; (5) significant changes in laws or government regulations; and (6) the cyclical nature of the steel industry. ■

Source: Nucor Corporation 2011 Annual Report, p. 3.

In the last chapter we explored how budgets are developed before a period begins. In this chapter, we explain how budgets can be adjusted to help guide actual operations and influence the performance evaluation process. For example, an organization's actual expenses will rarely equal its budgeted expenses as estimated at the beginning of the period. The reason is that the actual level of activity (such as unit sales) will rarely be the same as the budgeted activity; therefore, many actual expenses and revenues will naturally differ from what was budgeted. Should a manager be penalized for spending 10% more than budgeted for a variable expense like direct materials if unit sales are 10% higher than budgeted? Of course not. After studying this chapter, you'll know how to adjust a budget to enable meaningful comparisons to actual results.

The Variance Analysis Cycle

Companies use the *variance analysis cycle,* as illustrated in Exhibit 10–1, to evaluate and improve performance. The cycle begins with the preparation of performance reports in the accounting department. These reports highlight variances, which are the differences between the actual results and what should have occurred according to the budget. The variances raise questions. Why did this variance occur? Why is this variance larger than it was last period? The significant variances are investigated so that their root causes can be either replicated or eliminated. Then, next period's operations are carried out and the cycle begins again with the preparation of a new performance report for the latest period. The emphasis should be on highlighting superior and unsatisfactory results, finding the root causes of these outcomes, and then replicating the sources of superior achievement and eliminating the sources of unsatisfactory performance. The variance analysis cycle should not be used to assign blame for poor performance.

Managers frequently use the concept of *management by exception* in conjunction with the variance analysis cycle. Management by exception is a management system that compares actual results to a budget so that significant deviations can be flagged as exceptions and investigated further. This approach enables managers to focus on the most important variances while bypassing trivial discrepancies between the budget and actual results. For example, a variance of $5 is probably not big enough to warrant attention, whereas a variance of $5,000 might be worth tracking down. Another clue is the size of the variance relative to the amount of spending. A variance that is only 0.1% of spending on an item is probably caused by random factors. On the other hand, a variance of 10% of spending is much more likely to be a signal that something is wrong. In addition to

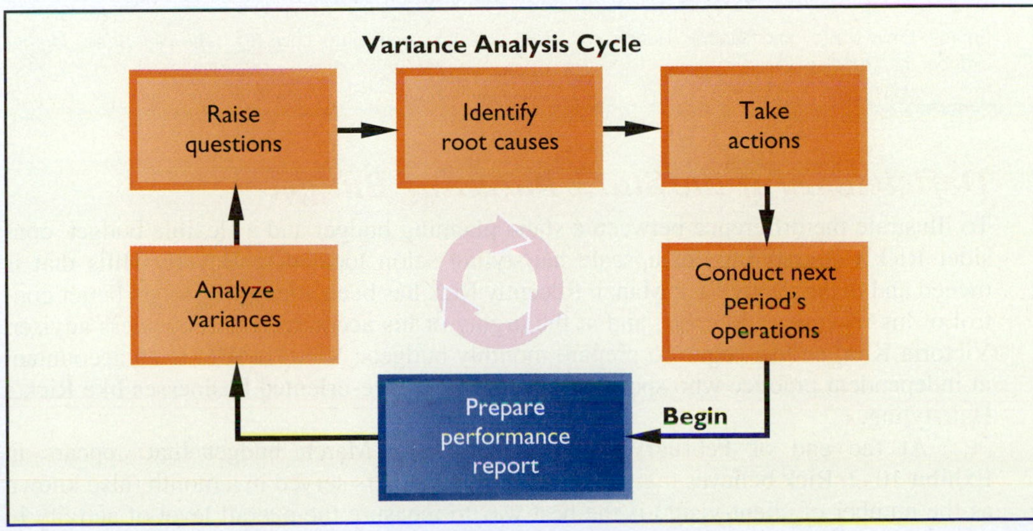

EXHIBIT 10–1
The Variance Analysis Cycle

watching for unusually large variances, the pattern of the variances should be monitored. For example, a run of steadily mounting variances should trigger an investigation even though none of the variances is large enough by itself to warrant investigation.

Next, we explain how organizations use flexible budgets to compare actual results to what should have occurred according to the budget.

Flexible Budgets

Characteristics of a Flexible Budget

LEARNING OBJECTIVE 10–1
Prepare a flexible budget.

The budgets that we explored in the last chapter were *planning budgets.* A **planning budget** is prepared before the period begins and is valid for only the planned level of activity. A static planning budget is suitable for planning but is inappropriate for evaluating how well costs are controlled. If the actual level of activity differs from what was planned, it would be misleading to compare actual costs to the static, unchanged planning budget. If activity is higher than expected, variable costs should be higher than expected; and if activity is lower than expected, variable costs should be lower than expected.

Flexible budgets take into account how changes in activity affect costs. A **flexible budget** is an estimate of what revenues and costs should have been, given the actual level of activity for the period. When a flexible budget is used in performance evaluation, actual costs are compared to what the costs *should have been for the actual level of activity during the period* rather than to the static planning budget. This is a very important distinction. If adjustments for the level of activity are not made, it is very difficult to interpret discrepancies between budgeted and actual costs.

IN BUSINESS

WINNERS AND LOSERS FROM THE NBA LOCKOUT

A company's actual net operating income can deviate from the budget for numerous and often uncontrollable reasons. For example, when the National Basketball Association (NBA) decided to suspend play because of a dispute between its team owners and players, many small businesses suffered—caterers, sports bars, apparel retailers, and parking lot owners all experienced a drop in revenues. BestSportsApparel.com experienced a substantial drop in NBA apparel sales due to the work stoppage. Rather than hiring 12 extra employees for the NBA season, the company reduced the size of its workforce.

While some companies lost revenues when the NBA shut down, others benefited from the situation. Andrew Zimbalist, professor of economics at Smith College, notes that "local economies are not impacted by sports work stoppages" because people choose to spend their entertainment dollars at other venues such as the theater, the zoo, or the museum.

Source: Emily Maltby and Sarah E. Needleman, "NBA Lockout: Local Firms Lose Big," *The Wall Street Journal,* October 13, 2011, p. B5.

Deficiencies of the Static Planning Budget

To illustrate the difference between a static planning budget and a flexible budget, consider Rick's Hairstyling, an upscale hairstyling salon located in Beverly Hills that is owned and managed by Rick Manzi. Recently Rick has been attempting to get better control of his revenues and costs, and at the urging of his accounting and business adviser, Victoria Kho, he has begun to prepare monthly budgets. Victoria Kho is an accountant in independent practice who specializes in small service-oriented businesses like Rick's Hairstyling.

At the end of February, Rick prepared the March budget that appears in Exhibit 10–2. Rick believes that the number of customers served in a month (also known as the number of client-visits) is the best way to measure the overall level of activity in

EXHIBIT 10–2
Planning Budget

Rick's Hairstyling Planning Budget For the Month Ended March 31	
Budgeted client-visits (*q*)	1,000
Revenue ($180.00*q*)	$180,000
Expenses:	
Wages and salaries ($65,000 + $37.00*q*)	102,000
Hairstyling supplies ($1.50*q*)	1,500
Client gratuities ($4.10*q*)	4,100
Electricity ($1,500 + $0.10*q*)	1,600
Rent ($28,500)	28,500
Liability insurance ($2,800)	2,800
Employee health insurance ($21,300)	21,300
Miscellaneous ($1,200 + $0.20*q*)	1,400
Total expense	163,200
Net operating income	$ 16,800

his salon. A customer who comes into the salon and has his or her hair styled is counted as one client-visit.

Note that the term *revenue* is used in the planning budget rather than *sales.* We use the term revenue throughout the chapter because some organizations have sources of revenue other than sales. For example, donations, as well as sales, are counted as revenue in nonprofit organizations.

Rick has identified eight major categories of costs—wages and salaries, hairstyling supplies, client gratuities, electricity, rent, liability insurance, employee health insurance, and miscellaneous. Client gratuities consist of flowers, candies, and glasses of champagne that Rick gives to his customers while they are in the salon.

Working with Victoria, Rick estimated a cost formula for each cost. For example, the cost formula for electricity is $1,500 + $0.10*q*, where *q* equals the number of client-visits. In other words, electricity is a mixed cost with a $1,500 fixed element and a $0.10 per client-visit variable element. Once the budgeted level of activity was set at 1,000 client-visits, Rick computed the budgeted amount for each line item in the budget. For example, using the cost formula, he set the budgeted cost for electricity at $1,600 (= $1,500 + $0.10 × 1,000). To finalize his budget, Rick computed his expected net operating income for March of $16,800.

At the end of March, Rick prepared the income statement in Exhibit 10–3, which shows that 1,100 clients actually visited his salon in March and that his actual net operating income for the month was $21,230. It is important to realize that the actual results are *not* determined by plugging the actual number of client-visits into the revenue and cost formulas. The formulas are simply estimates of what the revenues and costs should be for a given level of activity. What actually happens usually differs from what is supposed to happen.

The first thing Rick noticed when comparing Exhibits 10–2 and 10–3 is that the actual profit of $21,230 (from Exhibits 10–3) was substantially higher than the budgeted profit of $16,800 (from Exhibit 10–2). This was, of course, good news, but Rick wanted to know more. Business was up by 10%—the salon had 1,100 client-visits instead of the budgeted 1,000 client-visits. Could this alone explain the higher net operating income? The answer is no. An increase in net operating income of 10% would have resulted in net operating income of only $18,480 (= 1.1 × $16,800), not the $21,230 actually earned during the month. What is responsible for this better outcome? Higher prices? Lower costs? Something else? Whatever the cause, Rick would like to know the answer and then hopefully repeat the same performance next month.

EXHIBIT 10–3
Actual Results—Income Statement

Rick's Hairstyling
Income Statement
For the Month Ended March 31

Actual client-visits	1,100
Revenue	$194,200
Expenses:	
Wages and salaries	106,900
Hairstyling supplies	1,620
Client gratuities	6,870
Electricity	1,550
Rent	28,500
Liability insurance	2,800
Employee health insurance	22,600
Miscellaneous	2,130
Total expense	172,970
Net operating income	$ 21,230

In an attempt to analyze what happened in March, Rick prepared the report comparing actual to budgeted costs that appears in Exhibit 10–4. Note that most of the variances in this report are labeled unfavorable (U) rather than favorable (F) even though net operating income was actually higher than expected. For example, wages and salaries show an unfavorable variance of $4,900 because the actual wages and salaries expense was $106,900, whereas the budget called for wages and salaries of $102,000. The problem with the report, as Rick immediately realized, is that it compares revenues and costs at

EXHIBIT 10–4
Comparison of Actual Results to the Static Planning Budget

Rick's Hairstyling
Comparison of Actual Results to the Planning Budget
For the Month Ended March 31

	Actual Results	Planning Budget	Variances*
Client-visits	1,100	1,000	
Revenue	$194,200	$180,000	$14,200 F
Expenses:			
Wages and salaries	106,900	102,000	4,900 U
Hairstyling supplies	1,620	1,500	120 U
Client gratuities	6,870	4,100	2,770 U
Electricity	1,550	1,600	50 F
Rent	28,500	28,500	0
Liability insurance	2,800	2,800	0
Employee health insurance	22,600	21,300	1,300 U
Miscellaneous	2,130	1,400	730 U
Total expense	172,970	163,200	9,770 U
Net operating income	$ 21,230	$ 16,800	$ 4,430 F

*The revenue variance is labeled favorable (unfavorable) when the actual revenue is greater than (less than) the planning budget. The expense variances are labeled favorable (unfavorable) when the actual expense is less than (greater than) the planning budget.

one level of activity (1,000 client-visits) to revenues and costs at a different level of activity (1,100 client-visits). This is like comparing apples to oranges. Because Rick had 100 more client-visits than expected, some of his costs should be higher than budgeted. From Rick's standpoint, the increase in activity was good; however, it appears to be having a negative impact on most of the costs in the report. Rick knew that something would have to be done to make the report more meaningful, but he was unsure of what to do. So he made an appointment to meet with Victoria Kho to discuss the next step.

MANAGERIAL ACCOUNTING IN ACTION
The Issue

RICK'S Hairstyling Salon

Victoria: How is the budgeting going?
Rick: Pretty well. I didn't have any trouble putting together the budget for March. I also prepared a report comparing the actual results for March to the budget, but that report isn't giving me what I really want to know.
Victoria: Because your actual level of activity didn't match your budgeted activity?
Rick: Right. I know the level of activity shouldn't affect my fixed costs, but we had more client-visits than I had expected and that had to affect my other costs.
Victoria: So you want to know whether the higher actual costs are justified by the higher level of activity?
Rick: Precisely.
Victoria: If you leave your reports and data with me, I can work on it later today, and by tomorrow I'll have a report to show you.

How a Flexible Budget Works

A flexible budget approach recognizes that a budget can be adjusted to show what costs *should be* for the actual level of activity. To illustrate how flexible budgets work, Victoria prepared the report in Exhibit 10–5 that shows what the *revenues and costs should have been given the actual level of activity* in March. Preparing the report is straightforward. The cost formula for each cost is used to estimate what the cost should have been for 1,100 client-visits—the actual level of activity for March. For example, using the cost formula $1,500 + $0.10*q*, the cost of electricity in March *should have been* $1,610 (= $1,500 + $0.10 × 1,100). Also, notice that the amounts of rent ($28,500), liability insurance ($2,800), and employee health insurance ($21,300) in the flexible budget equal the corresponding amounts in the planning budget (see Exhibit 10–2). This occurs because fixed costs are not affected by the activity level.

EXHIBIT 10–5
Flexible Budget Based on Actual Activity

Rick's Hairstyling
Flexible Budget
For the Month Ended March 31

Actual client-visits (*q*)	1,100
Revenue ($180.00*q*)	$198,000
Expenses:	
Wages and salaries ($65,000 + $37.00*q*)	105,700
Hairstyling supplies ($1.50*q*)	1,650
Client gratuities ($4.10*q*)	4,510
Electricity ($1,500 + $0.10*q*)	1,610
Rent ($28,500)	28,500
Liability insurance ($2,800)	2,800
Employee health insurance ($21,300)	21,300
Miscellaneous ($1,200 + $0.20*q*)	1,420
Total expense	167,490
Net operating income	$ 30,510

We can see from the flexible budget that the net operating income in March *should have been* $30,510, but recall from Exhibit 10–3 that the net operating income was actually only $21,230. The results are not as good as we thought. Why? We will answer that question shortly.

To summarize to this point, Rick had budgeted for a profit of $16,800. The actual profit was quite a bit higher—$21,230. However, Victoria's analysis shows that given the actual number of client-visits in March, the profit should have been even higher—$30,510. What are the causes of these discrepancies? Rick would certainly like to build on the positive factors, while working to reduce the negative factors. But what are they?

Flexible Budget Variances

To answer Rick's questions concerning the discrepancies between budgeted and actual costs, Victoria broke down the variances shown in Exhibit 10–4 into two types of variances—activity variances and revenue and spending variances. We explain how she did it in the next two sections.

Activity Variances

LEARNING OBJECTIVE 10–2
Prepare a report showing activity variances.

Part of the discrepancy between the budgeted profit and the actual profit is due to the fact that the actual level of activity in March was higher than expected. How much of this discrepancy was due to this single factor? Victoria prepared the report in Exhibit 10–6 to answer this question. In that report, the flexible budget based on the actual level of

EXHIBIT 10–6
Activity Variances from Comparing the Flexible Budget Based on Actual Activity to the Planning Budget

Rick's Hairstyling
Activity Variances
For the Month Ended March 31

	Flexible Budget	Planning Budget	Activity Variances*
Client-visits	1,100	1,000	
Revenue ($180.00*q*)	$198,000	$180,000	$18,000 F
Expenses:			
Wages and salaries ($65,000 + $37.00*q*)	105,700	102,000	3,700 U
Hairstyling supplies ($1.50*q*)	1,650	1,500	150 U
Client gratuities ($4.10*q*)	4,510	4,100	410 U
Electricity ($1,500 + $0.10*q*)	1,610	1,600	10 U
Rent ($28,500)	28,500	28,500	0
Liability insurance ($2,800)	2,800	2,800	0
Employee health insurance ($21,300)	21,300	21,300	0
Miscellaneous ($1,200 + $0.20*q*)	1,420	1,400	20 U
Total expense	167,490	163,200	4,290 U
Net operating income	$ 30,510	$ 16,800	$13,710 F

*The revenue variance is labeled favorable (unfavorable) when the revenue in the flexible budget is greater than (less than) the planning budget. The expense variances are labeled favorable (unfavorable) when the expense in the flexible budget is less than (greater than) the planning budget.

activity for the period is compared to the planning budget from the beginning of the period. The flexible budget shows what should have happened at the actual level of activity, whereas the planning budget shows what should have happened at the budgeted level of activity. Therefore, the differences between the flexible budget and the planning budget show what should have happened solely because the actual level of activity differed from what had been expected.

For example, the flexible budget based on 1,100 client-visits shows revenue of $198,000 (= $180 per client-visit × 1,100 client-visits). The planning budget based on 1,000 client-visits shows revenue of $180,000 (= $180 per client-visit × 1,000 client-visits). Because the salon had 100 more client-visits than anticipated in the budget, actual revenue should have been higher than budgeted revenue by $18,000 (= $198,000 − $180,000). This activity variance is shown on the report as $18,000 F (favorable). Similarly, the flexible budget based on 1,100 client-visits shows electricity costs of $1,610 (= $1,500 + $0.10 per client-visit × 1,100 client-visits). The planning budget based on 1,000 client-visits shows electricity costs of $1,600 (= $1,500 + $0.10 per client-visit × 1,000 client-visits). Because the salon had 100 more client-visits than anticipated in the budget, actual electricity costs should have been higher than budgeted costs by $10 (= $1,610 − $1,600). The activity variance for electricity is shown on the report as $10 U (unfavorable). Note that in this case, the label "unfavorable" may be a little misleading. Costs *should* be $10 higher for electricity simply because business was up by 100 client-visits; therefore, is this variance really unfavorable if it was a necessary cost of serving more customers? For reasons such as this, we would like to caution you against assuming that unfavorable variances always indicate bad performance and favorable variances always indicate good performance.

Because all of the variances on this report are solely due to the difference between the actual level of activity and the level of activity in the planning budget from the beginning of the period, they are called **activity variances.** For example, the activity variance for revenue is $18,000 F, the activity variance for electricity is $10 U, and so on. The most important activity variance appears at the very bottom of the report; namely, the $13,710 F (favorable) variance for net operating income. This variance says that because activity was higher than expected in the planning budget, the net operating income should have been $13,710 higher. We caution against placing too much emphasis on any other single variance in this report. As we have said above, one would expect some costs to be higher as a consequence of more business. It is misleading to think of these unfavorable variances as indicative of poor performance.

On the other hand, the favorable activity variance for net operating income is important. Let's explore this variance a bit more thoroughly. First, as we have already noted, activity was up by 10%, but the flexible budget indicates that net operating income should have increased much more than 10%. A 10% increase in net operating income from the $16,800 in the planning budget would result in net operating income of $18,480 (= 1.1 × $16,800); however, the flexible budget shows much higher net operating income of $30,510. Why? The short answer is: Because of the presence of fixed costs. When we apply the 10% increase to the budgeted net operating income to estimate the profit at the higher level of activity, we implicitly assume that the revenues and *all* of the costs increase by 10%. But they do not. Note that when the activity level increases by 10%, three of the costs—rent, liability insurance, and employee health insurance—do not increase at all. These are all purely fixed costs. So while sales do increase by 10%, these costs do not increase. This results in net operating income increasing by more than 10%. A similar effect occurs with the mixed costs, which contain fixed cost elements—wages and salaries, electricity, and miscellaneous. While sales increase by 10%, these mixed costs increase by less than 10%, resulting in an overall increase in net operating income of more than 10%. Because of the existence of fixed costs, net operating income does not change in proportion to changes in the level of activity. There is a leverage effect. The percentage changes in net operating income are ordinarily larger than the percentage increases in activity.

LEARNING OBJECTIVE 10–3
Prepare a report showing revenue and spending variances.

Revenue and Spending Variances

In the last section we answered the question "What impact did the change in activity have on our revenues, costs, and profit?" In this section we will answer the question "How well did we control our revenues, our costs, and our profit?"

Recall that the flexible budget based on the actual level of activity in Exhibit 10–5 shows what *should have happened given the actual level of activity.* Therefore, Victoria's next step was to compare actual results to the flexible budget—in essence comparing what actually happened to what should have happened. Her work is shown in Exhibit 10–7.

Focusing first on revenue, the actual revenue totaled $194,200. However, the flexible budget indicates that, given the actual level of activity, revenue should have been $198,000. Consequently, revenue was $3,800 less than it should have been, given the actual number of client-visits for the month. This discrepancy is labeled as a $3,800 U (unfavorable) variance and is called a *revenue variance.* A **revenue variance** is the difference between the actual total revenue and what the total revenue should have been, given the actual level of activity for the period. If actual revenue exceeds what the revenue should have been, the variance is labeled favorable. If actual revenue is less than what the revenue should have been, the variance is labeled unfavorable. Why would actual revenue be less than or more than it should have been, given the actual level of activity? Basically, the revenue variance is favorable if the average selling price is greater than expected; it is unfavorable if the average selling price is less than expected. This could happen for a variety of reasons including a change in selling price, a different mix of products sold, a change in the amount of discounts given, poor accounting controls, and so on.

EXHIBIT 10–7
Revenue and Spending Variances from Comparing Actual Results to the Flexible Budget

Rick's Hairstyling
Revenue and Spending Variances
For the Month Ended March 31

	Actual Results	Flexible Budget	Revenue and Spending Variances*
Client-visits	1,100	1,100	
Revenue ($180.00*q*)	$194,200	$198,000	$3,800 U
Expenses:			
Wages and salaries ($65,000 + $37.00*q*)	106,900	105,700	1,200 U
Hairstyling supplies ($1.50*q*)	1,620	1,650	30 F
Client gratuities ($4.10*q*)	6,870	4,510	2,360 U
Electricity ($1,500 + $0.10*q*)	1,550	1,610	60 F
Rent ($28,500)	28,500	28,500	0
Liability insurance ($2,800)	2,800	2,800	0
Employee health insurance ($21,300)	22,600	21,300	1,300 U
Miscellaneous ($1,200 + $0.20*q*)	2,130	1,420	710 U
Total expense	172,970	167,490	5,480 U
Net operating income	$ 21,230	$ 30,510	$9,280 U

*The revenue variance is labeled favorable (unfavorable) when the actual revenue is greater than (less than) the flexible budget. The expense variances are labeled favorable (unfavorable) when the actual expense is less than (greater than) the flexible budget.

IN BUSINESS

STATE OF THE UNION SPEECH HURTS CORPORATE JET INDUSTRY

In December 2008, Detroit auto executives flew private corporate jets to Washington D.C. to plead for billions of taxpayer dollars to save their companies. The public outcry was loud and clear: How could companies on the verge of bankruptcy afford to transport their executives in private corporate jets? One month later President Obama's State of the Union speech included criticism of CEOs who "disappear on a private jet."

The impact of these events on the corporate jet manufacturing industry was swift and severe. Dassault Aviation had 27 more order cancellations than new orders in the first quarter of 2009. Cessna Aircraft had 92 first-quarter order cancellations and laid off 42% of its workforce. Approximately 3,100 jets flooded the resale market compared to 1,800 jets for resale in the first quarter of the prior year. The CEO of Cessna and the president of Gulfstream Aerospace went to the White House in May 2009 to seek an end to the rhetoric that was destroying their sales.

These facts illustrate how an activity variance can be affected by uncontrollable events. The actual first-quarter sales at these companies were substantially lower than their budgeted sales due to reasons that they could not foresee or control.

Source: Carol Matlack, "Public Flak Grounds Private Jets," *BusinessWeek,* June 8, 2009, p. 13.

© Francisco Cruz/Purestock/Superstock

Focusing next on costs, the actual electricity cost was $1,550; however, the flexible budget indicates that electricity costs should have been $1,610 for the 1,100 client-visits in March. Because the cost was $60 less than we would have expected for the actual level of activity during the period, it is labeled as a favorable variance, $60 F. This is an example of a *spending variance.* By definition, a **spending variance** is the difference between the actual amount of the cost and how much a cost should have been, given the actual level of activity. If the actual cost is greater than what the cost should have been, the variance is labeled as unfavorable. If the actual cost is less than what the cost should have been, the variance is labeled as favorable. Why would a cost have a favorable or unfavorable variance? There are many possible explanations including paying a higher price for inputs than should have been paid, using too many inputs for the actual level of activity, a change in technology, and so on. In the next chapter we will explore these types of explanations in greater detail.

Note from Exhibit 10–7 that the overall net operating income variance is $9,280 U (unfavorable). This means that given the actual level of activity for the period, the net operating income was $9,280 lower than it should have been. There are a number of reasons for this. The most prominent is the unfavorable revenue variance of $3,800. Next in line is the $2,360 unfavorable variance for client gratuities. Looking at this in another way, client gratuities were more than 50% larger than they should have been according to the flexible budget. This is a variance that Rick would almost certainly want to investigate further. He may find that this unfavorable variance is not necessarily a bad thing. It is possible, for example, that more lavish use of gratuities led to the 10% increase in client-visits.

Exhibit 10–7 also includes a $1,300 unfavorable variance related to employee health insurance, thereby highlighting how a fixed cost can have a spending variance. While fixed costs do not depend on the level of activity, the actual amount of a fixed cost can differ from the estimated amount included in a flexible budget. For example, perhaps Rick's employee health insurance premiums unexpectedly increased by $1,300 during March.

In conclusion, the revenue and spending variances in Exhibit 10–7 will help Rick better understand why his actual net operating income differs from what should have happened given the actual level of activity.

LEARNING OBJECTIVE 10–4
Prepare a performance report that combines activity variances and revenue and spending variances.

A Performance Report Combining Activity and Revenue and Spending Variances

Exhibit 10–8 displays Victoria's performance report that combines the activity variances (from Exhibit 10–6) with the revenue and spending variances (from Exhibit 10–7). The report brings together information from those two earlier exhibits in a way that makes it easier to interpret what happened during the period. The format of this report is a bit different from the format of the previous reports in that the variances appear between the amounts being compared rather than after them. For example, the activity variances appear between the flexible budget amounts and the planning budget amounts. In Exhibit 10–6, the activity variances appeared after the flexible budget and the planning budget.

Note two numbers in particular in the performance report—the activity variance for net operating income of $13,710 F (favorable) and the overall revenue and spending variance for net operating income of $9,280 U (unfavorable). It is worth repeating what those two numbers mean. The $13,710 favorable activity variance occurred because actual activity (1,100 client-visits) was greater than the budgeted level of activity (1,000 client-visits). The $9,280 unfavorable overall revenue and spending variance occurred because the profit was not as large as it should have been for the actual level of activity for the period. These two different variances mean very different things and call for different types of actions. To generate a favorable activity variance for net operating income, managers must take actions to increase client-visits. To generate a favorable overall revenue and spending variance, managers must take actions to protect selling prices, increase operating efficiency, and reduce the prices of inputs.

The performance report in Exhibit 10–8 provides much more useful information to managers than the simple comparison of budgeted to actual results in Exhibit 10–4. In Exhibit 10–4, the effects of changes in activity were jumbled together with the effects of how well prices were controlled and operations were managed. The performance report in Exhibit 10–8 clearly separates these effects, allowing managers to take a much more focused approach in evaluating operations.

EXHIBIT 10–8
Performance Report Combining Activity Variances with Revenue and Spending Variances

Rick's Hairstyling
Flexible Budget Performance Report
For the Month Ended March 31

	(1) Actual Results	Revenue and Spending Variances (1) – (2)	(2) Flexible Budget	Activity Variances (2) – (3)	(3) Planning Budget
Client-visits	1,100		1,100		1,000
Revenue ($180.00*q*)	$194,200	$3,800 U	$198,000	$18,000 F	$180,000
Expenses:					
Wages and salaries ($65,000 + $37.00*q*)	106,900	1,200 U	105,700	3,700 U	120,000
Hairstyling supplies ($1.50*q*)	1,620	30 F	1,650	150 U	1,500
Client gratuities ($4.10*q*)	6,870	2,360 U	4,510	410 U	4,100
Electricity ($1,500 + $0.10*q*)	1,550	60 F	1,610	10 U	1,600
Rent ($28,500)	28,500	0	28,500	0	28,500
Liability insurance ($2,800)	2,800	0	2,800	0	2,800
Employee health insurance ($21,300)	22,600	1,300 U	21,300	0	21,300
Miscellaneous ($1,200 + $0.20*q*)	2,130	710 U	1,420	20 U	1,400
Total expense	172,970	5,480 U	167,490	4,290 U	163,200
Net operating income	$ 21,230	$9,280 U	$ 30,510	$13,710 F	$ 16,800

To get a better idea of how the performance report accomplishes this task, look at hairstyling supplies in the performance report. The actual cost of hairstyling supplies was $1,620 for the period, whereas in the planning budget, this cost was $1,500. In the comparison of the actual results to the planning budget in Exhibit 10–4, this difference is shown as an unfavorable variance of $120. Exhibit 10–4 uses a static planning budget approach that compares actual costs at one level of activity to budgeted costs at a different level of activity. As we said before, this is like comparing apples to oranges. This variance is actually a mixture of two different effects. This becomes clear in the performance report in Exhibit 10–8. The $120 difference between the actual results and the budgeted amount is composed of two different variances—a favorable spending variance of $30 and an unfavorable activity variance of $150. The favorable spending variance occurred because less was spent on hairstyling supplies than one would have expected, given the actual level of activity for the month. The activity variance occurs because activity was greater than anticipated in the planning budget, which naturally resulted in a higher total cost for this variable cost.

The flexible budget performance report in Exhibit 10–8 provides a more valid assessment of performance than simply comparing actual costs to static planning budget costs because actual costs are compared to what costs should have been at the actual level of activity. In other words, apples are compared to apples. When this is done, we see that the spending variance for hairstyling supplies is $30 F (favorable) rather than $120 U (unfavorable) as it was in the original static planning budget performance report (see Exhibit 10–4). In some cases, as with hairstyling supplies in Rick's report, an unfavorable static planning budget variance may be transformed into a favorable revenue or spending variance when an increase in activity is properly taken into account. The following discussion took place the next day at Rick's salon.

MANAGERIAL ACCOUNTING IN ACTION
The Wrap-up

Victoria: Let me show you what I've got. [Victoria shows Rick the flexible budget performance report in Exhibit 10–8.] I simply used the cost formulas to update the budget to reflect the increase in client-visits you experienced in March. That allowed me to come up with a better benchmark for what the costs should have been.

Rick: That's what you labeled the "flexible budget based on 1,100 client-visits"?

Victoria: That's right. Your original budget was based on 1,000 client-visits, so it understated what some of the costs should have been when you actually served 1,100 customers.

Rick: That's clear enough. These spending variances aren't quite as shocking as the variances on my first report.

Victoria: Yes, but you still have an unfavorable variance of $2,360 for client gratuities.

Rick: I know how that happened. In March there was a big political fundraising dinner that I forgot about when I prepared the March budget. To fit all of our regular clients in, we had to push them through here pretty fast. Everyone still got top-rate service, but I felt bad about not being able to spend as much time with each customer. I wanted to give my customers a little extra something to compensate them for the less personal service, so I ordered a lot of flowers, which I gave away by the bunch.

Victoria: With the prices you charge, Rick, I am sure the gesture was appreciated.

Rick: One thing bothers me about the report. When we discussed my costs before, you called rent, liability insurance, and employee health insurance fixed costs. How can I have a variance for a fixed cost? Doesn't fixed mean that it doesn't change?

Victoria: We call these costs *fixed* because they shouldn't be affected by *changes in the level of activity*. However, that doesn't mean that they can't change for other reasons. Also, the use of the term *fixed* also suggests to people that the cost can't be controlled, but that isn't true. It is often easier to control fixed costs than variable costs. For example, it would be fairly easy for you to change your insurance bill by adjusting the amount of insurance you carry. It would be much more difficult for you to significantly reduce your spending on hairstyling supplies—a variable cost that is a necessary part of serving customers.

Rick: I think I understand, but it *is* confusing.

Victoria: Just remember that a cost is called variable if it is proportional to activity; it is called fixed if it does not depend on the level of activity. However, fixed costs can change for reasons unrelated to changes in the level of activity. And controllability has little to do with whether a cost is variable or fixed. Fixed costs are often more controllable than variable costs.

IN BUSINESS

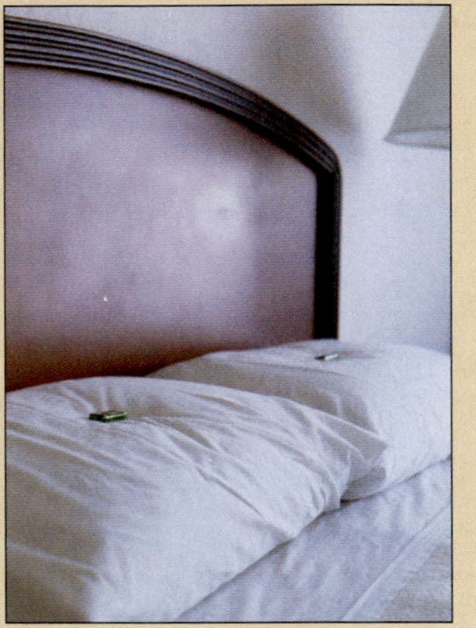

© Janis Christie/Photodisc/Getty Images

HOTELS MANAGE REVENUE AND COST LEVERS AMID RECESSION

When the economy spiraled downward in 2009, it forced hotel chains to make tough decisions in an effort to achieve their profit goals. For example, Wyndham Hotels and Resorts decided to take sewing kits, mouthwash, and showercaps out of its rooms—instead, requiring customers to ask for these amenities at the front desk. Intercontinental Hotels Group stopped delivering newspapers to loyalty-program members' rooms; Marriott International cut back its breakfast offerings; and the Ritz-Carlton reduced operating hours at its restaurants, spas, and retail shops. In addition, many hotel chains reduced their rental rates.

A flexible budget performance report can help hotel managers analyze how the changes described above impact net operating income. It isolates activity, revenue, and spending variances that help identify the underlying reasons for differences between budgeted and actual net operating income.

Source: Sarah Nassauer, "No Showercaps at the Inn," *The Wall Street Journal,* January 22, 2009, pp. D1–D2.

Performance Reports in Nonprofit Organizations

The performance reports in nonprofit organizations are basically the same as the performance reports we have considered so far—with one prominent difference. Nonprofit organizations usually receive a significant amount of funding from sources other than sales. For example, universities receive their funding from sales (i.e., tuition charged to students), from endowment income and donations, and—in the case of public universities—from state appropriations. This means that, like costs, the revenue in governmental and nonprofit organizations may consist of both fixed and variable elements. For example, the Seattle Opera Company's revenue in a recent year consisted of grants and donations of \$12,719,000 and ticket sales of \$8,125,000 (or about \$75.35 per ticket sold). Consequently, the revenue formula for the opera can be written as:

$$\text{Revenue} = \$12{,}719{,}000 + \$75.35q$$

where q is the number of tickets sold. In other respects, the performance report for the Seattle Opera and other nonprofit organizations would be similar to the performance report in Exhibit 10–8.

Performance Reports in Cost Centers

Performance reports are often prepared for organizations that do not have any source of outside revenue. In particular, in a large organization a performance report may be prepared for each department—including departments that do not sell anything to outsiders. For example, a performance report is very commonly prepared for production departments in manufacturing companies. Such reports should be prepared using the same principles we have discussed and should look very much like the performance report in Exhibit 10–8—with the exception that revenue, and consequently net operating income, will not appear on the report. Because the managers in these departments are responsible for costs, but not revenues, they are often called *cost centers.*

Flexible Budgets with Multiple Cost Drivers

LEARNING OBJECTIVE 10–5
Prepare a flexible budget with more than one cost driver.

At Rick's Hairstyling, we have thus far assumed that there is only one cost driver—the number of client-visits. However, in the activity-based costing chapter, we found that more than one cost driver might be needed to adequately explain all of the costs in an organization. For example, some of the costs at Rick's Hairstyling probably depend more on the number of hours that the salon is open for business than the number of client-visits. Specifically, most of Rick's employees are paid salaries, but some are paid on an hourly basis. None of the employees is paid on the basis of the number of customers actually served. Consequently, the cost formula for wages and salaries would be more accurate if it were stated in terms of the hours of operation rather than the number of client-visits. The cost of electricity is even more complex. Some of the cost is fixed—the heat must be kept at some minimum level even at night when the salon is closed. Some of the cost depends on the number of client-visits—the power consumed by hair dryers depends on the number of customers served. Some of the cost depends on the number of hours the salon is open—the costs of lighting the salon and heating it to a comfortable temperature. Consequently, the cost formula for electricity would be more accurate if it were stated in terms of both the number of client-visits and the hours of operation rather than just in terms of the number of client-visits.

Exhibit 10–9 shows a flexible budget in which these changes have been made. In that flexible budget, two cost drivers are listed—client-visits and hours of operation—where q_1 refers to client-visits and q_2 refers to hours of operation. For example, wages and salaries depend on the hours of operation and its cost formula is $\$65{,}000 + \$220q_2$. Because the salon actually operated 190 hours, the flexible budget amount for wages and salaries is $106,800 (= $65,000 + $220 × 190). The electricity cost depends on both client-visits and the hours of operation and its cost formula is $\$390 + \$0.10q_1 + \$6.00q_2$. Because the actual number of client-visits was 1,100 and the salon actually operated for 190 hours, the flexible budget amount for electricity is $1,640 (= $390 + $0.10 × 1,100 + $6.00 × 190). Notice that the net operating income in the flexible budget based on two cost drivers is $29,380, whereas the net operating income in the flexible budget based on one cost driver (see Exhibit 10–5) is $30,510. These two amounts differ because the flexible budget based on two cost drivers is more accurate than the flexible budget based on one driver.

EXHIBIT 10–9
Flexible Budget Based on More than One Cost Driver

Rick's Hairstyling Flexible Budget For the Month Ended March 31	
Actual client-visits (q_1)	1,100
Actual hours of operation (q_2)	190
Revenue ($\$180.00q_1$)	$198,000
Expenses:	
Wages and salaries ($\$65{,}000 + \$220q_2$)	106,800
Hairstyling supplies ($\$1.50q_1$)	1,650
Client gratuities ($\$4.10q_1$)	4,510
Electricity ($\$390 + \$0.10q_1 + \$6.00q_2$)	1,640
Rent ($28,500)	28,500
Liability insurance ($2,800)	2,800
Employee health insurance ($21,300)	21,300
Miscellaneous ($\$1{,}200 + \$0.20q_1$)	1,420
Total expense	168,620
Net operating income	$ 29,380

IN BUSINESS

© Comstock Images/Jupiter Images

HOSPITALS TURN TO FLEXIBLE BUDGETS

Mary Wilkes, a senior managing director with Phase 2 Consulting, says that hospitals may have to pay as much as $300,000 to install a flexible budgeting system, but the investment should readily pay for itself by enabling "more efficient use of hospital resources, particularly when it comes to labor." One of the keys to creating an effective flexible budgeting system is to recognize the existence of multiple cost drivers. Many hospitals frequently use patient volume as a cost driver when preparing flexible budgets; however, other variables can influence revenues and costs. For example, the percentage of patients covered by private insurance, Medicaid, or Medicare, as well as the proportion of uninsured patients all influence revenues and costs. A flexible budgeting system that incorporates patient volume and these other variables will be more accurate than one based solely on patient volume.

Source: Paul Barr, "Flexing Your Budget," *Modern Healthcare,* September 12, 2005, pp. 24–26.

The revised flexible budget based on both client-visits and hours of operation can be used exactly like we used the earlier flexible budget based on just client-visits to compute activity variances as in Exhibit 10–6, revenue and spending variances as in Exhibit 10–7, and a performance report as in Exhibit 10–8. The difference is that because the cost formulas based on more than one cost driver are more accurate than the cost formulas based on just one cost driver, the variances will also be more accurate.

Some Common Errors

LEARNING OBJECTIVE 10–6
Understand common errors made in preparing performance reports based on budgets and actual results.

We started this chapter by discussing the need for managers to understand the difference between what actually happened and what was expected to happen—formalized by the planning budget. To meet this need, we developed a flexible budget that allowed us to isolate activity variances and revenue and spending variances. Unfortunately, this approach is not always followed in practice—resulting in misleading and difficult-to-interpret reports. The most common errors in preparing performance reports are to implicitly assume that all costs are fixed or to implicitly assume that all costs are variable. These erroneous assumptions lead to inaccurate benchmarks and incorrect variances.

We have already discussed one of these errors—assuming that all costs are fixed. This is the error that is made when static planning budget costs are compared to actual costs without any adjustment for the actual level of activity. Such a comparison appeared in Exhibit 10–4. For convenience, the comparison of actual to budgeted revenues and costs is repeated in Exhibit 10–10. Looking at that exhibit, note that the actual cost of hairstyling supplies of $1,620 is directly compared to the budgeted cost of $1,500, resulting in an unfavorable variance of $120. But this comparison only makes sense if the cost of hairstyling supplies is fixed. If the cost of hairstyling supplies isn't fixed (and indeed it is not), one would *expect* the cost to go up because of the increase in activity over the budget. Comparing actual costs to static planning budget costs only makes sense if the cost is fixed. If the cost isn't fixed, it needs to be adjusted for any change in activity that occurs during the period.

EXHIBIT 10–10
Faulty Analysis Comparing Actual Amounts to Budgeted Amounts (Implicitly Assumes All Income Statement Items Are Fixed)

Rick's Hairstyling
For the Month Ended March 31

	Actual Results	Planning Budget	Variances
Client-visits	1,100	1,000	
Revenue	$194,200	$180,000	$14,200 F
Expenses:			
Wages and salaries	106,900	102,000	4,900 U
Hairstyling supplies	1,620	1,500	120 U
Client gratuities	6,870	4,100	2,770 U
Electricity	1,550	1,600	50 F
Rent	28,500	28,500	0
Liability insurance	2,800	2,800	0
Employee health insurance	22,600	21,300	1,300 U
Miscellaneous	2,130	1,400	730 U
Total expense	172,970	163,200	9,770 U
Net operating income	$ 21,230	$ 16,800	$ 4,430 F

EXHIBIT 10–11
Faulty Analysis That Assumes All Budget Items Are Variable

Rick's Hairstyling
For the Month Ended March 31

	(1) Actual Results	(2) Planning Budget × (1,100/1,000)	Variances (1) – (2)
Client-visits	1,100		
Revenue	$194,200	$198,000	$3,800 U
Expenses:			
Wages and salaries	106,900	112,200	5,300 F
Hairstyling supplies	1,620	1,650	30 F
Client gratuities	6,870	4,510	2,360 U
Electricity	1,550	1,760	210 F
Rent	28,500	31,350	2,850 F
Liability insurance	2,800	3,080	280 F
Employee health insurance	21,600	23,430	830 F
Miscellaneous	2,130	1,540	590 U
Total expense	172,970	179,520	6,550 F
Net operating income	$ 21,230	$ 18,480	$2,750 F

The other common error when comparing budgets to actual results is to assume that all costs are variable. A report that makes this error appears in Exhibit 10–11. The variances in this report are computed by comparing actual results to the amounts in the second numerical column where *all* of the budget items have been inflated by 10%—the percentage by which activity increased. This is a perfectly valid adjustment to make if an item is strictly variable—like sales and hairstyling supplies. It is *not* a valid adjustment if the item contains any fixed element. Take, for example, rent. If the salon serves 10% more customers in a given month, would you expect the rent to increase by 10%? The answer is no. Ordinarily, the rent is fixed in advance and does not depend on the volume of business. Therefore, the amount shown in the second numerical column of $31,350 is incorrect, which leads to the erroneous favorable variance of $2,850. In fact, the actual rent paid was exactly equal to the budgeted rent, so there should be no variance at all on a valid report.

IN BUSINESS

SNOW REMOVAL BUDGETS GET PLOWED UNDER

The District of Columbia budgeted $6.2 million for its annual snow removal needs based on an expectation of 15 inches of snow per year. So, when it received 28 inches of snow in one weekend, its snow removal budget got plowed under. During this same weekend, the Virginia Department of Transportation estimated that 500,000 tons of snow dropped on its northern Virginia roadways, leading to historic cost overruns in its $79 million snow removal budget.

In these types of situations, a flexible budget can help managers assess operational efficiency. For example, a manager could create a cost formula such as "the snow removal cost per inch of snow" to estimate what the total variable snow removal costs should be for the actual inches of snowfall. This "flexed" snow removal cost could be compared to the actual snow removal cost in an effort to identify sources of exceptional performance or opportunities for process improvement.

Source: Sudeep Reddy and Clare Ansberry, "States Face Big Costs to Dig Out From Blizzard," *The Wall Street Journal*, February 9, 2010, p. A6.

Summary

Directly comparing actual revenues and costs to static planning budget revenues and costs can easily lead to erroneous conclusions. Actual revenues and costs differ from budgeted revenues and costs for a variety of reasons, but one of the biggest is a change in the level of activity. One would expect actual revenues and costs to increase or decrease as the activity level increases or decreases. Flexible budgets enable managers to isolate the various causes of the differences between budgeted and actual costs.

A flexible budget is a budget that is adjusted to the actual level of activity. It is the best estimate of what revenues and costs should have been, given the actual level of activity during the period. The flexible budget can be compared to the budget from the beginning of the period or to the actual results.

When the flexible budget is compared to the budget from the beginning of the period, activity variances are the result. An activity variance shows how a revenue or cost should have changed in response to the difference between actual and budgeted activity.

When actual results are compared to the flexible budget, revenue and spending variances are the result. A favorable revenue variance indicates that revenue was larger than should have been expected, given the actual level of activity. An unfavorable revenue variance indicates that revenue was less than it should have been, given the actual level of activity. A favorable spending variance indicates that the cost was less than expected, given the actual level of activity. An unfavorable spending variance indicates that the cost was greater than it should have been, given the actual level of activity.

A flexible budget performance report combines activity variances and revenue and spending variances on one report.

Common errors in comparing actual costs to budgeted costs are to assume all costs are fixed or to assume all costs are variable. If all costs are assumed to be fixed, the variances for variable and mixed costs will be incorrect. If all costs are assumed to be variable, the variances for fixed and mixed costs will be incorrect. The variance for a cost will only be correct if the actual behavior of the cost is used to develop the flexible budget benchmark.

Review Problem: Variance Analysis Using a Flexible Budget

Harrald's Fish House is a family-owned restaurant that specializes in Scandinavian-style seafood. Data concerning the restaurant's monthly revenues and costs appear below (q refers to the number of meals served):

	Formula
Revenue	16.50q$
Cost of ingredients	6.25q$
Wages and salaries	$10,400
Utilities	$800 + 0.20q$
Rent	$2,200
Miscellaneous	$600 + 0.80q$

Required:

1. Prepare the restaurant's planning budget for April assuming that 1,800 meals are served.
2. Assume that 1,700 meals were actually served in April. Prepare a flexible budget for this level of activity.
3. The actual results for April appear below. Prepare a flexible budget performance report for the restaurant for April.

Revenue	$27,920
Cost of ingredients	$11,110
Wages and salaries	$10,130
Utilities	$1,080
Rent	$2,200
Miscellaneous	$2,240

Solution to Review Problem

1. The planning budget for April appears below:

Harralds Fish House Planning Budget For the Month Ended April 30	
Budgeted meals served(q)	1,800
Revenue (16.50q$)	$29,700
Expenses:	
Cost of ingredients (6.25q$)	11,250
Wages and salaries ($10,400)	10,400
Utilities ($800 + 0.20q$)	1,160
Rent ($2,200)	2,200
Miscellaneous ($600 + 0.80q$)	2,040
Total expense	27,050
Net operating income	$ 2,650

2. The flexible budget for April appears below:

Harralds Fish House Flexible Budget For the Month Ended April 30	
Actual meals served (q)	1,700
Revenue (16.50q$)	$28,050
Expenses:	
Cost of ingredients (6.25q$)	10,625
Wages and salaries ($10,400)	10,400
Utilities ($800 + 0.20q$)	1,140
Rent ($2,200)	2,200
Miscellaneous ($600 + 0.80q$)	1,960
Total expense	26,325
Net operating income	$ 1,725

3. The flexible budget performance report for April appears below:

Harralds Fish House
Flexible Budget Performance Report
For the Month Ended April 30

	(1) Actual Results	Revenue and Spending Variances (1) – (2)	(2) Flexible Budget	Activity Variances (2) – (3)	(3) Planning Budget
Meals served	1,700		1,700		1,800
Revenue ($16.50*q*)	$27,920	$130 U	$28,050	$1,650 U	$29,700
Expenses:					
Cost of ingredients ($6.25*q*)	11,110	485 U	10,625	625 F	11,250
Wages and salaries ($10,400)	10,130	270 F	10,400	0	10,400
Utilities ($800 + $0.20*q*)	1,080	60 F	1,140	20 F	1,160
Rent ($2,200)	2,200	0	2,200	0	2,200
Miscellaneous ($600 + $0.80*q*)	2,240	280 U	1,960	80 F	2,040
Total expense	26,760	435 U	26,325	725 F	27,050
Net operating income	$ 1,160	$565 U	$ 1,725	$ 925 U	$ 2,650

Glossary

Activity variance The difference between a revenue or cost item in the flexible budget and the same item in the static planning budget. An activity variance is due solely to the difference between the actual level of activity used in the flexible budget and the level of activity assumed in the planning budget. (p. 445)

Flexible budget A report showing estimates of what revenues and costs should have been, given the actual level of activity for the period. (p. 440)

Planning budget A budget created at the beginning of the budgeting period that is valid only for the planned level of activity. (p. 440)

Revenue variance The difference between the actual revenue for the period and how much the revenue should have been, given the actual level of activity. A favorable (unfavorable) revenue variance occurs because the revenue is higher (lower) than expected, given the actual level of activity for the period. (p. 446)

Spending variance The difference between the actual amount of the cost and how much the cost should have been, given the actual level of activity. A favorable (unfavorable) spending variance occurs because the cost is lower (higher) than expected, given the actual level of activity for the period. (p. 447)

Questions

10–1 What is a static planning budget?

10–2 What is a flexible budget and how does it differ from a static planning budget?

10–3 What are some of the possible reasons that actual results may differ from what had been budgeted at the beginning of a period?

10–4 Why is it difficult to interpret a difference between how much expense was budgeted and how much was actually spent?

10–5 What is an activity variance and what does it mean?

10–6 What is a revenue variance and what does it mean?

10–7 What is a spending variance and what does it mean?

10–8 What does a flexible budget performance report do that a simple comparison of budgeted to actual results does not do?

10–9 How does a flexible budget based on two cost drivers differ from a flexible budget based on a single cost driver?

10–10 What assumption is implicitly made about cost behavior when actual results are directly compared to a static planning budget? Why is this assumption questionable?

10–11 What assumption is implicitly made about cost behavior when all of the items in a static planning budget are adjusted in proportion to a change in activity? Why is this assumption questionable?

Multiple-choice questions are available with Connect.

Additional student resources are available with Connect. connect

Applying Excel

LEARNING OBJECTIVES 10–1, 10–2, 10–3, 10–4

The Excel worksheet form that appears below is to be used to recreate the Review Problem related to Harrald's Fish House. Download the workbook containing this from Connect. *On the website you will also receive instructions about how to use this worksheet form.*

You should proceed to the requirements below only after completing your worksheet.

Required:

1. Check your worksheet by changing the revenue in cell D4 to $16.00; the cost of ingredients in cell D5 to $6.50; and the wages and salaries in cell B6 to $10,000. The activity variance for net operating income should now be $850 U and the spending variance for total expenses should be $410 U. If you do not get these answers, find the errors in your worksheet and correct them.
   a. What is the activity variance for revenue? Explain this variance.
   b. What is the spending variance for the cost of ingredients? Explain this variance.

	A	B	C	D	E	F	G	H	I
1	Chapter 10: Applying Excel								
2									
3	**Data**								
4	Revenue			$16.50	q				
5	Cost of ingredients			$6.25	q				
6	Wages and salaries	$10,400							
7	Utilities	$800	+	$0.20	q				
8	Rent	$2,200							
9	Miscellaneous	$600	+	$0.80	q				
10									
11	Actual results:								
12	Revenue	$27,920							
13	Cost of ingredients	$11,110							
14	Wages and salaries	$10,130							
15	Utilities	$1,080							
16	Rent	$2,200							
17	Miscellaneous	$2,240							
18									
19	Planning budget activity	1,800	meals served						
20	Actual activity	1,700	meals served						
21									
22	*Enter a formula into each of the cells marked with a ? below*								
23	**Review Problem: Variance Analysis Using a Flexible Budget**								
24									
25	***Construct a flexible budget performance report***								
26						*Revenue*			
27						*and*			
28		*Planning*	*Activity*		*Flexible*	*Spending*		*Actual*	
29		*Budget*	*Variances*		*Budget*	*Variances*		*Results*	
30	Meals served	?			?			?	
31	Revenue	?	?		?	?		?	
32	Expenses:								
33	Cost of ingredients	?	?		?	?		?	
34	Wages and salaries	?	?		?	?		?	
35	Utilities	?	?		?	?		?	
36	Rent	?	?		?	?		?	
37	Miscellaneous	?	?		?	?		?	
38	Total expenses	?	?		?	?		?	
39	Net operating income	?	?		?	?		?	
40									

Chapter 10 Form / Filled in Chapter 10 Form / Chapter 10 Form

2. Revise the data in your worksheet to reflect the results for the following year:

Data			
Revenue			$16.50q
Cost of ingredients			$6.25q
Wages and salaries	$10,400		
Utilities	$800	+	$0.20q
Rent	$2,200		
Miscellaneous	$600	+	$0.80q
Actual results:			
Revenue	$28,900		
Cost of ingredients	$11,300		
Wages and salaries	$10,300		
Utilities	$1,120		
Rent	$2,300		
Miscellaneous	$2,020		
Planning budget activity	1,700 meals served		
Actual activity	1,800 meals served		

Using the flexible budget performance report, briefly evaluate the company's performance for the year and indicate where attention should be focused.

The Foundational 15

connect **Additional student resources are available with Connect.**

LEARNING OBJECTIVES 10–1, 10–2, 10–3,

Adger Corporation is a service company that measures its output based on the number of customers served. The company provided the following fixed and variable cost estimates that it uses for budgeting purposes and the actual results for May as shown below:

	Fixed Element per Month	Variable Element per Customer Served	Actual Total for May
Revenue		$5,000	$160,000
Employee salaries and wages	$50,000	$1,100	$88,000
Travel expenses		$600	$19,000
Other expenses	$36,000		$34,500

When preparing its planning budget the company estimated that it would serve 30 customers per month; however, during May the company actually served 35 customers.

Required:

1. What amount of revenue would be included in Adger's flexible budget for May?
2. What amount of employee salaries and wages would be included in Adger's flexible budget for May?
3. What amount of travel expenses would be included in Adger's flexible budget for May?
4. What amount of other expenses would be included in Adger's flexible budget for May?
5. What net operating income would appear in Adger's flexible budget for May?
6. What is Adger's revenue variance for May?
7. What is Adger's employee salaries and wages spending variance for May?
8. What is Adger's travel expenses spending variance for May?
9. What is Adger's other expenses spending variance for May?
10. What amount of revenue would be included in Adger's planning budget for May?
11. What amount of employee salaries and wages would be included in Adger's planning budget for May?
12. What amount of travel expenses would be included in Adger's planning budget for May?
13. What amount of other expenses would be included in Adger's planning budget for May?
14. What activity variance would Adger report in May with respect to its revenue?
15. What activity variances would Adger report with respect to each of its expenses?

Additional student resources are available with Connect. connect **Exercises**

EXERCISE 10–1 Prepare a Flexible Budget [LO 10–1]

Puget Sound Divers is a company that provides diving services such as underwater ship repairs to clients in the Puget Sound area. The company's planning budget for May appears below:

Puget Sound Divers Planning Budget For the Month Ended May 31	
Budgeted diving-hours (*q*)	100
Revenue ($365.00*q*)	$36,500
Expenses:	
Wages and salaries ($8,000 + $125.00*q*)	20,500
Supplies ($3.00*q*)	300
Equipment rental ($1,800 + $32.00*q*)	5,000
Insurance ($3,400)	3,400
Miscellaneous ($630 + $1.80*q*)	810
Total expense	30,010
Net operating income	$ 6,490

Required:

During May, the company's activity was actually 105 diving-hours. Prepare a flexible budget for that level of activity.

EXERCISE 10–2 Prepare a Report Showing Activity Variances [LO 10–2]

Flight Café is a company that prepares in-flight meals for airlines in its kitchen located next to the local airport. The company's planning budget for July appears below:

Flight Café Planning Budget For the Month Ended July 31	
Budgeted meals (*q*)	18,000
Revenue ($4.50*q*)	$ 81,000
Expenses:	
Raw materials ($2.40*q*)	43,200
Wages and salaries ($5,200 + $0.30*q*)	10,600
Utilities ($2,400 + $0.05*q*)	3,300
Facility rent ($4,300)	4,300
Insurance ($2,300)	2,300
Miscellaneous ($680 + $0.10*q*)	2,480
Total expense	66,180
Net operating income	$ 14,820

In July, 17,800 meals were actually served. The company's flexible budget for this level of activity appears below:

Flight Café Flexible Budget For the Month Ended July 31	
Budgeted meals (*q*)	17,800
Revenue ($4.50*q*)	$80,100
Expenses:	
Raw materials ($2.40*q*)	42,720
Wages and salaries ($5,200 + $0.30*q*)	10,540
Utilities ($2,400 + $0.05*q*)	3,290
Facility rent ($4,300)	4,300
Insurance ($2,300)	2,300
Miscellaneous ($680 + $0.10*q*)	2,460
Total expense	65,610
Net operating income	$14,490

Required:

1. Prepare a report showing the company's activity variances for July.
2. Which of the activity variances should be of concern to management? Explain.

EXERCISE 10–3 Prepare a Report Showing Revenue and Spending Variances [LO 10–3]

Quilcene Oysteria farms and sells oysters in the Pacific Northwest. The company harvested and sold 8,000 pounds of oysters in August. The company's flexible budget for August appears below:

Quilcene Oysteria Flexible Budget For the Month Ended August 31	
Actual pounds (*q*)	8,000
Revenue ($4.00*q*)	$32,000
Expenses:	
Packing supplies ($0.50*q*)	4,000
Oyster bed maintenance ($3,200)	3,200
Wages and salaries ($2,900 + $0.30*q*)	5,300
Shipping ($0.80*q*)	6,400
Utilities ($830)	830
Other ($450 + $0.05*q*)	850
Total expense	20,580
Net operating income	$11,420

The actual results for August appear below:

Quilcene Oysteria Income Statement For the Month Ended August 31	
Actual pounds	8,000
Revenue	$35,200
Expenses:	
Packing supplies	4,200
Oyster bed maintenance	3,100
Wages and salaries	5,640
Shipping	6,950
Utilities	810
Other	980
Total expense	21,680
Net operating income	$13,520

Required:

Prepare a report showing the company's revenue and spending variances for August.

EXERCISE 10–4 Prepare a Flexible Budget Performance Report [LO 10–4]

Vulcan Flyovers offers scenic overflights of Mount St. Helens, the volcano in Washington State that explosively erupted in 1982. Data concerning the company's operations in July appear below:

Vulcan Flyovers Operating Data For the Month Ended July 31	Actual Results	Flexible Budget	Planning Budget
Flights (q)	48	48	50
Revenue (320.00q$)	$13,650	$15,360	$16,000
Expenses:			
Wages and salaries ($4,000 + 82.00q$)	8,430	7,936	8,100
Fuel (23.00q$)	1,260	1,104	1,150
Airport fees ($650 + 38.00q$)	2,350	2,474	2,550
Aircraft depreciation (7.00q$)	336	336	350
Office expenses ($190 + 2.00q$)	460	286	290
Total expense	12,836	12,136	12,440
Net operating income	$ 814	$ 3,224	$ 3,560

The company measures its activity in terms of flights. Customers can buy individual tickets for overflights or hire an entire plane for an overflight at a discount.

Required:

1. Prepare a flexible budget performance report for July.
2. Which of the variances should be of concern to management? Explain.

EXERCISE 10–5 Prepare a Flexible Budget with More Than One Cost Driver [LO 10–5]

Alyeski Tours operates day tours of coastal glaciers in Alaska on its tour boat the Blue Glacier. Management has identified two cost drivers—the number of cruises and the number of passengers—that it uses in its budgeting and performance reports. The company publishes a schedule of day cruises that it may supplement with special sailings if there is sufficient demand. Up to 80 passengers can be accommodated on the tour boat. Data concerning the company's cost formulas appear below:

	Fixed Cost per Month	Cost per Cruise	Cost per Passenger
Vessel operating costs	$5,200	$480.00	$2.00
Advertising	$1,700		
Administrative costs	$4,300	$24.00	$1.00
Insurance	$2,900		

For example, vessel operating costs should be $5,200 per month plus $480 per cruise plus $2 per passenger. The company's sales should average $25 per passenger. The company's planning budget for July is based on 24 cruises and 1,400 passengers.

Required:

Prepare the company's planning budget for July.

EXERCISE 10–6 Critique a Variance Report [LO 10–6]

The Terminator Inc. provides on-site residential pest extermination services. The company has several mobile teams who are dispatched from a central location in company-owned trucks. The company uses the number of jobs to measure activity. At the beginning of April, the company budgeted for 100 jobs, but the actual number of jobs turned out to be 105. A report comparing the budgeted revenues and costs to the actual revenues and costs appears below:

The Terminator Inc. Variance Report For the Month Ended April 30	Actual Results	Planning Budget	Variances
Jobs	105	100	
Revenue	$20,520	$19,500	$1,020 F
Expenses:			
Mobile team operating costs	10,320	10,000	320 U
Exterminating supplies	960	1,800	840 F
Advertising	800	800	0
Dispatching costs	2,340	2,200	140 U
Office rent	1,800	1,800	0
Insurance	2,100	2,100	0
Total expense	18,320	18,700	380 F
Net operating income	$ 2,200	$ 800	$1,400 F

Required:

Is the above variance report useful for evaluating how well revenues and costs were controlled during April? Why, or why not?

EXERCISE 10–7 Critique a Variance Report [LO 10–6]

Refer to the data for The Terminator Inc. in Exercise 10–6. A management intern has suggested that the budgeted revenues and costs should be adjusted for the actual level of activity in April before they are compared to the actual revenues and costs. Because the actual level of activity was 5% higher than budgeted, the intern suggested that all budgeted revenues and costs should be adjusted upward by 5%. A report comparing the budgeted revenues and costs, with this adjustment, to the actual revenues and costs appears below.

The Terminator Inc. Variance Report For the Month Ended April 30	Actual Results	Adjusted Planning Budget	Variances
Jobs	105	105	
Revenue	$20,520	$20,475	$ 45 F
Expenses:			
Mobile team operating costs	10,320	10,500	180 F
Exterminating supplies	960	1,890	930 F
Advertising	800	840	40 F
Dispatching costs	2,340	2,310	30 U
Office rent	1,800	1,890	90 F
Insurance	2,100	2,205	105 F
Total expense	18,320	19,635	1,315 F
Net operating income	$ 2,200	$ 840	$1,360 F

Required:

Is the above variance report useful for evaluating how well revenues and costs were controlled during April? Why, or why not?

EXERCISE 10–8 Flexible Budgets and Activity Variances [LO 10–1, LO 10–2]

Jake's Roof Repair has provided the following data concerning its costs:

	Fixed Cost per Month	Cost per Repair-Hour
Wages and salaries	$23,200	$16.30
Parts and supplies		$8.60
Equipment depreciation	$1,600	$0.40
Truck operating expenses	$6,400	$1.70
Rent	$3,480	
Administrative expenses	$4,500	$0.80

For example, utilities should be $1,400 per month plus $0.05 per machine-hour. The company expects to work 5,000 machine-hours in June. Note that the company's direct labor is a fixed cost.

Required:
Prepare a report showing the company's activity variances for May.

EXERCISE 10–9 Flexible Budget [LO 10–1]
Wyckam Manufacturing Inc. has provided the following information concerning its manufacturing costs:

	Fixed Cost per Month	Cost per Machine-Hour
Direct materials		$4.25
Direct labor	$36,800	
Supplies		$0.30
Utilities	$1,400	$0.05
Depreciation	$16,700	
Insurance	$12,700	

For example, utilities should be $1,400 per month plus $0.05 per machine-hour. The company expects to work 5,000 machine-hours in June. Note that the company's direct labor is a fixed cost.

Required:
Prepare the company's planning budget for manufacturing costs for June.

EXERCISE 10–10 Flexible Budget [LO 10–1]

Lavage Rapide is a Canadian company that owns and operates a large automatic carwash facility near Montreal. The following table provides data concerning the company's costs:

	Fixed Cost per Month	Cost per Car Washed
Cleaning supplies		$0.80
Electricity	$1,200	$0.15
Maintenance		$0.20
Wages and salaries	$5,000	$0.30
Depreciation	$6,000	
Rent	$8,000	
Administrative expenses	$4,000	$0.10

For example, electricity costs are $1,200 per month plus $0.15 per car washed. The company expects to wash 9,000 cars in August and to collect an average of $4.90 per car washed.

Required:
Prepare the company's planning budget for August.

EXERCISE 10–11 Flexible Budget [LO 10–1]

Refer to the data for Lavage Rapide in Exercise 10–10. The company actually washed 8,800 cars in August.

Required:

Prepare the company's flexible budget for August.

EXERCISE 10–12 Prepare a Report Showing Activity Variances [LO 10–2]

Refer to the data for Lavage Rapide in Exercise 10–10. The actual operating results for August appear below.

Lavage Rapide Income Statement For the Month Ended August 31	
Actual cars washed	8,800
Revenue	$43,080
Expenses:	
Cleaning supplies	7,560
Electricity	2,670
Maintenance	2,260
Wages and salaries	8,500
Depreciation	6,000
Rent	8,000
Administrative expenses	4,950
Total expense	39,940
Net operating income	$ 3,140

Required:

Prepare a report showing the company's activity variances for August.

EXERCISE 10–13 Prepare a Report Showing Revenue and Spending Variances [LO 10–3]

Refer to the data for Lavage Rapide in Exercise 10–10 and Exercise 10–12.

Required:

Prepare a report showing the company's revenue and spending variances for August.

EXERCISE 10–14 Prepare a Flexible Budget Performance Report [LO 10–4]

Refer to the data for Lavage Rapide in Exercises 10–10 and Exercises 10–12.

Required:

Prepare a flexible budget performance report that shows the company's revenue and spending variances and activity variances for August

EXERCISE 10–15 Flexible Budget Performance Report in a Cost Center [LO 10–1, LO 10–4]

Packaging Solutions Corporation manufactures and sells a wide variety of packaging products. Performance reports are prepared monthly for each department. The planning budget and flexible budget for the Production Department are based on the following formulas, where q is the number of labor-hours worked in a month:

	Cost Formulas
Direct labor	15.80q$
Indirect labor	$8,200 + 1.60q$
Utilities	$6,400 + 0.80q$
Supplies	$1,100 + 0.40q$
Equipment depreciation	$23,000 + 3.70q$
Factory rent	$8,400
Property taxes	$2,100
Factory administration	$11,700 + 1.90q$

The actual costs incurred in March in the Production Department are listed below:

	Actual Cost Incurred in March
Direct labor	$134,730
Indirect labor	$19,860
Utilities	$14,570
Supplies	$4,980
Equipment depreciation	$54,080
Factory rent	$8,700
Property taxes	$2,100
Factory administration	$26,470

Required:

1. The company had budgeted for an activity level of 8,000 labor-hours in March. Prepare the Production Department's planning budget for the month.
2. The company actually worked 8,400 labor-hours in March. Prepare the Production Department's flexible budget for the month.
3. Prepare the Production Department's flexible budget performance report for March, including both the spending and activity variances.
4. What aspects of the flexible budget performance report should be brought to management's attention? Explain.

EXERCISE 10–16 Flexible Budgets and Revenue and Spending Variances [LO 10–1 , LO 10–3]

Via Gelato is a popular neighborhood gelato shop. The company has provided the following data concerning its operations:

	Fixed Element per Month	Variable Element per Liter	Actual Total for June
Revenue		$12.00	$71,540
Raw materials		$4.65	$29,230
Wages	$5,600	$1.40	$13,860
Utilities	$1,630	$0.20	$3,270
Rent	$2,600		$2,600
Insurance	$1,350		$1,350
Miscellaneous	$650	$0.35	$2,590

While gelato is sold by the cone or cup, the shop measures its activity in terms of the total number of liters of gelato sold. For example, wages should be $5,600 plus $1.40 per liter of gelato sold and the actual wages for June were $13,860. Via Gelato expected to sell 6,000 liters in June, but actually sold 6,200 liters.

Required:

Prepare a report showing Via Gelato revenue and spending variances for June.

EXERCISE 10–17 Flexible Budget Performance Report [LO 10–1, LO 10–4]

AirQual Test Corporation provides on-site air quality testing services. The company has provided the following data concerning its operations:

	Fixed Component per Month	Variable Component per Job	Actual Total for February
Revenue		$360	$18,950
Technician wages	$6,400		$6,450
Mobile lab operating expenses	$2,900	$35	$4,530
Office expenses	$2,600	$2	$3,050
Advertising expenses	$970		$995
Insurance	$1,680		$1,680
Miscellaneous expenses	$500	$3	$465

The company uses the number of jobs as its measure of activity. For example, mobile lab operating expenses should be $2,900 plus $35 per job, and the actual mobile lab operating expenses for February were $4,530

The company expected to work 50 jobs in February, but actually worked 52 jobs.

Required:

Prepare a flexible budget performance report showing AirQual Test Corporation's revenue and spending variances and activity variances for February.

EXERCISE 10–18 Working with More Than One Cost Driver [LO 10–4, LO 10–5]

The Gourmand Cooking School runs short cooking courses at its small campus. Management has identified two cost drivers that it uses in its budgeting and performance reports—the number of courses and the total number of students. For example, the school might run two courses in a month and have a total of 50 students enrolled in those two courses. Data concerning the company's cost formulas appear below:

	Fixed Cost per Month	Cost per Course	Cost per Student
Instructor wages		$3,080	
Classroom supplies			$260
Utilities	$870	$130	
Campus rent	$4,200		
Insurance	$1,890		
Administrative expenses	$3,270	$15	$4

For example, administrative expenses should be $3,270 per month plus $15 per course plus $4 per student. The company's sales should average $800 per student.

The actual operating results for September appear below:

	Actual
Revenue	$32,400
Instructor wages	$9,080
Classroom supplies	$8,540
Utilities	$1,530
Campus rent	$4,200
Insurance	$1,890
Administrative expenses	$3,790

Required:

1. The Gourmand Cooking School expects to run three courses with a total of 45 students in September. Prepare the company's planning budget for this level of activity.
2. The school actually ran three courses with a total of 42 students in September. Prepare the company's flexible budget for this level of activity.
3. Prepare a flexible budget performance report that shows both revenue and spending variances and activity variances for September.

Additional student resources are available with Connect. connect **Problems**

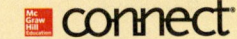

PROBLEM 10–19 Activity and Spending Variances [LO 10–1, LO 10–2, LO 10–3]

You have just been hired by FAB Corporation, the manufacturer of a revolutionary new garage door opening device. The president has asked that you review the company's costing system and "do what you can to help us get better control of our manufacturing overhead costs." You find that the company has never used a flexible budget, and you suggest that preparing such a budget would be an excellent first step in overhead planning and control.

After much effort and analysis, you determined the following cost formulas and gathered the following actual cost data for March:

	Cost Formula	Actual Cost in March
Utilities	$20,600 plus $0.10 per machine-hour	$24,200
Maintenance	$40,000 plus $1.60 per machine-hour	$78,100
Supplies	$0.30 per machine-hour	$8,400
Indirect labor	$130,000 plus $0.70 per machine-hour	$149,600
Depreciation	$70,000	$71,500

During March, the company worked 26,000 machine-hours and produced 15,000 units. The company had originally planned to work 30,000 machine-hours during March.

Required:

1. Prepare a report showing the activity variances for March. Explain what these variances mean.
2. Prepare a report showing the spending variances for March. Explain what these variances mean.

PROBLEM 10–20 More than One Cost Driver [LO 10–4, LO 10–5]

Milano Pizza is a small neighborhood pizzeria that has a small area for in-store dining as well as offering take-out and free home delivery services. The pizzeria's owner has determined that the shop has two major cost drivers—the number of pizzas sold and the number of deliveries made.

Data concerning the pizzeria's costs appear below:

	Fixed Cost per Month	Cost per Pizza	Cost per Delivery
Pizza ingredients		$3.80	
Kitchen staff	$5,220		
Utilities	$630	$0.05	
Delivery person			$3.50
Delivery vehicle	$540		$1.50
Equipment depreciation	$275		
Rent	$1,830		
Miscellaneous	$820	$0.15	

In November, the pizzeria budgeted for 1,200 pizzas at an average selling price of $13.50 per pizza and for 180 deliveries.

Data concerning the pizzeria's operations in November appear below:

	Actual Results
Pizzas	1,240
Deliveries	174
Revenue	$17,420
Pizza ingredients	$4,985
Kitchen staff	$5,281
Utilities	$984
Delivery person	$609
Delivery vehicle	$655
Equipment depreciation	$275
Rent	$1,830
Miscellaneous	$954

Required:

1. Prepare a flexible budget performance report that shows both revenue and spending variances and activity variances for the pizzeria for November.
2. Explain the activity variances.

PROBLEM 10–21 Critique a Report; Prepare a Performance Report [LO 10–1, LO 10–4, LO 10–6]

TipTop Flight School offers flying lessons at a small municipal airport. The school's owner and manager has been attempting to evaluate performance and control costs using a variance report that compares the planning budget to actual results. A recent variance report appears below:

TipTop Flight School
Variance Report
For the Month Ended July 31

	Actual Results	Planning Budget	Variances
Lessons	155	150	
Revenue	$33,900	$33,000	$900 F
Expenses:			
Instructor wages	9,870	9,750	120 U
Aircraft depreciation	5,890	5,700	190 U
Fuel	2,750	2,250	500 U
Maintenance	2,450	2,330	120 U
Ground facility expenses	1,540	1,550	10 F
Administration	3,320	3,390	70 F
Total expense	25,820	24,970	850 U
Net operating income	$ 8,080	$ 8,030	$ 50 F

After several months of using such variance reports, the owner has become frustrated. For example, she is quite confident that instructor wages were very tightly controlled in July, but the report shows an unfavorable variance.

The planning budget was developed using the following formulas, where q is the number of lessons sold:

	Cost Formulas
Revenue	220q$
Instructor wages	65q$
Aircraft depreciation	38q$
Fuel	15q$
Maintenance	$ 530 + 12q$
Ground facility expenses	$1,250 + 2q$
Administration	$3,240 + 1q$

Required:

1. Should the owner feel frustrated with the variance reports? Explain.
2. Prepare a flexible budget performance report for the school for July.
3. Evaluate the school's performance for July.

PROBLEM 10–22 Performance Report for a Nonprofit Organization [LO 10–1, LO 10–4, LO 10–6]

The St. Lucia Blood Bank, a private charity partly supported by government grants, is located on the Caribbean island of St. Lucia. The blood bank has just finished its operations for September, which was a particularly busy month due to a powerful hurricane that hit neighboring islands causing many injuries. The hurricane largely bypassed St. Lucia, but residents of St. Lucia willingly donated their blood to help people on other islands. As a consequence, the blood bank collected and processed over 20% more blood than had been originally planned for the month.

A report prepared by a government official comparing actual costs to budgeted costs for the blood bank appears below. Continued support from the government depends on the blood bank's ability to demonstrate control over its costs.

St. Lucia Blood Bank Cost Control Report For the Month Ended September 30	Actual Results	Planning Budget	Variances
Liters of blood collected	620	500	
Medical supplies	$ 9,250	$ 7,500	$1,750 U
Lab tests	6,180	6,000	180 U
Equipment depreciation	2,800	2,500	300 U
Rent	1,000	1,000	0
Utilities	570	500	70 U
Administration	11,740	11,250	490 U
Total expense	$31,540	$28,750	$2,790 U

The managing director of the blood bank was very unhappy with this report, claiming that his costs were higher than expected due to the emergency on the neighboring islands. He also pointed out that the additional costs had been fully covered by payments from grateful recipients on the other islands. The government official who prepared the report countered that all of the figures had been submitted by the blood bank to the government; he was just pointing out that actual costs were a lot higher than promised in the budget.

The following cost formulas were used to construct the planning budget:

	Cost Formulas
Medical supplies	$15.00*q*
Lab tests	$12.00*q*
Equipment depreciation	$2,500
Rent	$1,000
Utilities	$500
Administration	$10,000 + $2.50*q*

Required:

1. Prepare a new performance report for September using the flexible budget approach.
2. Do you think any of the variances in the report you prepared should be investigated? Why?

PROBLEM 10–23 Critiquing a Report; Preparing a Performance Budget [LO 10–1, LO 10–4, LO 10–6]

Exchange Corp. is a company that acts as a facilitator in tax-favored real estate swaps. Such swaps, know as 1031 exchanges, permit participants to avoid some or all of the capital gains taxes that would otherwise be due. The bookkeeper for the company has been asked to prepare a report for the company to help its owner/manager analyze performance. The first such report appears below:

Exchange Corp Analysis of Revenues and Costs For the Month Ended May 31	Actual Unit Revenues and Costs	Planning Budget Unit Revenues and Costs	Variances
Exchanges completed	50	40	
Revenue	$385	$395	$10 U
Expenses:			
Legal and search fees	184	165	19 U
Office expenses	112	135	23 F
Equipment depreciation	8	10	2 F
Rent	36	45	9 F
Insurance	4	5	1 F
Total expense	344	360	16 F
Net operating income	$ 41	$ 35	$ 6 F

Note that the revenues and costs in the above report are *unit* revenues and costs. For example, the average office expense is $135 per exchange completed on the planning budget; whereas, the average actual office expense is $112 per exchange completed.

Legal and search fees is a variable cost; office expenses is a mixed cost; and equipment depreciation, rent, and insurance are fixed costs. In the planning budget, the fixed component of office expenses was $5,200.

All of the company's revenues come from fees collected when an exchange is completed.

Required:

1. Evaluate the report prepared by the bookkeeper.
2. Prepare a performance report that would help the owner/manager assess the performance of the company in May.
3. Using the report you created, evaluate the performance of the company in May.

PROBLEM 10–24 Critiquing a Variance Report; Preparing a Performance Report [LO 10–1, LO 10–4, LO 10–6]

Several years ago, Westmont Corporation developed a comprehensive budgeting system for planning and control purposes. While departmental supervisors have been happy with the system, the factory manager has expressed considerable dissatisfaction with the information being generated by the system.

A typical departmental cost report for a recent period follows:

Assembly Department
Cost Report
For the Month Ended March 31

	Actual Results	Planning Budget	Variances
Machine-hours	35,000	40,000	
Variable costs:			
Supplies	$ 29,700	$ 32,000	$ 2,300 F
Scrap	19,500	20,000	500 F
Indirect materials	51,800	56,000	4,200 F
Fixed costs:			
Wages and salaries	79,200	80,000	800 F
Equipment depreciation	60,000	60,000	—
Total cost	$240,200	$248,000	$ 7,800 F

After receiving a copy of this cost report, the supervisor of the Assembly Department stated, "These reports are super. It makes me feel really good to see how well things are going in my department. I can't understand why those people upstairs complain so much about the reports."

For the last several years, the company's marketing department has chronically failed to meet the sales goals expressed in the company's monthly budgets.

Required:

1. The company's president is uneasy about the cost reports and would like you to evaluate their usefulness to the company.
2. What changes, if any, should be made in the reports to give better insight into how well departmental supervisors are controlling costs?
3. Prepare a new performance report for the quarter, incorporating any changes you suggested in requirement 2.
4. How well were costs controlled in the Assembly Department in March?

PROBLEM 10–25 Critiquing a Cost Report; Preparing a Performance Report [LO 10–1, LO 10–4, LO 10–6]

Frank Weston, supervisor of the Freemont Corporation's Machining Department, was visibly upset after being reprimanded for his department's poor performance over the prior month. The department's cost control report is given below:

Freemont Corporation–Machining Department Cost Control Report For the Month Ended June 30	Actual Results	Planning Budget	Variances
Machine-hours	38,000	35,000	
Direct labor wages	$ 86,100	$ 80,500	$ 5,600 U
Supplies	23,100	21,000	2,100 U
Maintenance	137,300	134,000	3,300 U
Utilities	15,700	15,200	500 U
Supervision	38,000	38,000	0
Depreciation	80,000	80,000	0
Total	$380,200	$368,700	$11,500 U

"I just can't understand all of these unfavorable variances," Weston complained to the supervisor of another department. "When the boss called me in, I thought he was going to give me a pat on the back because I know for a fact that my department worked more efficiently last month than it has ever worked before. Instead, he tore me apart. I thought for a minute that it might be over the supplies that were stolen out of our warehouse last month. But they only amounted to a couple of hundred dollars, and just look at this report. Everything is unfavorable."

Direct labor wages and supplies are variable costs; supervision and depreciation are fixed costs; and maintenance and utilities are mixed costs. The fixed component of the budgeted maintenance cost is $92,000; the fixed component of the budgeted utilities cost is $11,700.

Required:

1. Evaluate the company's cost control report and explain why the variances were all unfavorable.
2. Prepare a performance report that will help Mr. Weston's superiors assess how well costs were controlled in the Machining Department.

Additional student resources are available with Connect. connect

Cases

CASE 10–26 Ethics and the Manager [LO 10–3]

Tom Kemper is the controller of the Wichita manufacturing facility of Prudhom Enterprises, Inc.

The annual cost control report is one of the many reports that must be filed with corporate headquarters and is due at corporate headquarters shortly after the beginning of the New Year. Kemper does not like putting work off to the last minute, so just before Christmas he prepared a preliminary draft of the cost control report. Some adjustments would later be required for transactions that occur between Christmas and New Year's Day. A copy of the preliminary draft report, which Kemper completed on December 21, follows:

Wichita Manufacturing Facility Cost Control Report December 21 Preliminary Draft	Actual Results	Flexible Budget	Spending Variances
Labor-hours	18,000	18,000	
Direct labor	$ 326,000	$ 324,000	$ 2,000 U
Power	19,750	18,000	1,750 U
Supplies	105,000	99,000	6,000 U
Equipment depreciation	343,000	332,000	11,000 U
Supervisory salaries	273,000	275,000	2,000 F
Insurance	37,000	37,000	0
Industrial engineering	189,000	210,000	21,000 F
Factory building lease	60,000	60,000	0
Total expense	$1,352,750	$1,355,000	$ 2,250 F

Melissa Ilianovitch, the general manager at the Wichita facility, asked to see a copy of the preliminary draft report. Kemper carried a copy of the report to her office where the following discussion took place:

Ilianovitch: Ouch! Almost all of the variances on the report are unfavorable. The only favorable variances are for supervisory salaries and industrial engineering. How did we have an unfavorable variance for depreciation?

Kemper: Do you remember that milling machine that broke down because the wrong lubricant was used by the machine operator?

Ilianovitch: Yes.

Kemper: We couldn't fix it. We had to scrap the machine and buy a new one.

Ilianovitch: This report doesn't look good. I was raked over the coals last year when we had just a few unfavorable variances.

Kemper: I'm afraid the final report is going to look even worse.

Ilianovitch: Oh?

Kemper: The line item for industrial engineering on the report is for work we hired Ferguson Engineering to do for us. The original contract was for $210,000, but we asked them to do some additional work that was not in the contract. We have to reimburse Ferguson Engineering for the costs of that additional work. The $189,000 in actual costs that appears on the preliminary draft report reflects only their billings up through December 21. The last bill they had sent us was on November 28, and they completed the project just last week. Yesterday I got a call from Laura Sunder over at Ferguson and she said they would be sending us a final bill for the project before the end of the year. The total bill, including the reimbursements for the additional work, is going to be . . .

Ilianovitch: I am not sure I want to hear this.

Kemper: $225,000

Ilianovitch: Ouch!

Kemper: The additional work added $15,000 to the cost of the project.

Ilianovitch: I can't turn in a report with an overall unfavorable variance! They'll kill me at corporate headquarters. Call up Laura at Ferguson and ask her not to send the bill until after the first of the year. We have to have that $21,000 favorable variance for industrial engineering on the report.

Required:

What should Tom Kemper do? Explain.

CASE 10–27 Plantwide versus Departmental Overhead Rates; Underapplied or Overapplied Overhead [LO 10–3, LO 10–5, LO 10–6]

Boyne University offers an extensive continuing education program in many cities throughout the state. For the convenience of its faculty and administrative staff and to save costs, the university operates a motor pool. The motor pool's monthly planning budget is based on operating 20 vehicles; however, for the month of March the university purchased one additional vehicle. The motor pool furnishes gasoline, oil, and other supplies for its automobiles. A mechanic does routine maintenance and minor repairs. Major repairs are performed at a nearby commercial garage.

The following cost control report shows actual operating costs for March of the current year compared to the planning budget for March.

Boyne University Motor Pool
Cost Control Report
For the Month Ended March 31

	March Actual	Planning Budget	(Over) Under Budget
Miles	63,000	50,000	
Autos	21	20	
Gasoline	$ 9,350	$ 7,500	$(1,850)
Oil, minor repairs, parts	2,360	2,000	(360)
Outside repairs	1,420	1,500	80
Insurance	2,120	2,000	(120)
Salaries and benefits	7,540	7,540	0
Vehicle depreciation	5,250	5,000	(250)
Total	$28,040	$25,540	$(2,500)

The planning budget was based on the following assumptions:

a. $0.15 per mile for gasoline.
b. $0.04 per mile for oil, minor repairs, and parts.
c. $75 per automobile per month for outside repairs.
d. $100 per automobile per month for insurance.
e. $7,540 per month for salaries and benefits.
f. $250 per automobile per month for depreciation.

The supervisor of the motor pool is unhappy with the report, claiming it paints an unfair picture of the motor pool's performance.

Required:

1. Prepare a new performance report for March based on a flexible budget that shows spending variances.
2. What are the deficiencies in the original cost control report? How does the report that you prepared in requirement 1 overcome these deficiencies?
(CMA, adapted)

CASE 10–28 Performance Report with More than One Cost Driver [LO 10–4, LO 10–5]

The Little Theatre is a nonprofit organization devoted to staging plays for children. The theater has a very small full-time professional administrative staff. Through a special arrangement with the actors' union, actors and directors rehearse without pay and are paid only for actual performances.

The costs from the current year's planning budget appear below. The Little Theatre had tentatively planned to put on six different productions with a total of 108 performances. For example, one of the productions was *Peter Rabbit,* which had a six-week run with three performances on each weekend.

The Little Theatre Costs from the Planning Budget For the Year Ended December 31	
Budgeted number of productions	6
Budgeted number of performances	108
Actors' and directors' wages	$216,000
Stagehands' wages	32,400
Ticket booth personnel and ushers' wages	16,200
Scenery, costumes, and props	108,000
Theater hall rent	54,000
Printed programs	27,000
Publicity	12,000
Administrative expenses	43,200
Total	$508,800

Some of the costs vary with the number of productions, some with the number of performances, and some are fixed and depend on neither the number of productions nor the number of performances. The costs of scenery, costumes, props, and publicity vary with the number of productions. It doesn't make any difference how many times *Peter Rabbit* is performed, the cost of the scenery is the same. Likewise, the cost of publicizing a play with posters and radio commercials is the same whether there are 10, 20, or 30 performances of the play. On the other hand, the wages of the actors, directors, stagehands, ticket booth personnel, and ushers vary with the number of performances. The greater the number of performances, the higher the wage costs will be. Similarly, the costs of renting the hall and printing the programs will vary with the number of performances. Administrative expenses are more difficult to pin down, but the best estimate is that approximately 75% of the budgeted costs are fixed, 15% depend on the number of productions staged, and the remaining 10% depend on the number of performances.

After the beginning of the year, the board of directors of the theater authorized expanding the theater's program to seven productions and a total of 168 performances. Not surprisingly, actual costs were considerably higher than the costs from the planning budget. (Grants from donors and ticket sales were also correspondingly higher, but are not shown here.) Data concerning the actual costs appear below:

The Little Theatre Actual Costs For the Year Ended December 31	
Actual number of productions	7
Actual number of performances	168
Actors' and directors' wages	$341,800
Stagehands' wages	49,700
Ticket booth personnel and ushers' wages	25,900
Scenery, costumes, and props	130,600
Theater hall rent	78,000
Printed programs	38,300
Publicity	15,100
Administrative expenses	47,500
Total	$726,900

Required:

1. Prepare a flexible budget for The Little Theatre based on the actual activity of the year.
2. Prepare a flexible budget performance report for the year that shows both spending variances and activity variances.
3. If you were on the board of directors of the theater, would you be pleased with how well costs were controlled during the year? Why, or why not?
4. The cost formulas provide figures for the average cost per production and average cost per performance. How accurate do you think these figures would be for predicting the cost of a new production or of an additional performance of a particular production?

Chapter 11

Standard Costs and Variances

Managing Materials and Labor

BUSINESS FOCUS

© Fabrice Dimier/Bloomberg/Getty Images

Schneider Electric's Oxford, Ohio, plant manufactures *busways* that transport electricity from its point of entry into a building to remote locations throughout the building. The plant's managers pay close attention to direct material costs because they are more than half of the plant's total manufacturing costs. To help control scrap rates for direct materials such as copper, steel, and aluminum, the accounting department prepares direct materials quantity variances. These variances compare the amount of direct materials that were actually used to the standard quantity of direct materials that should have been used to make a product (according to computations by the plant's engineers). Keeping a close eye on these differences helps to identify and deal with the causes of excessive scrap, such as an inadequately trained machine operator, poor quality raw material inputs, or a malfunctioning machine.

Because direct labor is also a significant component of the plant's total manufacturing costs, the management team daily monitors the direct labor efficiency variance. This variance compares the actual amount of labor time used to the standard amount of labor time allowed to make a product. When idle workers cause an unfavorable labor efficiency variance, managers temporarily move workers from departments with slack to departments with a backlog of work to be done. ■

Source: Author's conversation with Doug Taylor, plant controller, Schneider Electric's Oxford, Ohio, plant.

LEARNING OBJECTIVES

After studying Chapter 11, you should be able to:

LO 11–1 Compute the direct materials price and quantity variances and explain their significance.

LO 11–2 Compute the direct labor rate and efficiency variances and explain their significance.

LO 11–3 Compute the variable manufacturing overhead rate and efficiency variances and explain their significance.

LO 11–4 (Appendix 11A) Compute and interpret the fixed overhead budget and volume variances.

In the last chapter, we investigated flexible budget variances. These variances provide feedback concerning how well an organization performed in relation to its budget. The impact on profit of a change in the level of activity is captured in the overall net operating income activity variance. The revenue and spending variances indicate how well revenues and costs were controlled—given the actual level of activity. In the case of many of the spending variances, we can get even more detail about how well costs were controlled. For example, at Rick's Hairstyling, an unfavorable spending variance for hairstyling supplies could be due to paying too much for the supplies or to using too many supplies, or some combination of the two. It would be useful to separate those two different effects, particularly if different people are responsible for purchasing the supplies and for using them. In this chapter, we learn how to use standard costs to decompose spending variances into two parts—a part that measures how well the acquisition prices of resources were controlled and a part that measures how efficiently those resources were used.

Standard Costs—Setting the Stage

A *standard* is a benchmark for measuring performance. Standards are found everywhere. Auto service centers like Firestone and Sears, for example, often set specific labor time standards for the completion of certain tasks, such as installing a carburetor or doing a valve job, and then measure actual performance against these standards. Fast-food outlets such as McDonald's and Subway have exacting standards for the quantity of meat going into a sandwich, as well as standards for the cost of the meat. Your doctor evaluates your weight using standards for individuals of your age, height, and gender. The buildings we live in conform to standards set in building codes.

Standards are also widely used in managerial accounting where they relate to the *quantity* and acquisition *price* of inputs used in manufacturing goods or providing services. *Quantity standards* specify how much of an input should be used to make a product or provide a service. *Price standards* specify how much should be paid for each unit of the input. If either the quantity or acquisition price of an input departs significantly from the standard, managers investigate the discrepancy to find the cause of the problem and eliminate it.

Next we'll demonstrate how a company can establish quantity and price standards for direct materials, direct labor, and variable manufacturing overhead and then we'll discuss how those standards can be used to calculate variances and manage operations.

MANAGERIAL ACCOUNTING IN ACTION
The Issue

Colonial Pewter Company

The Colonial Pewter Company makes only one product—an elaborate reproduction of an 18th century pewter statue. The statue is made largely by hand, using traditional metal-working tools. Consequently, the manufacturing process is labor intensive and requires a high level of skill.

Colonial Pewter has recently expanded its workforce to take advantage of unexpected demand for the statue as a gift. The company started with a small cadre of experienced pewter workers but has had to hire less experienced workers as a result of the expansion. The president of the company, J. D. Wriston, has called a meeting to discuss production problems. Attending the meeting are Tom Kuchel, the production manager; Janet Warner, the purchasing manager; and Terry Sherman, the corporate controller.

J. D.: I've got a feeling that we aren't getting the production we should out of our new people.

Tom: Give us a chance. Some of the new people have been with the company for less than a month.

Janet: Let me add that production seems to be wasting an awful lot of material—particularly pewter. That stuff is very expensive.

Tom: What about the shipment of defective pewter that you bought—the one with the iron contamination? That caused us major problems.

Janet: How was I to know it was off-grade? Besides, it was a great deal.
J. D.: Calm down everybody. Let's get the facts before we start attacking each other.
Tom: I agree. The more facts the better.
J. D.: Okay, Terry, it's your turn. Facts are the controller's department.
Terry: I'm afraid I can't provide the answers off the top of my head, but if you give me about a week I can set up a system that can routinely answer questions relating to worker productivity, material waste, and input prices.
J. D.: Let's mark it on our calendars.

Setting Direct Materials Standards

Terry Sherman's first task was to prepare quantity and price standards for the company's only significant raw material, pewter ingots. The **standard quantity per unit** defines the amount of direct materials that should be used for each unit of finished product, including an allowance for normal inefficiencies, such as scrap and spoilage.[1] After consulting with the production manager, Tom Kuchel, Terry set the quantity standard for pewter at 3.0 pounds per statue.

The **standard price per unit** defines the price that should be paid for each unit of direct materials and it should reflect the final, delivered cost of those materials. After consulting with purchasing manager Janet Warner, Terry set the standard price of pewter at $4.00 per pound.

Once Terry established the quantity and price standards he computed the standard direct materials cost per statue as follows:

$$3.0 \text{ pounds per statue} \times \$4.00 \text{ per pound} = \$12.00 \text{ per statue}$$

IN BUSINESS

MANAGING RAW MATERIAL COSTS IN THE APPAREL INDUSTRY

A company's raw material costs can rise for numerous and often uncontrollable reasons. For example, severe weather in China, which is the world's largest producer of cotton, can influence the cotton prices paid by Abercrombie & Fitch. Rising fuel costs can influence what Maidenform Brands pays for its petroleum-based synthetic fabrics. When farmers stop producing cotton in favor of soybeans, it increases the price Jones Apparel Group pays for a shrinking supply of cotton.

When faced with rising raw material costs, companies can respond three ways. First, they can maintain existing selling prices and consequently operate with lower margins. Second, they can pass the cost increases along to customers in the form of higher prices. Third, they can try to lower their raw material costs. For example, Hanesbrands buys hedging contracts that lock in its cotton prices, thereby insulating the company from future cost increases. JCPenney is changing the blend of raw materials used in its garments, whereas Maidenform has started buying some of its raw materials from lower-cost producers in Bangladesh.

Source: Elizabeth Holmes and Rachel Dodes, "Cotton Tale: Apparel Prices Set to Rise," *The Wall Street Journal*, May 19, 2010, p. B8.

© David Sucsy/Getty Images

Setting Direct Labor Standards

Direct labor quantity and price standards are usually expressed in terms of labor-hours or a labor rate. The **standard hours per unit** defines the amount of direct labor-hours that should be used to produce one unit of finished goods. One approach used to determine this standard is for an industrial engineer to do a time and motion study, actually

[1] Although companies often create "practical" rather than "ideal" materials quantity standards that include allowances for normal inefficiencies such as scrap, spoilage, and rejects, this practice is often criticized because it contradicts the zero defects goal that underlies many process improvement programs. If these types of allowances are built into materials quantity standards, they should be periodically reviewed and reduced over time to reflect improved processes, better training, and better equipment.

clocking the time required for each task. Throughout the chapter, we'll assume that "tight but attainable" labor standards are used rather than "ideal" standards that can only be attained by the most skilled and efficient employees working at peak effort 100% of the time. Therefore, after consulting with the production manager and considering reasonable allowances for breaks, personal needs of employees, cleanup, and machine downtime, Terry set the standard hours per unit at 0.50 direct labor-hours per statue.

The **standard rate per hour** defines the company's expected direct labor wage rate per hour, including employment taxes and fringe benefits. Using wage records and in consultation with the production manager, Terry Sherman established a standard rate per hour of $22.00. This standard rate reflects the expected "mix" of workers, even though the actual hourly wage rates may vary somewhat from individual to individual due to differing skills or seniority.

Once Terry established the time and rate standards, he computed the standard direct labor cost per statue as follows:

0.50 direct labor-hours per statue × $22.00 per direct labor-hour = $11.00 per statue

Setting Variable Manufacturing Overhead Standards

As with direct labor, the quantity and price standards for variable manufacturing overhead are usually expressed in terms of hours and a rate. The *standard hours per unit* for variable overhead measures the amount of the allocation base from a company's predetermined overhead rate that is required to produce one unit of finished goods. In the case of Colonial Pewter, we will assume that the company uses direct labor-hours as the allocation base in its predetermined overhead rate. Therefore, the standard hours per unit for variable overhead is exactly the same as the standard hours per unit for direct labor—0.50 direct labor-hours per statue.

The *standard rate per unit* that a company expects to pay for variable overhead equals *the variable portion of the predetermined overhead rate.* At Colonial Pewter, the variable portion of the predetermined overhead rate is $6.00 per direct labor-hour. Therefore, Terry computed the standard variable manufacturing overhead cost per statue as follows:

0.50 direct labor-hours per statue × $6.00 per direct-labor hour = $3.00 per statue

This $3.00 per unit cost for variable manufacturing overhead appears along with direct materials ($12 per unit) and direct labor ($11 per unit) on the *standard cost card* in Exhibit 11–1. A **standard cost card** shows the standard quantity (or hours) and standard price (or rate) of the inputs required to produce a unit of a specific product. The **standard cost per unit** for all three variable manufacturing costs is computed the same way. The standard quantity (or hours) per unit is multiplied by the standard price (or rate) per unit to obtain the standard cost per unit.

EXHIBIT 11–1
Standard Cost Card—Variable Manufacturing Costs

Inputs	(1) Standard Quantity or Hours	(2) Standard Price or Rate	Standard Cost (1) × (2)
Direct materials.	3.0 pounds	$4.00 per pound	$ 12.00
Direct labor	0.50 hours	$22.00 per hour	11.00
Variable manufacturing overhead	0.50 hours	$6.00 per hour	3.00
Total standard cost per unit			$26.00

Using Standards in Flexible Budgets

Once Terry Sherman created the standard cost card shown in Exhibit 11–1, he was ready to use this information to calculate direct materials, direct labor, and variable manufacturing overhead variances. Therefore, he gathered the following data for the month of June:

Originally budgeted output in June	2,100 statues
Actual output in June	2,000 statues
Actual direct materials cost in June*	$24,700
Actual direct labor cost in June?	$22,680
Actual variable manufacturing overhead cost in June	$7,140

*The revenue variance is labeled favorable (unfavorable) when the actual revenue is greater than (less than) the planning budget. The expense variances are labeled favorable (unfavorable) when the actual expense is less than (greater than) the planning budget.

Using the above data and the standard cost data from Exhibit 11–1, Terry computed the spending and activity variances shown in Exhibit 11–2. Notice that the actual results and flexible budget columns are each based on the actual output of 2,000 statues. The planning budget column is based on the planned output of 2,100 statues. The standard costs of $12.00 per unit for materials, $11.00 per unit for direct labor, and $3.00 per unit for variable manufacturing overhead are each multiplied by the actual output of 2,000 statues to compute the amounts in the flexible budget column. For example, the standard direct labor cost per unit of $11.00 multiplied by 2,000 statues equals the direct labor flexible budget of $22,000. Similarly, the three standard variable cost figures are multiplied by 2,100 units to compute the amounts in the planning budget column. For example, the direct labor cost for the planning budget is $23,100 (= $11.00 per unit × 2,100 units).

The spending variances shown in Exhibit 11–2 are computed by taking the amounts in the actual results column and subtracting the amounts in the flexible budget column. For all three variable manufacturing costs, this computation results in a positive number because the actual amount of the cost incurred to produce 2,000 statues exceeds the standard cost allowed for 2,000 statues. Because, in all three instances, the actual cost incurred exceeds the standard cost allowed for the actual level of output, the variance is labeled unfavorable (U). Had any of the actual costs incurred been less than the standard cost allowed for the actual level of output, the corresponding variances would have been labeled favorable (F).

The activity variances shown in the exhibit are computed by taking the amounts in the flexible budget column and subtracting the amounts in the planning budget column. For all three variable manufacturing costs, these computations result in negative numbers and what are labeled as favorable (F) variances. The label favorable is used in these instances because the standard cost allowed for the actual output is less than the standard cost allowed for the planned

EXHIBIT 11–2
Flexible Budget Performance Report for Variable Manufacturing Costs

Colonial Pewter
Flexible Budget Performance Report—Manufacturing Costs Only
For the Month Ended June 30

	Actual Results	Spending Variances	Flexible Budget	Activity Variances	Planning Budget
Statues produced (*q*).	2,000		2,000		2,100
Direct materials ($12.00*q*).	$24,700	$ 700 U	$24,000	$1,200 F	$25,200
Direct labor ($11.00*q*)	$22,680	$ 680 U	$22,000	$ 1,100 F	$23,100
Variable manufacturing overhead ($3.00*q*).	$7,140	$1,140 U	$6,000	$300 F	$6,300

output. Had the actual level of activity been greater than the planned level of activity, all of the computations would have resulted in positive numbers and unfavorable (U) activity variances.

While the performance report in Exhibit 11–2 is useful, it would be even more useful if the spending variances could be broken down into their price-related and quantity-related components. For example, the direct materials spending variance in the report is $700 unfavorable. This means that, given the actual level of production for the period, direct materials costs were too high by $700—at least according to the standard costs. Was this due to higher than expected prices for materials? Or was it due to too much material being used? The standard cost variances we will be discussing in the rest of the chapter are designed to answer these questions.

A General Model for Standard Cost Variance Analysis

Standard cost variance analysis decomposes spending variances from the flexible budget into two elements—one due to the price paid for the input and the other due to the amount of the input that is used. A **price variance** is the difference between the actual amount paid for an input and the standard amount that should have been paid, multiplied by the actual amount of the input purchased. A **quantity variance** is the difference between how much of an input was actually used and how much should have been used and is stated in dollar terms using the standard price of the input.

Why are standards separated into two categories—price and quantity? Price variances and quantity variances usually have different causes. In addition, different managers are usually responsible for buying and using inputs. For example, in the case of a raw material, the purchasing manager is responsible for its price and the production manager is responsible for the amount of the raw material actually used to make products. Therefore, it is important to clearly distinguish between deviations from price standards (the responsibility of the purchasing manager) and deviations from quantity standards (the responsibility of the production manager).

Exhibit 11–3 presents a general model that can be used to decompose the spending variance for a variable cost into a *price variance* and a *quantity variance*.[2] Column (1) in this exhibit corresponds with the Actual Results column in Exhibit 11–2. Column (3) corresponds with the Flexible Budget column in Exhibit 11–2. Column (2) has been inserted into Exhibit 11–3 to enable separating the spending variance into a price variance and a quantity variance.

EXHIBIT 11–3
A General Model for Standard Cost Variance Analysis—Variable Manufacturing Costs

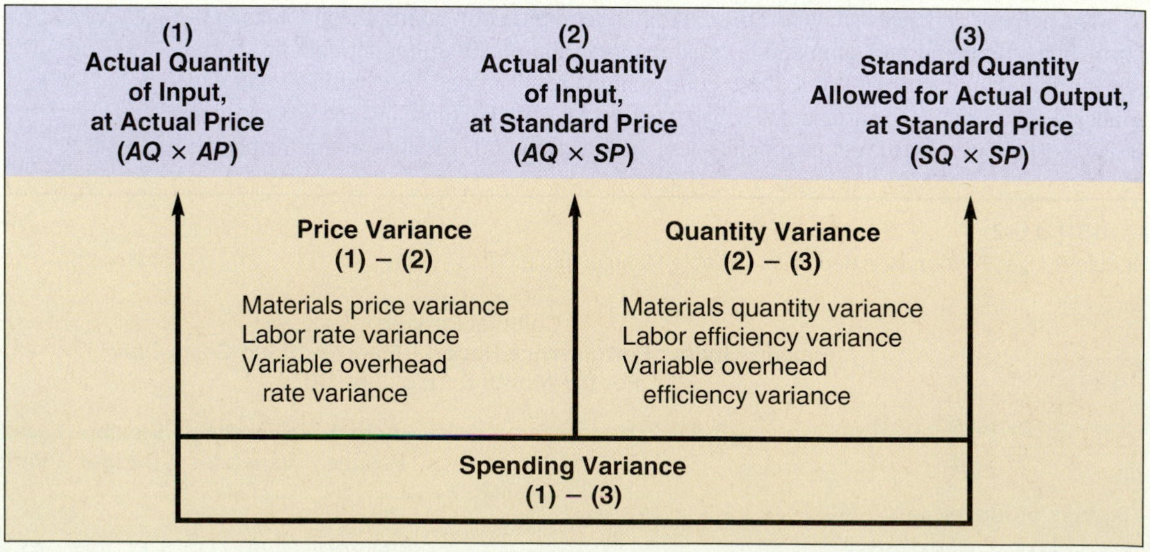

[2] This general model can always be used to compute direct labor and variable manufacturing overhead variances. However, it can be used to compute direct materials variances only when the actual quantity of materials purchased equals the actual quantity of materials used in production. Later in the chapter, we will explain how to compute direct materials variances when these quantities differ.

Three things should be noted from Exhibit 11–3. First, it can be used to compute a price variance and a quantity variance for each of the three variable cost elements—direct materials, direct labor, and variable manufacturing overhead—even though the variances have different names. A price variance is called a *materials price variance* in the case of direct materials, a *labor rate variance* in the case of direct labor, and a *variable overhead rate variance* in the case of variable manufacturing overhead. A quantity variance is called a *materials quantity variance* in the case of direct materials, a *labor efficiency variance* in the case of direct labor, and a *variable overhead efficiency variance* in the case of variable manufacturing overhead.

Second, all three columns in the exhibit are based on the *actual amount of output* produced during the period. Even the flexible budget column depicts the standard cost allowed for the *actual amount of output* produced during the period. The key to understanding the flexible budget column in Exhibit 11–3 is to grasp the meaning of the term *standard quantity allowed (SQ)*. The **standard quantity allowed** (when computing direct materials variances) or **standard hours allowed** (when computing direct labor and variable manufacturing overhead variances) refers to the amount of an input *that should have been used* to manufacture the actual output of finished goods produced during the period. It is computed by multiplying the actual output by the standard quantity (or hours) per unit. The standard quantity (or hours) allowed is then multiplied by the standard price (or rate) per unit of the input to obtain the total cost according to the flexible budget. For example, if a company actually produced 100 units of finished goods during the period and its standard quantity per unit of finished goods for direct materials is 3 pounds, then its *standard quantity allowed (SQ)* would be 300 pounds (= 100 units × 3 pounds per unit). If the company's standard cost per pound of direct materials is $2.00, then the total direct materials cost in its flexible budget would be $600 (= 300 pounds × $2.00 per pound).

Third, the spending, price, and quantity variances—regardless of what they are called—are computed exactly the same way regardless of whether one is dealing with direct materials, direct labor, or variable manufacturing overhead. The spending variance is computed by taking the total cost in column (1) and subtracting the total cost in column (3). The price variance is computed by taking the total cost in column (1) and subtracting the total cost in column (2). The quantity variance is computed by taking the total cost in column (2) and subtracting the total cost in column (3). In all of these variance calculations, a positive number should be labeled as an unfavorable (U) variance and a negative number should be labeled as a favorable (F) variance. An unfavorable price variance indicates that the actual price (AP) per unit of the input was greater than the standard price (SP) per unit. A favorable price variance indicates that the actual price (AP) of the input was less than the standard price per unit (SP). An unfavorable quantity variance indicates that the actual quantity (AQ) of the input used was greater than the standard quantity allowed (SQ). Conversely, a favorable quantity variance indicates that the actual quantity (AQ) of the input used was less than the standard quantity allowed (SQ).

With this general model as the foundation, we will now calculate Colonial Pewter's price and quantity variances.

Using Standard Costs—Direct Materials Variances

LEARNING OBJECTIVE 11–1
Compute the direct materials price and quantity variances and explain their significance.

After determining Colonial Pewter Company's standard costs for direct materials, direct labor, and variable manufacturing overhead, Terry Sherman's next step was to compute the company's variances for June. As discussed in the preceding section, variances are computed by comparing actual costs to standard costs. Terry referred to the standard cost card in Exhibit 11–1 that shows the standard direct materials cost per statue was computed as follows:

3.0 pounds per statue × $4.00 per pound = $12.00 per statue

Colonial Pewter's records for June showed that the actual quantity (AQ) of pewter purchased was 6,500 pounds at an actual price (AP) of $3.80 per pound, for a total cost of $24,700. All of the material purchased was used during June to manufacture

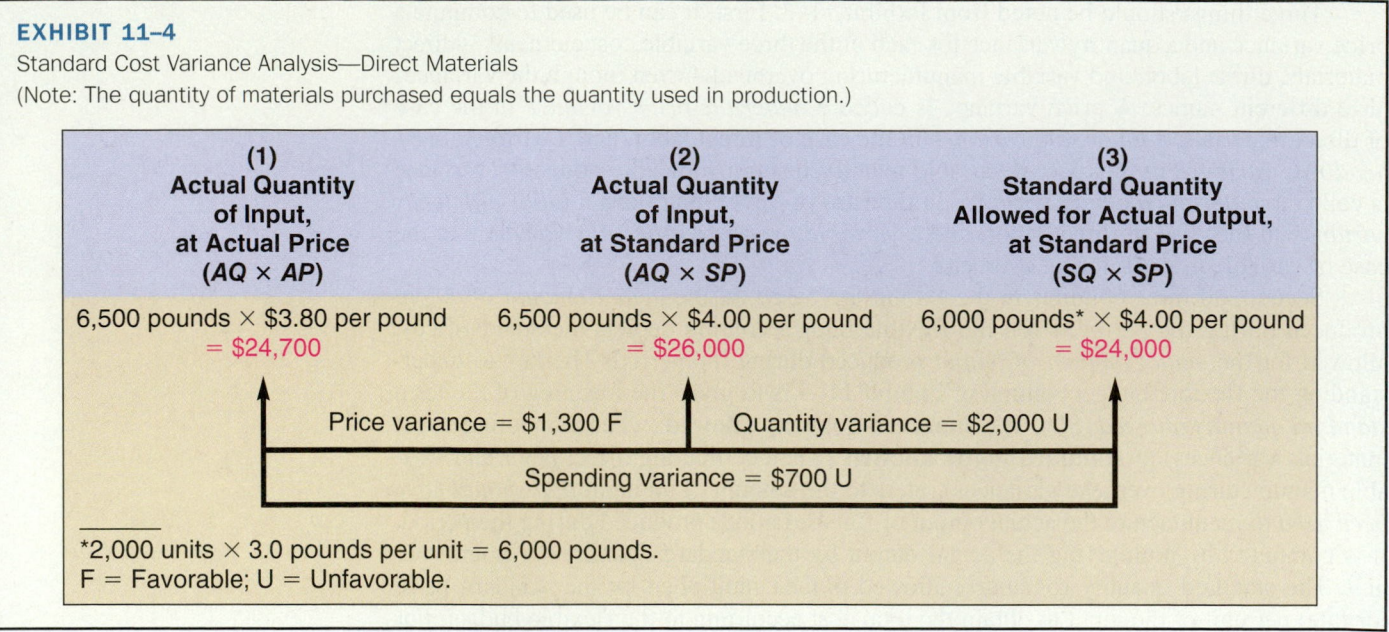

EXHIBIT 11–4
Standard Cost Variance Analysis—Direct Materials
(Note: The quantity of materials purchased equals the quantity used in production.)

(1) Actual Quantity of Input, at Actual Price (*AQ* × *AP*)	(2) Actual Quantity of Input, at Standard Price (*AQ* × *SP*)	(3) Standard Quantity Allowed for Actual Output, at Standard Price (*SQ* × *SP*)
6,500 pounds × $3.80 per pound = $24,700	6,500 pounds × $4.00 per pound = $26,000	6,000 pounds* × $4.00 per pound = $24,000

Price variance = $1,300 F
Quantity variance = $2,000 U
Spending variance = $700 U

*2,000 units × 3.0 pounds per unit = 6,000 pounds.
F = Favorable; U = Unfavorable.

2,000 statues.[3] Using these data and the standard costs from Exhibit 11–1, Terry computed the price and quantity variances shown in Exhibit 11–4.

Notice that the variances in this exhibit are based on three different total costs—$24,700, $26,000, and $24,000. The first, $24,700, is the actual amount paid for the actual amount of pewter purchased. The third total cost figure, $24,000, refers to how much should have been spent on pewter to produce the actual output of 2,000 statues. The standards call for 3 pounds of pewter per statue. Because 2,000 statues were produced, 6,000 pounds of pewter should have been used. This is referred to as the *standard quantity allowed* for the actual output and its computation can be stated in formula form as follows:

Standard quantity allowed for actual output = Actual output × Standard quantity

If 6,000 pounds of pewter had been purchased at the standard price of $4.00 per pound, the company would have spent $24,000. This is the amount that appears in the company's flexible budget for the month. The difference between the $24,700 actually spent and the $24,000 that should have been spent is the spending variance for the month of $700 U. This variance is unfavorable (denoted by U) because the amount that was actually spent exceeds the amount that should have been spent.

The second total cost figure in Exhibit 11–4, $26,000, is the key that allows us to decompose the spending variance into two distinct elements—one due to price and one due to quantity. It represents how much the company should have spent if it had purchased the actual amount of input, 6,500 pounds, at the standard price of $4.00 a pound rather than the actual price of $3.80 a pound.

The Materials Price Variance

Using the $26,000 total cost figure in column (2) of Exhibit 11–4, we can make two comparisons—one with the total cost of $24,700 in column (1) and one with the total cost of $24,000 in column (3). The difference between the $24,700 in column (1) and the $26,000 in column (2) is the *materials price variance* of $1,300, which is labeled as favorable (denoted by F). A **materials price variance** measures the difference between an input's actual price and its standard price, multiplied by the actual quantity purchased.

[3] Throughout this section, we assume zero beginning and ending inventories of materials and that all materials purchased during the period are used during that period. The more general case in which there are beginning and ending inventories of materials and materials are not necessarily used during the period in which they are purchased is considered later in the chapter.

To understand the price variance, note that the actual price of $3.80 per pound of pewter is $0.20 less than the standard price of $4.00 per pound. Because 6,500 pounds were purchased, the total amount of the variance is $1,300 (= $0.20 per pound × 6,500 pounds). This variance is labeled favorable (F) because the actual purchase price per pound is less than the standard purchase price per pound. A price variance is labeled unfavorable (U) if the actual purchase price exceeds the standard purchase price.

Generally speaking, the purchasing manager has control over the price paid for goods and is therefore responsible for the materials price variance. Many factors influence the prices paid for goods including how many units are ordered, how the order is delivered, whether the order is a rush order, and the quality of materials purchased. If any of these factors deviates from what was assumed when the standards were set, a price variance can result. For example, purchasing second-grade materials rather than top-grade materials may result in a favorable price variance because the lower-grade materials may be less costly. However, the lower-grade materials may create production problems. It also bears emphasizing that someone other than the purchasing manager could be responsible for a materials price variance. For example, due to production problems beyond the purchasing manager's control, the purchasing manager may have to use express delivery. In these cases, the production manager should be held responsible for the resulting price variances.

IN BUSINESS

DIRECT MATERIAL PURCHASES: A RISK MANAGEMENT PERSPECTIVE

Shenzhen Hepalink manufactures heparin, a blood-thinning medication that is injected directly into the bloodstream of some surgical patients. The company relies on suppliers to extract its raw material, called crude heparin, from the intestines of slaughtered pigs. The harvesting of crude heparin is susceptible to contamination if the process is improperly managed and monitored. For example, Baxter International recently recalled tainted heparin that some people believe caused illnesses, allergic reactions, and deaths in some patients in the United States and Germany.

Shenzhen Hepalink strives to reduce contamination risks by buying crude heparin only from Chinese government-regulated slaughterhouses instead of rural unregulated slaughterhouses. The company also maintains quality assurance laboratories on each supplier's premises to ensure compliance with applicable rules. These safeguards increase Shenzhen Hepalink's raw materials cost, but they also reduce the risk of contaminated heparin eventually being injected into a patient's bloodstream.

Source: Gordon Fairclough, "How a Heparin Maker in China Tackles Risks," *The Wall Street Journal*, March 10, 2009, pp. B1 and B5.

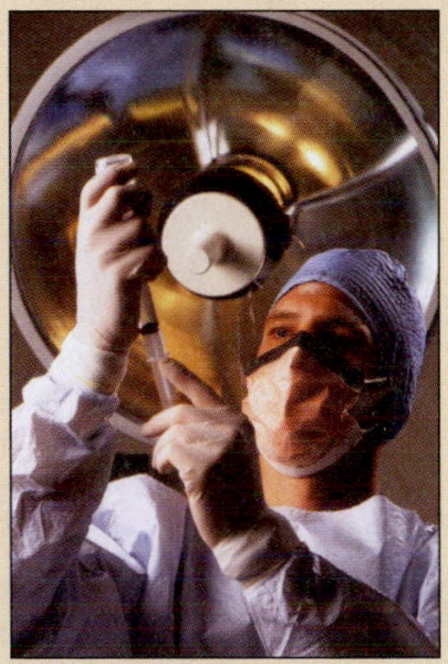

The Materials Quantity Variance

Referring again to Exhibit 11–4, the difference between the $26,000 in column (2) and the $24,000 in column (3) is the *materials quantity variance* of $2,000, which is labeled as unfavorable (denoted by U). The **materials quantity variance** measures the difference between the actual quantity of materials used in production and the standard quantity of materials allowed for the actual output, multiplied by the standard price per unit of materials. It is labeled as unfavorable (favorable) when the actual quantity of material used in production is greater than (less than) the quantity of material that should have been used according to the standard.

To understand the materials quantity variance, note that the actual amount of pewter used in production was 6,500 pounds. However, the standard amount of pewter allowed for the actual output is 6,000 pounds. Therefore, too much pewter was used to produce the actual output—by a total of 500 pounds. To express this in dollar terms, the 500 pounds is multiplied by the standard price of $4.00 per pound to yield the quantity variance of $2,000 U. Why is the standard price of pewter, rather than the actual price, used in this calculation? The production manager is ordinarily responsible for the quantity variance. If the actual price were used in the calculation of the quantity variance, the production

EXHIBIT 11–5
Direct Materials Variances: The Equations-Based Approach

Materials Price Variance:

Materials price variance = $(AQ \times AP) - (AQ \times SP)$
Materials price variance = $AQ(AP - SP)$
Materials price variance = 6,500 pounds($3.80 per pound − $4.00 per pound)
Materials price variance = $1,300 F

Materials Quantity Variance:

Materials quantity variance = $(AQ \times SP) - (SQ \times SP)$
Materials quantity variance = $SP(AQ - SQ)$
Materials quantity variance = $4.00 per pound(6,500 pounds − 6,000 pounds)
Materials quantity variance = $2,000 U
where:
AQ = Actual quantity of pounds purchased and used in production
SQ = Standard quantity of pounds allowed for the actual output
AP = Actual price per unit of the input
SP = Standard price per unit of the input

manager's performance evaluation would be unfairly influenced by the efficiency or inefficiency of the purchasing manager.

Excessive materials usage can result from many factors, including faulty machines, inferior materials quality, untrained workers, and poor supervision. Generally speaking, it is the responsibility of the production manager to see that material usage is kept in line with standards. There may be times, however, when the *purchasing* manager is responsible for an unfavorable materials quantity variance. For example, if the purchasing manager buys inferior materials at a lower price, the materials may be unsuitable for use and may result in excessive waste. Thus, the purchasing manager rather than the production manager would be responsible for the quantity variance.

Thus far, we have shown how to compute direct materials variances using the general model depicted in Exhibit 11–4; however, these variances can also be calculated using basic mathematical equations. Exhibit 11–5 shows how Colonial Pewter can compute its direct materials variances using the equations-based approach.

IN BUSINESS

CUSTOMERS SPEAK LOUD AND CLEAR

When ConAgra Foods raised the price of its Banquet frozen dinners from $1.00 to $1.25, many customers stopped buying the product. The resulting drop in sales contributed to a 40% decline in the company's stock price. It also presented ConAgra with an interesting challenge—lowering its raw material costs so that Banquet frozen dinners could be profitable at the customer-mandated price of $1.00. ConAgra responded by replacing expensive entrees such as barbecued chicken and country-fried pork with less costly choices such as meat patties and rice and beans. It also shrank standard portion sizes and expanded the use of cheaper side items such as mashed potatoes and brownies. However, the company did not sacrifice on variety—it still offers more than 100 Banquet-branded products.

Source: Joseph Weber, "Over a Buck for Dinner? Outrageous," *BusinessWeek,* March 9, 2009, p. 57.

Using Standard Costs—Direct Labor Variances

LEARNING OBJECTIVE 11–2
Compute the direct labor rate and efficiency variances and explain their significance.

Terry Sherman's next step in determining Colonial Pewter's variances for June was to compute the direct labor variances for the month. Recall from Exhibit 11–1 that the standard direct labor cost per statue is $11, computed as follows:

$$0.50 \text{ hours per statue} \times \$22.00 \text{ per hour} = \$11.00 \text{ per statue}$$

EXHIBIT 11–6
Standard Cost Variance Analysis—Direct Labor

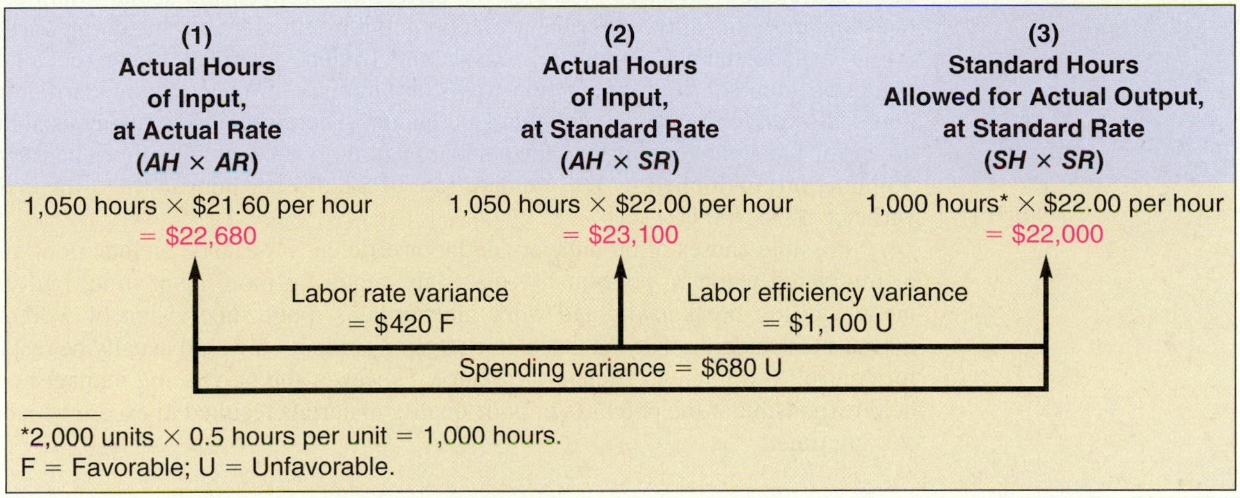

In addition, Colonial Pewter's records for June showed that 1,050 direct labor-hours were actually worked. Given that the company paid its direct labor workers a total of $22,680 (including payroll taxes and fringe benefits), the average actual wage rate was $21.60 per hour (= $22,680 ÷ 1,050 hours). Using these data and the standard costs from Exhibit 11–1, Terry computed the direct labor rate and efficiency variances that appear in Exhibit 11–6.

Notice that the column headings in Exhibit 11–6 are the same as those used Exhibits 11–3 and 10–4, except that in Exhibit 11–6 the terms *rate* and *hours* are used in place of the terms *price* and *quantity*.

The Labor Rate Variance

Using the $23,100 total cost figure in column (2) of Exhibit 11–6, we can make two comparisons—one with the total cost of $22,680 in column (1) and one with the total cost of $22,000 in column (3). The difference between the 22,680 in column (1) and the $23,100 in column (2) is the *labor rate variance* of $420 F. The **labor rate variance** measures the difference between the actual hourly rate and the standard hourly rate, multiplied by the actual number of hours worked during the period.

To understand the labor rate variance, note that the actual hourly rate of $21.60 is $0.40 less than the standard rate of $22.00 per hour. Because 1,050 hours were actually worked, the total amount of the variance is $420 (= $0.40 per hour × 1,050 hours). The variance is labeled favorable (F) because the actual hourly rate is less than the standard hourly rate. If the actual hourly rate had been greater than the standard hourly rate, the variance would have been labeled unfavorable (U).

In most companies, the wage rates paid to workers are quite predictable. Nevertheless, rate variances can arise based on how production supervisors use their direct labor workers. Skilled workers with high hourly rates of pay may be given duties that require little skill and call for lower hourly rates of pay. This will result in an unfavorable labor rate variance because the actual hourly rate of pay will exceed the standard rate specified for the particular task. In contrast, a favorable rate variance would result when workers who are paid at a rate lower than specified in the standard are assigned to the task. However, the lower-paid workers may not be as efficient. Finally, overtime work at premium rates will result in an unfavorable labor rate variance if the overtime premium is charged to the direct labor account.

The Labor Efficiency Variance

Referring back to Exhibit 11–6, the difference between the $23,100 in column (2) and the $22,000 in column (3) is the *labor efficiency variance* of $1,100 unfavorable (U). The **labor efficiency variance** measures the difference between the actual hours used and the standard hours allowed for the actual output, multiplied by the standard hourly rate.

To understand Colonial Pewter's labor efficiency variance, note that the actual amount of hours used in production was 1,050 hours. However, the standard amount of hours allowed for the actual output is 1,000 hours. Therefore, the company used 50 more hours for the actual output than the standards allow. To express this in dollar terms, the 50 hours are multiplied by the standard rate of $22.00 per hour to yield the efficiency variance of $1,100 U.

Possible causes of an unfavorable labor efficiency variance include poorly trained or motivated workers; poor-quality materials, requiring more labor time; faulty equipment, causing breakdowns and work interruptions; poor supervision of workers; and inaccurate standards. The managers in charge of production would usually be responsible for control of the labor efficiency variance. However, the purchasing manager could be held responsible if the purchase of poor-quality materials resulted in excessive labor processing time.

IN BUSINESS

CASHIERS FACE THE STOPWATCH

© Rob Melnychuk/Photodisc/Getty Images

Operations Workforce Optimization (OWO) writes software that uses engineered labor standards to determine how long it should take a cashier to check out a customer. The software measures an employee's productivity by continuously comparing actual customer checkout times to pre-established labor efficiency standards. For example, the cashiers at Meijer, a regional retailer located in the Midwest, may be demoted or terminated if they do not meet or exceed labor efficiency standards for at least 95% of customers served. In addition to Meijer, OWO has attracted other clients such as Gap, Limited Brands, Office Depot, Nike, and Toys "R" Us, based on claims that its software can reduce labor costs by 5–15%. The software has also attracted the attention of the United Food and Commercial Workers Union, which represents 27,000 Meijer employees. The union has filed a grievance against Meijer related to its cashier monitoring system.

Source: Vanessa O'Connell, "Stores Count Seconds to Cut Labor Costs," *The Wall Street Journal,* November 17, 2008, pp. A1–A15.

Another important cause of an unfavorable labor efficiency variance may be insufficient demand for the company's products. Managers in some companies argue that it is difficult, and perhaps unwise, to constantly adjust the workforce in response to changes in the amount of work that needs to be done. In such companies, the direct labor workforce is essentially fixed in the short run. If demand is insufficient to keep everyone busy, workers are not laid off and an unfavorable labor efficiency variance will often be recorded.

If customer orders are insufficient to keep the workers busy, the work center manager has two options—either accept an unfavorable labor efficiency variance or build inventory. A central lesson of Lean Production is that building inventory with no immediate prospect of sale is a bad idea. Excessive inventory—particularly work in process inventory—leads to high defect rates, obsolete goods, and inefficient operations. As a consequence, when the workforce is basically fixed in the short term, managers must be cautious about how labor efficiency variances are used. Some experts advocate eliminating labor efficiency variances in such situations—at least for the purposes of motivating and controlling workers on the shop floor.

Direct labor variances can also be computed using equations instead of the general model depicted in Exhibit 11–6. Exhibit 11–7 shows how Colonial Pewter can compute its direct labor variances using the equations-based approach.

EXHIBIT 11–7
Direct Labor Variances: The Equations-Based Approach

Labor Rate Variance:

Labor rate variance = $(AH \times AR) - (AH \times SR)$
Labor rate variance = $AH(AR - SR)$
Labor rate variance = 1,050 hours($21.60 per hour − $22.00 per hour)
Labor rate variance = $420 F

Labor Efficiency Variance:

Labor efficiency variance = $(AH \times SR) - (SH \times SR)$
Labor efficiency variance = $SR(AH - SH)$
Labor efficiency variance = $22.00 per hour(1,050 hours − 1,000 hours)
Labor efficiency variance = $1,100 U
where:
AH = Actual quantity of hours used in production
SH = Standard quantity of hours allowed for the actual output
AR = Actual rate per direct labor-hour
SR = Standard rate per direct labor-hour

Using Standard Costs—Variable Manufacturing Overhead Variances

LEARNING OBJECTIVE 11–3
Compute the variable manufacturing overhead rate and efficiency variances and explain their significance.

The final step in Terry Sherman's analysis of Colonial Pewter's variances for June was to compute the variable manufacturing overhead variances. The variable portion of manufacturing overhead can be analyzed using the same basic formulas that we used to analyze direct materials and direct labor. Recall from Exhibit 11–1 that the standard variable manufacturing overhead is $3.00 per statue, computed as follows:

0.50 hours per statue × $6.00 per hour = $3.00 per statue

Also recall that Colonial Pewter's cost records showed that the total actual variable manufacturing overhead cost for June was $7,140 and that 1,050 direct labor-hours were worked in June to produce 2,000 statues. Terry's analysis of this overhead data appears in Exhibit 11–8.

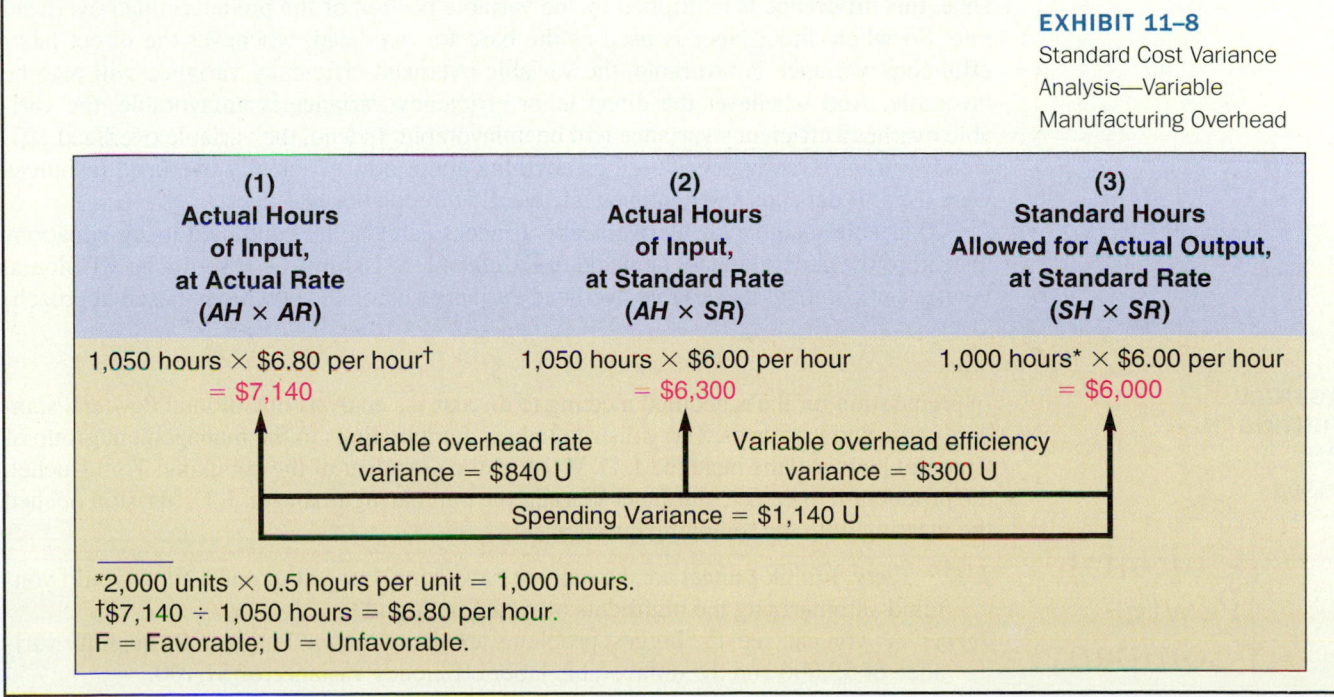

EXHIBIT 11–8
Standard Cost Variance Analysis—Variable Manufacturing Overhead

(1) Actual Hours of Input, at Actual Rate ($AH \times AR$)	(2) Actual Hours of Input, at Standard Rate ($AH \times SR$)	(3) Standard Hours Allowed for Actual Output, at Standard Rate ($SH \times SR$)
1,050 hours × $6.80 per hour† = $7,140	1,050 hours × $6.00 per hour = $6,300	1,000 hours* × $6.00 per hour = $6,000

Variable overhead rate variance = $840 U (between columns 1 and 2)

Variable overhead efficiency variance = $300 U (between columns 2 and 3)

Spending Variance = $1,140 U (between columns 1 and 3)

*2,000 units × 0.5 hours per unit = 1,000 hours.
†$7,140 ÷ 1,050 hours = $6.80 per hour.
F = Favorable; U = Unfavorable.

Notice the similarities between Exhibits 11–6 and 11–8. These similarities arise from the fact that direct labor-hours are being used as the base for allocating overhead cost to units of product; thus, the same hourly figures appear in Exhibit 11–8 for variable manufacturing overhead as in Exhibit 11–6 for direct labor. The main difference between the two exhibits is in the standard hourly rate being used, which in this company is much lower for variable manufacturing overhead than for direct labor.

The Variable Manufacturing Overhead Rate and Efficiency Variances

Using the $6,300 total cost figure in column (2) of Exhibit 11–8, we can make two comparisons—one with the total cost of $7,140 in column (1) and one with the total cost of $6,000 in column (3). The difference between the $7,140 in column (1) and the $6,300 in column (2) is the *variable overhead rate variance* of $840 U. The **variable overhead rate variance** measures the difference between the actual variable overhead cost incurred during the period and the standard cost that should have been incurred based on the actual activity of the period. The difference between the $6,300 in column (2) and the $6,000 in column (3) is the *variable overhead efficiency variance* of $300 U. The **variable overhead efficiency variance** measures the difference between the actual level of activity and the standard activity allowed for the actual output, multiplied by the variable part of the predetermined overhead rate.

To understand Colonial Pewter's variable overhead efficiency variance, note that the actual amount of hours used in production was 1,050 hours. However, the standard amount of hours allowed for the actual output is 1,000 hours. Therefore, the company used 50 more hours for the actual output than the standards allow. To express this in dollar terms, the 50 hours are multiplied by the variable part of the predetermined overhead rate of $6.00 per hour to yield the variable overhead efficiency variance of $300 U.

The interpretation of the variable overhead variances is not as clear as the direct materials and direct labor variances. In particular, the variable overhead efficiency variance is exactly the same as the direct labor efficiency variance except for one detail—the rate that is used to translate the variance into dollars. In both cases, the variance is the difference between the actual hours worked and the standard hours allowed for the actual output. In the case of the direct labor efficiency variance, this difference is multiplied by the standard direct labor rate. In the case of the variable overhead efficiency variance, this difference is multiplied by the variable portion of the predetermined overhead rate. So when direct labor is used as the base for overhead, whenever the direct labor efficiency variance is favorable, the variable overhead efficiency variance will also be favorable. And whenever the direct labor efficiency variance is unfavorable, the variable overhead efficiency variance will be unfavorable. Indeed, the variable overhead efficiency variance really doesn't tell us anything about how efficiently overhead resources were used. It depends solely on how efficiently direct labor was used.

Variable manufacturing overhead variances can also be computed using equations instead of the general model depicted in Exhibit 11–8. Exhibit 11–9 shows how Colonial Pewter can compute its variable overhead variances using the equations-based approach.

MANAGERIAL ACCOUNTING IN ACTION

The Wrap-Up

Colonial Pewter Company

In preparation for the scheduled meeting to discuss his analysis of Colonial Pewter's standard costs and variances, Terry distributed his computations to the management group of Colonial Pewter. This included J. D. Wriston, the president of the company; Tom Kuchel, the production manager; and Janet Warner, the purchasing manager. J. D. Wriston opened the meeting with the following question:

J. D.: Terry, I think I understand what you have done, but just to make sure, would you mind summarizing the highlights of what you found?

Terry: As you can see, the biggest problems are the unfavorable materials quantity variance of $2,000 and the unfavorable labor efficiency variance of $1,100.

EXHIBIT 11–9
Variable Manufacturing Overhead Variances: The Equations-Based Approach

Variable Overhead Rate Variance:

Variable overhead rate variance = $(AH \times AR) - (AH \times SR)$
Variable overhead rate variance = $AH(AR - SR)$
Variable overhead rate variance = 1,050 hours($6.80 − $6.00)
Variable overhead rate variance = $840 U

Variable Overhead Efficiency Variance:

Variable overhead efficiency variance = $(AH \times SR) - (SH \times SR)$
Variable overhead efficiency variance = $SR(AH - SH)$
Variable overhead efficiency variance = $6.00 per hour(1,050 hours − 1,000 hours)
Variable overhead efficiency variance = $300 U
where:
AH = Actual quantity of hours used in production
SH = Standard quantity of hours allowed for the actual output
AR = Actual rate per direct labor-hour
SR = Standard rate per direct labor-hour

J. D.: Tom, you're the production boss. What do you think is causing the unfavorable labor efficiency variance?

Tom: It has to be the new production workers. Our experienced workers shouldn't have much problem meeting the standard of half an hour per unit. We all knew that there would be some inefficiency for a while as we brought new people on board. My plan for overcoming the problem is to pair up each of the new guys with one of our old-timers and have them work together for a while. It would slow down our older guys a bit, but I'll bet the unfavorable variance disappears and our new workers would learn a lot.

J. D.: Sounds good. Now, what about that $2,000 unfavorable materials quantity variance?

Terry: Tom, are the new workers generating a lot of scrap?

Tom: Yeah, I guess so.

J. D.: I think that could be part of the problem. Can you do anything about it?

Tom: I can watch the scrap closely for a few days to see where it's being generated. If it is the new workers, I can have the old-timers work with them on the problem when I team them up.

J. D.: Janet, the favorable materials price variance of $1,300 isn't helping us if it is contributing to the unfavorable materials quantity and labor efficiency variances. Let's make sure that our raw material purchases conform to our quality standards.

Janet: Will do.

J. D.: Good. Let's reconvene in a few weeks to see what has happened. Hopefully, we can get those unfavorable variances under control.

An Important Subtlety in the Materials Variances

Most companies use the *quantity of materials purchased* to compute the materials price variance and the *quantity of materials used* in production to compute the materials quantity variance. There are two reasons for this practice. First, delaying the computation of the price variance until the materials are used would result in less timely variance reports. Second, computing the price variance when the materials are purchased allows materials to be carried in the inventory accounts at their standard cost. This greatly simplifies bookkeeping.

When we computed materials price and quantity variances for Colonial Pewter in Exhibit 11–4, we assumed that 6,500 pounds of materials were purchased and used in production. However, it is very common for a company's quantity of materials purchased to differ from its quantity used in production. When this happens, the materials price variance is computed using the *quantity of materials purchased,* whereas the materials quantity variance is computed using the *quantity of materials used* in production.

To illustrate, assume that during June Colonial Pewter purchased 7,000 pounds of materials at $3.80 per pound instead of 6,500 pounds as assumed earlier in the chapter. Also assume that the company continued to use 6,500 pounds of materials in production and that the standard price remained at $4.00 per pound.

Given these assumptions, Exhibit 11–10 shows how to compute the materials price variance of $1,400 F and the materials quantity variance of $2,000 U. Note that the price variance is based on the amount of the input purchased whereas the quantity variance is based on the quantity of the input used in production. Column (2) of Exhibit 11–10 contains two different total costs for this reason. When the price variance is computed, the total cost used from column (2) is $28,000—which is the cost of the input *purchased,* evaluated at the standard price. When the quantity variance is computed, the total cost used from column (2) is $26,000—which is the cost of the actual input *used,* evaluated at the standard price.

Exhibit 11–10 shows that the price variance is computed on the entire amount of material purchased (7,000 pounds), whereas the quantity variance is computed only on the amount of materials used in production during the month (6,500 pounds). What about the other 500 pounds of material that were purchased during the period, but that have not yet been used? When those materials are used in future periods, a quantity variance will be computed. However, a price variance will not be computed when the materials are finally used because the price variance was computed when the materials were purchased.

Because the price variance is based on the amount purchased and the quantity variance is based on the amount used, the two variances do not generally sum to the spending variance from the flexible budget, which is wholly based on the amount used. We would also like to emphasize that the variances depicted in Exhibit 11–10 can also be computed

EXHIBIT 11–10

Standard Cost Variance Analysis—Direct Materials

(Note: The quantity of materials purchased does not equal the quantity used in production.)

(1) Actual Quantity of Input, at Actual Price ($AQ \times AP$)	(2) Actual Quantity of Input, at Standard Price ($AQ \times SP$)	(3) Standard Quantity Allowed for Actual Output, at Standard Price ($SQ \times SP$)
7,000 pounds × $3.80 per pound = $26,600	7,000 pounds × $4.00 per pound = $28,000	6,000 pounds* × $4.00 per pound = $24,000
	6,500 Pounds × $4.00 per pound = $26,000	

Price variance = $1,400 F

Quantity variance = $2,000 U

In this case, the price variance and the quantity variance do not sum to the spending variance because the price variance is based on the quantity purchased whereas the quantity variance is based on the quantity used in production, and the two numbers differ.

*2,000 units × 3.0 pounds per unit = 6,000 pounds.

F = Favorable; U = Unfavorable.

EXHIBIT 11–11
Direct Materials Variances: The Equations-Based Approach (when the quantity of materials purchased does not equal the quantity used in production)

Materials Price Variance:

Materials price variance = $(AQ \times AP) - (AQ \times SP)$
Materials price variance = $AQ(AP - SP)$
Materials price variance = 7,000 pounds($3.80 per pound − $4.00 per pound)
Materials price variance = $1,400 F
where:
AQ = Actual quantity of pounds *purchased*
AP = Actual price per unit of the input
SP = Standard price per unit of the input

Materials Quantity Variance:

Materials quantity variance = $(AQ = SP) - (SQ \times SP)$
Materials quantity variance = $SP(AQ - SQ)$
Materials quantity variance = $4.00 per pound(6,500 pounds − 6,000 pounds)
Materials quantity variance = $2,000 U
where:
AQ = Actual quantity of pounds *used in production*
SQ = Standard quantity of pounds allowed for the actual output
SP = Standard price per unit of the input

using the equations shown in Exhibit 11–11. The approaches shown in *Exhibits 11–10 and 11–11 can always be used to compute direct materials variances.* However, *Exhibits 11–4 and 11–5 can only be used in the special case when the quantity of materials purchased equals the quantity of materials used.*

Standard Costs—Managerial Implications

Advantages of Standard Costs

Standard cost systems have a number of advantages.

1. Standard costs are a key element in a management by exception approach as defined in the previous chapter. If costs conform to the standards, managers can focus on other issues. When costs are significantly outside the standards, managers are alerted that problems may exist that require attention. This approach helps managers focus on important issues.
2. Standards that are viewed as reasonable by employees can promote economy and efficiency. They provide benchmarks that individuals can use to judge their own performance.
3. Standard costs can greatly simplify bookkeeping. Instead of recording actual costs for each job, the standard costs for direct materials, direct labor, and overhead can be charged to jobs.
4. Standard costs fit naturally in an integrated system of "responsibility accounting." The standards establish what costs should be, who should be responsible for them, and whether actual costs are under control.

Potential Problems with Standard Costs

The improper use of standard costs can present a number of potential problems.

1. Standard cost variance reports are usually prepared on a monthly basis and often are released days or even weeks after the end of the month. As a consequence, the

information in the reports may be so outdated that it is almost useless. Timely, frequent reports that are approximately correct are better than infrequent reports that are very precise but out of date by the time they are released. Some companies are now reporting variances and other key operating data daily or even more frequently.

2. If managers use variances only to assign blame and punish subordinates, morale may suffer. Furthermore, subordinates may be tempted to cover up unfavorable variances or take actions that are not in the best interests of the company to make sure the variances are favorable.
3. Labor-hour standards and efficiency variances make two important assumptions. First, they assume that the production process is labor-paced; if labor works faster, output will go up. However, output in many companies is not determined by how fast labor works; rather, it is determined by the processing speed of machines. Second, the computations assume that labor is a variable cost. However, direct labor may be essentially fixed. If labor is fixed, then an undue emphasis on labor efficiency variances creates pressure to build excess inventories.
4. In some cases, a "favorable" variance can be worse than an "unfavorable" variance. For example, McDonald's has a standard for the amount of hamburger meat that should be in a Big Mac. A "favorable" variance would mean that less meat was used than the standard specifies. The result is substandard Big Macs and possibly numerous dissatisfied customers.
5. Too much emphasis on meeting the standards may overshadow other important objectives such as maintaining and improving quality, on-time delivery, and customer satisfaction. This tendency can be reduced by using supplemental performance measures that focus on these other objectives.
6. Just meeting standards is not sufficient because companies need to continually improve to remain competitive. For this reason, some companies focus on the trends in the standard cost variances—aiming for continual improvement rather than just meeting the standards. In other companies, engineered standards are replaced either by a rolling average of actual costs, which is expected to decline, or by very challenging target costs.

In sum, managers should exercise considerable care when using a standard cost system. It is particularly important that managers go out of their way to focus on the positive, rather than just on the negative, and to be aware of possible unintended consequences.

Summary

A standard is a benchmark for measuring performance. Standards are set for both the quantity and the cost of inputs needed to manufacture goods or to provide services. Quantity standards indicate how much of an input, such as labor time or raw materials, should be used to make a product or provide a service. Cost standards indicate what the cost of the input should be.

When standards are compared to actual performance, the difference is referred to as a *variance.* Variances are computed and reported to management on a regular basis for both the quantity and the price elements of direct materials, direct labor, and variable overhead. Price variances are computed by taking the difference between actual and standard prices and multiplying the result by the amount of input purchased. Quantity variances are computed by taking the difference between the actual amount of the input used and the amount of input that is allowed for the actual output, and then multiplying the result by the standard price of the input.

Standard cost systems provide companies with a number of advantages, such as supporting the management by exception approach, simplifying bookkeeping, and providing a benchmark that employees can use to judge their own performance. However, critics of standard cost systems argue that they provide information that is outdated, they can motivate employees to make poor decisions in an effort to generate favorable variances, and they fail to adequately embrace the mindset of continuous process improvement.

Traditional standard cost variance reports are often supplemented with other performance measures to ensure that overemphasis on standard cost variances does not lead to problems in other critical areas such as product quality, inventory levels, and on-time delivery.

Review Problem: Standard Costs

Xavier Company produces a single product. Variable manufacturing overhead is applied to products on the basis of direct labor-hours. The standard costs for one unit of product are as follows:

Direct material: 6 ounces at $0.50 per ounce	$ 3.00
Direct labor: 0.6 hours at $30.00 per hour	18.00
Variable manufacturing overhead: 0.6 hours at $10.00 per hour	6.00
Total standard variable cost per unit	$27.00

During June, 2,000 units were produced. The costs associated with June's operations were as follows:

Material purchased: 18,000 ounces at $0.60 per ounce	$10,800
Material used in production: 14,000 ounces	—
Direct labor: 1,100 hours at $30.50 per hour	$33,550
Variable manufacturing overhead costs incurred	$12,980

Required:
Compute the direct materials, direct labor, and variable manufacturing overhead variances.

Solution to Review Problem

Direct Materials Variances

Actual Quantity of Input, at Actual Price (*AQ* × *AP*)	Actual Quantity of Input at Standard Price (*AQ* × *SP*)	Standard Quantity Allowed for Actual Output, at Standard Price (*SQ* × *SP*)
18,000 ounces × $0.60 per ounce = $10,800	18,000 ounces × $0.50 per ounce = $9,000	12,000 ounces* × $0.50 per ounce = $6,000

Price variance = $1,800 U

14,000 ounces × $0.50 per ounce = $7,000

Quantity variance = $1,000 U

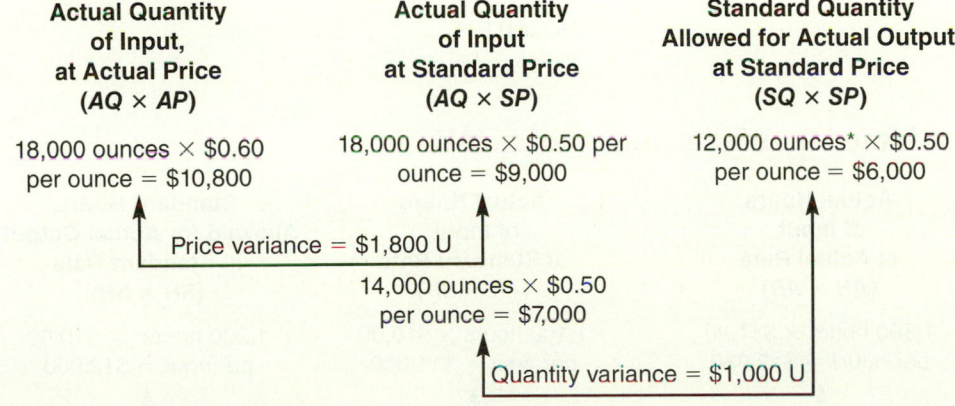

*2,000 units × 6 ounces per unit = 12,000 ounces.

Using the formulas in the chapter, the same variances would be computed as follows:

Materials price variance = (AQ × AP) − (AQ × SP)
= AQ(AP − SP)
= 18,000 ounces ($0.60 per ounce × $0.50 per ounce)
= $1,800 U

$$
\begin{aligned}
\text{Materials quantity variance} &= (\text{AQ} \times \text{SP}) - (\text{SQ} \times \text{SP}) \\
&= \text{SP}(\text{AQ} - \text{SQ}) \\
&= \$0.50 \text{ per ounce } (14{,}000 \text{ ounces} \times 12{,}000 \text{ ounces}) \\
&= \$1{,}000 \text{ U}
\end{aligned}
$$

Direct Labor Variances

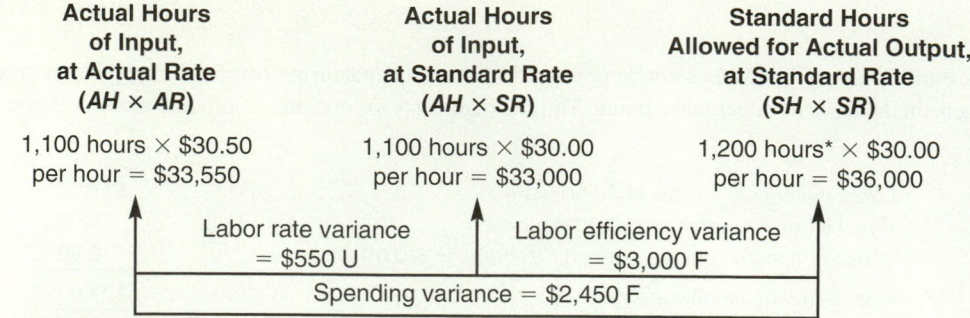

Actual Hours of Input, at Actual Rate (*AH* × *AR*)	Actual Hours of Input, at Standard Rate (*AH* × *SR*)	Standard Hours Allowed for Actual Output, at Standard Rate (*SH* × *SR*)
1,100 hours × $30.50 per hour = $33,550	1,100 hours × $30.00 per hour = $33,000	1,200 hours* × $30.00 per hour = $36,000

Labor rate variance = $550 U

Labor efficiency variance = $3,000 F

Spending variance = $2,450 F

*2,000 units × 0.6 hours per unit =1,200 hours.
F = Favorable; U = Unfavorable.

Using the formulas in the chapter, the same variances can be computed as follows:

$$
\begin{aligned}
\text{Labor rate variance} &= (AH \times AR) - (AH \times SR) \\
&= \text{AH}(\text{AR} - \text{SR}) \\
&= 1{,}100 \text{ hours } (\$30.50 \text{ per hour} - \$30.00 \text{ per hour}) \\
&= \$550 \text{ U}
\end{aligned}
$$

$$
\begin{aligned}
\text{Labor efficiency variance} &= (\text{AH} \times \text{SR}) - (SH \times SR) \\
&= \text{SR}(\text{AH} - \text{SH}) \\
&= \$30.00 \text{ per hour } (1{,}100 \text{ hours} - 1{,}200 \text{ hours}) \\
&= \$3{,}000 \text{ F}
\end{aligned}
$$

Variable Manufacturing Overhead Variances

Actual Hours of Input, at Actual Rate (*AH* × *AR*)	Actual Hours of Input, at Standard Rate (*AH* × *SR*)	Standard Hours Allowed for Actual Output, at Standard Rate (*SH* × *SR*)
1,100 hours × $11.80 per hour† = $12,980	1,100 hours × $10.00 per hour = $11,000	1,200 hours* × $10.00 per hour = $12,000

Variable overhead rate variance = $1,980 U

Variable overhead efficiency variance = $1,000 F

Spending variance = $980 U

*2,000 units × 0.6 hours per unit = 1,200 hours.
†$12,980 ÷ 1,100 hours = $11.80 per hour.
F = Favorable; U = Unfavorable.

Using the formulas in the chapter, the same variances can be computed as follows:

$$\text{Variable overhead rate variance} = (AH \times AR) - (AH \times SR)$$
$$= \text{AH(AR} - \text{SR)}$$
$$= 1{,}100 \text{ hours } (\$11.80 \text{ per hour} - \$10.00 \text{ per hour})$$
$$= \$\ 1{,}980 \text{ U}$$

$$\text{Variable overhead efficiency variance} = (AH \times SR) - (SH \times SR)$$
$$= \text{SR(AH} - \text{SH)}$$
$$= \$10.00 \text{ per hour } (1{,}100 \text{ hours} - 1{,}200 \text{ hours})$$
$$= \$1{,}000 \text{ F}$$

Glossary

Labor efficiency variance The difference between the actual hours taken to complete a task and the standard hours allowed for the actual output, multiplied by the standard hourly labor rate. (p. 486)

Labor rate variance The difference between the actual hourly labor rate and the standard rate, multiplied by the number of hours worked during the period. (p. 485)

Materials price variance The difference between the actual unit price paid for an item and the standard price, multiplied by the quantity purchased. (p. 482)

Materials quantity variance The difference between the actual quantity of materials used in production and the standard quantity allowed for the actual output, multiplied by the standard price per unit of materials. (p. 483)

Price variance A variance that is computed by taking the difference between the actual price and the standard price and multiplying the result by the actual quantity of the input. (p. 480)

Quantity variance A variance that is computed by taking the difference between the actual quantity of the input used and the amount of the input that should have been used for the actual level of output and multiplying the result by the standard price of the input. (p. 480)

Standard cost card A detailed listing of the standard amounts of inputs and their costs that are required to produce one unit of a specific product. (p. 478)

Standard cost per unit The standard quantity allowed of an input per unit of a specific product, multiplied by the standard price of the input. (p. 478)

Standard hours allowed The time that should have been taken to complete the period's output. It is computed by multiplying the actual number of units produced by the standard hours per unit. (p. 481)

Standard hours per unit The amount of direct labor time that should be required to complete a single unit of product, including allowances for breaks, machine downtime, cleanup, rejects, and other normal inefficiencies. (p. 477)

Standard price per unit The price that should be paid for an input. (p. 477)

Standard quantity allowed The amount of an input that should have been used to complete the period's actual output. It is computed by multiplying the actual number of units produced by the standard quantity per unit. (p. 481)

Standard quantity per unit The amount of an input that should be required to complete a single unit of product, including allowances for normal waste, spoilage, rejects, and other normal inefficiencies. (p. 477)

Standard rate per hour The labor rate that should be incurred per hour of labor time, including employment taxes and fringe benefits. (p. 478)

Variable overhead efficiency variance The difference between the actual level of activity (direct labor-hours, machine-hours, or some other base) and the standard activity allowed, multiplied by the variable part of the predetermined overhead rate. (p. 488)

Variable overhead rate variance The difference between the actual variable overhead cost incurred during a period and the standard cost that should have been incurred based on the actual activity of the period. (p. 488)

Questions

11–1 What is a quantity standard? What is a price standard?

11–2 Why are separate price and quantity variances computed?

11–3 Who is generally responsible for the materials price variance? The materials quantity variance? The labor efficiency variance?

11–4 The materials price variance can be computed at what two different points in time? Which point is better? Why?

11–5 If the materials price variance is favorable but the materials quantity variance is unfavorable, what might this indicate?

11–6 Should standards be used to identify who to blame for problems?

11–7 "Our workers are all under labor contracts; therefore, our labor rate variance is bound to be zero." Discuss.

11–8 What effect, if any, would you expect poor-quality materials to have on direct labor variances?

11–9 If variable manufacturing overhead is applied to production on the basis of direct labor-hours and the direct labor efficiency variance is unfavorable, will the variable overhead efficiency variance be favorable or unfavorable, or could it be either? Explain.

11–10 Why can undue emphasis on labor efficiency variances lead to excess work in process inventories?

Multiple-choice questions are available with Connect.

Applying Excel

LEARNING OBJECTIVES 11–1, 11–2, 11–3

The Excel worksheet form that follows is to be used to recreate the main example in the text related to the Colonial Pewter Company. Download the workbook containing this from Connect. *On the website you will also receive instructions about how to use this worksheet form.*

You should proceed to the requirements below only after completing your worksheet.

Required:

1. Check your worksheet by changing the direct materials standard quantity in cell B6 to 2.9 pounds, the direct labor quantity standard quantity in cell B7 to 0.6 hours, and the variable manufacturing overhead in cell B8 to 0.6 hours. The materials spending variance should now be $1,500 U, the labor spending variance should now be $3,720 F, and the variable overhead spending variance should now be $60 F. If you do not get these answers, find the errors in your worksheet and correct them.
   a. What is the materials quantity variance? Explain this variance.
   b. What is the labor rate variance? Explain this variance.

	A	B	C	D	E	F	G
1	**Chapter 11: Applying Excel**						
2							
3	**Data**						
4	***Exhibit 11-1: Standard Cost Card***						
5	*Inputs*	*Standard Quantity*		*Standard Price*			
6	Direct materials	3.0	pounds	$4.00	per pound		
7	Direct labor	0.50	hours	$22.00	per hour		
8	Variable manufacturing overhead	0.50	hours	$6.00	per hour		
9							
10	Actual results:						
11	Actual output	2,000	units				
12	Actual variable manufacturing overhead cost	$7,140					
13		*Actual Quantity*		*Actual price*			
14	Actual direct materials cost	6,500	pounds	$3.80	per pound		
15	Actual direct labor cost	1,050	hours	$21.60	per hour		
16							
17	*Enter a formula into each of the cells marked with a ? below*						
18	**Main Example: Chapter 11**						
19							
20	***Exhibit 11-4: Standard Cost Variance Analysis–Direct Materials***						
21	Standard Quantity Allowed for the Actual Output, at Standard Price	?	pounds ×	?	per pound =	?	
22	Actual Quantity of Input, at Standard Price	?	pounds ×	?	per pound =	?	
23	Actual Quantity of Input, at Actual Price	?	pounds ×	?	per pound =	?	
24	Direct materials variances:						
25	Materials quantity variance	?					
26	Materials price variance	?					
27	Materials spending variance	?					
28							
29	***Exhibit 11-6: Standard Cost Variance Analysis–Direct Labor***						
30	Standard Hours Allowed for the Actual Output, at Standard Rate	?	hours ×	?	per hour =	?	
31	Actual Hours of Input, at Standard Rate	?	hours ×	?	per hour =	?	
32	Actual Hours of Input, at Actual Rate	?	hours ×	?	per hour =	?	
33	Direct labor variances:						
34	Labor efficiency variance	?					
35	Labor rate variance	?					
36	Labor spending variance	?					
37							
38	***Exhibit 11-8: Standard Cost Variance Analysis–Variable Manufacturing Overhead***						
39	Standard Hours Allowed for the Actual Output, at Standard Rate	?	hours ×	?	per hour =	?	
40	Actual Hours of Input, at Standard Rate	?	hours ×	?	per hour =	?	
41	Actual Hours of Input, at Actual Rate	?	hours ×	?	per hour =	?	
42	Variable overhead variances:						
43	Variable overhead efficiency variance	?					
44	Variable overhead rate variance	?					
45	Variable overhead spending variance	?					
46							

Chapter 11 Form | Filled in Chapter 11 Form | Chapter 11 Formulas

2. Revise the data in your worksheet to reflect the results for the subsequent period:

Data **Exhibit 11–1: Standard Cost Card**		
Inputs	Standard Quantity	Standard Price
Direct materials	3.0 pounds	$4.00 per pound
Direct labor.	0.50 hours	$22.00 per hour
Variable manufacturing overhead	0.50 hours	$6.00 per hour
Actual results:		
Actual output	2,100 units	
Actual variable manufacturing overhead cost . . .	$5,100	
	Actual Quantity	Actual Price
Actual direct materials cost	6,350 pounds	$4.10 per pound
Actual direct labor cost	1,020 hours	$22.10 per hour

a. What is the materials quantity variance? What is the materials price variance?

b. What is the labor efficiency variance? What is the labor rate variance?

c. What is the variable overhead efficiency variance? What is the variable overhead rate variance?

The Foundational 15

Additional student resources are available with Connect.

LEARNING OBJECTIVES 11–1, 11–2, 11–3

Preble Company manufactures one product. Its variable manufacturing overhead is applied to production based on direct labor-hours and its standard cost card per unit is as follows:

Direct materials: 5 pounds at $8.00 per pound	$40.00
Direct labor: 2 hours at $14 per hour	28.00
Variable overhead: 2 hours at $5 per hour	10.00
Total standard cost per unit	$78.00

The planning budget for March was based on producing and selling 25,000 units. However, during March the company actually produced and sold 30,000 units and incurred the following costs:

a. Purchased 160,000 pounds of raw materials at a cost of $7.50 per pound. All of this material was used in production.
b. Direct laborers worked 55,000 hours at a rate of $15.00 per hour.
c. Total variable manufacturing overhead for the month was $280,500.

Required:

1. What raw materials cost would be included in the company's planning budget for March?
2. What raw materials cost would be included in the company's flexible budget for March?
3. What is the materials price variance for March?
4. What is the materials quantity variance for March?
5. If Preble had purchased 170,000 pounds of materials at $7.50 per pound and used 160,000 pounds in production, what would be the materials price variance for March?
6. If Preble had purchased 170,000 pounds of materials at $7.50 per pound and used 160,000 pounds in production, what would be the materials quantity variance for March?
7. What direct labor cost would be included in the company's planning budget for March?
8. What direct labor cost would be included in the company's flexible budget for March?
9. What is the labor rate variance for March?
10. What is the labor efficiency variance for March?
11. What is the labor spending variance for March?
12. What variable manufacturing overhead cost would be included in the company's planning budget for March?
13. What variable manufacturing overhead cost would be included in the company's flexible budget for March?
14. What is the variable overhead rate variance for March?
15. What is the variable overhead efficiency variance for March?

Exercises

Additional student resources are available with Connect.

EXERCISE 11–1 Direct Materials Variances [LO11–1]

Bandar Industries Berhad of Malaysia manufactures sporting equipment. One of the company's products, a football helmet for the North American market, requires a special plastic. During the quarter ending June 30, the company manufactured 35,000 helmets, using 22,500 kilograms of plastic. The plastic cost the company $171,000.

According to the standard cost card, each helmet should require 0.6 kilograms of plastic, at a cost of $8 per kilogram.

Required:

1. According to the standards, what cost for plastic should have been incurred to make 35,000 helmets? How much greater or less is this than the cost that was incurred?

2. Break down the difference computed in requirement 1 into a materials price variance and a materials quantity variance.

EXERCISE 11–2 Direct Labor Variances [LO11–2]

SkyChefs, Inc., prepares in-flight meals for a number of major airlines. One of the company's products is grilled salmon in dill sauce with baby new potatoes and spring vegetables. During the most recent week, the company prepared 4,000 of these meals using 960 direct labor-hours. The company paid these direct labor workers a total of $9,600 for this work, or $10.00 per hour.

According to the standard cost card for this meal, it should require 0.25 direct labor-hours at a cost of $9.75 per hour.

Required:

1. According to the standards, what direct labor cost should have been incurred to prepare 4,000 meals? How much does this differ from the actual direct labor cost?
2. Break down the difference computed in requirement 1 into a labor rate variance and a labor efficiency variance.

EXERCISE 11–3 Variable Overhead Variances [LO11–3]

Logistics Solutions provides order fulfillment services for dot.com merchants. The company maintains warehouses that stock items carried by its dot.com clients. When a client receives an order from a customer, the order is forwarded to Logistics Solutions, which pulls the item from storage, packs it, and ships it to the customer. The company uses a predetermined variable overhead rate based on direct labor-hours.

In the most recent month, 120,000 items were shipped to customers using 2,300 direct labor-hours. The company incurred a total of $7,360 in variable overhead costs.

According to the company's standards, 0.02 direct labor-hours are required to fulfill an order for one item and the variable overhead rate is $3.25 per direct labor-hour.

Required:

1. According to the standards, what variable overhead cost should have been incurred to fill the orders for the 120,000 items? How much does this differ from the actual variable overhead cost?
2. Break down the difference computed in requirement 1 into a variable overhead rate variance and a variable overhead efficiency variance.

EXERCISE 11–4 Direct Labor and Variable Manufacturing Overhead Variances [LO11–2, LO11–3]

Erie Company manufactures a small mp3 player called the Jogging Mate. The company uses standards to control its costs. The labor standards that have been set for one Jogging Mate mp3 player are as follows:

Standard Hours	Standard Rate per Hour	Standard Cost
18 minutes	$12.00	$3.60

During August, 5,750 hours of direct labor time were needed to make 20,000 units of the Jogging Mate. The direct labor cost totaled $73,600 for the month.

Required:

1. According to the standards, what direct labor cost should have been incurred to make 20,000 units of the Jogging Mate? By how much does this differ from the cost that was incurred?
2. Break down the difference in cost from requirement 1 into a labor rate variance and a labor efficiency variance.
3. The budgeted variable manufacturing overhead rate is $4 per direct labor-hour. During August, the company incurred $21,850 in variable manufacturing overhead cost. Compute the variable overhead rate and efficiency variances for the month.

EXERCISE 11–5 Working Backwards from Labor Variances [LO11–2]

The auto repair shop of Quality Motor Company uses standards to control the labor time and labor cost in the shop. The standard labor cost for a motor tune-up is given below:

Job	Standard Hours	Standard Rate	Standard Cost
Motor tune-up	2.5	$9.00	$22.50

The record showing the time spent in the shop last week on motor tune-ups has been misplaced. However, the shop supervisor recalls that 50 tune-ups were completed during the week, and the controller recalls the following variance data relating to tune-ups:

Labor rate variance	$87 F
Labor spending variance	$93 U

Required:

1. Determine the number of actual labor-hours spent on tune-ups during the week.
2. Determine the actual hourly rate of pay for tune-ups last week.

(*Hint:* A useful way to proceed would be to work from known to unknown data either by using the variance formulas in Exhibit 11–7 or by using the columnar format shown in Exhibit 11–6.)

EXERCISE 11–6 Direct Materials and Direct Labor Variances [LO11–1, LO11–2]

Huron Company produces a commercial cleaning compound known as Zoom. The direct materials and direct labor standards for one unit of Zoom are given below:

	Standard Quantity or Hours	Standard Price or Rate	Standard Cost
Direct materials	4.6 pounds	$2.50 per pound	$11.50
Direct labor	0.2 hours	$12.00 per hour	$2.40

During the most recent month, the following activity was recorded:

a. Twenty thousand pounds of material were purchased at a cost of $2.35 per pound.
b. All of the material purchased was used to produce 4,000 units of Zoom.
c. 750 hours of direct labor time were recorded at a total labor cost of $10,425.

Required:

1. Compute the materials price and quantity variances for the month.
2. Compute the labor rate and efficiency variances for the month.

EXERCISE 11–7 Direct Materials Variances [LO11–1]

Refer to the data in Exercise 11–6. Assume that instead of producing 4,000 units during the month, the company produced only 3,000 units, using 14,750 pounds of material. (The rest of the material purchased remained in raw materials inventory.)

Required:

Compute the materials price and quantity variances for the month.

EXERCISE 11–8 Direct Materials and Direct Labor Variances [LO11–1, LO11–2]

Dawson Toys, Ltd., produces a toy called the Maze. The company has recently established a standard cost system to help control costs and has established the following standards for the Maze toy:

Direct materials: 6 microns per toy at $0.50 per micron
Direct labor: 1.3 hours per toy at $8 per hour

During July, the company produced 3,000 Maze toys. Production data for the month on the toy follow:

Direct materials: 25,000 microns were purchased at a cost of $0.48 per micron. 5,000 of these microns were still in inventory at the end of the month.

Direct labor: 4,000 direct labor-hours were worked at a cost of $36,000.

Required:

1. Compute the following variances for July:
   a. The materials price and quantity variances.
   b. The labor rate and efficiency variances.
2. Prepare a brief explanation of the possible causes of each variance.

Problems

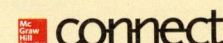

PROBLEM 11–9 Comprehensive Variance Analysis [LO11–1, LO11–2, LO11–3]

Marvel Parts, Inc., manufactures auto accessories. One of the company's products is a set of seat covers that can be adjusted to fit nearly any small car. The company has a standard cost system in use for all of its products. According to the standards that have been set for the seat covers, the factory should work 2,850 hours each month to produce 1,900 sets of covers. The standard costs associated with this level of production are:

	Total	Per Set of Covers
Direct materials	$42,560	$22.40
Direct labor	$17,100	9.00
Variable manufacturing overhead (based on direct labor-hours)	$6,840	3.60
		$35.00

During August, the factory worked only 2,800 direct labor-hours and produced 2,000 sets of covers. The following actual costs were recorded during the month:

	Total	Per Set of Covers
Direct materials (12,000 yards)	$45,600	$22.80
Direct labor	$18,200	9.10
Variable manufacturing overhead	$7,000	3.50
		$35.40

At standard, each set of covers should require 5.6 yards of material. All of the materials purchased during the month were used in production.

Required:

Compute the following variances for August:

1. The materials price and quantity variances.
2. The labor rate and efficiency variances.
3. The variable overhead rate and efficiency variances.

PROBLEM 11–10 Multiple Products, Materials, and Processes [LO11–1, LO11–2]

Mickley Corporation produces two products, Alpha6s and Zeta7s, which pass through two operations, Sintering and Finishing. Each of the products uses two raw materials, X442 and Y661. The company uses a standard cost system, with the following standards for each product (on a per unit basis):

	Raw Material		Standard Labor Time	
Product	X442	Y661	Sintering	Finishing
Alpha6	1.8 kilos	2.0 liters	0.20 hours	0.80 hours
Zeta7	3.0 kilos	4.5 liters	0.35 hours	0.90 hours

Information relating to materials purchased and materials used in production during May follows:

Material	Purchases	Purchase Cost	Standard Price	Used in Production
X442	14,500 kilos	$52,200	$3.50 per kilo	8,500 kilos
Y661.	15,500 liters	$20,925	$1.40 per liter	13,000 liters

The following additional information is available:

a. The company recognizes price variances when materials are purchased.
b. The standard labor rate is $19.80 per hour in Sintering and $19.20 per hour in Finishing.
c. During May, 1,200 direct labor-hours were worked in Sintering at a total labor cost of $27,000, and 2,850 direct labor-hours were worked in Finishing at a total labor cost of $59,850.
d. Production during May was 1,500 Alpha6s and 2,000 Zeta7s.

Required:

1. Prepare a standard cost card for each product, showing the standard cost of direct materials and direct labor.
2. Compute the materials price and quantity variances for each material.
3. Compute the labor rate and efficiency variances for each operation.

PROBLEM 11–11 Direct Materials and Direct Labor Variances; Computations from Incomplete Data [LO11–1, LO11–2]

Sharp Company manufactures a product for which the following standards have been set:

	Standard Quantity or Hours	Standard Price or Rate	Standard Cost
Direct materials	3 feet	$5 per foot	$15
Direct labor.	? hours	? per hour	?

During March, the company purchased direct materials at a cost of $55,650, all of which were used in the production of 3,200 units of product. In addition, 4,900 hours of direct labor time were worked on the product during the month. The cost of this labor time was $36,750. The following variances have been computed for the month:

Materials quantity variance.	$4,500 U
Labor spending variance	$1,650 F
Labor efficiency variance	$800 U

Required:

1. For direct materials:
   a. Compute the actual cost per foot for materials for March.
   b. Compute the price variance and the spending variance.
2. For direct labor:
   a. Compute the standard direct labor rate per hour.
   b. Compute the standard hours allowed for the month's production.
   c. Compute the standard hours allowed per unit of product.

(*Hint:* In completing the problem, it may be helpful to move from known to unknown data either by using the columnar format shown in Exhibits 11–4 and 11–6 or by using the variance formulas in Exhibits 11–5 and 11–7.)

PROBLEM 11–12 Variance Analysis in a Hospital [LO11–1, LO11–2, LO11–3]

John Fleming, chief administrator for Valley View Hospital, is concerned about the costs for tests in the hospital's lab. Charges for lab tests are consistently higher at Valley View than at other hospitals and have resulted in many complaints. Also, because of strict regulations on amounts reimbursed for lab tests, payments received from insurance companies and governmental units have not been high enough to cover lab costs.

Mr. Fleming has asked you to evaluate costs in the hospital's lab for the past month. The following information is available:

a. Two types of tests are performed in the lab—blood tests and smears. During the past month, 1,800 blood tests and 2,400 smears were performed in the lab.
b. Small glass plates are used in both types of tests. During the past month, the hospital purchased 12,000 plates at a cost of $28,200. 1,500 of these plates were unused at the end of the month; no plates were on hand at the beginning of the month.
c. During the past month, 1,150 hours of labor time were recorded in the lab at a cost of $13,800.
d. The lab's variable overhead cost last month totaled $7,820.

Valley View Hospital has never used standard costs. By searching industry literature, however, you have determined the following nationwide averages for hospital labs:

Plates: Two plates are required per lab test. These plates cost $2.50 each and are disposed of after the test is completed.

Labor: Each blood test should require 0.3 hours to complete, and each smear should require 0.15 hours to complete. The average cost of this lab time is $14 per hour.

Overhead: Overhead cost is based on direct labor-hours. The average rate for variable overhead is $6 per hour.

Required:

1. Compute a materials price variance for the plates purchased last month and a materials quantity variance for the plates used last month.
2. For labor cost in the lab:
   a. Compute a labor rate variance and a labor efficiency variance.
   b. In most hospitals, one-half of the workers in the lab are senior technicians and one-half are assistants. In an effort to reduce costs, Valley View Hospital employs only one-fourth senior technicians and three-fourths assistants. Would you recommend that this policy be continued? Explain.
3. Compute the variable overhead rate and efficiency variances. Is there any relation between the variable overhead efficiency variance and the labor efficiency variance? Explain.

PROBLEM 11–13 Basic Variance Analysis; the Impact of Variances on Unit Costs [LO11–1, LO11–2, LO11–3]

Koontz Company manufactures a number of products. The standards relating to one of these products are shown below, along with actual cost data for May.

	Standard Cost per Unit		Actual Cost per Unit
Direct materials:			
Standard: 1.80 feet at $3.00 per foot	$ 5.40		
Actual: 1.80 feet at $3.30 per foot			$ 5.94
Direct labor:			
Standard: 0.90 hours at $18.00 per hour	16.20		
Actual: 0.92 hours at $17.50 per hour			16.10
Variable overhead:			
Standard: 0.90 hours at $5.00 per hour	4.50		
Actual: 0.92 hours at $4.50 per hour			4.14
Total cost per unit	$26.10		$26.18
Excess of actual cost over standard cost per unit		$0.08	

The production superintendent was pleased when he saw this report and commented: "This $0.08 excess cost is well within the 2 percent limit management has set for acceptable variances. It's obvious that there's not much to worry about with this product."

Actual production for the month was 12,000 units. Variable overhead cost is assigned to products on the basis of direct labor-hours. There were no beginning or ending inventories of materials.

Required:

1. Compute the following variances for May:
   a. Materials price and quantity variances.
   b. Labor rate and efficiency variances.
   c. Variable overhead rate and efficiency variances.
2. How much of the $0.08 excess unit cost is traceable to each of the variances computed in requirement 1?
3. How much of the $0.08 excess unit cost is traceable to apparent inefficient use of labor time?
4. Do you agree that the excess unit cost is not of concern?

PROBLEM 11–14 Basic Variance Analysis [LO11–1, LO11–2, LO11–3]

Becton Labs, Inc., produces various chemical compounds for industrial use. One compound, called Fludex, is prepared using an elaborate distilling process. The company has developed standard costs for one unit of Fludex, as follows:

	Standard Quality	Standard Price or Rate	Standard Cost
Direct materials	2.5 ounces	$20.00 per ounce	$50.00
Direct labor............................	1.4 hours	$12.50 per hour	17.50
Variable manufacturing overhead	1.4 hours	$3.50 per hour	4.90
			$72.40

During November, the following activity was recorded related to the production of Fludex:

a. Materials purchased, 12,000 ounces at a cost of $225,000.
b. There was no beginning inventory of materials; however, at the end of the month, 2,500 ounces of material remained in ending inventory.
c. The company employs 35 lab technicians to work on the production of Fludex. During November, they worked an average of 160 hours at an average rate of $12 per hour.
d. Variable manufacturing overhead is assigned to Fludex on the basis of direct labor-hours. Variable manufacturing overhead costs during November totaled $18,200.
e. During November, 3,750 good units of Fludex were produced.

Required:

1. For direct materials:
   a. Compute the price and quantity variances.
   b. The materials were purchased from a new supplier who is anxious to enter into a long-term purchase contract. Would you recommend that the company sign the contract? Explain.
2. For direct labor:
   a. Compute the rate and efficiency variances.
   b. In the past, the 35 technicians employed in the production of Fludex consisted of 20 senior technicians and 15 assistants. During November, the company experimented with fewer senior technicians and more assistants in order to save costs. Would you recommend that the new labor mix be continued? Explain.
3. Compute the variable overhead rate and efficiency variances. What relation can you see between this efficiency variance and the labor efficiency variance?

PROBLEM 11–15 Comprehensive Variance Analysis [LO11–1, LO11–2, LO11–3]

Miller Toy Company manufactures a plastic swimming pool at its Westwood Plant. The plant has been experiencing problems as shown by its June contribution format income statement below:

	Budgeted	Actual
Sales (15,000 pools)	$450,000	$450,000
Variable expenses:		
Variable cost of goods sold*	180,000	196,290
Variable selling expenses	20,000	20,000
Total variable expenses	200,000	216,290
Contribution margin	250,000	233,710
Fixed expenses:		
Manufacturing overhead	130,000	130,000
Selling and administrative	84,000	84,000
Total fixed expenses	214,000	214,000
Net operating income	$ 36,000	$ 19,710

*The revenue variance is labeled favorable (unfavorable) when the revenue in the flexible budget is greater than (less than) the planning budget. The expense variances are labeled favorable (unfavorable) when the expense in the flexible budget is less than (greater than) the planning budget.

Janet Dunn, who has just been appointed general manager of the Westwood Plant, has been given instructions to "get things under control." Upon reviewing the plant's income statement, Ms. Dunn has concluded that the major problem lies in the variable cost of goods sold. She has been provided with the following standard cost per swimming pool:

	Standard Quantity or Hours	Standard Price or Rate	Standard Cost
Direct materials	3.0 pounds	$2.00 per pound	$ 6.00
Direct labor	0.8 hours	$6.00 per hour	4.80
Variable manufacturing overhead	0.4 hours*	$3.00 per hour	1.20
Total standard cost			$12.00

*The revenue variance is labeled favorable (unfavorable) when the actual revenue is greater than (less than) the flexible budget. The expense variances are labeled favorable (unfavorable) when the actual expense is less than (greater than) the flexible budget.

During June the plant produced 15,000 pools and incurred the following costs:

a. Purchased 60,000 pounds of materials at a cost of $1.95 per pound.
b. Used 49,200 pounds of materials in production. (Finished goods and work in process inventories are insignificant and can be ignored.)
c. Worked 11,800 direct labor-hours at a cost of $7.00 per hour.
d. Incurred variable manufacturing overhead cost totaling $18,290 for the month. A total of 5,900 machine-hours was recorded.

It is the company's policy to close all variances to cost of goods sold on a monthly basis.

Required:

1. Compute the following variances for June:
   a. Materials price and quantity variances.
   b. Labor rate and efficiency variances.
   c. Variable overhead rate and efficiency variances.
2. Summarize the variances that you computed in requirement 1 by showing the net overall favorable or unfavorable variance for the month. What impact did this figure have on the company's income statement? Show computations.
3. Pick out the two most significant variances that you computed in requirement 1. Explain to Ms. Dunn possible causes of these variances.

PROBLEM 11–16 Comprehensive Variance Analysis [LO11–1, LO11–2, LO11–3]

Highland Company produces a lightweight backpack that is popular with college students. Standard variable costs relating to a single backpack are given below:

	Standard Quantity or Hours	Standard Price or Rate	Standard Cost
Direct materials.	?	$6 per yard	$?
Direct labor	?	?	?
Variable manufacturing overhead	?	$3 per direct labor-hour	?
Total standard cost.			$?

Overhead is applied to production on the basis of direct labor-hours. During March, 1,000 backpacks were manufactured and sold. Selected information relating to the month's production is given below:

	Materials Used	Direct Labor	Variable Manufacturing Overhead
Total standard cost allowed*	$16,800	$10,500	$4,200
Actual costs incurred	$15,000	?	$3,600
Materials price variance	?		
Materials quantity variance	$1,200 U		
Labor rate variance		?	
Labor efficiency variance		?	
Variable overhead rate variance			?
Variable overhead efficiency variance			?

*For the month's production.

The following additional information is available for March's production:

Actual direct labor-hours.	1,500
Difference between standard and actual cost per backpack produced during March	$0.15 F

Required:

1. What is the standard cost of a single backpack?
2. What was the actual cost per backpack produced during March?
3. How many yards of material are required at standard per backpack?
4. What was the materials price variance for March if there were no beginning or ending inventories of materials?
5. What is the standard direct labor rate per hour?
6. What was the labor rate variance for March? The labor efficiency variance?
7. What was the variable overhead rate variance for March? The variable overhead efficiency variance?
8. Prepare a standard cost card for one backpack.

Cases

CASE 11–17 Working Backwards from Variance Data [LO11–1, LO11–2, LO11–3]

You have recently accepted a position with Vitex, Inc., the manufacturer of a popular consumer product. During your first week on the job, the vice president has been favorably impressed with your work. She has been so impressed, in fact, that yesterday she called you into her office and asked you to attend the executive committee meeting this morning for the purpose of leading a discussion on the variances reported for last period. Anxious to favorably impress the executive committee, you took the variances and supporting data home last night to study.

On your way to work this morning, the papers were laying on the seat of your new, red convertible. As you were crossing a bridge on the highway, a sudden gust of wind caught the papers and blew them over the edge of the bridge and into the stream below. You managed to retrieve only one page, which contains the following information:

Standard Cost Card

Direct materials, 6 pounds at $3 per pound	$18.00
Direct labor, 0.8 direct labor-hours at $15 per direct labor-hour	$12.00
Variable manufacturing overhead, 0.8 direct labor-hours at $3 per direct labor-hour	$2.40

	Total Standard Cost*	Variances Reported: Price or Rate	Variances Reported: Quantity or Efficiency
Direct materials	$405,000	$6,900 F	$9,000 U
Direct labor	$270,000	$14,550 U	$21,000 U
Variable manufacturing overhead	$54,000	$1,300 F	$?† U

*Applied to Work in Process during the period.
†Entry obliterated.

You recall that manufacturing overhead cost is applied to production on the basis of direct labor-hours and that all of the materials purchased during the period were used in production. Work in process inventories are insignificant and can be ignored.

It is now 8:30 A.M. The executive committee meeting starts in just one hour; you realize that to avoid looking like a bungling fool you must somehow generate the necessary "backup" data for the variances before the meeting begins. Without backup data it will be impossible to lead the discussion or answer any questions.

Required:

1. How many units were produced last period?
2. How many pounds of direct material were purchased and used in production?
3. What was the actual cost per pound of material?
4. How many actual direct labor-hours were worked during the period?
5. What was the actual rate paid per direct labor-hour?
6. How much actual variable manufacturing overhead cost was incurred during the period?

Appendix 11A: Predetermined Overhead Rates and Overhead Analysis in a Standard Costing System

LEARNING OBJECTIVE 11–4
Compute and interpret the fixed overhead budget and volume variances.

In this appendix, we will investigate how the predetermined overhead rates that we discussed in the job-order costing chapter earlier in the book can be used in a standard costing system. Throughout this appendix, we assume that an absorption costing system is used in which *all* manufacturing costs—both fixed and variable—are included in product costs.

Predetermined Overhead Rates

The data in Exhibit 11A–1 pertain to MicroDrive Corporation, a company that produces miniature electric motors. Note that the company budgeted for 50,000 machine-hours based on production of 25,000 motors. At this level of activity, the budgeted variable manufacturing overhead was $75,000 and the budgeted fixed manufacturing overhead was $300,000.

Recall from the job-order costing chapter that the following formula is used to set the predetermined overhead rate at the beginning of the period:

$$\text{Predetermined overhead rate} = \frac{\text{Estimated total manufacturing overhead cost}}{\text{Estimated total amount of the allocation base}}$$

The estimated total amount of the allocation base in the formula for the predetermined overhead rate is called the **denominator activity**.

As discussed in the job-order costing chapter, once the predetermined overhead rate has been determined, it remains unchanged throughout the period, even if the actual level of activity differs from what was estimated. Consequently, the amount of overhead applied to each unit of product is the same regardless of when it is produced during the period.

EXHIBIT 11A–1
MicroDrive Corporation Data

Budgeted production	25,000 motors	
Standard machine-hours per motor		2 machine-hours per motor
Budgeted machine-hours (2 machine-hours per motor 3 25,000 motors)	50,000 machine-hours	
Actual production	20,000 motors	
Standard machine-hours allowed for the actual production (2 machine-hours per motor × 20,000 motors)	40,000 machine-hours	
Actual machine-hours	42,000 machine-hours	
Budgeted variable manufacturing overhead	$75,000	
Budgeted fixed manufacturing overhead	$300,000	
Total budgeted manufacturing overhead	$375,000	
Actual variable manufacturing overhead	$71,400	
Actual fixed manufacturing overhead	$308,000	
Total actual manufacturing overhead	$379,400	

MicroDrive Corporation uses budgeted machine-hours as its denominator activity in the predetermined overhead rate. Consequently, the company's predetermined overhead rate would be computed as follows:

$$\text{Predetermined overhead rate} = \frac{\$375{,}000}{50{,}000 \text{ MHs}} = \$7.50 \text{ per MH}$$

This predetermined overhead rate can be broken down into its variable and fixed components as follows:

$$\text{Variable component of the predetermined overhead rate} = \frac{\$75{,}000}{50{,}000 \text{ MHs}} = \$1.50 \text{ per MH}$$

$$\text{Fixed component of the predetermined overhead rate} = \frac{\$300{,}000}{50{,}000 \text{ MHs}} = \$6.00 \text{ per MH}$$

For every standard machine-hour recorded, work in process is charged with $7.50 of manufacturing overhead, of which $1.50 represents variable manufacturing overhead and $6.00 represents fixed manufacturing overhead. In total, MicroDrive Corporation would apply $300,000 of overhead to work in process as shown below:

$$\text{Overhead applied} = \frac{\text{Predetermined}}{\text{overhead rate}} \times \frac{\text{Standard hours allowed}}{\text{for the actual output}}$$
$$= \$7.50 \text{ per machine–hour} \times 40{,}000 \text{ machine–hours}$$
$$= \$300{,}000$$

Overhead Application in a Standard Cost System

To understand fixed overhead variances, we first have to understand how overhead is applied to work in process in a standard cost system. Recall that in the job-order costing chapter we applied overhead to work in process on the basis of the actual level of activity. This procedure was correct because at the time we were dealing with a normal cost system.[1] However, we are now dealing with a standard cost system. In such a system, overhead is applied to work in process on the basis of the *standard hours allowed for the actual output of the period* rather than on the basis of the actual number of hours worked. Exhibit 11A–2 illustrates this point. In a standard cost system, every unit of a particular product is charged with the same amount of overhead cost, regardless of how much time the unit actually requires for processing.

Normal Cost System		Standard Cost System	
Manufacturing Overhead		**Manufacturing Overhead**	
Actual overhead costs incurred.	Applied overhead costs: Actual hours × Predetermined overhead rate.	Actual overhead costs incurred.	Applied overhead costs: Standard hours allowed for actual output × Predetermined overhead rate.
Underapplied or overapplied overhead		Underapplied or overapplied overhead	

EXHIBIT 11A–2
Applied Overhead Costs: Normal Cost System versus Standard Cost System

Budget Variance

Two fixed manufacturing overhead variances are computed in a standard costing system—a *budget variance* and a *volume variance.* These variances are computed in Exhibit 11A–3. The **budget variance** is simply the difference between the actual fixed manufacturing overhead and the budgeted fixed manufacturing overhead for the period. The formula is:

$$\text{Budget variance} = \text{Actual fixed overhead} + \text{Budgeted fixed overhead}$$

If the actual fixed overhead cost exceeds the budgeted fixed overhead cost, the budget variance is labeled unfavorable. If the actual fixed overhead cost is less than the budgeted fixed overhead cost, the budget variance is labeled favorable.

Applying the formula to the MicroDrive Corporation data, the budget variance is computed as follows:

$$\text{Budget variance} = \$308{,}000 - \$300{,}000 = \$8{,}000 \text{ U}$$

According to the budget, the fixed manufacturing overhead should have been $300,000, but it was actually $308,000. Because the actual cost exceeds the budget by $8,000, the

[1] Normal cost systems are discussed in the job-order costing chapter.

EXHIBIT 11A–3
Fixed Overhead Variances

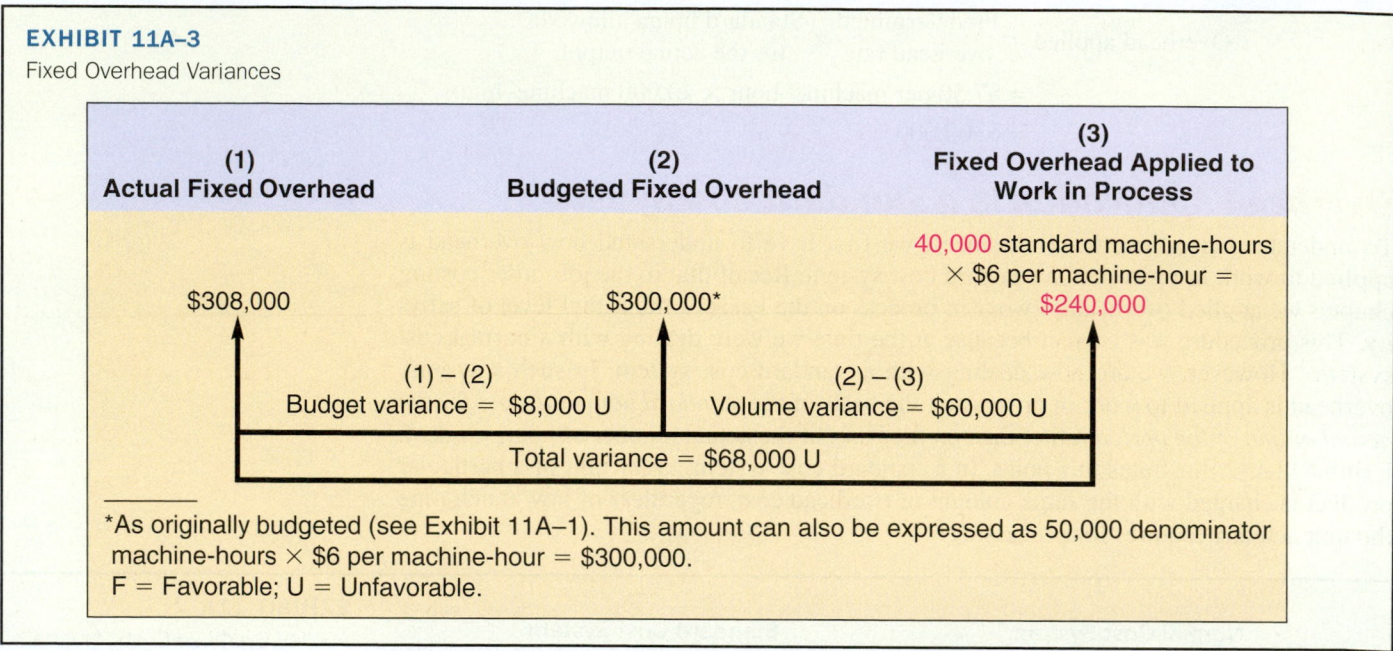

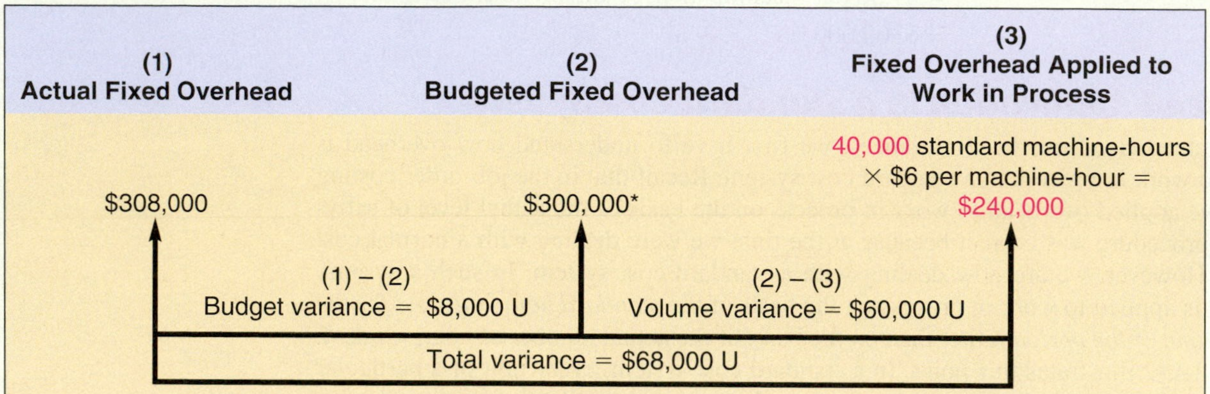

*As originally budgeted (see Exhibit 11A–1). This amount can also be expressed as 50,000 denominator machine-hours × $6 per machine-hour = $300,000.
F = Favorable; U = Unfavorable.

variance is labeled as unfavorable; however, this label does not automatically signal ineffective managerial performance. For example, this variance may be the result of waste and inefficiency, or it may be due to an unforeseen yet prudent investment in fixed overhead resources that improves product quality or manufacturing cycle efficiency.

Volume Variance

The **volume variance** is defined by the following formula:

$$\text{Volume variance} = \begin{matrix}\text{Budgeted fixed}\\ \text{overhead}\end{matrix} - \begin{matrix}\text{Fixed overhead applied}\\ \text{to work in process}\end{matrix}$$

When the budgeted fixed manufacturing overhead exceeds the fixed manufacturing overhead applied to work in process, the volume variance is labeled as unfavorable. When the budgeted fixed manufacturing overhead is less than the fixed manufacturing overhead applied to work in process, the volume variance is labeled as favorable. As we shall see, caution is advised when interpreting this variance.

To understand the volume variance, we need to understand how fixed manufacturing overhead is applied to work in process in a standard costing system. As discussed earlier, fixed manufacturing overhead is applied to work in process on the basis of the standard hours allowed for the actual output of the period. In the case of MicroDrive Corporation, the company produced 20,000 motors and the standard for each motor is 2 machine-hours. Therefore, the standard hours allowed for the actual output is 40,000 machine-hours (= 20,000 motors × 2 machine-hours). As shown in Exhibit 11A–3, the predetermined fixed manufacturing overhead rate of $6.00 per machine-hour is multiplied by the 40,000 standard machine-hours allowed for the actual output to arrive at $240,000 of fixed manufacturing overhead applied to work in process. Another way to think of this is that the standard for each motor is 2 machine-hours. Because the predetermined fixed manufacturing overhead rate is $6.00 per machine-hour, each motor is assigned $12.00 (= 2 machine-hours × $6.00 per machine-hour) of fixed manufacturing overhead.

Consequently, a total of $240,000 of fixed manufacturing overhead is applied to the 20,000 motors that are actually produced. Under either explanation, the volume variance according to the formula is:

$$\text{Volume variance} = \$300{,}000 - \$240{,}000 = \$60{,}000\ \text{U}$$

The key to interpreting the volume variance is to understand that it depends on the difference between the hours used in the denominator to compute the predetermined overhead rate and the standard hours allowed for the actual output of the period. While it is not obvious, the volume variance can also be computed using the following formula:

$$\begin{matrix}\text{Volume} \\ \text{variance}\end{matrix} = \begin{matrix}\text{Fixed component of the} \\ \text{predetermined overhead rate}\end{matrix} \times \left(\begin{matrix}\text{Denominator} \\ \text{hours}\end{matrix} - \begin{matrix}\text{Standard hours allowed} \\ \text{for the actual output}\end{matrix}\right)$$

In the case of MicroDrive Corporation, the volume variance can be computed using this formula as follows:

$$\begin{aligned}\text{Volume variance} &= \begin{matrix}\$6.00\ \text{per} \\ \text{machine-hour}\end{matrix} \times \left(\begin{matrix}50{,}000 \\ \text{machine-hours}\end{matrix} - \begin{matrix}40{,}000 \\ \text{machine-hours}\end{matrix}\right) \\ &= \$6.00\ \text{per machine-hour} \times (10{,}000\ \text{machine-hours}) \\ &= \$60{,}000\ \text{U}\end{aligned}$$

Note that this agrees with the volume variance computed using the earlier formula.

Focusing on this new formula, if the denominator hours exceed the standard hours allowed for the actual output, the volume variance is unfavorable. If the denominator hours are less than the standard hours allowed for the actual output, the volume variance is favorable. Stated differently, the volume variance is unfavorable if the actual level of activity is less than expected. The volume variance is favorable if the actual level of activity is greater than expected. It is important to note that the volume variance does not measure overspending or underspending. A company should incur the same dollar amount of fixed overhead cost regardless of whether the period's activity was above or below the planned (denominator) level.

The volume variance is often viewed as a measure of the utilization of facilities. If the standard hours allowed for the actual output are greater than (less than) the denominator hours, it signals efficient (inefficient) usage of facilities. However, other measures of utilization—such as the percentage of capacity utilized—are easier to compute and understand. Perhaps a better interpretation of the volume variance is that it is the error that occurs when the level of activity is incorrectly estimated and the costing system assumes fixed costs behave as if they are variable. This interpretation may be clearer in the next section that graphically analyzes the fixed manufacturing overhead variances.

Graphic Analysis of Fixed Overhead Variances

Exhibit 11A–4 shows a graphic analysis that offers insights into the fixed overhead budget and volume variances. As shown in the graph, fixed overhead cost is applied to work in process at the predetermined rate of $6.00 for each standard hour of activity. (The applied-cost line is the upward-sloping line on the graph.) Because a denominator level of 50,000 machine-hours was used in computing the $6.00 rate, the applied-cost line crosses the budget-cost line at exactly 50,000 machine-hours. If the denominator hours and the standard hours allowed for the actual output are the same, there is no volume variance. It is only when the standard hours differ from the denominator hours that a volume variance arises.

EXHIBIT 11A–4
Graphic Analysis of Fixed Overhead Variances

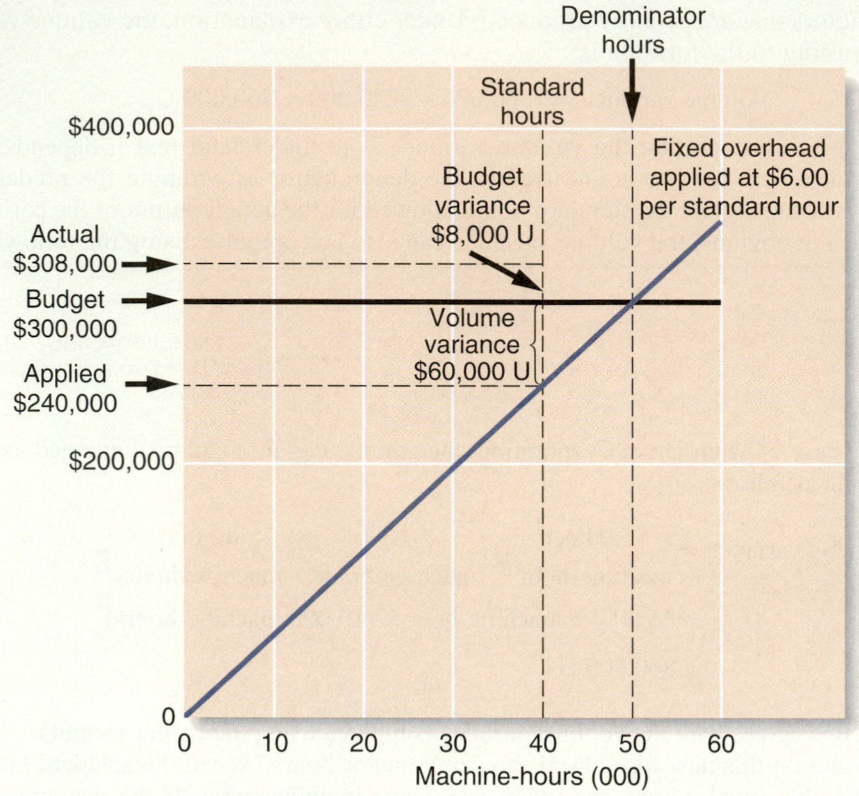

In MicroDrive's case, the standard hours allowed for the actual output (40,000 hours) are less than the denominator hours (50,000 hours). The result is an unfavorable volume variance because less cost was applied to production than was originally budgeted. If the situation had been reversed and the standard hours allowed for the actual output had exceeded the denominator hours, then the volume variance on the graph would have been favorable.

Cautions in Fixed Overhead Analysis

A volume variance for fixed overhead arises because when applying the costs to work in process, we act *as if* the fixed costs are variable. The graph in Exhibit 11A–4 illustrates this point. Notice from the graph that fixed overhead costs are applied to work in process at a rate of $6 per hour *as if* they are variable. Treating these costs as if they are variable is necessary for product costing purposes, but some real dangers lurk here. Managers can easily be misled into thinking that fixed costs are *in fact* variable.

Keep clearly in mind that fixed overhead costs come in large chunks. Expressing fixed costs on a unit or per hour basis, though necessary for product costing for external reports, is artificial. Increases or decreases in activity in fact have no effect on total fixed costs within the relevant range of activity. Even though fixed costs are expressed on a unit or per hour basis, they are *not* proportional to activity. In a sense, the volume variance is the error that occurs as a result of treating fixed costs as variable costs in the costing system.

Reconciling Overhead Variances and Underapplied or Overapplied Overhead

In a standard cost system, the underapplied or overapplied overhead for a period equals the sum of the overhead variances. To see this, we will return to the MicroDrive Corporation example.

As discussed earlier, in a standard cost system, overhead is applied to work in process on the basis of the standard hours allowed for the actual output of the period. The following table shows how the underapplied or overapplied overhead for MicroDrive is computed.

Predetermined overhead rate (a)	$7.50 per machine-hour
Standard hours allowed for the actual output [Exhibit 11A–1] (b)	40,000 machine-hours
Manufacturing overhead applied (a) × (b).	$300,000
Total Actual manufacturing overhead [Exhibit 11A–1]	$379,400
Manufacturing overhead underapplied or overapplied	$79,400 underapplied

We have already computed the budget variance and the volume variance for this company. We will also need to compute the variable manufacturing overhead variances. The data for these computations are contained in Exhibit 11A–1. Recalling the formulas for the variable manufacturing overhead variances from Exhibit 11–9, we can compute the variable overhead rate and efficiency variances as follows:

$$\text{Variable overhead rate variance} = (AH \times AR) - (AH \times SR)$$

$$= AH(AR - SR)$$

$$= \frac{42{,}000}{\text{machine-hours}} - \left(\frac{\$1.70 \text{ per}}{\text{machine-hours}^2} - \frac{\$1.50 \text{ per}}{\text{machine-hours}}\right)$$

$$= \$8.400 \text{ U}$$

$$\text{Variable overhead efficiency variance} = (AH \times SR) - (SH \times SR)$$

$$= SR(AH - SH)$$

$$= \frac{\$1.50 \text{ per}}{\text{machine-hours}} - \left(\frac{42{,}000}{\text{machine-hours}} - \frac{40{,}000 \text{ per}}{\text{machine-hours}}\right)$$

$$= \$3{,}000 \text{ U}$$

We can now compute the sum of all of the overhead variances as follows:

Variable overhead rate variance	$ 8,400 U
Variable overhead efficiency variance	3,000 U
Fixed overhead budget variance	8,000 U
Fixed overhead volume variance.	60,000 U
Total of the overhead variances	$79,400 U

Note that the total of the overhead variances is $79,000, which equals the underapplied overhead of $79,000. In general, if the overhead is underapplied, the total of the standard cost overhead variances is unfavorable. If the overhead is overapplied, the total of the standard cost overhead variances is favorable.

---

[2] AR = $780,400 ÷ 42,000 machine-hours = $1.70 per machine-hour.

Glossary

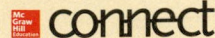

Budget variance The difference between the actual fixed overhead costs and the budgeted fixed overhead costs for the period. (p. 509)

Denominator activity The level of activity used to compute the predetermined overhead rate. (p. 508)

Volume variance The variance that arises whenever the standard hours allowed for the actual output of a period are different from the denominator activity level that was used to compute the predetermined overhead rate. It is computed by multiplying the fixed component of the predetermined overhead rate by the difference between the denominator hours and the standard hours allowed for the actual output. (p. 510)

Appendix 11A Exercises and Problems

Additional student resources are available with Connect.

EXERCISE 11A–1 Fixed Overhead Variances [LO11–4]

Primara Corporation has a standard cost system in which it applies overhead to products based on the standard direct labor-hours allowed for the actual output of the period. Data concerning the most recent year appear below:

Total budgeted fixed overhead cost for the year	$250,000
Actual fixed overhead cost for the year	$254,000
Budgeted standard direct labor-hours (denominator level of activity)	25,000
Actual direct labor-hours	27,000
Standard direct labor-hours allowed for the actual output	26,000

Required:

1. Compute the fixed portion of the predetermined overhead rate for the year.
2. Compute the fixed overhead budget variance and volume variance.

EXERCISE 11A–2 Predetermined Overhead Rate; Overhead Variances [LO11–3, LO11–4]

Norwall Company's variable manufacturing overhead should be $3.00 per standard machine-hour and its fixed manufacturing overhead should be $300,000 per month.

The following information is available for a recent month:

a. The denominator activity of 60,000 machine-hours is used to compute the predetermined overhead rate.
b. At the 60,000 standard machine-hours level of activity, the company should produce 40,000 units of product.
c. The company's actual operating results were:

Number of units produced	42,000
Actual machine-hours	64,000
Actual variable manufacturing overhead cost	$185,600
Actual fixed manufacturing overhead cost	$302,400

Required:

1. Compute the predetermined overhead rate and break it down into variable and fixed cost elements.
2. Compute the standard hours allowed for the actual production.
3. Compute the variable overhead rate and efficiency variances and the fixed overhead budget and volume variances.

EXERCISE 11A–3 Applying Overhead in a Standard Costing System [LO11–4]

Privack Corporation has a standard cost system in which it applies overhead to products based on the standard direct labor-hours allowed for the actual output of the period. Data concerning the most recent year appear below:

Variable overhead cost per direct labor-hour	$2.00
Total fixed overhead cost per year	$250,000
Budgeted standard direct labor-hours (denominator level of activity)	40,000
Actual direct labor-hours	39,000
Standard direct labor-hours allowed for the actual output	38,000

Required:

1. Compute the predetermined overhead rate for the year.
2. Determine the amount of overhead that would be applied to the output of the period.

EXERCISE 11A–4 Fixed Overhead Variances [LO11–4]

Selected operating information on three different companies for a recent year is given below:

	Company		
	A	B	C
Full-capacity machine-hours	10,000	18,000	20,000
Budgeted machine-hours*	9,000	17,000	20,000
Actual machine-hours	9,000	17,800	19,000
Standard machine-hours allowed for actual production	9,500	16,000	20,000

*Denominator activity for computing the predetermined overhead rate.

Required:

For each company, state whether the company would have a favorable or unfavorable volume variance and why.

EXERCISE 11A–5 Using Fixed Overhead Variances [LO11–4]

The standard cost card for the single product manufactured by Cutter, Inc., is given below:

Standard Cost Card—per Unit	
Direct materials, 3 yards at $6.00 per yard	$ 18
Direct labor, 4 hours at $15.50 per hour	62
Variable overhead, 4 hours at $1.50 per hour	6
Fixed overhead, 4 hours at $5.00 per hour	20
Total standard cost per unit	$106

Manufacturing overhead is applied to production on the basis of standard direct labor-hours. During the year, the company worked 37,000 hours and manufactured 9,500 units of product. Selected data relating to the company's fixed manufacturing overhead cost for the year are shown below:

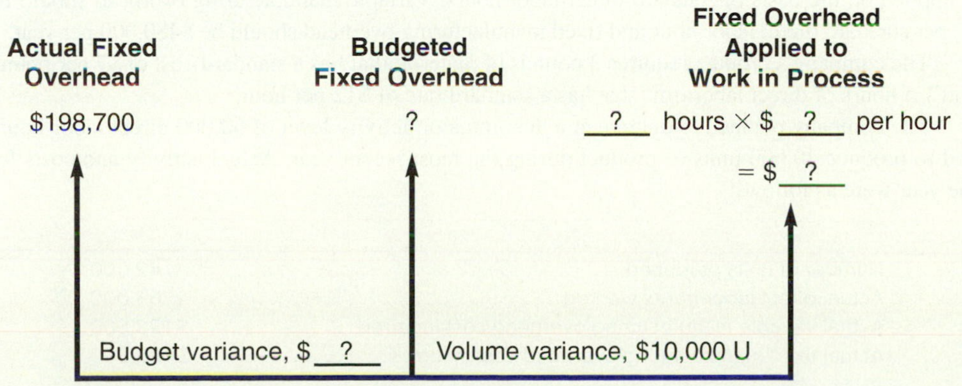

Required:

1. What were the standard hours allowed for the year's production?
2. What was the amount of budgeted fixed overhead cost for the year?
3. What was the fixed overhead budget variance for the year?
4. What denominator activity level did the company use in setting the predetermined overhead rate for the year?

EXERCISE 11A–6 Predetermined Overhead Rate [LO11–4]

Operating at a normal level of 30,000 direct labor-hours, Lasser Company produces 10,000 units of product each year. The direct labor wage rate is $12 per hour. Two and one-half yards of direct materials go into each unit of product; the material costs $8.60 per yard. Variable manufacturing overhead should be $1.90 per standard direct labor-hour. Fixed manufacturing overhead should be $168,000 per period.

Required:

1. Using 30,000 direct labor-hours as the denominator activity, compute the predetermined overhead rate and break it down into variable and fixed elements.
2. Complete the standard cost card below for one unit of product:

Direct materials, 2.5 yards at $8.60 per yard	$21.50
Direct labor, ?	?
Variable manufacturing overhead, ?	?
Fixed manufacturing overhead, ?	?
Total standard cost per unit	$?

EXERCISE 11A–7 Relations Among Fixed Overhead Variances [LO11–4]

Selected information relating to Yost Company's operations for the most recent year is given below:

Activity:	
Denominator activity (machine-hours)	45,000
Standard hours allowed per unit	3
Number of units produced	14,000
Costs:	
Actual fixed overhead costs incurred	$267,000
Fixed overhead budget variance	$3,000 F

The company applies overhead cost to products on the basis of standard machine-hours.

Required:

1. What were the standard machine-hours allowed for the actual production?
2. What was the fixed portion of the predetermined overhead rate?
3. What was the volume variance?

PROBLEM 11A–8 Applying Overhead; Overhead Variances [LO11–3, LO11–4]

Lane Company manufactures a single product that requires a great deal of hand labor. Overhead cost is applied on the basis of standard direct labor-hours. Variable manufacturing overhead should be $2 per standard direct labor-hour and fixed manufacturing overhead should be $480,000 per year.

The company's product requires 3 pounds of material that has a standard cost of $7 per pound and 1.5 hours of direct labor time that has a standard rate of $12 per hour.

The company planned to operate at a denominator activity level of 60,000 direct labor-hours and to produce 40,000 units of product during the most recent year. Actual activity and costs for the year were as follows:

Number of units produced	42,000
Actual direct labor-hours worked	65,000
Actual variable manufacturing overhead cost incurred	$123,500
Actual fixed manufacturing overhead cost incurred	$483,000

Required:

1. Compute the predetermined overhead rate for the year. Break the rate down into variable and fixed elements.
2. Prepare a standard cost card for the company's product; show the details for all manufacturing costs on your standard cost card.
3. Do the following:
   a. Compute the standard direct labor-hours allowed for the year's production.
   b. Complete the following Manufacturing Overhead T-account for the year:

Manufacturing Overhead

?	?
?	?

4. Determine the reason for any underapplied or overapplied overhead for the year by computing the variable overhead rate and efficiency variances and the fixed overhead budget and volume variances.
5. Suppose the company had chosen 65,000 direct labor-hours as the denominator activity rather than 60,000 hours. State which, if any, of the variances computed in requirement 4 would have changed, and explain how the variance(s) would have changed. No computations are necessary.

PROBLEM 11A–9 Applying Overhead; Overhead Variances [LO11–3, LO11–4]

Chilczuk, S.A., of Gdansk, Poland, is a major producer of classic Polish sausage. The company uses a standard cost system to help control costs. Manufacturing overhead is applied to production on the basis of standard direct labor-hours. According to the company's flexible budget, the following manufacturing overhead costs should be incurred at an activity level of 35,000 labor-hours (the denominator activity level):

Variable manufacturing overhead cost. . . .	$ 87,500
Fixed manufacturing overhead cost	210,000
Total manufacturing overhead cost.	$ 297,500

During the most recent year, the following operating results were recorded:

Activity:	
Actual labor-hours worked	30,000
Standard labor-hours allowed for output	32,000
Cost:	
Actual variable manufacturing overhead cost incurred.	$78,000
Actual fixed manufacturing overhead cost incurred.	$209,400

At the end of the year, the company's Manufacturing Overhead account contained the following data:

Manufacturing Overhead

Actual	287,400	Applied	272,000
	15,400		

Management would like to determine the cause of the $15,400 underapplied overhead.

Required:

1. Compute the predetermined overhead rate. Break the rate down into variable and fixed cost elements.
2. Show how the $272,000 Applied figure in the Manufacturing Overhead account was computed.
3. Analyze the $15,400 underapplied overhead figure in terms of the variable overhead rate and efficiency variances and the fixed overhead budget and volume variances.
4. Explain the meaning of each variance that you computed in requirement 3.

PROBLEM 11A–10 Comprehensive Standard Cost Variances [LO11–1, LO11–2, LO11–3, LO11–4]

"Wonderful! Not only did our salespeople do a good job in meeting the sales budget this year, but our production people did a good job in controlling costs as well," said Kim Clark, president of Martell Company. "Our $18,300 overall manufacturing cost variance is only 1.2% of the $1,536,000 standard cost of products made during the year. That's well within the 3% parameter set by management for acceptable variances. It looks like everyone will be in line for a bonus this year."

The company produces and sells a single product. The standard cost card for the product follows:

Standard Cost Card—per Unit	
Direct materials, 2 feet at $8.45 per foot	$16.90
Direct labor, 1.4 direct labor-hours at $16 per direct labor-hour	22.40
Variable overhead, 1.4 direct labor-hours at $2.50 per direct labor-hour	3.50
Fixed overhead, 1.4 direct labor-hours at $6 per direct labor-hour	8.40
Standard cost per unit	$51.20

The following additional information is available for the year just completed:

a. The company manufactured 30,000 units of product during the year.

b. A total of 64,000 feet of material was purchased during the year at a cost of $8.55 per foot. All of this material was used to manufacture the 30,000 units. There were no beginning or ending inventories for the year.

c. The company worked 43,500 direct labor-hours during the year at a direct labor cost of $15.80 per hour.

d. Overhead is applied to products on the basis of standard direct labor-hours. Data relating to manufacturing overhead costs follow:

Denominator activity level (direct labor-hours)	35,000
Budgeted fixed overhead costs	$210,000
Actual variable overhead costs incurred	$108,000
Actual fixed overhead costs incurred	$211,800

Required:

1. Compute the materials price and quantity variances for the year.
2. Compute the labor rate and efficiency variances for the year.
3. For manufacturing overhead compute:
   a. The variable overhead rate and efficiency variances for the year.
   b. The fixed overhead budget and volume variances for the year.
4. Total the variances you have computed, and compare the net amount with the $18,300 mentioned by the president. Do you agree that bonuses should be given to everyone for good cost control during the year? Explain.

PROBLEM 11A–11 Comprehensive Standard Cost Variances [LO11–1, LO11–2, LO11–3, LO11–4]

Flandro Company uses a standard cost system and sets predetermined overhead rates on the basis of direct labor-hours. The following data are taken from the company's budget for the current year:

Denominator activity (direct labor-hours)	5,000
Variable manufacturing overhead cost	$25,000
Fixed manufacturing overhead cost	$59,000

The standard cost card for the company's only product is given below:

Direct materials, 3 yards at $4.40 per yard	$13.20
Direct labor, 1 hour at $12 per hour	12.00
Manufacturing overhead, 140% of direct labor cost	16.80
Standard cost per unit	$42.00

During the year, the company produced 6,000 units of product and incurred the following costs:

Materials purchased, 24,000 yards at $4.80 per yard.	$115,200
Materials used in production (in yards).	18,500
Direct labor cost incurred, 5,800 hours at $13 per hour.	$75,400
Variable manufacturing overhead cost incurred.	$29,580
Fixed manufacturing overhead cost incurred	$60,400

Required:

1. Redo the standard cost card in a clearer, more usable format by detailing the variable and fixed overhead cost elements.
2. Prepare an analysis of the variances for direct materials and direct labor for the year.
3. Prepare an analysis of the variances for variable and fixed overhead for the year.
4. What effect, if any, does the choice of a denominator activity level have on unit standard costs? Is the volume variance a controllable variance from a spending point of view? Explain.

PROBLEM 11A–12 Selection of a Denominator; Overhead Analysis; Standard Cost Card [LO11–3, LO11–4]

Morton Company's variable manufacturing overhead should be $4.50 per standard direct labor-hour and fixed manufacturing should be $270,000 per year.

The company manufactures a single product that requires two direct labor-hours to complete. The direct labor wage rate is $15 per hour. Four feet of raw material are required for each unit of product; the standard cost of the material is $8.75 per foot.

Although normal activity is 30,000 direct labor-hours each year, the company expects to operate at a 40,000-hour level of activity this year.

Required:

1. Assume that the company chooses 30,000 direct labor-hours as the denominator level of activity. Compute the predetermined overhead rate, breaking it down into variable and fixed cost elements.
2. Assume that the company chooses 40,000 direct labor-hours as the denominator level of activity. Repeat the computations in requirement 1.
3. Complete two standard cost cards as outlined below.

Denominator Activity: 30,000 Direct Labor-Hours	
Direct materials, 4 feet at $8.75 per foot.	$35.00
Direct labor, ?	?
Variable manufacturing overhead, ?	?
Fixed manufacturing overhead, ?	?
Standard cost per unit	$?

Denominator Activity: 40,000 Direct Labor-Hours	
Direct materials, $4 feet at $8.75 per foot.	$35.00
Direct labor, ?	?
Variable manufacturing overhead, ?	?
Fixed manufacturing overhead, ?	?
Standard cost per unit	$?

4. Assume that the company actually produces 18,000 units and works 38,000 direct labor-hours during the year. Actual manufacturing overhead costs for the year are:

Variable manufacturing overhead cost.	$174,800
Fixed manufacturing overhead cost	271,600
Total manufacturing overhead cost.	$446,400

Do the following:

a. Compute the standard direct labor-hours allowed for this year's production.

b. Complete the Manufacturing Overhead account below. Assume that the company uses 30,000 direct labor-hours (normal activity) as the denominator activity figure in computing predetermined overhead rates, as you have done in requirement 1.

Manufacturing Overhead

Actual costs	446,400	Applied	?
	?		?

c. Determine the cause of the underapplied or overapplied overhead for the year by computing the variable overhead rate and efficiency variances and the fixed overhead budget and volume variances.

5. Looking at the variances you have computed, what appears to be the major disadvantage of using normal activity rather than expected actual activity as a denominator in computing the predetermined overhead rate? What advantages can you see to offset this disadvantage?

Performance Measurement in Decentralized Organizations

Performance Measures That Drive Financial Results

BUSINESS FOCUS

© ZUMA Press, Inc/Alamy

Companies that wish to achieve strong financial results need to be responsive to employee and customer needs. For example, Papa John's uses mystery shoppers and a 10-point scale to measure the quality of 10,000 pizzas per month. The mystery shopper scores, which are tied to executive bonuses, help Papa John's meet the customers' need for high-quality pizza. American Express asked its 26,000 call-center employees what they needed to achieve higher job satisfaction—then it responded by delivering flexible schedules, more career development, and higher pay. Collectively, these changes increased the company's service margins by 10%.

This chapter discusses financial measures that companies use to track performance. It also introduces some nonfinancial performance measures, related to customers, employees, and business processes, that companies use to drive financial results. ■

Sources: Scott Cendrowski, "Papa John's John Schnatter," *Fortune*, September 28, 2009, p. 34; Christopher Tkaczyk, "No. 73: American Express," *Fortune*, August 16, 2010, p. 14.

LEARNING OBJECTIVES

After studying Chapter 12, you should be able to:

LO 12–1 Compute return on investment (ROI) and show how changes in sales, expenses, and assets affect ROI.

LO 12–2 Compute residual income and understand its strengths and weaknesses.

LO 12–3 Compute delivery cycle time, throughput time, and manufacturing cycle efficiency (MCE).

LO 12–4 Understand how to construct and use a balanced scorecard.

LO 12–5 (Appendix 12A) Determine the range, if any, within which a negotiated transfer price should fall.

LO 12–6 (Appendix 12B) Charge operating departments for services provided by service departments.

Except in very small organizations, top managers must delegate some decisions. For example, the CEO of the Hyatt Hotel chain cannot be expected to decide whether a particular hotel guest at the Hyatt Hotel on Maui should be allowed to check out later than the normal checkout time. Instead, employees at Maui are authorized to make this decision. As in this example, managers in large organizations have to delegate some decisions to those who are at lower levels in the organization.

Decentralization in Organizations

In a **decentralized organization**, decision-making authority is spread throughout the organization rather than being confined to a few top executives. As noted above, out of necessity all large organizations are decentralized to some extent. Organizations do differ, however, in the extent to which they are decentralized. In strongly centralized organizations, decision-making authority is reluctantly delegated to lower-level managers who have little freedom to make decisions. In strongly decentralized organizations, even the lowest-level managers are empowered to make as many decisions as possible. Most organizations fall somewhere between these two extremes.

Advantages and Disadvantages of Decentralization

The major advantages of decentralization include:

1. By delegating day-to-day problem solving to lower-level managers, top management can concentrate on bigger issues, such as overall strategy.
2. Empowering lower-level managers to make decisions puts the decision-making authority in the hands of those who tend to have the most detailed and up-to-date information about day-to-day operations.
3. By eliminating layers of decision making and approvals, organizations can respond more quickly to customers and to changes in the operating environment.
4. Granting decision-making authority helps train lower-level managers for higher-level positions.
5. Empowering lower-level managers to make decisions can increase their motivation and job satisfaction.

The major disadvantages of decentralization include:

1. Lower-level managers may make decisions without fully understanding the company's overall strategy.
2. If lower-level managers make their own decisions independently of each other, coordination may be lacking.
3. Lower-level managers may have objectives that clash with the objectives of the entire organization.[1] For example, a manager may be more interested in increasing the size of his or her department, leading to more power and prestige, than in increasing the department's effectiveness.

---

[1] Similar problems exist with top-level managers as well. The shareholders of the company delegate their decision-making authority to the top managers. Unfortunately, top managers may abuse that trust by rewarding themselves and their friends too generously, spending too much company money on palatial offices, and so on. The issue of how to ensure that top managers act in the best interests of the company's owners continues to challenge experts. To a large extent, the owners rely on performance evaluation using return on investment and residual income measures, as discussed later in the chapter, and on bonuses and stock options. The stock market is also an important disciplining mechanism. If top managers squander the company's resources, the price of the company's stock will almost surely fall—possibly resulting in a loss of prestige, bonuses, and a job. And, of course, particularly outrageous self-dealing may land a CEO in court.

4. Spreading innovative ideas may be difficult in a decentralized organization. Someone in one part of the organization may have a terrific idea that would benefit other parts of the organization, but without strong central direction the idea may not be shared with, and adopted by, other parts of the organization.

Responsibility Accounting

Decentralized organizations need *responsibility accounting systems* that link lower-level managers' decision-making authority with accountability for the outcomes of those decisions. The term **responsibility center** is used for any part of an organization whose manager has control over and is accountable for cost, profit, or investments. The three primary types of responsibility centers are *cost centers, profit centers,* and *investment centers.*

Cost, Profit, and Investment Centers

Cost Center The manager of a **cost center** has control over costs, but not over revenue or the use of investment funds. Service departments such as accounting, finance, general administration, legal, and personnel are usually classified as cost centers. In addition, manufacturing facilities are often considered to be cost centers. The managers of cost centers are expected to minimize costs while providing the level of products and services demanded by other parts of the organization. For example, the manager of a manufacturing facility would be evaluated at least in part by comparing actual costs to how much costs should have been for the actual level of output during the period. Standard cost variances and flexible budget variances, such as those discussed in earlier chapters, are often used to evaluate cost center performance.

Profit Center The manager of a **profit center** has control over both costs and revenue, but not over the use of investment funds. For example, the manager in charge of a Six Flags amusement park would be responsible for both the revenues and costs, and hence the profits, of the amusement park, but may not have control over major investments in the park. Profit center managers are often evaluated by comparing actual profit to targeted or budgeted profit.

Investment Center The manager of an **investment center** has control over cost, revenue, and investments in operating assets. For example, General Motors' vice president of manufacturing in North America would have a great deal of discretion over investments in manufacturing—such as investing in equipment to produce more fuel-efficient engines. Once General Motors' top-level managers and board of directors approve the vice president's investment proposals, he is held responsible for making them pay off. As discussed in the next section, investment center managers are often evaluated using return on investment (ROI) or residual income measures.

Evaluating Investment Center Performance—Return on Investment

LEARNING OBJECTIVE 12–1
Compute return on investment (ROI) and show how changes in sales, expenses, and assets affect ROI.

An investment center is responsible for earning an adequate return on investment. The following two sections present two methods for evaluating this aspect of an investment center's performance. The first method, covered in this section, is called *return on investment* (ROI). The second method, covered in the next section, is called *residual income.*

The Return on Investment (ROI) Formula

Return on investment (ROI) is defined as net operating income divided by average operating assets:

$$\text{ROI} = \frac{\text{Net operating income}}{\text{Average operating assets}}$$

The higher a business segment's return on investment (ROI), the greater the profit earned per dollar invested in the segment's operating assets.

Net Operating Income and Operating Assets Defined

Note that *net operating income,* rather than net income, is used in the ROI formula. **Net operating income** is income before interest and taxes and is sometimes referred to as EBIT (earnings before interest and taxes). Net operating income is used in the formula because the base (i.e., denominator) consists of *operating assets.* To be consistent, we use net operating income in the numerator.

Operating assets include cash, accounts receivable, inventory, plant and equipment, and all other assets held for operating purposes. Examples of assets that are not included in operating assets (i.e., examples of nonoperating assets) include land held for future use, an investment in another company, or a building rented to someone else. These assets are not held for operating purposes and therefore are excluded from operating assets. The operating assets base used in the formula is typically computed as the average of the operating assets between the beginning and the end of the year.

Most companies use the net book value (i.e., acquisition cost less accumulated depreciation) of depreciable assets to calculate average operating assets. This approach has drawbacks. An asset's net book value decreases over time as the accumulated depreciation increases. This decreases the denominator in the ROI calculation, thus increasing ROI. Consequently, ROI mechanically increases over time. Moreover, replacing old depreciated equipment with new equipment increases the book value of depreciable assets and decreases ROI. Hence, using net book value in the calculation of average operating assets results in a predictable pattern of increasing ROI over time as accumulated depreciation grows and discourages replacing old equipment with new, updated equipment. An alternative to using net book value is the gross cost of the asset, which ignores accumulated depreciation. Gross cost stays constant over time because depreciation is ignored; therefore, ROI does not grow automatically over time, and replacing a fully depreciated asset with a comparably priced new asset will not adversely affect ROI.

Nevertheless, most companies use the net book value approach to computing average operating assets because it is consistent with their financial reporting practices of recording the net book value of assets on the balance sheet and including depreciation as an operating expense on the income statement. In this text, we will use the net book value approach unless a specific exercise or problem directs otherwise.

Understanding ROI

The equation for ROI, net operating income divided by average operating assets, does not provide much help to managers interested in taking actions to improve their ROI. It only offers two levers for improving performance—net operating income and average operating assets. Fortunately, ROI can also be expressed in terms of **margin** and **turnover** as follows:

$$\text{ROI} = \text{Margin} \times \text{Turnover}$$

where

$$\text{Margin} = \frac{\text{Net operating income}}{\text{Sales}}$$

and

$$\text{Turnover} = \frac{\text{Sales}}{\text{Average operating assets}}$$

Note that the sales terms in the margin and turnover formulas cancel out when they are multiplied together, yielding the original formula for ROI stated in terms of net operating income and average operating assets. So either formula for ROI will give the same answer. However, the margin and turnover formulation provides some additional insights.

Margin and turnover are important concepts in understanding how a manager can affect ROI. All other things the same, margin is ordinarily improved by increasing selling prices, reducing operating expenses, or increasing unit sales. Increasing selling prices and reducing operating expenses both increase net operating income and therefore margin. Increasing unit sales also ordinarily increases the margin because of operating leverage. As discussed in a previous chapter, because of operating leverage, a given percentage increase in unit sales usually leads to an even larger percentage increase in net operating income. Therefore, an increase in unit sales ordinarily has the effect of increasing margin. Some managers tend to focus too much on margin and ignore turnover. However, turnover incorporates a crucial area of a manager's responsibility—the investment in operating assets. Excessive funds tied up in operating assets (e.g., cash, accounts receivable, inventories, plant and equipment, and other assets) depress turnover and lower ROI. In fact, excessive operating assets can be just as much of a drag on ROI as excessive operating expenses, which depress margin.

IN BUSINESS

A STRATEGY OF SCARCITY

Old Rip Van Winkle Distillery employs two people, Julian Van Winkle III and his son Preston. Its annual sales of $2 million pale in comparison to larger competitors such as Makers' Mark and Wild Turkey. Although the company could easily triple its sales volume, it chooses to limit sales to 7,000 cases of bourbon per year. Given that the company's 20-year-old aged whiskey once achieved an unprecedented "99" rating from the Beverage Tasting Institute of Chicago, demand for the company's products far exceeds its supply—thereby enabling regular price increases. For example, a fifth of 20-year-old Pappy Van Winkle bourbon sells for $110. In accounting terms, the Old Rip Van Winkle Distillery purposely foregoes turnover in favor of earning large margins on its award-winning products.

Source: Brian Dumaine, "Creating the Ultimate Cult Brand," *Fortune,* February 28, 2011, pp. 21–24.

© John Burke/Getty Images

Many actions involve combinations of changes in sales, expenses, and operating assets. For example, a manager may make an investment in (i.e., increase) operating assets to reduce operating expenses or increase sales. Whether the net effect is favorable or not is judged in terms of its overall impact on ROI.

For example, suppose that the Montvale Burger Grill expects the following operating results next month:

Sales	$100,000
Operating expenses	$90,000
Net operating income	$10,000
Average operating assets	$50,000

The expected return on investment (ROI) for the month is computed as follows:

$$\text{ROI} = \frac{\text{Net operating income}}{\text{Sales}} \times \frac{\text{Sales}}{\text{Average operating assets}}$$

$$= \frac{\$10{,}000}{\$100{,}000} \times \frac{\$100{,}000}{\$50{,}000}$$

$$= 10\% \times 2 = 20\%$$

Suppose that the manager of the Montvale Burger Grill is considering investing \$2,000 in a state-of-the-art soft-serve ice cream machine that can dispense a number of different flavors. This new machine would boost sales by \$4,000, but would require additional operating expenses of \$1,000. Thus, net operating income would increase by \$3,000, to \$13,000. The new ROI would be:

$$\text{ROI} = \frac{\text{Net operating income}}{\text{Sales}} \times \frac{\text{Sales}}{\text{Average operating assets}}$$

$$= \frac{\$13{,}000}{\$104{,}000} \times \frac{\$104{,}000}{\$52{,}000}$$

$$= 12.5\% \times 2 = 25\% \text{ (as compared to 20\% originally)}$$

In this particular example, the investment increases ROI, but that will not always happen.

E.I. du Pont de Nemours and Company (better known as DuPont) pioneered the use of ROI and recognized the importance of looking at both margin and turnover in assessing a manager's performance. ROI is now widely used as the key measure of investment center performance. ROI reflects in a single figure many aspects of the manager's responsibilities. It can be compared to the returns of other investment centers in the organization, the returns of other companies in the industry, and to the past returns of the investment center itself. DuPont also developed the diagram that appears in Exhibit 12–1. This exhibit helps managers understand how they can improve ROI.

EXHIBIT 12–1
Elements of Return on Investment (ROI)

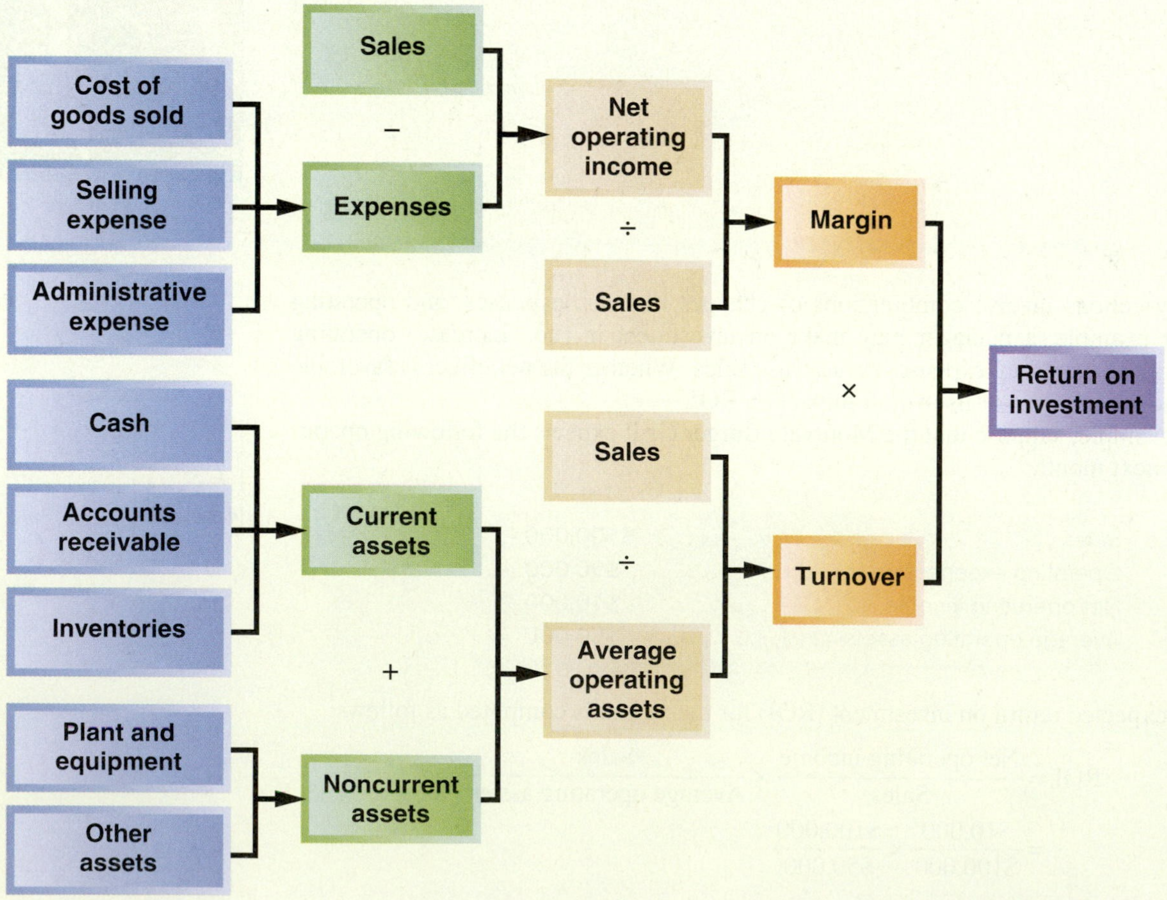

IN BUSINESS

MICROSOFT MANAGES IN AN ECONOMIC DOWNTURN

Microsoft responded to tough economic times by lowering its prices, thereby accepting lower margins per unit sold in exchange for higher turnover. For example, Microsoft lowered the price of its Office software from $150 to $100 (after promotional discounts) and realized a 415% increase in unit sales. In China, the company combated huge piracy problems by dropping the price of Office to $29, resulting in an 800% increase in sales. Microsoft established a selling price of $200 for its Windows 7 PC operating system, which was $40 less than the price the company charged for its predecessor Vista PC operating system.

Source: Peter Burrows, "Microsoft's Aggressive New Pricing Strategy," *BusinessWeek*, July 27, 2009, p. 51.

Criticisms of ROI

Although ROI is widely used in evaluating performance, it is subject to the following criticisms:

1. Just telling managers to increase ROI may not be enough. Managers may not know how to increase ROI; they may increase ROI in a way that is inconsistent with the company's strategy; or they may take actions that increase ROI in the short run but harm the company in the long run (such as cutting back on research and development). This is why ROI is best used as part of a balanced scorecard, as discussed later in this chapter. A balanced scorecard can provide concrete guidance to managers, making it more likely that their actions are consistent with the company's strategy and reducing the likelihood that they will boost short-run performance at the expense of long-term performance.
2. A manager who takes over a business segment typically inherits many committed costs over which the manager has no control. These committed costs may be relevant in assessing the performance of the business segment as an investment but they make it difficult to fairly assess the performance of the manager.
3. As discussed in the next section, a manager who is evaluated based on ROI may reject investment opportunities that are profitable for the whole company but would have a negative impact on the manager's performance evaluation.

Residual Income

LEARNING OBJECTIVE 12–2
Compute residual income and understand its strengths and weaknesses.

Residual income is another approach to measuring an investment center's performance. **Residual income** is the net operating income that an investment center earns above the minimum required return on its operating assets. In equation form, residual income is calculated as follows:

$$\text{Residual income} = \text{Net operating income} - \left(\text{Average operating assets} \times \text{Minimum required rate of return}\right)$$

Economic Value Added (EVA®) is an adaptation of residual income that has been adopted by many companies.[2] Under EVA, companies often modify their accounting principles in various ways. For example, funds used for research and development are often treated as investments rather than as expenses.[3] These complications are best dealt

[2] The basic idea underlying residual income and economic value added has been around for over 100 years. Economic value added has been popularized and trademarked by the consulting firm Stern Stewart & Co.

[3] Over 100 different adjustments could be made for deferred taxes. LIFO reserves, provisions for future liabilities, mergers and acquisitions, gains or losses due to changes in accounting rules, operating leases, and other accounts, but most companies make only a few. For further details, see John O'Hanlon and Ken Peasnell, "Wall Street's Contribution to Management Accounting: the Stern Stewart EVA® Financial Management System," *Management Accounting Research* 9, 1998. pp. 421–444.

with in a more advanced course; in this text we will not draw any distinction between residual income and EVA.

When residual income or EVA is used to measure performance, the objective is to maximize the total amount of residual income or EVA, not to maximize ROI. This is an important distinction. If the objective were to maximize ROI, then every company should divest all of its products except the single product with the highest ROI.

A wide variety of organizations have embraced some version of residual income or EVA, including Bausch & Lomb, Best Buy, Boise Cascade, Coca-Cola, Dun and Bradstreet, Eli Lilly, Federal Mogul, Georgia-Pacific, Hershey Foods, Husky Injection Molding, J.C. Penney, Kansas City Power & Light, Olin, Quaker Oats, Silicon Valley Bank, Sprint, Toys R Us, Tupperware, and the United States Postal Service.

For purposes of illustration, consider the following data for an investment center—the Ketchikan Division of Alaskan Marine Services Corporation.

Alaskan Marine Services Corporation Ketchikan Division Basic Data for Performance Evaluation	
Average operating assets	$100,000
Net operating income	$20,000
Minimum required rate of return	15%

Alaskan Marine Services Corporation has long had a policy of using ROI to evaluate its investment center managers, but it is considering switching to residual income. The controller of the company, who is in favor of the change to residual income, has provided the following table that shows how the performance of the division would be evaluated under each of the two methods:

Alaskan Marine Services Corporation
Ketchikan Division

	Alternative Performance Measures	
	ROI	Residual Income
Average operating assets (a)	$100,000	$100,000
Net operating income (b)	$20,000	$20,000
ROI, (b) ÷ (a)	20%	
Minimum required return (15% × $100,000)		15,000
Residual income		$ 5,000

The reasoning underlying the residual income calculation is straightforward. The company is able to earn a rate of return of at least 15% on its investments. Because the company has invested $100,000 in the Ketchikan Division in the form of operating assets, the company should be able to earn at least $15,000 (15% × $100,000) on this investment. Because the Ketchikan Division's net operating income is $20,000, the residual income above and beyond the minimum required return is $5,000. If residual income is adopted as the performance measure to replace ROI, the manager of the Ketchikan Division would be evaluated based on the growth in residual income from year to year.

Motivation and Residual Income

One of the primary reasons why the controller of Alaskan Marine Services Corporation would like to switch from ROI to residual income relates to how managers view new investments under the two performance measurement methods. The residual income approach encourages managers to make investments that are profitable for the entire company but that would be rejected by managers who are evaluated using the ROI formula.

To illustrate this problem with ROI, suppose that the manager of the Ketchikan Division is considering purchasing a computerized diagnostic machine to aid in servicing marine diesel engines. The machine would cost $25,000 and is expected to generate additional operating income of $4,500 a year. From the standpoint of the company, this would be a good investment because it promises a rate of return of 18% ($4,500 ÷ $25,000), which exceeds the company's minimum required rate of return of 15%.

If the manager of the Ketchikan Division is evaluated based on residual income, she would be in favor of the investment in the diagnostic machine as shown below:

Alaskan Marine Services Corporation
Ketchikan Division
Performance Evaluated Using Residual Income

	Present	New Project	Overall
Average operating assets	$100,000	$25,000	$125,000
Net operating income	$20,000	$4,500	$24,500
Minimum required return	15,000	3,750*	18,750
Residual income	$ 5,000	$ 750	$ 5,750

*The revenue variance is labeled favorable (unfavorable) when the actual revenue is greater than (less than) the planning budget. the expense variances are labeled favorable (unfavorable) when the actual expense is less than (greater than) the planning budget.

Because the project would increase the residual income of the Ketchikan Division by $750, the manager would choose to invest in the new diagnostic machine.

Now suppose that the manager of the Ketchikan Division is evaluated based on ROI. The effect of the diagnostic machine on the division's ROI is computed below:

Alaskan Marine Services Corporation
Ketchikan Division
Performance Evaluated Using ROI

	Present	New Project	Overall
Average operating assets (a)	$100,000	$25,000	$125,000
Net operating income (b)	$20,000	$4,500	$24,500
ROI, (b) ÷ (a)	20%	18%	19.6%

The new project reduces the division's ROI from 20% to 19.6%. This happens because the 18% rate of return on the new diagnostic machine, while above the company's 15% minimum required rate of return, is below the division's current ROI of 20%. Therefore, the new diagnostic machine would decrease the division's ROI even though it would be a good investment from the standpoint of the company as a whole. If the manager of the division is evaluated based on ROI, she will be reluctant to even propose such an investment.

Generally, a manager who is evaluated based on ROI will reject any project whose rate of return is below the division's current ROI even if the rate of return on the project is above the company's minimum required rate of return. In contrast, managers who are evaluated using residual income will pursue any project whose rate of return is above the minimum required rate of return because it will increase their residual income. Because it is in the best interests of the company as a whole to accept any project whose rate of return is above the minimum required rate of return, managers who are evaluated based on residual income will tend to make better decisions concerning investment projects than managers who are evaluated based on ROI.

Divisional Comparison and Residual Income

The residual income approach has one major disadvantage. It can't be used to compare the performance of divisions of different sizes. Larger divisions often have more residual income than smaller divisions, not necessarily because they are better managed but simply because they are bigger.

As an example, consider the following residual income computations for the Wholesale Division and the Retail Division of Sisal Marketing Corporation:

	Wholesale Division	Retail Division
Average operating assets (a)	$1,000,000	$250,000
Net operating income	$120,000	$40,000
Minimum required return: 10% × (a)	100,000	25,000
Residual income	$ 20,000	$15,000

Observe that the Wholesale Division has slightly more residual income than the Retail Division, but that the Wholesale Division has $1,000,000 in operating assets as compared to only $250,000 in operating assets for the Retail Division. Thus, the Wholesale Division's greater residual income is probably due to its larger size rather than the quality of its management. In fact, it appears that the smaller division may be better managed because it has been able to generate nearly as much residual income with only one-fourth as much in operating assets. When comparing investment centers, it is probably better to focus on the percentage change in residual income from year to year rather than on the absolute amount of the residual income.

Operating Performance Measures

LEARNING OBJECTIVE 12–3
Compute delivery cycle time, throughput time, and manufacturing cycle efficiency (MCE).

In addition to financial performance measures, organizations use many nonfinancial performance measures. While financial measures pick up the *results* of what people in the organization do, they do not measure what *drives* organizational performance. For example, activity and revenue variances pick up the results of efforts aimed at increasing sales, but they do not measure the actions that actually drive sales such as improving quality, exposing more potential customers to the product, filling customer orders on time, and so on. Consequently, many organizations use a variety of nonfinancial performance measures in addition to financial measures. In this section we will discuss three examples of such measures that are critical to success in many organizations—delivery cycle time, throughput time, and manufacturing cycle efficiency (MCE). Note that while these examples focus on manufacturers, very similar measures can be used by any service organization that experiences a delay between receiving a customer request and responding to that request.

Delivery Cycle Time

The amount of time from when a customer order is received to when the completed order is shipped is called **delivery cycle time**. This time is an important concern to many customers, who would like the delivery cycle time to be as short as possible. Cutting the delivery cycle time may give a company a key competitive advantage—and may be necessary for survival. The formula for computing delivery cycle time is as follows:

Delivery cycle time = Wait time + Throughput time

Throughput (Manufacturing Cycle) Time

The amount of time required to turn raw materials into completed products is called **throughput time**, or *manufacturing cycle time*. The relation between the delivery cycle time and the throughput (manufacturing cycle) time is illustrated in Exhibit 12–2.

As shown in Exhibit 12–2, the throughput time, or manufacturing cycle time, is made up of process time, inspection time, move time, and queue time. *Process time* is the amount of time work is actually done on the product. *Inspection time* is the amount of time spent ensuring that the product is not defective. *Move time* is the time required to move materials or partially completed products from workstation to workstation. *Queue time* is the amount of time a product spends waiting to be worked on, to be moved, to be inspected, or to be shipped.

As shown at the bottom of Exhibit 12–2, only one of these four activities adds value to the product—process time. The other three activities—inspecting, moving, and queuing—add no value and should be eliminated as much as possible. The formula for computing throughput (manufacturing cycle) time is as follows:

Throughput (manufacturing cycle) time =
Process time + Inspection time + Move time + Queue time

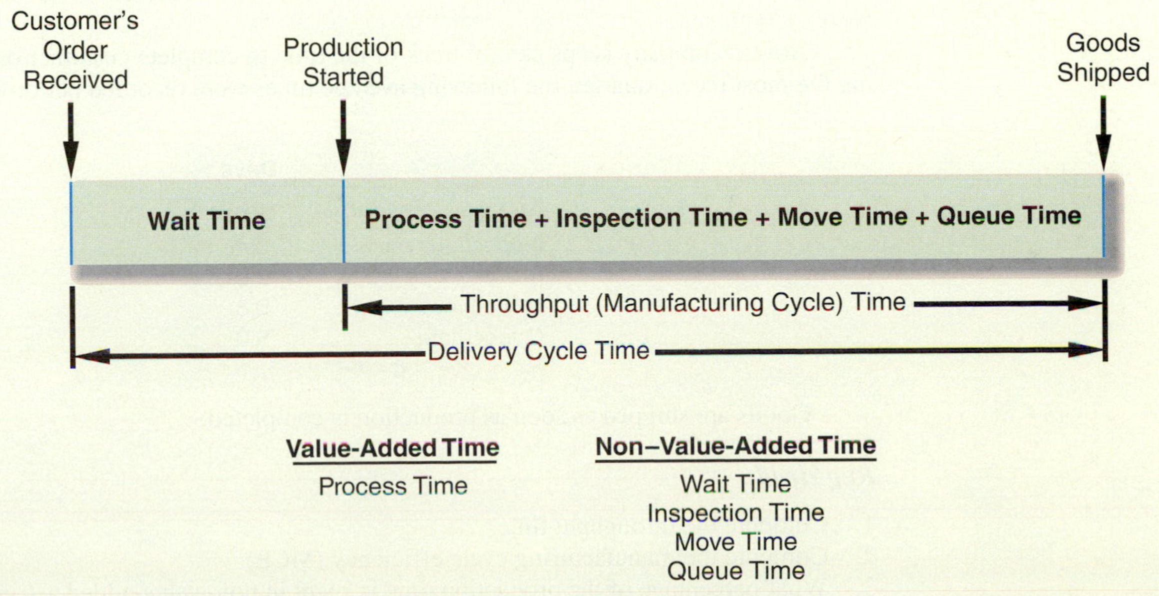

EXHIBIT 12–2
Delivery Cycle Time and Throughput (Manufacturing Cycle) Time

IN BUSINESS

THE DOCTOR WILL SEE YOU . . . LATER

When medical care reimbursement rates drop, doctors often respond by packing more patients into each day, thereby increasing patient wait times. Press Ganey Associates surveyed 2.4 million patients at more than 10,000 locations and determined an average wait time to see a doctor of 22 minutes. While these delays inconvenience patients, they also have financial implications for doctors. For example, Laurie Green, an obstetrician-gynecologist in San Francisco, prides herself on running an efficient medical practice because "she needs to bring in $75 every 15 minutes just to meet her office overhead."

If your doctor's office is overrun with delays, consider getting the first appointment of the day because the "early bird" not only gets the worm, but it also avoids wait time at the doctor's office!

Source: Melinda Beck, "The Doctor Will See You Eventually," *The Wall Street Journal,* October 19, 2010, pp. D1 and D4.

Manufacturing Cycle Efficiency (MCE)

Through concerted efforts to eliminate the *non–value-added* activities of inspecting, moving, and queuing, some companies have reduced their throughput time to only a fraction of previous levels. In turn, this has helped to reduce the delivery cycle time from months to only weeks or hours. Throughput time, which is a key measure in delivery performance, can be put into better perspective by computing the **manufacturing cycle efficiency (MCE)**. The MCE is computed by relating the value-added time to the throughput time. The formula is:

$$\text{MCE} = \frac{\text{Value-added time (Process time)}}{\text{Throughput (manufacturing cycle) time}}$$

Any non–value-added time results in an MCE of less than 1. An MCE of 0.5, for example, would mean that half of the total production time consists of inspection, moving, and similar non–value-added activities. In many manufacturing companies, the MCE is less than 0.1 (10%), which means that 90% of the time a unit is in process is spent on activities that do not add value to the product. Monitoring the MCE helps companies to reduce non–value-added activities and thus get products into the hands of customers more quickly and at a lower cost.

Example To provide an example of these measures, consider the following data for Novex Company:

Novex Company keeps careful track of the time to complete customer orders. During the most recent quarter, the following average times were recorded per order:

	Days
Wait time	17.0
Inspection time	0.4
Process time.	2.0
Move time.	0.6
Queue time.	5.0

Goods are shipped as soon as production is completed.

Required:

1. Compute the throughput time.
2. Compute the manufacturing cycle efficiency (MCE).
3. What percentage of the production time is spent in non–value-added activities?
4. Compute the delivery cycle time.

Solution

1. Throughput time = Process time + Inspection time + Move time + Queue time
   = 2.0 days + 0.4 days + 0.6 days + 5.0 days
   = 2.0 days
2. Only process time represents value-added time; therefore, MCE would be computed as follows:

$$\text{MCE} = \frac{\text{Value-added time}}{\text{Throughput time}} = \frac{2.0 \text{ days}}{8.0 \text{ days}}$$
$$= 0.25$$

Thus, once put into production, a typical order is actually being worked on only 25% of the time.

3. Because the MCE is 25%, 75% (100% − 25%) of total production time is spent in non–value-added activities.
4. Delivery cycle time = Wait time + Throughput time
   = 17.0 days + 8.0 days
   = 25.0 days

IN BUSINESS

LEAN OPERATING PERFORMANCE MEASURES

Watlow Electric Manufacturing Company implemented *lean accounting* to support its lean manufacturing methods. The company stopped providing standard cost variance reports to operating managers because the information was generated too late (at the end of each month) and it could not be understood by frontline employees. Instead, the company began reporting daily and hourly process-oriented measures that helped frontline workers improve performance.

Examples of lean operating performance measures are shown in the table below:

Measure	Description of Measure
On-time delivery percentage	Measures the percentage of orders that customers would define as being delivered on time.
Day-by-the-hour	Measures the quantity of production on an hourly basis to ensure that it is synchronized with customer demand.
First time through percentage	Measures the percentage of completed units that are free of defects.
Number of accidents and injuries	Measures the number of accidents and injuries on the manufacturing floor.
5S audit.	Measures the cell workers' ability to keep their work area organized and clean.

Note: 5S stands for Sort, Straighten, Shine, Standardize, and Sustain

Sources: Jan Brosnahan, "Unleash the Power of Lean Accounting," *Journal of Accountancy*, July 2008, pp. 60–66; and Brian Maskell and Frances Kennedy, "Why Do We Need Lean Accounting and How Does It Work?" *Journal of Corporate Accounting and Finance*, March/April 2007, pp. 59–73.

Balanced Scorecard

LEARNING OBJECTIVE 12–4
Understand how to construct and use a balanced scorecard.

Financial measures, such as ROI and residual income, and operating measures, such as those discussed in the previous section, may be included in a *balanced scorecard*. A **balanced scorecard** consists of an integrated set of performance measures that are derived from and support a company's strategy. A strategy is essentially a theory about how to achieve the organization's goals. For example, Southwest Airlines' strategy is to offer an *operational excellence* customer value proposition that has three key components—low ticket prices, convenience, and reliability. The company operates only one type of aircraft, the Boeing 737, to reduce maintenance and training costs and simplify scheduling. It further reduces costs by not offering meals, seat assignments, or baggage transfers and by booking a large portion of its passenger revenue over the Internet. Southwest also uses point-to-point flights rather than the hub-and-spoke approach of its larger competitors, thereby providing customers convenient, nonstop service to their final destination. Because Southwest serves many less-congested airports such as Chicago Midway, Burbank, Manchester, Oakland, and Providence, it offers quicker passenger check-ins and reliable departures, while maintaining high asset utilization (i.e., the company's average gate turnaround time of 25 minutes enables it to function with fewer planes and gates). Overall, the company's strategy has worked. At a time when Southwest Airlines' larger competitors are struggling, it continues to earn substantial profits.

Under the balanced scorecard approach, top management translates its strategy into performance measures that employees can understand and influence. For example, the amount of time passengers have to wait in line to have their baggage checked might be a performance measure for the supervisor in charge of the Southwest Airlines check-in counter at the Burbank airport. This performance measure is easily understood by the supervisor, and can be improved by the supervisor's actions.

Common Characteristics of Balanced Scorecards

Performance measures used in balanced scorecards tend to fall into the four groups illustrated in Exhibit 12–3: financial, customer, internal business processes, and learning and growth. Internal business processes are what the company does in an attempt to satisfy customers. For example, in a manufacturing company, assembling a product is an internal

EXHIBIT 12–3
From Strategy to Performance Measures: The Balanced Scorecard

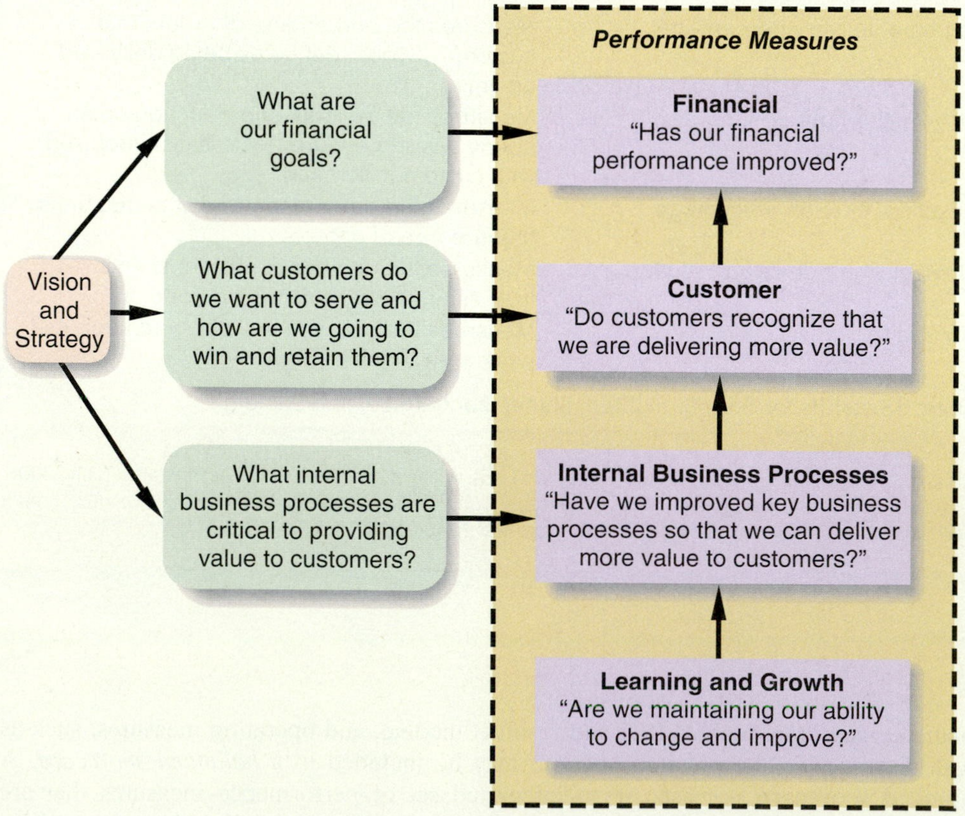

business process. In an airline, handling baggage is an internal business process. The idea underlying these groupings (as indicated by the vertical arrows in Exhibit 12–3) is that learning is necessary to improve internal business processes; improving business processes is necessary to improve customer satisfaction; and improving customer satisfaction is necessary to improve financial results.

Note that the emphasis in Exhibit 12–3 is on *improvement*—not on just attaining some specific objective such as profits of $10 million. In the balanced scorecard approach, continual improvement is encouraged. If an organization does not continually improve, it will eventually lose out to competitors that do.

Financial performance measures appear at the top of Exhibit 12–3. Ultimately, most companies exist to provide financial rewards to owners. There are exceptions. Some companies—for example, The Body Shop—may have loftier goals such as providing environmentally friendly products to consumers. However, even nonprofit organizations must generate enough financial resources to stay in operation.

For several reasons, financial performance measures are not sufficient in themselves—they should be integrated with nonfinancial measures in a well-designed balanced scorecard. First, financial measures are lag indicators that report on the results of past actions. In contrast, nonfinancial measures of key success drivers such as customer satisfaction are leading indicators of future financial performance. Second, top managers are ordinarily responsible for the financial performance measures—not lower-level managers. The supervisor in charge of checking in passengers can be held responsible for how long passengers have to wait in line. However, this supervisor cannot reasonably be held responsible for the entire company's profit. That is the responsibility of the airline's top managers.

IN BUSINESS

WHY DO COMPANIES FAIL TO EXECUTE THEIR STRATEGIES?

Robert Paladino served as the vice president and global leader of the Telecommunications and Utility Practice for the Balanced Scorecard Collaborative—a consulting organization that works with companies to implement balanced scorecards. He offers four reasons why nine out of ten organizations fail to execute their business strategies.

First, only 5% of a company's workforce understands their organization's strategy. Paladino commented "if employees don't understand the strategic objectives, then they could be focused on closing the wrong performance gaps." Second, 85% of management teams spend less than one hour per month discussing strategy. Managers cannot effectively implement strategies if they do not spend enough time talking about them. Third, 60% of organizations do not link their budgets to strategy. The inevitable result is that companies pursue "financial strategies that differ from or, worse, may be in conflict with their business and customer quality strategies." Finally, only 25% of managers have their incentives linked to strategy. Thus, most managers are working to maximize their compensation by improving strategically misguided metrics.

Paladino says the balanced scorecard overcomes these four barriers because it helps employees focus their actions on executing organizational strategies.

Source: Robert E. Paladino, "Balanced Forecasts Drive Value," *Strategic Finance,* January 2005, pp. 37–42.

Exhibit 12–4 lists some examples of performance measures that can be found on the balanced scorecards of companies. However, few companies, if any, would use all of these performance measures, and almost all companies would add other performance measures. Managers should carefully select performance measures for their own company's balanced scorecard, keeping the following points in mind. First and foremost, the performance measures should be consistent with, and follow from, the company's strategy. If the performance measures are not consistent with the company's strategy, people will find themselves working at cross-purposes. Second, the performance measures should be understandable and controllable to a significant extent by those being

EXHIBIT 12–4
Examples of Performance Measures for Balanced Scorecards

Customer Perspective	
Performance Measure	**Desired Change**
Customer satisfaction as measured by survey results	+
Number of customer complaints	–
Market share	+
Product returns as a percentage of sales	–
Percentage of customers retained from last period	+
Number of new customers	+

Internal Business Processes Perspective	
Performance Measure	**Desired Change**
Percentage of sales from new products	+
Time to introduce new products to market	–
Percentage of customer calls answered within 20 seconds	+
On-time deliveries as a percentage of all deliveries	+
Work in process inventory as a percentage of sales	–
Unfavorable standard cost variances	–
Defect-free units as a percentage of completed units	+
Delivery cycle time	–
Throughput time	–
Manufacturing cycle efficiency	+
Quality costs	–
Setup time	–
Time from call by customer to repair of product	–
Percent of customer complaints settled on first contact	+
Time to settle a customer claim	–

Learning and Growth Perspective	
Performance Measure	**Desired Change**
Suggestions per employee	+
Employee turnover	–
Hours of in-house training per employee	+

evaluated. Third, the performance measures should be reported on a frequent and timely basis. For example, data about defects should be reported to the responsible manager at least once a day so that problems can be resolved quickly. Fourth, the scorecard should not have too many performance measures. This can lead to a lack of focus and confusion.

While the entire organization will have an overall balanced scorecard, each responsible individual will have his or her own personal scorecard as well. This scorecard should consist of items the individual can personally influence that relate directly to the performance measures on the overall balanced scorecard. The performance measures on this personal scorecard should not be overly influenced by actions taken by others in the company or by events that are outside of the individual's control. And, focusing on the performance measure should not lead an individual to take actions that are counter to the organization's objectives.

With those broad principles in mind, we will now take a look at how a company's strategy affects its balanced scorecard.

IN BUSINESS

MEASURING CUSTOMER LOYALTY

Bain & Company consultant Fred Reichheld recommends measuring customer loyalty with one question—"On a scale of 0 to 10, how likely is it that you would recommend us to your friends and colleagues?" Customers who choose a score of 9 or 10 are labeled promoters. Those who choose a score of 0 to 6 are categorized as detractors, while those who select 7 or 8 are deemed passively satisfied. The net promoter score measures the difference between the percentages of customers who are promoters and detractors. Reichheld's research suggests that changes in a company's net promoter score correlate with (or move in tandem with) changes in its sales.

General Electric's Healthcare Division used net promoter scores to determine 20% of its managers' bonuses. The metric was eventually rolled out to all General Electric divisions. Other adopters of the net promoter score include American Express, consulting firm BearingPoint, and software maker Intuit.

Source: Jean McGregor, "Would You Recommend Us?" *BusinessWeek*, January 30, 2006, p. 94.

© TongRo Images Stock/Alamy

A Company's Strategy and the Balanced Scorecard

Returning to the performance measures in Exhibit 12–3, each company must decide which customers to target and what internal business processes are crucial to attracting and retaining those customers. Different companies, having different strategies, will target different customers with different kinds of products and services. Take the automobile industry as an example. BMW stresses engineering and handling; Volvo, safety; Jaguar, luxury detailing; and Honda, reliability. Because of these differences in emphasis, a one-size-fits-all approach to performance measurement won't work even within this one industry. Performance measures must be tailored to the specific strategy of each company.

Suppose, for example, that Jaguar's strategy is to offer distinctive, richly finished luxury automobiles to wealthy individuals who prize handcrafted, individualized products. To deliver this customer intimacy value proposition to its wealthy target customers, Jaguar might create such a large number of options for details, such as leather seats, interior and exterior color combinations, and wooden dashboards, that each car becomes virtually one of a kind. For example, instead of just offering tan or blue leather seats in standard cowhide, the company may offer customers the choice of an almost infinite palette of colors in any of a number of different exotic leathers. For such a system to work effectively, Jaguar would have to be able to deliver a completely customized car within a reasonable amount of time—and without incurring more cost for this customization than the customer is willing to pay. Exhibit 12–5 suggests how Jaguar might reflect this strategy in its balanced scorecard.

If the balanced scorecard is correctly constructed, the performance measures should be linked together on a cause-and-effect basis. Each link can then be read as a hypothesis in the form "If we improve this performance measure, then this other performance measure should also improve." Starting from the bottom of Exhibit 12–5, we can read the links between performance measures as follows. If employees acquire the skills to install new options more effectively, then the company can offer more options and the options can be installed in less time. If more options are available and they are installed in less time, then customer surveys should show greater satisfaction with the range of options available. If customer satisfaction improves, then the number of cars sold should increase. In addition, if customer satisfaction improves, the company should be able to

EXHIBIT 12–5
A Possible Strategy at Jaguar and the Balanced Scorecard

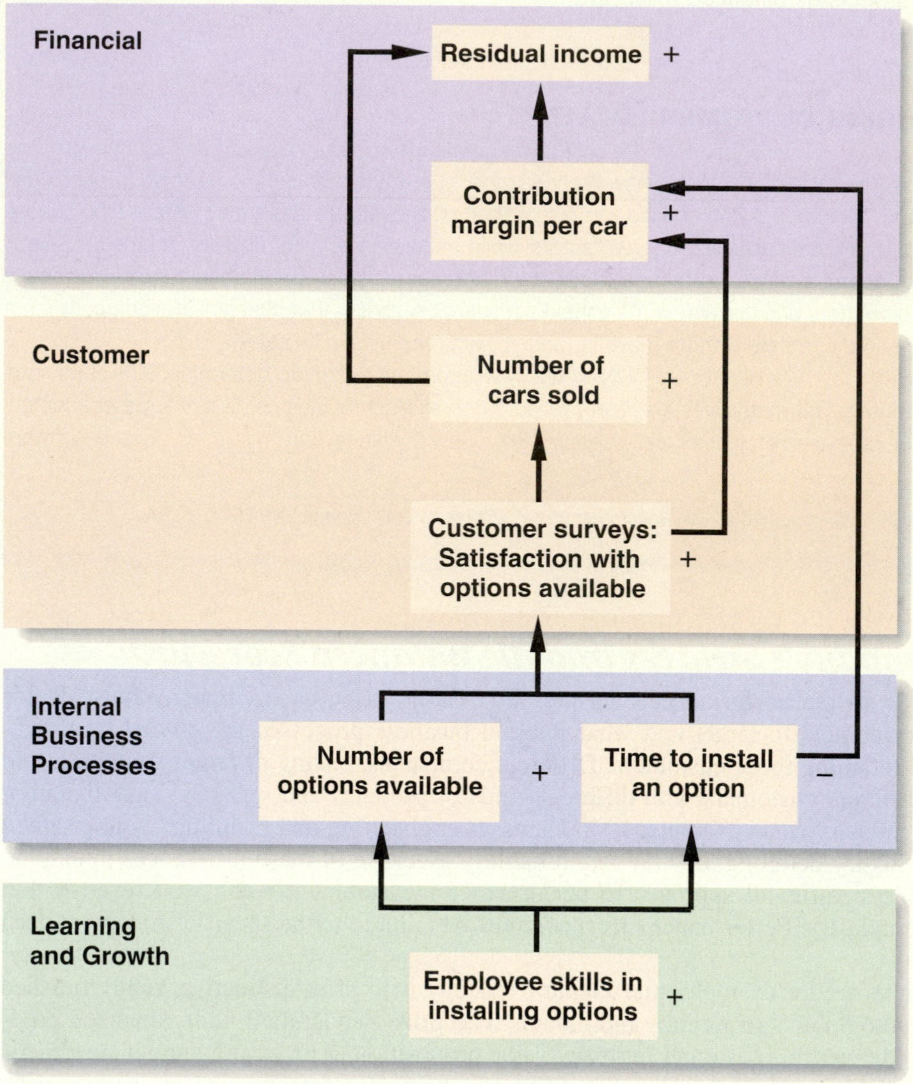

maintain or increase its selling prices, and if the time to install options decreases, the costs of installing the options should decrease. Together, this should result in an increase in the contribution margin per car. If the contribution margin per car increases and more cars are sold, the result should be an increase in residual income.

In essence, the balanced scorecard lays out a theory of how the company can take concrete actions to attain its desired outcomes (financial, in this case). The strategy laid out in Exhibit 12–5 seems plausible, but it should be regarded as only a theory. For example, if the company succeeds in increasing the number of options available and in decreasing the time required to install options and yet there is no increase in customer satisfaction, the number of cars sold, the contribution margin per car, or residual income, the strategy would have to be reconsidered. One of the advantages of the balanced scorecard is that it continually tests the theories underlying management's strategy. If a strategy is not working, it should become evident when some of the predicted effects (i.e., more car sales) don't occur. Without this feedback, the organization may drift on indefinitely with an ineffective strategy based on faulty assumptions.

IN BUSINESS

THE WELLNESS SCORECARD

Towers Watson estimates that America's average annual health care spending per employee now exceeds $10,000, up from $5,386 in 2002. However, companies that have implemented high-performing corporate wellness programs have annual health care costs that are $1,800 per employee less than other organizations. These high-performing companies create and track wellness performance measures as an important part of managing their programs.

The wellness scorecard is one framework for measuring corporate wellness performance. It has four categories of measures—attitudes, participation, physical results, and financial results—that are connected on a cause-and-effect basis. If employee attitudes toward the company's wellness program improve, then it should increase the rate of employee participation in wellness activities. If employees increase their participation rates, then it should produce physical results, such as lower obesity rates, lower incidents of diabetes, and increased smoking cessation rates. These physical improvements should produce positive financial results for the company, such as lower medical, pharmaceutical, and disability disbursements.

Sources: Towers Perrin, "2010 Health Care Cost Survey," www.towerswatson.com; and Peter C. Brewer, Angela Gallo, and Melanie R. Smith, "Getting Fit with Corporate Wellness Programs," *Strategic Finance,* May 2010, pp. 27–33.

© JGI/Tom Grill/Blend Images/Getty Images

Tying Compensation to the Balanced Scorecard

Incentive compensation for employees, such as bonuses, can, and probably should, be tied to balanced scorecard performance measures. However, this should be done only after the organization has been successfully managed with the scorecard for some time—perhaps a year or more. Managers must be confident that the performance measures are reliable, sensible, understood by those who are being evaluated, and not easily manipulated. As Robert Kaplan and David Norton, the originators of the balanced scorecard concept point out, "compensation is such a powerful lever that you have to be pretty confident that you have the right measures and have good data for the measures before making the link."[4]

IN BUSINESS

SUSTAINABILITY AND THE BALANCED SCORECARD

The Sustainable Investment Research Analyst Network (SIRAN) studied changes in the sustainability reporting practices of the Standard & Poor's (S&P) 100 companies from 2005 to 2007. Eighty-six of the S&P 100 companies had corporate sustainability websites as of 2007, an increase of 48% since 2005. Forty-nine of the S&P 100 companies published sustainability reports in 2007, up 26% from 2005.

Graham Hubbard, a professor at the University of Adelaide, recommends incorporating sustainability reporting into the balanced scorecard by adding two categories of measures related to social performance and environmental performance. Social performance measures focus on a company's philanthropic investments, community service, and employee safety and satisfaction. Environmental measures focus on a company's energy and water use per unit of output and its waste generation and disposal performance.

Sources: "Rise in Sustainability Reporting by S&P 100 Companies," *Business and the Environment with ISO14000 Updates,* October 2008, pp. 5–6; and Graham Hubbard, "Measuring Organizational Performance: Beyond the Triple Bottom Line," *Business Strategy and the Environment,* March 2009, pp. 177–191.

[4] Lori Calabro. "On Balance: A CFO Interview," *CFO*, February 2001, pp. 73–78.

Summary

For purposes of evaluating performance, business units are classified as cost centers, profit centers, and investment centers. Cost and profit centers are commonly evaluated using standard cost and flexible budget variances as discussed in prior chapters. Investment centers are evaluated using the techniques discussed in this chapter.

Return on investment (ROI) and residual income and its cousin EVA are widely used to evaluate the performance of investment centers. ROI suffers from the underinvestment problem—managers are reluctant to invest in projects that would decrease their ROI but whose returns exceed the company's required rate of return. The residual income and EVA approaches solve this problem by giving managers full credit for any returns in excess of the company's required rate of return.

A balanced scorecard is an integrated system of performance measures designed to support an organization's strategy. The various measures in a balanced scorecard should be linked on a plausible cause-and-effect basis from the very lowest level up through the organization's ultimate objectives. The balanced scorecard is essentially a theory about how specific actions taken by various people in the organization will further the organization's objectives. The theory should be viewed as tentative and subject to change if the actions do not in fact result in improvements in the organization's financial and other goals. If the theory changes, then the performance measures on the balanced scorecard should also change. The balanced scorecard is a dynamic measurement system that evolves as an organization learns more about what works and what doesn't work and refines its strategy accordingly.

Review Problem: Return on Investment (ROI) and Residual Income

The Magnetic Imaging Division of Medical Diagnostics, Inc., has reported the following results for last year's operations:

Sales	$25 million
Net operating income	$3 million
Average operating assets	$10 million

Required:

1. Compute the Magnetic Imaging Division's margin, turnover, and ROI.
2. Top management of Medical Diagnostics, Inc., has set a minimum required rate of return on average operating assets of 25%. What is the Magnetic Imaging Division's residual income for the year?

Solution to Review Problem

1. The required calculations follow:

$$\text{Margin} = \frac{\text{Net operating income}}{\text{Sales}}$$

$$= \frac{\$3{,}000{,}000}{\$25{,}000{,}000}$$

$$= 12\%$$

$$\text{Turnover} = \frac{\text{Sales}}{\text{Average operating assets}}$$

$$= \frac{\$25{,}000{,}000}{\$10{,}000{,}000}$$

$$= 2.5$$

$$ROI = \text{Margin} \times \text{Turnover}$$
$$= 12\% \times 2.5$$
$$= 30\%$$

2. The Magnetic Imaging Division's residual income is computed as follows:

Average operating assets	$10,000,000
Net operating income	$3,000,000
Minimum required return (25% × $10,000,000)	2,500,000
Residual income	$ 500,000

Glossary

Balanced scorecard An integrated set of performance measures that are derived from and support the organization's strategy. (p. 533)

Cost center A business segment whose manager has control over cost but has no control over revenue or investments in operating assets. (p. 523)

Decentralized organization An organization in which decision-making authority is not confined to a few top executives but rather is spread throughout the organization. (p. 522)

Delivery cycle time The elapsed time from receipt of a customer order to when the completed goods are shipped to the customer. (p. 530)

Economic Value Added (EVA®) A concept similar to residual income in which a variety of adjustments may be made to GAAP financial statements for performance evaluation purposes. (p. 527)

Investment center A business segment whose manager has control over cost, revenue, and investments in operating assets. (p. 523)

Manufacturing cycle efficiency (MCE) Process (value-added) time as a percentage of throughput time. (p. 532)

Margin Net operating income divided by sales. (p. 524)

Net operating income Income before interest and income taxes have been deducted. (p. 524)

Operating assets Cash, accounts receivable, inventory, plant and equipment, and all other assets held for operating purposes. (p. 524)

Profit center A business segment whose manager has control over cost and revenue but has no control over investments in operating assets. (p. 523)

Residual income The net operating income that an investment center earns above the minimum required return on its operating assets. (p. 527)

Responsibility center Any business segment whose manager has control over costs, revenues, or investments in operating assets. (p. 523)

Return on investment (ROI) Net operating income divided by average operating assets. It also equals margin multiplied by turnover. (p. 523)

Throughput time The amount of time required to turn raw materials into completed products. (p. 531)

Turnover Sales divided by average operating assets. (p. 524)

Questions

12–1 What is meant by the term *decentralization?*

12–2 What benefits result from decentralization?

12–3 Distinguish among a cost center, a profit center, and an investment center.

12–4 What is meant by the terms *margin* and *turnover* in ROI calculations?

12–5 What is meant by residual income?

12–6 In what way can the use of ROI as a performance measure for investment centers lead to bad decisions? How does the residual income approach overcome this problem?

12–7 What is the difference between delivery cycle time and throughput time? What four elements make up throughput time? What elements of throughput time are value-added and what elements are non–value-added?

12–8 What does a manufacturing cycle efficiency (MCE) of less than 1 mean? How would you interpret an MCE of 0.40?

12–9 Why do the measures used in a balanced scorecard differ from company to company?

12–10 Why does the balanced scorecard include financial performance measures as well as measures of how well internal business processes are doing?

Multiple-choice questions are available with Connect.

Applying Excel

connect **Additional student resources are available with Connect.**

LEARNING OBJECTIVES 12–1, 12–2

The Excel worksheet form that follows is to be used to recreate the Review Problem related to Medical Diagnostics, Inc. Download the workbook containing this from Connect. *On the website you will also receive instructions about how to use this worksheet form.*

	A	B	C	D	E
1	Chapter 12: Applying Excel				
2					
3	**Data**				
4	Sales	$25,000,000			
5	Net operating income	$3,000,000			
6	Average operating assets	$10,000,000			
7	Minimum required rate of return	25%			
8					
9	*Enter a formula into each of the cells marked with a ? below*				
10	**Review Problem: Return on Investment (ROI) and Residual Income**				
11					
12	***Compute the ROI***				
13	Margin	?			
14	Turnover	?			
15	ROI	?			
16					
17	***Compute the residual income***				
18	Average operating assets	?			
19	Net operating income	?			
20	Minimum required return	?			
21	Residual income	?			
22					

Chapter 12 Form | Filled in Chapter 12 Form

You should proceed to the requirements below only after completing your worksheet.

Required:

1. Check your worksheet by changing the average operating assets in cell B6 to $8,000,000. The ROI should now be 38% and the residual income should now be $1,000,000. If you do not get these answers, find the errors in your worksheet and correct them.

   Explain why the ROI and the residual income both increase when the average operating assets decrease.

2. Revise the data in your worksheet as follows:

Data	
Sales	$1,200
Net operating income	$72
Average operating assets	$500
Minimum required rate of return	15%

a. What is the ROI?
b. What is the residual income?
c. Explain the relationship between the ROI and the residual income?

Additional student resources are available with Connect. connect **The Foundational 15**

LEARNING OBJECTIVES 12–1, 12–2

Westerville Company reported the following results from last year's operations:

Sales	$1,000,000
Variable expenses	300,000
Contribution margin	700,000
Fixed expenses	500,000
Net operating income	$ 200,000
Average operating assets	$625,000

This year, the company has a $120,000 investment opportunity with the following cost and revenue characteristics:

Sales	$200,000
Contribution margin ratio	60% of sales
Fixed expenses	$90,000

The company's minimum required rate of return is 15%.

Required:

1. What is last year's margin?
2. What is last year's turnover?
3. What is last year's return on investment (ROI)?
4. What is the margin related to this year's investment opportunity?
5. What is the turnover related to this year's investment opportunity?
6. What is the ROI related to this year's investment opportunity?
7. If the company pursues the investment opportunity and otherwise performs the same as last year, what margin will it earn this year?
8. If the company pursues the investment opportunity and otherwise performs the same as last year, what turnover will it earn this year?
9. If the company pursues the investment opportunity and otherwise performs the same as last year, what ROI will it earn this year?
10. If Westerville's chief executive officer will earn a bonus only if her ROI from this year exceeds her ROI from last year, would she pursue the investment opportunity? Would the owners of the company want her to pursue the investment opportunity?
11. What is last year's residual income?
12. What is the residual income of this year's investment opportunity?
13. If the company pursues the investment opportunity and otherwise performs the same as last year, what residual income will it earn this year?

14. If Westerville's chief executive officer will earn a bonus only if her residual income from this year exceeds her residual income from last year, would she pursue the investment opportunity?
15. Assume that the contribution margin ratio of the investment opportunity was 50% instead of 60%. If Westerville's chief executive officer will earn a bonus only if her residual income from this year exceeds her residual income from last year, would she pursue the investment opportunity? Would the owners of the company want her to pursue the investment opportunity?

Additional student resources are available with Connect. connect

Exercises

EXERCISE 12–1 Compute the Return on Investment (ROI) [LO 12–1]

Alyeska Services Company, a division of a major oil company, provides various services to the operators of the North Slope oil field in Alaska. Data concerning the most recent year appear below:

Sales	$7,500,000
Net operating income	$600,000
Average operating assets	$5,000,000

Required:

1. Compute the margin for Alyeska Services Company.
2. Compute the turnover for Alyeska Services Company.
3. Compute the return on investment (ROI) for Alyeska Services Company.

EXERCISE 12–2 Residual Income [LO 12–2]

Juniper Design Ltd. of Manchester, England, is a company specializing in providing design services to residential developers. Last year the company had net operating income of $600,000 on sales of $3,000,000. The company's average operating assets for the year were $2,800,000 and its minimum required rate of return was 18%.

Required:

Compute the company's residual income for the year.

EXERCISE 12–3 Measures of Internal Business Process Performance [LO 12–3]

Management of Mittel Rhein AG of Köln, Germany, would like to reduce the amount of time between when a customer places an order and when the order is shipped. For the first quarter of operations during the current year the following data were reported:

Inspection time	0.3 days
Wait time (from order to start of production)	14.0 days
Process time	2.7 days
Move time	1.0 days
Queue time	5.0 days

Required:

1. Compute the throughput time.
2. Compute the manufacturing cycle efficiency (MCE) for the quarter.
3. What percentage of the throughput time was spent in non–value-added activities?
4. Compute the delivery cycle time.
5. If by using Lean Production all queue time during production is eliminated, what will be the new MCE?

EXERCISE 12–4 Building a Balanced Scorecard [LO 12–4]

Lost Peak ski resort was for many years a small, family-owned resort serving day skiers from nearby towns. Lost Peak was recently acquired by Western Resorts, a major ski resort operator. The new owners have plans to upgrade the resort into a destination resort for vacationers. As part of this plan, the new owners would like to make major improvements in the Powder 8 Lodge, the resort's on-the-hill cafeteria. The menu at the lodge is very limited—hamburgers, hot dogs, chili, tuna fish sandwiches, pizzas, french fries, and packaged snacks. With little competition, the previous owners of the resort had felt no urgency to upgrade the food service at the lodge. If skiers want lunch on the mountain, the only alternatives are the Powder 8 Lodge or a brown bag lunch brought from home.

As part of the deal when acquiring Lost Peak, Western Resorts agreed to retain all of the current employees of the resort. The manager of the lodge, while hardworking and enthusiastic, has very little experience in the restaurant business. The manager is responsible for selecting the menu, finding and training employees, and overseeing daily operations. The kitchen staff prepare food and wash dishes. The dining room staff take orders, serve as cashiers, and clean the dining room area.

Shortly after taking over Lost Peak, management of Western Resorts held a day-long meeting with all of the employees of the Powder 8 Lodge to discuss the future of the ski resort and the new management's plans for the lodge. At the end of this meeting, management and lodge employees created a balanced scorecard for the lodge that would help guide operations for the coming ski season. Almost everyone who participated in the meeting seemed to be enthusiastic about the scorecard and management's plans for the lodge.

The following performance measures were included on the balanced scorecard for the Powder 8 Lodge:

a. Weekly Powder 8 Lodge sales
b. Weekly Powder 8 Lodge profit
c. Number of menu items
d. Dining area cleanliness as rated by a representative from Western Resorts management
e. Customer satisfaction with menu choices as measured by customer surveys
f. Customer satisfaction with service as measured by customer surveys
g. Average time to take an order
h. Average time to prepare an order
i. Percentage of kitchen staff completing basic cooking course at the local community college
j. Percentage of dining room staff completing basic hospitality course at the local community college

Western Resorts will pay for the costs of staff attending courses at the local community college.

Required:

1. Using the above performance measures, construct a balanced scorecard for the Powder 8 Lodge. Use Exhibit 12–5 as a guide. Use arrows to show causal links and indicate with a + or − whether the performance measure should increase or decrease.
2. What hypotheses are built into the balanced scorecard for the Powder 8 Lodge? Which of these hypotheses do you believe are most questionable? Why?
3. How will management know if one of the hypotheses underlying the balanced scorecard is false?

EXERCISE 12–5 Return on Investment (ROI) [LO 12–1]

Provide the missing data in the following table for a distributor of martial arts products:

	Division		
	Alpha	Bravo	Charlie
Sales	$?	$11,500,000	$?
Net operating income	$?	$920,000	$210,000
Average operating assets	$800,000	$?	$?
Margin	4%	?	7%
Turnover	5	?	?
Return on investment (ROI)	?	20%	14%

EXERCISE 12–6 Contrasting Return on Investment (ROI) and Residual Income [LO 12–1, LO 12–2]

Meiji Isetan Corp. of Japan has two regional divisions with headquarters in Osaka and Yokohama. Selected data on the two divisions follow:

	Division	
	Osaka	Yokohama
Sales	$3,000,000	$9,000,000
Net operating income	$210,000	$720,000
Average operating assets	$1,000,000	$4,000,000

Required:

1. For each division, compute the return on investment (ROI) in terms of margin and turnover. Where necessary, carry computations to two decimal places.
2. Assume that the company evaluates performance using residual income and that the minimum required rate of return for any division is 15%. Compute the residual income for each division.
3. Is Yokohama's greater amount of residual income an indication that it is better managed? Explain.

EXERCISE 12–7 Creating a Balanced Scorecard [LO 12–4]

Ariel Tax Services prepares tax returns for individual and corporate clients. As the company has gradually expanded to 10 offices, the founder Max Jacobs has begun to feel as though he is losing control of operations. In response to this concern, he has decided to implement a performance measurement system that will help control current operations and facilitate his plans of expanding to 20 offices.

Jacobs describes the keys to the success of his business as follows:

"Our only real asset is our people. We must keep our employees highly motivated and we must hire the 'cream of the crop.' Interestingly, employee morale and recruiting success are both driven by the same two factors—compensation and career advancement. In other words, providing superior compensation relative to the industry average coupled with fast-track career advancement opportunities keeps morale high and makes us a very attractive place to work. It drives a high rate of job offer acceptances relative to job offers tendered."

"Hiring highly qualified people and keeping them energized ensures operational success, which in our business is a function of productivity, efficiency, and effectiveness. Productivity boils down to employees being billable rather than idle. Efficiency relates to the time required to complete a tax return. Finally, effectiveness is critical to our business in the sense that we cannot tolerate errors. Completing a tax return quickly is meaningless if the return contains errors."

"Our growth depends on acquiring new customers through word-of-mouth from satisfied repeat customers. We believe that our customers come back year after year because they value error-free, timely, and courteous tax return preparation. Common courtesy is an important aspect of our business! We call it service quality, and it all ties back to employee morale in the sense that happy employees treat their clients with care and concern."

"While sales growth is obviously important to our future plans, growth without a corresponding increase in profitability is useless. Therefore, we understand that increasing our profit margin is a function of cost-efficiency as well as sales growth. Given that payroll is our biggest expense, we must maintain an optimal balance between staffing levels and the revenue being generated. As I alluded to earlier, the key to maintaining this balance is employee productivity. If we can achieve cost-efficient sales growth, we should eventually have 20 profitable offices!"

Required:

1. Create a balanced scorecard for Ariel Tax Services. Link your scorecard measures using the framework from Exhibit 12–5. Indicate whether each measure is expected to increase or decrease. Feel free to create measures that may not be specifically mentioned in the chapter, but make sense given the strategic goals of the company.
2. What hypotheses are built into the balanced scorecard for Ariel Tax Services? Which of these hypotheses do you believe are most questionable and why?

3. Discuss the potential advantages and disadvantages of implementing an internal business process measure called *total dollar amount of tax refunds generated.* Would you recommend using this measure in Ariel's balanced scorecard?
4. Would it be beneficial to attempt to measure each office's individual performance with respect to the scorecard measures that you created? Why or why not?

EXERCISE 12–8 Computing and Interpreting Return on Investment (ROI) [LO 12–1]

Selected operating data for two divisions of Outback Brewing, Ltd., of Australia are given below:

	Division	
	Queensland	New South Wales
Sales	$4,000,000	$7,000,000
Average operating assets	$2,000,000	$2,000,000
Net operating income	$360,000	$420,000
Property, plant, and equipment (net)	$950,000	$800,000

Required:
1. Compute the rate of return for each division using the return on investment (ROI) formula stated in terms of margin and turnover.
2. Which divisional manager seems to be doing the better job? Why?

EXERCISE 12–9 Return on Investment (ROI) and Residual Income Relations [LO 12–1, LO 12–2]

A family friend has asked your help in analyzing the operations of three anonymous companies operating in the same service sector industry. Supply the missing data in the table below:

	Company		
	A	B	C
Sales	$9,000,000	$7,000,000	$4,500,000
Net operating income	$?	$280,000	$?
Average operating assets	$3,000,000	$?	$1,800,000
Return on investment (ROI)	18%	14%	?
Minimum required rate of return:			
Percentage	16%	?	15%
Dollar amount	$?	$320,000	$?
Residual income	$?	$?	$90,000

EXERCISE 12–10 Cost-Volume-Profit Analysis and Return on Investment (ROI) [LO 12–1]

Posters.com is a small Internet retailer of high-quality posters. The company has $1,000,000 in operating assets and fixed expenses of $150,000 per year. With this level of operating assets and fixed expenses, the company can support sales of up to $3,000,000 per year. The company's contribution margin ratio is 25%, which means that an additional dollar of sales results in additional contribution margin, and net operating income, of 25 cents.

Required:
1. Complete the following table showing the relation between sales and return on investment (ROI).

Sales	Net Operating Income	Average Operating Assets	ROI
$2,500,000	$475,000	$1,000,000	?
$2,600,000	$?	$1,000,000	?
$2,700,000	$?	$1,000,000	?
$2,800,000	$?	$1,000,000	?
$2,900,000	$?	$1,000,000	?
$3,000,000	$?	$1,000,000	?

2. What happens to the company's return on investment (ROI) as sales increase? Explain.

EXERCISE 12–11 Effects of Changes in Profits and Assets on Return on Investment (ROI) [LO 12–1]

Fitness Fanatics is a regional chain of health clubs. The managers of the clubs, who have authority to make investments as needed, are evaluated based largely on return on investment (ROI). The company's Springfield Club reported the following results for the past year:

Sales............................	$1,400,000
Net operating income.............	$70,000
Average operating assets..........	$350,000

Required:

The following questions are to be considered independently. Carry out all computations to two decimal places.

1. Compute the Springfield club's return on investment (ROI).
2. Assume that the manager of the club is able to increase sales by $70,000 and that, as a result, net operating income increases by $18,200. Further assume that this is possible without any increase in operating assets. What would be the club's return on investment (ROI)?
3. Assume that the manager of the club is able to reduce expenses by $14,000 without any change in sales or operating assets. What would be the club's return on investment (ROI)?
4. Assume that the manager of the club is able to reduce operating assets by $70,000 without any change in sales or net operating income. What would be the club's return on investment (ROI)?

EXERCISE 12–12 Evaluating New Investments Using Return on Investment (ROI) and Residual Income [LO 12–1, LO 12–2]

Selected sales and operating data for three divisions of different structural engineering firms are given as follows:

	Division A	Division B	Division C
Sales............................	$12,000,000	$14,000,000	$25,000,000
Average operating assets..........	$3,000,000	$7,000,000	$5,000,000
Net operating income	$600,000	$560,000	$800,000
Minimum required rate of return	14%	10%	16%

Required:

1. Compute the return on investment (ROI) for each division using the formula stated in terms of margin and turnover.
2. Compute the residual income for each division.
3. Assume that each division is presented with an investment opportunity that would yield a 15% rate of return.
   a. If performance is being measured by ROI, which division or divisions will probably accept the opportunity? Reject? Why?

b. If performance is being measured by residual income, which division or divisions will probably accept the opportunity? Reject? Why?

EXERCISE 12–13 Effects of Changes in Sales, Expenses, and Assets on ROI [LO 12–1]

CommercialServices.com Corporation provides business-to-business services on the Internet. Data concerning the most recent year appear below:

Sales	$3,000,000
Net operating income	$150,000
Average operating assets	$750,000

Required:

Consider each question below independently. Carry out all computations to two decimal places.

1. Compute the company's return on investment (ROI).
2. The entrepreneur who founded the company is convinced that sales will increase next year by 50% and that net operating income will increase by 200%, with no increase in average operating assets. What would be the company's ROI?
3. The chief financial officer of the company believes a more realistic scenario would be a $1,000,000 increase in sales, requiring a $250,000 increase in average operating assets, with a resulting $200,000 increase in net operating income. What would be the company's ROI in this scenario?

Problems

PROBLEM 12–14 Measures of Internal Business Process Performance [LO 12–3]

DataSpan, Inc., automated its plant at the start of the current year and installed a flexible manufacturing system. The company is also evaluating its suppliers and moving toward Lean Production. Many adjustment problems have been encountered, including problems relating to performance measurement. After much study, the company has decided to use the performance measures below, and it has gathered data relating to these measures for the first four months of operations.

	Month			
	1	2	3	4
Throughput time (days)	?	?	?	?
Delivery cycle time (days)	?	?	?	?
Manufacturing cycle efficiency (MCE)	?	?	?	?
Percentage of on-time deliveries	91%	86%	83%	79%
Total sales (units)	3,210	3,072	2,915	2,806

Management has asked for your help in computing throughput time, delivery cycle time, and MCE. The following average times have been logged over the last four months:

	Average per Month (in days)			
	1	2	3	4
Move time per unit	0.4	0.3	0.4	0.4
Process time per unit	2.1	2.0	1.9	1.8
Wait time per order before start of production	16.0	17.5	19.0	20.5
Queue time per unit	4.3	5.0	5.8	6.7
Inspection time per unit	0.6	0.7	0.7	0.6

Required:

1. For each month, compute the following:
   a. The throughput time.
   b. The MCE.
   c. The delivery cycle time.
2. Evaluate the company's performance over the last four months.
3. Refer to the move time, process time, and so forth, given above for month 4.
   a. Assume that in month 5 the move time, process time, and so forth, are the same as in month 4, except that through the use of Lean Production the company is able to completely eliminate the queue time during production. Compute the new throughput time and MCE.
   b. Assume in month 6 that the move time, process time, and so forth, are again the same as in month 4, except that the company is able to completely eliminate both the queue time during production and the inspection time. Compute the new throughput time and MCE.

PROBLEM 12–15 Return on Investment (ROI) and Residual Income [LO 12–1, LO 12–2]

Financial data for Joel de Paris, Inc., for last year follow:

Joel de Paris, Inc.
Balance Sheet

	Beginning Balance	Ending Balance
Assets		
Cash	$ 140,000	$ 120,000
Accounts receivable	450,000	530,000
Inventory	320,000	380,000
Plant and equipment, net	680,000	620,000
Investment in Buisson, S.A.	250,000	280,000
Land (undeveloped)	180,000	170,000
Total assets	$2,020,000	$2,100,000
Liabilities and Stockholders' Equity		
Accounts payable	$ 360,000	$ 310,000
Long-term debt	1,500,000	1,500,000
Stockholders' equity	160,000	290,000
Total liabilities and stockholders' equity	$2,020,000	$2,100,000

Joel de Paris, Inc.
Income Statement

Sales		$4,050,000
Operating expenses		3,645,000
Net operating income		405,000
Interest and taxes:		
Interest expense	$150,000	
Tax expense	110,000	260,000
Net income		$ 145,000

The company paid dividends of $15,000 last year. The "Investment in Buisson, S.A.," on the balance sheet represents an investment in the stock of another company.

Required:

1. Compute the company's margin, turnover, and return on investment (ROI) for last year.

2. The board of directors of Joel de Paris, Inc., has set a minimum required rate of return of 15%. What was the company's residual income last year?

PROBLEM 12–16 Creating a Balanced Scorecard [LO 12–4]

Mason Paper Company (MPC) manufactures commodity grade papers for use in computer printers and photocopiers. MPC has reported net operating losses for the last two years due to intense price pressure from much larger competitors. The MPC management team—including Kristen Townsend (CEO), Mike Martinez (vice president of Manufacturing), Tom Andrews (vice president of Marketing), and Wendy Chen (CFO)—is contemplating a change in strategy to save the company from impending bankruptcy. Excerpts from a recent management team meeting are shown below:

Townsend: As we all know, the commodity paper manufacturing business is all about economies of scale. The largest competitors with the lowest cost per unit win. The limited capacity of our older machines prohibits us from competing in the high-volume commodity paper grades. Furthermore, expanding our capacity by acquiring a new paper-making machine is out of the question given the extraordinarily high price tag. Therefore, I propose that we abandon cost reduction as a strategic goal and instead pursue manufacturing flexibility as the key to our future success.

Chen: Manufacturing flexibility? What does that mean?

Martinez: It means we have to abandon our "crank out as many tons of paper as possible" mentality. Instead, we need to pursue the low-volume business opportunities that exist in the nonstandard, specialized paper grades. To succeed in this regard, we'll need to improve our flexibility in three ways. First, we must improve our ability to switch between paper grades. Right now, we require an average of four hours to change over to another paper grade. Timely customer deliveries are a function of changeover performance. Second, we need to expand the range of paper grades that we can manufacture. Currently, we can only manufacture three paper grades. Our customers must perceive that we are a "one-stop shop" that can meet all of their paper grade needs. Third, we will need to improve our yields (e.g., tons of acceptable output relative to total tons processed) in the nonstandard paper grades. Our percentage of waste within these grades will be unacceptably high unless we do something to improve our processes. Our variable costs will go through the roof if we cannot increase our yields!

Chen: Wait just a minute! These changes are going to destroy our equipment utilization numbers!

Andrews: You're right Wendy; however, equipment utilization is not the name of the game when it comes to competing in terms of flexibility. Our customers don't care about our equipment utilization. Instead, as Mike just alluded to, they want just-in-time delivery of smaller quantities of a full range of paper grades. If we can shrink the elapsed time from order placement to order delivery and expand our product offerings, it will increase sales from current customers and bring in new customers. Furthermore, we will be able to charge a premium price because of the limited competition within this niche from our cost-focused larger competitors. Our contribution margin per ton should drastically improve!

Martinez: Of course, executing the change in strategy will not be easy. We'll need to make a substantial investment in training because ultimately it is our people who create our flexible manufacturing capabilities.

Chen: If we adopt this new strategy, it is definitely going to impact how we measure performance. We'll need to create measures that motivate our employees to make decisions that support our flexibility goals.

Townsend: Wendy, you hit the nail right on the head. For our next meeting, could you pull together some potential measures that support our new strategy?

Required:

1. Contrast MPC's previous manufacturing strategy with its new manufacturing strategy.
2. Generally speaking, why would a company that changes its strategic goals need to change its performance measurement system as well? What are some examples of measures that would have been appropriate for MPC prior to its change in strategy? Why would those measures fail to support MPC's new strategy?

3. Construct a balanced scorecard that would support MPC's new manufacturing strategy. Use arrows to show the causal links between the performance measures and show whether the performance measure should increase or decrease over time. Feel free to create measures that may not be specifically mentioned in the chapter, but nonetheless make sense given the strategic goals of the company.
4. What hypotheses are built into MPC's balanced scorecard? Which of these hypotheses do you believe are most questionable and why?

PROBLEM 12–17 Comparison of Performance Using Return on Investment (ROI) [LO 12–1]

Comparative data on three companies in the same service industry are given below:

	Company		
	A	B	C
Sales	$600,000	$500,000	$?
Net operating income	$84,000	$70,000	$?
Average operating assets	$300,000	$?	$1,000,000
Margin	?	?	3.5%
Turnover	?	?	2
ROI	?	7%	?

Required:

1. What advantages are there to breaking down the ROI computation into two separate elements, margin and turnover?
2. Fill in the missing information above, and comment on the relative performance of the three companies in as much detail as the data permit. Make *specific recommendations* about how to improve the ROI.

(Adapted from National Association of Accountants, *Research Report No. 35,* p. 34)

PROBLEM 12–18 Return on Investment (ROI) and Residual Income [LO 12–1, LO 12–2]

"I know headquarters wants us to add that new product line," said Dell Havasi, manager of Billings Company's Office Products Division. "But I want to see the numbers before I make any move. Our division's return on investment (ROI) has led the company for three years, and I don't want any letdown."

Billings Company is a decentralized wholesaler with five autonomous divisions. The divisions are evaluated on the basis of ROI, with year-end bonuses given to the divisional managers who have the highest ROIs. Operating results for the company's Office Products Division for the most recent year are given below:

	Total
Sales	$10,000,000
Variable expenses	6,000,000
Contribution margin	4,000,000
Fixed expenses	3,200,000
Net operating income	$ 800,000
Divisional operating assets	$ 4,000,000

The company had an overall return on investment (ROI) of 15% last year (considering all divisions). The Office Products Division has an opportunity to add a new product line that would require an additional investment in operating assets of $1,000,000. The cost and revenue characteristics of the new product line per year would be:

Sales	$2,000,000
Variable expenses	60% of sales
Fixed expenses	$640,000

Required:

1. Compute the Office Products Division's ROI for the most recent year; also compute the ROI as it would appear if the new product line is added.
2. If you were in Dell Havasi's position, would you accept or reject the new product line? Explain.
3. Why do you suppose headquarters is anxious for the Office Products Division to add the new product line?
4. Suppose that the company's minimum required rate of return on operating assets is 12% and that performance is evaluated using residual income.
   a. Compute the Office Products Division's residual income for the most recent year; also compute the residual income as it would appear if the new product line is added.
   b. Under these circumstances, if you were in Dell Havasi's position, would you accept or reject the new product line? Explain.

PROBLEM 12–19 Internal Business Process Performance Measures [LO 12–3]

Tombro Industries is in the process of automating one of its plants and developing a flexible manufacturing system. The company is finding it necessary to make many changes in operating procedures. Progress has been slow, particularly in trying to develop new performance measures for the factory.

In an effort to evaluate performance and determine where improvements can be made, management has gathered the following data relating to activities over the last four months:

	Month			
	1	2	3	4
Quality control measures:				
Number of defects	185	163	124	91
Number of warranty claims	46	39	30	27
Number of customer complaints	102	96	79	58
Material control measures:				
Purchase order lead time	8 days	7 days	5 days	4 days
Scrap as a percent of total cost	1%	1%	2%	3%
Machine performance measures:				
Machine downtime as a percentage of availability	3%	4%	4%	6%
Use as a percentage of availability	95%	92%	89%	85%
Setup time (hours)	8	10	11	12
Delivery performance measures:				
Throughput time	?	?	?	?
Manufacturing cycle efficiency (MCE)	?	?	?	?
Delivery cycle time	?	?	?	?
Percentage of on-time deliveries	96%	95%	92%	89%

The president has read in industry journals that throughput time, MCE, and delivery cycle time are important measures of performance, but no one is sure how they are computed. You have been asked to assist the company, and you have gathered the following data relating to these measures:

	Average per Month (in days)			
	1	2	3	4
Wait time per order before start of production	9.0	11.5	12.0	14.0
Inspection time per unit	0.8	0.7	0.7	0.7
Process time per unit	2.1	2.0	1.9	1.8
Queue time per unit	2.8	4.4	6.0	7.0
Move time per unit	0.3	0.4	0.4	0.5

Required:

1. For each month, compute the following performance measures:
   a. Throughput time.
   b. MCE.
   c. Delivery cycle time.
2. Using the performance measures given in the main body of the problem and the performance measures computed in requirement 1, do the following:
   a. Identify areas where the company seems to be improving.
   b. Identify areas where the company seems to be deteriorating.
3. Refer to the inspection time, process time, and so forth, given for month 4.
   a. Assume that in month 5 the inspection time, process time, and so forth, are the same as for month 4, except that the company is able to completely eliminate the queue time during production using Lean Production. Compute the new throughput time and MCE.
   b. Assume that in month 6 the inspection time, process time, and so forth, are the same as in month 4, except that the company is able to eliminate both the queue time during production and the inspection time using Lean Production. Compute the new throughput time and MCE.

PROBLEM 12–20 Return on Investment (ROI) Analysis [LO 12–1]

The contribution format income statement for Huerra Company for last year is given below:

	Total	Unit
Sales	$4,000,000	$80.00
Variable expenses	2,800,000	56.00
Contribution margin	1,200,000	24.00
Fixed expenses	840,000	16.80
Net operating income	360,000	7.20
Income taxes @ 30%	108,000	2.16
Net operating income	$ 252,000	$ 5.04

The company had average operating assets of $2,000,000 during the year.

Required:

1. Compute the company's return on investment (ROI) for the period using the ROI formula stated in terms of margin and turnover.

   For each of the following questions, indicate whether the margin and turnover will increase, decrease, or remain unchanged as a result of the events described, and then compute the new ROI figure. Consider each question separately, starting in each case from the data used to compute the original ROI in requirement 1.
2. Using Lean Production, the company is able to reduce the average level of inventory by $400,000. (The released funds are used to pay off short-term creditors.)
3. The company achieves a cost savings of $32,000 per year by using less costly materials.
4. The company issues bonds and uses the proceeds to purchase $500,000 in machinery and equipment at the beginning of the period. Interest on the bonds is $60,000 per year. Sales remain unchanged. The new, more efficient equipment reduces production costs by $20,000 per year.
5. As a result of a more intense effort by salespeople, sales are increased by 20%; operating assets remain unchanged.

6. Obsolete inventory carried on the books at a cost of $40,000 is scrapped and written off as a loss.
7. The company uses $200,000 of cash (received on accounts receivable) to repurchase and retire some of its common stock.

PROBLEM 12–21 Creating Balanced Scorecards that Support Different Strategies [LO 12–4]

The Midwest Consulting Group (MCG) helps companies build balanced scorecards. As part of its marketing efforts, MCG conducts an annual balanced scorecard workshop for prospective clients. As MCG's newest employee, your boss has asked you to participate in this year's workshop by explaining to attendees how a company's strategy determines the measures that are appropriate for its balanced scorecard. Your boss has provided you with the excerpts below from the annual reports of two current MCG clients. She has asked you to use these excerpts in your portion of the workshop.

Excerpt from Applied Pharmaceuticals' annual report:

> The keys to our business are consistent and timely new product introductions and manufacturing process integrity. The new product introduction side of the equation is a function of research and development (R&D) yield (e.g., the number of marketable drug compounds created relative to the total number of potential compounds pursued). We seek to optimize our R&D yield and first-to-market capability by investing in state-of-the-art technology, hiring the highest possible percentage of the "best and the brightest" engineers that we pursue, and providing world-class training to those engineers. Manufacturing process integrity is all about establishing world-class quality specifications and then relentlessly engaging in prevention and appraisal activities to minimize defect rates. Our customers must have an awareness of and respect for our brand image of being "first to market and first in quality." If we deliver on this pledge to our customers, then our financial goal of increasing our return on stockholders' equity should take care of itself.

Excerpt from Destination Resorts International's annual report:

> Our business succeeds or fails based on the quality of the service that our front-line employees provide to customers. Therefore, it is imperative that we strive to maintain high employee morale and minimize employee turnover. In addition, it is critical that we train our employees to use technology to create one seamless worldwide experience for our repeat customers. Once an employee enters a customer preference (e.g., provide two extra pillows in the room, deliver fresh brewed coffee to the room at 8:00 A.M., etc.) into our database, our worldwide workforce strives to ensure that a customer will never need to repeat it at any of our destination resorts. If we properly train and retain a motivated workforce, we should see continuous improvement in our percentage of error-free repeat customer check-ins, the time taken to resolve customer complaints, and our independently assessed room cleanliness. This in turn should drive improvement in our customer retention, which is the key to meeting our revenue growth goals.

Required:

1. Based on the excerpts above, compare and contrast the strategies of Applied Pharmaceuticals and Destination Resorts International.
2. Select balanced scorecard measures for each company and link the scorecard measures using the framework from Exhibit 12–5. Use arrows to show the causal links between the performance measures and show whether the performance measure should increase or decrease over time. Feel free to create measures that may not be specifically mentioned in the chapter, but nonetheless make sense given the strategic goals of each company.
3. What hypotheses are built into each balanced scorecard? Why do the hypotheses differ between the two companies?

PROBLEM 12–22 Perverse Effects of Some Performance Measures [LO 12–4]

There is often more than one way to improve a performance measure. Unfortunately, some of the actions taken by managers to make their performance look better may actually harm the organization. For example, suppose the marketing department is held responsible only for increasing the performance measure "total revenues." Increases in total revenues may be achieved by working harder and smarter, but they can also usually be achieved by simply cutting prices. The increase in volume from cutting prices almost always results in greater total revenues; however, it does not always lead to greater total profits. Those who design performance measurement systems need to keep in mind that managers who are under pressure to perform may take actions to improve performance measures that have negative consequences elsewhere.

Required:

For each of the following situations, describe actions that managers might take to show improvement in the performance measure but which do not actually lead to improvement in the organization's overall performance.

1. Concerned with the slow rate at which new products are brought to market, top management of a consumer electronics company introduces a new performance measure—speed-to-market. The research and development department is given responsibility for this performance measure, which measures the average amount of time a product is in development before it is released to the market for sale.
2. The CEO of an airline company is dissatisfied with the amount of time that her ground crews are taking to unload luggage from airplanes. To solve the problem, she decides to measure the average elapsed time from when an airplane parks at the gate to when all pieces of luggage are unloaded from the airplane. For each month that an airport's ground crew can lower its "average elapsed time" relative to the prior month, the CEO pays a lump-sum bonus to be split equally among members of the crew.
3. A manufacturing company has been plagued by the chronic failure to ship orders to customers by the promised date. To solve this problem, the production manager has been given the responsibility of increasing the percentage of orders shipped on time. When a customer calls in an order, the production manager and the customer agree to a delivery date. If the order is not completed by that date, it is counted as a late shipment.
4. Concerned with the productivity of employees, the board of directors of a large multinational corporation has dictated that the manager of each subsidiary will be held responsible for increasing the revenue per employee of his or her subsidiary.

Cases

connect Additional student resources are available with Connect.

CASE 12–23 Balanced Scorecard [LO 12–4]

Haglund Department Store is located in the downtown area of a small city. While the store had been profitable for many years, it is facing increasing competition from large national chains that have set up stores on the outskirts of the city. Recently the downtown area has been undergoing revitalization, and the owners of Haglund Department Store are somewhat optimistic that profitability can be restored.

In an attempt to accelerate the return to profitability, management of Haglund Department Store is in the process of designing a balanced scorecard for the company. Management believes the company should focus on two key problems. First, customers are taking longer and longer to pay the bills they incur using the department store's charge card, and the company has far more bad debts than are normal for the industry. If this problem were solved, the company would have more cash to make much needed renovations. Investigation has revealed that much of the problem with late payments and unpaid bills results from customers disputing incorrect charges on their bills. These incorrect charges usually occur because salesclerks incorrectly enter data on the charge account slip. Second, the company has been incurring large losses on unsold seasonal apparel. Such items are ordinarily resold at a loss to discount stores that specialize in such distress items.

The meeting in which the balanced scorecard approach was discussed was disorganized and ineffectively led—possibly because no one other than one of the vice presidents had read anything about how to build a balanced scorecard. Nevertheless, a number of potential performance measures were suggested by various managers. These potential performance measures are:

a. Percentage of charge account bills containing errors.
b. Percentage of salesclerks trained to correctly enter data on charge account slips.

c. Average age of accounts receivables.
d. Profit per employee.
e. Customer satisfaction with accuracy of charge account bills from monthly customer survey.
f. Total sales revenue.
g. Sales per employee.
h. Travel expenses for buyers for trips to fashion shows.
i. Unsold inventory at the end of the season as a percentage of total cost of sales.
j. Courtesy shown by junior staff members to senior staff members based on surveys of senior staff.
k. Percentage of suppliers making just-in-time deliveries.
l. Sales per square foot of floor space.
m. Written-off accounts receivable (bad debts) as a percentage of sales.
n. Quality of food in the staff cafeteria based on staff surveys.
o. Percentage of employees who have attended the city's cultural diversity workshop.
p. Total profit.

Required:

1. As someone with more knowledge of the balanced scorecard than almost anyone else in the company, you have been asked to build an integrated balanced scorecard. In your scorecard, use only performance measures listed previously. You do not have to use all of the performance measures suggested by the managers, but you should build a balanced scorecard that reveals a strategy for dealing with the problems with accounts receivable and with unsold merchandise. Construct the balanced scorecard following the format used in Exhibit 12–5. Do not be concerned with whether a specific performance measure falls within the learning and growth, internal business process, customer, or financial perspective. However, use arrows to show the causal links between performance measures within your balanced scorecard and explain whether the performance measures should show increases or decreases.
2. Assume that the company adopts your balanced scorecard. After operating for a year, some performance measures show improvements, but not others. What should management do next?
3. *a.* Suppose that customers express greater satisfaction with the accuracy of their charge account bills but the performance measures for the average age of accounts receivable and for bad debts do not improve. Explain why this might happen.
   b. Suppose that the performance measures for the average age of accounts receivable, bad debts, and unsold inventory improve, but total profits do not. Explain why this might happen. Assume in your answer that the explanation lies within the company.

Appendix 12A: Transfer Pricing

Divisions in a company often supply goods and services to other divisions within the same company. For example, the truck division of Toyota supplies trucks to other Toyota divisions to use in their operations. When the divisions are evaluated based on their profit, ROI, or residual income, a price must be established for such a transfer—otherwise, the division that produces the good or service will receive no credit. The price in such a situation is called a *transfer price.* A **transfer price** is the price charged when one segment of a company provides goods or services to another segment of the same company. For example, most companies in the oil industry, such as Shell, have petroleum refining and retail sales divisions that are evaluated on the basis of ROI or residual income. The petroleum refining division processes crude oil into gasoline, kerosene, lubricants, and other end products. The retail sales division takes gasoline and other products from the refining division and sells them through the company's chain of service stations. Each product has a price for transfers within the company. Suppose the transfer price for gasoline is $0.80 a gallon. Then the refining division gets credit for $0.80 a gallon of revenue on its segment report and the retailing division must deduct $0.80 a gallon as an expense on its segment report. Clearly, the refining division would like the transfer price to be as high as possible, whereas the retailing division would like the transfer price to be as low as possible. However, the transaction has no direct effect on the entire company's reported profit. It is like taking money out of one pocket and putting it into the other.

Managers are intensely interested in how transfer prices are set because they can have a dramatic effect on the reported profitability of their divisions. Three common approaches are used to set transfer prices:

1. Allow the managers involved in the transfer to negotiate the transfer price.
2. Set transfer prices at cost using either variable cost or full (absorption) cost.
3. Set transfer prices at the market price.

We will consider each of these transfer pricing methods in turn, beginning with negotiated transfer prices. Throughout the discussion, keep in mind that *the fundamental objective in setting transfer prices is to motivate the managers to act in the best interests of the overall company.* In contrast, **suboptimization** occurs when managers do not act in the best interests of the overall company or even in the best interests of their own division.

Negotiated Transfer Prices

LEARNING OBJECTIVE 12–5
Determine the range, if any, within which a negotiated transfer price should fall.

A **negotiated transfer price** results from discussions between the selling and buying divisions. Negotiated transfer prices have several important advantages. First, this approach preserves the autonomy of the divisions and is consistent with the spirit of decentralization. Second, the managers of the divisions are likely to have much better information about the potential costs and benefits of the transfer than others in the company.

When negotiated transfer prices are used, the managers who are involved in a proposed transfer within the company meet to discuss the terms and conditions of the transfer. They may decide not to go through with the transfer, but if they do, they must agree to a transfer price. Generally speaking, we cannot predict what transfer price they will agree to. However, we can confidently predict two things: (1) the selling division will agree to the transfer only if its profits increase as a result of the transfer, and (2) the buying division will agree to the transfer only if its profits also increase as a result of the transfer. This may seem obvious, but it is an important point.

Clearly, if the transfer price is below the selling division's cost, the selling division will incur a loss on the transaction and it will refuse to agree to the transfer. Likewise, if the transfer price is set too high, it will be impossible for the buying division to make any profit on the transferred item. For any given proposed transfer, the transfer price has both a lower limit (determined by the situation of the selling division) and an upper limit (determined by the situation of the buying division). The actual transfer price agreed to by the two division managers can fall anywhere between those two limits. These limits determine the **range of acceptable transfer prices**—the range of transfer prices within which the profits of both divisions participating in a transfer would increase.

An example will help us to understand negotiated transfer prices. Harris & Louder, Ltd., owns fast-food restaurants and snack food and beverage manufacturers in the United Kingdom. One of the restaurants, Pizza Maven, serves a variety of beverages along with pizzas. One of the beverages is ginger beer, which is served on tap. Harris & Louder has just purchased a new division, Imperial Beverages, that produces ginger beer. The managing director of Imperial Beverages has approached the managing director of Pizza Maven about purchasing Imperial Beverages' ginger beer to sell at Pizza Maven restaurants rather than its usual brand of ginger beer. Managers at Pizza Maven agree that the quality of Imperial Beverages' ginger beer is comparable to the quality of their regular brand. It is just a question of price. The basic facts are as follows:

Imperial Beverages:	
Ginger beer production capacity per month	10,000 barrels
Variable cost per barrel of ginger beer	$8 per barrel
Fixed costs per month	$70,000
Selling price of Imperial Beverages ginger beer on the outside market	$20 per barrel
Pizza Maven:	
Purchase price of regular brand of ginger beer	$18 per barrel
Monthly consumption of ginger beer	2,000 barrels

The Selling Division's Lowest Acceptable Transfer Price The selling division, Imperial Beverages, will be interested in a proposed transfer only if its profit increases. Clearly, the transfer price must not fall below the variable cost per barrel of $8. In addition, if Imperial Beverages does not have sufficient capacity to fill the Pizza Maven order while supplying its regular customers, then it would have to sacrifice some of its regular sales. Imperial Beverages would expect to be compensated for the contribution margin on any lost sales. In sum, if the transfer has no effect on fixed costs, then from the selling division's standpoint, the transfer price must cover both the variable costs of producing the transferred units and any opportunity costs from lost sales.

Seller's perspective:

$$\text{Transfer price} \geq \text{Variable cost per unit} + \frac{\text{Total contribution margin on lost sales}}{\text{Number of units transferred}}$$

The Buying Division's Highest Acceptable Transfer Price The buying division, Pizza Maven, will be interested in a transfer only if its profit increases. In cases like this where a buying division has an outside supplier, the buying division's decision is simple. Buy from the inside supplier if the price is less than the price offered by the outside supplier.

Purchaser's perspective:

$$\text{Transfer price} \leq \text{Cost of buying from outside supplier}$$

Or, if an outside supplier does not exist:

$$\text{Transfer price} \leq \text{Profit to be earned per unit sold (not including the transfer price)}$$

We will consider several different hypothetical situations and see what the range of acceptable transfer prices would be in each situation.

Selling Division with Idle Capacity Suppose that Imperial Beverages has sufficient idle capacity to satisfy Pizza Maven's demand for ginger beer without sacrificing sales of ginger beer to its regular customers. To be specific, let's suppose that Imperial Beverages is selling only 7,000 barrels of ginger beer a month on the outside market. That leaves unused capacity of 3,000 barrels a month—more than enough to satisfy Pizza Maven's requirement of 2,000 barrels a month. What range of transfer prices, if any, would make both divisions better off with the transfer of 2,000 barrels a month?

1. The selling division, Imperial Beverages, will be interested in the transfer only if:

$$\text{Transfer price} \geq \text{Variable cost per unit} + \frac{\text{Total contribution margin on lost sales}}{\text{Number of units transferred}}$$

Because Imperial Beverages has enough idle capacity, there are no lost outside sales. And because the variable cost per unit is \$8, the lowest acceptable transfer price for the selling division is \$8.

$$\text{Transfer price} \geq \$8 + \frac{\$0}{2{,}000} = \$8$$

2. The buying division, Pizza Maven, can buy similar ginger beer from an outside vendor for \$18. Therefore, Pizza Maven would be unwilling to pay more than \$18 per barrel for Imperial Beverages' ginger beer.

$$\text{Transfer price} \leq \text{Cost of buying from outside supplier} = \$18$$

3. Combining the requirements of both the selling division and the buying division, the acceptable range of transfer prices in this situation is:

$$\$8 \leq \text{Transfer price} \leq \$18$$

Assuming that the managers understand their own businesses and that they are cooperative, they should be able to agree on a transfer price within this range.

Selling Division with No Idle Capacity Suppose that Imperial Beverages has *no* idle capacity; it is selling 10,000 barrels of ginger beer a month on the outside market at \$20 per barrel. To fill the order from Pizza Maven, Imperial Beverages would have to divert 2,000 barrels from its regular customers. What range of transfer prices, if any, would make both divisions better off transferring the 2,000 barrels within the company?

1. The selling division, Imperial Beverages, will be interested in the transfer only if:

$$\text{Transfer price} \geq \begin{array}{c}\text{Variable cost}\\ \text{per unit}\end{array} + \frac{\text{Total contribution margin on lost sales}}{\text{Number of units transferred}}$$

Because Imperial Beverages has no idle capacity, there *are* lost outside sales. The contribution margin per barrel on these outside sales is \$12 (\$20 − \$8).

$$\text{Transfer price} \geq \$8 + \frac{(\$20 - \$8) \times 2{,}000}{2{,}000} = \$8 + (\$20 - \$8) - \$20$$

Thus, as far as the selling division is concerned, the transfer price must at least cover the revenue on the lost sales, which is \$20 per barrel. This makes sense because the cost of producing the 2,000 barrels is the same whether they are sold on the inside market or on the outside. The only difference is that the selling division loses the revenue of \$20 per barrel if it transfers the barrels to Pizza Maven.

2. As before, the buying division, Pizza Maven, would be unwilling to pay more than the \$18 per barrel it is already paying for similar ginger beer from its regular supplier.

$$\text{Transfer price} \leq \text{Cost of buying from outside supplier} = \$18$$

3. Therefore, the selling division would insist on a transfer price of at least \$20. But the buying division would refuse any transfer price above \$18. It is impossible to satisfy both division managers simultaneously; there can be no agreement on a transfer price and no transfer will take place. Is this good? The answer is yes. From the standpoint of the entire company, the transfer doesn't make sense. Why give up sales of \$20 to save costs of \$18?

Basically, the transfer price is a mechanism for dividing between the two divisions any profit the entire company earns as a result of the transfer. If the company as a whole loses money on the transfer, there will be no profit to divide up, and it will be impossible for the two divisions to come to an agreement. On the other hand, if the company as a whole makes money on the transfer, there will be a profit to share, and it will always be possible for the two divisions to find a mutually agreeable transfer price that increases the profits of both divisions. If the pie is bigger, it is always possible to divide it up in such a way that everyone has a bigger piece.

Selling Division Has Some Idle Capacity Suppose now that Imperial Beverages is selling 9,000 barrels of ginger beer a month on the outside market. Pizza Maven can only sell one kind of ginger beer on tap. It cannot buy 1,000 barrels from Imperial Beverages and 1,000 barrels from its regular supplier; it must buy all of its ginger beer from one source.

To fill the entire 2,000-barrel a month order from Pizza Maven, Imperial Beverages would have to divert 1,000 barrels from its regular customers who are paying $20 per barrel. The other 1,000 barrels can be made using idle capacity. What range of transfer prices, if any, would make both divisions better off transferring the 2,000 barrels within the company?

1. As before, the selling division, Imperial Beverages, will insist on a transfer price that at least covers its variable cost and opportunity cost:

$$\text{Transfer price} \geq \begin{matrix}\text{Variable cost}\\ \text{per unit}\end{matrix} + \frac{\text{Total contribution margin on lost sales}}{\text{Number of units transferred}}$$

   Because Imperial Beverages does not have enough idle capacity to fill the entire order for 2,000 barrels, there *are* lost outside sales. The contribution margin per barrel on the 1,000 barrels of lost outside sales is $12 ($20 – $8).

$$\text{Transfer price} \geq \$8 + \frac{(\$20 - \$8) \times 2{,}000}{2{,}000} = \$8 + (\$20 - \$8) = \$20$$

   Thus, as far as the selling division is concerned, the transfer price must cover the variable cost of $8 plus the average opportunity cost of lost sales of $6.
2. As before, the buying division, Pizza Maven, would be unwilling to pay more than the $18 per barrel it pays its regular supplier.

$$\text{Transfer price} \leq \text{Cost of buying from outside supplier} = \$18$$

3. Combining the requirements for both the selling and buying divisions, the range of acceptable transfer prices is:

$$\$14 \leq \text{Transfer price} \leq \$18$$

   Again, assuming that the managers understand their own businesses and that they are cooperative, they should be able to agree on a transfer price within this range.

No Outside Supplier If Pizza Maven has no outside supplier for the ginger beer, the highest price the buying division would be willing to pay depends on how much the buying division expects to make on the transferred units—excluding the transfer price. If, for example, Pizza Maven expects to earn $30 per barrel of ginger beer after paying its own expenses, then it should be willing to pay up to $30 per barrel to Imperial Beverages. Remember, however, that this assumes Pizza Maven cannot buy ginger beer from other sources.

Evaluation of Negotiated Transfer Prices As discussed earlier, if a transfer within the company would result in higher overall profits for the company, there is always a range of transfer prices within which both the selling and buying division would also have higher profits if they agree to the transfer. Therefore, if the managers understand their own businesses and are cooperative, then they should always be able to agree on a transfer price if it is in the best interests of the company that they do so.

Unfortunately, not all managers understand their own businesses and not all managers are cooperative. As a result, negotiations often break down even when it would be in the managers' own best interests to come to an agreement. Sometimes that is the fault of the way managers are evaluated. If managers are pitted against each other rather than against their own past performance or reasonable benchmarks, a noncooperative atmosphere is almost guaranteed. Nevertheless, even with the best performance evaluation system, some people by nature are not cooperative.

Given the disputes that often accompany the negotiation process, many companies rely on some other means of setting transfer prices. Unfortunately, as we will see below, all of the alternatives to negotiated transfer prices have their own serious drawbacks.

Transfers at the Cost to the Selling Division

Many companies set transfer prices at either the variable cost or full (absorption) cost incurred by the selling division. Although the cost approach to setting transfer prices is relatively simple to apply, it has some major defects.

First, the use of cost—particularly full cost—as a transfer price can lead to bad decisions and thus suboptimization. Return to the example involving the ginger beer. The full cost of ginger beer can never be less than $15 per barrel ($8 per barrel variable cost + $7 per barrel fixed cost at capacity). What if the cost of buying the ginger beer from an outside supplier is less than $15—for example, $14 per barrel? If the transfer price were set at full cost, then Pizza Maven would never want to buy ginger beer from Imperial Beverages because it could buy its ginger beer from an outside supplier at a lower price. However, from the standpoint of the company as a whole, ginger beer should be transferred from Imperial Beverages to Pizza Maven whenever Imperial Beverages has idle capacity. Why? Because when Imperial Beverages has idle capacity, it only costs the company $8 in variable cost to produce a barrel of ginger beer, but it costs $14 per barrel to buy from outside suppliers.

Second, if cost is used as the transfer price, the selling division will never show a profit on any internal transfer. The only division that shows a profit is the division that makes the final sale to an outside party.

Third, cost-based prices do not provide incentives to control costs. If the actual costs of one division are simply passed on to the next, there is little incentive for anyone to work to reduce costs. This problem can be overcome by using standard costs rather than actual costs for transfer prices.

Despite these shortcomings, cost-based transfer prices are often used in practice. Advocates argue that they are easily understood and convenient to use.

Transfers at Market Price

Some form of competitive **market price** (i.e., the price charged for an item on the open market) is sometimes advocated as the best approach to the transfer pricing problem—particularly if transfer price negotiations routinely become bogged down.

The market price approach is designed for situations in which there is an *outside market* for the transferred product or service; the product or service is sold in its present form to outside customers. If the selling division has no idle capacity, the market price is the correct choice for the transfer price. This is because, from the company's perspective, the real cost of the transfer is the opportunity cost of the lost revenue on the outside sale. Whether the item is transferred internally or sold on the outside market, the production costs are exactly the same. If the market price is used as the transfer price, the selling division manager will not lose anything by making the transfer, and the buying division manager will get the correct signal about how much it really costs the company for the transfer to take place.

While the market price works well when the selling division has no idle capacity, difficulties occur when the selling division has idle capacity. Recalling once again the ginger beer example, the outside market price for the ginger beer produced by Imperial Beverages is $20 per barrel. However, Pizza Maven can purchase all of the ginger beer it wants from outside suppliers for $18 per barrel. Why would Pizza Maven ever buy from Imperial Beverages if Pizza Maven is forced to pay Imperial Beverages' market price? In some market price-based transfer pricing schemes, the transfer price would be lowered to $18, the outside vendor's market price, and Pizza Maven would be directed to buy from Imperial Beverages as long as Imperial Beverages is willing to sell. This scheme can work reasonably well, but a drawback is that managers at Pizza Maven will regard the cost of ginger beer as $18 rather than the $8, which is the real cost to the company when the selling division has idle capacity. Consequently, the managers of Pizza Maven will make pricing and other decisions based on an incorrect cost.

Unfortunately, none of the possible solutions to the transfer pricing problem are perfect—not even market-based transfer prices.

Divisional Autonomy and Suboptimization

The principles of decentralization suggest that companies should grant managers autonomy to set transfer prices and to decide whether to sell internally or externally. It may be very difficult for top managers to accept this principle when their subordinate managers are about to make a suboptimal decision. However, if top management intervenes, the purposes of decentralization are defeated. Furthermore, to impose the correct transfer price, top managers would have to know details about the buying and selling divisions' outside market, variable costs, and capacity utilization. The whole premise of decentralization is that local managers have access to better information for operational decisions than top managers at corporate headquarters.

Of course, if a division manager consistently makes suboptimal decisions, the performance of the division will suffer. The offending manager's compensation will be adversely affected and promotion will become less likely. Thus, a performance evaluation system based on divisional profits, ROI, or residual income provides some built-in checks and balances. Nevertheless, if top managers wish to create a culture of autonomy and independent profit responsibility, they must allow their subordinate managers to control their own destiny—even to the extent of granting their managers the right to make mistakes.

International Aspects of Transfer Pricing

The objectives of transfer pricing change when a multinational corporation is involved and the goods and services being transferred cross international borders. In this context, the objectives of international transfer pricing focus on minimizing taxes, duties, and foreign exchange risks, along with enhancing a company's competitive position and improving its relations with foreign governments. Although domestic objectives such as managerial motivation and divisional autonomy are always important, they often become secondary when international transfers are involved. Companies will focus instead on charging a transfer price that reduces its total tax bill or that strengthens a foreign subsidiary.

For example, charging a low transfer price for parts shipped to a foreign subsidiary may reduce customs duty payments as the parts cross international borders, or it may help the subsidiary to compete in foreign markets by keeping the subsidiary's costs low. On the other hand, charging a high transfer price may help a multinational corporation draw profits out of a country that has stringent controls on foreign remittances, or it may allow a multinational corporation to shift income from a country that has high income tax rates to a country that has low rates.

Review Problem: Transfer Pricing

Situation A

Collyer Products, Inc., has a Valve Division that manufactures and sells a standard valve:

Capacity in units	100,000
Selling price to outside customers	$30
Variable costs per unit	$16
Fixed costs per unit (based on capacity)	$9

The company has a Pump Division that could use this valve in one of its pumps. The Pump Division is currently purchasing 10,000 valves per year from an overseas supplier at a cost of \$29 per valve.

Required:

1. Assume that the Valve Division has enough idle capacity to handle all of the Pump Division's needs. What is the acceptable range, if any, for the transfer price between the two divisions?
2. Assume that the Valve Division is selling all of the valves that it can produce to outside customers. What is the acceptable range, if any, for the transfer price between the two divisions?
3. Assume again that the Valve Division is selling all of the valves that it can produce to outside customers. Also assume that \$3 in variable expenses can be avoided on transfers within the company, due to reduced selling costs. What is the acceptable range, if any, for the transfer price between the two divisions?

Solution to Situation A

1. Because the Valve Division has idle capacity, it does not have to give up any outside sales to take on the Pump Division's business. Applying the formula for the lowest acceptable transfer price from the viewpoint of the selling division, we get:

$$\text{Transfer price} \geq \begin{array}{c}\text{Variable cost}\\ \text{per unit}\end{array} + \frac{\text{Total contribution margin on lost sales}}{\text{Number of units transferred}}$$

$$\text{Transfer price} \geq \$16 + \frac{\$0}{10{,}000} = \$16$$

   The Pump Division would be unwilling to pay more than \$29, the price it is currently paying an outside supplier for its valves. Therefore, the transfer price must fall within the range:

$$\$16 \leq \text{Transfer price} \leq \$29$$

2. Because the Valve Division is selling all of the valves that it can produce on the outside market, it would have to give up some of these outside sales to take on the Pump Division's business. Thus, the Valve Division has an opportunity cost, which is the total contribution margin on lost sales:

$$\text{Transfer price} \geq \begin{array}{c}\text{Variable cost}\\ \text{per unit}\end{array} + \frac{\text{Total contribution margin on lost sales}}{\text{Number of units transferred}}$$

$$\text{Transfer price} \geq \$16 + \frac{(\$30 - \$16) \times 10{,}000}{10{,}000} = \$16 + \$14 = \$30$$

   Because the Pump Division can purchase valves from an outside supplier at only \$29 per unit, no transfers will be made between the two divisions.
3. Applying the formula for the lowest acceptable transfer price from the viewpoint of the selling division, we get:

$$\text{Transfer price} \geq \begin{array}{c}\text{Variable cost}\\ \text{per unit}\end{array} + \frac{\text{Total contribution margin on lost sales}}{\text{Number of units transferred}}$$

$$\text{Transfer price} \geq (\$16 - \$3) + \frac{(\$30 - \$16) \times 10{,}000}{10{,}000} = \$16 + \$14 = \$30$$

   In this case, the transfer price must fall within the range:

$$\$27 \leq \text{Transfer price} \leq \$29$$

Situation B

Refer to the original data in situation A above. Assume that the Pump Division needs 20,000 special high-pressure valves per year. The Valve Division's variable costs to manufacture and ship the special valve would be $20 per unit. To produce these special valves, the Valve Division would have to reduce its production and sales of regular valves from 100,000 units per year to 70,000 units per year.

Required:

As far as the Valve Division is concerned, what is the lowest acceptable transfer price?

Solution to Situation B

To produce the 20,000 special valves, the Valve Division will have to give up sales of 30,000 regular valves to outside customers. Applying the formula for the lowest acceptable transfer price from the viewpoint of the selling division, we get:

$$\text{Transfer price} \geq \begin{matrix}\text{Variable cost}\\ \text{per unit}\end{matrix} + \frac{\text{Total contribution margin on lost sales}}{\text{Number of units transferred}}$$

$$\text{Transfer price} \geq \$20 + \frac{(\$30 - \$16) \times 30{,}000}{20{,}000} = \$20 + \$21 = \$41$$

Glossary (Appendix 12A)

Market price The price charged for an item on the open market. (p. 562)

Negotiated transfer price A transfer price agreed on between buying and selling divisions. (p. 558)

Range of acceptable transfer prices The range of transfer prices within which the profits of both the selling division and the buying division would increase as a result of a transfer. (p. 558)

Suboptimization An overall level of profits that is less than a segment or a company is capable of earning. (p. 558)

Transfer price The price charged when one division or segment provides goods or services to another division or segment of an organization. (p. 557)

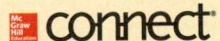

connect Appendix 12A Exercises and Problems

Additional student resources are available with Connect.

EXERCISE 12A–1 Transfer Pricing Basics [LO 12–5]

Sako Company's Audio Division produces a speaker that is used by manufacturers of various audio products. Sales and cost data on the speaker follow:

Selling price per unit on the intermediate market	$60
Variable costs per unit	$42
Fixed costs per unit (based on capacity)	$8
Capacity in units	25,000

Sako Company has a Hi-Fi Division that could use this speaker in one of its products. The Hi-Fi Division will need 5,000 speakers per year. It has received a quote of $57 per speaker from another manufacturer. Sako Company evaluates division managers on the basis of divisional profits.

Required:

1. Assume that the Audio Division is now selling only 20,000 speakers per year to outside customers.
   a. From the standpoint of the Audio Division, what is the lowest acceptable transfer price for speakers sold to the Hi-Fi Division?
   b. From the standpoint of the Hi-Fi Division, what is the highest acceptable transfer price for speakers acquired from the Audio Division?

c. If left free to negotiate without interference, would you expect the division managers to voluntarily agree to the transfer of 5,000 speakers from the Audio Division to the Hi-Fi Division? Why or why not?

d. From the standpoint of the entire company, should the transfer take place? Why or why not?

2. Assume that the Audio Division is selling all of the speakers it can produce to outside customers.
   a. From the standpoint of the Audio Division, what is the lowest acceptable transfer price for speakers sold to the Hi-Fi Division?
   b. From the standpoint of the Hi-Fi Division, what is the highest acceptable transfer price for speakers acquired from the Audio Division?
   c. If left free to negotiate without interference, would you expect the division managers to voluntarily agree to the transfer of 5,000 speakers from the Audio Division to the Hi-Fi Division? Why or why not?
   d. From the standpoint of the entire company, should the transfer take place? Why or why not?

EXERCISE 12A–2 Transfer Pricing from the Viewpoint of the Entire Company [LO 12–5]

Division A manufactures electronic circuit boards. The boards can be sold either to Division B of the same company or to outside customers. Last year, the following activity occurred in Division A:

Selling price per circuit board	$125
Variable cost per circuit board	$90
Number of circuit boards:	
Produced during the year	20,000
Sold to outside customers	16,000
Sold to Division B	4,000

Sales to Division B were at the same price as sales to outside customers. The circuit boards purchased by Division B were used in an electronic instrument manufactured by that division (one board per instrument). Division B incurred $100 in additional variable cost per instrument and then sold the instruments for $300 each.

Required:

1. Prepare income statements for Division A, Division B, and the company as a whole.
2. Assume that Division A's manufacturing capacity is 20,000 circuit boards. Next year, Division B wants to purchase 5,000 circuit boards from Division A rather than 4,000. (Circuit boards of this type are not available from outside sources.) From the standpoint of the company as a whole, should Division A sell the 1,000 additional circuit boards to Division B or continue to sell them to outside customers? Explain.

EXERCISE 12A–3 Transfer Pricing Situations [LO 12–5]

In each of the cases below, assume that Division X has a product that can be sold either to outside customers or to Division Y of the same company for use in its production process. The managers of the divisions are evaluated based on their divisional profits.

	Case	
	A	B
Division X:		
Capacity in units	200,000	200,000
Number of units being sold to outside customers	200,000	160,000
Selling price per unit to outside customers	$90	$75
Variable costs per unit	$70	$60
Fixed costs per unit (based on capacity)	$13	$8
Division Y:		
Number of units needed for production	40,000	40,000
Purchase price per unit now being paid to an outside supplier	$86	$74

Required:

1. Refer to the data in case A above. Assume in this case that $3 per unit in variable selling costs can be avoided on intracompany sales. If the managers are free to negotiate and make decisions on their own, will a transfer take place? If so, within what range will the transfer price fall? Explain.
2. Refer to the data in case B above. In this case, there will be no savings in variable selling costs on intracompany sales. If the managers are free to negotiate and make decisions on their own, will a transfer take place? If so, within what range will the transfer price fall? Explain.

PROBLEM 12A–4 Transfer Price with an Outside Market [LO 12–5]

Hrubec Products, Inc., operates a Pulp Division that manufactures wood pulp for use in the production of various paper goods. Revenue and costs associated with a ton of pulp follow:

Selling price		$70
Expenses:		
Variable	$42	
Fixed (based on a capacity of 50,000 tons per year)	18	60
Net operating income		$10

Hrubec Products has just acquired a small company that manufactures paper cartons. This company will be treated as a division of Hrubec with full profit responsibility. The newly formed Carton Division is currently purchasing 5,000 tons of pulp per year from a supplier at a cost of $70 per ton, less a 10% purchase discount. Hrubec's president is anxious for the Carton Division to begin purchasing its pulp from the Pulp Division if an acceptable transfer price can be worked out.

Required:

For requirements 1 and 2, assume that the Pulp Division can sell all of its pulp to outside customers for $70 per ton.

1. Are the managers of the Carton and Pulp Divisions likely to voluntarily agree to a transfer price for 5,000 tons of pulp next year? Why or why not?
2. If the Pulp Division meets the price that the Carton Division is currently paying to its supplier and sells 5,000 tons of pulp to the Carton Division each year, what will be the effect on the profits of the Pulp Division, the Carton Division, and the company as a whole?

For requirements 3–6, assume that the Pulp Division is currently selling only 30,000 tons of pulp each year to outside customers at the stated $70 price.

3. Are the managers of the Carton and Pulp Divisions likely to voluntarily agree to a transfer price for 5,000 tons of pulp next year? Why or why not?
4. Suppose that the Carton Division's outside supplier drops its price (net of the purchase discount) to only $59 per ton. Should the Pulp Division meet this price? Explain. If the Pulp Division does *not* meet the $59 price, what will be the effect on the profits of the company as a whole?
5. Refer to requirement 4. If the Pulp Division refuses to meet the $59 price, should the Carton Division be required to purchase from the Pulp Division at a higher price for the good of the company as a whole?
6. Refer to requirement 4. Assume that due to inflexible management policies, the Carton Division is required to purchase 5,000 tons of pulp each year from the Pulp Division at $70 per ton. What will be the effect on the profits of the company as a whole?

PROBLEM 12A–5 Market-Based Transfer Price [LO 12–5]

Stavos Company's Screen Division manufactures a standard screen for high-definition televisions (HDTVs). The cost per screen is:

Variable cost per screen	$ 70
Fixed cost per screen*	30
Total cost per screen	$100

*Based on a capacity of 10,000 screens per year.

Part of the Screen Division's output is sold to outside manufacturers of HDTVs and part is sold to Stavos Company's Quark Division, which produces an HDTV under its own name. The Screen Division charges $140 per screen for all sales.

The costs, revenue, and net operating income associated with the Quark Division's HDTV are given below:

Selling price per unit		$480
Variable cost per unit:		
Cost of the screen	$140	
Variable cost of electronic parts	210	
Total variable costs		350
Contribution margin		130
Fixed costs per unit		80*
Net operating income per unit		$ 50

*Based on a capacity of 3,000 units per year.

The Quark Division has an order from an overseas source for 1,000 HDTVs. The overseas source wants to pay only $340 per unit.

Required:

1. Assume that the Quark Division has enough idle capacity to fill the 1,000-unit order. Is the division likely to accept the $340 price or to reject it? Explain.
2. Assume that both the Screen Division and the Quark Division have idle capacity. Under these conditions, would it be advantageous for the company as a whole if the Quark Division rejects the $340 price? Show computations to support your answer.
3. Assume that the Quark Division has idle capacity but that the Screen Division is operating at capacity and could sell all of its screens to outside manufacturers. Compute the profit impact to the Quark Division of accepting the 1,000-unit order at the $340 unit price.
4. What conclusions do you draw concerning the use of market price as a transfer price in intracompany transactions?

PROBLEM 12A–6 Basic Transfer Pricing [LO 12–5]

Alpha and Beta are divisions within the same company. The managers of both divisions are evaluated based on their own division's return on investment (ROI). Assume the following information relative to the two divisions:

	Case 1	Case 2	Case 3	Case 4
Alpha Division:				
Capacity in units	80,000	400,000	150,000	300,000
Number of units now being sold to outside customers	80,000	400,000	100,000	300,000
Selling price per unit to outside customers	$30	$90	$75	$50
Variable costs per unit	$18	$65	$40	$26
Fixed costs per unit (based on capacity)	$6	$15	$20	$9
Beta Division:				
Number of units needed annually	5,000	30,000	20,000	120,000
Purchase price now being paid to an outside supplier	$27	$89	$75*	–

*Before any purchase discount.

Managers are free to decide if they will participate in any internal transfers. All transfer prices are negotiated.

Required:

1. Refer to case 1 shown above. Alpha Division can avoid $2 per unit in commissions on any sales to Beta Division. Will the managers agree to a transfer, and if so, within what range will the transfer price be? Explain.
2. Refer to case 2 shown above. A study indicates that Alpha Division can avoid $5 per unit in shipping costs on any sales to Beta Division.
   a. Would you expect any disagreement between the two divisional managers over what the transfer price should be? Explain.
   b. Assume that Alpha Division offers to sell 30,000 units to Beta Division for $88 per unit and that Beta Division refuses this price. What will be the loss in potential profits for the company as a whole?
3. Refer to case 3 shown above. Assume that Beta Division is now receiving an 8% price discount from the outside supplier.
   a. Will the managers agree to a transfer? If so, what is the range within which the transfer price would be?
   b. Assume that Beta Division offers to purchase 20,000 units from Alpha Division at $60 per unit. If Alpha Division accepts this price, would you expect its ROI to increase, decrease, or remain unchanged? Why?
4. Refer to case 4 shown above. Assume that Beta Division wants Alpha Division to provide it with 120,000 units of a *different* product from the one that Alpha Division is now producing. The new product would require $21 per unit in variable costs and would require that Alpha Division cut back production of its present product by 45,000 units annually. What is the lowest acceptable transfer price from Alpha Division's perspective?

CASE 12A–7 Transfer Pricing; Divisional Performance [LO 12–5]

Weller Industries is a decentralized organization with six divisions. The company's Electrical Division produces a variety of electrical items, including an X52 electrical fitting. The Electrical Division (which is operating at capacity) sells this fitting to its regular customers for $7.50 each; the fitting has a variable manufacturing cost of $4.25.

The company's Brake Division has asked the Electrical Division to supply it with a large quantity of X52 fittings for only $5 each. The Brake Division, which is operating at 50% of capacity, will put the fitting into a brake unit that it will produce and sell to a large commercial airline manufacturer. The cost of the brake unit being built by the Brake Division follows:

Purchased parts (from outside vendors)	$22.50
Electrical fitting X52	5.00
Other variable costs	14.00
Fixed overhead and administration	8.00
Total cost per brake unit	$49.50

Although the $5 price for the X52 fitting represents a substantial discount from the regular $7.50 price, the manager of the Brake Division believes that the price concession is necessary if his division is to get the contract for the airplane brake units. He has heard "through the grapevine" that the airplane manufacturer plans to reject his bid if it is more than $50 per brake unit. Thus, if the Brake Division is forced to pay the regular $7.50 price for the X52 fitting, it will either not get the contract or it will suffer a substantial loss at a time when it is already operating at only 50% of capacity. The manager of the Brake Division argues that the price concession is imperative to the well-being of both his division and the company as a whole.

Weller Industries uses return on investment (ROI) to measure divisional performance.

Required:

1. Assume that you are the manager of the Electrical Division. Would you recommend that your division supply the X52 fitting to the Brake Division for $5 each as requested? Why or why not? Show all computations.
2. Would it be profitable for the company as a whole for the Electrical Division to supply the fittings to the Brake Division if the airplane brakes can be sold for $50? Show all computations, and explain your answer.

3. In principle, should it be possible for the two managers to agree to a transfer price in this particular situation? If so, within what range would that transfer price lie?
4. Discuss the organizational behavior problems, if any, inherent in this situation. What would you advise the company's president to do in this situation?

(CMA, adapted)

Appendix 12B: Service Department Charges

LEARNING OBJECTIVE 12–6
Charge operating departments for services provided by service departments.

Most large organizations have both *operating departments* and *service departments.* The central purposes of the organization are carried out in the **operating departments**. In contrast, **service departments** do not directly engage in operating activities. Instead, they provide services or assistance to the operating departments. Examples of service departments include Cafeteria, Internal Auditing, Human Resources, Cost Accounting, and Purchasing.

Service department costs are charged to operating departments for a variety of reasons, including:

- To encourage operating departments to make wise use of service department resources. If the services were provided for free, operating managers would be inclined to waste these resources.
- To provide operating departments with more complete cost data for making decisions. Actions taken by operating departments have impacts on service department costs. For example, hiring another employee will increase costs in the human resources department. Such service department costs should be charged to the operating departments, otherwise the operating departments will not take them into account when making decisions.
- To help measure the profitability of operating departments. Charging service department costs to operating departments provides a more complete accounting of the costs incurred as a consequence of activities in the operating departments.
- To create an incentive for service departments to operate efficiently. Charging service department costs to operating departments provides a system of checks and balances in the sense that cost-conscious operating departments will take an active interest in keeping service department costs low.

In Appendix 12A, we discussed *transfer prices* that are charged within an organization when one part of an organization provides a product to another part of the organization. The service department charges considered in this appendix can be viewed as transfer prices that are charged for services provided by service departments to operating departments.

Charging Costs by Behavior

Whenever possible, variable and fixed service department costs should be charged to operating departments separately to provide more useful data for planning and control of departmental operations.

Variable Costs

Variable costs vary in total in proportion to changes in the level of service provided. For example, the cost of food in a cafeteria is a variable cost that varies in proportion to the number of persons using the cafeteria or the number of meals served.

A variable cost should be charged to consuming departments according to whatever activity causes the incurrence of the cost. For example, variable costs of a maintenance department that are caused by the number of machine-hours worked in the operating departments should be charged to the operating departments on the basis of machine-hours. This will ensure that these costs are properly traced to departments, products, and customers.

Fixed Costs

The fixed costs of service departments represent the costs of making capacity available for use. These costs should be charged to consuming departments in *predetermined lump-sum amounts* that are determined in advance and do not change. The lump-sum amount charged to a department can be based either on the department's peak-period or long-run average servicing needs.

The logic behind lump-sum charges of this type is as follows: When a service department is first established, its capacity will be determined by the needs of the departments that it will serve. This capacity may reflect the peak-period needs of the other departments, or it may reflect their long-run average or "normal" servicing needs. Depending on how much servicing capacity is provided for, it will be necessary to make a commitment of resources, which will be reflected in the service department's fixed costs. These fixed costs should be borne by the consuming departments in proportion to the amount of capacity each consuming department requires. That is, if available capacity in the service department has been provided to meet the peak-period needs of consuming departments, then the fixed costs of the service department should be charged in predetermined lump-sum amounts to consuming departments on that basis. If available capacity has been provided only to meet "normal" or long-run average needs, then the fixed costs should be charged on that basis.

Once set, charges should not vary from period to period, because they represent the cost of having a certain level of service capacity available for each operating department. The fact that an operating department does not need the peak level or even the "normal" level of service every period is immaterial; the capacity to deliver this level of service must be available. The operating departments should bear the cost of that availability.

Should Actual or Budgeted Costs Be Charged?

The *budgeted,* rather than actual, costs of a service department should be charged to operating departments. This ensures that service departments remain solely responsible for explaining any differences between their actual and budgeted costs. If service departments could base their charges on actual costs, then operating departments would be unfairly held accountable for cost overruns in the service departments.

Guidelines for Service Department Charges

The following summarizes how service department costs should be charged to operating departments:

- Variable and fixed service department costs should be charged separately.
- Variable service department costs should be charged using a predetermined rate applied to the actual quantity of services consumed.
- Fixed costs represent the costs of having service capacity available. These costs should be charged in lump sums to each operating department in proportion to their peak-period needs or long-run average needs. The lump-sum amounts should be based on budgeted fixed costs, not actual fixed costs.

Example

Seaboard Airlines has two operating divisions: a Freight Division and a Passenger Division. The company has a Maintenance Department that services both divisions. Variable servicing costs are budgeted at $10 per flight-hour. The department's fixed costs are budgeted at $750,000 for the year. The fixed costs of the Maintenance Department are budgeted based on the peak-period demand, which occurs during the Thanksgiving to New Year's holiday period. The airline wants to make sure that none of its aircraft are grounded during this key period due to unavailability of maintenance facilities. Approximately 40% of the maintenance during this period is performed on the Freight Division's equipment, and 60% is performed on the Passenger Division's equipment. These figures and the budgeted flight-hours for the coming year are as follows:

	Percent of Peak Period Capacity Required	Budgeted Flight-Hours
Freight Division	40%	9,000
Passenger Division	60	15,000
Total	100%	24,000

Year-end records show that actual variable and fixed costs in the aircraft Maintenance Department for the year were $260,000 and $780,000, respectively. One division logged more flight-hours during the year than planned, and the other division logged fewer flight-hours than planned, as shown below:

	Flight-Hours	
	Budgeted	Actual
Freight Division	9,000	8,000
Passenger Division	15,000	17,000
Total flight-hours	24,000	25,000

The amount of Maintenance Department cost charged to each division for the year would be as follows:

		Actual activity	Division	
			Freight	Passenger
	Variable cost charges:			
Budgeted variable rate	$10 per flight-hour ×	8,000 flight-hours	$ 80,000	
	$10 per flight-hour ×	17,000 flight-hours		$170,000
	Fixed cost charges:			
Peak-period capacity required	40% × $750,000		300,000	
	60% × $750,000			450,000
	Total charges		$380,000	$620,000
	Budgeted fixed cost			

Notice that variable servicing costs are charged to the operating divisions based on the budgeted rate ($10 per hour) and the *actual activity* for the year. In contrast, the charges for fixed costs are based entirely on budgeted data. Also note that the two operating divisions are *not* charged for the actual costs of the service department, which are influenced by how well the service department is managed. Instead, the service department is held responsible for the actual costs not charged to other departments as shown below:

	Variable	Fixed
Total actual costs incurred	$260,000	$780,000
Total charges to operating departments	250,000*	750,000
Spending variance—responsibility of the Maintenance Department	$ 10,000	$ 30,000

*$10 per flight-hour × 25,000 actual flight-hours = $250,000.

Some Cautions in Allocating Service Department Costs

Pitfalls in Allocating Fixed Costs

Rather than charge fixed costs to operating departments in predetermined lump-sum amounts, some companies allocate them using a *variable* allocation base that fluctuates from period to period. This practice can distort decisions and create serious inequities between departments. The inequities arise from the fact that the fixed costs allocated to one department are heavily influenced by what happens in *other* departments.

Sales dollars is an example of a variable allocation base that is often used to allocate fixed costs from service departments to operating departments. Using sales dollars as a base is simple, straightforward, and easy to work with. Furthermore, people tend to view sales dollars as a measure of ability to pay, and, hence, as a measure of how readily costs can be absorbed from other parts of the organization.

Unfortunately, sales dollars are often a very poor base for allocating or charging costs because sales dollars vary from period to period, whereas the costs are often largely *fixed.* Therefore, a letup in sales effort in one department will shift allocated costs from that department to other, more successful departments. In effect, the departments putting forth the best sales efforts are penalized in the form of higher allocations. The result is often bitterness and resentment on the part of the managers of the better departments.

For example, let's assume that a large men's clothing store has one service department and three sales departments—Suits, Shoes, and Accessories. The service department's costs total $60,000 per period and are allocated to the three sales departments according to sales dollars. A recent period showed the following allocation:

	Departments			
	Suits	Shoes	Accessories	Total
Sales by department.	$260,000	$40,000	$100,000	$400,000
Percentage of total sales.	65%	10%	25%	100%
Allocation of service department costs, based on percentage of total sales.	$39,000	$6,000	$15,000	$60,000

In the following period, let's assume the manager of the Suits Department launched a successful program to expand sales in his department by $100,000. Furthermore, let's assume that sales in the other two departments remained unchanged, total service department costs remained unchanged, and the sales departments' expected usage of service department resources remained unchanged. Given these assumptions, the service department cost allocations to the sales departments would change as shown below:

	Departments			
	Suits	Shoes	Accessories	Total
Sales by department.	$360,000	$40,000	$100,000	$500,000
Percentage of total sales.	72%	8%	20%	100%
Allocation of service department costs, based on percentage of total sales.	$43,200	$4,800	$12,000	$60,000
Increase (or decrease) from prior allocation	$4,200	$(1,200)	$(3,000)	$0

After seeing these allocations, the manager of the Suits Department is likely to complain, because by growing sales in his department, he is being forced to carry a larger share of the service department costs. In essence, this manager is being punished for his outstanding performance by being saddled with a greater proportion of service department costs. On the other hand, the managers of the departments that showed no sales growth are being relieved of a portion of the costs they had been carrying. Yet, there was no change in the amount of services provided for any department across the two periods.

This example shows why a variable allocation base such as sales dollars should only be used as a base for allocating or charging costs in those cases where service department costs actually vary with the chosen allocation base. When service department costs are fixed, they should be charged to operating departments according to the guidelines mentioned earlier.

Glossary (Appendix 12B)

Operating department A department in which the central purposes of the organization are carried out. (p. 570)

Service department A department that does not directly engage in operating activities; rather, it provides services or assistance to the operating departments. (p. 570)

Appendix 12B Exercises and Problems connect

Additional student resources are available with Connect.

EXERCISE 12B–1 Service Department Charges [LO 12–6]

Hannibal Steel Company has a Transport Services Department that provides trucks to haul ore from the company's mine to its two steel mills—the Northern Plant and the Southern Plant. Budgeted costs for the Transport Services Department total $350,000 per year, consisting of $0.25 per ton variable cost and $300,000 fixed cost. The level of fixed cost is determined by peak-period requirements. During the peak period, the Northern Plant requires 70% of the Transport Services Department's capacity and the Southern Plant requires 30%.

During the year, the Transport Services Department actually hauled the following amounts of ore for the two plants: Northern Plant, 130,000 tons; Southern Plant, 50,000 tons. The Transport Services Department incurred $364,000 in cost during the year, of which $54,000 was variable cost and $310,000 was fixed cost.

Required:

1. Determine how much of the $54,000 in variable cost should be charged to each plant.
2. Determine how much of the $310,000 in fixed cost should be charged to each plant.
3. Should any of the $364,000 in the Transport Services Department cost not be charged to the plants? Explain.

EXERCISE 12B–2 Sales Dollars as an Allocation Base for Fixed Costs [LO 12–6]

Konig Enterprises, Ltd., owns and operates three restaurants in Vancouver, B.C. The company allocates its fixed administrative expenses to the three restaurants on the basis of sales dollars. During 2013, the fixed administrative expenses totaled $2,000,000. These expenses were allocated as follows:

	Restaurants			
	Rick's Harborside	Imperial Garden	Ginger Wok	Total
Total sales—2013	$16,000,000	$15,000,000	$9,000,000	$40,000,000
Percentage of total sales	40%	37.5%	22.5%	100%
Allocation (based on the above percentages)	$800,000	$750,000	$450,000	$2,000,000

During 2014, the following year, the Imperial Garden restaurant increased its sales by $10 million. The sales levels in the other two restaurants remained unchanged. The company's 2014 sales data were as follows:

	Restaurants			
	Rick's Harborside	Imperial Garden	Ginger Wok	Total
Total sales—2014	$16,000,000	$25,000,000	$9,000,000	$50,000,000
Percentage of total sales	32%	50%	18%	100%

Fixed administrative expenses remained unchanged at $2,000,000 during 2014.

Required:

1. Using sales dollars as an allocation base, show the allocation of the fixed administrative expenses among the three restaurants for 2014.
2. Compare your allocation from requirement 1 to the allocation for 2013. As the manager of the Imperial Garden, how would you feel about the amount that has been charged to you for 2014?
3. Comment on the usefulness of sales dollars as an allocation base.

EXERCISE 12B–3 Service Department Charges [LO 12–6]

Korvanis Corporation operates a Medical Services Department for its employees. Charges to the company's operating departments for the variable costs of the Medical Services Department are based on the actual number of employees in each department. Charges for the fixed costs of the Medical Services Department are based on the long-run average number of employees in each operating department.

Variable Medical Services Department costs are budgeted at $80 per employee. Fixed Medical Services Department costs are budgeted at $400,000 per year. Actual Medical Services Department costs for the most recent year were $41,000 for variable costs and $408,000 for fixed costs. Data concerning employees in the three operating departments follow:

	Cutting	Milling	Assembly
Budgeted number of employees	170	100	280
Actual number of employees for the most recent year	150	80	270
Long-run average number of employees	180	120	300

Required:

1. Determine the Medical Services Department charges for the year to each of the operating departments—Cutting, Milling, and Assembly.
2. How much, if any, of the actual Medical Services Department costs for the year should not be charged to the operating departments?

PROBLEM 12B–4 Service Department Charges [LO 12–6]

Sharp Motor Company has two operating divisions—an Auto Division and a Truck Division. The company has a cafeteria that serves the employees of both divisions. The costs of operating the cafeteria are budgeted at $40,000 per month plus $3 per meal served. The company pays all the cost of the meals.

The fixed costs of the cafeteria are determined by peak-period requirements. The Auto Division is responsible for 65% of the peak-period requirements, and the Truck Division is responsible for the other 35%.

For June, the Auto Division estimated that it would need 35,000 meals served, and the Truck Division estimated that it would need 20,000 meals served. However, due to unexpected layoffs of employees during the month, only 20,000 meals were served to the Auto Division. Another 20,000 meals were served to the Truck Division as planned.

Cost records in the cafeteria show that actual fixed costs for June totaled $42,000 and that actual meal costs totaled $128,000.

Required:

1. How much cafeteria cost should be charged to each division for June?
2. Assume that the company follows the practice of allocating *all* cafeteria costs incurred each month to the divisions in proportion to the number of meals served to each division during the month. On this basis, how much cost would be allocated to each division for June?
3. What criticisms can you make of the allocation method used in requirement 2?
4. If managers of operating departments know that fixed service costs are going to be allocated on the basis of peak-period requirements, what will be their probable strategy as they report their estimate of peak-period requirements to the company's budget committee? As a member of top management, what would you do to neutralize such strategies?

PROBLEM 12B–5 Service Department Charges [LO 12–6]

Tasman Products, Ltd., of Australia has a Maintenance Department that services the equipment in the company's Forming Department and Assembly Department. The cost of this servicing is charged to the operating departments on the basis of machine-hours. Cost and other data relating to the Maintenance Department and to the other two departments for the most recent year are presented below.

Data for the Maintenance Department follow:

	Budget	Actual
Variable costs for lubricants	$96,000*	$110,000
Fixed costs for salaries and other.	$150,000	$153,000

*Budgeted at $0.40 per machine-hour.

Data for the Forming and Assembly departments follow:

	Percent of Peak-Period Capacity Required	Machine-Hours	
		Budget	Actual
Forming Department.	70%	160,000	190,000
Assembly Department . . .	30%	80,000	70,000
Total.	100%	240,000	260,000

The level of fixed costs in the Maintenance Department is determined by peak-period requirements.

Required:

Management would like data to assist in comparing actual performance to planned performance in the Maintenance Department and in the other departments.

1. How much Maintenance Department cost should be charged to the Forming Department and to the Assembly Department? Show all computations.
2. Should any portion of the actual Maintenance Department costs not be charged to the other departments? If all costs should be charged, explain why; if a portion should not be charged, compute the amount and explain why it should not be charged.

Appendix

A

Pricing Products and Services

LEARNING OBJECTIVES

After studying Appendix A, you should be able to:

LO A–1 Compute the profit-maximizing price of a product or service using the price elasticity of demand and variable cost.

LO A–2 Compute the selling price of a product using the absorption costing approach.

LO A–3 Compute the target cost for a new product or service.

Introduction

Some products have an established market price. Consumers will not pay more than this price and there is no reason for a supplier to charge less—the supplier can sell all that it produces at this price. Under these circumstances, the supplier simply charges the prevailing market price for the product. Markets for basic raw materials such as farm products and minerals follow this pattern.

In this appendix, we are concerned with the more common situation in which a business is faced with the problem of setting its own prices. Clearly, the pricing decision can be critical. If the price is set too high, customers won't buy the company's products. If the price is set too low, the company's costs won't be covered.

The usual approach in pricing is to *mark up* cost.[1] A product's **markup** is the difference between its selling price and its cost and is usually expressed as a percentage of cost.

$$\text{Selling price} = (1 + \text{Markup percentage}) \times \text{Cost}$$

For example, a company that uses a markup of 50% adds 50% to the costs of its products to determine selling prices. If a product costs $10, then the company would charge $15 for the product. This approach is called **cost-plus pricing** because a predetermined markup percentage is applied to a cost base to determine the selling price.

Two key issues must be addressed with the cost-plus approach to pricing. First, what cost should be used? Second, how should the markup be determined? Several alternative approaches are considered in this appendix, starting with the approach generally favored by economists.

IN BUSINESS

THE BUSINESS OF ART SCULPTURE

Shidoni Foundry, located in Tesuque, New Mexico, is a fine art casting and fabrication facility. The process of creating a bronze or other metal sculpture is complex. The artist creates the sculpture using modeling clay and then hires a foundry such as Shidoni to produce the actual metal sculpture. Shidoni craftspeople make a rubber mold from the clay model then use that mold to make a wax version of the original. The wax is in turn used to make a ceramic casting mold, and finally the bronze version is cast. Both the wax and the ceramic casting mold are destroyed in the process of making the metal casting, but the rubber mold is not and can be reused to make additional castings.

The surface of the metal sculpture can be treated with various patinas. One of the accompanying photos shows Harry Gold, the shop's patina artist, applying a patina to a metal sculpture with brush and blowtorch. The other photo shows a finished sculpture with patinas applied.

The artist is faced with a difficult business decision. The rubber mold for a small figure such as the seated Indian in the accompanying photo costs roughly $500; the mold for a life-size figure such as the cowboy costs $3,800 to $5,000. This is just for the mold! Fortunately, as discussed above, a number of metal castings can be made from each mold. However, each life-size casting costs $8,500 to $11,000. In contrast, a casting of the much smaller Indian sculpture would cost about $750. Given the fixed costs of the mold and variable costs of the casting, finish treatments, and bases, the artist must decide how many castings to produce and how to price them. The fewer the castings, the greater the rarity factor, and hence the higher the price that can be charged to art lovers. However, in that case, the fixed costs of making the mold must be spread across fewer items. The artist must make sure not to price the sculptures so high that the investment in molds and in the castings cannot be recovered.

Source: Conversations with Shidoni personnel, including Bill Rogers and Harry Gold, and Shidoni literature. See www.shidoni.com for more information concerning the company.

© Eric Noreen

© Eric Noreen

[1] There are some legal restrictions on prices. Antitrust laws prohibit "predatory" prices, which are generally interpreted by the courts to mean a price below average variable cost. "Price discrimination"—charging different prices to customers in the same market for the same product or service—is also prohibited by the law.

The Economists' Approach to Pricing

LEARNING OBJECTIVE A–1
Compute the profit-maximizing price of a product or service using the price elasticity of demand and variable cost.

If a company raises the price of a product, unit sales ordinarily fall. Because of this, pricing is a delicate balancing act in which the benefits of higher revenues per unit are traded off against the lower volume that results from charging a higher price. The sensitivity of unit sales to changes in price is called the *price elasticity of demand.*

Elasticity of Demand

A product's price elasticity should be a key element in setting its price. The **price elasticity of demand** measures the degree to which a change in price affects the unit sales of a product or service. Demand for a product is said to be *inelastic* if a change in price has little effect on the number of units sold. The demand for designer perfumes sold by trained personnel at cosmetic counters in department stores is relatively inelastic. Raising or lowering prices on these luxury goods has little effect on unit sales. On the other hand, demand for a product is *elastic* if a change in price has a substantial effect on the volume of units sold. An example of a product whose demand is elastic is gasoline. If a gas station raises its price for gasoline, unit sales will drop as customers seek lower prices elsewhere.

Price elasticity is very important in determining prices. Managers should set higher markups over cost when customers are relatively insensitive to price (i.e., demand is inelastic) and lower markups when customers are relatively sensitive to price (i.e., demand is elastic). This principle is followed in department stores. Merchandise sold in the bargain basement has a much lower markup than merchandise sold elsewhere in the store because customers who shop in the bargain basement are much more sensitive to price (i.e., demand is elastic).

The price elasticity of demand for a product or service, ε_d, can be estimated using the following formula.[2,3]

$$\varepsilon_d = \frac{\ln(1 + \%\text{ change in quantity sold})}{\ln(1 + \%\text{ change in price})}$$

For example, suppose that the managers of Nature's Garden believe that a 10% increase in the selling price of their apple-almond shampoo would result in a 15% decrease in the number of bottles of shampoo sold.[4] The price elasticity of demand for this product would be computed as follows:

$$\varepsilon_d = \frac{\ln[1 + (-0.15)]}{\ln[1 + (0.10)]} = \frac{\ln(0.85)}{\ln(1.10)} = -1.71$$

For comparison purposes, the managers of Nature's Garden believe that another product, strawberry glycerin soap, would experience a 20% drop in unit sales if its price is increased by 10%. (Purchasers of this product are more sensitive to price than the purchasers of the apple-almond shampoo.) The price elasticity of demand for the strawberry glycerin soap is:

$$\varepsilon_d = \frac{\ln[1 + (-0.20)]}{\ln[1 + (0.10)]} = \frac{\ln(0.80)}{\ln(1.10)} = -2.34$$

Both of these products, like other normal products, have a price elasticity that is less than –1.

---

[2] The term "ln()" is the natural log function. You can compute the natural log of any number using the LN or In*x* key on your calculator. For example, In(0.85) = –0.1625.

[3] This formula assumes that the price elasticity of demand is constant. This occurs when the relation between the selling price, *p,* and the unit sales, *q* can be expressed in the following form: $\text{In}(q) = a + \varepsilon_d$. Even if this is not precisely true, the formula provides a useful way to estimate a product's price elasticity.

[4] The estimated change in unit sales should take into account competitors' responses to a price change.

Note that the price elasticity of demand for the strawberry glycerin soap is larger (in absolute value) than the price elasticity of demand for the apple-almond shampoo. This indicates that the demand for strawberry glycerin soap is more elastic than the demand for apple-almond shampoo.

In the next subsection, the price elasticity of demand will be used to compute the selling price that maximizes the profits of the company.

The Profit–Maximizing Price

Under certain conditions, the profit-maximizing price can be determined by marking up *variable cost* using the following formula:[5]

$$\text{Profit-maximizing markup on variable cost} = \frac{-1}{1 + \varepsilon_d}$$

Using the above markup, the selling price would be set using the formula:

$$\text{Profit-maximizing price} = (1 + \text{Profit-maximizing markup on variable cost}) \times \text{Variable cost per unit}$$

The profit-maximizing prices for the two Nature's Garden products are computed below using these formulas:

Apple-Almond Shampoo

$$\text{Profit-maximizing markup on variable cost} = \left(\frac{-1}{1 + (-1.71)}\right) = 1.41$$

$$\text{Profit-maximizing price} = (1 + 1.41)\$2.00 = \$4.82$$

Strawberry Glycerin Soap

$$\text{Profit-maximizing markup on variable cost} = \left(\frac{-1}{1 + (-2.34)}\right) = 0.75$$

$$\text{Profit-maximizing price} = (1 + 0.75)\$0.40 = \$0.70$$

Note that the 75% markup for the strawberry glycerin soap is lower than the 141% markup for the apple-almond shampoo. The reason for this is that the purchasers of strawberry glycerin soap are more sensitive to price than the purchasers of apple-almond shampoo. Strawberry glycerin soap is a relatively common product with close substitutes available in nearly every grocery store.

Exhibit A–1 shows how the profit-maximizing markup is generally affected by how sensitive unit sales are to price. For example, if a 10% increase in price leads to a 20% decrease in unit sales, then the optimal markup on variable cost according to the exhibit is 75%—the figure computed above for the strawberry glycerin soap. Note that the optimal markup drops as unit sales become more sensitive to price.

Caution is advised when using these formulas to establish a selling price. The formulas rely on simplifying assumptions and the estimate of the percentage change in unit sales that would result from a given percentage change in price is likely to be inexact. Nevertheless, the formulas can provide valuable clues regarding whether prices should be increased or decreased. Suppose, for example, that the strawberry glycerin soap is currently being sold for $0.60 per bar. The formula indicates that the profit-maximizing price

[5] The formula assumes that (a) the price elasticity of demand is constant; (b) Total cost = Total fixed cost + Variable cost per unit × Quantity sold: and (c) the price of the product has no effect on the sales or costs of any other product. The formula can be derived using calculus.

EXHIBIT A–1
The Optimal Markup on Variable Cost as a Function of the Sensitivity of Unit Sales to Price

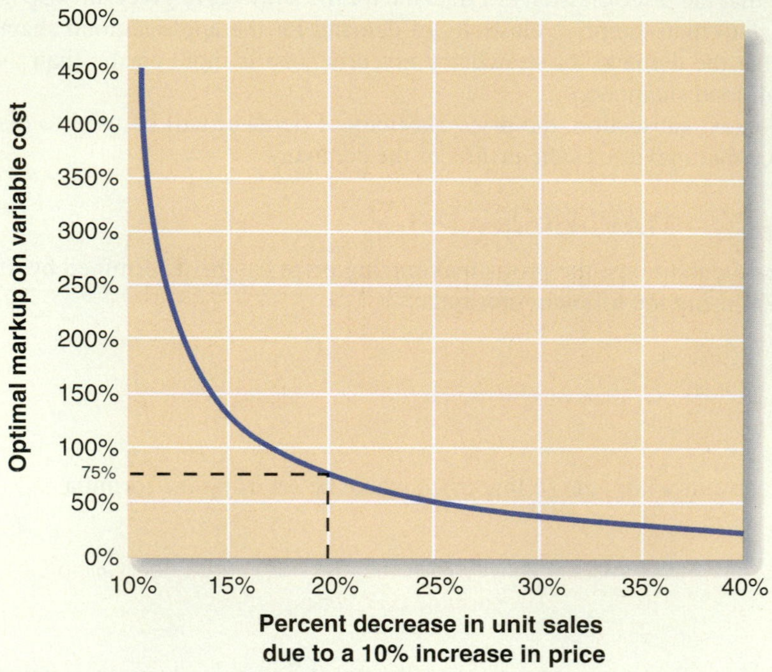

is $0.70 per bar. Rather than increasing the price by $0.10, it would be prudent to increase the price by a more modest amount to observe what happens to unit sales and to profits.

The formula for the profit-maximizing price conveys a very important lesson. If the total fixed costs are the same whether the company charges $0.60 or $0.70, they cannot be relevant in the decision of which price to charge for the soap. The optimal selling price should depend on two factors—the variable cost per unit and how sensitive unit sales are to changes in price. Fixed costs play no role in setting the optimal price. Fixed costs are relevant when deciding whether to offer a product but are not relevant when deciding how much to charge for the product.

We can directly verify that an increase in selling price for the strawberry glycerin soap from the current price of $0.60 per bar is warranted, based just on the forecast that a 10% increase in selling price would lead to a 20% decrease in unit sales. Suppose, for example, that Nature's Garden is currently selling 200,000 bars of the soap per year at the price of $0.60 a bar. If the change in price has no effect on the company's fixed costs or on other products, the effect on profits of increasing the price by 10% can be computed as follows:

	Present Price	Higher Price
Selling price (a)	$0.60	$0.60 + (0.10 × $0.60) = $0.66
Unit sales (b)	200,000	200,000 – (0.20 × 200,000) = 160,000
Sales (a) × (b)	$120,000	$105,600
Variable cost ($0.40 per unit)	80,000	64,000
Contribution margin	$ 40,000	$ 41,600

Despite the apparent optimality of prices based on marking up variable costs according to the price elasticity of demand, surveys consistently reveal that most managers approach the pricing problem from a completely different perspective. They prefer to mark up some version of full, not variable, costs, and the markup is based on desired profits rather than on factors related to demand. This approach is called the *absorption costing approach to cost-plus pricing*.

The Absorption Costing Approach to Cost-Plus Pricing

LEARNING OBJECTIVE A–2
Compute the selling price of a product using the absorption costing approach.

The absorption costing approach to cost-plus pricing differs from the economists' approach both in what costs are marked up and in how the markup is determined. Under the absorption approach to cost-plus pricing, the cost base is the absorption costing unit product cost, as defined in Chapter 3, rather than variable cost.

Setting a Target Selling Price Using the Absorption Costing Approach

To illustrate, assume that the management of Ritter Company wants to set the selling price on a product that has just undergone some design modifications. The accounting department has provided cost estimates for the redesigned product as shown below:

	Per Unit	Total
Direct materials	$6	
Direct labor	$4	
Variable manufacturing overhead	$3	
Fixed manufacturing overhead		$70,000
Variable selling and administrative expenses	$2	
Fixed selling and administrative expenses		$60,000

The first step in the absorption costing approach to cost-plus pricing is to compute the unit product cost. For Ritter Company, this amounts to $20 per unit at a volume of 10,000 units, as computed below:

Direct materials	$ 6
Direct labor	4
Variable manufacturing overhead	3
Fixed manufacturing overhead ($70,000 ÷ 10,000 units)	7
Unit product cost	$20

Ritter Company has a general policy of marking up unit product costs by 50%. A price quotation sheet for the company prepared using the absorption approach is presented in Exhibit A–2. Note that selling and administrative expenses are not included in the cost base. Instead, the markup is supposed to cover these expenses.

EXHIBIT A–2
Price Quotation Sheet—Absorption Basis (10,000 Units)

Direct materials	$ 6
Direct labor	4
Variable manufacturing overhead	3
Fixed manufacturing overhead (based on 10,000 units)	7
Unit product cost	20
Markup to cover selling and administrative expenses and desired profit—50% of unit manufacturing cost	10
Target selling price	$30

Determining the Markup Percentage

Ritter Company's markup percentage of 50% could be a widely used rule of thumb in the industry or just a company tradition that seems to work. The markup percentage may also be the result of an explicit computation. As we have discussed, the markup over cost should be largely determined by market conditions. However, many companies base their markup on cost and desired profit. The reasoning goes like this. The markup must be large enough to cover selling and administrative expenses and provide an adequate return on investment (ROI). Given the forecasted unit sales, the markup can be computed as follows:

$$\text{Markup percentage on absorption cost} = \frac{(\text{Required ROI} \times \text{Investment}) + \text{Selling and administrative expenses}}{\text{Unit product cost} \times \text{Unit sales}}$$

To show how this formula is applied, assume Ritter Company invests $100,000 in operating assets such as equipment to produce and market 10,000 units of the product each year. If Ritter Company requires a 20% ROI, then the markup for the product would be determined as follows:

$$\text{Markup percentage on absorption cost} = \frac{(20\% \times \$100{,}000) + (\$2 \text{ per unit} \times 10{,}000 \text{ units} + \$60{,}000)}{\$20 \text{ per unit} \times 10{,}000 \text{ units}}$$

$$= \frac{(\$20{,}000) + (\$80{,}000)}{\$200{,}000} = 50\%$$

As shown earlier, this markup of 50% leads to a target selling price of $30 for Ritter Company. *If the company actually sells 10,000 units* of the product at this price, the company's ROI on this product will indeed be 20%. This is verified in Exhibit A–3. However,

EXHIBIT A–3
Income Statement and ROI Analysis—Ritter Company Actual Unit Sales = 10,000 Units; Selling Price = $30

Direct materials	$ 6
Direct labor	4
Variable manufacturing overhead	3
Fixed manufacturing overhead ($70,000 ÷ 10,000 units)	7
Unit product cost	$20

Ritter Company
Absorption Costing Income Statement

Sales ($30 per unit × 10,000 units)	$300,000
Cost of goods sold ($20 per unit × 10,000 units)	200,000
Gross margin	100,000
Selling and administrative expenses ($2 per unit × 10,000 units + $60,000)	80,000
Net operating income	$ 20,000

ROI

$$\text{ROI} = \frac{\text{Net operating income}}{\text{Average operating assets}}$$

$$= \frac{\$20{,}000}{\$100{,}000}$$

$$= 20\%$$

if it turns out that more than 10,000 units are sold at this price, the ROI will be greater than 20%. If less than 10,000 units are sold, the ROI will be less than 20%. *The required ROI will be attained only if the forecasted unit sales volume is attained.*

Problems with the Absorption Costing Approach

The absorption costing approach makes pricing decisions look deceptively simple. All a company needs to do is compute its unit product cost, decide how much profit it wants, and then set its price. It appears that a company can ignore demand and arrive at a price that will safely yield whatever profit it wants. However, as noted above, the absorption costing approach relies on a forecast of unit sales. Neither the markup nor the unit product cost can be computed without such a forecast.

The absorption costing approach essentially assumes that customers *need* the forecasted unit sales and will pay whatever price the company decides to charge. However, customers have a choice. If the price is too high, they can buy from a competitor or they may choose not to buy at all. Suppose, for example, that when Ritter Company sets its price at $30, it sells only 7,000 units rather than the 10,000 units forecasted. As shown in Exhibit A–4, the company would then have a loss of $25,000 on the product instead of a profit of $20,000.[6] Some managers believe that the absorption costing approach to pricing is safe. This is an illusion. The absorption costing approach is safe only if customers choose to buy at least as many units as managers forecasted they would buy.

EXHIBIT A–4
Income Statement and ROI Analysis—Ritter Company Actual Unit Sales = 7,000 Units; Selling Price = $30

Direct materials	$ 6
Direct labor	4
Variable manufacturing overhead	3
Fixed manufacturing overhead ($70,000 ÷ 7,000 units)	10
Unit product cost	$23

Ritter Company
Absorption Costing Income Statement

Sales ($30 per unit × 7,000 units)	$210,000
Cost of goods sold ($23 per unit × 7,000 units)	161,000
Gross margin	49,000
Selling and administrative expenses ($2 per unit × 7,000 units + $60,000)	74,000
Net operating loss	$ (25,000)

ROI

$$\text{ROI} = \frac{\text{Net operating income}}{\text{Average operating assets}}$$

$$= \frac{-\$25{,}000}{\$100{,}000}$$

$$= -25\%$$

[6] It may be *impossible* to break even using an absorption costing approach when the company has more than one product—even when it would be possible to make substantial profits using the economists' approach to pricing. For details, see Eric Noreen and David Burgstahler. "Full Cost Pricing and the Illusion of Satisficing," *Journal of Management Accounting Research* 9 (1997).

Target Costing

LEARNING OBJECTIVE A–3
Compute the target cost for a new product or service.

Our discussion thus far has presumed that a product has already been developed, has been costed, and is ready to be marketed as soon as a price is set. In many cases, the sequence of events is just the reverse. That is, the company already *knows* what price should be charged, and the problem is to *develop* a product that can be marketed profitably at the desired price. Even in this situation, where the normal sequence of events is reversed, cost is still a crucial factor. The company can use an approach called *target costing*. **Target costing** is the process of determining the maximum allowable cost for a new product and then developing a prototype that can be profitably made for that maximum target cost figure. A number of companies have used target costing, including Compaq, Culp, Cummins Engine, Daihatsu Motors, Chrysler, Ford, Isuzu Motors, ITT Automotive, Komatsu, Matsushita Electric, Mitsubishi Kasei, NEC, Nippodenso, Nissan, Olympus, Sharp, Texas Instruments, and Toyota.

The target cost for a product is computed by starting with the product's anticipated selling price and then deducting the desired profit, as follows:

Target cost = Anticipated selling price − Desired profit

The product development team is then given the responsibility of designing the product so that it can be made for no more than the target cost.

Reasons for Using Target Costing

The target costing approach was developed in recognition of two important characteristics of markets and costs. The first is that many companies have less control over price than they would like to think. The market (i.e., supply and demand) really determines price, and a company that attempts to ignore this does so at its peril. Therefore, the anticipated market price is taken as a given in target costing. The second observation is that most of a product's cost is determined in the design stage. Once a product has been designed and has gone into production, not much can be done to significantly reduce its cost. Most of the opportunities to reduce cost come from designing the product so that it is simple to make, uses inexpensive parts, and is robust and reliable. If the company has little control over market price and little control over cost once the product has gone into production, then it follows that the major opportunities for affecting profit come in the design stage where valuable features that customers are willing to pay for can be added and where most of the costs are really determined. So that is where the effort is concentrated—in designing and developing the product. The difference between target costing and other approaches to product development is profound. Instead of designing the product and then finding out how much it costs, the target cost is set first and then the product is designed so that the target cost is attained.

An Example of Target Costing

To provide a simple example of target costing, assume the following situation: Handy Company wishes to invest $2,000,000 to design, develop, and produce a new hand mixer. The company's Marketing Department surveyed the features and prices of competing products and determined that a price of $30 would enable Handy to sell an estimated 40,000 hand mixers per year. Because the company desires a 15% ROI, the target cost to manufacture, sell, distribute, and service one mixer is $22.50 as computed below:

Projected sales (40,000 mixers × $30 per mixer)	$1,200,000
Less desired profit (15% × $2,000,000)	300,000
Target cost for 40,000 mixers	$ 900,000
Target cost per mixer ($900,000 ÷ 40,000 mixers)	$22.50

This $22.50 target cost would be broken down into target costs for the various functions: manufacturing, marketing, distribution, after-sales service, and so on. Each functional area would be responsible for keeping its actual costs within target.

Summary

Pricing involves a delicate balancing act. Higher prices result in more revenue per unit but drive down unit sales. Exactly where to set prices to maximize profit is a difficult problem, but, in general, the markup over cost should be highest for those products where customers are least sensitive to price. The demand for such products is said to be price inelastic.

Managers often rely on cost-plus formulas to set target prices. From the economists' point of view, the cost base for the markup should be variable cost. In contrast, in the absorption costing approach the cost base is the absorption costing unit product cost and the markup is computed to cover both nonmanufacturing costs and to provide an adequate return on investment. With the absorption approach, costs will not be covered and return on investment will not be adequate unless the unit sales forecast used in the cost-plus formula is accurate. If applying the cost-plus formula results in a price that is too high, the unit sales forecast will not be attained.

Some companies take a different approach to pricing. Instead of starting with costs and then determining prices, they start with prices and then determine allowable costs. Companies that use target costing estimate what a new product's market price is likely to be based on its anticipated features and prices of products already on the market. They subtract desired profit from the estimated market price to arrive at the product's target cost. The design and development team is then given the responsibility of ensuring that the actual cost of the new product does not exceed the target cost.

Glossary

Cost-plus pricing A pricing method in which a predetermined markup is applied to a cost base to determine the target selling price. (p. 579)

Markup The difference between the selling price of a product or service and its cost. The markup is usually expressed as a percentage of cost. (p. 579)

Price elasticity of demand A measure of the degree to which a change in price affects the unit sales of a product or service. (p. 580)

Target costing The process of determining the maximum allowable cost for a new product and then developing a prototype that can be profitably made for that maximum target cost figure. (p. 586)

Questions

A–1 What is cost-plus pricing?

A–2 What does the price elasticity of demand measure? What is inelastic demand? What is elastic demand?

A–3 According to the economists' approach to setting prices, the profit-maximizing price should depend on what two factors?

A–4 Which product should have a larger markup over variable cost, a product whose demand is elastic or a product whose demand is inelastic?

A–5 When the absorption costing approach to cost-plus pricing is used, what is the markup supposed to cover?

A–6 What assumption does the absorption costing approach make about how consumers react to prices?

A–7 Discuss the following statement: "Full cost can be viewed as a floor of protection. If a company always sets its prices above full cost, it will never have to worry about operating at a loss."

A–8 What is target costing? How do target costs enter into the pricing decision?

Multiple-choice questions are available with Connect.

Exercises

connect® Additional student resources are available with Connect.

EXERCISE A–1 The Economists' Approach to Pricing [LO A–1]

Maria Lorenzi owns an ice cream stand that she operates during the summer months in West Yellowstone, Montana. Her store caters primarily to tourists passing through town on their way to Yellowstone National Park.

Maria is unsure of how she should price her ice cream cones and has experimented with two prices in successive weeks during the busy August season. The number of people who entered the store was roughly the same each week. During the first week, she priced the cones at $1.89 and 1,500 cones were sold. During the second week, she priced the cones at $1.49 and 2,340 cones were sold. The variable cost of a cone is $0.43 and consists solely of the costs of the ice cream and of the cone itself. The fixed expenses of the ice cream stand are $675 per week.

Required:

1. Did Maria make more money selling the cones for $1.89 or for $1.49?
2. Estimate the price elasticity of demand for the ice cream cones.
3. Estimate the profit-maximizing price for ice cream cones.

EXERCISE A–2 Absorption Costing Approach to Setting a Selling Price [LO A–2]

Martin Company is considering the introduction of a new product. To determine a selling price, the company has gathered the following information:

Number of units to be produced and sold each year	14,000
Unit product cost	$25
Projected annual selling and administrative expenses	$50,000
Estimated investment required by the company	$750,000
Desired return on investment (ROI)	12%

Required:

The company uses the absorption costing approach to cost-plus pricing.

1. Compute the markup required to achieve the desired ROI.
2. Compute the selling price per unit.

EXERCISE A–3 Target Costing [LO A–3]

Shimada Products Corporation of Japan is anxious to enter the electronic calculator market. Management believes that in order to be competitive in world markets, the price of the electronic calculator that the company is developing cannot exceed $15. Shimada's required rate of return is 12% on all investments. An investment of $5,000,000 would be required to purchase the equipment needed to produce the 300,000 calculators that management believes can be sold each year at the $15 price.

Required:

Compute the target cost of one calculator.

EXERCISE A–4 The Economists' Approach to Pricing [LO A–1]

The postal service of St. Vincent, an island in the West Indies, obtains a significant portion of its revenues from sales of special souvenir sheets to stamp collectors. The souvenir sheets usually contain several high-value St. Vincent stamps depicting a common theme, such as the life of

Princess Diana. The souvenir sheets are designed and printed for the postal service by Imperial Printing, a stamp agency service company in the United Kingdom. The souvenir sheets cost the postal service $0.80 each. St. Vincent has been selling these souvenir sheets for $7.00 each and ordinarily sells about 100,000 units. To test the market, the postal service recently priced a new souvenir sheet at $8.00 and sales dropped to 85,000 units.

Required:

1. Does the postal service of St. Vincent make more money selling souvenir sheets for $7.00 each or $8.00 each?
2. Estimate the price elasticity of demand for the souvenir sheets.
3. Estimate the profit-maximizing price for souvenir sheets.
4. If Imperial Printing increases the price it charges to the St. Vincent postal service for souvenir sheets to $1.00 each, how much should the St. Vincent postal service charge its customers for the souvenir sheets?

Problems

PROBLEM A–5 Standard Costs; Absorption Costing Approach to Setting Prices [LO A–2]

Wilderness Products, Inc., has designed a self-inflating sleeping pad for use by backpackers and campers. The following information is available about the new product:

a. An investment of $1,350,000 will be necessary to carry inventories and accounts receivable and to purchase some new equipment needed in the manufacturing process. The company's required rate of return is 24% on all investments.

b. A standard cost card has been prepared for the sleeping pad, as shown below:

	Standard Quantity or Hours	Standard Price or Rate	Standard Cost
Direct materials	4.0 yards	$2.70 per yard	$ 10.80
Direct labor.	2.4 hours	$8.00 per hour	19.20
Manufacturing overhead (⅕ variable).	2.4 hours	$12.50 per hour	30.00
Total standard cost per jacket			$60.00

c. The only variable selling and administrative expense will be a sales commission of $9 per pad. Fixed selling and administrative expenses will be (per year):

Salaries.	$ 82,000
Warehouse rent.	50,000
Advertising and other.	600,000
Total.	$732,000

d. Because the company manufactures many products, no more than 38,400 direct labor-hours per year can be devoted to production of the new sleeping pads.

e. Manufacturing overhead costs are allocated to products on the basis of direct labor-hours.

Required:

1. Assume that the company uses the absorption approach to cost-plus pricing.
   a. Compute the markup that the company needs on the pads to achieve a 24% return on investment (ROI) if it sells all of the pads it can produce.
   b. Using the markup you have computed, prepare a price quotation sheet for a single sleeping pad.
   c. Assume that the company is able to sell all of the pads that it can produce. Prepare an income statement for the first year of activity and compute the company's ROI for the year on the pads, using the ROI formula from Chapter 11.

2. After marketing the sleeping pads for several years, the company is experiencing a falloff in demand due to an economic recession. A large retail outlet will make a bulk purchase of pads if its label is sewn in and if an acceptable price can be worked out. What is the minimum acceptable price for this special order?

PROBLEM A–6 Missing Data; Markup Computations: Return on Investment (ROI); Pricing [LO A–2]

South Seas Products, Inc., has designed a new surfboard to replace its old surfboard line. Because of the unique design of the new surfboard, the company anticipates that it will be able to sell all the boards that it can produce. On this basis, the following incomplete budgeted income statement for the first year of activity is available:

Sales (? boards at ? per board)	$?
Cost of goods sold (? boards at ? per board)	1,600,000
Gross margin	?
Selling and administrative expenses	1,130,000
Net operating income	$?

Additional information on the new surfboard follows:

a. An investment of $1,500,000 will be necessary to carry inventories and accounts receivable and to purchase some new equipment. The company's required rate of return is 18% on all investments.

b. A partially completed standard cost card for the new surfboard follows:

	Standard Quantity or Hours	Standard Price or Rate	Standard Cost
Direct materials	6 feet	$4.50 per foot	$27
Direct labor	2 hours	? per hour	?
Manufacturing overhead	? hours	? per hour	?
Total standard cost per surfboard			$?

c. The company will employ 20 workers to make the new surfboards. Each will work a 40-hour week, 50 weeks a year.

d. Other information relating to production and costs follows:

Variable manufacturing overhead cost (per board)	$5
Variable selling expense (per board)	$10
Fixed manufacturing overhead cost (total)	$600,000
Fixed selling and administrative expense (total)	$?
Number of boards produced and sold (per year)	?

e. Overhead costs are allocated to production on the basis of direct labor-hours.

Required:

1. Complete the standard cost card for a single surfboard.
2. Assume that the company uses the absorption costing approach to cost-plus pricing.
   a. Compute the markup that the company needs on the surfboards to achieve an 18% return on investment (ROI).
   b. Using the markup you have computed, prepare a price quotation sheet for a single surfboard.
   c. Assume, as stated, that the company is able to sell all of the surfboards that it can produce. Complete the income statement for the first year of activity, and then compute the company's ROI for the year.

3. Assuming that direct labor is a variable cost, how many units would the company have to sell at the price you computed in (2) above to achieve the 18% ROI? How many units would have to be sold to just break even?

PROBLEM A–7 The Economists' Approach to Pricing; Absorption Costing Approach to Cost-Plus Pricing [LO A–1, LO A–2]

Software Solutions, Inc., was started by two young software engineers to market SpamBlocker, a software application they had written that screens incoming e-mail messages and eliminates unsolicited mass mailings. Sales of the software have been good at 50,000 units a month, but the company has been losing money as shown below:

Sales (50,000 units × $25 per unit)	$1,250,000
Variable cost (50,000 units × $6 per unit)	300,000
Contribution margin	950,000
Fixed expenses	960,000
Net operating loss	$ (10,000)

The company's only variable cost is the $6 fee it pays to another company to reproduce the software on CDs, print manuals, and package the result in an attractive box for sale to consumers. Monthly fixed selling and administrative expenses are $960,000.

The company's marketing manager has been arguing for some time that the software is priced too high. She estimates that every 5% decrease in price will yield an 8% increase in unit sales. The marketing manager would like your help in preparing a presentation to the company's owners concerning the pricing issue.

Required:

1. To help the marketing manager prepare for her presentation, she has asked you to fill in the blanks in the following table. The selling prices in the table were computed by successively decreasing the selling price by 5%. The estimated unit sales were computed by successively increasing the unit sales by 8%. For example, $23.75 is 5% less than $25.00 and 54,000 units is 8% more than 50,000 units.

Selling Price	Estimated Unit Sales	Sales	Variable Cost	Fixed Expenses	Net Operating Income
$25.00	50,000	$1,250,000	$300,000	$960,000	$(10,000)
$23.75	54,000	$1,282,500	$324,000	$960,000	$(1,500)
$22.56	58,320	?	?	?	?
$21.43	62,986	?	?	?	?
$20.36	68,025	?	?	?	?
$19.34	73,467	?	?	?	?
$18.37	79,344	?	?	?	?
$17.45	85,692	?	?	?	?
$16.58	92,547	?	?	?	?
$15.75	99,951	?	?	?	?

2. Using the data from the table, construct a chart that shows the net operating income as a function of the selling price. Put the selling price on the *X*-axis and the net operating income on the *Y*-axis. Using the chart, determine the approximate selling price at which net operating income is maximized.
3. Compute the price elasticity of demand for the SpamBlocker software. Based on this calculation, what is the profit-maximizing price?

4. The owners have invested $2,000,000 in the company and feel that they should be earning at least 2% per month on these funds. If the absorption costing approach to pricing were used, what would be the target selling price based on the current sales of 50,000 units? What do you think would happen to the net operating income of the company if this price were charged?
5. If the owners of the company are dissatisfied with the net operating income and return on investment at the selling price you computed in requirement 3, should they increase the selling price? Explain.

PROBLEM A–8 Target Costing [LO A–3]

National Restaurant Supply, Inc., sells restaurant equipment and supplies throughout most of the United States. Management is considering adding a machine that makes sorbet to its line of ice cream making machines. Management will negotiate the price of the sorbet machine with its Swedish manufacturer.

Management of National Restaurant Supply believes the sorbet machine can be sold to its customers in the United States for $4,950. At that price, annual sales of the sorbet machine should be 100 units. If the sorbet machine is added to National Restaurant Supply's product lines, the company will have to invest $600,000 in inventories and special warehouse fixtures. The variable cost of selling the sorbet machines would be $650 per machine.

Required:

1. If National Restaurant Supply requires a 15% return on investment (ROI), what is the maximum amount the company would be willing to pay the Swedish manufacturer for the sorbet machines?
2. The manager who is flying to Sweden to negotiate the purchase price of the machines would like to know how the purchase price of the machines would affect National Restaurant Supply's ROI. Construct a chart that shows National Restaurant Supply's ROI as a function of the purchase price of the sorbet machine. Put the purchase price on the *X*-axis and the resulting ROI on the *Y*-axis. Plot the ROI for purchase prices between $3,000 and $4,000 per machine.
3. After many hours of negotiations, management has concluded that the Swedish manufacturer is unwilling to sell the sorbet machine at a low enough price so that National Restaurant Supply is able to earn its 15% required ROI. Apart from simply giving up on the idea of adding the sorbet machine to National Restaurant Supply's product lines, what could management do?

Appendix

B

Profitability Analysis

LEARNING OBJECTIVES

After studying Appendix B, you should be able to:

LO B–1 Compute the profitability index and use it to select from among possible actions.

LO B–2 Compute and use the profitability index in volume trade-off decisions.

LO B–3 Compute and use the profitability index in other business decisions.

Introduction

Perhaps more than any other information, managers would like to know the profitability of their products, customers, and other business segments. They want this information so that they know what segments to drop and add and which to emphasize. This appendix provides a coherent framework for measuring profitability, bringing together relevant materials from several chapters. After studying this appendix you should have a firm grasp of the principles underlying profitability analysis. The first step is to distinguish between *absolute profitability* and *relative profitability.*

Absolute Profitability

Absolute profitability is concerned with the impact on the organization's overall profits of adding or dropping a particular segment such as a product or customer—without making any other changes. For example, if Coca-Cola were considering closing down its operations in the African country of Zimbabwe, managers would be interested in the absolute profitability of those operations. Measuring the absolute profitability of an existing segment is conceptually straightforward—compare the revenues that would be lost from dropping the segment to the costs that would be avoided. When considering a new potential segment, compare the additional revenues from adding the segment to the additional costs that would be incurred. In each case, include only the additional costs that would actually be avoided or incurred. All other costs are irrelevant and should be ignored.

In practice, figuring out what costs would change and what costs would not change if a segment were dropped (or added) can be very difficult. Activity-based costing can help in identifying such costs, but all costs should be carefully analyzed to determine whether they would really change. For example, an activity-based costing study of Coca-Cola's Zimbabwe operations might include charges for staff support provided to the Zimbabwe operations by Coca-Cola's corporate headquarters in Atlanta. However, if eliminating the Zimbabwe operations would have no impact on actual costs in Atlanta, then these costs are not relevant and should be excluded when measuring the absolute profitability of the Zimbabwe operations.

For examples of the measurement of absolute profitability, see "Appendix 6A: ABC Action Analysis," the section "Segmented Income Statements and the Contribution Approach" in Chapter 5, and the section "Adding and Dropping Product Lines and Other Segments" in Chapter 7.

Relative Profitability

LEARNING OBJECTIVE B–1
Compute the profitability index and use it to select from among possible actions.

Even when every segment is *absolutely* profitable, managers often want to know which segments are most and least profitable. **Relative profitability** is concerned with ranking products, customers, and other business segments to determine which should be emphasized.

Why are managers interested in ranking segments or determining the relative profitability of segments? The answer to this deceptively simple question provides the key to measuring relative profitability. The only reason to rank segments is if something forces you to make trade-offs among them. If trade-offs are not necessary, the solution is simple—keep every segment that is absolutely profitable. What would force a manager to make trade-offs among profitable segments? There is only one answer—a *constraint.* In the absence of a constraint, all segments that are absolutely profitable should be pursued. On the other hand, if a constraint is present, then by definition the company cannot pursue every profitable opportunity. Choices have to be made. Thus, measuring relative profitability makes sense only when a constraint exists that forces trade-offs. This point cannot be overemphasized; constraints are fundamental to understanding and measuring relative profitability.

How should relative profitability be measured? Divide each segment's measure of absolute profitability, which is the incremental profit from that segment, by the amount of the constraint required by the segment. For example, refer to the data below for two of the many segments within a company:

	Segment A	Segment B
Incremental profit	\$100,000	\$200,000
Amount of constrained resource required.	100 hours	400 hours

Segment B may seem more attractive than Segment A because its incremental profit is twice as large, but it requires four times as much of the constrained resource. In fact, Segment B would not be the best use of the constrained resource because it generates only \$500 of incremental profit per hour (\$200,000 ÷ 400 hours), whereas Segment A generates \$1,000 of incremental profit per hour (\$100,000 ÷ 100 hours). Another way to look at this is to suppose that 400 hours of the constrained resource are available. Would you rather use the hours on four segments like Segment A, generating a total incremental profit of \$400,000, or on one segment like Segment B, which generates \$200,000 in incremental profit?

In general, the relative profitability of segments should be measured by the **profitability index** as defined below:

$$\text{Profitability index} = \frac{\text{Incremental profit from the segment}}{\text{Amount of the constrained resource required by the segment}}$$

The profitability index is computed below for the two segments in the example:

	Segment A	Segment B
Incremental profit (a).	\$100,000	\$200,000
Amount of constrained resource required (b)	100 hours	400 hours
Profitability index (a) ÷ (b)	\$1,000 per hour	\$500 per hour

We have already encountered several examples of the profitability index in previous chapters. For example, in Chapter 8 the project profitability index was defined as:

$$\text{Project profitability index} = \frac{\text{Net present value of the project}}{\text{Amount of investment required by the project}}$$

The project profitability index is used when a company has more long-term projects with positive net present values than it can fund. In this case, the incremental profit from the segment is the net present value of the project. And because the investment funds are the constraint, the amount of the constrained resource required by the segment is the amount of investment required by the project.

As an example of the use of the profitability index, consider the case of Quality Kitchen Design, a small company specializing in designing kitchens for upscale homes. Management is considering the 10 short-term projects listed in Panel A of Exhibit B–1. The incremental profit from each project is listed in the second column. For example, the incremental profit from Project A is $9,180. This incremental profit consists of the revenues from the project less any costs that would be incurred by the company as a consequence of accepting the project. The company's constraint is the lead designer's time. Project A would require 17 hours of the lead designer's time. If all of the projects were accepted, they would require a total of 100 hours. Unfortunately, only 46 hours are available. Consequently, management will have to turn down some projects. The profitability index will be used in deciding which projects to accept and which to turn down. The profitability index for a project is computed by dividing its incremental profit by the amount of the lead designer's time required for the project. In the case of Project A, the profitability index is $540 per hour.

EXHIBIT B–1
Ranking Segments Based on the Profitability Index

Panel A: Computation of the Profitability Index

	Incremental Profit (A)	Amount of the Constrained Resource Required (B)	Profitability Index (A) ÷ (B)
Project A	$9,180	17 hours	$540 per hour
Project B	$7,200	9 hours	$800 per hour
Project C	$7,040	16 hours	$440 per hour
Project D	$5,680	8 hours	$710 per hour
Project E	$5,330	13 hours	$410 per hour
Project F	$4,280	4 hours	$1,070 per hour
Project G	$4,160	13 hours	$320 per hour
Project H	$3,720	12 hours	$310 per hour
Project I	$3,650	5 hours	$730 per hour
Project J	$2,940	3 hours	$980 per hour
		100 hours	

Panel B: Ranking Based on the Profitability Index

	Profitability Index	Amount of the Constrained Resource Required	Cumulative Amount of the Constrained Resource Used
Project F	$1,070 per hour	4 hours	4 hours
Project J	$980 per hour	3 hours	7 hours
Project B	$800 per hour	9 hours	16 hours
Project I	$730 per hour	5 hours	21 hours
Project D	$710 per hour	8 hours	29 hours
Project A	$540 per hour	17 hours	46 hours
Project C	$440 per hour	16 hours	62 hours
Project E	$410 per hour	13 hours	75 hours
Project G	$320 per hour	13 hours	88 hours
Project H	$310 per hour	12 hours	100 hours

Panel C: The Optimal Plan

	Incremental Profit
Project F	$ 4,280
Project J	2,940
Project B	7,200
Project I	3,650
Project D	5,680
Project A	9,180
	$32,930

The projects are ranked in order of the profitability index in Panel B of Exhibit B–1. The last column in that panel shows the cumulative amount of the constrained resource (i.e., lead designer's time) required to do the projects at that point in the list and higher. For example, the 7 hours listed to the right of Project J in the cumulative column represents the sum of the 4 hours required for Project F plus the 3 hours required for Project J.

To find the best combination of projects within the limits of the constrained resource, go down the list in Panel B to the point where all of the available constrained resource is used. In this case, because 46 hours of lead designer time are available, that would be the point above the solid line drawn in Panel B of Exhibit B–1. Projects F, J, B, I, D, and A lie above that line and would require a total of exactly 46 hours of lead designer time. The optimal plan consists of accepting these six projects and turning down the others. The total incremental profit from accepting these projects would be $32,930 as shown in Panel C of Exhibit B–1. No other feasible combination of projects would yield a higher total incremental profit.[1]

We should reinforce a very important point that may be forgotten in the midst of these details. The profitability index is based on *incremental* profit. When computing the incremental profit for a segment such as a product, customer, or project, only the *incremental* costs of the segment should be included. Those are the costs that could be avoided—whether fixed or variable—if the segment is eliminated. All other costs are not relevant and should be ignored—including allocations of common costs.

Volume Trade-Off Decisions

LEARNING OBJECTIVE B–2
Compute and use the profitability index in volume trade-off decisions.

Earlier we stated that you have already encountered several examples of the profitability index in this book. One was the project profitability index in Chapter 8. The other example of the profitability index is in the section "Utilization of a Constrained Resource" in Chapter 7. That section deals with situations in which a company does not have enough capacity to satisfy demand for all of its products. Therefore, the company must produce less than the market demands of some products. This is called a volume trade-off decision because the decision, at the margin, consists of trading off units of one product for units of another. Fixed costs are typically unaffected by such decisions—capacity will be fully utilized, it is just a question of how it will be utilized. In volume trade-off decisions where fixed costs are irrelevant, the profitability index takes the special form:

$$\text{Profitability index for a volume trade-off decision} = \frac{\text{Unit contribution margin}}{\text{Amount of the constrained resource required by one unit}}$$

This profitability index is identical to the "contribution margin per unit of the constrained resource" that was used in Chapter 7 to decide which products should be emphasized. An example of a volume trade-off decision is presented in Exhibit B–2. In this example, the company makes three products that use the constrained resource—a machine that is available 2,200 minutes per week. As shown in Panel B of Exhibit B-2, producing all

[1] In this example, the top projects exactly consumed all of the available constrained resource. That won't always happen. For example, assume that only 45 hours of lead designer lime are available. This small change complicates matters considerably. Because of the "lumpiness" of the projects, the optimal plan isn't necessarily to do projects F, J, B, I, and D—slopping at Project D on the list and a cumulative requirement of 29 hours. That would leave 16 hours of unused lead designer time. The best use of this time may be Project C, which has an incremental profit of $7,040. However, other possibilities exist too. Finding and evaluating all of the most likely possibilities can take a lot of lime and ingenuity. When the constrained resource is not completely exhausted by the top projects on the list, some tinkering with the solution may be necessary. For this reason, the list generated by ranking based on the profitability index should be viewed as a starting point rather than as a definitive solution when the projects are "lumpy" and take big chunks of the constrained resource.

EXHIBIT B–2
Using the Profitability Index in a Volume Trade-Off Decision

Panel A: Product Data

	Products RX200	VB30	SQ500
Unit contribution margin	$15 per unit	$10 per unit	$16 per unit
Demand per week	300 units	400 units	100 units
Amount of the constrained resource required	5 minutes per unit	2 minutes per unit	4 minutes per unit

Panel B: Total Demand on the Constrained Resource

	Products RX200	VB30	SQ500	Total
Demand per week (a)	300 units	400 units	100 units	
Amount of the constrained resource required (b)	5 minutes per unit	2 minutes per unit	4 minutes per unit	
Total amount of the constraint required per week to meet demand (a) × (b)	1,500 minutes	800 minutes	400 minutes	2,700 minutes

Panel C: Computation of the Profitability Index

	Products RX200	VB30	SQ500
Unit contribution margin (a)	$15 per unit	$10 per unit	$16 per unit
Amount of the constrained resource required (b)	5 minutes per unit	2 minutes per unit	4 minutes per unit
Profitability index (contribution margin per unit of the constrained resource) (a) × (b)	$3 per minute	$5 per minute	$4 per minute

Panel D: The Optimal Plan

Amount of constrained resource available	2,200 minutes
Less: Constrained resource required for production of 400 units of VB30	800 minutes
Remaining constrained resource available	1,400 minutes
Less: Constrained resource required for production of 100 units of SQ500	400 minutes
Remaining constrained resource available	1,000 minutes
Less: Constrained resource required for production of 200 units of RX200*	1,000 minutes
Remaining constrained resource available	0 minutes

*1,000 minutes available ÷ 5 minutes per unit of RX200 = 200 units of RX200.

Panel E: The Total Contribution Margin under the Optimal Plan

	Products RX200	VB30	SQ500	Total
Unit contribution margin (a)	$15 per unit	$10 per unit	$16 per unit	
Optimal production plan (b)	200 units	400 units	100 units	
Contribution margin (a) × (b)	$3,000	$4,000	$1,600	$8,600

three products up to demand would require 2,700 minutes per week—500 more minutes than are available. Consequently, the company cannot fully satisfy demand for these three products and some product or products must be cut back.

The profitability index for this decision is computed in Panel C of Exhibit B–2. For example, the profitability index for product RX200 is $3 per minute. The comparable figure for product VB30 is $5 per minute and for product SQ500 is $4 per minute. Consequently, the correct ranking of the products is VB30 followed by SQ500, then followed by RX200.

The optimal production plan is laid out in Panel D of Exhibit B–2. The most profitable products, VB30 and SQ500, are produced up to demand and the remaining time on the constraint is used to make 200 units of RX200 (1,000 available minutes ÷ 5 minutes per unit).

The total contribution margin from following this plan is computed in Panel E of Exhibit B–2. The total contribution margin of $8,600 is higher than the contribution margin that could be realized from following any other feasible plan. Assuming that fixed costs are not affected by the decision of which products to emphasize, this plan will also yield a higher total profit than any other feasible plan.

Managerial Implications

LEARNING OBJECTIVE B–3
Compute and use the profitability index in other business decisions.

In addition to the add-or-drop and volume trade-off decisions discussed above, the profitability index can be used in other ways. For example, which products would you rather have your salespersons emphasize—those with a low profitability index or those with a high profitability index? The answer is, of course, that salespersons should be encouraged to emphasize sales of the products with the highest profitability indexes. However, if salespersons are paid commissions based on sales, what products will they try to sell? The selling prices of products RX200, VB30, and SQ500 appear below:

		Products	
	RX200	VB30	SQ500
Unit selling price	$40	$30	$35

If salespersons are paid a commission based on gross sales, they will prefer to sell product RX200, which has the highest selling price. But that is the *least* profitable product given the current constraint. It has a profitability index of only $3 per minute compared to $5 per minute for VB30 and $4 per minute for SQ500.

This suggests that salespersons should be paid commissions based on the profitability index and the amount of constraint time sold rather than on sales revenue. This would encourage them to sell the most profitable products, rather than the products with the highest selling prices. How would such a compensation system work? Prior to making a sales call, a salesperson would receive an up-to-date report indicating how much of the constrained resource is currently available and a listing of all products showing the amount of the constraint each requires and the profitability index. Such a report would appear as follows:

Marketing Data Report		Products	
	RX200	VB30	SQ500
Unit selling price	$40	$30	$35
Unit variable cost	25	20	19
Unit contribution margin (a).	$15	$10	$16
Amount of the constrained resource required per unit (b).	5 minutes	2 minutes	4 minutes
Profitability index (a) ÷ (b).	$3 per minute	$5 per minute	$4 per minute

Total available time on the constrained resource: 100 minutes

The key here is to realize that the salesperson is, in essence, selling time on the constraint. A salesperson who is paid based on the profitability index will prefer to sell product VB30 because the salesperson would get credit for sales of $500 if all 100 minutes are used on product VB30 ($5 per minute × 100 minutes), whereas the credit would be only $300 for product RX200 or $400 for product SQ500.[2]

The profitability index also has implications for pricing new products. Suppose that the company has designed a new product, WR6000, whose variable cost is $30 per unit and that requires 6 minutes of the constrained resource per unit. Because the company is currently using all of its capacity, the new product would necessarily displace production of existing products. Consequently, the price of the new product should cover not only its variable cost, but it should also cover the opportunity cost of displacing existing products. What product would be displaced? Production of RX200 should be cut first because it is the least profitable existing product. And how much is a minute of the constrained resource worth if it would otherwise be used to make product RX200? A minute of the constrained resource is worth $3 per minute, the profitability index of product RX200. Therefore, the selling price of the new product should at least cover the costs laid out below:[3]

$$\begin{array}{c}\text{Selling price of}\\\text{new product}\end{array} \geq \begin{array}{c}\text{Variable cost of}\\\text{the new product}\end{array} + \left(\begin{array}{c}\text{Opportunity}\\\text{cost per unit of}\\\text{the constrained}\\\text{resource}\end{array} \times \begin{array}{c}\text{Amount of the}\\\text{constrained resource}\\\text{required by a unit of}\\\text{the new product}\end{array}\right)$$

In the case of the new product WR6000, the calculations would be:

$$\text{Selling price of WR6000} \geq \$ + (\$3 \text{ per minute} \times 6 \text{ minutes}) = \$30 + \$18 = \$48$$

WR6000 should sell for at least $48 or the company would be better off continuing to use the available capacity to produce RX200.[4]

[2] Equivalent incentives would be provided by commissions based on total coniribution margin. If all 100 available minutes are used to make product VB30, 50 units could be produced (100 minutes ÷ 2 minutes per unit), for which the total contribution margin would be $500 ($10 per unit × 50 units). Likewise, the total contribution margin for products RX200 and SQ500 would be $300 and $400. Respectively, if all available minutes were used to make just those products.

[3] In addition, the selling price of a new product should cover any avoidable fixed costs of the product. This is easier said than done, however, because achieving this goal involves estimating how many units will be sold—which in turn depends on the selling price.

[4] If production of WR6000 eventually completely displaces production of RX200. the opportunity cost would change. It would increase to $4 per minute, the profitability index of the next product in line to be cut back.

Summary

A strong distinction should be made between absolute profitability and relative profitability. A segment is considered profitable in an absolute sense if dropping it would result in lower overall profits. Absolute profitability is measured by the segment's incremental profit, which is the difference between the revenues from the segment and the costs that could be avoided by dropping the segment.

A relative profitability measure is used to rank segments. Such rankings are necessary only if a constraint forces the organization to make trade-offs among segments. To appropriately measure relative profitability, three things must be known. First, the constraint must be identified. Second, the incremental profit associated with each segment must be computed. Third, the amount of the constrained resource required by each segment must be determined. Relative profitability is measured by the profitability index, which is the incremental profit from the segment divided by the amount of the constrained resource required by the segment. The profitability index can be used in a variety of situations, including selections of projects and volume trade-off decisions.

Glossary

Absolute profitability The impact on the organization's overall profits of adding or dropping a particular segment such as a product or customer—without making any other changes. (p. 594)

Profitability index The measure of relative profitability, which is computed by dividing the incremental profit from a segment by the amount of the constrained resource required by the segment. (p. 595)

Relative profitability A ranking of products, customers, or other business segments for purposes of making trade-offs among segments. This is necessary when a constraint exists. (p. 594)

Questions

B–1 What is meant by *absolute* profitability?

B–2 What is meant by *relative* profitability?

B–3 A successful owner of a small business stated: "We have the best technology, the best products, and the best people in the world. We have no constraints." Do you agree?

B–4 What information is needed to measure the *absolute* profitability of a segment?

B–5 What information is needed to measure the *relative* profitability of a product?

B–6 How should the relative profitability of products be determined in a volume trade-off decision?

B–7 What costs should be covered by the selling price of a new product?

Multiple-choice questions are available with Connect.

Exercises

Additional student resources are available with Connect.

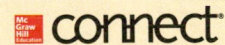

EXERCISE B–1 Ranking Projects Based on the Profitability Index [LO B–1]

MidWest Amusements is in the process of reviewing 10 proposals for new rides at its theme parks in cities scattered throughout the American heartland. The company's only experienced safety engineer must carefully review plans and monitor the construction of all new rides. However, she is only available to work on new rides for 1,590 hours during the year. The net present values and the amount of safety engineer time required for the proposed rides are listed below:

Proposed Ride	Net Present Value	Safety Engineer Time Required (hours)
Ride 1	$1,268,200	340
Ride 2	1,152,000	360
Ride 3	649,600	320
Ride 4	644,100	190
Ride 5	540,000	250
Ride 6	539,200	160
Ride 7	462,000	110
Ride 8	457,200	360
Ride 9	403,200	180
Ride 10	387,500	250
Total	$6,503,000	2,520

Required:

1. Which of the proposed rides should the company build this year? (Note: The incremental profit of a long-term project such as constructing a new ride is its net present value.)
2. What would be the total net present value of the rides built under your plan?

EXERCISE B–2 Volume Trade-Off Decision [LO B–2]

Heritage Watercraft makes reproductions of classic wooden boats. The bottleneck in the production process is fitting wooden planks to build up the curved sections of the hull. This process requires the attention of the shop's most experienced craftsman. A total of 1,800 hours is available per year in this bottleneck operation. Data concerning the company's four products appear below:

Adirondack	Adirondack	Lake Huron	Oysterman	Voyageur
Unit contribution margin.	$485	$268	$385	$600
Annual demand (units)	80	120	100	140
Hours required in the bottleneck operation per unit	5	4	7	8

No fixed costs could be avoided by modifying how many units are produced of any product or even by dropping any one of the products.

Required:

1. Is there sufficient capacity in the bottleneck operation to satisfy demand for all products?
2. What is the optimal production plan for the year?
3. What would be the total contribution margin for the optimal production plan you have proposed?

EXERCISE B–3 Pricing a New Product [LO B–3]

Seattle's Top Coffee owns and operates a chain of popular coffee stands that serve over 30 different coffee-based beverages. The constraint at the coffee stands is the amount of time required to fill an order, which can be considerable for the more complex beverages. Sales are often lost because customers leave after seeing a long waiting line to place an order. Careful analysis of the company's existing products has revealed that the opportunity cost of order filling time is $2.70 per minute.

The company is considering introducing a new product, praline cappuccino, to be made with pecan extract and molasses. The variable cost of the standard size praline cappuccino would be $0.30 and the time required to fill an order for the beverage would be 40 seconds.

Required:

What is the minimum acceptable selling price for the new praline cappuccino product?

Problems

Additional student resources are available with Connect.

PROBLEM B–4 Customer Profitability and Managerial Decisions [LO B–1, LO B–3]

Advanced Pharmaceuticals, Inc., is a wholesale distributor of prescription drugs to independent retail and hospital-based pharmacies. Management believes that top-notch customer representatives are the key factor in determining whether the company will be successful in the future. Customer representatives serve as the company's liaison with customers—helping pharmacies monitor their stocks, delivering drugs when customer stocks run low, and providing up-to-date information on drugs from many different companies. Customer representatives must be ultra-reliable and are highly trained. Good customer representatives are hard to come by and are not easily replaced.

Customer representatives routinely record the amount of time they spend serving each pharmacy. This time includes travel time to and from the company's central warehouse as well as time spent replenishing stocks, dealing with complaints, answering questions about drugs, informing pharmacists of the latest developments and newest products, reviewing bills, explaining procedures, and so on. Some pharmacies require more hand-holding and attention than others and consequently they consume more of the representatives' time.

Recently, customer representatives have made more frequent complaints that it is impossible to do their jobs without working well beyond normal working hours. This has led to an alarming increase in the number of customer representatives quitting for jobs in other organizations. As a consequence, management is considering dropping some customers to reduce the workload on customer representatives. Data concerning a representative sample of the company's customers appears below:

	Leafcrest Pharmacy	Providence Hospital Pharmacy	Madison Clinic Pharmacy	Jenkins Pharmacy
Total revenues	$272,650	$2,948,720	$1,454,880	$155,280
Cost of drugs sold	$211,470	$2,234,480	$1,119,440	$115,920
Customer service costs	$10,640	$74,400	$42,000	$4,480
Customer representative time	190	1,240	560	80

Customer service costs include all of the costs—other than the costs of the drugs themselves—that could be avoided by dropping the customer. These costs include the hourly wages of the customer representatives, their sales commissions, the mileage-related costs of the customer representatives' company-provided vehicles, and so on.

Required:

1. Rank the four customers in terms of their profitability.
2. Customer representatives are currently paid $25 per hour plus a commission of 1% of sales revenues. If these four pharmacies are indeed representative of the company's customers, could the company afford to pay its customer representatives more in order to retain them?

PROBLEM B–5 Volume Trade-Off Decision; Managing the Constraint [LO B–2, LO B–3]

Sammamish Brick, Inc., manufactures bricks using clay deposits on the company's property. Raw clays are blended and then extruded into molds to form unfired bricks. The unfired bricks are then stacked onto movable metal platforms and rolled into the kiln where they are fired until dry. The dried bricks are then packaged and shipped to retail outlets and contractors. The bottleneck in the production process is the kiln, which is available for 2,000 hours per year. Data concerning the company's four main products appear below. Products are sold by the pallet.

	Traditional Brick	Textured Facing	Cinder Block	Roman Brick
Gross revenue per pallet	$756	$1,356	$589	$857
Contribution margin per pallet	$472	$632	$376	$440
Annual demand (pallets)	90	110	100	120
Hours required in the kiln per pallet	8	8	4	5

No fixed costs could be avoided by modifying how much is produced of any product.

Required:

1. Is there sufficient capacity in the kiln to satisfy demand for all products?
2. What is the production plan for the year that would maximize the company's profit?
3. What would be the total contribution margin for the production plan you have proposed?
4. The kiln could be operated for more than 2,000 hours per year by running it after normal working hours. Up to how much per hour should the company be willing to pay in overtime wages, energy costs, and other incremental costs to operate the kiln additional hours?
5. The company is considering introducing a new product, glazed Venetian bricks, whose variable cost would be $820 per pallet and that would require 10 hours in the kiln per pallet. What is the minimum acceptable selling price for this new product?
6. Salespersons are currently paid a commission of 5% of gross revenues. Will this motivate the salespersons to make the right choices concerning which products to sell most aggressively?

PROBLEM B–6 Interpreting Common Practice [LO B–1]
In practice, many organizations measure the relative profitability of their segments by dividing the segments' margins by their revenues. The segment margin for this purpose is the segment's revenue less its fully allocated costs—including allocations of fixed common costs. For example, a hospital might compute the relative profitability of its major segments as follows:

St. Ignatius Hospital
Profitability Report
(in thousands of dollars)

	Emergency Room	Surgery	Acute Care	Total
Revenue.	$10,630	$21,470	$18,840	$50,940
Fully allocated cost.	10,060	21,090	18,550	49,700
Margin	$ 570	$ 380	$ 290	$ 1,240
Profitability (Margin ÷ Revenue)	5.4%	1.8%	1.5%	2.4%

The hospital's net operating income for this period was $1,240,000.

Required:

1. Evaluate the use of the margin, as defined above, in the numerator of the profitability measure.
2. Evaluate the use of revenue in the denominator of the profitability measure.

PROBLEM B–7 Ranking Alternatives and Managing with a Constraint [LO B–1, LO B–3]
Luxus Baking Company has developed a reputation for producing superb, one-of-a-kind wedding cakes in addition to its normal fare of breads and pastries. While the wedding cake business is a major moneymaker, it creates some problems for the bakery's owner, Kari Therau, particularly in June. The company's reputation for wedding cakes is largely based on the skills of Regina Yesterman, who decorates all of the cakes. Unfortunately, last year the company accepted too many cake orders for some June weekends, with the result that Regina was worked to a frazzle and almost quit. To prevent a recurrence, Kari has promised Regina that she will not have to work more than 27 hours in any week to prepare the wedding cakes for the upcoming weekend. (Regina also has other duties at the bakery, so even with the 27-hour limitation, she would be working more than full-time in June.)

A number of reservations for wedding cakes for the first weekend in June had already been received from customers by early May. When a customer makes a reservation, Ms. Therau gets enough information concerning the size of the wedding party and the desires of the customer to determine the cake's price, the cost to make it, and the amount of time that Regina will need to spend decorating it. The reservations for the first weekend in June are listed below:

Customer	Incremental Profit	Reginas Time Required (hours)
Afonso.	$ 195	5
Carloni.	259	7
Cullins	105	3
Frese	170	5
Gerst	117	3
Jelovich.	124	4
Klarr	192	6
Melby.	144	4
Rideau.	150	5
Towner	256	8
Total.	$1,712	50

For example, the Afonso cake would require 5 hours of Regina's time and would generate a profit of $195 for the bakery. Following industry practice, pricing for the cakes is based on their size and standard formulas and does not reflect how much decorating would be required.

Required:

1. Ms. Therau feels that she must cancel enough cake reservations to reduce Regina's workload to the promised level. She knows that customers whose reservations have been cancelled will be disappointed, but she intends to refer all of those customers to an excellent bakery across town. If the sole objective is to maximize the company's total profit, which reservations should be cancelled?
2. What would be the total profit if your recommendation in requirement 1 is followed?
3. Assume that for competitive reasons it would not be practical for Luxus Bakery to change the pricing of its wedding cakes. What recommendations would you make to Ms. Therau concerning taking reservations in the future?
4. Assume that Luxus Bakery could change the way it prices its wedding cakes. What recommendations would you make to Ms. Therau concerning how she should set the prices of wedding cakes in the future?
5. What might Ms. Therau be able to do to keep both Regina and her customers happy while increasing her profits? Be creative. (Hint: Review the section on managing constraints in Chapter 7.)

Additional student resources are available with Connect. connect **Cases**

CASE B–8 Redirecting Effort [LO B–2]

Vectra Corporation recently suffered its fourth straight decline in quarterly earnings—despite a modest increase in sales. Unfortunately, Vectra's industry is highly competitive, so the company is reluctant to increase its prices. However, management believes that profits would improve if the efforts of its sales force were redirected toward the company's most profitable products.

Several years ago Vectra decided that its core competencies were strategy, design, and marketing and that production should be outsourced. Consequently, Vectra subcontracts all of its production.

Vectra's salespersons are paid salaries and commissions. All of the company's salespersons sell the company's full line of products. The commissions are 5% of the revenue generated by a salesperson and average about 60% of a salesperson's total compensation. There has been some discussion of increasing the size of the sales force, but management prefers for the present to redirect the efforts of salespersons toward the more profitable products. While management is reluctant to tinker with the sales compensation scheme, revenue targets for the various products will be set for the regional sales managers based on the products that management wants to push most aggressively. The regional sales managers will be paid a bonus if the sales targets are met.

The company computes product margins for all of its products using the following formula:

Selling price
Less: Sales commissions
Less: Cost of sales
Less: Operating expenses
Product margin

The cost of sales in the product margin formula is the amount Vectra pays to its production subcontractors. The operating expenses represent fixed costs. Each product is charged a fair share of those costs, calculated this year as 34.6% of the product's selling price.

Management is convinced that the best way to improve overall profits is to redirect the efforts of the company's salespersons. There are no plans to add or drop any products.

Required:

How would you measure the relative profitability of the company's products in this situation? Assume that it is not feasible to change the way salespersons are compensated. Also assume that the only data you have available are the selling price, the sales commissions, the cost of sales, the operating expenses, and the product margin for each product.

Index

D